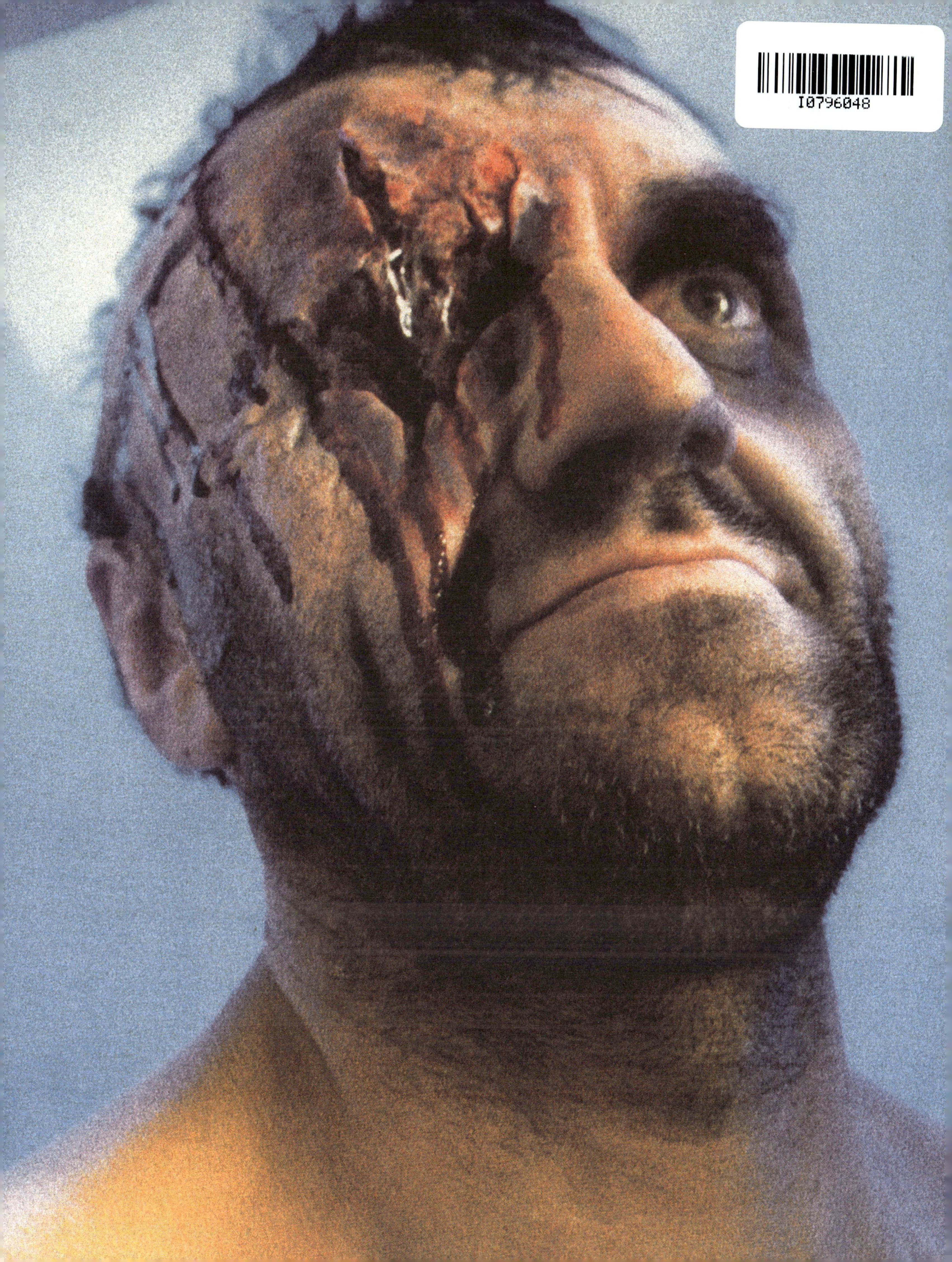

BEYOND TERROR
THE FILMS OF LUCIO FULCI

First edition published in both hardback and paperback by FAB Press, May 1999.
Second pressing published in paperback only by FAB Press, October 2002.
Hardback first edition ISBN 978-0-9520260-5-4
Paperback first edition (both pressings) ISBN 978-0-9529260-6-1

Revised & expanded second edition first published in hardcover only by FAB Press, November 2017

This fourth pressing of the revised & expanded second edition published by FAB Press, June 2025

FAB Press Ltd.
2 Farleigh
Ramsden Road
Godalming
GU7 1EY
England, UK

www.fabpress.com

Designed and Typeset by Harvey Fenton and Stephen Thrower,
with thanks to CoCo and Francis Brewster for production assistance.

A CIP catalogue record for this book is available from the British Library.

Hardcover
ISBN 978-1-903254-90-5

Printed in India

EU Safety Representative
Easy Access System Europe
Mustamäe tee 50,
10621 Tallinn, Estonia
gpsr.requests@easproject.com

Beyond Terror

The Films of Lucio Fulci

Stephen Thrower

acknowledgements

Special acknowledgement goes to Julian Grainger for his valuable proof-reading of the manuscript, for tracking down obscure titles and for permission to reproduce credits from his personal database of European actors and actresses. His assistance in compiling and annotating the filmography was also essential.

The author wishes to thank the following for their help and encouragement during the preparation, writing and editing of this book: **Luca Palmerini** (for the Dardano Sacchetti material), **Pete Tombs** (for good advice on the first draft), **Barrie Dwyer** (for the essential summer retreat), **Marc Morris** (for help in tracing many of these films over the years and for providing the *Zombie Flesh-Eaters* DVD frame-grabs), **Martin Coxhead** (for elusive titles and some visual material), **Kris Gavin** (for assistance to Julian Grainger), **Deborah Bacci** (for translation assistance), **Mark Ashworth** (for advice on obscure Italiana and frequent help with translation), **Patrizia Milazzo** (for help in translation), **Trevor Barley** and **Paul Brown** (for bringing Lucio Fulci over here in 1994 to present his films), **Marcelle Perks** (for a chat about *The New York Ripper*), **Francis Brewster** and **Martin Brooks** (for bringing the actor and actress filmographies up to date for this edition), **Adrian Smith** (for proof-reading the *initial* final version and additional research), **Scott Grantham** (for clearing up some confusion in the credits for *The New York Ripper*), **John Martin** (for the special edition bonus chapter Lucio Fulci interview text), **Robin Bougie** (for drafting the Eibon corner embellishments on the Special Edition case), **Jake West** (for his dazzling Indiegogo promotional film and his invaluable support and advice), **Nigel Hooper** and **Arianna Mantovani** (for translation of Italian-language press sources) and **David Knight** (for the author's photograph).

Stills and illustrations are from the author's collection and from: **Martin Beine**, **Bill Bennett**, **Francis Brewster**, **Nigel Burrell**, **Mitch Davis**, **Max Décharné**, **Kenneth Eriksen**, **Harvey Fenton**, **Antonella Fulci**, **Alan Jones**, **John Martin**, **Bob Murawski**, **Gary Needham**, **Kim Newman**, **Salvatore Pazzi** (Thriller, Torino), **Adrian Smith** and **Andy Waller**.
Frontispiece: French artwork for *City of the Living Dead*.

For their kind participation in interviews, thanks to:
Michele De Angelis, **Fabio Frizzi**, **Antonella Fulci**, **Catriona MacColl**, **Anselmo Parrinello** and **Dardano Sacchetti**.

For sheer hard work and focus, thanks to **Harvey Fenton**.

For taking me to my first 'horror' movie (David Lynch's *The Elephant Man*) and for her valued encouragement of my writing, special thanks to **Diane Newby**.

For communicating his enthusiasm so strongly in those early *Starburst* reviews, thanks to **Alan Jones**, the first writer to recognise the power of Fulci's Gothic horrors.

Dedicated to my partner **Ossian Brown**, who drew the Eibon symbol for the book cover and who weathered my manias and depressions (not to mention a period when I was speaking cod-Italian in my sleep) during the long haul to publication.
At last it's done!

In memory of Lucio Fulci, whose films taught me to love the Italian cinema, and David Warbeck, the handsomest devil in the Beyond.

contents

* Films are dated by the year of their release. Dates are only listed in the text for the first reference to each title per chapter, or when pertinent.
* Lucio Fulci's films are referred to first under their original language release titles followed by the most common English-language variant, e.g. *Una sull'altra/One on Top of the Other* (1969). Thereafter only the English-language variant is used.
* Where several different English-language titles have proliferated, the author has tried to select the most common British one, except where personal prejudice forbids! (e.g. Fulci's *Manhattan Baby* was released in both Italy and America as such, but appeared on video in the UK blandly retitled as *Possessed*.) Common American titles stand in for films released in the States but not in Great Britain.
* In the absence of any English-language release, the films are referred to under their original language titles only.
* Films by other directors are referred to by their most common English-language title, except where they were either undistributed in Britain/America or distributed under their Italian names (as is the case with sundry art cinema releases). Even then, inconsistencies occur. For instance, Federico Fellini's *La Dolce Vita* is usually referred to as such in English-speaking countries, but Luchino Visconti's *The Damned* is rarely listed as *La caduta degli Dei*, its actual Italian title. Where such contradictions occur, I've opted for the more immediately recognisable choice. Basically, the use of titles reflects my wish to make the flow of this book as smooth as possible. Therefore I've opted not to list Italian + English titles, as some critics prefer. Purists may object, but if the pattern is to be consistent one ends up with absurdities like *Zombi holocaust/Zombie Holocaust*, *Diabolik/Danger: Diabolik*, and great traffic pile-ups like *Perchè quelle strane gocce di sangue sul corpo di Jennifer?/Why Those Strange Drops of Blood on the Body of Jennifer?*

foreword by antonella fulci

Antonella Fulci on her grandmother, Lucio's mother:

"Your question about her ever working in the film industry puts a smile on my face, because Lucia always hated it. She thought every film-maker was a crazy bugger who should go and find a real job. She wanted dad to become a lawyer instead! In this picture she's about 20 and still living in Sicily. Now that you mention it, she could have become a movie star with her natural beauty. But if she were here and heard me say that she'd question my sanity and grumble: 'Me among all those dirty crazy people? No way!'

Daddy kept an old issue of *Variety* in his writing table drawer. He really loved its obituary page and often talked about how it showed chance is more revealing than pure facts: the page was dedicated to Louis B. Mayer, the Leo.

The divine Orson used to call him the biggest clown in America, Bad Billy Wilder told him bitterly to fuck off when Louis accused him of ungratefulness to the hand that feeds, after the premiere of *Sunset Boulevard*, but this wasn't reported in the celebration article. Everybody was there to glorify the legend and daddy was sincerely touched until he saw a very short paragraph, at the bottom of the page:
'The wife and the daughter of Edgar G. Ulmer fondly remember their husband and father, on the anniversary of his death'.

Once again the movie that always obsessed him for its perfection was talking to his heart.

Fate was the thread of Ulmer's masterpiece *Detour* (1945), with its five days of shooting and Tom Neal's death from drug abuse shortly after it, and fate too was uniting the King of Hollywood and the genius of no-budgeted movies. I suggested that daddy was like the hitchhiker of the movie, but he laughed behind his tiny glasses, as always.

Printed paper and celluloid preserve a man from death in other people's hearts, and sometimes a tiny little film can change your life. Daddy could turn any movie conversation into a praise for Ann Savage's cheap skirt waving in the dust, at the gas station. He said she could have been the second Bette Davis, and I think he was right. He loved to remember his only experience on the set with his true mentor. Ulmer was directing the third unit crew of Siodmak's *The Crimson Pirate* (1952) and daddy was the substitute for 'an athletic assistant', in his own words.

They became friends, I can bet daddy did everything to make it so anyway, and Edgar told him about the many Yiddish movies he directed and some amusing stories about his friends Carl (Jung) and Isaac (Singer). I never discovered what he said about *Detour*, if I think about it. Well, that was dad!

I think for the film maker in Lucio, *Detour* meant five days of hard sweaty work on the road, twenty four hours a day; he always wondered how such a movie, almost totally shot in open spaces, could give him such claustrophobia. That was probably what made him fall in love forever. Norma Desmond and her magnificence were miles away from the gas station but her spirit was there, clear in Lucio's young mind. I'm talking about cinema, he had it in his blood!

Once he was being questioned about *The Beyond*. He compared the movie to a poem by Antonin Artaud just to provoke the interviewer, but the guy seemed to take it seriously because I'm reading about *The Beyond*'s 'Artaudian' atmosphere over and over. It's touching how people keep searching for a common thread in daddy's frequent genre-mutations. Take a breath folks, if there's a thread in daddy's career, it's a small b-movie from the past.

In *One on Top of the Other*, for example, and just to praise my favourite thriller once more, the weak George D. enjoys a more positive twist of fate than the pessimistic Tom Neal, with the help of a favourable time zone and a big stroke of luck. (No spoilers here!) Daddy said he'd been inspired by his dream girl Susan Hayward as Barbara Graham (*I Want to Live!*, Robert Wise, 1958) for the gas chamber sequence. About Susan he used to say: *'She's queer, but she really drives me crazy!'*

I'd rather tell you about our wonderful summer vacations than about death and the casualties of time; if you wanted to see Lucio's very best you should have seen him on the ocean. Our departures were worthy of Jerome's *Three Men in a Boat*, but daddy's commander's instinct made it great fun. Every year we sailed from port to port for a month, met friends and had late night parties on the open sea. It was fun to see daddy flirt with every girl, making jokes. Once I saw him reading a girl's fortune in the palm of her hand, like a real gypsy. He was so serious that I laughed nearly to death. Later when we recalled the story he said, grinning:
'When you want someone and you've exhausted any other chance you only have two ways to reach your goal: Play her a song on the guitar, and I'm unable to; so I was using the second sure-fire way'.
'Pretend you can read her fortune?'
'Sure!'
'What did you tell her?'
'Everything she wanted to hear... but now please fuck off cause you're making me screw up my marine knot!'
'It was ok', he added with a much bigger grin, then paid all his attention to the knot.

Daddy hated the jerk-nauts and their motor boats. The three of us went where the wind blew, stopping at times by the little islands around the Argentario promontory and proceeding in random directions.
It was beautiful and a sort of miracle potion for our moods. The beauty of the places we discovered day by day healed every neurosis, me and Camilla cooked fantastic meals aboard while daddy read his books and wrote his things. He said he loved the southeast wind because it made him think better.

Krzysztof Kieslowski had an unpronounceable name and entitled most of his movies like the ten commandments. The eleventh commandment was his last triad: *Three Colours: Blue, White* and *Red*. The three colours of France; the country he moved to from his native Poland. He was constantly hailed as a genius.
In his films Miss Binoche merged with the dominating colour, delighting the eyes of a large audience of aesthetes and intellectuals. The young director (45 years old) passed away on 13 March 1996, the same day as my dad. I wasn't in the best mood to appreciate the irony of fate when I saw the macabre 'double feature' on newspapers the next day, a sort of 'Fulci vs. Kieslowski' (full of crocodile tears for the artisan and literary orgasms for the Polish aesthete), but I'm sure that daddy was laughing loud, wherever he was.

That was the day I pulled out *Variety* from the drawer...

...One of those God-blessed summers, we saw Tony Curtis standing still on a dock in Porto Ercole. Daddy started blessing him out loud:
'Look at that man! Remember that he kissed Marilyn! What a man!'
Who knows what Tony Curtis was doing there, but I guess he wasn't thinking about Miss Monroe in the cool breeze that cleared the most wonderful of sunsets, as he didn't even turn his white head to look at the bearded man who was praising him so loud.

In my mind's eye, a merciful fate re-united Louis B. Mayer and Edgar G. Ulmer in the same place, and they were looking at the same sunset. It was magic...
I looked around for Madame Desmond but she wasn't there with them at all, and I felt wonderfully good.

"voices from beyond"

a personal introduction

Like many British horror fans who grew up in the seventies, I spent the decade reading about films it was impossible to see. My fascination for the genre was fuelled entirely by books about cinema, and by horror fiction. Thankfully, there was a good supply of Edgar Allan Poe and H.P. Lovecraft at my local library, along with the standards like Bram Stoker's *Dracula*. Anthologies of ghost stories (M.R. James, Sheridan Le Fanu and many others) provided traditionally crafted scares, and there was always the BBC's *Doctor Who* – going through a particularly nerve-jangling Gothic spell – to cement my attraction to the vicarious sensations of terror. Lovecraft in particular mutated my childhood with his dank and cosmically distorted world-view. My taste for the fantastic and grotesque was well established, thanks to the inhabitants of Dunwich, Arkham and Innsmouth...

These dark and morbid pleasures were barely tolerated in 'serious' literary circles, but it mattered not to me. By the time I found out that Lovecraft was disdained by the literary establishment, he'd already become a major part of my interior life. As for another of my teenage influences, a long-running anthology series called *The Pan Books of Horror Stories*, which concentrated on the gruesome and grotesque, it was seemingly beneath contempt. Easily available in high street booksellers like Woolworths or W.H. Smith, they sold by the cart-load, and to my knowledge escaped without censure. I never saw a single tabloid scare about the content of these 'paperback-nasties', although the stories were often hyperbolically grisly, with sexual violence and perversion present too. Their extreme imagery sent this horror-obsessed teenager into paroxysms of near-nausea. A delighted nausea, I would have queasily admitted, after sitting alone with *Flame!* by Norman Kaufman, or *Ashes to Ashes* by Alan Hillery. The earlier volumes interspersed stomach-churning tales with work of a more reputable pedigree, but while Patricia Highsmith and David Case may have shown greater prose abilities it was usually the likes of Kaufman whose work ended up being quoted on the back covers, which featured choice glimpses of the nastiness inside: *"Great chunks of bone kept bouncing up from where the hammer was splintering his skull"*. Browsing through older books about horror cinema, it struck me what a difference there was, between the classic Universal Pictures movies – Frankenstein, Dracula, The Mummy, The Wolf Man – and these shocking tales! Could the cinema ever match their explicit horror?

It soon would. Thanks to David Pirie's book *The Vampire Cinema* which turned up providentially in my local library, I became aware of the existence of a new horror cinema that was sweeping the dusty, cobwebbed Gothics of the thirties and sixties aside. Breathlessly anticipating the day when I might see these shockingly violent films, I read about them avidly and gloated over the stills that promised even worse in store. I felt a thrilling anxiety at the thought of what ninety minutes of such unrelieved mayhem might be like.

Adding to my pleasurable anticipation was an awareness that these newer films marked the passing of a critical order. Established horror film pundits, for whom James Whale and Val Lewton, *Nosferatu* and *Dr. Jekyll and Mr. Hyde* constituted the acceptable canon, were sneeringly disdainful about them, expressing disapproval and outright disgust at their new excesses. Never mind that they were reacting just as previous critical cabals had done when they slammed Tod Browning's *Freaks*. Even some admirers of Hammer, who not so long ago had been considered utterly depraved for championing Terence Fisher, scorned the more recent films, whose titles – *The Last House on the Left*, *The Texas Chain Saw Massacre*, *Night of the Living Dead*, *Twitch of the Death Nerve*, *Shivers* – were mentioned with high-handed deprecations and dark hints of declining moral standards. The same scorn that had been poured on the shockers of yesteryear was being recycled, without irony, to attack a new generation of filmmakers. Needless to say, all this was grist for the mill of adolescent infatuation. Suddenly, horror's more elderly icons seemed too pallid, and not just because of the sepulchral murk of their habitat.

above:
David Warbeck, star of *The Beyond*

For most of the seventies and the early nineteen-eighties I lived in or around Wakefield in West Yorkshire. The city's only cinema was an 'ABC' three-screener which I'd begun to visit after leaving school at sixteen. It was here, in February 1982, that I first encountered one of the key films discussed in this book, on a double bill that was to influence my viewing habits for decades to come: *The Beyond* by Lucio Fulci, plus *Shock* by Mario Bava. I had the cineaste's formative experience that week; returning three times, dragging friends along the third time, then catching the same two films again twelve miles away in Leeds, where they played for a further fortnight. I treasure my recollections of this period, when Eagle Films – the UK distributors of many great Italian horrors – were in the ascendant on provincial cinema screens. Other Fulci films such as *City of the Living Dead*, *The House by the Cemetery* and a re-released *Zombie Flesh-Eaters* turned up in quick succession, along with work by Italian directors like Ruggero Deodato, Umberto Lenzi and Bruno Mattei.

Suddenly it was vital that I find out what was playing across the whole sprawling county of Yorkshire. I learned of the trend for horror all-nighters, often in places I'd never visited before. Harrogate, a staunchly conservative North Yorkshire town, played host to a Saturday night bill of David Cronenberg's *Shivers* and *Rabid*, George Romero's *Dawn of the Dead* and *Night of the Living Dead* and Bob Clark's excellent *Dead of Night*. These films matched the gory delights of the Pan horror stories yet added a startling sophistication all their own.

below:
Portrait of the artist as an old corpse: Schweik, warlock and painter of *The Beyond*.

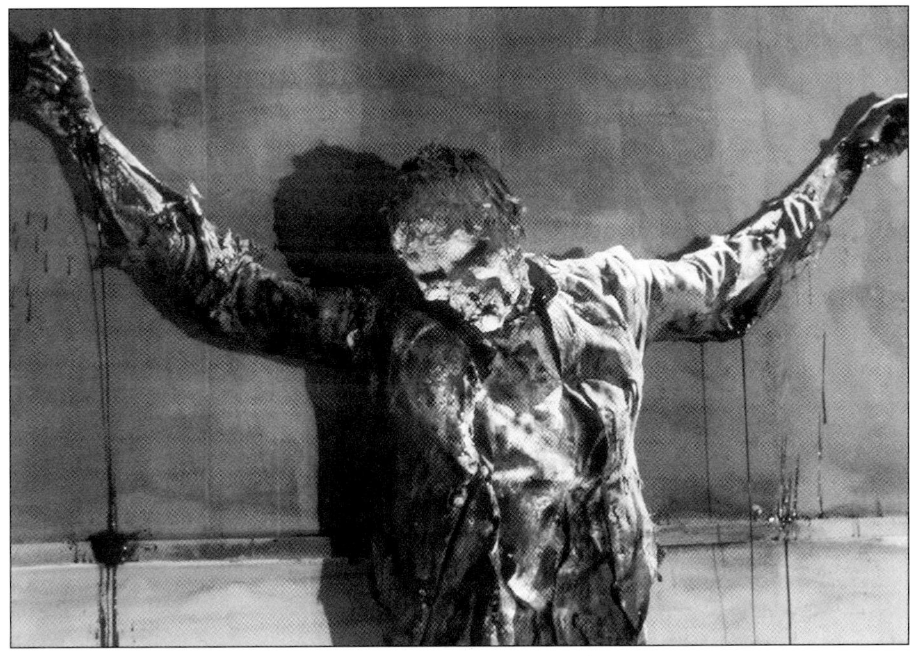

above:
Fulci directing *The House by the Cemetery.* Cinematographer Sergio Salvati is to the right of Fulci (pointing).

British film censorship was in its imperial phase throughout the nineteen-seventies. The British Board of Film Censors banned certain movies outright and reduced many more to splicy truncated travesties before gracing them with that all-important 'X' (a symbol now more redolent of a pair of scissors than a hallmark of the forbidden). But as the decade turned, for a brief, glorious period – no longer than four or five years – everything changed. A revolution swept through our high streets, all over the country: video stores, packed to the ceiling with films over which the censor had no jurisdiction. It was bliss.

Horror films enjoyed an immediate prominence in these stores (the 'return of the repressed' theory vindicated) The shelves were full of low-budget, splashily packaged horror items. Some films that had been cut in British cinemas were now available in their brazen entirety. Legendary shockers whose visibility had been limited to a few festival screenings were prominently displayed, and whole national cinematic identities were there to be mapped thanks to a surge of hitherto unsuspected foreign works. The popular cinema of America, Spain and Italy accounted for most of the new material, although films made in France, Greece, Switzerland, Sweden, Indonesia, Japan, Hong-Kong, The Philippines and Mexico turned up too. Suddenly there were five video stores in Wakefield's town centre alone ('mom and pop' stores, to use the American term for small privately owned shops, and much the better for it). Most of these were eventually squeezed out of the market by giant American-owned chains like Blockbuster Video but for a while the film industry felt wonderfully open and pluralistic.

This explosion of gruesomeness, in a plethora of weird styles, was a welcome shock to my system. I would watch three or four films in a night with friends at their VCR-equipped houses, before grabbing an hour or two's sleep. A line of speed, off to work, then out in the late afternoon to catch whatever horror movie was unspooling at the cinema. It was an exciting time to be a fan.

I was seeing a lot of films, but that Italian double bill was a pivotal experience for me. Something I hadn't yet the vocabulary or the background reading to define was apparently linking the films: not merely their presence on a bill together, more like some shared, arcane aspect of their style. But what was it? I hadn't led the traditional cinephile's home life. My parents hated films, or indeed anything which required sustained concentration. TV was 'rationed', (there for brief bursts of light entertainment); anything which smacked of darkness, created palpable tension, or induced an air of contemplation was scorned and switched off. Nonetheless, I had enough sense of the prevailing cultural norms to find these two Italian films immediately wild and disorientating. Was it the music? The wonderful soundtracks to *The Beyond* and *Shock* made a major impression on me. Was it the lavish photography... or the way in which mundane events were transformed into the macabre by the camera's dwelling attention? Or was it this – that the extraordinary violence and gruesomeness on show took such a cavalier attitude to plausibility and taste that one sensed *anything* could happen? I came to feel that all these things and more make the films of Lucio Fulci special and exciting. His best work offers the viewer strange, exotic pleasures that are available nowhere else. Lucio Fulci became a key name in my personal pantheon of greats. I hope that this book will communicate that initial excitement, as well as drawing upon the more considered evaluation I've tried to develop in the years since my first contact with Italy's most outrageous and controversial director!

Stephen Thrower, Spring 1999

below:
Two Italian movie maestros together. Lucio Fulci (left) with Mario Bava.

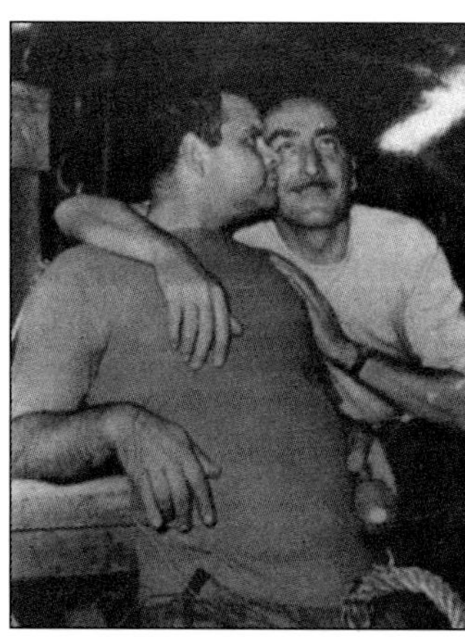

That's where I signed off, back in 1999, and it seemed a decent conclusion. But there's another story: a tale I didn't tell, a door I didn't open. So come with me, if you will, through this cracked and gaping tombstone, down this narrow staircase twisting in the dark, to a cellar, and a table, and a book I've left for you to read...

"I wanted to spare you,
but now I'll have to tell you everything"
Emily

It can be nerve-wracking to meet a filmmaker whose work you adore, even more so when you're planning to write a book about him. Unfortunately, in the case of my meeting with Lucio Fulci, 'nerve-wracking' doesn't really cover it. In fact the experience so badly disappointed me that it almost derailed the book altogether. My original intention had been to base the endeavour around a detailed account of the director's views and recollections, as much a biographical work as a study of the films themselves. Regrettably, what transpired made this impossible, and I lost heart for a while before resuming the project from a different standpoint.

I finished *Beyond Terror* in 1999 and decided not to describe my encounter with Fulci; it seemed too negative. But things have moved on, tales of Fulci's volatile temperament are well known, and *Beyond Terror* has had plenty of time to assert itself on its own terms. It can do no harm to Lucio to relate the story now; if accounts of his unreasonable behaviour could derail his credibility it would have happened long ago. Nor can it harm the book, which was well received on first publication despite the drastic change of direction I was forced to take. I've decided to include it here because I think it has some anecdotal value, if only as a rather forlorn comedy of trashed expectations. So here it is, my sorry tale. Keep your hankies ready...

I first met Lucio Fulci on Sunday 11th December 1994 at the Everyman Cinema, London. The occasion was Eurofest, a weekend film festival in Fulci's honour organised by Trevor Barley and Paul Brown. The great man's dangerous reputation preceded him – temperamental, impatient, ill-humoured – and I was braced to encounter him on these difficult terms. According to Barley, this aspect of Fulci was indeed apparent, as the honoured guest grumbled and griped his way through the amenities and arrangements, none of which he seemed to find satisfactory. Nevertheless, by the time I was introduced to this Italian 'mostro' on the second afternoon of his visit, he seemed positively mellow. Sitting in the Everyman bar, surrounded by admirers bearing trophies from their film collections, he was in high spirits. He sipped mineral water, marker pen in hand, and beamed at all comers, quite at home with the ardent attention.

It was this jocular, twinkly-eyed version of Fulci who agreed to be interviewed at length for my book. His early return to Italy the following day made such an interview impractical at the time, so we exchanged telephone numbers and made tentative arrangements for the following year. I suggested visiting him at his home in Italy, for a detailed discussion that would range through the length and breadth of his career, and to my delight he said yes. In the summer we spoke on the phone and set a date for my visit to Rome. I would fly out on the 30th of July, meet Fulci on the 31st and spend two days in discussion with him, then return home on the 2nd of August.

The trip excited my imagination. There's a magic and romance to the city of Rome, and here I was, paying my first visit, on a mission to interview the director of some of the greatest horror films ever made. Journalistic ennui be damned, this was going to be a thrill. Fulci even suggested to me on the phone that we could discuss his work during a walk around Lake Bracciano, the chief beauty spot in his home town. I dallied with this lovely image for days afterwards. Could the prospect be any more enticing? I decided that Lucio Fulci's reputation for hostility was either undeserved or needed reassessing. Arriving in Rome late Sunday evening, I felt a pleasurable anticipation that even an astonishingly humid heat-wave, broiling the city at the blistering height of summer, couldn't spoil. As arranged, I telephoned Fulci the following day, around noon, at which point (cue downward-sliding violins) everything changed:

"Who? Who? Oh... yes. Yes, well, no, I don't know. No, I don't want to talk... no, not this week. I talk to RAI TV at the weekend, and I'm tired... I already talk about my films to RAI. No, it is not a good time..."

Would tomorrow be better? *"No! I told you, I already talk about my films to RAI..."*

You can imagine my mood, jammed into a telephone booth on the plaza of an infernally hot rail terminus, listening to an obdurate, cantankerous Fulci giving me the bum's rush back to Blighty, with no interview and minus the price of an airline ticket. I reminded him that I was booked to return to London just two days later. As I tried to remain calm while protesting that now was hardly the fairest time to have a change of mind, Fulci's tone became more resentful and he slid increasingly into rapid Italian. Then he hung up.

Oh dear. Bucolic images of a stroll beside Lake Bracciano discussing flesh-eating zombies and *Beatrice Cenci* curled up and burned in my mind like celluloid in a faulty projector. Our rendezvous had been set up weeks in advance but my 'host' was pulling the plug with not even an apology, just resentment at my shocked objections. I stewed on the situation for twenty minutes, then called him again. I asked him to reconsider, and pressed home the fact that the trip had cost me personally. I allowed myself to sound aggrieved. At last a grudging and less than cordial invitation was extended, providing the business could be wrapped up quickly. I accepted, despite realising that the brief interview now on offer could just as easily have taken place at the Everyman Cinema the previous December. With a heavy heart I set off for Bracciano, a distance of some fifty or so miles.

Having rushed into agreeing a time, I discovered that one train had just left and the next required a dash from one railway station to another. After a fraught journey across Rome on a packed, sauna-like underground train, and a slow journey over land through countryside that events had turned sour to my eyes, I finally arrived in Bracciano an hour later than agreed. With Fulci in the mood he was in, I had a foreboding sense that this delay would cause further antagonism. Sure enough, calling from the village station for the directions he couldn't be bothered to give me back in Rome, I encountered the legendary rage of the man in full flight. To say that Fulci was screaming at me down the phone may create an undignified impression, but it's not far from the truth. No, I could *not* have the interview. Where had I been? How dare I hold up his plans? Once again I found myself having to argue, this time more strenuously, for an interview of any sort. Relenting at last, he told me the address and insisted I hurry up so the whole odious business could be terminated as soon as possible. I arrived exhausted, dripping with sweat, beneath a crushing weight of disappointment and suppressed anger.

The interview was mediated by Antonella Fulci who translated where necessary. It seems to me she must have soothed her father's temper because when we finally spoke in person he was quieter and less aggressive. As it was, I did not conduct a very structured or coherent interview. I was too hot, too distressed, too disappointed, and I struggled, practically speaking, to condense my extensive notes down to fit the conversation. I now wish I'd opted to talk about just two or three films; instead we wandered around his filmography impulsively. We spoke for longer than an hour, maybe two. As I left, Antonella explained that her father had been unwell recently. She also told me he'd been surprised that I asked about his early work when most people only wanted to talk about zombies. Bitterly, I remembered my plans for a career-long discussion. I rang the following day to see if there was a chance of returning: Antonella was sympathetic, but there was to be no second interview.

Looking back, it's clear that Fulci's poor health was indeed a factor in his behaviour that day. And reaching further back, to the testimony of various actors over the years, it's also clear that even in good health there was no guarantee that Fulci would not take against you and give you hell. I suspect he forgot that I was even coming, and when faced with his lapse of memory, lashed out at me. I speak from experience: my own memory fails me more often than I like to admit, and I've lashed out too rather than take the embarrassment on the chin. Loss of memory entails loss of pride, which isn't easy to accept.

Pride afflicted me too when I got back home. I spent many weeks unable to even look at the folder on my computer labelled 'Fulci'. All of this occurred in the days before e-mail (for most of us) and after a brief telephone conversation with Antonella I gave up on the idea of trying again. I now regret this. Fulci died just seven months later, felled by the diabetes which blighted his latter years. By the time I received the sad news, I'd parcelled away my experience in Italy and made serious inroads into the book you now hold. I'd written enough, in fact, to wish I could have started earlier, and shared some of the material with him.

The one thing that mattered to Lucio Fulci, it seems to me, more than anything else in his professional life, was respect. Money and success and international sales were very important, but it's respect I think he desired the most. And despite my unfortunate experience, I have enormous respect for Lucio Fulci: for his wild creativity, his canny intelligence, his inventiveness, his passion, his perseverance, and his wit. When I think of the sweep of that extraordinary career I feel enormous admiration, and I hope that it shines through in these pages. This book is for you, Lucio; it was always for you. Speaking as an atheist with a love of the fantastic, I hope that you find a copy one day as you browse through the libraries of the Beyond...

In Braille, naturally.

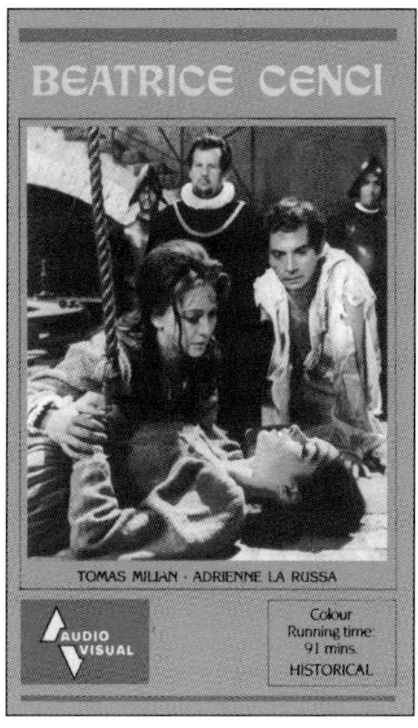

above:
Rare UK pre-cert video cover for Fulci's *Beatrice Cenci*, one of only two titles issued on the obscure Audio Visual label.

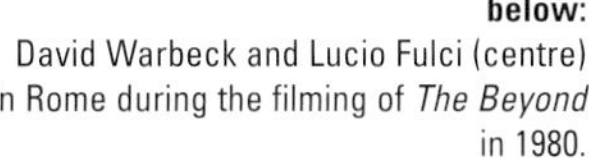

below:
David Warbeck and Lucio Fulci (centre) in Rome during the filming of *The Beyond* in 1980.

chapter one

Introduction to the films of Lucio Fulci

For lovers of the grisly and macabre, 'Lucio Fulci' will always be a name to savour. His death in 1996, after a long struggle with diabetes, was a sad loss for the horror genre, and marked the end of an era for Italian exploitation cinema.

Although Fulci's death was duly noted by the major Italian dailies, the film industry paid scant regard to the loss of one of its most colourful and notorious figures, a fact which came as no surprise to his admirers. No matter how revered he may be in horror fandom, in the wider culture Fulci will probably always remain deliciously disreputable. His best known films indulge bloodthirsty audiences to the hilt with their gruesome excesses, and his deliberately goading approach ("Violence *is* Italian art!") makes him an uncomfortable fit for mainstream acceptance. To some, for whom the horror film can never be too timid, he was a reprehensible panderer, offering his sick-minded audience nothing but blood and guts. To others, he was a bold and anarchic horror specialist, willing to go ever further in search of the ultimate set-piece.

Lucio Fulci was an art critic and medical student before entering Italy's prestigious film school, the Centro Sperimentale di Cinematografica, after the Second World War. This was a fertile period for the institution, as both Michelangelo Antonioni and Luchino Visconti were teaching there. Obtaining a diploma, he entered the movie business in 1948 as assistant second unit director on a version of *The Last Days of Pompeii* by Marcel L'Herbier; a much re-made story dating back to the earliest days of Italian cinema. This led to frequent assignments as assistant director and co-scriptwriter on a slew of films in the comic genre and a stint as editor of the film journal *La Settimana Incom*. The majority of his script work was for Totò, a leading light of Italy's comedy cinema who would star in Fulci's directing debut, *I ladri*.

Fulci began his directing career with a stream of light-hearted comedies for the home market. Some of these (*I ragazzi del juke box*, 1959; *Urlatori alla sbarra*, 1960; *Uno strano tipo*, 1963) tapped into the emerging rock'n'roll scene, connecting with young audiences and bringing Fulci his earliest commercial successes. Between 1962 and 1967 he specialised in farcical comedy, directing nine films starring the hugely popular Sicilian comedy duo Franco [Franchi] & Ciccio [Ingrassia] and featuring them as guests in four more.

At the end of the sixties, Fulci turned to the darker environs of the murder mystery, or giallo, and enjoyed his first sustained period of artistic achievement. His marvellous thrillers *Una sull'altra / One on Top of the Other* (1969), *Una lucertola con la pelle di donna / A Lizard in a Woman's Skin* (1971), *Non si sevizia un paperino / Don't Torture a Duckling* (1972) and *Sette note in nero / The Psychic* (1977) are widely regarded today as some of the finest in the genre. Goodness knows how many giallo films were made in Italy in the 1970s, but Fulci's stylish and brooding works stand head and shoulders above the crowd, on a par with the thrillers of Dario Argento.

One on Top of the Other offered suspense, sexiness and languid melancholy, but Fulci's subsequent gialli also featured a more notorious flourish of his fiery temperament – a fascination with brutality. Sex and violence were chillingly combined in his second thriller *A Lizard in a Woman's Skin*, conveyed with a dreamy surrealism that showed a more daring cinematic persona. His next thriller was a masterpiece: *Don't Torture a Duckling* demonstrated Fulci's increasingly ferocious attitude toward the Catholic Church, through a tale of serial child murders, rural black magic and hypocrisy. Most memorably, he filmed a protracted chain-whipping that would set the seal on his shocking approach to violence in the years to come.

Like most commercial Italian directors, Fulci's output varied from genre to genre. He tried his hand at westerns (*Le colt cantarono la morte e fu tempo di massacro / Massacre Time*, 1966; *I quattro dell'apocalisse / The Four of the Apocalypse*, 1975; *Sella d'argento / Silver Saddle*, 1978), children's adventures (*Zanna Bianca / White Fang*, 1973; *Il ritorno di Zanna Bianca / Challenge to White Fang*, 1974), period costume drama (*Beatrice Cenci*, 1969), sword and scorcery fantasy (*Conquest*, 1983), dystopian sci-fi (*I guerrieri dell'anno 2072 / Rome 2033 – The Fighter Centurions*, 1984) and crime thrillers (*Luca il contrabbandiere / The Smuggler*, 1980). However, he eventually found himself identified with a single genre – horror. Throughout a career spanning five decades, he worked in a remarkable variety of styles, but it was the shameless grandstanding of viscera, maggots and mutilation in the classic *Zombi 2 / Zombie Flesh-Eaters* (1979) that guaranteed him lasting recognition.

Of all the scenes that Lucio Fulci directed, perhaps the central image he's remembered for is the scene in *Zombie Flesh-Eaters* in which a long wooden splinter pierces the wide-open eye of a terrified woman. As a zombie drags this victim by the hair through a smashed doorframe, to her date with cinema destiny, the audience is confronted with one of the most shocking images in horror. Fulci's other films are packed with scenes at least as impressive as this, but, questions of authorship aside, it's perhaps the ultimate tribute that this scene should have stuck in the mind's eyes of so many people.

Made in 1979 when Fulci was fifty-one, *Zombie Flesh-Eaters* was a huge international success, and a tonic to the middle-aged director. Brazenly pursuing his flair for explicit violence he entered a period of feverish inspiration. These were the golden years for Lucio Fulci, in which he thrilled devotees of the horror genre by embarking on a series of outlandish journeys into metaphysical madness and grotesque physical repulsion. *Paura nella città dei morti viventi / City of the Living Dead* (1980), *Black Cat / The Black Cat* (1981), *L'aldilà / The Beyond* (1981) and *Quella villa accanto al cimitero / The House by the Cemetery*

facing page:
Lucio Fulci on location in Louisiana for *The Beyond*.

below:
A portrait of Lucio Fulci age 20.

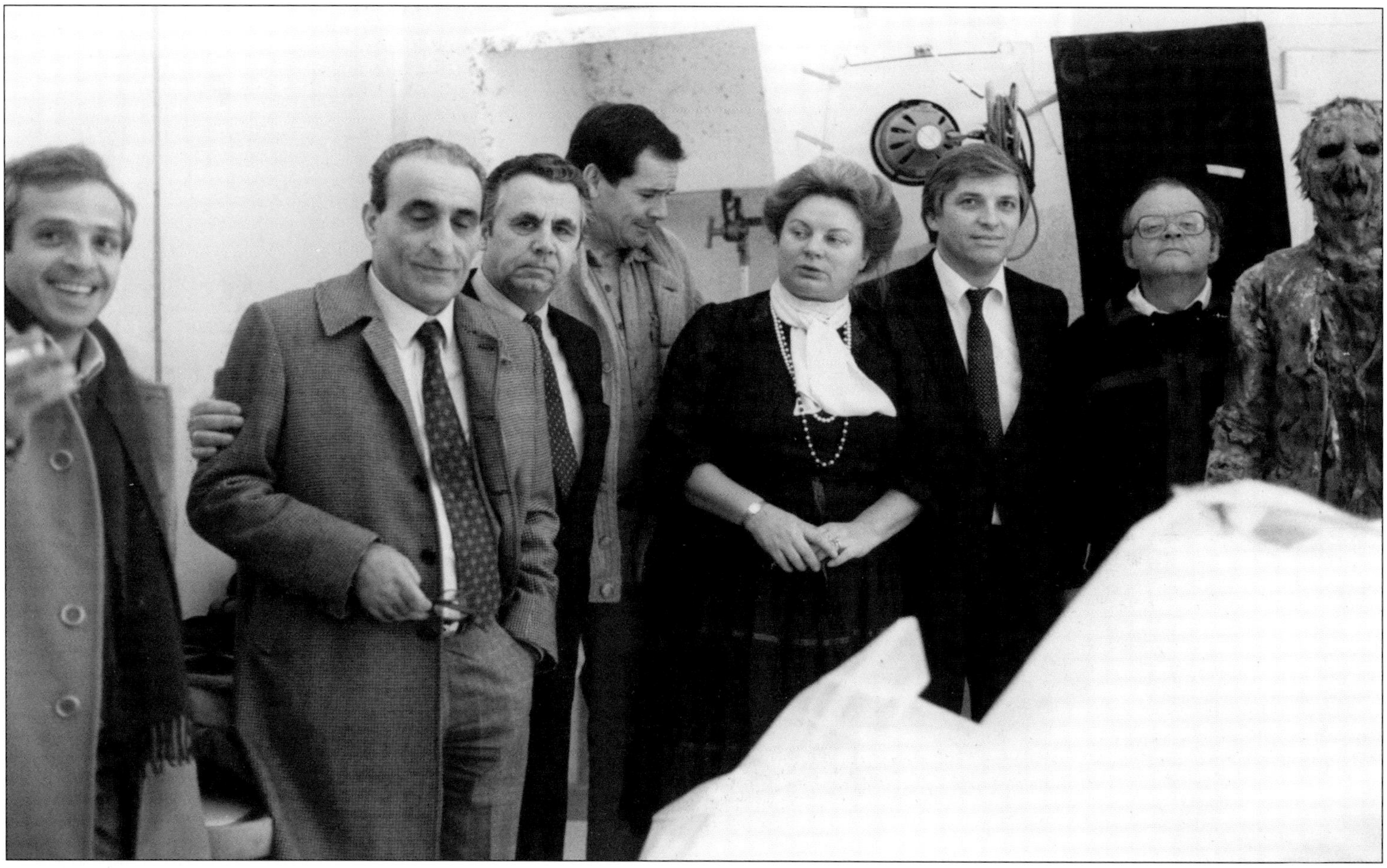

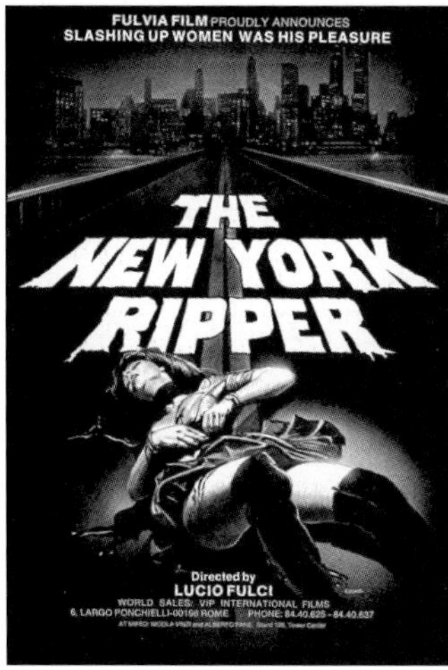

top:
Fulci (far right) on the set of *The Beyond*, with David Warbeck (behind) and Fabrizio De Angelis (far left).

above and right:
Controversy on the way... Fulci's later career would be characterised by debates around screen violence, particularly with regard to *The New York Ripper*, which was marketed to generate maximum shock value, as amply demonstrated by the full page ad placed by Fulvia Film in the Wednesday, October 14, 1981 edition of *Variety*.

(1981) are among the very best that Italian horror has to offer. Supernatural themes and weird logic collide with flesh-ripping gore to breathtaking effect. Bleak and brutal horrors are transformed into bloody poetry. Bodily disintegration, outlandish attacks on the integrity of the human face, the morbid menacing of child characters – all this could have been unbearably grim. And yet the whispers of a strange sadness, captured through loving camera technique and a decayed mottled splendor in the art design, designate these films as more than just an endurance test. Fulci became notorious for bloodshed, but he also achieved subtler effects. A melancholy lyricism in the face of mounting dread characterises these marvellous Gothic horrors. Their success helped trigger a rash of similarly violent Italian horror movies, ranging from the absurd and trashy to the harshly sadistic. It seemed that every commercial director in Rome wanted a bit of the action; few besides Fulci, though, would imbue their sordid visions with the same feel for elegance amid the offal.

Fulci's star was in the ascendant in the early 1980s, and many of the films from this period have attracted lasting admiration. Ever the iconoclast, though, he returned to the giallo format in 1982 with a film so brutal that it alienated even some of the hard-core horror audience. *Lo squartatore di New York/The New York Ripper* (1982) was a gruelling, downbeat and hideously violent affair, made all the more disturbing by its refusal of fantastic or supernatural elements. The story of a razor-slashing maniac carving his way through sexually active young women in a grimy urban setting, it generated a few positive notices, and brisk business in Italy and the United States. But it also made Fulci a target for an unsavoury alliance of censors and feminists, who were unwilling to tolerate the film's violence and unable to credit its ironies. Whether he'd intended to or not, Fulci marked himself out as dangerous. He was portrayed as a misogynous panderer to the lowest of audience desires. The film, a bitter trawl through depravity and hypocrisy, is actually very clever in its manipulation of our responses; our urge to judge it as reprehensible is constantly being problematised. For many, though, no amount of irony or rhetorical gamesmanship could make up for the lingering mutilation of women it depicted. Fulci's horror thriller, intended mainly to jangle the nerves of jaded horror consumers, ended up arousing their moral indignation, not to mention the outright hostility of the censors.

After this scandalous high-water mark, Fulci's sensibility began to falter. Films like *Murderock uccide a passo di danza/Murder-Rock Dancing Death* (1984) and *Ænigma* (1987) were failed stabs at making entertainments that fitted in with the new criteria for horror in the 1980s. The master of morbidity's strongest suits – illogical dread, downbeat moods and gruesome graphic violence – were becoming less popular with audiences who were retreating from the confrontational. Horror films in the mid-to-late 1980s were more concerned with cartoonish 'kick-ass' *resistance* to fear. Fulci was left high and dry, trying to match the dwindling guts and shrinking nerve of the eighties horror film.

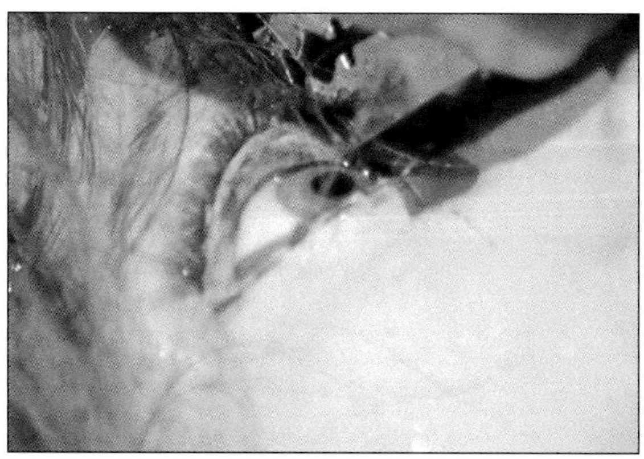

Health problems began to take a toll on Fulci during this period. Viral hepatitis struck the embattled director after completion of *Murder-Rock Dancing Death*; as the condition worsened into cirrhosis, rumours abounded that he was near death. In fact he fought back, recovering sufficiently to direct *Il miele del diavolo/The Devil's Honey* (1986), a steamy erotic drama á là *9½ Weeks* that showed he could still respond to current commercial trends outside the horror genre.

Then came a disappointment on a grand scale. *Zombi 3* (1988), a supposed sequel to *Zombie Flesh-Eaters*, emerged as a charmless chaotic mess, completely devoid of the director's previous merits. Different accounts have been given for this failure, but what's certain is that Fulci did not finish the film. After shooting on location in the Philippines, he was either released from the project or taken ill, with work completed by producer Claudio Fragasso and Grade Z exploitation director Bruno Mattei. Were it not for commercial expediency, Fulci would probably have taken his name off the project.

The *Zombi 3* debacle didn't prevent Fulci from giving his by then dubious commercial blessing to films by other directors; a slate of quickie low-budget Italian horrors shot in 1988 and 1989 were released on video with an ad-line proclaiming 'Lucio Fulci presents...' In most cases Fulci had little or nothing to do with the making of these films, although he did step in to co-direct *Hansel e Gretel* (1988) when credited helmer Giovanni Simonelli proved incapable of finishing. As part of the same production deal Fulci also delivered two new films as director: *Quando Alice ruppe lo specchio/Touch of Death* and *Sodoma's Ghost/The Ghosts of Sodom* (1988).

With the Italian exploitation film industry shrivelling away in the late 1980s, Fulci turned briefly to television. The success of Lamberto Bava's *Brivido Giallo* series for Silvio Berlusconi's Reteitalia TV company led to the commissioning of a four-part film series called *Houses of Doom*, comprising two Lucio Fulci projects – *La dolce casa degli orrori/The Sweet House of Horrors* (1989), and *La casa nel tempo/The House of Clocks* (1989) – plus two films by exploitation stalwart Umberto Lenzi. Sadly, although the films were completed, they were deemed unsuitable for transmission. Bloodied but unbowed, Fulci pressed on, obtaining finance for a supernatural horror film about evil nuns, *Demonia* (1990), before creating *Un gatto nel cervello (I volti del terrore)/Nightmare Concert* (1990), the weirdest film of his later years. A kind of 'greatest hits' hotch-potch of his recent work, concocted in a hurry to avoid a lawsuit from a previous producer, it took the form of a self-portrait, with Fulci playing himself, a director plagued by grisly visions of horror and mutilation. It was his last film to receive an Italian cinema release.

Fulci's output between 1988 and 1991 saw little or no release abroad. Tiredness, cynicism and sheer lack of inspiration dogged his efforts, and even the terribly low budgets can't take all the blame. Fulci was by now churning out horror films because he had to: a director capable of many different shades of creativity had become typecast as a 'goremonger' at a time when the Italian film industry had virtually given up on horror. There was an eleventh hour glitch in Fulci's downward spiral – the reasonably professional *Voci dal profondo/Voices from Beyond* in 1991 – but the weak and overpadded ghost story *Le porte del silenzio/Door to Silence* (also 1991) proved to be his last film.

Following *Door to Silence*, Fulci entered a final period of decline. Sadly, his death in 1996 came after a painstaking three year period trying to get a new project off the ground. Plans were afoot for him to collaborate with Dario Argento on a lavish re-make of André De Toth's 1953 film *House of Wax*, itself a re-make of the earlier *Mystery of the Wax Museum* (1933). But it was not to be. Fulci died while still waiting for production to begin. The film eventually appeared in 1997 as *M.D.C. Maschera di cera/The Wax Mask*, directed by Argento's special fx maestro Sergio Stivaletti, from a Daniele Stroppa script which bore little relation to Fulci's own. Fate was merciless, robbing Lucio Fulci of the opportunity to mount a final prestige production. He died at the age of 68, frustrated and undervalued in the industry to which he'd given his life-time's endeavour.

R.I.P. Lucio Fulci

Born in Rome, 17th June 1927
Died in Rome, 13th March 1996

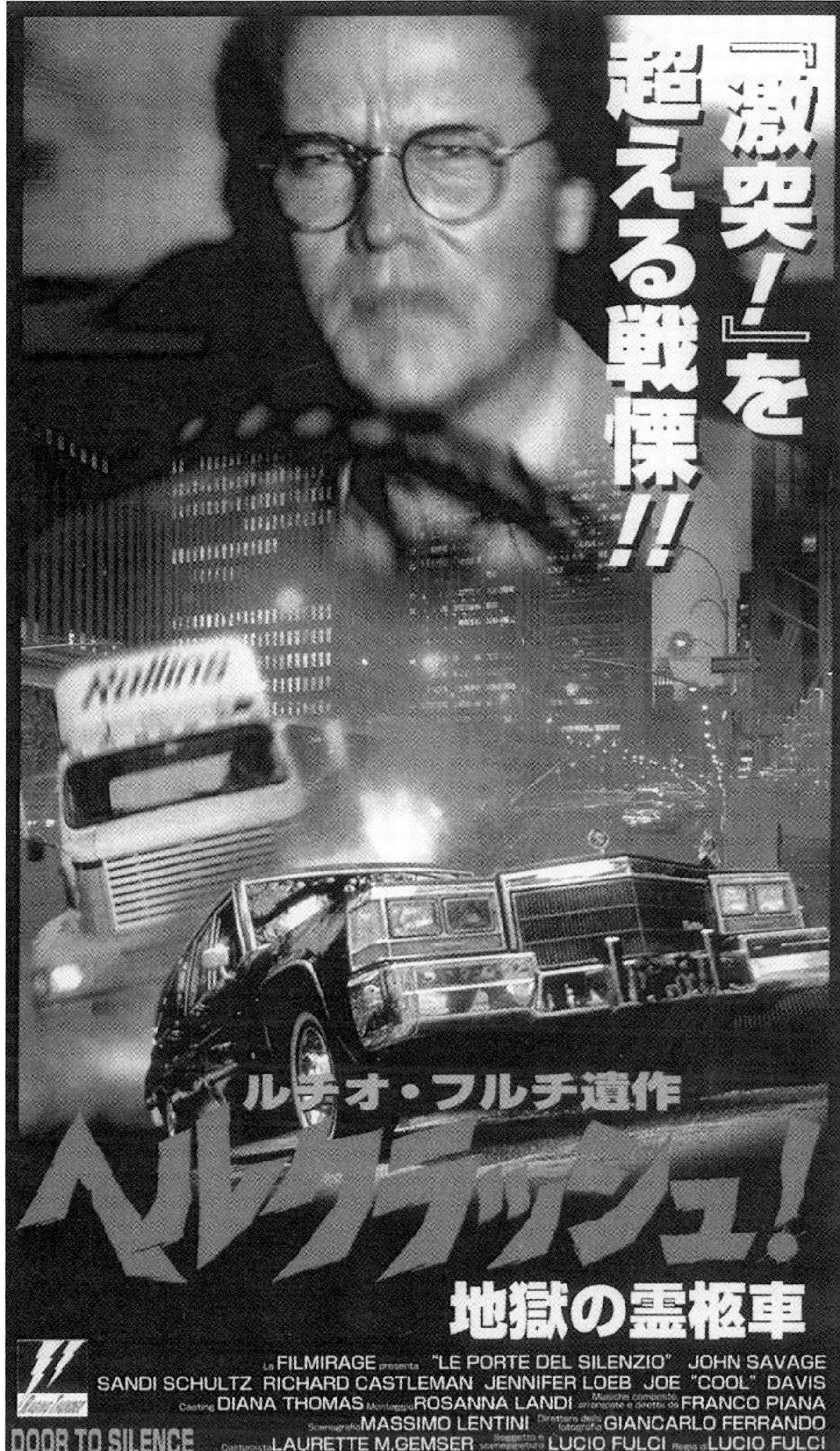

above:
Japanese video cover artwork for *Door to Silence*, Fulci's poorly received final film.

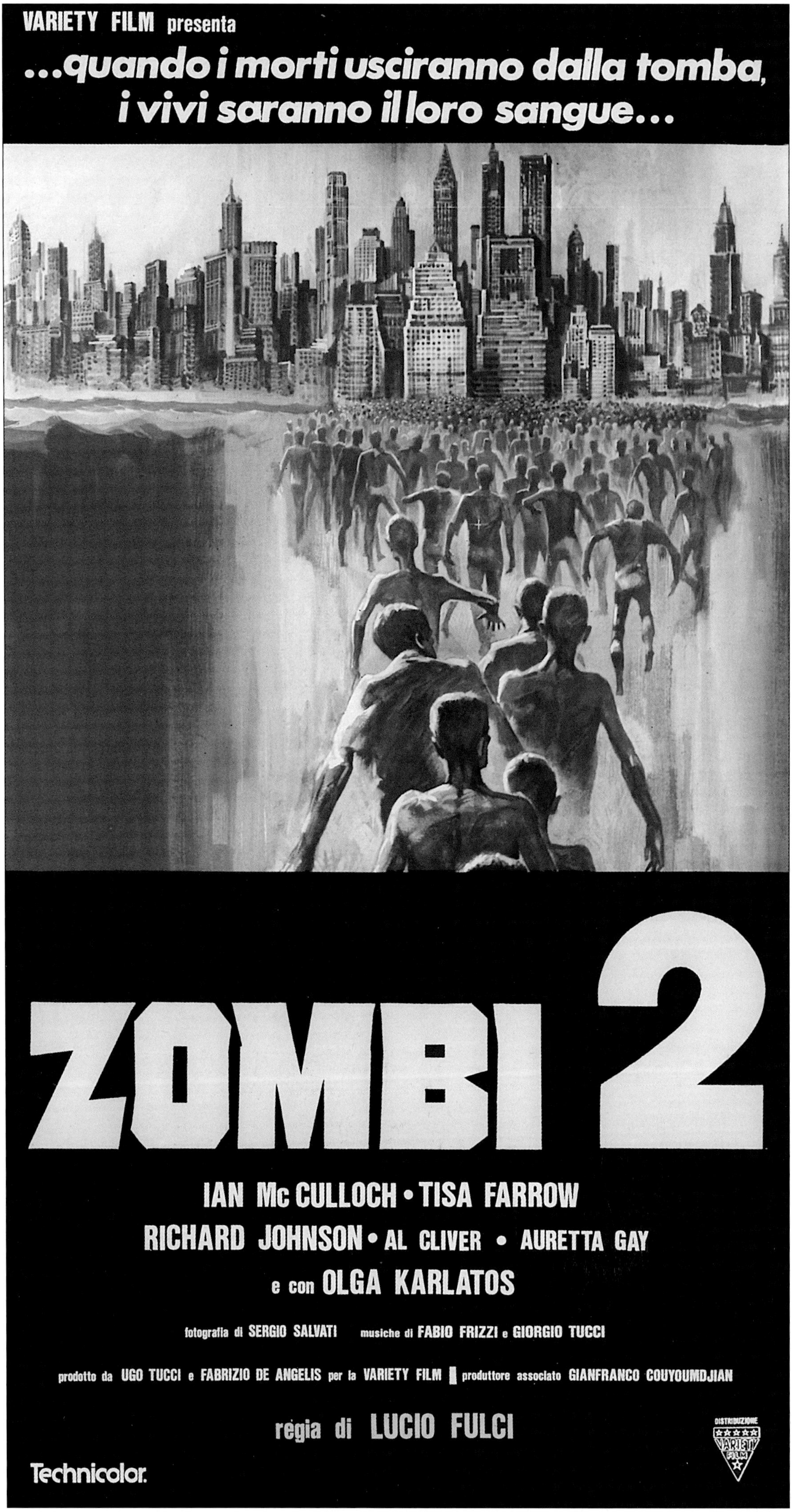

VARIETY FILM presenta

...quando i morti usciranno dalla tomba, i vivi saranno il loro sangue...

ZOMBI 2

IAN Mc CULLOCH • TISA FARROW

RICHARD JOHNSON • AL CLIVER • AURETTA GAY

e con **OLGA KARLATOS**

fotografia di SERGIO SALVATI musiche di FABIO FRIZZI e GIORGIO TUCCI

prodotto da UGO TUCCI e FABRIZIO DE ANGELIS per la VARIETY FILM | produttore associato GIANFRANCO COUYOUMDJIAN

regia di **LUCIO FULCI**

Technicolor.

chapter two

Zombie!

featuring:

Zombie Flesh-Eaters aka *Zombi 2* (1979)

1979 was a revitalising year for Italian horror, and Lucio Fulci was the director most responsible. Yet on the face of it, his commercial smash hit *Zombi 2* (aka *Zombie Flesh-Eaters*) had all the hallmarks of a quickie rip-off. It was bankrolled by producers Fabrizio De Angelis and Ugo Tucci to cash in, quite blatantly, on George A. Romero's *Dawn of the Dead*, which came out in Rome during September 1978 as *Zombi*. Romero's grisly horror masterpiece went through the roof in Italy, earning $1million in its first six weeks, which gave De Angelis the 'inspiration' to finance something along similar lines. But whom should he invite to direct?

Just prior to *Zombi 2*, De Angelis had been working with sexploitation director Joe D'Amato, on the lurid sex-and-horror flick *Emanuelle and the Last Cannibals* (1977) and the straightforward sex opus *Emanuelle and the White Slave Trade* (1978). However, D'Amato and De Angelis parted company after these pictures, leaving De Angelis in search of a new slate of projects. (Later De Angelis wound up directing exploitation flicks himself, including *Deadly Impact* in 1984 and *Cobra Mission* in 1986).

To stand a chance of matching the success of the Romero film, De Angelis needed a seasoned professional at the wheel. His first choice was action helmer Enzo G. Castellari, director of *The Heroin Busters* (1977) and *The Inglorious Bastards* (1978), but when Castellari declared no interest in making horror pictures De Angelis drafted in Lucio Fulci, on the basis of two of his thrillers, *Don't Torture a Duckling* (1972) and *The Psychic* (1977), both of which featured graphic, high-impact violence.

The Psychic was written by Dardano Sacchetti, from whom De Angelis had recently bought a script called "Nightmare Island". This became *Zombie Flesh-Eaters* (although the screen credit went to Sacchetti's wife Elisa Briganti).[1] Re-teaming the writer and director of *The Psychic* proved a canny decision by De Angelis, as the next few years would prove...

Flagrant imitation of American hit movies was a long-standing characteristic of Italian popular cinema, and yet it's wrong to paint the relationship as purely parasitical. The commercial impetus may have been to copy, but once the money was in place there was room for maverick creativity and imagination. What's more, detractors of so-called 'spaghetti horror' often neglect to mention that the process was one of cultural cross-pollination, a two-way street. Throughout the sixties and seventies there were numerous occasions when commercial ideas were exchanged, on a more or less visible level, between the two countries' cinematic cultures.[2] While the commercialism of the Italian industry often propelled 'hired gun' directors into projects designed to exploit American box-office trends, the results often displayed a divergent, even ironic character. National variations in moral attitudes, and different cultural sensibilities, meant that what may have started out as a rip-off often emerged from the Italian studios bearing scant similarity – in either form or content – to the alleged model. The most celebrated example is the spaghetti western, a genre in which directors like Sergio Corbucci and Sergio Leone drew critical admiration for the way in which they tampered with the formula of a quintessentially American genre.

Fulci and Sacchetti took full advantage of the opportunity De Angelis offered to them, turning a projected rip-off into something more unusual. Sacchetti ingeniously set up the story as more of a prequel than a sequel to Romero's hit, and by choosing to depict the 'genesis of the living dead' the production displayed an amusing insouciance. *Zombie Flesh-Eaters* drew upon older horror imagery (from Hammer's 1966 *Plague of the Zombies* and the Val Lewton horrors of the 1940s), pointing to the redundancy of any simple notion of an 'original'. In addition, Fulci's zombies – far more revolting and putrescent than Romero's – exuded a foreboding reek of Death beyond the cerebral allegory of the American hit. Whether conceived as a 'rip-off' or not, the film turned out to have its own quite unique identity.

Zombie Rivalry

Dawn of the Dead had been bankrolled as an American/Italian co-production, with Romero's producer Richard Rubinstein forging a deal with Italian horror specialists Dario and Claudio Argento. *Dawn* hit Italian cinemas first, on 1 September 1978, but Rubinstein was unable to snare an American release until 20 April 1979, nearly eight months later. This was due to serious problems with the US ratings board, the MPAA, who indicated that there was no way *Dawn of the Dead* would secure an 'R' certificate without massive cuts. As a result, Romero's film had difficulty securing a Stateside distributor.

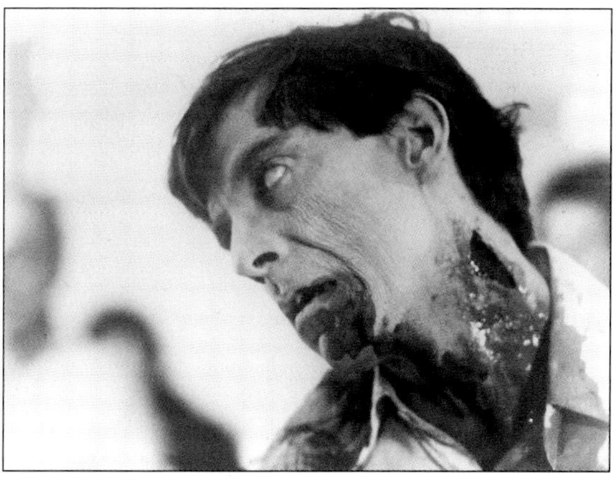

left:
David Emge as Steven the unfortunate helicopter pilot in George A. Romero's *Dawn of the Dead*.

above and below: *Zombie Flesh-Eaters*, German poster (*above*), and Dutch VHS cover (*below*).

right: UK poster for *Dawn of the Dead.*

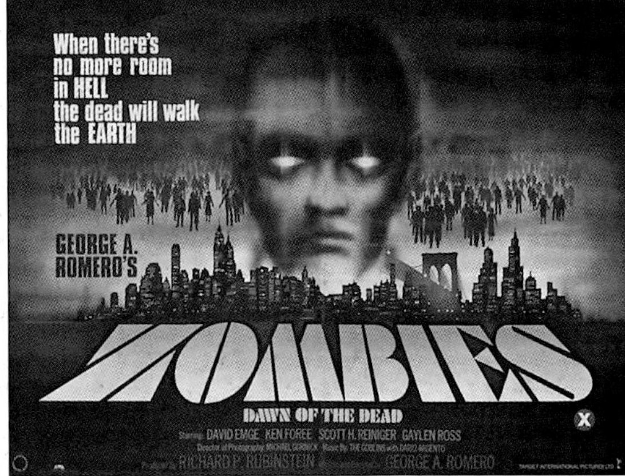

Warner Bros, for instance, had expressed interest in the film, but they needed an 'R' rating. They would risk neither an unrated release nor an 'X', the reason being that newspapers refused to run ads for 'X' films, which were inextricably associated with pornography. The MPAA had never bothered to copyright the 'X' symbol, and by the mid-seventies the tag had been owned by porno film producers, who ramped up the impact with unofficial extensions such as the 'Triple 'X" rating. Romero eventually opted to release *Dawn of the Dead* unrated, rather than cut it for an 'R', but he was taking a serious gamble: many newspapers refused to run ads for unrated films too.

Zombie Flesh-Eaters was shot in June and July of 1979, and then rushed into Italian cinemas by the end of August. The film did very well, thanks in part to its impertinent echo of the Romero film's title. In Italy, *Dawn of the Dead* was known as *Zombi*; thanks to a quirk of the Italian legal system Fulci's movie could be released there with the brazenly exploitative title *Zombi 2*. However, such flagrant implication of a direct link was only possible in the home market. Another strategy was required to sell the film in America. *"Dario Argento was the Italian producer of* Dawn of the Dead, *and neither Dario nor any of his people were involved in* Zombi 2. *If the American distributor claims otherwise, he's likely to find himself in a lawsuit"*, said Richard Rubinstein.[3] Ironically, the Romero film's American title allowed Fulci's opus to present itself there as *Zombie*. In July 1980, American exploitation entrepreneur Jerry Gross successfully released Fulci's zombie epic unrated, following the lead of George Romero's film. In a cat-and-mouse manoeuvre, Romero's film was re-titled *Zombies – Dawn of the Dead* in the UK, so the Fulci film had to be re-named again; this time as the less definitive, but more viscerally charged *Zombie Flesh-Eaters*.

Made for substantially less than $500,000, *Zombi 2* performed modestly in Italy in the summer of '79 but raked in more than $30 million worldwide, and it was this eye-popping payday that provided Italian horror with an essential booster shot of producer confidence.The result was a gory tidal wave of Italian horror epics. Despite the success of the film, however, Fulci and Dardano Sacchetti were apparently paid very little. What's more, Sacchetti stated that: *"Even after the success obtained by* Zombi 2, *neither Fulci nor I worked for a year... It's very difficult to work in the Italian cinema, especially if you do horror films... often you find yourself on the breadline"*.[4]

Amongst the Living

On the acting front, Fulci was well served by two British performers, Richard Johnson and Ian McCulloch. Johnson turned in a sweaty, shifty performance in a tantalising but underwritten role. (It can be a thankless task playing the male lead in a Fulci film). He began as a stage actor at 17, before his good looks ensured him leading man status in a string of movies (he was married for a short while to Hitchcock actress Kim Novak, glacial star of *Vertigo*). An early showing in Robert Wise's masterful *The Haunting* (1963) lent him genre credibility, as did his frequent forays into Italian horror for directors like Damiano Damiani (*The Witch*, 1966), Massimo Dallamano (*The Cursed Medallion*, 1975), and Sergio Martino (*Island of the Fishmen*, 1979 and *The Great Alligator*, 1979). His other genre work includes *Beyond the Door* (Ovidio Assonitis, 1974), *The Comeback* (Pete Walker, 1978) and *The Monster Club* (Roy Ward Baker, 1980). Johnson also turned his hand to film production, on *Turtle Diary* (John Irvin, 1985) and *Castaway* (Nicolas Roeg, 1986). The production honoured him with favoured billing in the credits for *Zombie Flesh-Eaters* – and reportedly Fulci was rather in awe of the man. The credit is well justified; Johnson serves the film with a sort of thumbnail sketch gravitas, a hard thing to pull off when the script is so simplistic.

McCulloch, a seasoned veteran of low-budget production, was given little in the way of scintillating dialogue to play with either, but scraped through with a likeable performance when even the unexplained ambiguities of Johnson's character were denied him.

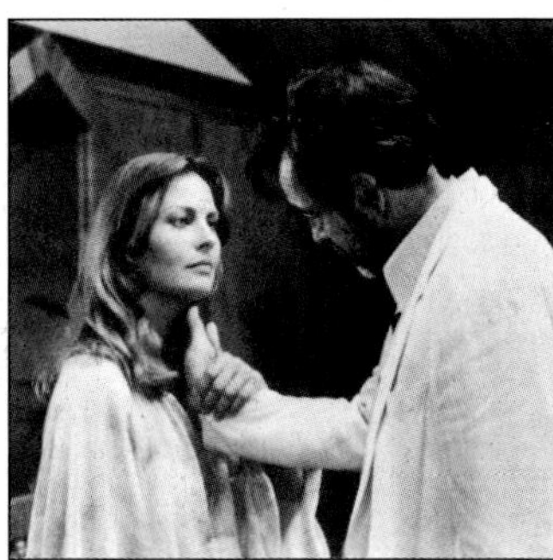

A Glaswegian, McCulloch was born in 1940. He trained at RADA, worked with the Royal Shakespeare Company and made his first horror film appearance in 1967; *It!* for Herbert J. Leder. That was indeed 'it' for McCulloch as far as the horror genre was concerned, until he accepted a role alongside John Hurt and Peter Cushing in Freddie Francis' *The Ghoul* (1974) for the Tyburn stable. Between the two films he'd gained a high profile role in the BBC's *Colditz* serial, and went on to further TV prominence as the star of Terry Nation's science fiction drama series, *Survivors*. He also contributed to the production of this landmark cult series, and even gained the uncommon leeway to write and direct his own death scene. His success with *Survivors* was instrumental in his casting for Fulci's living dead opus. Co-producer Ugo Tucci offered McCulloch the lead because of the success the series had enjoyed in Italy. Indeed, Tucci was the main co-ordinator as far as McCulloch was concerned. It was he who explained the rough outline of the story, apparently because of Fulci's limited ability to communicate in English.

McCulloch was subsequently roped into producer Fabrizio De Angelis' next project, then known as *Queen of the Cannibals* (released as *Zombie Holocaust* in the UK). This was written by De Angelis himself to cash in on his own success with Fulci's zombie film, and directed by venerable old-timer of Italian exploitation Marino Girolami. A final Italian assignment for McCulloch came with a leading role in Luigi Cozzi's daft but engaging sci-fi/horror effort, *Contamination* (1980). He is candid about the scant importance given to actors' performances in Italian exploitation: *"These films were almost in profit before a frame was shot. They were pre-sold all over the world on a title, storyboards, poster artwork, synopsis".*[5]

Fulci's lead actress was Tisa Farrow, sister of Mia. Unlike her famous sister, acting did not seem to agree with her, and although Fulci's zombie film made few demands on her abilities, she barely registered as a screen presence. After a role in Joe D'Amato's *Anthropophagous the Beast* in 1980, Farrow disappeared from view, with tales of her

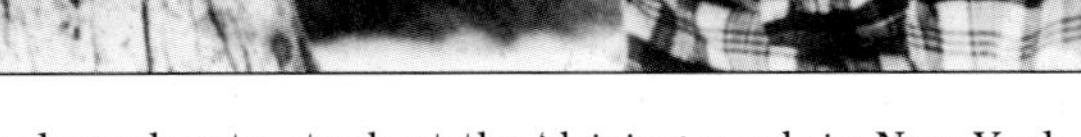

whereabouts stuck at the 'driving a cab in New York City' level of credibility.

Of the others to populate the island of Matul in Fulci's epic, perhaps the most unusual are the Romano kids, seven boys and a girl who performed as European circus acrobats before turning to film stunt-work. They donned torn, soily garments and submitted their faces to the attentions of make-up effects designer Giannetto De Rossi, emerging to play the horde of rotten-faced, tottering zombies.

above:
Olga Karlatos as Mrs. Menard.

top left:
Farrow and McCulloch in mid-flight.

below:
The poster artwork for *Zombie Flesh-Eaters* was re-used by Vipco for the film's successful UK video release.

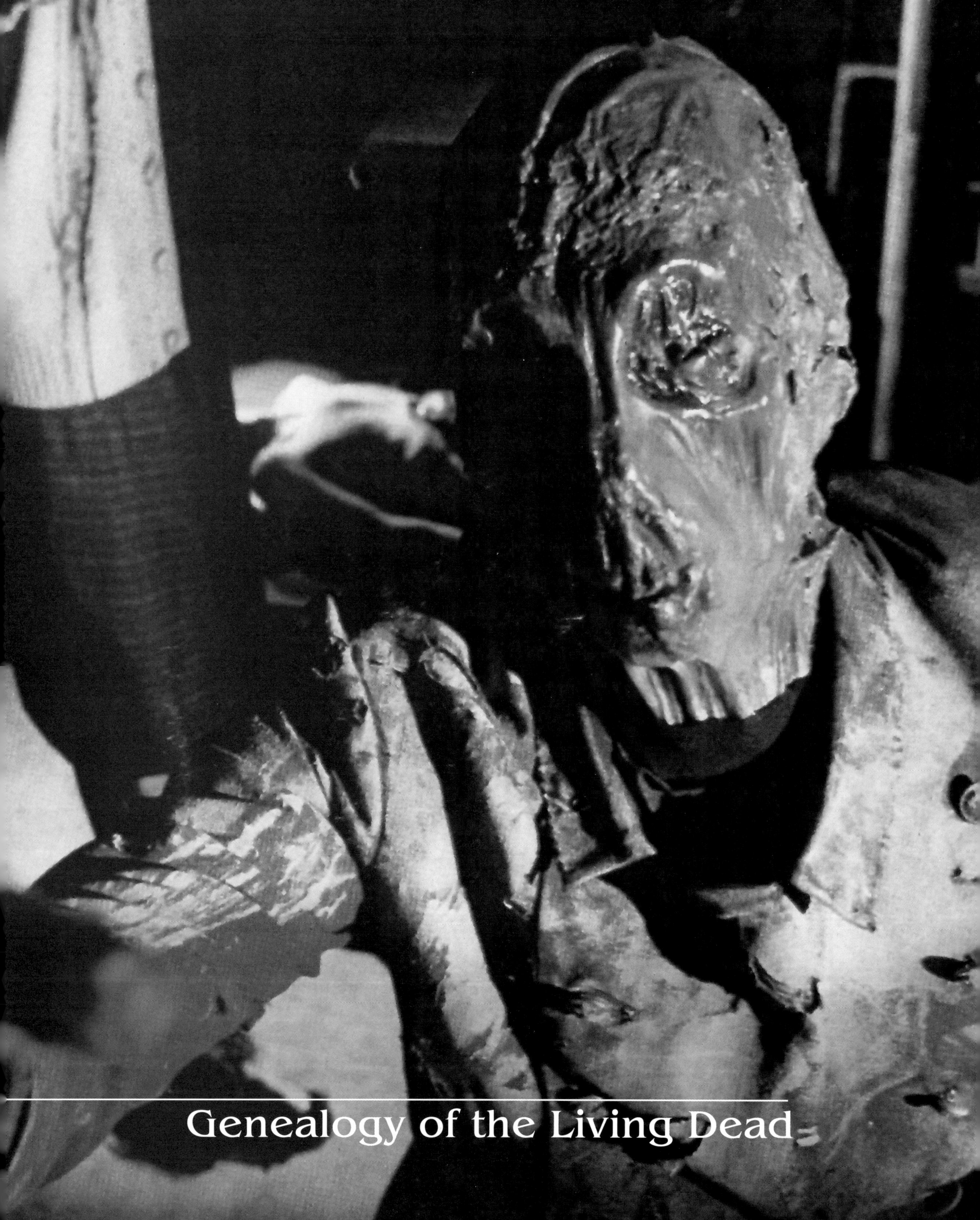

Genealogy of the Living Dead

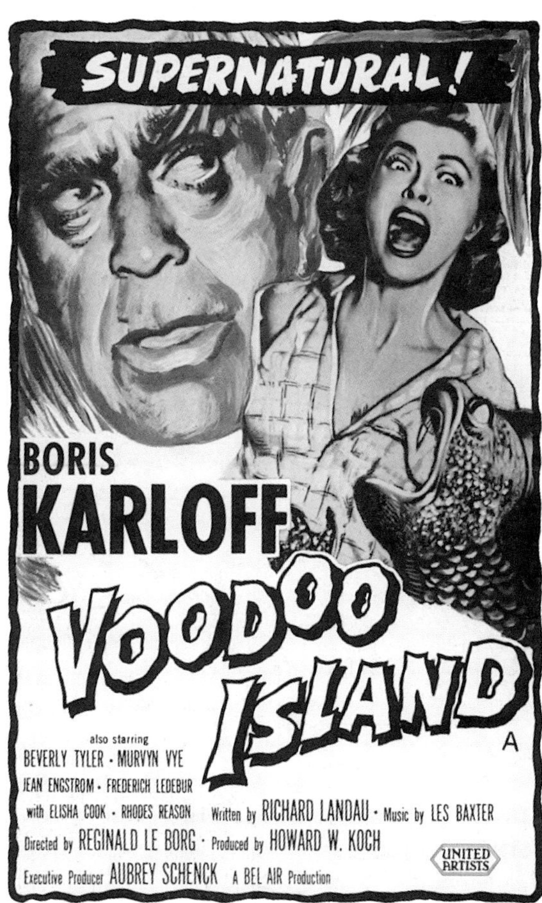

Zombie Flesh-Eaters owed its financial existence to the opportunism of its producer, but what of the subject matter? Romero is not the only source of imagery for Fulci's rendering of the zombie mythos, and it is worth looking back to see how the motifs he applies emerged through the horror films of previous generations.
In an interview with Jim Wynorski for *Fangoria* in 1980, Fulci said: *"I wanted to recapture the moody atmosphere of witchcraft and paganism that must have been prevalent when Europeans first settled in the Caribbean during the 1700s. That's when the concept of zombies – human slaves brought back from the dead – first became popularly known to western civilisation. I've always held great admiration for the marvellous horror classics made in America... Fright films such as* I Walked with a Zombie, Voodoo Island *and* The Walking Dead *were all in the back of my mind as I made this picture."*[6]

Unlike those other horror staples Dracula, Frankenstein and The Wolf-Man, the shambling ghoul or zombie has no original text to draw from. Literature was bereft of zombie tales until well after they appeared in the cinema.[7] Whilst the ghoul has affinities with the vampire, it has distinct differences too. The vampire creates a sort of perversely desirable elite status for his undead victims, as they join him in his moonlit limbo, but zombies reflect instead the fear of depersonalisation, alienation, physical decay. They are presented without even a whisper of eroticism. The only real link between the two is the way in which they pass on their condition through bites.

The Zombie first lurched into cinema's pantheon of horror in 1932, with the Bela Lugosi vehicle *White Zombie*, a film now regarded as something of a cult item, despite – if not because of – its cheapness and incoherence. It was directed by minor horror practitioner Victor Halperin, and starred Bela Lugosi as a voodoo master enslaving the Haitian dead, amidst a welter of Gothic surrealism. Halperin's film may have provided the genre with its first use of the word 'zombie', but these were not 'the living dead' as subsequent horror fans would come to know them – in *White Zombie*, the zombiefied slaves are actually Haitian islanders under a voodoo spell.

At the time, *White Zombie* was criticized for its poor acting and confused storyline, demonstrating, then as now, the commentators' preferences for conventional storytelling values. It's interesting to note just how swiftly the culture of cinema was being cut into rigid shapes for providing 'reliable' information in recognizable formats. Nonetheless the horror genre was already generating striking examples of rebellion against these expectations. *White Zombie*'s preference for dreamlike visuals and atmosphere ignored such mundane preoccupations as story cohesion, and in consequence was scornfully described in the New York "World Telegram" as

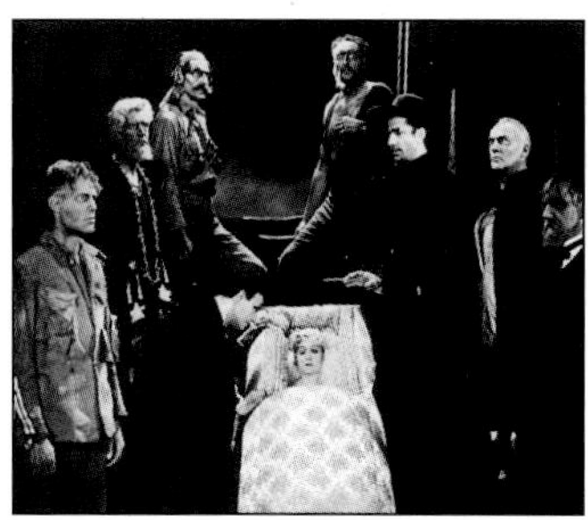

above:
High strangeness from *White Zombie* (1932).

left:
Living dead capers from *The Dead That Walk* aka *Zombies of Mora Tau* (1957).

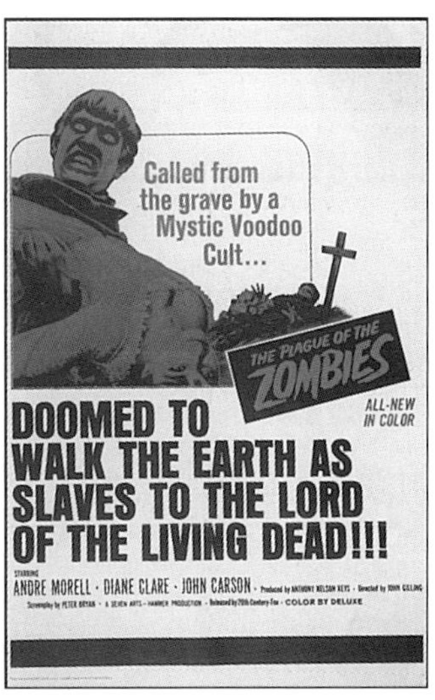

"a potpourri of zombies, frightened natives, witch doctors, leering villains, sinister shadows, painted sets and banal conversation... as entertainment it is nil". Such a description alone would surely have attracted devotees of the weird and surreal. The same attitude would emerge, almost fifty years later, in critical appraisal of Lucio Fulci's zombie films; once again a film-maker's preference for atmosphere over logic would be attacked from the standpoint of 'proper' film-making, based on rigid storytelling conventions.

Garnett Weston's screenplay for *White Zombie* was suggested by *The Magic Island*, a 1929 book about voodoo written by William Seabrook, who is credited with having introduced the word 'zombie' into the horror genre's terminology. (The volume was later abridged, in 1966, to a racier read under the name of *Voodoo Island*.) In a tone of breathless reportage, he offers the curious reader a 'you-are-there' account of Haitian ritual, an approach to the topic which owes its tone to a deeper relationship, between the Imperialist European colonisers and their mysteriously motivated native work-forces. There's an almost sadomasochistic quality to the fears expressed in these inflamed accounts of what the slave underclass were doing in their secret societies. Whilst Europeans may have held the upper hand in terms of fire-power and wealth, they were on shakier ground when it came to the realm of the symbolic, where the 'native' appeared as a figure of awe and potency in the eyes of a decadent 'civilised' class. So-called 'primitive' religious ritual makes demands upon adherents, demands of self-abnegation and daring feats of prowess in the face of pain. These black 'devils' must have seemed appallingly committed, to observers who could feel their Judaeo-Christian beliefs crumbling under the onslaught of atheist malcontents. The voodoo energy witnessed could hardly be matched by the enervated tatters of Christian ritual. These fears of a secret energy, sullenly amassing itself beneath a tissue of subservience, present us with an image of the insecurities of power.[8]

Halperin returned to the zombie theme in 1936 with *Revolt of the Zombies* but failed to re-capture *White Zombie*'s ambience. For nearly thirty years thereafter, zombies remained virtually unexploited as figures of terror. Michael Curtiz's *The Walking Dead* (1936) saw horror icon Boris Karloff try his hand at the theme, although his status as a zombie is questionable – he retains the presence of mind to play the piano and revenge himself on his enemies. 1943's *I Walked with a Zombie*, directed by Jacques Tourneur and produced by Val Lewton, made it even less clear what the ontological status of a zombie might be. It is revealed that a central female character, who has supposedly been turned into a zombie, never actually died and may in fact merely be mad. The Lewton/Tourneur collaborations – *I Walked with a Zombie*, *Cat People* (1942) and *The Leopard Man* (1943) – have of course amassed critical praise over the years for their poetic restraint. It's ironic that Fulci should have claimed he was influenced by these films. Over the years they've been held aloft, as if from the mire, by critics who use Lewton's low-key mannerisms as a benchmark of excellence, in opposition to the kind of visceral horror practised by Fulci himself.

The forties and fifties provided little to focus the concept of the living dead, as various titles from the cheapie Monogram Studios shuffled out. *King of the Zombies* (1941) by Jean Yarbrough and *Revenge of the Zombies* (1943) by Steve Sekely did nothing to expand the territory, re-treading without vitality the existing motifs. At least 1957 saw the first aquatic zombies – an idea that would return in Fulci's *Zombie Flesh-Eaters* – in the cheap but bizarre *Zombies of Mora Tau* (1957) directed by Edward L. Cahn.

It wasn't until the sixties that 'things' really started to move. The Hammer studios were the first to offer a genuinely stylish variation on the traditional voodoo curse story. John Gilling's *Plague of the Zombies* (1966) dispensed with the comfortable bamboo-zling blinds of exoticism and depicted a more English form of slave injustice. The creatures were of a similar mould as before but Gilling spun the tale into a more directly political cloth. Here the zombies are slaves of a local squire (and voodoo master) working down a Cornish tin mine. Instead of locating the basis for fear in the rituals of a foreign country, the squire's actions are the real issue. His villainy combines the unsavoury practises of voodoo with the exploitative habits of the feudal aristocracy.

The status of these zombies is explicitly clarified once and for all – they are definitely *re-animated cadavers*. Gilling also grants them a far more alarming appearance. No longer passive, remote creatures, or silly, bathetic shamblers, they lurch menacingly into view, jangling the viewers' nerves thanks to sudden, shockingly edited appearances. Facially they also ring the changes, bearing expressions of ghastly, leering malice in place of the traditional blank look. Most importantly of all, *Plague of the Zombies* boasts a brilliant resurrection scene, where the dead emerge from soily graves. Fulci's *Zombie Flesh-Eaters* explicitly re-stages this for a bravura sequence in an ancient *conquistadores* graveyard.

But it was the Pittsburgh independent George Romero who gave the zombie theme a truly radical twist, in the seminal modern horror film *Night of the Living Dead* (1968). Suddenly, the living dead had a simple but terrifying purpose. Their one aim, propelling them into grisly attacks, was to eat the flesh of the living. At a stroke they became not just scary but horribly dangerous, whilst the breaking of the deep-seated taboo surrounding cannibalism provided an even greater shock. Romero's zombies were not content merely to lurk menacingly and shamble around in obedience to an occult Master. The trappings of Voodoo ritual, and the panic they inspired in Western imaginations stripped of belief in their own religious iconography, provided no basis to the Pittsburgh director's vision. Indeed, *Night of the Living Dead* showed an almost total disinterest in providing cause-and-effect explanations for the eruption of the living dead into our world. This was to prove Romero's truly modern innovation. (Indeed it

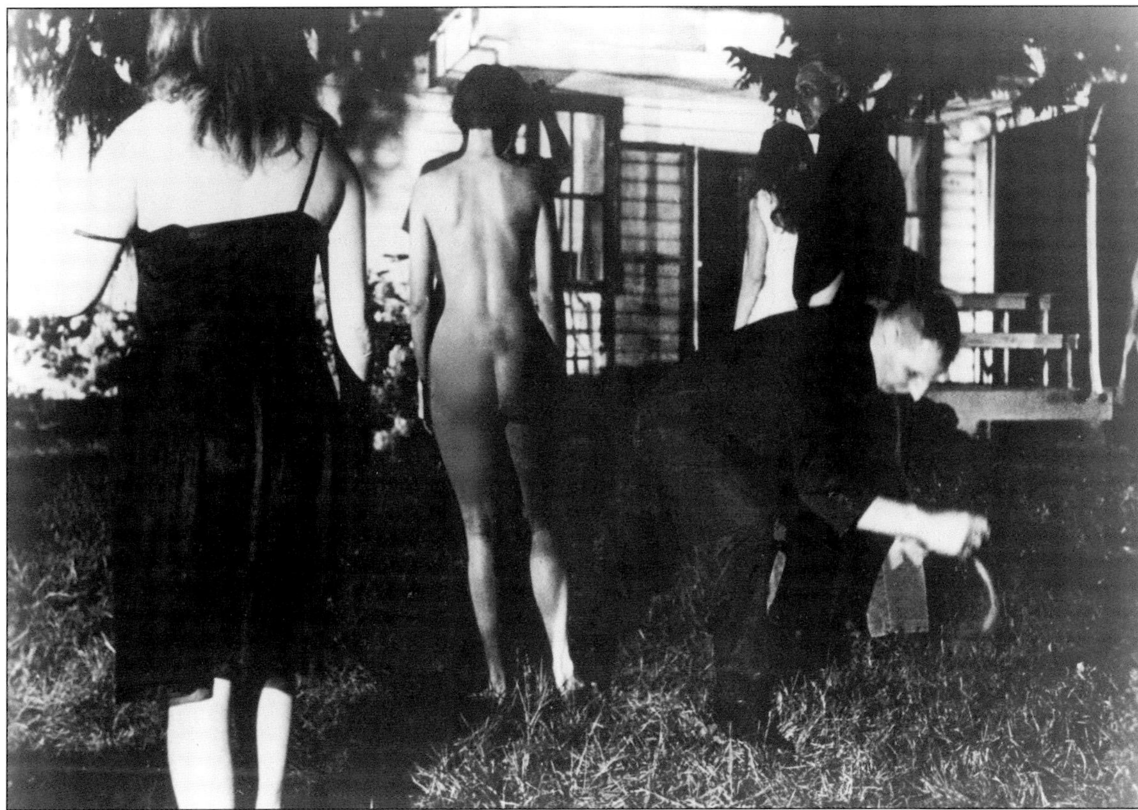

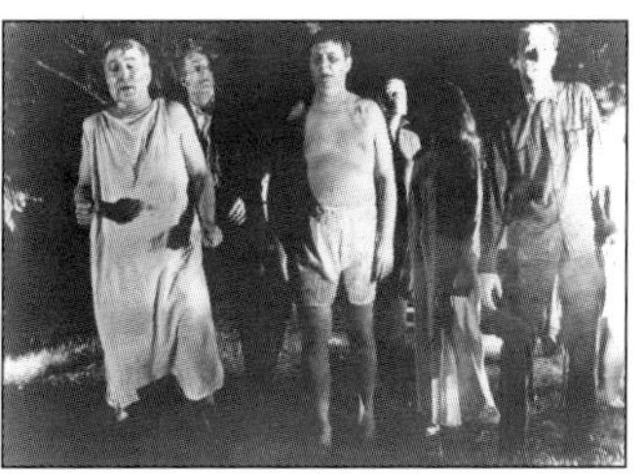

may have been too modern even for him – subsequent entries in his 'zombie trilogy' re-introduce theological speculations through a focus on the less critically examined religious beliefs of black characters).

Over the years, much has been made of *Night of the Living Dead*'s fleeting science-fiction 'explanation' for the horrific events depicted. But if we leave aside the erotic connections between post-Atom Bomb guilt and the mention of radiation from a returning "Venus-probe"(!), Romero's zombies best exemplify the horror of senseless, unmotivated attack. The hysteria, panic and despair of *Night of the Living Dead* is generated by a pervading sense of meaninglessness. The absence of any real answers to the audiences' questions – 'what's happening?', 'how – and why?' – gave the film its shattering impact, just as much as the emergence of a new level of visceral horror.

To some extent, graphic murder and mutilation were already visible in the horror films of the 1960s. Drive-in audiences had the pleasure of Herschell Gordon Lewis's *Blood Feast* (1963), *Two Thousand Maniacs!* (1964) and *The Gruesome Twosome* (1967) to prepare them, whilst continental audiences could experience Mario Bava's gaudy aria of brutality *Blood and Black Lace* (1964); but *Night of the Living Dead* cut through in a particularly shocking way. A new era of horror cinema was beginning – relentless, grim, nihilistic, tailored to an age of unreason – and either filled with a sense of dismay at the corruption of all conventions of moral behaviour – be it personal, social or global – or aware of the fast-increasing fragmentation of the categories of value and meaning themselves. Many of the directors who spearheaded the US independent horror 'scene' – Tobe Hooper, Wes Craven, Larry Cohen, Romero – were disillusioned liberals or ex-radical activists. The early seventies were a bitter time for such people. Civil rights and anti-war protests were met with hysterical State violence, whilst the increasing grotesquerie of assassination and serial murder gnawed away at America's saturated consciousness, via lurid tabloids and television. Too much reality?

Influential though it was, *Night of the Living Dead* was not immediately taken up as a fixed template for zombie movies. Instead it was followed by a ragtag and bobtail assortment of diverse American oddities. *Messiah of Evil* (Willard Huyck, 1973) took a 'hippie dream goes sour' theme and smashed it into a 'consumer society goes crazy' riff, well before Romero's *Dawn of the Dead* played with the same ideas. *Children Shouldn't Play with Dead Things* (Bob Clark, 1972) begins as a send-up about graverobbing but turns genuinely creepy when the ghouls appear; *Garden of the Dead* (John Hayes, 1972) strikes out on its own with its talking, formaldehyde-addicted chain-gang zombies; and *The Child* (Robert Voskanian, 1977) likewise plays by its own obscure rules, featuring a nasty little girl who uses psychic powers to terrorise her family and tutor, before introducing them to her 'friends' from the graveyard. Best of all was Bob Clark's under-rated chiller *Deathdream* (1972) featuring one of the earliest examples of a soon-to-be American movie cliché, the psycho Vietnam vet; except that this one was a zombie, brought back to his unsuspecting family by the fervent prayers of his mother, in a variation on the classic ghost story "The Monkey's Paw".

The special effects for *Deathdream* were created by a young man called Tom Savini, soon to be famous for another, more gruesome project: George Romero's apocalyptic *Dawn of the Dead*. The visceral and emotional impact of this grisly masterpiece is hard to overstate: it ushers in a massive escalation of graphic violence, opens out the claustrophobic drama of *Night of the Living Dead* to depict an entire civilisation on the brink of collapse, and steeps a complex narrative with a heavy dose of political and social commentary. A handful of survivors, besieged in a giant shopping mall by the living dead, bicker and lose their heads, surrounded by empty symbols of western extravagance and menaced by zombiefied 'shoppers'. While *Night* ended with total negation, *Dawn* left a couple of its likeable characters standing, but declined to offer much hope for a new civilisation... That pessimism then turns to despair in the third of the series: *Day of the Dead* (1985) is a bleak, exhausting film with lots of shouting, a plethora of disgusting characters, and some extraordinary 'top-that!' effects work. Sadly, the series ran out of steam with *Land of the Dead* (2005), which let down the side with its corny supervillain and bland hero. What's more, by suggesting that the zombies are now

this page:
Night of the Living Dead,
the turning point for screen horror.

facing page:
Images from Hammer's
Plague of the Zombies.

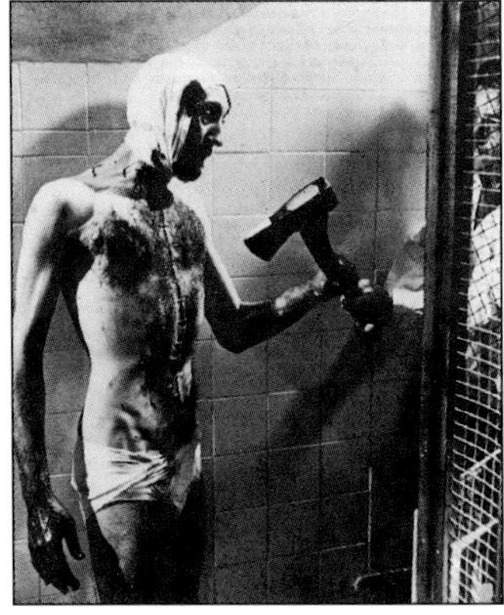

above:
Stranger on these shores: Jorge Grau's marvellous zombie film, *The Living Dead at Manchester Morgue.*

right:
On the other hand... a different slant on the flesh-eating theme from Ruggero Deodato's infamous *Cannibal Holocaust.*

the real locus of sympathy, yet failing to explore them in detail, Romero left us with a half-cooked theoretical abstraction which may have looked good on paper but failed to ignite onscreen.

Between *Night of the Living Dead* and *Dawn of the Dead*, two Spanish filmmakers kept the zombie subgenre genre alive and kicking. The first salvo came from Amando de Ossorio, who delivered the beguiling *Tombs of the Blind Dead* (1971), featuring sightless skeletal zombie Knights Templar on horseback. Bringing to his movie the virtues of a genuinely creepy ghost story, Ossorio then lifted it toward the sublime with his fantastically effective eyeless ghouls, sculpted and created by the director himself. Surely the scariest-looking zombies ever to grace a horror picture, they seem to have risen straight from the pages of an especially hair-raising EC comic-strip. So effective (and internationally saleable) was the film that it sired three sequels: *Return of the Evil Dead* (1973), *The Ghost Galleon* aka *Horror of the Zombies* (made in 1973 but released 1975) and *Night of the Seagulls* (1975). Although none of the subsequent films quite matched the first, either aesthetically or commercially, the second and fourth were moody and highly enjoyable, with only the third, the talky and tedious *Horror of the Zombies*, outstaying its welcome.

Vying with the films of Lucio Fulci for the title of best European zombie film, Jorge Grau's Spanish/Italian co-production *The Living Dead at Manchester Morgue* (1974) is a real gem. Its evergreen charm is down to a constellation of factors, including the warmth and friendship that blossoms in extremis between the two likeable leads (Raymond Lovelock and Cristina Galbó), the excellent soundtrack by Giuliano Sorgini, some amusing irregularities of accent and dialogue, copious eruptions of glistening gore, and the juxtaposition of zombies with the glorious landscape of the Derbyshire Peak District. In the 1960s and '70s the North of England hardly ever appeared in genre movies; Hammer, for instance, rarely strayed beyond the Home Counties. It took a Spanish director inspired by an American film (*Night of the Living Dead*) to look further afield and realise that England's beauty extends well beyond the cluster of counties adjacent to London. Grau's direction singles out odd details of landscape and locale, and finds evocative ways of framing simple scenes which, combined with the explicit ripping of flesh and glistening red organs, announces a distinctive Mediterranean identity. Talented special make-up artist Giannetto De Rossi, soon to become an essential contributor to Lucio Fulci's films, treats us to a variety of exotic sights: the ripping out of an English bobby's liver and the plucking of his eyeballs, the evisceration of a receptionist plus a handful of breast pulled from her cleavage, and a doctor's spectacular demise from an axe-blow to the head. *The Living Dead at Manchester Morgue* thus anticipates the glorious carnage of Lucio Fulci's zombie tales.

below:
More flesh-eating from Deodato's *Cannibal* (aka *Last Cannibal World*).

Staying with Spanish horror: having already turned his hand to cannibal movies (*Devil Hunter*, 1980; *Cannibals*, 1980) and slasher films (*Bloody Moon*, 1981), it was inevitable that Spain's most prolific director, Jess Franco, would direct a zombie film too. At the request of French production company Eurociné, Franco bashed out *Oasis of the Zombies* (1982), a film of less than stellar quality that would nevertheless linger around for years in a variety of retitlings and repackagings. Though the film is undeniably awful, its desert-roaming goggle-eyed zombies have a fibrous, sand-blasted quality all their own, and in deference to Fulci's vision of putrefaction it's good to see a few worms squirming around in their facial mulch. Better by far was Franco's *Mansion of the Living Dead* (1982) which took the scantily clad airheads-in-peril of *Bloody Moon* and dropped them into a surpassingly weird story of sex slavery and living dead priests (the latter a nod to the Knights Templar of Amando de Ossorio although visually the ghouls are just men smeared with dirty shaving foam!). With zombies very much *au courant* in the film markets of the early 1980s, Eurociné asked French horror specialist Jean Rollin to film Romero-esque inserts designed to 'up-date' Jess Franco's *A Virgin Among the Living Dead* (1971), a truly poetic film which hitherto had featured a more rarefied breed of 'zombies' who tell jokes, play the piano and enjoy sexual perversion. Rollin also accepted Eurociné's plea to step in and rescue a film which Franco had abandoned on the weekend before shooting was due to begin – a peculiar sequence of events for which we all should be grateful, as it gave us the charmingly awful *Zombie Lake* (1980). Although Rollin's adventures in Francoland were far from his best work, he did have his own prior history with the living dead. In 1978 he'd taken a vacation from vampire-themed tales and directed the picturesque, sombre and sorely under-rated *Les raisins de la mort* (1978). This came out three months before *Dawn of the Dead*, featured zombies created by pesticides sprayed on French vineyards, and as such appears to have been inspired mainly by *The Living Dead at Manchester Morgue*. He later returned to the zombie theme with a gruesome – yet gentle and poetic – film called *The Living Dead Girl*

(1982), which incorporated his enduring fascination with close female friendships.

Meanwhile, in backyards and scrublands across America, the ultra-low-budget 'spawn-of-*Dawn*' staggered shakily, and a tad unconvincingly, across the screen. Tony Malanowski's minimalistic *Night of Horror* (1980) and its 'deluxe' variant *Curse of the Screaming Dead* (1982) rated zero for thrills but scored high for eccentricity and dimestore dedication. Fred Olen Ray's inept but amusing *The Alien Dead* (1980) was worth a look for diehards, and Don Dohler's *Fiend* (1980) was a rare example of a post-*Dawn* zombie film that owed nothing to Romero, with a reanimated cadaver, possessed by a demon, giving violin tutorials in deepest Baltimore. *The Dark Power* (Phil Smoot, 1985) unleashed zombie Toltec Indians and shoehorned them into a sorority slasher film; *Forest of Fear* (Chuck McCrann, 1979) showed hippies turning into zombies when their marijuana field is sprayed with an experimental poison by 'The Man'; and the ultra-weird *Frozen Scream* (Frank Roach, 1980) gave us dead people stored in cryogenic suspension who are sent out to kill by radio control.

In the 21st Century, Danny Boyle's *28 Days Later* (2002) and Zack Snyder's *Dawn of the Dead* remake (2004) gave us running zombies, for which I'm sure we're all eternally grateful. (Boyle distanced his movie from the subgenre, and it's true that his screeching sprinting 'rage' victims aren't zombies, strictly speaking, but his film borrows liberally from the post-Romero zombie subgenre.) From then on, the living dead were back with a vengeance: in fact the deluge of zombie movies that have run amok in the last fifteen years dwarfs the smattering of earlier titles mentioned so far. Even the British joined the fray, for only the second time since *Plague of the Zombies* in 1966 (1998's *I, Zombie: Chronicles of Pain* being the other). Picking up cues from splatstick horror films like Dan O'Bannon's *Return of the Living Dead* (1985) and Peter Jackson's *Braindead* (1990), Edgar Wright's *Shaun of the Dead* (2004) grafted lads'-night-in comedy material onto a heartfelt pastiche of Romero's originals (social critique and all). The result was funny and intelligent, but its play-for-laughs combo of the humdrum and the gruesome paved the way for a series of less and less skilful 'zom-coms'.

Back in the mid-1990s, video game designers had turned to Romero (and to a lesser degree Fulci) for inspiration, hence the hugely popular "Resident Evil" and "House of the Dead" shoot-'em-ups. Seizing upon the (heavily ironic) gunplay of the Romero films and turning it into a gung-ho *raison d'être*, such games made a fortune, which led to a slew of movies based on video games based on movies. Blending zombie attacks with the asskicking attitude of James Cameron's *Aliens* (1986) these generally irksome products mark the rise of what we might call zombie overkill (there have been six *Resident Evil* films since 2002). In 2010 the American TV series *The Walking Dead* began its seven-seasons-and-counting march across our screens, while the ease and affordability of zombie make-up birthed a slew of 'let's all go to the woods and pretend to be zombies' fan movies. The result? A once-thrilling subgenre became a crowded thoroughfare, the zombie not so much a symbol of abjection or apocalypse, more an off-the-peg fantasy role-play icon. In the 1980s it was still quite peculiar to see fans queueing for hours at Romero casting calls, desperately wanting to be zombies. Nowadays your mum probably goes on 'zombie walks', while the fans prefer to make their own found-footage zombie videos. By 2020 it seems we will all have either been in a zombie film, or directed one. Essentially, the 'zombie apocalypse' has been bought out, franchised, and exhausted. How else to describe a genre that has given the world *Zombies vs Strippers* (2008), *Milfs vs. Zombies* (2015) or – please God make it stop – *Undead or Alive: A Zombedy* (2007)?

above:
Fulci's vision of the dead denied their earthly identities, casting them as metaphysical derelicts.

Anthropophagy in the UK

Zombi 2 was released in the UK in 1980 as *Zombie Flesh-Eaters* and given an 'X' certificate after the removal of several key scenes by the BBFC. It would be another eighteen months before British audiences would, thanks to the video revolution, be able to enjoy Fulci's outrageous excesses in their entirety. *Vipco*, the company who had initially released the 'X' print of the film on videocassette shortly after its theatrical release, took the unusual step of re-issuing the film to retailers as a "Strong Uncut Version" the following year. Whilst the original version did well enough, the latter proved to be a huge rental success.

It's a shame that subsequent releases of Fulci's were not made available in the same fashion. For the censor, zombies became *persona non grata* on British cinema screens. *City of the Living Dead*, *The Beyond* and *The House by the Cemetery* were all heavily cut both in the cinema and later on videocassette, as were numerous other efforts by Italian directors shuffling in Fulci's wake: *Zombie Holocaust*, *The Nights of Terror*, *Zombie Creeping Flesh* and *Nightmare City* all suffered similar fates. After Government legislation in 1984, when submission of videos to the censor became mandatory, Fulci's films were released again, shorn of even the most fleeting violence by companies wishing to avoid the costly process of re-submitting them. Unbelievably, some of these versions were subjected to even more cuts by the scissor-happy BBFC. Anyone in the UK buying a censor-approved copy of *The Beyond*, *The House by the Cemetery* or *City of the Living Dead* between 1985 and 1999, as sold by companies such as Elephant Video, would have seen these films at their most toothless and humiliated, stripped of anything even remotely visceral by a censorship regime eager to placate the right-wing press.

Does *Zombie Flesh-Eaters* steal anything from Romero's *Dawn of the Dead*? Apart from some of its marketing thunder, the answer is not really. Sacchetti's script sets itself up as, if anything, a prequel to Romero's hit – particularly for an audience that may never have seen Romero's *Night of the Living Dead*. Let's now have a detailed look at the film that put Lucio Fulci on the map.

below:
Violence erupts on the island of Matul...

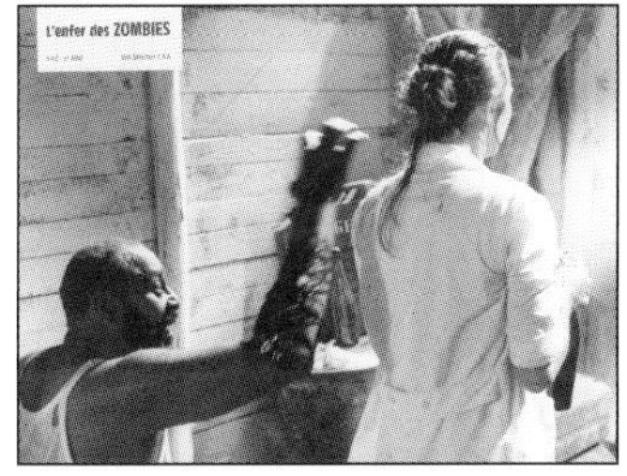

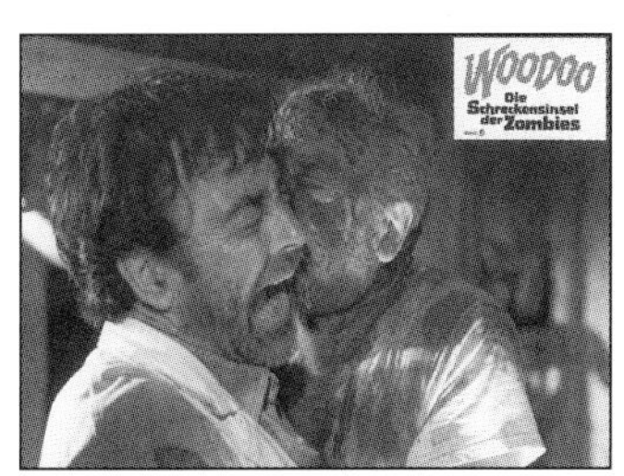

Italian theatrical title
Zombi 2

Italy

International theatrical titles
Zombie Flesh-Eaters (UK)
Zombie (USA)
Woodoo Die Schreckensinsel der Zombies (WG)
('Voodoo – Horror Island of the Zombies')
L'enfer des Zombies (BEL poster)
('Hell of the Zombies')
De Hel van der Zombies (BEL poster)
Yüzde 99 Ölüm (TUR)
('99 percent Death')
Ölüm Bölgesine Dönüş (TUR alt.)
('Return to the Death Zone')
Los muertos vivientes (MEX)
('The Living Dead')
Sanguelia (JAP poster title)
Nueva York bajo el terror de los zombi (SP)
('New York Under Terror of the Zombies')

Other titles
Nightmare Island (pre-shooting script)
The Island of the Living Dead (shooting script)

Video titles
Zombie 2 (NL)
Noche de panico (SP)
('Night of Panic')
La noche de los muertos vivos (VNZ)
('Night of the Living Dead') sic

DVD titles
Zombie A volta dos mortos (BRZ)
('Zombie The Return of the Dead')
Raedslernes grønne Ø (NOR)
('Terrors of the Green Island')

Production company
Variety Film (Rome)

Theatrical distributors
Variety Film (Italy)
Jerry Gross Organization (USA)
Miracle Films (UK)

Theatrical running time
Italy 94m
UK cut version 88m 57s
90m 43s before cuts

Video/DVD/Blu-ray times (adjusted)
Blue Underground Blu-ray 91m 11s
Vipco video (UK) 90m 39s

Censorship
Italian censor certificate 73936
issued 23 August 1979
UK 'X' certificate
issued 02 January 1980

Shooting period
April-May 1979

Release information
Rome 25 August 1979
Bari 31 August 1979
UK (London) 08 February 1980
USA (Flint, MI) 02 July 1980

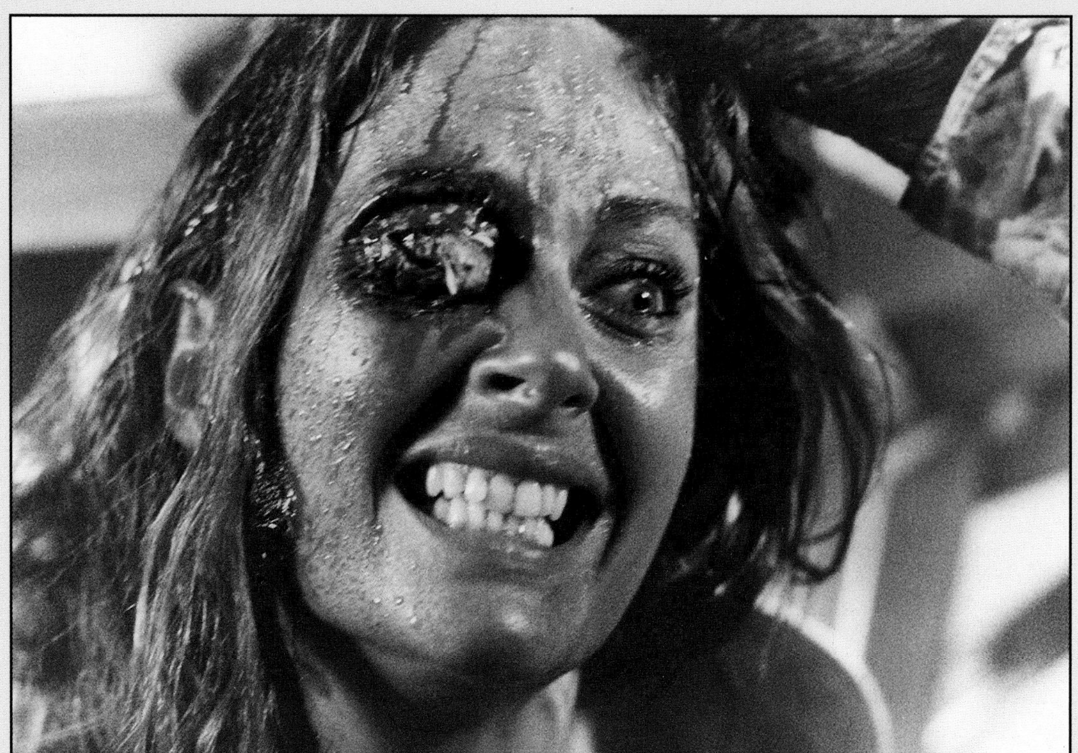

Zombie Flesh-Eaters

1979

Directed by Lucio Fulci. produced by Ugo Tucci & Fabrizio De Angelis for Variety Film. screenplay: Elisa Briganti & [uncredited] Dardano Sacchetti. director of photography: Sergio Salvati. music: Fabio Frizzi & Giorgio Tucci; published by Variety. editor: Vincenzo Tomassi. special effects & make-up supervisor: Giannetto De Rossi. associate producer: Gianfranco Couyoumdjian. production designer & costumes: Walter Patriarca. production co-ordination: Giorgio Chessari. production manager: Antonio Mazza. unit managers: Walter Massi, Tullio Lullo. assistant director: Robert Giandalia. script continuity: Daniela Tonti. underwater photography: Ramon Bravo, with collaboration from Paolo Curfo. camera operator: Franco Bruni. assistant cameraman: Fabrizio Vicari. gaffer: Fernando Massaccesi. key grip: Ennio Brizzolari. make-up: Maurizio Trani. hairstylist: Mirella Sforza. seamstress: Fiorella De Simone. props: Romano Chessari. set dresser: Carlo Ferri. set construction: Giovanni Corridori. action stills: Sergio Strizzi & David Cagnazzo. production accountant: Walter Massi. titles: Studio Mafera. 1st assistant editor: Carlo Della Corte. sound recordist: Ugo Celani. boom operator: Giuliano Gramaccioni. dubbing editor: Nick Alexander. re-recording: Bruno Moreal @ Fono Roma, for Cinitalia.

Cast: Tisa Farrow (Anne Bowles). Ian McCulloch (Peter West). Richard Johnson (Dr. David Menard). Al Cliver (Brian Hull). Auretta Gay (Susan Barrett). Stefania d'Amario (nurse at Menard's hospital). Olga Karlatos (Paola Menard). *Uncredited:* Dakar (Lucas, Menard's assistant). Ugo Bologna (Anne's father). Leslie Thomas (coroner). James Sampson (James, coroner's assistant). Leo Gavero (Fritz, Menard's friend). Franco Fantasia (Father Matthias). Rámon Bravo (underwater zombie). Omero Capanna (zombie). Alberto Dell'Acqua (zombie). Arnaldo Dell'Acqua (zombie). Ottaviano Dell'Acqua (worm-eye zombie). Lucio Fulci (West's news editor). Arthur 'Captain' Haggerty (boat zombie).

Synopsis: Two New York harbour patrolmen investigating an apparently abandoned ship are attacked by a zombie which bursts from the hold. Peter West, a reporter, teams up with Anne Bowles, the daughter of the boat's missing owner, and together they fly to the Antilles in search of Matul, the island where Anne's father had been working with a colleague, Dr. Menard. At a harbour they meet Susan Barrett and Brian Hull, who own a small sailing boat. They agree to help Anne and Peter find Matul ... On the island, tensions between Menard and his wife Paola are running high. She wants to leave, terrified by reports of zombie attacks. He insists on staying to research the phenomenon. Leaving her alone at their beach-house, Menard drives to his tumbledown 'hospital' based in a converted wooden church on the other side of the island ... During a scuba dive en-route to Matul Susan is attacked, first by a shark and then by an underwater zombie ... On the island, Paola is attacked by a zombie and dies horribly when her eye is impaled on a spike of wood. The visitors land on Matul and meet Menard, who informs them that Anne's father died of a strange disease. He tells them about the living dead, whose appearance is blamed by locals on a voodoo curse. Menard asks the others to go and check on his wife. They find her dead, with zombies gorging on her remains. Revolted, the visitors drive back to the hospital but after a crash they are forced to finish the journey on foot. Resting briefly in a clearing, they realise they are in a 16th century graveyard for the Spanish Conquistadores. An ancient zombie rises from the soil, killing Susan. The others make it to the hospital and barricade the doors and windows, but the patients are dying and returning as zombies too. Menard and his two remaining nurses are attacked and killed. Peter, Anne and Brian escape by setting fire to the creatures, but when Brian is confronted by the walking corpse of Susan, he is badly bitten. Making it back to the boat, the trio set sail for the USA. Brian dies and Peter locks his body in the hold. As the corpse revives, Anne and Peter hear terrible news on the radio: New York is now over-run with zombies...

About the production: *Zombie Flesh-Eaters* is so often referred to as a rip-off of George Romero's *Dawn of the Dead* that it's worth looking, first of all, at the time-line of events leading to the production of this pivotal Italian horror film.

Dawn of the Dead was shot on location in Pennsylvania, USA between November 1977 and February 1978. In March '78 Romero's rough cut arrived in Rome, so that music by Goblin could be added under the supervision of *Dawn*'s co-producer Dario Argento. This was therefore the earliest that *Dawn* could possibly have been seen by Italian industry insiders. In July '78 Dardano Sacchetti wrote a script called 'Nightmare Island' for Gianfranco Couyoumdjian's company, Flora Film. The Italian edit of Romero's *Dawn* was completed in August 1978, and in September it was released there as *Zombi*, making a million dollars for distributors Titanus in its first six weeks. A month later, in October '78, a trade ad appeared in *Variety* proclaiming a forthcoming Flora Film production called 'Island of the Living Death' – this was in fact Sacchetti's 'Nightmare Island' script, retitled (and badly translated) to refer to zombies. Come December, 'Nightmare Island'/'Island of the Living Death' was announced in *Variety* again, this time by Variety Film, a company belonging to Ugo Tucci and Fabrizio De Angelis. (As part of the handover deal from Flora to Variety, Gianfranco Couyoumdjian received an 'associate producer' credit on the Italian version of the film and its posters). De Angelis first offered the project to action specialist Enzo Castellari, but Castellari wasn't interested. Enter Lucio Fulci (although apparently Umberto Lenzi had also been offered the gig, according to a 1979 news item in *Variety*: *"Lucio Fulci, not Umberto Lenzi, is set to helm "Zombi 2" late March, according to latest info from Variety Film"*.[9]

Now at last the film went into production, with Fulci installed as director. Shooting began in April 1979, on location in New York and Santo Domingo. In an e-mail sent to the author, Dardano Sacchetti asserted, *"Fulci shot the script exactly as written eight months earlier. He said no to nothing, and took out maybe a comma. The scene of the eye was described frame by frame."*[10]

Rush-released in August 1979, *Zombi 2* performed modestly in Italy but went on to enormous success worldwide, in the process transforming Fulci's career and installing him forever as the king of Italian splatter.

Review: *Zombie Flesh-Eaters* starts very strongly with a nerve-shattering incident aboard a deserted schooner drifting into the New York Harbour. Fulci declares a different identity to Romero's *Dawn of the Dead* almost immediately, thanks to the bizarre appearance of the first zombie encountered by two harbour patrolmen on the vessel. Bald, hugely obese, plastered with flaking skin and drooling blood, it lurches up onto the deck to be backlit by the sun hanging low in the sky. The effect is incredibly alarming, a combination of menace, repulsiveness and out-and-out weirdness.

Presaging the attack is a detail that's quintessential Fulci, utterly alien to the film's American model but a sign of things to come in the next few years. As a patrolman explores the cabin of the schooner, we're shown various details of squalor and chaos amidst the cramped quarters. Rotting food on paper plates is accompanied by the sound of buzzing flies. The air, we can well imagine, is thick with nauseating odour. This queasy atmosphere is amplified by a completely unexpected image. On the keys of a tiny old pianola in the corner of the cabin, we see a tangled mess of filthy black gunge and writhing worms. The soundtrack blares with a deep, flatulent synthesizer sound, increasing our disorientation. The information contained in the shot is negligible, yet the forceful rudeness of the sound and the almost childish grossness of the image suggest that the audience beware – the film will have as much to do with gut-level repulsion as with violence. When a zombie bursts out of the hold and attacks the police officer, Fulci assaults us with another morbid image. Struggling beneath the monster, the victim tears away from it a strip of rotten, scab-like flesh. We see intense disgust on his face. Seconds later his throat is savaged in a welter of gore.

As the zombie falls into the harbour waves, propelled by the force of the second officer's gun, Sergio Salvati's camera rises slowly from the rippling waters to dwell, ominously, upon the skyline of New York. A buzzing, threatening synthesiser underscores the shot, leading us to expectations of an imminent urban apocalypse. Indeed, the film almost loses its momentum after this tease, because it subsequently veers away for half an hour, before delivering the anticipated eruption of zombie mayhem somewhere else entirely. The chief flaw of *Zombie Flesh-Eaters* is its fluctuating tension during the first thirty minutes; Fulci allows the audience a little too much time to breathe. However, the following scene at the morgue – a white medical examiner treating his black assistant with ill-concealed contempt – points again to the beginnings of urban destruction.

Getting there

The narrative momentum of *Zombie Flesh-Eaters* is at first hampered by the tiresome business of getting the principal cast out of New York – with its expensive shooting permits and rubbernecking passers-by – and off to Santo Domingo in the Antilles where much of the action unfolds. Although the pace is allowed to sag, McCulloch and Farrow do at least have some fun in a scene where a cop finds them illegally searching the mysterious boat for clues to the fate of Farrow's missing father. By posing as a bickering couple trying to 'make out' on the empty vessel, they enjoy a brief spell of comedy business before being hurled into the grislier action.

En-route to the island of Matul, sexploitation thrusts its helmet above the parapet, with some ogling shots of Auretta Gay's topless scuba-diving preparations. Such t&a frivolity is swiftly forgotten though, as it leads into one of the film's craziest, funniest and most dreamlike ideas; an encounter with an underwater zombie...

above:
Fulci added three signatures to this Australian poster, such was his pleasure at seeing it for the first time when it was shown to him at Eurofest in London, 1994.

opposite, main picture:
A moment of cinema legend: Mrs. Menard (Olga Karlatos) gets something in her eye...

below:
Auretta Gay as Susan, after her terrifying encounter with a shark and a zombie.

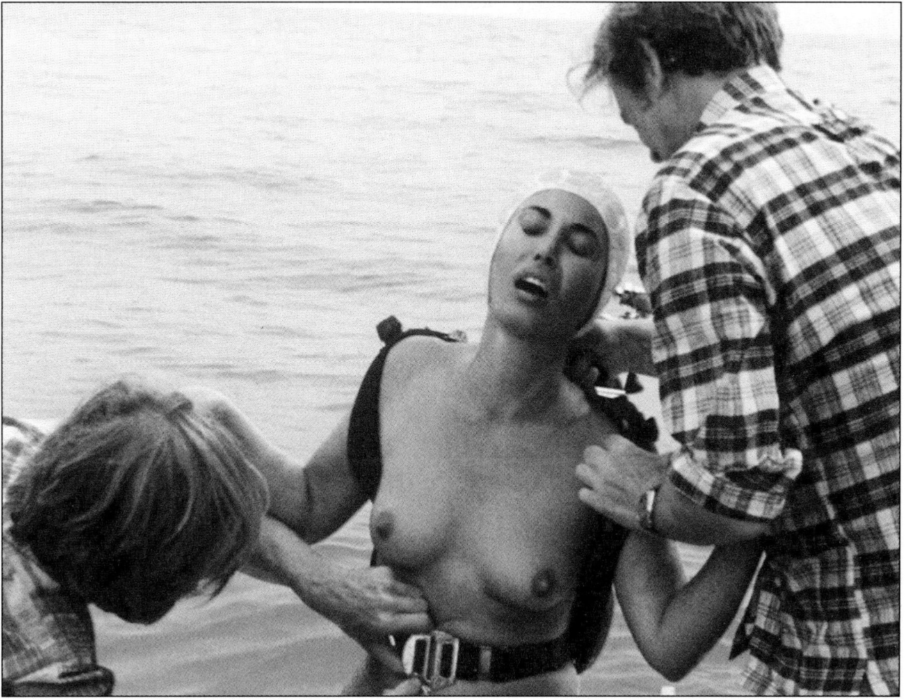

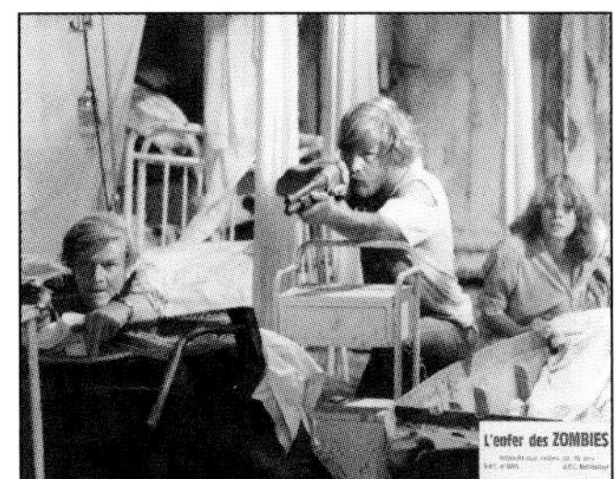
L'enfer des ZOMBIES

WOODOO
Die Schreckensinsel der Zombies
Ian McCulloch
Tisa Farrow
Richard Johnson
Best.-Nr.
VU-3003
ca. 85 Minuten Spieldauer
VIDEO
COLOR-CASSETTE
marketing-film

サンゲリア
SANGUELIA

WOODOO
Die Schreckensinsel der Zombies

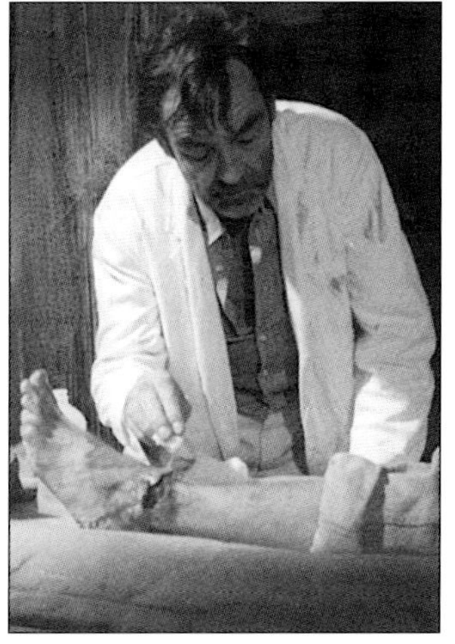

...quando i morti usciranno dalla tomba,
i vivi saranno il loro sangue...
ZOMBI 2
IAN McCULLOCH · TISA FARROW · RICHARD JOHNSON
OLGA KARLATOS
LUCIO FULCI

The initially random though picturesque diving scenes turn gloriously surreal as Susan is menaced by an approaching shark, and then attacked by a bizarre, ragged ghoul which reaches out to grab her from the dark recesses of a coral outcrop. What follows is a triumph of the ridiculous that nevertheless seems to have stayed in the minds of all who've seen the film. A slow-motion fight ensues between zombie and shark, with the latter emerging victorious, tearing at rotting limbs with much gratuitous crunching on the soundtrack. The crowning touch to this balletic confrontation is the score; a gorgeously calm yet patently loopy composition by the incomparable Fabio Frizzi. Such weird underwater diversion combines the *Jaws* franchise with the zombie mythos, yet seems to have sprung almost without precedent onto the screen. There *was* a sort of underwater zombie sequence in the bedraggled shambles of *Zombies of Mora Tau* (1957); nevertheless, Fulci's perversely detailed nonsense is no idle plagiarism. It's an idea that may well be unique because no one in their right minds would film it, but it's cause for celebration nonetheless. Another sequence beginning with sexploitation-style nudity occurs during the prelude to the film's most celebrated sequence; the grisly fate of Mrs. Menard...

"A splinter in the eye is the best magnifying glass"
Theodor Adorno

If one image were to act as the pinnacle of Lucio Fulci's contribution to cinema, it would have to be the fate of Mrs. Menard, whose terrified, wide-open right eye is impaled on a giant splinter in glorious close-up. The scene is as deeply lodged in the memory of horror fans as the splinter itself is wedged in the victim's cornea. It's the culmination and climax of a particular kind of confrontational movie imagery, the crunch point of a game horror films have always played with their audiences, delivering on the threat instead of backing down. We talk of horror films 'going for the jugular' but of course what really makes sense is to go for the eyes.

So what is going on here? It's a curious game to play, embracing contradictory urges, attraction and repulsion, mastery and submission...

Voices hostile to the horror genre would claim that it's all about pathological hatred of women, as if one is thrilling to the penetration/obliteration of a woman's identity, represented by her eye. And yet one could easily counter that male audience-members are themselves being penetrated by this assaultive image. The victim may be a woman, but gender is redundant when you consider that we are all watching with the same organs: we're united by our eyes. As rough and tough as anyone may be, we all have soft eyeballs, and we all understand that to stick a needle into the core of someone's sense of self, you aim for the eyes. Male or female, we're equally likely to flinch (and maybe cheer) as the spike goes in. We can all feel the horror, the transgression and the shock; it really doesn't matter that the victim is a woman. We experience common humanity through this nightmarish penetration. I find it unlikely that a male viewer could displace his anxieties about the 'soft' parts of his body merely by attributing this 'exorbitant' mutilation to a plight suffered by the feminine. I think what we're mostly saying, if we like this sort of movie, is that we want the director to make it *hurt*. It's not so much about audience sadism, it's more the masochistic thrill of letting the image overwhelm your senses. In modern-day parlance, the scene is 'fucked up', and guess who's doing the fucking...

Money and notoriety aside, what did Fulci get out of filming this scene? Where did his mind wander during lunch that day? Tormented Catholic that he was, you wonder if he saw it as rebellion: if you're watching everything I do, Holy Father, get a load of this! Given that Fulci was struggling at the time to make ends meet, one suspects also a certain amount of subliminal aggression, a desire once and for all to make an impression (a *deep* impression), on his audience. And being a cultured man very familiar with the films of Buñuel, he no doubt relished the idea of doing what only the Spaniard had done on screen before: attacking the very organs required to enjoy movies...

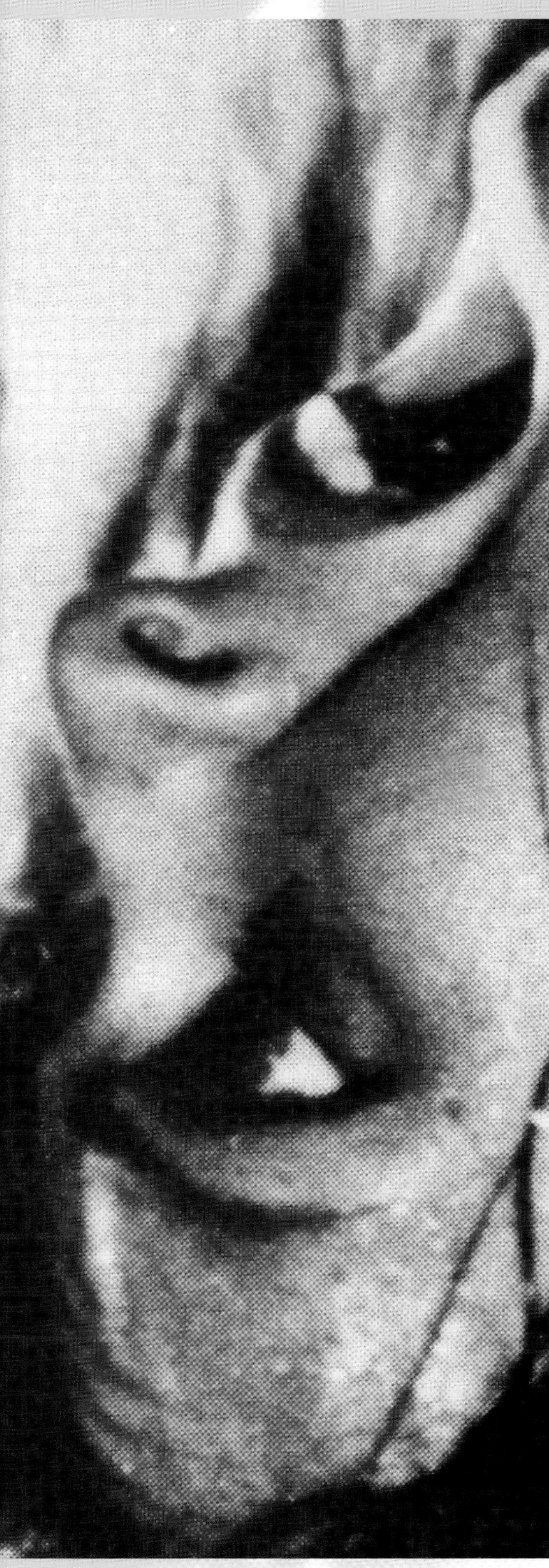

Cynics, meanwhile, might read the sequence as a portrait of Fulci, whose identity had already been 'splintered' by varying degrees of compromise to the factors of commercial necessity and 'hired gun' expediency. This was, after all, not a project he had nurtured from the beginning. One thing's for sure: the famous 'eye scene' was Fulci's chance, once and for all, after thirty years in the industry, to make an unforgettable impression on an audience.

You have to admire the boldness of the challenge. The sequence targets the viewer dead-centre, homing in on the 'rite of passage' aspect of horror cinema; by making the whole act of seeing the subject of attack, a powerful *frisson* is generated. The scene is a deliciously cruel, painfully astute mocking of the voyeuristic urge to gaze, and if the piercing of the eye isn't *quite* the final word in screen dialectics it's certainly a good try! Ultimately however, the scene releases a liberating energy, inspiring laughter with its sheer relentlessness.

Aftermath

From this fantastic outburst of violence, the film returns to its preoccupation with physical disgust. The unfortunate Mrs. Menard's body is eventually discovered by Anne, Peter, Susan and Brian, surrounded by sluggish, indifferent ghouls. She is being lazily picked over by these creatures, as if on a self-service rack in a restaurant. Her flesh is unaccountably slimy, wet, almost jellied. Liquescent and undifferentiated, her organs, skin and muscle tissue are reduced to a slippery pulp. One detail keeps us aware of what we're witnessing; above this horrid tableau, her mutilated face is visible. The reactions of the four characters are vital to the effect. As if in confirmation of our response they back off, not with expressions of shock or fear, but of revulsion. Their loathing is generated by the sight of the human body as nothing but food.

It's worth drawing attention here to the writing of Julia Kristeva whose theories of abjection could be applied to this scene and others like it in Fulci's work. Barbara Creed's book on horror films, *The Monstrous Feminine*, builds a considerable critical edifice out of reference to Kristeva's work, and readers interested in recent psychoanalytical perspectives on the genre may find it stimulating (although as usual the films discussed are almost without fail American; even radical feminist critics are disinclined to examine films that fall outside the established critical boundaries for textual analysis).

On the subject of food loathing, Creed relates Kristeva's position:

"In relation to the horror film, it is relevant to note that food loathing is frequently represented as a major source of abjection, particularly the eating of human flesh ... The ultimate in abjection is the corpse ... Within a religious context, the corpse is also utterly abject. It signifies one of the basic forms of pollution – the body without a soul. As a form of waste it represents the opposite of the spiritual..."[11]

Thus do we recognise Mrs. Menard's body, abject in its loss of form and integrity, a repulsive sight which challenges our own bodily integrity. The fact that some may be sickened enough to retch, or even vomit, demonstrates the power of the image. And of course the zombies themselves are 'bodies without souls', their abject corruption far more visually apparent than their Romero counterparts. As an early ad, placed by Wizard Video in the American horror magazine *Fangoria*, proudly stated: *"The oozing pustulent horror of* Zombie *makes* Dawn of the Dead *look like Rebecca of Sunnybrook Farm!"*

To represent Creed's arguments more closely is not my intention here. Suffice to say that for the climax of the film, as the remaining humans are coralled in a wooden chapel under seige from hordes of zombies, these putrified corruptions of the flesh are attacked with cleansing fire. (Fulci's subsequent zombie film *City of the Living Dead* takes the same route.) This ties in closely to the Kristevan idea which Creed espouses, that the popular horror film is a modern defilement rite, seeking *"the purification of the abject through a descent into the foundations of the symbolic construct."*[12]

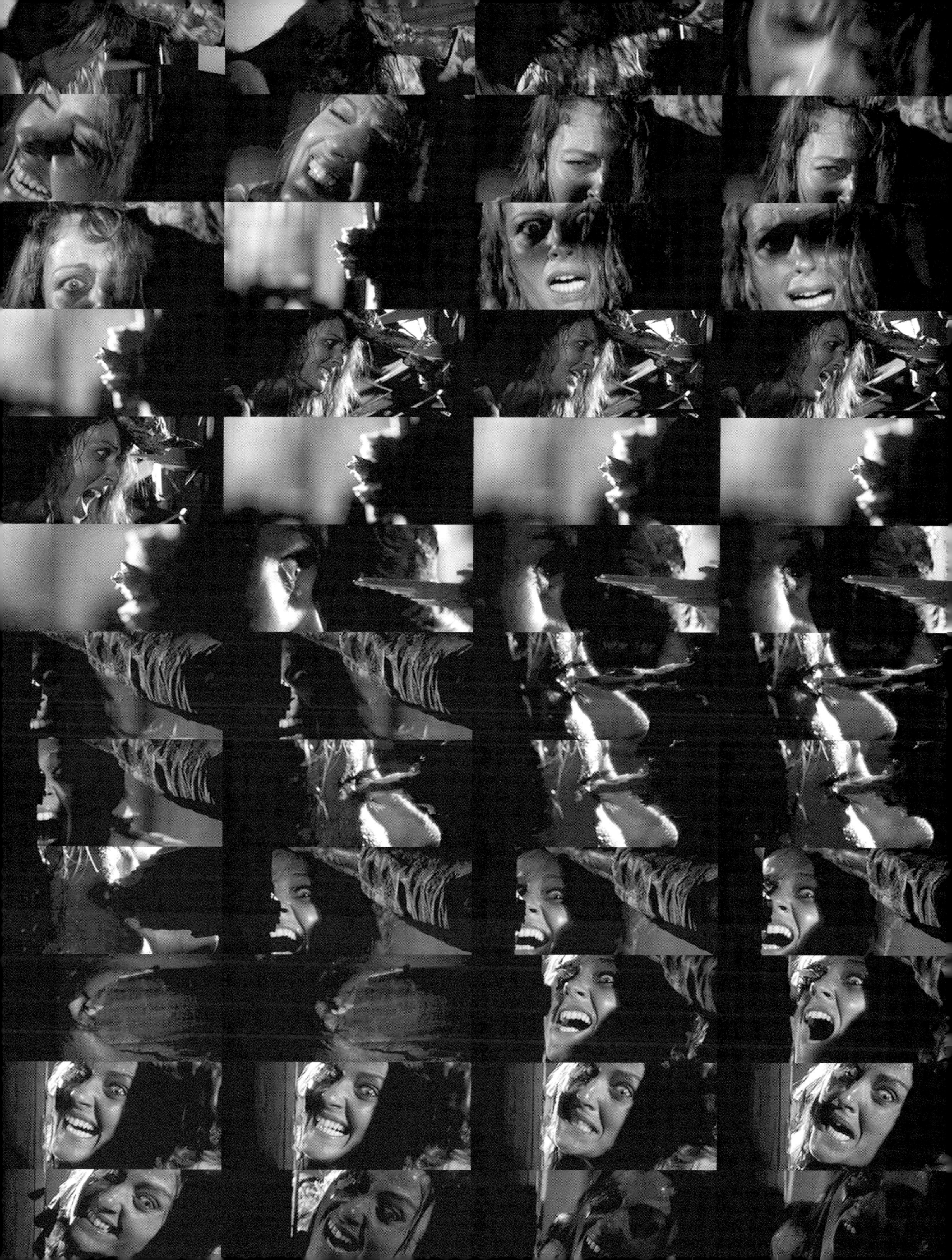

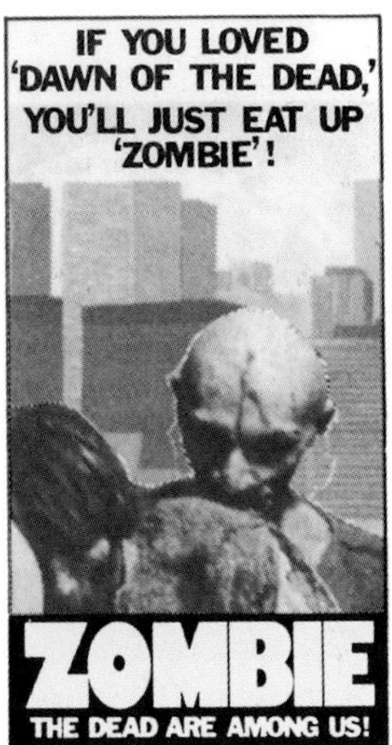

above, opposite, below right and bottom:
The film's distributors made sure their target audience got the message with a variety of memorable strap lines.

Italian independence, American influence

So there is a distinction to be made between Fulci's approach to the gruesome and Romero's. In *Dawn of the Dead* the violence, however shocking, is remarkably clean, well-defined; and the ghouls are, almost without fail, nothing more than pasty-faced versions of their old living selves. This ironically feeds Romero's allegorical preoccupations. His zombies have to represent *something*, in the name of either political or (in the case of a zombiefied Hare Krishna devotee) frivolous irony. Too much decay and they would – horror of horrors! – become indistinguishable from each other. (This may well be why *Day of the Dead* – Romero's third installment – was less of a commercial success in America; the director started to follow through his own logic and had the creatures looking vague, messy and decayed). Fulci's cadavers dispense with the conceits of allegory and perambulate around as Dead Things At Large. Only two sequences demand specific identity. The first is when the *conquistadores* emerge from their ancient burial ground, and the second is when Susan returns from the dead and bites Brian.

The most famous zombie in the film – thanks to the superb American poster – is undoubtedly the one that rises from the leaf-mould of an ancient *conquistadores* graveyard to bite Susan. Tall, ugly and very strange, it lurches from a shallow grave with a nest of worms dangling from its eye sockets. Never mind that a dead *conquistadore* would probably be a mere skeleton, this is how zombies looked in the classic 'EC Comics' of the early fifties, published in America by William M. Gaines. What follows, as the *conquistadores* rise from their graves and attack the Matul hospital, shows a zest for the appearance of rotting ghouls which is typical of both the EC artists (Jack Davis, Graham 'Ghastly' Ingels and others) and the Italian *fumetti* (popular and violent comic-strip pamphlets). This visual approach is maintained throughout. Look at the composition when Mrs. Menard is pulled through the doorframe for her date with the splinter of destiny; the arrangement of diagonals and jagged zigzags bears striking resemblance to a good frame of comic strip art.

Zombie Flesh-Eaters is not a masterpiece, but a sort of 'pop classic' of Italian horror. In terms of its construction it's neither suspenseful enough to bear comparison with Fulci's gialli, nor oblique enough to be considered as visual poetry, as his next few movies deserved. It's also lumbered with a bathetic, laughable coda, remembered almost as often as the classic eye impalement scene. The surviving characters sail back to New York, but tune in to a radio announcer screaming, *"I've just been informed that zombies have entered the building, they're at the door... they're coming in... Aaarrgh!"* In a campy sort of way this is quite funny, but is likely to leave casual audiences laughing at, and not with, the film. Nonetheless Fulci had crafted a memorable experience, sure to excite connoisseurs of extreme imagery. The action in the second half of the film cracks along with the energy a good horror comic should have. Ultimately, *Zombie Flesh-Eaters* is sensational without being particularly complex. But thanks to a wonderful score and the outrageous invention of the gore effects, it stays in the hearts and minds of those who love Italian exploitation cinema.

Footnotes

1 Although for years it was thought that Sacchetti had given the credit to his wife, possibly for tax purposes, Briganti's commentary track on the Arrow Films Blu-ray of *Zombie Flesh-Eaters*, released in 2012, establishes that she genuinely co-authored the script.

2 It is now commonly upheld that the American slasher film owes a major stylistic and narrative debt to Italian horror maestro Mario Bava's *A Bay of Blood*, where a strikingly similar series of gruesome murders to those of the early *Friday the 13th* films can be seen. The Bava film circulated regularly in the US, trailing a variety of re-titlings which effaced its Continental origins – including a notorious reselling as the bizarre and inappropriate *Last House on the Left Part 2* (see Chapter 4). Bava's 1965 sci-fi outing, *Planet of the Vampires* influenced the 1979 smash hit *Alien*, as *Alien*'s writer Dan O'Bannon admitted in an interview with David Konow: *"I was aware of* Planet of the Vampires. *I don't think I had seen it all the way through [...] I had seen clips from it and it struck me as evocative. It had the curious mixture that you get in these Italian films of spectacularly good production design with an aggressively low budget mentality."* Outside of horror, early Italian spectacles such as *The Last Days of Pompeii* (1913) and *Cabiria* (1914) were massive influences on Hollywood's own epic historical tales. See Chapter Three.

3 Richard Rubinstein, Romero's *Dawn of the Dead* producer, interviewed by Jim Wynorski in *Fangoria* #8, October 1980.

4 Sacchetti may be right about his own situation at the time, but Fulci's next film after *Zombi 2 – The Smuggler* – went into production in December of 1979. It was released the following August.

5 Ian McCulloch interview by Martin Coxhead, *Fangoria* #52, March 1986.

6 Lucio Fulci, interviewed by Jim Wynorski in *Fangoria* #8, October 1980.

7 Richard Matheson's 1950s novel *I Am Legend* has been cited by George Romero as an influence on his *Night of the Living Dead*. Boris Sagal's *The Omega Man* (1971) is an adaptation of Matheson's story but fails to bring much of the uncanny to its 'last man under siege from vampires' premise.

8 These assumptions, which are both insulting and potentially useful to the perceived 'underclass', extend into the mercantile and 'upper class' notion of the fearsome virility and animalistic passions of the working class.

9 *Variety*, 7 February 1979.

10 Dardano Sacchetti, from an e-mail to the author dated 18 June 2012. The original Italian is as follows: *"Fulci girò esattamente lo script che era pronto da otto mesi. Non aggiunse e non tolse una virgola. La scena dell'occhio era descritta fotogramma per fotogramma."*

11 From Barbara Creed, *The Monstrous Feminine*, pp9-10 (Routledge, 1993).

12 From Barbara Creed, *The Monstrous Feminine*, p14 (Routledge, 1993).

ZOMBIE FLESH EATERS ARE HERE!
ZOMBIE
WHAT HAPPENS LATER IN
NEW YORK IS EVEN MORE TERRIFYING!

right:
Zombies rise from the shallow graves of Matul's *conquistadores*.

WE ARE GOING TO EAT YOU!

ZOMBIE

...THE DEAD ARE AMONG US!

Jerry Gross presents "ZOMBIE" starring Tisa Farrow • Ian McCulloch • Richard Johnson • Al Cliver
Story and Screenplay by Elisa Briganti • Produced by Ugo Tucci and Fabrizio De Angelis for Variety Film
Color by Metro Color • Directed by Lucio Fulci • Distributed by The Jerry Gross Organization

There is no explicit sex in this picture.
However, there are scenes of violence which may be considered shocking.
No one under 17 will be admitted.

THE ISLAND
OF THE
LIVING DEAD
(ZOMBI 2)

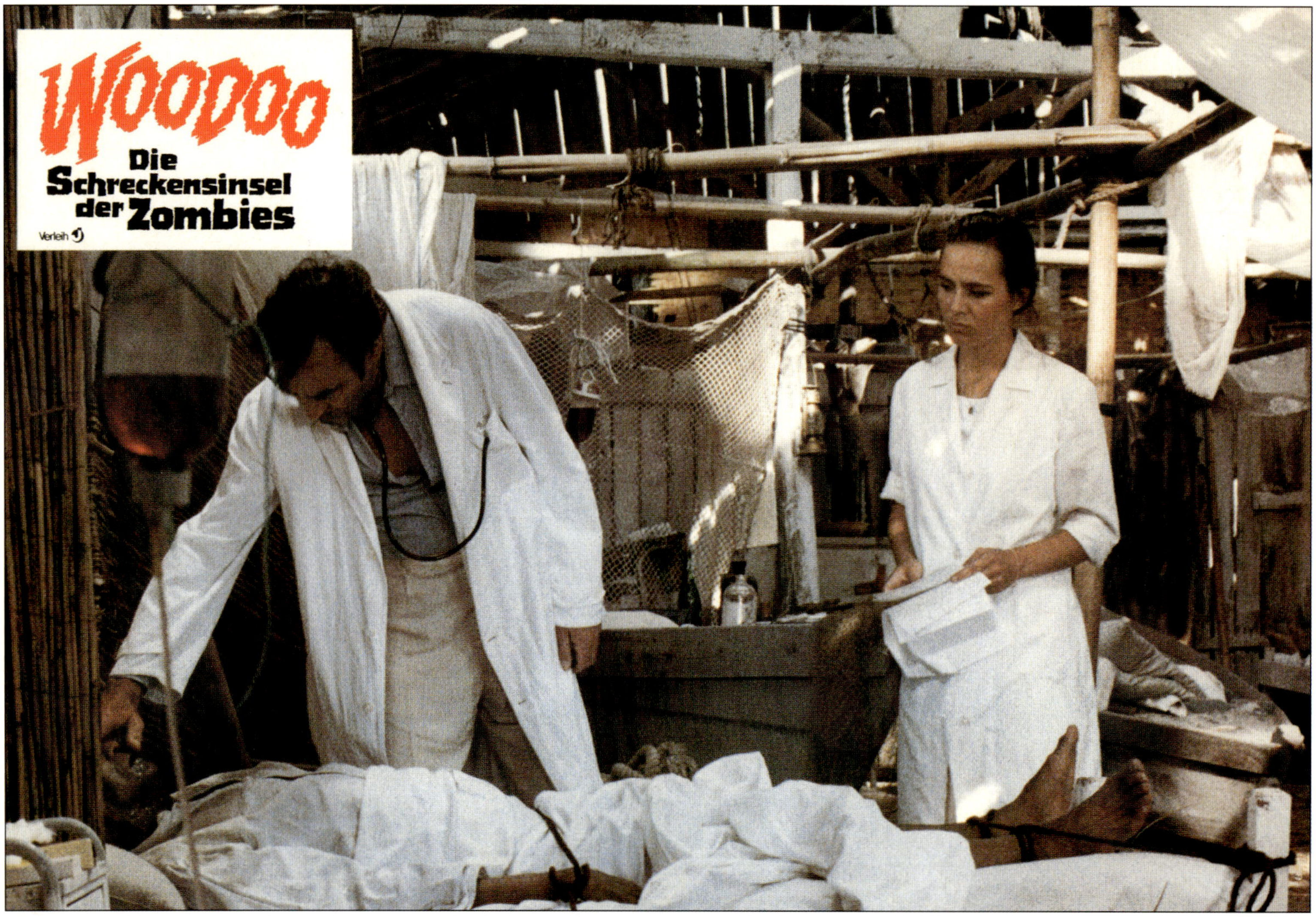

WOODOO
Die Schreckensinsel der Zombies
Verleih

WOODOO
Die Schreckensinsel der Zombies
Verleih

WOODOO

Die Schreckensinsel der Zombies

Verleih

WOODOO

Die Schreckensinsel der Zombies

Verleih

above: Ahoy there maties! Actor and dog-trainer Arthur 'Captain' Haggerty as the first of Fulci's 'character' zombies.

left: The most famous snaggle-toothed grin in zombiedom: seen here on the original Italian poster.

below: Zombies stagger through a deserted village on the island of Matul – a scene of Lewtonesque desolation beautifully photographed by Fulci's regular cameraman of the period, Sergio Salvati.

opposite anticlockwise from top left: Anne (Tisa Farrow), Peter (Ian McCulloch) and Brian (Al Cliver) get aquainted in the Antilles; Dr. Menard's assistant Lucas (Dakar) rises from the dead to attack Anne; a seemingly deserted schooner drifts into New York under the Brooklyn Bridge; cops versus zombies on an Italian fotobusta.

Woodoo
Die Schreckensinsel der Zombies

Woodoo
Die Schreckensinsel der Zombies

VARIETY FILM presenta

...quando i morti usciranno dalla tomba,
i vivi saranno il loro sangue...
ZOMBI 2
IAN Mc CULLOCH • TISA FARROW • RICHARD JOHNSON · AL CLIVER · AURETTA GAY
e con OLGA KARLATOS regia di LUCIO FULCI fotografia di SERGIO SALVATI musica di FABIO FRIZZI e GIORGIO TUCCI
prodotto da UGO TUCCI e FABRIZIO DE ANGELIS per la VARIETY FILM \ produttore associato GIANFRANCO COUYOUMDJIAN Technicolor

กรีทาทัพตามกัด.... สยดกว่า! มันเขี้ยวกว่า! และดำโตกว่า!
ตัดสินใจแต่เดี๋ยวนี้จะหนีหรือสู้
กัดยับ
และแหลก
กว่าภาคแรก
โดยผลงาน
ของทีมสร้างเดิม
คนกัดคน
ซอมบี้ 2
ZOMBI 2
ภาค 2
ริชาร์ด จอห์นสัน
ทิช่า ฟาร์โรว์ นำ.
โคบราเดอร์สฟิล์ม
CO-BROTHERS FILM

ฉายที่ วันที่

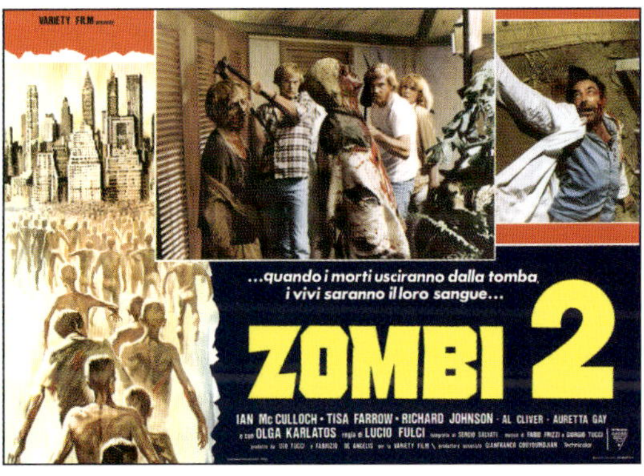

this page: Although Fulci withheld a New York apocalypse until the last few minutes of *Zombie Flesh-Eaters*, it didn't stop the poster designers from choosing Manhattan under siege as the key artwork to be used around the world: in Thailand (poster on facing page); in Italy (for this *Zombi 2* fotobusta); in Mexico (as *Los muertos vivientes*, above); in Venezuela (cheekily retitled *La noche de los muertos vivos* or 'Night of the Living Dead'!) and in Spain (as *Nueva York bajo el terror de los zombi* or 'New York Under Terror of the Zombies').

top: An image more representative of the film's visual pallette – dishevelled corpses roaming a poverty-stricken shanty village on a Caribbean island.

GAUMONT présente

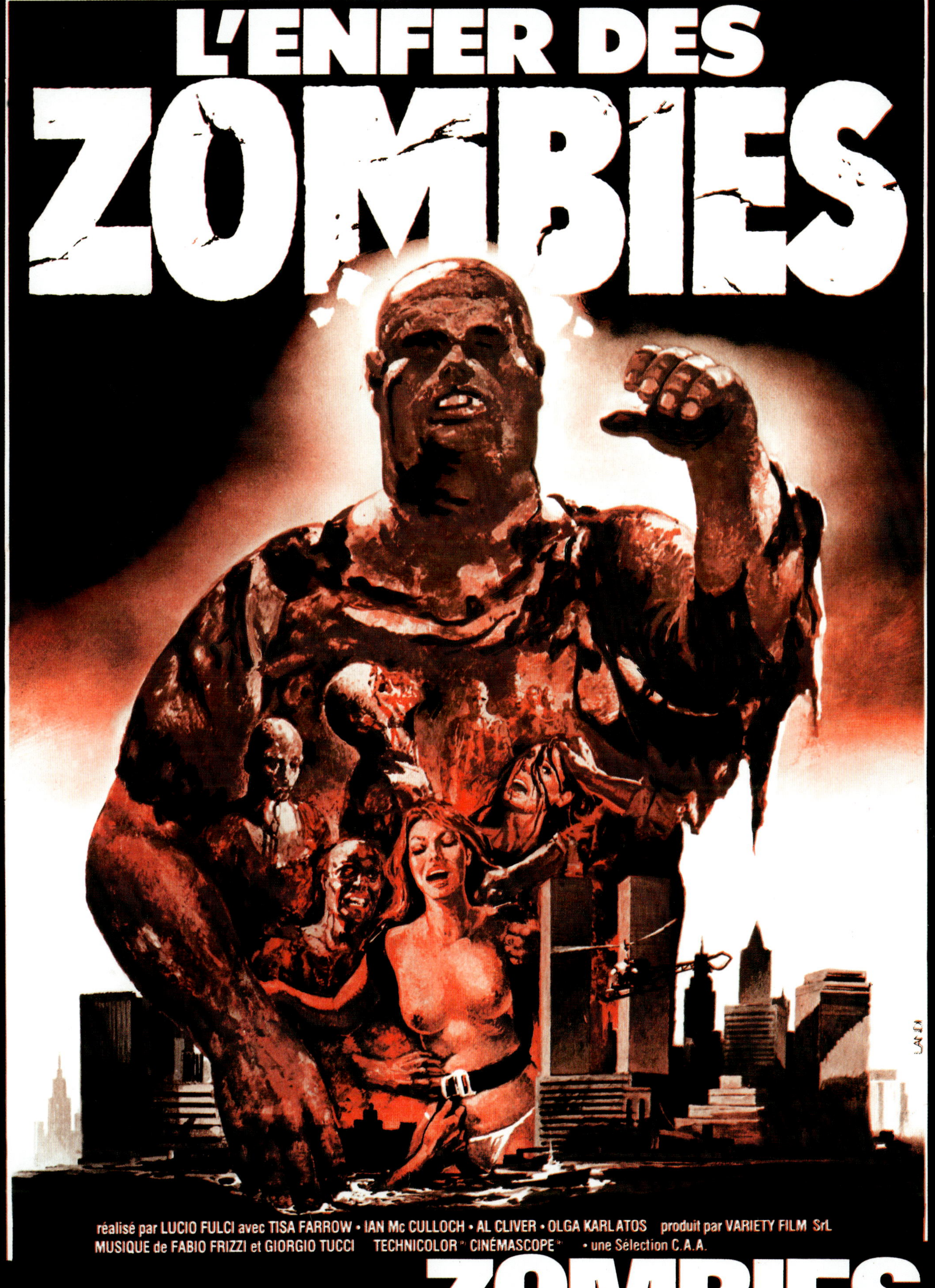

DE HELVAN DE ZOMBIES

(THE ISLAND OF THE LIVING DEAD)

Imprimé en Belgique

EDICOLOR - Bruxelles - Tél. 343.63.49 . 343.87.43

FILIMPEX- EXCELSIOR

MADAME LA PRÉSIDENTE EST PEU FAROUCHE!

avec met EDWIGE FENECH
en/et RAF LUCA
GIANCARLO DETTORI

REGIE LUCIO FULCI

MIJN ZUSTER EN IK

VERANTWOORDELIJKE UITGEVER : EXCELSIOR

DRUK. LICHTERT - 1070 Brussel

this page: top: Belgian poster for Fulci's *La Pretora*; **bottom left:** Spanish pressbook cover for *Young Dracula*; **bottom right:** Spanish pressbook for *The Eroticist*.

WANTED
Four numbskulls who stole a $50,000,000 statue from the Vatican, and sold it for $80.
For further information, see
IS THIS ANY WAY TO RUN A VATICAN?
OPERATION ST. PETER
REWARD (IN HEAVEN)
LANDO BUZZANCA · JEAN-CLAUDE BRIALY · HEINZ RUHMANN
CHRISTINE BARCLAY · UTA LEVKA · ANTONELLA DELLA PORTA · PINUCCIO ARDIA · UGO FANGAREGGI · DANTE MAGGIO
EDWARD G. ROBINSON AS "JOE VENTURA"
AN ULTRA FILM PRODUCTION · LUCIO FULCI · IN COLOR
AN ITALO-FRANCO-GERMAN CO-PRODUCTION
ULTRA FILM—MARIANNE PRODUCTIONS—ROXY FILM · A PARAMOUNT PICTURE
COPYRIGHT © 1969 PARAMOUNT PICTURES CORPORATION

Cea
DISTRIBUCION
MARIO CAROTENUTO
ANDREA CECCHI
MARISA MERLINI
HELENA CHANEL
LA RUBIA TUVO LA CULPA
JANO,
DIRECTOR
LUCIO FULCI

chapter three

The Comedies

(1959 - 1976)

Lucio Fulci's career from the late 1960s onwards has received a lot of attention from fans and historians of Italian genre cinema. His earlier work, however, has not. It can come as quite a surprise to discover that before Fulci had even begun to create the macabre tales of horror for which he was internationally famous, he'd made an astonishing sixteen comedy films, interspersed with three rock'n'roll musicals or 'musicarellos'. Unfortunately, these earlier films are mostly unavailable in English and so have tended to fall by the wayside in English-language studies of his work. In 1999, when this book was first published, very few of Fulci's early films were available commercially. They played on Italian TV from time to time, but there was little one could do to track them down. Since then, of course, the media landscape has changed enormously, and it is now possible to see every one of Fulci's films. This new edition therefore covers all of the titles missing from the original text.

Cinema d'Italia

From the beginning, Italy has had a love affair with the cinema. Even before there were any Italian films, exhibitors were plying audiences with the earliest available titles from France. These movies were shown in theatres, travelling carnivals, and – in the big cities – in specially built movie-houses. The first Italian fiction film was made in 1905 (*The Capture of Rome, 20th September 1870*, by Filoteo Alberini), and marked Italy's early preference for historical spectacle. Other titles proliferated to satisfy this taste. *Quo Vadis* (1912), *The Fall of Troy* (1913), *The Last Days of Pompeii* (1913) – the latter remade repeatedly right up to the late 1950s; these films combined grand spectacle with literary respectability. Unlike most other countries, where the cinema was considered, for many years, as a vulgar diversion for the lower classes, Italian films were immediately incorporated into the fabric of the arts. Some early titles were subsidized by wealthy Italian aristocrats, eager to demonstrate their appreciation of the new art-form and to bask in the reflected glory of these expensive evocations of ancient times.

At first, the historically-based films were a means to propagate traditional aesthetics from literature. Even poetry was allied to the early Italian cinema, with Gabriele D'Annunzio being invited to write the intertitles for one of the period's most prestigious epics, Giovanni Pastrone's *Cabiria* (1914).[1] This three-hour cornerstone of Italian cinema, detailing the travails of the eponymous Sicilian slave girl during the Second Punic War, introduced the popular strong-man character Maciste (played here for the first time by Bartolomeo Pagano, a dock-worker chosen simply for his physique). Maciste appeared in a few more adventures in the following years, before spawning the hugely popular peplum genre of the 1950s and '60s. Although related to the old historical spectacles, these later films ditched close ties to literature and the exhaustive recreation of history-book events. Instead the peplum emphasised fantastical feats of physical prowess, mixing musclebound Olympian heroics with sometimes weird mythical action. The films blurred the line between mythology and history, creating a realm of popular myth incorporating them both.[2]

Prior to World War I, film production flourished in several cities (chiefly Rome, Naples, Milan and Turin) and Italian producers enjoyed considerable success exporting their entertainments around Europe and the United States. But this initial fecundity was limited by the problem of distribution during the war, and by the start of the 1920s Italy was experiencing a wave of American dominance, thanks to the rapidly growing popularity of Hollywood movies. Throughout the 1920s a downward trend emerged. Between 1923-29 production figures were particularly poor – 15 films a year or less. By then, 80% of movies screened were American. Italian producers were failing to move with the times and attempting to sell audiences on formulas from pre-war production.

Fortunately, throughout the 1930s there was a slow recovery in Italy's film production. This was actually due to the Fascist government of the time who encouraged a nationalized co-ordination of cinema enterprise, backing the construction of the Centro Sperimentale film school in 1932 and the most famous of Italy's film studios, Cinecittà, in 1937. The studio was soon able to boast high-level facilities on a scale unrivalled outside the USA, and its soundstages were occupied constantly.[3]

opposite:
This beautiful Spanish poster for *Colpo gobbo all'italiana* bears the Spanish release title *La rubia tuvo la culpa*, which translates as 'The Blonde Was to Blame'. In defiance of the title, however, the artist (Francisco Fernandez Zarza-Pérez, aka 'Jano') has chosen as his subject the relatively minor character of Silvana (Ombretta Colli), a brunette! 'Jano' also created the gorgeous Spanish poster for Jess Franco's *Los ojos siniestros del Doctor Orloff.* Note Fulci's signature on this poster, to the left of his director credit.

below:
Early days, before the rise of the *comedia all'italiana*... dock-worker Bartolomeo Pagano, the first man to portray Italy's popular heroic archetype Maciste, launched the *peplum* genre in the epic *Cabiria* (1914).

Whilst the political intention may have been to fix and manipulate, through cultural 'engineering', a distinct, protected national identity, the government's initiatives would thankfully bear less tainted fruit. The Fascists stimulated the growth of the industry, but they failed to really control the tenor of the stories told by filmmakers (unlike the more drastic controls exerted by Stalin in the Soviet Union).

Mussolini's death came in 1945 at the end of the Second World War, and the following years saw the development of a new and important movement in Italian cinema – Neo-Realism. Luchino Visconti's *Ossessione* (1943), a movie based on James M. Cain's novel *The Postman Always Rings Twice*, with its censor-baiting sexuality and gritty rural realism, was the precursor of a new cinema focusing on ordinary lives and hardships, frequently peopled by non-actors and filmed on location. Addressing the turmoil and economic misery of the collapsed nation, Neo-Realist film was epitomised by Roberto Rossellini's *Rome, Open City* (1945).

Around 65 Italian films were being made each year as the 1940s ended. Producers from the United States began to mount productions at Cinecittà too, thanks to relaxed financial arrangements. By the time the 1950s – a significant, lucrative decade for Italian cinema – were underway, production was up to between 130-140 films a year. The number of cinema seats sold also reached a peak. 1955 saw ticket sales reach a phenomenal 819 million. The American studio 20th Century Fox elected to film their Frank Sinatra vehicle *Three Coins in the Fountain* at Cinecittà in 1954, and soon the studio was being dubbed 'Hollywood on the Tiber'. Cheap facilities, good weather and cheaper labour attracted more and more American productions. Add to this the fact that up-and-coming Italian directors like Federico Fellini and Michelangelo Antonioni – as well as established figures Roberto Rossellini and Vittorio De Sica – were gaining international recognition, and the 1950s can undoubtedly be considered a boom time full of opportunity and activity for Rome's film industry.

Funny business Italian style

The success of the industry was not, however, solely based on the artistic credibility of its emerging international directors. Italy was churning out its own brand of mainstream cinema, keenly attuned to audience demand, and it was this type of product that made the industry so robust, providing the financial security necessary to make Italy's 'art' cinema viable. Producers could afford to gamble on critically lauded but 'difficult' directors like Michelangelo Antonioni because the home market provided a steady flow of cash from the less esoteric, more populist entertainments. Production companies like the Lombardo family's 'Titanus' evolved a strategy which balanced popular films, by comedy specialists like Dino Risi, with auteurist work by Fellini (*Il bidone*, 1955) and Luchino Visconti (*Rocco and His Brothers*, 1960).[4]

Over the years, a constantly evolving chain of genres proliferated: historical epics, muscleman spectacles, espionage capers, westerns, science fiction sagas, giallo murder mysteries, regurgitated exorcism movies, violent cop thrillers, Gothic horror fantasies, hard gore films, post-Apocalyptic adventures, erotic thrillers; all have swum intricately around in the 'exploitation' pool, sometimes consuming each other or mating to produce exotic, short-lived mutations. But one type of movie would remain a constant, decade after decade – the homegrown Italian comedy. Throughout the fifties and on into the sixties, it was comedy, not the Gothic horror or the peplum, that ruled Italian production. A phenomenal number, ranging from pure slapstick to jaundiced political satire, were produced to meet the demands of an eager cinema-going populace.

In his book "Italian Films", Robin Buss explains some of the key qualities of Italian comic cinema: *"...the comedies of the post-war period are not mere farce. In fact, it is characteristic of Italian comedy that its subjects are often decidedly unfunny (war, especially; crime, seduction and adultery; even rape) and that it lurches often from farce to tragedy. It derives... from an inability to keep out the unpleasant realities of life, and an awareness that fate has a habit of turning clowns into emperors, heroes into corpses and cowards into heroes. It is to do with insecurity about identity, an uncertainty about what one is engaged in, which blurs distinctions of genre."*

Italian film comedy was originally based on theatre's *commedia dell'arte* and the bawdy satirical romps of writers like Boccaccio. However, it soon became a host for the growing influence of Hollywood. The culture's stockpile of comedy archetypes expanded in the late 1930s to incorporate a 'high-class' aesthetic drawn from sophisticated Hollywood comedies and drawing-room melodrama. This was the birth of the so-called 'white telephone' subgenre of Italian film comedy. Bourgeois in social alignment, it was preoccupied with wit, wealth and manners rather than slapstick, satire and absurdity.

The Italian cinema's love affair with broader comedy reasserted itself with the *commedia all'italiana* of the late 1950s. This 'comedy-Italian style' arose from the *neo-realisma rosa* or 'rose-tinted' neo-realism of the late 1940s and early 1950s. After the socially challenging but sometimes depressing neo-realist films began to pall, this more sentimental variant arrived, sweetening the hardships depicted with a greater emphasis on humour and optimism. Even De Sica, whose *Bicycle Thieves* (1948) was a touchstone of Italian Neo-Realism, indulged in the *neo-realisma rosa* in films like *The Gold of Naples* (1954). However, the emerging *commedia all'italiana* could be a few shades darker than this rather mawkish forerunner. The 1950s were a period of great change in Italian society, with the economy booming but the political direction of the country stagnating. The stage was set for a comedy with greater satirical emphasis, ridiculing both the 'modernity' of Italy's vulgar, TV-stimulated consumerism and the surviving dogmas of the 'old' Italy (on sexual matters, for instance), whilst importing elements of moral and social criticism.

Totò, i Re di Commedia

It is impossible to discuss the *commedia all'italiana* without referring to Italy's most loved and revered comedic figure; Totò, and yet even today he remains largely unknown outside his native land. In 2007 the Italian novelist Umberto Eco wrote, *"In this globalised universe where it seems that everybody's watching the same movies and eating the same food, there are still abysses and overwhelming fractures separating one culture from another. How can two peoples, one of which is oblivious of Totò, truly understand each other?"*[5] Eco was discussing the difficulty of translating Italian novels into Chinese, but it's not just in China that Totò remains obscure. The king of Italian comedy made over a hundred films in his homeland but he's a virtual unknown in the English-speaking world. Only in France has he received anything like the attention his work enjoys in Italy. (*Cahiers du Cinema* devoted two consecutive issues to the Neapolitan comic, in February and March 1979.) Lucio Fulci cut his teeth as a writer and assistant director on a string of Totò films during the 1950s but most of them are out of sight across one of the cultural fractures described by Eco. There has never been a London retrospective devoted to the comic at the National Film Theatre, and most of his work remains untranslated...

Totò was born Antonio De Curtis (aka Antonio De Curtis Gaglardi Ducas Commeno Di Bisanzio) in Naples on 15 February 1898. In the 1940s he staged comedy revues at theatres specialising in the *commedia dell'arte*, and throughout his career he would continue to draw on this highly stylized form: gestures of proclamation and denunciation, contorted emotional outbursts, parodic demonstrations of carnival cunning, *faux-naïf* jollity; all emerge in the *commedia dell'arte*'s ritualized movements. Bordering the areas of mime and dance, and with a weird similarity to puppeteering, it's something of an acquired taste for those whose culture doesn't include it as part of the background noise of familiar entertainment.

Totò's career prefigures and predates the *commedia all'italiana* – his first film, *Fermo con le mani!* by Gero Zambuto, was released in 1937. Early efforts like this and *Animali pazzi* (1939), by Carlo Ludovico Bragaglia, attempted to forge a whimsical persona for the comedian, but his aggressive, pleasure-seeking stage character was unsuited to these softer films. Gradually his performances were allowed to flourish as he wished, and Totò was able to attract writers willing to explore his style. He favoured an exaggerated form of physical absurdity, tending to the proletarian in class orientation and aggressively anarchic in spirit. By the time the young Lucio Fulci encountered him in the early fifties, he had become established as a major figure in Italian cinema. His films were made with a variety of directors, although he preferred working with the esteemed comedy specialist Stefano Vanzina, aka Steno.[6]

Steno's films, and others by directors like Mario Monicelli,[7] were part of a regular output featuring the Neapolitan comic, who would insert his own persona into parodies of then popular trends; hence his peplum entry *Totò contro Maciste* (1962, d: Fernando Cerchio) and the horror tale *Totò all'inferno* (1955, d: Camillo Mastrocinque). The appeal of this wily clown in Italy was far-reaching. *Guardie e ladri*, directed by Steno and Mario Monicelli in 1951, was one of many Totò films to enjoy critical success as well as entertaining the 'uneducated masses' of rural Italy.

Lucio Fulci gained precious early experience writing for the famous comedian under Steno's tutelage. Steno became his mentor, and the two worked together on fifteen films in as many years.

Prior to being taken under the famous director's wing, Fulci had worked as second unit assistant director on Paolo Moffa and Marcel L'Herbier's *The Last Days of Pompeii* (shot 1948-49, released 1950) and made a number of short documentaries. As the fifties progressed, he graduated to assistant director on Steno's *Totò e i re di Roma* ('Totò and the King of Rome', 1952), *Totò e le donne* ('Totò and the Women', 1952) and *Totò a colori* ('Totò in Colour', 1952; Italy's very first colour film); then worked as co-scriptwriter on *Totò all'inferno* ('Totò in Hell', 1955), *Totò nella Luna* ('Totò on the Moon', 1958) and *Totò, Peppino e la dolce vita* ('Totò, Peppino and the Sweet Life', 1961). The culmination of these collaborations came in 1959, when Totò agreed to star in Fulci's directorial debut, *I ladri* ('The Thieves'). Despite it being quite a coup for the neophyte director to have a big star like Totò onboard, the film itself proved inauspicious – or as Fulci once described it, "a dazzling failure".[8]

Totò also acted in films by Italy's 'art cinema' directors, including Roberto Rossellini and Federico Fellini. (The latter stepped in to direct scenes for 1954's *Dov'è la libertà...?* after Rossellini fell ill.)[9] His performance in Pier Paolo Pasolini's *Hawks and Sparrows* (1966) was critically lauded, and he went on to appear in *Che cosa sono le nuvole?*, Pasolini's segment of *Capriccio all'italiana*. Totò was working in the cinema right up to his death in 1967. He left behind a body of work that is still beloved by Italian audiences today.

Foundations of Sordi

When it came to Italian comedy in the 1950s, second only to Totò was Alberto Sordi – and as a young, energetic scriptwriter Fulci wrote for this much-loved actor too. Born in Rome in 1920, Sordi began his career in the 1940s when he dubbed Oliver Hardy's voice for Italian releases of the Laurel and Hardy films. Early performances of note included the eponymous lead in Fellini's *The White Sheik* (1952) and 'Alberto' in Fellini's next film *I vitelloni* (1953). These credits led director Steno, and a scripting team including the young Lucio Fulci, to invent a character for Sordi to play in Steno's portmanteau film *Un giorno in pretura* (1953). Together with the actor, they created a suave, glib but immaculately dressed rogue, coasting on the new freedom and prosperity of post-war Rome, and revelling in the imported manners of the American 'liberators'. It was to become a regular, popular persona for him. Fulci and Steno would elaborate on it in their 1954 collaboration for Sordi, *Un americano a Roma* and 1955's *Piccola posta*. Fulci's contribution is frequently overlooked in favour of Steno's, but the fcat that Sordi went on to become one of Italy's most

above left:
Lobby card image for *00-2 agenti segretissimi* (1964).

above:
Locandina for Fulci's first film, and a scene from *I ladri* depicting Totò (right).

opposite and bottom left:
Various posters for films headlined by the ubiquitous Italian comedy star *Totò*.

below:
Fulci's second film followed swiftly on from his debut; both were made in 1959. *I ragazzi del juke box* (or 'Jukebox Boys') faired better at the box-office, so Fulci returned again to the rock'n'roll musical format, with one of the 'Jukebox Boys' – Adriano Celentano – as his star. See *Urlatori alla sbarra* and *Uno strano tipo*.

above:
lobby card from Fulci's *I due pericoli pubblici* (1964).

Locandina for a celebratory title in the Franco & Ciccio filmography.

Lucio Fulci working on set with his mentor Steno (Stefano Vanzina).

top right:
Locandina for *L'amore primitivo* (1964), featuring the two Sicilian clowns cavorting with American import Jayne Mansfield, whose career took in stints at Cinecittà and Hollywood (see *The Wild, Wild World of Jayne Mansfield*).

bottom right:
Franco & Ciccio in *002 operazione Luna*.

facing page:
The times they were a-changing; Fulci responded to the liberalism of '60s Italy with films like *Le massaggiatrici* (1962) and *Gli imbroglioni* (1963, pictured), which offered fleeting nudity in a light comedy setting.

successful actors, his profile at home comparable to more internationally reknowned figures such as Marcello Mastroianni and Vittorio Gassman, owes much to Fulci's scriptwriting skills.

Fulci and the Two Cine-Idiots

In 1962 Lucio Fulci embarked on a run of thirteen films with comedians Franco Franchi and Ciccio Ingrassia, aka Franco & Ciccio. Like Totò, the duo were enormously popular in Italy (and to a lesser degree in Spain) but their appeal elsewhere was virtually non-existent. While a few films in which they appeared as minor players were released internationally (Mario Bava's *Dr. Goldfoot and the Girl Bombs* for instance), this was rarely ever true of the films they headlined. A short-lived attempt by one distributor to introduce them to the American public (see entry on *00-2 agenti segretissimi*) reaped little reward, and so the duo remained almost exclusively an Italian phenomenon. Even today, not a single genuine 'Franco and Ciccio' film is officially available on DVD in the UK or USA.

And yet, although they've remained out of sight of the English-speaking world, the films are not totally alien. Comparison can be made to the British music hall tradition, in particular the farcical physical comedy of Norman Wisdom. Like Franco and Ciccio, Wisdom was never highly thought of by critics but he was very popular with working class audiences: his run of seventeen 'star vehicles' between 1955 and 1969, many for the Rank Organisation, can be seen as one of the most sustained box-office success stories of the post-war period. The big difference is that whereas Wisdom always played 'honest' working characters, Franco and Ciccio tended to play petty criminals or conmen; both, however, relied on the pricking of others' pomposity to generate sympathy. The 'Carry On' comedy films also come to mind, on account of their taste for pastiche and their fondness for absurd facial contortions, although the Franco and Ciccio films are not so relentlessly fixated on sexual innuendo: there's a certain amount of impudent lechery, but the undercurrent of sexual repression and embarrassment so characteristic of the Carry Ons is not evident. That said, it's not difficult to imagine the two Sicilians appearing in a scene with Carry On star Kenneth Williams, an actor whose comic snobbery would have played well against the exaggerated crudity of Franchi.

Franchi and Ingrassia began their careers together, performing open-air theatre and variety shows in Sicily (both were born in Palermo). After being discovered by a popular singer of the time, Domenico Modugno, they were offered small parts in Mario Mattoli's *Appuntamento a Ischia* (1960) and Vittorio De Sica's *The Last Judgement* (1961). Their first starring roles were for Neapolitan writer/comedian Riccardo Pazzaglia, who chose them for his film *L'onorata società* (1961), and from here they set their screen personas down in stone, relentlessly reproducing a stock range of expressions through over a hundred films. Franco would play the rough, rubber-faced working class clown, all flailing limbs and idiot grimacing, whilst Ciccio – gaunt and pseudo-dignified – played the arrogant superior, driven to distraction by his 'crazy' companion.

Their involvement in Italy's art cinema was limited, although they did appear, with Totò, in *Cappriccio all'italiana*, playing puppets in Pasolini's segment of the 1967 film (*Che cosa sono le nuvole?*). Ingrassia also appeared as the mad uncle Teo in Federico Fellini's *Amarcord* (1973). They remained bound to each other throughout the 1960s and early 1970s, and despite frequent rows they once claimed, *"Dividing us would be like tearing a photograph in half"*. This they proceeded to do, however, in the mid-seventies after a series of increasingly violent

clashes. During this period Ingrassia directed two films – *Paolo il freddo* (1974) and *L'esorciccio* (1975), which contained gags at the expense of his one-time partner. Franchi, meanwhile, approached Lucio Fulci – who at the time was experiencing difficulty getting film projects together – to help him make a comedy series for Italian TV called *Un uomo da ridere* (1978).[10] It was only a brief hiatus though, and the two comics were together again a few years later to work with the Taviani Brothers in the 'jar' episode of their internationally acclaimed Pirandello adaptation, *Kaos* (1984).

Comedy is notoriously prone to subjective judgement; if a joke doesn't make you laugh it can feel like nails down a blackboard to persist any further. But while my pain threshold is low for Franco and Ciccio (even, if I may blaspheme outrageously, for Totò), I've tried where possible to put personal taste aside. Besides, as I've persisted through these films I find that I've enjoyed a few of them more than I expected. Onwards, then, through commedia alla Fulci!

Translation
'The Thieves'

Italy/Spain

International theatrical title
Contrabando en Ñapóles (SP)
'Smuggling in Naples'

Production companies
I.C.M. [Industria Cinematografica Mondiale] (Rome)
Fénix Films (Madrid)

Theatrical distributors
Regional distribution in Italy
Cinematográfica Fénix (Spain)

Running time
Italy 95m
Spain (SMC) 95m
Spain (Gremesi book) 82m

DVD running time (adjusted)
RHV DVD (Italy) 85m 57s

Censorship
Italian censor certificate 29694 issued 20 June 1959

Release information
Turin 25 August 1959
Rome 06 September 1959
Bari 10 September 1959
Barcelona 17 April 1960
Madrid 12 December 1960
Chicago, IL 16 December 1963 (Italian language, billed as 'Toto Commissario (I ladri)')

filmed in black and white

I ladri

1959

Directed by Lucio Fulci. produced by Roberto Capitani & Luigi Mondello for I.C.M. [Industria Cinematografica Mondiale] (Roma) / Fénix Film (Madrid). story & screenplay: Marcello Coscia, Nanni Loy, Ottavo Jemma, Marino Onorati, Vittorio Vighi & Lucio Fulci. director of photography: Manuel Berenguer. music: Carlo Innocenzi, conducted by Franco Ferrara; published by Nazionalmusic (Milan). editor: Gino Talamo. set designer: Ugo Pericoli. set decorator: Carlo Gentili. production manager: Ignazio Luceri. unit manager: Augusto Dolfi. assistant director: Felice D'Alisera. continuity: Franca Carotenuto. cameraman: Carlo Fiore. assistant cameraman: Angelo Lotti. costume designer: Giulia Deriu. make-up: Cesare Gambarelli. assistant make-up: Franco Gambarelli. production secretary: Remo De Angelis. assistant editor: Tita Perozzi. sound: Bruno Moreal. boom operator: Tullio Petricca. recording: Augusto Troiani. songs (including "Che notte!") written & performed by Fred Buscaglione. Interiors filmed at Incir-De Paolis Studios (Rome).

Cast: Giovanna Ralli (Maddalena Scognamiglio). Armando Calvo (Giuseppe 'Joe' Castagnato). Totò (Commissario Di Savio). Giacomo Furia (Vincenzo Scognamiglio, Maddalena's husband). Enzo Turco (Brigadiere Lanocella, Di Savio's sidekick). Maria Luisa Rolando (Concetta Improta, hula hoop dancer). Rafael Luis Calvo [as 'Rafael Calvo'] (don Antonio Ciardella, a mafioso). Juanjo Menéndez [as 'Juan José Menéndez'] (Salvatore Scognamiglio, Vincenzo's brother). Roberto De Simone (Alberto Scognamiglio, Vincenzo's uncle). *Uncredited:* Leopoldo Valentini (moustachioed policeman who interrupts interview with stripper). Félix Fernández (Dr. Ascione, forensics expert). Fred Buscaglione (himself). Mara Laso (woman irritated by Joe at New Year's Eve party).

Synopsis: Naples. As a cargo ship from America discharges its contents, a jam-jar rolls out of a packing case and is picked up by a dock worker, Vincenzo Scognamiglio. Opening it, he finds the jar is stuffed with coins. Slow-witted Vincenzo is puzzled but his shrewd wife Maddalena realises that the coins are part of a bigger consignment being smuggled into the country. After reading in a newspaper that Joe Castagnato, an American counterfeiter and thief, has recently arrived in Naples, she puts two and two together, and accompanied by her buffoonish family visits the American, insisting that he cut them in. Meanwhile, the garrulous and vain Commissioner Di Savio of Naples is on the case, and an odd-looking agent from the FBI is monitoring his investigation...

About the production: Fulci had not intended *I ladri* to be his feature directing debut, but as a recently married man he found that he badly needed the money and so was persuaded to hop into the big chair for the first time. An Italian-Spanish co-production, the project started out with the working title "Madrid at night", and was correspondingly set in the Spanish capital. By the time of filming, however, a decision had been taken to relocate the story to Naples. (If, as seems likely, the change came about when Fulci signed on as director, it would suggest that "Madrid at night" was originally intended for a Spanish helmsman.) Despite the change of story location, the shoot went ahead in Madrid, although further scenes were filmed on the outskirts of Naples to help with the new setting. Interiors were shot in Rome, chiefly to accommodate the wishes of the star, Totò, who was reluctant to leave the city. Totò's agreement to participate in the film was quite a coup for the first-time director, and a sign of the close friendship that Fulci had built up with the star during his tenure as screenwriter and assistant director.

Review: Every journey must have a beginning, innocuous words which cannot prepare one for the trudge that is *I ladri*, a comedy crime caper as threadbare in charm as its simplistic title. Whilst many of Fulci's later comedies have pleasurable qualities which open up under scrutiny, *I ladri* remains stubbornly dull and unengaging. Resting its laurels upon a hectoring, relentless performance by headlining star Totò, this visually unappealing film is set for too much of the time in drab little offices, from which the revered comedian declaims page after page of histrionic dialogue to a succession of forgettable flunkies. Playing a highly strung Neapolitan police commissioner who pits his wits against an American counterfeiter, Totò dominates the film, and one has to say not to its benefit. (In fact he appears to have taken over behind the scenes too, probably directing his own scenes. Fulci told Robert Schlockoff in *L'Écran Fantastique*, *"I did twenty-two films with [Totò], as a writer or assistant director, and he helped me direct my first film, I ladri."*)[11] It seems that Fulci, at this very early juncture, lacked the confidence to rein in his star; the scenes in which Totò appears are allowed to run indiscriminately while time ticks away and little of narrative importance is established. There is an occasional twinkle in the dialogue; (Di Savio: *"You're the king of the alibi, the king of ubiquity. You're ubiquitous, admit it! What did your friends call you?"* Castagnato: *"Elsewhere."*) but most of the surrounding material feels weak and insubstantial, and with Fulci's camera seemingly fixed to the floor much of the time there's not a lot of visual interest either. Armando Calvo, as the American criminal Joe Castagnato, is stiff and unconvincing, the bumbling Scognamiglio family are from stock, and only Giovanna Ralli as the glamorous Maddalena really shines.

I ladri has little to recommend it besides the simple fact that it marks Fulci's debut. One notes, more in desperation than enthusiasm, that it features the first corpse in the Fulci canon; an elderly watchman found dead from barbiturate abuse. There's also a slightly risqué strip routine, which climaxes with a neat little lighting trick to cover the actress's boobs; the only pleasurable twitch of technique (too brief to call it a flourish) in the film. The trick was not enough to avoid trouble with the censor: the striptease sequence was cut for the original release, although fortunately it remains intact on the Italian DVD. *I ladri* was, by Fulci's own admission, not a success (*"[it] turned out to be a big flop"*[12]), playing for a single week in Turin's Lux Cinema, and for just three days in Rome, at a cinema called the America. It was, however, more cordially received in Spain, where it played in June 1961 as *Contrabando en Nápoles*. The reviewer for ABC Madrid was moderately amused: *"Smiles, if not laughter, dominate the story, which is handled with agility by director Lucio Fulci."*[13]

The character of 'Joe Castagnato' was inspired by the song "Ciao Joe" by Fred Buscaglione, which can be heard over the opening credits. In addition, Buscaglione himself appears in the film during the New Year's Eve party sequence, singing "Che notte!" ('What a night!'). The two songs were released on a single together in 1959, with the disc label announcing they were *"from the film I ladri"*. I can find no evidence of an earlier release for either song, which suggests that Fulci first encountered "Ciao Joe" at a live performance by Buscaglione, and incorporated the idea into his script before the record was cut ... Fred (Ferdinando) Buscaglione's stage persona drew heavily on old American gangster movies, with the singer adopting a cynical drawl and exaggerated 'cool' intended to evoke the Chicago mobsters of the Hollywood films he loved. He favoured a romantic vision of the gangster as a sort of violent dandy, hat at a rakish angle and a Clark Gable moustache pencilled on his lip, with a gun in one hand and a whiskey in the other. Fulci evidently got along well with the singer; he signed him up again for *I ragazzi del juke box*, for which Buscaglione sang three songs onscreen ("Sofisticata", "Il dritto di Chicago" and "Bambole d'Italia"). These were to be among his last recordings; tragically he was killed at dawn on 3 February 1960, at the age of 38, when his car, a pink Ford Thunderbird, collided with a truck directly outside the American embassy in Rome.

top left:
The Commissario gets to grips with sexy hula hoop dancer Concetta Improta (Maria Luisa Rolando)...

above:
...and confers with forensics expert Dr. Ascione (Félix Fernández, left) while Brigadiere Lanocella (Enzo Turco) looks on.

opposite, main picture:
Commissario Di Savio (Totò) squares off against American smuggler 'Joe' Castagnato (Armando Calvo) in this staged (or missing) shot from *I ladri*.

opposite, bottom left:
Spanish poster for Fulci's first movie.

left:
Fred Buscaglione (as himself) in full Chicago gangster mode during a live performance of his song "Che notte".

below:
Enzo Turco (left) as the Commissario's sidekick, Brigadiere Lanocella.

Translation
'The Juke Box Kids'

Italy

Shooting title
Ti dirò... che tu mi piaci

International theatrical title
Con Pullover y Blue Jeans (ARG)
'With Pullover and Blue Jeans'

An Italian Production by
Era Cinematografica (Rome)

Theatrical distributors
Lux Film (Italy)

Running time
Italy 102m

TV & DVD running times (adjusted)
Italian TV 96m 26s
Medusa DVD (Italy) 98m 31s

Censorship
Italian censor certificate 30036
issued 13 August 1959

Release information
Rome 28 August 1959
Turin 01 September 1959
Brindisi 26 September 1959
Bari 12 November 1959

filmed in black and white

I ragazzi del juke box

1959

Directed by Lucio Fulci. produced by Giovanni Addessi for Era Cinematografica. production manager: Elios Vercelloni. story & screenplay: Lucio Fulci, Piero Vivarelli & Vittorio Vighi. director of photography: Carlo Montuori. music: Eros Sciorilli, conducted by Giorgio Fabor. editor: Gabriele Varriale. set designer: Ottavio Scotti. unit manager: Franco Di Mauro. assistant director: Felice D'Alisera. continuity: Franca Carotenuto. cameraman: Goffredo Bellisario. costume designer: Grazia Lusignoli. make-up: Giulio Scarozza. set decorator: Arrigo Breschi. production assistant: Saverio Scriponi. sound: Franco Groppioni. interiors filmed at Incir-De Paolis Studios (Rome).

Cast: Tony Dallara (Tony Bellaria, a singer). Elke Sommer (Giulia Cesari). Betty Curtis (Betty Dorys, a singer, Cesari's secretary). Antonio de Teffé (Paolo Macelloni, Tony's manager). Mario Carotenuto (Cesari, a record company mogul). Fred Buscaglione (Fred, a singer). Adriano Celentano (Adriano, a singer). Gianni Meccia (singer of "Odio tutte le vecchie signore"). Giacomo Furia (Gennarino, Cesari's chief associate). Benedetta Rutili [as 'Benny Rutili'] (Rosalba Bergonzoni, Cesari's mistress). Ivette [Yvette] Masson (Maria Davanzale). Giuliano Mancini (Jimmy, the bodybuilder). Milion Chery. Renato Tagliani (TV presenter introducing 'Appio Claudio'). Loretta Capitoli. Gianni Riommi. Mara Fiè (brunette girl in plaid shirt at la Fognia). Andrea Scotti (dark-haired man in striped t-shirt at La Fogna). Mario Ambrosino (Viscontelli). Rossella D'Aquino (Rossella, brunette in hooped black top). Paola Patrizi. Gianni Loti. Renato Mambor (Bill, youth who throws dart without looking at the board). Sergio Calò. Juan Santacreu. Bands appearing as themselves: The Asternovas. The Modern Jazz Gang. I Campioni. *Uncredited:* Lucio Fulci (Salomone, a promoter). Claudio Villa (Appio Claudio). Lars Bloch ('Dracula', Jimmy's blond friend at La Fogna). *Unconfirmed (from IMDb):* Karin Well. Nino Musco. Paolo Fiorino. Vera Napi. Ornella Vanoni (barmaid at La Fogna). Gianni Dei (a dancer at La Fogna).

Synopsis: In a café bar called The Sewer, young people congregate to listen to American-style rock'n'roll on the venue's gleaming new jukebox. The club is run by Paolo Macelloni, an ambitious hustler on the lookout for musical talent. His girlfriend, Giulia, is the daughter of Cesari, head of a successful record label. Giulia's father wants nothing to do with the rock'n'roll scene, preferring the sort of middle-of-the-road crooner typified by his latest signing, Appio Claudio, whom he is currently promoting heavily. When Tony Bellaria, a talented but old-fashioned crooner from the South, wins a coveted singing spot at The Sewer by throwing a bullseye dart at a picture of Mr. Cesari, Paolo is mortified: Tony's style is far more conservative than the usual Sewer fare. However, when Adriano Celentano takes control of the musical arrangements and Tony performs Figaro's aria from The Barber of Seville to a rock'n'roll beat, the crooner earns the respect of the club and Paolo becomes his manager. A visiting journalist, Salomone, suggests that the best way to combat the major labels is to put on a music festival at the club so Paolo arranges for the cream of the new crop to play there: Adriano Celentano and his Modern Jazz Gang, Fred Buscaglione and the Asternovas, eccentric singer-guitarist Gianni Meccia, and Giulia's friend Betty Dorys (who is also Cesari's secretary). Incensed by the Cesari empire's hardball business approach, which keeps the new music off jukeboxes around the country, clubgoers from The Sewer deface all the posters of Appio Claudio currently on display around the city. This does not go down well with the Mafia, who are heavily subsidising the star's career. At a showcase for Tony Bellara at The Sewer, a group of mafiosi in the audience deliberately provoke a brawl. The police are called and arrests made. Tony decides this is too much and boards a bus back to his village, but Paolo and Giulia persuade him to stay. On the night of Appio Claudio's 'coronation', a glitzy promotional bash arranged by Cesari with saturation TV coverage, the 'sewer gang' invade the stage, install a jukebox, and bop to the music while a stripper mimes to Betty's song "Troppo timidà" ('Too Shy'). The nationwide press outrage is too much for Cesari, who suffers a nervous collapse. While he's away, Giulia takes over the family business and swiftly uses her position to sign Betty and Tony. When Cesari returns he finds that Giulia's signings are outselling all of his other acts and decides to embrace the 'new wave'...

About the production: Unlike *I ladri*, the exuberant *I ragazzi del juke box* made quite a splash on release in the summer of 1959. Not only did it rake in the lira, it inaugurated a brand new Italian genre – the 'musicarello' – and provided Fulci with the template for a further two films in the same vein; *Urlatori alla sbarra* (1960) and *Uno strano tipo* (1963). The premiere screening in Rome was announced in the press on 28 August 1959, and the advertisement took no prisoners: *"Today, we mark the beginning of Lux Film's 1959-60 season, and the reopening of the Capitol cinema, with an exceptional first. Forget the 'H' bomb! Forget the arrival of Martians! Forget that trip to the moon! Look Out! Look Out! Here come the most famous 'Howlers' of the day, appearing for the first time as actors in an explosive film!"*[14] 'Howlers' or 'screamers' (a term not unlike 'ravers' in London's beatnik parlance) were a fairly recent phenomenon in Italy, and Fulci was ahead of the curve bringing the newly minted youth movement to the screen (*Rock Around the Clock* opened in Italy in October 1956; Adriano Celentano, Italy's Elvis Presley, released his first single, a cover of Little Richard's 'Rip It Up', in 1958). Fulci's timing was perfect: the alleged link between juvenile delinquency and rock'n'roll was a current hot topic in the press. Italy's left-wing newspaper *l'Unità* (founded by Antonio Gramsci in 1924) ran a full-page article on the phenomenon on the day the Fulci film opened, under the headline 'But who are these Teddy Boys?', which led off with the following strapline: *"Their escapades fill the pages of newspapers. From the acts of professional delinquents to the stunts of boorish youngsters, everything is attributed to 'Teddy-Boys' ... Is there any truth in the psychosis that seems to grip the minds of the 'right-thinking'? Is there really a problem of a resurgence of juvenile delinquency?"*[15] With press 'synergy' like that, *I ragazzi del juke box* had no trouble finding an audience...

Review: This slender but engaging story (narrated by a sentient jukebox no less) depicts a nascent rock'n'roll scene in the fictitious country of 'Festivalia', centred around a dancing club and café called La Fogna ('The Sewer'). A sign on the steps warns customers, "Please do not ask for songs from the festivals because the band that plays here is armed", which seems at first glance to reinforce the notion that these 'howlers' are a social menace. However, the film soon establishes that it's a playful pose, taken foolishly at face value by the press. The kids in the film are energetic, vivacious and naive, while the forces massed against them, represented chiefly by an uncomprehending music industry, are at best out of touch, at worst positively malicious. The stage is therefore set for a light and breezy kids-versus-squares face-off, delivered with lots of frivolous energy by Fulci. The film is positively crammed with musical interludes, from Elvis-inspired rock'n'roll to close-harmony songs showing the influence of the Everly Brothers and The Platters. A bubblegum toe-tapper and some old-time crooner material round out the bill for those who find the 'new music' too hectic.

Adriano Celentano is the key selling point, thanks to the singer's then-recent ascent to pop-idol status in Italy. His Bill Haley-soundalike song "Il ribelle" ('The Rebel') was released just a month before the film opened, making it the chart-topper uppermost in viewers' minds as they took their seats. As a consequence it gets pride of place in the film, played 'unplugged' by Celentano on a semi-acoustic guitar, in a vigorous performance surrounded by clapping children (a choice which shows how lightly he wore his rock'n'roll 'cool'). Two of his songs here, the title track and "Il tuo bacio è come un rock" ('Your kiss is like a rock'), were released off the back of the film as a single in November 1959; a third, "Vorrei saper perchè" ('I'd like to know why') was written by Fulci, Celentano and Piero Vivarelli but recorded and released by female pop sensation Mina the same year. Fulci later wrote another hit for Celentano, "24 Mila Baci", which turned up in Piero Vivarelli's film *Io bacio... tu baci* and scored a respectable second place in competition at the 1961 San Remo Festival.

Gianni Meccia, meanwhile, ensures that his female fans will abandon him in their later years, despite his Tony Curtis good looks, by grimacing his way through the frankly weird "Odio tutte le vecchie signore" ('I hate all old ladies'), performed onstage to a spotlit table of four elderly women playing cards. Prominent among the more traditional acts is Tony Dallara, whose 'Tony Bellaria' forms an unlikely partnership with Celentano's rock'n'rollers. Netting him for the film was really quite a coup: Dallara's first single "Come prima" was released in December 1957 and became the biggest selling single in Italy to that date. He went on to win a major prize at the San Remo Music Festival in 1960 and two more on the Italian TV singing contest Canzonissima in 1960-61. (Look out too for prominent soundtrack composer Berto Pisano who plays double bass during Betty Curtis's rendition of "Dimmelo con un disco".) Another singer with a traditional approach, and a major commercial profile at the time, was mellifluous tenor Claudio Villa, who plays music industry favourite 'Appio Claudio'. Strangely, given that he was a big star who'd won the San Remo music festival in 1955 and 1957 (and would go on to win it again in 1962 and 1967), Villa goes unmentioned in the credits, although he deserves a nod for gamely poking fun at his own reputation as a purveyor of patriotic tearjerkers (in this case performing a lachrymose number about a homesick miner in a foreign land dreaming of his mother, complete with train whistles and tolling bells).

Fulci himself has a speaking role in the film, playing Salomone, a journalist who takes an interest in the new music and suggests to the youngsters that they fight back against negative press by arranging their own music festival. He shows himself to be a natural comedian, playing the journalist with a wandering eye and making it perfectly clear what attracts this older man to the scene; namely the bosoms of young women in tight sweaters! As director, meanwhile, the attitude he takes to the rock'n'roll milieu is essentially sympathetic: scenes like the one in which Adriano Celentano, guitar slung around his neck, serenades horrified old ladies in the town square while gangs of children gather round and dance, are played for laughs at the expense of the uptight older generation, and the machinations and ignorance of the music establishment are held up for ridicule too.

Standout scenes include the massive ruck that breaks out in La Fogna, which begins when a gang of Cosa Nostra troublemakers deliberately trip up a young barman: tables are smashed, bottles are thrown, the bar is totalled, and the entire clientele join in (including mild-mannered Tony Dallara) until the arrival of the police brings an end to the chaos (notice how the extras playing cops can't wipe the goofy grins off their faces as they pile into the melée). The dramatic highlight, however, comes when the kids gatecrash a pompous televised music industry shindig and interrupt the 'investiture' of Appio Claudio by staging a rock'n'roll protest, complete with juke-box hauled onto the stage and a sexy girl stripping down to her underwear.

Reviewers were fairly kind to the film, with *l'Unità* declaring, *"There is not much to say about this string of songs filling a whole movie, interrupted by at most fifteen minutes of narrative. The 'shouters' criticise the 'melodic singers' because they are selling out for publicity, but in the end they too will join the chorus. The movie is smoothly directed by the young Lucio Fulci. Jukebox aficionados will love it: if they compare the price of the cinema ticket to the price for each song bought at the juke box, audiences might even say this is money well spent!"*[16]

this page, from top:
Elke Sommer and Fred Buscaglione; Gianni Meccia sings his song of hate to a group of old ladies; Betty Curtis with Celentano and his group; Tony Dallara sings the old-fashioned way but remains popular at "The Sewer"; Giulia runs the show at her father's company in this dreamy sequence; Fred (Fred Buscaglione) chats to Maria (Yvette Masson) at "The Sewer".

opposite, main picture:
Adriano Celentano rocks the shopping centre, while Paolo (Antonio de Teffé aka Anthony Steffen, left), Jimmy (Giuliano Mancini, centre) and Giulia (Elke Sommer, right) drop some foot.

opposite, bottom left:
This Italian locandina concentrates on the most glamorous juke box girl, Elke Sommer.

Translation
'Howlers in the Dock'

Italy

Alternative theatrical title
Metti, Celentano e Mina... (IT)

Production companies
Era Cinematografica (Rome)

Theatrical distributors
Lux Film (Rome)

Note: The Italian cinema archive lists CIC as distributor, although this is not borne out by the numerous posters now available for scrutiny.

Theatrical running time
Italy 83m

TV running time (adjusted)
Italian TV 82m 18s

Censorship
Italian censor certificate 31243 issued 16 February 1960

Release information
Bari 23 March 1960
Turin 21 April 1960
Rome 28 May 1960

filmed in black and white

Urlatori alla sbarra

1960

Directed by Lucio Fulci. produced by Giovanni Addessi for Era Cinematografica. production manager: Gino Millozza. story & screenplay: Giovanni Addessi, Lucio Fulci, Vittorio Vighi & Piero Vivarelli. director of photography: Gianni Di Venanzo. music: Piero Umiliani with the participation of Chet Baker. editor: Gabriele Varriale. art director: Ottavio Scotti. art director – dancing: Giancarlo Catucci for Alfonso Ferrara. unit manager: Felice D'Alisera. assistant director: Piero Vivarelli. continuity: Franca Carotenuto. cameraman: Erico Menczer. costume designer: Vera Marzot. actresses wardrobe: Luisa Spagnoli. set decorator: Camillo Del Signore. dancing & choreography: Gino Landi. sound: Mario Del Pezzo. songs "Ritroviamoci", "Moto rock", "Milioni di scintille" & "non sò parlare" performed by Joe Sentieri, courtesy of Dischi Juke-box; "Vorrei saper perchè", "Nessuno", "Wisky" & "Tintarella di luna" performed by Mina [Mina Mazzini], courtesy of Dischi Italdisc; "Rock matto", "Blue jeans rock", "Nikita rock", "Impazzivo per te", "Il tuo bacio è come un rock" performed by [Adriano] Celentano, courtesy of Dischi Jolly; "Arrivederci" performed by Chet Baker; "Precipito" & "Beby rock" performed by Brunetta, courtesy of Dischi Ricordi; "Odio" performed by Umberto Bindi, courtesy of Dischi Ricordi; "Soldati delicati" performed by Gianni Meccia, courtesy of Dischi R.C.A.; "Carina" performed by Corrado Ioiacono, courtesy of Dischi Fontana; "Io" & "Brivido blù" performed by I Brutos. music publishers: Colonna Sonora Film – Ariston – Nazional Music – Ricordi – Mascotte – Accordo – Curci.

Cast: Adriano Celentano (Adriano, 'The Springer'). Mina (Mina). Joe Sentieri (Joe 'The Red'). Elke Sommer (Giulia Giommarelli). Chet Baker (Chet Baker aka "The American"). Giacomo Furia (L'onorevole Gubellini). Giuliano Mancini (Marione, leather-jacketed gang-member). Turi Pandolfini (Senator Bucci, old man who befriends the gang). Nico Pepe. Jocelyn Lane [as 'Jakie Lane']. Elisabetta Velinski. Cristine Martel. Benedetta [Benny] Rutili (Belisaria). Marilù Tolo (Marilù). Martita de Balle. Lucia Modugno. Carlotta Barilli (Carlotta, girl who canoodles with Chet Baker at Giulia's house). Maggiora Vergano. Corrado Lojacono (Corrado). Brunetta (herself, singer of "Precipito" and "Beby Rock"). Umberto Bindi (singer in dark glasses performing "Odio"). Gianni Meccia (Gianni aka "Satan"). I Brutos [lead singer: Jack Guerrini. Backing singers: Gerry Brown, Elio Piatti, Gianni Zullo, Aldo Maccione.]. La Moderna Jazz Gang. Mario Carotenuto (Professor Giommarelli). Mimmo Billi (President of 'Blue Jeans' company). Fazio Salvatore (old man crossing road). Enzo Garinei (Carimei). Gianni Minervini. Ignazio Leone. Carlo Alighiero. Renato Mambor ("Comanche", gang-member with Davy Crockett hat). Lars Bloch [as 'Lars Block'] ('Jesse', darker of two blonds in cowboy gear). Vincenzo Bizzotto. *Uncredited:* Peppino Di Capri (singer of "Io sono mio"). Corrado Loiacono (singer of "Carina"). Umberto Bindi (singer of "Odio"). Bruno Martino. Lino Banfi (doorman at Senator Bucci's apartment). Sandro Giovannini (Giuseppini). Gorni Kramer (Bremer, 'The Maestro', an accordionist). Mario Landi (the director, Lando).

Synopsis: The adventures of a band of friends, teddy boys and rock'n'roll chicks whose crazy, fun-loving habits inspire jiving from some citizens and bitter complaints from others. A prominent jeans company feels that the kids' 'bad reputation' is adversely affecting the sales and public image of their product. Prevailing upon the youths to help, they engineer a series of promotional stunts to lighten the public's opinion of these good-hearted rock'n'roll naifs – and their lovely blue jeans. Unscrupulous politicians make things difficult for the youngsters, but all turns out well – after helping a few women across the road and carrying elderly men bodily up flights of stairs (hey, he lives on the ground floor, you crazy knuckleheads!), the film ends with the solid Roman bourgeoisie dancing in the streets, seduced by the wonders of rock and roll music.

Review: This primitive comedy plays out a musical scenario in episodic fashion. Whilst clearly intended as a showcase for the talents of Italian celebrities Adriano Celentano and Mina (making criticism of its limitations somewhat redundant), there is frankly little to get excited about. Of course American International Pictures were churning out similar pics across the Atlantic, in the wake of Universal's 1956 hit *Rock Around the Clock* (the first film about rock'n'roll, produced by trendsetting New Yorker Stan Katzman and featuring Bill Haley and the Comets). Crude though *Urlatori alla sbarra* is, it's not really any worse than the AIP flicks it's responding to.

Having said that, the lack of even the most basic jiving talents among the featured cast betray the hurried and rather amateurish nature of the production. Whoever cast the film must have been impatient with the whole idea of rock'n'roll; these youths dance like embarrassed epileptics, hopelessly trying to suppress an oncoming fit. Sadly it's the star, Adriano Celentano, who's the worst offender. Watching him twitch in such a grotesque fashion it's difficult, quite honestly, to see here what the basis of his charm was meant to be. The inarticulate spasms of a neurotic in the throes of a nervous breakdown would make a sexier spectacle than this alleged Elvis-imitator, who handles a guitar like an alien forced into karaoke bondage. One is reminded of old punk clubs, full of people expressing their 'irony' and 'alienation' by simulating mental handicap on the dancefloor. (To be fair though, *Uno strano tipo*, his next collaboration with Fulci, gives a more favourable account of his appeal.)

The modest popular success of the film was due mainly to the fact that it brought together Celentano and Mina (full name Mina Mazzini), two enduringly popular figures in the Italian pop scene. The latter, who performs her own songs but is dubbed for dialogue, is reputedly possessed of a great singing voice, although her range sounds pretty ordinary on the songs performed here. Nonetheless, she occupies a cult position in Italy to this day, and her propensity for risqué material and eccentric scat-singing of the Cleo Laine variety has apparently enshrined her in the hearts of the country's multitude of transvestites. A recent Italian 'TV' film consists of performances by a host of cross-dressers lip-synch'ing to Mina's more outré hits; for one number she sings the contents of a menu, climaxing with another kind of scat-singing as she runs out of dishes and orders "ka-ka".

Other well-known faces of the period include Mario Carotenuto, a very prolific comic actor who'd appeared in Fulci's *I ragazzi del juke box* the year before and also wrote and starred in his 1962 film *Colpo gobbo all'italiana*: a nineteen-year-old Elke Sommer (famous to all fans of Italian horror as the star of Mario Bava's wonderful *Lisa and the Devil* and the engaging *Baron Blood*) who tags along with the gang to indulge in a spot of sitting-room bop: and American trumpet legend Chet Baker, who turns up in an enigmatic (or undeveloped) performance (he also contributed one song to the soundtrack, 'Arrivederci'). Baker's melancholic musical style was fuelled by personal misfortune and a massive heroin problem: seen sprawled in the bathtub with trumpet in hand at a party, and briefly later, as a blank-eyed, mumbling apparition in a lift, he is weirdly adrift in a film he seems almost oblivious to the making of.

Urlatori alla sbarra has dated, like so many similar examples of the period, making anything but the most cursory of critical assessment now something of a waste of time. It shares the fate of British responses to the rock'n'roll phenomenon such as *Rock Around the World* (1957) starring Tommy Steele and *Expresso Bongo* (1959) with Cliff Richard, both of whom were touted as the 'British Elvis', or American surf/pop items like AIP's *Beach Party* (1963) starring Annette Funicello and Frankie Avalon. Designed to appeal to a transient youth phenomenon, ephemeral and made on the cheap, *Urlatori* is only likely to have significance today for a nostalgic Italian audience who remember the period's naiveté with fondness. There's a glimmer of the mature Fulci in the story's cynical emphasis on corporate manipulation, but it wouldn't do to labour the observation. The light, inconsequential humour is too thin to support camp reappraisal and, apart from the aforementioned hoofing, there is little in it to amuse a modern audience; a fact which one imagines would cause little consternation to either the performers or the film-makers.

above:
Celentano's band in full swing at a house party held by Mina.

left:
Locandina.

opposite, main picture:
Jazz prodigy, idol and drug casualty Chet Baker (pictured here in Bruce Weber's documentary biopic *Let's Get Lost*); an enigmatic addition to the cast of *Urlatori alla sbarra*.

opposite, bottom left:
Italian poster under the film's alternative release title.

below:
Fotobusta which emphasises the involvement of the popular singer Mina.

Translation
'Smart Move Italian-Style'

Italy

International theatrical titles
La rubia tuvo la culpa (SP)
'The Blonde Was to Blame'
Colpe bajo a la italiana (MEX)
'Below the Belt Italian Style'

Production companies
Mirafilm (IT)
Marcus Produzione Cinematografica (IT)

Theatrical distributors
Mirafilm (IT)

Running time
Italy 100m
Spain 90m

TV running time (adjusted)
Italy 97m 45s

Censorship
Italian censor certificate 37415
issued 04 May 1962

Release information
Turin 11 May 1962
Bari 11 May 1962
Rome 09 June 1962
Barcelona 02 February 1965
Seville 28 May 1965

filmed in black and white

Colpo gobbo all'italiana

1962

Directed by Lucio Fulci. a Mira Film / Marcus Cinematografica production. production manager: Roberto Fabbri. story: Mario Carotenuto. screenplay: Bruno Corbucci & Giovanni Grimaldi. director of photography: Alfio Contini. music: Piero Umiliani; published by R.C.A. editor: Franco Fraticelli. production designer: Giuseppe Ranieri. set dresser: Franco Fontana. production supervisor: Giorgio Gravina. unit manager: Bruno Sassaroli. assistant director: Leo Lenoir [Leonardo Scavino]. 2nd assistant director: Stefano Rolla. continuity: Franca Carotenuto. cameraman: Maurizio Scanzani. assistant cameraman: Remo Grisanti. 2nd assistant cameraman: Roberto Brega. assistant production designer: Franco Callapietra. production secretaries: Laura Vignola & Piero De Luca. songs "La nottola di notte", "Quello che bolle in pentola" by Piero Umiliani & Gianni Meccia, performed by Gianni Meccia. sax & flute soloist: Marcello Boschi.

Cast: Mario Carotenuto (Nando Paciocchi). Andrea Checchi (Orazio Menicotti). Hélène Chanel (the French blonde). Gina Rovere (Gina, Paciocchi's wife). Gabriele Antonini (Ennio, the youngest gang-member). Aroldo Tieri ("Titillo" ['The Tickler'], the safecracker). Ombretta Colli (Silvana, Ennio's girlfriend). Mario De Simone ("Occhio di bue" ['Bullseye'], fair-haired gang member). Nino Terzo (Maggiola, moustachioed gang-member). Marisa Merlini (Nunziata, Maggiola's wife). Gino Bramieri (Panza, rival hood questioned by Paciocchi). Burt Nelson (the American). End credits: Silla Bettini (Bullone, car repair shop boss). Luigi Bonos [as 'Gigi Bonos'] (drunk outside cinema). Giangaetano Gabella. Giulio Calì (costumier). Vittorio Daverio ('Fischio', pickpocket gang-member). Peppino De Martino (insomniac accountant). Ignazio Dolce [as Ignazio Dolci] ("The Algerian"?). Ugo Fangareggi (Busaccia, worker at car repair shop). Jole Fierro (Ines, a prostitute and friend of Orazio). Giacomo Furia (Brigadiere, Orazio's superior on moped). Antonio Gerini (hotel receptionist greeting the Paciocchis). Zoe Incrocci. Henry Martial (black American on bus). Lionello Morandi. Nino Nini (desk sergeant at police station). Mario Passante (Tuttabirra, man questioned by Ennio at pool-hall). Gianni Perelli. Carlo Pisacane (Bullseye's grandfather). Mimmo Poli (The host). Arturo Valentin. Alfredo Venturi. *Uncredited:* 'Jimmy il Fenomeno' [Luigi Origene Soffrano] (man claiming 'mental infirmity' at police station).

Synopsis: Orazio Menicotti, an ex-thief turned straight now employed as a night watchman, witnesses a violent quarrel between a husband and wife while cycling on his rounds one Friday night. After the husband, an American, storms off, the woman, who's French, persuades Orazio to accompany her to the police station to register a complaint. En-route, she seduces Orazio into an embrace, then suddenly turns angry and dumps him out on the street. When he returns to his patch he finds the door of a small bank ajar, and the safe inside empty. At first Orazio suspects the robbery is the work of his old friends, a group of local thieves: Bullseye, Maggiola and Fischio. However, they plausibly deny involvement, explaining that such a job would be too big for them. Orazio and the gang visit another ex-criminal, Nando Paciocchi, for advice. Sympathising with Orazio's predicament, and also concerned because his now-legitimate business savings are with the bank in question, Paciocchi devises a plan to track down the real culprits, recover the dough, and return it before the bank reopens on Monday. Bullseye and Ennio question the local villains, while Fischio goes so far as to get himself arrested for pickpocketing in order to fish for information among the prison inmates. His information leads to a French criminal known as 'The Algerian' who's in league with the American whom Orazio saw on the night of the robbery. Retrieving all four suitcases of money, and sending 'The Algerian' packing, Paciocchi and the gang return home to stash the dough until it can be returned to the safe the next night. Despite the entreaties of their various girlfriends and relatives, they mostly resist the temptation to help themselves to a cut, with the exception of Maggiola, whose wife grabs some of the money to feed their numerous children and kicks her husband in the crotch when he tries to retrieve it. All that remains is to get the remaining cash back in the safe – but how? Orazio had accidentally knocked the safe door shut when he arrived on the scene. To reopen it, Paciocchi cons 'The Tickler', a top-flight safecracker, into assisting them by committing a 'robbery in reverse'...

About the production: The initial impetus for this film came not from Fulci but from its star, Mario Carotenuto. Interviewed by *La Stampa* before the film's release, in a feature titled "Carotenuto tries to discover the true face of Rome by night", he said: "My thieves do not look like those you see in Pasolini or Fellini. It's a good-natured view of Rome, they 'work' like good people, so director Lucio Fulci was able to choose them as the protagonists of the film."[17] The film did good business, staying on release through the summer of 1962; in fact it was still playing on eight Roman screens in September that year. Yet for some reason the official takings reported in *Dizionario del Cinema Italiano* don't reflect this (L116, 630,000 – half as much as *I ladri*, which was a flop by Fulci's own admission). Perhaps we ought not to set too much store by the official figures!

Review: Opening with no less than four quotations about Rome after dark, from Stendhal, François-René de Chateaubriand, Cesare Pascarella and Giuseppe Gioachino Belli (the latter two rendered in the Romanesco dialect), *Colpo gobbo all'italiana*[18] comes on strong with its ambition to convey the flavour of the city at night. Fortunately what follows is a confident and engaging comic drama that delivers on that promise. We spend lots of time exploring the moonlit streets of Rome, from back-alleys and crumbling stairwells to shadowy tramyards and prison walls, in the company of various night-owl characters; petty thieves, prostitutes, shop-owners, drunks, young lovers, and the black-clad "bats" or nightwatchmen, whose job it is to keep an eye on the safety of their districts.

Beautifully filmed in moody black and white, *Colpo gobbo all'italiana* is the first of Fulci's films to seduce the eye as well as simply telling a story. It revisits the criminal milieu of *I ladri* but improves on that film in every way; the scenario moves as smoothly as the camera and we spend plenty of time on the streets, resulting in an almost Nouvelle-Vague air of freedom and verisimilitude. Conversations take place on stairwells and street corners, and Rome's beauty, its juxtaposition of ancient and modern, is captured in shot after shot. The camera tracks along busy streets with the characters, hopping onto trams and buses to emphasise the working reality of the city in daytime, then shifts to an almost dreamlike atmosphere of glistening beauty at night. While *I ragazzi del juke box* and *Urlatori alla sbarra* rely on the charm of their soundtracks and the energetic frivolity of their scenarios, this is a film that appeals to the eyes. Compositionally it's Fulci's first really accomplished work, with some arresting sequences drawing creatively upon deep focus to enhance the emotional architecture of the story. The sequence in which Maggiola returns to his wife and five hungry children, with a suitcase of money that he cannot spend, is ravishingly composed, as well as being performed to perfection by Nino Terzo (soon to be a Fulci regular, with seven roles in the next six years) and Marisa Merlini (star of one of the most famous 'neorealisma rosa' films, Luigi Comencini's *Pane, amore e fantasia*). Fulci is greatly supported in all this by his cinematographer, Alfio Contini. *Colpo gobbo all'italiana* was the first of their six alliances, followed by *I due della legione*, *Gli imbroglioni*, *I maniaci* (another highlight), *I due pericoli pubblici* and *Operazione San Pietro*. Contini, who was the same age as Fulci when he made *Colpo gobbo all'italiana*, went on to shoot major pictures such as Michelangelo Antonioni's *Zabriskie Point* (1970) and Liliana Cavani's *The Night Porter* (1974), and worked with Dino Risi, Gillo Pontecorvo, Vittorio De Sica, Sergio Leone and Michael Cacoyannis. In the horror/thriller genres he shot Umberto Lenzi's *Oasis of Fear* (1971), Gianfranco Mingozzi's *Flavia the Heretic* (1974) and Ugo Liberatore's *Damned in Venice* (1978) and remained in the industry into the 2000s, shooting *Ripley's Game* (2002) for Cavani.

left:
Fotobusta showing Checchi's exploration of the scene of the robbery (top right), the safecracking scene (bottom right) and Hélène Chanel as a phony French damsel in distress.

Although this is basically a comedy, Fulci ensures that the performances stay on the right side of plausibility even as the situation turns comical. Central to the film is the quiet suavity of Andrea Checchi's nightwatchman, a reformed criminal trying to go straight, doing his job with good grace and an eye for the underdog. Checchi's character is not lampooned, nor does he get entangled in slapstick situations (in fact, unusually for a Fulci comedy, slapstick is not a facet of the film). The comedic aspects, when they do emerge, are played with a light touch: I loved the sequence in which Bullseye's grandfather steals money from one of the suitcases then covers his tracks by filling it with newspaper, only to be found dangling from the toilet cistern, desperately attempting to stuff the money out of sight. Also amusing is the sequence in which 'The Tickler', safecracker extraordinaire, works his arcane magic and springs the lock, only to discover, to his horror and disbelief, that the purpose of their visit is not to empty the safe but to fill it.

One could say that *Colpo gobbo all'italiana* is Fulci's contribution to the oft-reviled 'neorealisma rosa' or 'pink neorealism' genre of Italian cinema. Certainly if the film has a flaw it's the script's unwillingness to countenance any kind of negativity or darkness (although admittedly this is rather like criticising an orange for not being a lemon). Even the French bank-robber, 'The Algerian', responds to being deprived of his swag with just a smile and a shrug. The story is populated by gentleman thieves and lovable rogues who can be prevailed upon eventually to do the right thing, a conceit which takes some believing, and if you're in a cynical mood you may find that this sentimentality about crime – the notion that criminals, a 'culture of the night', are basically decent and reasonable – undermines the story. An indulgent fascination with small-time criminals, bordering on sentimentality, runs through most of Fulci's comedies, especially those featuring Franco and Ciccio who nearly always play rogues, and it was a facet of his work that persisted into the 1980s (see for instance the heroic cigarette smugglers in *The Smuggler*). Less seriously, it's also a stretch to believe that the pickpocket, Fischio, can get himself arrested, charged and imprisoned in the space of twenty-four hours: however, the conceit is worth indulging as it cues up the amusing and atmospheric scene in which the gang sing stanzas of popular songs over the prison wall to their incarcerated comrade, while he sings back to them the information he's gleaned. Speaking of songs, the soundtrack leads off with "La nottola di notte" ('The Owl of the Night'), an agreeably hummable tune written and performed by Gianni Meccia (see *I ragazzi del juke box* and *Urlatori alla sbarra*). It subsequently appeared on a 7" EP in 1962, along with two instrumental cuts by Piero Umiliani and Meccia's other song for the film, the manic "Quello che bolle in pentola" ('What's Cooking?').

above:
Promotional photomontage featuring Rovere (top) and Carotenuto, Antonini and Tieri (bottom, left to right).

opposite, main picture:
Photomontage featuring (clockwise from top left): Andrea Checchi, Gabriele Antonini, Aroldo Tieri, Gina Rovere and Mario Carotenuto.

opposite, bottom left:
The cover of the 7" EP released on RCA Victor featuring four tracks from the film: two written and sung by Gianni Meccia, two instrumentals by Piero Umiliani.

Translation
'Those Two in the Legion'

Italy

Production companies
Titanus (Rome)
Ultra Film (Rome)
Sicilia Cinematografica (Palermo)

Theatrical distributors
Titanus (Rome)
Jumbo Cinematografica (IT)

Running time
Italy 97m

DVD running time (adjusted)
Hobby & Work Publishing (IT) 88m 41s

Censorship
Italian censor certificate 38006
issued 27 July 1962

Release information
Turin 17 August 1962
Rome 19 August 1962
Bari 25 August 1962
Petersham, NSW, AUS 05 February 1966
(Italian language screening)
Philadelphia, PA 10 October 1966
(Italian language screening)
Bridgeport, CT 24 May 1969
(Italian language screening)

filmed in black and white

I due della legione

1962

Directed by Lucio Fulci. produced by Danilo Marciani for Ultra Film / Sicilia Cinematografica (Palermo) / Titanus (Rome). story: Antonio Leonviola & Roberto Bianchi Montero. screenplay: Antonio Leonviola, Roberto Bianchi Montero, Lucio Fulci, Dino Di Palma, Arnaldo Marrosu, Giancarlo Del Re, Bruno Corbucci & Giovanni Grimaldi. director of photography: Alfio Contini. music: Luis Enriquez Bacalov. editor: Mario Serandrei. production designer & costume designer: Walter Patriarca. unit manager: Giorgio Baldi. assistant director: Adolfo Dragone. 2nd assistant director: Stefano Rolla. continuity: Bruna Malaguti Sarti. cameraman: Maurizio Scanzani. make-up: Marcello Di Paolo. weapons: Franco Zini. production secretaries: Dino Di Salvo & Franco Mancini. still photography: Fratelli Colombo. sound: Mario Messina. sound recording: Giorgio Pallota. song "Saida" by Borelli & Tomasini, performed by Maria Tonini Rigel with the Ennio Morricone Orchestra and the Franco Potenza Choir.

Cast: Franco Franchi (Franco Cocuzza). Ciccio Ingrassia (Ciccio Fisichella). Rosalba Neri (Lina, Sadrim Bey's lover). Alighiero Noschese (The Sultan, Mustafa Abdul Bey). Maria Teresa Vianello (Cigarette seller at the Scrum Tavern). Aldo Giuffrè (Sadrim Bey, the Sultan's cousin). Aldo Bufilandi. Nino Terzo (Sergeant Trafford). Jo Garsò (Saida, Roger's lover). Carlo Lombardi (Commandant of the Legion). Gianni Rizzo (Sadrim Bey's Arab associate). Rosario Borelli (Roger, officer of the legion in love with Saida). Gianni Crosio (Naples police sergeant tracking Pasqualino). Aldo Pini [as 'Aldo Dini']. Cesare Polacco (Inspector, Neapolitan police). *Uncredited:* Lucio Fulci (vagrant on cattle-train).

Synopsis: Franco Cocuzza and Ciccio Fisichella, two Sicilian card-sharps, arrive in Naples but discover they are no match for the wily Neapolitan locals, who soon figure out how their trick is done and pass the news around. Soon the crooks are penniless and despairing. After a complicated interaction with the local police involving the death of Pasqualino, a member of a local clan of the Camorra (Neapolitan 'mafia'), the two decide to flee Naples, and following the advice of a vagrant they meet on a cattle train they head for a place where they can really lay low; North Africa, and the Foreign Legion. Naturally, all does not go smoothly. Whilst the bullying Sergeant Trafford sees them for the morons they really are, the Commandant of the Legion believes them to be dangerous criminals. Impressed, he employs them as spies for the Legion and sends them to infiltrate the court of a local Arab sheikh, Mustafa Abdul Bey. The two dumbells find themselves embroiled in a power-play between the randy Sheik, who thinks of nothing but sexual novelty, and his conniving cousin Sadrim Bey, who plans to assassinate him. When a vacancy for two new wives arises, Franco and Ciccio don silks and veils to spy on the royal court. Unfortunately, the Sheik finds them irresistible...

About the production: The first film in which comic duo Franco Franchi (born Francesco Benenato) and Ciccio Ingrassia (born Francesco Ingrassia) appeared as top-of-the-bill stars was Riccardo Pazzaglia's *L'onorata società* (1961). Fulci's *I due della legione* was the second, and the first to proclaim their presence in the title. Fulci worked with them thirteen times in all, until *Il lungo il corto il gatto* in 1967. By comparison, Giorgio Simonelli made eleven films with the duo (mostly gangster/mafiosi comedies) and Marino Girolami made nine. (It should be noted, however, that Franco and Ciccio have smaller parts in Fulci's *Le massaggiatrici*, *I maniaci* and *Gli imbroglioni*.) On the production side, funding was partially provided by Palermo's Sicilia Cinematografica, a company with close business links to the larger Rome-based set-up, Ultra Film. Oddly, however, Sicilia Cinematografica habitually went uncredited on prints, posters and promotional materials, and *I due della legione* was no exception.

Review: Setting the stamp on future Franco and Ciccio outings, *I due della legione* is so typical of their 'brand' that it could just as easily be the fifteenth in the series, rather than the first. The

humour arises from fixed constants; Franco is the rubber-faced buffoon, a concentration of primitive energy at constant war with his own limited intelligence, and Ciccio is the exasperated would-be 'brains' of the operation, who is nevertheless perpetually unable to steer the two of them out of trouble. For anyone new to Franco and Ciccio, Franchi's performance is the most likely sticking point. If you find his exaggerated face-pulling difficult to accept you will always struggle with these films; there really is no respite. One has to concede, however, that there's a fair amount of detail tucked up inside his facial and bodily gymnastics. Though illiterate and uncultured, the 'Franco' of these films possesses traces of instinctual wiliness (tripped up by a lack of sustained thought), a propensity for 'buttering up' authority figures (which rarely succeeds), and an underlying childlike quality which is sometimes genuine, sometimes switched on full-blast to beguile opponents. He is quick to anger and quick to run, and in social situations affects an ingratiating manner, offering the most obsequious remarks with a grin so cheesily accomodating that it makes your jaw ache to look at it. The most irritating of his tics, for me at least, is a facial expression of disbelief or dismay shared with an imaginary onlooker (eyebrows slanted upwards in the middle, eyes wildly seeking agreement left or right). This sense of an appeal to an imaginary observer is something carried over from the duo's roots in live vaudeville; one of the oddities of the Franco and Ciccio style is a sense that they are only partially 'inside' the drama, that they are onlookers of their own performance. Other Franco characteristics include the basic drives of hunger and lust, and the prideful enjoyment of mimickry and charade. He's like a perpetually grinning dog, performing tricks and looking for applause; whether you find this appealing or alienating is a matter of taste, but irrespective of personal preference I have at least come to appreciate him as a skilful vaudeville performer. By comparison, Ingrassia is the soul of restraint, never overdoing it even when he must express total frustration (which is approximately every two minutes). The secret of their success was consistency; never try to feed your audience a dish they didn't ask for. *I due della legione* therefore sees Fulci drawing up the recipe for one of the biggest success stories in Italian popular cinema...

I due della legione is a fast-moving farce with some incidental visual pleasures along the way. Fulci chooses attractively ramshackle locations in Naples and captures a sense of the city's proletarian street life: pretty girls selling bread and ricotta from baskets carried through the streets, fishermen at the bay, the massed crowds at a major football stadium, and rough-looking barber-shops with not a hair-model glamour photo in sight. Franco and Ciccio set up their card-trick scam in a crumbling back-alley, using a folding wooden table that looks very much as if it's been passed down from street entertainer to street entertainer since the 1890s. When the petty crooks are ruined by an influx of clued-in customers (one of the funniest sequences has the details of their scam broadcast over the tannoy at a major sporting event, leading to a mass exodus as thousands rush from the stadium to exploit the hapless duo), they leave town by hiding in a cattle-train, which leads to an encounter with a garrulous and jovial vagrant played by Fulci himself. Once again, as in *I ragazzi del juke box*, Fulci shows himself to be a real comic talent and a genuinely good actor. It's such a pleasure to see him in these early films, playing characters far more interesting and amusing than the peripheral authority figures he chose in the horror films of the early 1980s.

The vagrant's advice to the fleeing crooks is to join the Foreign Legion, and the style of humor that ensues from here on is not unlike the British Carry On films: our two idiots find army life either incomprehensible or unbearable, leading to inevitable conflict with a sadistic Sergeant (Nino Terzo, making the most of his sneering character). Fulci is happy to depict the top brass as dimwitted too, and the Commandant who decides the Sicilian duo are criminal geniuses (*"Exactly what the legion needs!"*) is lampooned as enthusiastically as the unfortunate 'grunts'. The remaining storyline is a grab-bag of sight gags and borderline bawdiness. Sent hiking across the desert to infiltrate the court of a randy local Sultan (Alighiero Noschese, having a ball with the sexual innuendo), Franco and Ciccio suffer heat exhaustion and start hallucinating. When they see a soft-drinks vendor with an iced truck of Coca Colas they decide not to be suckered by such an obvious illusion, even as the man protests: *"I've been wandering around this desert for six months but everyone thinks I'm a mirage so I haven't made a dime."* At the Sultan's court we reach the comic centrepiece of the film, the harem sequence, and once again the Carry Ons come to mind: you could be forgiven for expecting Bernard Bresslaw, Charles Hawtrey and Sid James to pop up. Although this sort of thing rarely appeals to me, I have to admit that the sight of Franco and Ciccio fending off a randy Arab nobleman while holding veils acoss their faces did stir a few smiles, with the lanky Ingrassia turning in some sterling 'eye acting' and resembling at times a brunette version of Bea Arthur. And speaking of real women, sultry Rosalba Neri looks pretty stunning as the conniving lover of the Sultan's cousin, plotting his downfall from beneath a veritable landslide of raven hair. Obscure Italian singer Jo Garsò is likewise visually impressive, playing a woman imprisoned by the Sultan, although Fulci seems to avoid giving her much dialogue, which suggests perhaps that she found the transition to the screen difficult.

There is, to state the blindingly obvious, nothing of weight or significance to this film, but still it's worth a look if you're a dedicated Fulci watcher. In the staging of visual gags, in his brisk pacing, and his amusing cameo, Fulci demonstrates considerable skill within the boundaries of the form. There's a breezy good cheer to *I due della legione*, a professional confidence which makes it abundantly clear how he came to enjoy such an sustained homeland career in comedy.

above:
Italian poster.

top left:
Franco and Ciccio drive their Sergeant (Nino Terzo, left) to distraction.

opposite, main picture:
Promotional image for the film.

opposite, bottom left:
The Italian DVD release.

left:
The Sultan (Alighiero Noschese) lusts after the two latest additions to his harem.

below:
Arduous parade ground duties reduce our two idiots to tears.

Translation
'The Masseuses'

Italy/France

International theatrical titles
Les Faux Jetons (FR)
('The Phonies')
...mit Damenbedienung (WG)
('Operation Ladies')

Production companies
Panda Società per L'Industria Cinematografica S.p.A. (Rome)
Gallus Films (Paris)

Theatrical distributors
Warner Brothers (Italy)
Interfrance (France)

Note: The Italian Cinema Archive lists Dear International as distributor, although this is not borne out by the numerous posters and locandinas available for scrutiny.

Running time
Italy 95m
France 83m

DVD running time (adjusted)
Videa/Eagle Pictures 91m 50s

Censorship
Italian censor certificate 38283
issued 20 September 1962
French Visa 28107
issued 13 July 1965

Shooting completed
late August 1962

Release information
Bari 27 September 1962
Turin 17 October 1962
Rome 12 January 1963
France 19 July 1965

filmed in black and white

Le massaggiatrici

1962

Directed by Lucio Fulci. produced by Ermanno Donati & Luigi Carpentieri for Panda Società per l'Industria Cinematografica (Roma) / Gallus Film (Paris). story & screenplay: Oreste Biancoli, Vittorio De Tuddo, Italo De Tuddo, Antoinette Pellevant. director of photography: Guglielmo Mancori. music: Lallo [Coriolano] Gori. editor: Ornella Micheli. production designer: Piero Filippone. production supervisor: Piero Donati. production manager: Lucio Bompani. cameraman: Sandro Mancori.

Cast: Sylva Koscina (Marisa, fair-haired 'masseuse'). Cristina Gajoni (Iris, blonde 'masseuse'). Valeria Fabrizi (Milena, brunette 'masseuse'). Marisa Merlini (Bice Petroni, a qualified masseuse). Ernesto Calindri (Parodi, a businessman). Philippe Noiret (Bellini, Paoloni's business secretary). Laura Adani (Mrs. Parodi). Luigi Pavese (Manzini, Parodi's business associate). Louis Seigner (Cipriano Paoloni, President of The Association for Protection of the Young). Franco Franchi (Franco, nightwatchman #1). Ciccio Ingrassia (Ciccio, nightwatchman #2). Nino Taranto (Professor Gaspare Petroni, Bice's husband). Gianni Bonagura (Cerrocchi, accountant who crashes into Bellini's car). Nello Ascoli. Marisa Quattrini. Nino Terzo (Brigadiere Calascione). Bruno Scipioni (Hotel doorman who calls Mrs. Parodi's cab). Mario Frera (heavy-set officer arresting Professor Petroni). Francesco Sormano. Carla Morosini. Augusto Pesarini. Marcello Simoni. Enrica Caperchi. Consalvo Dell'Arti (Hotel receptionist greeting Mrs. Parodi).

Synopsis: When her car is stolen by a customer, Milena, a gorgeous young woman working the streets of Milan as a prostitute, decides it would be safer to set up a call-girl agency from her apartment. To this end, she and two similarly glamorous friends, Iris and Marisa, advertise their services euphemistically as 'masseuses' in the press... Parodi, a businessman in the construction industry, is sent to Milan by his wife (who runs the firm) to finalise a contract for the construction of a hostel for 'fallen women', commissioned by a philanthropic organisation called 'The Association for Protection of the Young'. He is accompanied on the trip by his friend Manzini, an engineer. Once in Milan the two men meet the Association's president, Cipriano Paoloni, and his business secretary Bellini. Back at the hotel, Manzini is overcome with the flu, but Parodi spots Milena's newspaper advert and arranges a visit. However, when he arrives at the girls' apartment block he presses the wrong buzzer and finds himself attempting to negotiate terms with their neighbour, the matronly Mrs. Petroni, an authentic masseuse who does not offer 'extras' at all. When the penny drops, Mrs. Petroni orders her husband Gaspare to go and remonstrate with the three girls, but they are more than a match for him and send him packing... Bellini, meanwhile, demands a bribe from Parodi (for the ruling political party and himself) before giving Parodi's company the contract. Manzini, now recovered, calls the masseuses and arranges for Marisa to visit him at the hotel. Bellini drops by unexpectedly and Manzini passes Marisa off as his wife. Between them, Marisa and Bellini hatch a plan to cream off even more money from the proposed deal. Further complications ensue when Parodi's suspicious wife arrives in town. Despite his exalted moral position (and quite coincidentally) Paoloni too is a customer of the phony masseuses. He visits the girls but has to hide in a closet when a policeman, Calascione, drops by to investigate Mrs. Petroni's complaint, and must hide again when Bellini calls by to see Marisa. The terror of exposure is too much for him and he dies of a heart attack in the closet. Paoloni's death threatens to ruin things for everyone: it transpires that he had signed the construction contract but post-dated it for superstitious reasons. If his death is reported, the contract is useless. Smuggling Paoloni's corpse back into his office, Parodi, Manzini and Bellini hope to delay the discovery of his death long enough for the contract to become valid. However, their attempts are compromised by the intervention of two buffoonish nightwatchmen at the dead man's offices...

above, first picture:
Fotobusta showing (from left to right) Valeria Fabrizi, Ernesto Calindri, Philippe Noiret and Luigi Pavese.

above, second picture:
Cipriano Paoloni (Louis Seigner, left), President of the Association for Protection of the Young, meets Marisa, a sexy masseuse (Sylva Koscina, right).

top left:
Fotobusta depicting Marisa Merlini as a genuine masseuse and Ernesto Calindri as the businessman looking for a certain something 'extra'.

opposite, main picture:
Franco ingratiates himself with Milena (Valeria Fabrizi).

opposite, bottom left:
Italian artwork for the film.

Review: Subtitled "A farce in modern tempo", *Le massaggiatrici* tells the story of a collision between two different strands of society, reputable and disreputable, with Fulci coming down firmly on the side of the latter. Quite risqué for its time, with a trio of loveable hookers setting themselves up in business in a respectable apartment block, this plays almost like a prototype for the films Pedro Almodóvar was making in the early 1980s, and just like Almodóvar Fulci depicts his working girls with as much respect and sympathy as he offers the rest of society, if not more so. The representatives of 'decency' meanwhile are consistently lampooned and criticised: they are either corrupt (Bellini), priggish (Mrs. Petroni) or hypocritical (Paoloni), whilst even the leading male characters, Parodi and Manzini, are a pair of mercenary philanderers who refuse to let a mere setback like a man's death get in the way of a lucrative contract.

While at the time it was made the story may have felt quite cheeky and irreverent, *Le massaggiatrici* is neither risqué enough to work as titillation, nor exciting enough to work as a thriller, and the giddiness of high farce is summoned too late in the day to make this more than a minor entry in the Fulci canon. That said, the last twenty minutes of this film, in which Parodi, Manzini and Bellini decide to delay discovery of Paoloni's death in order to clinch a business deal, give this light but meandering film some added zest. The men smuggle the corpse back into his office while the 'masseuses' distract the nightwatchmen (played by Franco and Ciccio in relatively modest supporting roles). When Franco, not to be distracted, goes to check Paolini's office, the conspirators hide the corpse behind a curtain and switch out the lights; Franco, unlucky as ever, sees shoes beneath the curtain, and believing it's a burglar smashes a bottle over the corpse's head. Naturally, when the body of the company president slumps to the ground Franco thinks that he's killed him. The attempts of Franco and Ciccio to get rid of the body, and the equally persistent attempts of Bellini and Parodi to put it back, bring much needed vigour and farcical energy to the final reel. It's all quite neatly done, and makes you wish that the rest of the film had been so engaging.

Fulci draws upon some significant French acting talent in this, his first French-Italian co-production: one of the mainstays of French drama, Philippe Noiret, plays the oily and insinuating Bellini. The actor once said that this was the worst film he'd ever made, and I'm afraid I'm not familiar enough with his career to contradict him, but really he has nothing (onscreen at least) to feel aggrieved about; he is good in his role, and the film, whilst not so serious, has some deliciously irreverent icing to make it worth his while. Also among the French contingent, Louis Seigner at least *appears* to be having fun as the hypocritical philanthropist Paoloni; a veteran of French cinema, he'd worked with Robert Bresson (*Les anges du péché*, 1943), Max Ophüls (*Le plaisir*, 1952) and Henri-Georges Clouzot (*La vérité*, 1960), and whilst in Italy in 1962 added a part in Antonioni's *L'eclisse* to his CV, which may explain his availability for *Le massaggiatrici*.

Variety, reviewing a Lucio Fulci film for the first time, were enthusiastic about *Le massaggiatrici*, calling it *"A fast-paced and exploitable comedy with strong prospects in depth. Surefire title for Italy, where the scandal of call girls disguising themselves as masseuses made recent headlines should help. Abroad, it should play well on the strength of broad comedy strongly laced with double entendres."*[19] Reviewed in Italy by *l'Unità*, however, the film was dismissed: *"Intended for fun without ever reaching the vigour and nobility of satire, whilst often even lacking the energy of vulgarity"*.[20] *La Stampa* were equally hard to impress, stating, *"As so often, a 'little film' designed to take your mind off your troubles instead leads one to brood over the sad future of our comedy films,"* before adding, *"Needless to say, the odd giggle escapes."*[21]

left:
Franco and Ciccio find themselves in trouble trying to hide a corpse.

Translation
'A Strange Type'

Italy

Production company
Giovanni Addessi Produzione Cinematografica S.p.A.

Theatrical distributors
Panta Cinematografica Distribuzione (IT)
Cabaret Film Distribuzione (IT)
Paramount Films of Italy Inc. (IT)
Lux Film (IT)

Running time
Italy 90m

DVD running time (adjusted)
Raro/Nocturno (IT) 98m 54s

Censorship
Italian censor certificate 39560 issued 18 February 1963

Release information
Bari 06 March 1963
Turin 04 April 1963
Rome 27 July 1963
Chicago, IL, 18 May 1965*
Philadelphia, PA, 03 October 1965*

filmed in black and white

* The Italian-language version of *Uno strano tipo* was shown in the USA by two cinemas specialising in films for Italian-American audiences. There is, however, no evidence that the film was ever subtitled or dubbed into English.

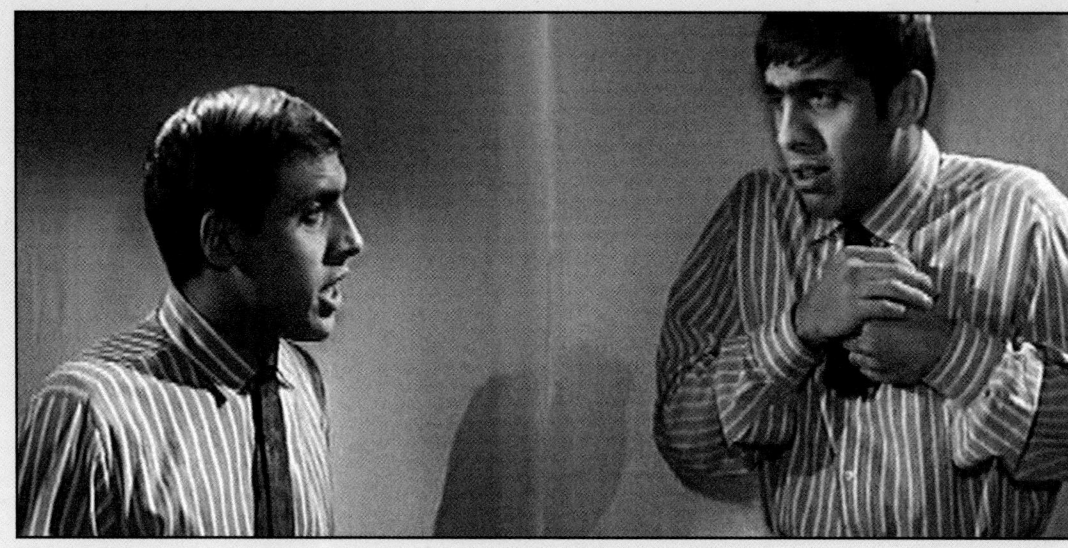

Uno strano tipo

1963

Directed by Lucio Fulci. executive producer: Giovanni Addessi for Giovanni Addessi Produzione Cinematografica S.p.A. produced by Franco Belotti & Walter Zarghetta. story: Vittorio Metz. screenplay: Vittorio Metz & Lucio Fulci. director of photography: Guglielmo Mancori. incidental music, arrangements & orchestra conductor: Detto Mariano; published by American Jank. editor: Ornella Micheli. set designer & set decorator: Gastone Carsetti. production supervisor: Mario Silvestri. production manager: Alberto Puccini. unit manager: Remo Odevaine. assistant director: Nino Zanchin. 2nd assistant director: Stefano Rolla. continuity: Mirta Corbucci. cameraman: Sandro Mancori. assistant cameraman: Enrico Cortese. costume designer: Antonia Quilici. make-up: Romolo De Martino. hairdresser: Italia Marini. sound: Adriano Taloni. post-synchronisation: N.I.S. Studios. technical equipment: G.S.C. songs "Stai lontana da me" by Hilliard & Mogol, "Pregherò" by Ricki Gianco & Don Backy, "Amami e baciami" by Celentano & Micki Del Prete, "Il tangaccio" by Marchetti, Mogol & Micki Del Prete, "Grazie, prego, scusi" by Massara, Mogol & Micki Del Prete, "Ombra nel sole" by Detto Mariano, Don Backy & Micki Del Prete – all performed by Adriano Celentano & "I Ribelli". format: Totalscope. processing, prints & optical effects: S.P.E.S., director: E. Catalucci. filmed on location on the Amalfi Coast & in Capri with interiors at GSC Studios.

Cast: Adriano Celentano (Peppino/Adriano Celentano). Claudia Mori (Carmelina). Donatella Turi (Manuela Mazzolani). Luigi Pavese (Mazzolani). Carlo Campanini (monk). Giacomo Furia (hotel manager). Gianni Agus (Gastone). Rosalba Neri (Marina, his wife). Franco Giacobini (journalist). Rafaella De Carolis [Miss Italia 1962] ('captain club'). Antonella Murgia [la bella d'italia 1962] (kid in Capri).Mario Brega (garage attendant). Renato Terra. Marco Morandi (kid in Capri). Anna Maria Surdo. Nino Di Napoli. Nunzia Fumo. "I Ribelli" [Don Backy, Micki Del Prete & Memo Dittongo]. Nino Taranto (Cannarulo). Erminio Macario (Giovanni). *Uncredited:* (Carmelina's brother). Valentino Macchi (young man at fiesta). Gino Santercole (himself).

Synopsis: Adriano Celentano, the rock'n'roll star, is looking forward to a quiet vacation in the coastal resort of Amalfi, accompanied by his group and his manager Giovanni, but when he arrives he finds that everyone in the town seems to hate him. A gas station attendant calls him a crook and threatens him, he gets into a fight with locals at a roadside café, and the staff at the hotel are downright hostile. When he goes for a walk on the beach, a young woman called Carmelina threatens him with a gun and demands he take care of the child he has sired with her. What he doesn't know is that a local idiot called Peppino, a dead ringer for Adriano, has been posing as the singer to make money and seduce young women, spurred on by an unscrupulous fraudster, Cannarulo. Meanwhile, Adriano is trying to have fun with Manuela Mazzolani, his fiancée, and impress her wealthy father, a snob who believes the rock'n'roll singer is wrong for his daughter. Returning to his hotel room, Adriano finds a baby: his supposed 'son', Pasqualino. The enraged Carmelina has left the child there for him to care for. If Manuela or Mr. Mazzolani see the baby they will conclude that Adriano is a philanderer, so he desperately tries to prevent its discovery. At the urging of a monk, Peppino meets with Carmelina and confesses the truth: it is he, not Adriano Celentano, who is the father. Carmelina forgives him, and together they resolve to retrieve the baby. Giovanni has booked Adriano to perform at the hotel, to offset the cost of the vacation: the singer invites along Manuela and her father, promising a more 'sophisticated' show. However, Cannarulo has also promised a 'Celentano' gig on the same night, in nearby Salerno, for a tough gang of female superfans called 'The Jaguars' who run a venue called 'Club Celentano'. The Jaguars are furious when they hear about the Amalfi gig, so they kidnap the real Celentano, take him back to their club, and make him perform for them. Simultaneously, the talentless Peppino is bullied into performing at the hotel, where he mimes to a Celentano record before a less than impressed Mr. Mazzolani. When the record sticks, the well-to-do crowd storm the stage, throwing napkins. Peppino flees. The real Celentano arrives back to save the evening, and his reputation, with a passionate rock'n'roll tango number. Peppino meanwhile resolves to reclaim his baby from the singer's room. He is genuinely eager to care for the child: his apparent neglect was instigated by the bullying Cannarulo. Farce erupts as Peppino enters room after room looking for the baby, leaving a trail of disaster for which Adriano is blamed when he comes offstage. Carmelina arrives and a row breaks out between her and Adriano – right in front of Manuela and her outraged father. Disaster is finally averted when the assembled crowd see Adriano and Peppino bump into each other. All becomes clear, and Peppino leaves with Carmelina and the baby.

About the production: *Uno strano tipo* was screened at the Bordighera Festival Internazionale del Film Comico e Umoristico, which ran from 10-19 March 1963. Adriano Celentano and Claudia Mori met while working on this film; they were married the following year and have remained together to this day.

Review: Adriano Celentano plays a dual role as himself and a buffoonish double in this fast-moving comedy, which takes some well-aimed pot-shots at the absurdities of fan worship, the myths about 'anti-social' rock'n'rollers, and the venality of the music business. The story, by veteran Totò screenwriter Vittorio Metz, boasts a string of inventive situations, and the confident cast have fun with it, not least Celentano who delivers a likeably casual performance as himself and a grotesquely simian Jerry Lewis routine as Peppino.

The first twenty minutes involve a hilarious inversion of expectations, as the dreamboat star of a thousand Italian bedroom posters is greeted by a sustained torrent of abuse and hostility. The gas station attendant refuses to fill up his sports car, a passer-by lobs a tomato at his windscreen, even the maid at the hotel sticks out her mop to trip him up as he walks through the lobby. *"Do you have Milanese plates? Milan played Naples last night, and Naples lost"*, offers the hotel manager, the only person who doesn't seem to harbour a feral hatred of the star. (He's from out of town, so he hasn't encountered the obnoxious and idiotic Peppino.)

Another thorn in Celentano's side is his manager, a snob who expresses disdain for rock'n'roll: *"When I produced operas like Carmen, that was real music"*, he moans. *"And the money I pay you is fake?"* snaps Celentano. It turns out the manager has booked his star to play a gig at the hotel, to recoup the costs of his holiday! So much for coddled celebrities...

The hotel concert, in which Peppino passes himself off as Celentano, is the comic centrepiece of the film, even though some of the gags are a tad predictable. Fulci has a gentle poke at the gullibility of pop audiences; at first no one spots that 'Peppino' is miming to a record, even when he shamefacedly tries to mimic the fade-out. It's strange, though, that when conniving Cannarulo ineptly plays the same disc a second time, we hear it sung by a woman. If the record is meant to be at the wrong speed, why do we not hear the 'Pinky and Perky' voice one expects from a speeded up record? It seems the switch to a female voice is straining, rather laboriously, to tie in with a gag about the singer's 'sophistication', for which we may read homosexuality: as Adriano/Peppino mimes to a female voice, the contemptuous Mr. Mazzolani runs a wettened finger camply over his eyebrows and rolls his eyes at his dismayed daughter. The funniest twist comes later, when the real Celentano leaps onstage to sing his new song only to find that no one wants to hear it, as they've already heard it twice from Peppino!

With the film's hide-the-baby routine, Fulci emulates the style of Frank Tashlin (whose rock'n'roll satire *The Girl Can't Help It* Fulci probably had in mind). *Uno strano tipo* however, lacks the manic intensity of Tashlin's work. Fulci is on firmer ground when depicting Celentano's hard-as-nails female fans. The girls have turned a café into a shrine to the star's image, but their attitude brooks no argument from the mere mortal himself. These tough cookies act like precursors of the film fanatics in John Waters' *Cecil B. Demented* (2000), abducting the star from his hotel and ordering him to perform at their club. *"Stay away from me!"* he cries, to be told *"Okay, do 'Stay Away from Me'"*, a reference to Celentano's hit song, *'Stai lontano da me'*. To underline the point, one of the girls manoeuvres the reluctant star onstage using her formidably jutting breasts, wearing a sweater emblazoned with the title in question! Talk about mixed messages...

this page, above, top left and bottom left:
Fotobusta artwork and poster art, all which emphasises the role of Adriano Celentano.

opposite, main picture:
Adriano Celentano as himself (left) and lookalike imposter Peppino (right).

opposite, bottom left:
A locandina, typeset so misleadingly that one might assume the film is called 'Rock'n'roll Black & White'.

below:
Celentano and his group 'The Rebels' rehearse for their upcoming show.

Translation
'The Swindlers'

Italy/Spain

International theatrical title
Los mangantes (SP) 'The Crooks'

Production companies
Produzione D.S. (Rome)
Tecisa Film (Madrid)

Theatrical distributors
Cineriz (Italy)
Rosa Films (Spain)

Running time
Italy 98m
Spain 90m

DVD running time (adjusted)
CG Home Video (Italy) 89m 15s

Censorship
Italian censor certificate 40974
issued 13 September 1963

Shooting period
June 1963

Release information
Turin 25 September 1963
Rome 30 October 1963
Barcelona 21 November 1964
Madrid 18 April 1965

filmed in black and white

Gli imbroglioni

1963

Directed by Lucio Fulci. produced by Dario Sabatello for Produzione D.S. (Roma) / Tecisa Film (Madrid). story & screenplay by Mario Guerra, Vittorio Vighi, Lucio Fulci & [episode 5 "Medico e fidanzata"] Castellano [Franco Castellano] & Pipolo [Giuseppe Moccia]. directors of photography Alfio Contini & Tino Santoni. music: Carlo Rustichelli, conducted by Roberto Pregadio; published by C.A.M. editor: Gisa Radicchi Levi. production designer: Sergio Canevari. set dresser: Dante Ferretti. set designer: Francisco Canet. production manager: Sergio Iacobis. unit manager: Lucio Trentini. 1st assistant directors: Giovanni Fago & Luis Enciso. 2nd assistant director: Stefano Rolla. continuity: Franca Carotenuto. cameraman: Maurizio Scanzani. costume designer: Anna Maria Tucci. make-up: Amato Garbini & Duilio Scarozza. hairdresser: Rosa Luciani. production secretary: Alberto Brama. assistant editor: Marina Sacco. technical development: Enzo Verzini. accountant: Nucci Cicogna. sound: Fernando Pescetelli. sound recording: Fono Roma. songs: "La ballata degli imbroglioni" music by Giorgo Gaber, lyrics by Umberto Simonetta, performed by Giorgio Gaber, disco-ricordi. "Roma nun fà la stupida stasera" by Garinei, Giovannini & Trovajoli, performed by Nino Manfredi & Lea Massari. "Ciumachella de Trastevere" by Garinei, Giovannini & Trovajoli, performed by Nora Orlandi's "4+4", published by C.A.M. "Go-kart twist" by Ennio Morricone & Pilantra, performed by Gianni Morandi, published by R.C.A. processing & prints: Istituto Nazionale Luce. negatives: Dupont S.A. positives: Ferrania p.14. Interiors filmed at Titanus Studios (Rome).

Cast: Walter Chiari (Dr. Mario Corti). Antonella Lualdi (Sister Celestina). Raimondo Vianello (Luciano Tabanelli). Dominique Boschero (Mrs. Taverna). Franco Franchi (Salvatore Di Carmine aka Rizzo aka Esposito). Ciccio Ingrassia (Napoleone Palumbo aka Nostradomine aka Roccanera). Aroldo Tieri (Orazio Taverna, football agent). Luciana Gilli (Liliana Ferri, Corti's lover). Mario Scaccia (Dr. Corti's lawyer). Umberto D'Orsi (Lucarini, lawyer wearing dark glasses). Xenia Valderi (Mrs. Ferri, Liliana's mother). Alberto Bonucci (football club manager). Pietro De Vico (Court chancellor with stammer). Lucia Modugno (Franca, customer at boutique). Elio Crovetto (Gustavo Schultz, German tourist). Nino Terzo (Guard at Egyptian tomb). Margaret Lee (Nurse Adelina, Corti's assistant). Franco Giacobini (Ovidio, Taverna's lawyer). Claudio Gora (Commendator Spianella, the first defendant). Camillo Mastrocinque (Spianella's Lawyer). José Calvo [as 'Pepe Calvo'] (Ludovico Marchioli, a tax officer). José Luis Lopez Vazquez [as ' José Lopez Vazquez'] (Judge). Nerio Bernardi (Monsignor). Maria Pia Luzi. Anna Maria Bottini (Boutique Owner). Oreste Lionello (Ciocchi, a store detective). Giampiero Littera (Coffee vendor). Fanfulla [aka Luigi Visconti]. Xan De Bolas (Antonio Monterosi, antique dealer). Francesco Merino (Pallavicini, snoozing court clerk). Giorgio Gaber (himself, singing the title song). "And the exotic beauties": Seyna Seyn. Elisabetta Wu-Tak. Mao Tai. Margaret Rose Keil (Schultz's daughter). Corinne Fontaine. Rosita Palomar (Nun with Sister Celestina). *Uncredited:* Stefania Sandrelli (Bellina, Corti's first patient). Mario De Simone (man whom Corti squirts with milk).

Synopsis: A story centred around the cases heard in a Rome courtroom during one day. *"La pretura" ('The Judge')*; On his way to court, Spianella beats a man to a parking space and then abuses him during an argument. On reaching the courtroom he realises that the man he has antagonised is the judge in charge of his case. *"Siciliani" [Pt.1]*: Two Sicilian buffoons are charged with selling stolen goods; in their 'defence' they explain that no sooner had they received the money than they were conned out of it again by a man posing as a government official demanding payment for a street vending license. *"La società calcistica" ('The football club')*; When negotiating a deal to sell a major football player to the Rome squad, Bolognan football manager Luciano Tabanelli makes lewd comments to Orazio Taverna, the agent for the Rome bid, about a woman he sees from his office window. The woman is in fact Taverna's wife, but rather than remonstrate, Taverna bites his lip in order not to endanger the deal. Things become difficult, however, as Tabanelli obsesses over the woman. The next day, Tabanelli describes an erotic dream he had about her: he and Taverna were Eskimos and the woman was Taverna's wife; unable to control his lust he blatantly seduced the woman and then ravished her in Taverna's igloo. He describes another dream the next day: in it he is Fletcher Christian, sitting astride the back of the defeated Captain Bligh, 'played' by Taverna, while 'the woman' performs a sexy Tahitian dance for him. On the third day Taverna can take no more and attacks Tabanelli with a football trophy... *"Suore" ('Sisters')*: Two nuns who bring a hamper of reconditioned clothes from their convent to sell to a boutique are persuaded by the shop-owner not to hand over the garments until after a tax official has left the premises; unfortunately for the honour of the two sisters, this means they are left holding a variety of sexy undergarments they feel obliged to pretend are theirs. When the sisters can take the tax official's snide questions no more, they attack him... *"Medico e fidanzata"* ('Doctor and Girlfriend'): Doctor Mario Corti is charged with abuse of his position by Mrs. Ferri, mother of Liliana, his girlfriend. She maintains that Corti is a sex maniac who first molested her daughter, then seduced her, after which he shamelessly proceeded to chase after other women; Corti maintains that it was Liliana who seduced him, that he is in fact a nervous fellow easily intimidated by beautiful women. *"Siciliani" [Pt.2]*: The two buffoons return to court charged with yet more offences: this time it's claimed that they tried to defraud Gustavo Schultz, a rich German tourist, by selling him a 'genuine' Etruscan mummy (in fact Franco wrapped in bandages). When Schultz informs the press, a camera crew arrives at the burial site, only to be 'attacked' by Franco who escapes from the tomb and runs amok... *"Medico e fidanzata"* Pt.2: Dr. Corti attends the funeral of his girlfriend's aunt under duress, as it clashes with a major football match. With a radio and earpiece he listens to the game during the procession but his involuntary gasps attract the attention of other male mourners, leading to mounting frenzy and a runaway hearse. The day ends with the judge adjourning the Corti case, and arranging for Corti and his girlfriend to get stuck in the court's broken lift. As sounds of an amorous nature rise from the shaft it becomes clear that the case of Ferri vs. Corti has resolved itself...

About the production: Drawing on *Un giorno in pretura*, a film he'd devised for Steno in 1953, Fulci created this, the first of his *films a episodi* (the term refers to the portmanteau multi-story comedy films that were all the rage in Italy in the 1950s and 1960s). *Un giorno in pretura* boasted Sophia Loren, Alberto Sordi and Walter Chiari in its stellar cast; Fulci couldn't afford Loren or Sordi but he did net Chiari again, and the talented comic actor stayed on board for *I maniaci* immediately afterwards. Described by Fulci rather pretentiously in *La Stampa* as a 'film-lampo' (a term borrowed from Cesare Zavattini's writing on neo-realism, meaning 'lightning-film'), *Gli imbroglioni* lacks the defining characteristic of the form (a story based on an aspect of contemporary life acted out by the real-life participants) but it was indeed shot 'lightning fast', in just twenty-four days, circa June 1963.[22] Fulci explained, *"Before starting filming we went through the script preparing ourselves in the most minute detail in order to avoid any problems that might delay our work [...] without compromising either the artistic aspects of the events making up the film, or the special care that we devoted to its creation."*[23] The script was the work of Fulci and two writing teams: Castellano and Pipolo, who wrote the segment "Medico e fidanzata", and Mario Guerra and Vittorio Vighi who worked on the Franco and Ciccio material. (Although not strictly speaking a team, inasmuch as they made more films apart than together, Guerra and Vighi combined their talents on seventeen films and a handful of TV episodes.)

Review: This is an episodic comedy based around a single day's courtroom hearings, with the defendants' stories dramatised at length. They include a young doctor accused of 'inappropriate' behaviour, a pair of nuns accused of assaulting a tax officer, a football agent nursing a grudge, and a pair of petty swindlers. The latter, of course, are played by Franco and Ciccio, who feature in two episodes. The second of these is enlivened by Fulci's first playful dabble with horror iconography: in order to con money out of a gullible German tourist, Ciccio shows the man around an Etruscan burial site while Franco dresses up as a mummy; not exactly side-splitting, but it's fun to see Fulci touching on territory that would define his later career. The humour is broad but engaging; for instance, the opening scene depicts an argument between two men vying for the same parking space outside a courtroom, only for the victor to find that the man he's humiliated is the judge in charge of his case. Aroldo Tieri is very funny as a football agent doing a slow burn as a business associate unwittingly lusts after his wife (he evidently relished playing the jealous husband, as he does it again in Fulci's *00-2 agenti segretissimi*). Walter Chiari, meanwhile, shows his versatility by playing the same character, a doctor, in two *Rashomon*-like facets: one a grotesque philanderer, deliberately dropping banana-skins outside his surgery in order to get injured women onto his surgical couch; the other a nervous virgin, terrified of women. The story wraps up with an episode in which the male members of a funeral cortége surreptitiously monitor the progress of a football match via a radio fitted with an earpiece; they keep it a secret from their solemn, grieving wives until their team wins the match, upon which the entire male contingent – including the carriage driver – explodes with jubilation. The horses bolt, the cortége accelerates, and the scene concludes with a frantic chase after the accelerating coffin. It's not unlike the gently irreverent humour of Irish comedian Dave Allen, a popular fixture on British TV in the 1960s and 1970s, or the early slapstick of Woody Allen (the scene would not be out of place in *Bananas*), although of course it precedes both.

So what's the underlying point of these stories? If there's any conclusion to draw, it's the banal observation that truth remains elusive even in the courtroom. The judge, well played with a light dusting of suppressed irritation by the Spanish actor José Luis Lopez Vazquez (rather unfairly low in the cast list despite having lots of screen time) is portrayed as essentially decent, if somewhat tart, exhibiting for instance a variation on the wisdom of Solomon when telling inveterate liars Franco and Ciccio that their sentence is not so harsh when one considers that it is shared by the six different personas they have tried to present in court. Essentially, the film is a bourgeois confection that sides with the authorities in their attempt to fathom the lies and chicanery of the publc, and as such is one of Fulci's most Establishment-friendly films; certainly the Lucio Fulci we encounter here is a long way from the man who directed *Beatrice Cenci*, *Don't Torture a Duckling* and *The Eroticist*, in which authorities of varying stripes are castigated and derided.

On the musical side, one can hear "Go-Kart Twist" (written by Ennio Morricone and sung by Gianni Morandi) playing at the beach during the scenes with Chiari and Luciana Gilli, while Giorgio Gaber opens the film with the cheery title song, "Gli imbroglioni". Disappointingly, however, he re-recorded the song before releasing it as a single later in 1963, and to my ears the second arrangement is less fluid and lacks the energetic singalong quality of the film version. Note too the introduction of a piece of music to accompany Franco and Ciccio, used again in *I due evasi di Sing Sing*, which blatantly mimics the famous Laurel and Hardy theme tune...

Gli imbroglioni received better Italian reviews than Fulci's previous two or three films, with *l'Unità* declaring: *"It is a movie divided into episodes, whose common thread is a courtroom and whose characters (either victims or felons) are all extremely colourful and interesting [...] The stories don't lack for wit and there are several enjoyable moments."*[24]

above: Locandina.

opposite, main picture: Napoleone Palumbo (Ciccio Ingrassia) grifts a German tourist (Elio Crovetto) and his wife, while Salvatore Di Carmine (Franco Franchi) pretends to be a reanimated mummy: a sign of things to come in Fulci's cinema!

opposite, bottom left: The 7" single release of the film's title song, sung by Giorgio Gaber.

below: Franco and Ciccio selling their ill-gotten goods; and attempting a con-trick in an Etruscan tomb.

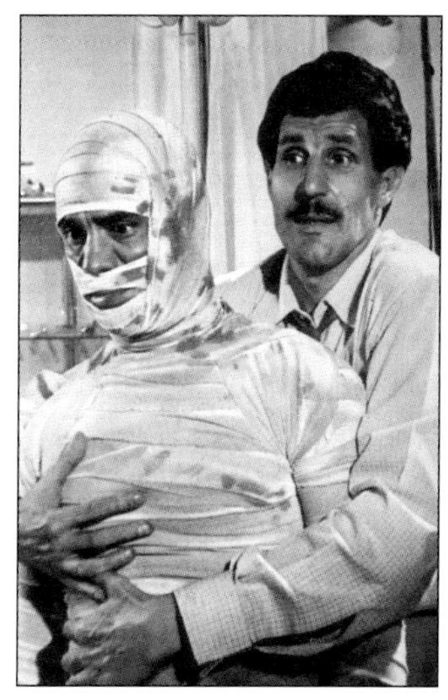

Translation
'The Maniacs'

Italy

Production company
Hesperia Cinematografica S.p.A. (IT)

Note: not to be confused with the Spanish production company Hesperia Films S.A.

Theatrical distributor
Cinedistribuzione Astoria (IT)

Running time
Italy 90m

DVD running time (adjusted)
CG Home Video (Italy) 94m 02s

Censorship
Italian censor certificate 42526 issued 26 March 1964

Shooting period
January 1964

Release information
Rome 28 March 1964
Lecce & Brindisi 02 April 1964
Turin 30 April 1964

filmed in black and white

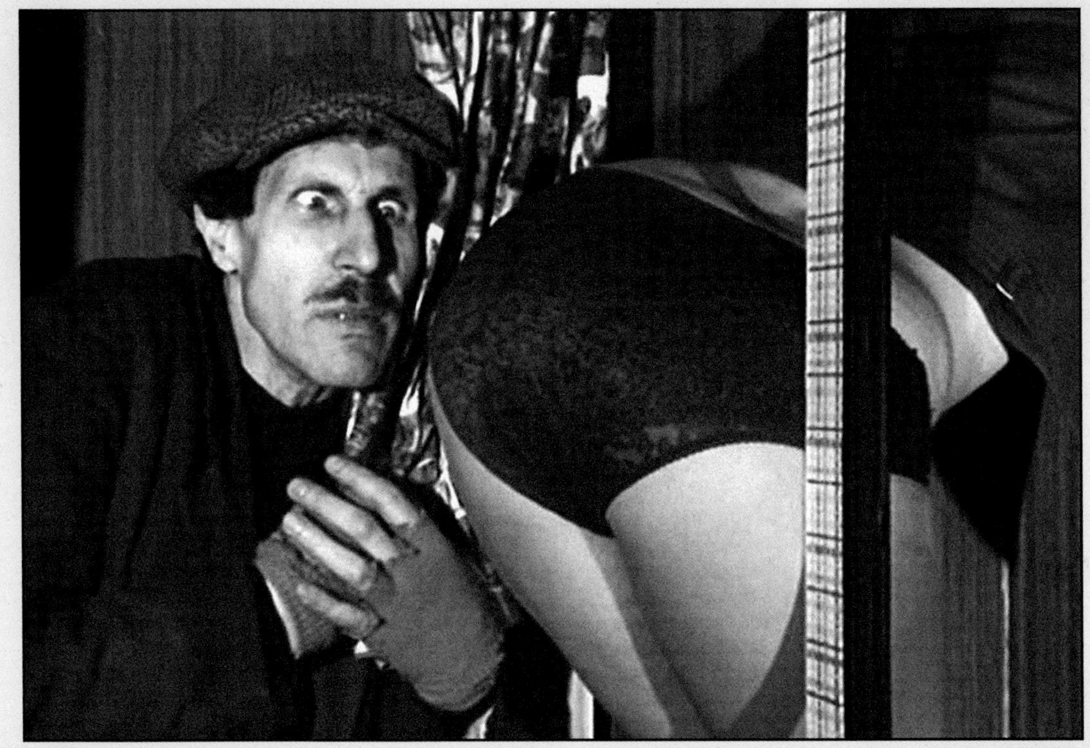

I maniaci

1964

Directed by Lucio Fulci. producer: Ferruccio Brusarosco. story & screenplay: Castellano [Franco Castellano] & Pipolo [Giuseppe Moccia], [Vittorio] Vighi, [Ugo] Guerra & [Lucio] Fulci; from an idea by Castellano [Franco Castellano] & Pipolo [Giuseppe Moccia]. director of photography: Riccardo Pallottini. music: Ennio Morricone; recorded & published by RCA Italiana. editor: Ornella Micheli Donati. set designer: Aurelio Crugnola. associate producer: Giancarlo Marchetti. production supervisor: Gianni Minervini. unit manager: Toto Mignone. 1st assistant director: Mariano Laurenti. 2nd assistant director: Giorgio Gallizio. cameraman: Gastone Di Giovanni. assistant cameraman: Gianni Bonivento. continuity: Franca Carotenuto. costume designer: Giuliano Papi. set dresser: Dik Dominici. make-up: Giannetto De Rossi. hairstylist: Maria Miccinilli. production secretary: Marcello Papaleo. assistant editor: Bruno Micheli. sound: Dino Fronzetti. sound re-recording: Renato Cadueri. post-synchronization recorded at International Recording Studios [on the] Westrex System with the collaboration of CID. songs: "La mie mania" sung by Gianni Morandi; "Ma neanche per idea" sung by Michele; "Sono un ragazzo" sung by Roby Ferranei; "Stelle e sogni" sung by Barbara Baldassare; "Eravamo amici" sung by Dino; "Cosa rimane alle fine di un amore" [composed &] sung by Nico Fidenco; "Pel di carota" [composed by Migliacci & Ennio Morricone], sung by Rita Pavone; "Mezzanotte" sung by Los Hermanos Riguad; "Ogni volta" [composed by Rossi & Roby Ferrante], sung by Paul Anka – all available on RCA Records. negatives & positives: Effetti Ottici S.P.E.S., director: E. Catalucci. raw stock: Dupont.

Cast: Pt. 1 – L'elaborazione: Loris Bazzocchi (Mechanic). Silla Bettini (hearse driver). Pt. 2 – Lo sport: Raimondo Vianello (Giulio Errani, the boss). Franco Fabrizi (Sita, Errani's employee/nemesis). Edy Biagetti (Biagetti, an employee). Ignazio Leone (Migliardi, Errani's dark-haired friend). Salvo Libassi (Errani's hat-wearing friend). Lisa Gastoni (Mrs. Errani). Pt. 3 – Il Sorpasso ('Overtaking'): Walter Chiari (maniacal motorist). Pt. 4 – L'hobby ('The Hobby'): Barbara Steele (Barbara, Enrico's wife). Mary Arden (tall blonde party guest). Gigi Ballista (Count). Gaia Germani (Carla, Enrico's lover). Nico Fidenco (Guitarist). Pt. 5 – I Consigli ('Advice'): Raimondo Vianello (Paolo, driver with bickering wife). Sandra Mondaini (Paolo's wife). Pt. 6 – La Protesta ('The Protest'): Walter Chiari (Pasquale Taddei). Aroldo Tieri (Mario, Pasquale's friend). Pt. 7 – Il pezzo antico ('The Antique Piece'): Franca Valeri (antique-hunter). Vittorio Caprioli (antique-hunter's husband). Umberto D'Orsi (Father Egisto). Pt. 8 – La Parolaccia ('The Swear Word'): Umberto D'Orsi (Ilario Baietti, struggling author). Enrico Maria Salerno (Professor Castelli, established author). Isarco Ravaioli (Eros, Castelli's manservant). Gustavo D'Arpe (heavy, balding literary critic). Antonio Acqua (older bespectacled critic). Pt. 9 – Lo Strip: Walter Chiari (Strip-club client). Corinne (Jazz club stripper). Gora de Paris (Mambo club stripper). Pery Han (stripper in veils). Pt. 10 – Le Interviste ('The Interview'): Raimondo Vianello (Micozzi, a politician). Pt. 11 – L'autostop ('The Hitch-hiker'): Walter Chiari (Sicilian hitchhiker). Umberto D'Orsi (motorist from Milan). Pt. 12 – La Cambiale ('The Promissory Note'): Barbara Steele (Mrs. Brugnoli). Raimondo Vianello (Mr. Brugnoli). Ingrid Schoeller (Mrs Bonfanti). Aroldo Tieri (Mr. Bonfanti). Pt. 13 – La comica finale: Il weekend (The final joke: the weekend'): Franco Franchi (thief). Ciccio Ingrassia (thief #2). Alicia Brandet (Rosetta, the maid). Ugo Fangareggi (Antonio, a soldier). Margaret Lee (Rosalynn). Corrado Olmi (Rosalynn's lover).

Synopsis: A film of thirteen parts. *L'elaborazione* ('Processing'): A hearse driver is obsessed ensuring that his vehicle gives 'passengers' the ultimate in driving comfort. *Lo sport* ('Sport'). Giulio Errani, a bullying office manager, loses a bet with some friends and must put his wife to work on the streets. When one of his employees finds out, he uses the knowledge to turn the tables at work. *Il sorpasso* ('Overtaking'): A motorist obsessed with other drivers speeding, refuses to allow a car to overtake, ending up driving more maniacially than anyone else. *L'hobby* ('The hobby'): Barbara becomes anxious that her rich husband Enrico has another woman, even though she already knows and accepts his 'secret' lover, Carla. *I consigli* ('Councils'): A married couple argue and wrangle constantly while driving. *La protesta* ('The protest'): Mario and Pasquale are two friends, whom we see in different historical periods. In each period they express dissatisfaction with the status quo but never lift a finger to change anything, instead repeatedly

backing down and kow-towing to authority. *Il pezzo antico* ('The Antique Item'): A couple obsessed with buying rustic antiques clear a monastery of its rough-hewn furniture, paying vast sums of money. The monks play along, then telephone for more cheap tat to take the place of their 'priceless antiques'. *La parolaccia* ('The Word'): A writer having difficulty writing his first novel visits a successful author who advises him to dredge his imagination for the seamiest and most depraved fantasies. When the writer finishes his new novel he presents it to a major literary society for whom the established author is a patron: he savages the work and humiliates the writer. *Lo strip* ('The strip'): A man obsessed with strippers watches them intently, but his reasons are not so straightforward. *Le interviste* ('Interviews'): A career politician finds that the same evasions and vague non-answers work in all situations. *L'autostop* ('Hitchhiking'): A poor Southern worker hitches a lift with an affluent Milanese businessman. In the course of the journey, although neither says or does anything wrong, they both become increasingly paranoid and hostile. *La cambiale* ('The promissory note'): Two bourgeois couples become obsessed with appearing wealthier than each other, but the only way they can keep up the race is to sink deeper and deeper into debt. *La comica finale: Il weekend* (The final joke: the weekend'): Two thieves break into a mansion believing that the owners are away for the weekend. However, the place is soon buzzing with activity as the woman of the house sneaks back with her lover, and the husband returns with his mistress.

About the production: *"Not a horror film! An explosion of laughter Italian-style!"* bellowed the pre-release ads for this portmanteau comedy film. Announced as forthcoming in *Variety* in December 1963, *I maniaci* started shooting in January of 1964 for Hesperia Cinematografica and was ready for review in the Italian press by the end of March 1964; an impressive velocity of production indeed.

Review: This, the second of Fulci's *films a episodi*, is easily the best of the two, in fact it's one of the highlights of his entire comedy output; it's varied enough not to weary the palate, and although some of the satirical barbs are so obvious you can see them coming a mile away, in other aspects Fulci shows flashes of the intelligent pessimism that would emerge in his films of the 1970s. The fourteen segments range from a comic one-hander about a mild-mannered driver who turns nasty when another car tries to overtake him, to a fairly detailed short story about a struggling writer who takes advice on how to 'épater-le-bourgeoisie' from a successful but pretentious colleague. This segment, *La Parolaccia* ('The Swear Word') is the most memorable in that it advances the film's most sophisticated premise. The intellectual pontificates on the need for art that is purposefully aggressive and destructive against society; yet he lives in a beautiful house with great works by the Flemish masters on the walls. Whilst affecting no concern for his worldly wealth he boasts that the more violently he rejects society's values the more they pay him for it. There is a deliberate attack here on the anti-establishment credentials of the Marxist wing of the Italian industry: when the unfortunate student is attacked by the censor board for the repugnance and obscenity of the art he's created, his intellectual 'friend' promptly decries the work as vulgar and immature, leading to the student's 'excommunication' by his peers (suggesting that the capitalist creed of competition so derided by Marxists springs back into play when their comfortable 'rebel' niche is threatened by new blood).

Also impressive is a segment in which we hear the unspoken thoughts of a liberal motorist from the north of Italy and a peasant hitch-hiker from the south to whom he gives a lift, as they progress from mutual appreciation to seething resentment and ultimately overwhelming paranoia (the peasant becomes convinced that the driver is a homosexual who intends to seduce him; the driver starts out mulling over the affluent north's shoddy treatment of the rural south and ends up leaping from the car convinced that the man is a psychopath determined to rob and kill him).

Overall, the themes are quickly and easily sketched in; vanity, foolishness, avarice, two-facedness. People bitch about injustice but do nothing when the time comes to make a stand, or take absurd stands on pointless matters of 'principle' (like the man who declares to his friends that if his football team misses a penalty he'll pimp his own wife, and who then feels compelled to honour his word); they act like 'maniacs' on the road whilst blaming their excesses on other drivers; and they kvetch about authority in private but suck up to it in person. There are some amusing sight-gags too – I enjoyed the skit about a strip-show patron whose face twitches with what we assume is suppressed lust, but who returns home instead to prance before a mirror fantasising that he's a stripper too. Euro-horror queen Barbara Steele appears twice, playing a society wife who discovers that even a mutually agreed open relationship isn't enough to keep her rich hubby satisfied (he's sneaking off to play amateur football with his friends), and who later drives him to penury by insisting on reckless hire-purchases (to fund an escalating feud with a couple who are likewise sinking into debt). Whether 'The Maniacs' is ultimately light in touch or simply light-weight ('The Fools' would be a more appropriate title), it's brisk and playful enough to sustain its ninety minute running time and has some interesting ideas amid the comic fluff.

above:
Fotobusta depicting (anti-clockwise from top left) Walter Chiari as a suspicious southern hitch-hiker; Umberto D'Orsi as the opportunistic Father of a Monastery, Raimondo Vianello as a man whose determination to 'keep up with the Joneses' leads to penury in old age, and Barbara Steele as a wife who suspects her husband of having an affair without her permission.

top left:
Giulio Errani (Raimondo Vianello, centre) flanked by his work colleagues (Salvo Libassi, left, and Edy Biagetti, right), loses a bet on his football team and must pimp his wife as forfeit.

opposite, main picture:
Words cannot convey...

opposite, bottom left:
Two bungling burglars (Franco and Ciccio) debate where to draw the line.

below:
The film's locandina.

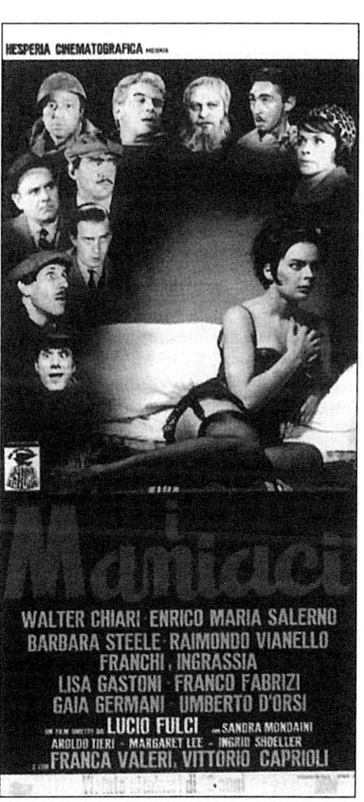

Translation
'Two Escapees from Sing Sing'

Italy

International theatrical title
Das Grossmaul (WG)
'The Loudmouth'

Other listed titles
2 Sing Sing Jailbreakers
(from a *Variety* news item)
Runaways from Sing Sing
(from a *Variety* news item)

Production companies
Mega Film (Bari/Rome)
Turris Film (Rome)

Theatrical distributors
Panta Cinematografica Distribuzione (IT)

Running time
Italy 99m

DVD running time (adjusted)
Avofilm (IT) 91m 14s

Shooting period
30 June through July 1964

Censorship
Italian censor certificate 43570
issued 12 August 1964

Release information
Turin 27 August 1964
Rome 04 September 1964
Bari 22 September 1964

filmed in black and white

I due evasi di Sing Sing

1964

Directed by Lucio Fulci. a Mega Film (Bari/Rome) / Turris Film (Rome) co-production. production supervisor: Antonio Colantuoni. story: Marcello Ciorciolini. screenplay: Marcello Ciorciolini & Lucio Fulci. director of photography: Adalberto Albertini. editor: Ornella Micheli. music: Ennio Morricone. production designers: Saverio D'Eugenio & Giuseppe Ranieri. production manager: Jacopo Comin. assistant director: Giovanni Fago. unit manager: Albino Morandin. continuity: Franca Carotenuto. cameraman: Carlo Fiore. costume designer: Vera Marzot. special effects: Sergio Canevari. sound: Franco Groppioni.

Cast: Franco Franchi (Franco Bacalone). Ciccio Ingrassia (Ciccio Bacalone). Arturo Dominici (Alfredo Attanasia, Mafia boss). Gloria Paul (Molly Smith, brunette 'given' to Ciccio). Alicia Brandet (Ruth Allenby, blonde moll 'given' to Franco). Attilio Dottesio (Tony Agnello, Attanasia's henchman). Omero Gargano (Joe Pastrano, Attanasia's henchman). Poldo Bendandi (Joachin Enriquez, 'La Sfregiato' ['Scarface'], Tristano's bald heavy). Renato Terra (Jim Doris). Vittorio Bonos (Hugh Ebertin, Governor of Sing Sing). Freddy Mack (Frederick Jones aka 'Cassius Pistol', boxer). Livio Lorenzon (Lemmy Tristano, Attanasia's chief rival). Enzo Andronico (Tristano's henchman first seen in passenger seat of his limousine). Mary Arden (tall woman with blonde bouffant at Attanasia's place). Marilù Asaro. Adolfo Belletti. Laura Bindi as 'Laura Bini']. Fausto Bombelli. Gustavo D'Arpe (Attanasia's lawyer). Vincenzo Falanga. Guido Giuseppone. Claire Gordon. Carlo Marcolini (Franco's would-be assassin killed by hidden gun). Fausto Parravano. Mimmo Poli. Franco Ricciardi. Luisa Rispoli. Francesco Sormano. Luca Sportelli (man electrocuted by slot machine in Attanasia's apartment). Nino Terzo (Thompson, moustachioed prison officer at Sing Sing). Walter Williams. *Uncredited:* Alfonso Giganti (Judge). Alfredo Rizzo (Sauna Director). Lat Shonibare (himself [Nigerian boxer k-o'd by his trainer]). Piero Morgia (blond prison officer teamed with Thompson). Lino Banfi (sobbing man who comes to Franco's dressing room).

Synopsis: Two Sicilian cousins, Franco and Ciccio Bacalone, are due to be executed in the gas chamber at Sing Sing. Avoiding execution by tampering with the gas supply – and almost succeeding in gassing their gaolers – the two buffoons are returned to their cell where Franco undertakes to write his prison memoir... In flashback we see that while working with Ciccio as an attendant at a Turkish bath-house in New York, Franco accidentally saved the life of Alfred Attanasia, a mafia boss taking a sauna, who came under attack from Lemmy Tristano, a bitter rival. In gratitude, Attanasia fixes the two cousins up with girlfriends, Molly and Ruth, and launches Franco's career as a boxer (with Ciccio as his trainer). Thanks to constant match-fixing Franco wins fight after fight. However, when it's time for the so-called 'Franco the Beast' to take a fall he manages to win by accident, which is a disaster since Attanasia and Tristano, now reconciled, have placed huge bets on his opponent. The gang bosses blame each other for cheating, and kill one another in a shoot-out on the scenery-strewn backlot of a television studio owned by Attanasia. Franco and Ciccio are blamed for the murders and find themselves on Death Row, but manage to get themselves caught up in an escape plan hatched by another prisoner, Joachin Enriquez, one of Tristano's heavies. Emerging as the only successful escapees, in a welter of confusion, they hook up again with Molly and Ruth, only to find themselves tricked into a cellar-bound rendezvous with Agnello and Pastrano, two henchmen of the deceased Attanasia who are now running his operation. Once again they survive the shoot-out, while Agnello and Pastrano shoot each other by accident. Just as Franco and Ciccio pick up the villains' guns they are caught 'red-handed' by the police and returned to await execution in Sing Sing. The flashback ends... The prison and court authorities, having examined the Bacalones' case, and furthermore having grown utterly sick of the duo, decide to offer them their freedom. Now barricaded in their cell, with the iron door wired to the mains, they refuse to come out, suspecting a trap. Even a telephone call from the Pentagon office fails to dislodge them: Franco responds to the President's offer of clemency with a colossal raspberry. In a flash forward to 1990, we see the two idiots, now doddering old men, still barricaded in their cell...

About the production: Shooting of *I due evasi di Sing Sing* must have been well underway by July of '64: a newspaper dated Tuesday 14 July 1964 is visible during a montage announcing the launch of Franchi's boxing career, and the same date can be seen twice again on subsequent news headline shots. It's likely that these inserts were collected towards the end of filming, suggesting mid-June to mid-July as the shooting period (on average, Fulci's Franco and Ciccio films were shot in approximately four weeks) ... This is the only Lucio Fulci film co-written by Marcello Ciorciolini, a writer who more frequently worked on Giorgio Simonelli's Franco & Ciccio films, seven of them in all. He also went on to direct five himself: *I barbieri di Sicilia* (1967), *Ciccio perdona... Io no!* (1968), *I nipoti di Zorro* (1968), *Indovina chi viene a merenda?* (1969) and *Franco e Ciccio... ladro e guardia* (1969), the timing of which suggests that he was drafted in to take up the slack when Fulci bowed out of the Franco & Ciccio business in 1967. (For more about *I due evasi di Sing Sing*, see the production entry for *00-2 agenti segretissimi*.)

Review: A knockabout comedy set on Death Row, in one of America's toughest, meanest prisons? Welcome to *I due evasi di Sing Sing*, Lucio Fulci's gangster comedy based on scenarios plucked from hardboiled crime fiction and Hollywood thrillers. He doesn't mess about either, jumping in feet first with a macabre skit set in the gas chamber (a location we'll be visiting again in 1969's superlative *One on Top of the Other*). Franco and Ciccio, petty criminals wrongly convicted of murder, manage to avoid being gassed by kicking away the tray of water into which the killing mechanism drops poison pellets. When prison officials enter the chamber to see what's wrong, Franco discovers the errant pellet and accidentally drops it in the water. In the confusion, he and Ciccio escape and the prison officials are locked in. Which is all very funny, so I suppose we ought not to care that in fact Sing Sing did not have a gas chamber, but was instead infamous for 'Old Sparky', its electric chair. A total of 614 men and women were electrocuted in Sing Sing, the first in 1891 and the last in 1963, just a year before *I due evasi di Sing Sing* was made. Fulci must surely have known this, so the decision to film a gas chamber instead of the electric chair would seem to be his idea of tact and good taste...

Sing Sing Prison, located up the Hudson River from New York, has a long history, stretching back to the 1820s. In the 19th century it was notorious for brutal punishments (water torture and "bucking", in which men were hung upside down in agonising positions), thankfully brought to an end in 1914 by the intervention of prison reformists. The place has long fascinated filmmakers: it was the setting for *Thunderbolt* (Josef von Sternberg, 1929), *The Big House* (George W. Hill, 1930), *Up the River* (John Ford, 1930) with Spencer Tracy and Humphrey Bogart, *20,000 Years in Sing Sing* (Michael Curtiz, 1932) starring Spencer Tracy, *Castle on the Hudson* (Anatole Litvak, 1940) with John Garfield, and of course *Angels with Dirty Faces* (Michael Curtiz, 1938) starring James Cagney. More recently, in 1962, it had been the setting for *Convicts 4* (released in Italy as *Tre passi dalla sedia elettrica* or 'Three steps from the electric chair'). In real life, Sing Sing had 'housed' famous gangsters like Willie Sutton, Lucky Luciano, and members of the infamous 'Murder Incorporated', a contract-killing operation composed of Italian-American and Jewish gangsters. Five 'Murder Inc.' members were executed at Sing Sing between 1942-44, and Fulci was evidently interested in the case: the character played by Arturo Dominici in *I due evasi di Sing Sing* – Mafia boss Alfredo Attanasia – is clearly named after real-life gangster Albert Anastasia, referred to by the press as the 'Lord High Executioner of Murder Inc.' (He avoided the electric chair but was assassinated in a barber shop in Manhattan in 1957.

So what do we get when we put aside the troubles of the real world? It turns out quite a lot. In terms of comedy set-pieces, there's an amusing slapstick routine in a men's sauna, involving Franco and Ciccio accidentally dowsing mafia bigwigs in hot mud as they try to relax in the steam room, which has the hallmarks of silent comedy and would not shame Laurel and Hardy. Afterwards, big-shot mobster Attanasia demonstrates his awesome influence to Franco and Ciccio by having a flunky call his TV station, which is currently showing a jaunty 'Freddy and the Dreamers' style pop group: with a terse *"Mr. Attanasia says 'No'"* the programme grinds to a halt and the band are ordered off! Now that's power. The real highlights, however, are provided by Franchi's exploits in the boxing ring. Even if the Franco and Ciccio 'brand' tends to curl your toes, it's hard not to laugh when Franco – aka 'Frankie the Beast' – first steps into the ring at a training gym, with one glove so heavily weighted that he can barely lift it: having managed to start windmilling his arm he finds he can't stop, punching out his trainer, demolishing the ring and finally knocking himself out too. Also very cleverly played is a scene in which Franco fights the imposing 'Cassius Pistol' (the name of course echoing Cassius Clay aka Muhammad Ali). Ciccio's accomplice pours glue in the grit-box into which the players step before fighting, which swiftly leaves Franco's adversary stuck to the ring canvas, swinging his fists and leaning back and forth at surreal angles. Franco then mimics this 'style', even though he is free to move as he wishes, until the two of them are swaying around like characters in a David Lynch dream sequence. At his best, in scenes such as this, Franchi brings a sort of Tex Avery quality to his physical comedy, and you come to realise that it makes just as much sense to look upon him as a live-action cartoon character as it does to see him as a vaudeville performer, or to reference the commedia dell'arte.

Fulci has plenty of fun with the fight scenes, giving them lots of fizz and vitality, but he really pulls out the stops for a bravura sequence at a TV station. A running battle between the Attanasia and Tristano gangs spills out onto the studio backlot, and thanks to the bungling of Franco and Ciccio the gunfighters find themselves dowsed in studio rain and smothered in fake snow before being buffetted by a powerful wind machine, all of which takes place in a partially dismantled studio lot dotted with camera cranes, lights and mismatched scenery. It's a playful deconstruction of a venerable tradition, the cinematic shoot-out, not quite Godardian but certainly very witty. The result is an enjoyable romp, one of the best Franco and Ciccio films, which if given a sympathetic English translation would probably win over a few sceptics.

above:
The Italian poster, a tad misleadingly, portrays the duo as full-on gangsters. (And is that the ghost of Fred Buscaglione in the background?)

opposite, main picture:
A posed publicity shot for *I due evasi di Sing Sing*.

opposite, bottom left:
This Italian locandina takes a witty 'poster within a poster' approach.

below left:
Eyeballs have always been important in the films of Lucio Fulci...

below:
Poldo Bendandi, playing thuggish prisoner 'Scarface' in his first of three consecutive roles in Fulci's Franco and Ciccio films, menaces the stars of the show.

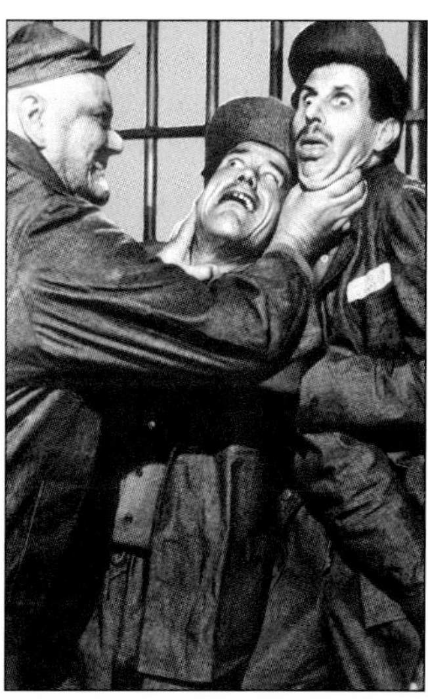

Translation
'00-2 Secret Agents'

Italy

International theatrical titles
00-2 Most Secret Agents (USA)
Oh! Those Most Secret Agents (USA re-release)
00-2 Agent (USA – Variety listing)
002 – Operação Bikini (POR)
'002 – Bikini Operation'
Wir, die Trottel vom Geheimdienst (WG) 'We, The Idiots of the Secret Service'

Production companies
Mega Film (Bari/Rome)

Theatrical distributors
Panta Cinematografica Distribuzione (IT)
Sherpix (USA)
Allied Artists (USA) re-release

Running time
Italy 90m

DVD running time (adjusted)
Medusa (IT) 93m 14s

Censorship
Italian censor certificate 43943 issued 08 October 1964

Release information
Bari 28 October 1964
Turin 03 November 1964
Rome 04 November 1964
USA (Texas) 23 June 1966 (as Oh! Those Most Secret Agents)
Germany 02 February 1970

00-2 agenti segretissimi

1964

Directed by Lucio Fulci. a Mega Film (Bari/Rome) production. production supervisor: Antonio Colantuoni. story: Vittorio Metz. screenplay: Metz, Fulci & Amedeo Sollazzo. director of photography: Adalberto Albertini. editor: Ornella Micheli. music: Piero Umiliani. production designer: Giuseppe Ranieri. set designer & special effects: Sergio Canevari. production manager: Jacopo Comin. unit managers: Orlando Orsini & Albino Morandin. assistant director: Nino Zanchin. 2nd assistant director: Giorgio Galizia. continuity: Franca Carotenuto. cameraman: Carlo Fiore. costume designer: Vera Marzot. make-up: Telemaco Tilli. hairdresser: Maria Miccinelli. production secretary: Stefano Amoroso. sound: Franco Groppioni. colour by Eastmancolor.

Cast: Franco Franchi (Franco Passalacqua). Ciccio Ingrassia (Ciccio Passalacqua). Ingrid Schoeller (Giulia Cirillo, wife of jealous husband). Carla Calò (Russian spy chief). Poldo Bendandi (Dimitri Tovarisc, bald Russian spy chief). Luca Sportelli (Fred, American Secret Service Chief). Aroldo Tieri (Dr. Nicola [aka 'Carlo'] Cirillo, the jealous husband). Enzo Andronico (Blond Russian agent with pinstripe suit). Nando Angelini (moustachioed American agent at the beach). Mary Arden (Nadja, blonde Russian agent who tries to seduce Franco). Marilù Asaro (). Pietro Ceccarelli [as 'Puccio Ceccarelli'] (head Chinese torturer). Anna Maria Checchi. Franz Colangeli [as 'Franz Colangelo']* (Maurice, bald Russian assassin with moustache). Mario Del Vago (bespectacled radio operator working for the Chinese). Rita Forzano. Annie Gorassini (blonde room-service maid). Connie Jorgensen. Viviana Larice. Carlo Marcolini (Grey-suited heavy zapped by Franco's electric touch). Piero Morgia (Joe, handsome blond American agent). Maria Luisa Rispoli. Selina Seyn [aka Seyna Seyn] (Chinese agent seducing Ciccio at restaurant). Alessandro Tedeschi (Ivan, bald Russian assassin wearing dark glasses). Anita Todesco (dark-haired woman in black dress who dances with Ciccio at The Ritz). Nino Terzo (Russian agent with moustache and wavy hair [paired with Enzo Andronico]). *Uncredited:* Harold Bradley (black bodybuilder). Pietro Torrisi** (white bodybuilder). János [John] Bartha (electroshock doctor). Amerigo Santarelli (stocky dark-haired agent with gun who interrupts torture session). Nicola Di Gioia (torturer with goat). Veriano Ginesi (2nd torturer with goat). Alfonso Giganti (waiter). * *IMDb wrongly credit him as Ralf Colangelo.* ** *wrongly credited onscreen as Francesco Torrisi.*

Synopsis: Acting on bogus information so intentionally ridiculous that only imbeciles would fall for it, burglars Franco and Ciccio break into a mansion in Rome. Having therefore proved that they are stupid enough to make ideal decoys for an espionage sting, they are drugged by an American spy boss, on the orders of an espionage computer, and microfilm containing bogus military information is inserted into one of Franco's molars. The two are then revived and sent on a 'holiday' to the French Riviera. The plan is for the two decoys to be seized by either the Russians or the Chinese, both of whom are hunting for the real military secrets, but through a series of comic happenstances the two idiots elude their intended captors and head off to the beach. Unfortunately for the Americans, it transpires that instead of decoy information a genuine secret formula has been accidentally implanted. Soon, spies of all the major superpowers are hunting the duo down, determined to pull out Franco's teeth...

About the production: *00-2 agenti segretissimi* was the first Franco and Ciccio film – indeed the first Lucio Fulci film – to get a release in the USA. It was picked up in December 1964 by Louis K. Sher, head of a national circuit of cinemas called the Art Theatre Guild. Sher had recently decided to enter the film distribution business, feeling dissatisfied with what he regarded as a lack of suitable product for his cinemas. He went on a reconnaisance trip to Rome and returned with the US and Canadian theatrical and TV rights to two of Fulci's Franco and Ciccio films: *00-2 agenti segretissimi* and *I due evasi di Sing Sing* (along with *I fuorilegge del matrimonio*, a sketch-comedy film starring Ugo Tognazzi and Annie Giradot). With a new title, *00-2 Secret Agent*, and the addition of English subtitles, the film was the first to be released by Sher's fledgling distribution company Sherpix, formed in March 1965. Sherpix would go on to become a fixture of the sexploitation market in the early 1970s, with a series of lucrative purchases surfing the wave of explicit sex films. When it came to knockabout comedy all'italiana, however, business was light, and the following year saw Sherpix offloading *00-2 agenti segretissimi* to Allied Artists, who promptly stuck it out again under the title *Oh! Those Most Secret Agents*. Records do not indicate if they went to the trouble of dubbing the film, although surely it would have been the sensible option for a quick-fire lowbrow comedy? Sadly, no one took a punt on Louis Sher's other Franco and Ciccio acquisition, *I due evasi di Sing Sing*. It's referred to only in passing in *Variety* (once as '2 Sing Sing Jailbreakers' and once as 'Runaways from Sing Sing'), so evidently Sher was so discouraged by the colourful *00-2 agenti segretissimi*'s failure to find an audience that he left the black-and-white half of the deal on the shelf.

Review: *00-2 agenti segretissimi* is a film of firsts. To begin with, it's Fulci's first film in colour, and the bright blue skies and sunny beach scenes make the most of this new opportunity. Then there's the first drop of blood in a Lucio Fulci film (emanating from a head-wound, no less: a Russian spy is shot in the back of the skull). And there's more; how about the first torture scene in a Fulci film? Okay, so it involves rubber-faced Franco Franchi having his feet tickled by the tongue of a salt-licking goat – not the most brutal scene in Fulci's library of pain – but he's then forced to consume vast quantities of water, which although comical is also faintly nauseating. With a blow to his massively swollen stomach the water jets back out, dowsing the red hot coals that were about to be applied to Ciccio. To cap it all in this parade of debuts, we have the first appearance of a power tool used aggressively on a human being; well, almost, as the Chinese secret service threaten to sever Franco's arm with an electric wood-saw. It may be a long way from here to the fate of poor Bob in *City of the Living Dead*, but the element of implied sadism adds spice to this genial spy romp, and taken along with the attractive location work make it my personal favourite of the Franco and Ciccio films.

00-2 agenti segretissimi was not universally admired at the time. *l'Unità*'s critic struck a weary tone that shaded into a rather odd complaint: *"Nowadays every film stars Franchi and Ingrassia, this time as secret agents chosen to divert Soviet intelligence (you can just imagine how the Soviet agents are depicted). Our two "heroes", despite their gullibility and thanks to a series of lucky circumstances, outwit everybody, even two extremely ferocious Chinese agents. This filmetto is rather dull, and sometimes objectionable and vulgar."*[25] Objectionable and vulgar? Thus far in Fulci's career he'd been attacked mainly for the perceived frivolity and inconsequence of his films. Here we see the stirrings of a different complaint, one that would colour the critical response to so much of his later work: a feeling that the director lacks decorum. So what's so 'objectionable' about this film? Putting aside the caricature depiction of Russians, to which the reviewer simply rolls his eyes, perhaps he was unnerved by the constant threat of crude dental attack, as various spies attempt to extract Franco's teeth to remove the sought-after microfilm? A wonderful comedy set-piece has implacable Russian agents pulling out molars from a cascade of unfortunates at a beach resort. KGB intelligence informs them that the bearer of the microfilm tooth has a limp: knowing that this is what the agents are looking for, Franco and Ciccio hide underneath a beach table and bash the feet of passers-by, leading to a cavalcade of limping holiday-makers, each of whom is dragged into a beach hut to have a tooth yanked out. If you're squeamish about dentists, I suppose this constant emphasis on pulling teeth out by the roots could bring on a hot flush or two. But 'objectionable'? Perhaps, then, the reviewer was dismayed by the Russians' pragmatic decision to ply the comedy duo with two hunky musclemen when it becomes apparent that they're not interested in the seductive women sent to their hotel room? In truth it's a blistering sunburn that renders the comedy duo impervious to female wiles, which leads to a hilarious scene in which Franco and Ciccio apply cooling lotion to one another's backs while the Russians listen in via a hidden microphone: from the groans and sighs of relief, the eavesdroppers get completely the wrong idea about what's going on!

00-2 agenti segretissimi is not enormously different to the other films Fulci made at the time: many of the gags and set-ups are corny in the extreme (especially those involving a sex-mad talking computer), and there are times when slipshod choreography makes the already implausible action impossible to believe (for instance, an escalating series of murders in a posh restaurant gets so silly that by the end we're asked to believe a chandelier can crash to the ground without anyone noticing). Nevertheless the film has an engaging, sunny, optimistic air to it, and there's enough going on to prevent it from turning into just another series of comedy pratfalls and facial contortions. It's dumb, it's silly, it's still a Franco and Ciccio movie, but it's actually not so hard to watch. Some of the gags stand up well: believing themselves threatened with death, the two idiots plead for their lives... *"I'm the father of seven children!"* claims Ciccio. *"I'm the son of seven fathers!"* tries Franco. And when, as mentioned earlier, the two get horrendously sunburned after overdoing it on their first day at the beach, their agonised attempt to get dressed in a minuscule changing booth without rubbing against one another leads to some inspired physical comedy. If you only watch one Franco and Ciccio movie, I suggest you make it this one.

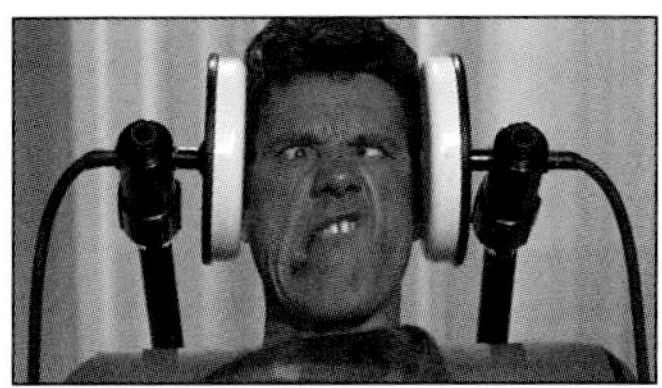

top:
Secret messages Italian-style from an agent masquerading as a hotel cleaner: "Go to the beach from 10 o'clock and improve your tan".

above:
'Franco Passalacqua' ('Franco Passing Water') has his 'brains' fried by electro-shock treatment. No appreciable damage occurs.

opposite, main picture:
Cheerful artwork for the film emphasising Franco and Ciccio's facility for disguise. Fifth-credited Annie Gorassini must have had a great agent; she plays the hotel maid who passes secret messages written on her panties and appears for maybe two minutes in the finished film!

opposite, bottom left:
Those double-0 screwballs aim for the American market. Annie Gorassini (pictured) makes her mark here too.

left:
This Italian locandina uses the same stylistic device (a poster within a poster) and overall visual design as Fulci's previous Franco and Ciccio comedy, *I due evasi di Sing Sing*; a risky strategy considering that they were released just two months apart.

below:
Franco undergoes water torture administered by a Russian agent (Poldo Bendandi).

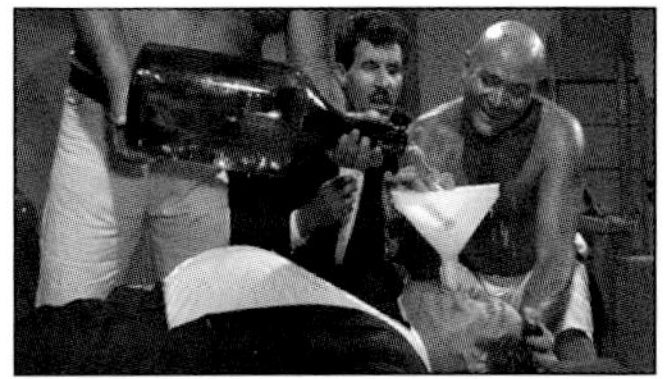

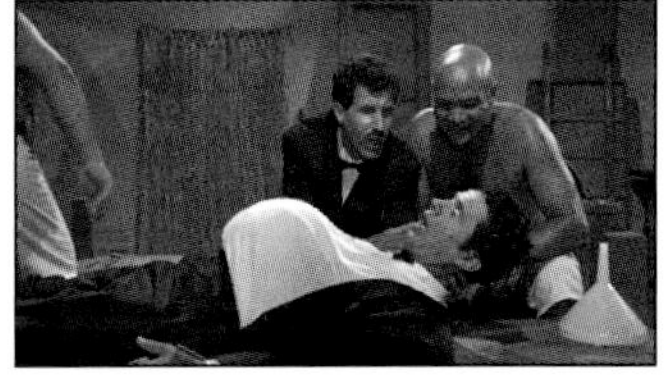

Translation
'Two Public Menaces'

Italy

Unconfirmed titles
I due nemici pubblici (IT)
'Those Two Public Menaces'
Two Dangerous Agents
(possible export title)

Production companies
Aster Film

Theatrical distributors
Medusa Distribuzione (Rome)

Running time
Italy 90m

DVD running time (adjusted)
CG (Italy) 89m 04s

Censorship
Italian censor certificate 44516
issued 30 December 1964

Release information
Rome 29 January 1965
Turin 27 February 1965
Fasano 21 March 1965
Bari 25 March 1965

filmed in black and white

I due pericoli pubblici

1965

Directed by Lucio Fulci. a Five Film (Rome) production. production manager: Piero Ghione. story: Adolfo [Alfonso] Brescia & Franco D'Este. screenplay: Roberto Gianviti & Amedeo Sollazzo. director of photography: Angelo Lotti. music: Enzo Leoni; published by Nazionalmusic (Milan). editor: Ornella Micheli. costume designer & set designer: Mario Giorsi. unit manager: Albino Morandin. assistant director: Giovanni Fago. continuity: Filiberto Fiaschi. cameraman: Gaetano Valle. assistant cameramen: Antonio Orlandini & Salvatore Caruso. make-up: Andrea Riva. hairdresser: Eugenio Guidi. still photography: Giannini & [Ermanno] Serto. assistant editor: Bruno Micheli. sound: Vittorio Massi. post-synchronization: Fono Roma. costume suppliers: Tigano – Lo Faro. props & weapons: Rancati. set furnishings: Supermercato Mobili S.p.A. shoes: Pompei. wigs: Rocchetti. processing & prints: S.P.E.S. director: E. Catalucci. interiors filmed at De Paolis – Incir Studios (Rome). *Uncredited:* Franchi and Ingrassia sing the title song "Sempre insieme" ('Always Together')

Cast: Franco Franchi (Franco Introlia). Ciccio Ingrassia (Ciccio Introlia). Margaret Lee (Floriana). Linda Sini (Dora). Riccardo Garrone ("The Baron"). Luciana Angiolillo (wife of the deceased). Mino Doro (Giorgio's father). Poldo Bendandi ("Mancino"). Ignazio Leone (insurance lawyer). Gianni Dei (Giorgio). Franco Morici. Corrado Olmi (Galanti, financier). Nino Nini (municipal police commander). Salvo Libassi (museum guard). Tullio Altamura (hospital doctor). Ugo Fangareggi (radio operator at the ministry). Nino Marchetti (Marshal). *Uncredited:* János [John] Bartha (man in whose car Floriana hides).

Synopsis: Franco and Ciccio Introlia, two ham-fisted swindlers, are sick of the criminal life and want to go straight. To this end they sign on at the labour exchange and get themselves hired as servants for 'The Baron', a rich diplomat who needs extra staff for a lavish reception. However, the two crooks soon realise that 'The Baron' is not a genuine diplomat but in fact a master criminal whom they once met in prison. The reception party is simply window-dressing designed to con money from a rich industrialist. Also in on the scam is the seductive Floriana, the Baron's lover. In the course of the evening the duo make a complete mess of the Baron's plan, landing him in prison, and worse still, leaving him massively out of pocket. The Baron's wife Dora and his hulking enforcer 'Mancino' threaten the hapless duo with death unless they repay the money. To this end, Franco and Ciccio stage a series of robberies and confidence tricks in a desperate attempt to steal their way out of trouble, but their efforts lead to yet more disaster. Posing as brothers of a Holy Order they try to extort a legacy from relatives of a recently deceased businessman. When this fails they attempt an art robbery from a museum, disguising themselves in the suits of armour on display. Before they can put the plan into operation, delivery men arrive to move the suits of armour to another location and the unlucky thieves are forced to jump out of a lorry onto the streets of Rome, still in their armour. Undeterred, they try to stage a mock car crash to claim insurance. Still, nothing works. Posing as cops they break into a gambling den, only for the real cops to show up too. This last screw-up at least has the lucky side-effect of landing Floriana, Dora and Mancino in jail; they were at the gaming tables when the police arived. Penniless, and ready to return to Sicily, the two dumbells decide to attempt an old favourite before leaving: they pose as policemen at a busy road junction and demand gifts from passing goods suppliers for 'La Befana' (a mythical benevolent witch with magical powers who brings presents to the children of Italy on the eve of Epiphany). Unfortunately, a superior officer arrives and takes their ill-gotten gains to distribute among the city's children. Finally, they pose as General Tornabuoni and General Franken at the Ministry of War and attempt to scam a rich man who wishes to buy his son's way out of National Service. However, Franco gets carried away in his role as 'General Franken' and with insane patriotic fervor persuades the ex-military man to force his son to sign up. The scheme is ruined, but Ciccio notices a safe in the

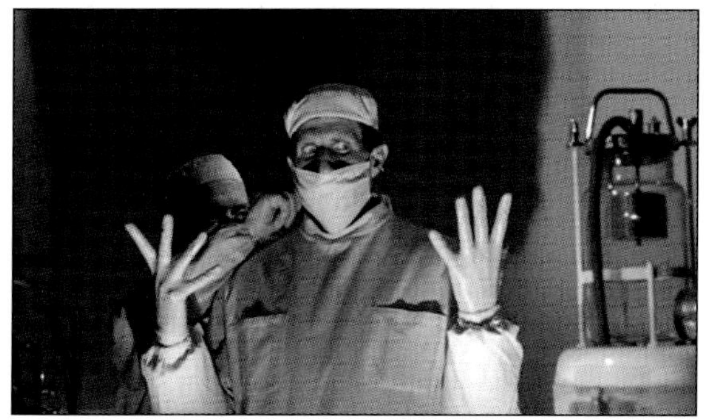

office and sets about opening it. While working, he asks Franco to get him something to eat from the bar: Franco sees a telephone with the letters B.A.R. on it, and uses it to place an order. The phone is in fact the hotline to "Bombardamento Aereo Rappresaglia" (Air Bombardment Retaliation) and Franco inadvertently orders them to detonate a hydrogen bomb on the Ministry of Defence. The two idiots end up in heaven, having rigged a fake pair of wings to fool St. Peter. Even now, the urge to steal proves overwhelming...

Review: Any movie that ends with two deceased crooks at the gates of heaven trying to steal Saint Peter's shiny halo can't be all bad... This is another film handsomely shot in black and white by Alfio Contini, who had previously given Fulci the benefit of his talent on *Colpo gobbo all'italiana*. The stand-out scene this time has Franco and Ciccio smoking grass, with each seeing the other as a beautiful belly-dancer, leading to a passionate drug-fueled smooch (observed by none other than Lucio Fulci as a fisherman on the quayside who shouts *"Hey, dopes!"* at the tripping couple). It's amusing to see the 'two idiots' getting high so early in the 1960s, although it's worth mentioning that Totò's *Che fine ha fatto Totò Baby?* (a parody of *What Ever Happened to Baby Jane?*) beat them to it (released in August 1964, it features Totò as two brothers, one mean and vicious, the other weak and vapid, with the former fueling his psychosis with lungfuls of home-grown cannabis). It's also interesting to see the duo perform a scene (dressed in suits of armour) in the midst of heavy traffic at a busy road junction in Rome, with a crowd of onlookers lining the pavement; the scene was shot 'guerilla style' with real people in the background, which has the virtue of framing the two clowns in front of their likely contemporary audience, many of whom appear thoroughly entranced. I also liked the scene in which the 'two public menaces' hide in a mental asylum, where they adopt the personas (and out of nowhere, the elaborate costumes) of Marie Antoinette and Napoleon Bonaparte to throw pursuers off the scent. In fact costume changes are at the heart of this outing, with the duo appearing elsewhere as phony monks, traffic police and military top brass, leading to a bravura comic turn from Franchi as a ranting fascist leader modelled on Chaplin's *The Great Dictator*. How do Franco and Ciccio manage to set themselves up as Generals in the War Ministry? They gain access on a Sunday, of course, when the Ministry is completely deserted except for two officers listening to football on the early warning radio system! The best laid plans of fumbling con-men are finally undone by the detonation of an atomic bomb (very au courant, as *Dr. Strangelove* hit Roman cinemas six months earlier) which leads to the heavenly pilfering mentioned earlier.

The script bubbles with word-play and absurdity, and some if not all of the lines inspire genuine laughs. For instance, when Franco steals a bulb from a light fitting at the labour exchange and Ciccio insists that he recall their promise to turn over a new leaf, Franco protests, *"Remember our new motto? 'There is a light in our future.'"* Later, when ruefully discussing the failure of their recent confidence tricks, he says, *"Enough of this life of dishonesty and scams... Let's steal!"* While these are not what you'd call 'zingers' there's enough liveliness to the delivery to keep things rolling, and the succession of sight-gags (Ciccio attempting to rescue a heavily drugged Franco from hospital for instance) keep the film afloat when the episodic plotting begins to meander. Last but not least, it's worth mentioning a great scene for the lovely Margaret Lee as Floriana, the Baron's lover. As the Baron's con-trick falls apart she hides in a diplomat's car boot to escape, not realising that the man is heading home to deliver a present, which is also in the boot, for his son. When the boy opens the boot to find Lee, curled up in skimpy lingerie, he goggles at her and declares, *"Thank you dad, it's really a fabulous gift!"* Sadly, the reviewer for *l'Unità* was less impressed with the film as a whole: *"The main characters are two thieves who, just out of prison, despite their good intentions, go back to robbing [...] They will never achieve their dreams of wealth, destined to disintegrate in an atomic explosion. They will meet in Heaven, where they finally steal the golden halo of St. Peter (and also the time and money of the paying audience)."*[26]

clockwise from top left:

Ciccio prepares to operate on Franco;

The Italian poster depicting Franco and Ciccio, rather misleadingly, as two gentleman thieves (among the few roles they do *not* play in the film);

Franco and Ciccio adopt cunning disguises to hide in a lunatic asylum.

opposite, main picture:
Publicity montage featuring Franco, Ciccio and Margaret Lee.

opposite, bottom left:
The film's Italian locandina.

bottom left:
Italian fotobusta for the film.

below:
Lucio Fulci in his cameo, watching Franco and Ciccio kissing.

Translation
'How We Got in Trouble with the Army'

Italy

Production companies
Five Film (Rome)

Theatrical distributors
Euro International Films

Theatrical running time
Italy 89m

DVD running time (adjusted)
Italian TV (PAL adjusted) 89m 02s

Censorship
Italian censor certificate 45538
issued 18 August 1965

Release information
Rome 21 August 1965
Turin 27 August 1965
Taranto 25 September 1965
Bari 01 October 1965

filmed in black and white

Come inguaiammo l'esercito

1965

Directed by Lucio Fulci. a Five Film (Rome) production. production manager: Piero Ghione. story: Adolfo [Alfonso] Brescia & Franco D'Este. screenplay: Roberto Gianviti & Amedeo Sollazzo. director of photography: Angelo Lotti. music: Enzo Leoni; published by Nazionalmusic (Milan). editor: Ornella Micheli. costume designer & set designer: Mario Giorsi. unit manager: Albino Morandin. assistant director: Giovanni Fago. continuity: Filiberto Fiaschi. cameraman: Gaetano Valle. assistant cameramen: Antonio Orlandini & Salvatore Caruso. make-up: Andrea Riva. hairdresser: Eugenio Guidi. still photography: Giannini & [Ermanno] Serto. assistant editor: Bruno Micheli. sound: Vittorio Massi. post-synchronization: Fono Roma. costume suppliers: Tigano – Lo Faro. props & weapons: Rancati. set furnishings: Supermercato Mobili S.p.A. shoes: Pompei. wigs: Rocchetti. processing & prints: S.P.E.S., director: E. Catalucci. interiors filmed at De Paolis – Incir Studios (Rome).

Cast: Remo Germani (Nick Moroni). Alicia Brandet (Catherine Swan, Moroni's wife). Gina Rovere (Mariuccia, Franco's girlfriend). Umberto D'Orsi (Hamlet, Moroni's manager). Luigi Pavese (General MacKee). Andrea Scotti (Captain who orders Franco and Ciccio to join manoeuvres). Alvaro Alvisi. Consalvo Dell'Arti (interviewer). Edy Nogara. Francesco Sormano [Franco Sormani] (Bearded Colonel). Nino Terzo (Convoy driver). Moira Orfei (Thaide Bonafini, Camilloni's fiancée). Franco Franchi (Franco Piscitello). Ciccio Ingrassia (Sgt. Ciccio Camilloni). *Uncredited:* Attilio Dottesio (hotel manager). Alfonso Giganti (Officer Percuoco). Filippo Perego (night club customer). Luca Sportelli (police inspector). Gustavo D'Arpe (Captain of the 18th Italian Regiment). John Bartha (Army officer who gives Ciccio a medal).

above, main picture:
Franco causes havoc during military manoeuvres.

below:
Poster featuring the strongest element of the film, the relationship between Franco's lowly private and Ciccio's social-climbing sergeant.

Synopsis: Nick Moroni, an Italian nightclub singer doing his national service, finds out that his estranged American wife Catherine Swan, an actress, plans to return to the USA and take their baby son with her. Incensed, Nick discusses the problem with his exploitative manager Hamlet, who seems interested only in arranging press junkets for his client, no matter how inconvenient. After performing at a night club on leave, Nick steals his baby son from Catherine's apartment and asks Hamlet to help him hide the child. However, he realises that Hamlet envisages claiming a reward for finding it, so he takes the baby to the barracks instead. He hides it in the storeroom, with the assistance of his idiotic friend Franco Piscitello, who is hoping Nick will help him to forge a career as an opera singer when they leave the army. Before Franco can find a more suitable hiding place, the bullying Sergeant Camilloni insists that he leave camp to help him with a deception: he is to dress as a waiter at the Sergeant's home and receive a visitor, Camilloni's wealthy fiancée Thaide Bonafini, without letting on that they are both just lowly soldiers. Franco attempts to conceal the child at Camilloni's house while the Sergeant's tryst proceeds, but he bungles his role as waiter and drives the poor woman away. Camilloni's furious remonstrations wake the baby, and its cries lead him to the bedroom where it is hidden. Puzzled, he asks Franco where the child has come from, but at that very moment receives a phone call from Thaide, saying that she's leaving for Bologna but has left him a reminder of their love: "A reminder you must keep close to you for the rest of your life." Dropping the telephone in shock, Camilloni assumes that she means the baby. He begs Franco to keep the baby hidden, a turn of events which Franco uses to blackmail his superior in return for preferential treatment. Meanwhile, Nick returns to the barracks and finds the child has gone. After confronting Catherine, whom he suspects of stealing the boy back, the two of them come to the conclusion that their son has been kidnapped. They inform the police, and in doing so discover that they are still in love. Returning to the barracks they find that neither the baby nor Franco can be found. Everything comes to a head during the next day's military manoeuvres run by the tightly wound General MacKee. Franco and Camilloni bring chaos to the proceedings, Nick and Catherine try to retrieve their son, and General MacKee is driven to a nervous breakdown, until at last the baby is reunited with its parents and Thaide arrives to assure Camilloni that he is not really a father.

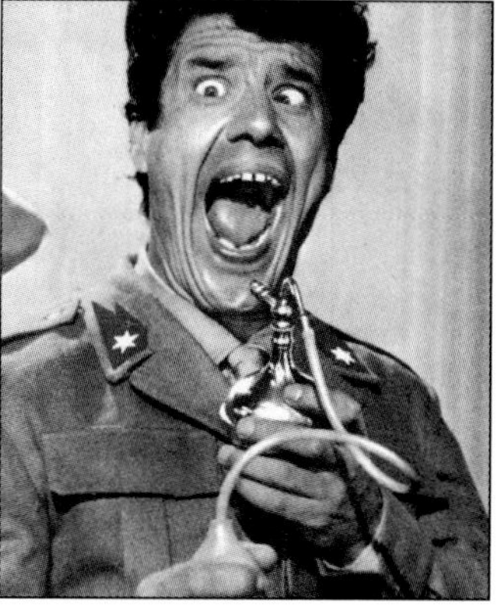

Review: *Come inguaiammo l'esercito* suffers from an uncertain tone, quite schizophrenic inasmuch as it runs a straightforward narrative about the troubled love life of a young man in the army alongside the maniacal antics of Franco and Ciccio. When the two strands intersect, for instance when the young hero tries to convince Franco to help him hide a baby, the mismatch in acting styles is too jarring, and Fulci never really synthesises a solution to this problem. Despite rallying comedically in the last reel, with an absurdist chase during military manoeuvres, there's a generally lacklustre feel to the proceedings, as if Fulci himself had lost faith in the project. What fun there is to be had relies on the interaction of Franco and Ciccio, with the former playing a lowly army private, and the latter a bullying, hectoring Sergeant prone to nonsensical tirades and impossible orders, screeching *"Silence!"* when no one is speaking and giving a bald private a drubbing for having long hair. The script, with contributions from Roberto Gianviti, a collaborator of great significance in Fulci's later career, can offer just a few amusing exchanges: for instance, when Ciccio as Sergeant Camilloni bellows, *"You're the worst soldier in this regiment! A month ago you were second to worst, but now you're the last,"* Franco replies, *"It's not my fault the other guy was kicked out!"*

It's tempting to lay the blame for the failings of *Come inguaiammo l'esercito* on its star, the pop singer turned actor Remo Germani (real name Remo Speroni). He's an unimpressive performer here, with little to offer the screen except a bland workaday earnestness. This was his only attempt at a cinema career, which shows that he too felt he was not cut out for the job, so we must not criticise too much; he's simply trying out for the wrong vocation. As a singer he was put under contract in 1962 by the Italian record company Jolly, and scored a hit in 1963 with a cheesy MOR number called "Baci" ('Kisses'), followed the same year with a top ten hit, "Non andare col tamburo" ('Do not leave with the drum'), which at least had the virtue of a jaunty arrangement. Evidently Fulci was hoping, after his success with Adriano Celentano, that casting another pop singer as leading man would help the film, but whereas Celentano proved to be a decent actor the gamble did not pay off here. Realisation evidently dawned on the producers that Germani was an insufficient 'hook' upon which to hang the film – all three Italian poster designs relegate him to also-ran status in the lower credits, with top-billed Franco and Ciccio the focus of attention. The best one can say about Germani is that he gave the film a naggingly catchy title song, "Ma cosa devo fare", which was released as a single in 1965, backed with another song from the film, "Ritornerai un'altra volta da me".

Really, though, it's the conception of the film that's at fault. The love story angle is weak and insipid, the story strand concerning Nick's exploitative manager Hamlet never develops any teeth, which means that any time spent away from Franco and Ciccio feels like padding. If there's a way to tell a love story and a Franco and Ciccio farce at the same time, Fulci doesn't find it. The highlights therefore come when the duo get enough screen time to develop their usual dynamic, in particular an excruciating and very funny sequence in which Franco has to act as Ciccio's waiter to impress the latter's rich fiancée; the results may be predictable, as Franco embarrasses Ciccio and terrorises his horrified girlfriend, but the sequence is nonetheless confident and effective, built as it is around that venerable comedy tradition, the humiliation of a would-be social climber. Also worthy of note, enriching the last reel with a twitchily amusing comic performance, is Luigi Pavese as General MacKee, whose brittle confidence is shattered when Franco and Ciccio take over radio operations during army manoeuvres. As the tension mounts he mutters *"Self control... self control..."* under his breath, until finally these are the only words he can say, having witnessed such non-sequitur delights as the Cavalry riding to the rescue and a Red Indian attack, neither of which can be dismissed as a dream, not even after a pinch from his underlings.

above, from top:
A selection of Franco Franchi grimaces; try them at home if you dare.

above centre, main image:
This locandina for *Come inguaiammo l'esercito* prominently features Alicia Brandet and the baby she's trying to take from her husband, played by Remo Germani. Whatever the outcome of the custody battle, Alicia certainly won the war of the film posters: Germani is nowhere to be seen.

top left:
Franco Franchi demonstrates careful baby handling to Gina Rovere.

Translation
'002 Operation Moon'

Italy/Spain

International theatrical title
Dos cosmonautas a la fuerza (SP)
'Two Astronauts Under Duress'

Production companies
Ima Film (Rome)
Agata Film (Madrid)

Theatrical distributors
Medusa Distribuzione (Italy)
Cinesco … "Una exclusiva Cooperativa Films" (Spain)

Running time
Italy 90m
Spain 89m

DVD running time (adjusted)
Videa/Eagle Pictures (IT) 88m 28s

Censorship
Italian censor certificate 46054
issued 25 November 1965

Release information
Turin 25 November 1965
Taranto & Foccia 01 December 1965
Rome 19 March 1966
Bilbao 19 July 1967
Barcelona 05 November 1967
Madrid 16 July 1969

filmed in black and white

002 operazione Luna

1965

Directed by Lucio Fulci. an IMA Film (Roma) / Agata Film (Madrid) co-production. production manager: Renato Jaboni. story & screenplay by Vittorio Metz & Amedeo Sollazo. director of photography: Tino Santoni. editor: Pedro Del Rey. music composed & conducted by Lallo [Coriolano] Gori. art director & costume designer: Nedo Azzini. set designer: Adolfo Cofiño. assistant director: Giovanni Fago. unit manager: Dino Di Salvo. continuity: Filiberto Fiaschi. cameraman: Giovanni Bergamini. assistant cameraman: Giuseppe Tinelli. assistant art director: Francesco Bronzi & Cesare Giuseppe Monello. make-up: Andrea Riva. still photography: Enrico Appetito. sound: Mario Ronchetti & Massimo Jaboni. optical effects: S.P.E.S.; director: E. Catalucci. dubbing studio: C.D.C. negative: Ferrania. interiors filmed at Cinecittà Studios (Rome).

Cast: Franco Franchi (Franco Messina / Colonel Paradowsky). Ciccio Ingrassia (Ciccio Cacace / Major Borovin). Linda Sini (Comrade Lemidova aka 'Madame Renò'). María Silva (Dr. Frauensen, bespectacled associate of Lemidova). Mónica Randall (Anna Borovin, the Major's wife). Elena Sedlak [as 'Hélène Sedlak'] (Nadia Paradowsky, the Colonel's wife). Emilio Rodríguez (Scordiakov, Russian space advisor). Chiro Bermejo (Mussorsky, Minister of Cosmonautics [or Astronautics]). Ignazio Leone (Sergio, dark-haired clinic henchman). Enzo Andronico (blond clinic henchman). Franco Moruzzi [as 'Franco Morici']. Piero Morgia (young Lieutenant who detains Paradowsky and Borovin). Lino Banfi [as 'Pasquale Zagaria'] (nightwatchman who catches Franco and Ciccio). *Uncredited:* János [John] Bartha (Doctor Gadrinsky, controller of gravity experiment). Francesca Romana Coluzzi (Sonia, masseuse who spots Franco and Ciccio photograph in newspaper).

Synopsis: When Russian cosmonauts Colonel Paradowsky and Major Borovin go missing in space, the Kremlin refuses to concede the fact, afraid of losing face with the Americans. Instead they set about searching for lookalikes to be fired into space in a second rocket, who can then be passed off as the missing cosmonauts when they return, thus saving the Kremlin from embarrassment. Sonia, a woman working for a Soviet spy ring in Rome, spots two Sicilian thieves, currently in the newspapers after a bungled robbery, who are identical to the missing cosmonauts. Springing the duo from prison, the Russians take them to their Rome base in a female health spa run by the fearsome Comrade Lemidova aka 'Madame Renò. The two attempt to escape by disguising themselves as women, but are recaptured and fired into space in the second rocket. In the meantime, Paradowsky and Borovin are found alive, having made an emergency splashdown, and are not best pleased to discover that on their safe return the two Sicilian goons have been sent for a quiet recuperative vacation with their Russian wives, Nadia Paradowsky and Anna Borovin. The wives are puzzled by their husbands' odd behaviour but put it down to 'space sickness' and hope that they will eventually return to normality. Eveyrthing comes to a head during a night of chaos and confusion, in which both the Russians and the two Sicilians hop in and out of bed with the bewildered wives. At last, the two Sicilian goons are sent back to Rome: but have the Russians deported the right people? Of course not! Franco and Ciccio must now ply their criminal trade in the snowy streets of Moscow....

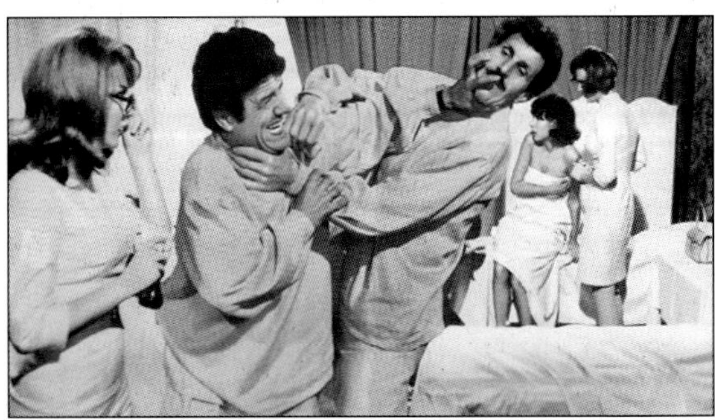

About the production: In March 1965, Soviet cosmonaut Alexei Leonov made the first spacewalk in history, beating the Americans by almost three months. Given that this story was so hot at the time, it seems likely that the script for *002 operazione Luna* – which sends Franco and Ciccio up in a rocket to become the first *morons* in space – was conceived and written quickly, in April of 1965, with shooting commencing by June at the latest. Allowing four to five weeks for shooting as usual, this gives the film a three month post-production period in which a distribution slot can be arranged, in time for a November release.

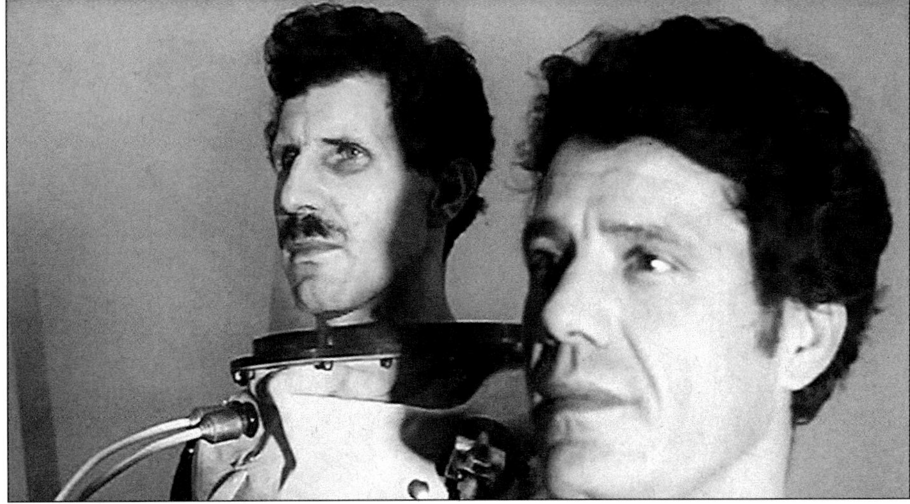

Review: Without a doubt, *002 operazione Luna* begins with the most disconcerting and disorientating sequence in any of Fulci's 'Franco and Ciccio' movies. We see the two comics playing Russian cosmonauts, surrounded by press and army officials en route to a rocket for take-off into orbit around the moon. What's so strange about it? The answer is simple: Franco Franchi's face is at rest. For two or three minutes we see him calm and composed, with not a trace of his usual grimacing. The effect is bizarre – like seeing Salvador Dali without his moustache. Of course it doesn't last: we discover that these Russian cosmonauts merely *look* like Franco and Ciccio. Enter the genuine articles, manic grimaces intact, as two Sicilian thieves whom we first meet as they attempt a robbery of an electrical goods store.

The first thing to note is that Fulci had evidently seen and admired Jules Dassin's *Rififi* (1955): the robbery sequence near the beginning of the film takes place without dialogue, just like the famous bank heist in Dassin's classic, and Fulci sends up the premise by having the two comics trying to communicate with absurd hand signals, or better still, in their vehicle at the beginning, pulling significantly charged expressions at each other which quickly degenerate into weird non-sequitur grimaces. With typical misfortune, the two hapless thieves emerge from the store to find their vehicle has been stolen, and when they leave their swag on the pavement to look for the van, their rivals drive up in it and grab the stolen goods too. All that's left for the Sicilian buffoons is the job of explaining to a passing nightwatchman (a young Lino Banfi) why the shop door has been forced open. Needless to say, all does not go well...

I had higher hopes for this one given its sci-fi setting and engagingly daft premise, but it's actually one of the weaker examples of the Franco and Ciccio brand. Earthbound much of the time, *002 operazione Luna* fails to exploit the sci-fi possibilities and instead settles for generic spy-movie pastiche and plenty of running around in corridors. (Indeed it's interesting to note that in a career spanning five decades, during which time science fiction achieved market domination, Fulci never once filmed an alien being: his one 'serious' science fiction film, *Rome 2033 – The Fighter Centurions*, is of the 'dystopian future Earth' variety, and with the exception of the unexplained creatures that pop up in his sword-and-sorcery film *Conquest* the only monsters he seemed to care about were human, whether living or undead.) The space rocket scenes are actually a bit of a trial, with a static camera pointed at the two actors strapped in their seats, a requirement which curtails much of their manic visual inventiveness. It just doesn't achieve lift-off, so thank goodness for a few fleetingly bizarre moments like the scene in which pieces of a human skeleton float past the two idiots during a seemingly endless (and largely chuckle-free) space walk.

That's not to say that there's nothing to enjoy. Comedic use is made of the facial distortion caused by extreme gravitational pressure, although in the case of Franco Franchi this must surely rank as one of the most redundant sight-gags in movie history. The highlight, if you're in the mood for 'Carry On' style humour, is a sequence in which Franco is hunted through the corridors of a health club by nurses wielding huge syringes, intent on giving him female hormones (having fallen for his current disguise as a woman and diagnosed him with serious hormonal problems). Rather like *00-2 agenti segretissimi*, in which the threat of torture felt poised to turn nasty, this sequence involving repeated injections hovers on the brink between pure slapstick and queasiness.

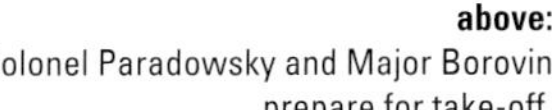

above:
Colonel Paradowsky and Major Borovin prepare for take-off.

left:
Scordiakov (Emilio Rodríguez) and Comrade Lemidova (Linda Sini) at Soviet mission control.

opposite, main picture:
Italian fotobusta featuring Francesca Romana Coluzzi as the Russian masseuse who spots Franco and Ciccio as doubles for the missing cosmonauts.

opposite, bottom left:
The film's locandina poster.

opposite, bottom right:
María Silva (left) watches Franco and Ciccio.

bottom left (fotobusta collage):
Sonia prepares a giant hypodermic to inject Franco with female hormones; the two cosmonuts are fêted by the Russian top brass.

below:
Doctor Gadrinsky (Janos Bartha) and Comrade Lemidova discuss putting Franco into their gravity simulator.

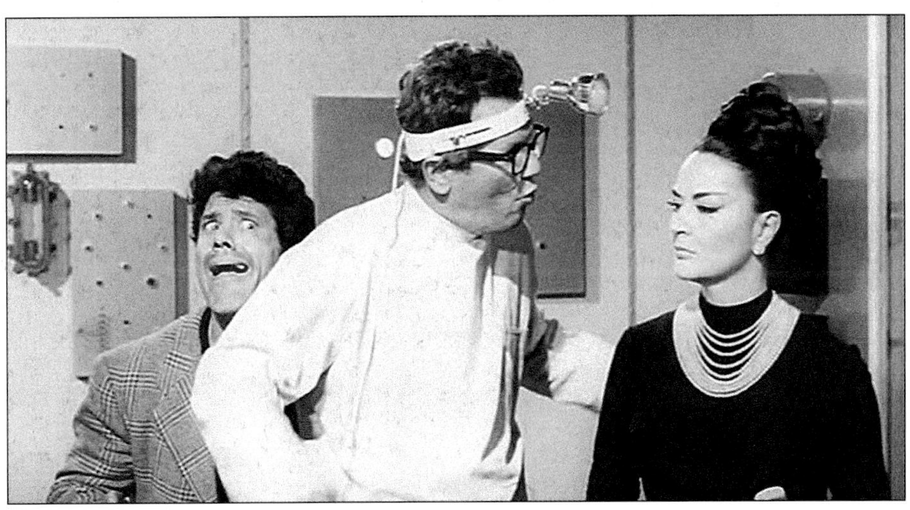

Translation
'Those Two Paratroopers'

Italy/Spain

Production companies
Ima Film (Rome)
Agata Film (Madrid)

Theatrical distributors
Medusa Distribuzione (Italy)

Unusually, although the film was an Italian-Spanish co-production, I can find no record of a Spanish title or release.

Running time
Italy 90m

DVD running time (adjusted)
Medusa (IT) 90m 56s

Censorship
Italian censor certificate 46214
issued 24 November 1965

Release information
Bitonto 30 December 1965
Turin 28 January 1966
Rome 19 March 1966

filmed in black and white

I due parà

1965

Directed by Lucio Fulci. an IMA Film (Rome) / Agata Film (Madrid) co-production. production manager: Renato Jaboni. story: Vittorio Metz & Amedeo Sollazzo. screenplay: Vittorio Metz, Amedeo Sollazzo & Lucio Fulci. director of photography: Tino Santoni. music: Piero Umiliani. editor: Pedro Del Rey. production designer: Adolfo Cofino. set dresser: Nedo Azzini. unit manager: Dino Di Salvo. assistant director: Giovanni Fago. continuity: Filiberto Fiaschi. cameraman: Giovanni Bergamini. assistant cameraman: Giuseppe Tinelli. costume designer: Mario Giorsi. make-up: Andrea Riva. wardrobe: Rosa Luciani. assistant production designer: Francesco Bronzi & Cesare Monello. assistant editor: Bruno Micheli. sound: Massimo Jaboni & Mario Ronchetti. colour by Eastmancolor.

Cast: Franco Franchi (Franco Impallomeni). Ciccio Ingrassia (Ciccio Impallomeni). Linda Sini (Consuelo). Umberto D'Orsi (American ambassador). María Silva (Santa). Roberto Camardiel (General José Limar). Mónica Randall (Rosita). Luis Peña (Alvardo Garcia, the rebel leader). Chiro Bermejo (). Ignazio Leone (Sergeant Sullivan, Italian-American paratrooper involved in 'rescue mission'). Emilio Rodríguez (Colonel Smith, US military in charge of 'rescue mission'). Enzo Andronico (Café owner). Tano Cimarosa (Garcia's right-hand man). Lino Banfi [as 'Pasquale Zagaria'] (Tequinho). Piero Morgia (Jack, young parachute lieutenant with Sullivan on 'rescue mission'). Luciano Bonanni (Villager with the rifles). Franco Moruzzi [as 'Franco Morici']. Francesca Romana Coluzzi (Passion Flower, a 'sbarbudo').

above, main picture:
Into battle with the two idiots.

below:
Italian locandina movie poster.

Synopsis: Franco and Ciccio Impallomeni, two Sicilian street entertainers who find it hard to make money among the peasant workers of their home town, decide to emigrate to America. After stowing away on the wrong boat they find themselves in an immigration camp in New Quiracao, capital of the republic of Santa Prisca, a South American country under control of the brutal dictator General José Limar. They swiftly make enemies of the military controllers of the camp who can't wait to get rid of them. Limar's regime is supported to some extent by the USA, which has business interests in the region. The country is embroiled in a bitter civil war: guerilla attacks are being mounted by rebels ('baffudos') and rebel women ("sbarbados") operating from hidden training camps in the countryside. Limar wants American military support, but a US ambassador sent to the region declares that American forces will only attack the rebels if they are attacked first. General Limar arranges a subterfuge to inveigle the Americans into helping: two prisoners will be taken from the immigration camp, disguised as American paratroopers, and dropped behind enemy lines into a rebel encampment. When the 'baffudos' kill or abuse them it will coax the Americans into retaliation. To this end, Franco and Ciccio are dressed up and parachuted into the rebel camp. Rebel chief Alvardo Garcia orders their immediate execution by hanging, but after the intervention of a gang of female rebels Franco and Ciccio are saved. Franco explains to the rebels that they are in fact Sicilians. Realising that the two idiots are part of a plan to inflame American feeling, the rebels mount an attack on the town where the immigration camp is located, but the US ambassador has already sent US paratroopers into the area. A gun battle breaks out between the rebels and Americans: Garcia sends Franco and Ciccio to explain to the US soldiers but instead they get themselves 'rescued'. Back at base, Colonel Smith realises they are not American soldiers because they have no dog-tags, and releases them into the custody of General Limar, who quizzes them for information about the rebels. Before he can torture them, the interview is terminated when the rebels burst in, led by Garcia. They overpower Limar and stage a coup. Garcia swiftly proves as power-mad as his predecessor, and a series of counter-revolutions and counter-counter-revolutions follow. When the US ambassador (now safely back in in Washington) sends American forces to restore General Limar to power, a mix-up results in Franco and Ciccio being anointed as the rulers of Santa Prisca. Finally, after much foolishness, the rebel women headed by Consuelo take control and impose a female dictatorship. Disguised as paratroopers, Franco and Ciccio board an American military plane believing they are at last on their way to the United States, only to discover they are headed for Vietnam.

About the production: This appears to have been made virtually back-to-back with *002 operazione Luna*; of the thirteen credited actors who appeared in that film, only one – Elena Sedlak – fails to show up again for *I due parà*. It's curious that the film appears not to have been released in Spain, despite being an Italian-Spanish co-production. One is left to speculate that the film's satirical depiction of a tyrannical fascist ruler who is deposed by leftist revolutionaries ran afoul of the Spanish censor, cautious of anything that might be seen as an attack on the country's own tyrant-in-residence, Generalissimo Franco...

Review: Six years before Woody Allen explored the comic potential of South American revolutionary politics in *Bananas*, Lucio Fulci essayed his own parodic spin on the topic, *I due parà*. It's prone to lethargy in places, and lacks some of the freewheeling maniacal invention that characterises the best of Franco and Ciccio, but it also provides an early indication of Fulci's underlying pessimism, depicting a world where everyone is simply reaching for power: whether they're at the top of the totem pole or trying to rise from beneath they're all the same when they get their hands on the controls. Even Franco and Ciccio are not exempt; the only difference with them is their lack of wiles, their inability to manoeuvre support for themselves. The two 'cretinos' are just as susceptible as anyone else to the corruption of power, although if you don't like this rather bleak point of view I suppose you could argue that it's really just an excuse for Franco Franchi to strut around in a silly uniform yelling orders like Charlie Chaplin in *The Great Dictator*. The approach is reminiscent of the kind of thing we see in surrealistic/anarchistic cartoons like *Ren & Stimpy*, in which 'lovable' characters suddenly stoop to the most atrocious behaviour. For Franchi and Ingrassia themselves, the delirium of performance itself is enough of a reason to clown around as monsters; they are raiding the costume box for anything that glitters. For Fulci, though, there's an underlying edge to his use of the characters. Their 'innocence' as hapless idiots is not sentimentalitised, as was the case, for instance, in the films of Norman Wisdom; given the opportunity he's perfectly willing to depict them as bullies and despots, restricted only by their utter stupidity.

Is it sustainable to argue that *I due parà* is a cut above the usual Franco and Ciccio fare, owing to its satire of American imperialism and jaundiced take on revolution? I think it's true that these facets lend *I due parà* some ballast to its frivolity here and there. The send-up of American involvement in South America is barbed and unambiguous, and the obsequious ambassador, played by Fulci regular Umberto D'Orsi, is a contemptuous caricature of American self-interest and duplicity. In the furtherance of a generally anarchistic worldview, in which all who aspire to authority are inherently flawed and not to be trusted, the film scorns its revolutionaries too, drawing on Orwell's notion (espoused in *Animal Farm*) that when slaves overthrow their masters they can become every bit as bad as their oppressors. This is all very well, but it's here that the film could do with a bit more substance: if we are to credit the film as a cautionary satire we need to see evidence of specific crimes committed by the new leadership. The ruling dictator General Limar was portrayed as an out-and-out monster, yet we see little of the rebel leader Garcia's wrong-doing 'after the revolution'. Seduced by the General's old squeeze Santa (the gorgeous María Silva, playing a woman who'll sleep with whoever's in charge) he tries on the General's uniforms and struts around in them for a while. Later we see him conducting himself like a martinet to his followers. It would surely have been worth putting some flesh on the bones of the satire, here, to give it more weight. It's not as if the point would be hard to make: one need only think of Fidel Castro's hatred and repression of homosexuals in the wake of the Cuban revolution to see how easily the rebel hero becomes a monster (and Fulci was definitely thinking of Cuba when he co-wrote this script: the "baffudos" in *I due parà* are clearly a parody of the Cuban revolutionaries known as "Barbudos").

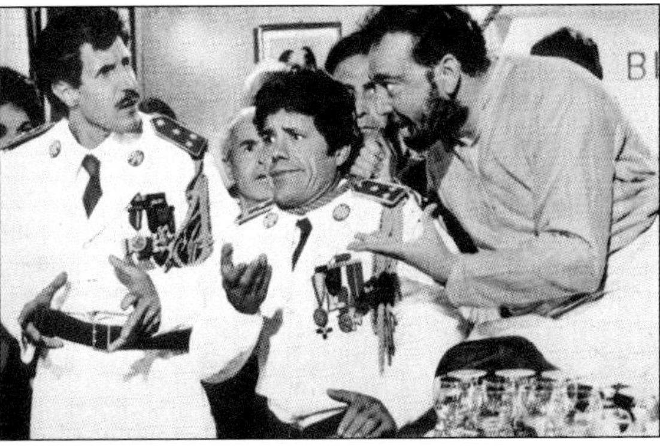

So there's a bit going on beneath the surface – but is the film funny? Well, yes, at times, but it's noticable that many of the gags have a macabre touch to them, whether frivolous (Franco cooking barbed wire and lightbulbs at the immigration camp) or fairly dark. Roberto Camardiel's sadistic General Limar is played for laughs but he's a thoroughly monstrous character, a jolly psychopath whom we first see casually burning a peasant rebel to death with a flame thrower built into a cigarette lighter. It's a Bond-villain contrivance (Limar himself mentions Bond when boasting of his various gadgets) but as staged by Fulci the gag sits uneasily between comical and nasty. The most shocking sequence is one in which the rebels, having caught Franco and Ciccio, proceed to hang them by the neck. Amazingly for a 'light comedy' they really do hang there, with no visible means of support, quite a grotesque image that is leavened for a while by a bevy of South American beauties who lift them up to relieve the pressure – but then drop them again when the rebels protest. Rather like the comic tortures in *00-2 agenti segretissimi* and the repeated surgical injections of *002 operazione Luna* it's a breezy bit of fun with 'something of the night' to it, although to what degree may depend on how much one knows about Fulci's later career...

Looking at the film purely as a comedy, I find that I didn't laugh very much. It's shot with less visual flair than the best of the Fulci comedies, has fewer really memorable set-pieces, and in the antics of the leading men there's an air of make-do-and-mend. Its chief interest lies in its darker undercurrents, the glimpse it offers of Fulci's gradually coalescing pessimism and cynicism. Beneath the smiles of this comic tale we can see the skull-teeth of an attitude that will flourish in the darkness of Fulci's later work: or as Benjamin the Donkey says in *Animal Farm*, *"Life will go on as it has always gone on – that is, badly."*

above:
Roberto Camardiel as the evil dictator, General José Limar.

left:
Enzo Andronico, with black hair this time, as the communist café owner who confronts Franco and Ciccio.

bottom left:
Franco and Ciccio are nearly hanged after landing in enemy territory.

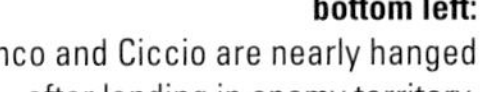

below:
Franco gets a taste for despotism after the revolution.

Translation
'How We Robbed the Bank of Italy'

Italy

Unconfirmed alternative title
I due uomini d'oro
(IT – this may just be a feature of the Italian poster) 'The Two Gold Men'

International TV title
How to Rob the Bank of Italy
(CAN/USA)

Production companies
Anteos Film
Fono Roma (Rome)

Theatrical distributors
Rank Film (IT)
Honda Cinematografica (IT)

Running time
Italy 100m

DVD running time (adjusted)
Italian TV 99m 18s

Censorship
Italian censor certificate 46663
issued 18 March 1966

Release information
Palermo 20 March 1966
Rome 26 March 1966
Turin 30 March 1966
Bari 07 April 1966
Canada, TV 01 November 1967
USA, TV 13 October 1968

Come svaligiammo la Banca d'Italia

1966

Directed by Lucio Fulci. an Anteos Film (Rome) / Fono Roma (Rome) co-production. production manager: Piero Ghione. story: Alfonso Brescia. screenplay: Roberto Gianviti, Lucio Fulci & Amedeo Sollazzo. director of photography: Fausto Rossi. editor: Nella Nannazzi. music: Lallo [Coriolano] Gori, with Alessandro Alessandroni's "Cantore Moderni". production designer: Franco Calabrese. set dresser & costume designer: Mario Giorsi. unit manager: Albino Morandin. assistant director: Giovanni Fago. continuity: Filiberto Fiaschi. cameraman: Luigi Filippo Carta: assistant cameraman: Mario Pastorini. assistant costume designer: Silvano Giorsi & Berenice Sparano. assistant production designer: Umberto Turco. make-up: Andrea Riva. still photography: Giannini. colour by Technicolor. format: Techniscope.

Cast: Franco Franchi (Franco). Ciccio Ingrassia (Ciccio). Lena Von Martens (Marilina, Franco's 'moll'). Mirella Maravidi (Rosalina, Ciccio's 'moll'). Mario Pisu (Paolo, il 'Maestro'). Maria Luisa Rispoli [as 'Luisa Rispoli']. Adriana Ambesi (Paolo's girlfriend). Alfredo Adami (Geremia, Paolo's bald associate). Enzo Andronico (man with a tic). Umberto D'Orsi (Commissioner). Mirko Ellis (Mirko). Fiorenzo Fiorentini (Romoletto aka 'The Evil Genius'). Furio Pellerani (Ferdinando Marconi, electrical 'expert'). Mino Pellerani (Fabio, drilling 'expert'). Carlo Taranto (Agnello Pasquale, explosives 'expert'). Giulio Saturnino (Filippo the plumbing 'expert'). The cat Venandro. *Uncredited:* Angelo Casadei (Policeman). Alfonso Giganti (Policeman). Alessandro Tedeschi (Policeman in civilian clothes).

Synopsis: Franco and Ciccio are two brothers who aspire to be thieves but seem destined to screw up. Their older brother Paolo, on the other hand, is a criminal mastermind known as 'The Maestro' who uses ultra-modern video gadgetry to supervise the actions of a crack gang of heisters without leaving his home, providing him with a perfect alibi. Franco and Ciccio are arrested for a bungled hold-up and Paolo uses his influence to get them freed. He decides the best thing to do is to give them money and women to keep them out of trouble, but none of his female friends will have anything to do with the two imbeciles. At last Paolo finds two suitable 'escorts' in the form of a ditsy pop duo; Marilina and Rosalina. Paolo leaves on a trip abroad after which he will commit his most ambitious crime yet: to rob the Bank of Italy. However, Ciccio manages to steal Paolo's detailed plans from his safe, and sick of being failures, he and Franco decide to commit the robbery themselves. To this end they assemble a crack team of experts; or so they believe. In fact the men they assemble are as clueless as themselves. They begin by seeking a criminal mastermind and opt for a ten-time loser, the self-styled 'Evil Genius'. He recommends Ferdinando, an electrical expert first seen blowing the lights in his own home; Joe Filippo, an obese plumber who can't fix a toilet without water jetting out of every fixture; Fabio, a dangerously unstable drill operator; and Agnello Pasquale, an explosives expert so easily confused that he can't decide which way round his first and second names should go. The team of losers set about digging under the bank vault but a variety of disasters befall them. The police get wind of the plan and arrest Paolo, marching him along to the vault where they expect to find the robbery in progress. To their surprise the vault is intact. The bewildered Commissioner decides that their intelligence is mistaken and orders the vault to be closed. Much later, Franco and Ciccio's gang finally break in. Accidentally bursting a water main they soak millions of lira in banknotes in muddy water. Nevertheless, the duo retreat to a secret hideaway and with the help of their two 'molls' dry the banknotes on washing lines.

About the production: Anteos Film were likely also known as Antheo Cinematografica or Anteo Cinematografica; in any case, they rarely produced anything, with only two more films, a Franco and Ciccio film *Il clan dei due Borsalini* (1971) and a lesbian-themed drama *Le rempart des Béguines* (1972) to their roster.

Review: Lucio Fulci's second film in colour, this middling Franco and Ciccio effort plays out a heist scenario modelled on *7 uomini d'oro* (1965), an Italian crime thriller by Marco Vicario which did good business on the Continent and impressed reviewers with its hour-long bank robbery sequence ('borrowed', it has to be said, from a similarly prolonged and beautifully staged bank robbery in Jules Dassin's 1955 classic *Rififi* – see also *002 operazione Luna*). On a Franco and Ciccio budget Fulci can't really match the stylish and inventive Vicario film (although admats for the film proclaimed *"I due omini d'oro!"* just to hammer home the connection), but the wordless opening sequence depicting a jewelry store robbery is shot efficiently and stylishly; the robbers are strange masked figures with lights and cameras attached to their foreheads who look more like sci-fi androids than the usual stocking-masked villains. The presence in Lallo Gori's score of some faux-Swingle Singers arrangements also takes a lead from Vicario's film (Armando Trovajoli did the Swingle-stylings in *7 uomini d'oro*, and Fulci would one-up the trend by getting the actual Ward Swingle Singers to provide music for *Operazione San Pietro* in 1967). As in *Come inguaiammo l'esercito*, the tone of the acting before the appearance of Franco and Ciccio is sober and restrained, entirely in keeping with a lightweight but straight-faced heist drama. Once the two comics are installed, however, the film plays out much as one would expect, and there's not a lot to report in the subsequent catalogue of scrapes and misunderstandings.

The sole surprise here is the appearance, around the half-way point, of Franco and Ciccio dressed as comic-strip super-criminals: surprising because instead of being simply another movie pastiche, of a kind so common in the Franco and Ciccio films, the sequence actually predates the Italian cinema's vogue for comic-strip adaptation. The cartoon-strips to which the film alludes were launched in 1962 ("Diabolik"), 1964 ("Kriminal") and 1966 ("Killing"). *Come svaligiammo la Banca d'Italia* was released in March 1966; shooting must have been completed by December 1965, or January 1966 at the latest. Umberto Lenzi's *Kriminal* was released in December 1966; the character known as 'Killing' (yes, that's his actual name) didn't make it to celluloid until the Turkish director Yilmaz Atadeniz ripped him off for *Kilink Istanbul'da* in 1967, while Mario Bava's *Danger: Diabolik* didn't reach the screen until 1968. Yet here are Franchi and Ingrassia, caped and masked, clad in black body stockings, with Ciccio's costume depicting a skeleton in gleaming white on black (á là 'Killing') and Franco's emblazoned with a giant letter 'K' for 'Kriminal'. Just in case there was any doubt, they sign themselves "Ciccio Diabolik" and "Franco Criminal" (the latter spelled with a 'c' presumably as a joke, Franco being such a chump that he can't even *mis*-spell properly).

There is, however, a sense of fatigue creeping into the comedy here. One can sense Fulci as a filmmaker beginning to shift and change: the straightforward crime aspect of the story seems more seductive to his sense of style than the clowning of his leading men. He is discovering visual techniques and motifs that would become more and more important to him: rack-focus composition, the placement of characters at the very edges of the widescreen frame, deliberately wild and blurry hand-held shots during the performance of an (otherwise rather staid) pop band, a sort of crypto-split-screen effect during the long-range video sequences, and a striking segue from a darkened tunnel, where stolen money floats in dirty water, to a succession of impressionistically hazy shots of the banknotes drying in the sun. All of these are purely pictorial pleasures, added to a story that scarcely demands them. With the earlier Franco and Ciccio comedies, Fulci spent much of his time focused on conveying the scripted gags, capturing the physical clowning of his stars, and maintaining a manic pace. With the thrillers and horror films for which he would later become best known, he embraced the opportunity for greater technical and pictorial extravagance, and one can sense that taste for visual excess beginning to assert itself here.

P.S. Fulci fans with an eye for the finer details will be interested to know that *Come svaligiammo la Banca d'Italia* marks the first appearance of a characteristic title font and a typographical style that Fulci would use for many of his later films, including *The Eroticist*, *Don't Torture a Duckling*, *The Psychic* and *City of the Living Dead*.

above:
Franco turns on the charm.

opposite, main picture:
In the tunnels beneath the Bank of Italy, Franco and Ciccio get to grips with some space-age technology.

opposite, bottom left:
The Italian poster which references Marco Vicario's *7 uomini d'oro*.

bottom left:
The face of a bungler.

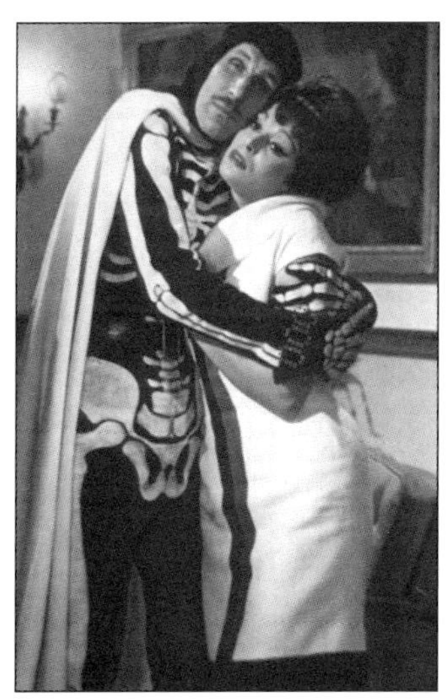

below:
Ciccio in a "Killing" costume.

Translation
'How We Stole the Atomic Bomb'

Italy/Egypt

International theatrical title
كيف تسرق القنبلة الذرية
(Egypt) 'How To Steal the Atomic Bomb'

Production companies
Five Film (Rome)
Fono Roma (Rome)
Copro Film (Cairo)

Theatrical distributors
Euro International Films (IT)

Theatrical running time
Italy 98m

DVD running time (adjusted)
Italian TV 93m 45s

Censorship
Italian censor certificate 48577
issued 01 February 1967

Release information
Turin 09 February 1967
Rome 03 March 1967
Bari 11 March 1967

Come rubammo la bomba atomica

1967

Directed by Lucio Fulci. a Five Film / Fono Roma (Rome) / Coprofilm (Cairo) co-production. production manager: Piero Ghione. story & screenplay: Sandro Continenza, Roberto Gianviti & Amedeo Sollazzo. director of photography: Fausto Rossi. editor: Nella Nannuzzi. music: Lallo [Coriolano] Gori; published by Nazionalmusic (Rome). production designer: Mario Giorsi. set dresser: Umberto Turco. unit manager: Albino Morandin. assistant director: Giovanni Fago. continuity: Filiberto Fiaschi. cameraman: Mario Pastorini. assistant cameraman: Antonio Orlandini. costume designer: Berenice Sparano. make-up: Andrea Riva. assistant costume designer: Silvano Giusti. still photography: Giannini & [Ermanno] Serto. sound: Alessandro Sarandrea. boom operator: Guido Felicioni. costumes supplier: Tigano Lo Faro. wigs: Rocchetti. colour by Technicolor. format: Techniscope. filmed on location in Egypt with interiors at Incir-De Paolis Studios (Rome).

Cast: Franco Franchi (Franco). Ciccio Ingrassia (Ciccio). Julie [Ann] Menard (Cinzia). Youssef Wahby (Doctor Yes). Eugenia Litrel (Modesty Bluff). Franco Bonvicini (Derek Flit). Adel Adham (James Bomb). Gianfranco Morici (Doctor Yes's assistant). Leda Palma. Bruno Ukmar. Silvana Bacci. Mario Barboni. Enzo Andronico (Spectrales henchman). Rodolfo Scarchilli. Mario Guizzardi. Abdul El Menem Ibrahim. *Uncredited:* Lucio Fulci (man smoking at waterfront café).

Synopsis: Franco (Franco Franchi) is a fisherman working off the Egyptian coast. His crew are casting their nets when an American plane crashes into the sea, scaring Franco's crewmates off in a rowboat. Franco, who cannot steer the boat, is stranded. Immediately, the incident alerts the secret services of the major nations, as well as Spectralis, an Italian underground spy group headed by Pasqualino aka Numero Uno. It also attracts the attention of the sinister Dr. Yes (Youssef Wahby). When Franco is washed up on an Egyptian beach, he is abducted by No. 87 (Ciccio Ingrassia), playing a minor Spectralis agent trying to improve his position. He has been despatched to investigate the missing bomb, and believes that the fisherman has vital information of its whereabouts. At first, Ciccio is unable to extract information from the buffoonish fisherman. His attempt to threaten Franco with torture on a mechanical arse-kicking device backfires (so to speak) when he lets himself be talked into demonstrating the necessary posture himself. Franco makes his escape and, too dim to understand that he is in Egypt, indeed unaware of any such country, attempts to purchase a rail ticket back to Palermo. A priest in line at the window helps him out and Franco treats the man to a cappuccino at a station bar. As he explains his predicament in detail to the padre, his hollering voice attracts the attention of a beautiful woman, Cinzia (Julie Menard), who joins in the conversation and seduces Franco. Back at the base, Ciccio is being attacked by three persistent but inept spies; James Bomb (Adel Adham), Modesty Bluff (Eugenia Litrel) and Derek Flit (Franco Bonvicini) (parodies, need one add, of Bond, Blaise and Flint). Fortunately for Ciccio, they are so fixated on depriving each other of the catch that they let him escape unnoticed while they brawl it out.

Meanwhile, Cinzia has lured Franco back to her hotel with the promise of an erotic liaison. Unbeknownst to him, she is an agent for Dr. Yes. While her back is turned, however, Bomb, Bluff and Flit attempt to abduct Franco, with the same side-splitting results as before. Ciccio grabs his prisoner back, and spirits him away to the base. This time he uses a lie detector to probe Franco's mind (sic). This convinces him that the fisherman knows nothing. It also means that he faces a fate worse than death (being fed to a pool of idle carp) for his failure. Franco talks Ciccio into teaming up and hatches a plot to plant a fake atomic bomb where it can be found. The pair make contact with Cinzia, who believes they know where the bomb is. She tricks them into a meeting with Dr. Yes. At his headquarters beneath a large villa, the 'mad genius' is attempting to revive an Egyptian mummy of Nabuco Sonor, the Queen of the Dead. He requires the atomic bomb to achieve her reanimation. His insane experiments appear to be successful when he achieves a twitch of the thumb from a specimen. Franco and Ciccio let him have the fake bomb, only to be told they will be sacrificed to the Queen of the Dead on her revival. The duo laugh, knowing the bomb is not real. Their hilarity turns to terror when the mummy stands up and advances upon them. The mad doctor's plans are thwarted, however, when the 'mummy' turns out to be Derek Flit in disguise. With the aid of Bomb and Bluff, he beats up the Yes men and abducts Franco and Ciccio. In the desert, the three superspies fall out again, and only stop fighting when a report from the car-radio announces that the nations involved have given up their search; America has claimed that no bomb was actually on board. Franco takes the disgraced Ciccio aboard his fishing boat. When they pull up the nets, what should they find but the real atomic bomb. The film concludes with Franco and Ciccio living in the lap of luxury, the atomic bomb pointing across the sea, and the world offering them untold riches by telephone to avert destruction. The last shot is of Ciccio's fingers stroking 'the button' that could trigger a nuclear catastrophe.

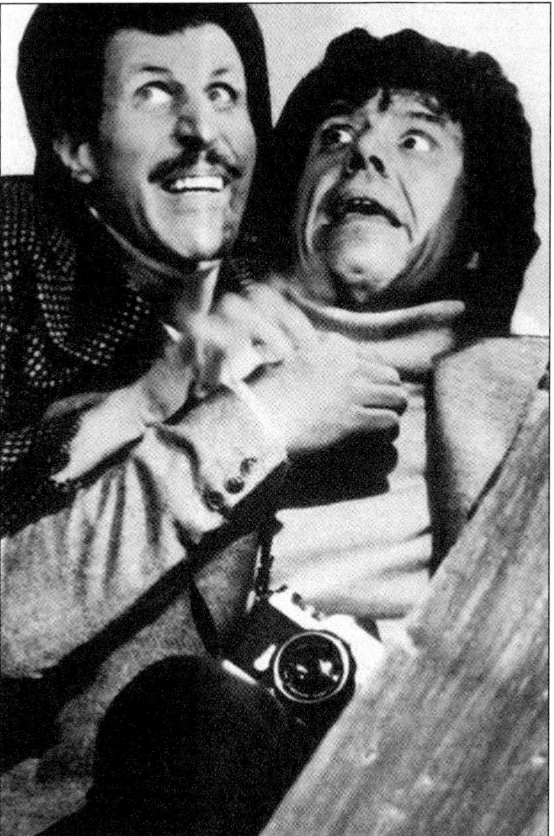

Review: *Come rubammo la bomba atomica* is, frankly, a dreadful film. The level of humour would disgrace an end-of-term school play, and the punning references to popular spy stories of the day leave the viewer aghast at the knowledge that Franco and Ciccio made scores of similar genre parodies. The script attempts to send up big-budget spy capers like the 'Bond' series, *Modesty Blaise* (1966) and *Our Man Flint* (1965), but fails dismally because much of the target material is already parodic. In the UK perhaps the only comedy duo to sink to the depths seen here were Cannon and Ball, in their unwatchable film outing *The Boys in Blue* (1983, directed – if you can believe it – by Val Guest, who in the fifties and sixties was responsible for excellent work like *The Quatermass Xperiment*, *Quatermass 2* and *Hell Is a City*).

Of the two leads Franco Franchi is by far the worst offender. His jabbering performance, accompanied by repetitive facial contortions, strives for chaos and absurdity but falls way short. Franchi plays a common role in the *commedia all'italiana* – the fool whose foolishness exposes the failings of others. This means he has the chance to play a buffoon *pretending* (and boy, does he labour the italics) to be more stupid than he already is. Watching an idiot expose the stupidity of a moron by acting like a cretin apparently formed the basis of his appeal, but partner Ciccio Ingrassia is capable of greater variation, and deserved better. He comes over like a sort of eviscerated Oliver Hardy, gangly, pompous and comically self-important. That said, any talent he may have possessed is thrown away by his willingness to yoke himself so repeatedly to Franchi.

Fulci's fans will find little to excite them here, unless they care to note that *Come rubammo la bomba atomica* features the director's second depiction of the dead returning to life. Sadly, if inevitably, the mummy that Dr. Yes 're-animates' turns out to be a disguised secret agent. Records indicate that this was not one of the more lucrative films Fulci made during the sixties; the fair commercial heights scaled by efforts such as *002 operazione Luna* were starting to elude him, a fact which no doubt whetted the director's appetite for giallo pastures.

above:
The film's original locandina.

left:
Promotional photo-montage for the film.

top left:
Franco and Ciccio meet the seductive Cinzia (Julie Menard) at an Egyptian nightclub.

bottom left:
Franco and Ciccio – the Italian Morecambe and Wise?

opposite, main picture:
Derek Flit (Franco Bonvicini) scrutinises stolen microfilm while James Bomb (Adel Adham, left) prepares to steal it from him.

opposite, bottom left:
Promotional artwork for the film.

below:
Cover of an Italian bootleg DVD release.

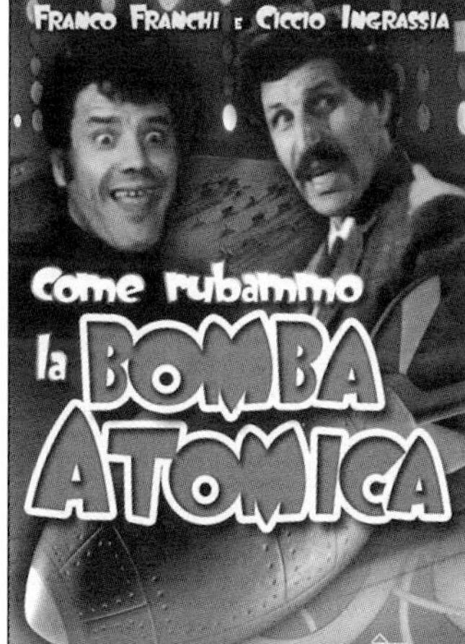

Translation
'The Long, the Short, the Cat'

Italy

Production companies
Five Film (Rome)
Fono Roma (Rome)

Theatrical distributors
Rank Film (IT)

Running time
Italy 90m

DVD running time (adjusted)
De Agostini (IT) 87m 52s

Censorship
Italian censor certificate 49093
issued 27 April 1967

Release information
Bari 05 May 1967
Rome 20 May 1967
Turin 03 June 1967

Il lungo il corto il gatto

1967

Directed by Lucio Fulci. a Five Film (Rome) / Fono Roma (Rome) co-production. production manager: Piero Ghione. story & screenplay: Gianpaolo Callegari, Roberto Gianviti, Marino Girolami & Amedeo Sollazzo. director of photography: Guglielmo Mancori. music by Lallo [Coriolano] Gori with Nora Orlandi's "4+4"; published by Nazionalmusic (Milan). editor: Nella Nannuzzi. set decorator: Umberto Turco. unit manager: Albino Morandin. assistant director: Giovanni Fago. continuity: Adolfo Cagnacci. cameraman: Mario Sbrenna. assistant cameraman: Antonio Orlandini. costume designer: Berenice Sparano. make-up: Raffaele Cristini. hairdresser: Martina Patacca. assistant costume designer: Silvano Giusti. production secretary: Mario Barboni. production assistant: Mario Barboni. still photography: Giannini & [Ermanno] Serto. sound: Allesandro Sarandrea. costume suppliers: Tigano – Lo Faro. shoes: Pompei. colour by Technicolor. format: Techniscope interiors filmed at Incir-De Paolis Studios (Rome).

Cast: Franco Franchi (Franco Pipitone). Ciccio Ingrassia (Ciccio La Capra). Ivy Holzer (Gina, Mrs. Comenda's maidservant). Giusi Raspani Dandolo (Countess La Rosa Capellini, widow of Archibaldo). Ivano Staccioli ("The Cat", an assassin). Daniele Vargas (Joe Smith of the CIA). Julie Ann Menard (Evelyn, Smith's assistant). Elsa Vazzoler (Countess De Vita). Gianni Agus (Count Alfonso De Vita). Enzo La Torre (Commissioner Proietti). Andrea Scotti (Martinez, Ordoñez's secretary). Mirella Panfili (). Enzo Andronico (Ferdinando, the news vendor). Ugo Attanasio (Guaramy's ambassador). Silvio Bagolini (the notary). Adolfo Belletti (Duke who refuses to dine with Ciccio). Rossella Bergamonti. Renato Chiantoni (doctor who declares the widow dead). Gaetano Cimarosa (nightwatchman). Anni Degli Uberti. Ugo Fangareggi (Delicatessen owner). Tom Felleghi (Professor Cagnetti). Adriana Giuffré (Antonietta, the Marquis' maidservant). Ignazio Leone (pool-hall owner). Giovanni Materassi (Marquis De Blanche, party guest wearing glasses). Barbara Nelli. Annamaria Panaro. Giulio Saturnino. Luigi Scavran (Count De Vita's balding manservant). Ignazio Spalla [Pedro Sanchez] (His Excellency, Prime Minister Ordoñez of Guaramy). Giulio Cesare Tomei. *Uncredited:* Alessandro Tedeschi (party-guest in dark glasses).

Synopsis: A wealthy widow, the Countess La Rosa Capellini, believes that the soul of her dear departed husband Archibaldo has entered her Siamese cat, and therefore demands that the feline be treated like a prince. As long as Archibaldo is looked after properly, the widow declares that when she dies she will leave her estate to her servants: Ciccio the butler, Gina the maidservant, and Franco the general dogsbody. Tasked with taking the cat for walks, Franco and Ciccio frequently lose the animal but it usually comes back. These incidents occur so frequently that local businesses have worked out a scam: whenever Franco and Ciccio turn up looking for the cat, the butcher claims that it has eaten his sausages, the delicatessen owner claims it has stolen salamis, and Ciccio duly stumps up the widow's cash. When the Countess dies, the notary informs the servants of their good fortune: unfortunately Archibaldo has gone missing, this time seemingly for good... Meanwhile, at a neighbouring mansion the Count and Countess De Vita are appalled to discover that a prestigious dinner party they are hosting has thirteen guests. The Countess is extremely superstitious so when Ciccio arrives, searching for Archibaldo, he is greeted effusively and invited to dine. However one of the guests, a Duchess, recognises him as a servant and refuses to eat at the same table. The Duchess and her husband leave in disgust, various guests cancel or arrive unexpectedly, and chaos ensues. Franco meanwhile has picked up a gold-digger in the form of Antonietta, the Count's maidservant, who becomes very flirtatious when she hears of the pending inheritance. The next morning, Gina spots Archibaldo in the grounds of the nearby Embassy of the [fictitious] Republic of Guaramy, which is currently hosting a visit from His Excellency, Prime Minister Ordoñez of Guaramy. In attendance is Joe Smith of the CIA, Ordoñez's secretary Mr. Martinez, and an inept Italian police chief, Commissioner Proietti. When Franco and Ciccio claim to have seen 'the cat' on the premises, Smith and Proietti mistakenly assume the two idiots are referring to a notorious criminal known as 'The Cat' whom they believe plans to assassinate Ordoñez. Thinking that Franco and Ciccio are somehow involved, Smith has them bugged and orders Proietti to arrest everyone to whom they talk. Soon all the local businessfolk who defrauded the widow are

above:
Franco and Ciccio perform Romeo and Juliet for the amusement of their rich employer, the Countess La Rosa Capellini (Giusi Raspani Dandolo), while Gina looks on.

top left:
Franco and Ciccio with 'Archibaldo'.

opposite, main picture:
"The Cat" (Ivano Staccioli) holds Franco, Ciccio and Gina (Ivy Holzer) prisoner.

opposite, bottom left:
Italian locandina.

locked up. Meanwhile, Martinez – who is plotting against his boss – passes photos of Franco and Ciccio, whom he perceives as a threat, to a group of hoods who undertake to kill them. However, it is 'The Cat' himself who deals with the situation, using Gina to lure Franco and Ciccio back to the widow's house and then tying them all to chairs in an upstairs room, with a time-bomb on the dresser. 'The Cat' tries to leave but realises his car-keys are missing; they have been stolen by Archibaldo, who is attracted to the furry key-ring. Franco and Ciccio manage to roll the bomb to the edge of the window balcony and Archibaldo finishes the job, nudging it off the ledge into the assassin's open-topped car below. 'The Cat' retrieves his car-keys and tries to drive away but the bomb explodes and kills him. Franco, Ciccio and Gina are left to enjoy a life of luxury in the widow's mansion.

Review: Shot partially at the gorgeous, run-down Villa Parisi in Frascati near Rome (familiar to horror fans as the home of the De Fiori family in Paul Morrissey's *Blood for Dracula* and the country house in Andrea Bianchi's peerlessly goofy *Burial Ground*), *Il lungo il corto il gatto* possesses some pictorial appeal but it lacks the freewheeling energy and wide range of location settings which enliven the better Franco and Ciccio films. The script too seems less playful, although I did find some of the interaction between Ciccio's status-obsessed butler and Franco's lowly factotum fairly amusing. Take this exchange for instance: Franco: *"Why don't you do it?"* Ciccio: *"I can't lower myself."* Franco: *"Back problems?"* The comic set-pieces are stretched a bit thin too, in particular the party sequence in which a superstitious Countess is so utterly fixated on avoiding thirteen guests at the dinner table that she forces her husband to include first Ciccio and then Franco as dinner guests, despite their 'lowly' status and poor manners. The scene is a chance for Ingrassia to shine, as he tries and fails to fit in with the etiquette of the occasion: first he suffers the indignity of being sent to eat in the kitchen when a snobbish Duchess recognises him as a servant, then he's shunted back to the main table after various departures and arrivals bring the number back to thirteen again. The whole scenario of outrageous snobbery and foolish superstition evidently appealed to Fulci as he makes quite a meal of it, drawing it out over sixteen minutes of screen time, but it doesn't really work for such a marathon stretch and could have done with pruning.

The cat gets a few good scenes, including, for me, probably the funniest sight gag of the film. The notary handling the Countess's will, responding to Ciccio's attempts to pass off a different moggy as the missing Archibaldo, pulls out a film projector and shows them a series of black-and-white police photo ID shots of the real cat, complete with face-on, left and right profile shots, and height markings on the backdrop. The cat gets to save the day too, despite having been banished after what seems to me a rare miscalculation in the characterisation of Franco: when the Countess dies, and he realises he will no longer have to attend to the pampered beast, he ejects it from the house with a running rugby kick! Don't worry, it's all done in the editing, but this casual violence against a cat, played as comedic by a sympathetic character, runs counter to the eager-to-please manner in which Franchi's 'idiot' is usually portrayed.

What's most puzzling about *Il lungo il corto il gatto* is the way it drops an entire sub-plot involving the planned assassination of Prime Minister Ordoñez, a deed that's being arranged by Ordoñez's own secretary, Martinez. We see Martinez speak to an associate of 'The Cat', the assassin tasked with doing the job, yet afterwards the story gets diverted and the plot-line never pays off. We see 'The Cat' capture Franco and Ciccio, we see his failure to kill them and his death in an explosion, but the conniving Martinez is never seen or mentioned again, nor the cowardly Odoñez. It's as though the script was filmed too quickly, without a second draft, leaving various plot strands up in the air. The death of Countess Capellini, established as a major character in the first third of the film, is not shown but merely reported to the two lead comics by a passing doctor, and the story thread involving the De Vitas' gold-digging maidservant Antonietta, who appears keen to exploit Franco when she hears about his inheritance, likewise fizzles out and goes nowhere.

It's clear from the film's lacklustre direction and half-baked exposition that Fulci had grown tired of making Franco and Ciccio films. Given that this is the last of their features together, it's tempting to read the final shot, of the duo waving goodbye, as their good-natured meta-response to Fulci's decision. Fulci remained appreciative of Franchi and Ingrassia; when I spoke to him in 1995 he told me he regarded his time with them as enjoyable and satisfying. And judging by that onscreen farewell, and the wink that Franchi gives to camera, it seems that the two Sicilians held no bitterness towards Fulci either, as he moved on to other challenges...

Having now seen all of Fulci's 'Franco and Ciccio' films, I'm happy to concede, despite my earlier antipathy, that they are not without wit and imagination (*00-2 agenti segretissimi*, *I due evasi di Sing Sing* and *I due pericoli pubblici* being the highlights for me). I've laughed here and there at the duo's antics, and my previous point of view has been tempered by an appreciation of their phenomenal energy and ferocious work ethic. Vaudeville slapstick is never going to mean that much to me, and I speak as someone brought up in the 1970s when the British version was a regular part of TV viewing, but from time to time while watching these films I've felt more than a glimmer of what it is about Franchi and Ingrassia that inspired such affection in Italy.

below:
The Countess's notary (Silvio Bagolini) informs the servants of their mistress's post-mortem demands.

Italian theatrical title:
Operazione San Pietro

Italy/France/West Germany

International theatrical titles
Au diable les anges! (FR)
'Damn the Angels!'
Die Abenteuer des Kardinal Braun (GER) 'The Adventures of Cardinal Brown'
Operation St. Peter (UK/Australia)
Operation St. Peter's (UK)
Operation St. Peter (Australia)
Operacion San Pedro (ARG)
A Szent Péter hadmüvelet (HUN)

Production companies
Ultra Film (Rome)
Marianne Productions (Paris)
Roxy Film (Munich)

Theatrical distributors
Interfilm (Italy)
Paramount (France/UK/Australia)

Running time
Italy 96m
France 100m
West Germany 96m
UK 95m 53s (before cuts)

DVD running time (adjusted)
01/RAI (Italy) 98m 27s

Shooting period
August 1967

Censorship
Italian censor certificate 50501
issued 22 December 1967
French Visa No. 33503
issued 28 June 1968
UK 'A' certificate
issued 05 December 1968

Release information
Rome 20 January 1968
Berlin 13 February 1968
Turin 22 February 1968
France 08 August 1968
UK (BBC TV) 27 September 1975

Operation St. Peter's

1968

Directed by Lucio Fulci. produced by Turi Vasile for Ultra Film (Rome) / Marianne productions (Paris) / Roxy Film (Munich). story & screenplay: Adriano Bolzoni, Ennio De Concini, Lucio Fulci & Roberto Gianviti. director of photography: Erico Menczer. editor: Ornella Micheli. music: The Ward Swingle Singers, published by C.A.M. (Rome). production designer: Giorgio Giovannini. production manager: Danilo Marciani. unit managers: Rodolfo Martello & Antonio Mazza. production assistant: Nicola Venditti. assistant director: Francesco Massaro. continuity: Rita Agostini. stunt co-ordinator: Remy Julienne. cameraman: Elio Polacchi. assistant cameramen: Federico Del Zoppo & Luigi Sbrizzi. make-up: Giulio Natalucci. set dresser: Dario Micheli. weapons: Vincenzo Lucarini. still photography: Giovan Battista Poletto. colour by Eastmancolor.

Cast: Lando Buzzanca (Napoleone). Edward G. Robinson (Joe Ventura). Jean-Claude Brialy (Cajella, a gigolo). Heinz Rühmann (Cardinal Erik Braun). Christine Barclay (Marisa). Uta Levka (Samantha, Ventura's associate). Antonella Della Porta (Giuliana, Cajella's wife). Pinuccio Ardia ('The Baron'). Ugo Fangareggi ('Agonia'). Dante Maggio ('The Captain'). Giovanni Ivan Scratuglia. Herbert Fux (Targout, an accomplice of Ventura). Wolfgang Kieling ('Frenchie' aka Poulain, an accomplice of Ventura). *Uncredited:* Virgilio Gazzolo (Father Siegfried Schulz, Braun's chief secretary). John Bartha (pinstriped attacker in Ventura's flashback). Carlo Pisacane (Sacristan with incense burner at wedding). Filippo Perego (elderly tourist in grey suit and black tie on the San Pietro guided tour). Franco Castellani (red jacketed barman in singles bar). Mario Castellani (jailer who witnesses Napoleone's escape). Pietro Tordi (Head of the order of Franciscan monks). Pietro Gerlini (tour-guide in San Pietro). Alessandro Tedeschi (tourist wearing dark glasses on the San Pietro guided tour). John Stacy (Englishman who pays the Baron for a private viewing of the Pietà).

Synopsis: Naples. Napoleone (Lando Buzzanca) is a small-time crook with big ideas. He is sprung from prison by accident when a foppish villain calling himself 'The Baron' (Pinuccio Ardia), and his two cohorts 'Agonia' (Ugo Fangareggi) and 'The Captain' (Dante Maggio), tunnel under his cell, having lost their way to the expected bank vault. Napoleone escapes with his 'rescuers' and discovers that the three are flat broke, despite the affected appearance of the Baron. Napoleone swiftly asserts himself as leader by posing as a master criminal and suggests they move to Rome and richer pickings. The four are forced to travel there in the back of a cattle wagon. On the outskirts of Rome the gang fall in with a seedy crook and gigolo who calls himself 'Il Cajella' (Jean-Claude Brialy). He owns a dilapidated used-car lot – Napoleone elects the place as a hide-out. At first his criminal activities are unambitious and he is soon spotted stealing a woman's purse at a modern shopping mall. Before the security guards can call the police Marisa (Christine Barclay), the woman whose purse he'd stolen, comes forward and announces that she knows him and saves him from arrest. She insists on calling Napoleone 'Filiberto', as it turns out merely because he resembles her dead husband. Meanwhile 'Il Cajella' encounters the beautiful Samantha (Uta Levka) whilst cruising for trade at a singles bar mainly patronized by wealthy older women. He is at first unaware that she 'belongs' to criminal big cheese Joe Ventura (Edward G. Robinson). The increasingly starved gang of crooks attempt to raise money by conning American tourists, offering them a private view of Michelangelo's famous Pietà, which is currently shielded from dust by a huge curtain during renovations. When a Vatican employee leaves a forklift truck unattended, Napoleone sees a way to pull off a job he believes could place him amongst the giants of crime. He will steal the famous statue of Madonna and Christ from The Vatican. This huge edifice, some fifteen feet high and weighing several tons, can be sold for a fortune. To the horror and admiration of his cohorts, Napoleone swathes the statue in a blanket and brazenly carries it on the forklift truck out onto the streets of Rome. The heist is successful, and the hungry crooks are jubilant, resolving to sell the priceless work for the meagre sum of thirty million lira. Cajella lets slip to Samantha that they have the Pietà – Joe Ventura overhears and forces him to betray his friends by revealing its whereabouts. Napoleone brings Marisa to the hide-out but before he can make love with her he accidentally dislodges the sheet to reveal the Pietà. Marisa, a strict Catholic, falls to her knees in prayer and shames Napoleone into doing likewise. Dragging him off to confession, she insists the statue be returned. Napoleone concedes but claims to have found the statue, leading Vatican officials to the hide-out in order to gain a reward. However, in the meantime Ventura and his gang have bribed the Baron and the others with food, making off with the statue themselves. Wanted posters depicting Ventura and Cajella are distributed throughout Italy. Ventura's gang head for Sicily, the statue in tow in a caravan, with the Vatican police and diverse Cardinals, priests and monks in hot pursuit. Ventura is forced to stop for a small village parade dramatizing the Stations of the Cross. 'Jesus' spots Cajella and climbs down from the cross to alert the 'centurions', before grabbing a child's bicycle and chasing after the thieves. Napoleone and his gang accompany Cardinal Braun (Heinz Rühmann), a Vatican official with particular interest in the thieves, who drives like a maniac after the fleeing criminals. Braun drives off the pier and crashes the car on board the gang's boat just as it sets off for Sicily. Ventura hands over his gun to Braun – it seems they were old friends in the Mafia before Braun saw the light. Samantha escapes on water skis and Cajella tries to swim after her to escape a group of female clients waiting for him on the pier.

top:
A mystery play being enacted during the climactic chase scene.

above:
Hungarian theatrical release poster.

top left:
Edward G. Robinson, always happy to pack some lead.

opposite, main picture:
Joe Ventura (Edward G. Robinson) and his thugs Targout (Herbert Fux) and 'Frenchie' (Wolfgang Kieling) prepare to sieze the Pietà.

opposite, bottom left:
The film's Italian locandina.

Review: *Operazione San Pietro* taunts the curiosity in a number of ways. Firstly, it stars cinema legend Edward G. Robinson in one of his last roles. Secondly, it is an unofficial sequel to a well-received Dino Risi film, *Operazione San Gennaro* (1966), a heist comedy featuring a late appearance by Totò that played as the lower half of a double bill in Britain in the early seventies, courtesy of Miracle Films. Risi's reputation here is negligible, although he is one of the most respected figures in Italian cinema. (Rumours that Risi completed a film called *Il gaucho* which was actually begun by Lucio Fulci in 1964 are untrue according to Fulci's daughter Antonella).

Operazione San Pietro was never released theatrically in the USA but an English-language print called *Operation St. Peter's* was released in the UK, having been granted an 'A' certificate on 5 December 1968 (precise release date unknown). This version was later aired on television by the BBC, on 27 September 1975. It features several actors from the Risi film reprising their roles: Pinuccio Ardia, Ugo Fangareggi, Dante Maggio and Giovanni Ivan Scratuglia – some of whom had anyway worked on Lucio Fulci comedies before – all returned for this attempt to cash in on the phenomenal domestic success of the Risi film. *Operazione San Gennaro* made 1,542 million lira, not far behind the takings for Argento's smash-hit debut *The Bird with the Crystal Plumage*, three years later.[27] *Operation St. Peter's* made less than half of that (643 million lira) but was nonetheless one of Fulci's biggest home-market earners of the '60s (the most successful being his pair of Franco and Ciccio sci-fi spy capers, *00-2 agenti segretissimi* and *002 operazione Luna*, which made a phenomenal 1,600 million and 888 million lira respectively, and *I due evasi di Sing Sing*, which netted 902 million lira).

Lando Buzzanca, speaking in his characteristic Southern Italian dialect, contributes the first of three performances for Fulci. He plays a character whose arrogance and delusions of grandeur are simultaneously sent up and indulged by the film. Comparing himself to Napoleon and aspiring to the status of super-criminal, he plays a kind of pampered buffoon, chided and yet mothered by other characters, and by the script. (Buzzanca frequently chose to play unsympathetic characters in comedies where he would be the butt of many of the jokes.)

Edward G. Robinson, as the head of a professional gang who steal the Pièta from Buzzanca, is wheeled through a series of gags that refer obliquely to his esteemed past in gangster movies like *Key Largo* (1948). His 1940s persona – the terrifying, psychopathic gangster – is lampooned in a scene where he subdues an unruly pack of minor hoods by enacting a rat-a-tat-tat machine-gun 'routine' empty-handed, aping his fearsome screen presence and providing his own sound effects into the bargain. As a generic aside, Robinson's gangster is propelled into neurotic, flailing rages by repetitive tapping and banging sounds, which – it is revealed – remind him of a particularly severe gangland beating at the start of his career.

Buzzanca's reprobates are portrayed, seemingly affectionately, as 'naughty boys'; their theft of the priceless Pièta is presented as a playful act of bravado, as 'cute' as it is audacious. However, the subject of Art's relationship to the Church could have offered scope for a more militant portrayal. The Vatican has a bad record when it comes to dealings with artists. Whether waiting for a death before moving in on someone's works, or manipulating poverty-stricken artists by offering huge commissions for devoutly-themed works, it has played a less-than-innocent game in the development of Italian art. Ventura's scheme, stealing the statue from the Vatican and then selling it back, is more amusing but in narrative terms the script-jokers are out of their league. As presented in *Operation St. Peter's*, the Church has a symbolic advantage: this priceless work of antiquity, Michelangelo's most important sculpture, and arguably the first such work to achieve a genuinely sensual curvature in its representation of the flesh, is to be sold back for avowedly less than its real value; which would be considered hard to define. Any price the criminals ask for the work will automatically be designated as less than its 'real' value, by a system that feels able to 'trump' Art by reference to an intangible standard of holiness beyond material value.

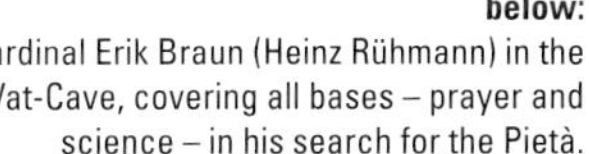

below:
Cardinal Erik Braun (Heinz Rühmann) in the Vat-Cave, covering all bases – prayer and science – in his search for the Pietà.

above:
Lando Buzzanca as the ambitious thief, Napoleone.

top right:
Herbert Fux as Ventura's sinister sidekick Targout.

What Fulci and his team of writers (including *Don't Torture a Duckling* co-writer Roberto Gianviti) have delivered with this scam is little more than a catch-me-if-you-can, hide-and-seek game with Catholicism – and the final third of the film is devoted to a repetitive pattern of chase and recovery.

The 'naughtiness' of *Operation St. Peter's* is underlined by the chosen music. Take for instance an extended sequence of clerics, nuns, and robed Vatican 'police' running in a frenzy to their battle-stations, after the news of the robbery has broken. Panoramic overhead shots of all this fevered activity are rendered satirical, in a saccharine fashion, by the use of The Swingle Singers' music on the soundtrack. Faintly loopy, yet immaculately precise, these vocal paradiddles inject little but the gentlest of ribbing to the righteousness of the Church.

After the intervention of Marisa, a beautiful, devout woman who, in a fit of Stendhal's Syndrome, faints at the sight of the stolen Pièta, Napoleone goes to confession and tells a priest that he is the thief responsible for stealing possibly the greatest work of Catholic art. Of course the priest is unable to reveal this to anyone without breaking his vows. It's probably the best joke in the film. Yet Napoleone's naive double standard creates further distance from this criminal. His character is not amoral so there's no way he can be conferred the status of anti-hero, but neither is he desperate enough in his pursuance of redemption to be likeable.

Operation St. Peter's attempts humour based on degrees of criminality, and distributes moral culpability in a similar way to *The Smuggler*, a later Fulci crime story. The gang of small-time thieves who helped Buzzanca pull off his daring heist are relieved of their treasure by a more ruthless gang of hoods, but even these hardened criminals achieve their aim by manipulative rather than brutal methods. In fact, their tactics reflect the Church's attitude to Art. They bribe the poor thieves with the offer of instant gain – partly with money, but more tellingly with food – implying that the lower echelons of crime are to be distinguished from 'hardened gangsters' by their poverty – forgiveness on the principle of need. This socialist, humanist view of human behaviour is unfortunately compromised by a refusal to challenge a major offender – the organised Catholic church – with anything more than gentle satire. It isn't really credible to portray criminal behaviour as socially determined when the power structures responsible for unequal distribution (and blatant stockpiling) of wealth are also tolerated in the same film.

Fulci's humour in *Operation St. Peter's* is ultimately quite frivolous, prepared to use cultural erudition for the sake of light humour, but unwilling to follow up into any kind of real commitment to satire. What's frustrating here is the sense that Fulci wants to mount a social critique while, at the same time, maintaining a sunny disposition that such ambitions can't fail to jar with. The scene where the poor thieves are bribed away from their ill-gotten gains by the offer of food could have come from a humanist parable on crime's roots in poverty, inequality and bad education by Vittorio De Sica (e.g. *Bicycle Thieves*), or a nihilistic piece of passionate realism by Luis Buñuel (eg. *Land Without Bread*). What to outsiders may seem a rather uneven blend of ambitions is actually typical of the *commedia all'italiana* and will have been coherent to Italian audiences. Yet the contrast could not be sharper when this last Fulci comedy of the '60s is compared with another of his religiously themed works, the scathing *Beatrice Cenci*, made just two years later.

Note: In 1964 the Vatican lent the Pietà to the New York World's Fair. People viewed the sculpture by standing on a conveyor belt moving past it. It was returned to the Vatican after the fair. On 21 May 1972 (Pentecost Sunday), a deranged geologist, Laszlo Toth, walked into the chapel and attacked the Pietà with a hammer while shouting "I am Jesus Christ; I have risen from the dead!" Raining down fifteen blows he severed Mary's arm at the elbow, knocked off her nose, and chipped one of her eyelids. Many of the pieces of marble that flew off were spirited away by onlookers: some were returned later but many were not, including Mary's nose, which had to be reconstructed from a chunk cut out of her back. The Pietà is now protected by a bulletproof glass panel.

opposite, main picture:
Italian locandina.

opposite, picture strip, from top:
The Chicago gangsters who traumatised Ventura, seen in flashback;
Napoleone (Lando Buzzanca);
Ventura and Frenchie spy on 'Il Cajella' during his tryst with Samantha;
The gigolo Il Cajella (Jean-Claude Brialy) dresses as a centurion at the request of the manipulative Samantha (Uta Levka);
Vatican priests on motorbikes;
'The Baron' (Pinuccio Ardia), an inept pseudo-gentleman criminal, accidentally springs Napoleone from prison.

right:
Napoleone prepares to pinch the Pietà.

LA ULTRA FILM PRESENTA

OPERAZIONE SAN PIETRO

CON LANDO BUZZANCA JEAN-CLAUDE BRIALY
HEINZ RUHMAN CHRISTINE BARCLAY
UTA LEVKA ANTONELLA DELLA PORTA

E CON I PERSONAGGI DI OPERAZIONE SAN GENNARO
PINUCCIO ARDIA (IL BARONE) DANTE MAGGIO (IL CAPITANO)
UGO FANGAREGGI (AGONIA) E CON EDWARD G. ROBINSON (NEL RUOLO DI JOE VENTURA)

REGIA DI LUCIO FULCI

UNA COPRODUZIONE ITALO-FRANCO-TEDESCA
ULTRA FILM-MARIANNE PRODUCTIONS-ROXY FILM
REALIZZATA DALLA ULTRA FILM DISTRIBUZIONE INTERFILM EASTMANCOLOR

Prima Edizione Italiana Anno 1967

LITO-P. RAGIONI Roma Via Prenestina 738 Printed in Italy

The Eroticist

1972

Directed by Lucio Fulci. produced by Edmondo Amati for New Film production S.r.l. (Rome) / Productions Jacques Roitfeld (Paris). story: Lucio Fulci & Alessandro Continenza. screenplay: Lucio Fulci, Alessandro Continenza & Ottavio Jemma. director of photography: Sergio D'Offizi. music: Fred Bongusto, arranged by Josè Mascolo; published by Prima Edizioni Musicali (Rome). editor: Vincenzo Tomassi. sets: Nedo Azzini. production organiser: Maurizio Amati. production supervisors: Fabrizio De Angelis & Roberto Onorati. assistant director: Giorgio Gentili. script girl: Rita Agostini. cameramen: Giovanni Bergamini, Enrico Lucidi, Sergio Melaranci & Alberto Serroni. costumes: Luciana Marinucci. make-up: Giannetto De Rossi & Alfio Naniconi. hair styles: Mirella Sforza. special effects: Ascani. decorator: Osvaldo Desideri. production secretary: Donato Bitetto. sound: Umberto Picistrelli. boom: Claudio Belladonna. special sound effects: Renato Marinelli. wigs: Maggi. costumes supplier: Tigano Lo Faro de Ma. set dressing: Cimino/Inter Office/ Rancati. jewels: Lembo. rugs & curtains: Sanchini. technical assistance: A.R.C.O.; E.C.E.; Schuller. titles: Studio 1. dream sequence realised with the co-operation of De Rossi. still photography: Photographic Team. unit publicists: [Enrico] Lucherini – [Margherita] Rossetti – [Matteo] Spinola. sound synchronization: Calpini. negative: Eastmancolor. positive: Telecolor S.p.A. (Rome). song "Dormi serena" by Fred Bongusto & Calfiano, performed by Bruno Martino. colour by Eastmancolor. widescreen.

Cast: Lando Buzzanca (Senator Gianni Puppis). Laura Antonelli (Nurse Hildegarde, a nun). Lionel Stander (Cardinal Maravidi). Agostina Belli (Nurse Brunhilde, a nun). Renzo Palmer (Father Lucian). Corrado Gaipa (don Gesualdo). Josè Quaglio (Pietro Fornari). Arturo Dominici (His Excellency). Eva Czemerys (fantasy woman). Anita Strindberg (French ambassador's wife). Francis Blanche (Father Schirer). Armando Bandini (Bardolino, Maravidi's secretary). Christian Alegny (Puppis' secretary). Aldo Puglisi (Carmelino, Puppis' chauffeur). Claudio Nicastro (Baddoni, police captain). Guglielmo Spoletini (Antonio Gazza, quiz show contestant). Fedor [Feodor] Chaliapin (Senator Torsello). Luigi Zerbinati (the general). Quinto Parmeggiani (Leonardi, army captain). Pupo De Luca (bugging officer). Giovanni Fago. Helen Parker. Filippo De Gara (TV announcer). Giuseppe Fortis (TV reporter). Claudio Dani. Umberto Bellucci. Umberto Di Grazia. Irio Fantini. *Uncredited:* Janos Bartha (film editor).

Original Italian title
Nonostante le apparenze...
e purchè la nazione non lo sappia...
all'onorevole piacciono le donne

Translation
'Notwithstanding appearances...
and as long as the country doesn't
know... the honorable gentleman
likes women'

Italy/France

International theatrical titles
The Eroticist (export title)
Obsédé malgré lui (FR)
'Obsessed Despite Himself'
The Senator Likes Women (alt. USA)
A su excelencia le gustan las mujeres
(SP) 'His Excellency Likes Women'
Der lange Schwarze mit dem Silberblick
(WG) 'The Cross-Eyed Man in Black'

Video titles
Les femmes du député (FR)
'The Deputy for Women'
Le député plait aux femmes (FR)
'The Hon. Member Appeals to Women'
El senador (ARG) 'The Senator'

Production companies
New Film Production s.r.l. (Rome)
Productions Jacques Roitfeld (Paris)

Theatrical distributors
Fida Cinematografica (Italy)
Etoile Distribution (France)

Running time
Italy 108m
France 85m

Video/DVD running times (adjusted)
VPD video (UK) 88m 47s
Severin DVD (USA) 109m 25s

Censorship
Italian censor certificate 59693
issued 01 March 1972
French Visa No. 39066
issued 04 June 1975

Release information
Potenza 11 February 1972
Bari 01 April 1972
Rome 12 May 1972
USA (Albuquerque) 24 January 1975
France (CNC) 30 July 1975

Synopsis: Senator Gianni Puppis, a hot contender for the next Italian Chief of State, is captured on unedited, untransmitted news-film furtively groping the bottom of the esteemed lady President of the Republic of Urania as she greets Italian dignitaries. A TV film editor studies the film with a colleague and remarks, "But he's queer!" Pictures of the incident fall into the hands of a highly unorthodox Dominican priest called Father Lucian, an old college friend of Puppis. He arranges a meeting with the bemused politician in a confessional booth, and demands money for the pictures. Puppis is furious but mystified – he can remember nothing of the incident. He refuses to pay up, but that night has a dream in which a naked woman beckons him, superimposed over St Peter's and The Vatican. Puppis telephones Father Lucian and offers him the money. In return, his 'friend' offers a consultation with a German psychiatrist. Puppis describes his recent affliction – his dreams and waking thoughts are becoming obsessed with bottoms. Mainly female ones, despite his usual preference for fey young men like his chauffeur Carmelino. He suffers black-outs, during which he commits terrible acts of bottom-pinching. "We've got to lick this thing, so to speak", says Father Lucian. Puppis leaves, vowing to maintain his self-control, but his hands wander while standing behind a young woman in a lift at the Senate Office.

The next day he announces that he is going to a "spiritual retreat" until the forthcoming election results are announced. Father Lucian drives the frantic man to a cloister run by his friend Father Schirer, a Dominican priest and psychiatrist. On the way, Puppis sees a veritable fusillade of ladies bottoms in a filling station forecourt. Before Father Lucian can stop him he has lurched zombie-like over to one tartan-frocked figure bent over examining the engine of a car; only to find himself face to face with a furious Scotsman. By the time the two men arrive at their destination, Puppis is blind drunk. Father Schirer welcomes the esteemed patient and informs the barely conscious man that his many skilled young nurses will help him. The clinic is staffed by nuns, all of them young and beautiful. Puppis is carried off to bed, but whilst unconscious grips the buttocks of a nun left to watch over him.

Back in Rome, Senator Puppis's absence is the subject of heated discussion. His opponents have been bugging his telephone, puzzling over coded conversations between Puppis and Father Lucian. The army are bugging their phones, in the hope of learning something that will ensure the planned military coup stays on course (with Puppis as next Chief of State they're confident of this). The Vatican secret police are bugging the military's phones, and Cardinal Maravidi is sitting in the Vatican cinema watching the film footage of Puppis, in a rage. Puppis owes his political success to shady deals with the Vatican and military hierarchy, and Maravidi – a manipulative monster willing to commit murder to facilitate 'divine will' – has groomed him for the position of President. Even Puppis's preference for young men is tolerated – the Cardinal prefers that he should be queer, expecting less scandal from this than the customary womanizing of Italian politicians. At the "spiritual retreat" Puppis describes a dream to Father Schirer whilst under hypnosis. It features the devout 'nurses' at the clinic, and visions of a Garden of Eden where foliage bursts with naked female bottoms. The next night Puppis sleepwalks to Schirer's room and molests him whilst fast asleep. Protesting his vow of chastity, the priest/analyst manages to wake the randy politician. Once fully awake, Puppis professes to feel much better, claiming that his dreams have liberated his mind. He returns to Rome full of optimism about his 'cure'. However, when Father Schirer takes confession from the nuns, he discovers that Puppis's rampaging sexual dreams have actually been enacted for real. The libidinous sisters all recount sexual encounters with Puppis.

Father Schirer storms into Puppis's house and demands an explanation, but is forced to hide when The Cardinal arrives unexpectedly. Cringing in the shower cubicle, he suffers a fatal heart attack when he thinks he is going to be discovered. Unaware of this, Puppis leaves with the Cardinal and attends a garden party prior to the celebration of the Founding of the Republic. After experiencing erotic visions, he swiftly seduces an ambassador's wife in the bushes. Carmelino discovers the body of Father Schirer and rushes to tell him, but is intercepted by the Vatican secret police. Returning home, Puppis is visited by Nurse Hildergarde, the only one of the cloistered order not to have been ravished by him. Begging him to relieve her of temptation and simultaneously scolding him for wickedness, she implores that they whip each other. Just as the twisted couple get down to it, the Vatican thugs arrive. The lovers escape through a back window but they are tracked to a secluded apartment and the nun is dragged away. Puppis confronts the Cardinal and says that he wants out of politics. The Cardinal replies that he won't allow it. Too much time and effort has been expended behind the scenes to hoist Puppis into position as a puppet Chief of State for his feelings to matter now. The Cardinal takes Puppis into the bowels of the Vatican to view waxworks of recently 'canonized' saints. They include Carmelino and Father Lucian. The threat is made explicit when he is told to look carefully at an unfinished wax model. Staring at the shapeless features, Puppis imagines a waxwork of himself. At a ceremony to accept his appointment as President, Puppis genuflects before a wax statue of Nurse Hildergarde. "The new President is remarkably religious", whispers an onlooker. The televised ceremony is switched off by a customer in a bar, who chooses instead to watch an asinine game show.

Review: Having made two dramatic and unusual thrillers and a well-crafted historical drama, Fulci returned to the ribald farce of his sixties comedies for more sexy comedy *all'Italiana*. Made just prior to *Don't Torture a Duckling*, the film is well photographed, for the often visually drab comedy genre, by *Duckling*'s exemplary cameraman Sergio D'Offizi. The film received a brief British video release in the early 1980s under its export title *The Eroticist*, a labelling adopted, presumably, in the wake of *The Exorcist* (1973). Despite this association, the film has no supernatural overtones and is instead a satire on the hypocrisies of Italy's politicians. Lest the topic become too 'heavy' for its audience, the action is liberally sprinkled with naughty nuns, bizarre sexy dream sequences and plenty of that once infamous Italian pastime, bottom pinching.

Surprisingly, this comedy is pretty enjoyable. For years, its reputation as 'Fulci's movie about bottom-pinching' led one to expect the worst. It draws a jaundiced picture of the corrupt relations between Church and State, and its combination of sex farce and bitter political commentary is a strange brew. However, the combination fits neatly into the *commedia all'italiana*, where such improbable dualisms were quite common (and succeeds where *Operation St. Peter's* failed by allowing the cynicism full reign). Whilst the Church gets hauled over the coals in uncompromising fashion, the closing moments explicitly blame the indifference of the Italian people for the chicanery of their politicians. This abrupt formulation ends the film on a sour note, which although arguably true is not integrated into either the subject matter or the tone of the rest of the film. It's doubtful whether bitter observations like this, attached to such a farcical premise, lead to anything more than further indifference.

That said, certain elements work very well. Buzzanca plays a thoroughly dislikeable character; starting out as a bourgeois buffoon, he runs the gamut from whining wretch to calculating political cynic, prepared to be manipulated into a power which will not even truly be his. As cowardly as Gianni Puppis is as a character, it's hard to think of another comic actor who would dare to take on a central role like this. Buzzanca skilfully animates him without appealing to audience sympathy at all. American comics like Steve Martin and Bill Murray have tackled similar parts, but can never resist giving their comic creations 'redeeming features'. Such sentimentality is nowhere to be found in Fulci's *The Eroticist*.

above:
Locandina.

opposite, main picture:
Senator Puppis dreams of giving in to his bottom-pinching urges.

opposite, bottom left:
British video cover art from the 1980s.

below:
Another image of licentious abandon beckons the disturbed politician.

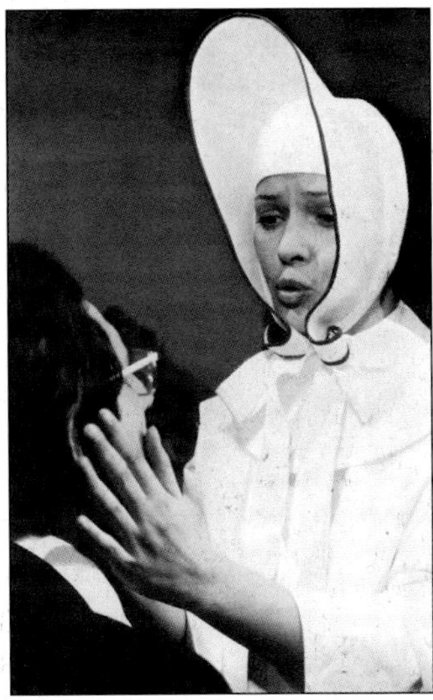

above:
Laura Antonelli consoles and seduces the neurotic Puppis.

"Politics to me is like the priesthood", Puppis pompously remarks, when someone asks why he's never married. It's not long before we see just how ironic that statement was. Fulci introduces a Vatican Cardinal of utter wickedness, played by the gravel-voiced American Lionel Stander (whose Stateside career as a comedian and supporting actor was interrupted after he fell foul of the Un-American Activities Committee in the early fifties). Cardinal Maravidi's attitude to holy office is that of the free-loading power-seeker, with a streak of the violent Mafia Don thrown in for good measure. His habit of 'canonizing' (slaughtering) enemies, then installing their wax replicas in a dingy cellar of the Vatican, is both hilarious and appalling. What a contrast in attitude between this and the gentle ribbing Fulci gave the Church in 1967's *Operation St. Peter's*!

Perhaps because of Fulci's prior success with *A Lizard in a Woman's Skin* (1971), he enriches this comedy with highly unusual dream sequences. One such, featuring a naked woman hovering in blackness, resembles the vision of lesbian erotica experienced by Florinda Bolkan in that marvellous film (discussed in the next chapter). But it's the extended dream Puppis has whilst under therapy at the 'clinic' that parades the most bizarre directorial styling. A freewheeling camera pans around a cemetery where a brimstone priest is ranting about the animalistic lust of women, warning Puppis not to fall into their evil traps. The scene cuts to a row of fetishistically veiled nuns, all with *derrières* exposed. Puppis fondles them one by one. Observing figures include political rivals and the Cardinal. His alleged 'friend' Lucian follows events with a film camera (could this character be meant to remind us of another behind-the-camera lurker?). Cut to a psychedelic vision of the Garden of Eden. Lucian assumes a devilish countenance, and hides behind a tree encoiled by the Serpent. A giant apple dangles from the tree, but Lucian points to the tree-trunk. Emerging from the folds of bark, as if from giant knotholes, are a host of female bottoms. The imagery conflates the Apple of Temptation, the Tree of Knowledge and the curvaceous buttocks of Woman. Giant apples fall to the ground and Puppis rolls around like a baby beneath. Cut to a double row of white hospital beds, each with a giant red apple placed upon it. In ecstacy, Puppis runs from bed to bed, squeezing at the inflated apples until they rupture like deflated beachballs... Later hallucinations, such as a woman taking the place of a horse beneath a monument of a mounted officer, or the hilarious sequence where Puppis explains fiscal policy whilst visualising an ambassador's wife nude except for dollars covering her nipples and vagina, are enjoyable diversions, but it's the Garden of Eden sequence which surprises the viewer most. It manages to be weird, 'kinky' and amusing all at once.

opposite page:
Lando Buzzanca as the sexually repressed politician Senator Puppis.

right:
The Senator loses control again, this time in the lifts at the Italian parliament.

below:
During analysis with Father Schirer (Francis Blanche) Puppis's sexual compulsions take yet another turn.

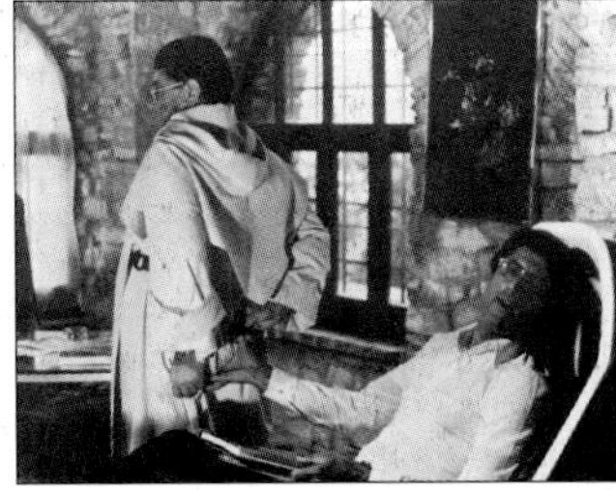

The liberation imagery here is contingent on the lead character's nominal homosexuality. Interestingly, Fulci would go on to cast Buzzanca as the lead in his 1975 horror-comedy *Young Dracula* (often referred to as *Dracula in the Provinces*), another homosexual-themed role – in which he plays a man who, after being bitten by a camp vampire, believes he's been turned queer and struggles comically to regain his sense of 'machismo'. The ironic reversal that *The Eroticist* presents, of a politician haunted by heterosexual fantasies running counter to his prosaic homosexuality, functions both as a tip of the hat to the topsy-turvy values of the Italian political scene and as an attempt to examine the distortions imposed on sexuality by the Catholic Church. Gianni Puppis's homosexuality appears to have developed through the Catholic installation of sexual disgust.

Catholic Christianity's biggest problem is sex, and by implication women. Priests and nuns take vows of chastity and abstinence to demonstrate their wish for 'pure' union with the Holy Spirit. Sex between men and women is viewed as impure. Explicit statements to this effect are rife in Catholic teaching. On the other hand, of course, the Church presents these 'acts' as a duty; 'go forth and multiply'. Unfortunately, the positive message is not passed on as forcefully as the negative, it being much easier for the Church to pour scorn on womankind than to discuss the natural condition of desire. Consequently, Puppis – as shown in the Eden dream where a priest warns him about 'evil' women – has developed into a repressed heterosexual, attempting to assuage his desires through political power and occasional sex with young men whilst harboring a deeply repressed fascination for women. Because Catholic society also *venerates* the female in the form of the Madonna, we may infer that Puppis has become obsessed with women's bottoms because they represent the most extreme paradox of femininity – they are both sacred and profane.

The way in which Puppis is persuaded into sexual passion by Nurse Hildergarde's lightning shifts of temperament (from guilt to arousal and from disgust to lubriciousness) indicate the circuitous routes desires must travel when they've been cramped, diverted and confused by religious teaching. *"You must find my body disgusting"*, the young nun demands as she exposes her breasts lasciviously (i.e. her arousal acts upon language to defy its restraints). The affirmation of desire through terms meant to suppress it recalls the strategies of Gay Liberation in the late eighties and nineties, when the word 'queer' was embraced as part of a contingent assault on prejudice. Whilst full self-knowledge is denied these characters, they are for a while wrestling with their Catholic oppression.

The Eroticist is one of the funniest of the Fulci comedies but it's best not to get too carried away with its reputation as political satire: a scene where a nun is rendered immobile by Buzzanca's tight grip on her bottom is at least as central to the writers' concerns as subverting the Italian parliament! When told that St. Paul taught that suffering rendered the sufferer divine, the nun responds *"I don't think St. Paul ever had to suffer this! His epistles would have touched on it"*. Like some Italian variation on the wit of Frankie Howerd, perhaps it is in such preposterous innuendos that we should look for *The Eroticist*'s real charm.

Democracy notwithstanding... and as long as the country doesn't know...

The dishonorable gentlemen vs. Lucio Fulci

It may seem difficult to believe, but in the early weeks of 1972 the satirical aspects of *All'onorevole piacciono le donne* sent the ruling Italian political party of the day, the Christian Democrats, into a panic, leading to a sordid chain of events involving corruption, manipulation of the censor board, and illegal film screenings for the party's political elite. Here is the whole story as it played out in the pages of the left-leaning newspaper *l'Unità*.

The first hint that Fulci was in for a rough ride with the film came in 1972, when he and producer Edmondo Amati noticed that the censor board were mysteriously dragging their heels instead of granting a certificate. *l'Unità* reported the situation on 3 February:

"All'onorevole piacciono le donne has not yet been passed by the censorship commission. It is going to be reconsidered, but has been in limbo for quite some time. The film attempts to describe [...] in a farcical manner the career of a Christian Democrat executive. It seems that this has bothered executives of the Christian Democrats because the actor Lando Buzzanca is made up in order to look similar to the very notorious – and very much discussed these days – exponent of the party. This, it is believed, is the real motive behind the consequent prohibition via censorship. It should be noted that the producer and distributor of the film is Edmondo Amati, brother of Giovanni, the most recent regional councillor of the Christian Democrats in Lazio, who is also the proprietor and manager of the most important chain of Roman cinemas ... The producer has instructed his legal representative, Masaro, and has put out a press release. This seems to support the hypothesis that behind the usual pretexts of censorship (obscenity and foul language et al) can be discerned, in essence, a political veto."[1]

A few days later, producer Edmondo Amati called a press conference. He screened the film for the assembled journalists, after which he and Lucio Fulci answered questions. Amati was quoted in *l'Unità*, saying: *"After the screening at the Ministry of Culture for a censor certificate, the president of the [censorship] commission, Dr. Vigorita, expressed to us his bewilderment about the theme of the film, which could represent a heavy attack on the Establishment. And yet the commission's motivation for refusing censor clearance, they say, is ostentatious obscenity and licentiousness of language."*[2]

So was the film really to be banned because of bad language and sexual scenes? Or was the censor doing someone else's bidding? *l'Unità*'s journalist reported, *"The producer and director are saying that the censors have fallen back on this formula – the only one to which the censor can cling in the face of the law – in order to conceal a political veto."*[3]

Adding more fuel to the fire, the article continued, *"The producer and director went on to inform journalists that they had been warned by voices from various Italian cities, north and south, of a 'private viewing' of the film reserved for other Christian Democrat personalities ... The producer has also been asked to shed light on a claim that he had been propositioned to sell the film so it would not be circulated in cinemas."*[4]

Obviously, if a political party in a democratic country were to attempt to buy a film from its producer in order to suppress it, it would be a very serious matter. So was there any truth to the rumour that a decision to do so was taken after a private screening for the Christian Democrat elite?

On the 10th of February *l'Unità* reported that the issues raised by the case had attracted the attention of an independent censorship watchdog organisation, Il Comitato unitario di agitazione del cinema italiano ('The Joint Action Committee for Italian Cinema'), who announced: *"[The committee] have determined that they see in the censorial measures a clear intention to punish the satirical and political content of the film itself. Seeing as this repressive measure has been accompanied by national news coverage in strange 'circumstances' the committee has given a mandate to the lawyer Giovanni Arnone to forward a complaint to the Director of Prosecutions to ascertain whether it is true that: at the projection of the film for the members of the censor board there were illegally present political personalities of the majority party and exponents of the security services of the state; that the projection itself had taken place outside the only administratively competent site; that following such a projection a police investigation was requested into the private affairs of the makers of the film themselves."*[5]

l'Unità followed up the story in an article dated 16 February 1972, beneath the headline 'Who is the secret viewer of via della Ferratella?': *"Intervening in the argument about the "No" verdict of the censorship board for the film All'onorevole piacciono le donne by Lucio Fulci, the minister of tourism and culture, Matteotti, specified – in a notification yesterday – that the film has been screened at the Ministry by special arrangement with the censorship board. Backing up rumours from other sources, Matteotti let it slip that in addition to the censor board screening, there was indeed another screening elsewhere, which took place inside the Ministry itself, at via della Ferratella. Now, the copy of a film that a producer deposits at the Ministry of Culture is available, solely and specifically, for the censorship commission. Matteotti admits instead that a second projection took place (in fact he let us know that such a thing has happened previously on other occasions) but did not tell us who participated and has not dispelled rumours that among those allegedly present at this projection were political personalities of the majority party and members of the State security service. Therefore, even if it might be legal for the Minister of Culture to see a film which has failed to pass the censor, it is absolutely illegal that a request of this type should be made and accepted for other persons who have nothing to do with the Ministry of Culture or the Government."*[6]

If the Christian Democrat party really did attempt to suppress Fulci's film, the situation blew up in their faces causing acute political embarrassment. Edmondo Amati lodged an appeal against the censor's decision, and a few days later the decision was reversed: almost certainly because of the scandal hitting the news. *l'Unità* reported the appeal's success on 2 March 1972: *"After having listened to the submissions of [...] the producer Edmondo Amati, the lawyer Gianni Massaro, and the director Lucio Fulci, as well as screenwriter Sandro Continenza, the joint commission of appeal has decided to give a favourable ruling, without cuts. Amati's lawyer Gianni Massaro said that the commission has judged correctly by not allowing themselves to be influenced by politics and limiting themselves to accepting the total lack of obscenity in the film, and stressed that such an assessment represents the only task required of the commission themselves according to the law of 1962."*[7]

Finally, when all the hoo-hah died down, reviewers were less than impressed with the film, and despite having zealously reported the censorship controversy *l'Unità* were especially caustic. After claiming that the movie had finally passed censorship in part due to a lack of *"social dangerousness, the film contained no reference to real facts,"* the reviewer went on to assert: *"The supposed comedy is boring, and uses heavy and outdated language. It lacks any kind of imagination that could highlight the contradictions and political 'intrigues' of our times, anything that could make it truly productive or satirical. The vice of Puppis (a puppet manoeuvred by mafia bishops) is a mere pretext to show bums and boobs."*[8] One wonders how anyone could castigate a film for lacking 'social dangerousness' after everything that had happened! It certainly looks as if *someone* in power felt threatened by the film, so maybe one question still remains: were reviewers paid to pour scorn on the film as part of a damage limitation strategy?

1 from *l'Unità*, 3/2/1972, p7: "Censura politica al film di Fulci?"
2 from *l'Unità*, 5/2/1972, p9: "L'onorevole non piace alla DC".
3 ibid.
4 ibid.
5 from *l'Unità*, 10/2/1972, p7: "Protesta per il veto al film di Fulci".
6 from *l'Unità*, 16/2/1972, p7: "Chi è il revisore segreto di via della Ferratella?"
7 from *l'Unità*, 2/3/1972, p9: "La Cassazione blocca i sequestri arbitrari di film".
8 from *l'Unità*, 12/5/1972.

Original Italian title
Il cavaliere Costante Nicosia demoniaco... ovvero Dracula in Brianza

Translation
'The Honorable and Demonic Costante Nicosia... or Dracula in Brianza'

Italy

International theatrical titles
Il cav. Costante Nicosia demoniaco ovvero Dracula in Brianza (IT stills/poster)
Muerdame Sr. Conde (SP)
'Bite Me, Señor Count'
Muerdame señor conde (SP poster)
El joven Dracula (SP alt.)
'Young Dracula'
Las picaras aventuras de Dracula (ARG) 'The Naughty Adventures of Dracula'
Young Dracula (export title)
The Young Dracula (US stills)

Other titles
Dracula in the Provinces (pre-release)

Production companies
Coralta Cinematografica S.r.l. (Rome)

Theatrical distributors
Titanus (IT)

Theatrical running time
Italy 100m

Video running time (adjusted)
VCG video (Germany) 92m 37s

Censorship
Italian censor certificate 67018 issued 21 August 1975

Release information
Rome 21 August 1975
Bari 28 August 1975

Young Dracula

1975

Directed by Lucio Fulci. a Coralta Cinematografica S.r.l. (Rome) production. story: Lucio Fulci. screenplay: Pupi Avati, Bruno Corbucci, Mario Amendola & Lucio Fulci. additional dialogue by Enzo Jannacci & Giuseppe Viola. director of photography: Sergio Salvati. music: [Franco] Bixio, [Fabio] Frizzi & [Vincente] Tempera. editor: Ornella Micheli. art director: Pierluigi Basile. production manager: Alfonso Donati. unit managers: Ennio Di Meo, Franco Mancarella & Romualdo Buzzanca. assistant directors: Victor Tourjansky & Giuseppe Pollini. script supervisor: Roberto Giandalia. cameramen: Franco Bruni & Enzo Tosi. assistant cameramen: Maurizio Lucchini & Bernardo Valli. key grip: Luciano Micheli. gaffer: Eugenio Raimondi. costumes: Massimo Lentini. Sylva Koscina's clothes by 'Mila Schon' of "I vergottini". make-up: Maria Luisa Tilli. hairstylist: Luisa Piovesan. wardrobe: Bertilla Silvestrin. clothes: Roberta Di Camerino & Marcello Rubinacci. furs: Viscardi. property master: Mario Gentilini. trovarobe: Duilio Caltabellotta. assistant editor: Bruno Micheli. publicity: Maria Ruhle. still photography: Gianfranco Massa. sound: Mario Attavi. boom operator: Marco Donati. sound recording: Cinemontaggio on the Westrex System. leather creations: Cesare Ricinni. costume house: G.P. 11. parrucche & acconciature: Ditta Maggi. set furnishings by "Larredamento" di Bagnolo Cremasco & by G.R.P.-SET-Cimino, Sanchini-Rancati. photography studio: Leo Massa. songs "Vampiro S.p.A." by Franco Nebbia, Franco Bixio, Fabio Frizzi & Vincent Tempera, sung by Franco Nebbia, released by Cinevox Record. "Lady Pamela" by Franco Bixio, Fabio Frizzi & Vincent Tempera, performed by Franco Nebbia; "O sole mio" by Di Capua; "Creola" by Ripp. prints & processing: Stacofilm. negative: Eastmancolor. interiors filmed at R.P.A. Elios Film Studios (Rome).

Cast: Lando Buzzanca (Costante Nicosia). Rossano Brazzi (Doctor Paluzzi). Sylva Koscina (Mariù Nicosia). Moira Orfei ('Bestia Assatanatà, dominatrix). Christa Linder (Liù). John Steiner (Count Dragulescu). Francesca Romana Coluzzi (Wanda Torsello). Grazia Di Marzà. Franco Nebbia (Meniconi, night club client). Michele Cimarosa (Salvatore). Grazia Spadaro (Aunt Maria). Giampaolo Rossi (Colombo). Ciccio Ingrassia (The Wizard of Noto). Valentina Cortese (Olghina Franchetti). Antonio Allocca (Peppino). Michele Cimarosa (Salvatore Cannata). Franca Martelli (Gia). Mauro Vestri. Ugo Fangareggi (Battai, Count's servant). Dorika Dori (singer). Carlo Bagno (head worker). Renato Malavasi (Arnaldo, the masochist's husband). John [Janos] Bartha (concierge, Romanian hotel). Barbara Musci (Georgia). Gianfranco Bocca (Colombo). Belsana Arfenone (Nicosia's domestic). Grazia Di Marzà. Giampaolo Rossi. *Uncredited:* Ilona Staller [aka Cicciolina].

Synopsis: Constantino (Costante) Nicosia is boorish, irascible and rich; having married into wealth, he is now the boss of a recently inherited toothpaste factory, and the owner of a basketball team. "The only reason I own this bunch of dippy dribblers is to push toothpaste to those sports nuts out there", he declares to his hunchbacked side-kick, Peppino. He is also extremely superstitious. Peppino is less of a friend than a good luck charm as far as the insensitive Nicosia is concerned. He believes that it brings good luck to rub a hunchback's hump. However, he is routinely rude to his human talisman: "Do you know who my father was?", demands Peppino after one insult. "A camel", snaps Nicosia. The signs and omens are all against this wealthy rat: a black cat crosses his path, and worse still he breaks a mirror at his apartment. Superstition demands that he persuade a virgin to piss over the broken shards of glass, in order to halt the tide of bad luck. Abusively, he presses the decrepit old spinster next door into service, assuming – mistakenly – that she has never 'done the deed'. His relationship with his wife Mariù is scarcely more convivial. "I always have good luck with things that rhyme with the letter 'u' – except you" he tells her. Reluctantly bowing to family pressure, Nicosia employs his brother-in-law in a menial post at the factory, but fires him after catching the man asleep on the job, snoring loudly – "The voice of the proletariat!" he sneers. At a family gathering that evening, he is accosted by his in-laws who attempt to shame him into giving the feckless man his job back. Instead of acquiescing to family practise, he bursts into an escalating tirade of rudeness against the sinister figure of Great Aunt Maria. The old woman responds by uttering a curse. Nicosia spits with derision at first, that is until the "old hag" threatens to pour oil onto the floor; this heavy duty bit of magical business breaks Nicosia's nerve, and he recants in a babbling panic. Too late – as Nicosia grovels for the curse to be lifted, the old woman has the last laugh.

A couple of days later, Nicosia is on a plane bound for Romania, to attend a business conference. A suave, gaunt figure seated nearby introduces himself as Count Dragulescu, and invites the troubled industrialist to visit him at his castle whilst in the region. On arriving, Nicosia discovers that the conference has been postponed, leaving him stranded at the hotel for the weekend. Another businessman, Meniconi, tells him that there are no prostitutes to be had in the region, and he has failed to seduce any of the local women, even after buying sexy lingerie to bribe them. He confides to Nicosia that he has taken to wearing the lingerie himself. Rather than spend the weekend in this wretched resort, Nicosia decides to call on the Count. The castle is very much what one would expect from a Romanian nobleman's abode, and the weather conditions amplify the Gothic effect. Dragulescu greets his guest in the cavernous dining hall – and we notice a certain feyness about this ironical nobleman. Suddenly, a gay bunch of revellers stagger down the stairs into the dining hall. The Count introduces his companions – three female, one male – to the wary visitor. They greet him in a lavish, tactile manner. When Boris, the screamingly camp male of the party, tries to greet Nicosia too, he backs nervously away and declines. Laughing, the Count sends Nicosia up to his room to prepare for dinner. When he comes back down, starchily tucked into a tuxedo, he finds himself over-dressed for the occasion: "Dinner in Transylvania is in the nude!", purrs Dragulescu. The evening becomes drunken and debauched. Nicosia strips off, cavorts with some of the assembled throng and then passes out cold. The next morning he wakes up in bed next to the mirthfully grinning Dragulescu. Running in horror from the castle, he returns to Italy...

Back in his little empire, Nicosia is uptight. He greets all who speak to him with a clenched, furious "Up yours! Up yours!" At the basketball practises, he is knocked off balance when a coach tells the team "You've got to make this the big one". Nicosia repeats the phrase 'big one' over and over, and then collapses when he sees a row of naked men's bottoms in the shower stall. Doctor Paluzzi suggests he try making out with his mistress – if he can't do that, the professional adds, then he must have been "deflowered" whilst drunk. This attempt to re-establish heterosexuality fails, however, because the tormented Nicosia feels compelled to bite her and suck blood from the wound. Ever more stricken, first with anxiety and then with self-pity, Nicosia calls on Great Aunt Maria. He begs her to remove the curse which, he assumes, is responsible for his misfortune. However, she claims it wasn't her curse which has caused his bloodsucking urge. She recommends that he visit the Magician of Noto in Sicily, and he complies in desperation. The 'magician' is clearly a fake, but Nicosia accepts his advice; the curse will only be lifted if he re-employs the brother-in-law he sacked. This 'suggestion' is actually a deliberate stunt organised by the family. Returning home far from being cured, he responds to his wife's sexual advances by plunging his teeth into her bare bottom. All seems lost to the once arrogant entrepreneur. Nicosia adopts a devil-may-care aggression; re-sacking his lazy relative, arranging to visit whores to satisfy his urge to bite, and isolating himself from his family and friends. Finally, he satisfies his craving by setting up a blood-bank at his factory-site, and compelling all employees to attend. Just as he seems to have surrendered to total cynicism, his wife arrives at the factory with a baby – his son. Rejoicing at this proof of his potency, he throws off the shackles of his superstitious paranoia and goes to greet his baby son – only to discover that the baby sports a protruding pair of fangs...

About the production: In January 1975, Giulio Sbarigia's Coralta Cinematografica had two comedies lined up: one was *Buttiglione diventa capo del servizio segreto* ('Buttiglione Becomes Head of the Secret Service') to be directed by Mino Guerrini; the other was *Il cavaliere Costante Nicosia demoniaco... ovvero Dracula in Brianza*, to be helmed by Lucio Fulci and starring Lando Buzzanca.[28] Filming was under way by 9 April 1975, with *Variety* reporting, *"Rossano Brazzi makes a guest appearance in the Lando Buzzanca sex comedy 'Dracula in the Province' [sic] now in production under Lucio Fulci's direction for Coralta."* A follow-up report dated 7 May 1975 declared that the film was still rolling, meaning that Fulci was shooting for at least a month, possibly closer to six weeks.

As a title, *Il cavaliere Costante Nicosia demoniaco... ovvero Dracula in Brianza* is something of a mouthful, and it's also pretty impenetrable in translation, with its use of an unusual character name (Costante Nicosia) and mention of an obscure region of Italy (Brianza). Little wonder that for English speaking markets some bright spark hit on the idea of *Young Dracula*. However, despite an English-language print under that name surfacing on Greek video in the 1980s, and an American stills set bearing the careless variant title 'The Young Dracula', there appears to have been no US release for the film. So what went wrong? Well, by the time the Fulci film was under consideration there were already two other films circulating in the USA with the same monicker; the execrable Harry Nilsson/Ringo Starr comedy *Son of Dracula* (1974), directed by Freddie Francis, which played as *Young Dracula* on its 1975 re-release, and Paul Morrissey's *Blood for Dracula* (1974), re-released as *Young Dracula* in 1976. In both cases the inspiration for this change in title was, of course, Mel Brooks's *Young Frankenstein* (1974), a sizeable international hit. It would seem that between them these two re-issues put the kibosh on a Stateside release for the Fulci film.

Review: This comedy was dismissed by the usually self-aggrandising Fulci as a lame effort. Although it has some entertainment value, it also provides evidence that the much-lauded Pupi Avati (who co-scripted) leaves the occasional clay footprint on his projects.[29] *Young Dracula* once again features Lando Buzzanca, this time as a wealthy industrialist who encounters a camp Romanian vampire. So what sort of perspective does this satire of 'homosexual panic' offer?

The prevailing theme is one of sexual anxiety. Costante Nicosia's absurd libidinal worries are the chief area of fascination, and the comedy is a combination of sacrificial satire – Nicosia as idiot to the sexual slaughter – and 'masculine' hysteria in the face of the intransigent demons of femininity and homosexuality (as usual these 'demons' are merged through the repressive faculty of conventional gender codes). The focus for this process is Count Dragulescu, who brings to a crisis the suggestions of unmanliness gathering around Nicosia. The seeds of this revelation are clear in the preceding sequences. For a start, Nicosia is a man whose social standing is the result of a fortunate wedding into a rich family. Italian masculinity is predicated, in this initial irony, as a matter of independent financial provision. Dependence of any sort, especially upon a woman, is seen as unmale. Secondly, Nicosia's short temper suggests a not-so-latent hysteria. Instead of his tantrums being imposing, they are silly and neurotic. Which leads on to his third problem, as the film would have it – superstitious belief in the paranormal. For all of his social power, Nicosia is prone to fits of absurd anxiety at the sight of cats crossing his path, mirrors breaking, all the paraphernalia of superstition. It's scarcely necessary

above:
Spanish admat for *Young Dracula*.

opposite, main picture:
Detail taken from the film's due foglie poster design.

opposite, bottom left:
Detail from the locandina, showing the film's full original theatrical title.

below:
Fulci directs Buzzanca on the set of *Young Dracula*.

bottom:
Nicosia (Lando Buzzanca) consults The Wizard of Noto (Ciccio Ingrassia).

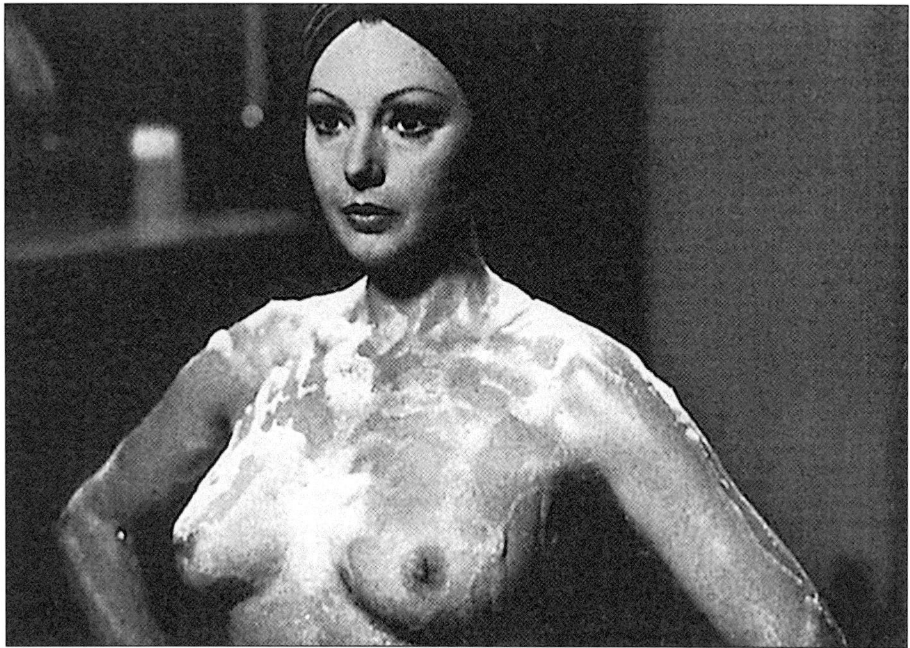

above:
Sylva Koscina as Nicosia's wife, Mariù bares her endowments.

right:
Nicosia experiments unsuccessfully with kinky sex.

facing page:
Spanish poster for Fulci's sex farce *La pretora*, starring the indefatigable Edwige Fenech (famous for her gialli and a slew of distinctly Italian sexy comedies in the 1970s).

below:
Sylva Koscina and Lando Buzzanca in frivolous mood during a set-up used for the film's promotional artwork.

to remark that belief of this sort has traditionally been identified as a feminine characteristic.

Even Nicosia's turn of phrase reveals 'unmanly' thought processes. As the businessman-owner of a basketball team, one might expect him to allocate a link of phallic virility between enterprise and the masculine prowess of 'his' team. Instead, he dismisses the connection, boasting about his exploitative attitude and deriding the team as a bunch of "dippy dribblers". He sees his role as the cynical purveyor of a product – toothpaste, with all its associations of falsity, insincerity, and routine mechanical squirting – aimed at men whose fascination with sport makes them 'nuts'. It is unfortunate for Nicosia that the phrase 'sports nuts' should emerge at this point; by using terms that suggest the testicles, he emerges as subject to the dominance of his consumers. His role as toothpaste manufacturer then suggests a ministration to an almost universal power-symbol – teeth. This dismissive attitude is punished when Nicosia returns from his Romanian trauma. The sight of the basketball team's naked masculinity, shown in a lingering shower-room pan across male buttocks, sends the humiliated business tycoon into a faint.

Nicosia's failure to engage with female characters is drawn through the convention of a loveless marriage. Furthermore, his cruel and exploitative attitude to an elderly woman neighbour marks him as a victim-in-waiting. The bluster and bragadaccio of Nicosia's character is satirized during the confrontation with Great Aunt Maria. Although prone to bouts of superstition, he attempts to 'fight' his lowly relatives on the basis of a 'sophisticated' denial of belief in spells and incantations. This pathetic resistance collapses, hilariously, when the spell attains a symbolic intensity strong enough to fell his shaky sense of superiority. The 'magic' practised by Great Aunt Maria is analogous to the commonly depicted omnipotence that 'the family' exerts on Italians. Interestingly, in this film Fulci keeps us 'ahead of the game' as far as any supposedly magical forces are concerned. Great Aunt Maria's incantation is designed merely to pursue a matter of family interest, and is no more 'mystical' than the operations of the Mafia. Indeed, her actions are equated with the Mafia when she hears Nicosia's metaphysical anxieties and dispatches him to the so-called Wizard residing in Sicily – 'spiritual' home of that cabbalistic crime syndicate.

Young Dracula treats its bigoted lead character contemptuously, and yet – by using the macho male's image of the simpering, vampiristic homosexual as a demon to taunt the man – it flirts with bad taste in a way which sours the comedy elements. Ultimately I don't think of this film as a homophobic exercise, as some writers have done, but its combination of fantastical satire and mundane comedy-of-manners is unsuccessful. Fulci's cynicism risked being lost in a murky union with the lead character's own bitter-mindedness.

In Italy, *l'Unità*'s response to this satire of a social climber's greed was measured but highly critical: *"The story is set in the industrial region of Brianza. The main character is Costante Nicosia, a crafty "terrone"* [a person from the South of Italy] *who has arrived in the North, dressed in rags, only to suddenly become an extremely wealthy entrepreneur. He quickly assimilates the manners of high society and the financial world, however, Costante can't shake certain picturesque archetypical aspects. These include his maniacal superstition, exasperated sexual appetite, a connection with the mafia and an arrogance towards the weak (specifically towards his employees) and his rough and demanding relatives. Both his employees and his relatives curse him, and these curses take effect during a trip to Transylvania, where he ends up sleeping with Count Dracula's heir. The entrepreneur-vampire will find no use in amulets and spells, and will have to start to suck people's blood literally rather than leech from them metaphorically. Pilfering from Polanski and Mel Brooks, Fulci and friends have stretched an idea that could have been funny in principle. However it has been realised with shallow and coarse methods. When Fulci tries to create a social parable, he inexorably fails to do so."*[30]

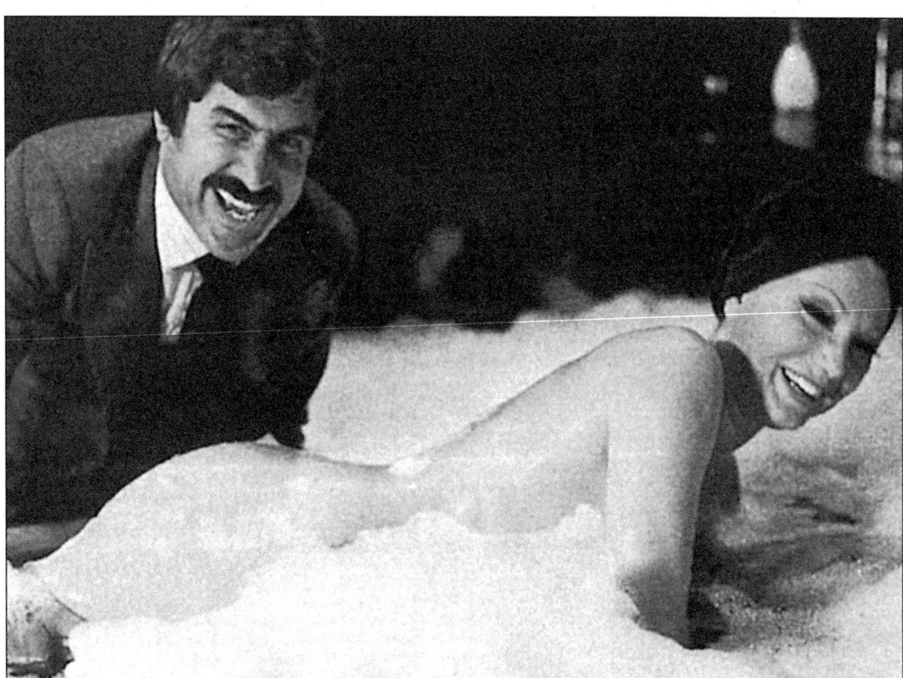

ALIANZA
CINEMATOGRAFICA
ESPAÑOLA

EDWIGE
FENECH

RAF LUCA

GIANCARLO
DETTORI

ORESTE
LIONELLO

LA JUEZ Y SU EROTICA HERMANA

Director: Lucio Fulci

color

Translation
'The Lady Magistrate'

Italy

International theatrical titles
My Sister and I (Pakistan)
La juez y su erotica hermana (SP)
'The Judge and Her Sexy Sister'
La main de ma soeur (FR)
'My Sister's Hand'
Ne Sevimli (TUR) 'What a Cutie'

Other titles
Juge ou putain (FR alt. video)
'Judge or Whore'

Production companies
Coralta Cinematografica S.r.l. (Rome)

Theatrical distributors
Dear International (Rome)

Running time
Italy 98m

DVD running time (adjusted)
IIF (IT) 98m 26s

Censorship
Italian censor certificate 69229
issued 28 October 1976

Shooting period
from 28 June 1976

Release information
Lecce 11 November 1976
Bari 15 December 1976
Florence 12 November 1976
Genova 19 November 1976
Rome 06 January 1977

La pretora

1976

Directed by Lucio Fulci. A Coralta Cinematografica production. producer: Roberto Sbarigia. screenplay: Franco Marotta & Laura Toscano. dialogue collaboration: Franco Mercuri. director of photography: Luciano Trasatti. editor: Ornella Micheli. music: Nico Fidenco, directed by G. [Giacomo] Dell'Orso; published by Stero Oceania S.r.l. (Rome). art director: Eugenio Liverani. unit manager: Ennio Di Meo. assistant director: Roberto Giandalia. continuity: Daniela Puccini. cameraman: Alessandro Ruzzolini. assistant cameramen: Maurizio Lucchini & Claudio Farinelli. costume designer: Vera Cozzolino. make-up: Gianni Morosi. hairstylist: Paolo Borzelli. production secretaries: Vittorio Fornasiero, Massimo Rossetti & Gianni Spedicato. still photography: Gianfranco Massa. assistant editors: Bruno Micheli & Mario D'Ambrosio. titles by Studio Mafera. sound: Mario Attavi. Italian version by S.A.S. – Società Attori Sincronizzatori; recorded at Elettronica Calpini. wardrobe supplied by Annamode. jewelry by Nino Lembo. wigs by Maggi. shoes by Pompei. set furnishings by Cimino-Dedalo-Sanchini. handbag & suitcase supplied by Ditta Fendi. Edwige Fenech's shoes by Casuccio & Scalera. Edwige Fenech's underwear by Ditta Paoletti. song "La pretora: Rosa o Viola?" by Nico Fidenco, vocal solo by Ernesto Brancucci. negatives by Eastmancolor. colour by Stacofilm. interiors filmed at Centro Cinematografico Dear (Rome).

Cast: Edwige Fenech (Judge Viola Orlando / Rosa Orlando, Viola's twin sister [two roles]). Raf Luca (Raffaele Esposito). Giancarlo Dettori (Count Renato Altero). Mario Maranzana (Bortolon, lawyer). Carlo Sposito (state prosecutor). Walter Valdi (Zaganella). Gianni Agus (Angelo Scotti). Oreste Lionello (Francesco Lo Presti). Gianni Solaro (Magni, lawyer). Piero Palermini (car salesman). Luca Sportelli. Galliano Sbarra. Pietro Tordi (Pavanin). Enrico Marciani. Michele Malaspina (maître d'hotel). *Uncredited:* Marina Frajese. Lucio Fulci (Esso gas station attendant).

Synopsis: Con-man and all-round scuzzball Rafaelle Esposito finds himself in court in the small town of Bellignano, charged with selling dog-food as gourmet goulash. His seedy lawyer Bortolon informs him that the local magistrate, Viola Orlando, is feared for her harsh sentences. After a disastrous initial hearing, Esposito visits a nearby hotel leisure complex and is shocked to see a woman he believes to be Viola walking around nearly nude, with flowers stuck to her nipples. He swiftly discovers that this is actually Rosa, Viola's promiscious and free-spirited identical twin. He and Rosa end up in bed together, and after a wild night of passion Esposito persuades Rosa to take part in a charade that will discredit her sister and hopefully get him off the hook with the court. Posing as Viola, Rosa sleeps with a few local crooks who are in trouble with the magistrate; thus, word begins to spead that Viola is a whore. Esposito steps up the pressure, arranging for Rosa to take part in a pornographic photo shoot based on Snow White and the Seven Dwarfs. Viola's fiancé Count Renato Altero manages to close down the shoot and buys some negatives, but the pictures are published anyway. When Esposito has the incriminating sex mag distributed among the public at his next court hearing, it seems that Viola's days as the scourge of the criminal classes are over...

About the production: Lucio Fulci was a busy man in the summer of 1976. While preparing to shoot *The Stepdaughter* (see Unmade Projects) he also had *La pretora* lined up for Coralta Cinematografica, and there was even a third film coming into view, 'Seven Black Notes', which was planned for July, to be produced by Dino De Laurentiis's older brother Luigi De Laurentiis. However some time during May – possibly because his schedule was becoming impossible – Fulci dropped *The Stepdaughter* and jumped straight into *La pretora*, which entered production towards the end of June 1976.

above:
Count Renato Altero in bed with Rosa ...or is it Viola? (It's Rosa).

left:
Rosa takes part in a porno version of Snow White and the Seven Dwarfs.

opposite, main picture:
Judge Viola Orlando is wooed by Count Renato Altero (Giancarlo Dettori).

opposite, bottom left:
French poster.

Review: Kicking off with an idea recycled from *Gli imbroglioni*, in which a defendant in an upcoming court case makes an enemy of the magistrate en-route to his hearing, this is a poorly written comedy with a muddled, unconvincing storyline (courtesy of husband-and-wife writing team Franco Marotta and Laura Toscano). It is however pretty much critic-proof, thanks to its gorgeous and vivacious star Edwige Fenech, who plays two roles: Viola Orlando, a stern, imperious magistrate, and Rosa her ditsy sex-mad twin. The reason just about anyone will want to see *La pretora* is to check out Fenech in a series of revealing outfits, or better still, in the nude, both of which demands are regularly satisfied; the question of whether or not the comedy is well crafted or the storyline convincing is probably academic. However, for the purposes of a book about Lucio Fulci *La pretora* must be assessed on more than just its willingness to expose la Fenech, so....

Why does Viola keep her twin sister secret? How is that even possible when she lives just a short drive away? *"You're leading a double life!"* says Viola's fiancé Count Renato Altero, and he's right – but we never discover why. As for Rosa, why is she so willing to ruin her sister? Sibling rivalry is the obvious assumption but it's not supported by the script, and it would need to have been one hell of a feud for Rosa to smear her sister's reputation like this. With no motive for either Viola's secretiveness or Rosa's maliciousness, the story completely lacks plausibility. Then there's the plot to humiliate Viola by having Rosa appear in a porno mag: it would take just a few words from the victim to discredit it, but it's set up in the film as successful blackmail; so why is Viola so reluctant to name her sister as the culprit? As a story, *La pretora* is incredibly half-cocked.

Structurally the film may flounder, but there are some funny lines here and there (probably thanks to Franco Mercuri, who gets sole credit for dialogue). After Rosa exhausts Esposito with her voracious sexual appetite she calls for him to 'come again', at which he sighs: *"What can I say? If I ever meet a girl who likes it limp, I'll destroy her."* When Altero sees the dwarfs in their underwear climbing on the bed for Rosa's photo-session, he demands, *"Isn't this supposed to be a kids' tale?"* Esposito replies, *"Even the kids are screwing these days, they don't believe in fairytales... Nowadays you need to demythologise, out with the old forms, the old taboos..."* Fulci also has fun with the shoot itself: *"It's time to work, we're not in Rome,"* says Esposito to the assembled set-dressers and lighting technicians, a spiky little joke considering where the film was being shot! I also liked Rosa's knickers with 'Kiss Me' embroidered on the front, and there's some choice dialogue when she poses as Viola to seduce the magistrate's locum (who's been lusting after his boss for years): *"Do you love justice?"* she demands, revealing her nudity beneath her robes of office; *"I revere it!"* says he, before sinking to his knees with his face in her crotch.

It's possible to view the film as Fulci letting off steam after a series of run-ins with the Italian censor; he was hauled before the court for cruelty to animals in *A Lizard in a Woman's Skin* (case dismissed), and accused of libel against a prominent politician for his political satire *The Eroticist* (case dismissed again). There was more trouble with the censor on *Don't Torture a Duckling*, so it's hardly a coincidence that one of Viola's responsibilities (unusually for a small town magistrate) is to censor adult films; I suspect the real reason that Rosa is willing to ruin Viola is simply that Lucio Fulci wants this woman to suffer! Interestingly, a male magistrate's 'crusade against pornography' was in the news at the time of filming. Under the headline *"The antiporno magistrate resumes his battle against the newsagents"*, an article in *La Gazzetta del Mezzogiorno* reported that Palermo magistrate Dr. Salmeri was appealing against a law exempting newsagents from criminal responsibility for the sale of obscene publications. On the facing page, rather spookily, was a small feature announcing the shooting of *La pretora*![31]

left:
Probably the only image for which this film will be remembered...

below:
Rosa goes to confession.

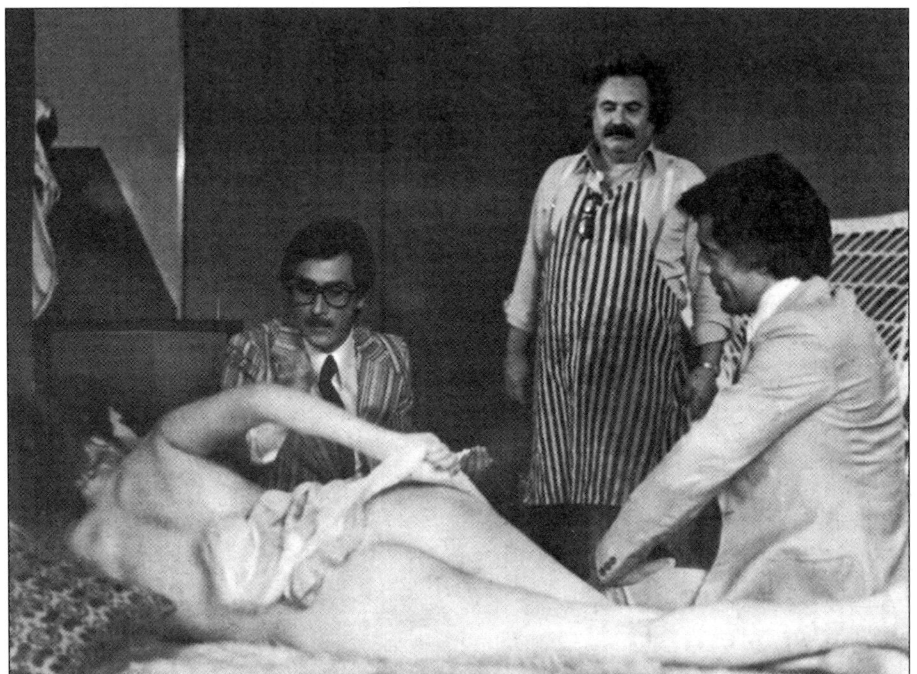

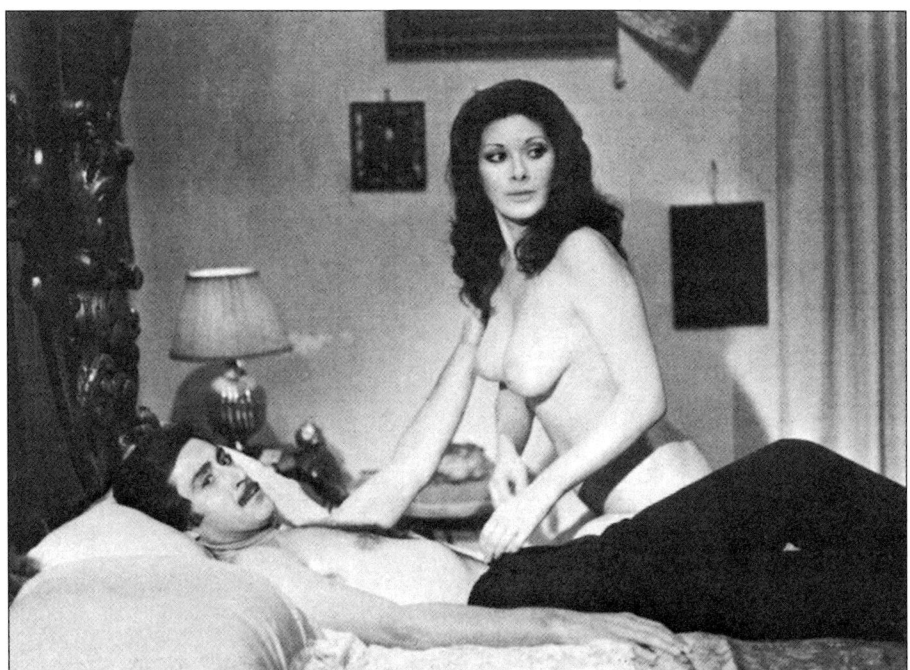

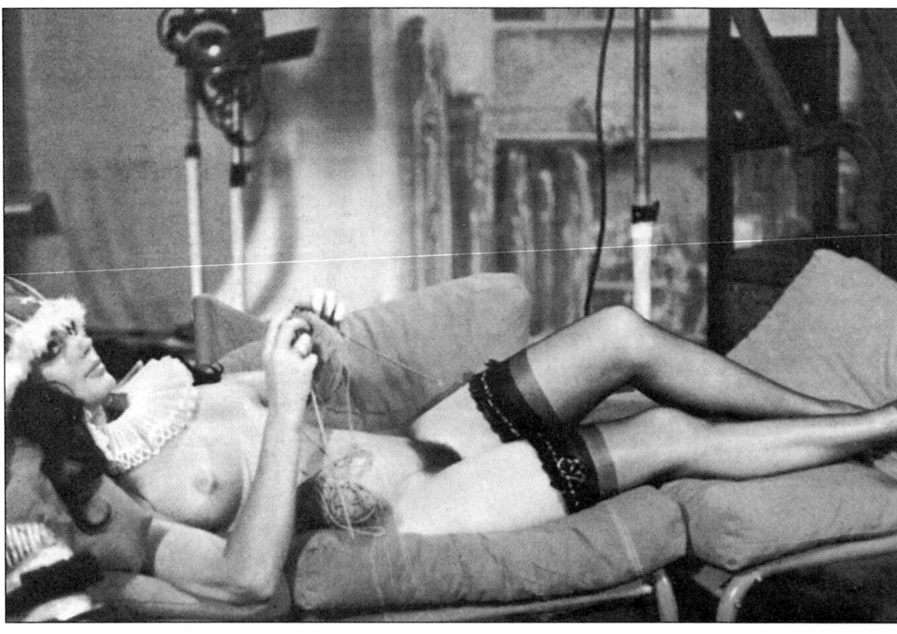

this page:
Fulci's last sex-comedy, *La pretora* (1976) starring Edwige Fenech.

Footnotes

1 D'Annunzio's patronage of the project assured its success, but did its director no personal favour. Pastrone, who worked under the pseudonym Piero Fosco, remained unknown for many years due to the attention given the far more famous poet's involvement.

2 It is reported that Benito Mussolini – who is quoted as having called the cinema "The strongest weapon" – was a fan of Maciste. The dictator enjoyed having his corpulent physique photographed, oiled and stripped to the waist in emulation of the iconic strongman.

3 Built after a mysterious fire destroyed the Cines studios in 1935, this huge 'cinema city' was constructed on the outskirts of Rome. Mussolini laid a ceremonial corner stone to commence the project and also opened the complex in 1937. By 1942, the number of soundstages had grown from ten to twelve (with a further two at the neighbouring Centro Sperimentale). After a public image problem in the wake of the demise of Italian Fascism, it recovered to become the dominant home of Italian cinema, playing host to Fellini and the giant peplum productions of the 1950s and 1960s.

4 Titanus handled Fulci's *Challenge to White Fang* (1974). After a cash crisis in the 1960s due to production of two expensive flops (*The Leopard*, 1963, and Robert Aldrich's disastrous epic, *Sodom and Gomorrah*, 1962), it recovered and made it into the 1980s before being asset-stripped and scaled down, concentrating mostly on TV productions.

5 'Ma che capirà il cinese?' by Umberto Eco, published 9 November 2007 in L'espresso online (http://espresso.repubblica.it/opinioni/la-bustina-di-minerva/2007/11/09/news/ma-che-capira-il-cinese-1.5989, sourced 3 February 2015).

6 Full name Stefano Vanzina, Steno was born January 9th, 1915, and died in 1988. He was a student at the Centro Sperimentale di Cinematografia during its earliest years whilst simultaneously reading Law at the University of Rome. After working for a while as a cartoonist he co-directed his first film – *Al diavolo la celebrità* – with Mario Monicelli in 1949. His filmography ran to 76 theatrical releases, of which seven featured Totò. After a rare venture into horror-comedy in 1979 (*Dottor Jekyll e gentile signora*) he directed his last feature, *Banana Joe*, in 1982. He was the father of *Nothing Underneath* director Carlo Vanzina.

7 Mario Monicelli was born in Viareggio in 1915. Raised in Milan, he attained early recognition when his co-directed amateur film *I ragazzi della via Paal* won a prize at the 1935 Venice Film Festival. He made his professional debut in the late 1940s, co-directing (with Steno) films for Totò, such as *Totò cerca casa* (1949), *Guardie e ladri* (1951) and *Totò e Carolina* (1954). Fulci worked with him (and Steno) on *Totò e i re di Roma* and *Totò e le donne*. Monicelli became known for piercing the pure entertainment parameters of the *commedia* with acute, sometimes aggressive social and political comment. His 1959 film *The Great War* shared the Golden Lion award at Venice with Roberto Rossellini's *Il generale della rovere*. This was the first time that a 'mere comedy' had been recognised in Italy as having 'serious' merits.

8 To Robert Schlockoff, as recorded in *Fangoria* #29.

9 Totò's spoof *Totò, Peppino e la dolce vita* (1961) reportedly angered Fellini when it was released in the wake of his classic *La Dolce Vita*. The two had apparently gotten on badly whenever they met. The doddering comedian who appears on stage to accept an award in Fellini's brilliant *Toby Dammit* (his superior segment of the Poe anthology film *Tre passi nel delirio*, 1968) is a parody of the ageing Totò, played by his music-hall rival Polidor (Ferdinand Guillaume).

10 In an interview conducted by Howard Berger in Manhattan at the Fangoria Weekend of Horrors, January 1996, Fulci described *Un uomo da ridere* as "...about an Ed Wood-like character, Italy's worst director. The kind of man who finds he's run out of film but says 'Let's shoot it anyway!'" The whole interview, printed in *Fangoria* #154, is well worth seeking out – it's billed as his last (the truth as far as I'm aware) and sees Fulci far more relaxed and forthcoming than usual.

11 The interview was translated into English by Frederic Levy and appeared in the UK genre magazine *Starburst* #48, August 1982.

12 ibid.

13 ABC Sevilla, 22 June 1961.

14 *l'Unità*, 28 August 1959.

15 *l'Unità*; 'But Who Are These Teddy-Boys?', 29 August 1959.

16 *l'Unità*, 29 August 1959.

17 *La Stampa*, 9-10 April 1962.

18 The title combines *Colpo gobbo*, the Italian 'aka' for Mickey Spillane's novel *The Big Kill*, and *Divorzio all'italiana*, a 1961 hit movie by Piero Germi starring Marcello Mastroianni.

19 *Variety*, 23 January 1963.

20 *l'Unità*, 13 January 1963.

21 *La Stampa*, 18 October 1962.

22 *La Stampa*, 22 June 1963.

23 *La Stampa*, 29 June 1963.

24 *l'Unità*, 31 October 1963.

25 *l'Unità*, 5 November 1964.

26 *l'Unità*, 30 January 1965.

27 *The Bird with the Crystal Plumage* made 1,650 million lira on its Italian release.

28 *Variety* reported the project on 22 January 1975 under the even more peculiar title 'Honourable Costante Bosisio, Satirist and Dracula in the Provinces'! Perhaps there was some confusion in the translation...

29 Writer, director and producer Giuseppe [Pupi] Avati was born 3rd November 1938. He is best known to horror fans for his brilliant *La casa dalle finestre che ridono* (1976) and *Zeder* (1983). He also co-scripted Lamberto Bava's impressive debut *Macabre* (1980). Something of an enigma to English-speaking film-goers, much of Avati's work is rarely seen outside of Italy. In 1996 he returned to the horror genre with a subtle supernatural tale, *The Arcane Enchanter*.

30 *l'Unità*, 22 August 1975

31 *La Gazzetta del Mezzogiorno*, 1 July 1976.

above:
Franco and Ciccio are led to the gas chamber (stop cheering, it's only a movie)... from *I due evasi di Sing Sing*.

left:
Commissioner Di Savio (Totò) gets to the bottom of Castagnato's smuggling racket in *I ladri*.

bottom left:
Paolo Macelloni (Antonio de Teffé) talks business with his two singing sensations, Tony Bellaria (Tony Dallara) and Fred (Fred Buscaglione) in *I ragazzi del juke box*.

below:
Spanish poster art for *The Eroticist*.

STELLOR FILMS présente

FLORINDA BOLKAN / IRENE PAPAS DANS

LA LONGUE NUIT DE L'EXORCISME

AVEC
BARBARA BOUCHET
TOMAS MILIAN
MARC POREL
GEORGE WILSON
DANS UN FILM DE
LUCIO FULCI

TECHNICOLOR

DE LANGE NACHT VAN DE DUIVEL

Imprimé en Belgique

EDICOLOR - Bruxelles - Tél. 343 63.49 - 343.87.43

chapter four

Build My Giallos High!

featuring:

One on Top of the Other aka *Una sull'altra* (1969)

A Lizard in a Woman's Skin aka *Una lucertola con la pelle di donna* (1971)

Don't Torture a Duckling aka *Non si sevizia un paperino* (1972)

The Psychic aka *Sette note in nero* (1977)

Throughout the sixties, Lucio Fulci concentrated on a parochial brand of comedy and few of the resulting movies were exhibited abroad. By 1968, his career had settled into a rut with the seemingly endless Franco & Ciccio series. All this was to change, however, when in 1969 he embraced a new genre enabling him to reach audiences further afield – the Italian murder mystery or giallo. It proved to be a great vehicle for his emerging talent; Fulci's brooding, visually rich thrillers are as fascinating in their own way as the horror films he made a decade later. Lust, violence, amorality and guilt, bloodshed and eroticism; all are intermingled in their lavish narratives. Compared to most other films of the genre (and there were *lots* of giallo films), Fulci's contributions stand apart as the work of a genuine talent.

Blood on the Tiber

The giallo crossbreeds the murder mystery with aspects of the horror genre, chiefly a lingering relish in the depiction of fear and bloodshed. It's a form where murder and intrigue, those staple features of popular drama, are taken to baroque extremes, frequently bordering on the ridiculous. Suspicion in the giallo is ubiquitous because *everyone* is hiding something. The general tone is one of moral decay and cynicism, with ever more convoluted plots emphasising morbid details in a Janus-faced world of paranoia and betrayal. The killer, often either masked and gloved or replaced by a proxy camera, flits with credulity-straining ease from crime scene to blood-caked crime scene, whilst reliable plot information is obstinately deferred; the scriptwriter will try just about anything to thwart our attempts at deduction (and the giallo is not above cheating either, as devotees of classic detective fiction will find to their frustration). Armchair psychoanalysts too are baited by the genre's habits; the killer's motivation is usually as tenuous as his methods are elaborate.

The horror ingredient comes from the giallo's frankly perverse dwelling upon violence, and the voyeur in us is likely to be well served by a similarly blatant dose of sleazy sex. Women are by far the most likely victims on the giallo hit-list, but the form's overall misanthropy (and desperation to out-manoeuvre its audience) throws up a significant number of female killers too. Thanks to the opportunities offered by this stylistically over-heated genre, it can be a port of call to both the driven mavericks and the dull misogynists of Italian cinema.

The roots go back to thirties Italy, where the word giallo – meaning 'yellow' – was applied to popular crime fiction, published in distinctive yellow covers. Bracketed as giallo by publication in Italy were such diverse literary figures as Agatha Christie and Cornell Woolrich, a factor that continues to cause argument about what precisely does and does not constitute a giallo film. A key cinematic influence on the form was Alfred Hitchcock, although the importance of his 1960 shocker, *Psycho* (which, along with Clouzot's *Les Diaboliques*, stimulated Hammer's run of murder thrillers) can be overstated. *Psycho*'s biggest influence on giallo manners was its show-stopping shower murder; Hitchcock suddenly

facing page:
The Belgian poster for Fulci's brilliant 1972 thriller *Don't Torture a Duckling*, released to French-speaking countries as *The Long Night of Exorcism*. This alternative title circulated in English-language publications for several years in the early 1980s, creating the mistaken impression that it was a different film altogether.

below:
Erotic goings-on at Julia Durer's London flat in *A Lizard in a Woman's Skin* (1971).

right and below:
Beautiful admat artwork for Mario Bava's seminal *Blood and Black Lace* (1964). Note the chilling matter-of-factness of the French title! An English print bearing the title *Six Women for the Murderer* was prepared for export although it subsequently became better known under its American title *Blood and Black Lace*; the American print was eventually released in Britain.

bottom:
Another woman for the murderer; death strikes once again in *Blood and Black Lace*.

pushed his unsuspecting audience into treacherous new territory where the most brutal acts could occur. The rest of the film is less pertinent here; if anything Hitchcock's later classic, *Frenzy* (1972), is the closest in spirit to the Italian thrillers, and by then the genre was already at its peak.

The giallo soon developed its own stylistic trademarks, going much further than American or British thrillers in the presentation of human malice, sleazy eroticism and the blatant use of cinematic technique. The kinetic style, cynicism and audience manipulation typical of Hitchcock was important; but whereas he employed narrative devices as elaborate blinds and bluffs to subvert the sometimes pedantic logic of Hollywood scripts, the better Italian directors turned the image itself into an aspect of perverse contemplation. Nowhere was this more extraordinarily achieved than in Mario Bava's *Blood and Black Lace*, (1964); perhaps the most stunning Italian thriller of the 1960s, it is also the best example of this primarily visual narrative style. Bava's earlier film *The Evil Eye* (1963) (the Italian title – *La ragazza che sapeva troppo* – was a nod to Alfred Hitchcock's *The Man Who Knew Too Much*) is generally accepted as the first example of the giallo form, but *Blood and Black Lace* eclipses it. An Italian/West German co-production, it glancingly resembles the German-produced krimis, crime thrillers derived from the novels of Edgar Wallace. West Germany was in the grip of 'Wallace-mania' at the time, and the producers wanted a suitable contribution from Bava. However, the relatively staid, b/w krimis paled in comparison to the Italian director's chillingly violent, colour-drenched delirium.

Playing with the audience in a daringly avant-garde manner, Bava saturated the sets with garish, ominous colour lighting, cluttered the *mise-en-scène* with antique bric-a-brac and scanned across the mayhem with grandiose, unmotivated camera movements. The viewer finds his eyes almost skidding along the surface of the screen (if you'll forgive the image), and the plot – a complicated bit of frippery – is nearly lost to the delirious appreciation of spectacle. Even now it remains an incredible experience; oppressive yet carnivalesque. When, for a couple of brief scenes, we see characters outdoors in daylight locations we feel disorientated; because the natural light of day has been usurped by a new dominion – of glowering reds, shimmering greens, arctic blues and jostling hordes of deep shadows. It's a shame then that this bold and innovative Italian's example was so infrequently followed up by subsequent giallo practitioners (although Fulci at least would later express a debt of gratitude).[1]

Bava may have started the ball rolling, and provided the genre with its first masterpiece, but *Blood and Black Lace* spawned few sixties imitators compared to the swollen ranks of the peplum and western; the glory days of the giallo wouldn't really arrive until the turn of the decade. Fulci was one of the earliest to feel the magnetic attraction of the format when he made *One on Top of the Other* in 1969, even though it was another proto-giallo mystery, Romolo Guerrieri's *The Sweet Body of Deborah* (1968), that stimulated his imagination. Between Bava's classic in 1964 and Fulci's initial foray a few such thrillers did crop up, but they were so varied in style that it's a dubious pursuit to identify them as part of a trend: Dino Tavella's *The Embalmer* (1965) mixes morbid horror and thriller motifs; Luigi Bazzoni and Franco Rossellini's *La donna del lago* (1965) is a haunting and hallucinatory giallo-inflected thriller shot beautifully in black and white; Ernesto Gastaldi and Vittorio Salerno's *Libido* (1965), Lionello De Felice and Elio Scardamaglia's *The Murder Clinic* (1966) and Angelo Dorigo's *Assassino senza volto* (1967) are Gothic horror/murder mystery hybrids; Giulio Questi's *Death Laid an Egg* (1967) disobeys so many film-making rules it probably deserves to be considered *sui generis* but is at least tenuously a murder thriller; Tinto Brass's *Col cuore in gola* (1967) is an attempt at an arty giallo floundering under the desire to emulate Jean-Luc Godard; Mino Guerrini's *Date for a Murder* (1967) is a flashily filmed thriller which teeters at the edge of the spy subgenre; Massimo Dallamano's *A Black Veil for Lisa* (1968) is an early culprit in the 'endless police-investigation' stakes; while Antonio Margheriti's *The Young, the Evil and the Savage* (1968), though facetious in tone, anticipates several trademarks of the mature giallo form, including questions of gender surrounding the identification of a black gloved killer.

Giallo Frenzy

Things didn't really take off though until the format was fuel-injected by a brilliant young newcomer, Dario Argento. His powerful, inventive debut, *The Bird with the Crystal Plumage* (1970), gave Italian directors plenty to think about, both thematically and commercially. A bravura use of subjective camera to menace victims, corkscrew plotting, and the electrifying tension of Argento's murder scenes, refined the giallo style into something sharper, more menacing and contemporary. He was in real terms the prime mover in the field; establishing hallmarks that would influence the best efforts of others and escape the prosaic ambitions of the rest. (The commercial consideration is important – innovative it may have been but sadly *Blood and Black Lace* made little impact on the Italian box-office, netting a lowly 123 million lira. Argento's debut was a definite hit, making 1,650 million lira on its home release, a sum that hiked the film up towards the commercial league occupied by Sergio Leone, for whose 1969 epic *Once Upon a Time in the West* Argento – with Bernardo Bertolucci – had co-written the screenplay.)

This box-office killing was the signal that unleashed the giallo hordes – soon the Italian film market was awash with densely-plotted miasmas of murder; some equipped with style to burn, others disappearing into an unappetizing stodge of ludicrous red herrings and stupid motivations. Fulci's contributions to this burgeoning cycle were definitely among the former category, as were such gems as *The Fifth Cord* (1971) by Luigi Bazzoni, *Crimes of the Black Cat* (1972) by Sergio Pastore, *Short Night of Glass Dolls* (1971) by Aldo Lado and *Plot of Fear* (1976) by Paolo Cavara. On a tackier but no less enjoyable note, the overheated excesses of the giallo style offered plenty of scope for campy melodrama (whether intentional or not): *In the Folds of the Flesh* (1970) by Sergio Bergonzelli, *Why Those Strange Drops of Blood on the Body of Jennifer?* (1972) by Giuliano Carnimeo, *In the Eye of the Hurricane* (1971) by José María Forqué and *L'occhio dietro la parete* (1977) by Giuliano Petrelli are all of a glossy, cheerfully tasteless persuasion, depicting maniacal disruptions in the lives of the sleazoid rich.

above: Dario Argento's first film, *The Bird with the Crystal Plumage* demonstrated many of the women-in-peril motifs picked up by later giallo films, not to mention the American slasher films of the late 1970s and early '80s.

Fulci wasn't the only director to specialize: others such as Sergio Martino, Armando Crispino and Massimo Dallamano demonstrated a taste for the slashing blades and sexual heat of the format. Martino's numerous efforts include sexy giallo frolics (*Gently Before She Dies*, 1972) and taut, salacious thrillers (*Torso*, 1973), whilst Crispino's enjoyable contributions are disorganized but compellingly odd (*The Etruscan Kills Again*, 1972, and *Autopsy*, 1975). Massimo Dallamano's *What Have You Done to Solange?* (1972) and *What Have They Done to Your Daughters?* (1974) also stand out, although they tend to over-emphasize police procedure.

The most dedicated *gialliste* of the period, perhaps best described as a poor man's Lucio Fulci, was the prolific exploitation director Umberto Lenzi (born 6th August 1931). It's interesting to note that Lenzi's career intersected with Fulci's on several occasions (their first association was on the production of *San Remo: la grande sfida* in 1960) although his achievements are mostly of a cruder calibre. Unlike Fulci, Lenzi concentrated heavily on pseudo-historical actioners during the sixties (involving characters like Sandokan the Great, Robin Hood, Katherine of Russia, Zorro and the inevitable Maciste), before amplifying his talents – as Fulci had done – with a clutch of satisfying thrillers: *Paranoia* (1969), *So Sweet... So Perverse* (1969), *A Quiet Place to Kill* (1970) and *Knife of Ice* (1972). All four featured American *Baby Doll* actress Carroll Baker as the wealthy, neurotic focus of the supporting cast's malice. These well-mounted mysteries combine a skilful, manipulative approach to plotting with an emphasis on the suffering of their endlessly troubled leading lady. *Seven Blood-Stained Orchids* (1972) continued the director's run of thrillers, this time with *One on Top of the Other* star Marisa Mell as the

bottom left: Umberto Lenzi's *Paranoia* played another of the giallo's favourite games – the torment and degradation of the idle (preferably female) rich.

below: US artwork for a reissue of Dario Argento's *Deep Red* (also known there as *The Hatchet Murders*).

above:
French artwork for Bava's masterful murder-thriller *A Bay of Blood.*

female focus. The Fulci connection was also amplified by the presence of Roberto Gianviti as co-scripter (Gianviti, responsible for co-writing *One on Top of the Other*, *A Lizard in a Woman's Skin* and *Beatrice Cenci*, worked with Fulci on *Don't Torture a Duckling* the same year). Unfortunately, Lenzi failed to maintain his aptitude for the giallo, blotting his filmography with a couple of amusing but wretched efforts that exemplify the fag-end of the Italian thriller – *Spasmo* (1974) and *Eyeball* (1974).

In the early 1970s a genre known as the *poliziesco or poliziotteschi* (influenced by American hits like *Dirty Harry*, *Bullitt* and *The French Connection*) embraced the police procedural aspect of the giallo but replaced murder and mystery with cop shoot-outs, car chases, vigilantism and police corruption. Meanwhile the giallo hovered at the brink of sexploitation in such erotically fixated films as *Cold-Blooded Beast* aka *Slaughter Hotel* (Fernando Di Leo, 1971), *Amuck!* (Silvio Amadio, 1971), *So Sweet, So Dead* aka *The Slasher Is the Sex Maniac* (Roberto Montero, 1972), *Strip Nude for Your Killer* (Andrea Bianchi, 1975) and *Giallo a Venezia* (Mario Landi, 1979).

Dario Argento continued to cut a swathe through much of the competition with a series of brutal, byzantine thrillers: *The Cat O'Nine Tails* (1971) and *Four Flies on Grey Velvet* (1971) were the work of an inventive, technology-addicted aesthete already tiring of straightforward thriller mechanisms and seeking an escape into weird pseudo-science and abnormal psychology. The transcendant title in his early career was *Deep Red* (1975); a jaw-dropping theatre of cruelty and the director's first masterpiece. Perhaps more than any other film in the giallo tradition, it takes the bloodied gauntlet thrown down by Mario Bava's *Blood and Black Lace* and achieves an even greater level of intensity. Art design turned positively fetishistic, and the plot showed reason threatened on all sides by parapsychology, synchronicity, madness, cognitive delirium and (for Argento) the first whisperings of the supernatural. *Deep Red* is an exotic mutant strain of giallo, a deliberately jarring assault on the senses: as demonstrated by the way it swaps the previous thrillers' (highly effective) Ennio Morricone scores for a blend of chilling string/percussion orchestration (from Giorgio Gaslini) and supercharged high-volume progressive rock (from Italian band Goblin).

What the best of these Italian films lacked in sense or character depth they more than made up for in dazzling displays of technique, turning sinister what could have been merely prosaic. In the hands of Lucio Fulci and Dario Argento, the giallo was virtually a horror film; packed with narrative convolution to be sure, but also revelling in purely grotesque and disturbing images in a way that blurred the edges of the two genres.

The saleability these gialli enjoyed would have been unthinkable in the British film industry. Figures for the early 1970s illustrate the strength of the Italian film market in comparison to the UK. In 1972, Italy's total population was around 54.8 million. Cinema admissions for that year totalled 553.6 million, meaning that on average each citizen attended the cinema ten times a year! Compare that with the figures for the UK in 1972: the population was approximately 55.7 million, almost the same as Italy; but with cinema admissions reaching a mere 156.6 million, the average number of visits for the year per head of population was only 2.81 (figures source: S.I.A.E. Italy). Small wonder that the Italian industry, with its propensity for plagiarism, imitation, pastiche and parody of whatever was popular, was able to flourish on such a hyperactive scale. Added to this fertile situation, Italy's state television service, RAI (who operated a monopoly before de-regulation in 1976), were required by law to co-operate with the film industry.

below:
Pornography and horror are the only genres where it's important to specify precisely what you mean by 'double penetration'...

Was Mario Bava Jason's father?

Eventually the giallo settled down into a stylistic rut. By the late seventies the trend had been exhausted, in Italy at least, with only Dario Argento capable of transcending its clichés with his superb *Tenebrae* (1982); a recursive narrative about a writer of murder thrillers that both rewrites the genre's sexual politics and comments on its roots. However, reverberations were still to be felt in the development of the American slasher films of the late seventies and early eighties, thanks once again to the influence of giallo patriarch Mario Bava. *Ecologia del delitto/A Bay of Blood* (1971), the most gruesome work of all by the influential director, was released to the US drive-ins and grindhouses three times in the mid-seventies. At first it was cut to receive an 'R' rating and re-titled as *Carnage*, then as *Twitch of the Death Nerve*: but it did even better when unscrupulous distributors Hallmark restored the missing slaughter scenes and changed its title again to *Last House on the Left Part II*, enticing audiences with the promise of more sick thrills in the style of Wes Craven's milestone sex-and-sadism opus (itself a Hallmark release). Sean Cunningham, producer of the real *The Last House on the Left* (1972), later 'borrowed' two distinctively outlandish Bava murder scenes from *A Bay of Blood* (including a couple having sex being impaled on a spear) for his low-budget mega-hit sequel *Friday the 13th Part 2* (1981). Cunningham's chief inspiration for the first *Friday the 13th* in 1980 was undoubtedly John Carpenter's hugely successful *Halloween* (1978) but Carpenter's film was an almost bloodless exercise in traditional suspense – not a gaping flesh-wound in sight. Cunningham's old buddies at Hallmark had financial input to the *Friday the 13th* deal too, so it's not much of a stretch to speculate that Bava's film, with its string of showy, vicious murders set around a moody lakeland location, might have figured in the planning of one of the highest-yielding cash-cows in exploitation cinema history.

There were plenty more Italian gialli released on the American exploitation circuit during the seventies. Hucksterish US distributors soon realised there was money to be made in the wake of home-grown independents like *Night of the Living Dead* and *The Last House on the Left*. Cheap, bloodthirsty horror films, though generally despised by Hollywood and the mainstream press, were doing just fine, both in the big cities where high levels of blue-collar custom kept the grindhouses open and down in the southern states where the drive-ins flourished on a similar basis. Enterprising distributors found the parallel excesses of the Italian horror/thriller genres a handy (and relatively cheap) source of shock-milking revenue. They could be marketed aggressively under lurid new titles, with attention-grabbing ad-copy that promised ever more traumatic sights in store for the curious; and of course the Italian films tended to stir plentiful nudity into the equation too.

Among those to play the US independent circuit were Sergio Martino's *Torso* and Umberto Lenzi's *Eyeball* (both from Joseph Brenner associates, who regularly re-jigged Italian films for US release), Silvio Amadio's *Amuck!* (as *Maniac Mansion* from Group 1, who also handled Fulci's *The Psychic*), Fernando Di Leo's *Slaughter Hotel* (Hallmark again), Roberto Montero's *The Slasher Is the Sex Maniac* (released a second time with hardcore porn inserts and re-titled *Penetration* by exploitation veteran William Mishkin), Emilio P. Miraglia's *The Night Evelyn Came Out of the Grave* (1971, released by Phase One) and *The Lady in Red Kills Seven Times* (1972 by Tower Film Corp.), and Dario Argento's *Deep Red* (re-titled by Howard Mahler Films as *The Hatchet Murders*). Lucio Fulci had the good fortune to deal with the more reputable American International Pictures for the US release of *A Lizard in a Woman's Skin*. Even they could be mercenary with foreign properties, though, often going so far as to re-score films as well as re-titling them (a practise which resulted in Bava's *Baron Blood* wilting under a strident Les Baxter score and *Black Sabbath* having its dialogue changed to remove a lesbian subtext). AIP actually released *A Lizard in a Woman's Skin* twice, once with the original lavish title intact, and then again with the terse, punchy and post-Hitchcockian *Schizoid*.

Once the body-count formula Bava bequeathed to *Friday the 13th* had been established, and the pros and cons of a rural versus urban setting weighed up by competitors (urban proving more popular), a steady stream of mysterious killers hacked their way through early eighties horror. America was having its own giallo-style craze with studio-backed stalk-and-slash films like *Night School* (aka *Terror Eyes*), *He Knows You're Alone*, *Happy Birthday to Me* and *The Prowler* (aka *Rosemary's Killer*) all aiming to slice off a bit of the low-budget action during 1980. Some slashers provided sleazier thrills, though, and these tended to feature the killer onscreen from the word go, without the element of mystery surrounding his identity. Prominent examples of this nastier strain include *Maniac* (1980) by William Lustig, *Don't Answer the Phone!* (1980) by Robert Hammer and *Don't Go in the House* (1980) by Joseph Ellison. (Interestingly, although the mystery-slashers occasionally revealed the killer to be a woman, thus following the lead of numerous gialli, these psycho-portrait slashers did not: the only exception I can think of being Abel Ferrara's avowedly 'feminist' *Ms.45* in 1980. This would seem to suggest that the main reason for having a female killer was to exploit the element of surprise.) One of the grisliest of all these psycho-portrait efforts was actually directed by an Italian living in the States: *Nightmare* (aka *Nightmares in a Damaged Brain*) was made by Romano Scavolini, a one-time *enfant-terrible* of Italian cinema whose lauded work for TV included a 1966 documentary about Søren Kierkegaard!

Into this fevered atmosphere Lucio Fulci essayed two further giallo films, both of them set in New York City; *The New York Ripper* (1982) and *Murder-Rock Dancing Death* (1984). The former is perhaps the most horrific and disturbing film of Fulci's career and is considered at length in Chapter Seven. The latter bears evidence of Fulci's wavering talents during the mid-to-late eighties and is also discussed in Chapter Seven, along with the other problematic films of that period.

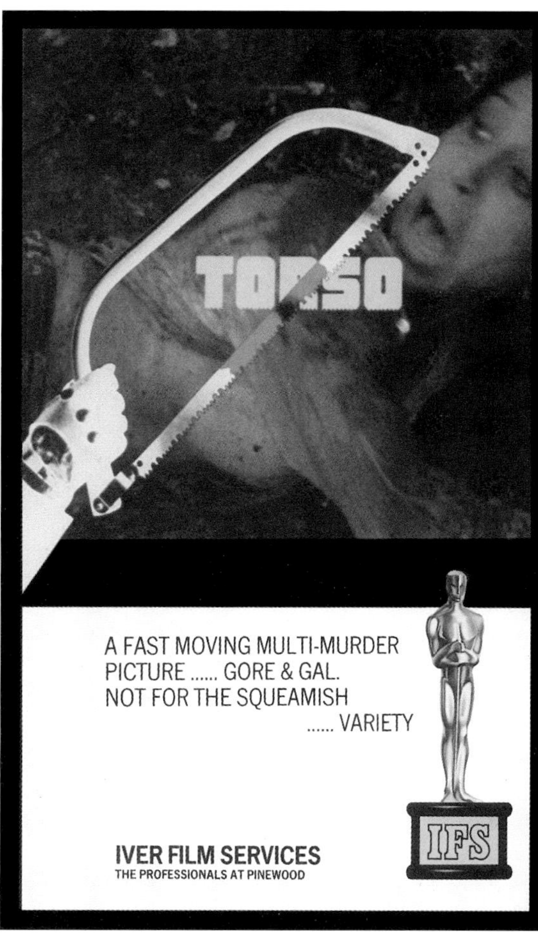

left: Sergio Martino's well crafted 1973 thriller *I corpi presentano tracce di violenza carnale* (which translates as 'The Body Bears Traces of Carnal Violence') underwent considerable truncation for its US release as *Torso*. The British video release artwork suggests – rather misleadingly – a hard gore film.

below: Claudio Volonté as Simon, illegitimate heir to the eponymous bay; just one of the murderous characters in Mario Bava's *A Bay of Blood*, caught up in a chain reaction of slaughter.

bottom: Fernando Di Leo's 1971 giallo *La bestia uccide a sangue freddo* was opportunistically marketed to remind audiences of the Richard Speck killings, re-titled as *Slaughter Hotel*.

Giallo alla Fulci

Lucio Fulci's first giallo, 1969's *Una sull'altra/One on Top of the Other*, is a brooding mixture of tension and melancholy, perhaps suffering in retrospect from a lack of violent or shocking scenes but expertly handled, with a sleazy air of perversity. The horrific pre-occupations of later work are present in just a handful of brief scenes, but a disturbing fatalism makes this blend of mystery and malice Fulci's first classic. It also shows the beginning of his adept handling of technical matters, demonstrating visual imagination through startling focus on unusual details; something that would inform all of his best work.

Fulci cited the 1968 film *The Sweet Body of Deborah* – directed by Romolo Guerrieri[2] and starring Carroll Baker and Jean Sorel – as an influence, calling it the first giallo.[3] Although his statement is an historical error, the remark suggests his interest was strongly piqued by the film. *The Sweet Body of Deborah* starred Sorel as a person suspected of murder struggling to prove his innocence, and when Fulci set about making *One on Top of the Other* he was to cast him in the lead role. But if the stylish air of murder, duplicity and romance in Guerrieri's film suggested a change of emphasis to Fulci – then embroiled in yet another Franco & Ciccio flick – the eventual outcome would owe as much to Hitchcock as it would to Guerrieri's drama.

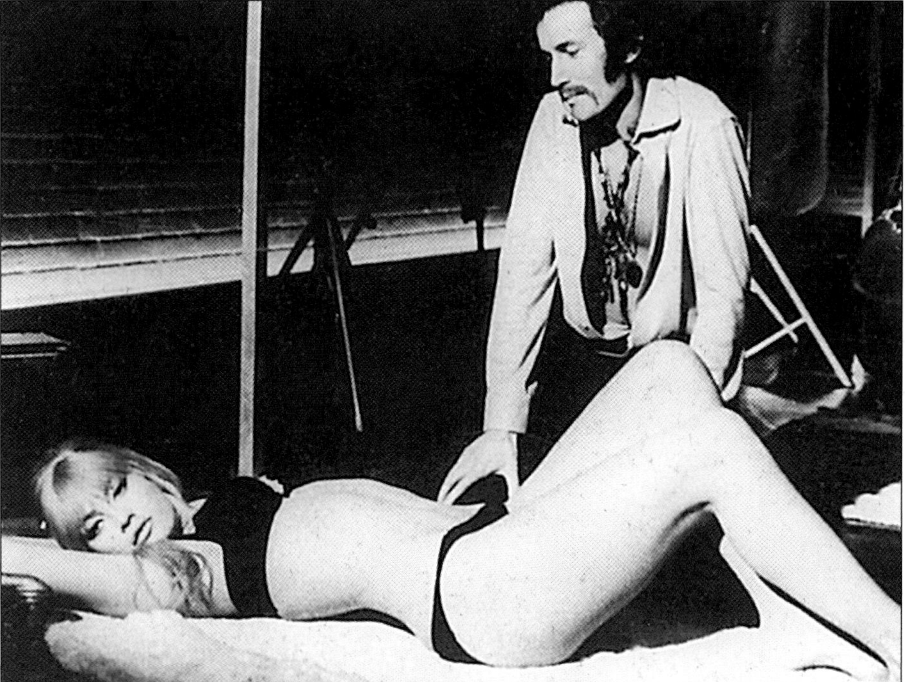

Both *The Sweet Body of Deborah* and *One on Top of the Other* are more concerned with the entanglements of sinister romance, popularized by Hitchcock's *Suspicion* (1941) and *Vertigo* (1958), than the murderous nightmares of Mario Bava's *Blood and Black Lace*. Fulci plunders twists from *Vertigo* and builds a suspenseful climax around a character's imminent demise in the San Quentin gas chamber that draws heavily on Hitchcock's approach to audience manipulation. In fact, if the giallo film is considered as principally a *murder* thriller with a parade of multiple victims, Fulci's drama barely enters the category. (As already noted, though, the giallo's original literary roots are something of a mishmash anyway, and the application of the term is fraught with ambiguities). A possible literary influence on the story is Cornell Woolrich's novel *Phantom Lady*, which also featured a race-against-time to save an innocent man condemned to death for the murder of his wife.

For his first venture into thriller territory, Fulci was able to call upon the assistance of Spanish-born photographer Alejandro Ulloa, whose efforts lift this melodrama in a way the sometimes over-leisurely pacing cannot. He shot the film beautifully; luminous clarity for interiors, sombre, rain-clouded moodiness for the often spectacular San Francisco-lensed exteriors. (Ulloa's best genre work prior to *One on Top of the Other* was for Spanish director Jess Franco, on his 1965 horror film *The Diabolical Dr. Z.*)

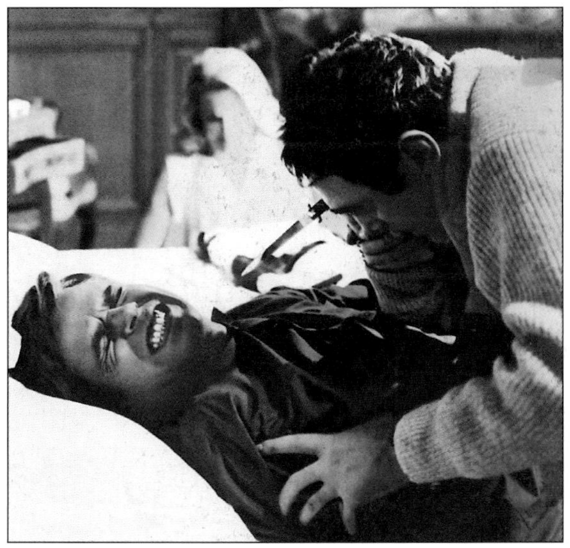

After a diversion into historical drama (1969's *Beatrice Cenci* – see Chapter Five), *Una lucertola con la pelle di donna/A Lizard in a Woman's Skin* (1971) showed Fulci's taste for violence and sexual explicitness increasing, along with his visual flamboyance. Although *Lizard* is densely plotted to the point of absurdity, it contains many stunning sequences constructed with an eye for the weird and hallucinatory. Again, one of the key strengths of the film was the photography, this time by Luigi Kuveiller. Kuveiller, later to shoot *The New York Ripper*, applies a full panoply of distorting devices – wide-angle lenses, jittery, hand-held work and numerous other techniques – which make the film an almost psychedelic affair at times. Kuveiller and Fulci also milk classic scenes from a wide array of well-chosen locations, most impressively at the deserted Alexandra Palace in North London. Whilst the mood of the film may be influenced by Antonioni's pessimistic treatment of swinging London in *Blow-Up* (1966), the plot is less derivative than Fulci's previous giallo, and the level of violence is much higher.

American interest in Fulci's work really began here, with the 1973 releases of *One on Top of the Other* and particularly *A Lizard in a Woman's Skin* gaining appreciative coverage in American movie bible *Variety*. The former was perhaps damned with faint praise: *"If one is willing to overlook the script's implausibilities and just watch the scenery – geographical and sexual – it's a relaxing way to spend an hour and a half"*. (It would be a long time before another Lucio Fulci film could be called 'relaxing'!) *Lizard*'s reception was far more positive: *"...an unusually well-mounted suspense thriller that should draw an audience from among filmgoers on the prowl for sensational stimulation"*. Going on to commend Fulci's imaginative staging of *"the surrealist fantasy of dreams and mental derangement"*, the reviewer draws particular attention to the *"first rate technical credits"*, principally Kuveiller's photography, Roman Calatayud's interior sets and the Ennio Morricone score.[4] All of which must have contributed to the success of the film; it was one of Fulci's top earners, and entered US distribution through American International Pictures, who re-titled it as the terse but genre-specific *Schizoid*. Particularly tantalizing to fans of the film is this assertion terminating *Variety*'s review: *"press book indicates AIP will be able to jack*

facing page:
Jennifer O'Neill's terrible fate unfolds in Fulci's labyrinthine thriller *The Psychic.*

above:
Marisa Mell as Monica Weston reveals her charms to photographer Larry (Jean Sobieski), in Fulci's first great thriller *One on Top of the Other.*

bottom left:
Jean Sorel pays heavily for interfering with *The Sweet Body of Deborah.*

below top:
Cary Grant menacing his paranoiac wife Joan Fontaine, in Hitchcock's classic *Suspicion* (1941).

below bottom:
Luigi Kuveiller, director of photography on *A Lizard in a Woman's Skin* (and the later *The New York Ripper*).

above:
Rich, neurotic repressed lesbian Carol Hammond (Florinda Bolkan) is taunted by her provocative neighbour Julia Durer (Anita Strindberg). Note the PR distributor's addition to Ms. Strindberg's wardrobe!

up screen time with extra erotic-porno footage self-censored in the Italo version. The orgy itself could run at least five minutes longer in more permissive markets." With a quoted running time of 99 minutes, one wonders what the truth of this rather exaggerated statement was, once the film festival buyers had calmed down. No longer version of this film with "extra erotic porno footage" has turned up to my knowledge, but what *is* there to see is impressive enough.

Too impressive, in fact, for some contemporary viewers. Fulci had called upon the services of special effects designer Carlo Rambaldi for certain sequences, including a bat attack and an encounter with a roomful of eviscerated dogs, bodies clamped open for medical experiments. The scene demanded that actress Florinda Bolkan stagger into the closed wing of a private sanatorium, only to be confronted with this gruesome sight, fainting in horror when she realises the dogs are actually still alive. To achieve the fearsome spectacle Fulci required, Rambaldi employed puppeteering and prosthetic techniques well in advance of their general exposure in hit films like *The Exorcist*, *Alien* and *The Thing*. By using inflatable 'bladder' devices, the heart and entrails of the flayed dog puppets could be made to pulsate, resembling living organs. Italian audiences were shocked and suddenly Fulci found himself on the sharp end of a legal indictment for cruelty to animals! Things looked bleak for a while as he stared a two-year prison sentence in the face, but all was not lost. Much to the director's relief, Rambaldi was able to retrieve one of the prosthetic model dogs he'd made for the film and produce it in court.

Fulci's most outstanding film of the period is *Non si sevizia un paperino/Don't Torture a Duckling* (1972), a film said to have been 'banned' at one time in Italy due to a scene where Barbara Bouchet exposes herself nude to a young boy. (Fulci speculated that the controversy was a politically motivated response to his previous film, *The Eroticist*; one particular Italian politician had apparently seen it as a scathing attack on himself.) A step on from the convoluted narratives of the earlier thrillers, with outstanding photography and landmark moments of brutal violence, it demonstrates what was fast becoming a characteristically pessimistic world-view. Here we see perhaps the most advanced degree of innovation exhibited by Fulci during his tenure as thriller specialist. The film bears little relation to any of the previously cited models, which makes it impossible to dismiss Fulci as a mere copyist. Despite their almost ubiquitous sway elsewhere in the giallo field, none of Argento's three films to that date had any significant influence on the content or style of this excellent movie (although the eccentric title sounds – along with *Lizard* – like a commercial nod to

right:
Florinda Bolkan again, suffering a savage chain-whipping attack in *Don't Torture a Duckling.*

below:
Stanley Baker in the Hammer Studio's war film *Yesterday's Enemy*, directed by Val Guest in 1959.

Argento's *Bird/Cat/Flies* triptych). Looking back at the 1970s, at the frantic proliferation of giallo clichés and sexploitation titillation, it's hard to see any convenient source of ideas that could have been plundered by Fulci and Gianviti. The film is that rare thing for the period; a highly imaginative, beautifully realised thriller without obvious precedent.

Don't Torture a Duckling has been criticized in some quarters for painting a bigoted picture of rural life. This is debatable, but Fulci was certainly not alone in depicting the South of Italy as rife with outmoded attitudes and intolerant violence. The perceived dichotomy between educated, sophisticated Northern Italy and the corrupt and threatening South is one which occurs frequently in Italian films. In Fulci's favour is the fact that numerous ironies accumulate around the idea of 'sophisticated' city-dwellers, whose detachment from the problems of rural life is pointedly attacked.

After a pause of five years, during which he essayed contributions to diverse genres, Fulci returned to the thriller format with *Sette note in nero/The Psychic* (1977). This sombre tale of a psychic who seems to have mentally 'witnessed' a perplexing murder is often unfairly dismissed, although the violent prologue (actually a reprise of a similar effect from *Don't Torture a Duckling*) was enough to convince *Zombie Flesh-Eaters* producer Fabrizio De Angelis that Fulci was the best director for the job. It's another well-shot film; the star – Jennifer O'Neill – gives a credibly nervous performance, and the central plot twist is reasonably well disguised until late in the day. *The Psychic*'s only drawbacks are a perhaps too-leisurely pace and the repeated shots of the heroine's eyes in tight close-up, which proved irritating to some viewers and critics. However, its failure to generate box-office success is inexplicable.

International Names

The four films discussed in this chapter are notable for the presence of high calibre international performers, including Stanley Baker, Leo Genn, Florinda Bolkan and Jennifer O'Neill. Whilst the roles don't always stretch their thespian talents very far, such actors lent the films a certain gravity. Their mainstream connections helped too; Italian movies often gained extra finance through co-production agreements with other countries. The contracts would usually demand the presence of a recognizable star, or at least a familiar face, for the international market. American producer David O. Selznick had once offered Vittorio De Sica co-production money if he would star Cary Grant in his next film, *Bicycle Thieves*. De Sica declined and cast a non-professional instead, but others were happy to accept the conditions foreign co-producers required, in return for their cash. Looking back, some of these stipulations can seem obtuse; the actors favoured may have passed into historical neglect, chosen because of one or two transient continental hits.

Stanley Baker, the top-line star of *A Lizard in a Woman's Skin*, was born in Wales on 28 February 1928 and died, of lung cancer, on 28 June 1976. He made his name in the fifties and sixties with roles emphasizing his hard, contemptuous looks and suppressed aggression. His persona became gradually more sophisticated, thanks to strong performances in three Joseph Losey films. One of them, *Blind Date* (1959), in which he plays the stubborn Inspector Morgan (with a cold), seems to have inflected his appearance as the stone-faced, whistling Inspector Corvin for Fulci. He essayed just one excursion into the horror genre with a short adaptation of Poe's *The Tell-Tale Heart* (J.B. Williams, 1953) but made three films for the Hammer Studio: a murder drama, *The Rossiter Case* (Francis Searle, 1951), a war film, *Yesterday's Enemy* (Val Guest, 1959), and a crime thriller, *Hell Is a City* (Val Guest, 1960). His other Italian credits were few; *La ragazza con la pistola* (Mario Monicelli, 1968) and *Zorro* (Duccio Tessari, 1975). After *Lizard*, Baker became a familiar face to British television viewers, taking a leading role in the popular drama series *How Green Was My Valley*. He was knighted in 1976, just a month before his death.

Leo Genn, who played Carol's misguided father in *A Lizard in a Woman's Skin*, was born in London on 9 August 1905 and died on 26 January 1978 after a varied, distinguished life. He gave up a law career to pursue acting, beginning on the stage in 1930. His first credit of interest here was *The Squeaker* (William K. Howard, 1937) from a story by Edgar Wallace, the German adaptations of whose work would play a formative role in the development of the Italian giallo film. Genn's thespian activities were combined with true life dramatics during World War II when he served as a colonel, though he was granted leave to act in ten films between 1939-45. After the war he worked with the prosecution at the Nuremberg and Belsen War Crimes trials. Genn's on-screen persona was distinguished and gentlemanly in the classic British style, and his refined English tones were in great demand for documentary narration. A part in Laurence Olivier's *Henry V* (1944) led to an upswing in film and stage roles both here and in the USA. The majority of his horror/fantastique credits are concentrated in the '60s: *Dr. Mabuse's Rays of Death* (Hugo Fregonese, 1964), one of producer Harry Alan Towers's stabs at *Ten Little Indians* (George Pollock, 1965), *Circus of Fear* (John Moxey, 1966), and *The Bloody Judge* (Jess Franco, 1970). He also appeared in two films for British horror specialist Pete Walker: in *Die Screaming, Marianne* (1970) he reprised his old occupation to play a particularly sleazy character, a corrupt judge with incestuous longings; whilst in the brilliant *Frightmare* (1974), he took a small guest role as a psychiatrist.

Many actors appearing in Fulci's gialli worked maybe once or twice with internationally famous directors but never emerged into fully fledged stardom. Fans of genre cinema often celebrate such figures, appreciating the highs *and* lows of their careers, admiring their dogged persistence almost as much as their brief blasts of talent. Some actors, like Jean Sorel, gained employment in Fulci's films for the very impassiveness and emotional torpor that may have killed their mainstream careers. Sorel, born in Marseilles on 25 September 1934, made his screen debut in 1959 with the ultra-obscure *J'irai cracher sur vos tombes* directed by Michel Gast, before going on to appear in a spate of 'prestige' engagements in the sixties; from Yves Allégret's adaptation of Emile Zola's novel *Germinal* (1963) and Roger Vadim's sexually souped-up version of *La Ronde* (1964) to more successful works like Luchino Visconti's *Vaghe stelle dell'orsa* (1965) and Luis Buñuel's *Belle de Jour* (1967).

Reviewers, though, tended to find Sorel inexpressive in these settings and his career instead shifted gear into thriller territory, where more often than not he was required simply to provide rakish, playboy good looks. Success with *The Sweet Body of Deborah* by Romolo Guerrieri (1968) propelled him into Fulci's first two gialli, and then on into assignments for Umberto Lenzi (*A Quiet Place to Kill*, 1970), Aldo Lado (*Short Night of Glass Dolls*, 1971), José María Forqué (*In the Eye of the Hurricane*, 1971) and Eloy de la Iglesia (*Clockwork Terror*, 1973). Now in his eighties, Sorel remains intermittently active, having recently appeared in the Italian mini-series *Una buona stagione* (2014) and the French Holocaust drama *L'origine de la violence* (2016).

The Psychic's Jennifer O'Neill has become a born-again Christian and motivational speaker, as reflected in her choice of roles since 1994: a faith-based

above:
Locandina for *Don't Torture a Duckling.* Note that the artwork de-emphasises the word 'un'. A possible reason for this is that Fulci actually intended the film's Italian title to be 'Don't Torture Donald Duck'! 'Paperino' is the name given to the popular Disney character in Italy. Obviously, such a title would meet with a frosty reception at the Disney Corporation, hence the amended title; 'Un Paperino' means simply 'a duckling'...

below:
Leo Genn, the distinguished English gentleman actor who plays Florinda Bolkan's lawyer father in *A Lizard in a Woman's Skin,* was no stranger to risqué material, as shown by this poster for the 1960 British crime flick *Too Hot to Handle.*

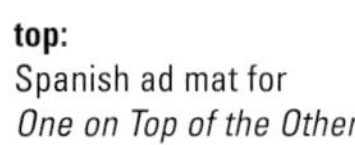

top:
Spanish ad mat for *One on Top of the Other.*

middle:
Elsa Martinelli remains aloof at the strip-joint.

above and right:
Monica Weston (Marisa Mell) performs her erotic dance show for an audience of West Coast sophisticates at The Roaring Twenties nightclub – *One on Top of the Other.*

sci-fi film *Time Changer* (2002), in which a bible professor from 1890 time-travels into the godless future of 2002 and witnesses such horrors as an unmarried couple kissing on television; a Billy Graham biopic, *Billy: The Early Years* (2008) starring Armie Hammer, a 'don't let them ban Christmas' tub-thumper called *Last Ounce of Courage* (2012) and *I'm Not Ashamed* (2016), a Christian polemic about the Columbine massacre.

Marisa Mell's starring role in *One on Top of the Other* followed just a year after she wowed audiences in Mario Bava's wonderful *Danger: Diabolik*, playing alongside John Phillip Law's eponymous supervillain as the leggier half of the most glamorous criminal duo of sixties cinema. Mell (born Marlies Moitzi in Graz on 24 February 1939) first appeared on the big screen in 1954 in the Austrian-made *Das Licht der Liebe*, and for the next ten years or so she worked principally in Austrian or West German productions. The sixties saw her turning to these shores for work, including an appearance in Ken Russell's less-than-successful comedy debut, *French Dressing* (1963), and a cloak-and-dagger spoof tale, *Masquerade* (1965) by Basil Dearden, director of the framing story for British horror museum-piece *Dead of Night* (1945). Italy too became a regular port of call, with acting assignments for comedy specialist and one-time Fulci associate Mario Monicelli (*Casanova '70*, 1965), *Mill of the Stone Women* maestro Giorgio Ferroni (*New York chiama Superdrago*, 1966), exploitation workhorse Umberto Lenzi (*Seven Blood-Stained Orchids*, 1972, and *Milano rovente*, 1973) and *Night Train Murders* director Aldo Lado (*L'ultima volta (Gli scippatori)*, 1976).

1973's *Pena de muerte* saw Mell working in Spain, for *The Living Dead at Manchester Morgue* director Jorge Grau. Yet despite her glamorous appearance, her only major Stateside credit was the risible Diana Ross vehicle *Mahogany* (Berry Gordy, 1975). By the eighties her ambitions were (depending on your viewpoint) either faltering or branching out into exciting new territory; she appeared in hardcore pornographic photo-stories for magazines like Italy's *Men*. Things reached their nadir (as for so many actors!) with an assignment for sleaze veteran Aristide Massaccesi (in his 1990 clunker *Ator III: The Hobgoblin*), but by then such tawdry credits were the least of her worries. Touchingly, her last work was an Austrian film called *I Love Vienna* in 1992. Mell succumbed to throat cancer in Vienna later that year, leaving behind a small but dedicated cult following who revere her as the slinky star of *Danger: Diabolik* and the devious *femme fatale* of Fulci's *One on Top of the Other*.

One particular actress who shone through in Fulci's early seventies work was former model and high society paparazzi favourite Florinda Bolkan. Born Florinda Bulcao (pronounced Bolkan) on 5 February 1941, she moved from her birthplace, Uruburetama in North-Eastern Brazil, to Rio de Janeiro when she was still very young. Her father, a poet who became active in politics and the growing ecological movement, died when she was still a girl – Florinda was thus forced to seek employment from an early age. Her first media exposure came when she was featured on a poster advertising a Brazilian airline (having been spotted whilst working as a hostess for the same company). In 1963 she married ageing playboy Francis Forbes, a liaison which didn't last but nonetheless helped propel her into the international socialite arena. From there she went on to Paris where for two years she studied art at the Sorbonne.

In 1967, a chance meeting with acclaimed Italian director Luchino Visconti launched her movie career – he recommended Bolkan to his director acquaintances before casting her as Helmut Berger's prostitute lover Olga in his epic exposé of German pre-war decadence *The Damned* (1969). Most of Bolkan's screen credits were amassed in the following five year period, as she was drawn to the bosom of Countess Marina Cicogna, a flamboyant Venetian film producer rumoured to have seduced her Brazilian protégé into a lesbian love affair. Cicogna established the dark, intense young actress through assignments for key directors like Vittorio De Sica (*Una breve vacanza*, 1973) and Elio Petri (*Investigation of a Citizen Above Suspicion*, 1970) for which she received international praise.

Bolkan's brace of performances for Fulci (in *A Lizard in a Woman's Skin* and *Don't Torture a Duckling*) are substantial successes; she captures a strained, neurotic quality that improves with each viewing. In both films she projects a cold, estranged facade, shot through with guilt and anguish in the former and rage and madness in the latter. Her ambiguous sexuality also fans the flames of certain erotic scenes with Anita Strindberg in *Lizard* – the choice of role revealing an admirably insouciant attitude to the gossip surrounding her alliance with la Cicogna. She obviously relished work that pushed the boundaries of good taste too. Having suffered a grisly fate in Fulci's *Duckling*, she was to go on to even more violent escapades in Gianfranco Mingozzi's brutal 'feminist allegory', *Flavia the Heretic* (1974), culminating in a graphic flaying scene that matches and perhaps even exceeds Fulci's excesses of the time.

Brutalist, fatalist, eroticist

Fulci's thrillers (and later his horror films) are coloured by persistent feelings of sadness, pessimism and despair. Entropic sexual relationships and dysfunctional emotional relationships are the norm, breeding misery, isolation and corruption. His work in the giallo arena vibrates uneasily between narrative pleasure (afforded by his well-calibrated plotting) and a downbeat *ennui* which almost smothers the excitement on offer. And yet his films are not just angsty endurance tests; they resonate with audiences who find them gripping and compelling. So how does Fulci generate life and energy and propulsion in his work, while painting in such dark emotional hues? With the exception of his first giallo, *One on Top of the Other*, the balance is maintained by the emergence of his most notorious cinematic hallmark – long, drawn out scenes of extreme violence. This ingredient, which would become the core focus of Fulci's work in years to come, provides a shocking and visceral counterbalance to his sombre emotional pallette. Instead of 'light relief' to offset the darkness, he gives us images of sheer horror so powerful and so extreme that they act as a sort of electric jolt to the system. By pursuing the unsettling and disturbing implications of his stories to their grisly end points, he achieves catharsis; the violence is both the inevitable outgrowth of his pessimistic world-view and his escape route from despair into a kind of savage celebration. Fulci's screen violence is the expression of both negative brutality and a positive vitality, and this peculiar oscillation is what gives his films their unique magnetism.

Exploitation cinema often treats its audiences to the very sights and sensations the sometimes blatantly moralistic films themselves deplore. The giallo film tends towards both cynicism and decadence, which goes for both the characters and the way they are depicted. The heyday of the giallo was the early seventies, and what we can see in some cases is a step back into conservatism after the liberal idealism of the late sixties. A film like Roberto Montero's *So Sweet, So Dead*, for instance, castigates women for adultery whilst observing their amorous affairs with hypocritical prurience. Fulci's thrillers occasionally border on the same hypocrisy: his films are both attracted and repelled by sexual freedom, but they display a crucial degree of self-consciousness about the paradox, which places them in a more thoughtful and responsible framework than many of their fellows in the giallo arena.

Before moving on to the reviews, it's important to mention that Fulci suffered a terrible personal tragedy in 1969, when his wife Maria took her own life in response to an erroneous diagnosis of cancer. The exact date of her death is difficult to ascertain (Fulci was understandably reluctant to go into details); however he once said that his wife's favourite of his films was *Beatrice Cenci*, which was made after *One on Top of the Other* in the summer of 1969. Maria's suicide was not the only agony to afflict Lucio: it was followed, a few years later, by the death of one of his daughters in a road accident. Tragedy was laid upon tragedy. It's therefore inescapable that we should think of these matters when looking at the development of Fulci's career. Although we should not lean too heavily on biographical 'explanations', the films discussed in this chapter possess a much darker emotional energy than the majority of giallo films by other directors, and it's notable that having specialised in knockabout comedies throughout the 1960s, Fulci veered away from them in the 1970s and 1980s (three films excepted) towards ever more dark and disturbing subjects. It therefore seems very likely that this sea change in Fulci's creativity was wrought by a prolonged period of emotional pain, in the wake of two harrowing personal tragedies.

above: Florinda Bolkan starring in the 1969 film *Love Circle* (aka *Metti una sera a cena*) by Giuseppe Petroni Griffi.

below: Florinda Bolkan with Gianmaria Volonté in *Investigation of a Citizen Above Suspicion* (1970).

Italian theatrical title
Una sull'altra

Italy/France/Spain

Alternative titles
The Perversion Story (*Variety* article)
One on the Other (*Variety* article)

International theatrical titles
Perversion Story (FR)
Una historia perversa (SP)
'A Perverse Story'
Nackt über Leichen (WG)
'Naked on top of Corpses'
One on Top of the Other (UK/USA/AUS)
Jedna žena je nestala (YUG)
'A Woman Is Missing'

Video titles
La machination (FR) 'The Set-Up'
Η Πλεκτανη (GRE) 'Body of Lies'

Production company
Empire Films (Rome)
Productions Jacques Roitfeld (Paris)
CC Trebol Film (Madrid)

Theatrical distributors
Fida Cinematografica (Italy)
Alpha France (France)
Atlantida Films S.A. (Spain)
GGP Releasing (USA)
Border Film Productions Ltd. (UK)
Filmways (Australia)

Theatrical running time
Italy 99m
UK 108m 06s before cuts
France 87m
Spain 95m

Video/DVD/Blu-ray times (adjusted)
Inter-Ocean video (UK) 102m 54s
Severin DVD (USA) 97m 10s
'Fan edit' DVD (USA) 107m 45s

Censorship
Italian censor certificate 54245
issued 08 August 1969
UK 'X' certificate
issued 14 January 1971

Shooting period
January-February 1969

Release information
Rome 22 August 1969
Bisceglie 05 September 1969
Bari 10 September 1969
Turin 11 October 1969
France 23 August 1970
UK (Liverpool, et al) 7 February 1971
USA (San Francisco – unconfirmed)
January 1972
USA (Raleigh, NC) 24 March 1972

One on Top of the Other

1969

Directed by Lucio Fulci. produced by Edmondo Amati for Fida Cinematografica (Rome) / Productions Jacques Roitfeld (France) / Coop. Trébol Films (Madrid). story: Lucio Fulci & Roberto Gianviti. screenplay: Lucio Fulci, Roberto Gianviti & José Luis Martinez Molla. director of photography: Alejandro Ulloa. music: Riz Ortolani; published by Beat-Prima. editor: Ornella Micheli. art director: Nedo Azzini. set designer: Roman Calatayud. production supervisor: Renato Jaboni. production managers: Alvin [Albino] Cocco & Luis Mendez. production secretary: Paolo Vandini. production assistants: Massimo Manasse & Francisco Tudela. assistant director: Max [Massimo] Castellani. continuity: Vittoria Vigorelli. camera operator: Gianni Bergamini. assistant cameraman: Gianni Bonivento. assistant set designer: Alessandro De Santis. costume designer: Lucia Mirisola. make-up: Peppino Banchelli. hairdresser: Jole Cecchini. set dresser: Pier Luigi Basile. still photography: Tonino Benetti. collaborator – New York shoot: Gray Frederickson. assistant editor: Concetta Pacini. sound: Mario Li Gobbi. sound studio: C.D.C. synchronisation: C.D.S.

Cast: Jean Sorel (Dr. George Dumurrier). Marisa Mell (Susan Dumurrier/Monica Weston). Elsa Martinelli (Jane Bleeker). Alberto de Mendoza (Henry Dumurrier). John Ireland (Inspector Wald). Jean Sobieski (Larry, the photographer). Faith Domergue (Martha, Susan's sister). Riccardo Cucciolla (Benjamin Wormser). Wilhelm ['Bill'] Vanders (Chief insurance agent). Franco Balducci (Loveday, cop wearing glasses at Monica's apartment). Giuseppe Addobbati [as 'John Douglas'] (Brent). Félix Dafauce [as 'Felix De Fauce'] (insurance agent in steel-rimmed glasses). Jesús Puente (Sgt. Rodriguez). George Rigaud (Arthur Mitchell, George's lawyer). *Uncredited:* Lucio Fulci (Graphologist). Malisa Longo (Elizabeth O'Neill, nurse/model). Raffaele Mottola (State Governor). Bobby Rhodes (black prison guard). Geoffrey Copleston (gas chamber doctor).

Synopsis: San Francisco: George Dumurrier, a businessman-doctor, runs a clinic with his brother Henry, but leaves care of Susan, his asthma-stricken wife, to her sister Martha and a nurse. George is having an affair with Jane, assistant to Larry, a trendy photographer. They travel out of town for a romantic break but on arriving at a casino George receives a phone call telling him that his wife has suffocated during a violent asthma attack. Returning home, he is consoled by his brother and frozen out by the hostile Martha. Susan's life insurance policy of a million dollars is a timely bonus for George's recklessly extended business enterprise. Perhaps too timely, the insurance agent suggests to Inspector Wald. An anonymous tip-off leads George and Jane to 'The Roaring Twenties', a Reno strip club. There they see Monica, a stripper who, although blonde not brunette and with different-coloured eyes, bears an uncanny resemblance to Susan. George is morbidly attracted and goes to bed with her. The police, who've been trailing George, arrest Monica. In her apartment they find a slip of paper on which Susan's signature is repeated over and over. In return for her freedom, Monica tells police she discovered that George had poisoned his wife (something the police already suspect) and was blackmailing him: she directs them to an envelope containing $10,000 hidden in her apartment. The envelope bears George's fingerprints. He is arrested, convicted of murder, and sent to the gas chamber. A visit from Henry reveals what is really happening; 'Monica' is in fact Susan. She and Henry are in love. They faked her death, bribed a coroner, and framed George for murder in order to get rid of him and claim his half of the estate. Police exhume the corpse of the fake Susan and match the teeth to her dental records (forged by Henry). George's fate appears sealed...

above: American distributors GGP literally made a splash with this eye-catching one-sheet for the film on its 1972 US release.

opposite: George Dumurrier (Jean Sorel) and his lover Jane (Elsa Martinelli) are a couple unable to find much warmth in each other's arms.

below: Jean Sorel and Marisa Mell.

About the production: Preparation for the shooting of Fulci's debut thriller *Una sull'altra* began late in 1968. A short feature in the newspaper *l'Unità* announced, *"Lucio Fulci has begun shooting* Una sull'altra *on the Cinecittà soundstages, starring Marisa Mell, Jean Sorel, Elsa Martinelli and Jean Sobieski. It will be shot mostly in the USA, in New York and California. The troupe, having finished stage work in Rome, will depart for the USA in early January and in America they will enjoy the benefits of permission to film in places that until now have never been used in movies, including the death cell in San Quentin prison, the inside of the Statue of Liberty in New York. and a lot of scenes to be shot at the ranch which Marilyn Monroe bought shortly before she committed suicide, and which since then has remained uninhabited."* Faith Domergue's casting was announced in *Variety* on 14 January 1969. The film, referred to as 'The Perversion Story', was scheduled to begin shooting in San Francisco late January, a dateline confirmed when supporting actor John Ireland was later reported to have flown there in early February to shoot his scenes. An article in *La Stampa* on 11 February 1969 described Marisa Mell as having *"recently starred in* Una sull'altra *by Lucio Fulci"* so it would seem that her scenes at least were finished earlier that month. The production was listed as 'recently completed' (i.e. edited and scored) in a *Variety* news item dated 7 May 1969, by which point it was being referred to simply as *Perversion Story*. This title did not survive in English-language territories, probably because a 1969 film by Spaniard Julio Buchs grabbed it first, but it did emerge, oddly enough, as the Fulci film's French theatrical release title. By November 1969 *Variety* were referring to the film as 'One on the Other' (a literal translation of *Una sull'altra*), but this was during a period when the film had yet to score an American distribution deal. Finally settling on *One on Top of the Other* as the English language title, the producers sold the film to UK distributors Border Films, who submitted it to the British Board of Film Censors and received an 'X' certificate on 14 January 1971. In November 1971 it was picked up for American distribution by GGP Releasing, a Boston-based production and distribution company. Reviewed in *Variety* on 19 January 1972, it went into regional release in May of that year.

Review: *One on Top of the Other* is a morbid mystery in the manner of Hitchcock's *Vertigo* first, and a borderline giallo film second. Unlike most giallos, the film does not pursue a murder enquiry through an ever increasing body-count, nor does the spectacle of murder itself occupy the sort of no-holds-barred attention that was typical of the genre after Mario Bava set the standard with *Blood and Black Lace*. What it does share with the giallo is a frantic shuffling of plot information, designed to conceal the identity of those responsible for a murderous intrigue. However, at its core the film is a mystery of the heart, a dark anti-romance, trading in paranoia, self-doubt and creeping anxiety, with the attacking blade not the physical kind employed by the giallo genre's razor-slashing killers, but instead a metaphorical dagger to the heart. Hatred, revenge and humiliation are the watchwords, chillingly enfolded within a terminally defective human relationship.

Although the film is set in San Francisco at the height of 'free-love', the specific milieu that we see is rather 'square', given the time and place. The hippie scene, with its orgiastic revels turning darker as the decade drew to a close, is largely ignored; the film instead focuses upon the way the more 'reputable' members of society were taking advantage of the spirit of the times. The social scene depicted is wealthy, professional and middle-aged, with little sign of any 'swinging' youth on the prowl. (By the time Fulci turned his attention to hippies, and a very morning-after version of 'swinging London', in 1971's *A Lizard in a Woman's Skin*, his jaded gaze was more suited to the time.) What insulates the characters from the social upheavals around them is their tendency to stubborn self-contemplation; Dr. George Dumurrier hardly needs the intoxicants and hallucinogens of the 'love generation' to fuel his introspective withdrawal into personal anomie. The overall feel of the story is both sensational and sombre, a tonal conflict paralleled by Riz Ortolani's alternately blaring and sorrowful jazz score.

The film opens with overhead shots of the San Quentin prison facility, a location the story eventually leads remorselessly back to, as George is well and truly 'stitched up' for his wife's murder. This circularity is a sign of the gloomy fatalism which pervades much of the action.

We can tell that George Dumurrier's wife Susan will be a strange, elusive character by the way that she's first relayed to us; as a gliding apparition, seen through reflections-in-reflections at the glass-doored Dumurrier household. Their palatial residence,

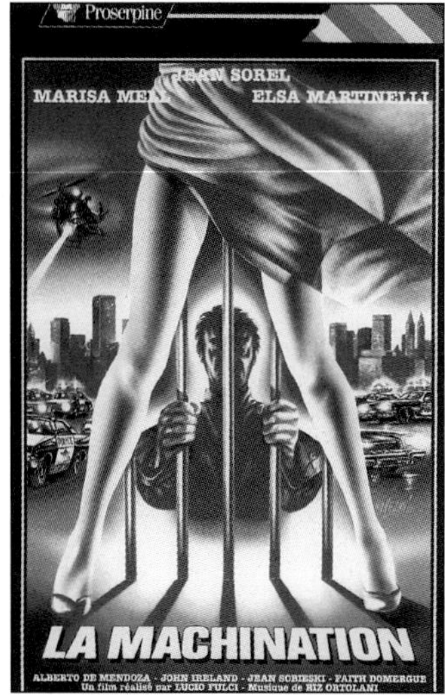

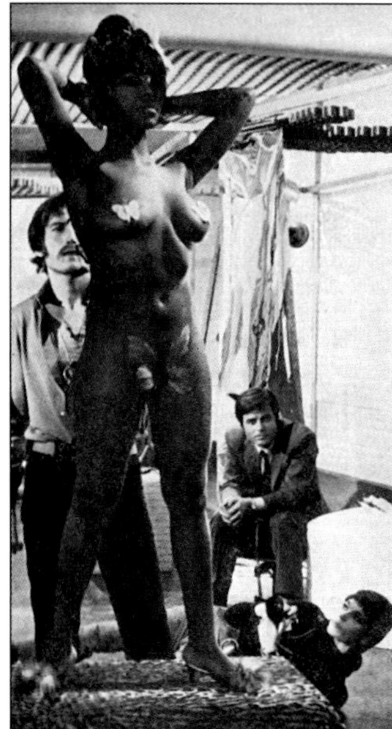

top left: French video cover under the alternative title *La machination*.

middle left: Fun at the stripjoint where Monica Weston performs.

bottom left: Sobieski, Sorel, Martinelli and mystery nude have a *Blow-Up* style photo-session.

above, main picture: Jean Sorel is pensive after sleeping with his lover Jane – sadly this lovely composition does not appear in the actual film.

right: Sorel and Mell get acquainted – or is it reacquainted?

indicative of great wealth, nevertheless has something of the tomb to it. We swiftly realise that Susan loathes her husband, and the atmosphere of feminine hostility is amplified by the presence of Susan's sister and constant companion, Martha. Martha looks ready to spit whenever George comes near; both she and Susan vibrate with suppressed menace. Evidently, while money can buy you marble inlay flooring and classical statuary, it can't buy a happy marriage. It's a cliché that was seized upon by many a subsequent giallo film: the lives of the very rich are nearly always depicted as cold and cynical, with lovelessness, misery and paranoia the price the wealthy have to pay for all those sumptuous interiors, expensive cars and ornamental gardens.

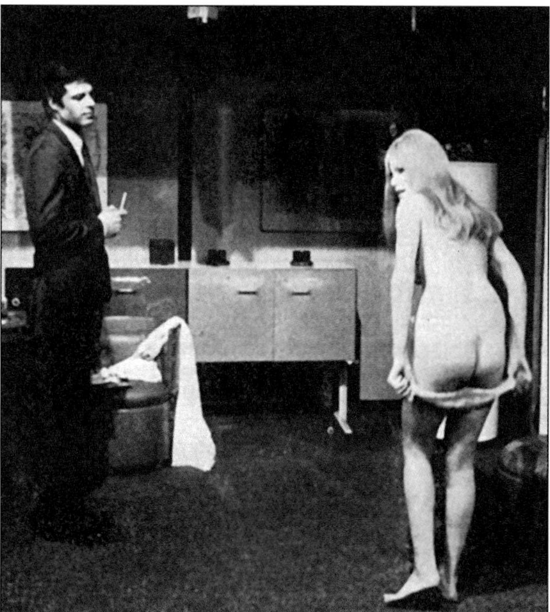

George's relationship with his wife is dead on its feet, and yet he lacks the courage to finish it. *"We lie out of necessity"* he claims, in feeble justification to Jane, his lover. Whether or not the first bloom of illicit passion with Jane had been invigorating to George we don't really know: by the time we meet her it's obvious he's been stringing her along for quite some time. But at least their relationship is not bitter and hateful, like his marriage: the sex, though lacking passion, is affectionate. (When George and Jane make love, Fulci films them from below through semi-transparent red sheets, as if the camera were lurking in the mattress, an unusual visual choice that adds the first twist of eccentric style to the film.) Such is the overall pessimism of the scenario, however, that a listless pall of *ennui* soon follows. After a weary lovers' quarrel, Jane decides to leave George and return by train to her father's house in Reno. *"Let's part here. I hate these tearful farewells on railway platforms,"* she says. George drives to Reno ahead of her; overhead shots of his car racing to beat the train on a parallel road allow us to consider him capable of vigour after all. Yet when he smilingly greets Jane outside the station in Reno, her response hints that this same scenario, or something like it, has happened before: *"One day I'll get off the train and you won't be there."*

The story kicks into gear soon afterwards, when Susan is found dead, having apparently overdosed on her asthma medication. Lead actress Marisa Mell then disappears from the narrative for a while, before returning as ostensibly a different character, a laconic high-class stripper called Monica. (You can tell she's high-class, because in a room full of topless waitresses she performs a strip-tease without actually exposing her breasts.) Her first encounter with George and Jane, in the 'Roaring Twenties' strip salon, is a *tour-de-force* of edgy unease by Fulci. George's staring and Jane's distrust inspire a plausible perplexity from 'Monica', as the uncomfortable trio sit around a table surrounded by topless babes trailing party streamers and bouncing beachballs. Mell is doubly impressive in this film; she's compelling as both the icy contemptuous wife and the earthy no-nonsense whore. Her double role is a variation, of course, on Hitchcock's *Vertigo*, in which a man's obsession with a glacial mysterious woman leads to trauma when it's revealed that she has never really existed, instead being the creation of a far more 'ordinary' actress. Here, the glacial woman is George's wife, and the accessible woman is the 'fake' personality, who has never independently existed.

The film's title suggests different things. There's the notion of masked or doubled identity: the Susan/Monica question is the central duplicity, although other aspects, such as George's affair with Jane, and George's manipulative brother, add variations on the theme. In a cruder sense, the title also suggests what was, for the time, a sustained emphasis on sexual coupling. There is throughout a general air of decadence and casual voluptuousness: nude shows at naughty night clubs are staffed by naked waitresses, sex scenes between the leads are rendered in a mannerist fashion popular among the artier echelons of erotic film-making, and the paraphernalia of the permissive sixties is much in evidence, as signified by a classic *Blow-Up*-style photo session.

All things considered, however, the 'Other' here is principally the duplicitous and unknowable female, whose guile, trickery and manipulation of facade constitutes a threat to the male hero. Male, but not masculine: George is the first of Fulci's explicitly passive male leads. He's victimised by his wife's charade and backed into an impossible situation: labelled a murderer and sent to the gas chamber, with no one who believes him able to save him.

George's passivity has two aspects. On the one hand, he's a quiet, withdrawn man, who exudes a constantly troubled air. His good looks suggest a tinge of rakishness, but a sadness is perpetually present. On the other hand, his reserve has a streak of coldness. His reactions to emotional stress bend inwards to a cloaked, almost dormant state of mind. His enervated response to the death of his wife, to the anxieties of his lover Jane, and even the apparition of Monica, point to a self-regarding, insular personality. The woman who calls herself 'Monica' (a pun on the word 'monicker'?) lies around at her apartment, telling George to get the door, answer the phone; generally exuding a casual sense of control over the man who is supposedly 'investigating' her. Add to this the fact that he's really her husband, first duped and then demoted to the status of a whore's manservant, and George's immersion in a humiliating power game is exascerbated.

The second aspect of George's passivity extends into the intimate space of his relations with women. He's diffident and reserved during lovemaking with Jane, and later too with Monica. *"You're a quiet lover"*, Monica says. This uncanny sense of restraint in a situation ripe for frankness and revelation marks George as yet another masked character, in a drama which posits human affairs as a series of lies and obscurations. When George is finally made aware of the coils of his wife's deceit, his reactions become more inflamed; and yet still there's an odd sort of low-intensity fatalism about him.

The sensations offered to us by this interplay of concealed aggressions and bland surfaces are stifling and disquieting. Although the story seems initially to be that of a victimised man suffering at the hands of a callous woman, the tale really offers us a representation of love's bitter ironies wherein no party can be said to hold the moral high ground. George's obsession with his work, and his less than romantic love affair, place him in the story's firing line. Although the plot against him is cruel and appalling – he is framed exquisitely for murder – his lack of passion or emotional honesty make him fair game in an unfair world.

The fact that George's fate is ultimately decided not by his own agency but by a lovesick client of 'Monica', Benjamin Wormser, is the final twist of the knife. Wormser is designated as pathetic, a man without self-respect who worships women to an extreme. And let's not forget he's also a man who has fastened with masochistic longing on George's wife. That it's he who acts decisively at the end leaves George, in Hollywood leading man terms, in a kind of living death. The film ends with a TV reporter speaking from the gas chamber, explaining how the last few minutes of George's ordeal played out. Incredibly, we never see George after this, as if the film itself has dismissed him from its concerns. For all that Fulci set this story in the United States, it's hard to imagine an American filmmaker willing to so drastically undercut the heroic male archetype.

One on Top of the Other mitigates its downbeat vibe with a plethora of creative flourishes. There are two gorgeous split-screen sequences, one depicting chemical tests performed on the alleged corpse of Susan Dumurrier, and the other a montage of multiple Monicas stripping against psychedelic back-projections. Marisa Mell's first strip sequence is a lurid highlight, part sixties camp, part genuine sexiness, and as for the movement and position of the camera, Fulci's choices are often strikingly elegant. Overall this is a very beautiful film. If it has a problem, it's that we struggle to believe Susan could deceive her husband simply by wearing a blonde wig and contact lenses. George has ample opportunity to scrutinise 'Monica' yet still he's taken in. It must be said, though, that Fulci attacks the problem with admirable bloody-mindedness, by choosing to stage a sex scene between George and 'Monica' in which George, though haunted by flashbacks to his wife, nevertheless remains convinced that Monica is another woman. We therefore have to assume that the Dumurriers' relationship was a total sham, because not even the intimacy of lovemaking blows Susan's cover. Such, then, is Lucio Fulci's first dissertation on the joys of love and marriage...

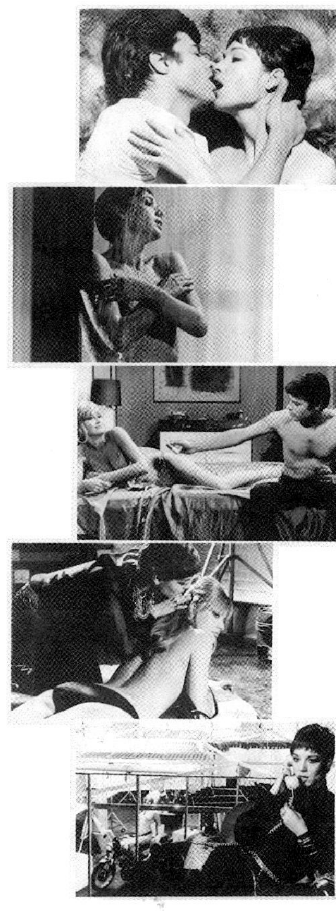

above: Series of stills showing Jean Sorel, Elsa Martinelli and Marisa Mell.

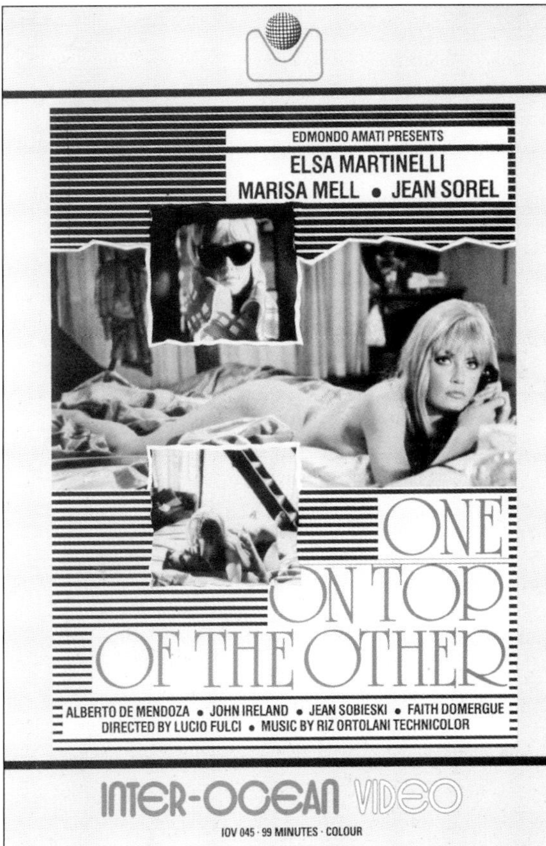

left: British pre-cert video cover.

below: As *Una historia perversa*, Fulci's proto-giallo played Spain in a 70mm version.

Italian theatrical title
Una lucertola con la pelle di donna

Italy/Spain/France

Alternative titles
The Cage (shooting title)
Femme serpent (FR unknown source)
'Serpent Woman'

International theatrical titles
Una lagartija con piel de mujer (SP)
Carole (FR)
La venin de la peur (FR alt.)
'The Venom of Fear'
Les salopes vont en enfer (FR alt.)
'Sluts Go to Hell'
Lizard in a Woman's Skin (UK)
A Lizard in a Woman's Skin (US)
Schizoid (US re-release)
Snovi zločina (YUG) 'Dream crimes'
Kâbus (TUR) 'Nightmare'
Un reptil con piel de mujer (MEX)
'A Reptile with a Woman's Skin'
La serpiente con piel de mujer (ARG)
'The Serpent with a Woman's Skin'

Production companies
International Apollo Films S.r.l. (Rome)
Atlantida Film S.A. (Madrid)
Les Films Corona (Paris)

Theatrical distributors
Fida Cinematografica (Italy)
A.I.P. (USA)
Gala Film Distributors (UK)
Filmways (Australia)

Theatrical running times
Italy 95m
UK theatrical 99m 11s
France (as 'Les salopes...') 102m
Spain (SMC) 89m

Video/DVD/Blu-ray times (adjusted)
Federal DVD (Italy) 102m 22s

Shooting period
September-October 1970

Censorship
Italian censor certificate 57694
issued 17th February 1971
Classified "X" by the BBFC
06 February 1973
French visa 38271 issued 15 June 1976
(as 'Les salopes vont en enfer')
France (CNC) 21 July 1976
(as 'Les salopes vont en enfer')

Release information
Rome 18 February 1971
Genova 23 February 1971
Bari 05 March 1971
USA (Los Angeles, CA) 29 Sept 1971
(as 'A Lizard in a Woman's Skin')
USA (Lubbock, TX) 14 April 1972
(as 'Schizoid')
UK (London) 25 May 1973

A Lizard in a Woman's Skin

1971

Directed by Lucio Fulci. produced by Edmondo Amati for International Apollo Films S.r.l. (Rome) / Atlántida Films S.A. (Madrid) / Les Films Corona (Paris). story: Lucio Fulci & Roberto Gianviti. screenplay: Lucio Fulci, Roberto Gianviti, José Luis Martinez Molla & André Tranché. director of photography: Luigi Küveiller. music: Ennio Morricone, conducted by Bruno Nicolai; published by General Music (Rome). supervising editor: Vincenzo Tomassi. editor: Jorge Serralonga. set designer & costume designer: Maurizio Chiari. production manager: Renato Jaboni. unit managers: Agostino Pane & José Garillo. assistant director: Giorgio Gentili. continuity: Roberto Giandalia. cameramen: Ubaldo Terzano & Saturnino Pita. assistant cameramen: Santiago Gomez, Antonio Annunziata & Gianni Bonivento. costumes for Mrs. Bolkan: Lancetti (Rome). make-up supervisor: Franco Di Girolamo. assistant make-up: Gloria Fava. hairdresser: Rosa Luciani. special effects: Giovanni Rambaldi & Eugenio Ascani. set decorator: Nedo Azzini. assistant set designer: Roman Calatayud. assistant set dresser: Claudio De Santis. assistant production manager: Luis Mendez. production secretaries: Roberto Carpentieri & Enrique Bellot. assistant editors: Rita Antonelli & Lea Piras. sound: Massimo Jaboni. synchronization: Pinewood Studios. the producers thank The Duke and The Duchess of Bedford for their co-operation and permission to photograph their property of "Woburn Abbey". with special thanks to Scotland Yard for the kind assistance given the troupe during shooting. vocal soloist: Edda Dell'Orso. filmed on location at London & Woburn Abbey (England) with interiors at Dear Center (Rome). colour by Technicolor.

Cast: Florinda Bolkan (Carol Hammond). Stanley Baker (Inspector Corvin). Jean Sorel (Frank Hammond). Leo Genn (Edmund Brighton). Silvia Monti (Deborah, Frank's lover). Alberto de Mendoza (Sgt. Brandon). Penny Brown (Jenny, a hippie). Mike Kennedy (Harry Smith, a hippie). Ely Galleani [as 'Edy Gall'] (Joan Hammond, Carol's stepdaughter). George Rigaud (Dr. Kerr). Ezio Marano (Lowell, scientific squad). Franco Balducci (McKenna, fair-haired detective in dark raincoat). Luigi Antonio Guerra (moustached policeman). Erzsi Paál [as 'Ersi Pond'] (Mrs. Gordon). Gaetano Imbró (Policeman). *Uncredited:* Anita Strindberg (Julia Durer). Tony Adams (young policeman wearing glasses). Jean Degrave (clinic director). Basil Dignam (Chief Inspector McCloud). Erni ['Ursel'] Eberz (Policewoman Bennett). Piero Nistri (Mrs. Gordon's chauffeur/lover).

Synopsis: Carol Hammond is the daughter of a wealthy lawyer, Edmund Brighton. Her husband Frank is a lawyer too, with Brighton's practice. Carol has been visiting a psychoanalyst to whom she relates a spate of disturbing dreams featuring her neighbour, Julia Durer. The dreams involve a lesbian encounter that ends with Carol stabbing Julia to death, observed by two hippies who watch without intervening. Later, Julia is found murdered in circumstances identical to those described by Carol. Inspector Corvin takes charge of the investigation and focuses on Carol. Her fingerprints match those on the murder weapon and she's arrested. But why would she describe the murder to her analyst? Could it be that someone has read her dream diary and is using it to frame her? Whilst awaiting trial Carol is sent to a sanitorium. She sees one of the hippies: fleeing, she stumbles into a room in which gruesome experiments are being conducted on living dogs. She faints in horror and when she recovers the hippie has disappeared... Carol's father posits a theory that Frank is the killer. He is having an affair: maybe Julia Durer was blackmailing him? Whilst out on bail, Carol is contacted by one of the hippies. At a rendezvous he tries to kill her but she's rescued by the police. Edmund Brighton commits suicide in a last effort to clear Carol's name, leaving a note claiming responsibility for the murder. But too late: Inspector Corvin deduces Carol's guilt from a slip of the tongue. She did indeed kill Julia Durer, who'd threatened to blackmail her about their lesbian relationship. Carol thought that the two hippies at the murder scene would describe her to the police, so she wrote up the crime in her dream diary. She'd hoped to avoid a murder sentence by producing the diaries in court as evidence of a split personality. She hadn't realised that the 'witnesses' were high on LSD, unable to comprehend what they saw, remembering her only as "a lizard... in a woman's skin".

About the production: *A Lizard in a Woman's Skin* began life as a script called 'The Cage', first mention of which can be traced back to *Variety*, 29 April 1970. Florinda Bolkan arrived in Rome on 3 August that year, ready to begin work, and leading man Jean Sorel was signed up around the same time, with shooting due to begin on the 20th. Reporting Bolkan's arrival, the Italian press referred to the forthcoming film as 'Donna dalla pelle di serpente' ('Woman with a snake's skin') – could this have been an early script title, or was Bolkan misremembering when speaking off the cuff to journalists?[5]

For reasons unknown, production was delayed by several weeks. On 26 August 1970 *Variety* declared that location filming would now take place in early September, and on the 30th of that month it was reported that Leo Genn had recently arrived in Rome to shoot his scenes, so it seems that English location work occupied most of September with the Rome studio scenes mounted in October.

A cast list published in September 1970 lists Nadia Cassini (or 'Nadia Cassim') alongside Silvia Monti, Jean Sorel, Florinda Bolkan and Stanley Baker, although as it turned out she was not to appear in the film. Perhaps Cassini, looking every inch the vivacious 'hippie-chick' in photos published elsewhere that year, had been lined up to play Jenny, the acid-loving eye-witness, before dropping out of the running for some reason? (She turned to sexploitation the same year, starring in Piero Vivarelli's *Il dio serpente* as a young woman who surrenders herself to a Caribbean snake god.)

By October 1970 the Fulci production was being referred to in *Variety* as 'The Cage (Una lucertola con la pelle di donna)', indicating that it was about to shed its original, rather dull title in favour of brighter, more vivid colours, inspired of course by Dario Argento's *The Bird with the Crystal Plumage*, which opened to rave reviews and bulging box office in February 1970. Years later, having often been accused of band-wagon jumping with *Lizard*, Fulci explained the roots of the giallo craze to an Italian newspaper, and stressed that neither he nor Argento could claim precedence: *"You want to know if I really feel like the inventor of the Italian giallo movie? Fine, let me tell you that the real creator is a distinguished unknown, Romolo Guerrieri, who in 1966* [actually 1967] *shot* The Sweet Body of Deborah. *A year after, I made* One on Top of the Other, *but no one even noticed: with that title it had been taken for an erotic film. It was only in 1969 that Dario Argento arrived with* The Bird with the Crystal Plumage *and everyone was shouting about this miracle."*[6]

above: Carol runs in terror from a mystery assailant.

opposite: Carol Hammond (Florinda Bolkan): victim or manipulator?

left: Lesbian seductress Julia Durer (Anita Strindberg) makes her move on the unstable Carol.

below: Admat designed for the AIP release of *Lizard...* in the US, retitled *Schizoid*.

above:
Locandina poster.

top right:
Scenes of hippie sex-and-drugs decadence taking place at the home of Julia Durer are assembled into a number of exciting psychedelic montages by Fulci and editor Jorge Serralonga. Whilst the screen time they enjoy is fairly short, the stills photographer seems to have been told to snap as many rolls as possible; see the rest of this section for further 'views'.

below:
Carol surrounded by the corpses of her family, faces mutilated in a style reminiscent of British artist Francis Bacon, whose paintings are seen hanging in the Hammond's London flat.

Review: One of Lucio Fulci's strongest films, *A Lizard in a Woman's Skin* is a mind-bendingly complex, beautifully shot and dazzlingly inventive psycho-thriller. Set in a strangely muted vision of swinging London, it's about a woman beset by nightmares, or perhaps hallucinations, who is accused of a murder which bears all the hallmarks of a dream she recently described to her psychoanalyst. Is she the killer? Or is someone trying to make it seem that way? The details of the murder match up perfectly with the notes she kept in her dream diary: has someone read those notes and then staged the murder to implicate her? Or is she actually insane, acting out her dreams with no conscious memory of doing so?

In some ways *A Lizard in a Woman's Skin* feels like a response to Roman Polanski's *Repulsion*, given that both films are set in London, place a strong emphasis on dreamlike imagery, and feature a central character called Carol. But whereas *Repulsion* sought to convey the subjective visions of a genuinely disturbed woman, *Lizard*, like its central character, plays a trickier game: we must unravel the truth of what we're seeing even as the relationship between the camera and the mind of the protagonist grows obscure, ambiguous, and misleading. The film is about perception, deceit and culpability. The story of a woman who may either be faking or losing her mind, it takes what appears to be an open and shut case and then bends over backwards to create doubt. We must constantly re-evaluate what we've seen, as the deviously clever plot twists and turns.

For the sake of clarity, therefore, let us drop any further ambiguity: Carol Hammond, it turns out, is lying. She did indeed kill her neighbour, Julia Durer, because the woman was about to reveal their lesbian affair, a scandal that Carol, a rich married socialite, could not bear. However, after entering Julia's boudoir and stabbing her on the bed, she sees two naked hippies, left over from an all-night party, watching and smiling enigmatically. Convinced that she's been caught red-handed, she runs away and then writes up her crime in her dream diary. This, she believes, will help mitigate her actions and lead to a verdict of "not guilty by reason of insanity". The enormous irony of her situation is that the two hippie 'witnesses' were high on LSD and couldn't have identified her anyway.

> *"I did one thing in* [Stage Fright] *that I never should have done; I put in a flashback that was a lie."*
> ~ Alfred Hitchcock, interviewed by François Truffaut.

In Hitchcock's *Stage Fright* (1950), a man on the run from the police tells a trusting female friend that a woman in a bloodstained dress had turned up at his house earlier, asking for his help. Although we're shown, in a flashback, the situation he describes, it later turns out that he was lying; his lady friend has been conned, and so have we. Hitchcock later regretted this 'cheat', which violated an unwritten rule requiring flashbacks to tell the truth. Lucio Fulci,

above:
Carol Hammond descends into an erotic maelstrom which may be dream, hallucination, or reality.

left:
Carol in the midst of more emotional trauma.

a devotee of Hitchcock, was no doubt familiar with *Stage Fright*, and he'd probably read the interview in which Hitchcock 'fessed up', so it's safe to assume, given his approach in *A Lizard in a Woman's Skin*, that he did not share Hitchcock's qualms!

As it happens, it's not a flashback that lies in this film; it's a dream sequence. The precise locus of truth is a thorny issue in *Lizard*, because Fulci does precisely what Carol is trying to do: both he and his lead character play the same game of deceit. The film's visual field is a tangled web of dreams, lies, hallucinations, and elements of the truth, and we are constantly buffeted by competing explanations for what we're seeing. The fact that all these various possibilities are operating at the same time makes the film's epistemology slippery and uncertain. How can a woman's murderous dream come true the following day? Is she insane, or hallucinating? Has someone read her dream diaries? Is her husband, or her psychoanalyst, trying to make her believe she did it? Is she being drugged? Is there a paranormal influence at work? Like Hitchcock, Fulci shows us things that a liar *wants* us to believe – making him, as much as Carol, the unreliable narrator. Not all of the surreal imagery we see is false; we can assume, for instance, that the opening dream sequence with its train imagery and slow motion lesbian seduction is genuine. At this point Carol is simply dreaming, and we are privy to her unconscious visions. For the actual murder, however, Fulci shows us the cocktail of truth and phony dream imagery that Carol concocts after the fact to convince a future jury she's insane. We see ingredients from Carol's earlier dream (the train; the slow motion; the wind that ripples her plush fur coat) and additional dream imagery not seen before (the screaming seated figures á là Francis Bacon; the giant winged bird á là Salvador Dali) leading up the murder itself. For the viewer, the only possible clue that we're seeing a fabrication is the use of Bacon and Dali imagery. Paintings by these artists adorn the walls of the Durer house, and a suspicious viewer might suppose that Carol – like Roger "Verbal" Kint in *The Usual Suspects* – is spinning a web of deceit using images drawn from her immediate environment; a mishmash of truth, deceit and fanciful decoration. However, the fact remains that we are shown this fabrication on screen, with nothing to indicate that it's false until much later in the narrative. (Cleverly, and very sneakily, Fulci cuts from this supposed 'dream sequence' to a shot of Carol lying on the psychiatrist's couch. We therefore assume we've been watching the dream that she's describing to her analyst, but it turns out that what we've really seen is the cunning patchwork of truth and lies she intends to use in her legal defence.)

If you want to pin an out-and-out lie on Fulci, one that does *not* involve ambiguous dream imagery, then consider the scene in which a gossipy friend of Carol's telephones to inform her that Julia Durer was not strangled, as first reported, but stabbed with a paper knife. Carol takes the call alone, with her family safely out of sight in an adjoining room, and yet Fulci shows her eyes widening in shock at the 'news'. But Carol *knows* how Julia Durer was killed –

below:
Poster advertising the Spanish theatrical release of *A Lizard in a Woman's Skin* in a 70mm print.

above:
Julia Durer seduces wealthy repressed lesbian Carol Hammond.

this page and opposite:
More imagery and promo artwork for *A Lizard in a Woman's Skin.*

below:
Variety advertisement dated May 1971 inviting prospective buyers to arrange a meeting with producer Edmondo Amati.

bottom:
Although the film was a co-production with Spain and France, the Spanish saw fit to slash Fulci's erotic thriller down to 88 minutes for its Iberian release – some 13 minutes shorter than the version playing in France as *Carole* (the French re-release *La venin de la peur* remains the longest version currently known to exist, although the British theatrical version ran just slightly shorter at 100 mins).

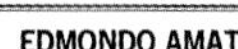

Wednesday, May 12, 1971 VARIETY

EDMONDO AMATI
Announces Completion of
THREE EXCEPTIONAL BOX-OFFICE HITS
MONICA VITTI
in
12 TIMES FEMALE
In a Film By
DINO RISI
The amazing versatility of Italy's leading comedy and dramatic actress

FLORINDA BOLKAN
STANLEY BAKER
JEAN SOREL
in
A LIZARD IN A WOMAN'S SKIN
Directed by LUCIO FULCI
". . . a well-mounted suspense thriller that should draw an audience from among filmgoers on the prowl for sensational stimulation . . ." VARIETY

Horror of Sexy Horrors
THE HORRIBLE SEXY VAMPIRE
Guaranteed to provide two hours of hair-raising entertainment

AND OTHER VERY IMPORTANT PICTURES AVAILABLE FOR SELECTED TERRITORIES

World Sales:
At Cannes: Edmondo Amati and his Foreign Department will be happy to receive friends and clients at the Hotel Martinez—from May 16
In Rome: Via Varese 4—Rome 00185—Tel: 491052/491059

above:
British pre-cert video cover.

she's the one who did it! Her reaction is not staged for the benefit of another character – there's no one else in the room. It's for our eyes only.

It's interesting that Fulci gives the imaginings and fabrications of his central character such bare-faced exposure on screen, because it ties in with several interesting British films of the period such as *Billy Liar* (1963), *If...* (1968) and *Deep End* (1970). As we oscillate between thinking that Carol is the killer and believing she's being victimised, we may even entertain a third possibility: perhaps, in trying to fake madness, she has succumbed to the real thing? It would explain the bizarre sequence with the split dogs at the sanitorium. Like Rock Hudson in *Shock Corridor* (1963), did Carol start out thinking she could simulate madness, only to end up crazy for real? (It certainly makes more sense than a private psychiatric clinic doing animal vivisection on the side!)

Putting aside the issue of truth, *Lizard* has many additional points of interest. For instance we can gauge from her first dream that Carol experiences sexual desire not as an arena for freedom of self-expression (as was the predominant 'riff' of the liberated late sixties/early seventies) but as a frightening, even nauseating experience. Her dreams are characterised by claustrophobia and sexual loathing – she finds herself bottled in by naked couples cavorting *en masse* in a train corridor. This claustrophobic image suggests the more oppressive demands of the counterculture. The ideal of 'free love' was taken to ludicrous theoretical extremes, and if you were not willing to 'put out' there were those who would label you selfish, bourgeois and counter-revolutionary. For some exploitative individuals, free love merely meant that one could expect unchallenged access to the bodies of 'liberated' women.

It's worth pointing out an underlying antipathy in the film towards psychoanalysis, although Fulci and Gianviti create something of a straw man here. Carol's analyst is a comically didactic fellow, not terribly realistic, who helpfully explains Carol's dreams to her, as though the job of the analyst were simply to translate an unfamiliar language into easily consumed clichés. *"In your dreams you always see her (Julia Durer) dressed as a strip-tease artist, or a prostitute,"* he says, *"In fact, that woman for you represents degradation and vice. The flat next door is a symbol of vice. You've referred to this woman before as someone who is not quite respectable... Your conscience forces you to disapprove of that woman's way of life, but at the same time her freedom excites your curiosity. You feel attracted"*. Such 'explanations' have more to do with writers juggling text and subtext in a screenplay than with psychoanalysis! But while the over-riding point seems to be that analysts are easily duped by criminal patients, the conflict the analyst describes is true enough: Carol was *very* attracted to her neighbour. Later, Fulci's witty use of split-screen juxtaposes a wild party at the Durer residence with a staid, formal dinner party at the Hammonds'. The assembled 'squares' joke uneasily about the noise from next door, but in a deliciously camp moment we see Carol's teenage step-daughter secretly tapping her foot to the 'far-out' sounds of Ennio Morricone filtering through from next door. Meanwhile, in an effective counterpoint to Carol's stiff-necked middle class dinner party, the walls of the Hammond residence are adorned with paintings by Francis Bacon, whose fantastical distortions of human flesh ironically underline the repressiveness of the household.

The use of Bacon's imagery in the art design is clever and creative throughout. For instance, Carol's bed is a modernist metal cube-outline, without curtains or canopy. Its chromium skeleton resembles a cage (echoing the film's original title and the cage-like structures applied by Francis Bacon to his paintings of tortured, twisted flesh). The Bacon works are also well incorporated into the imagery of Carol's second dream: the assembled dinner guests seen earlier are enthroned upon palatial chairs, their eyes gouged, faces ripped and bleeding guts exposed, mimicking Bacon's savage paintings. Fulci plays slyly with our credulity here: we accept the Bacon imagery as dream imagery and assume that these disturbing paintings have influenced Carol at an unconscious level, when it turns out she has simply used them to add verisimilitude to her lies.

As for the murder of Julia Durer, it's an extraordinary spectacle which extends a giallo taste for violence into the realm of outright horror. When Carol stabs her lesbian seductress, Fulci really lets rip, delivering a full-frontal display of close-up mutilation. His camera has already dwelt upon Durer's firm and jutting breasts, shown bobbing towards the camera in teasing slow motion. Now we see them penetrated by the blade of Carol's knife, in a shocking sequence which dwells obscenely on the gory details. Blood oozes in celebratory slow-motion from convincingly fleshy mounds, and the threateningly dynamic Durer expires in a welter of gore. It's a vivid and pungent depiction of slaughter that equals anything in Fulci's later Gothic horrors.

A Lizard in a Woman's Skin is a film about worlds colliding: the staid upper middle class world of outwardly 'respectable people' versus the wild orgiastic world of the counterculture. In 'swinging London', high and low culture came together: working class and upper class, druggies and duchesses, low criminals and the landed gentry found themselves cheek by jowl at the same all-night parties. The UK was perceived from the continent as a country steeped in tradition, which must have made it all the more fascinating for outsiders when it morphed into the crucible for an entirely new culture. This dualism is evident in Fulci's choice of locations, many of which, though symbolic of the establishment, had also recently doubled as settings for counter-culture 'happenings'. The Royal Albert Hall, home of the Proms, hosted the distinctly hippieish "International Poetry Incarnation" in 1965; Woburn Abbey welcomed the 1967 "Festival of the Flower Children"; and the Alexandra Palace, home of the first BBC transmissions, was the venue for "The 14 Hour Technicolor Dream", also in 1967.

Carol and her moneyed family are heavily critiqued in the film, not so much for murder as for hypocrisy and selfishness. But what about the parallel youth culture we see? In his 1959 rock 'n' roll film *I ragazzi del juke box*, Fulci sided very much with 'the kids'; here he's far more ambivalent. By the early 1970s he was a middle-aged man, and sure enough, his portrait of the hippies is mostly unsympathetic. The counter-culture dream of a revolution in the head leading to a revolution in everyday life was already beginning to fade, and Fulci is completely cynical on the topic, depicting the acid-tripping hippies who 'witness' Carol's crime with cataracted eyes: LSD, he's saying, far from opening the doors of perception, merely cuts the user off from meaningful engagement with the world.

With this film, Fulci proved himself a skilled craftsman with a morbid but commercially viable take on the world. *A Lizard in a Woman's Skin* may have concerned itself with a lead character who conceals her innermost thoughts, but it revealed a great deal more of the talent of its director than any other film to that date. Fulci once said: *"My first true fantastic film was* Una lucertola con la pelle di donna. *You could have two endings, one fantastic, the other in the line of a detective story. The producer insisted that the end be a logical one."*[7] To anyone familiar with the film's brutal, erotic and surrealistic thrills, it's clear that Fulci found a way of thwarting that producer: despite settling in the end for the conventional closure of detective fiction, he gave us a film that sits just as well in the *fantastique*.

below and facing page:
The American advertising artwork concept for *A Lizard in a Woman's Skin* makes a literal interpretation of the film's title.

in the annals of the abnormal there is no more erotic nightmare than the strange lusts of a...

"LIZARD IN A WOMAN'S SKIN"

Edmondo Amati presents

FLORINDA BOLKAN · STANLEY BAKER · JEAN SOREL

in **"LIZARD IN A WOMAN'S SKIN"** R RESTRICTED Under 17 Requires Accompanying Parent or Adult Guardian

with Alberto De Mendoza · Silvia Monti · Mike Kennedy · George Rigaud · Anita Strindberg

and with **LEO GENN** · Directed by LUCIO FULCI · Music by ENNIO MORRICONE

Co-production: Apollo Films, Rome · Les Films Corona, Paris · Atlantida Film, Madrid

TECHNICOLOR® · An American International Release

MARISA MELL · JEAN SOREL
ELSA MARTINELLI · JOHN IRELAND
in
ONE ON TOP OF THE OTHER
'X'
music by RIZ ORTOLANI TECHNICOLOR®

above:
British poster artwork for *One on Top of the Other*.

right, from top: *The Psychic* – Virginia (Jennifer O'Neill) searches for the corpse seen in her vision; feeling claustrophobic; traumatized by the truth; Signora Casati (Veronica Michielini) pays for her attempts to contact Virginia.

facing page:
The American poster.

Suddenly she could see into the future . . .
. . . and saw her own murder . . .

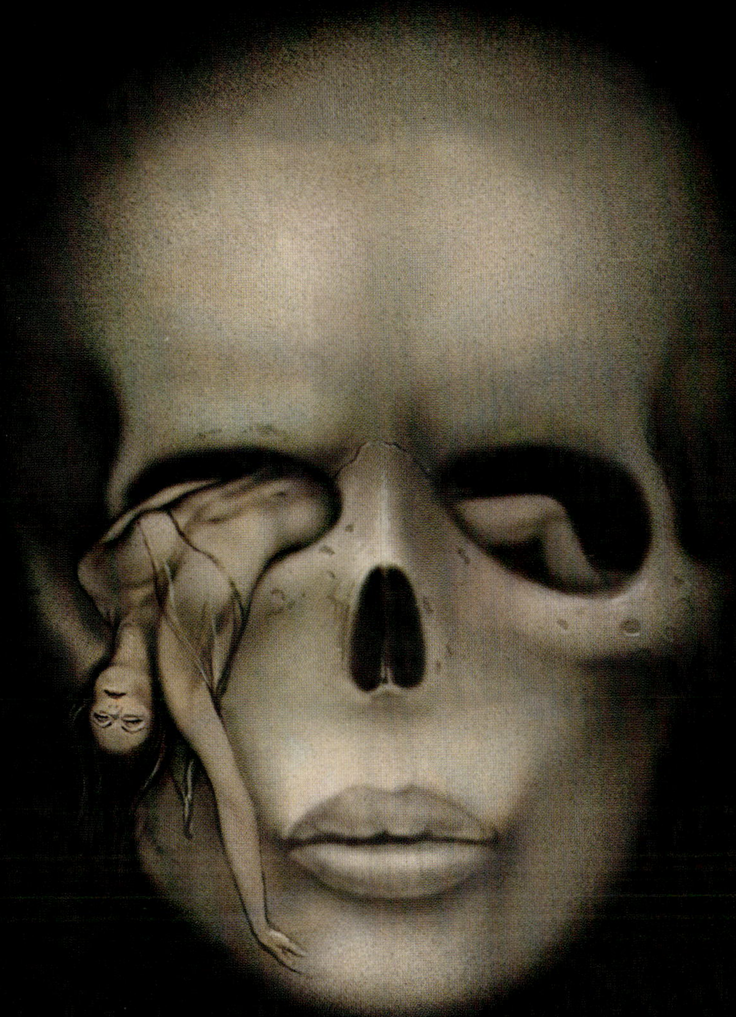

Jennifer O'Neill
is

THE PSYCHIC

Brandon Chase presents Jennifer O'Neill "THE PSYCHIC"
Starring Marc Porel Evelyn Stewert Jenny Tamburi Gabriele Ferzetti
Produced by Cinecompany Directed by Lucio Fulci Color by Deluxe
A Group 1 Release A Rizzoli Film R RESTRICTED

"THE PSYCHIC"

BITING, GNAWING
TERROR
CLAWS AT YOUR
BRAIN!
WARNING!
NOT RECOMMENDED
VIEWING FOR PERSONS
WITH SCHIZOPHRENIC
TENDENCIES!
SCHIZOID
R RESTRICTED
Under 17 Requires Accompanying
Parent or Adult Guardian
starring
FLORINDA BOLKAN · STANLEY BAKER · JEAN SOREL and with LEO GENN
Produced by
EDMONDO AMATI · Executive Producer
RENATO JABONI · Written and Directed by
LUCIO FULCI · TECHNICOLOR® · An American International Release
COPYRIGHT ©1972 AMERICAN INTERNATIONAL PICTURES, INC.
72/41

METROPOLITAN FILMS presents
JENNIFER O'NEILL
JOHN GARCO
MARC POREL
in
A FILM by
LUCIO FULCI
SEVEN BLACK NOTES

HOLLYWOOD VIDEO
présente
une sélection METROPOLITAN EXPORT
LE VENIN DE LA PEUR
écrit et réalisé : LUCIO FULCI

présente
MARISA MELL - JEAN SOREL
ELSA MARTINELLI
dans
PERVERSION Story
ALBERTO de MENDOZA
JOHN IRELAND
avec JEAN SOBIESKI
et FAITH DOMERGUE
un film de LUCIO FULCI
TECHNICOLOR - PANORAMIQUE
INTERDIT AUX MOINS DE 18 ANS

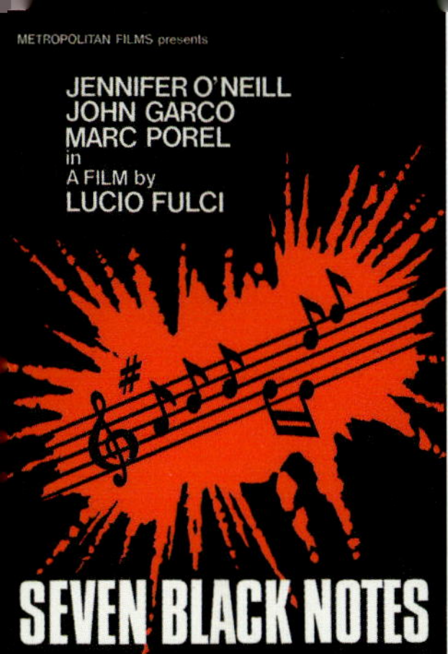

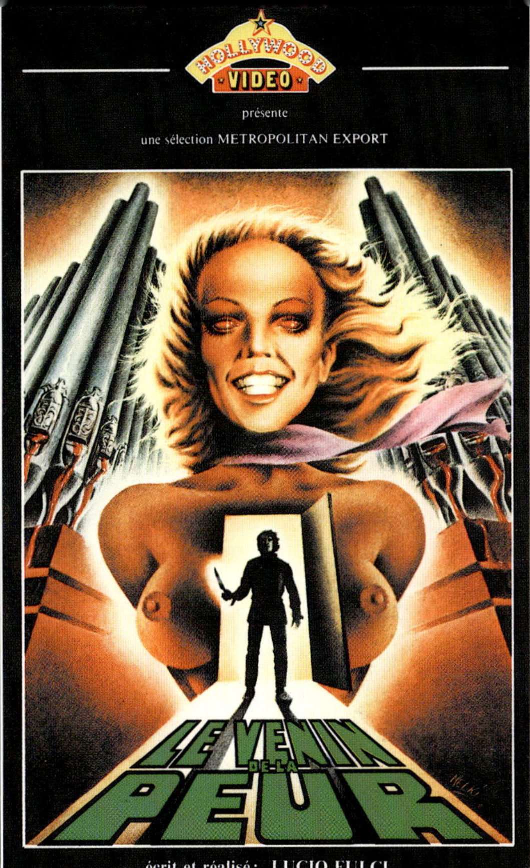

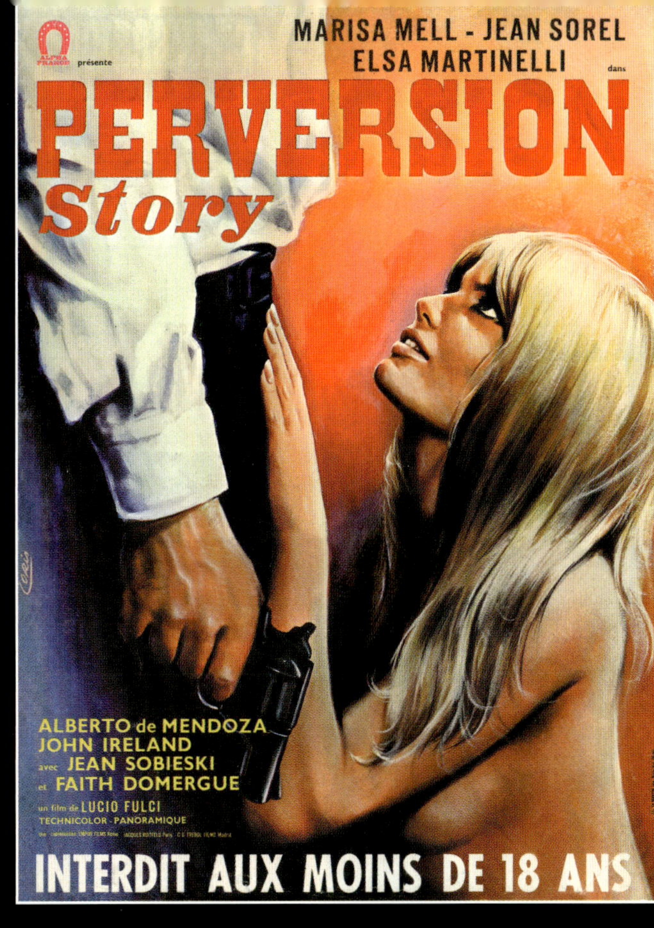

bove: A rare North European poster.

ight: French video cover art for a release of *A Lizard in a Woman's Skin* (as 'The Venom of Fear').

ar right: Stylish but somewhat misleading rtwork for *One on Top of the Other*, also eleased in France under the alternative itle *Perversion Story.*

acing page: American poster for *A Lizard n a Woman's Skin.*

elow: A striking Mexican lobby card for *A Lizard in a Woman's Skin.*

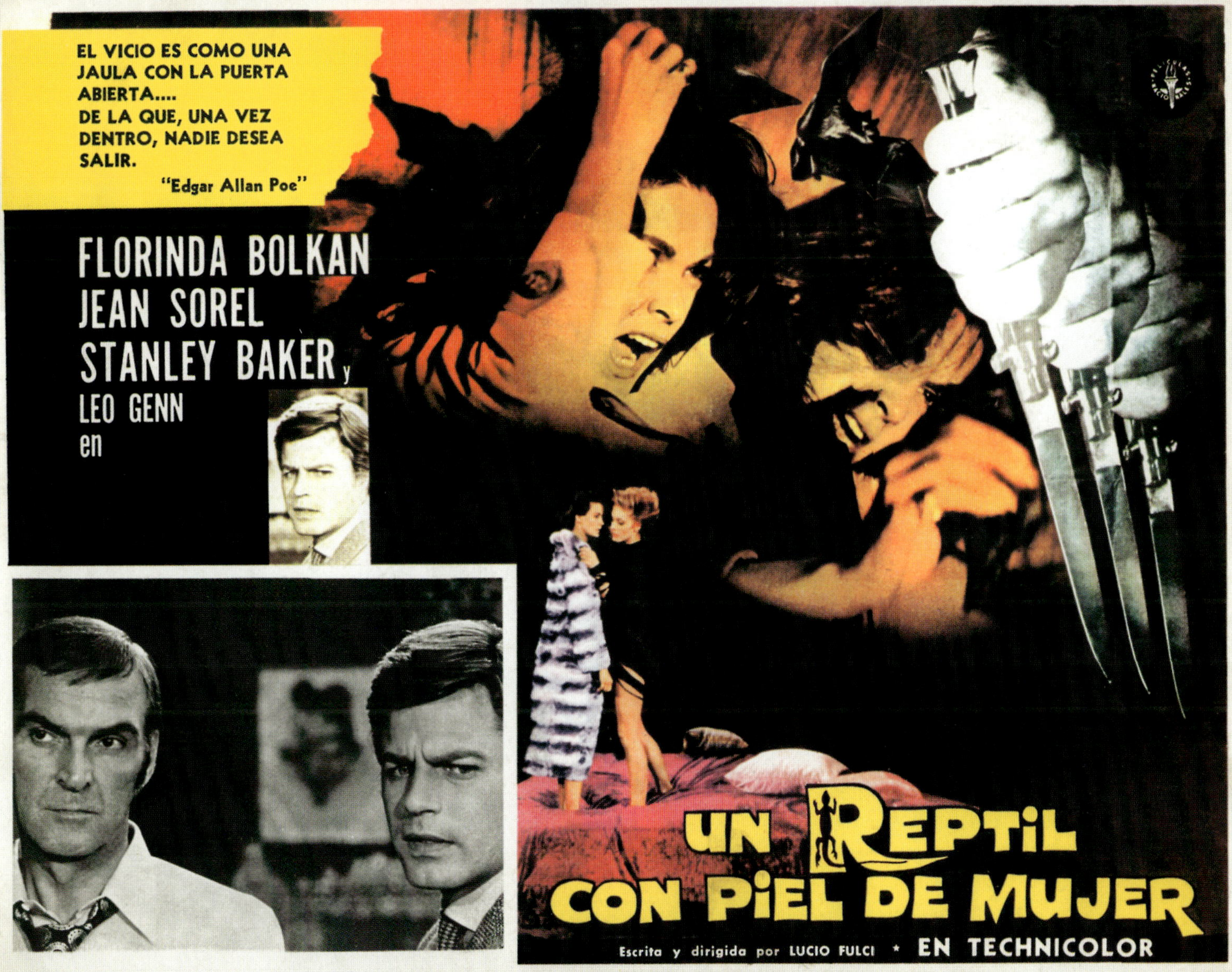

EL VICIO ES COMO UNA JAULA CON LA PUERTA ABIERTA.... DE LA QUE, UNA VEZ DENTRO, NADIE DESEA SALIR.
"Edgar Allan Poe"
FLORINDA BOLKAN
JEAN SOREL
STANLEY BAKER y
LEO GENN
en
UN REPTIL CON PIEL DE MUJER
Escrita y dirigida por LUCIO FULCI • EN TECHNICOLOR

this page:
Florinda Bolkan as Carol Hammond, the repressed lesbian whose neuroses are the subject of *A Lizard in a Woman's Skin.*

facing page:
Spanish press sheet for *One on Top of the Other.*

ATLANTIDA FILMS, S.A
DISTRIBUCION
MARISA
MELL
JEAN
SOREL
ELSA
MARTINELI
UNA
HISTORIA
PERVERSA
JANO
DIRECTOR
LUCIO FULCI
UNA COPRODUCCION HISPANO-ITALIANA
DE TREBOL FILMS
PANORAMICA
Technicolor
70 m/m
CON LA MARAVILLA DEL
SONIDO ESTEREOFONICO

Don't Torture A Duckling
Florinda Bolkan - Tomas Milian Regie: Lucio Fulci
ca. 1½ uur speelfilm

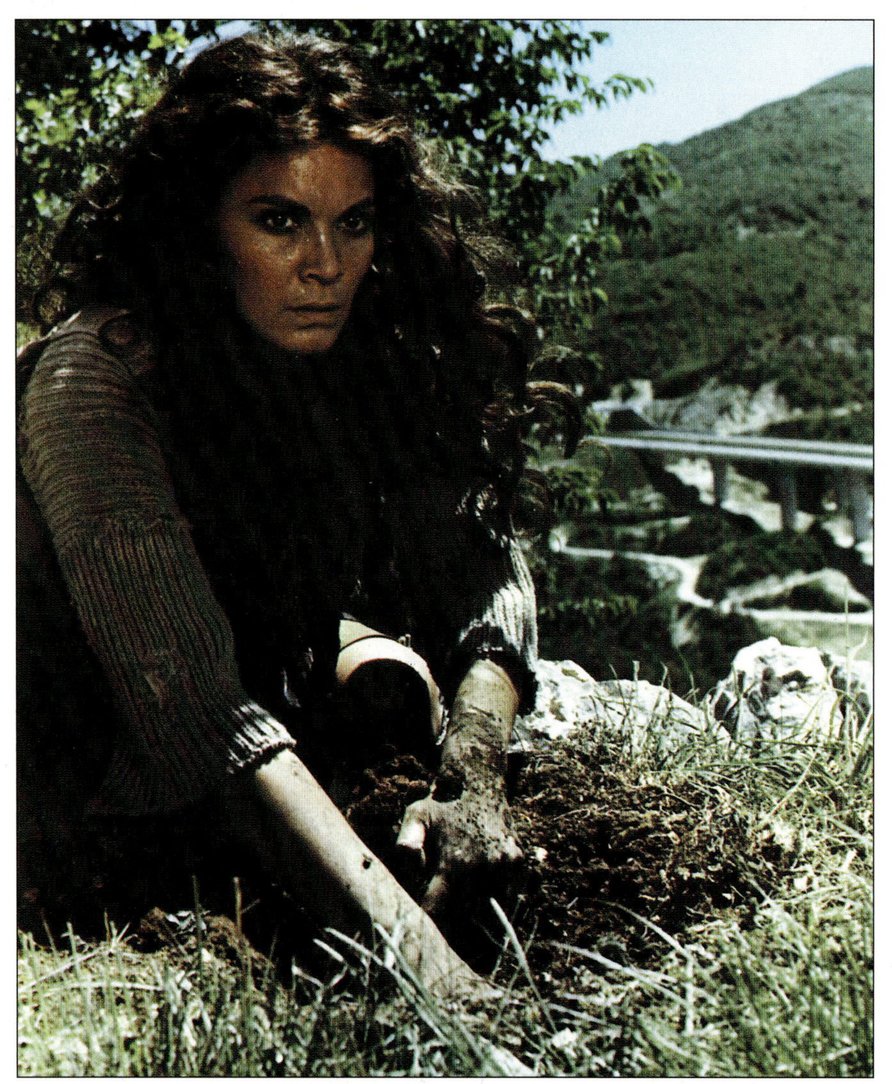

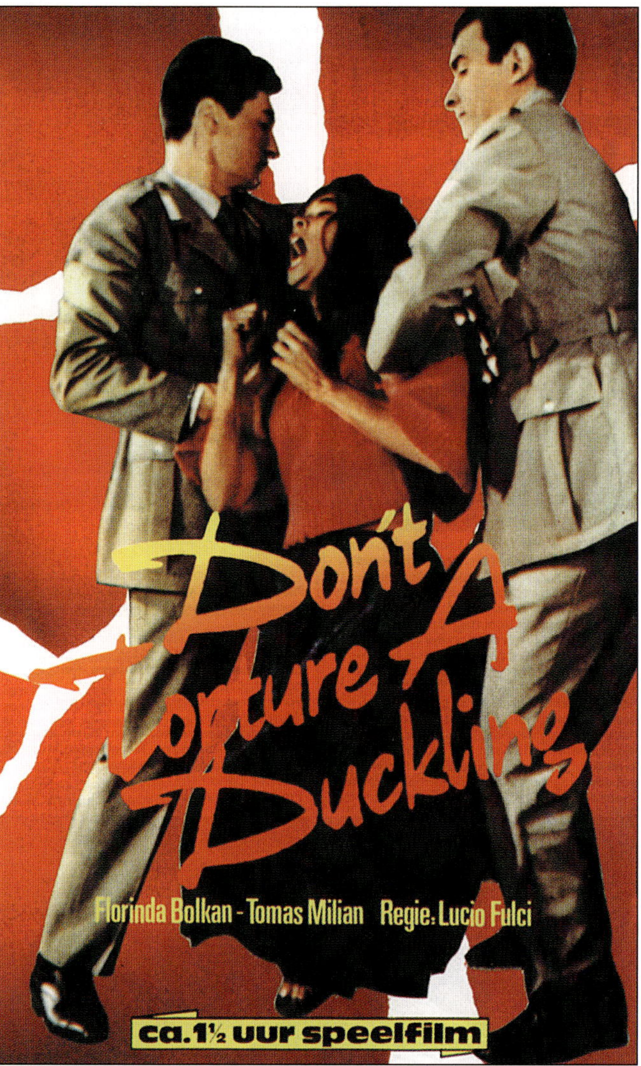

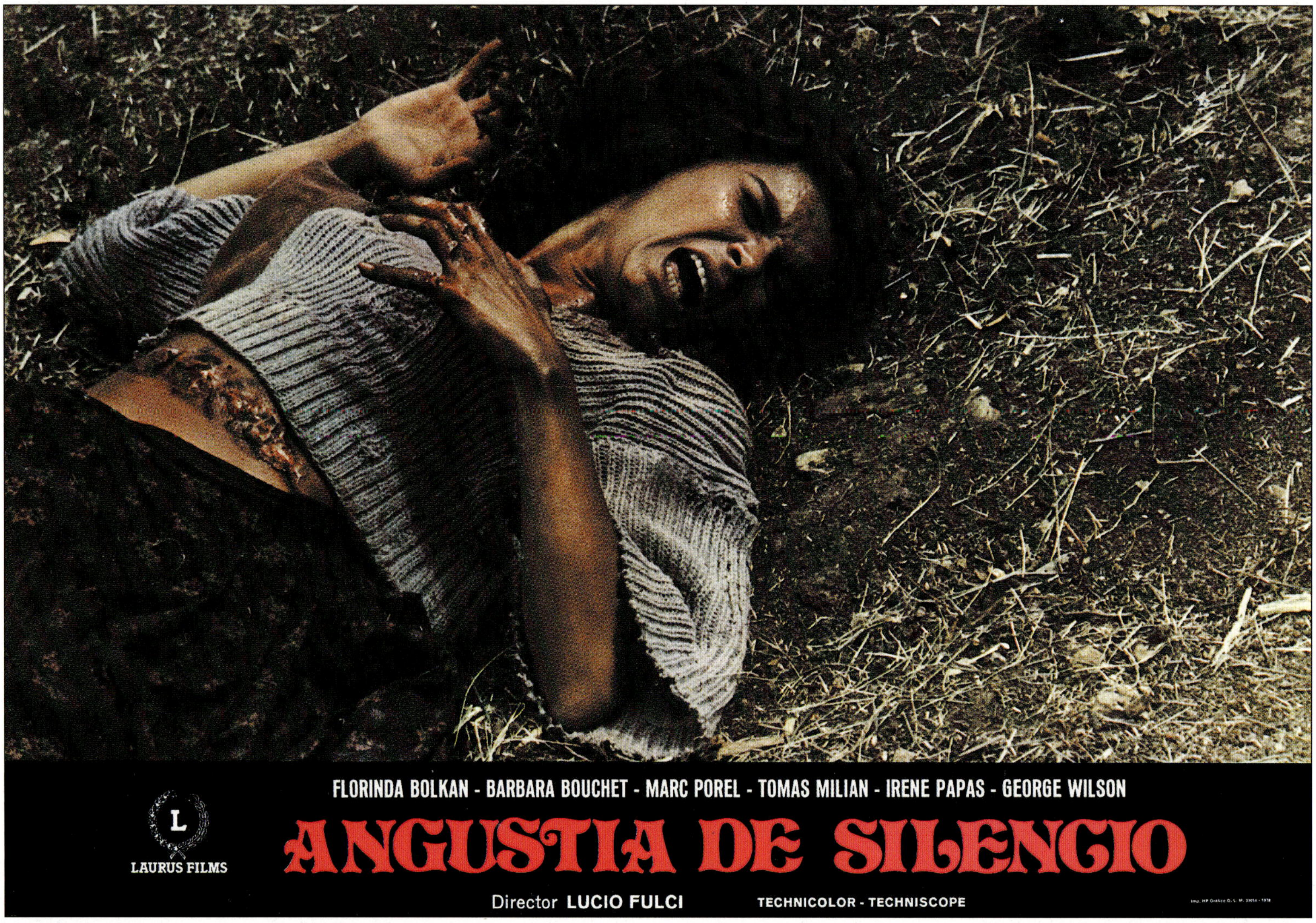
FLORINDA BOLKAN - BARBARA BOUCHET - MARC POREL - TOMAS MILIAN - IRENE PAPAS - GEORGE WILSON
L
LAURUS FILMS
ANGUSTIA DE SILENCIO
Director LUCIO FULCI
TECHNICOLOR - TECHNISCOPE

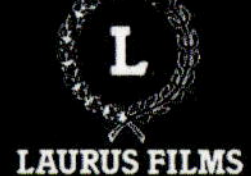

facing page top left: The 'witch' known only as 'la maciara' (Florinda Bolkan) in *Don't Torture a Duckling.*

facing page top right: The Dutch VHS cover for the film.

facing page bottom and this page below: The horrific fate of la maciara.

Don't Torture a Duckling

1972

Directed by Lucio Fulci. produced by Renato Jaboni for Medusa Distribuzione. story: Lucio Fulci & Roberto Gianviti. screenplay: Lucio Fulci, Roberto Gianviti & Gianfranco Clerici. director of photography: Sergio D'Offizi. music: Riz Ortolani; published by General Music, (Rome). editor: Ornella Micheli. set designer: Pierluigi Basile. production manager: Agostino Pane. assistant director: Francesco Cinieri. continuity: Roberto Giandalia. cameraman: Gianni Bergamini. assistant cameraman: Enrico Lucidi. costumes: Marisa Crimi. special make-up: Franco Di Girolamo & Nilo Iacoponi. hair styles: Rosetta Luciani. costumer's assistant: Elisabetta Pocioni. assistant make-up: Maurizio Trani. production assistants: Donato Bitetto & Massimo Civilotti. paymaster: Valerio Ferri. still photographer: G.B. Schwarze. editor's assistant: Bruno Micheli. sound engineer: Massimo Laboni. sound effects editors: Aurelio Pennacchia & Ezio Marcorin. synchronization: C.D.S. set furnishings: "Habitat", Via Cristoforo Colombo (Rome). Production wishes to thank the headquarters of the Carabinieri of the town of Monte S. Angelo for their valuable co-operation. song "Quei giorni insieme a te" by Riz Ortolani, performed by Ornella Vanoni. colour by Eastmancolor. negative: Technicolor. format: Techniscope. filmed on location in the town of Monte S. Angelo (Italy).

Cast: Florinda Bolkan (la maciara). Barbara Bouchet (Patrizia). Tomas Milian (Andrea Martelli). Irene Papas (Aurelia Avallone). Marc Porel (Don Alberto Avallone). Georges ['George'] Wilson (Francesco). Antonello Campodifiori (Young lieutenant with moustache). Ugo D'Alessio (Captain Modesti, balding police officer). Virgilio Gazzolo [as 'Virginio Gazzolo'] (police commissioner, wearing glasses). Vito Passeri (Giuseppe Barra). Rosalia Maggio (Mrs. Spriano, Michele's mother). Andrea Aureli (Mr. Lo Cascio, Bruno's father). Linda Sini (Mrs. Lo Cascio, Bruno's mother). Franco Balducci (Mr. Spriano, Michele's father). *Uncredited:* Fausta Avelli (Malvina Avallone). Gianfranco Barra (Impallomeni, older moustachioed policeman). Janos ['John'] Bartha (policeman at desk after Barra's arrest). Duilio Cruciani (Mario, boy found dead beside stream).

Italian theatrical title
Non si sevizia un paperino

Italy

Alternative titles
Don't Torture Donald Duck (shooting title/literal translation)
Fanatismo (IT alt. theatrical/video) 'Bigotry'

International theatrical titles
Don't Torture a Duckling (English-language export title)
La longue nuit de l'exorcisme (FR) 'The Long Night of Exorcism'
Angustia de silencio (SP) 'Anguish of Silence'
No tortures esa muñeca (SP) 'Don't Torture the Doll'
Les poupées de sang (CAN québécois) 'Dolls of Blood'
O estranho segredo do bosque dos sonhos (BRZ) 'Strange Secret of the Wood of Dreams'
O segredo do bosque dos sonhos (POR) 'The Secret Wood of Dreams'
Linç (TUR) 'Lynched'

Video titles
La nuit de l'exorcisme (FR) 'The Night of Exorcism'
Fureur meurtrière (FR) 'Murderous Rage'
Woodoo (DEN) 'Voodoo'
Kauhujen Dylä (FIN) 'The Village of Horrors'
To Trigono Tis Mavris Mageias (GRE) 'The Triangle of Black Magic'
Satanades tis akolasias (GRE) 'Satanic Debauchery'
Boyntoy (GRE) 'Voodoo'
Paperino (FR) 'Duckling'
Ne zaklasd a kiskacsát! (HUN) 'Don't Harass a Duckling!'

Production companies
Medusa Distribuzione

Theatrical distributors
Medusa Distribuzione

Theatrical running times
Italy 110m
Spain (SMC) 113m

Video/DVD/Blu-ray running times (adjusted)
Anchor Bay DVD (USA) 102m 00s
Medusa DVD (Italy) 102m 05s

Shooting period
Shooting from 02 May 1972

Censorship
Italian censor certificate 61046 issued 22 September 1972

Release information
Rome 29 September 1972
Melissano 10 November 1972
Bari 01 December 1972

Synopsis: A series of child murders is taking place in a remote village of Southern Italy. The victims are young boys on the cusp of puberty. At first, suspicion falls upon Giuseppe, a local simpleton and 'peeping tom' who has been repeatedly taunted by the boys. In the hills, la maciara – a woman who claims to be a witch – conducts black magic ceremonies, using mud dolls to represent the boys of the village. They have angered her by disturbing a burial mound which contains a dead baby's skeleton. Also a suspect is Patrizia, a young woman from the city lying low in the village after a drug scandal. Despite their young ages she offers sexual favours to the local adolescents. She is befriended by Martelli, a journalist from the North who is investigating the killings. Amid increasing local hysteria, Giuseppe is arrested for the first murder, but it soon transpires that he's innocent: he did however find one of the bodies and attempt to use the information to extort a pitiful sum of money from the parents. Seeking la maciara, Martelli and the police go to meet with 'old Francesco', an eccentric living in a stone hut in the hills. He too practises black magic, and sells charms and potions. He is close to la maciara, with whom he is rumoured to have had (and then disposed of) a baby. He is also friendly with Patrizia, who gets a kick out of black magic. The police hunt down and arrest la maciara, who gleefully confesses to the crimes. However, it transpires that she believes her incantations have merely 'brought about' the deaths, and has no awareness of the physical methods used. An alibi provided by a policeman miles away from the murder scene clinches her innocence, and she is set free. However, the fathers of the dead boys are unconvinced and beat her to death with chains. Patrizia and Martelli's investigations lead them to the village's amiable young priest, Don Alberto Avallone, and his strange, silent mother Aurelia. Don Alberto encourages the local boys to play football beside the church. Aurelia has another child, a girl of about five who was born retarded. Martelli intuits that the child has witnessed the murders when he sees her pulling the heads off her dolls. One such doll's head, that of Donald Duck, was found at one of the crime scenes. Martelli's theory is correct: Don Alberto is the killer. He strangles the boys to rescue them from their future carnal sins. He takes the little girl, witness to his crimes, and tries to throw her off a cliff. After a fist-fight with Martelli, Don Alberto falls to a gruesome death on the rocks below.

above:
Irene Papas as Aurelia Avallone, the priest's mother in *Don't Torture a Duckling.*

left and below:
Andrea Matelli (Tomas Milian) and Patrizia (Barbara Bouchet) investigating the mysterious serial killings that plague a small rural village in Southern Italy.

opposite:
Tomas Milian and Barbara Bouchet discover the awful truth...

About the production: *Non si sevizia un paperino* was announced to the trades in March 1972 as 'Don't Torture Donald Duck', a title which was soon withdrawn, presumably after a threatening phone call from the Disney Studio! When first announced in the pages of *Variety*, *Duckling*'s cast included Italian exploitation regular Raymond Lovelock alongside Florinda Bolkan and Tomas Milian. With Milian already on board playing the film's investigative reporter, it would seem that Lovelock was initially slated for the part of Don Alberto (the only other significant role for a younger male actor). However at some point between March and May, Lovelock was replaced by Marc Porel (though not before another actor was briefly mooted, Italian singer Massimo Ranieri, a former child pop prodigy who'd recently represented Italy in the 1971 Eurovision Song Contest). Shooting began on 2 May 1972 and continued into June.

Review: *Don't Torture a Duckling* is one of Lucio Fulci's most striking achievements. It combines outstanding photography, clever plotting, some shocking eruptions of violence, and a pessimistic world view which shades into tenderness when it comes to the suffering of children. Fulci co-wrote the screenplay with his regular writing colleague Roberto Gianviti (the two men had already written eight screenplays together, including *One on Top of the Other* and *A Lizard in a Woman's Skin*). Between them they came up with a story well beyond the norm for the increasingly crowded giallo market. While all around were frantically trying to mimic the icy cosmopolitan chic of Dario Argento, Fulci opted instead to set his next giallo in a poor rural area, and made the murder victims young boys instead of the customary parade of beautiful women. A sick and twisted murderer is at large and, as per usual for the giallo genre, the suspects include just about everyone we meet – but that's just about the only point of similarity with the rest of the giallo genre.

The film has three major themes: the way in which rural insularity fosters prejudice, the relationship between Italy's North and South, and the way the Catholic Church's perverse veneration of 'innocence' generates monsters. Packed, then, with ideas not generally associated with the giallo, *Don't Torture a Duckling* is as ambitious as it is unusual.

The first two themes come together in the film's most brutal and memorable set-piece: the chain-whipping of a self-professed witch, known only as la maciara ('the witch'), whom local villagers believe is responsible for the child-killings afflicting the region. The killing of la maciara is designed to make the argument against vigilante violence (the killers are the fathers of the murdered boys) and as savage as it is it's also a marvellous piece of cinema, bringing all of Fulci's skills together. Creative camerawork, intelligent use of music, punchy editing and grotesque special effects coalesce with Florinda Bolkan's terrified performance to create a scene that's almost operatically horrific. The brutality of chain-whipping had never been captured before with such shocking intensity. Fulci would return to the idea later, in the gothique gloom of *The Beyond*, but

above:
Greek actress Irene Papas plays Aurelia, mother of the village priest Don Alberto.

here the naturalistic settings, bright sunlight and superior make-up effects lend the victim's slow death an astonishing intensity. The perpetrators, their faces set impassively, surround the unfortunate 'witch' like a pack of wolves, backing her into an isolated country graveyard. When she tries to pull the wrought-iron gates shut, they are slammed viciously on her fingers. She retreats, but her chain-wielding assailants encircle her, fetching ferocious swipes across her face and body. The detail here is truly repellant, as the flesh not only bleeds but also 'sweats' with the clear fluid which bad wounds exude in reality. Fulci employs two contrasting pieces of music on the soundtrack: an uptempo belter called "Crazy" by Wess and the Airedales (a library track previously used in Dino Risi's 1969 comedy *Vedo nudo*) and a soaring lament by Italian pop singer Ornella Vanoni called "Quei giorni insieme a te" ('Those Days with You'). The songs emerge from a radio turned up loud by one of the attackers to drown out the victim's screams, which adds a painfully ironic quality to the suffering onscreen.

Despite the victim's black magic ravings earlier, her status as an ultimately tragic figure is forcefully underlined in the aftermath of her beating. While many Fulci sequences depict physical violence, it's rare to see the victim cling to life afterwards; once the violence is over the victim usually dies. Here, though, after the chain-whipping has shocked us with its savagery, we remain with the victim as she crawls to the highway seeking help. Just as she makes it to the busy road skirting the village, she dies. Fulci fills half of the frame with her sightless face as deep focus traffic whizzes past behind, and then holds the shot for twelve seconds. La maciara's futile attempt to gain the attention of passing motorists is therefore clearly intended as a metaphor for the social isolation endemic to Southern Italy in the 1970s.

below:
A somewhat carelessly designed Spanish poster for the film.

As a result, *Don't Torture a Duckling* has been attacked by some critics for painting a reactionary portrait of rural life, with Fulci accused of perpetuating a common stereotype in Italian culture, in which the South clings to outmoded moral attitudes rejected by the modern, free-thinking North. A contemporary review in the left-leaning newspaper *l'Unità* homed in on this aspect of the story and found the film lacking in subtlety: "Non si sevizia un paperino *deals with peculiar aspects of the Italian deep South, namely magic and superstition, which flourish alongside the modern motorways. Maybe the only image that is convincing in this movie is the metaphor of false progress, emerging from the contrast between the material poverty and morality of the little town of Accendura (where the lurid events and mysterious murders take place, where the witch is accused of having killed three young boys with her black magic spells) and the smooth tarmac of the motorways on which new cars travel indifferently. But this image on its own cannot make a movie, neither can certain 'topics', even the most courageous. In this movie there is no trace of any socio-ideological analysis that can justify the choice of such a topic. Instead one finds only irritating oversimplified attitudes towards the villagers, the prostitutes, sexual repression, the police's narrow-mindedness, the village idiot, the inhumanity of the mob. This does not allow any dialogue to explore or illuminate the backwardness and incivility of the South. If you add to all this scenes of sadistic violence (the witch's massacre with chains and axes),* Non si sevizia un paperino *clearly and fully reveals its commercial intent rather than its social engagement.*"[8]

Putting aside the critic's facile distinction between 'commercial' and 'socially engaged' cinema, is it fair to accuse Fulci of 'oversimplified attitudes' in his depiction of the South? It rather depends on whether you believe that a film has to offer "socio-ideological analysis" in order to justify telling a story such as this. Perhaps the script by Fulci and Gianviti employs broad strokes compared to, say, the work of Francesco Rosi, but it surely counts for something that they chose to offset their critique of Southern attitudes with a parallel critique of the indifference and decadence of sophisticated urbanites. Yes, the attitude of local villagers to the slaying of their children is depicted as ugly and indiscriminate. When news leaks out that the local 'witch' has been arrested, crowds surround the police station baying for her blood. After police questioning she is deemed to be merely mad, and released without charge, but the locals are not satisfied and take the law into their own hands. Their violent and wrongful 'retribution' is depicted with disgust by Fulci, which seems to me no worse than the sort of sociological special pleading that would blame iniquity on inequity. If the film fails to present a sociological case-study about rural mob vigilantism, it does at least show that when you add fear, panic and superstition together, terrible and unjust things can happen. Meanwhile the image of tourists from the wealthier regions cruising past these pockets of rural poverty tells us all we need to know about the director's political sympathies. If Fulci really was a supercilious metropolitan, taking potshots at the yokels, he would scarcely have constructed such a striking and caustic visual metaphor, one which even *l'Unità*'s reviewer was forced to concede had metaphorical impact.

The fact that the villagers buy spells and potions from an old 'magician' (Francesco, played by Georges Wilson), while also accepting the ministrations of the Catholic Church, documents an interesting side to rural affairs in Italy, not unlike the duality present in Haiti, where African magic and Catholicism blend together. Given *Duckling*'s perceived socio-geographical divide, between Northern rationalism and Southern superstition, it's interesting that Fulci actually gives a lot of dramatic weight to la maciara's spells (the film opens with her burying a voodoo doll). Although the narrative ultimately favours a rational explanation, it includes a scene in which la maciara claims that her magic may have worked through someone else: that the 'real' killer may have been the instrument of vengeance she had sought with her spells. Nothing that occurs after la maciara's death takes this supernatural notion any further, therefore it's hardly a robust reading of the film, but in view of Fulci's later dalliance with the supernatural (e.g. *Zombie Flesh-Eaters*) it's worth bearing in mind...

Someone whose belief-system is *not* embraced, directly or indirectly, is the killer priest Don Alberto. Indeed the central point of the film is to reject the priest's Catholic hatred of the flesh. Alberto claims that he's 'saving' boys from the sin of desire, but then he also attempts to murder his baby sister, who has seen enough to betray him. Any claim to a 'spiritual' justification is therefore totally undermined.

Does the film imply that Don Alberto is a paedophile? It has to be said there's not a lot of support for this theory in the dialogue, and when the coroner examines the victims he finds no evidence of sexual abuse. So is it a step too far to consider the priest a paedophile as well as a murderer? I think not, as there are clues elsewhere to suggest that his 'higher reasons' hide a secret lust. For instance, it's significant that he never shows the slightest interest in saving *girls* from sin, a spiritual 'oversight' which suggests that it's desire which drives his actions. Then there's the way Fulci films the boys when showing them as Don Alberto sees them: playing football in rhapsodic slow motion, the boys leap around in white football kits which glow with kitsch romantic radiance. It's like a lovers' flashback, or a dream of romantic paradise. Schmaltzy music plays as Don Alberto eulogises in voice-over: *"They are my brothers, and I love them"*. Finally, there's the priest's preferred method of killing, strangulation, often regarded as one of the most sexual of killing techniques, with its squeezing of flesh, physical intimacy, and sustained manual pressure.

So why not just go ahead and specify molestation, if that's what Fulci is hinting at? Perhaps because the subject was just too controversial; going the extra yard in order to nail the priest's sexual motives would have been a massively provocative step for an Italian filmmaker in the early 1970s, especially someone outside the charmed circle of 'art cinema'. Commercially too, it may just have been too ugly and depressing a topic. Sensitivity to the child actors could also have played a part. Fulci shows very little of the murders themselves, concentrating on the discovery of the corpses, probably to avoid putting children through distressing situations on set.

Some paedophiles are drawn to sexually precocious children; some presume to initiate the young into sexual knowledge; and others see sex as spiritually unclean and think that sex with an innocent child is somehow pure. Although Don Alberto abstains from sexual behaviour, it's this latter group to which he seems to belong 'in spirit'. There is, in his veneration of innocence, something perverse and unhealthy. For Don Alberto (and Catholicism in general) the ultimate sin is sexual pleasure, and when 'his boys' begin to lust after women, he fears they will drift away and turn their backs on the sanctification he offers. But whether or not the intention was to characterise him as a paedophile, there's no doubt that Don Alberto is one of Fulci's unmitigated monsters: when he falls to his death from a clifftop, his face smashing repeatedly against the rocks on the way down, you get the distinct feeling that Fulci is cheering his demise every step of the way.

Perhaps the film's most unusual character is Patrizia, a city girl lying low in the rural backwater of Accendura after a minor drugs scandal. Her low-cut necklines and short skirts meet with disapproval from the villagers, and the scene in which we first encounter her seems calculated to provoke our disapproval too. A young boy, Michele, brings

above:
Patrizia and Martelli believe the priest's mother Aurelia could be shielding her son, or may even be responsible for the murders herself...

below:
Mexican lobby card.

above:
Danish video cover.

facing page:
Italian sales sheet for the film under the alternative title *Fanatismo*. Note that this was another of Fulci's films to be made available in 70mm.

below:
'Old Francesco' (Georges Wilson), a hermit living in the hills who is said to have schooled la maciara in the black arts.

Patrizia a glass of orange juice as she reclines nude in her room, luxuriating beneath a sun-lamp. She taunts the nervous boy, showing off her body, asking him if he'd like to make love to her, and telling him he's "full of shit" when he swears that he's already had lots of girls. But despite this mean and disturbing characterisation, Patrizia is shown in a gradually more sympathetic light. Her boredom with village life is understandable, given the hedonistic life she's been forced to give up, and her efforts to assist the investigation prove valuable. But we're faced with a difficult hurdle: she too shows an unhealthy interest in children, although it's presented as an idiosyncrasy more than a sickness. Patrizia and Don Alberto are therefore linked, but whereas he negates his sexual desire for boys through a brutally repressive drive to purity, she indulges sexual power over them by her brazen exhibitionism.

In Italy there's a greater degree of tolerance for the sexual adventurism of adolescents and this extends to homosexual as well as heterosexual activity. If boys 'fool around' with each other, the Italian response is more 'so what' than 'what's wrong?' It's only when boys engage in sex with older men, or when men live with other men 'like man and wife' that Italian morality resembles that of the British and Americans, and the weight of taboo comes crashing down. On the other hand, a great many Italian films (by exploitation *and* art-house directors, like Fellini, Visconti, Malle, Bertolucci) present the early sexual experiences of teenage boys with older women as episodes of fun. These encounters are typically shown as occasions for celebration, humour, nostalgia and farce. *Don't Torture a Duckling* contrasts a murderous male pervert with a manipulative female who gets a kick out of boys' inexperience. The former is clearly defined as a monster. The latter, because of a much higher tolerance towards the idea of seduction by women, is barely questioned in her 'unusual tastes'. No one would argue that it is better for a boy to be murdered by a paedophile than be seduced by a woman, but to portray Patrizia as, essentially, a fun gal who likes to give the boys a treat, is a tad more 'broad-minded' than seems entirely justifiable. Certainly, it's difficult to imagine a man in the same role being accepted with quite so much sangfroid.

If ethical discrepancies arise, it's still a tribute to Fulci that such uncomfortable subject matter has been grappled with at all. *Don't Torture a Duckling* is a genuine one-off: it looks great, sounds great, and tackles a number of prickly, off-the-wall subjects. It may occasionally veer into the pedantic (with a few scenes too many of the police investigation) but its idiosyncrasies and jawdropping violence make it a memorable and challenging experience.

Fulci remained proud of this movie until the end of his career, calling it *"my favourite of my own films"*.[9] In an article called "The tricks of the trade, according to Lucio Fulci", which appeared in *l'Unità* in May 1982, he used an example from the film to illustrate his commitment to the search for creative technical solutions and to explain why he regarded special effects as a valid medium for his creativity:

"Do you remember the end of Don't Torture a Duckling *with the head of Marc Porel that smashed against jagged rocks? Lots of people have asked me how I shot that scene, even Nanni Loy did not manage to understand the technique used. But it was easy. The fake sharp edges of the rock had been placed horizontally and each hit (in the rubber head there were ten little explosive charges) was filmed separately. Then I edited the whole into a sequence making the scene vertical. I would have also liked to insert superimposed some real shots of the look in Porel's eyes, but the producer refused me the 300,000 lira necessary for that small enrichment."*[10]

FLORINDA BOLKAN - BARBARA BOUCHET - MARC POREL - TOMAS MILIAN - IRENE PAPAS - GEORGE WILSON
LAURUS FILMS
ANGUSTIA DE SILENCIO
Director LUCIO FULCI
TECHNICOLOR - TECHNISCOPE

70 m/m
TECHNICOLOR

FLORINDA BOLKAN
TOMAS MILIAN
IRENE PAPAS
FANATISMO
(NON SI SEVIZIA UN PAPERINO)
Director
Lucio FULCI

Italian theatrical title
Sette note in nero

Translation
'Seven Notes in Black'

Italy

Alternative title
Seven Black Notes (Dolce come morire) (shooting title)

International theatrical titles
The Psychic (USA)
L'emmurée vivante (FR)
'The One Buried Alive'
Murder to the Tune of 7 Black Notes (Pakistan)

Video titles
Prediction (FR)
Demoniac (FR alt.)

Production company
Cinecompany S.r.l.

Theatrical distributor
Cineriz ("Rizzoli Film presents") (Italy)
Group 1 (USA)

Theatrical running time
Italy 95m

Video/DVD/Blu-ray running times (adjusted)
Domo video (Italy) 97m 26s
Columbia video (Japan) 96m 21s
Severin DVD (USA) 97m 14s

Shooting period
Shooting from 04 October 1976

Censorship
Italian censor certificate 70296 issued 18 May 1977

Release information
Rome 26 August 1977
Bari 31 August 1977
USA (Indianapolis, IN) 19 January 1979

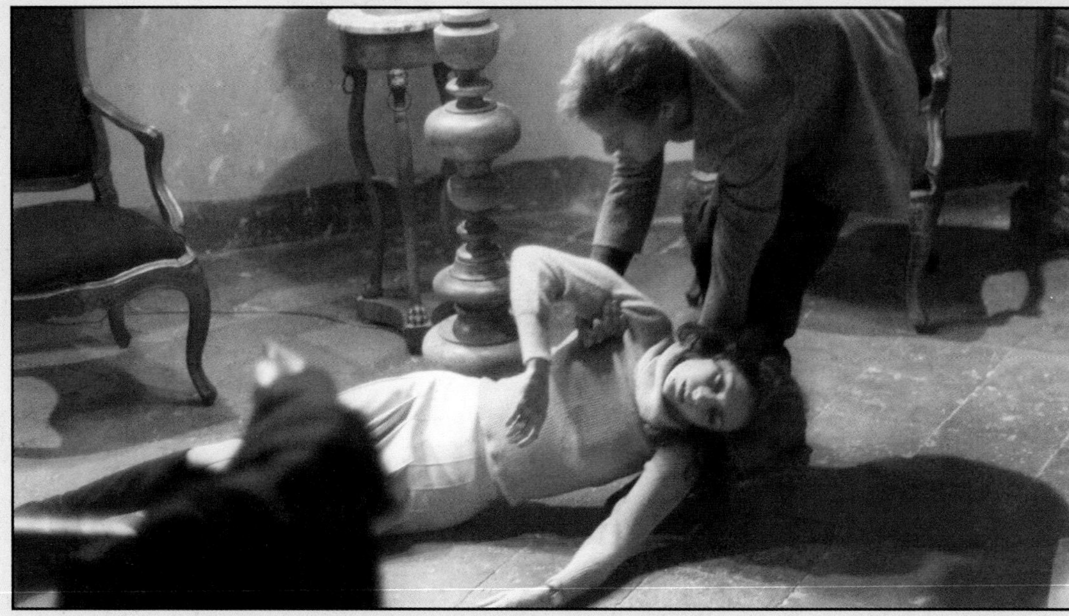

The Psychic

1977

Directed by Lucio Fulci. a film produced by Cinecompany S.r.l. story & shooting script: Lucio Fulci, Roberto Gianviti & Dardano Sacchetti. director of photography: Sergio Salvati. music score [Franco] Bixio, [Fabio] Frizzi & [Vincenzo] Tempera; published by Bixio C.E.M.S.A. / Rizzoli Film. editor: Ornella Micheli. set designer: Luciano Spadoni. production manager: Franco Cuccu. assistant director: Roberto Giandalia. continuity: Rita Agostini. cameraman: Franco Bruni. assistant cameramen: Maurizio Lucchini & Claudio Farinelli. chief electrician: Alfredo Fedeli. key grip: Luciano Micheli. costume designer: Massimo Lentini. make-up artist: Maurizio Giustini. assistant make-up artist: Antonio Maltempo. wardrobe: Carmen Pericolo. property master: Goffredo Massetti. assistant set designer: Roberta Tomassetti. assistant production manager: Carlo Cucchi. production secretary: Marco Giannoni. business manager: Roberto Penna. production secretary: Marco Giannoni. stills: Luciano Adiutori. assistant cutter: Bruno Micheli. assistant editor: Mario D'Ambrosio. sound technician: Raul Montesanti. boom: Alfonso Montesanti. sound effects: Renato Marinelli. synchronization: Cinefonico Palatino. international soundtrack produced at Cinefonico Palatino. English version dubbing director: Tony La Penna at CDS Via Margutta. Jennifer O'Neill's jewelry: Bulgari; her furs by Fendi. hats by Venturi. shoes by Salato. theme recorded by Gil Ventura. "With You" by Ernest, Franco Bixio, Fabio Frizzi & Vincenzo Tempera, performed by Linda Lee. colour by Telecolor. format: Vistavision.

Cast: Jennifer O'Neill (Virginia Ducci). Gabriele Ferzetti (Emilio Rospini). Marc Porel (Luca Fattori). Gianni Garko (Francesco Ducci). Ida Galli [as 'Evelyn Stewart'] (Gloria Ducci). Jenny Tamburi [Luciana Della Robbia] (Bruna, Fattori's secretary). Luigi Diberti (chief investigator). Fabrizio Jovine (Commissioner D'Elia). Riccardo Parisio Perrotti (Melli, Ducci's lawyer). Loredana Savelli (Giovanna Rospini). Salvatore Puntillo (2nd cab driver). Bruno Corazzari (Canevari, stable boy). Vito Passeri (caretaker). Francesco Angrisano (1st cab driver). Veronica Michielini (Giuliana Casati). Paolo Pacino (Inspector Russi). Fausta Avelli (Virginia as a girl). Elizabeth Turner (Virginia's mother). Ugo D'Alessio (gallery owner).

Synopsis: Virginia Ducci, a wealthy young English woman newly married to an Italian husband, suffers from confusing, fragmented psychic visions: a broken mirror, a lamp, a yellow cigarette, a magazine with a young woman on the cover, the bloody corpse of an old lady, a man with a limp, and someone being walled up in a dark hole... She turns for advice to her friend Dr. Luca Fattori, who has an interest in the paranormal. Afterwards she goes to examine a villa owned by her husband Francesco. The couple are planning to move into the building, which Francesco hasn't used for four years. Seeing the place for the first time, Virginia is disturbed to notice items from her vision. In a plastered-over recess she uncovers skeletal human remains. Police identify the victim as Agneta Bignardi, a young woman killed four years ago. When shown a photo of the girl, Virginia recognises her as the girl on the magazine cover in her vision. Francesco is arrested when he admits that he'd had an affair with the girl. Virginia discusses the case with Francesco's sister Gloria and the two of them go to the villa. Gloria says that it was she who had bought the furniture (which Virginia has seen in her visions) *after* Francesco's departure. A magazine runs a picture of Agneta Bignardi on the cover of their current issue – it's the same cover that Virginia saw in her vision. Luca points out that the magazine has only existed for a year, therefore Virginia's visons are premonitions rather than past events. They find further evidence that appears to clear Francesco. Gloria, meanwhile, gives Virginia a watch that plays a haunting tune on the hour. When Francesco arrives at the villa, Virginia is alarmed to see that he's limping, due to a twisted ankle sustained just a few hours ago. She becomes more and more frightened by the confluence of elements from her vision. The last crucial link occurs when Francesco, who did in fact kill Agneta Bignardi, sees an incriminating letter on the dresser. Virginia hasn't read it, but he believes she has. He attacks her with a poker, breaking the mirror in the process. As she lies dazed, he bricks her up in the recess where Bignardi's body was found. Finally all the details in the room fit with the vision. Luca arrives, followed by two cops who are trying to arrest him for speeding. Francesco invites them in, but despite his conviction that Virginia is in danger Luca cannot break Francesco's facade of innocence. As Luca turns to leave, escorted by the police, the haunting tune played by Virginia's watch emerges from the bricked up wall...

above:
Jennifer O'Neill as reluctant psychic Virginia Ducci, discussing her fears with her husband's sister Gloria (Evelyn Stewart).

About the production: From the germ of its initial idea to completion and release of the film, *Sette note in nero* was an unusually long and complicated experience for Fulci. The trail began in 1975 when Fulci and his regular co-scripter Roberto Gianviti were paid to write a treatment of a 1973 book by Vieri Razzini called "Terapia mortale" ('Deadly Therapy') for producer Dino De Laurentiis. After six months they were in trouble, having failed to come up with a decent version of the story. At this point De Laurentiis introduced Fulci to Dardano Sacchetti, who was then working primarily in the 'poliziotteschi' genre (ruthless urban cop thrillers) for Stelvio Massi and Umberto Lenzi. Sacchetti claims to have told Fulci that the story he'd been working on so far was no good. Instead they decided to write something else, and Sacchetti came up with the idea for *Sette note in nero*. He then wrote the script with Gianviti and Fulci.

This new story was initially announced, in May 1976, as a late-summer production for Luigi De Laurentiis's Aurofilm. Oddly, it was also described simultaneously in *Variety* as a project for Cinecompany, a set-up owned and run by director/producer Luciano Ercoli and his business partner Alberto Pugliese, and indeed it was Cinecompany who eventually emerged as producers of the finished film. Aurofilm seem to have dropped out, which fits with Sacchetti's assertion that De Laurentiis (if not Dino then Luigi) turned it down. (Rumour has it that De Laurentiis found Fulci too "vulgar" while Fulci regarded De Laurentiis as a huge bore; whatever the reasons, the two men clearly didn't hit it off.)

Even with the money on board, and a script at the ready, production did not run smoothly. Shooting was put back from the summer to the autumn, specifically 4 October 1976. Location filming in Siena, Tuscany, was completed by the end of October, after which production moved to Rome for more location work and the filming of studio interiors. *Variety* declared shooting "recently completed" on 5 January 1977, suggesting that the schedule had extended at least as far as December. Delays hit post-production too; whereas many Fulci films were ready for release three months after shooting, *Sette note in nero* did not come out for eight months, an unusually long wait. Whether the difficulties lay with the material or the financial stability of the production company is unclear, although the fact that Cinecompany never released another film after this may be significant.

There is an interesting footnote to this story. In a wide-ranging interview for *Video Watchdog* in 1997, veteran scriptwriter and giallo specialist Ernesto Gastaldi claimed that *he* provided source material for *Sette note in nero*. Referring to Lucio Fulci, he said: *"We worked together many times on thriller stories, but none were ever filmed, for various reasons. One of his films,* Sette note in nero, *was based on an idea of mine, but I did not write the script."*[11] In an interview for *Nocturno* magazine[12], Gastaldi claimed that *Sette note in nero* was based on an unpublished script of his called "Pentagramma in nero" ('Black Pentagram'). (The script does exist: it is currently held by a library in Milan whose records indicate it was written by Gastaldi and Guido Leoni.) Dardano Sacchetti, however, bitterly rejected Gastaldi's claim. He agreed that Fulci came up with the *title* of *Sette note in nero*, but in an angry response sent to *Nocturno*'s online forum, he declared that Gastaldi had nothing to do with the actual writing; at best he may have inspired Fulci's choice of the film's eventual title ('Pentagram in Black' leading to 'Seven Notes in Black').

In a 1995 interview with Massimo Lavagnini published in the American magazine *Draculina*, Fulci's description of the division of labour between the three credited writers was the opposite of Sacchetti's. When asked by Lavagnini, *"Who had the original idea for the script, you or Dardano Sacchetti?"*, Fulci responded: *"Me and Gianviti. Sacchetti gave us a great idea for the ending of the movie, the sound of the carillon... I remember I had great troubles with the screenplay which our producers Luigi and Aurelio De Laurentiis didn't like. They asked me 'can we turn it into a counterespionage movie?' (laughs) But then I came to an agreement with Fulvio Frizzi, who was the commercial director of Rizzoli. He took the responsibility to produce my movie."*[13]

opposite main image:
Married life between Virginia Ducci (Jennifer O'Neill) and her husband Francesco (Gianni Garko) is far from blissful.

opposite bottom left:
French poster.

below:
Japanese video cover.

top:
The body of Signora Casati (Veronica Michielini) is discovered.

above:
Virginia experiences an ever-increasing sense of foreboding...

below:
The full horror of Virginia's fate is made clear when her husband launches a vicious attack, clubbing her unconscious and walling her up in their own home.

Review: For a long time *The Psychic* was an unjustly maligned work in Fulci's career. Described as dull and repetitious in Phil Hardy's *Aurum Film Encyclopedia: Horror*, perhaps the real problem was that it tended to be viewed and found wanting alongside the gory Gothics Fulci produced in the early eighties. Screened at the Rex Cinema Fantastic Films Festival along with *City of the Living Dead* in 1980, it failed to provide equal gruesomeness and suffered as a consequence, being apparently booed at the time. Seen on its own terms, however, *The Psychic* – aka *Seven Notes in Black* – deserves consideration as one of Fulci's best

The plot, whilst mechanically contrived, has a definite power, a gloomy menace which exemplifies Fulci's fatalism. Time is the trap which closes inexorably around Virginia. Her waking visions of bloody death are ironic torments, frustrating her desire for autonomy. The theme of a vision misunderstood by the victim of unwanted psychic powers recalls Nicolas Roeg's masterly supernatural thriller *Don't Look Now* (1973). The visions themselves may remind the viewer of similar scenes in Mario Bava's excellent *A Hatchet for the Honeymoon* (1969), with their rippling, distorted perspectives, not to mention their recurrence as tantalising new details are added. Bava's film, however, was a black satire on a murderer's maternal hang-ups, and the visions were fixed in the character's traumatized past. Here we are teased by different ambiguities.

Virginia is ably portrayed by Jennifer O'Neill as an innocent abroad. Her predicament is emphasized by the heavily accented English spoken by the Italian cast. At one point, she trails all over town in a cab looking for an address which turns out to be virtually in the next street to her point of departure, merely because she fails to pronounce the destination with the correct stress! This causes problems for the viewer as well; several complicated passages of exposition are delivered in accents that occlude the script. Rospini's hospital-bed scene is particularly difficult to fathom, which is a shame because he delivers some vital information.

Virginia remains something of a cypher throughout. She has psychic powers, but no control over them, no apparent opinions about them, and no real insight into them until it's virtually too late. In fact she is barely a 'real character' at all. She's a weirdly fascinating automaton, propelled by Fate towards a destiny she cannot change. This is a deeply pessimistic extension of the film's theme. Fate decrees all, so who cares what idiosyncrasies we think we have? Apart from the fact that she's psychic, all that we learn about Virginia is contained in a few terse symbols. She drives a Rolls Royce. (Rich). She rides a white horse. (Innocent). Her mother committed suicide. (Tragic). Although she becomes obsessed with uncovering the meaning of her visions, her intelligence is apparently untouched by paranormal talent. The first sign she has that her visions may not be set in the past – the sighting of Signora Casati – is interpreted mystically. She must be seeing a ghost.

Her most ambiguous action occurs during one of the film's best scenes. Whilst hiding in terror at the house of Signora Casati, she spies an ornamental bust placed upon a cabinet and recognises it as one of the elements in her vision. However, in the vision it was lying on its side. Possessed either by a dangerous misunderstanding of her predicament, or a particularly daring taste for brinkmanship, she turns the bust over, revealing a concealed letter the appropriation of which almost leads to her undoing. However, whilst Virginia's knowledge of her destiny extends no further than the image of incarceration behind a brick wall, the plot eventually works in favour of the capture of her murderous husband. If she hadn't discovered the letter, Francesco wouldn't have seen it in her possession. Therefore he wouldn't have tried to entomb her alive. Therefore he wouldn't have been exposed as a psychopath. Virginia has participated in the process of which she is a prisoner. At least this submission ultimately saves her from married life with Francesco, a man quite willing to murder her in the most horrible fashion to protect himself.

Does Virginia act to save herself or does she acquiesce to the inexorable demands of her vision? A moment of existential freedom or submission to the death drive? It's difficult to tell. Were it not for Luca's decision to speed away from the traffic cops who pulled him over, Virginia would have died. The (Sartrean) suggestion is that only in moments of impulsive action are we really free.

The different existential decisions made by Virginia and Luca are worth comparing. While she acts on impulse to *further* destiny (by making a divergent element – the upright bust – agree with her premonition), he *transcends* the fatalistic death-drive of the plot through an act of resistance. Virginia, so central throughout the story, ends up 'holding her breath' for rescue from a secondary male. This passive, pathetic state is reminiscent of Lando Buzzanca's characters in *The Eroticist* and *Young Dracula*, albeit without the harsh mockery of those films.

But the agency of Virginia's rescue is only patriarchal in a deeply ambivalent way. The chimes of the watch go off as she lies unconscious in her intended tomb. The watch was a present from her husband's sister... who was given it by a man she'd once had an affair with; a man from The Vatican. On the one hand, Virginia is saved by the intervening grace of the church (a veritable *deus ex machina*). On the other, she is saved by the seductive power of a woman, who obtained gifts from a Cardinal by tempting him into carnal delights. Ultimately, Virginia emerges from her premature burial through the agency of both Luca and Gloria. She is rendered child-like by this, returned to the helpless state of awareness she experienced in the prologue. This circularity suggests the conundrum of nature vs. nurture, the frying pan and fire to our tenuous sense of free will.

The Psychic bears telling relations to other Italian films, most notably to the Dario Argento films *The Cat O'Nine Tails* (1971) and *Deep Red* (1975). The former is invoked in a sequence where deduction hinges on the discovery of a full version of a cropped photograph. Sacchetti received a co-writing credit on *The Cat O'Nine Tails*, which perhaps explains the device's reoccurrence here. The reference to *Deep Red* on the other hand is entirely opportunistic, as the

soundtrack mutates into a Goblin pastiche for the fevered scene of Virginia discovering a skeletal corpse behind a plastered wall. Bearing clear similarities to David Hemmings's excavations in the Argento film, it also incorporates a subtext of Sacchetti's by having a layer of bricks beyond the plaster resemble those that imprison Dora and the corpse of her first husband in *Shock* (also 1977), written by Sacchetti for Mario Bava.

Virginia's attempt to hide in a church is given away when her watch chimes go off, a scene which recalls a very similar set-up in the 1971 giallo *A Lizard in a Woman's Skin* (in which a terrorised Florinda Bolkan gives away her location by leaning on the stoppers of a giant pipe organ). The film also indulges Fulci's taste for lighting horrific tableaux with stark flashbulb exposures, as police photograph the pathetic remnants of the murdered Agneta Bignardi. A glancing cue from a painting by Vermeer suggests an appreciation of the Dutch painter's uncanny ability to accumulate hints and insinuations within the most apparently ordered of canvasses.

The Psychic has never received credit for its powerful scenes of tension and unease. The first of these begins as Virginia enters a room soon to be revealed as the one in her vision. Left alone by the caretaker, she sits among the vague shapes of furniture, their forms draped in dust-covers. Idly she removes them until the room yields up its secret face. Pacing, music and ominous visual suggestion all combine here, creating a wonderfully morbid *frisson*. This is well amplified when the characters deduce that Virginia's second sight is actually a glimpse into the future. An edgy, faintly hysterical dread develops in the handling of mood from hereon. This is no longer a mystery, but a horror story. Helplessness is emphasized by things like the pointlessly circuitous cab journey Virginia endures, only to find that the real destination is just a few streets away from where she started. As the final movement gets underway, each of the fateful fragments Virginia perceived in her visions start to coalesce in the present. Francesco's casual delivery of the correct magazine-cover to the table, and his 'accidentally' twisted ankle, along with his meaningless but portended act of taking Virginia's cigarette and placing it just-so on the ash-tray, contribute to a dense atmosphere of doom. The last detail – a mirror broken as Francesco pulls back the poker to bash his wife's brains in – carries a chill of psychological horror.

Fulci called this film mechanical, correctly alluding to the closed nature of the narrative. For all its pleasures *The Psychic* keeps its audience at bay with a highly selective, manipulative disclosure of information. We may think our ability to guess the villain's identity makes us active participants in the diegetic process, but we are in fact kept very much in the dark about salient features of the plot. Our fixed position in relation to this closed text is most tellingly shown when Fulci has the camera zoom in on a magazine cover featuring Agneta Bignardi. Unlike Luca and Virginia, we can easily see that the magazine is only one year into publication. Fulci's blatant zoom robs us of the possibility of merely noticing the errant detail. Instead he notices for us, and our position in relation to the text is confirmed as secondary. Despite such restrictions, however, this elegantly constructed murder mystery confirms Fulci as a director of skill and sophistication, more than able to deal with complex narratives (a fact critics of his horror films often tried to deny).

Footnotes

1 Discussing the bat attack in *A Lizard in a Woman's Skin*, Fulci said *"I remember Bava was much impressed when he saw the sequence, though I am sure he would have done it better than me"* (to Robert Schlockoff, *Starburst* #48, reprinted from an original *L'Écran Fantastique* article). This indicates the sort of respect with which Mario Bava (1914-1980) – director, cinematographer and genuine Italian innovator – was regarded by horror specialists. It's impossible to reduce Bava's achievements to a footnote; suffice to say that along with Dario Argento and Lucio Fulci he is responsible for the best fantastic films of the Italian cinema. Outstanding credits include *The Mask of Satan* (1960), *The Whip and the Body* (1963), *Black Sabbath* (1963), *Blood and Black Lace* (1964), *Kill, Baby, Kill!* (1966), *Danger: Diabolik* (1968), *A Bay of Blood* (1971), *Lisa and the Devil* (1973) and *Shock* (1977).

2 Romolo Guerrieri is the pseudonym of Romolo Girolami (born 5 December 1931), one of a dynasty of Italian directors. His brother Marino Girolami (born 1 February 1914) directed *Zombie Holocaust* (1980), a rip-off of *Zombie Flesh-Eaters*. Marino's son Enzo Girolami (aka Enzo G. Castellari, born 29 July 1938) directed *Quel maledetto treno blindato* aka *The Inglorious Bastards* (1978) and *Bronx Warriors* (1982). Renzo Girolami (aka Renzo Spaziani, born 12 January 1939) directed the 'western grottesco' *Più forte, sorelle* in 1976, and is the son of Romolo and Marino's brother Francesco: Francesco was the only one not to have taken up directing.

3 *"Perversion Story was the first title put on the clapperboard by producer Edmondo Amati, an excellent producer who didn't know then what 'giallo' was because, after all, that film was only the second giallo produced in Italy. The first was* The Sweet Body of Deborah*..."* – Lucio Fulci speaking to Luca Palmerini, *Giallo Pages* #1. Note: Lucio Fulci is sometimes rumoured to have co-written *The Sweet Body of Deborah*.

4 Ennio Morricone was born in Rome in 1928. Classically trained, he studied composition with Goffredo Petrassi at the Conservatoria di Santa Cecilia, Rome. He first worked as an arranger and orchestral conductor for the record industry, before developing as a specialist in music for TV, radio, theatre and cinema. He transcended classical convention early on, attending seminars at the International Summer School at Darmstadt-Kranichstein, in Germany. Here he was exposed to the influence of Karlheinz Stockhausen, who was directing courses in composition and analysis. This was his cue for a startling venture into the avant-garde. He joined the Gruppo di Improvvisazione Nuova Consonanza, an improvisation group of composer/musicians formed in 1964. (Of their available recordings, the best is *Musica su schemi*, Cramps Records, Milan.) Morricone's distinctive strangulated trumpet playing was to feature in many of his scores for film, including Argento's *The Bird with the Crystal Plumage* and Fulci's *A Lizard in a Woman's Skin*, which benefit from his inventive combination of melodic and dissonant elements.

5 *La Stampa*, 3 August 1970.

6 *l'Unità*, 29 June 1984.

7 To Robert Schlockoff, as printed in *Starburst* #48.

8 *l'Unità*, 30 September 1972.

9 To *Fangoria*'s January 1996 'Weekend of Horrors' in Manhattan, USA. (Howard Berger).

10 "The tricks of the trade, according to Lucio Fulci", *l'Unità*, 1 May 1982.

11 "What Are Those Strange Drops of Blood in the scripts of Ernesto Gastaldi?" Gastaldi interviewed by Tim Lucas, *Video Watchdog* #39, May/June 1997.

12 Ernesto Gastaldi, interviewed in *Nocturno* #100.

13 Lucio Fulci interviewed by Massimo Lavagnini for *Draculina* #24, 1995.

above:
Gianni Garko as the evil husband, willing to inter his wife alive to prevent her from revealing his crimes to the police.

top left:
Virginia tells the police about the body she's discovered walled up at her house.

below:
Locandina.

สหมงคลฟิล์ม
เสนอ
ความมหัศจรรย์สุดขอบฟ้า
ธนูวิเศษ.. มนุษย์หมาป่า..
จักรพรรดิเสือหยก.. ปีศาจหิน..
ราชินีหน้ากากทอง..
มนุษย์ผีดิบ..
ธนูไฟ
CONQUEST
ยอร์จ ริเวโร • อังเดร อ๊อกชิพินติ
พบ
ซาบรีน่า เซลเลอร์
ลูซิโอ ฟุลซี

ฉายที่ วันที่

chapter five

The Ghoul Can't Help It

Violent holidays from horror

featuring:

Massacre Time aka *Le colt cantarono a morte e fu... tempo di massacro* (1966)

Beatrice Cenci (1969)

White Fang aka *Zanna Bianca* (1973)

Challenge to White Fang aka *Il ritorno di Zanna Bianca* (1974)

The Four of the Apocalypse aka *I quattro dell'apocalisse* (1975)

Silver Saddle aka *Sella d'argento* (1978)

The Smuggler aka *Luca il contrabbandiere* (1980)

Conquest (1983)

Rome 2033 – The Fighter Centurions aka *I guerrieri dell'anno 2072* (1984)

Complicating the usual picture of Fulci's career, which tends to privilege his horror films, are his numerous excursions into other genres. In this chapter we'll be looking at these diverse works, from *Massacre Time* in 1966 to *Rome 2033 – The Fighter Centurions* in 1984. Three of the nine films discussed in this chapter are westerns (the aforementioned *Le colt cantarono la morte e fu tempo di massacro/Massacre Time*, 1966; plus *I quattro dell'apocalisse/The Four of the Apocalypse*, 1975; and *Sella d'argento/Silver Saddle*, 1978). Two children's adventure films (*Zanna Bianca/White Fang*, 1973 and *Il ritorno di Zanna Bianca/Challenge to White Fang*, 1974) take us perhaps furthest away from Fulci's reputation for the horrific: whilst the remaining oddities are a period costume drama (*Beatrice Cenci*, 1969), a savage crime thriller (*Luca il contrabbandiere/The Smuggler*, 1980), a sword and scorcery fantasy (*Conquest*, 1983), and a dystopian sci-fi tale (*I guerrieri dell'anno 2072/Rome 2033 – The Fighter Centurions*, 1984).

These films, then, fall into genres for which the director is scarcely well known. That said, there is still a great deal of pleasure to be felt in watching them. Fulci was a seasoned professional who was able to make a go of at least half these tales. What's more, horror buffs will be amused to see that in each there is *some* form of engagement with violence, ranging from the casual and generically obvious (gun and fist-fights in the westerns for instance) to the explosive and virulently excessive (scenes of rape and torture in *The Smuggler*). Somehow, it seems Lucio Fulci just couldn't help it...

A Fistful of Fulcis

The 1960s was the decade that saw Italy's 'spaghetti' westerns emerge and flourish. When Sergio Leone scored a massive hit with *A Fistful of Dollars* in 1964 every producer in Rome wanted a bit of the action. Leading the field after the trailblazing Leone was Sergio Corbucci, whose impressive *Django* (1966) inspired even more imitation. Many of the industry's journeymen directors were pressed into service to try their luck, with varying degrees of success. Talents such as Tonino Cervi (*Today It's Me... Tomorrow You!*, 1968), Giulio Questi (*Django, Kill!*, 1967), Enzo Castellari (*Any Gun Can Play*, 1967), Giuliano Carnimeo (*C'è Sartana... vendi la pistola e comprati la bara!*, 1970), Sergio Sollima (*The Big Gundown*, 1967), Luigi Bazzoni (*Man, Pride and Vengeance*, 1967) and even Mario Bava (*Roy Colt & Winchester Jack*, 1970), were among the galloping hordes to descend on whatever stretches of dusty European scrubland could be made to simulate the Wild West. (Yugoslavia, Spain and even Austria were regularly used as stand-ins for Texas, Arizona and New Mexico.)

Fulci joined the posse early on with his 1966 film *Massacre Time*, starring a 24-year-old Franco Nero. The handsome young star was still hot from the saddle of Corbucci's *Django* (also 1966), perhaps his most famous role, so Fulci had landed himself something of a catch. Nero was born Franco Sparanero in Parma Italy, on the 23rd November 1941. His career began in 1963 with an arty exercise for Italian director Damiano Damiani called *The Empty Canvas*, alongside Bette Davis in her first

facing page:
Poster for Fulci's sword-and-sorcery saga, *Conquest* (1983).

below:
Fabio Testi and Lynne Frederick take to the wagon-trail in *The Four of the Apocalypse*.

above:
Admat for Fulci's *Massacre Time* from AIP under its US theatrical release title.

right:
Franco Nero in Sergio Corbucci's *Django* (1966), the spaghetti western that made him famous. Nero won the role when the wife of the film's assistant director Ruggero Deodato convinced Corbucci that the handsome young actor was a better choice than rival Mark Damon.

below:
Tomas Milian in Michelangelo Antonioni's *Identification of a Woman* (1982), playing a troubled film director trying to find the ideal woman to star in his new film.

foreign film role.[1] Then, after a couple of sci-fi flicks for Antonio Margheriti (*Wild, Wild Planet* and *War of the Planets*, both 1965) he took the lead in *Django*, before embarking on a slew of roles in hard-boiled crime thrillers, cop sagas and more spaghetti westerns. Nero seemed to favour narratives which revolved around elaborate revenge scenarios, often with a pronounced sado-masochistic quality, and *Massacre Time*'s tale of warring brothers offered plenty of scope for humiliation and payback.

The star's career continued to oscillate between action adventure engagements, art projects and the occasional thriller. He worked with Luis Buñuel (*Tristana*, 1970), Claude Chabrol (*Les magiciens*, 1975) and Rainer Werner Fassbinder (*Querelle*, 1982), then turned up in Renny Harlin's *Die Hard 2* (1990). His Italian thriller choices were distinguished; both *The Fifth Cord* by Luigi Bazzoni (1971) and *Hitch-Hike* by Pasquale Festa Campanile (1977) are outstanding, featuring Nero in what amounts to the same persona, an alcoholic reporter portrayed at two increasingly cynical stages.

Of Fulci's westerns, the second – *The Four of the Apocalypse* – was the most brutal, thanks to a harrowing rape scene missing from most prints. It's also the best, being able – unlike *Massacre Time* – to support Fulci's claims that he brought a dream-like quality to his vision of the Wild West.[2] *The Four of the Apocalypse* starred Fabio Testi and one-time wife of Peter Sellers, Lynne Frederick, in a rambling odyssey both sentimental and cruel. It also saw Tomas Milian cast for the third time in a Fulci film, after leading roles in *Beatrice Cenci* and *Don't Torture a Duckling*.

Born Tomás Quintin Rodriguez to Italian/Cuban parents on 3 March 1937 in Havana, the good-looking, dark-featured actor made his debut in two films scripted by Pier Paolo Pasolini for satirical director Mauro Bolognini; 1959's *La notte brava* and 1960's *Il bell'Antonio*. Pasolini himself was later to cast Milian in *La ricotta*, his infamous segment of *Ro.Go.Pa.G* (1963), a quartet of short films by Roberto Rossellini, Jean-Luc Godard, Pier Paolo Pasolini and Ugo Gregoretti.[3] Like just about everyone in Rome, Milian went on to appear in Luchino Visconti's sprawling epic *The Leopard* (1963), but he soon became associated with more commercial ventures, beginning with classic spaghetti westerns like Sergio Sollima's *The Big Gundown* (1967) and *Face to Face* (1967), the bizarre *Django, Kill!* (1967) by oddball director Giulio Questi, and Sergio Corbucci's *Vamos a matar, companeros!* (1970). Milian's Cuban roots meant he was often cast as a Mexican, in the so-called 'Zapata' strain of spaghetti western. His role as the villainous Chaco in Fulci's *The Four of the Apocalypse* was no exception, and indeed seems to have been inspired by his part in *The Big Gundown*. Sollima's film had Milian wrongly blamed for a terrible rape-murder purely on the basis of his race and his petty thievery; Fulci inverts this characterisation to make Milian the genuine sadist responsible for raping a prostitute.

A handful of roles in art projects show evidence of Milian's wide-ranging appeal (1969's *The Cannibals* by Liliana Cavani; 1971's *The Last Movie* for a drug-frazzled Dennis Hopper; 1979's *La luna* for Bernardo Bertolucci; and most notably – as Niccolò, a film-maker – in Michelangelo Antonioni's *Identification of a Woman*, 1982), but it was his association with exploitation director Umberto Lenzi that made most impact on Italian audiences in the seventies. He starred in a run of Lenzi cop thrillers, starting in 1974 with *Almost Human*, swiftly followed by *One Just Man* (1975), *Free Hand for a Tough Cop* (1976), *Brutal Justice* (1976), *Violent Naples* (1976), *The Cynic, the Rat and the Fist* (1977) and *Angry Vengeance* (1977). These are brutal, astonishingly cynical tales of jaded, vicious cops taking the law into their own hands to smash even more sadistic criminals. Politically odious and often distinctly misogynistic, Lenzi's right-wing fantasies of social cleansing were inspired by Clint Eastwood's role in Don Siegel's *Dirty Harry* (making it, after *A Fistful of Dollars*, the second time an Eastwood persona had triggered Italian passions). The *poliziesco*, as it's known, is one of the guiltier pleasures of Italian exploitation; Lenzi's efforts in particular quicken the pulse with their brash energy even as the mind recoils at their politics. Nevertheless, these savage, unsympathetic dramas – often starring either Milian, Henry Silva or John Saxon – are Lenzi's most significant contribution to Italian exploitation, and act as precursors of the cynical excess Fulci went all out to achieve in *The Smuggler*.

Milian had played weaker, scummier characters in some of these dramas and he was no stranger to material that sent up masculinity (see the curious 1971 giallo, *Murder By Design* by Maurizio Lucidi). But he must eventually have started to chafe at the limitations of the cop series,

because he burlesqued them in a series of films for another regular collaborator, Bruno (brother of Sergio) Corbucci, including the action comedy *Delitto al "Blue Gay"* aka *Cop in Drag* (1984). He maintained a strong professional reputation well into the 21st century, working with Steven Spielberg (*Amistad*, 1997) and Steven Soderbergh (*Traffic*, 2000), and often specialising in deeply unlikable characters such as the Dominican dictator Rafael Trujillo in Luis Llosa's *La fiesta del Chivo*, 2005. He died in 2017 at the age of 84.

Despite the better qualities of *The Four of the Apocalypse*, it also betrayed a sentimental streak, with the music ladling sickly emotion over scenes already verging on the mawkish. Unfortunately this misjudgement was to continue, dominating Fulci's last western *Silver Saddle*. The star this time was Giuliano Gemma, whose spaghetti western roots went back to 1965 and the series of titles featuring 'Johnny Ringo' (eg. 1965's *A Pistol for Ringo* and *The Return of Ringo*, by Duccio Tessari). These were knockabout, humorous affairs without the darkness of the *Django* films, and *Silver Saddle* seems to have been conceived as a lighter confection in the same style. The story centres around a little boy, played by Sven Valsecchi, a child actor known mainly for heart-string pullers on Italian TV, but an overall air of lassitude ensures even the most susceptible will find themselves dry-eyed. Perhaps Fulci wanted to lighten up after the fatalistic bleakness of his previous film *The Psychic*, in 1977. Instead he ended his dalliance with the Wild West on a distinctly moribund note, just as the whole genre was grinding to a halt. The following year saw Fulci at an uncharacteristically low ebb professionally, accepting work on lowly musical revues for TV. Thankfully this was not for long; soon he was reaping the rewards of his sterling work in the giallo field, with the offer of director's seat on a modestly budgeted horror flick called *Zombie Flesh-Eaters*...

Family Viewing à la Fulci

Jack London (1876-1916) wrote his most famous book, *The Call of the Wild*, in 1903, when he was still in his twenties. A silent screen adaptation was filmed by the Pathe studio in 1923 but the first major version came later, in 1935. *The Call of the Wild* starred Clark Gable and Loretta Young and was directed by William "Wild Bill" Wellman, a hard-drinking maverick ex-soldier who'd lived the sort of life London's adventure stories could have taken as material (Wellman also directed James Cagney in the classic gangster picture *The Public Enemy* in 1931). It was a resounding hit, inspiring producers at Hollywood's 20th Century Fox to look again at London's work. The result was the first adaptation of London's other well-known tale, *White Fang*. It was made (a year after Wellman's *Call of the Wild*) by David Butler, a proficient but minor director of comedy and musical material later known for helming the Bob Hope vehicle *Road to Morocco* (1942). His *White Fang* was another success, despite featuring lower magnitude stars Michael Whalen and Jean Muir (the latter one of those whose career was ruined when she was 'exposed' as a Communist sympathizer in the 1950s).

Lucio Fulci's *White Fang* (1973) was produced by veteran film entrepreneur Harry Alan Towers as one of a number of multi-national tax dodges he was pulling at the time (money from Italy, France and Spain went into the pot for Fulci's version). Towers's first Jack London adaptation, *The Call of the Wild* (directed by Ken Annakin, 1972), had been a great success thanks to the presence of top-line star Charlton Heston and the beautiful Maria Rohm. Fulci's film was also reasonably well-received, particularly in Italy. In the UK it became one of only three Fulci titles of the seventies (along with *A Lizard in a Woman's Skin* and *Zombie Flesh-Eaters*) to get proper distribution. *White Fang* was quite fairly reviewed on its 1974 release here by Verina Glaessner in the *Monthly Film Bulletin* as: *"An unambitious comic-strip adaptation of Jack London's superb novel, that nevertheless manages to capture something of the essence of London's world – the purity of the struggle with (not against) nature in the icy wastes, the corruption of the money-grabbing mining towns"*. The profits were substantial enough for Fulci to embark immediately on a sequel, *Challenge to White Fang* (1974), though unfortunately this follow-up was denied a UK release, despite performing almost as well as the first in Italy.

clockwise this page:
Tomas Milian as Olimpio, the doomed love interest in *Beatrice Cenci*...

A montage from the publicity material for Fulci's *White Fang*...

Virna Lisi (the female lead in both of Fulci's *White Fang* films) began her career as a glamorous young actress in films like *Four Kinds of Love* (1965)... before maturing into powerful character roles like her ferocious Catherine de Medici in *La Reine Margot* (1994).

above:
Maurizio Pradeaux followed Fulci's lead with *I figli di Zanna Bianca*.

above right:
White Fang villain John Steiner pays a severe penalty for his fascistic revels in the nazisploitation tale *Deported Women of the SS Special Section*.

The two films have a slightly anachronistic feel to them, as if they were made in the early sixties instead of the mid-seventies. Perhaps this is due to their melodramatic soundtracks by Carlo Rustichelli. However, even here unexpected moments of very 'seventies' violence occur. Both films turn up regularly on Italian TV at Christmas-time, yet their gritty action style would certainly exclude them from rubbing shoulders with *E.T.* and the Queen's Speech in this country.

Jack London's story was the subject of numerous re-interpretations by Italian directors in the wake of Fulci's success. Maurizio Pradeaux, the director of two lightweight gialli, *Death Carries a Cane* (1972) and *Death Steps in the Dark* (1976), made *I figli di Zanna Bianca* in 1974. Tonino Ricci, hack director of *Thor the Conqueror* (1982) turned in *Zanna Bianca alla riscossa* in 1975. Alfonso Brescia, another hack who dabbled in 'sexy' and giallo films (e.g. *Naked Girl Killed in Park*, 1972) made *Zanna Bianca e il cacciatore solitario* (1975). To cap it all, in a fit of Wolfmania Harry Alan Towers himself produced a *further* treatment of London's tale, Gianfranco Baldanello's *Cry of the Wolf* (1975), with Jack Palance and Joan Collins!

The mythic resonance of Jack London's novel persisted into the 1990s, with the big budget *White Fang* (Randall Kleiser, 1990), starring Ethan Hawke; and a sequel, *White Fang 2: Myth of the White Wolf* (Ken Olin, 1994) starring Scott Bairstow. Since then, the limelight has shifted to London's similarly themed *Call of the Wild*, with a film adaptation starring Rutger Hauer in 1997, an Emmy-nominated mini-series in 2000, and a 3D adaptation starring Christopher Lloyd in 2007. It would seem that London's tales of the great outdoors will always hold a certain magic for young imaginations.

The principal villain in *White Fang* is manipulative property tycoon Charles 'Beauty' Smith, and Fulci chose his bad-guy well, casting the sly-eyed British actor John Steiner for the part (John Carradine had played the role in the 1936 version). Fulci was to employ Steiner again in the 1975 horror comedy *Young Dracula*, recognizing in the gaunt actor's features a wicked glint of camp; ideal for the role of a homosexual Count Dracula. Steiner got his

start in film with a clutch of small roles in eccentric Brit productions; Peter Brook's *The Persecution and Assassination of Jean-Paul Marat as Performed By the Inmates of the Asylum of Charenton Under the Direction of the Marquis de Sade* (1966), *Bedazzled* by Stanley Donen (1967), and *Work Is a Four Letter Word* by Thomas Clyde (1968).

Following his roles for Fulci he continued to work in Italy, dabbling in some of the country's most controversial entertainments. He demonstrated an entirely un-British willingness to embrace the wild side of acting life, by accepting a role as a Nazi officer in Rino Di Silvestro's *Deported Women of the SS Special Section* (1976). For some, films like this are a sub-genre too far. The mid-seventies saw a short vogue for stories set in the prison camps of Nazi Germany, a trend initiated by the commercial success of Liliana Cavani's arthouse shocker *The Night Porter*, American items such as Robert Frost's sleazy little S&M flick *Love Camp 7* (1968) and particularly the infamous *Ilsa, She Wolf of the SS*, directed in 1974 by American Don Edmonds. These latter two were aimed at the jaded, sensation-seeking crowds who frequented the fleapits of New York's Times Square (sadly gone forever since the Disney Corporation bought up the real estate). Nowadays one can easily discern a farcical quality to films such as *Ilsa, She Wolf* (and its two sequels), but on release they must have seemed pretty far out. Not to be outdone, the Italians took the poor taste of *Ilsa* as a challenge, and mounted a series of ever-more freakish variants. *Deported Women of the SS Special Section* is actually one of the more restrained, despite its ominously verbose title. John Steiner obviously enjoyed himself though – he'd made the similarly themed *Salon Kitty* for erotic specialist Tinto Brass in 1975 (and signed up for the same director's epic shagfest *Caligula*).

After a commendable performance in Paolo Cavara's 1976 giallo *Plot of Fear* came *Shock* (1977) directed by the great Mario Bava, with Steiner top-lining alongside Dario Argento's partner of the time, actress Daria Nicolodi. This led to Argento casting Steiner as the maniacal film journalist Cristiano Berti in his 1982 masterpiece *Tenebrae*; a twitchy, bizarre performance that remains Steiner's most celebrated film credit.

Past Tense to Future Nonsense

Lucio Fulci is not a name many people associate with historical drama but, artistically speaking, his study of medieval Catholic hypocrisy, *Beatrice Cenci*, was one of his earliest real successes. Historical accounts of the events that befell the troubled Cenci family had previously been adapted by the English Romantic poet Shelley in 1819 and the French writer Stendhal in 1839, as well as Fulci's favourite art rebel Antonin Artaud (in a play called *The Cenci*, 1935). Ex-sculptor and art critic Riccardo Freda directed a film version the year before his creaky

below:
The bandit Catalano (Pedro Sanchez) lives down to expectations in *Beatrice Cenci*.

but influential horror film *I vampiri* in 1957, but there's little of Freda's coolness about Fulci's interpretation, with its humid fervour for the spectacle of suffering. A vicious torture sequence conducted by the clergy and a ripe patricidal eye-stabbing are shown to us unflinchingly. However, the script places emphasis firmly on the story and characters, without foregrounding the several violent scenes quite as gleefully as Fulci's later, more notorious works. The man himself sometimes referred to this handsomely shot film as his personal favourite (though at other times *Don't Torture a Duckling* would be singled out).

As mentioned earlier, Italy's exploitation directors had, during the seventies, turned from the labyrinthine narrative excesses of the giallo to the right-wing law enforcement wet dreams of the *poliziesco*, with Umberto Lenzi making the biggest impact in the latter form. But Fulci was too much of an anarchist to embrace the *poliziesco* wholesale. Attracted by the viciousness he may have been, but the rebel in Fulci wanted no part in the more fascistic implications of the post-*Dirty Harry* spaghetti crime flick. Interviewed by Robert Schlockoff for *L'Écran Fantastique* in 1980 he made indirect reference to the phenomenon when challenged on the question of his horror movies' 'gratuitous' violence. Describing the approach in his horror films as one where *"the viewer doesn't participate in the violence, but, on the contrary, is relieved from it"*, he went on to say: *"I think the police films with Clint Eastwood are much more dangerous for young people."* Fulci was demonstrating his unease with masturbatory authoritarian dramas such as *Death Wish*, *Dirty Harry* and *Magnum Force*; but he also knew very well that subsequent Italian crime thrillers had played the same games. His one straight crime story, *The Smuggler*, is at times unbelievably brutal, however it restricts extreme cruelty to the actions of the villains and doesn't endorse eye-for-an-eye responses from the law – from other criminals perhaps but not the *carabinieri*.

Despite the often grubby realism employed visually, the Italian *poliziesco* is an almost fantastical arena in which the police are shown taking out society's incoherent frustrations on evil criminals (and their lackeys in public life). The prevailing high-level corruption endemic to Italy's political landscape of the 1970s is repeatedly attacked; however, the point is usually made just to reinforce the case for giving a *Free Hand for a Tough Cop*, to quote one title. Fulci wanted none of this: instead, by adding *Mafiosi* motifs (with a nod to Francis Ford Coppola's *The Godfather*), he devised a crime story where the cops are kept at bay; in *The Smuggler* it's the old-guard Mafia who act as intervening authority figures, curbing the brutal excesses of younger nuovo-hoodlums. He even injected a hint of quixotic (not to say nationalistic) idealism by having his 'decent' Neapolitan crooks (whose crimes of contraband tobacco and liquor smuggling are forgiven by the film) struggling to resist the blandishments of heroin-pushing degenerates from Marseilles.

Fulci cast a likeable star to lead his good-guy smugglers. Fabio Testi (having already starred in Fulci's *The Four of the Apocalypse* with Tomas Milian) plays Luca with engaging heroic qualities, as he enacts a vendetta in response to his brother's murder. Good-looking and lean in build, Testi embodies an Italian machismo that is slanted to the harder side of *L'uomo vogue*. As well as the usual western and action credits (a part in *Once Upon a Time in the West* for example), Testi performed capably for Andrzej Zulawski (the Polish cine-magician best known for the uniquely strange horror/art film *Possession*), in his moving psychodrama *L'important c'est d'aimer* (1975). Like Zulawski, Fulci required the handsome actor to simulate beatings and trauma, but the script of *The Smuggler* demands less of him. (*The Heroin Busters*, Testi's 1977 cops vs. drug-runners flick by Enzo G. Castellari is more likely to have caught his eye.)

top:
Ocron (Sabrina Siani) reclines in Cleopatran splendor in Fulci's sword-and-sorcery saga *Conquest*.

above:
Beatrice (Adrienne Larussa) is tortured to obtain a confession for the murder of her abusive father, in *Beatrice Cenci*.

Fulci's lowest ebb as a jack of all trades came when he attempted to craft a *Conan the Barbarian* rip-off, with *Conquest* (1983). Receiving an apparently tempting financial offer from producer Giovanni Di Clemente whilst filming *Manhattan Baby* for Fabrizio De Angelis in 1982, he rushed off to start filming, believing that a lucrative new production deal was in the bag. However Clemente soon disappointed Fulci, who found the experience so dispiriting that he refused to make the second of the two pictures he'd signed up for. The ensuing lawsuit was eventually discarded in Fulci's favour, but the pressure meant he had little to do with the finishing of *Conquest*. Indeed, Fulci claimed he left post-production under the supervision of his regular editor Vincenzo Tomassi, only bothering to turn up at the end to check the results. It was here that Fulci began burning bridges, cutting himself off from associates in a way that laid the seeds of his isolation in the late eighties and early nineties. *Beyond* producer Fabrizio De Angelis was the first casualty, spurned in a graceless fashion by Fulci's defection to Clemente.

Despite also having alienated collaborator Dardano Sacchetti with his brusque dismissal of previous joint efforts (see Chapter Six), Fulci had one further Sacchetti script ready to go. *Rome 2033 – The Fighter Centurions* (1984) bears marks of the strain, as it's a rather tired effort, despite featuring turns from dependable exploitation stars like Fred Williamson, Howard Ross (aka Renato Rossini) and Jared Martin. Its real problem is lack of money, a factor which, though it had nearly always dogged Fulci's career, was finally beginning to tell. Previous films such as *The Beyond*, *The Black Cat* or *The Psychic* had managed, despite low budgets, to look marvellous, their style reasonably uncramped by the financial realities. Science fiction spectacle on the other hand is a film genre virtually predicated on the availability of big money. Even though the film drew on the *Mad Max* films more than mega-buck Spielberg sci-fi, it still required both spectacular model effects (a spaceship flying over Rome) and extensive post-production (action sequences in need of tight editing). In fact it got neither; the model-work was unconvincing and the fight scenes botched,

below:
Fred Williamson, Hal Yamanouchi, Al Cliver and Jared Martin in high spirits filming Fulci's sci-fi adventure *Rome 2033 – The Fighter Centurions*.

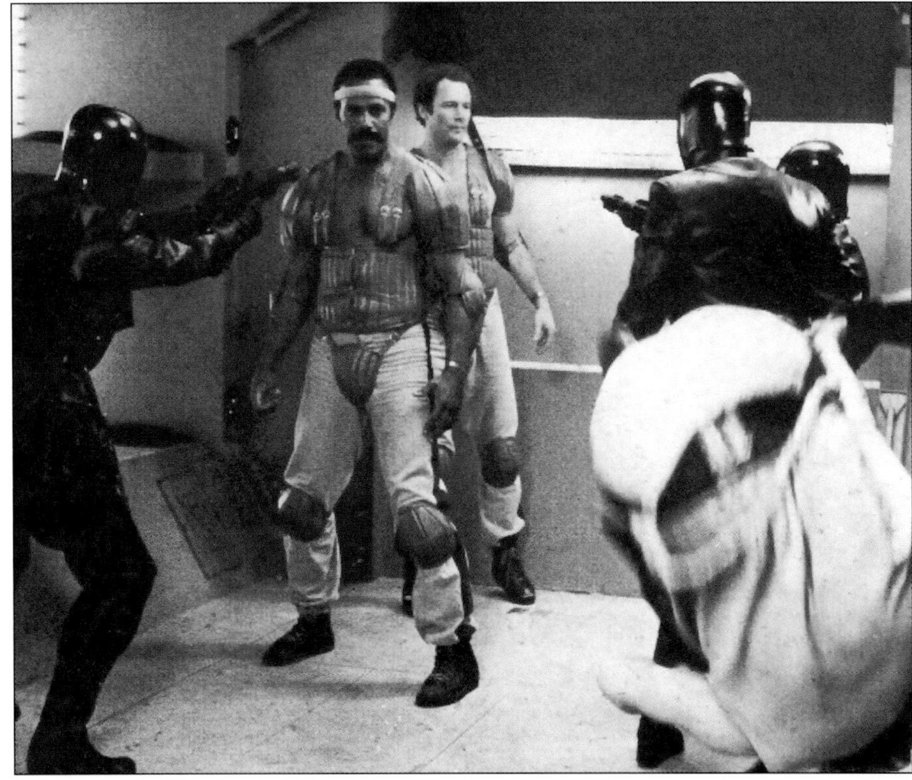

slow-moving fiascos. Fulci would have been better off abandoning the unnecessary sci-fi hardware and concentrating on the futuristic gladiatorial aspects, which given the right attention could have been exciting – after all, Fulci had once shown himself to be adept at kinetic action sequences in films like the two *White Fang* projects.

Fulci Goes To Hollywood?

The whirling camera and smooth editing of the *White Fang* films, with their action film dynamics, suggest how Fulci could have played the Hollywood field if his morbid preoccupations had been buoyed by American big budget finance. Dutch director Paul Verhoeven made the transition so well from European eccentric to Stateside purveyor of bone-crunching thrills that he upstaged many an American 'action specialist' with his ironic, nihilistic sensibility. Fulci told me he'd been offered the chance to move to the States and direct movies there during the seventies. When I quizzed him he seemed ambivalent about the decision he made. By refusing, and staying in the Italian industry, he remained attached to the familiar environs of Italian production. On the other hand, his gradual fade from prominence in Italy during the 1980s coincided with American culture's swamping of Italian cinemas.

How bitterly Fulci must have run the sequence back through his mind. The offer to make films in America could have seen him importing some of Italy's daring into American productions. Instead, he remained 'true to his roots'; and saw the whole edifice of Italian production eroded by fickle younger audiences with a trendy preference for American style. A style, let's remember, that is principally built upon the availability of large amounts of money, and the unthinking, almost primitive arrogance of the casually powerful. Directors like Verhoeven have it in them to become a sort of virus – at least an irritant – in the system of American entertainment (see *Starship Troopers* for evidence of his discomfiting technique). Fulci, an older man than the Dutch *wunderkind*, would have found his fatalism less saleable than Verhoeven's twisted jocularity but his professionalism could have ensured him some prominence. Films like *White Fang*, and many others, demonstrate Fulci's flexibility and willingness to shift genres in search of success. It's for this reason that we can hardly consider Fulci an *auteur*. He bears more relation to the directors of the Hollywood studio system than the American independent horror specialists of the 1970s.

With this in mind then, let's now explore the less travelled hinterlands of Lucio Fulci's talent.

this page: Action superstar Fred Williamson and leading man Jared Martin take on the forces of corporate evil in *Rome 2033 – The Fighter Centurions.* **bottom picture:** The gladiatorial motorcyclists.

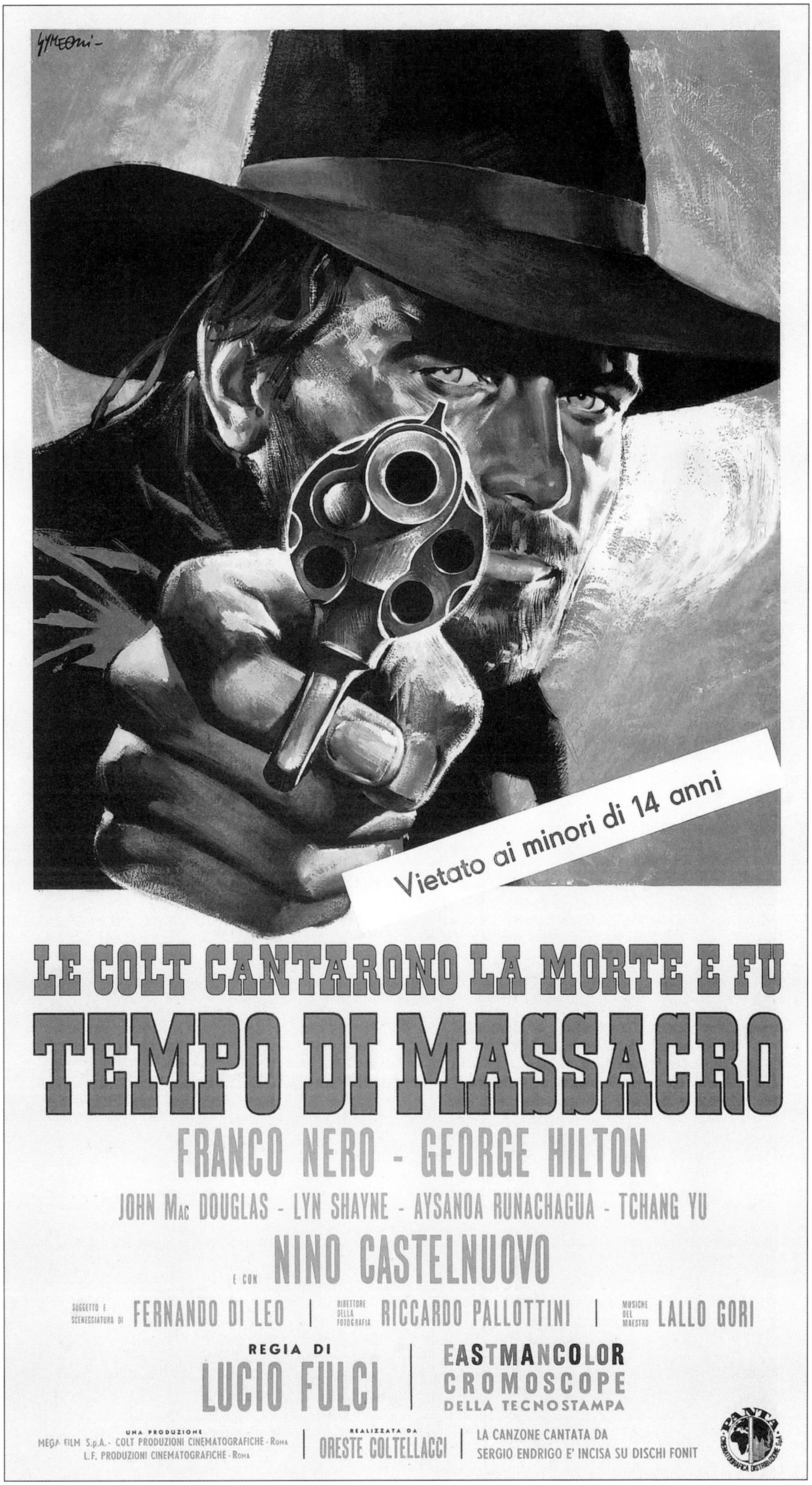
Vietato ai minori di 14 anni
LE COLT CANTARONO LA MORTE E FU
TEMPO DI MASSACRO
FRANCO NERO - GEORGE HILTON
JOHN MAC DOUGLAS - LYN SHAYNE - AYSANOA RUNACHAGUA - TCHANG YU
E CON NINO CASTELNUOVO
SOGGETTO E SCENEGGIATURA DI FERNANDO DI LEO
DIRETTORE DELLA FOTOGRAFIA RICCARDO PALLOTTINI
MUSICHE DEL MAESTRO LALLO GORI
REGIA DI LUCIO FULCI
EASTMANCOLOR CROMOSCOPE DELLA TECNOSTAMPA
UNA PRODUZIONE MEGA FILM S.p.A. - COLT PRODUZIONI CINEMATOGRAFICHE - ROMA L.F. PRODUZIONI CINEMATOGRAFICHE - ROMA
REALIZZATA DA ORESTE COLTELLACCI
LA CANZONE CANTATA DA SERGIO ENDRIGO E' INCISA SU DISCHI FONIT
PANTA CINEMATOGRAFICA DISTRIBUZIONE S.p.A.

THE
SMUGGLER
met als bendeleider
FABIO TESTI

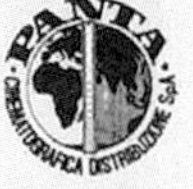

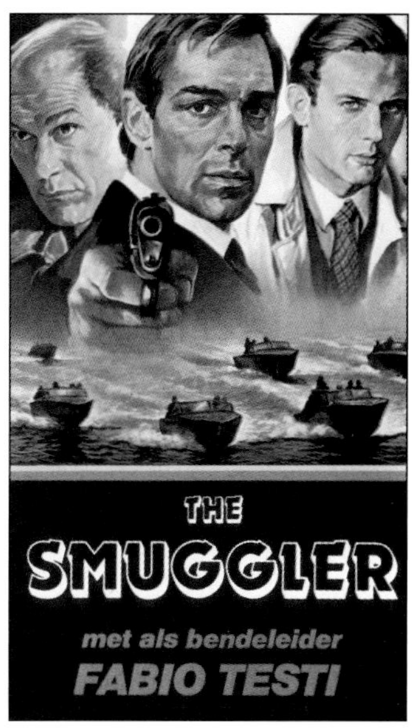

above:
Dutch video cover for *The Smuggler* (1980).

left:
Italian locandina poster for *Massacre Time*, aka *The Brute and the Beast* (1966).

ADRIENNE LA RUSSA · TOMAS MILIAN
BEATRICE CENCI
GEORGE WILSON · ANTONIO CASAGRANDE · MAVIE · PEDRO SANCHEZ
RAYMOND PELLEGRIN
LUCIO FULCI
EASTMANCOLOR

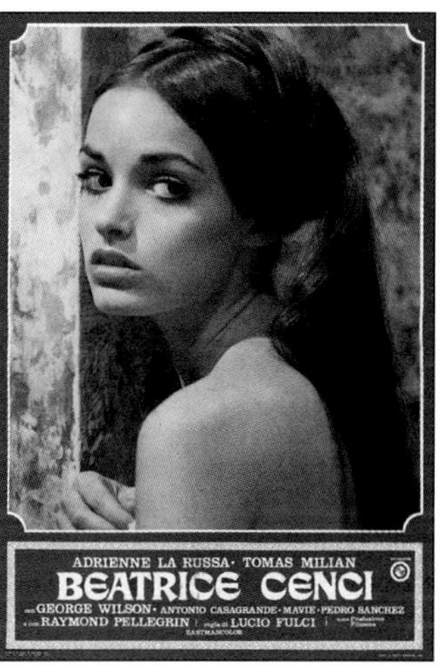

above:
Artwork for *Beatrice Cenci* (1969).

below:
French admat for *White Fang* (1973).

20th CENTURY-FOX présente
Une production OCÉANIA P.I.C.
FRANCO NERO
DANS
CROC BLANC
Tiré du roman du même nom de
JACK LONDON
AVEC
VIRNA LISI - FERNANDO REY - JOHN STEINER
RAIMUND HARMSTORF
DANIEL MARTIN
RICK BATTAGLIA
DANIELE DUBLINO
AVEC
pour la première fois à l'écran dans le rôle de MITSAH
MISSAELE
ET AVEC
CAROLE ANDRÉ
Mise en scène de
LUCIO FULCI

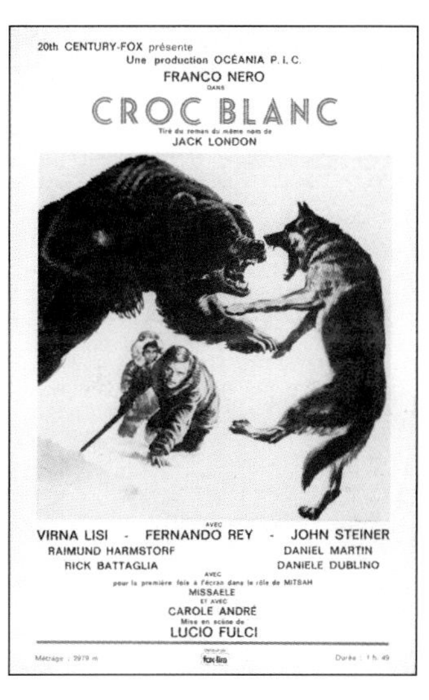

Italian theatrical title
Le colt cantarono la morte e fu...
Tempo di massacro

Translation
'The gun sang of death and it was...
Massacre Time'

Italy

International theatrical titles
The Brute and the Beast (USA)
La ville sans sheriff (FR)
'The Town Without a Sheriff'
Django – sein Gesangbuch war der Colt (WG) 'Django – His Hymnbook was the Colt'
Django's Seksløber Er Lov (DEN)
'Django's Six-Shooter is the Law'

Video/DVD titles
Colt Concert (NL)
Kolt Concert (NL alt.)
Concerto para un Colt (SP)
'Concert for a Colt'
En Dollar per Skott (SWE)
'A Dollar a Shot'
Αγριες Αποκαλυψεις (GRE)
'Wild Revelations'
Las pistolas cantaron la muerte (SP DVD) 'The pistols sing of death'
Massacre Time (USA alt. DVD)

Production companies
Mega Film S.p.A. (Bari/Rome)
Colt - L.F. Produzioni Cinematografiche (Rome)

Theatrical distributors
Panta Cinematografica (Italy)
Colt Distributors S.R.L. (Italy)
American International Pictures (USA)

Theatrical running times
Italy 83m
France 82m

Video/DVD/Blu-ray running times (adjusted)
Cinehollywood video 92m 09s
Wild East DVD (as 'Les temps du massacre') 92m 01s

Shooting period
May 1966

Censorship
Italian censor certificate 47469
04 August 1966

Release information
Rome 19 August 1966
Turin 25 August 1966
Bari 24 August 1966
USA (Detroit) 27 November 1968

Massacre Time

1966

Directed by Lucio Fulci. Panta Distribution presents a Joint Production / Mega Film (Bari/Rome) / Colt Produzioni Cinematografiche / L.F. Produzioni Cinematografiche production. general organizer: Oreste Coltellacci. story & screenplay: Fernando Di Leo. director of photography: Riccardo Pallottini. music: Lallo [Coriolano] Gori, conducted by the composer; published by Nazionalmusic (Milan). film editor: Ornella Micheli. art director: Sergio Canevari. assistant director: Giovanni Fago. continuity: Filiberto Fiaschi. cameraman: Gastone Di Giovanni. assistant cameramen: Sergio Martinelli & Carlo Tafani. production manager: Livio Maffei. unit manager: Albino Morandin. costumes: Silvano Giusti. set dresser: Mario Giorsi. special effects: Eros Baciucchi. make-up: Andrea Riva. hairdressers: Marcella De Marzi & Lina Cassini. production secretaries: Mario Barboni & Enzo Mazzucchi. assistant film editor: Bruno Micheli. sound engineer: Fernando Pescetelli. boom operator: Corrado Volpicelli. English voices by E.L.D.A. of Rome. song "A Man Alone (Back Home, Someday)" by [Sergio] Bardotti, [Lucio] Fulci & [Sergio] Endrigo; performed by Sergio Endrigo, recorded by Fonit. colour: Eastmancolor. printing/development: Tecnostampa using Cromoscope system. Kodak film. interiors filmed at Elios Film Studios (Rome).

Cast: Franco Nero (Tom Corbett). George Hilton (Jeffrey Corbett). Linda Sini [as 'Lynn Shane'] (Brady, bar owner). Giuseppe Addobbati [as 'John M. Douglas'] (Mr. Scott). Nino Castelnuovo (Jason 'Junior' Scott). Tom Felleghy (Murray, chief prospector). Franco Moruzzi [as 'Franco Morici']. Rina Franchetti (Mercedes). Tchang Yu [as 'Yu Tchang'] (Undertaker). Aysanoa Runachagua (Sonko, Scott's Indian henchman). *Uncredited:* Attilio Severini (older Scott henchman). Romano Puppo (tall Scott henchman). Roberto Alessandri. Mario Dionisi. Salvatore Borghese (short Scott henchman). Janos ['John'] Bartha (Carradine). Gino Barbacane (Jason's blond henchman). Franco Cobianchi (Chubby, the barman). Franco Gulà (old farmer). Franco Ukmar (Jason's henchman shot by Jeff on stairs).

Synopsis: New Mexico. Tom Corbett, a prospector, receives a message from Carradine, a family friend, telling him to return immediately to Laramie Town, and the home where he'd lived with his widowed mother. When she died she left the house and land to Tom's brother Jeff, and insisted that young Tom be sent away. Money was sent to him but her dying wish was that he should never return. When he arrives he finds the family house derelict. The land now belongs to a Mr. Scott, and he's warned to beware whenever he sees the Scott sign. In town, Tom sees Scott, with his sadistic son Jason, aka 'Junior', apprehending a family who are moving out of town because of Scott's low wages. Junior shoots the son in cold blood. Tom then visits Jeff, who is now a drunkard living in a shack on the edge of town with Mercedes, the family's old Indian servant. Both Jeff and Mercedes insist that Tom should leave, and refuse to discuss why he's been summoned. Determined to find out what's going on, Tom rides into town, observed by a group of Scott's men. Jeff follows Tom and joins him in the bar. A brawl breaks out and Jeff handles himself admirably, despite being rolling drunk. The brothers stagger out together, but Jeff once again insists Tom should leave. Instead, Tom visits the Carradines to find out why the letter was sent. Before he can discuss it, the Carradines are killed by shadowy assailants. Tom resolves to go to the Scott ranch. Jeff joins him, and shoots Scott's guards to help his brother approach the isolated ranch, after gaining a promise that Tom will take responsibility for having killed them. Tom walks into the Scott ranch to find a garden party in progress. He confronts Scott, but the old man refuses to talk. Jason is not so diffident, giving Tom a protracted whipping in front of the guests. Back at Jeff's shack, Tom is tended to by Mercedes, but a gunman at the window kills her. Jeff resolves to join his brother and seek vengeance. Jeff tells Tom the truth: Scott is Tom's real father. They encounter Scott at a remote shack and the old man admits that it was he who sent for Tom. He'd had no part in the killings of the Carradines or Mercedes. He tremblingly informs Tom that Jason, Tom's younger brother, is insane. Before he can go on, Jason shoots him, and with his henchmen pulls back to the ranch. Jeff accompanies Tom on a mission to bring down Junior. They kill Jason's men and Jeff saves Tom's life by blasting the gun out of Jason's hand as he prepares to shoot his older brother in the back. Jason chickens out of a bare-handed fight to the death but Tom grapples with him, pitching him from a gantry to his death.

Review: Scripted by Fernando Di Leo, Fulci's first western is something of a disappointment to anyone looking for an early classic in his repertoire. Rather than revelling in the parodic excesses suggested by Sergio Leone's then current work, the story follows a fairly standard stylistic furrow, with just a few touches of baroque violence and familial collapse to mark it out. Unlike Sergio Corbucci's *Django*, there is little sense of a dark, mocking re-take of American manners, and the technical aspects of the production are only infrequently impressive. This can come as a surprise to anyone who has read interviews in which Fulci claimed that *Massacre Time* was an "oneiric western", referring to a supposed dreamlike quality that I for one can barely perceive.

Massacre Time begins with a *Hounds of Zaroff* style manhunt led eagerly by young Jason Scott, aka 'Junior'. Tell-tale signs of psychosis are quickly apparent as he watches his human quarry (possibly Jeff's father?) splashing frantically around in the river, being torn apart by hunting dogs. His eyes roll back and he appears to be at the point of orgasm. In one of the film's more imaginative strokes, the credits then appear over the victim's blood washing downstream, until lost in a foaming torrent leading many miles downstream to the hero, Tom (Franco Nero), who is panning the shallows for gold.
Junior is the most excessively portrayed character in the film, the handsome spoiled favourite of a father whose indulgence has nurtured a monster. The young man has slowly exerted his dominance over the old; son has become master.

As remarked by Fulci in various interviews, the relationship is designated as Oedipal in a scene where he plays the piano with his father accompanying alongside. Scott Senior is shamed by his weakness, covertly arranging for his supposedly banished older son to return and sort things out. However, for a while it looks as if Junior will assert victory over his big brother too. Only when he backs down from Tom's challenge to fight without weapons does the young maniac lose face. His attempt to shoot Tom in the back condemns him, in western terms, to ignominy, while Tom's honour is intact.

Amongst the actors, Nino Castelnuovo is striking as the sadistic younger brother who gets to humiliate Franco Nero on the end of his whip. Nero of course went on to star in countless westerns and crime thrillers, his contract seemingly stipulating at least one scene of beating and degradation per film. (The victim-hero type he portrays here would re-surface in Fulci's early gialli, with Jean Sorel's roles.) The confrontation between brothers at the Scott ranch, which takes place before an audience of dandified onlookers, is as prolonged a demonstration as could be wished of the Italian westerns' sado-masochistic drives.

As Tom's half-brother Jeff, George Hilton also makes a good sized meal out of his performance, as the sly drunk who can still pack a punch and a pistol. The requisite bar-room brawl is well-staged around his tequila-soaked demeanour, which fools adversaries into thinking him an easy conquest. Fulci shows some early traces of his mature style as he frames Nero and Hilton's sweating, stubble-cheeked faces in tight close-up whilst picking out other characters in deep focus. (The technique would be followed up in the 1969 film *Beatrice Cenci* and emerge later as part of the humid atmospherics of *The Beyond*). The action often takes place in darkened locations, at night, or in dimly lit interiors. The surreal quality alluded to by Fulci is admittedly present in a few brief images; Tom's return to the family ranch only to discover it reduced to a wind-lashed open-roofed habitat of foraging pigs being the main example. But there is no real commitment to heightening the plot-line with technical exaggeration, and no attempt to render the format ironic with its own clichés.

On a more 'positive' note, perhaps the degree of damage done to the basic family unit in this film shows Fulci's nascent taste for the blighted and pessimistic. Tom is forced to kill his insane younger brother, and their father dies at the younger man's hand, precipitating the classic need to avenge the murdered father. The topic of madness makes its debut in a Fulci story (as opposed to the madcap antics of the comedies), whilst the blatancy of Junior's erotic pleasure in cruelty would raise a few eyebrows had it emerged in an American oater of the period. Although sentiment is allowed to reveal itself in the eventual loyalty between Tom and Jeff, the majority of the time their relationship is one of mutual mistrust. As with many of the films made by Fulci away from the horror/thriller fold, the importance of women is virtually extinguished, with the mother already dead at the story's beginning and the only other female role occupied by Mercedes, the family's servant. But such darkness is only chewing away at the edges. For spaghetti western fans, *Massacre Time* may hold the attention, but otherwise it merely marks time before Fulci's transition to a more inventive style in the late sixties and early seventies.

top:
Franco Nero finds the company frosty in his home town.

above:
Dutch video cover.

left:
Nero approaches the ranch belonging to his estranged father and brother.

below:
Mercedes (Rina Franchetti) tries to stop Tom (Franco Nero) from confronting his troubled past.

Italian theatrical title
Beatrice Cenci

Italy

Alternative titles
The True Story of Beatrice Cenci (pre-shooting title)
Conspiracy (title used in 'Cinema X' magazine)

International theatrical titles
Liens d'amour et de sang (FR)
'Bonds of Love and Blood'
Die Nackte und der Kardinal (GER)
'The Nude and the Cardinal'

Video/DVD title
Conspiracy of Torture (USA DVD)

Production company
Filmena S.r.l. (Rome)

Theatrical distributors
CIDIF (Italy)
Les Films Jacques Leitienne (France)

Theatrical running time
Italy 99m

Video/DVD/Blu-ray running times (adjusted)
Audio-Visual video (UK) 93m 29s
Midnight Choir DVD (USA) 93m 03s

Shooting period
August-Sept 1969

Censorship
Italian censor certificate 55002
13 November 1969

Release information
Rome 14 November 1969
Taranto 21 November 1969
Parma 24 November 1969
Bari 28 November 1969

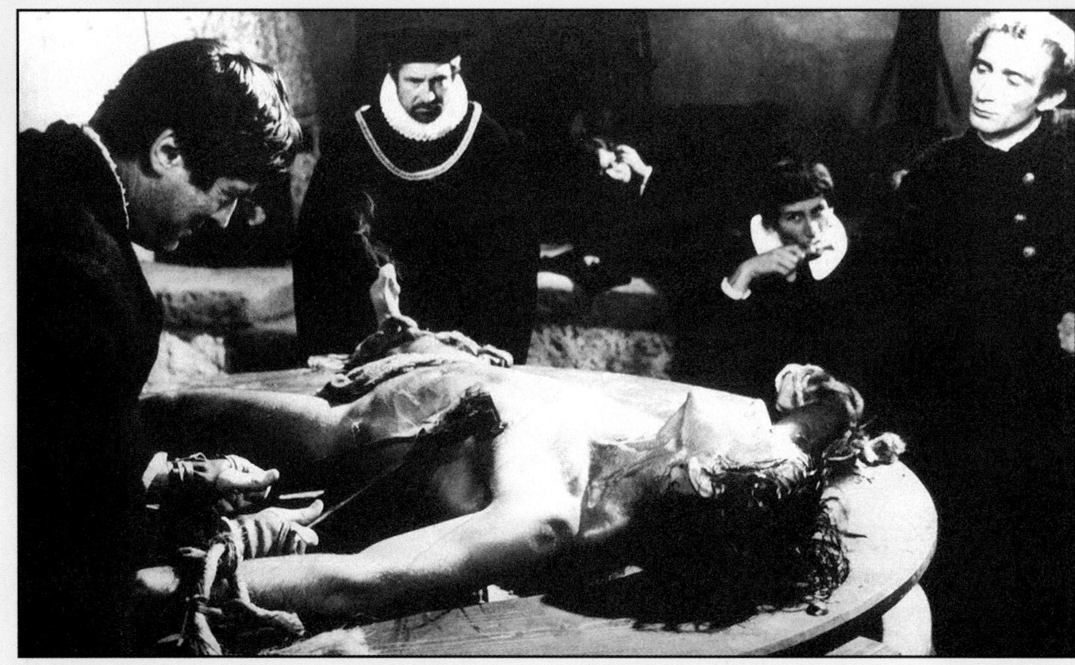

Beatrice Cenci

1969

Directed by Lucio Fulci. produced by Giorgio Agliani for Filmena S.r.l. (Rome). story & screenplay: Lucio Fulci & Roberto Gianviti. director of photography: Erico Menczer. music by Angelo [Francesco] Lavagnino & Silvano Spadaccino; published by Nazionalmusic (Milan). editor: Antonietta Zita (Fono Roma S.p.A.). art director: Umberto Turco. production manager: Adriano Merkel. unit manager: Elio Di Pietro. assistant director: Tiziano Cortini. continuity: Roberto Giandalia. cameraman: Silvio Fraschetti. costume designer: Mario Giorsi. make-up: Otello Sisi. hair stylist: Antonietta Caputo. assistant costumes: Silvano Giusti. production secretaries: Bruno Ridolfi & Mario Campolunghi. administration: Giuseppe Franciosi. still photography: Ermanno Serto. assistant editor: Giuliano Mattioli. sound: Leopoldo Rosi & Carlo Diotallevi. dubbing: S.A.S. [Società Attori Sincronizzazione]. costume house: Tigano-Lo Faro. wigs: Rocchetti. set furnishings: Rancati. shoes: Pompei. optical effects: S.P.E.S., director: E. Catalucci. cantano i cantastorie di Silvano Spadaccino. Eastmancolor. colour, negatives & positives by S.P.E.S. interiors filmed at De Paolis Studios (Rome).

Cast: Tomas Milian (Olimpio Calvetti). Adrienne La Russa (Beatrice Cenci). Georges ['George'] Wilson (Francesco Cenci). Mavie Bardanzellu [as 'Mavi'] (Lucrezia, Beatrice's stepmother). Antonio Casagrande (Giacomo Cenci, Beatrice's older brother). Ignazio Spalla [as 'Pedro Sanchez'] (Catalano, the bandit). Max Steffen Zacharias (Prospero Farinaccio, counsel for the defence). Raymond Pellegrin (Cardinal Lanciani). Massimo Sarchielli (Gasparro, Francesco's bearded associate). Mirko Ellis (fair-haired bearded inquisitor). Janos ['John'] Bartha (heavy-jowled inquisitor). Calogero Micciché. Gustavo D'Arpe (Farinaccio's fat colleague). Umberto D'Orsi (murder investigator). Alfio Petrini. Giuseppe Fortis (chaplain). Maciej Rayzacher [as 'Jerzy Rayzacher'] (notekeeper during Olimpio's torture). Stefano Oppedisano (soldier who identifies Gasparro's corpse). *Uncredited:* Giancarlo Badessi (bearded inquisitor who confronts Beatrice with Olimpio). Angelo Casadei. Ernesto Colli (gaunt inquisitor at Olimpio's torture). Amedeo Trilli (balding man reporting Francesco to official). Renato De Carmine (The Pope).

top right:
Olimpio (Tomas Milian) undergoes torture by the Church Inquisitors, played by Mirko Ellis (bearded), Maciej Rayzacher (eating chicken) and Ernesto Colli (far right).

below:
German press book cover.

Synopsis: Francesco Cenci, a rich nobleman and landowner, is hated by everyone, including his family. He's vicious, conniving, tyrannical and miserly, and has made numerous enemies in Church and State. His beautiful young daughter Beatrice plans to enter a convent, as much to escape her father as for spiritual reasons. When Francesco hears of this he imprisons Beatrice in the dungeon of his castle, only releasing her to attend a party which he has thrown to celebrate the death of two of his sons, whom he has long resented for the financial weight they place upon him. Beatrice defies him by attending the party in a black funeral dress. In an upstairs bedroom Francesco drunkenly rips off his daughter's dress and rapes her. Beatrice changes drastically after this horror. She coerces her besotted servant Olimpio with sexual favours, and embroils him in her plans for revenge. He is told to seek the assistance of a local bandit, Catalano, and pay him to murder Francesco Cenci. However, when the time comes the bandit cannot do the deed: he is a killer "in reputation only". Olimpio too finds he cannot stomach killing. In a fury, Beatrice snatches the knife, Olimpio restrains the victim, and she herself stabs her father in the eye. Beatrice is aglow, but Olimpio is stricken with guilt. The whole of the Cenci household, including the dead man's wife Lucrezia and oldest son Giacomo, are complicit in Beatrice's act. Beatrice even encourages her little brother Bernardo to help carry his father's body onto the ramparts of the castle. There they contrive to make it look as though Francesco has been killed in a drunken fall from the battlements. However, a wily investigator despatched from Rome soon deduces that the fall was no accident. Suspicion closes around Olimpio, who is taken into custody and tortured for information about the slaying. Cardinal Lanciani attempts to extract a statement from him implicating Beatrice, but Olimpio maintains that she is innocent. He dies, after much suffering, without admitting her guilt. Torture proves more effective against Beatrice's mother and brother, though not Beatrice herself. Nevertheless, the court decrees death to them all, except Bernardo who will be sold into slavery. However, the planned execution causes great unrest amongst the people, who feel that Beatrice was justified in killing the father who molested her. To satisfy public opinion, the Pope decides to absolve Beatrice of her sins – but only *after* she has been beheaded.

About the production: In the summer of 1969 Lucio Fulci's *Beatrice Cenci* was one of two competing versions of the famous historical tale battling to make it into production. Fulci's script, co-written with Roberto Gianviti, was called 'The True Story of Beatrice Cenci' in pre-production, and marked the debut of newcomers Filmena Productions; the other, lined up for director Florestano Vancini and *Elvira Madigan* star Pia Degermark[4] from a script by Fabio Pittorru and Massimo Felisatti, was being nurtured by one of the giants of Italian filmmaking, Dino De Laurentiis. *Variety* referred to this 'battle of the Cencis' on 16 July 1969: *"Director Lucio Fulci assigned Adrienne La Russa, Tomas Milian and George Wilson to principal roles in 'Beatrice Cenci' and the Filmena project seems ready to jump the gun for De Laurentiis, who is rushing preparations for his version at Dinocitta."* The two films were neck-and-neck for a while, with a *Variety* report dated 13 August 1969 suggesting that De Laurentiis had signed Christopher Plummer for his version (Plummer had appeared in the De Laurentiis production *Waterloo* earlier that year). However, just a few days later Fulci started shooting. Adrienne La Russa and Tomas Milian were pictured in a brief news article in *La Stampa*, dated 20 August 1969, which declared that filming had been under way *"in questi giorni"* ('these recent days'). By 17 September, *Variety* were reporting that the De Laurentiis production had been shelved because, *"Lucio Fulci got his to the starting line first"*, and the 'David and Goliath' aspect of the news story was so juicy that as late as April 1970 they were still referring to it: *"Filmena opened shop last year rather conspicuously by beating Laurentiis to the punch on 'Beatrice Cenci'"*.[5] (Incidentally, Dino De Laurentiis must have been pretty aggrieved when exactly the same thing happened again on another 1969 project: he was forced to shelve his production 'The Iron Outlaws' – which would have starred Rod Taylor[6] as the antipodean criminal/hero Ned Kelly – when the United Artists production *Ned Kelly* starring Mick Jagger went into production first.)

Review: Impressively mounted and generally well acted (especially by Georges Wilson as Francesco Cenci and Umberto D'Orsi as a sly murder investigator), *Beatrice Cenci* enlivens its historical subject matter with a pleasingly grotty 'realism' and much carnal emphasis amid the ruffs and bodices. The opening scene of the construction and preparation of a gallows is strongly conceived and carried out, pulling from the lavish spectacle – so beloved of Italian period drama – a disconcerting fixation on prosaic details. For instance, we first see an apprehensive group of the Cenci family's supporters, dripping with sweat as they deliberate, plucking irritably at their costumes. The same attention to sticky, uncomfortable atmospheric detail is apparent in the torture scene later, not least as it involves a sadistic branding.

The heat extends to Fulci's directorial style too, something that would come to characterise his best work. Indeed the violent torture of Olimpio – and several other passages, such as one in which a man is savaged to death by Francesco Cenci's dogs – provides the first real evidence of Fulci's taste for brutality. The bilious portrayal of Don Francesco's patriarchal excess is well achieved by actor Georges Wilson. When a visiting servant of the Pontiff protests at his blasphemous remarks, the irate Cenci remarks: *"Let Him plug His ears"*. Even the camera marks obeisance to this bully; in a scene where the enraged patriarch kicks a dog-dish across the floor, the camera drops down to mutt's eye level as if flinching. In fact the action is generally well-attended by the camera and occasionally recalls the sterling work of Michael Reeves (director of *The Sorcerers*, 1967, and *Witchfinder General*, 1968). The film gains an air of seriousness from this technical virtuosity, which probably helps account for Fulci's opinion that it was his best film.

With Beatrice, Fulci has the opportunity to depict the suffering of an archetypal victim. But whilst this once-demure young woman is finally executed, we see little of her physical sufferings. Instead the film concentrates on the torture of her lover Olimpio. A sequence involving the naked man stretched on a wheel until his veins and tendons rupture, followed by the repeated branding of his flesh by hot irons, makes a meal of the sado-masochistic pleasure to be had observing the excrutiating process of Inquisition. Skilled use is made in these scenes of the affected boredom of the torturers, whose indifferently repeated questions and threats are delivered in a way which mocks the victim's screams. Olimpio's fate is pre-figured by his declaration to Beatrice after making love: *"There are moments of happiness that one could pay for with one's life; but mine is not enough to repay your love's worth."* Mixed with the tale of Beatrice's deep familial trauma, then, is a whiff of the *'belle dame sans merci'*.

Fulci and Gianviti structured their film in an unusual way, turning the story into a mystery. This mirrors the heroine's selective disclosure of information in the cause of her revenge. We are placed at the unfortunate Olimpio's side by the delayed revelation of the 'last straw' that motivated Beatrice's fury. The affair she embarks upon with her lover, one of the servant classes, is perhaps borne of cynical expediency. Beatrice may deliberately have offered her body to Olimpio, whom she knew was infatuated with her, as a 'honey trap' to obtain his promise to kill Francesco. As Olimpio sprawls dying on the floor, physically broken by the torturers, he maintains total responsibility for the murder. Thus, he believes, his statement will set Beatrice free – as long as she can conceal her love for him when she is shown his wrecked body by the officials.

"It's not the first time a dependent claims to have loved his mistress", Beatrice calmly pronounces, gazing at Olimpio with a softly derisive smile. As she leaves the dungeon, Olimpio gazes after her in rapturous despair. The scene is constructed so we can believe that even a parting glance would result in the exposure of the lovers' plot. And yet we wonder, as does the tormented Olimpio, whether true love could walk away without a flicker, however surreptitious. The haunting suggestion (made explicit by the torturers as they mock their victim) is that he has been made a 'fool for love', by a woman whose piety before rape has been transformed into an equally intense cynicism after it. Has Beatrice manipulated the passion of others in the name of her haughty vengeance? Fulci's film leaves the question un-answered.

The concern with Catholic hypocrisy is continued from *Operation St. Peter's*, made the previous year; but whereas that film's attitude was lightly elaborated through farce, this time the attack on the Church's cynicism – the conferring of sainthood upon a murderess to avoid civil unrest – is harsh and uncompromised. The theme of a woman's unfathomable duplicity is also a feature of two further collaborations with scriptwriter Gianviti; *One on Top of the Other* and the superlative *A Lizard in a Woman's Skin*. *Beatrice Cenci* may lack the psychedelic charms of the contemporary stories, but it remains one of the strongest early works, and an especially hard-hitting entry in the Italian costume drama stakes. Fans of the horror/thriller films of Lucio Fulci may be pleasantly surprised by the qualities he brings to this project.

top:
Although later excised from the UK video, this orgy sequence characteristically caught the attention of Britain's *Cinema X* magazine when it was screened under its export title *Conspiracy.*

above:
Beatrice and her father Francesco (Georges Wilson).

below:
Olimpio and Beatrice.

bottom:
Francesco Cenci bathes with an emissary from Rome.

Italian theatrical title
Zanna Bianca

Italy Spain & France

International theatrical titles
Croc blanc (FR) 'White Fang'
Colmillo blanco (SP) 'White Fang'
Wolfsblut (WG) 'Wolfblood'

Video/DVD titles
White Fang (Call of the Wild II) (NL)
Ulvehunden (DEN) 'Wolfdog'

Production companies
Oceania Produzioni Internazionali Cinematografiche s.r.l. (Rome)
Incine Compania Industrial Cinematografica s.a. (Madrid)
Les Productions Fox Europa (Paris)

Theatrical distributors
Titanus Distribuzione (Italy)
In-Cine Distribuidora Cinematografica s.a. (Spain)
20th Century Fox (France)

Theatrical running times
Italy 105m
Spain (SMC) 105m
France 98m
UK 101m

Video/DVD/Blu-ray running times (adjusted)
Ascot Elite DVD (Germany) 103m 28s

Shooting and release information
Shooting from 13 June 1973
Italian censor certificate 63706
19 December 1973
Rome 22 December 1973
Bari 03 January 1974
French visa 41939 issued
07 October 1974
UK (London) 13 December 1974
France (CNC) 27 June 1975
USA (Cedar Rapids, IA)
31 October 1975

White Fang

1973

Directed by Lucio Fulci. produced by Harry Alan Towers for Oceania Produzioni Internazionali Cinematografiche (Rome) / In-Cine Compañia Industrial Cinematográfica (Madrid) / Production Fox-Europa (Paris). presented by American Cinema. based on the novel White Fang by Jack London. adaptation: Roberto Gianviti, Piero Regnoli, Peter Welbeck [Harry Alan Towers], Guy Elmes, Thom Keyes & Guillaume Roux. dialogue Peter Welbeck & Guillaume Roux. supervisor of photography Erico Menczer. director of photography: Pablo Ripoli. music: Carlo Rustichelli, conducted by Alessandro Blonksteiner; published by Zita. editor: Ornella Micheli. art director: Emilio Ruiz. set designer & costume designer: Enzo Bulgarelli. production manager: Piero Donati. unit manager: Ennio Di Meo. 2nd unit director: Tonino Ricci. assistant directors: Francesco Cinieri, Victor Tourjansky, Giuseppe Leoni & Roberto Sbarigia. continuity: Roberto Giandalia. cameraman: Mario Mazzoni. assistant cameraman: Roberto Brega. 2nd unit cameramen: Otello Spila & Giovanni Bergamini. collaborators – location photography: Elisabeth Klaus & Hans Musek. make-up: Dante Trani. assistant costume designer: Ernestina Pacifico Hess. assistant art director: Mario Dentici. assistant set designer: Emilio Ruiz. production secretary: Donato Bitetto. still photography: Mario Mazzoni. stills laboratory: Leo Massa (Rome). unit publicists: Enrico Lucherini, Margherita Rossetti, Matteo Spinola. assistant editor: Bruno Micheli. sound: Aldo De Martini. synchronization: Fono Roma. colour by Eastmancolor. laboratory: Technospes (Rome). filmed on location in Norway, Spain & Italy with interiors at Cinecittà Studios (Rome).

Cast: Franco Nero (Jason Scott). Virna Lisi (Sister Evangelina). Fernando Rey (Father Oatley). John Steiner (Charles 'Beauty' Smith). Missaele (Mitsah). Daniel Martín (Charlie, Mitsah's father). Raimund Harmstorf (Kurt Jansen). Daniele Dublino (Chester, a killer). Carole André (Krista Oatley). Rik Battaglia (Jim Hall, Smith's well-dressed henchman). Janos ['John'] Bartha (corrupt Mountie). Luigi Antonio Guerra. Carla Mancini. Maurice Poli (chief Mountie). *Uncredited:* Alfonso Giganti (saloon bartender).

Synopsis: When Charlie, a Native American fur-trader, discovers that his son Mitsah has befriended a wolf, he scares the beast away. He changes his mind, however, when the animal (actually a wolf/dog cross-breed) arrives at the hut, barking furiously. Mitsah has fallen through the ice on a nearby lake and the animal has come to raise the alarm. Mitsah is saved but falls seriously ill and Charlie must seek help in nearby Dawson City. There he meets Jason Scott, a writer, and Sister Evangelina, a nun who has arrived with funds to set up a hospital. Alcoholic priest Father Oatley shows suspicious interest in her money. He is under the thumb of Dawson City's most powerful resident, Beauty Smith, who has bought his way into prominence with cash and promisory notes. Flanked by a posse of thugs he lords it up around town. Evangelina takes care of Mitsah, but as the boy lies barely conscious his father is threatened outside by Smith's thugs. A vicious fight is provoked between White Fang and Smith's champion hound; White Fang wins. Smith tries to buy the beast, but Charlie refuses. Furious, Smith orders his gang to murder Charlie. White Fang is captured by Smith's men and put to service earning money in a public fight against a captive wild bear. White Fang is injured but Scott and Sister Evangelina manage to rescue him. Returning him to Mitsah, they avoid telling the boy about his father's death. In the meantime, Scott takes care of the youngster. Smith's business plans falter and he decides to escape with his ill-gotten gains, intending to start again in another town where gold has recently been discovered. He tries to persuade Oatley's daughter Krista, a 'dancer' at a notorious bar, to leave with him as his wife. When she refuses he kills her. Father Oatley sees what Smith has done and reveals his secret to the townsfolk. The whole town prepares to move on in search of gold. Chester, the assassin who murdered Charlie, is released from prison by a corrupt Mountie and at Smith's orders attempts to murder Jason Scott. White Fang leaps through the window and savages him. Scott, White Fang and a horde of villagers pursue Beauty Smith, who has taken Mitsah hostage after shooting Father Oatley in the head. White Fang saves the day by gnashing at the villain's wrist. Beauty Smith is taken back to face justice, but White Fang is apparently lost. A tearful Mitsah sails downriver, distraught at the loss of his father and beloved hound. At the last minute White Fang reappears, swimming from the riverbank after the departing boat.

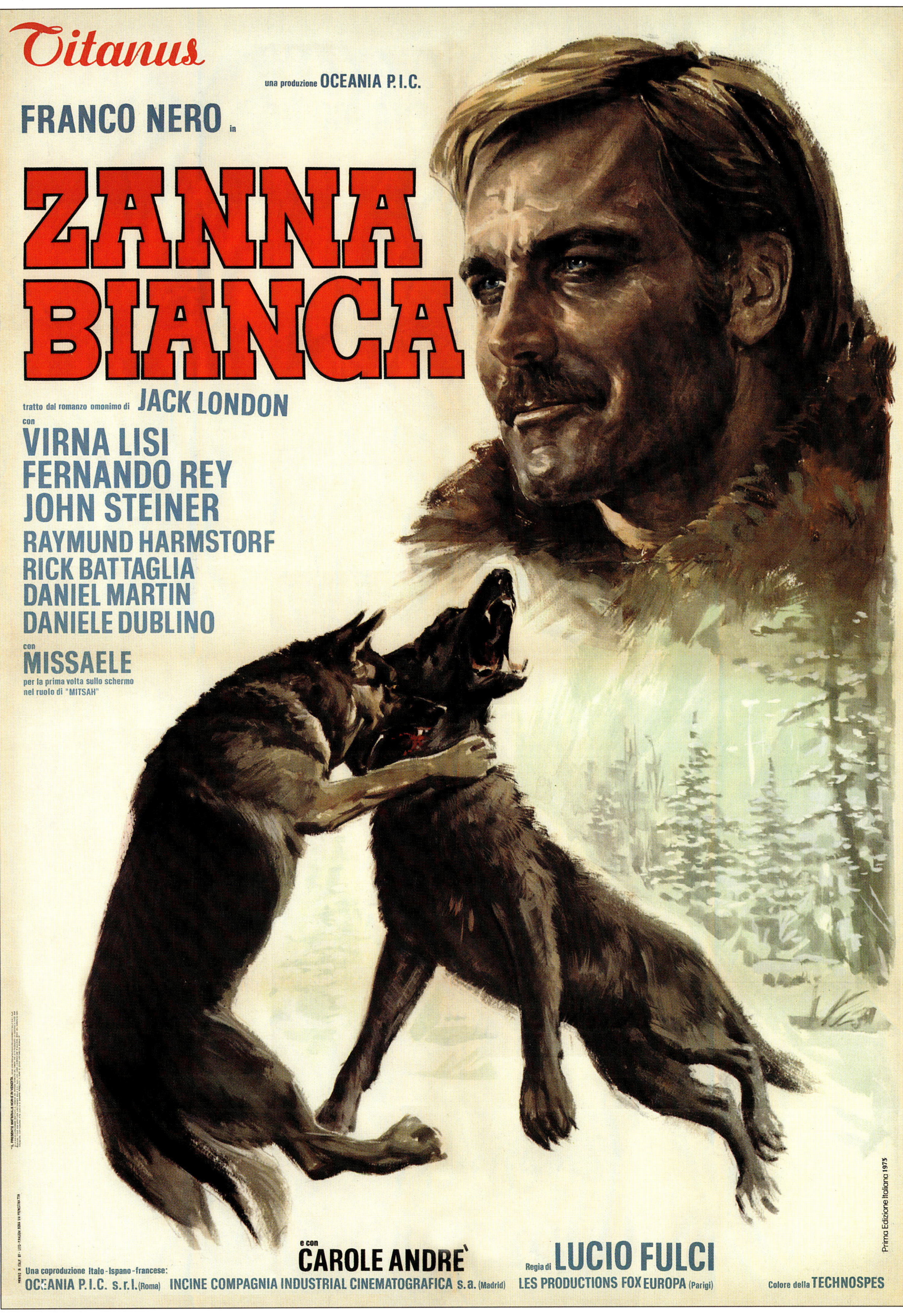
Titanus
una produzione OCEANIA P.I.C.
FRANCO NERO in
ZANNA BIANCA
tratto dal romanzo omonimo di JACK LONDON
con
VIRNA LISI
FERNANDO REY
JOHN STEINER
RAYMUND HARMSTORF
RICK BATTAGLIA
DANIEL MARTIN
DANIELE DUBLINO
con
MISSAELE
per la prima volta sullo schermo
nel ruolo di "MITSAH"
e con
CAROLE ANDRE'
Regia di LUCIO FULCI
Una coproduzione Italo-Ispano-francese:
OCEANIA P.I.C. s.r.l. (Roma) INCINE COMPAGNIA INDUSTRIAL CINEMATOGRAFICA s.a. (Madrid) LES PRODUCTIONS FOX EUROPA (Parigi)
Colore della TECHNOSPES
Prima Edizione Italiana 1973

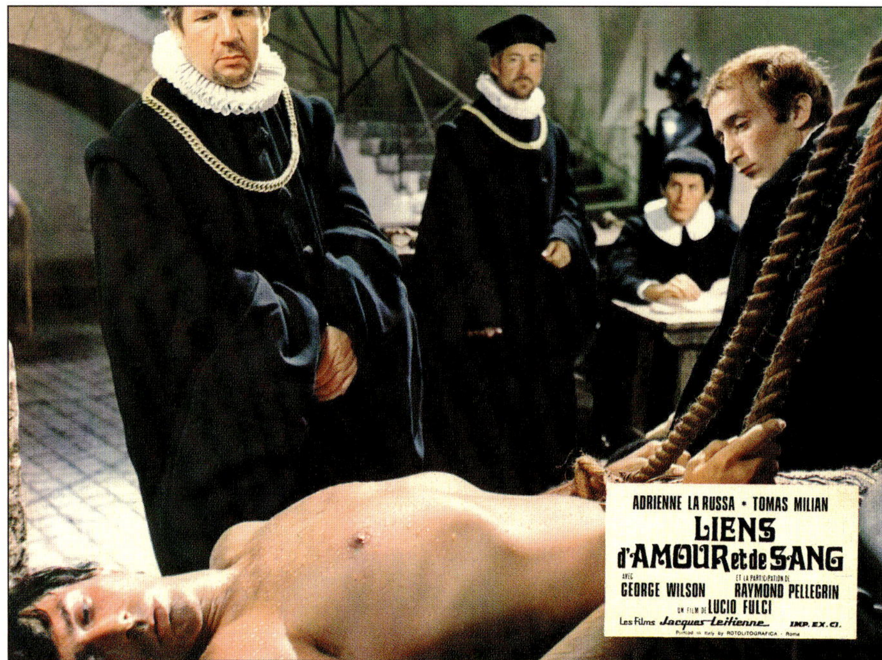

this page left (top to bottom):
Beatrice Cenci: Tomas Milian about to be tortured by order of the Vatican; Beatrice (Adrienne La Russa) attended by her young brother Giacomo (Antonio Casagrande) and family friends; Beatrice's lecherous father Francesco (Georges Wilson) indulges his passions in a scene trimmed from the UK video release.

this page right (top to bottom):
Massacre Time aka *The Brute and the Beast:* Two lobby cards; lower depicts the hero's brother Jeff (George Hilton) on the right, alongside Tom (Franco Nero) on the left; *Beatrice Cenci:* Poster from Belgium.

opposite page: Typically inventive and stark graphic design on this Polish poster.

Beatrice Cenci
Włoski film historyczny
Reżyseria: Lucio Fulci
W głównych rolach:
TOMAS MILIAN
ADRIENNE LA RUSSA
Georges Wilson
Raymond Pelegrin
Produkcja
FILMENA
W. GÓRKA 71
CWF

top: Tomas Milian exudes Mansonesque menace as the villainous Chaco in *The Four of the Apocalypse*.
left: The West German theatrical release: 'Condemned to Life – Condemned to Death'.
above: Stubby Preston (Italian heartthrob Fabio Testi) in a tight spot in *The Four of the Apocalypse*.

The Four of the Apocalypse – **top left:** Spanish pressbook; **top right:** Clem (Michael J. Pollard) begs for some booze from the sadistic Chaco.
below: Italian fotobusta; **left pic:** Chaco (Tomas Milian) humiliates Clem; and **right pic:** Stubby (Fabio Testi) is appalled at the slaughter of a wagon-train of Christian pilgrims.

IN A PLACE BEYOND TIME, COMES A TERRIFYING CHALLENGE BEYOND IMAGINATION!

CONQUEST

GIOVANNI DI CLEMENTE Presents

"CONQUEST" Starring GEORGE RIVERO • ANDREW OCCHIPINTI • CONRADO SAN MARTIN • VIOLETA CELA JOSE GRAS PALAU • MARIA SCOLA • Also starring SABRINA SELLERS • Story by GIOVANNI DI CLEMENTE Screenplay by GINO CAPONE • JOSE DE LA LOMA Sr. • CARLOS VASALLO • Music by CLAUDIO SIMONETTI Produced by GIOVANNI DI CLEMENTE • Directed by LUCIO FULCI

Released By UFDC UNITED FILM DISTRIBUTION COMPANY

R RESTRICTED UNDER 17 REQUIRES ACCOMPANYING PARENT OR ADULT GUARDIAN

DOLBY STEREO™ IN SELECTED THEATRES

Rome 2033 – The Fighter Centurions

far right: Spanish pressbook cover

Conquest

right: Spanish pressbook cover.

bottom right: Ocron (Sabrina Siani) pleads with The Great Zora (Conrado San Martin) to help her kill Mace.

bottom left: Impressive monsters enliven the murk of Fulci's sword-and-sorcery tale.

below: Mace (Jorge Rivero) swears to avenge his friend Ilias.

JACK LONDON'S
GREATEST ADVENTURE STORY
Challenge To
White Fang
DOG SLED TEAMS RACE FOR GOLD
THROUGH AVALANCHES...
LANDSLIDES... BLIZZARDS...
STARRING
FRANCO NERO • VIRNA LISI • HARRY CAREY, JR.
PG PARENTAL GUIDANCE SUGGESTED
Some material may not be suitable for pre-teenagers
WRITTEN BY ALBERT SILVESTRI DIRECTED BY LUCIO FULCI COLOR PRINTS BY CFI
A CREATIVE ENTERTAINMENT PRESENTATION / A SIERRA ASSOCIATES FILM / DISTRIBUTED BY PREMIERE RELEASING ORGANIZATION

About the production: In 1972, veteran exploitation producer Harry Alan Towers bankrolled and co-wrote an adaptation of Jack London's *The Call of the Wild*, starring Charlton Heston. Heston himself was not impressed with the resulting film (in his journal he wrote, *"I fear I've fallen in with amateurs and con men. This had not been a picture really but a production deal, patched together with incredible adroitness and negotiating skill – and no film-making talent whatsoever"*[7]), but *The Call of the Wild* made enough money for Towers to consider financing a second Jack London adaptation the following year. In February 1973 *Variety* reported that Towers was prepping London's *White Fang*, with plans to shoot it in Spain with Peter Collinson (*The Italian Job*) lined up to direct. However, Collinson dropped out (he moved on to shoot the Agatha Christie adaptation *And Then There Were None* for Towers in 1974) and instead *White Fang* went before the cameras in June 1973 with Lucio Fulci at the helm. The crew left for Salzburg in Austria on 23 June 1973, and a few days later began shooting for a month on Austria's snowy mountain slopes. Further filming was then scheduled for Madrid, after which production returned to Rome.

So was Harry Alan Towers still attached as producer of the Fulci film? The Italian credits certainly show him as co-writer but there's no indication that he produced it. Three companies are named – Oceania Produzioni Internazionali Cinematografiche s.r.l. (Rome), Incine Compania Industrial Cinematografica S.A. (Madrid) and Les Productions Fox Europa (Paris) – but none of these are Towers's. Neither Italian nor English-language credits mention a production company associated in any way with Towers (bear in mind that Towers was a master of the complicated production deal). It therefore seems that he sold his script to Giulio Sbarigia (of Oceania) after Collinson dropped out, and decided for some reason not to produce the film. This makes it unique in Tower's career, as the only example of him selling a script he'd written to another company without in some way participating in production.

Review: Beginning in a snow-covered forest created on an Italian soundstage, Fulci's first stab at Jack London's gritty children's adventure – like its follow-up, *Challenge to White Fang* – feels curiously adult in tone. As Verina Glaessner noted in a 1974 Monthly Film Bulletin review, *"the hound is mercifully un-Lassie-like, making the film one any kid with an ounce of imagination should enjoy"*.

White Fang was a well-financed affair, with the big Dawson City set populated by hordes of extras in period dress. Fulci's direction of this lavish mainstream adventure is competent, if less stylized than his previous thrillers. The spectacular snow-covered settings are photographed very well, however, and the principal actors are always engaging, with particular credit due to Franco Nero in heroic mode and John Steiner as the villainous Beauty Smith. Steiner's performance is lively and dramatic, but thankfully avoids the moustache-twirling pantomime frequently trotted out by adults to amuse children. A blaring, old-fashioned soundtrack from Carlo Rustichelli features a bit too prominently at times, although some will delight in recognizing themes from the composer's scores for Mario Bava (*Blood and Black Lace* and *Kill, Baby, Kill!*).

Considering that the film is ostensibly a boy's adventure story, very little action is dished out for the young actor Missaele. He's laid up in bed for most of the time, and this leads to a lack of focus in some sections of the story. Because he isn't immediately told about his father's death, the few scenes where we do see him, recovering and playing with his canine companion, are incongruous. The reason for witholding such vital knowledge is revealed fairly late in the day. It can seem as if the boy has barely registered the tragic event, and prefers to fool around with his dog rather than grieve. Women don't get much scope for activity in the story, either. In fact, we only encounter two – one is a nun and the other a whore. A very nice nun, of course, and a very nice whore too, but the allotted roles are simpler than Jack London's writing suggested.

So much for the film's faults. Fulci scores more highly during the numerous scenes of conflict. The first sign of Fulcine passion is a vicious and protracted dog fight, witnessed as father and son arrive in Dawson. The editing here is excellent, and the soundtrack's montage of amplified growls and furious barks effectively winds up the viewers' nerves. The same goes for an even more alarming fight between White Fang and a giant bear. We may occasionally be able to spot the substitution of a man in a rug for the actual beast, but the scene is quite scary and intense enough for this technical lapse to be forgiven. Fulci emphasized that, despite appearances, no animal was injured or maltreated during the making of his *White Fang* films. (He'd already been hauled before the Italian courts on a false charge of mistreating animals after the shocking 'split dogs' scene in 1971's *A Lizard in a Woman's Skin*.)

As one might cheerfully expect, Fulci's concept of material suitable for children differs considerably from British or American entertainments. Here we are treated to numerous acts of violence: a stabbing, the aforementioned animal fights, and even a dog gnawing at the flesh of a felled man's throat. All exceed the parameters normally set for kids' fare here. The priest receives 'communion' with a bullet through the cranium, and the villain has his wrist chewed extravagantly by the heroic beast. These scenes aren't as extreme as others in Fulci's more adult concoctions, but in context, Fulci's roughhouse approach to children's drama can be startling.

It would be unfair though to suggest that Fulci's only achievement with this film was to inject dubious levels of violence into children's drama. Many action sequences are skilfully mounted, and the general tenor of the drama has a refreshingly unpatronizing air to it. When a henchman of the evil Beauty Smith creeps through the night into good-natured journalist Jason Scott's hut, the cultivated menace compares with similar scenes in his more 'adult' films. Likewise the climactic chase through the woods. This latter seems to be a favourite scenario for Fulci. He also included vigorous, kinetic woodland chases in the earlier films *Massacre Time* and *Don't Torture a Duckling*. (Perhaps a version of *The Most Dangerous Game* would have suited him?)

Of course, many a British child would delight at the bloodthirstiness of the film, and it's a fact that these two – *White Fang* and its sequel – are Fulci's most frequently televised in Italy, having been major hits in the cinema. Their fame in his native country is assumed by their inclusion on the cover of Fulci's collection of articles and memoirs, *Miei mostri adorati*, published in Italy, which lists a number of his best-known films. To understand their appeal further, let's now look at the second title.

above:
Spanish art for *White Fang*.

left:
Detail from the artwork for the Danish VHS release of *White Fang*.

facing page:
US theatrical poster for Fulci's sequel.

Italian theatrical title
Il ritorno di Zanna Bianca

Translation
'The Return of White Fang'

Italy, West Germany & France

International theatrical titles
Der Teufelsschlucht der Wilden Wölfe (WG) 'The Devil's Ravine of Wild Wolves'
La revanche de croc-blanc (BEL, French-language release) 'Revenge of White Fang'
Goudzoekers in Alaska (BEL, Dutch-language release) 'Prospectors in Alaska'
Challenge to White Fang (USA/AUS)
La carrera del oro (SP) 'The Gold Rush'
Izazov Bele Šape (YUG) 'The Challenge of White Fang'

Video/DVD titles
Les aventuriers du grand nord (FR alt. video) 'Ticket to the Great North'
Wolfsblut 2 (WG) 'Wolfblood 2'
Desafio en la nieve (ARG) 'Challenge in the Snow'
Ulvehunden vender tilbage (DEN) 'Wolfdog Returns'
Le retour de Buck le loup (FR DVD) 'The Return of Buck the Wolf'
Le retour de croc-blanc (FR DVD) 'The Return of White Fang'
Wolfsblut kehrt zurück (GER DVD) 'Wolfsblood Returns'

Production companies
Coralta Cinematografica S.r.l. (Rome)
Les Films Corona (Paris)
Terra Filmkunst GmbH (Berlin)

Theatrical distributors
Titanus Distribuzione (Italy)
Constantin Film (West Germany)
No French distributor ascertained.
Premiere Releasing Organisation (USA) ("A Creative Entertainment Presentation" / "A Sierra Associates Film")

Theatrical running times
Italy 100m
France 98m
West Germany 98m

Video/DVD/Blu-ray running times (adjusted)
Ascot Elite DVD (Germany) 97m 55s

Shooting period
April-May 1974

Censorship
Italian censor certificate 65323 issued 09 October 1974

Release information
Rome 31 October 1974
Bari 31 October 1974
USA (Sioux City, IA) 23 July 1975

Challenge to White Fang

1974

Directed by Lucio Fulci. a Coralta Cinematografica (Rome) / Terra Filmkunst GmbH (Berlin) / Les Films Corona (Paris) co-production. story Roberto Silvestri & Roberto Gianviti. screenplay Roberto Silvestri, Roberto Gianviti & Lucio Fulci. director of photography: Silvano Ippoliti. music Carlo Rustichelli. editor: Ornella Micheli. production designer: Giovanni Natalucci. production co-ordinator: Roberto Sbarigia. production manager: Piero Donati. unit manager: Ennio Di Meo. 2nd unit director: Tonino Ricci. assistant directors: Victor Tourjansky & Stefano Sbarigia. continuity: Roberto Giandalia. stunt co-ordinator: Goffredo Unger. camera operators: Enrico Sasso & Maurizio Luchhini. 2nd unit director of photography: Sergio Salvati. scenes in Canada shot by Aristide Massaccesi. costume designer: Massimo Lentini. make-up: Dante Trani. hairstylist: Giusy Bovina. special effects: Gino De Rossi. production assistant on location: Verena Baldeo. action stills: Mario Mazzoni. assistant to the editor: Bruno Micheli. sound recordist: Mario Ottavi. wigs: Maggi (Rome). costumes supplied by Cinecostume (Rome). footwear: Pompei (Rome). weapons: S.T.A.C.C. (Rome). photographic laboratory: Leo Massa (Rome). White Fang was trained by Sebastiano Arcifa. colour by Eastmancolor. processing laboratory: Technospes (Rome). filmed on location in Canada with interiors at Cinecittà Studios (Rome)

Cast: Franco Nero (Jason Scott). Virna Lisi (Sister Evangelina). John Steiner (Beauty Smith/Charles Forth). Raimund Harmstorf (Kurt Jansen). Yanti Somer (Liverpool's sister). Werner Pochath (Harvey). Hannelore Elsner (Jane LeClerq). Renato De Carmine (Lt. Charles LeClerq). Harry Carey Jr. (John Tarwater). Renato Cestiè (Bill Tarwater). Donald O'Brien (Liverpool). Rolf Hartmann (Carter). Janos ['John'] Bartha (Mountie). Paolo Magalotti (Ted, Smith's grey-bearded henchman). Sergio Smacchi (Smith's black-bearded henchman). Ezio Marano (card-sharp). Stanislaus Gunawan. Vittorio Fanfoni (man who raises fire alarm). Carla Mancini. *Uncredited:* Missaele (Mitsah). Riccardo Petrazzi (man who attacks card-sharp). Goffredo Unger (bearded barman).

Synopsis: [Characters from *White Fang* in italics]. *Mitsah* is killed by *Beauty Smith* during a raid on two fur traders. *White Fang* is taken to a nearby town by John Tarwater, an old trader, and befriends Bill, John's fatherless grandson. The beast helps John win money from a crooked card-sharp, so he embarks on an expedition in search of gold ... Smith is now living under the name of 'Charles Forth'. *Sister Evangelina* meets him and recognises him immediately. She contacts *Jason Scott* and his friend *Kurt Jansen*, but the town's corrupt Inspector Leclerq claims to have known 'Forth' for six years. Scott tries to expose 'Forth' with the help of a man called Liverpool who then dishonestly leaves town with money given to him by Scott. Scott meets Bill and John, who have returned empty handed from their search for gold. White Fang remembers Scott from their previous adventure. Liverpool returns shamefacedly, after finding two men, one dead the other sick, who were sold insufficient supplies by Smith. The survivor, Carter, has gangrene and Scott has to amputate his legs. Smith's henchmen frame White Fang for killing a man, and a posse drives the beast out of town. When Bill hunts for him in the forest he's attacked by an eagle but White Fang defends him. Bill smuggles the animal back. Carter tells John the location of a gold-seam in the mountains, but Harvey, a secret associate of Smith's, overhears and informs Smith. Evangelina is lured away, leaving Carter alone. Smith tortures the sick man for information then kidnaps John and heads for the mine, setting fire to the hut with Bill inside. Carter dies in the flames but Bill is rescued by Evangelina, who dies in the attempt. The townspeople riot and Leclerq shoots himself. Scott organizes a posse to give chase. White Fang locates Beauty Smith and attacks him. Smith tries to shoot the animal but his gunshots trigger an avalanche. Smith is crushed to death. John also dies, but asks that Bill inherit the gold seam Carter told him about. Harvey shows his true colours and says that the legal owner will be the first to register the claim in town. He suggests a sled-race to settle the dispute. He attempts dirty tricks to win, but dies when he's run over by Scott's sled-team headed by White Fang. Scott reaches town first and enters Bill's name in the ledger. Saying farewell to Bill and White Fang, who will both be staying with Kurt, Scott returns to the city with new stories to write.

UNIVERSAL FILMS ESPAÑOLA, S. A. PRESENTA

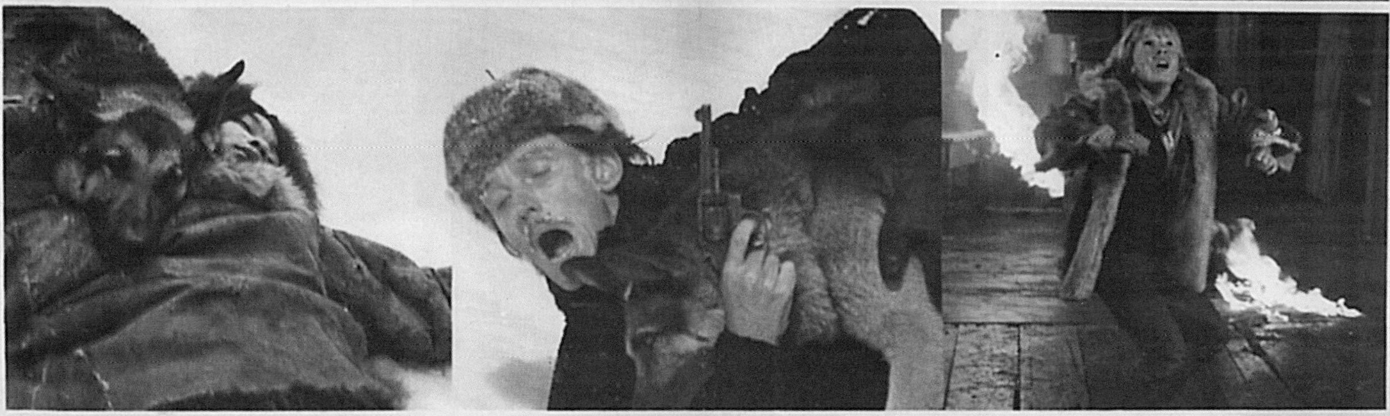

CORALTA CINEMATOGRAFICA PRESENTA

FRANCO NERO EN

COLOR technospes

LA CARRERA DEL ORO

EMEGE D.L. B 13.047-76

VIRNA LISI · JOHN STEINER · RAIMUND HARMSTORF

YANTI SOMER · WERNER POCHATH · HANNELORE ELSNER

CON RENATO DE CARMINE · HARRY CAREY Jr. Y RENATO CESTIE COMO "BILL"

Director LUCIO FULCI

GUION ALBERTO SILVESTRI, ROBERTO GIANVITI Y LUCIO FULCI

UNA COPRODUCCION ITALO-FRANCO-ALEMANA CORALTA CINEMATOGRAFICA S.r.l. (ROMA) LES FILMS CORONA (PARIS) TERRA FILMKUNST G.m.b'h. (BERLIN)

both images to the right:
Spanish advertising artwork and accompanying still.

About the production: Delighted by the commercial success of *White Fang*, Italian producer Giulio Sbarigia (whose company Oceania were top-billed on the first film) swiftly conceived a follow-up. *Variety* reported that *"Nationwide returns for Christmas entry 'White Fang' of $1,500,000 [have] prompted producer Giulio Sbarigia to recall director Lucio Fulci and rush out 'The Return of White Fang.'"*[8] A cast was duly assembled featuring three stars of the first film – Franco Nero as the hero Jason Scott, Virna Lisi as Sister Evangelina, and John Steiner as the hissable villain Beauty Smith. Rather shockingly, the new script began by killing off the boy hero of the first film, leaving the way open for a more bankable moppet, Renato Cestiè, to step in. (Cestiè, already a veteran of three giallo films having appeared in Sergio Sollima's *Il diavolo nel cervello*, Mario Bava's *A Bay of Blood* and Sergio Martino's *Torso*, had recently proven himself a thoroughbred tearjerker in the lucrative weepie melodrama *L'ultima neve di primavera* aka *The Last Snows of Spring*.)

At a press conference in Rome in March 1974, Fulci was at pains to point out that the sequel – though inspired by the first film's financial success – was intended respectfully to the author of the original. *"I would like to state that this film does not seem to me to represent an abuse or an offence against the London novel. The film, in fact, has been conceived with a 'Londonesque' atmosphere perfectly adhering to the spirit of his work, and as for the rest, there are some clear references to other works by famous writers: a key figure of the story, for example, is none other than the protagonist of the story 'The Matches'.*[9] *I am a craftsman and I think first of all about the public, so I was happily surprised with the wide acclaim they bestowed on White Fang. Il ritorno di Zanna Bianca begins where the previous one ends and tends to focus more upon the unique relationship between man and animal. The film ends with a spectacular epilogue: a gold rush on snow with sixty sledges".*[10] With that in mind, production got under way early in April, with shooting taking place in the Austrian Alps (for the aforementioned sledging scene, twenty-two racing huskie dogs were brought over specially from Manitoba). The film was ready in time for a showcase of Titanus productions in Caracas in late October 1974, and although it didn't quite match the success of *Zanna Bianca* it proved to be another hit.

Review: Again bearing a few telling signs of its lineage as a Lucio Fulci film, this adventure for resilient children is well-mounted at the Cinecittà studios, and the dramatic Canadian exteriors are handsomely shot, by a crew including Tonino Ricci, Sergio Salvati and Aristide Massaccesi (aka Joe D'Amato) in the second unit. So important was their contribution that their credits are printed in large type, indicating that a significant amount of work was captured by the three independently of Fulci. Whatever the arrangement, Ricci – who also performed second unit duties on Fulci's first *White Fang* – went on to direct his own entry in the lupine saga, *Zanna Bianca alla riscossa*, in 1975.

The plot again seems ambiguous as to where its loyalties lie, with adult viewers or children. (Rather mirroring the plight of the titular beast, whose recognition of Franco Nero from the previous film is used to put the dog's friendship with young Bill into occasional tear-jerking doubt.) Many of the subsidiary themes are fairly adult, bearing more resemblance to the western genre. Jack London's novel was indeed slanted towards older children, but here the themes – including gambling, corruption, business extortion and blackmail – are somewhat obscurely developed.

bottom right:
Danish video cover.

below:
Fire at the mission.

left:
John Steiner as the villainous Beauty Smith.

far left:
Young Bill (Renato Cestiè) and his four-legged pal.

On balance though the material is handled very well – Fulci's *White Fang* films date back to a time when the attitude of film-makers working for children wasn't entirely washed out into patronising blandness, or foolishly premature 'irony'. A degree of sentimentality is also held reasonably in check. The harsh terrain of the locations and the predominantly adult cast surround the 'boy and his wolf' with enough jeopardy and brisk masculine pursuits to balance the affectionate heart of the tale.

Violence is once again to the fore (beginning with the fate of the first film's boy star, who is unceremoniously shot at the start of this sequel!) Several scenes of hostility towards the heroic mutt could rattle the nerves of adults, never mind kids eager to see their canine hero triumph. During a fearsome battle with a huge eagle which attacks the vulnerable young hero, the wolf's eyes appear to be pecked out. A shocked and tearful Bill guides the animal back to Franco Nero's fatherly care. The man discovers that although White Fang's eyes are caked shut with blood from the fight, the orbs are actually still intact. However, this is not ascertained without some tense and faintly nauseating probing between the animal's gore-smeared eyelids.

Then there's Carter, the gold prospector whose legs have to be cut off because of the onset of gangrene. Whilst we never actually see the decaying flesh being hacked from the whisky-sedated sufferer, or get more than a glimpse of the truncated shape of the stumps through a bedsheet, the heavy atmosphere of foreboding prior to the operation is excrutiating in itself. The idea of the man so helplessly and drunkenly waiting for someone to pluck up the nerve to perform the task of severing his legs – combined with the highly suggestive reluctance of all concerned to do this most odious of men's tasks – makes the dramatic situation one which Freud would undoubtedly have had something to say about (to coin a phrase).

It also creates an interesting conflict with the macho slapstick of earlier bar-room scenes, where the consumption of alcohol is seen as part of the usual displays of manly brawling. Suddenly, a man is being plied with alcohol to secure his participation in the removal of his legs! The anaesthetic effects of booze may be hard to fathom for a youngster whose experience of drink has hitherto been associated purely with male license and horseplay. Carter's subsequent fate adds further to the horror of helplessness, as he becomes the target of an extortion bid by the film's chief villain. Lying in bed recuperating after his ordeal, he is tortured for information by having his freshly bandaged stumps beaten! His immolation in the burning timber house in the aftermath of Smith's visit completes this character's descent into a demasculinized, helpless state of passivity.

Further horror is generated by the death of the only significant female character in the film. Sister Evangelina is set aflame whilst trying to rescue Carter, and rushes out into the snowy street, flames billowing from her wimple. Her death is disturbing in a film where female concerns and characteristics are contained within a single figure.

For children, perhaps the most drawn-out sequence of horror occurs when White Fang is attacked by the whole village for a death he didn't cause. Lackeys of the evil Smith throw the body of a man they've killed into a husky-dog's enclosure. The townsfolk, aware that the boy is harboring a pet wolf, claim that the damage could not have been wrought by their beloved dogs, and turn on White Fang. A posse of enraged villagers advance, and young Bill must try to save White Fang by driving him away, beating him with a plank of wood. Confused, hurt, then finally afraid, White Fang flees, but not without being chased, cornered, partially beaten and tormented, before at last making his escape. Fulci manages to make the sequence so hard-hitting and protracted that even cynical adults might care.

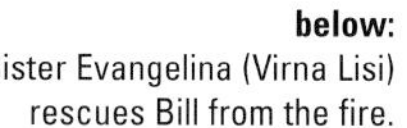

below:
Sister Evangelina (Virna Lisi) rescues Bill from the fire.

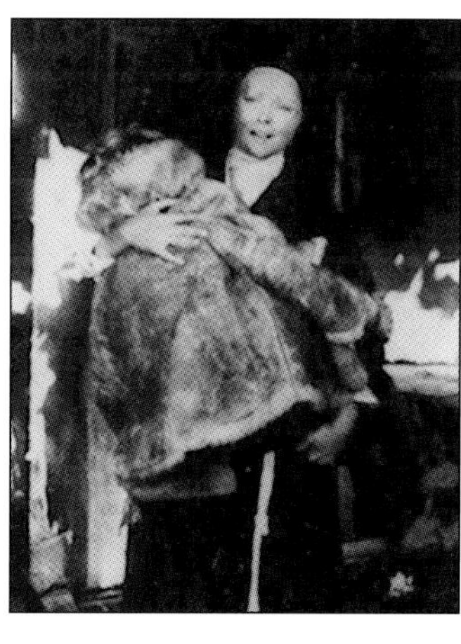

Italian theatrical title
I quattro dell'apocalisse

Italy

International theatrical title
Verdammt zu Leben – Verdammt zu Sterben (WG) 'Condemned to life – Condemned to Death'

Video/DVD titles
Four of the Apocalypse (USA DVD)
Prärie des Todes (GER)
'Prairie of Death'

Production company
Coralta Cinematografica S.r.l. (Rome)

Theatrical distributor
Cineriz (Italy)

Theatrical running times
Italy 105m

Video/DVD/Blu-ray running times (adjusted)
Anchor Bay DVD (USA) 104m 01s

Shooting and release information
Shooting from 02 December 1974
Italian censor certificate 66945
04 August 1975
Rome 12 September 1975
Bari 25 September 1975

The Four of the Apocalypse

1975

Directed by Lucio Fulci. produced by Piero Donati for Coralta Cinematografica S.r.l. adapted for the screen by Ennio De Concini from the stories of Brett Harte. director of photography: Sergio Salvati. music: Franco Bixio, Fabio Frizzi & Vince Tempera. editor: Ornella Micheli. art director: Giovanni Natalucci. production manager: Roberto Sbarigia. unit manager: Ennio Di Meo. location managers: Julio Parra & Verena Baldeo. assistant directors: Giuseppe Pollini & Claudio Bondì. script continuity: Roberto Giandalia. stunt co-ordinator: Goffredo Unger. camera operator: Enrico Sasso. assistant operators: Maurizio Lucchini & Emilio Bestetti. costumes: Massimo Lentini. make-up supervision: Massimo De Rossi. make-up assistant: Feliziano Ciriaci. hairstylist: Agnese Panarotto. assistant to the art director: Luigi Quintili. assistant editor: Bruno Micheli. cutting room assistant: Rossanna Landi. sound recordist: Mario Ottavi. boom operator: Marco Donati. English version recorded at Fono Roma for Cinitalia (Rome). costume house: Cinecostume (Rome). wigs: Maggi (Rome). footwear: Arditi (Rome). gunsmiths: CI.PA (Rome). action stills: Leo Massa (Rome). unit publicists: M.L. (Rome). songs "Movin' On", "Was It All in Vain", "Bunny (Let's Stay Together)", "Let Us Pray", "Stubby (You're Down and Out)" music by Franco Bixio, Fabio Frizzi & Vince Tempera, words by Greenfield Cook, performed by Cook and The Benjamin Franklin Group. musicians – keyboard: Vince Tempera. guitar: Massimo De Luca. bass: Michele Seffer. harmonica: Franco Di Lelio & featuring Tony Esposito's Numero Uno as rhythm section. colour by Eastmancolor. processing laboratory: Technospes (Rome). filmed on location in Austria with interiors filmed at Cinecittà Studios S.p.A. (Rome) & R.P.A. Elios Studios (Rome).

Cast: Fabio Testi (Stubby Preston). Lynne Frederick (Emanuelle 'Bunny' O'Neill). Michael J. Pollard (Clem). Harry Baird (Butt). Tomas Milian (Chaco). Adolfo Lastretti (Rev. Sullivan). Bruno Corazzari (Lemmy, cigar-smoking Altaville resident). Giorgio Trestini (Mel, Altaville man who names baby). Donald O'Brien (Sheriff of Salt Flat). *Uncredited:* Charles Borromel (Montana, blond Altaville resident). Lorenzo Robledo (man tortured by Chaco). Claudio Ruffini (man shot in saloon doorway). Goffredo Unger (bearded Altaville man who places $10 bet). Lone Fleming (blonde Christian woman). Duilio Cruciani (Christian boy in straw hat). Alfonso Rojas (man giving orders to Salt Flat gunmen). Edward Mannix (Narrator [English version]).

Synopsis: Salt Flat, Utah, 1873. Stubby Preston, a card-sharp, arrives in town. However, the sheriff recognises him, destroys his cards and throws him in a cell. His cell-mates are Emmanuelle 'Bunny' O'Neill, a young prostitute; Butt, a mentally disturbed black man obsessed with the dead; and Clem, an alcoholic. During the night a masked posse wreak havoc in the town. Fearing for their safety, the sheriff allows the prisoners to leave town next morning, pointing them to an abandoned wagon. The four decide to travel together, and Stubby takes a shine to Bunny. As they travel, Bunny reveals that she is pregnant by a client. After an encounter with a group of Swiss Christian missionaries, the four meet a Mexican called Chaco. He is welcomed into the group but soon shows a wicked side when he persuades the group to take peyote with him. Stubby spits it out, his suspicions alerted, but the rest of the party accept. Chaco humiliates the alcoholic Clem by ordering him to crawl and bark like a dog for liquor. Chaco ties the travellers up at gunpoint, and rapes Bunny. Stubby swears to kill him. The bandit rides off with their gear, leaving them tied up in the desert, except for Clem whom he shot in the leg. Clem frees the others and they continue on foot. Later they see the aftermath of another attack by Chaco. The Christian wagoners, children and all, have been slaughtered. Eventually the four friends see buildings ahead. They arrive in the pouring rain, but discover a ghost town. Butt is ecstatic when he discovers a graveyard full of 'friends' to talk to. Clem dies from his gunshot wounds, his dying request that Stubby and Bunny be married. Butt elects to stay in the ghost town: Stubby and Bunny leave him to his 'city of the dead'. After bumping into Stubby's old friend the (pseudo) Reverend Sullivan, Bunny's labour pains begin and Sullivan recommends taking her to Altaville, a town populated entirely by men. The men of Altaville are excited at the prospect of a birth, and celebrations break out when it's a boy, but tragedy strikes: Bunny dies after giving birth. Mel, the man who delivered the baby, persuades Stubby to leave the child with the men of Altaville. He is given a horse and a gun, and rides away. A chance encounter in the next town delivers Chaco to Stubby's vengeance. Stubby shoots him dead. Alone again, he rides off into the evening. At the last minute, a stray dog joins him on his way.

About the production: Lucio Fulci's success on the *White Fang* films put him in good stead with Italian producer Giulio Sbarigia, who in the early months of 1974 was expanding his operations (he was now the head of *two* sizeable Italian production companies, Coralta and Oceania). Very impressed by the international sales of the *White Fang* films, Sbarigia hired Fulci to direct a third project, a spaghetti western called *The Four of the Apocalypse*. This had been on Sbarigia's mind as early as 27 February 1974 (prior to the shooting of *Challenge to White Fang*), when it was mooted in *Variety* as a forthcoming Coralta title along with a planned Terence Hill-Bud Spencer comedy, 'Giuro e Spergiuro' (aka 'I Swear... It's Perjury'). The latter project fell by the wayside, but *The Four of the Apocalypse* became one of two Coralta productions to be shot back-to-back in Austria in late 1974. Joe D'Amato started filming *Giubbe rosse* (aka *Killers of the Savage North*) on 11 November, and Fulci rolled *The Four of the Apocalypse* immediately afterwards, commencing 2 December. Both films were not only bankrolled by the same company but also starred the same topliners, Fabio Testi and Lynne Frederick.

Meanwhile, Sbarigia was looking for a director to helm a plum project he was hawking around called *Salon Kitty*. Although it was originally intended for Giuseppe Patroni Griffi to direct, *Variety* announced in July 1974 that Sbarigia had offered the film to Sidney Lumet! Sadly the director of *12 Angry Men* and *Serpico* turned down the chance to shoot a film about sex in a Nazi brothel and made *Dog Day Afternoon* instead. One wonders if Sbarigia offered it to Fulci. (*Salon Kitty* was eventually directed by Tinto Brass.)

Note: For some reason, the Internet Movie Database claims that Edmondo Amati was the uncredited producer of *The Four of the Apocalypse*. Amati's production company at the time was Fida Cinematografica, and they have never been linked to the production of the Fulci film; I can only assume that some anecdotal source has been relied upon, but I can find no documented back-up for the assertion.

Review: *The Four of the Apocalypse* shows a more developed pictorial sense than Fulci's previous western, *Massacre Time*, along with a pleasingly melancholic disposition. However, despite indulging his wistful, almost sentimental qualities, Fulci once again goes for the jugular with some shocking scenes of violence and degradation. It's this mixture of sadness and sickness that elevates the film into the company of his best work and distinguishes it as one of the most unusual of all spaghetti westerns. The cruelty exhibited by Chaco (played by the ever-reliable Tomas Milian) is an essential factor. Without the streak of evil he delivers, the film might almost have been gentle. Fulci's emphasis on sadism complicates the overall atmosphere in a way that mere gunplay could never have done. When Fulci has Chaco capture a sheriff and, motivated purely by sadism, flay a portion of skin from his stomach with a hunting knife, before pinning the hapless lawman's badge directly onto his bared chest, we know we're in the hands of a cinematic sensationalist, eager to terrorize his audience. This scene, along with the subsequent humiliation of the alcoholic Clem and the rape of the teenage girl Bunny, feels like a variation on the sick torture scenes of *The Last House on the Left*, although after the brutality meted out to the sheriff the rape is perhaps less graphically unpleasant than might have been expected.

Although this really is Lucio Fulci's best western, it suffers – like many of his ventures into different genres – from a lack of affect. It's only when one reflects on the story that its more bizarre qualities take hold. Problems include the crass soundtrack songs and a somewhat mawkish last reel. The story – based on a pulp-literary source – depicts a string of encounters on a journey through the wilderness of North America (represented by Austrian locations). This episodic quality is quite pleasant, but leaves the viewer with the sense of something lacking. At no point does the narrative actually become unhinged, or fragmented. Its chain structure is *ad-hoc* without being experimental. Because of the

above:
Chaco (Tomas Milian) rapes a drugged and bound 'Bunny' (Lynne Frederick).

opposite main image:
Butt (Harry Baird) explores the cemetery of a ghost town.

opopsite bottom left:
French video cover.

left:
Bunny and Stubby (Fabio Testi) hear gunshots outside the jail and fear for their lives.

below:
Danish video cover.

right:
Chaco indulges in sadistic torture and disembowelling, another scene missing from most prints of the film.

failure to detach from convention, we become critical of the film's superficial play with form; there is no complexity or intertwining of plot strands apparent here. For instance, a revenge motif is introduced when Stubby witnesses Bunny's rape, and yet the 'pay-off' is cursory in the extreme. Even Chaco seems aware of this, when he mocks Stubby for shooting without warning. We expect western treatments of revenge to make a lavish meal of the dramatic situation, and Italian westerns usually play the card of vengeance all the more prominently. Somehow, though, the film's enthusiasm seems to falter after the death of Bunny, and the bitterly avowed revenge, when it happens, feels tagged on. Sergio Leone brought a canny regard for the bitter epiphanies of audience fantasy into his revenge scenarios, but Fulci leaves us feeling that one of the genre's most potent pieces of 'business' has been thrown away.

Much better though are some of the self-contained episodes along the way; particularly the ghost town sequence, and the highly unusual scenes in Altaville. The former is just great cinema, and marks the beginning of Fulci's successful relationship with director of photography Sergio Salvati. The idea of the ghost town is actually one of the film's most coherent elaborations. Butt, the black man we are introduced to in the Salt Flat prison-cell, finds his macabre yet beautiful home there. *"I'm a friend of all the dead people, I see them all the time"*, he declares to Stubby when they meet; *"Sometimes they're a-screamin' an' a-shoutin'"*. Stubby good-naturedly responds, *"And that makes people crazy..."* Butt wholeheartedly agrees. When the four companions arrive at the deserted settlement, its wooden boards collapsing beneath a barrage of gorgeously filmed rain, they camp out for the night in the draughty environs of a disused house, bereft of all but the walls, ceiling and beams. Bunny demonstrates a nervousness about stripping off her wet garments which betrays her inexperience as a 'whore'. Maybe she really is just nineteen, as she claimed earlier. Making as if to disrobe, she opens a door to discover the adjacent room is a roofless shell, full of rain. It is a fleeting yet beautiful image.

The morning after, Butt is seen running from tombstone to tombstone in a chaotically unkempt graveyard, full of stone crosses and slippery, rain-soaked vegetation. He reads from the stone engravings and we see mania grip him as he invests the name of the dead with the energy of his own voice. A relationship between mental disturbance and the supernatural is drawn swiftly and concisely. Butt conjures ghosts who offer him splendour and wealth without bigotry and hatred. For him ghosts are marvels, company for a black man struggling to be free in the abandoned spaces of white frontier individualism. *"Stubby, this town's full of folks, you know. Real fine folks! I thought those houses were as empty as old tin cans, but in the evening they're full of gentlemen in checkered jackets, elegant gentlemen! And their ladies, in brightly coloured skirts... real fine folk... they don't care if you're black or white"*.

below:
Milian, Frederick and Testi.

The death of Clem is handled with tenderness, thanks to an excellent performance by Michael J. Pollard. Fulci greatly respected this gifted character actor who first caught the eye of critics with an eccentric role in the controversial gangster film *Bonnie and Clyde*. His willingness to throw himself into this role, which involves some very physical interaction with Tomas Milian's villainous Chaco (at one point, Milian spits beer into Pollard's upturned mouth, in a single uninterrupted shot) lends the film an intensity that even more celebrated Fulci masochists like Franco Nero and Giovanni Lombardo Radice might have balked at.

Just as we think we've seen the last of his character, Fulci unleashes a startling coda. As the remaining 'three of the apocalypse' mourn their friend, Butt picks up Clem's body and tenderly carries it away, intoning a litany of comfort to the deceased man's soul. He returns later with meat for the three to stave off their hunger. Stubby and Bunny tuck into what they believe is an animal Butt has caught outside. However, there's a shock for them (and us) when Stubby finds Clem's corpse in an adjoining room, a tell-tale chunk of flesh missing from one buttock! This act of unwitting cannibalism is another example of Fulci's taste for combining horror and tenderness, an aesthetic that was to achieve full bloom in films like *The Beyond* and *The House by the Cemetery*.

Stubby and Bunny opt to leave the ghost town and head off in search of civilisation. Butt refuses to go and the couple set off without him, assured of his ability to fend for himself by his recent capture of a rabbit. Fulci films their departure from several different angles, with numerous hand-held point-of-view shots. We hear Stubby explaining Butt's madness to his future bride, and watch as he repeatedly points to camera, suggesting where Butt may be hiding. Each shot apparently represents Butt's point of view, and yet the different positions make this impossible. This creates an eerie, schizophrenic effect, supporting Fulci's claim that *The Four of the Apocalypse* is his most surreal western.

The sequence in the all-male town of Altaville is another triumph of the irrational. Snow-bound after the previous dust-bowl settings, it seems immediately bizarre. Whilst there is no overt suggestion of homosexuality in the demeanor of Altaville's residents, their implacable refusal of female company seems almost a satire on the lines of Paul Morrissey/ Andy Warhol's *Lonesome Cowboys* (1968). Their acceptance of Bunny's presence (and pregnancy) is only really procured by the birth of a male child. The men of Altaville, high atop a mountain – and perhaps intended to be close to God and far from the scourge of Woman – have to initiate town birth records in honour of the boy child. The idyll of caring masculinity they represent is given an unconditional seal of approval by the film when Stubby opts to leave the child to the male enclave.

The Four of the Apocalypse is stranger the further one gets away from it, slipping by quite casually on first viewing but staying in the mind for some time afterwards. Of all Fulci's most 'masculine' films (the westerns, the White Fang diptych) it is undoubtedly the most unusual. The sadism involved links it to Fulci's horror films, whilst the intermittent harshness of the narrative suggests how little love he had for the American West. Unlike Hawks, Ford or even Leone, he presents it as a land of unremitting cruelty and hate, making his viewpoint more akin to that of Giulio Questi, director of the bleakly nihilistic *Django, Kill!* As in *Challenge to White Fang*, the only woman dies, and if the child lives on it is in a motherless world. Typically, Fulci foregoes the more standard appeals of heroic adventure for a bleak vision of a land without hope, except through the delirious visions of madness or the eccentric fantasia of Altaville's womanless society. Perhaps Butt is correct in his preference; maybe the Wild West was more a land of the dead than the living.

this page:
After setting up for the night in a ghost town, the four travellers get to know each other better...

Italian theatrical title
Sella d'argento

Italy

International theatrical titles
Montura de plata (SP) 'Silver Saddle'
Silbersattel (WG) 'Silver Saddle'
Srebrno Sedlo (YUG) 'Silver Saddle'

Video/DVD title
Sie sterben in Stiefeln (GER DVD)
'They Die with Their Boots On'

Production company
Rizzoli Film

Theatrical distributor
Cineriz ("Rizzoli Film presents")

Theatrical running time
Italy 94m

Video/DVD/Blu-ray running times (adjusted)
Filmlab video (Denmark) 98m 06s
Sunfilm Blu-ray (Germany) 98m 14s

Shooting period
Shooting from mid-December 1977

Censorship
Italian censor certificate 71727
issued 01 April 1978

Release information
Rome 21 April 1978
Taranto 22 April 1978
Bari 19 May 1978

Silver Saddle

1978

Directed by Lucio Fulci. a Rizzoli Film production. story & shooting script: Adriano Bolzoni. director of photography: Sergio Salvati. music: [Franco] Bixio, [Fabio] Frizzi & [Vincente] Tempera; published by Bixio / C.E.M.S.A. – Rizzoli Film. editor: Ornella Micheli. scenic designer & costumes: Carlo Simi. set dresser: Carlo Centilil. production supervisor: Bruno Gallo. production managers: Carlo Bartolini & Ennio Di Meo. unit manager: Gilberto Carbone. assistant director & stunt co-ordinator: Nazzareno Zamperla. continuity: Roberto Giandalia. cameraman: Enrico Cortese. assistant operator: Maurizio Lucchini. make-up: Walter Cossu. hairdresser: Giuseppina Bovino. wardrobe: Nera Caporali. production secretaries: Mauro Miraglia & Nestore Baratella. production accountant: Giancarlo Ciotti. assistant editors: Bruno Micheli & Mario D'Ambrosio. sound technician: Mario Ottavi. boom operator: Giovanni Fratarcangeli. sound recording: Doppiaggio C.D., supervised by Pino Locchi. Italian version: Mario Milani. English language edition: Tony La Penna. dubbing studio: Santini Edizioni (Rome). the songs "Silver Saddle" & "Two Hearts" by Franco Bixio, Fabio Frizzi, Vincente Tempera & Ken Tobias, performed by Ken Tobias. colour by Technicolor. format: Techniscope. negatives: Kodak Eastmancolor. interiors filmed at Dear International Studios (Rome).

Cast: Giuliano Gemma (Roy Blood). Sven Valsecchi (Thomas Barrett, Jr.). Ettore Manni (Thomas Barrett). Gianni De Luigi (Turner). Cinzia Monreale (Margaret Barrett). Licinia Lentini (Miss Sheba, brothel madame). Aldo Sambrell [as 'Aldo Sanbrell'] (Garrincha). Philippe Hersent (Sheriff). Donald ['Donal'] O'Brien (Fletcher). Sergio Leonardi (Butch the bartender). Karina Verlier [as 'Karine Stampfli'] (Peggy). Agnes Kalpagos (one of Sheba's women). Maria Tinelli [as 'Anna Maria Tinelli'] (one of Sheba's women). Geoffrey Lewis (Two-Strike Snake). *Uncredited:* Juan Antonio Rubio (gunman).

Synopsis: The South Texas border. A poor man, conned out of money by a powerful landowner called Barrett, confronts Luke, a crook in Barrett's employ. Luke shoots him in front of his young son. The boy picks up his father's gun, shoots the killer and mounts the man's horse with its ornate silver-trimmed saddle. He grows up to be an outlaw: Roy Blood ... Roy rides into the Texan town of Cerritos on his silver-saddled horse accompanied by Two-Strike Snake, an amusing but treacherous fellow he's recently met. Snake tells Roy that he knows the story of the Silver Saddle. He also knows that Roy leaves a trail of the dead in his wake, which is why he tags along – to collects valuables from the corpses. Roy meets Sheba, an old flame who runs the whorehouse. She tells Roy that a Mexican named Garrincha is extorting money from her. Roy obligingly shoots Garrincha's chief lackey, Shep. A man called Turner offers Roy a payday: $2,000 for a hit. He accepts when he hears the name of the intended victim: Thomas Barrett. However, instead of the old man Roy was hoping for, a young boy turns up. As the child approaches, several men try to shoot him. Roy shoots the would-be assassins and rescues the boy: Thomas Barrett Jr, son of the now-deceased Richard Barrett who'd swindled Roy's father. Young Tom is currently in the care of his uncle, Thomas Barrett Sr. Disgusted, Roy leaves the boy in the hills with just a knife and blanket. Tom's older sister Margaret is distraught about his disappearance. Thomas Sr. discusses the search with his estate manager – Turner – who announces that the kidnapper is Roy Blood. A $5,000 price is put on Roy's head. Meanwhile, Snake has a proposition for Roy. He has found Tom and plans to ask a huge ransom. Roy hears that it was Turner who set up the hit as a way to kill both Tom and he while blaming Roy for the child's death. Sheba tells Roy that Tom and Margaret stand to inherit the family fortune, and the rest of the Barrett clan are plotting against them. Roy shoots Turner but Garrincha's men abduct the boy. The sheriff arrests Roy, claiming he's an accomplice. Garrincha demands a huge ransom: Barrett Sr. despatches a rider with the money but the courier is murdered after handing it over. Roy escapes jail, and thanks to Tom, who flies a kite to attract attention, he tracks down Garrincha. Roy and Snake shoot it out with Garrincha's men. The rescue is successful but Snake dies in the struggle. At the Barrett ranch, Roy exposes Thomas Sr., who in league with Turner had been planning to dispose of Tom and Margaret. The kidnapping stunt with Garrincha was part of a plan to avert suspicion. Roy shoots the treacherous uncle. As the lone outlaw returns to the plains, he's joined by Tom, riding a pony.

above:
Aldo Sambrell as the evil Garrincha flogging the film's child star Sven Valsecchi.

left:
Giuliano Gemma and Geoffrey Lewis; Licinia Lentini as brothel madame Sheba.

About the production: *Sella d'argento* aka *Silver Saddle* was first announced in *Variety* in September 1977: *"Following 'Mareth'*[11]*, Giuliano Gemma will appear in 'The Silver Saddle' on a steep budget in the US, Spain and on Rome interiors for Rizzoli Productions."*[12] The film went swiftly into production mid-December 1977, and shooting continued through January 1978 in Almería, Spain. (In October 1977 *Variety* announced that Gemma was due to star in a Lucio Fulci film called 'They Died with Their Boots On' supposedly set for late October. A subsequent article dated 21 December 1977 refers to *Silver Saddle* as *"ex-They Died with Their Boots On"* so it would seem that this was a pre-shooting title. Many years later it was used (in translation) as the German DVD release title: *Sie sterben in Stiefeln*.)

Review: Fulci's third western was also one of Italy's last. Unfortunately it's easy to see why – the film looks and even sounds like the last gasp. It begins with a slow trudge through flat, ugly countryside and ends on a note of cloying sentimentality. The surreal elements of *The Four of the Apocalypse* are nowhere to be found in *Silver Saddle*, which can't even boast the dark, sweaty look or psychotic family strife of *Massacre Time* to lift it from the mire. The presence of an irritating blond-haired moppet tests the patience, and the title song sugars the action throughout, compounding the felony by laboriously recapping plot developments in the lyrics.

Of the few enjoyable scenes, a shoot-out in a dusty old barn slatted with sunlight, achieves some pictorial beauty, and at least the encounter with a militant bunch of priests is amusing. When hero Roy Blood asks the padre whether he can guarantee young Thomas's safety, the latter remarks that it was, after all, a friar who invented gunpowder. *"If anyone with bad intentions shows their face here, we shall give them our benediction"*, he says, toting his gun. Of course, the bandits get the better of them, and for a few seconds the film turns into an out-take from Alejandro Jodorowsky's *El Topo* as Roy finds the monks bloodily murdered and the padre nailed to the door of the monastery. Unfortunately, the locations for this film have all the attractiveness and drama of a land-fill site. The preponderance of crumbling, run-down buildings could have been atmospheric, but instead they make the film look half-dead, and the usually inspired Fulci-Salvati camera team fail to wring any striking compositions from them.

The performances are pretty mundane too. Gemma makes a bland hero, neither effectively impassive nor likeably eccentric. The script calls for both shadings from the actor, but he remains vague and detached from the proceedings throughout, like a minor male model on his weekend off. Lewis, who appeared in Tonino Valerii's western spoof *My Name Is Nobody* (and turned up with Clint Eastwood in *Every Which Way But Loose* in 1978), tries to bring something creepier to his role as the vulturous Snake, but he's fighting a losing battle in a film which gives him no support. Even the villains are a forgettable bunch. Violence is infrequent, although a man gets a bullet to the face in one brief close-up, and stunt work is desultory too. One explosion is so unconvincing that a Mexican bandit actually flies through the air *towards* the blast.

Perhaps this film was intended for younger children, although the presence of little Sven Valsecchi – child star of a string of popular tear-jerkers – suggests that Fulci may also have been attempting a 'woman's film' here! The plot places lots of emphasis on the boy's enjoyment of the stock situations. It's as if the writers, having decided that a child hero would appeal to youngsters, inadvertently made him a western fan rather than a character. Even the prostitutes are friendly to him when he's hidden upstairs in the whore-house. Not a trace of cynicism or world-weariness from these gals; come the kid's bedtime, they're getting all gooey about tucking him in (and without any innuendo either). By the end of the film you're really quite sick of the little tyke, and the last shot of him riding a pony after the 'outlaw' hero will induce profanities from viewers with low saccharine tolerance. Fans of Fulci's horror films should rejoice that this limp effort failed at the Italian box-office – at least it discouraged him from trying the format again.

below:
Sven Valsecchi as Thomas Barrett Jr.

Italian theatrical title
Luca il contrabbandiere

Translation
'Luca the smuggler'

Italy

Alternative titles
Il contrabbandiere (IT alt. theatrical)
Contraband (export title/USA DVD)
The Smuggler (export title/USA video)

Video/DVD titles
The Naples Connection (UK)
Das Syndikat des Grauens (GER)
'The Syndicate of Terror'
El contrabandista (ARG)
'The Smuggler'
La guerre des gangs (FR)
'The Gang War'
Lucas el contrabandista (SP)
'Lucas the Smuggler'
Smugleren (NOR) 'The Smuggler'
Lucas le contre-bandier (FR alt. video)
'Lucas the Smuggler'
Brennpunkt Napoli (DEN DVD)
'Focal Point Napoli'

Production companies
Primex Italiana
C.M.R. Cinematografica

Theatrical distributors
Cinedaf (Italy)

Theatrical running times
Italy 97m

Video/DVD/Blu-ray running times (adjusted)
Blue Underground DVD (USA) 96m 39s

Shooting period
Shooting from 03 December 1979

Censorship
Italian censor certificate 75421
issued 07 August 1980

Release information
Rome 21 August 1980
(as Il contrabbandiere)
Naples September 1980
Fasano 11 September 1980
Bari 12 September 1980

The Smuggler

1980

Directed by Lucio Fulci. produced by Sandra Infascelli for Primex Italiana/C.M.R. Cinematografica. screenplay: Ettore Sanzo, Gianni Di Chiara, Fulci & Giorgio Mariuzzo. director of photography: Sergio Salvati. music: Fabio Frizzi, published by Nationalmusic (Milan). editor: Vincenzo Tomassi. set designer: Francesco Calabrese. director of production: Sergio Jacobis. unit managers: Nicola Venditti, Giulio Longo & Vittorio Bucci. ass. director: Roberto Giandalia. script supervisors: Daniela Tonti & Egle Guarino. masters of arms: Sergio Sagnotti & Nazzareno Cardinali. cameramen: Mari Sbrenna & Franco Bruni. ass. cameramen: Maurizio Lucchini, Daniele Cimini & Giovanni Brescini. ass. cameramen, underwater: Alessio Gelsini & Massimo Pan. chief electrician: Alfredo Fedeli. chief grip: Ennio Brizzolari. costume designer: Massimo Lentini. special effects make-up: Franco Di Girolamo. make-up: Fabrizio Sforza. hairstylist: Ida Gilda De Guilmi. special effects: Germano Natali & Roberto Pace. ass. art director: Luciano Tarquini. set dressing: Berta Betti. ass. make-up: Antonio Maltempo. production secretaries: Eliana Cipri, Dina Pallich & Matteo Marino. paymaster: Roberto Ornaro. ass. production secretary: Luca Garzotto. cashiers: Danilo Martelli & Romano De Francesco. still photographer: Francesco Bellomo. stills laboratory: Roberto Russo. 1st ass. editor: Giancarlo Tiburzi. 2nd ass. editor: Amando Pace. sound: Ugo Celani. boom operator: Eros Giustini. sound recording by C.D.S. mixage: Gianni D'Amico. special sound effects: Studio Sound. Thanks to "Motoscafi Blu" for their collaboration during the making of this film. "You Are Not the Same" by Lucio Fulci & Fabio Frizzi, performed by Cricket. colour by Staco Film. negative: Kodak. filmed on location in Naples, interiors at De Paolis Studios (Rome).

Cast: Fabio Testi (Luca Di Angelo). Ivana Monti (Adele Di Angelo). Marcel Bozzuffi (Francois Jacois, 'The Marsigliese'). Saverio Marconi (Luigi Perlante). Enrico Maisto (Mickey Di Angelo). Ferdinando Murolo (Scherino). Fabrizio Jovine (Chief of Police). Daniele Dublino (Prosecutor). Guido Alberti (Don Morrone). Giordano Falzoni (Charlie, shady doctor). Giulio Farnese (Alfredo, Perlante's associate). Ofelia Meyer (Ingrid, woman burned by Marsigliese). Tommaso Palladino (Capece, racehorse owner). Venantino Venantini (Captain Tarantino). Ajita Wilson (Luisa, Perlante's moll). Luciano Rossi (Marsigliese's chemist). Salvatore Billa. Romano Puppo (Marsigliese's chief assassin). Omero Capanna. Virgilio Daddi. Cintia Lodetti [as 'Cinzia Lodetti'] (Ursula, Perlante's blonde). Rita Frei (Philomena, Morrone's maid). Nello Pazzafini [as 'Giovanni Pazzafini'] (killer at sulphur pits). Aldo Massasso (Don Murolo, gang boss with disabled wife). Enzo D'Ausilio (smuggler boss who chairs meeting on boat). Antonio Mellino [aka Agostino O'Pazzo'] (Marsigliesi's driver). Angelo Boscariol. Marcello Filotico. Salvatore Puccinelli. *Stunts:* Giorgio Ricci, Attilio Severini, Romano Capanna, Giuseppe Mattei. *Uncredited:* Lucio Fulci (old capo). Alfonso Giganti (policeman who calls for Tarantino). Benito Pacifico (Scherino's moustached henchman).

Synopsis: Luca Di Angelo is a smuggler dealing in cigarettes and booze. After a run-in with the police, he and his brother Mickey suspect a rival, Scherino, of passing on information. They discuss their suspicions with Perlante, a playboy with Mafia connections. En route to a fire at Mickey's racing stables the brothers are stopped at a fake police roadblock. Mickey is murdered in a hail of bullets – Luca escapes. After his brother's funeral, Luca vows revenge. He goes after Scherino but he's overpowered and given a beating. However, Scherino tells Luca he had no part in Mickey's killing. A tip-off leads Luca to a derelict boat where a hood is making a drugs pick-up. Luca tortures him for information about his boss, known as The Marsigliese. Luca phones Perlante, who tells him that Jacois is muscling into the region to deal in hard drugs. At his hide-out, the Marsigliese punishes a woman trying to sell him cut drugs by burning her face. He then orders a series of hits against the region's gang bosses. Perlante's sidekick Alfredo triggers off a bomb hidden in Perlante's bed. Perlante calls Luca and sets up a meeting with The Marsigliese to discuss a merger. Luca talks to his fellow smugglers and persuades them not to accept. The next day the police launch a massive sweep of Naples, arresting many smugglers. Luca is saved by Scherino, who suggests an alliance. They call at Perlante's to discuss their plans with him, but the Marsigliese and his assassins burst in and mortally wound Scherino. Luca escapes, and Scherino manages to shoot the treacherous Perlante through the throat before dropping dead. The Marsigliese abducts Luca's wife and again insists that Luca should merge his smuggling network. To help him decide, the sound of Adele being anally raped is relayed down the phone. The old-guard mafia swing back into action from semi-retirement to deal with the French sadist. They shoot his henchmen during the handover of the traumatised Adele, and Luca himself shoots the Marsigliese.

About the production: Just as *Zombie Flesh-Eaters* had been offered first to action helmer Enzo Castellari, so too was *The Smuggler*. When the project appeared in *Variety* on 24 October 1979, Castellari was the proposed director, Franco Nero was the intended star, and Eleonora Vallone was the female lead. However, by the time the film went before the cameras, on 3 December 1979, all three had vacated the project, replaced by Fulci as director, Fabio Testi as star, and Ivana Monti as female lead.[13]

The company responsible for *The Smuggler*, Primex Cinematografia, had been inactive since the death of owner-producer Roberto Infascelli in a road accident in 1977. However, in the hands of his wife Sandra Infascelli (one of the very few female Italian producers of the period), Primex bounced back in 1979 with a new slate of releases, beginning in March with the Palermo-based project *Corleone a Brooklyn*, directed by Umberto Lenzi. *The Smuggler* then went into production from December 1979 to January 1980.

The film's subject matter, cigarette smuggling in the Naples bay area, was a hot topic at the time.[14] In January 1979 *Variety* had devoted an article to the subject: *"Cigarette smugglers, the backbone of Naples' sagging economy, are fast becoming the new antiheroes of Neapolitan cinema. A rash of films – often starring the real life 'guappi' (tough guys) of the local underground or the camorra (local Mafia) – are boxoffice hits in a city where unemployment, crime and human misery are rampant."* Citing a lucrative reissue of an old Neapolitan favourite *Zappatore* (1950) as the spark that inspired renewed interest, the article continued, *"The success of this Neapolitan revival [...] encouraged local producers to unspool their own Mafia adventures.* Onore e guapparia *starring Pino Mauro (said to be an ex-boss of the local Mafia) as a 'good-guy' smuggler was released in 1977, with modest success. The real boom came last August with the release of* L'ultimo guappo *featuring Mario Merola, an ex-longshoreman. Soon after with machine-gun speed (it was shot in a record 30 days) another film starring Mauro was shot:* I figli non si toccano. *Merola also kept pace with the release of* Serenata calibro 9. *Not to be outdone by 'guappo' kings Mauro and Merola, several film studios specializing in Neapolitan 'westerns' have cropped up in the city ... The formula is always the same, borrowing from the classic western. 'Instead of the prairie, there is the sea,' says Ciro Ippolito, an actor who has been specializing in these kinds of films, 'Instead of horses, there are the smugglers' motorboats and instead of the cowboy, there is the 'good guy' smuggler.'"*[15]

Review: As extreme as *Zombie Flesh-Eaters* had been the year before, an overarching fantasy context had prevailed. There's no such safety net in *The Smuggler*, a crime story in which sequences of astonishing sadism are made all the more alarming by the comparatively realistic *mise-en-scène*. Of course we expect some examples of violence in a film about organized crime; but what do mafia films serve up besides flashy, squib-laden shoot-outs and part-horrific, part-comical flourishes like *The Godfather*'s horse-head in the bed routine...? *The Smuggler* drastically oversteps these expectations.

Having seen the Eurocrime thrillers of cinematic bruisers like Ruggero Deodato and Umberto Lenzi we may think we know what to expect from the format: bitterly cynical plots, bleak ersatz characterization, sadistic beatings, and a revelling in the portrayal of the same sleaze the 'heroes' rail against. Fulci however can lay claim to having gone further than any of his contemporaries. *The Smuggler* is way, way over the top and sticks in the mind for its sheer raging hostility.

The story is gripping, although narrative is convoluted at the expense of clarity. Characters are introduced as related in one way or another, but the fleeting exposition sometimes leaves us wondering who the hell is who; and as the plot revolves around double crossings and sundry gangland trickery the film can ill afford to further cloud its logic. Sergio Salvati's camerawork is merely adequate here, with there being less call for the sort of languid tracking shots that usually feature in his work. The only sequence to demonstrate his slightly surrealistic brand of photography takes place at an industrial limepit given extra menace by fantastic curls of smoke rising from a chemical pool. A gunman's plunge into the corrosive liquid merits a brief but impressive overhead shot in slow motion, highlighting the strange colour and texture of the pool's scummed surface. Elsewhere, the scene where Luca extracts information from a terrified minion by sadistically twisting a knife into his armpit, benefits from a great location – a derelict ship lying tilted at a steep angle on its mooring.

All of these details, however, are mere niceties next to the meat of the movie's *raison d'être*. This is ultimately and unequivocally one violent, brutal bastard of a film. The film's sadistic *pièce de résistance* involves The Marsigliese (Marcel Bozzufi), a high level dealer in heroin and cocaine, who is pushing 'respectable' smugglers into plying his trade instead of contraband tobacco and booze. When a woman tries to trick this underworld monster into buying a huge consignment of cut drugs, he uses a bunsen burner to blowtorch her face. As the luckless drug-dealer screams, her features are reduced – in hideous detail and at great length – to a melted suppurating mess. The editing cuts between close ups of the grotesquely squawking victim and the tight-lipped sneering villain, coming back to the horror repeatedly and making the scene difficult to watch without squirming in astonished repulsion.

Few acts of cinematic sadism can compete with this alarming scene; along with a brutal anal rape scene featuring Ivana Monti it's a pinnacle of bad taste that would not go amiss in the more notorious *New York Ripper*. All the more bizarre, then, to see Marcel Bozzufi doing the dirty deed here. Himself a director (his first film being *The American* in 1969 starring Jean-Louis Trintignant and Simone Signoret), Bozzufi gained international recognition as an actor in William Friedkin's 1971 hit, *The French Connection*. An accomplished character player, he excelled as the mocking ex-lover in Robert Altman's amazing psychological thriller, *Images* (1972).

The Smuggler sees Fulci demonstrating both the necessary directing skills to compete with mainstream product and the pathological taste for violence that would exclude him. It's always been a problem for film-makers to tackle violent subject matter in a way which suggests a detachment from the acts depicted. Horror films enjoy a special status as they exist precisely to unsettle, upset and outrage; gratuitousness is a positive plus. Violence in other film genres tends to exist in a wider continuum of signification. Perhaps Fulci recognised the need for some personal angle or statement on the excesses of the story, because his cameo is an unusually active one. We see him pop up at the end as one of the old-guard *Mafiosi*, machine-gunning the sadistic drug-smuggling monsters whose nastiness has provided the film's main exploitation focus. This doesn't quite wash, unfortunately, because he's already brought so much relish to their cruelties. The question of whose side he's really on is posed rather than answered by his blithe gentleman-of-crime cameo. Horror specialist Dario Argento makes much of his predilection for donning the murderer's gloves for close-ups in his murder scenes. Fulci – whose cameo appearances are nearly always as peripheral authority figures – here makes a less credible artistic statement by ducking responsibility for the gruesomely saleable highlights of his films.

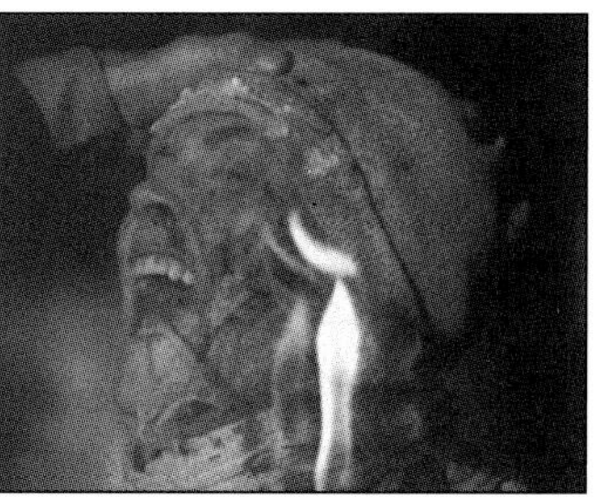

top:
A drug runner suffers The Marsigliese's brutal retribution for selling cut cocaine.

above:
German admats.

opposite top:
Fabio Testi as criminal hero Luca Di Angelo.

opposite bottom left:
British video cover.

below:
A rival Mafia Don is shot at the races by The Marsigliesi's henchmen.

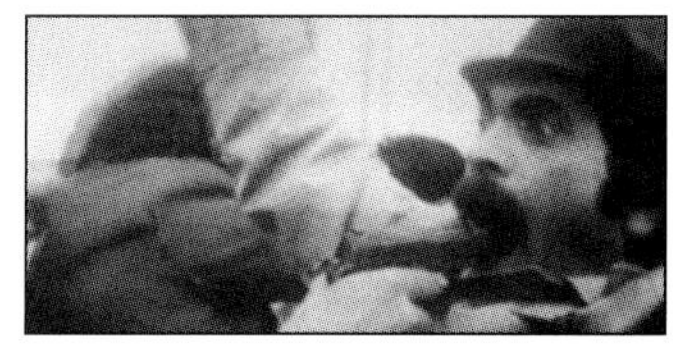

Original title
Conquest

Italy, Spain & Mexico

International theatrical titles
La conquista de la tierra perdida (SP) 'The conquest of the lost land'
El barbaro La conquista de la tierra perdida (MEX) 'The Barbarian: The Conquest of the Lost Land'
Osvajač (YUG) 'Conqueror'

Production companies
Clemi Cinematografica S.r.l.
Produciones Esme S.A. (Mexico)
Golden Sun (Barcelona)

Theatrical distributors
United Film Distribution (USA)
L.T. Técnicas Audiovisuales S.A.
Miracle Films (UK)

Theatrical running times
Italy 80m
Spain (SMC) 88m
UK 84m

Video/DVD/Blu-ray running times (adjusted)
Blue Underground DVD (USA) 88m 34s

Shooting period
October-November 1982

Censorship
Italian censor certificate 78895 issued 27 May 1983

Release information
Borgosesia (Turin) 07 July 1983
Taranto 04 August 1983
Bari 20 August 1983
UK '18' certificate granted (with cuts) 22 November 1983
UK (London) 18 May 1984
No Rome screenings

Conquest

1983

Directed by Lucio Fulci. produced by Giovanni Di Clemente for Clemi Cinematografica S.r.l. (Rome) / Golden Sun (Barcelona) / Produciones Esme S.A. (Mexico). story: Giovanni Di Clemente. screenplay: Gino Capone, José Antonio de la Loma Sr. & Carlos Vasallo. director of photography: Alejandro Alonso Garcia. music: Claudio Simonetti; published by GIPSY. film editing supervisor: Vincenzo Tomassi. editor: Emilio Rodriguez Oses. art director: Massimo Lentini. in charge of production: Pietro Innocenzi. Spanish production manager: José Antonio de la Loma Sr.. unit manager: Domenico Lo Zito. assistant directors: Filiberto Fiaschi, Roberto Tatti & José Antonio de la Loma Jr.. cameramen: Federico Del Zoppo & Claudio Morabito. assistant cameraman: Mario Bagnato. chief grips: Matteo Giordano & Roberto Pizzi. chief electrician: Gaetano Coniglio. continuity: Walter Marconi. make-up masks: Franco Rufini. hairdresser: Luigi Contini. wardrobe: Alvaro Grassi. equipment: Rodolfo Ruzza. assistant make-up: Mauro Meniconi. interior decorator: Mariangela Capuano. administration: Costantino Di Clemente. production secretary: Franco Anniballi. stills: Piero Caputi. assistant editors: Giancarlo Tiburzi, Rita Antonelli & Patrizia Innocenzi. post production: Vincenzo Santangelo. titles: Video Gamma. sound: Eros Giustini. boom operator: Ettore Mancini. synchronization: International Recording. mixage: Romano Pampaloni. special effects sound: Studio Anzellotti. wardrobe: Costumi Sat. wigs: Rocchetti / Carboni. colour by Telecolor S.p.A. (Rome). negative: Kodak. in Dolby Stereo. interiors filmed at R.P.A. Elios Studios (Rome).

Cast: Jorge Rivero [as 'George Rivero'] (Mace). Andrea Occhipinti (Ilias). Conrado San Martín (Zora). Violeta Cela (Sacrificial Victim). José Gras Palau (Fado). Gioia Scola [as 'Maria Escola'] (Girl Ilias saves from snake). Sabrina Siani [as 'Sabrina Sellers'] (Ocron). *Uncredited:* Olga Breeskin.

this page main image:
Mace (Jorge Rivero) finds himself in a vulnerable situation.

below:
Danish video cover.

Synopsis: Ilias, a handsome youth, embarks on a Quest, leaving his home for a fog-shrouded wilderness. He receives a magic bow to mark his passage into manhood and enters a strange land where people are terrorised by werewolves acting under the orders of Ocron, an evil masked woman. Ocron's marauders try to steal the bow and capture Ilias but are foiled when a rugged outlaw called Mace leaps to his defence. Soon the two are friends. Mace cares for animals and has a special bond with many species. Ocron sends Fado, the head of her brutal werewolves, to capture Ilias. When Ilias and Mace stop to eat, Ilias spots a young girl he recognises. Suddenly, masked attackers kill the girl, abduct Ilias and steal his bow. Mace tracks them, and in a bloody fight rescues his young friend. Ocron has Fado burned on a giant hot-plate as punishment for failure, and summons the Great Zora, a spirit who resides in the body of a white wolf. She offers herself body and soul to Zora if he can kill Ilias. Ilias declares that he will punish Ocron; Mace refuses to join him but agrees to escort his friend as far as the seashore. On the way, they are assailed by hundreds of tiny arrows: Ilias is hit, and breaks out in hideous boils. Mace locates a special plant that will cure his affliction. After an encounter with grotesque zombies, Mace has to do battle with a double of himself. He wins and the double is revealed as Zora, who disappears after reverting to humanoid form. The plant restores Ilias to health, but he has lost his nerve. He heads home, pleading with Mace to go with him. Mace refuses, and declines to take the youth's bow. No sooner have they parted than Mace is attacked by a band of cobweb-covered monsters. They tie him to a wooden cross and interrogate him for information about Ilias. Ilias appears and saves Mace from the creatures but the older man falls into the sea bound to a cross. Dolphins bite through the bonds and he is washed up on the shore. Ilias informs him that he's had a change of heart and decided to return to be with his friend and defeat Ocron. That night Ilias is sucked down into a lair of subterranean monsters. When Mace follows he finds the young man hanging upside down, his head cut off. Zora delivers the head to Ocron. Mace lights a funeral pyre and sits beside his friend's burning body. Ilias speaks inside his mind and tells him to anoint himself with the ashes. This will pass on the power Cronos gave to Ilias, and make the magic bow his. Mace confronts Ocron and the bow flies through the air into his hands. He fires a magic arrow which penetrates Ocron's mask, revealing the face of a ghoul. As Ocron dies, she turns into a wolf, and runs into the wilderness with the white wolf Zora.

About the production: On the same day that the Edmondo Amati project 'Siegfried's Sword' was reported as nixed in *Variety* (23 June 1982), Fulci's name was attached to another sword-and-sorcery title, 'Mace – the Outcast', under the auspices of writer/producer Giovanni Di Clemente. By October it was renamed *Conquest*, at which point it acquired a Mexican co-producer, Carlos Vasallo of Produciones Esme S.A., along with Esme's regular Spanish business partners Golden Sun. The script, too, bore the imprint of the new investors: Di Clemente was credited as writer along with Carlos Vasallo and José Antonio de la Loma. The latter was a director of multiple Esme pics starring Jorge Rivero, a handsome and muscular Mexican actor who was a big box-office draw on his home turf, so it's not surprising therefore that Rivero was signed up as the star of *Conquest*. He was not the only Mexican to join the cast; a list of Mexican productions in *Variety* also named Mexican showgirl Olga Breeskin – *"a bounteously-bosomed nitery queen"* – as a member of the *Conquest* cast.[16]

Shooting began 18 October 1982 and ran into November, with the film supposedly finished and ready for trade screenings in late January 1983. But along the way something went wrong. Come May 1983 the film was back in post-production, so evidently there was a crisis of confidence, and a decision to try and enhance the picture with post-production effects.

With the film completed, United Film Distribution picked up US distribution rights in December 1983. A showcase premiere was planned for February 1984 in New York. Steven Flynn, vice president in charge of advertising for UFD, declared that a spread of between 8 and 110 screens was envisioned for the film's release. (Judging by the film's subsequent low profile in the USA one suspects the final figure was at the lower end of this range.) *Conquest* was seen by a *Variety* reviewer in New York on 21 April 1984, after which it sank like a stone and failed to find a substantial audience.

Lucio Fulci often dismissed *Conquest* as a bad experience, and it seems at least part of the problem for him was a power struggle with the Mexican producers. Whatever went on behind the scenes, it seems to have impacted on the production as a whole. It's really the first Fulci picture in which the technical credits are poor. Here was a director who prided himself on his mastery of the technical side of filmmaking; can the failure of *Conquest*, with its eye-straining panoply of scrims, grainy soft focus and optical enhancements, be blamed on producer interference? Or was it a sign of something more ominous – namely, Fulci's faltering judgement and poor health?

Review: If films have a personality, someone slipped this one a Mickey Finn. Admittedly, half the fun of sleeping pills is in fighting the effects, staying awake to experience their weird pharmaceutical slurring; but few would want to feel that way whilst trying to crawl through a *Conan the Barbarian* rip-off. Here Lucio Fulci begs to differ. Adrift in a sulphurous gas, so apposite to the blurry lump of a story that it almost seems like a rude joke, *Conquest* – to paraphrase De Sade – is a frustrating experience. It could have been one of the few good sword and sorcery movies to emerge from the Italian exploitation scene, if Lucio Fulci – fresh from his Gothic triumphs – had given it his best shot. As it is, looking to discern the outlines of a possible hidden classic in this tale is an uncomfortable experience, akin to trying out mittens for the eyes. It could be a story 'visioned' by one of the cataracted characters who populate *The Beyond*. The anaesthetic quality of the drama challenges comprehension, and even though my viewing tape was of good quality, I seem to be recalling its world as though muffled by a poor transfer. Amongst the terrors lurking in the cotton wool of *Conquest*'s *mise-en-scène* are a clan of admittedly impressive-looking monsters, but even they fail to inject much energy into the proceedings.

After the surprise hit of Jean-Jacques Annaud's *Quest for Fire* (1981) in Italy, several films popped up on the exploitation circuit to mimic its style. Umberto Lenzi's *The Ironmaster* (1983) and *Master of the World* (1983) pathetically strove to emulate Annaud's alleged verisimilitude, and so, it would seem, does this particular mess. It's as if the scriptwriters started out trying to fuse the comic-strip mysticism of *Conan*, the pre-historic world of *Quest for Fire* and the monsters of Fulci's recent work into some warped new concoction… and then got bored and went out instead.

Conquest did receive some appreciation from British film critic and novelist Anne Billson, who commented in the London listings magazine *Time Out* that *"There is an inordinate amount of spurting wounds, severed heads and oozing poison pustules which jiffs up the action whenever the dumb dialogue and orange-filtered skies threaten to get tiresome"*. The verdict from La Stampa, however, was negative: *"It cannot be compared to other movies of the same genre, in which Excalibur, Conan and Kaan reign supreme. This movie, except for a few photographic impressions, is much worse than the previous work of this director. As a prehistoric fable it is tenuous, the story is told with difficulty, the two good characters are shallow, and the gruesome scenes (chopped heads, quartered bodies) are more clumsy than terrifying."*[17]

It's perverse and almost amusing that Fulci should enshroud his macho tale of derring-do in such a Stygian fog. *Conquest* mummifies its hero in an undifferentiated state, more evocative of a stifling nightmare of the archaic womb than the pre-civilized brute male 'freedom' more conventionally celebrated by the genre. That said, there is a homoerotic buddy-bonding quality to the relationship between Ilias and the older Mace, and some possible innuendo can be had reflecting on the significance of Ilias's magic bow. Rivero and Occhipinti seem to be checking each other out as the film progresses, but maybe I'm reading too heavily against the grain of this bland drama in an effort to sustain personal interest. No wonder Dardano Sacchetti mocked Fulci's conviction that this was to be his big break away from his regular collaborators. If *Conquest* was the only Lucio Fulci film in existence no one would mourn the absence of others.

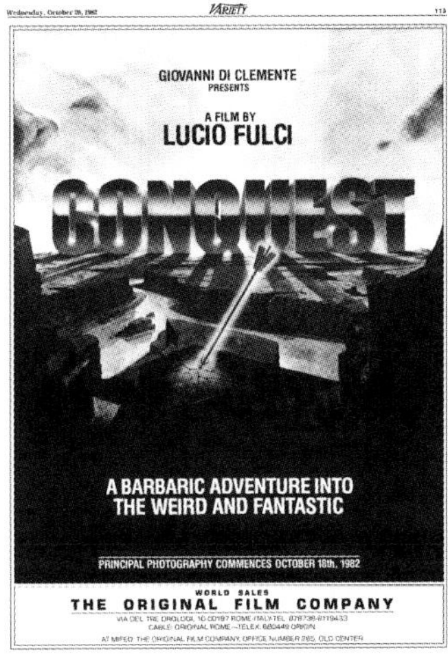

top:
Italian fotobusta (left) and Italian locandina poster (right).

above:
The locandina artwork was developed from this early concept art produced for a *Variety* advertisement dated October 1982.

below:
Detail from a Mexican lobby card.

Rome 2033 – The Fighter Centurions

1984

Directed by Lucio Fulci. executive producer: James Vaughan. A Regency Productions film from an original idea by Elisa [Livia] Briganti & Dardano Sacchetti. screenplay: Elisa [Livia] Briganti, Cesare Frugoni, Dardano Sacchetti & Lucio Fulci. director of photography: Joseph [Giuseppe] Pinori. music composed & conducted by Riz Ortolani; published by CAM. editor: Vincent Thomas [Vincenzo Tomassi]. art directors: Frank [Francesco] Vanorio & Jerry Mitchell. production manager: Peter Larson. unit manager: Enzo Nigro. 1st assistant director: Rinaldo Ricci. 2nd assistant director: Luciano Palermo. script continuity: Maria Gloria Eminente. 2nd unit continuity: Camilla Fulci. stunt co-ordinator: Sergio Mioni. 2nd unit cameraman: Aldo Tonti. camera operator: Silvano Tessicini. camera assistants: Giancarlo Granatelli & Sandro Rubeo. key grip: Antonio Marra. gaffer: Renato Sardini. costumes: Mario Giorsi. make-up artist: Franco Di Girolamo. hair stylists: Vitaliana Patacca & Martina Patacca. special effects: Corridori. optical effects & miniatures: Al Passeri & Joseph Natanson. seamstress: Lucia Baldacci. props: Agatino Fonti. motorcycle design: Joe Cancellara. make-up assistant: Rosario Prestopino. wardrobe assistant: Silvano Giusti. set dresser: Stefano Paltrinieri. set construction: Alvaro Belsole. accountant: Antonio Mastronardi. action stills: Tony Benetti. 1st assistant editor: Rita Antonelli. 2nd assistant editor: Carlo Della Porta. titles: Video Gamma. sound supervisor: Antonio Testa. boom operator: Giuseppe Testa. sound mixer: Eros Giustini. re-recording engineer: Bruno Moreal. post-sync director: Nick Alexander. dialogue editor: Michael Billingsley. sound effects: Cineaudio Effects. foley man: Alvaro Gramigna. camera & lighting equipment: Arco 2 – Roma Cine Service. costume houses: Costumi D'Arte & SAT. wigs: Rocchetti – Carboni. footwear: Arditi. set furnishings: E. Rancati. A.I.C. transport: Cinematografica Service. insurance: Cinesicurtà. the production thanks Farioli KTM; Moto Guzzi; Jawa Motorcycles. colour by Technicolor. processing laboratory: Telecolor S.p.A. filmed on location in Rome and at RPA Elios Studios (Rome) & Cinecittà (Rome).

Cast: Jared Martin (Drake). Fred Williamson (Abdul). Renato Rossini [as 'Howard Ross'] (Raven). Eleonora Brigliadori [as 'Eleonor Gold'] (Sarah, Cortez's assistant). Cosimo Cinieri (Professor Towman). Claudio Cassinelli (Cortez). Valéria Cavalli [as 'Valerie Jones'] (Susan Drake, née Harvard). Donald O'Brien [as 'Donal O'Brian'] (Monk). Penny Brown (Sybil, Cortez's blonde assistant). Pier Luigi Conti [as 'Al Cliver'] (Kirk). Mario Novelli [as 'Tony Sanders'] (Tango). Hal Yamanouchi [as 'Haruiko Yamanouchi'] (Akira). *Uncredited:* Matteo Corsini. Giovanni Di Benedetto (Sam). Cinzia Monreale (Linda Summers, Danger Game contestant). Franco Moruzzi (moustachioed gladiator).

Italian theatrical title
I guerrieri dell'anno 2072

Translation
'Warriors of the Year 2072'

Italy

Note – screen copyright is specified as 1983, although the film was not released until 1984.

Alternative titles
Roma 21° secolo Ben Hur contro Spartacus (pre-shooting title)
'Rome 21st Century Ben Hur Against Spartacus'
Rome 2033: The Centurions (pre-shooting title)
The Centurions (Roma anno 2033) (pre-shooting title)
Rome 2033: Fighter Centurions (pre-release sales title)
Rome 2033 A.D. The Fighter Centurions (pre-release sales title)
The Centurions: Rome 2033 (*Variety* reported sales title)

International theatrical titles
2072 Les mercenaires du futur (FR)
'2072 Mercenaries of the Future'
Die Schlacht der Centurions (WG)
'The Battle of the Centurions'
Roma año 2072 D.C. Los Gladiatores (SP) 'Rome year 2072 D.C.: The Gladiators'
Rome 2033: The Fighter Centurions (UK)
New Gladiators (AUS)
The New Gladiators (USA)
Fighting Force (DEN)
Año 2072 La ultima batalla (ARG)
'Year 2072, the Last Battle'
Gladiatorerna Fighting Centurions (SWE) 'Gladiators: Fighting Centurions'

Production company
Regency Productions (Rome)

Theatrical distributor
Titanus

Theatrical running times
Italy 89m
Spain (SMC) 96m

Video/DVD/Blu-ray running times (adjusted)
7 Keys video (Australia) 94m 10s
UFA video (Germany) 92m 40s

Censorship
Italian censor certificate 79146 issued 15 September 1983

Release information
Alessandria 06 March 1984
Rome 09 March 1984
Brindisi 06 April 1984
Fasano 08 June 1984
Bari 14 August 1984

Synopsis: Rome. The 21st Century. Cortez, WBS TV's chief of programming, is fuming at the ratings enjoyed by a rival American company's 'Kill-bike' show, which has made a hero out of unbeaten champion, Drake. Cortez and his assistants Sybil and Sarah receive a video message from station boss, 'Sam', demanding that they steal the format of gladiatorial contests on motorbikes and set them where it all began: the Colosseum. Contestants will be chosen from the Death Rows of the world. Drake, who's just been put on Death Row for killing the men who murdered his wife, is brought to the training compound. He must face sadistic chief guard Raven and the other contestants: Abdul, Akira and Kirk. All are fitted with electronic bracelets. He also meets an old friend, a man with a fibre-optic eye called Monk, now a WBS employee. Drake is strapped into a 'hate stimulator' device, designed to find out if a man can be provoked into murder. Drake does not crack. Sarah becomes attracted to him, and he earns the respect of the other prisoners after winning a battle of wits with Raven. Sarah shows Drake evidence that proves he was set up for murder to get him on the show. A device smuggled in by Monk facilitates an escape attempt: as soon as they are caught, footage mysteriously turns up on TV. Sarah visits Professor Towman, the inventor of the WBS computer system, looking for a way to access restricted files. The professor gives her a pass-key before he is murdered. As the WBS Gladiator Contest commences, she discovers that the computer will kill the survivors twenty minutes after the show by detonating their wrist bracelets. Riding into the arena on a motorcycle she stops the games and informs the men, who attack the control tower and kill Raven. Cortez is found to have plotted the death of the survivors to discredit Sam and take over the station. Abdul kills him. A computer image of 'Sam' reveals that 'he' is just the computer. The rebels force entry to an inner chamber with Sarah's pass-key. There they are attacked by the traitor Monk. Drake kills him and Sarah uses the destructor codes to blow up 'Sam' and de-activate the deadly bracelets. Sarah and Drake fly away together.

About the production: Although a massive falling out was just around the corner, in 1983 Lucio Fulci and Dardano Sacchetti were still good friends. In June of that year Fulci began work on another Sacchetti-scripted project, funded by Edmondo Amati's Regency Productions, and for a while it seemed like the trickiest thing they had to worry about was what to call it...

I guerrieri dell'anno 2072 was first referred to in *Variety*, on 4 May 1983, as 'Roma 21° secolo Ben Hur contro Spartacus' (aka 'Rome 21st Century Ben Hur vs. Spartacus'). A month later the title had changed to 'Rome 2033: The Centurions' and in July it was referred to as 'The Centurions (Roma anno 2033)'. By the time it was ready for foreign sales in March 1984 the film was being referred to as 'Rome 2033: Fighter Centurions', whilst Regency's own sales brochure went with 'Rome 2033 A.D. The Fighter Centurions'. At some point prior to the Italian theatrical release, '2033' fell out of favour, and in March 1984 the film turned up in cinemas as *I guerrieri dell'anno 2072*. However, a *Variety* article about Regency Productions in May 1984 revealed that the earlier date was back in fashion for other territories, with Regency seeking foreign sales for 'The Centurions: Rome 2033'. In France the film played briefly as *2072 Les mercenaires du futur*, and in the UK it came out, on video only, as *Rome 2033: The Fighter Centurions*. A few years later an Australian video company released the film as *New Gladiators*, a decision echoed by the American video release *The New Gladiators*. Finally, Troma's DVD release in 2001 bore the screen credit *Rome, 2072 A.D. The New Gladiators* – yet another variant! Since the title card looks authentic to the film's initial release period it seems likely that *Rome, 2072 A.D. The New Gladiators* was intended to be the original US theatrical title.

Review: Although *Rome 2033 – The Fighter Centurions* has its admirers in certain cult movie quarters, for me there is precious little to enjoy in this shoddily produced and routinely acted foray into dystopian sci-fi. It anticipates the plot of the Arnold Schwarzenegger star vehicle, *The Running Man* (1987), directed by Paul Michael Glaser and adapted from a Richard Bachman (aka Stephen King) novel of the same name. However, King's pseudonymous effort was published in 1982, which theoretically means that scripters Briganti, Sacchetti and Frugoni had the chance to plunder it for ideas. The chain goes back even further, though: *La decima vittima* (1965), an Italian/Spanish co-production directed by Elio Petri and starring Ursula Andress, Marcello Mastroianni and Elsa Martinelli, features much the same plot, with the added similarity of the story being set in Rome. The roots for both this film and King's Bachman novel are ultimately to be found in a Robert Sheckley short story, *The Seventh Victim*.

Part of the problem is the budget, which needs to be much higher for this sort of thing. Sad to say, the brave attempts of the model designers to come up with a futuristic tabletop version of Rome are a failure, and the scenes of the TV-station's flying saucer hovering over the Colosseum are very poor. The script is a cursory affair, leavened with the occasional unintended howler, like this exchange between Drake and TV boss Cortez: *"Go to Hell!"*; *"I would if I thought it would raise my ratings"*. Characters solemnly pronounce lines like *"Computers, we built them to be our slaves, but we're turning out to be theirs"*, whilst the limp action sequences waste the efforts of some dependable exploitation stalwarts.

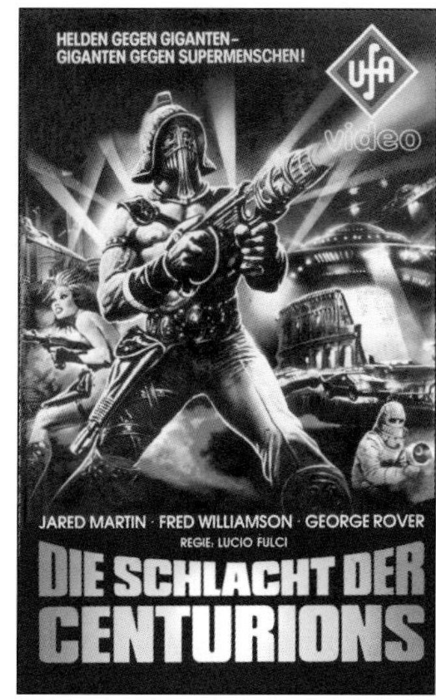

above:
German video cover.

opposite:
Raven's guards apprehend the escaped criminals.

below:
Drake (Jared Martin), Abdul (Fred Williamson), Sarah (Eleonora Brigliadori) and Kirk (Al Cliver) turn the tables.

itself can be traced to the Roman spectacles of death nearly two thousand years before!

Unfortunately, this promising concept is unceremoniously squelched by the film's failure to pull off its own spectacle, meaning that whilst the Italians may get first credit the Americans get the last laugh. Perhaps the only riposte capable of freezing that laugh is the film's depiction of an orbiting supercomputer manipulating events. Behind the illusory human face of power lies an impersonal, orbital, disembodied force, suggesting a view of global society dominated beyond the reach of individuals of any nation; a concept uncannily similar to the 'end-of-history' declarations of modern-day Cassandra, Jean Baudrillard.

above:
Danish video cover.

top and below:
Drake and Sarah.

Jared Martin makes a creditable attempt to take the film seriously, and his rugged features lend the underwritten heroic role more strength than it deserves. One sequence that Martin has to endure, featuring a group of white-clad oafs trying to project 'New Wave' menace as holograms of his wife's killers, really brings bile to the throat. However, Martin gives the film a square-jawed leading man's presence, and is assisted by the formidable action/exploitation star Fred Williamson and an amusingly camp turn from Howard Ross as the bullying Chief Guard, Raven. A scene where he tortures the gladiators by making them dangle from a metal bar above an electrified floor has some impact, and even Al Cliver's overdone electrocution works well. *"When you hit the floor you will sizzle like fried eggs"*, crows Raven, as the men struggle to maintain their hold.

Much of the rest of this tin-foiled turkey grates on the nerves, and the climactic gladiatorial spectacle is just embarrassing. The sight of men wheeling around a circuit like nervous Sunday-drivers, on 'futuristic' motorbike-chariots made from cardboard and silver-paper, really saps the action film momentum. The stunt work is cautious and unimpressive too. Production company Regency made the similarly over-extended *The Atlantis Interceptors* (directed by Ruggero Deodato) the same year.

Fulci's reputation as a purveyor of gory spectacle must have suggested the decadence of ancient Rome as a natural subject for him to dramatize, but this attempt to put a high-tech moral spin on the Roman Games is a complete let down. Nearly lost amidst the corner-cutting and carelessness of the project is the germ of an ambitious idea, to do with the relationship between Italian and American popular culture. Cortez's plan to rip off the American gladiator show, whilst setting it in The Colosseum to underline how the Americans stole the idea from Italy in the first place, seems pertinent to Fulci's experience. The dispute over who first innovated the kind of gory spectacle Fulci thrived on is pursued back beyond the medium of cinema itself. As if to settle the charges of plagiarism he'd been subjected to once and for all, *Rome 2033* boldly suggests that the roots of cinema

Footnotes

1 Nero clocked up several more roles for Damiani, whose varied work straddles both genre and 'art' cinema: *The Day of the Owl*, 1968; *Confessions of a Police Captain*, 1971; *L'istruttoria è chiusa dimentichi tante sbarra*, 1971; and *How to Kill a Judge*, 1974.

2 "Colt Concert [Massacre Time] *is an oneiric western. There are three elements: the mean brother who plays the piano with his father, expressing the oedipal nature of their relationship; a lost brother who doesn't know his identity; and a drunkard. I'm not a realist, like Leone. The French described my film as a western 'reve', which means 'dreamed'*." – to Luca Palmerini, *Giallo Pages* #1 and: "*A western which I feel belongs in the fantastique* [Massacre Time]. *It was very different from other Italian westerns one could see then: both soft-spoken and extremely violent. The confrontation of two brothers in an unreal climate.*" – to Robert Schlockoff, *L'Écran Fantastique*, reprinted in *Starburst* #48.

3 Pasolini's contribution earned him a four month suspended sentence for 'public defamation' following complaints about its contempt for the Church; *La ricotta* starred Orson Welles as a devout Christian director filming a biblical story amidst repeated cries of "Get those crucified characters out of here!"

4 Pia Degermark info from *The Las Vegas Sun*, 18 May 1969.

5 *Variety*, 29 April 1970.

6 Says Taylor himself, in an interview at www.rodtaylorsite.com

7 From *The Actor's Life: Journals 1956-1976* by Charlton Heston (Dutton, 1978).

8 *Variety*, 23 January 1974.

9 Perhaps a reference to the 1969 novel *Les allumettes suédoises* by Robert Sabatier, which was translated into Italian as *I fiammiferi* in 1972.

10 "Il film Zanna Bianca avrà un seguito", *l'Unità*, 22 March 1974.

11 'Mareth' was a shooting title for Umberto Lenzi's WW2 adventure *Il grande attacco*.

12 *Variety*, 7 September 1977.

13 This didn't stop a few mistaken references to Castellari as director of the film popping up later in *Variety*, one in January and one in May 1980. Castellari seems to have been going through a rough patch in 1979; he turned down *Zombi 2* in January, dropped out of *Speed Cross* for producer Giovanni Di Clemente in August, and in December he walked out on *The Smuggler*.

14 Among the directors contributing to this boom in Neapolitan production, by far the most prolific was Alfonso Brescia, who made ten films in the region within a three year period: *Napoli serenata calibro 9* (1978), *L'ultimo guappo* (1978), *Il mammasantissima* (1979), *Napoli... la camorra sfida, la città risponde* (1979), *I contrabbandieri di Santa Lucia* (1070), *Lo scugnizzo* (1979), *La tua vita per mio figlio* (1980), *Carcerato* (1981), *I figli... so' pezzi 'e core* (1981) and *Napoli, Palermo, New York – Il triangolo della camorra* (1981). All but one of these (*Lo scugnizzo*) starred ex-longshoreman Mario Merola. They were either crime thrillers about local gangsters, or 'sceneggiata' films, a term referring to a style of Neapolitan musical melodrama or 'musical soap opera' – action and dialogue interspersed with songs. Fulci, for his part, only shot this one crime film in Naples, but he did have connections there, having made so many films with Franco and Ciccio who had a huge following in the region. Connections aside, it's likely that he was approached by Primex Cinematografia because, after the grisly *Zombi 2*, he was perceived as a man who would bring the right sort of visceral punch to the project, an assessment that proved right on the money.

15 "Naples Translates Hollywood Westerns Into 'Bad Guy' Pix", *Variety*, 3 January 1979.

16 *Variety*, 25 May 1983. This is difficult to confirm as the extant cast lists are woefully underpopulated and the image quality of the film makes identification difficult.

17 *La Stampa*, 7 June 1983. Don Coscarelli's *The Beastmaster* (1982) was called *Kaan principe guerro* ('Kaan Warrior Prince') in Italy.

"Woe be unto him who opens one of the Seven Gateways to Hell, because through that Gateway Evil will invade the world..."

~ The Book of Eibon ~

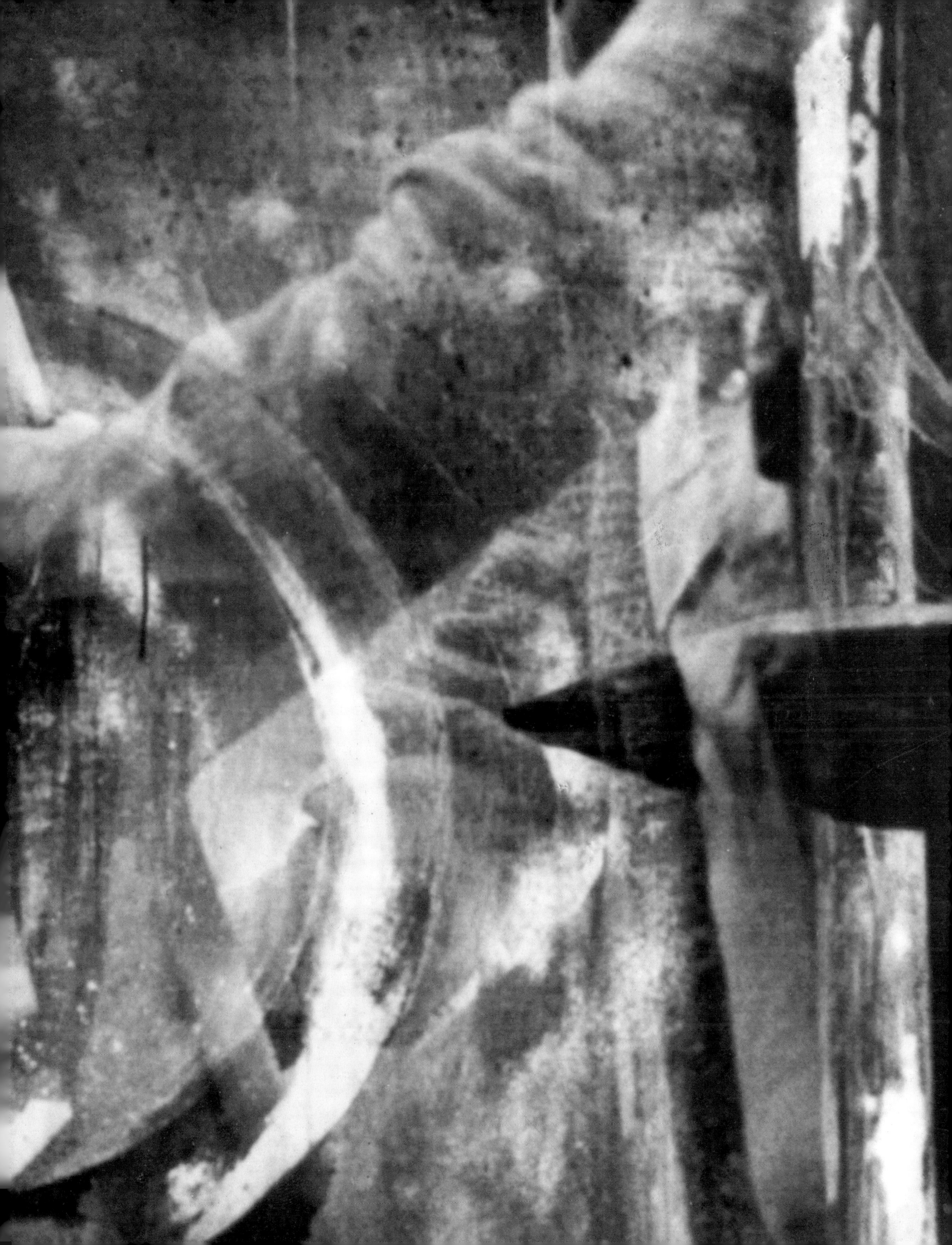

READ THE FINE PRINT.
YOU MAY HAVE JUST MORTGAGED YOUR LIFE.
House by the Cemetery
AN ALMI PICTURES PRESENTATION
Starring KATHERINE MACCOLL PAOLO MALCO
ANNA PIERONI SILVIA COLLATINA
AND WITH DAGMAR LASSANDER DIRECTED BY LUCIO FULCI
DUE TO THE GRAPHIC NATURE OF THIS FILM
NO ONE UNDER 17 WILL BE ADMITTED
©1984 ALMI PICTURES, INC. ALL RIGHTS RESERVED

chapter six

Gothic Hells, Gruesome Visions

featuring:

City of the Living Dead aka *Paura nella città dei morti viventi* (1980)

The Black Cat aka *Black Cat* (1981)

The Beyond aka *L'aldilà* (1981)

The House by the Cemetery aka *Quella villa accanto al cimitero* (1981)

Manhattan Baby (1982)

The years from 1980 to 1983 following the international success of *Zombie Flesh-Eaters* were the most creatively adventurous of Lucio Fulci's career. They also marked a rewarding period for Italian horror production in general; the Rome studios were awhirl with delirious activity. Genre kingpin Dario Argento was in the ascendant, producing his most brilliant work: *Inferno* in 1980 and *Tenebrae* in 1982 both belong in the ranks of the all-time classics of Italian horror. Even the less ambitious exploitation regulars (Umberto Lenzi, Joe D'Amato, Antonio Margheriti, Luigi Cozzi for example) were crafting outrageous and entertaining work. The horror genre, although never rivalling the popularity previously enjoyed by comedies or westerns, was achieving an increased level of success with Italian audiences. Despite appalling mishandling by 20th Century Fox elsewhere, Argento's *Inferno* was the ninth most popular film in Italy that year.[1]

Inferno was to play a significant role in the formation of Fulci's work at the time, a role which is explored later in this chapter. Having noted the influence, however, we can move on – Fulci's films of this period are also characterized by a clearly distinct style, arising from his own haunted, pessimistic sensibility. The narrative experimentation of his writing partner Dardano Sacchetti and the technical virtuosity of other regular collaborators, including his cinematographer of the period Sergio Salvati and the composer Fabio Frizzi, also contribute invaluably. These early eighties films are marked by the all-round success of their team efforts. The scripting was sketchy at times – as so often in the horror genre – but the films were aided immeasurably by the participation of performers like Catriona MacColl, David Warbeck, Patrick Magee and Paolo Malco, people who lent the films a presence which transcended the sometimes meagre dimensions of the dialogue.

Technical accomplishments aside, it's the way this rebellious director *privileged* his violent sequences that afforded the greatest pleasure to his fans (and proved the most objectionable quality to detractors). By now, the violence Lucio Fulci showed was gratuitous in the best sense of the word. It existed as a defiantly elaborated fundamental presence in its own right, with no apology and no contextual excuse. Horrendous physical trauma in films like *The Beyond* and *The House by the Cemetery* takes pride of place, and the surrounding technique draws the viewer inexorably into its contemplation. Fulci's splashy, multi-coloured depictions of decay and bodily mutilation are triumphs of *art-maudit*. Orbital rupture by glass shards, by giant splinter, by probing undead finger, by rusty nail, by beaks of stuffed birds; the vomiting of innards; the savage ripping of throats by possessed dogs, by ghoulish fingers and by ancient zombie teeth; the corroding of faces by acid or quicklime, and the eating of a man's tongue by spiders; all the horrors that befall the flesh are transformed into cruel leaps of the imagination. His strategy earned him both criticism and admiration for his 'nailed down camera' approach to visceral horror. This focus – the manner in which the clotted, stubbornly dominant gore scenes are allowed to interrupt the flow of the story – makes sense when considered as a distinctly Roman way of going about things. Just as we are accustomed to the demands of art objects, to be contemplated with lingering, almost

facing page: American poster.

below: Emily betrayed by her guide dog – one of the magnificently excessive scenes in *The Beyond*.

right:
Italian fotobuste.

below:
German poster for the Fabrizio De Angelis/Marino Girolami film *Zombie Holocaust.*

bottom:
French still – Ian McCulloch goes back to the beach... *Zombie Holocaust.*

ritual concentration – in galleries, in churches, or outside when encountering the phantasmagorias of architecture – so this Roman director wanted us, *dared* us, to slow down our cinematic 'step' and gaze, long and hard, at his gruesome creations.

Unfortunately, this fertile period seems doomed to have been the last appreciable heyday of Italian horror. Fulci himself suffered terrible neglect in his last few years – producers were no longer willing to venture through the domain he thrived in best, preferring to bankroll farces and romantic comedies instead. This drastically reduced the amount of production money his films could attract. Nonetheless, as we look back, aware that the Roman industry has now succumbed to the thrall of American values, its production roster shrunken almost beyond recognition, this period of Italian excess continues to occupy a special position in the hearts of genre devotees.

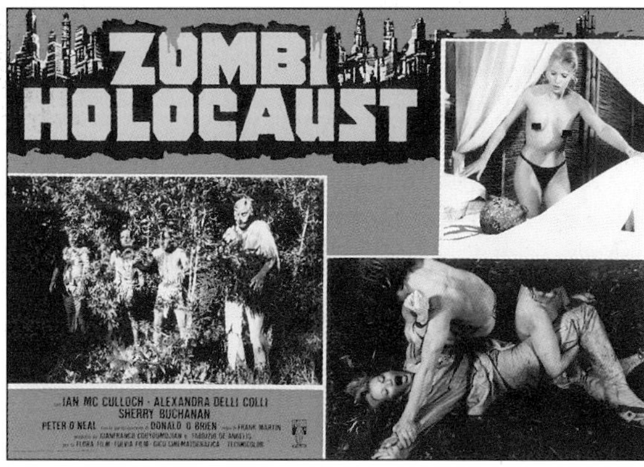

Roma: Città Sanguinosa! 1980-1983

So what was going on during this golden era? Certainly there were numerous movies that owed their existence to the unexpected success of *Zombie Flesh-Eaters*. Many were cheap but engagingly nasty affairs, peppered with idiosyncrasies and charged up with ham-fisted energy by the promise of quick box-office profit. Before going on to look in more detail at Fulci's very special films of this period, it's worth establishing the overall context of fevered activity triggered by Lucio Fulci's living dead epics.

Fulci's producer on *Zombie Flesh-Eaters*, Fabrizio De Angelis, was one of the first off the block, following through in true Italian exploitation manner with a further 'variation' on the theme. By scribbling a quick treatment for another veteran director (this time Marino Girolami) and conscripting a couple of *Flesh-Eaters*' cast members, including star Ian McCulloch, *Zombie Holocaust* was rushed into production on the same sets and locations as Fulci's film. It reached Italian screens in March 1980 and later hit cinemas worldwide, trailing re-titlings like so much eviscerated intestines. The film was made available to German audiences as *Zombies unter Kannibalen*, revealing its unique secret to the Teutonic market thanks to their characteristically blunt way with words. De Angelis, in one of those moments of producer 'inspiration' that makes a nonsense of the *auteur* theory, had decided to combine the flesh-eating ghouls of the Fulci film with a 'primitive cannibal tribe' idea ripped off from 1980's other gruesome hit, *Cannibal Holocaust*.

Zombie Holocaust boasts a plethora of gruesome special make-up effects by Giannetto De Rossi's assistant and frequent Fulci collaborator, Maurizio Trani, and Rosario Prestopino, make-up assistant on *City of the Living Dead* and *The New York Ripper*. It's a grotty but likeable film that has found favour with sleaze fans, especially Americans tempted in by the enterprising and unscrupulous US distributors. Exploitation entrepreneur Terry Levene of Aquarius Releasing edited on a new, unrelated prologue from an aborted Stateside production, and re-titled the film *Dr. Butcher M.D.* This may have obscured the film's 'themes' behind a typically billboard-grabbing title, but the ad campaign ensured the film a cult reputation: *"He's a depraved sadistic rapist, a bloodthirsty homicidal killer... and he makes house-calls!"* the posters gloated. It's one of the all-time great exploitation come-ons, though the addition of an awful synthesizer score to this US version blemishes the film throughout.

Girolami, the director hired to helm this excursion into deepest opportunism, was born in 1914, and directed his first film, *La strada buia* in 1950. Like many of the men responsible for Italy's most violent and shocking films of the seventies and eighties, he was born of a much older generation, a fact of Italian production which can seem surprising, given the youth-oriented market the films generally appealed to. He concentrated mainly on light, frivolous comedies in the 1960s, producing along the way three films with Fulci regulars Franco and Ciccio – *Due Rrringos nel Texas* (1967), *Franco, Ciccio e le vedove allegre* (1968), and *Don Franco e Don Ciccio nell'anno della contestazione* (1970) – picking up more or less where Fulci had left off with the Sicilian buffoons.

Then there was Aristide Massaccesi (better known as Joe D'Amato), a frequently good cinematographer who became a decidedly sleazy director. Massaccesi was born in 1936 and started off his career in the Italian cinema as assistant cameraman and eventually cinematographer, working on a slew of sixties productions. He began directing in 1973, with the incoherent but haunting horror item *Death Smiles At Murder*, but soon moved into sex films, where he pioneered an innovation of somewhat dubious merit – the porno/horror hybrid. After becoming enmeshed in a series of *Emmanuelle* cash-ins, he opted to merge his relentless cinematic obsessions for pudenda and sadistic horror; the hardcore *Emanuelle in America* (1976) contains simulated snuff scenes so rough they are rumoured to have inspired David Cronenberg's dark satire of decadent media overload, *Videodrome* (1983).

Massaccesi's personal acquaintance with Fulci began with a job as director of second-unit photography on 1974's *Challenge to White Fang*[2], and the two men remained aware of each other's work. Although up to his elbows in soft and hardcore porn movies at the time, *Zombie Flesh-Eaters* caught the sexploitation veteran's attention. He staggered in on the zombie phenomenon with *Erotic Nights of the Living Dead* (1980), a blatant cash-in featuring appallingly lit, cruddy zombies and dreary sex scenes on a Caribbean island. Surprisingly, even the obvious requirement of extreme gore was blown; the gut-churning elements were inept even by Massaccesi's frequently low standards. Ironically, his most impressive horror film – *Beyond the Darkness* (1979) – had been released the same year as *Zombie Flesh-Eaters* to a deafening silence from critics. An impressively downbeat, grisly affair, *Beyond the Darkness* was actually a gored-up re-tread of *Il terzo occhio* by Mino Guerrini, an obscure 1966 film starring the handsome young star of *Django*, Franco Nero.

Massaccesi's most notorious effort is 1980's *Anthropophagous the Beast*. It's a turgid, badly photographed slouch of a film (blown up from 16mm), featuring *Zombie Flesh-Eaters* star Tisa Farrow, which nonetheless perks up in the final reel to deliver a slew of horrific images – the eating of an unborn foetus, some bloody scalp twisting and so on. More important, though, is the film's dumb but deluxe gore climax: the cannibalistic monster of the title is eviscerated – and proceeds to consume his own entrails. The image is a perfect metaphor for the Italian exploitation cinema's feeding frenzy, all the better for being unintended as such.[3] D'Amato worked at an amazing clip throughout the seventies and eighties and, having expanded into production with his Filmirage company (scoring a critical and commercial success with Michele Soavi's 1987 directing debut *Stagefright*), he eventually acted as producer on Fulci's 1991 flop *Door to Silence*.

Not all Italian horror films of the period were as sleazy as Massaccesi's. In 1980 a youthful Luigi Cozzi (32 at the time), directing as usual under the pseudonym of Lewis Coates, turned in his best known film, the gory but oddly innocent *Contamination*. Despite some fashionable splatter, its atmosphere was more reminiscent of fifties sci-fi 'shockers' like *Fiend Without a Face* (1958). *Contamination* borrows heavily from 1979's smash hit *Alien*, but blatantly lifts its exciting prologue from *Zombie Flesh-Eaters*, and again – like *Zombie Holocaust* – drafts Ian McCulloch into the proceedings. *Contamination* boasts credulity-straining gore effects from Giovanni Corridori, and is professionally photographed by Giuseppe (*Murderock*, *Rome 2033*) Pinori. Carlo De Mejo (*City of the Living Dead*) makes an appearance, and the whole thing exudes a faintly hallucinatory air of the absurd. (One character menaced by an alien pod in the shower cries: "*Let me out of here! There's an Egg!!*")

Cozzi, a cosy remora to the shark of Dario Argento, achieves his own brief moments of pulp epiphany, and rarely fails to amuse (aficionados of the giallo film particularly recommend his 1975 thriller *The Dark Is Death's Friend*). Sadly, he went on to waste time on a pair of muscleman projects: his *Hercules* (1983) and *Hercules II* (1985) are – like most latterday attempts to return to that quintessentially Italian genre, the peplum – virtually unwatchable.

Umberto Lenzi, having recently stoked the exploitation pot with some grisly post-*Cannibal Holocaust* mayhem in *Eaten Alive* (1980), adopted the living dead formula in 1980's ludicrous yet thrilling *Nightmare City*. A Spanish-Italian co-production, Lenzi's gory confectionary boasted little thematic relation to Fulci's film, and yet existed almost entirely because of it. Indeed, *Nightmare City*, in its ham-fisted way, actually delivers on the promise of *Zombie Flesh-Eaters* by having most of its action take place in urban locales. Zombie attacks on airports, hospitals and TV stations (so frustratingly witheld in Romero's *Dawn of the Dead* and tantalizingly suggested in Fulci's film) explode here in a riot of ridiculous but thrilling bloodshed. The film climaxes, fittingly, with zombies attacking the dopey leading couple at an amusement park.[4]

The apotheosis of all this post-Fulci mayhem? For me it has to be Andrea Bianchi's *The Nights of Terror* (1980), a hilariously sleazy retread of the zombie theme set around a crumbling palatial villa. *The Nights of Terror* exerts a weird fascination as it boils the format down to a series of extended, implacable zombie attacks, spiced with sexploitation writhings and creepy intimations of incest. Bianchi, who brought the world

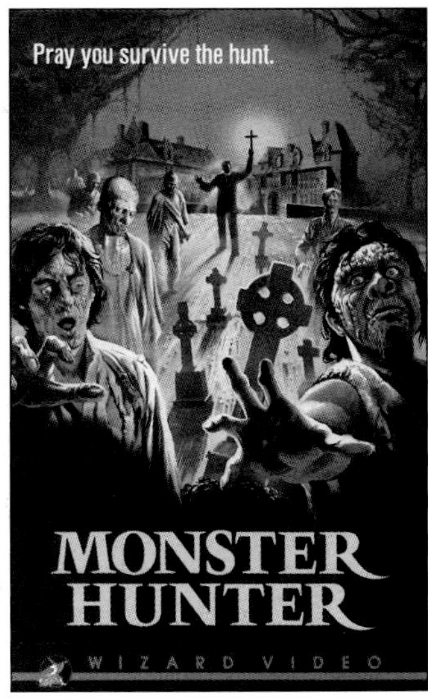

above:
Joe D'Amato's follow-up to *Anthropophagous the Beast* was released in Britain as *Absurd*. In America it got a video release as *Monster Hunter* with cover art trading on the popularity of Fulci's Gothic imagery.

above left:
A typically daft image from Joe D'Amato's *Erotic Nights of the Living Dead*.

below:
Another Italian actress receives the sacrament of eye impalement in Andrea Bianchi's weird and wonderful *The Nights of Terror* (German still).

above:
Spanish poster for Andrea Bianchi's *The Nights of Terror*, the *reductio ad absurdum* of Italian zombie flicks.

the giallo delights of *Strip Nude for Your Killer* (1975), marinates the loony action in Moog synthesizer and overdramatic string arrangements, tilts the camera at the slightest provocation, and conjures the kind of childish, regressive atmosphere that short-circuits sophistication. Yet there's so much for fans of the more *outré* horror cinema to enjoy. There's a quality of nightmare to it: brutal, disjointed and farcical, grindingly repetitive yet able to sneak whimsical, lunatic images into the fray. It's also gory in a singularly grubby fashion: the zombies (designed by Rosario Prestopino) are the sack-clothed plebeians of the sub-genre, toting garden tools (and a scythe!) when battering their way into a mansion to munch on the cowering good-lifers inside. The undead are so mouldering as to be virtually fossilized (they emerge from an Etruscan tomb so goodness knows how old they're meant to be). When hit by bullets their 'flesh' explodes like ancient pottery; yet their eyeballs are often untouched by decay. Best of all this is one of the surprisingly few horror films where *everyone* dies, an outcome that earns my unconditional admiration and makes it the ideal film to finish with here.

So the Italian exploitation industry was on a horror roll; but whilst producers, writers and directors undoubtedly remained willing to plunder American films for commercial plot skeletons, they could also, thanks to the success of *Zombie Flesh-Eaters*, lift ideas from Italian sources; just as they had earlier when Dario Argento's *The Bird with the Crystal Plumage* synergized the Italian thriller. *Zombie Holocaust* and *Erotic Nights of the Living Dead*, admittedly cheapskate productions with a much smaller audience than their model, both centred around the voodoo-island location of Fulci's film but failed to achieve the same resonance. What they lacked was the Fulci team's canny decision to look beyond Romero's zombie films towards the traditional undead of the early horror cinema; and yet further back, to the genre's roots in the European Gothic tradition.

Fulci and the Gothic tradition

The scripts Lucio Fulci filmed in the early eighties were all flavoured with references to classic horror literature, yet they were defiantly up-to-date in their graphic, visceral abandon. What does it mean to label these films 'Gothic', when they are set almost entirely in the modern world? The word, in its purest sense, conjures a period long gone. Originally it was used to denote architecture of Western Europe from the 12th to the 16th centuries; it came into its secondary usage when taken to describe a particularly over-ripe sort of literary work of the late 18th and early 19th century. Supernatural fiction, particularly that which exhibited an enhanced propensity for the grotesque, was labelled Gothic; books like Horace Walpole's *The Castle of Otranto* (1764), Matthew Lewis's *The Monk* (1796) and Mary Shelley's *Frankenstein; or, The Modern Prometheus* (1818) are noted examples. Gloomy in atmosphere and packed with eerie castles atop dark hillsides, cobwebbed vaults and all the morbid trappings of the tomb, such novels flourished as a popular form despite the deprecations of 'educated' readers. Gothic literature was often considered to be crude and barbarous; and these judgements are still among the connotations the word carries for some users. On the other hand, such unfettered morbidity excited the approval of rebel decadent writers in 19th century France and later the Surrealists, who were enraptured by the 'convulsive beauty' of the Gothic melodrama's 'vulgar' excitations.

The problem, especially for dour Protestants, seems to have been that it was one of the first literary forms to allow itself the joy of fevered exaggeration (although Bible writers like John the Apostle may take first credit there), and it's precisely the quality of over-excitability and excess – in both mood and incident – that makes it the ideal label for Fulci's horror tales. More than just evidence of crudity (a word which merely suggests the work is unhoned), Fulci's treatment of the physical takes acts of sadism and barbarity to the limit, deliberately to provide the viewer with a dizzying surplus of sensation. This aspect of carnal extremity characterises such astonishing scenes as the girl vomiting her innards in *City of the Living Dead* and the ecstatically morbid sight of Mrs. Menard being slowly eaten by ghouls in *Zombie Flesh-Eaters*. When Mrs. Gittleson is speared with a poker by the hideous Dr. Freudstein in *The House by the Cemetery*, Fulci isn't content to show a couple of percussive stabbings, as would normally be the case. Instead he draws the scene out almost in slow motion, distressing the viewer's sense of time almost as much as their stomach. There's actually something endearingly generous about Fulci's gore scenes; they allow us so much time to gawp that we are sometimes able to check the artificiality of the effects (as is the case with the notorious spider attack in *The Beyond*). It really is the thought that counts in such instances!

It's more conventionally felt that a 'Gothic' horror film is one with a period, preferably middle-European setting; Mario Bava's early films such as *The Mask of Satan* (17th century Moldavia) and *Kill, Baby, Kill!* (18th century Romania) are good examples of the form, as are many of the best-known Hammer horrors. This usage pays obedience to the idea of the term's historical origins. The stylistic concerns of the Gothic novel, however, can always be reconvened in fiction of a more up-to-date kind. The term 'Southern Gothic' for instance is taken to refer to a kind of melodramatic fiction set in the deep South of the USA, featuring characters with a high level of grotesquerie and eccentricity. Flannery O'Connor's *Wise Blood*, the plays of Tennessee Williams, William Faulkner's novels (*Sanctuary*, for example, with its impotent degenerate lead called 'Popeye', who gets off to a bad start in life cutting up kittens with scissors); all marinate their narratives in a dense gumbo of eroded wealth, decaying homesteads, failing dreams and moral/social/sexual disorder. *City of the Living Dead* and *The Beyond* both benefit from being set in Southern state locations that bring to mind this particular strain of Gothic drama.

European America

When looking at the commercial Italian cinema, it's possible to distinguish between productions that aim to mimic the style of American films, and those that take sustenance from their own visual traditions. Films in the former category can be fun (such as the Dardano Sacchetti co-scripted *Cannibal Apocalypse* directed by Antonio Margheriti in 1980) but the latter, as exemplified by the best work of Fulci, Argento and Bava, are of greater interest. American culture already saturates the UK so it's refreshing to see Italian films play their own cultural game, even if the realities of finance and production in a world marketplace demand certain contrivances to compete with American cinema. *Dawn of the Dead* may have started the ball rolling, but the particular interest that *Zombie Flesh-Eaters* received had shown producer Fabrizio De Angelis, writer Dardano Sacchetti and director Fulci that their version of zombie lore could survive in the international movie marketplace without harking back constantly to the same model. If sundry other Italian offerings were to take their cues more rigidly from the Romero tradition, Sacchetti and Fulci were less inclined to follow than to take advantage of their own innovations. *City of the Living Dead*, *The Beyond* and *The House by the Cemetery* owe virtually nothing to *Dawn of the Dead* (although other American influences do appear), and much more to Italian or Spanish horror. The other two films discussed in this chapter (*The Black Cat* and *Manhattan Baby*) refer to other works entirely.

The three principal films under consideration here – *City of the Living Dead*, *The Beyond* and *The House by the Cemetery* – are all ostensibly located in the United States; exteriors were filmed in Savannah, East Georgia; New Orleans, South-East Louisiana; and Concorde, near Boston, Massachusetts respectively. Mixed with these American locales are the interiors, shot at De Paolis Studios in Rome.[5] The canny – or fortuitous – choice of American locations adds to the ambiguity, with the New Orleans setting of *The Beyond* steeped in Mediterranean architecture (set up as a port by the French in 1718, it belonged to Spain between 1763 and 1803). Palms and exotic vegetation bloom in luxurious gardens belonging to houses of the Southern United States, their windows bedecked with Mediterranean-style shutters. In an interview with Luca Palmerini for his book *Spaghetti Nightmares*, set and costume designer Massimo Lentini indicated that the choice of Louisiana for the location shoot of *The Beyond* was a casual affair; in a meeting with Fulci and De Angelis, Lentini simply pointed at Louisiana when the question was raised, and De Angelis enthusiastically took the suggestion.

Detractors have carped occasionally about the use of American settings, throwing scorn on the integrity of these Italian productions for aiming to ingratiate themselves with American audiences. Certainly, whilst it should be obvious to most viewers that the films have a very distinct Italian style, commercial considerations – like the need for a Stateside release – will not have been discarded. It would be naive (and unnecessary) to construe the location choices as purely the evidence of an authorial imagination fixed on the literature of the Deep South. The pressure from producers to make the films viable for sale to the USA, a market notoriously fixated on the relentless consumption of its own image and a spurning of any suggestion of 'foreign-ness', will undoubtedly have played a major part.

Priority must anyway be given to the sensations experienced by the viewer, who may have little exposure to the film-makers' alleged intentions. This doesn't have to impede enjoyment; on the contrary it means that one can forge a personal, imaginative link with these irregularly designed, stimulatingly off-centre productions. Packed as they are with tangential relations and recalcitrant illogic, one is inclined anyway to give the filmmakers the benefit of the doubt, and assume that the dislocation is part of their effort to entertain us. Rather than taking them apart, the best response is to treat all the locations as parts of an *imaginary* geography. No matter if the scene shifts from American streets to lush apparently Mediterranean gardens, populated by Roman-nosed 'Americans' sweltering under the weight of flagrantly Italian interior design! Part of the thrill of these Fulci films is their elliptical construction.

For an American audience with a taste for distortions of the familiar, Fulci's cavalier use of clashing styles must be particularly bracing. They exude just enough Americana to make the subsequent deviations genuinely fantastical. Tobe Hooper, director of *The Texas Chain Saw Massacre*, whose vision of family life was as uncanny as it gets, endorsed the US video release of *The Beyond* with a hyperbolic quote.[6] Although Hooper's career in horror films fell into tragic disarray, his best work demonstrates a real grasp of the nightmare quality Fulci's horrors cultivate. *The Beyond*, with its American locations leading into a Roman studio Hell, must have impressed him for this reason, as well as perhaps reminding him of his own excellent, undervalued follow up to *Chain Saw*, *Death Trap* (1977).[7]

above:
Neville Brand gives his wildest performance (Wolfman Jack meets Charles Manson) as a psychopathic hotelier in Tobe Hooper's nightmarish *Death Trap*.

left:
These plebeian, tool-wielding Etruscan zombies are advancing on a villa full of decadent victims in Andrea Bianchi's *The Nights of Terror*.

Collaboration with Dardano Sacchetti

Eight of Fulci's fifty-four films were co-scripted with Dardano Sacchetti; from 1977's *The Psychic* to *Rome 2033 – The Fighter Centurions* in 1983. Sacchetti's influence on Fulci's career was almost entirely positive, with distinct evidence of his revitalizing perspective permeating the films of Fulci's commonly-regarded 'classic' period. Sadly, the collaboration was to end in acrimony and dispute over due credit. In this respect, Sacchetti's claim is strengthened by the immediate and lasting drop in quality that can be detected in the films Fulci directed after their split.

Sacchetti was born in Montenero di Bisaccia, Campobasso on 27 June 1944. He became secretary of the Bertrand Russell Peace Foundation in his early twenties, and his passage through college was marked by activism in the Rome students' movement. An early interest in film and theatre found expression in acting and writing; he worked on the magazines *Città futura* and *Cinema e film* and performed with the MKS theatre group. Despite the political upheavals felt throughout European youth culture in 1968, his interests followed a more 'classical' direction with a book of poems published in 1969. His real passion though was for the cinema, and two genres in particular appealed to him:*"I've always been fond of police and horror stories. I've been reading them since I was a kid; I used to go in the cemeteries during the night to give proof of my courage"*, he says. *"Italian cinema, when I started to work, was not interested in the horror field. In Italy the popular cinema almost always follows American or British trends: when I was a kid, there had been Bava and Freda's movies, which sort of cashed in on the Hammer productions".*

His big break into screen-writing came in 1971, when a friendship with Dario Argento, hot from the surprise international success of *The Bird with the Crystal Plumage*, blossomed into a creative collaboration on Argento's second film *The Cat O'Nine Tails*. Sacchetti is frank about who deserves the lion's share of this credit: *"We wrote the treatment for [*Il gatto*] which Dario transformed into one of sixty-five pages"*, he remarks.[8] Argento often seems to desire an escape from the post-Freudian motifs so apparent in his best work (*Deep Red*, *Tenebrae*), professing an admiration and espousal of the semi-mystic works of Carl Jung. In *The Cat O'Nine Tails* he seems to be striving to escape Freud in the direction of genetic pre-determination, which provides the lunatic pseudo-science upon which the film's implausible dynamics are built. It's unclear whether it was Sacchetti or Argento who initiated this, but Sacchetti's subsequent work would seem to have accepted the Freudian schemata, if and when psychoanalytical concepts play a part at all.

After *The Cat O'Nine Tails* came out, Sacchetti and co-scripter Luigi Collo had a brief but well-publicized row with the director, which caught the attention of Bruno Todini, then general manager of Dino De Laurentiis's film empire. Todini pointed out the fledgling writer, who was so publicly flying the coop, to horror maestro Mario Bava. In 1971 Bava approached Sacchetti with an offer to write his new film. It was to emerge as a triumph of Italian horror.

A Bay of Blood (the Italian title *Reazione a catena* translates as "Chain Reaction") was an essential Bava film, and one which was to have far reaching implications for the horror genre, inspiring as it did the American *Friday the 13th* series, and in turn the emergence of the 'horror franchise' syndrome. A 'Chain Reaction' indeed! The film won a prize at the Sitges festival on the year of its release, although it went the way of many Bava films, indifferently received in the cinemas, and failing to secure any respect for the seminal *auteur* until after his death. Immediately afterwards, Sacchetti worked on the script for Bava's *Shock*, although the film would not be made for another five years, by which point it had been augmented by three other writers (including Bava's son, Lamberto, soon to become a director himself). Its eventual release in 1977 marked the end of Bava's cinematic career.[9] *Shock* is a wonderful film, chilling and authentically terrifying at times, yet playful with its psychological references (a scene where a 'possessed' child has his crayon drawings 'analysed' by a psychiatrist *may* have been intended seriously – let's hope not, as instead it provides a hilarious pop simulation of analysis). Fraught with sinister atmosphere, dream logic and honest to goodness scares, it features Daria Nicolodi, the partner of Dario Argento for many years, in what is undoubtedly her best role. Although *Shock* was originally circulated in the UK as a double bill with Spaniard Vicente Aranda's *The Blood Spattered Bride* (1972), it is to Sacchetti's advantage that it reappeared on a double bill with *The Beyond*, when the latter hit our shores in 1981. Thanks to Sacchetti, there is a unity to the pairing which permeates the style of these thematically dissimilar but atmospherically congruent films. It would seem that Sacchetti was responsible for more than just the syphoning of dialogue into characters' mouths.[10]

above:
Daria Nicolodi suffers nightmares of confinement in the house of her dead junkie husband – *Shock.*

left:
Locandina for Mario Bava's *Shock.*

facing page, main picture:
Doctor McCabe (David Warbeck) discovers the Book of Eibon shrouded by cobwebs, in the burnt-out shell of 'Emily's house'... *The Beyond.*

facing page, inset:
Scriptwriter Dardano Sacchetti.

With his script for *Shock* completed but yet to be filmed, Sacchetti's next major encounter brought him into contact with Lucio Fulci. They first met in 1975, and soon set to work on a script together, creating a tale that would eventually emerge in 1977 as *Sette note in nero*, or *The Psychic*. Sacchetti explains: *"The story came from "Terapia mortale" by Vieri Razzini (now a well-known movie critic in Italian TV)... they wanted to make it more spectacular, so I worked with them and eventually we came to a different story. The movie became a story of the impossibility of going against Destiny: there's this woman who sees herself dead and tries to prevent it from actually happening. I still think it's maybe Lucio's masterpiece"*. So began a fruitful and prolific partnership. By all accounts the pair got

below:
Locandina for Dario Argento's *The Cat O'Nine Tails.*

above:
Theresa the medium is questioned by sceptical New York cops, in *City of the Living Dead.*

off to a harmonious start, although, as noted in Chapter Four, *The Psychic* did not meet with much acclaim or sympathetic response from audiences. It was over a year before they were able to work together again. During this period, Fulci was forced to earn money producing musical revues on Italian TV, and apart from his last western, the disastrous *Silver Saddle*, in 1978, he found himself without film work. Sacchetti was luckier, with a number of projects being filmed in 1977.

Then in 1979 came the zombie phenomenon: *"Things changed with the Italian success of Romero's* Zombi [Dawn of the Dead], *which pushed Italy's smaller producers towards horror"*, he notes. Collaborating, for personal and tax reasons, under his wife's name, Elisa Livia Briganti, he penned a treatment for a zombie story that both responded to the successful Romero film and established its own identity. "Zombi 2 *was a huge success in Italy and abroad. It made a lot of money in the USA and in Japan. The Japanese also used it in pirate productions: I once saw a Sony cassette, with fifteen minutes of the movie inserted, in an imitation Japanese zombie-movie!"*

Aware of the perennial criticisms levelled at the Italian exploitation scene (parasitical, mercenary), Sacchetti explains his attitude to the process good-humoredly: *"We have to thank American movies that give us something to eat!* [laughs]. *Obviously, it's easier for a producer to get money if he cashes in on the success of another film. So when they call you to make one of these movies, it's up to you to profit from the occasion to make something different and personal, or to choose to make a bad copy of the original; I always try to make something different. It's easier when you work with intelligent people: sometimes you write one way and then the movie comes out as a copy of the model, and then sometimes not. Take* Zombi 2, *which was based on Romero's* Dawn of the Dead, Zombi *in Italy. A producer decided to make a small horror film, although my inspiration came not from the Romero movie, but from the comic-strip hero Tex Willer. The idea was about someone dead, reanimated and remote-controlled by a crazy scientist through an electronic device put in the brain. My wife and I decided to return to the classic zombie tales, and we tried to use those clichés for a story which started as a mystery and became an adventure afterwards. So the zombie is the mystery murderer in the beginning, then it becomes an adventure; the zombie is like the Indian in the old westerns. It's just the bad guy, it's not, like in Romero, the dropout, the alien, the black, which rebels against society and destroys the supermarkets. The title was decided by the distributor!"*

The voracious wheeling and dealing of producer Fabrizio De Angelis made a substantial difference to Fulci and Sacchetti's fortunes in the industry.

right:
Hi-jinks in the props department? An early resurrection for this ghoul in *City of the Living Dead.*

His brash energy ensured the *Zombie Flesh-Eaters* project a sizeable slice of the market's attention, although the remunerative rewards were perhaps less to Sacchetti's benefit than they could have been. Sacchetti remains pragmatic about the cut-throat nature of the business however. Commenting on Fulvia Film, the De Angelis company responsible for many of the Fulci-Sacchetti titles, he insists: *"You can say anything against them: they exploited the horror genre as you would exploit a whore, but at least they got movies made! They were the 'August movies': since the big shots never come out before September 15th, these films could get a big theatre for an August week, and if things worked they would remain one whole month. Now the majors fill August with the left-overs of the American productions, those which they force you to buy if you want the good films, the big hits".* (August is often excruciatingly hot in Italy; many city-dwellers head for the hills and coasts, leaving the cinemas either closed – due to lack of air-conditioning – or half empty).

Next on the duo's list of achievements together was 1980's *City of the Living Dead*, which despite the big hit they'd scored the year before took some effort to get off the ground. At last Fulci was able to persuade production company Medusa to back the latest Sacchetti script, *Paura nella città dei morti viventi*. Sacchetti received a paltry four million lira, but this time Fulci was able to negotiate a rather more favourable slice of the cake for himself, emerging from the deal with around fifteen million. It was filmed in July and August 1980 in Savannah, Georgia, USA, with interiors added, as usual, at De Paolis Studios, Rome.

Surprisingly, Sacchetti expresses dissatisfaction with *City of the Living Dead*: *"One of our least successful films in as much as it had been thought out and filmed in desperation"*. Nonetheless, he maintains, *"From one point of view, the best results have come from Fulci, at least until he came to think that he was the only creator of his films"*. The degree of irregularity in *City*'s construction is explored more fully later, but however striking one finds the film's collapsing structure, its commercial achievement was again significant. The film enjoyed large audiences and worldwide distribution, as well as cementing Fulci's reputation as a purveyor of extreme physical horror.

The very same day that *City* made its debut in Roman cinemas Fulci was off again; *Black Cat* commenced photography in North-West London on the 11th August 1980 and ran through until late September, a surprisingly long shoot for what Fulci always called "a favour" directed for a producer friend. Sacchetti was not involved this time (the script, a casual adaptation of Edgar Allan Poe's story *The Black Cat*, was by Biagio Proietti). Having shot many scenes based around a wilful feline 'performer', Fulci was able to leave the complicated task of assembly in the capable hands of editor Vincenzo Tomassi (who did an excellent job). This allowed the hyperactive director to jump almost immediately into pre-production on yet another horror project.

Sacchetti's next assignment with Fulci, *The Beyond*, was to become the most celebrated of all their work together. In the summer of 1980 Fabrizio De Angelis again approached Sacchetti, impressed by the gory, money-spinning *City of the Living Dead*, and suggested that he and Fulci make a similar film for his Fulvia production company. *"At that time the young producer Fabrizio De Angelis sniffed the business and asked Lucio for a few films. We made four or five movies in about two years, one after another. Some were not such huge hits as* Zombi 2, *but all of them appeared in* Variety*'s top fifty"*, explains Sacchetti. After the struggle with Medusa to get backing for *City of the Living Dead*, the two men needed little coercion to work with De Angelis again. Sacchetti remembered a short treatment he'd written a couple of years earlier and then put aside; these few pages would provide the inspiration for *The Beyond*, a tale even more savage and poetic than *City*. De Angelis had very few stipulations about the content of the film he would bankroll – all he required to secure the deal was more of Fulci's extreme,

left:
Alternative Italian poster for *City of the Living Dead.*

below:
German admat for *City...*

bottom:
Sandra (Janet Agren) airs her tonsils as the living corpse of Emily (Antonella Interlenghi) grabs her.

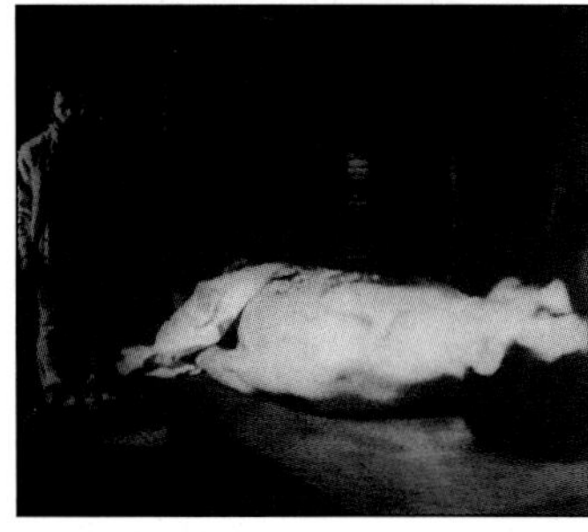

above:
Norman Boyle (Paolo Malco) discovers the awful truth in *The House by the Cemetery*.

right:
The Beyond; Catriona MacColl and Michele Mirabella with the seriously injured house painter (Larry Ray).

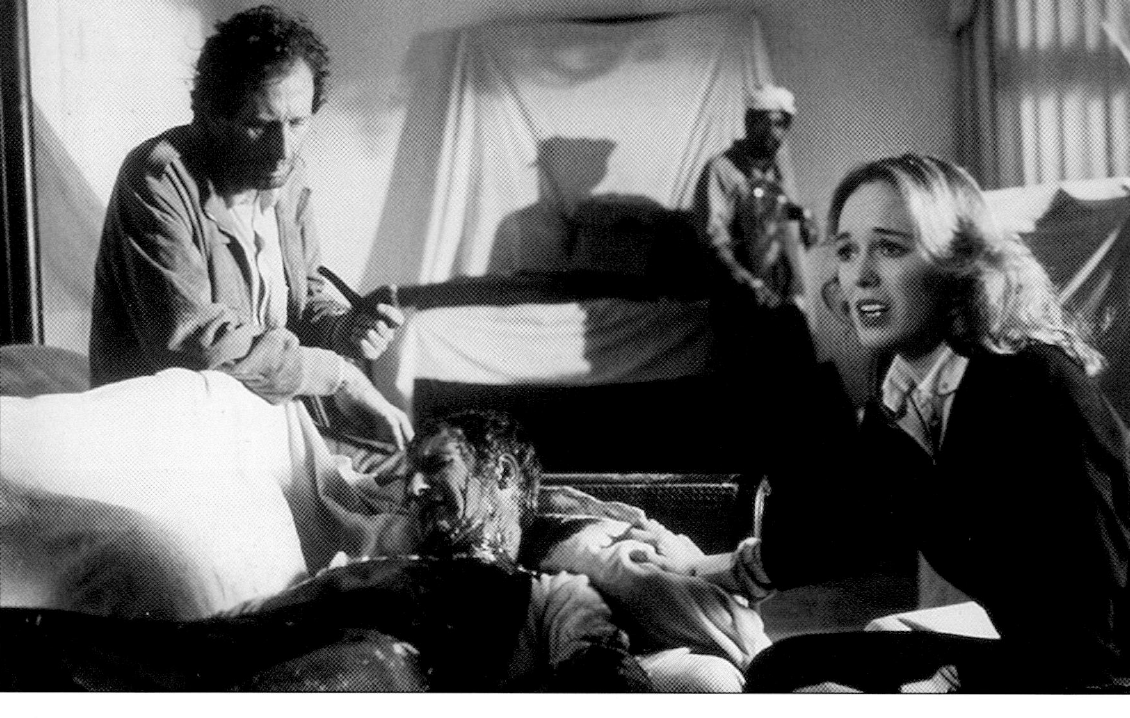

creative sadism... and some zombies. Sacchetti's story made no mention of zombies at first; but their presence was demanded by the German backers and so in they went. Although the film was not an out-and-out German co-production, a pre-sales deal was secured with German distributors, who were thus in a sufficiently powerful position to demand more of the same for their money.

The way in which these swiftly commissioned and rather hurriedly made films were financed is typical of the low-budget film industry of the seventies and eighties. The prevalent exploitation strategy was the 'pre-sale' – Sacchetti describes how De Angelis would work:*"They're made for foreign investors, because in Italy there's no market for them. Great Britain, Germany, Denmark, France, Japan, and even the USA are very hungry for strong horror movies, thrillers or adventures. The problem is the foreign market is tougher, there is greater competition; at MIFED, in the Cannes market, there are movies from everywhere in the world. So the producers go to the markets with a brochure, a title, a synopsis, saying: 'I've got this movie to sell'. Actually they sell the idea: when and if they find a buyer, they make him sign a contract promising to buy the movie for a certain amount of money. On the basis of this paper they are able to obtain the financing from the banks. They make the movie, sell it to the buyers and give back the money to the bank. So the budget of the movie depends upon the number of buyers and the amount they are willing to pay. (Fulvia) would go to MIFED with a couple of posters, ten lines of plot and a tentative title: when they found a buyer they would call me from Milano and say: 'Dardano, we've sold 'Watchacallit' – start writing now! You have six days, we're giving them the finished copy in three months!!"*

Sacchetti and co-scripter Giorgio Mariuzzo produced a script, based on Sacchetti's outline, that met the commercial requirements and also had the artistically-minded Fulci very excited. But financial limitations, as always, played a part in the subsequent mutation of the story. Several ideas the two had dreamed up were just too far out, too expensive for the production. Sacchetti was forced to re-write, virtually the night before location filming was due to begin, replacing scenes of a visionary (i.e. expensive) nature with even more gore than was already planned. Shooting eventually commenced on 20 October 1980, with Fulci forced by the ever-present budgetary restrictions to amend the script as he went.

The results were astounding, all the more so when the difficulties experienced in realising them are considered. The final cost of mounting this most beautiful of Fulci's horror stories was around 580 million lira (a mere $450,000, small change in Hollywood terms). Even George Romero, the Pittsburgh independent whose *Dawn of the Dead* was praised for its impressive achievement on a low budget, had over three times as much to play with for his zombie opus. Fulci and his technical crew – director of photography Sergio Salvati in particular – had performed a miracle.

Not that Fulci was one to rest on his laurels. *The Beyond* received its first public screening in Italy, on 29th April 1981, but by then the director had already completed principal photography on his next film, again from a Sacchetti script; a tale of childhood horror and spare-part surgery called 'Freudstein' in pre-production. The result was *The House by the Cemetery*, perhaps the most coherent storyline Sacchetti had given Fulci since *The Psychic*. It too was a financial success for De Angelis and Fulvia Film, and the turn-around this time was even faster – the film received its first screening on 14th August 1981, just four months after the crew had returned from the chilly New England locations. Indeed, Fulci shot another project co-written by Sacchetti the same month as *The House by the Cemetery*, flying to the Big Apple to venture the most controversial film of his career, *The New York Ripper* (known in its early stages as 'The Beauty Killer' – see Chapter Seven).

That any sort of style or accomplishment was visible in the results of such a hectic production schedule is astonishing. But eventually, as with all good scams, adverse pressure finally bore down on the show, changing the face of Italian independent production and squashing out the 'B-movie' practitioners who had so enterprisingly carved themselves a slice of the megalithic film industry pie. As fast as it had come, the horror boom of the early eighties faded in strength. *"In Italy, horror went on being considered as a 'B'-genre, so the market kept going down and down. The budgets became smaller and it became very difficult to compete with the expensive special effects of the Americans.*

below:
Emily suffers spontaneous bleeding after touching the warlock's painting in *The Beyond*.

bottom:
Janet Agren enjoys the glamour of a Lucio Fulci film shoot in this scene from *City of the Living Dead*.

Then in 1982 the Italian farce triumphed over everything else, and the horror market was closed".

The two men had just one further horror story to add to their joint credits in the genre, but sadly it emerged as something of a mess. *Manhattan Baby* commenced shooting on Manhattan island from 22 March 1982, and the resulting oddity was soaked in the fatigue that must have been stalking Fulci ever since he'd embarked on his frenzied Gothic journey, three furiously paced years ago. Arguments and disloyalties ate away at the producer-writer-director alliance, and the script itself seems to flag in its enthusiasm for the previous Gothic motifs (see review). An unwilling, resentful Fulci was forced by Fabrizio De Angelis to travel to Cairo, shooting an Egyptian prologue there that was not part of Sacchetti's script (presumably the producer thought this would serve both to remind audiences of the prologue to *The Exorcist* and attach the film to the less than vigorous coat-tails of recent Charlton Heston vehicle *The Awakening*). To further darken Fulci's glowering mood, the budget was slashed from 650 million to 450 million lira. It's perhaps understandable that he responded so enthusiastically to the overtures of a rival producer during the unhappy experience of filming *Manhattan Baby* (see Chapter Five). The film limped over the finish line to be exhibited in Rome on 12 August 1982, but no one was particularly happy with it; a breathtaking period of creativity had finally run out of steam.

"It was crazy, but sometimes you would manage to do a decent or even a good movie", Sacchetti reflects: *"It was a miracle if you think about the conditions that the fantasy cinema in Italy was made in. But then costs boomed: now America is less expensive than Italy for a movie troupe. The Italian product has lost its competitiveness and its economic convenience for the investors. Now they only do 'prestige' movies, auteur stuff. But the style is the same... I don't know if it's true, but they told me that Gianni Amelio's* Il ladro di bambini *originally finished with the kid shooting the carabiniere... but the ending wasn't shot because the producer had run out of money! And that's the movie that won the prize at Cannes..."*

Sacchetti has moved on since his collaboration with Fulci ended in 1983. His mood has changed from dismissive anger to a mellower, more casual position. There was a final bone of contention to deal with, when Fulci went on record in a French film magazine accusing Sacchetti of 'stealing a screenplay' from him. (In 1983 Sacchetti showed Fulci a script entitled 'Evil Comes Back' – *"a sequel in fantasy style to* Il postino suona sempre due volte*"* – Fulci loved it and was keen to direct. However, financial difficulties led to the project being shelved; until four years later, when *Demons* director Lamberto Bava used it for a Reteitalia TV thriller called *Per sempre* – 'Forever'. Fulci, who was having problems mounting new productions at the time, seems to have regarded this as a betrayal on Sacchetti's part, hence his unfairly exaggerated statements about a 'theft'.) Sacchetti meanwhile found Fulci's habit of attributing all the qualities of his successful films entirely to his own directorial prowess galling and dishonest. It was a familiar story in the collaborative hot-bed of film-making. The relationship between writers and directors is often fraught with ego-related tensions, and the thoughtless ease with which some critics append all credit to the director adds to a writer's resentment.

Sacchetti is naturally keen to take the credit for the offbeat plotting and avant-garde dismissal of conventional narrative in the films he wrote for the temperamental Fulci:*"Lucio's problem is that he's basically a logic man. He began as a "Giallista", so he gives great attention to the structures of the plot. Even if he's very cultured, he didn't update his culture. I'm a son of the comics, I love Moebius and Frazetta, Corto Maltese. Maltese never uses a neat plot, it's much more an atmosphere, less technical"*. Bearing in mind that the accrediting of inspiration between warring parties in the film business can be difficult, Sacchetti's next statement throws some doubt on the strict distinction he is trying to make between Fulci's straight-line professionalism and his own free-spirited inventiveness: *"To use the gore, [Fulci] wanted traditional logic connections: like* Paura nella città dei morti viventi *or* Lo squartatore di New York. *I like to go beyond rationality"*. Anyone who has witnessed the first of these two examples of 'rationality' and 'traditional logic connections' may consider even Sacchetti's division of the imaginative labour best taken with a pinch of salt! Despite his criticisms, though, Sacchetti remains willing to praise his late partner, stressing both the high quality of their collaborations and Fulci's undoubted professionalism.

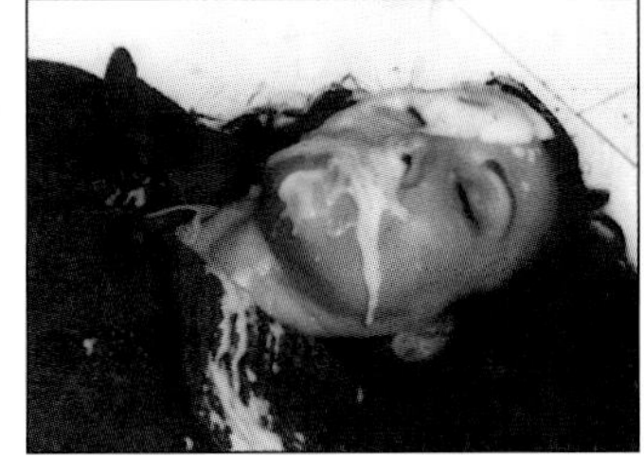

top: "Bob's always bringing home that trash!" – Catriona MacColl and Paolo Malco ponder their son's peculiarities in *The House by the Cemetery*;

above: Laura De Marchi dies horribly when a bottle of acid upturns itself onto her face in *The Beyond*;

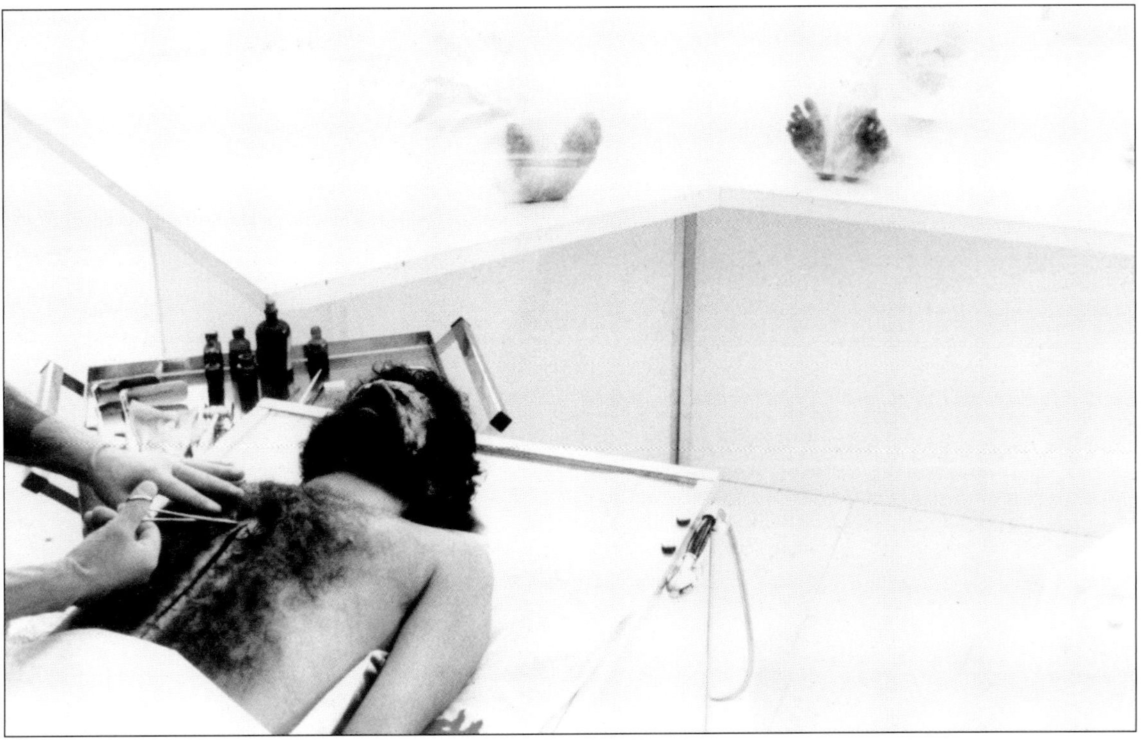

left: *The Beyond*; Joe the Plumber at the morgue.

below: Italian poster art for *Manhattan Baby*.

right:
The unfortunate child actor Giovanni Frezza, whose good performance in *The House by the Cemetery* is nearly ruined by one of Italian exploitation's worst dubbing performances.

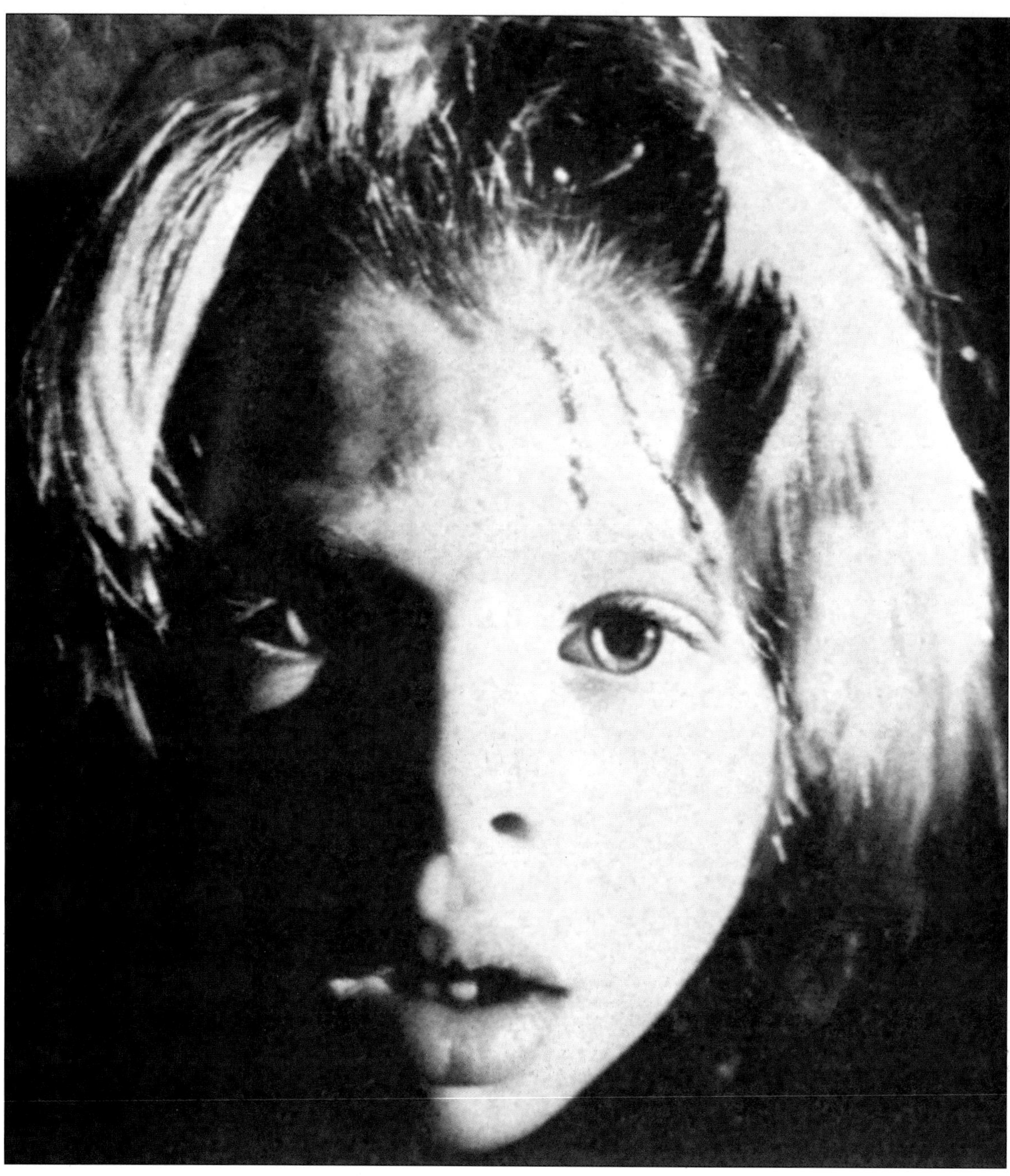

The trouble with dubbing

The pleasure of Fulci's Gothic films stems from two key factors – their visual style and the way in which they foreground violence. They propose a highly unusual set of relations to more conventional film practise. Whether this experience of difference is exhilarating or frustrating depends on how fixated the viewer is on the rites and manners of dominant cinema. Before looking at these differences, however, it is worth mentioning a factor which dogs audience response to nearly all Italian films; the habitual practise of sound dubbing.

Dubbing may in some cases determine a viewer's total resistance to the popular Italian cinema. It's a technique which attracts a great deal of flak from both audiences and cinema pundits alike, and demonstrates the hostility that a film in the commercial arena can always expect if it 'fails' to match the standards of 'realism' propagated by Hollywood.

The process originally came about because of technical limitations. The older film cameras were very noisy to run and even noisier to move. The fluidity of much Italian camerawork would have been impossible if the cameras had been 'blimped' (i.e. encased for sound-proofing) and thus made too heavy. Furthermore, the multi-national aspect of many Italian films/co-productions made dialogue recording on the set impractical. Last but by no means least, it is faster and therefore cheaper to shoot a film mute or with a guide-only soundtrack.

Dubbing can evoke an immediate sense of otherness, a detachment and sensory dislocation created by the mismatching of an actor's lips and the dubbed voice. We may also notice a discrepancy between the visual space represented and the acoustic properties of the dubbed sound. This otherness, of course, cannot simply be claimed as evidence of a deliberate challenge to Hollywood convention. Indeed, it's worth remembering that Italian audiences, whose appetite for cinema is voracious, are themselves completely adjusted to the process. Some may assume that dubbing is a practise used purely for non-Italian versions of Italian films, with the native language versions being recorded 'live on-set', as American films are assumed to be. In fact, Italian audiences accept without concern that their home-produced films are dubbed, by long-standing convention. Only in the 1980s did they start to experiment with 'direct sound'. This demonstrates that an audience's dislike of dubbing

left:
John Morghen (aka Giovanni Lombardo Radice) is murdered by intolerant Dunwich patriarch Venantino Venantini, in *City of the Living Dead.*

is merely a matter of resistance to unfamiliar modes, rather than an unchallengable rejection of a technical inferiority.

In fact, dubbing – or looping as the Americans call it – is common practice on many popular Hollywood films, especially those featuring noisy mechanical contrivances, explosions and special effects technology (that is, about three quarters of Hollywood's entire production). The difference is that it's far more common in America for an actor to dub his own lines. A lot of Italian films are sent to post-production studios to be dubbed by an in-house roster of voice artists (which has led some hard-core fans of Italian horror to champion not only the actors visible on screen but also a few of the recurrent 'voices' that recur in film after film). This, in combination with the generally lower budgets and hurried post-production schedules, results in a more easily detectable trace of the dubbing process.

It's this awareness of process which intrudes, unwelcomely for some, into the cosy flow of uninterrupted satisfaction. What the film theorist Laura Mulvey calls "the reinforcement of the ego" offered by pleasurable looking (and listening) is threatened by dubbing's aural 'stepping back' from the film's perceived unity. However, what mainstream audiences prefer is merely the *illusion* of realistic speech recording; verisimilitude, rather than actual fidelity to the 'moment' of performance. Such fidelity often creates another sort of alienation in the reluctant viewer, and is usually present only in the works of directors with a renegade sensibility. The films of American innovators like Paul Morrissey, John Cassavetes and Robert Altman often use 'documentary' sound recording. Ironically, this seems to offer a general audience 'too much' realism. Naturalistic dialogue recording allows for the occasional inaudibility of a voice, or the merging of multiple voices at the expense of individual clarity. It acknowledges the acoustics of particular spaces and environments as components rather than distortions of a sound, and treats the wider field of audibility (street sounds from open windows, etc) as part of a sought after presence within the representation. Such techniques of realism are hard for many audiences to accept, even though they make the dialogue presentation of mainstream films seem artificial and contrived in comparison.

Some directors achieve a warped and stylized disconnectedness in the dubbing of dialogue. In particular, one thinks of Dario Argento, who sets his actors' bland expressions grotesquely at odds with their weird vocal intonations. Fulci also plays creatively with strange inflections through this method, and I discuss his efforts in more detail in the reviews.

"Violence *is* Italian art"

The statement above was made by Lucio Fulci in an interview in the early 1980s, and he was then embroiled in making that statement truer than ever before. Before going on to look at the films he made at that time, it's worth pausing a moment to consider the extremely vexed question of violence and the morality – or otherwise – required in its representation.

To me, there is something strangely offensive about the idea of screen violence 'justified by the plot', or 'redeemed by context'. If all art is quite useless, as Oscar Wilde once stated, then all screen violence is gratuitous. There is only apologetic or unapologetic gratuitousness in the depiction of violence. Even then, we can be tricked into adopting a hierarchical system of judgement by prioritising the film of 'high moral seriousness' to the detriment of other, less didactic films. Take for instance Krzysztof Kieslowski's *A Short Film About Killing* (1988), which shows us the hideous human destruction that lies behind the grandiose phrase 'capital punishment'. The film's explicit horror includes such sights as excrement sliding from the hanged man's trouser leg into a tray, placed there especially for that purpose. The detail is disturbing as much for the acceptance it exposes as for the element of physical disgust. This is very provocative and skilful. Still, valuable though the film is as a challenge to society to reject such barbaric state crimes, it is best experienced in its details, devoid of the need for artistic 'justification'. To point to the film's political agenda and its moral seriousness as reason enough to 'allow' the detailed depiction of violence – as many critics tend to do – is to trade one serious point (Kieslowski's anger at the state's violence) for another; namely, the freedom of expression that all artists should have. Just because a filmmaker creates work where violence is the expression of a profound moral position doesn't mean that the absence of the latter precludes artistic engagement with the former.

below:
"I think I'm having a nervous breakdown" – psychiatrist Jerry (Carlo De Mejo) discovers his patient's paranoid fears are all too real in *City of the Living Dead.*

bottom:
The warlock artist, Schweik, is chain-whipped in the basement of The Seven Doors Hotel... *The Beyond.*

right:
The Beyond; Fulci finds yet another angle on his favourite imagery – here Martha (Veronica Lazar) experiences a sudden loss of stereoscopic resolution…

Cinematic violence can be the medium for a social, moral or political argument, but is never simply 'justified' by these aims.

The notion of there being a justified violence in art is one that rests on very shaky ground; ground that horror fans nonetheless often end up occupying, because we have allowed the terms of the argument to be defined by those who wish to censor artistic endeavor. We seem to find ourselves talking about this or that film's 'responsible' use of violence, there in the film to further a psychological or social 'point' that the 'responsible' film-maker is alleged to be making. As soon as we enter this discourse though, we are immediately on the defensive, with the onus upon us to 'justify' a sequence of film on criteria that many of us do not share. It would take more than Fulci's much-publicised remarks about the drill scene in *City of the Living Dead* (*"A cry I wanted to launch against a certain kind of fascism"*) to construct a 'defence' for the film on the grounds of high moral purpose.

The term 'gratuitous' carries such a negative weight of connotation (callous, thoughtless, slapdash, unjustified, exploitative, *wrong*), that often the unfortunate horror fan is reduced to playing down the genre's capacity to shock and outrage the senses, defensively labelling horror films 'harmless'; a qualifier that only means something because we have subliminally allowed ourselves to consider some of them 'harmful'! There are all sorts of ways in which fans are prevailed upon, by the surrounding discourses hostile to the genre, to assert that the very scenes they so like in these films don't really work, don't really disturb, or shock, or don't require us to take them seriously. Thus, fans might start to mutter about the unconvincing special effects, the bad dubbing, the cheesy music, the less than serious acting, or whatever. One is reminded of the way that newspapers manage to invest the word 'denies' with such contemptuous irony that it is virtually transformed into an admission of guilt.[11]

Any reference to the disposability or shoddiness of the spectacle is ingenuousness tricked into a double-talk disingenuousness. One may well feel that perhaps the special effects, in a scene taken to represent the full evil of the horror genre's vicious nature, fall short of the mark when it comes to 'shocking realism' – but pointing to this technical shortcoming, in response to a provocation to defend horror films, plays right into the hands of the enemy.

below:
Danish video cover for *City of the Living Dead.*

Illusion and Reality, Thought and Deed

What is needed in the debate about screen violence is a thorough recognition of the difference between thought and action. All screen violence is gratuitous, no matter how high-handed the contextual 'defence'. The only place for responsible violence is – dubiously – in the realm of *actions in the world*. As film-maker David Cronenberg asserts, an artist – and I believe that for these purposes we must include even the least imaginative purveyors of sensationalism – has no social responsibility to prove *in his work*. The realm of representation and the world of physical action are distinct provinces. This may seem a less than dialectical formulation, especially as much art has itself pursued a convoluted philosophical exploration of the *inter-relatedness* of art and reality. The difference is that artistic explorations of the theme take place, entirely – and entirely *appropriately* – at the level of discourse. Discourse is therefore the only conduit between the distinct regions of art and reality. If a film appears to indulge in sadistic displays and questionable representations of human behaviour, the appropriate response can be a dialectical one within discourse, but not 'without' it (in either sense of the word).

It is an absurd endeavour to attempt to establish thoughts as things. Art in all its forms requires that it be thought about (however casually) in order to exist. Without this, it would be nothing more than a philosophic tree falling in a forest with no one there to hear it. Cinematic images are *analagous* to projected thoughts in a technological lucid-dream-state, simultaneously ours and yet strangely other. The actual experience of watching is characterized by a willed suspension of disbelief (not just of the narrative's devices but of the whole technological simulation). Nonetheless, as we remember where we are and stand to leave the auditorium, this willed submission to the spectacle definitively ends. What we subsequently do with the recollections of what we have gazed at is the conscious responsibility of each individual.

"From words we passed to deeds", De Sade's libertines boast in *The 120 Days of Sodom*. Should an individual pass from images, through discourse on those images, and on into acts of physical violence in the real world, he has entered a domain of law; a law, let it be said, that need accept no

above:
Catriona MacColl's management agency placed this ad, revealing that *The House by the Cemetery*'s shooting title was *La casa di Freudstein.*

causal reference to consumed images in this person's defence. The *event* of cinema, or for that matter video, is consciously present to all viewers, before and after the 'dream state' of viewing. Physical actions in the real world take immediate and unmistakable precedence over the image the moment we stop watching; otherwise why stand up to leave the theatre, surely a blink/edit would take us where we wanted to go? No one thinks like that, and so there can be no credence given to absurd assertions that someone acted violently because they 'thought they were in a film', or because they were 'unable to distinguish illusion and reality' – to kidnap Woody Allen's gag, illusion is like death; try getting a good steak dinner there.

The only exceptions to this awareness are psychotics and schizophrenics, for whom *anything*, from the barking of a neighbour's dog ('The Son of Sam') to the lyrics of a Beatles song (Charles Manson), can appear as a directive to violent action. The use of such a minority, by advocates of draconian censorship, to curb the freedom of every individual is disgusting and dishonest. Typically, it's always someone else's pleasures that are responsible for social evils. Politicians who attack the cinema for directing impressionable minds to perform hideous violence are almost without fail utterly disinterested in film. Moral campaigners merely focus on the cinema because the real causes of violence in society are either too difficult to define or too close to home for them to want to address. As for the censors themselves; they have the oldest reason in the world to espouse the value of what they do – they get paid for it, whilst occupying a regal position towards a culture that they are impotent to contribute to.

It isn't that the law has no role to play in the realm of entertainment. Classification; the restriction of availability to minors; warning of extreme content in the packaging of entertainments; making the industry pay full attention to such restrictions; these are appropriate responses to social concern. Of course there are exceptions, some obvious, some less so. Advertising for instance, with its direct primary intention – unambiguously to provoke people into expenditure and consumption – entails social responsibilities; as does the filming of events taking place in the world that involve already defined criminal conduct like the use of force, real sexual violence etc. Child pornography is *ipso facto* subject to censure by law because it has a direct real-time contiguence with an already outlawed criminal activity. There is a place for the denial of a person's legal right to sell video recordings of a serious sex crime for profit. But the major crime is the sexual act, its recording is an admittedly disturbing secondary factor. Such real-life horrors are fittingly dealt with by criminal law. Again, it is with breathtaking cynicism that the advocates of censorship attempt to suggest that there is no way to prevent a flood of child pornography – without imposing censorship on *all films* of any kind! Vitally, no crime is truly committed before the cameras of a horror film. Social intolerance of aberrant human behaviour is a distinct and separate matter – let the law and the individual hammer that one out, and leave the projected worlds of the cinema, whose true relation is not to reality but to the imaginary and to thought itself, in the province of independent choice where they belong.

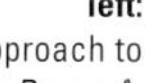

left:
The BBFC demonstrate their approach to horror film fans (*The Beyond*).

below:
Japanese video cover for *City of the Living Dead.*

above:
Variety reported excellent opening week ticket sales for screenings of *The Beyond* in America, where Aquarius Releasing put it out under the title *7 Doors of Death*.

right:
Veronica Lazar as Martha, luckless servant of The Beyond.

The birth of the Fulci cult

Fulci's success abroad in the early eighties was secured by some positive reviews, helping to spread word of his films to young audiences around the world. Fantastic cinema publications in Great Britain, France and America were responding, with more and more enthusiasm, to the 'spaghetti horror' genre. Audiences were developing for whom Fulci's new Italian Gothics were an exhilarating discovery. They enjoyed the way these unpredictable imports confounded expectation. A sense of connection built up as each new Fulci film appeared, giving his work an exciting air of territory unfolding. Many new fans of the Italian exploitation scene were captivated by the magical and grisly world these interlinked and consistently bizarre Fulci films presented. They possessed an outrageous rude health in the face of tiresome mainstream decorum, and delighted with lavish scenes of jaw-dropping violence. Startled film magazines seemed almost to apologize for covering them.

Early appreciation for the special piquancy of the field was generated first by *Starburst*'s Alan Jones in Great Britain, the staff of *L'Écran Fantastique* in France, and later the USA's teen-orientated *Fangoria*. The prominence they afforded the genre triggered new interest in earlier periods of Italian horror. Jones became instrumental in promoting Italian horror in Britain, penning auteurist love letters to Dario Argento, championing neglected maestro Mario Bava and offering praise to Fulci's work, modulated with a few pertinent reservations. Starting from a mixed review of *The Beyond* (*"the work of a talented but careless minor master"*) he warmed to the controversial director, until by the time *The House by the Cemetery* arrived he spoke as a committed champion: *"It really does seem that I am a minority in my growing admiration for Fulci. And as far as I am concerned, it is* still *growing. [*The House by the Cemetery*] builds to what is one of the best sustained climaxes of Gothique melodrama seen in recent memory." City of the Living Dead*, released here out of sequence with its fellows, also benefitted from Jones's increasing respect for Fulci's style: *"I've seen* City of the Living Dead *three times and wasn't bored for a moment on each occasion and that is surely what popular cinema is all about. [...] Shadowy, claustrophobic atmosphere full of menace is at the crux of this, and there is no doubt in my mind that Fulci is a master of such manipulation. It really does annoy me when dissenters call him a hack, because in each of the recent films he has made, there are so many individual worthwhile merits. At this stage in the game his talent cannot be called merely accidental"*. Fulci's profile in this country must have benefitted immensely from these articles, even though *Starburst*'s letters page saw squeamish malcontents attacking the very idea of advocating such grisly horrors.

In France, Fulci started to establish himself as a regular attraction at the Rex Cinema's annual festivals, where horror, fantastic, and science fiction films were premiered to an audience whose lively response, pro- or anti-, became a staple feature of the celebrations. Fulci was present on a number of occasions; to show *Zombie Flesh-Eaters*, *City of the Living Dead* and other older titles, such as his neglected 1977 thriller *The Psychic*.

right:
David Warbeck became an enthusiastic participant in fan-organised festivals in the UK and abroad.

The development of home video at the time was also vital. Fulci may never have enjoyed his precarious claim to *auteur*-style recognition, had it not been for the deluge of small video labels desperate for cheap films to add to a precipitously growing market. Of course, he made little immediate lucre from video releases – it's doubtful that the obscure UK video release of his crime story *The Smuggler*, for instance, ever made him a button – but as fans of Fulci's horror films, then appearing in the cinema, discovered bits and pieces of his diverse back catalogue on video, his reputation as a genre 'personality' was born.

Alan Jones may have spotted the special magic of Fulci's Gothics when they were released here but he was pretty much the exception. Geoff Andrew of London magazine *Time Out* spoke for the unhip community (i.e. able to appreciate 'low culture' forms like the horror film, but still shackled to fairly bourgeois notions of taste and accomplishment) when he called *The Beyond "a shamelessly artless horror story whose senseless story is merely an excuse for a poorly connected series of sadistic tableaux of torture and gore"*. Noting that *"suspense takes second place to repulsion"*, Andrew placed himself in a traditional position, viewing the modern horror film as some adjunct to Hitchcock's innovations in *Psycho*. By this measure, a horror movie is only validated if it applies itself to the techniques of suspense and psychological gamesmanship. Fulci's Gothic-styled horrors, like Bava's before them, show little interest in this tactical arrangement of plot information. His gialli proved that he was more than equipped to play such games when he felt it was suitable, but here in the realm of dreamlike disruption and fragmented violence, losing the plot was the desired effect.

The same critic waded a bit more daringly through the sludge of his own limited perceptions in a review of *City of the Living Dead*: *"It's laughably awful, though with its nonsensical 'plot', randomly constructed according to the illogic of fear, and its grotesque emphasis on physical mutability, fragmentation and decay, it could just conceivably be the sort of disreputable movie the Surrealists would have loved"*. So near and yet so far! Having grasped that something unusual was going on, the critic – with post-'Golden Turkey' 'bad movie' qualifiers dangling – promptly cringed back to the nearest 'high culture' reference point for protection; in this case the ever-reliable Surrealists. Padding their copy with nervous apologia in case of challenges from disgruntled 'real cinema' buffs, critics like these are the unwelcome gatecrashers at a feast for the genuinely adventurous viewer.

above:
Ticket for the UK press screening of *The Beyond*.

left:
Warbeck as Doctor McCabe (*The Beyond*).

left:
The leading players of *City of the Living Dead* are subjected to a storm of maggots.

Fulci – an actor's view

Among those best placed to describe Lucio Fulci as a man and as a director are the performers who have worked with him. Catriona MacColl is without doubt the actress most important to Fulci's success (having starred in *City of the Living Dead*, *The Beyond* and *The House by the Cemetery*), and the voluble, charming figure of the late David Warbeck (star of *The Black Cat* and *The Beyond*) was also a key witness to the on-set peccadilloes of this eccentric film-maker.

I interviewed both performers in 1995 and they were able to shed light on the collaborative aspect of the Italian film-making process, as well as the extent to which the actors are often left to make up their roles as the film is being shot. Warbeck explained the working relations on set:

"It's almost telepathic, unlike American or British unionized films. I can tell the cameraman how to fiddle with the lens, and I can tell when the lighting's not right. And they can equally tell me how to get the face right, how to catch the light there or whatever. And if they don't like something they tell me. As a consequence you all work together, and we're straining to get going each day and zap very fast through it. And an awful lot of people can't cope with that. Basically it's as crude as this: you turn up, you haven't seen the script, I'm lucky to get a script minutes before starting on the location! My agent will say 'Darling, darling, Lucio wants you to go off and make a film with him' and you say 'Oh great, what are the dates, where's the ticket – and I never know what the story's about, quite honestly, until I turn up. When I turn up I desperately try to get a script from the script girl, or someone. But as for 'Sit down let's discuss our intentions with this role – no! I do it in a matter of minutes. I whizz over it, say 'Right do you want anything particular?' – 'No darling just do it'. Invariably. It's time, you see. there's never any time for these things."

Under such circumstances the cast are free to devise – to some extent – their own approach to the roles. Warbeck:

"You always try to decorate what's there. If you've got a Janet and John script you have to really wrack your brains to make it interesting. The worst thing you can call a performance is boring; you can say anything else".

On the subject of Fulci's approach to briefing performers before shooting a film, Catriona MacColl says:

"I don't think he likes having to explain parts and psychological motivation to actors, he just likes one to get on with the job – which I do as a professional, and I think I'm quite good at it. I think he felt he could rely on me. To a degree I gave my own performance. If I had a question I wanted to ask I could ask him, but he was under a lot of pressure. The days were long and sometimes the effects were very difficult. I don't remember spending a lot of time discussing character with him, but that's OK. I've worked with a lot of directors in TV and in a way in film. It's quite surprising how few talk to actors. I went and met him – he's quite a character to meet first time round. But he made me laugh, far from being a tyrant like I'd been warned, although he does seem to find communication with his actresses quite difficult, I'm not sure why. He got on incredibly well with Paolo Malco (in House by the Cemetery*) who's a very cultured, intelligent and charming man, I don't think there was a problem there."*

Both Warbeck and MacColl felt that Fulci was gradually improving as the films of that hectic period rolled through the cameras. Warbeck recalled the difference between *Black Cat* and *The Beyond* as like:

"Chalk and cheese! Black Cat *was a mess. I couldn't see why that one wasn't coming together. Patrick Magee was a lovely guy to work with, although he was dying, sadly. I thought, with that face and that situation, that story – I'm just the... well, not the plonker but just the fairly boring policeman plodding around. It was a tricky film because Magee was so ill. It just didn't have the energy* The Beyond *had. Whereas* The Beyond *has absolute class to it. Fulci always had his own mad energy, but the problem – which you never really hear about – was all the backstage admin, money problems, problems with the producers and the cost of the labs, and 'Oh we can't shoot that bit tomorrow, you'll have to cancel it, re-write it, re-think it' – 'But we have to, it's crucial to the story' – 'No, there's no money... NO!' – and you're a week behind... and that's international. So much of this is done on a wing and a prayer."*

Catriona MacColl:

"I would have said that there was a natural evolution. The one I liked the least was the first one, City of the Living Dead*... although in Savannah, the fact that the mayor's daughter was working in the crew as second assistant or something opened a lot of doors for us. The mayor was hanging around the shoot and I guess he liked me because he presented me with the key to the city! I remember having a ball making* The Beyond*... The Italians are renowned for, well not ripping off exactly, but, you know... I remember having seen* The Shining *not long before that... I was saying to the guys who'd written it who were hanging around the set 'Oh you must have seen* The Shining*, yes?'. And they all went 'What is that?* The Shining*? Never heard of it' I thought 'Oh come on, pull the other one, you know?'*

Warbeck enjoyed his experience with the director, and delighted in recounting his eccentricities. He described Fulci's manner on set:

"When I was working with him, one of the things that would fascinate me is he would smoke this pipe of his upside down! So he was always on fire, all his jumpers were burned. Fulci had a wicked sense of humour, a very blunt mouth – 'Oh she's a bucket of shit', etc. So blunt. He's Roman you see, not Italian. Romans are like cockneys, they're proud of their heritage but they're not going to stand any of that smart stuff, you know, it's like 'Fuck 'em'. He gets cross and agitated when things haven't been arranged. He'd get very impatient if you couldn't keep up, like, we haven't got time to waste another three shots. Most of these films you only get two

below:
David and Catriona relax during the recording of their commentary for Grindhouse Releasing's edition of *The Beyond*. This session, in June 1997, was David's last recorded performance.

above:
Catriona MacColl is buried alive in one of *City of the Living Dead*'s most terrifying scenes.

takes, very rarely do you get three. The only fight I had on The Beyond *with Fulci, one of the few we've had, was when he wanted me to shoot someone point blank range in the face. I started off quietly saying 'I can't do that – even the blanks can maim, you know?' Knowing the mechanics he still said 'No I want you to do it'. I said, 'Change camera angles and it'll look like I'm doing it full on', but he wanted this one shot. Then it got very rowdy, I can speak enough Italian and I get very loud. I told the entire studio floor, for insurance reasons, what I was about to do... and shot him in the shoulder. I told the guy I was going to shoot him and he'd probably be hurt, or start bleeding. Fulci just didn't care. So I shot his shoulder – Bang! Blood, the whole lot... and Fulci said 'Didn't like that shot, do it again!'"*

This would seem to confirm the stories of Fulci's monstrous on-set furies but Warbeck went on to explain the wider picture:

"Actors and actresses in Italian films are generally regarded as less than prostitutes. They are regarded as scum. The bodies in The Beyond *at the end – they were literally street derelicts, winos. They brought them in from outside the studio, and the only way they could get them to lie down was to give them booze. But they were particularly derelict."*

I asked Catriona MacColl what she thought of the films now:

"I hadn't seen House by the Cemetery *for 15 years, and apart from the gory scenes which one expects, it's actually better made than my memory of it, the camera-work's actually quite good. It's wonderful-looking and very atmospheric. Someone asked me if I knew that the ones I was in were among the most popular. It's actually quite comforting that one's performance is appreciated, especially in something where perhaps originally no one cared too much about your performance, either on the set or when I got the job."*

The schedules for her three films were all much the same:

"I spent a lot of time in Italy, which I adore. City *was done in the spring, I think we were in the States in April or May. We would do two or three weeks in Georgia, or Boston or New Orleans, and then about six weeks in Rome. Fulci wasn't actually present at the dubbing, he had a dubbing director take care of it. On* City *he was still shooting when we dubbed it. On the whole I like to think that what I'd done on the set was right so I tried to match it – more often than not that's what I did. It always depends on the availability of the actors, but I seem to remember doing most of it on my own."*

She explains her absence from further Italian horrors thus:

"I did toy with the idea of moving to Rome. But then I thought if they wanted an English actress they'd probably come and look for me in England, so perhaps it would be better if I didn't go and live there. But then the bottom fell out of the industry, which had more to do with it."

As for the illogicality that makes the films so uniquely bizarre, MacColl speculates that much of it was accidental. Asked about the scene in *The House by the Cemetery* where she comes across Ann, the babysitter, cleaning up a giant bloodstain on the floor after a murder has been committed, she laughs:

"Yes, somehow very quickly there's no more blood on the floor. That's a rather kitsch aspect, although it does make it that bit more amusing. It wasn't deliberate – more to do with the speedy filming and perhaps not too much care with regards to the logic. Fulci's quite lucky I think with those mistakes – in that genre you can get away with more and it actually adds to the thing."

David Warbeck always maintained a positive opinion of Fulci, and as we approach the reviews for these special films, it's worth recalling his words:

"I said to Fulci – where do you get your ideas from, you must have a horrible mind, and horrible night-mares. He said, 'David, David, life is far worse than anything I can invent'. His life had been spent fighting – producers, distributors, censors, to get these ideas and images across... fighting, challenging... how far you can push violence, how far you can push storylines. He was always a wonderful rebel. And when you look at the sanitised nature of most American films, or popular films, it's a miracle he was able to do it at all."

right:
On the set of 'Schweik's painting' – *The Beyond.*

David Warbeck

aka David Mitchell: born 17th November 1941 in Christchurch, New Zealand; died 23rd July 1997 in London, UK

David Warbeck occupied a special position in the hearts of cult film devotees, both for his marvellous screen work and for his lively contribution to the film festival circuit. His particular skill, one which like most 'natural' performers he rendered invisible, was an ability to combine awareness of the magic he was creating with a complete absence of preciousness. He was a sophisticated man whose surprise at being suddenly lauded for films he'd made far from the glare of celebrity was tempered with a perpetual ability to meet the moment. Instead of emerging, blinking and bemused, into the arena of specialised cult attention, he responded as if for all the world he'd anticipated it. He played a game which to fans was seamless in its poise: David hadn't sought celebrity in the vulgar style of some performers, and he was sardonically aware of the narrow confines of this unexpected fame; yet he carried with him the savoir-faire of a man who took to praise like a cat to heat. His manner was that of cultivated ease.

I spent one uninterrupted afternoon in his company. We took a walk through the cemetery that provided Gothic peace (and extra market value) to his property nearby. It was a freezing winter's day, all too rare in London, with snow on the trees and underfoot. He showed me his glamorously eccentric Hampstead home and answered questions about his involvement with Lucio Fulci with a carefully calibrated blend of admiration and irony. Perhaps, as an actor, he was able to see Fulci, a man of rage and eccentricity, as a fellow performer – he certainly gave him his due respect whilst celebrating the most outrageous details of his personal behaviour. No doubt he knew all these difficult, thorny qualities were just Fulci's own way of coping with the need to perform as 'director'.

In Great Britain, actors are usually only prepared to enjoy themselves as part of the ongoing museum-ification of Britishness – whether it be as upper-middle class costume exhibits or gutter-snipe ordinary Joes on a slow train to Hollywood. David belonged to a different time, different class, different frame of mind. In many ways he was a truly European actor (Kiwi variety), beyond those tired old high-vs-low art arguments. Working for Sergio Leone or Lucio Fulci, for Russ Meyer or Antonio Margheriti, he simply revelled in the medium – if his art was accidental, it was a happy accident, and one he always had the good taste to celebrate.

Italian theatrical title
Paura nella città dei morti viventi

Translation
'Fear in the City of the Living Dead'

Italy

Alternative title
The Fear (shooting title)

International theatrical titles
City of the Living Dead (UK)
The Gates of Hell (USA)
Frayeurs (FR) 'Frights'
Miedo (SP) 'Fear'
Ein Zombie hing am Glockenseil (WG)
'A Zombie Hanging on the Bell-Rope'
Panico en la ciudad de los muertos vivientes (ARG) 'Panic in the City of the Living Dead'
Twilight of the Dead
(USA aborted theatrical)

Video/DVD titles
The City of the Living Dead (AUS)
Zombiernes by (NOR) 'Zombie City'
Entrada al infierno (SP)
'Entrance to Hell'
Pavor na cidade dos zumbis (BRZ)
'Fear in the City of Zombies'
Fear in the City of the Living Dead (LEB)
Ein Kadaver hing am Glockenseil (GER DVD) 'A Corpse Hanging on the Bell-Rope'
Zombik varosa (HUN DVD)
'Zombie City'

Production companies
National Cinematografica
Dania Film
Medusa Distribuzione

Theatrical distributors
Medusa Distribuzione (Italy)
Eagle Films (UK)
MPM (USA)

Theatrical running times
Italy 91m
UK 91m 51s (after cuts)
USA theatrical release (unrated) 93m

Video/DVD/Blu-ray running times (adjusted)
Anchor Bay DVD (USA) 92m 34s

Shooting period
July-August 1980

Censorship
Italian censor certificate 75480
issued 07 August 1980

Release information
Rome 22 August 1980
Foggia 04 September 1980
Bari 10 September 1980
UK (Birmingham, et al) 18 April 1982
UK (London) 07 May 1982
USA (Los Angeles, CA) 08 April 1983

City of the Living Dead

1980

Directed by Lucio Fulci for Dania Film / Medusa Distribuzione / National Cinematografica. producer: Mino Loy. executive producer in the U.S: Robert Warner. story & screenplay: Lucio Fulci & Dardano Sacchetti. director of photography: Sergio Salvati. music: Fabio Frizzi; published by Flipper – NC. editor: Vincenzo Tomassi. set designer & costumes: Massimo Antonello Geleng. production manager: Giovanni Masini. unit manager: Gianfranco Coduti. assistant director: Roberto Giandalia. continuity: Rita Agostini & Donatella Botti. stunt coordinator: Nazzareno Cardinali. cameraman: Roberto Forges Davanzati. assistant cameraman: Maurizio Lucchini. key grip: Giancarlo Serravalli. chief electrician: Roberto Belli. make-up: Franco Rufini. hairstyles: Luciano Vito. special effects: Gino De Rossi. props: Rodolfo Ruzza. assistant costumes: Luciana Morosetti. assistant make-up: Rosario Prestopino. assistant set designer: Ovidio Taito. set dressing: Giacomo Calò Carducci. production secretary: Franco Galizi. assistant production secretary: Alfredo Fornacini. stills: Garibaldi Schwarze. assistant editors: Pietro Tomassi & Armando Pace. sound engineer: Ugo Celani. boom: Eros Giustini. sound effects: Studio Sound. sound studios: N.C. mixage: Bruno Moreal. set furnishings: Rancati – Cimino. colour by LV – Luciano Vittori. filmed in Savannah, Georgia (USA) with interiors at Incir – De Paolis Studios (Rome).

Cast: Christopher George (Peter Bell). Catriona MacColl [as 'Katriona MacColl'] (Mary Woodhouse). Carlo De Mejo (Dr. Jerry Hill). Janet Agren (Sandra). Antonella Interlenghi (Emily Robbins). Giovanni Lombardo Radice (Bob). Daniela Doria (Rosie Kelvin). Fabrizio Jovine (Father William Thomas). Luca Venantini [as 'Luca Paisner'] (John-John Robbins). Michele Soavi (Tommy Fisher). Venantino Venantini (Mr. Ross). Enzo D'Ausilio (Sheriff Russell's deputy). Adelaide Aste (Theresa, a mystic). Luciano Rossi (blond policeman in Theresa's apartment). Robert Sampson (Sheriff Russell). *Uncredited:* Lucio Fulci (Dr. Joe Thompson). Michael Gaunt (Gravedigger). Perry Pirkanen (Blond Gravedigger). James Sampson (James McLuhan, black séance member). Martin Sorrentino (Sgt. Clay). Robert E. Warner (policeman outside apartment building).

Synopsis: New York. During a séance, Mary Woodhouse is pronounced dead after seeing a vision of a priest, Father Thomas, hanging himself in the graveyard of a town called Dunwich. Peter Bell, a journalist, visits Mary's burial site on the day of her internment. He hears screams from inside the casket and saves Mary from premature burial. Theresa, a mystic, warns Peter and Mary that the priest's suicide will open a door through which the dead can invade the world, commencing on All Saints' Day, just a few days away ... In Dunwich, strange events have been occurring. The intolerant Mr. Ross is inclined to blame Bob, a backward local boy. Jerry, a psychiatrist, is with a patient, Sandra, when his girlfriend Emily arrives to tells him she's going to meet Bob. They rendezvous at a disused garage, but unearthly groans scare Bob away. Emily is left alone to face the evil spirit of Father Thomas. A young couple making out in the vicinity also see the ghostly priest. They suffer a grisly fate, and Emily too is found dead. Meanwhile, Mary and Peter head for Dunwich. Bob sees Father Thomas hanging in a derelict house; a mortician is bitten by a female cadaver while trying to steal her jewellery; the decaying Emily pays a nocturnal visit to her little brother John-John; and a corpse appears on Sandra's kitchen floor. Sandra calls Jerry for help but the body disappears as mysteriously as it appeared. Mr. Ross catches Bob fraternising with his daughter and kills the boy with a drill. Mary and Peter arrive in Dunwich and meet Jerry and Sandra. At Jerry's office a sudden violent storm showers them with maggots. Jerry receives a distressing call from John-John who says that Emily has returned from the grave and killed his parents. The four rush over to the Robbins house and find the boy's story is true. Sandra tries to take the boy to her apartment but the zombie/ghost of Emily kills her. At the local bar, Mr. Ross, his friend Mike, and the barman are killed by marauding ghouls. Mary, Peter and Jerry head back to the graveyard as All Saints' Day begins. They descend into Father Thomas's family tomb, discovering an underground grotto of cobwebbed putrescence. Sandra reappears as a zombie, and kills Peter. Mary and Jerry confront Father Thomas. Before his evil gaze can destroy Mary, Jerry disembowels him with a rotting wooden cross. The evil priest and his massing zombies burst into flames and turn to dust. Mary and Jerry emerge from the tomb to see John-John running towards them, until the film ends as it began – on Mary's scream...

About the production: Compared to the other Fulci films of the period, *City of the Living Dead* received minimal pre-release fanfare. It was first announced in *Variety* on 9 April 1980 as 'The Fear' starring Christopher George. A few days later a follow-up article asserted that Stateside shooting would take place for four weeks in Atlanta, Georgia, before moving to Rome. Two days after that, came news that the US location had been changed to Savannah, Georgia. A *Variety* 'in production' listing appeared on July 1980, and that was essentially it.

The producer was initially announced as Mino Loy of National Cinematografica, and sure enough *City of the Living Dead* was eventually released as a co-production between National Cinematografica, Dania Film (a company run by Luciano Martino) and Medusa Distribuzione (a long established production and distribution house run by partners Felice Colaiacomo and Franco Poccioni). Oddly, however, no actual producer is credited on the film. Italian and English-language prints list Giovanni Masini as 'direttore di produzione' or 'in charge of production', his name appearing immediately before Fulci's directorial credit. This has led to various reference works erroneously crediting Masini as *producer* of the film (including, it must be admitted, the first edition of this book). In fact Masini's true role on *City of the Living Dead* (as it was on numerous other films, mainly for Ruggero Deodato) was that of production manager or production supervisor. These are hands-on jobs involving such tasks as co-ordinating preliminary shooting schedules, overseeing locations, completing the necessary arrangements with local authorities, and coordinating transportation of cast and crew. When it comes to the genuine producer on the film, there is a puzzling credit vaccum on all available prints. One could suggest the heads of the three co-production companies, Mino Loy (National), Luciano Martino (Dania), plus Felice Colaiacomo and Franco Poccioni (Medusa), although they would normally be considered executive producers. Since Loy was the first to be mentioned in *Variety* in relation to the film he would seem the most likely candidate for the credit.

Review: *City of the Living Dead* consolidates the brand of oozing pustulent horror that became the trademark of Fulci's work in the early eighties, whilst also extending beyond the visceral towards a distinctive brand of dream-like irrationality. The violence this time is even more grotesque and unlikely than the mayhem of *Zombie Flesh-Eaters* – at least there it was chiefly contained within the prescribed behaviour of its munching zombies. Here the best scenes are unrestrained by either taste or plausibility. Another sacrifice to Fulci's increased confidence is the notion of an establishing plot. In *Zombie Flesh-Eaters*, the process of getting to the island of Matul grounded the film, albeit shakily, in familiar terms of reference. *City of the Living Dead*, on the other hand, propels us straight away into humid atmospheres and mysterious occurrences, and in place of credible narrative we are submersed in the wanton details of illogic.

By conventional standards a jarringly arrhythmic film, *City*... upstages its simple 'race against time' plot with a welter of strangeness. Co-writer Dardano Sacchetti says that it was a rushed production, and lead actress Catriona MacColl agrees, indicating that shooting was hurried and uncoordinated. It is important, though, not to ground the film in these prosaic background details. Events are rendered discontinuous by tangible, on-screen methods: outrageous set-pieces foregrounding Franco Ruffini's gore prosthetics, perversely detailed cameo roles, cool flourishes of camera technique, and some striking art design; all of which suggest that Fulci, Sacchetti and cinematographer Sergio Salvati were applying lessons learned from the works of Mario Bava and Dario Argento.

Unlike others who have tried to emulate these formidable directors (Antonio Bido for example), Fulci grasped something very important; if narrative is to be de-emphasized in the horror genre, then the texture of even the most prosaic encounter should contain a thread of the bizarre and mysterious. Usually, the genre's thrills have to supercede each other in intensity and the story must advance with strong forward motion; this is recognised in the often-used analogy of the 'rollercoaster' of horror. The narrative 'motor' in most horror films is crude but very important – change emphasis from cumulative to floating or fragmented horror and you risk losing the audience. But if you suffuse the *mise-en-scène* with weird, eye-catching detail, and inflate the actual scenes of horror to grotesque proportions, there is room for narrative experiment. The film's *surfaces* can synthesize a continuous sense of form. In this respect, with regard to the narrative structure and unusual editing patterns, Fulci and Sacchetti were treading rare ground for the genre, and it is this aspect of the production which makes it especially compelling.

Conventional wisdom has it that "a narrative is a chain of events in cause-effect relationship occurring in time and space".[12] Fulci's Gothic films – *City of the Living Dead*, *The Beyond* and *The House by the Cemetery* – all use the supernatural as a means to subvert cause and effect, leading to situations where the very structures of the films seem to be under attack from the stories' otherworldly agents. It is interesting to compare them to *The Exorcist* (William Friedkin, 1973), Hollywood's most celebrated attempt at supernatural horror. Friedkin's film is doggedly stable in its structure – consider for instance the fixing of the demonic possession to Regan's bedroom – and for many viewers expecting to be assaulted with the film's notorious scenes of horror, the tale can seem slow and pedantic. It's over an hour before we become acquainted with the demon, and even then its purpose in turning a child into a gargoyle vision of sexuality is performative more than combative. The film allows us to visit her bedroom, ostensibly as if the demon were holding court. Actually it feels more as if we are being granted entry to a carnival tent freak show. It becomes hard to credit the demon's supposedly awesome power when it is so monotonously fixed in the one location. Of course, the film was a hit on such a grand scale partly

above:
Spanish and British video covers.

opposite, main picture:
Carlo De Mejo and Catriona MacColl explore the catacombs beneath Dunwich cemetery.

below:
Emily (Antonella Interlenghi) returns from the grave to haunt her little brother.

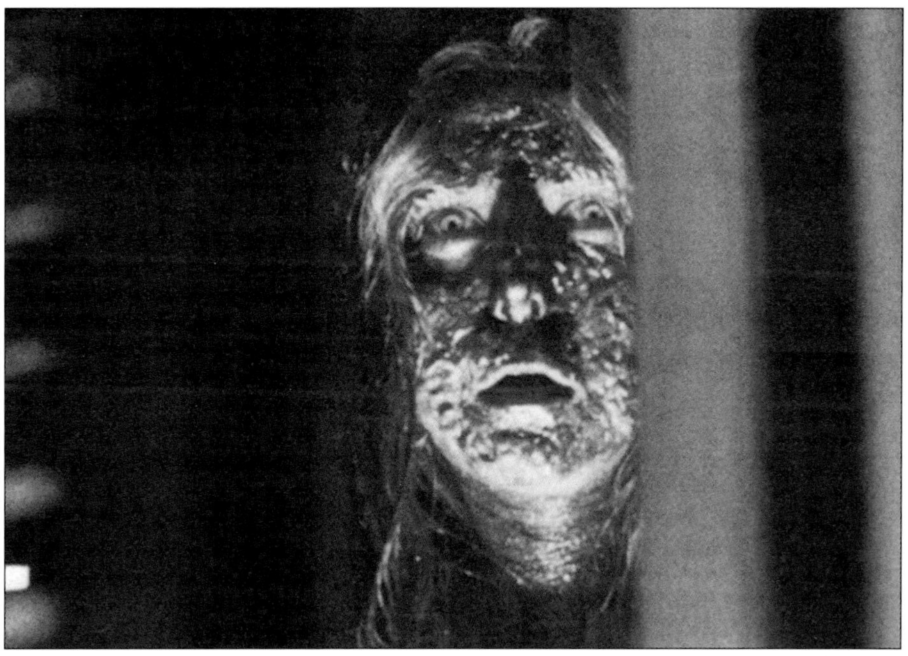

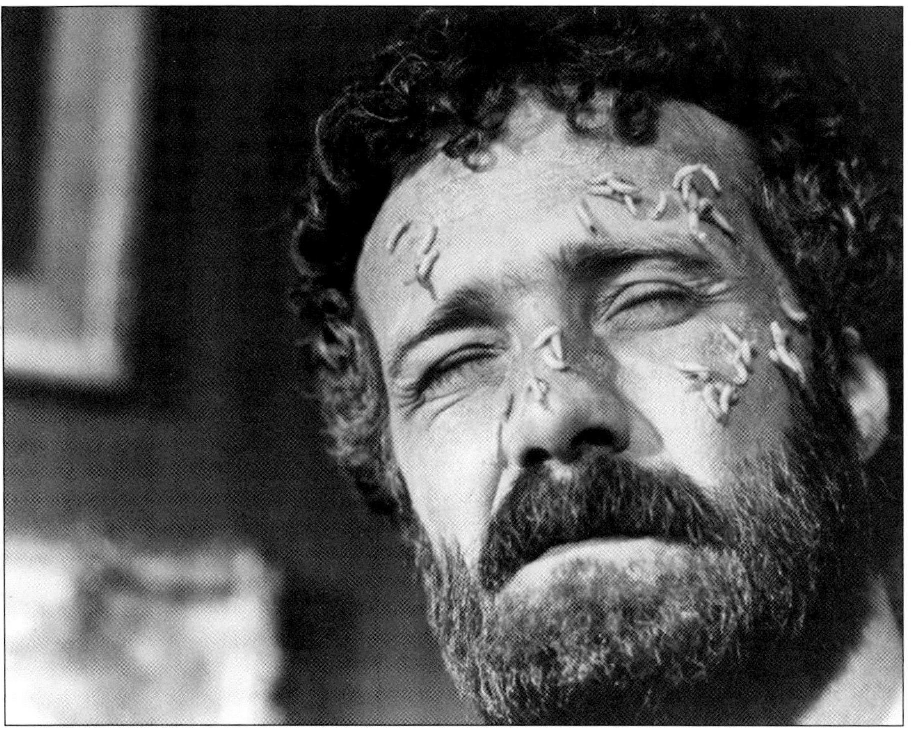

above:
Carlo De Mejo in a scene guaranteed to sour relations between director and cast.

below:
Evil Father Thomas (Fabrizio Jovine) hangs himself, thus opening the Gates of Hell.

bottom:
German admat.

bottom right:
Catriona MacColl, Carlo De Mejo and Christopher George enter the catacombs through Father Thomas's tomb.

because it brought the reassuringly solid values of straightforward storytelling to bear on the subject. No matter how much Pazuzu snarls and vomits, the demon is safely trapped, not so much by the framework of Christian religion – which is risibly elaborated in the film – but by the house; and even more so by the sensible, four-square plot structure itself. No chaos escapes from the events being described and into the actual texture of the film. This leaves it a deeply conservative work.

City does not pay off in the limited ambit of conventional narrative; mounting terror is not its objective. Fulci said that he wanted to make *"a nightmare film where horror is ubiquitous, even in apparently innocuous forms"*. This he achieves admirably with Sacchetti's script as the basis, and the supernatural manifestations that proliferate as All Saints' Day approaches are made all the more disturbing by the strangely shattered storyline. There *is* a linear thread to be found running through the story – Mary and Peter's attempts to reach the village of Dunwich, seen by Mary in her vision – but the degree of digression and the absence of coherently mounting tension subvert it. The effect is akin, in retrospect, to that of a collage. Our recollection of the story is characterized by the jostling of individual scenes, all fraught with weird tension and unease, some bursting into outright horror.

Fulci's way-out style steers the time-honoured parallel montage technique off into the beyond. I have personally seen this film at least thirty times, and I'm still not certain I could detail the succession of events accurately throughout. Some narrative lines are broken several times, returned to and explored until their (generally gory) conclusion: e.g. the story of Bob the young misfit, the inhabitants of the bar-room: others aren't really 'lines' at all but self-contained set-pieces, like the weird medium, corrupt mortician and unfortunate necking couple. Characters are introduced, subjected to strange events and then left in a limbo. Despite the 'investigative' thread of the two leads, the overall dynamic is discontinuous, not progressive, fragmentary instead of explicatory.

City of the Living Dead is saturated with technical exaggeration, teeming with oddball performances and high on its own outrageous contrivances. Elegant cross-fades and superimpositions add beauty, as do a handful of judicious, painterly details, like the petal seen dropping silently from a rose held by the catatonic Mary in her coffin. All these factors coalesce, and the film survives its thin story thanks to the eccentricity of its detail. The result, a pleasing paradox, is located in an overlapping zone between

spasmodic disruption and smooth languourous gloom. Even when the plot is ragged and the psychology rudimentary, we are overwhelmed by an eerie gracefulness amidst the carnage. Fabio Frizzi's slow, piano-based score is a vital factor here. Having set up the brooding atmosphere through sustained piano chords, the music supports the film's paradoxes by turning warm and serene for the undead's crusty perambulations. There is also an air of curdling sensuality in the flanged guitar music of some sequences, which reinforces a key component of Fulci's sensibility – the slide from sexual pleasure into disgust, and vice-versa.

According to Fulci, fear is *City*'s principle theme, but whilst a morbid dread permeates Fulci's work, it is physical disgust that drives his *Paura*. This broken *City* is a seething carnival; of vomit, worms, entrails, dead babies, squished brains and decaying flesh. Women spew up their intestines, eyes stream with blood, rats eat brains from splintered skull cavities; and in one knowingly gross moment a handful of worm-infested gloop is squelched (via a victim's point of view shot) into the audience's face. Fulci's Gothic horrors exhibit a definite aspect of corporeal revulsion: with mortality as a concept, with decay and deformity, with dysfunctionality in sexuality, with procreation and birth-process, and with death as a hideous fact.

The zombies, when they appear, are psychedelic and dishevelled, messy Jackson Pollock-faced entities possessed of both ghostly and ghoulish skills. Fulci has them brazenly appear and disappear in the wink of a frame-edit, only to grab fistfuls of hair, skull and bloody brains in defiantly physical style. They are ultimately show-cased in a beautifully designed cavern, located deep in the crumbling bowels of a cemetery.

Peppering this gruesome mulch are a variety of weird minor characters. A wild-eyed medium, who comes on like an emaciated Bette Midler and tilts the action immediately into the purple environs of parody; a pair of porn-obsessed gravediggers who whistle obtuse melodies whilst exhuming ancient skeletons, read dirty magazines and discuss the "hot lunches" depicted within (but assume a mechanical propriety when journalist Peter Bell asks to see inside the grave); a sleazy magpie mortician who pays dearly for his wandering fingers; and a lachrymose elderly couple whose unfortunate son is plagued by supernatural visitations from his dead sister. Most famously, a flinching misfit known as 'Bob' experiences miserable hallucinations before having his luckless brain skewered on a garage drilling lathe. Just about the only minor character not to exhibit bizarre character traits is a bland parish vicar who gives Mary and Peter directions to Dunwich. His only tic is an unaccountable complacency when pronouncing the route *"blocked – by a landslide – there you'll find Dunwich"*. One small flourish (he crosses himself after expressing concern about the couple's motives for seeking Dunwich) is the only distinguishing feature he is granted, along with his modern specs. The suggestion is that he is some kind of spiritually inadequate trendy vicar, aware that he's facilitating a descent into Hell but unequipped to intervene for Good.

Mary and Peter's journey by car to Dunwich is the closest thing to a structuring narrative the film has and even that is subverted at times. One of the most priceless moments in *City* comes when Mary pulls up en route to the 'cursed city' – and insists on finding somewhere for a bite to eat. Peter is surprised; after all, it's supposed to be of the utmost urgency to find Dunwich before the gates of Hell are opened.

Mary: "Oh, not now, do you mind?"
Peter: "You're the one who dragged me out here in the armpit of the world, chasing your *galloping* cadavers!"

I wish they *had* gone for that bite to eat, and taken time out to expand on their camp wit. Lurking off the slip road of their journey is another film, one

main picture:
Daniela Doria vomits her guts whilst boyfriend Michele Soavi retches, in one of Fulci's most extravagantly repulsive scenes.

middle:
Bob (John Morghen), lonely misfit in a doomed City...

above:
De Mejo and MacColl confront Father Thomas in his lair.

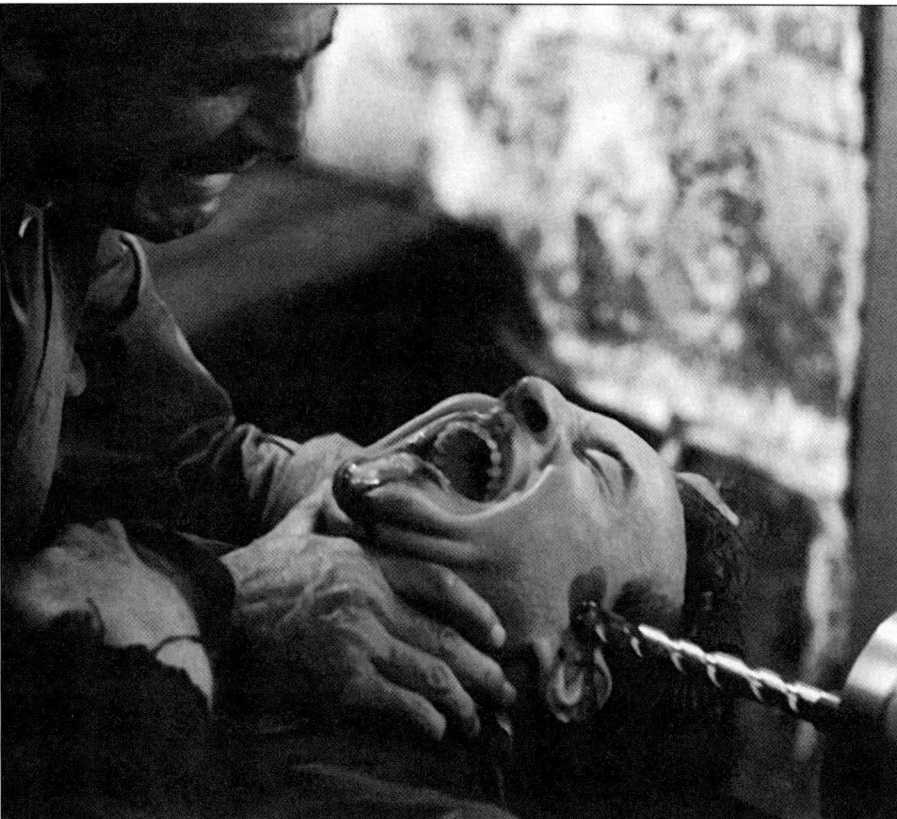

above:
Venantino Venantini and John Morghen enact Fulci's take on generational conflict.

below:
Fire down below – zombies burst into flames in the subterranean caverns.

bottom:
Emily (Antonella Interlenghi) is embalmed by a sinister mortician in *City of the Living Dead.*

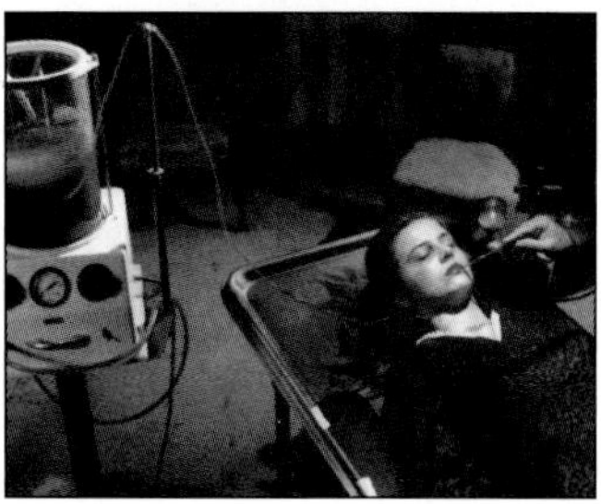

perhaps more character-based. This sensation is due entirely to the lead performers, who bring good humour to the film without sullying the sweaty, soily, wormy atmosphere. MacColl lends this quality to all of her Fulci films; her presence in all three is instrumental, and leavens the otherwise gleeful wallowing in violence. Although *City* is dark in theme and imagery, there's a psychedelic airiness around the edges that stops it from being a downer. No one could exactly call it a light-hearted romp; but neither would the informed horror fan bracket *City* with the harsher strain of Italian horror flick, exemplified by such rough rides as Ruggero Deodato's *House on the Edge of the Park* and *Cannibal Holocaust*... or Fulci's *The New York Ripper*.

The town of Dunwich is a triumph of atmosphere. Indeed, the scenes in which we see Dunwich are so successful it's a shame it wasn't more central to the action. The actual location of Savannah, Georgia, perhaps appealed to the lapsed Catholic in Fulci – it had once been the home of staunch Catholic Flannery O'Connor, writer of Southern Gothic dramas *Wise Blood* and *The Violent Bear It Away*, whose firm belief did nothing to dilute her caustic attacks on Christian hypocrisy (a subject close to Fulci's heart in earlier films such as *Beatrice Cenci* and *The Eroticist*). This seems especially likely given that the film concerns itself with an evil clergyman. Certain other aspects reveal Dardano Sacchetti's scrutiny of contemporary American horror films in the development of his script. One place that appears repeatedly is a dusty, wood-slatted bar, reassuringly normal inside but located inexplicably in the middle of nowhere. It acts as a barometer of encroaching supernatural phenomena, and the strange weather that envelops it – thick fog in broad daylight, a howling wind – soon invades its cosy bar-room rationality; a breeze-block wall cracks and a tendril of mist drifts ominously in. The barman's defiantly prosaic response, *"Damn building, new construction..."*, humorously suggests the lengths that people will go to shore up rational perceptions in the face of the inexplicable. Although tangentially reminiscent of Stephen King's novella *The Mist*, it more credibly recalls John Carpenter's excellent and under-rated *The Fog* (1979) – in which another small town is troubled by an ever-increasing spectral threat in the twenty four hours leading up to a significant date. (In Carpenter's film it is the anniversary of a shipwreck that offers the dead the opportunity to rise and take vengeance on the living.)

Another American independent release that Sacchetti may have drawn inspiration from is Don Coscarelli's *Phantasm* (1979). This marvellous and unusual film, packed with weird ideas and often defiantly incoherent, is also built around a small town whose geography is fragmented, partial and mysterious. It shares with *City of the Living Dead* a simultaneously morbid and colourfully deranged approach to its violence (as well as another strangely isolated bar). Central to the action is a rambling graveyard and spectacular mortuary/funeral home, whilst the appearance and disappearance of the recently dead ruptures logic and allows the narrative to digress in bizarre ellipses. This is all the more surprising and stimulating as *Phantasm*, despite Coscarelli's Libyan roots, is an American film. Episodic, arrhythmic, willing to sacrifice credibility for an extraordinary image – such qualities we've discussed in relation to Fulci are so rarely present in American horrors. Coscarelli's film provides a missing trans-cultural link.

Fulci was ever the tormented Catholic. He once claimed to a *L'Écran Fantastique* journalist: *"I am happier than somebody like Buñuel who says he is looking for God. I have found him in others' misery, and my torment is greater [...] for I have realized that God is a God of suffering. I envy atheists; they don't have all these difficulties."*

Theological matters are particularly prominent in *City of the Living Dead*. The film opens with a priest, Father Thomas, killing himself. For Christians, the notion of man's importance to God provides a dominant reality principle, with life on earth succeeded by eternal life with God. This lends value to living, but at the price of considering it a gift from above. According to Christians, original sin separates Man from The Almighty, but through faith in His mercy will come an eventual reconciliation. Life is thus to be valued because it offers the opportunity of coming to Him. Death, meanwhile, is subject to the Will of God and its apparent arbitrariness, its indifference to the wishes and feelings of the living, is characterized as part of a grand design, the overall sense of which is privileged only to Him.

Yet in suicide, a man takes control of this supposedly divine process – Christians preach that no believer must hasten his own demise unless he wishes to forfeit everything, to throw his eternal soul to damnation. As we've seen, cause-and-effect narrative is under threat in *City*, but the story presents the suicide of Father Thomas as the decisive event that precipitates the malevolence. As such, he assumes considerable importance.

In questioning the name of the priest we might recall Thomas the Doubter in New Testament lore, who required physical proof of the Resurrection. (Was Christ the first zombie or does that honour go to Lazarus?) Christ is said to have placed Thomas's finger in the wounds of his (undead) body to allay the disciple's doubts. The story seems more interested in presenting an image of Christ's feminine quality, and is perhaps an aspect of Christ's hermaphroditic appeal. (See Larry Cohen's excellent *God Told Me To* for an illustration of this.)

Father Thomas hangs himself: and suicide, the act of a despairing individual who has given up on life and God, is, as we have noted, one of the cardinal sins. The fact that he returns as a 'shade' to promote further evil suggests that suicidal impulses are a recruiting technique of the Devil's, although surely giving up on God must involve giving up on

Satan too. Despair is the least useful of emotions, and even the Devil himself would be hard pressed to make an enthusiastic acolyte out of a suicide case.

Another possibility is that Father Thomas is an evil priest from the outset, and hangs himself at the behest of his Evil God. After all, a suicidal priest makes a wonderful promotional tool for Satan. Imagine the despair, the falling-off of belief it would inspire in congregations! If despairing souls are hell-bound, spurned by a jealous God – that ultimate paranoiac who requires constant belief and adoration to bolster an apparently limitless insecurity – then a suicidal priest could truly spread the blight of disillusionment through his flock. More souls for Satan. So Thomas, far from doubting, has embraced the Fallen Angel and renounced the world to commit his eternal soul to Evil.

There's also the possibility that Father Thomas has anticipated the oncoming apocalypse, and has committed the 'sin' of suicide in a moment of "nearer my God to thee" weakness. If this is so – if the 'good' Father is failing in the face of encroaching Evil – he is characterized by fear; the quality that precedes all else in the original title: *Paura nella città dei morti viventi*.

Furthermore, Father Thomas induces horrific physical transformations in people merely by staring at them. Their eyes stream with blood. His presence is therefore 'fearful' and indulges a playfulness in respect of 'fear' as an entertainment. We are, after all, staring at the screen to be scared! His most extreme provocation is to make a young woman vomit her entrails out of her mouth. This posits the (malevolent) gaze as progenitor of gruesomeness; an amusing conceit, considering that we are likewise staring at the characters. It also suggests the notion of a link between feminity and death. Just as the zombies in these Gothic films are examples of Death being called upon to produce something visible, so too is the woman called upon by Father Thomas to 'produce' some visible extrusion from her mouth. Fear is clearly as much to do with what is produced by the look as it is to do with the look itself. Fear produces the fearful, and vice versa. The only thing to fear is fear itself.

As horror fans we obviously wish to see something horrible, and just as Father Thomas stares at the vomiting girl, so do we – in amazed, impressed revulsion. It's this quality of admiration that 'redeems' the reactive masochism being indulged. What many commentators on the genre fail to appreciate is the extent to which the viewer is playing quite intentionally with 'fear', not as an indulgence in the sensation, which would be reactive; but as a game, a challenge, to endure a sensation which might otherwise overwhelm. Part of the appeal of the horror genre is precisely the opportunity to (at least) rehearse the overcoming of fear.

In early Christian belief, the image was believed to be inherently evil, and medieval theologians The Iconoclasts considered any representation of the Divinity to be a sin. Perhaps they guessed that to externalize the metaphysical threat – upon which Christian religion depended – would result in the gradual rehearsal of resistance; a callousing, a hardening to the notion of fear, that most useful of religious tools.

Father Thomas makes his last appearance in the spectacular underground caverns at the end of the film. There, truly, is the 'City' of the title. What is he doing there? Feminist critic Barbara Creed discusses the notion of the 'monstrous feminine' in relation to men's fear of the womb; which, it is supposed, they identify with an abject absence of masculine power, with omnipresent feminine control, and by association death. *City*'s space beneath the cemetery is as abject as one could require in the furtherance of Creed's theory. But Fulci and Sacchetti put the figure of the monstrous priest at the epicentre of this particular abyss, which suggests Christian theology as the method by which men are rendered susceptible to the blandishments of fear-of-the-feminine. Deep within the supposed 'womb of death' lies the poisonous deceiver of religion, collapsed into a single putrid figure. The emphasis on disgust, rottenness and decay characteristic of *City* is here presented as a legacy of Christian teaching.

The priest is symbolically castrated (the symbolic is all he's got going for him), stabbed in the crotch with a rotting wooden crucifix; there's something satisfyingly pagan (and economical) about this outcome. At the same time we also see the destruction of the underground chamber, the 'womb of death', by fire – perhaps the destruction of the patriarchal Christian entails a new, less privileged position for Woman (once the Monster of the Abject) too. Combative feminism has embraced that which propels male fears as part of its identity. Given the continued collapse of Christianity, a matriarchal alternative will require more than male fears to support it.

In this context, Mary's emergence from the underground horror into yet another nightmare is curious. If the boy running towards her is a horrific apparition – a threat – the end of the film could be seen as challenging femininity with the presence of a new male being, an intransigent reminder of the inevitable relation between male and female. (Although Mary and Jerry both survive it is Mary's reaction to the final terror that is focused on.) Having survived the patriarchal abyss, Woman is not immune to the endless succession of life, any more than she can be 'mistress' of the anguish of death.

Though this paranoiac finale feels half-baked (and was apparently cobbled together in a last-minute emergency by editor Vincenzo Tomassi) the rest of Fulci's sumptuously repellent Gothic vision stays in the mind. Despite the occasional cliché (Sandra's neurosis for example), Fulci shows men and women joining forces to fight against supernatural menace (both here and in *The Beyond*). The final truth – beyond the semantic battleground which characterizes the interaction of the sexes – is that difference makes no difference. Long live death.

above:
De Mejo and Agren hear strange noises after the disappearance of Mrs. Holden's corpse.

below:
Jerry and Mary emerge from the horrors of the tomb.

Italian theatrical title
Black Cat

Italy

Alternative titles
Black Cat (Gatto nero)
(IT theatrical – inc. onscreen translation)
The Black Cat (Il gatto di Park Lane)
(shooting title)

Video/DVD title
The Black Cat
(UK/USA video/DVD/Blu-ray)

Production company
Selenia Cinematografica

Theatrical distributors
Distribuzione Lanciamento Film (Italy)
IIF (Italy)
Urania Film (Italy)
World Northal (USA)

Theatrical running time
Italy 92m

Video/DVD/Blu-ray running times (adjusted)
Anchor Bay DVD (USA) 91m 38s

Shooting period
Shooting August-September 1980

Censorship
Italian censor certificate 76321
issued 09 March 1981

Release information
Taranto 11 April 1981 (as 'Black Cat')
Rome 24 April 1981
Bari 20 May 1981

The Black Cat

1981

Directed by Lucio Fulci. produced by Giulio Sbarigia for Selenia Cinematografica (Rome). story & screenplay: Biagio Proietti; freely adapted from Edgar Allan Poe's short story The Black Cat. director of photography: Sergio Salvati. music: Pino Donaggio, conducted by Natale Massara. editor: Vincenzo Tomassi. art director: Massimo Antonello Geleng. production designer: Francesco Calabrese. production executive: Renato Angiolini. production manager: Ennio Onorati. unit managers: Antonio De Padova & Tommaso Pantano. 2nd unit director: Roberto Giandalia. assistant directors: Victor Tourjansky & David Del Bufalo. script continuity: Daniela Tonti. stunt co-ordinator: Nazzareno Cardinali. camera operators: Franco Bruni & Roberto Forges-Davanzati. assistant cameraman: Maurizio Lucchini. gaffer: Alfredo Fedeli. key grip: Ennio Brizzolari. costumes: by Massimo Lentini. make-up artist: Franco Di Girolamo. hair stylist: Maria Pia Crapanzano. special effects: Paolo Ricci. seamstress: Palmina Tacconi. make-up assistant: Rosario Prestopino. action stills: Gianfranco Massa. 1st assistant editor: Rita Antonelli. 2nd assistant editor: Pietro Tomassi. titles & optical effects: Penta Studio. sound recordist: Ugo Celani. boom operator: Eros Giustini. recorded at Fono Roma S.r.l. for Cinitalia (Rome). dubbing editor: Nick Alexander .additional sound effects: Fernando Caso & Alvaro Gramigna. set furnishings: GRP – Cimino. carpets & drapes: Alfredo D'Angelo. the cats were trained by Pasquale Martino, Rome. Animals Unlimited, London. the scenes filmed on location in England were shot with the collaboration of Filmex Ltd. (London). colour (Italy) by LV – Luciano Vittori. prints by Eastmancolor. processing laboratory: Telecolor S.p.A. (Rome). format: Technovision. shooting in North West London with interiors at R.P.A. Elios Studios (Rome), Cine International Studios & Incir De Paolis Studios, (Rome).

Cast: Patrick Magee (Robert Miles). Mimsy Farmer (Jill Travers). David Warbeck (Inspector Gorley). Pier Luigi Conti [as 'Al Cliver'] (Sgt. Wilson). Dagmar Lassander (Lillian Grayson). Bruno Corazzari (Ferguson, pub customer killed by cat). Geoffrey Copleston (Inspector Flynn). Daniela Doria (Maureen Grayson, Lillian's daughter). *Uncredited:* Vito Passeri (caretaker). Lucio Fulci (Doctor [scenes deleted]).

Synopsis: In a rural English village, strange Mr. Miles lives alone except for his black cat. He spends his time making tape recordings at the graves of the recently deceased. Jill Travers, an American photographer on vacation, finds a tiny microphone in a crypt... Maureen Grayson and her boyfriend Stan lock themselves in an airtight room behind a boathouse to have sex. The key mysteriously disappears and they are trapped. Maureen's mother Lillian alerts the police. Scotland Yard's Inspector Gorley arrives to head the investigation. Jill goes to see Miles, who talks about the barriers of perception and how to go beyond them. He tries to hypnotise her but is prevented by the black cat, which leaps and scratches him. That night, a local man called Ferguson is killed after leaving the pub; the cat menaces him and he falls to his death on metal spikes. Inspector Gorley asks Jill to photograph the corpse. She notices cat scratches on Ferguson's hands, which remind her of those suffered by Miles. Lillian (an old lover of Miles), begs him to help find her daughter. He enters a trance and describes the boathouse, and the location of the missing key. The police and Lillian rush to the scene. Battering down the door, locked from the inside, they discover the decomposed remains of Maureen and Stan. The key was outside, an impossible feat for a murderer, since the only way out of the room was a blocked air-vent ... The next victim is Lillian, burned to death in a fire started by the cat. Jill shows Miles the photographs of Ferguson's hand. She accuses him of exerting an evil influence over the cat, but Miles insists it's the cat which dominates him. That night, he hangs it by the neck from a tree branch. Supernatural forces are unleashed and the cat appears as a ghost. Gorley sees the creature, which hypnotises him into walking in front of a speeding car. Jill sneaks into Miles's home and snoops around. When he returns, she hides in the cellar and encounters the cat. Fleeing, she is cornered by Miles, who tells her that the cat picks up on his hatred for the villagers and acts without his control. He knocks her unconscious and walls her up alive in the cellar ... Gorley, now recovered from his accident, turns up at Miles's house with his colleague, Inspector Flynn, and insists on searching for Jill. He finds nothing and is about to leave when he hears the cat's cries. Miles has unwittingly walled up both Jill and the cat. Jill is rescued and Miles is arrested.

About the production: During preparations for *City of the Living Dead* in the spring of 1980, Fulci was also being lined up to direct another film, *Black Cat*. Interestingly, this was first described – in a full page ad in *Variety* dated 30 April 1980 – as an Anglo-Italian co-production. However, the only company named in the advert was Selenia Cinematografica, the latest production enterprise of Fulci's long-time associate Giulio Sbarigia (see *White Fang*) whose previous companies, Coralta and Oceania, had ceased activity around 1976. *Black Cat* marked Sbarigia's return to front-line production after a four year absence. Amusingly, it seems he came out of retirement through sheer boredom, as *Variety* explained: *"Sbarigia complained to this reporter that he got fed up with retirement ('How much canasta can you play a day?') and decided to produce again. His reinaugural effort is 'The Black Cat' from an Edgar Allan Poe tale, and it rolls soon under the direction of Lucio Fulci – an old hand at chillers – on extended location near London and in Italy as an Italo-British coproduction. Sbarigia, in the days when his companies, Oceana and Coralta, were active two or three years ago, was a big cog in Italian cinema. His activities then also extended to minority coproducer."*[13]

Who, then, was Sbarigia's mooted 'Anglo' co-producer? None other than Harry Alan Towers, whom you may recall had almost ended up co-producing *White Fang* with Sbarigia back in 1973. A *Variety* article referring to the Fulci project, in June 1980, placed Towers very much in the front seat with Sbarigia: *"Harry Alan Towers is re-knitting co-production ties in Italy but from his new base in Canada. In July, [Towers] will co-produce 'Southern Cross' with Fulvio Lucisano of Italian International under the direction of Enzo Castellari [...] With Giuliano [sic] Sbarigia of Selenia Cinematografica, Towers is co-producing 'The Cat' with Lucio Fulci directing mainly on location in Canada. Chiller starts in June with Donald Pleasence and Mimsy Farmer. 'If the Poe film does well,' Towers told Variety, 'Sbarigia and I will co-produce a series of Poe adaptations. I think we make a good marriage to produce films with a Northern American look and with Italian visual quality.'"*[14]

However, for reasons unknown (a clash of personalities?) Towers and Sbarigia once again parted company. In fact the 're-knitting' of Towers's Italo-production ties seems to have unravelled pretty quickly, because the Castellari project failed to ignite too. Towers would not seal another Italian co-production deal until 2002, when his company co-produced a pair of TV movies – *Un difetto di famiglia* and *Il destino ha 4 zampe* – with Italian International and RAI TV.

With Towers no longer involved, Canada was crossed off the *Black Cat* production schedule: English locations were back, and Donald Pleasence was replaced by Patrick Magee. Olga Karlatos, at one point announced among the cast, dropped out for reasons unknown. If, as seems likely, she was down for the role of Lillian, the role went to Dagmar Lassander instead. Mimsy Farmer, David Warbeck, and Al Cliver were all confirmed by July, and production finally began in England on 4 August 1980. Shooting took place in three Buckinghamshire villages, Hambledon, West Wycombe and Chalfont St. Giles, and was completed in the last week of September. *Variety* described the film as 'finished' by 15 October 1980 with prints expected by the end of November. If true this indicates a post-production period of around three weeks, which seems a trifle rapid even for Fulci! In the same article the film grew a longer (though short-lived) new title: *The Black Cat (Il gatto di Park Lane)*.

Interviewed in the pages of *l'Unità* in May 1982, Fulci used Sbarigia as an example of the unreasonable pressure placed on him by producers: *"Ahhh... the producers. You cannot imagine how tiring it is to work with some of them. In* Black Cat *for example there is a scene (a room that becomes animated) shot as a precise copy of* The Exorcist. *It did not fit in with the style of the film, I know, but it was imposed by the producer. He said that 'it fitted in well'. I do not want to be problematic, but the reality is this: my films cost the same amount to make as a sexy comedy by Bombolo, with the difference that* The New York Ripper *sells across the whole world and* Le fichissime *does not. Let's be aware of that!"*[15]

Review: *The Black Cat* is an immensely enjoyable supernatural tale, beautifully filmed by Sergio Salvati and packed with incidental pleasures. Although it can't compete with *The Beyond* or *The House by the Cemetery* for sheer horror, it can boast some credible shock moments and an endearingly lopsided set of British characters, reminiscent of Jorge Grau's classic *The Living Dead at Manchester Morgue* (1974).

We open with the star of the show (the cat of course, who else) prowling the streets of a lovely rural village (Hambledon in Buckinghamshire). Sergio Salvati's camera is slung low to convey a cat's eye perspective. We see the animal sneak into a parked car and hitch a secret ride before seemingly hypnotising the driver into crashing the vehicle. The credits then appear over shots of the unscathed feline exploring church grounds and farm yards, slate roofs and gables. The accompanying theme by Italian-born composer Pino Donaggio is reminiscent of medieval English pastorale, folk-tinged for a touch of pagan atmosphere. (It's interesting to note that in 1990 the same composer worked with Dario Argento on *his* Poe-pourri, *Two Evil Eyes*. Donaggio's scores for both films are memorable and creative, although it's notable that they are often quite a lot busier than the images: perhaps the music was composed in advance?)[16]

The Black Cat is a more relaxed, even mellow supernatural tale than one would have anticipated from Lucio Fulci during this period, falling as it does between two hyper-grisly shockers, *City of the Living Dead* and *The Beyond*. Fulci claimed that he directed the story quickly and cheaply as a favour to producer Giulio Sbarigia: if this is true, then the gift was handsomely delivered. The intimate scale of the film and its relatively low key style are suitably matched, while the technical credits, as with all of Fulci's films from this period, are excellent.

The credit sequence comes to an end as the cat enters a rambling house which belongs to a sinister old medium called Mr. Miles, played by veteran Irish actor Patrick Magee. For such a modest, low-budget film this was a triumph of casting. Magee – who sadly passed away just two years later – brings to the rather flimsy script the authentic mood of Poe. Hostile and threatening, yet haunted and fearful, he lends *The Black Cat* much through sheer thespian magnetism. We first see him listening to eerie voices playing on a reel-to-reel tape recorder in his gloomy oak-panelled study.[17] It turns out that Miles records these 'voices from beyond' at the gravesides of the recently deceased (a practise perhaps modelled on the example of Latvian psychologist and student of Jung, Dr. Konstantin Raudive, whose book *Breakthrough* – about 'electronic voice phenomena' – was published in 1971). Wandering through fog-shrouded tombstones, tape recorder in hand, Magee cuts a marvellously Gothic figure, and thanks to his characteristic air of brimstone and portent we can almost overlook the fact that this intriguing concept goes absolutely nowhere! Miles's graveside recordings add some atmospheric colour, but the idea never really ties in to the story as a whole. Which is a pity: the notion of a man communicating with the dead, while beset by the fury of an evil cat, suggests all sorts of strange possibilities which the story never explores.

above: French poster art.

opposite main image: Ferguson (Bruno Corazzari) is menaced by the sinister cat.

opposite bottom left: Italian video cover.

below: Japanese video cover.

top:
Bruno Corazzari makes an unlucky landing.

above:
Fiery death in the prologue sequence.

below:
Mr. Miles (Patrick Magee) under attack by the malevolent feline.

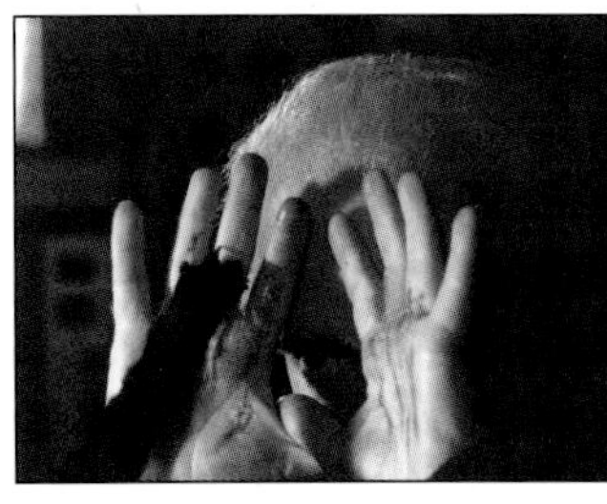

Magee's greatest asset as a performer, something he shared with other obliquely talented character actors such as Patrick McGoohan and Donald Pleasence, was the ability to transcend meagre scripting by suggesting an unusual personality *behind* the role. The horror genre is notorious for the folklorish simplicity of many of its premises – actors like Magee lend an essential depth through their fierce idiosyncrasy. Fulci obviously thought that this man could carry *The Black Cat* on personal menace alone, as shown by the frequent close-ups granted to the actor's eyes and beetling brow. And how right he was! Miles exchanges long glowering looks with the cat: *"We are bound together by hatred,"* he says. *"He wants to kill me"*. As a visual evocation of claustrophobic hatred these close-ups are highly effective, even if they do rather drastically abbreviate Poe's psychological insights.

Magee has always excelled at playing bilious, twisted and misanthropic characters: we need only recall Mr. Alexander in *A Clockwork Orange* (1971), or the perverted father, General Carew, in Borowczyk's *The Strange Case of Dr. Jekyll and Miss Osbourne* (1981). Best of all, to my mind, though sorely underrated elsewhere, was his appearance as the alcoholically riddled and morally corrupt Reverend Slodden in *Sir Henry at Rawlinson End* (made the same year as *The Black Cat*), a hilarious OTT performance which threatens to upstage even the great Trevor Howard, who starred as Sir Henry. (Perhaps only Patrick McGoohan's gin-soaked turn in the under-appreciated Canadian film *Kings and Desperate Men* compares for sheer ham-on-a-tightrope entertainment...)

It's just as well that Magee delivers an authentic blast of Poe because, without wishing to be churlish to a very enjoyable film, one has to say that Biagio Proietti's screenplay ignores or contradicts a lot of Poe's best ideas. In the original story, evil stems from the twisted heart of the (unnamed) narrator who, in a malevolent fury fuelled by acute alcoholism, mutilates and kills his beloved pet cat. When he encounters a second cat, similar in appearance, he takes it into his home, partly to salve his guilt for killing the first. After just a few days, however, in defiance of the animal's affection, he becomes convinced that it's a malevolent spirit out to destroy him. This perception is heavily implied by Poe – within the bounds of a first-person narrative – to be a paranoid delusion. The story the *narrator* wants to tell is about a supernatural feline punishing him for his earlier wickedness; the story *Poe* wants to tell is about the distorting effects of guilt, and the contortions of the spirit that arise when someone tries to escape it. Yet Poe's theme is nowhere to be found in Fulci's film. There's no indication that Miles suffers corrosive guilt: instead the film asserts that the cat is, indeed, a supernatural nemesis to be feared. In other words, Proietti completely inverts (or 'perverts') the original story.

In 1979, Proietti had written a number of Edgar Allan Poe adaptations for Italian television, including versions of "The House of Usher" and "William Wilson". Evidently he was an aficionado – and yet here, for reasons unknown, he chooses to discard a lot of what makes the original story work. Poe's "spirit of perverseness" – that strange and terrible urge to vex one's own soul – is left unexplored. In its place we get something much simpler (and let's face it, sillier): a battle of wills between man and malefic superfeline. Any ambiguity is kicked rudely out of the catflap when the heroic leads, Jill and Inspector Gorley, actually *see* the murderous moggy appearing and disappearing magically, before their very eyes. This just doesn't make sense: if Gorley believes in the supernatural it helps to exonerate Miles, and if the cat kills Gorley, Miles will evade justice!

Proietti also dispenses with Poe's denouement, in which the protagonist brings about his own downfall. In the story, when the police come in search of the narrator's missing wife, he raps with his cane on the newly built wall behind which he's interred her corpse. *"These walls are solidly put together,"* he boasts, at which point the second cat, which he'd unwittingly imprisoned with the corpse, yowls in response. The spirit of perverseness prevails twice: first in the destruction of a beloved pet, and then in this absurd act of self-sabotage. Mystifyingly, Proietti neglects this very dramatic twist: instead of being triggered by Miles's actions, the cat's wails are completely spontaneous.

Other questions accumulate. Why, when Miles has neither maimed nor hurt a cat, does it want to kill him? All that we learn about their relationship is that they are "bound together by hate", and that the cat acts out Miles's suppressed hostility to others. Does Miles believe that the cat will one day act out his *self*-hatred too? Maybe so, but we see little evidence. True, Miles seems disturbed by the cat's attack on Gorley, but his concern comes out of nowhere. He demonstrates no remorse when the other deaths occur; in fact he seems to regard the cat's behaviour as entirely acceptable, apart from its hatred of him!

The suggestion that the cat carries out Miles's subconscious wishes makes one wonder if Proietti was borrowing a motif from David Cronenberg's *The Brood*, released the previous year. But even then, there are questions. Why does the cat single out Maureen and her boyfriend? We never hear of anything they've done to anger Miles. It's implied that Maureen's mother Lillian used to be Miles's lover. So is Maureen the daughter of their liaison? Did she spurn her father? Fulci leaves this loose end dangling, along with many others. Why does the cat kill Ferguson, the villager? We saw the man spying on one of Miles's cemetery recording sessions, but Miles didn't seem to notice him. We're left to assume that this victim is just one of the many 'snooping villagers' whom Miles despises.

As Dario Argento would do in *Two Evil Eyes* ten years later, Fulci and Proietti incorporate elements from a variety of Poe stories. In the scene where two lovers are trapped in a boat-house, for instance, Fulci draws on one of Poe's central fears, being buried alive, while the fact that the victims lock themselves in, but the key turns up outside, is an example of the classic 'locked room mystery' invented by Poe in his story "Murders in the Rue Morgue". There are also echoes of "The Telltale Heart" and "The Imp of the Perverse" bouncing around in the story, and when Miles is revealed to be a hypnotist it echoes "The Facts in the Case of M. Valdemar". Such a gumbo of Poe ideas may not lash together coherently, but the collage effect is enjoyable nonetheless.

Aside from Magee's star turn, one has to admit there's a bit of a character vacuum in the film. It's sparsely populated enough as it is, but the absence of a likeable heroine really weakens it. In place of a lead character meaningfully tied to the action, the script introduces Jill, an American photographer on vacation (hence a vacant performance by Mimsy Farmer). We first see her walking through beautiful woodland before emerging beside a tomb, its lid skewed open. Our bland 'heroine' clambers down into a sepulchral chamber and suddenly we're back in the director's Gothic realm – underground mausoleums, cobweb strewn passages, and skeletal human remains. Sadly, however, the scene peters out: Jill does *not* encounter the living dead, which is a pity: she could do with a serious zombie attack to liven her up a bit.

Thankfully the next significant arrival fairs better. Inspector Gorley, a Scotland Yard investigator played by handsome David Warbeck. enters the film on a motorbike at high speed, shattering the sleepy village atmosphere with a burst of cartoon machismo. The Inspector has been called in to investigate a series of bizarre deaths baffling the local constabulary, as represented by Fulci regular Al Cliver in the role of a mild-mannered British bobby. Gorley promptly takes him to the local pub for a drink, but not before the local copper has issued him with a speeding ticket, an amusing little scene well played by Warbeck and Cliver.

Meanwhile, strange deaths continue apace with the less than Poe-like introduction of a necking teenage couple, who take to a windowless boat-shed to make out in true *Friday the 13th* fashion. As noted earlier, claustrophobia is the motif here: the couple lock themselves in for a bout of teenage sex only to discover they've 'lost' the key and can't escape from the increasingly stuffy, airless room. The girl in this scene is played by Daniela Doria, a pretty young actress who was Fulci's regular whipping girl of the period: in *The Black Cat* she dies foaming at the mouth and writhing half-naked on the floor; in *City of the Living Dead* she vomits up her internal organs; in *The House by the Cemetery* her cranium is skewered with a butcher knife; and in *The New York Ripper* she undergoes graphic evisceration by razor blade, including the slicing of an eyeball and a nipple. Quite a litany of screen abuse! Either something about her appearance brought out the sadist in Fulci, or (more likely) she was a trooper, happy to do such violent scenes no questions asked.

Throughout the film, Sergio Salvati's photography is outstanding. His elegant steadicam, equipped with a wide-angle lens, prowls the moody locations at ankle height, making the feline's frequent point-of-view shots exciting and pleasurable. Rather than encouraging sadistic identification with 'the killer' – who, after all, is clearly a cat – the camera's motion is an aesthetic, sensual pleasure in its own right, exploring unusual locations and offering interesting visual textures. We see this during the boat-house scenes, with their dilapidated woodwork and clean white tiling, and later, during the sequence in which the drunk Ferguson is stalked remorselessly through moonlit farm buildings by the black cat. The man panics and falls to his death on spiked machinery, but not before Fulci and Salvati have wrung plenty of suspense and visual impact from the location.

The rest of the film is a chequerboard of shocking or nasty images, leavened by unintentional absurdity. It's always amused me, for instance, that when Ferguson's body is discovered, Jill is drafted in as a forensic photographer by Inspector Gorley. Would Scotland Yard *really* ask a stray American tourist to photograph a corpse? Probably not, but at least it gives the principal characters the chance to get acquainted, in a story where relationships are tangential and underdeveloped! It also gives Fulci the opportunity to light up his gory effects with multiple flash exposures, a technique he'd utilised before in *One on Top of the Other*, *A Lizard in a Woman's Skin* and *The Smuggler* ... The demise of Mrs. Grayson is particularly odd, being both nasty and ridiculous: this time the fiendish pussycat knocks over a candelabra and the unfortunate woman awakens to find her house on fire. As she attempts to put out the blaze her nightdress catches light, and in a scene that quivers between risibly fake and grotesquely realistic she's enveloped in sheets of flame: cue hideous shots of dripping flesh, and a dummy effect that would embarrass Herschell Gordon Lewis ... More successful is the cat attack on Gorley, with some wince-inducing shots of claws dragging bloody furrows in the cop's outstretched palms, followed by a well-edited road accident (the second in the film) as the dazed detective wanders into the path of an oncoming car ... Bearing in mind the general attractiveness of the production, we can afford to forgive the few elements that don't work at all – the atrocious drawing of a hanged cat which appears on Miles's wall, for instance.

The Black Cat has languished for too long in the shadow of its immediate neighbours. It boasts a wealth of brooding atmosphere, gorgeous locations, some exciting images of horror, and a compelling central performance from Patrick Magee. It's another example of that special *frisson* which Continental directors can bring to horror stories set in the UK, joining José Larraz's *Vampyres* (1974), Jorge Grau's *The Living Dead at Manchester Morgue* (1974), Massimo Dallamano's *What Have You Done to Solange?* (1972) and of course Fulci's *A Lizard in a Woman's Skin*, on a roll-call of films that offer British viewers a pleasingly exotic spin on familiar terrain. All things considered, it's one of the most purely enjoyable films of Fulci's career.

above: *Variety* advert from 1 October 1980.

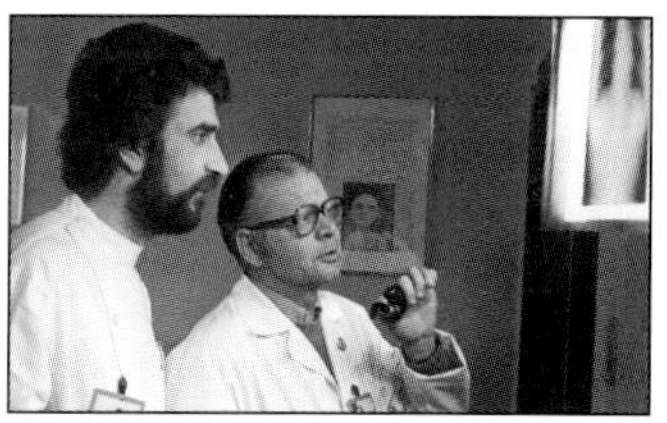

below: Fulci's cameo as a doctor was cut from the final version.

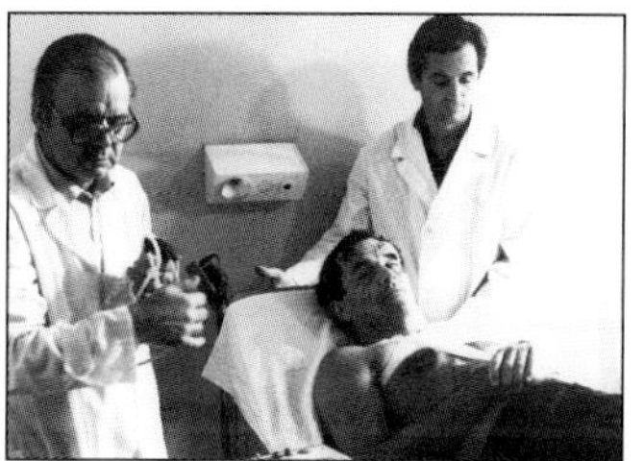

bottom: Mimsy Farmer as Jill Travers, an American tourist who helps the police with their murder enquiries.

Italian theatrical title
E tu vivrai nel terrore! L'aldilà

Translation
'And You Will Live in Terror! The Beyond'

Italy

Alternative title
L'aldilà (IT alt. theatrical)
The Hereafter (possible English pre-shooting title)

International theatrical titles
The Beyond (UK)
El más allá (SP) 'The Beyond'
7 Doors of Death (USA)
Die Geisterstadt der Zombies (WG) 'Ghost-Town of the Zombies'
The Beyond Hell Raiser (Pakistan poster)
L'au-delà (FR) 'The Beyond'
Über dem Jenseits (WG alt. theatrical/ video) 'Above the Beyond'
Las 7 puertas del infierno (MEX) 'The 7 Gates of Hell'

Video/DVD titles
Woodoo Rædslernes Hotel (DEN) 'Hotel of Voodoo Terrors'
Horrors Hotel (POL)
Vrata Pakla (YUG) 'Gates of Hell'
Terror nas trevas (BRZ) 'Terror in the Darkness'
A casa do além (alt. BRZ) 'The House from Beyond'
Η 7η Ιυλη Της Κολασεως (GRE) 'The 7th Gate of Hell'
Rædslernes Hotel (DEN DVD) 'Hotel of Terrors'
Eibon Die 7 Tore des Schreckens (GER DVD) 'The 7 Gates of Secrets'

Production company
Fulvia Film S.r.l.

Theatrical distributors
Medusa Distribuzione (Italy)
Eagle Films (UK)
Aquarius Releasing (USA)

Theatrical running times
Italy 88m
UK 85m 32s (after cuts)

Video/DVD/Blu-ray running times (adjusted)
Arrow Blu-ray (UK) 87m 25s
Anchor Bay DVD (USA) 87m 24s

Approximate shooting period
November-December 1980

Censorship
Italian censor certificate 76406 issued 23 March 1981

Release information
Molfetta 23 May 1981
Bari 28 May 1981
Rome 04 June 1981
UK (Hanley, Staffs) 1 November 1981
UK (London) 20 November 1981
USA (New York) 11 November 1983

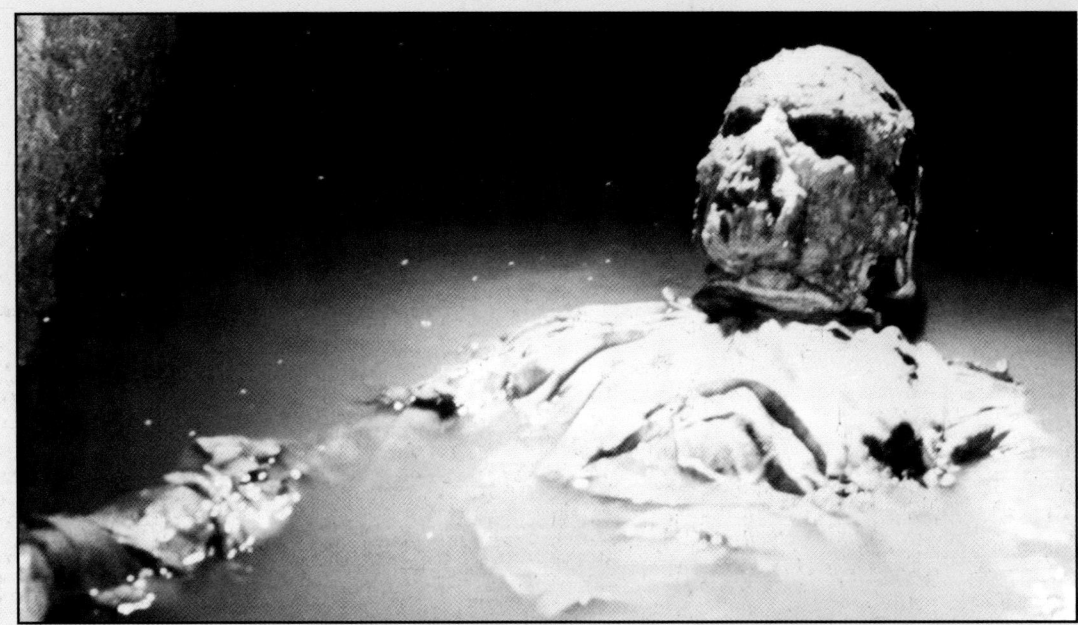

The Beyond

1981

Directed by Lucio Fulci. producer: Fabrizio De Angelis for Fulvia Film S.r.l. (Rome). story: Dardano Sacchetti. screenplay Dardano Sacchetti, Giorgio Mariuzzo & Lucio Fulci. director of photography: Sergio Salvati. music [Italian & UK versions]: Fabio Frizzi, © Deaf. music [US version] Mitch Tuspeh & Ira Tuspeh. editor: Vincenzo Tomassi. production designer & costumes: Massimo Lentini. special effects & make-up: Giannetto De Rossi. unit manager: Tullio Lullo. assistant director: Roberto Giandalia. continuity: Rita Agostini. stunt coordinator: Nazzareno Cardinali. cameraman: Franco Bruni. assistant cameraman: Maurizio Lucchini. key grip: Lamberto Del Bene. chief electrician: Alfredo Fedeli. make-up artist: Maurizio Trani. hairstylist: Luciana Palombi. special effects: Germano Natali. assistant designer: Claudia Giammona. property master: Rodolfo Ruzza. property assistant: Franco Rinaldi. production secretary: Fabrizio De Martino. stills: Alberto Cocchi. assistant editors: Pietro Tomassi & Armando Pace. titles & visual effects: Penta Studio. sound engineer: Ugo Celani. boom operator: Eros Giustini. sound studios: N.C. mixage: Bruno Moreal. special sound effects: Enzo Di Liberto, Studio sound. transportation: Romana Trasporti Cinematografici. costumes: S.A.F.A.S. cameras & equipment: Cinenoleggio. set furnishings: G.R.P. set dressings: Alfredo D'Angelo. wigs: Rocchetti Carboni. the production wishes to thank The Louisiana Film Commission for their kind collaboration. colour/film laboratory: Technicolor. negatives: Eastmancolor. filmed on location in New Orleans (U.S.A.) with interiors at IN.CI.R. De Paolis Studios (Rome).

Cast: Catriona MacColl [as 'Katherine MacColl'] (Liza Merrill). David Warbeck (Dr. John McCabe). Cinzia Monreale [as 'Sarah Keller'] (Emily). Antoine Saint-John (Schweik). Veronica Lazar (Martha). Larry Ray [as 'Anthony Flees'] (Larry, the house painter). Giovanni De Nava (Schweik zombie). Pier Luigi Conti [as 'Al Cliver'] (Dr. Harris). Michele Mirabella (Martin Avery, the architect). Gianpaolo Saccarola [as 'Giampaolo Saccarola'] (Arthur). Maria Pia Marsala (Jill, Joe's daughter). Laura De Marchi (Mary-Ann, Joe's wife). *Uncredited:* Tonino Pulci (Joe the Plumber). Lucio Fulci (town clerk). Calogero Azzaretto (2nd hospital zombie McCabe shoots after Harris says "Here they come!"). Roberto Dell'Acqua (hospital zombie who grabs Liza's hair). Gilberto Galimberti (dark-haired hospital zombie with mole on right cheek). Amedeo Salamon (bald elderly hospital zombie shot in chest).

Synopsis: New Orleans, 1927. An angry mob descends on The Seven Doors Hotel, Room 36. They seize an artist called Schweik, accused of being a warlock, and drag him to the cellar, where they torture and crucify him... New Orleans, 1981. Liza Merrill has inherited the Seven Doors Hotel (and its creepy servants Arthur and Martha). As soon as she moves in, a painter falls off a rig and is horribly injured. Dr. John McCabe takes him to hospital and offers Liza sympathy. Joe the plumber attempts to repair a major leak in the cellar but is murdered by a presence that emerges from behind a slime-caked wall. Martha finds Joe's body, and another much older cadaver: Schweik's. Liza meets a strange blind woman, Emily. At her opulent house Emily warns Liza to leave the hotel. Joe's wife is killed by a levitating bottle of acid at the hospital morgue and her daughter Jill is menaced by the re-animated Schweik. When Liza meets with John to discuss her anxieties, he says he knows everyone in the area but has never heard of Arthur and Martha. That night, Emily tells Liza that the hotel was built over one of the Seven Gateways to Hell. She's about to reveal more when her hands wander over a weird landscape painting Schweik was working on at the time of his death. She runs away into the night but Liza notices that she makes no footfalls. Venturing into Room 36, Liza finds an ancient book called 'Eibon'. In the bathroom she sees Schweik's corpse. When she returns with John the room is empty. He queries her story about Emily – there is no one living at the house she described. Liza's friend Martin Avery goes to the library in search of the hotel plans, but falls victim to a horde of giant spiders. John visits the house where Liza met Emily and finds it empty except for a copy of 'Eibon'. At the hotel, Martha is killed by Joe's corpse. Emily is summoned back to Hell by Schweik. Liza and John take refuge in the hospital, but zombies now walk the corridors. John's colleague Harris is killed by flying glass. John and Liza are trapped in the morgue with Jill who suddenly attacks Liza: John shoots the girl dead. The terrified couple flee down a staircase into what should be the hospital basement. Instead they find themselves in the hotel cellar. Through a cloud of smoke they walk into the landscape depicted in the warlock's painting...

above:
German video cover.

left:
Liza (Catriona MacColl), Dr. McCabe (David Warbeck) and Jill (Maria Pia Marsala) on the run from the living dead.

facing page:
The rotting corpse of Schweik, warlock, artist and Guardian of The Seven Doors Hotel.

below:
Liza suffers an hysterical fit when surprised by Dr. McCabe at the hotel.

bottom:
Liza and Joe (Tonino Pulci) discuss the waterlogged cellar.

About the production: *The Beyond* was first announced on 15 October 1980 in a full-page ad in *Variety*: *"Fulvia Film proudly announces a major production – After the worldwide success of Zombie II [sic] – Producer-Director-Special Effects-Screenplay are teamed again in The Beyond – Now in preparation."* By 12 November 1980 the four-week location schedule in Louisiana was said to be on the verge of an "upcoming start". However, two months later on 21 January 1981 the film was still "in preparation", making the actual production period difficult to pin down. A 1984 *Variety* article about producer Fabrizio De Angelis, referring to his production schedules on the Fulci films, said, *"De Angelis limited his overseas treks to four weeks of exteriors and two to three weeks in Italy."*[19] Assuming that production actually began some time in late January, a seven week shooting period would mean that post-production would have been under way by the end of March 1981, leaving just enough time for a late May opening in Italy.

Interestingly, Lamberto Bava has claimed that he was in the running to direct this project. Speaking to UK journalist Jay Slater in *The Dark Side* magazine, he said, *"Luciano Martino had previously offered me the role of director ... and I was on the contract do so. However, I didn't want to make* The Beyond *and gave it to Fulci instead."*[20]

Review: So here we are... at the threshold of the quintessential Lucio Fulci film. Gorgeous and vile, like a dream about a nightmare, it's a magical, elusive experience. Fulci's career had already merged beauty, horror and excitement, but for those who could appreciate its macabre poetry *The Beyond* seduced the imagination in a way that transcended comparison. Despite fleeting similarities to other films (Michael Winner's *The Sentinel* and Stanley Kubrick's *The Shining*), Fulci's special talent was now beyond the reach of such simple reductions. Arriving after the recent success of *Zombie Flesh-Eaters* and the striking weirdness of *City of the Living Dead*, *The Beyond* showed that a genuinely unique film could spring from the Italian cinema's network of commercial influences. The drift towards a fragmented, deserialised narrative, tantalisingly begun in *City*, here flourishes unchecked.

The elaborate set-pieces that Fulci unleashed in the earlier films are allowed to blossom freely and gruesomely, in a hot-house atmosphere of bodily disintegration and fevered dream-logic. *City*'s fragmentary road-movie structure is abandoned, because *The Beyond* is already in sight; a fatefully magnetic destination – out of reach yet inescapable – visible in the malefic geometry of the Seven Doors Hotel.

The characters here are either trapped, betrayed or merely spun disorientatingly around by the central location of *The Beyond*, a dilapidated old Louisiana hotel near the river. We sense the river's continual presence, thanks to the mysteriously waterlogged cellars and the mournful hooting of steamboats, but we only see it in the sepia-toned prologue. (New Orleans is largely below sea level, a geographical fact the film seems to acknowledge at every turn, with its sweltering actors, fluid camera movement and slow-motion physical action). All outward journeys turn into fatalistic ellipses, which eventually lead

above:
A workman falls from scaffolding outside The Seven Doors Hotel after glimpsing a presence inside the supposedly empty building.

insanely back to the bowels of the building. Liza goes out on a trip into old New Orleans but the journey yields nothing except the discovery of a sinister book connected with the Hotel (which disappears before it can be perused); whilst Martin the architect's trip to the library, to look at plans for the Hotel's foundations, results in spectacular spider madness erupting in broad daylight – not even this municipal sanctuary of reason is safe. The Knowledge to be found in the library is no protection from the Beyond's irrational onslaught.

At one of Fulci's most stunning locations, Liza drives down a coastal road's empty perspective as if pursuing the vanishing point of a metaphysical abstract; there is nothing to be seen except the road unrolling, until the moment is interrupted by a vision of a blind woman called Emily standing with her guide-dog in the middle of the road – *"I've been looking for you"*, Emily tells Liza. Once again, we sense a great expanse of river or lake or sea, at either side of the causeway walls, but we never see it.

Liza confides to friendly Doctor John that making a go of the Hotel is her last chance to succeed in life, over lunch-time drinks at a reassuringly melancholy jazz-bar, with clarinet and mournful trumpet improvising away in the background. Even there, the Doctor is called to the phone on hospital business and his shocked disbelief at what he's hearing is audible across the room. Liza's face registers a pessimistic recognition of the pattern. All escape bends back to – where? The warlock's painting of a grey, dusty landscape, subterranean yet exterior, populated by prone figures resembling stone ruins – people who have become their own crumbling graves? The figures recall pictures of the victims of Vesuvius, those residents of Pompeii and Herculaneum petrified in their postures of agony; a vision perhaps lingering in Fulci's mind since his work as assistant second unit director on *The Last Days of Pompeii* in 1950.

If forays away from the Hotel end up curling creepily back to it, what of the fate awaiting rash visitors? By attempting to intervene in Liza's fate, Dr. McCabe also enters the chilling world of the Hotel's influence. Checking up on Liza's assertion that she has encountered a living being, Emily, in a lavishly furnished version of what is supposed to be a derelict house, he discovers a copy of The Book of Eibon, containing dire threats about the dead emerging from The Hotel and walking the Earth. His attempt to telephone Liza is unsuccessful and he is forced to go back to the hotel to confront her. They flee from one supernatural assault in the hotel basement to another at the brightly lit hospital. *"No Liza, I'm a doctor; and I won't accept irrational explanations"*, he tells her, but it's too late for such square-jawed ignorance. The heroic doctor's subsequent slide into terror when finally confronted with a situation at the hospital that utterly defeats "rational explanation" benefits from Warbeck's acting talents, adding a tinge of psychic collapse to the picture.

A builder and plumber, reassuringly stolid figures of normality, also have their functionality rudely swept aside, with the latter figure, Joe, all working-class common-sense and laconic bandana-and-beard joviality, particularly abused. How sad for a plumber to end up inhabiting a tubful of rank, scurvy bathwater, manipulated in death to act as a slimy surprise when staff problems demand a sacrifice.

right:
Liza visits Emily's opulently furnished house. Yet when Dr. McCabe investigates later, he finds it an unoccupied, burnt-out shell.

below:
Warbeck and MacColl.

left:
Joe's wife prepares her husband's body for the funeral she'll never see...

At least the undead Joe gets to tie up an (arbitrary?) loose end by killing the housemaid Martha, whose sinister innuendo in the cellar – *"I've made this path to the far end – just for Joe"* – set her up for his almost touching 'revenge from beyond the grave'.

Then there's friendly, optimistic Martin, whose revolting fate is way out of proportion to his story function. We might imagine the headline: 'Architect Eaten by Spiders in Library Lunch-break' – as one of the lurid newspaper clippings awaiting an unwary researcher in the screenplay for an unmade *Beyond* sequel. This sardonic character enjoys a brief glimpse of the trans-dimensional architects' plans for the Seven Doors Hotel and a peremptory browse through local history – *"Three weeks of picketing – a great labour victory"* – before succumbing to the implacable demands of Fulci's notoriously static sadism. The following grisliness puts even the most hardened and generous viewer of Italian horror to the test, with its simultaneously repulsive and ridiculous special effects, involving an attack by several real tarantulas and several risibly fake clockwork pipe-cleaner mock-ups.

Once again, a character is stripped of all volition by the extra-diegetic demands of Fulci's gloating camera. Granted the victim is knocked unconscious to begin with, falling from a ladder onto a marble floor, but he's awake as the aforementioned spider attack gets under way. Viewer masochism must surely play a part in the pleasure to be had watching a mysteriously immobile figure having its face, tongue and eyes eaten by ravening arachnids. If the pursuit and murder of struggling, resisting victims mobilizes the sadistic component of the audience's gaze, Fulci's insistence on depicting victims who are devoid of opposition to their dissolution finds its analogue in the receptive face of the horror fan, strangely immobile also, before a repulsive spectacle of attack on the sense organs. The frequency with which Fulci homes in on victims who are seemingly paralyzed – physically and orally – by their gruesome impending fate can either be seen as a practical contingency (making the gore effects easier to operate and photograph) or more generously as a function of the peculiar fatalism expounded in the stories. Fulci's films often feature wooden, emotionally unresponsive and passive characters, and their eventual destruction follows this through. Despite the extreme horror they endure many of them are obscurely pinned, faces frozen in a gurgling, terrified rictus.

In most cases these early eighties films show even the most strenuous efforts of the characters leading nowhere. The survivors of *Zombie Flesh-Eaters* flee back to a collapsed western civilisation, *City of the Living Dead* disgorges its characters into a meta-narratological rupture – "the mirror breaks", as Fulci explains it – at the prospect of a zombiefied child; the reserved father and hysterical mother of *The House by the Cemetery*

below:
More gun heroics.

bottom:
"Attack, Dickie, attack!" – Emily's Alsation in deceptively heroic mode.

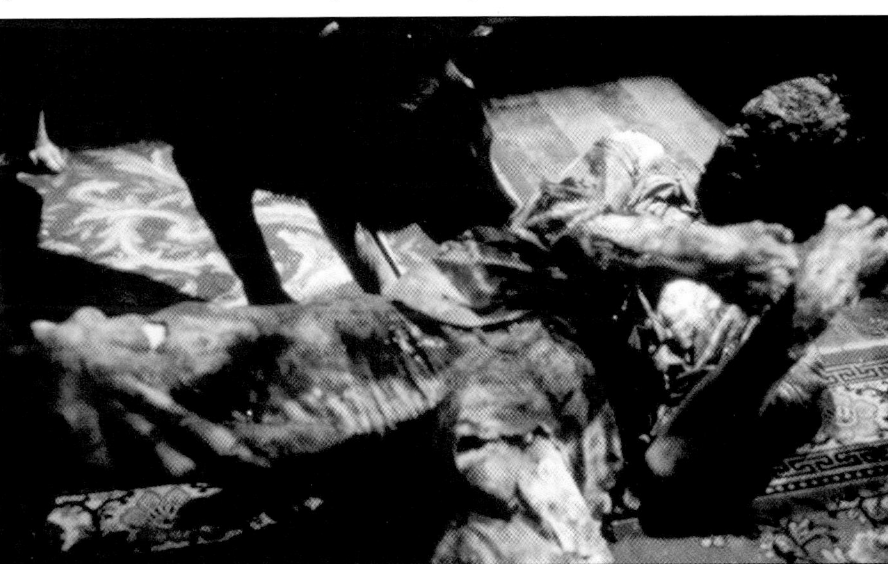

above:
Dutch video cover.

right:
During a zombie attack, Liza finds herself in the wrongest place at the wrongest time...

attempt heroics in the rescue of their child but fail gruesomely, their son 'adopted' into the past by a family destined to be slain by a paternal monster. John and Liza in *The Beyond* end up trapped in mono-directional limbo despite having established some kind of emotional contact, making their fate perhaps the most pessimistic of all.

Resistance isn't part of the vocabulary in *The Beyond*. Gross distortions and ruinations of flesh collapse out from the haze of the narrative, and a lavish pictorialism distends the image in preference to advancing the story – the film dominates the characters, whose flight from terror is as so much water, sluicing through a mildewed maze inexorably down to the Underworld. No one really *does* anything much – Liza shuffles a few towels around the dusty, uninviting hotel rooms, drives distractedly nowhere in particular, and gives a few terse orders to creepy Arthur and sullen, bedraggled Martha, the staff who *"came with the hotel"*. *"Arthur and Martha just can't seem to get it together"*, the excellent Catriona MacColl deadpans. Arthur exudes painful shyness, slight retardation and sweaty sexual repression as he explains, with a voice like Peter Lorre, that he's been instructed by Martha to clean the chimneys: *"Some of them are blocked"*, he stammers, sounding in much the same state himself. Arthur is one of a long line of pathetic male characters in Fulci's films. It's an

right:
Dr. McCabe tries to relax at a downtown bar but strange events at the hospital soon intrude.

below:
Pre-production advertising for *The Beyond* in the 15 October 1980 edition of *Variety*.

archetype familiar in Italian comedies, one which curdles when the comedic support is removed. Benjamin Wormser in *One on Top of the Other*, Giuseppe in *Don't Torture a Duckling*, and Bob in *City of the Living Dead* all bear similarities to Arthur, as does the sickly librarian in the following year's *The House by the Cemetery*.

The general air of lassitude is kind of appropriate given the famed laid-back aura of New Orleans. 'The Big Easy' is known as a haven for eccentrics unimpressed by the American Protestant work-ethic, unlike the high-rise Mormon stockpile of Salt Lake City or the blue-collar factory farm of Chicago. (When Joe the Plumber ambles down to start work on the flooded cellar, he assures an anxious Liza; *"It'll take... as long as it takes."*) Like Fulci, the residents of New Orleans are mainly Catholics who don't give a damn for the Pope; and no doubt the local popularity of a so-called 'voodoo saint', Expedite, appealed too, to the director of the voodoo-inflected *Zombie Flesh-Eaters*

It's in the nature of the modern horror film to depict hopeless situations, where all turns out as badly as we'd anticipated when we bought our ticket or paid our rental fee. Anyone looking to the horror film for happy endings, particularly in Fulci's work, has made a perverse, ill-informed choice of genre. However, it would seem that developments over the last few decades point to a restlessness among cinemagoers confronted with the genre's once-favoured mode of grim fatalism. Modern horror's commercial successes now deploy themes of character 'empowerment', in which horrific threats are conjured purely to facilitate subsequent identification with defiant wise-cracking heroes. Ironically, it may again have been George Romero (already responsible for changing horror's emphases in *Night of the Living Dead*) who was responsible for ushering in this

above:
The scene David Warbeck described earlier in this chapter...

below:
Warbeck and Fulci regular Al Cliver, as the terrified Doctor Harris.

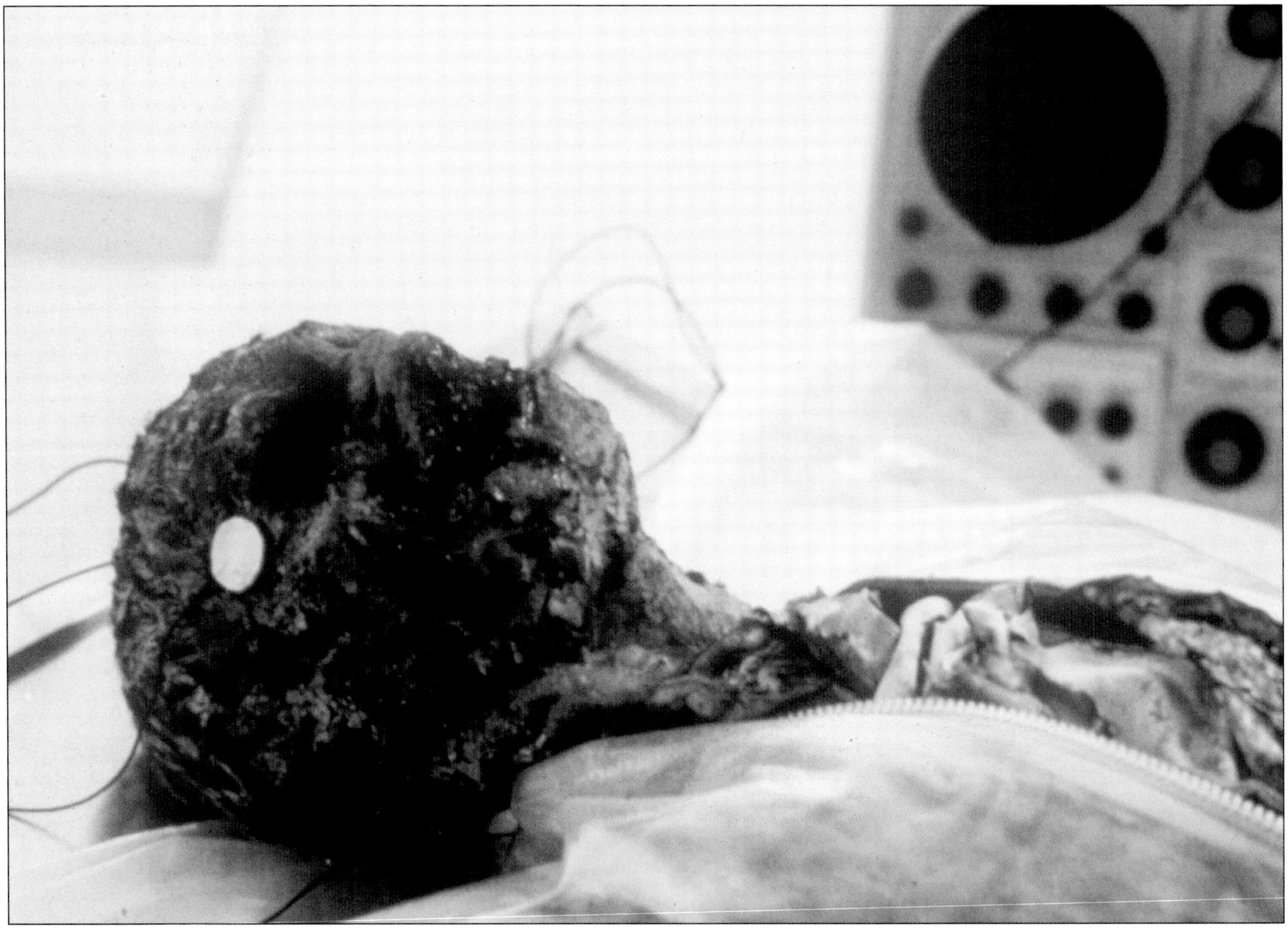

above:
Schweik is attached to an EEG machine by a whimsical Dr. Harris.

below:
Theatrical poster for the 1998 Miramax theatrical re-release of *The Beyond*. Quentin Tarantino's Rolling Thunder production company were instrumental in persuading Miramax to strike and distribute new prints; Tarantino is a committed fan of Fulci's work, and a true aficionado of the Italian 'exploitation' cinema.

(diametrically opposed) paradigm shift. *Dawn of the Dead* provided the genre's first example of fight-'em-back heroics, notwithstanding the film's careful undercutting of such archetypes. (The relatively luke-warm reception for his *Day of the Dead* being due largely, one assumes, to that film's far more ruthless and unambiguous rejection of its predecessor's popular gung-ho streak).

Whilst the macho horseplay and gun-toting of *Dawn of the Dead* did emerge in Italian variants (especially *Cannibal Apocalypse*, a hugely enjoyable 'cannibalization' of Romero's themes directed in 1980 by Antonio Margheriti – from yet another script by Dardano Sacchetti! – or in a hilariously scrambled form, Umberto Lenzi's *Nightmare City*, where it's the *zombies* who emerge as gun-toting, machete-wielding thugs!), its trace in *The Beyond* is confined to the final hospital scenes. David Warbeck's beefy Magnum heroics are undercut more by the character's frustrating lack of insight into the logic of zombie obliteration than any directorial irony. Despite accumulating evidence that a shot to the head is the only way to 'kill' the soporifically meandering undead – whose hospital corpse-garb adds to the sleepwalker impression by resembling pyjamas – Dr. John McCabe continues to use up bullets by stubbornly firing at their breast-pockets. *"I won't accept irrational explanations"*, indeed! Later, in a scene which offers an unintentional glimpse beyond-*The Beyond*, we see Warbeck sending himself up, as lift doors curtail a brief glimpse of the capable Dr. John attempting to reload his pistol by inserting a bullet down the barrel! Catriona MacColl's quick, disbelieving grin is a blink-and-you'll-miss-it pleasure that escapes the otherwise morbid atmosphere.

There's something excremental about the passageway into the Beyond as excavated by 'Joe the Plumber'. Scraping away slimy layers of dark brown gunge, kneeling in filthy water and examining the dank paste he's found by smearing it between his fingers, Joe's experience just prior to his violent demise is akin to the foreboding exploration of a sewer, complete with plopping wetness and lavatory trickling on the soundtrack. Is there a glancing awareness of the links between anality and death here, perhaps signalled by the character's almost too-macho presence? Scurvy old Martha, whose job seems to involve mopping up the mess that this other dimension oozes all over the place, finds 'Joe' dead or dying, eye-sockets collapsed into bloody gashes after the first of the film's numerous eyeball attacks. She swivels him round to the camera, which allows for another stomach-churning image – 'Joe's mouth dribbling a glutinous stream of diarrhetic orange slime. The camera enhances the excretory sense by tilting slowly to follow the body as it slides down the wall. Present in this image's connotational structure is the messy and uncoordinated dribbling of babies, a further pointer to the faecal fascinations of early childhood, where the inability to control eating and defecation generates a confusion of oral and anal.

We seem to be talking shit here… Martha explores the subterranean zone further and we see yet more scatological imagery. A corpse, mouldy and gnarled, pops sickeningly up to the surface from a trough of foul, discoloured water, and floats there like a turd in a toilet bowl. We assume that it must be the cadaver of Schweik, the artist-warlock so brutally repressed – crucified through the wrists and splattered with quicklime by torch-bearing ruffians – in the opening sequence. It's the Artist as waste product.

Transferred to the hospital nearby, Schweik's corpse catches the attention of Dr. McCabe's somewhat fanciful assistant, Harris, who decides to attach electrodes to its skull and check for blips on his oscilloscope. The situation reads like a joke about the value of Art Criticism. *"You wanna wire this old gonz up to your brain-wave machine?"*, queries a disbelieving McCabe, before leaving him to it. The implication is that analysis of the dead Artist is pointless. Then again, there is a single 'blip' which occurs on the oscilloscope screen when neither Harris nor McCabe are looking...

The Italian horror genre is haunted by the arch presence of Dario Argento, particularly in the wake of his smash hit *Suspiria* (1977) and its semi-sequel *Inferno* (1980). Furthermore, it was Dario Argento who, in his capacity as international co-producer of *Dawn of the Dead*, was responsible for the final cut of Romero's film in Italy. His influence also extended to the soundtrack, co-written with his regular collaborators Goblin. Romero notes that Argento's input was accepted because of his belief that the Italian was a man who would not violate the spirit of the work. This unusual degree of trust resulted in a five minute difference in length and a greater emphasis (read 'volume') given to the Goblin music; the shorter, louder Italian version is shorn of a few dialogue sequences, on the basis that the humour was unlikely to work with Italian audiences. So Romero's influential zombie opus arrived in Italian cinemas under the benevolent patronage of Dario Argento.

Although Fulci was by now shedding the influence of *Dawn*, features such as the gun-play at the climax of *The Beyond* are residual evidence of the debt. However, Dr. McCabe's shooting of Jill, the last shocking gore in the film – we see him blow a huge chunk of her skull clean off – indicates the frantic shorthand with which these resonances were incorporated. Jill is a young girl who, unbeknownst to the two leads, has been 'zombified' in an earlier attack. Young children are often the focus of a tender yet despairing gaze in Fulci's films, with the idea – or the fully realized spectacle – of their destruction remaining the site of an unambiguous horror. Even in the delirious world of a Fulci film, the swiftness of Dr. McCabe's reflex is shocking. Unmediated by the anguished doubts that Romero's characters face when they are attacked by 'familiar' zombies, this sacrifice of an admittedly depthless child to the exigencies of ultra-gory thrills is perhaps the film's only sour note.

More playful than the mere incorporation of guns and zombies is the casting of actress Veronica Lazar in the role of Martha. The way Lazar is handled in the plot suggests that audiences were expected to remember her as a central character in Dario Argento's hit *Inferno*, released the year before. (A similar cross-referencing with *Inferno* occurs in *The House by the Cemetery*, using Ania Pieroni). In the Argento film, Lazar plays a sinister nurse who turns out to be 'Mater Tenebrarum' (the Mother of Darkness), part of a female gestalt version of Death itself.

All of which loads Veronica Lazar's appearance in *The Beyond* with a certain amount of referential baggage. Again she plays a sinister character, glooming around in a mysterious building, with violent death and weird significance all around. And here too the sense is of a supernatural disposure hiding behind a mundane, functional facade. Martha's speech patterns combine surly deference with obscure threat; there's a staggered, edgy musicality in one exchange with Liza (as they ascend a spiral staircase), a weirdly stimulating 'wrongness' similar to Argento's.

She must be up to *something*, we surmise, must surely be in on the Hotel's secrets, however

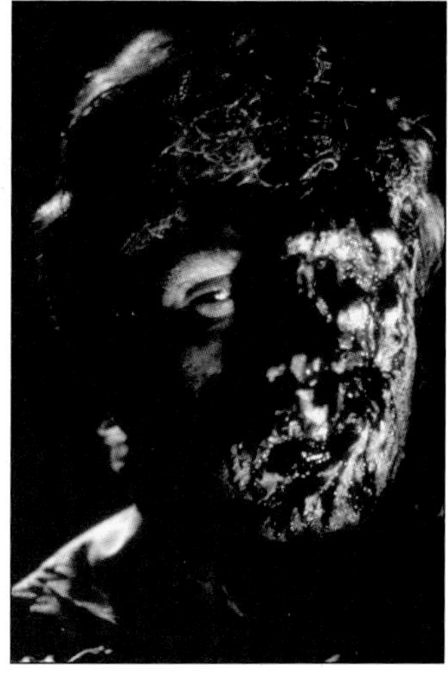

above:
A denizen of the underworld.

below:
A possessed Jill attends her parents' funerals.

bottom:
Dr. McCabe discovers a hieroglyph etched into the rotten flesh of the corpse found in the cellar.

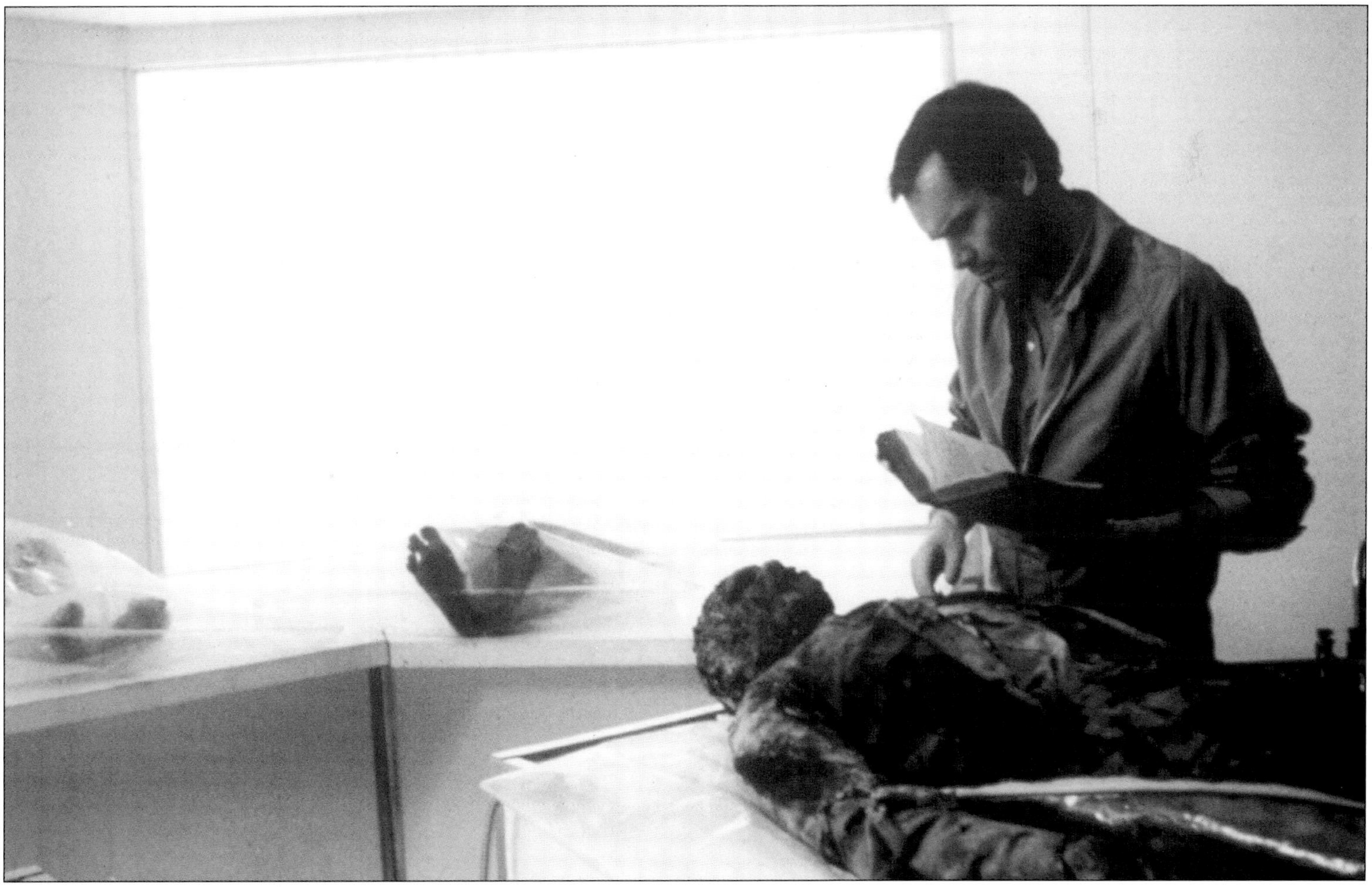

top:
Joe the Plumber gets his revenge on Martha.

above:
Mexican admat.

ambivalently. Yet Martha herself appears to be apprehensive of what the Hotel will throw up next. All of which turns out to be part of the film's remorseless illogic – sinister Martha meets a literally eye-popping demise at the hands of a zombie lying concealed in a bathful of dirty water. Defying the murmurous hints already dropped, the film turns against all of its characters, even the ones who appear to have been chosen for their iconic dimension. In truly pessimistic fashion, no one serves the Beyond and gains anything but the most fleeting and troubled of abeyances from their own inevitable doom.

The wraith of Dario Argento haunts the fate of Emily too. When the Alsation guide-dog turns unexpectedly upon its mistress, we are reminded of the savaging of *Suspiria*'s blind pianist (though Fulci of course takes the depiction of flesh-rending dog savagery even further). Then there's the soundtrack, featuring scale-permutated piano and exaggeratedly mock-Gothic choral pieces. Most derivative of all are the bizarrely redundant voices spitting the word "spider!" over an arachnid attack sequence, recalling the voices hissing "Witch!" over *Suspiria*'s score.

Fulci's interviews at the time are replete with asides that suggest Argento's influence. The phrase *"absolute film"* would arise when Fulci discussed *The Beyond*, perhaps lifted from Argento's ruminations on *Inferno*. (It also suggests François Truffaut's term 'pure film' in reference to Hitchcock's work: meaning generated by the unique fusion of image and sound that is cinema.) Fulci suggests that the term indicates a *"film without borders"* and a preference for the unrestrained quality of the image over narrative logic. Sure enough, the film privileges evocative incidents (instead of relegating them to brief moments of tightly constricted flamboyance). Inventive staging is brought to bear on details that wouldn't normally be considered important enough to warrant it (such as the elaborate crane shot pulling back from Emily as she plays the piano and the slow, gliding camera that tracks Emily and Liza through the bushes to Emily's door). Scenes like these bear out Fulci's remarks, and *The Beyond* is thus his most avant-garde film. In a way, he'd hit upon a formula that allowed him to have things both ways. The plot may disappear and the images may dominate the action, but the shocking excess of the many violent scenes provides a quality of dread in place of dramatic conflict, and encourages its popular horror film audience to keep watching.

The Beyond features many sequences where the application of technique appears spontaneously inspired rather than referential. One of the most imaginative is the sudden departure of Emily when a conversation with Liza about the haunted hotel is interrupted. The sequence plays daringly with the very conditions of cinema projection, and risks alienating the viewer with a technique simulating mechanical failure. Liza, already suspicious of the weird, alabaster-skinned woman, discusses with her the strange events she's experienced at the hotel. Emily tells her the story of Schweik, the warlock whose death we witnessed in the prologue.

Even this commonplace of narrative exposition – one character 'filling in' another with knowledge we've already been granted – is rendered eerie and magical. Instead of a prosaic fade from the beginning of an explanation to the end (arriving back in time for 'And that's how it all happened...'), we spend the period of explanation being swirled around the hotel stairs and corridors, to the accompaniment of Fabio Frizzi's deeply resonant choral Mellotron. The cue line is immaculately Gothic (*"But now I'll have to tell you everything..."*), the point of re-entry into the character's conversation compellingly askew. We return to hear Emily still offering metaphysical 'explanations' for the impossibilities Liza has found herself struggling with. Emily's unease, consistent with her depiction as a threshold denizen, is marked first by the sound of fluttering on the soundtrack, prompting her nervous enquiry about other presences in the room. Liza gets to make a speech about her defiantly down-to-earth views:

"Now listen: I've lived in New York all my life – and if there's one thing I've learned not to believe in it's ghosts. I was lucky to inherit this hotel; the first good break I've had. It'll take more than a faulty electrical contact or some crazy story to make me give it up."

Emily remains distressed, however, convinced that the evil Schweik is lurking nearby. As she runs her hands over the painting we saw Schweik working on in the prologue, the service bell for Room 36 rings abruptly. Room 36 was the warlock's room. Emily discovers her hands are covered in blood after touching the old painting, and panicked she runs out into the misty night, followed by her guide dog.

The next minute or so challenges the viewer in a truly bizarre way. Emily's sudden departure has been conveyed by an oddly restricted soundtrack, and just as the audience perhaps spotted something peculiar, so too does Liza. In diegetic terms the mystery is reassuringly familiar – surely, the mysterious blind girl made no footfalls as she ran across the bare wooden floor and out of the door? However, the suddenness of the auditory trick plays strangely on the ear. I suspect many viewers will have believed that for a short while the film print itself, or even the projector/speaker system, had been at technical fault.

What makes this scene so compelling is the fact that Liza then muses about the short sequence discussed, via a slow zoom to her thoughtfully closed eyes. As if in telepathic response to the viewer's suspicions, she imagines the 'shot' repeated twice, overlapping, as well as 'running it' again from a lower, previously unseen angle. In each case, the supernaturally silent footfalls are juxtaposed jarringly with shots of Liza enacting a 'test-run' across the floorboards, complete with harsh, clamorous footstep sounds. She never actually moves; instead the shots and sounds represent her deductive process – how could this girl and her dog run across bare boards without making a sound? In diegetic terms the function of the scene is merely to reinforce the character's realisation – Emily is a ghost! In a wider sense, though, the scene possesses the exhilarating air of a lucid dream.

top:
Liza is sprayed with blood whilst exploring beneath the hotel.

above:
The funeral of Jill's parents.

left:
Dr. McCabe and Liza are forced to flee the Hotel when a storm erupts in the cellar...

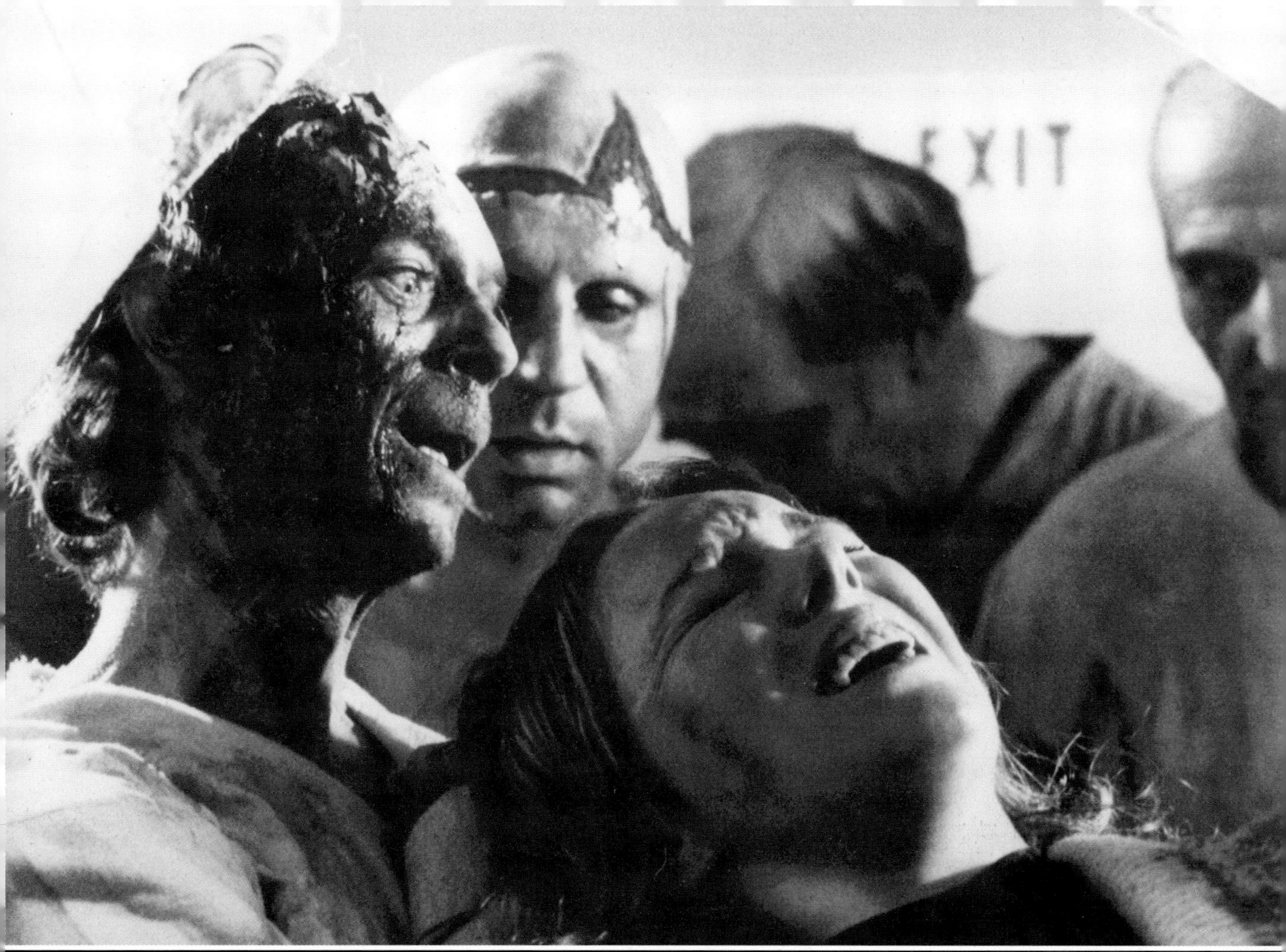

The Beyond is memorable, of course, for its outlandish scenes of violence, a quality fast becoming the key note of Fulci's style. Discussing special effects in an interview conducted a year later, in May 1982, Fulci gave a ringing defence of his focus on graphic violence, stressing the opportunity it gave him for creativity and visual surprise: *"There are those that call me the butcher of thrillers, but those who say that are making a mistake. The special effects, the make-ups that I use, are absolutely appropriate for the horror films that I like to make. It may not be a noble genre, but it is the only one that gives me the possibility to 'play' with the camera, to improvise new solutions, to invent disturbing atmospheres. You know what's the trouble with the young Italian directors? They frame the characters from the chest to the head for the whole film. They make them talk on and on and on (see Abatantuono) and they do not worry about anything else as long as they make a profit. Not me, I love the thousand little phases of the job that lie behind an effect [...] for example, the masks, the filters, the montage, swapping a wax head for a real one, the dissolve within a frame, the slowed down explosion, etc, etc. And if I forget the procedure I used for a film, all the better, it will mean that I will be forced to look for different solutions. The important thing, I repeat, is to have the curiosity and the will to experiment."*[21]

For many people, *The Beyond* is quintessential Lucio Fulci. Watching it now and trying to appreciate how such a beautiful piece of work could ever have been reviled as slapdash and inept by critics is difficult indeed. Its dreamlike fluctuations create a unique sense of delirium. *City of the Living Dead*'s collage effect has been massaged into a smooth, undulating continuity. Lyrical camerawork sweeps the eye across the feverish imagery for appointments with fascinating bouts of violence. Cinematic space is in total flux, narrative is eluded. The surreal New Orleans settings – a run-down hotel, a library, a harshly lit hospital and a public bar – are linked by spectral ruined houses and mysterious coastal roads across invisible seas. Spiders munch weirdly on human lips and devour a man's tongue, a plethora of eyeballs are ejected from their sockets in a variety of unexpected ways, a huge bottle of acid turns a woman's face into a microcosmic sea of red froth, and an Alsation dog rips huge strips of flesh from the face of a ghost. Nothing makes sense – in glorious detail – to the accompaniment of bizarre, orchestrated serenities from the incomparable Fabio Frizzi. No matter how often I watch this film, thinking I'll never return after so many visits, I still find myself returning once again: *The Beyond*, a magical epic of sensuous decay, is Fulci's masterpiece.

above, inset:
The petrified remains of those who died in Pompeii after the eruption of Vesuvius on 24 August AD 79.

above, main picture:
Inside the painting...

facing page top:
A cunning zombie (Roberto Dell'Acqua) breaks through a window to grab Liza.

facing page bottom:
"I don't want to go back..."
Emily is terrorized by assorted ghouls.

Italian theatrical title
Quella villa accanto al cimitero

Translation
'That House Beside the Cemetery'

Italy

Alternative title
The House Outside the Cemetery (pre-release title)

International theatrical titles
The House by the Cemetery (UK/USA)
House by the Cemetery (USA poster)
Das Haus an der Friedhofmauer (WG) 'The House at the Cemetery Wall'
Aquella casa al lado del cementerio (SP) 'That House Next to the Cemetery'
Slagtehuset ved Kirkegården (DEN) 'The Slaughterhouse by the Cemetery'
La maison pres du cimetiere (FR) 'The House near the Cemetery'

Video/DVD titles
Las casa cercana al cementario (ARG) 'The House near the Cemetery'
Revenge of the Ripper New York [sic] (onscreen title, Greek 'Starlight Video' release)
Ο Αντεϱοβγάλτης Τηε Νεας Υοϱκης 2 (GRE video cover) 'The Ripper New York 2' [sic]

Production company
Fulvia Film S.r.l.

Theatrical distributors
Medusa Distribuzione (Italy)
Almi Pictures (USA)

Theatrical running times
Italy 87m
UK 86m 15s (before cuts)

Video/DVD/Blu-ray running times (adjusted)
Anchor Bay DVD (USA) 86m 15s

Shooting and release information
Shooting June-July 1981
Italian censor certificate 76953 14 August 1981
Rome 21 August 1981
Brindisi 28 August 1981
Bari 04 September 1981
UK (Birmingham) 4 July 1982
UK (London) 15 October 1982
USA (Newark, NJ) 27 March 1984

The House by the Cemetery

1981

Directed by Lucio Fulci. producer: Fabrizio De Angelis for Fulvia Film S.r.l. (Rome). story: Elisa Livia Briganti. screenplay: Dardano Sacchetti, Giorgio Mariuzzo & Lucio Fulci. director of photography: Sergio Salvati. music: Walter Rizzati. music copyright: DEAF S.r.l.. editor: Vincenzo Tomassi. production designer & costumes: Massimo Lentini. unit managers: Paolo Gargano & Fabrizio De Martino. assistant director: Roberto Giandalia. continuity: Daniela Puccini & Daniela Tonti. stunt co-ordinator: Nazzareno Cardinali. cameraman: Franco Bruni. assistant cameraman: Maurizio Lucchini. key grip: Giacomo Tomaselli. chief electrician: Alfredo Fedeli. make-up & special effects make-up: Giannetto De Rossi & Maurizio Trani. hairstyles: Maria Pia Crapanzano. special effects: Gino De Rossi. seamstress: Bertilla Silvestrin. property master: Rodolfo Ruzza. assistant costumes: Claudia D'Obici. make-up assistant: Antonio Maltempo. set dressings: Mariangela Capuano. production secretary: Guglielmo Smeraldi. paymaster: Otello Tomassini. stills: Antonio Benetti. assistant editor: Pietro Tomassi. cutting room assistant: Armando Pace. sound engineer: Ugo Celani. boom: Eros Giustini. sound studios & sound synchronization: C.D.S.. mixage: Gianni Amico. equipment & cameras: Cinenoleggio S.p.A.. costumes: Safas / SAT Costumes. wigs: Rocchetti / Carboni. stills processing: Atelier Fotografico. set furnishings: Arredamenti Cineteatrali grp. L'Immaginoteca. E. Rancati. fabrics: D'Angelo. colour by LV – Luciano Vittori. negatives: Kodakcolor. filmed on location in New England (U.S.A.) with interiors filmed at De Paolis Studios (Rome).

Cast: Catriona MacColl [as 'Katherine MacColl'] (Lucy Boyle). Paolo Malco (Dr. Norman Boyle). Ania Pieroni (Ann, the babysitter). Giovanni Frezza (Bob Boyle). Silvia Collatina (Mae Freudstein). Dagmar Lassander (Laura Gittleson, estate agent). Giovanni De Nava (Dr. Jacob Tess Freudstein). Daniela Doria (first female victim). Gianpaolo Saccarola (Daniel Douglas, library assistant). Carlo De Mejo (Mr. Wheatley, head librarian). Kenneth A. Olsen [as 'John Olson'] (Harold, estate agent). Elmer Johnson (cemetery caretaker). Ranieri Ferrara (Steve, first male victim). Teresa Rossi Passante (Mary Freudstein). *Uncredited:* Lucio Fulci (Professor Muller).

Synopsis: Norman and Lucy Boyle and their young son Bob move into a sinister old house in New England, while Norman finishes off a research project begun by his deceased colleague Dr. Peterson, who reportedly killed his family at the house before committing suicide. The place is called Oak Mansion, but locals refer to it as 'that Freudstein house'... En-route to New England, Bob has a psychic encounter with a little girl called Mae, who warns him to stay away. Arriving at the house, which has gravestones in the garden, Norman finds the cellar door is nailed shut. A babysitter called Ann arrives, although no one seems to have sent for her. Heading to the local library, Norman meets head librarian Mr. Wheatley and his assistant Daniel Douglas, who informs Norman that Peterson had been conducting private research into 'Oak Mansion', none of which had any relevance to his official studies. Among Peterson's papers Norman finds an audio cassette. Meanwhile Bob has befriended Mae, who seems to live nearby. She shows him a tombstone in the garden bearing the name 'Mary Freudstein', whom she claims isn't really dead. Lucy finds another tombstone set into the sitting room floor and hears strange noises which scare her terribly. Norman tells her it's normal for houses in the area to have indoor tombs. Producing a set of keys he opens up the cellar to reassure her, but a giant bat attacks him. Spooked, the Boyles ask to be moved but the estate agent tells them it will take a few days. The following afternoon, when Mrs. Gittleson from the agency drops by, she finds the house empty. The indoor tombstone cracks, trapping her by the ankle, and a hulking figure stabs her to death with a poker. Next, Ann disappears. Bob finds her severed head in the cellar, and when he tries to escape the door slams shut. A rotting hand pushes his head against the door as Norman tries to axe it down. Narrowly avoiding killing Bob, the parents force entry to the cellar. Norman breathlessly explains to Lucy what he's learned from Peterson's cassette. The house originally belonged to a turn of the century surgeon called Dr. Freudstein who conducted illegal experiments in the cellar. Freudstein, who murdered Peterson's family, is still alive and needs human flesh to sustain himself. The rotting, pustulent creature attacks the Boyles, killing both Norman and Lucy. With the help of Mae and the ghost of Mary Freudstein, Bob escapes the cellar through the cracked tombstone, joining them in a spirit world outside time.

About the production: *The House by the Cemetery*, like *The Beyond*, was a relatively straightforward production for Fabrizio De Angelis's Fulvia Film. Paolo Malco's casting was announced in *Variety* on 1 April 1981 and the production was said to be "on the start line" by 13 May 1981, with shooting expected in Boston MA, Rome and *"other Italo locations"*. The film was then listed as "in production" on 29 July 1981. Two odd wrinkles can be found in the *Variety* coverage: a news item naming David Warbeck as a cast member (perhaps Fulvia's documentation for *The Beyond* and *The House by the Cemetery* was becoming tangled?), and an international product listing dated 4 November 1981 which refers to the film under its pre-shooting title 'Freudstein'.

Review: Lucio Fulci was definitely on a roll as *The House by the Cemetery* went before the cameras. His collaboration with Dardano Sacchetti was in full flight, and he was steadily becoming recognised as the purveyor of a distinctive new brand of horror cinema. His films of this period show a director finding renewed form among the rip-off merchants and money-chasers of the Italian exploitation scene.

The House by the Cemetery again indulges in the gruesome excesses of previous Fulci horrors, but this time the story unfolds in a controlled, slightly more conventional manner. After a pre-credits bout of spookiness, climaxing with a spectacular knife-demise for the ever-unfortunate Daniela Doria (already victimized in *City of the Living Dead* and *The Black Cat*), Walter Rizzati's pop-gothique, Bach-influenced organ theme creates a wonderful sense of anticipation over a shot of the eponymous house. An understated menace then presides for the first half hour, with Fulci showing a greater patience than usual, opting to let the mood build in slow and ominous increments, rather than hurling us headlong into madness.

More than any other Fulci film, *The House by the Cemetery* touches on family life and the home. In fact, the family as it is generally discussed – male and female parent with at least one child – is nearly always absent from Fulci's stories. Through a variety of scriptwriting collaborations over the years, no nuclear family had really been foregrounded before *The House by the Cemetery* (apart from the incest-ridden house of *Beatrice Cenci*). The script recalls Sacchetti's work for Mario Bava on the classic *Shock*, with the central presence of a family (mother-father-young son), and the focus of danger located in the cellar. Shades of Stanley Kubrick's *The Shining* (1980) and Stuart Rosenberg's *The Amityville Horror* (1979) are also present, along with motifs derived from horror literature.

Fulci had built key scenes around the threat of violence to 'innocent' children before (in *Don't Torture a Duckling*, *City of the Living Dead* and *The Beyond*). Here he strives, with only one limitation, to make a child the central concern of the narrative. The drawback, as I'm sure nearly all the film's fans will concede, is the terrible dubbing suffered by Giovanni Frezza, the young actor playing Bob, whose pivotal position in the story is so nearly ruined by a grotesque interpretation. The sound of an adult straining to simulate the voice of a pre-pubertal boy is likely to set viewers' teeth grinding. Nevertheless, it pays to persist with the film, not least for its sympathetic portrayal of the way children perceive the adult world.

Like Danny Torrance in Stephen King's novel *The Shining*, Bob swiftly emerges as the focus of supernatural events.[22] He sees the figure of a little girl gesturing him to stay away, in a photograph of an eerie house at his family's New York apartment. Bob's mother dismisses his story and continues with preparations to leave for their new home. On arriving in New Whitby, Bob again makes contact with the strange girl, called Mae, who clutches a battered doll and exudes the stubborn determination of the traumatized child. Their conversation, with Bob alone inside his parents' car and Mae about fifty yards away on the far side of the road, is played quietly with casual acting from the children. Bob talks to the girl without a flicker of perplexity, even though the car windows are closed and she is some considerable distance away; once again she warns him not to go to the new house. Bob protests that his wishes have been ignored: *"Parents never listen. They only do what they want"*.

His acceptance of their paranormal relationship draws on a commonplace assumption that kids

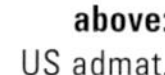

above:
US admat.

left:
Daniela Doria suffers one of Fulci's most absurd death scenes.

below:
Mae appears in an old photograph warning Bob to stay away.

above:
Lucy and Norman find moving house more stressful than anticipated.

right:
After opening up the cellar, Lucy (Catriona MacColl) and Norman (Paolo Malco) find they have a serious pest problem.

handle such disruptions of 'normality' more easily. If Bob is more perceptive, though, then his parents are quite staggeringly slow on the uptake. The soundtrack knows it, we know it, anyone with eyes to see should know it – and yet Lucy and Norman fail to fully register that the house they are moving into is identical to the one in the photograph which has presumably occupied their sitting room wall for the last few years! *"A typical example of the local architecture"*, mutters Norman, when his wife has a brief stab of recognition, *"There are probably hundreds like it in the area."*

For fans of Fulci's other films of the period, *House* unfolds in a way that makes casual but thrilling allusions to its predecessors. The casting of Catriona MacColl in this respect is vital. In each of MacColl's three roles for Fulci (*City*, *Beyond* and *House*) she contributes an engaging, intelligent presence through even the most minimal of script provision. Fulci's work has often been attacked for its neglect of character detail, but he certainly made up for this with some excellent casting.

You can't help but watch the early scenes with a certain amusement, however, as we see MacColl's 'Lucy Boyle' embark unsuspectingly on a further venture into Fulci's nightmare terrain. It's as if she's experienced the preceding horrors (of Dunwich and The Seven Doors Hotel) as nothing more than swiftly forgotten dreams; and yet these dreams burst once more into horrific reality as the story unfolds. Several times we see small frowns of apprehension cross Catriona MacColl's face as eerie details start to build up. It's as if her character is about to remember the other films... Such delirious perceptions are perhaps the stuff of lysergic experience, but the proximity of MacColl's three films for Fulci, their stylistic unity and confluence of mood, contribute powerfully to the process.

Fulci's triumph, whether it is accidental or not, is to have created a series of films that haunt each other. His productions at this time frequently overlapped, and their chronological sequence is subverted by the way in which each partly resembles the others, supplying extra cross-tensions. Factors such as the obsession with physical decay, the emphasis on worms and maggots, the alarming plasticity of flesh and bone, and Fulci's sheer doggedness in presenting drawn-out mutilation all help to connect the Gothic films; as does the repeated portrayal of a demonic dream-world beneath our own (the Dunwich cemetery catacombs, the haunted hotel basement leading to another dimension and, here, the labyrinthine charnel house of Dr. Freudstein). Add to this the overlapping qualities of design, music and Salvati's cinematography and Fulci's films between 1979 and 1983 can be seen as a weird continuum, exchanging energies in a demented mélange.

The interior set of the 'house by the cemetery' itself is hauntingly similar to the Seven Doors Hotel in *The Beyond*, with its wood-and-plaster boards, stained glass panelling, and even a spiral staircase seen briefly in the cellar. These grand but grotty settings, filmed by a caressing camera, make the approach of each threatening situation feel like the immanent eruption of an overarching meta-film, of which each separate title is just a fragment. This meta-film juts in through such images as the collapsed graves scattered casually around in the garden, and the pugnacious presence of a huge tombstone in the house itself. It's trying to get in through the soundtrack moanings and subjective camera wanderings we experience during the first few nights the Boyle family spend in the building. Set dressings and technical factors all add to the impression.

Paolo Malco's portrayal of Norman Boyle is another factor in *House*'s success. Thanks to his abilities, we are once again in a world where strange, lingering looks and inexplicable evasions haunt the characters' perceptions of each other. The basic family unit of father, mother and child isn't exactly riddled with tension, but it's certainly trailing a few ragged threads. Soon after the Boyles arrive in the small New England town where Norman has been despatched to do research, he is recognised by the female estate agent, even though he swears he's never been there before. The woman seems taken aback by his denial, and the seeds of doubt register as

below:
Paolo Malco tries to fight the formidable Dr. Freudstein.

suppressed anxiety on Lucy Boyle's face. A similarly tantalizing misrecognition occurs at the library, where the chief librarian, Mr. Wheatley, claims to recognise him as a previous visitor to Dr. Peterson.

For once a Fulci male projects a more intriguing sort of emotional restraint. Instead of being lumbered with blankness, Norman seems as if his thoughts are elsewhere – something of a step forward, inasmuch as we sense he is at least *having* thoughts. His furtive eye contact and numerous other evasive tics alert our suspicions. Dr. Boyle's distracted manner is especially foreboding when he barely reacts to the discovery of a tombstone in the floor of his new home. *"This ain't New York"*, he remarks, *"Most of the old houses in the area have tombstones in them, because in the winter it freezes here"*. It's all too much for his overstrung wife, and Norman is quick to offer pills to calm her sudden attack of nerves. Too quick? In a scene which unites sinister suggestion with a warping of reality, she rejects his offer saying she's *"heard that those pills can provoke hallucinations"*. A sinister pause is observed, before Norman quietly intones: *"Are you sure?"* Whether he's questioning the truth of what she's heard or the fact that she's heard it at all introduces a note of druggy ambiguity.

The ambivalent paternal figure is a link with Sacchetti's aforementioned Bava film, *Shock*. Norman may not prove as duplicitous as Bruno (John Steiner) in that film, but for a while we are taunted with the possibility that he could be an evil figure. The drug implications match the plot of *Shock*, too. In Bava's film, Dora (Daria Nicolodi) is regularly drugged by her husband... and Norman Boyle keeps insisting that his wife should take the medication he's had prescribed for her. It's implied during the build-up to the Boyles' discovery of Dr. Freudstein that Norman might be cheating on his devoted wife, obsessed with the morbid history of the house they've taken, and at the very least callous for taking them to the house of a mad colleague who murdered his family. Likewise, the suggestions of neurosis in Lucy echo the operatic suffering of Dora in *Shock*.[23]

And yet, as the story reaches a climax, we discover nothing to support our doubts about Norman Boyle. Every opportunity to make him an evil father is relinquished by the way the film ultimately portrays his actions. Strange eye contact, ominous music, the paranoia of his wife – all conspire to encourage our doubts, but Norman (even his name is generically loaded to connote *Psycho*) never actually freaks out. Recollections of other tales attempt to impinge on our view of him: Lovecraft's *The Case of Charles Dexter Ward* – a man who is affected by his researches into the past and comes to resemble more and more his ancestor, a black magician, for instance; but the expected avenues of negativity are ultimately rejected by Sacchetti's script.

The cluster of American cinematic influences, taking in Kubrick's *The Shining*, and Stuart Rosenberg's film of *The Amityville Horror*, also turn out to be misleading. Fulci even toys with our recollections of these two films, with their monstrous, axe-wielding fathers, when Norman grabs an axe to break down the cellar door. This time, though, the father-figure's intentions are honourable. Too bad that Dr. Freudstein is holding Bob's head flat against the inside of the cellar door. Fulci then reprises one of the most outstanding scenes from *City of the Living Dead*, as Norman's axe emerges through the splintering wood millimetres away from his son's skull. Dr. Boyle, however, never even tries to kill his wife and son. The genre's principle of symmetry and proliferation of evil would usually demand that Boyle – like *The Amityville Horror*'s Mr. Lutz, and *The Shining*'s Jack Torrance – should gradually be overcome with a desire to destroy his beloved family. This never happens, despite the near-overwhelming cinematic and literary pressure. But the family's fate is still grim, even if Norman and Lucy do turn out to be positive parental figures after all. The climax has them united in attempting to save their son from the voracious clutches of Dr. Freudstein, but they fail spectacularly, and gruesomely.

As in the previous films of this period, certain writers are glancingly invoked by a number of visual or written cues. In *City of the Living Dead* it was H.P. Lovecraft; *The Black Cat* drew on Edgar Allan Poe in a rather idiosyncratic manner; *The Beyond* touched on recollections of Clark Ashton Smith, and Lovecraft again, through the mysterious grimoire *Eibon* and the application of Lovecraft's impossible geometries; and here, in *The House by the Cemetery*, we encounter, along with the tirelessly persistent shade of Lovecraft, the British novelist Henry James. James may seem an unlikely touchstone for the hyperbole of Fulci's gore-drenched films, but *House* is a little different, concentrating most of the grisly scenes into the film's climax, and loitering moodily around the notion of supernatural congress between children. The grafting of a quotation from James's 1898 novella *The Turn of the Screw* (*"No one will ever know whether children are monsters or monsters are children"*) may admittedly seem opportunistic, an undigested idea on a par with the naming of Freudstein. But as Fulci pointed out, the monster does emit the sound of a child to lure visitors down to the cellar, and the analogy between monsters and children suggests we consider the unchanneled, amoral world of the child and it's contiguity with the state of mind of the psychopath.

It's impossible to discuss *The House by the Cemetery* without mentioning Ann, the baby-sitter, a character who seems to come pre-packed with her own chilling pauses: she's so enigmatic she may as well be trailing a slipstream of dot-dot-dots. Her arrival heralds another outbreak of the weird performance arrythmia that was so effective and bizarre in *The Beyond*. As with Veronica Lazar's 'Martha' it's through the casting of an actress used iconically in Dario Argento's *Inferno* that a special kind of staggered dialogue and top-heavy inference accumulates. Ann is played by Ania Pieroni, who made a lasting impression as 'Mater Lachrymarum' in the music lecture sequence of Argento's masterpiece.

above and below:
The violent death of Ann the babysitter (Ania Pieroni).

above:
American ad mat.

facing page:
Childhood trauma Fulci-style...

A marvellously creepy earlier sequence anticipated Ann's appearance. In it, we saw Mae looking wistfully into the gingerbread-style window of a dressmaker's store. Her attention is drawn by an oddly detailed tailor's dummy whose head suddenly falls to the floor, leaving a soggy stump oozing blood. The detached head lies grotesquely in a growing pool of dark gore and the soundtrack spasms ominously. Although at this point we've no idea who the girl is, we know she's experiencing some sort of vision; but one so loaded that it outdoes the borders normally allowed such a premonitory scene. Once again, Fulci's gory images rupture the expected flow of the story.

When Ann arrives in the Boyles' new house, Fulci slams the shop-window sequence forcefully back at us, by intercutting her strange smile with a shot of the severed dummy-head. Of course, the dummy bears an uncanny resemblance to this strange new arrival, but the excessive intercutting goes beyond overstatement, avoids clumsiness, and establishes his brand of jolting arrythmia. Despite this sudden conflation of significant flashback, sinister arrival and plangent music, the film then moves on to a quiet domestic sequence. No time is allowed for a winding down into normality, and yet we notice that an unaccountable complacency has taken over the family's response to this strange new arrival. As if the threatening portent had never happened, Ann has been granted the role of caring for the couple's young son.

There may just be similarities between the strange figure of Ann and the sensitive Governess in James's *The Turn of the Screw*. As with Martha in *The Beyond*, we assume she's implicated in the supernatural designs of 'Freudstein's place'; but instead she suffers decapitation at the hands of the ghoulish doctor. Perhaps her weird pseudo-complicity with the house is a perversion of the Governess's preternatural awareness in James's tale. If this is the case, Bob and Mae are like fragmented versions of the two children, whilst Freudstein and his creepily innocent wife are analogous to the sinister Peter Quint and Miss Jessel. Although the distribution of menace and innocence has been reshuffled and displaced, the characters in Sacchetti's script suggest a glancing degree of attention to James's narrative design.

Lest we get carried away praising the subtlety and restraint of *The House by the Cemetery*, it must be stressed that the film's physical violence, when it does occur, is top notch brutality in the grand Fulci/De Rossi tradition. First to really suffer the outrageous fortunes of death Italian style is Mrs. Gittleson, the friendly estate agent. Arriving when the family are out, she wanders into the house, unwisely letting herself in for a date with the lurking presence we've been expecting for thirty minutes. The film clicks into Fulci's inimitable trademark slow gear, the music swirls into flange-swamped life, and the subjective camera is finally allowed to go in for the kill. After a number of moody trick starts and false leads, we can tell that this encounter is going to pay off. A sharpened poker is thrust into the prone woman as she lies with her ankle trapped by the indoor tombstone. The repeated stabbing is drawn out to a hysterical degree. At the climax of the sequence, in a stunning moment of effects wizardry, the poker sinks deep into the flesh of Mrs. Gittleson's throat. As if this were not shocking enough, its brusque removal from the wound releases a ghastly slow motion gush of blood, as gross as the dog-attack on Emily in *The Beyond*. The victim is dragged away across the floor and we get a glimpse of *further* injuries to the head that seem to have been omitted. (As it turns out, they are all that is left of an effects sequence that was filmed but failed to meet with Fulci's requirements).

The day after this spectacular slaughter sees Lucy emerging into the kitchen after a good night's sleep, and blearily observing Ann scrubbing diligently at a huge bloodstain. Inexplicably unfazed by the gory mess, and the sight of the strange young woman quietly attempting to wipe away all trace of it, Lucy tries a half-hearted query, earning a stubbornly evasive response: *"I made coffee"*. At this stage of the game such moments, which should vibrate irritatingly with the taint of careless direction, just add to the general off-centredness. When Ann herself is decapitated, head sliced off at

right:
Lucy and Bob's fear at what lurks in the basement is etched on their faces; French lobby card.

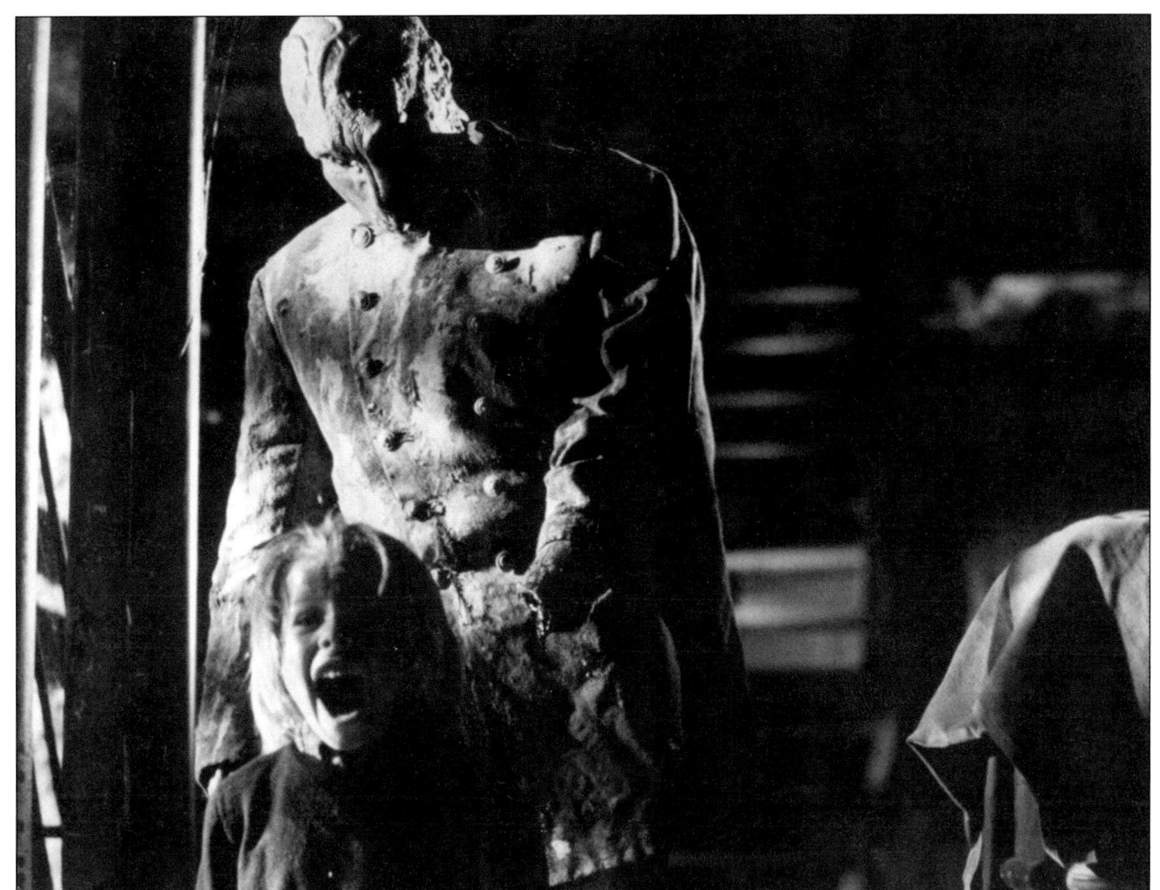

READ THE FINE PRINT.
YOU MAY HAVE
JUST MORTGAGED
YOUR LIFE.
DUE TO THE
GRAPHIC NATURE
OF THIS FILM, NO ONE
UNDER 17 WILL BE
ADMITTED
House
by the
Cemetery

above:
Locandina.

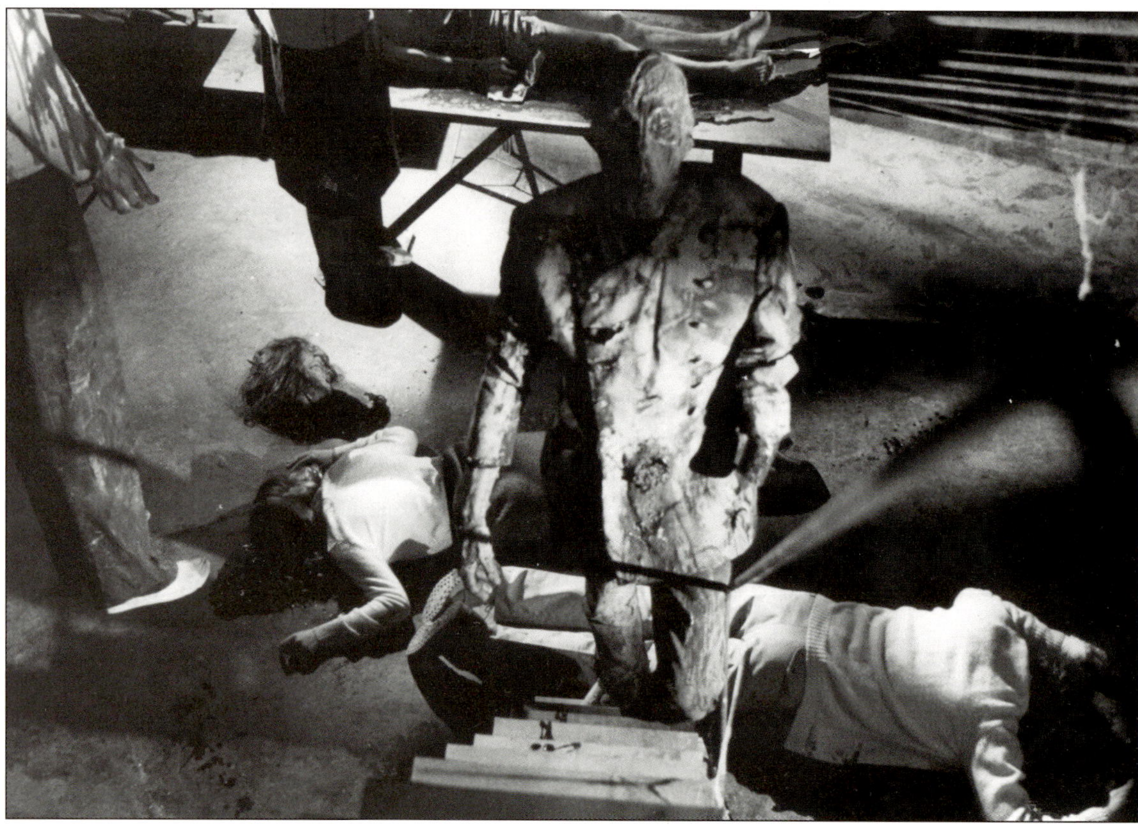

right:
Having slaughtered the boy's parents, Dr. Freudstein (Giovanni De Nava) advances on the hapless Bob.

the neck by repeated swipes of Freudstein's knife, the swift and merciless despatching of this mysterious character really knocks the viewer for six. So much for her, we think, as she bows right out of the supernatural running.

The monster of the film, despite the Henry James quote, is unquestionably the reeking cadaverous ghoul of Dr. Freudstein. Staggering around his charnel house lair, belching putrescence from his wounds, but still nightmarishly stronger than his healthy adversaries, he is a truly frightening creation. He looks almost insectoid, in fact, like a particularly nasty beetle, and more than lives up to the moment when he's finally revealed to our gaze. Twice we see Dr. Freudstein's horrific surgical left-overs; once to accompany Dr. Peterson's mad cassette recording (a fabulous sequence of pulp Gothic horror, like EC Comics without the yuck-yuck humour); and once again at the end of the line for the doomed Boyles. A really powerful blend of terror and disgust is captured in these scenes. Not simply repulsive, and not just creepy either, they capture something of our dread imaginings of *what actually goes on* inside the monster's lair.

No one who has written about this film has been able to stifle amazement at the monster's provocative name. The attachment of Freud and Frankenstein seems so pregnant with meaning, and yet nobody has ever stepped forward to deliver the phantom baby. Certainly we may look in vain for any suggestion of a link to Sigmund Freud in the barbaric butcher Dr. Freudstein! Before we burn off any needless energy looking for elusive significance, I believe I have discovered the source of this striking appellation: namely veteran Italian film exporter Michel *Freudenstein*, the head of foreign sales with Titanus International, who in 1979 set up Italian distribution giants Filmexport Group! One of the major players in Italian distribution, he will certainly have been a familiar name to Lucio Fulci, Fabrizio De Angelis and anyone else involved in selling Italian films for international distribution, meaning that the Freudstein name is almost certainly just an in-joke! (Whether he had a penchant for home surgery is *not* on record...)

So where does Bob really go at the end of the film? Earlier we saw Mae gazing out of the window from a cluttered Bava-esque room filled with antiques. The doll-like Mary Freudstein calls her away from the window, asking what she's been looking at. Mae answers *"The house"*, meaning the Freudstein house where her new friend Bob is in danger. *"Come away, you can't see it from here"*, Mrs. Freudstein softly tells her. And yet aren't they themselves in the Freudstein house, gazing out from another time, rather than another place? This is the ultimate example of the uncanny, searching for home *from* home and always failing to find it. When Mae and Mary Freudstein take young Bob with them at the end, they walk off down a wooded grove, trees bleak and denuded in winter light. The camera uses an extreme wide angle lens, and there is the sense that if they keep walking they'll soon be right back where they started – at the house by the cemetery. In a subtle way, the end is just as terrible a trap for Bob as it was for John and Liza in *The Beyond*; he's returning forever to a house that can never be home.

right:
Lucy and Bob try to escape from Freudstein's lair.

COB TESS
FREUDSTE

Original title
Manhattan Baby

Italy

Alternative title
L'occhio del male (shooting title)
'The Evil Eye'

International theatrical titles
Eye of the Evil Dead (USA)
Oči Zla (YUG) 'Evil Eyes'
Exorcismo en Manhattan Baby (ARG)
'Exorcism in Manhattan Baby'

Video/DVD titles
Possessed (UK)
La malediction du pharaon (FR DVD)
'The Curse of the Pharaoh'
Amulett des Bösen (GER DVD)
'Amulet of Evil'

Production company
Fulvia Film S.r.l.

Theatrical distributors
Fulvia Film S.r.l. (Italy)
Ferpi Film (Italy)
21st Century Distribution Corp. (USA)

Theatrical running times
Italy 85m

Video/DVD/Blu-ray running times (adjusted)
Anchor Bay DVD (USA) 88m 47s

Shooting period
March-April 1982

Censorship
Italian censor certificate 78081
issued 10 August 1982

Release information
Aosta & Vercelli 19 August 1982
Turin 21 August 1982
Bari 28 September 1982
Rome 26 November 1982
USA (New York) 17 October 1986
(1 day only)

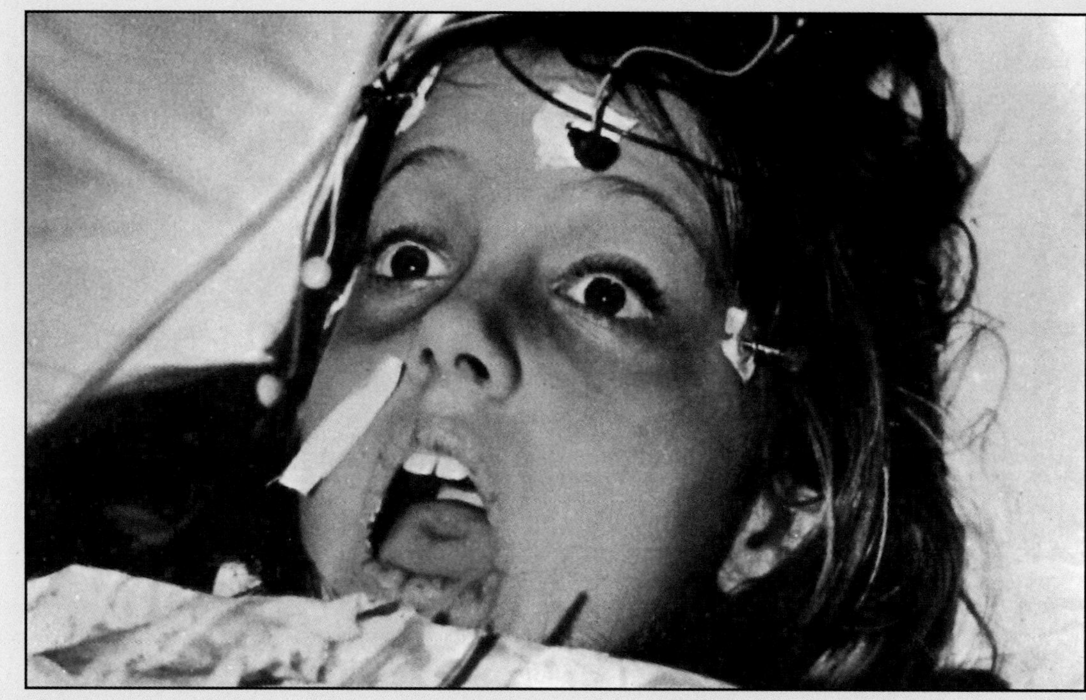

Manhattan Baby

1982

Directed by Lucio Fulci. produced by Fabrizio De Angelis for Fulvia Film. story & screenplay: Elisa Livia Briganti & Dardano Sacchetti. director of photography: Guglielmo Mancori. music: Fabio Frizzi; published by DEAF Edizioni Musicali S.r.l. (Rome). editor: Vincenzo Tomassi. production designer & costumes: Massimo Lentini. production manager: Palmira De Negri. unit manager: Paolo Gargano. assistant director: Roberto Giandalia. continuity: Rita Agostini. cameraman: Franco Bruni. assistant cameramen: Aldo Marchiori & Adriano Mancori. chief electrician: Franco Brescini. key grip: Ennio Brizzolari. make-up: Maurizio Trani. hairstylist: Luciano Vito. wardrobe: Maria Spigarelli. property master: Rodolfo Ruzza. assistant designer: Mariangela Capuano. assistant make-up: Antonio Maltempo. set construction: Fabio Traversari & Roberto Pace. production secretary: Luca Santolini. administration: Otello Tomassini. stills: Franco Bellomo. assistant editors: Pietro Tomassi & Rita Antonelli. sound recordist: Eros Giustini. boom operator: Guglielmo Smeraldi. sound studios: N.C. (Rome). mixage: Bruno Moreal. cameras & equipment: Cinenoleggio. wigs: Rocchetti/Carboni. photo lab. Antonio Benetti. set furnishings: GRP / L'Immaginoteca / E. Rancati. set dressings: D'Angelo. special optical effects: Studio 4. costumes: GP 11. colour/processing by Telecolor spa (Rome). negatives: Eastmancolor. filmed on location in Manhattan (U.S.A.) & Cairo (Egypt) with interiors filmed at De Paolis Studios (Rome).

Cast: Christopher Connelly (Professor George Hacker). Laura Lenzi [as 'Martha Taylor'] (Emily Hacker). Brigitta Boccoli (Susie Hacker). Giovanni Frezza (Tommy Hacker). Cinzia De Ponti (Jamie Lee, the au-pair). Cosimo Cinieri [as 'Laurence Welles'] (Adrian Marcato). Andrea Bosic (Phil, the eye specialist). Carlo De Mejo (Luke Anderson, Emily's colleague). Enzo Marino Bellanich [as 'Vincenzo Bellanich'] (Robert Wiler, George's colleague). Mario Moretti (Tennant). Lucio Fulci (Dr. Foster). Tonino ['Antonio'] Pulci (Orderly). *Uncredited:* Martin Sorrentino (Caretaker).

Synopsis: On holiday in Egypt, Susie Hacker – daughter of archaeologist George and his wife Emily – is approached by a mysterious old woman who gives her an amulet with a blue eye in the centre. Soon after, George is blinded, while exploring an ancient tomb, by a piercing blue light which emerges from a wall decoration. Back in New York, doctors inform him that the blindness is temporary. Susie begins to act strangely, and her younger brother Tommy too. The children disappear on "voyages" having gained access to supernatural doorways. George's eyesight returns, and he describes a design in the tomb to a colleague, Wiler, who claims it's a sign of terrible evil. Later, a scorpion appears in Hacker's desk drawer, the au-pair Jamie Lee is menaced by a snake in the cellar, and piles of sand cover the apartment floor. The caretaker dies in a weird lift accident, and Luke, a colleague of Emily's, disappears after going upstairs to open Susie's jammed bedroom door: he's transported to the desert of Egypt, and dies alone in the dunes. In Central Park, Jamie Lee takes a polaroid of Susie which shows nothing but the amulet against the grassy background. She throws it away but a woman picks it up, contacts a man called Adrian Marcato, and then passes the polaroid to Mrs. Hacker with Marcato's name on it. Jamie Lee disappears, and Wiler is killed by a cobra whilst examining the polaroid. George and Emily track down Marcato to his antique shop. He tells them about the evil symbolism of the jewel, and suggests that Susie has absorbed its energy. He warns them to ensure she doesn't have the amulet in her possession. When they find it in Susie's bedroom, she appears to them glowing with an unearthly blue light, then faints. Marcato visits the girl, but is assailed by her inner voice crying for help, and falls to the ground, foaming at the mouth. He regains consciousness and succeeds in linking minds with George, showing him the mystical Egypt his children have been visiting. At the hospital an X-ray shows the shape of a hooded cobra in Susie's chest. Tommy is affected too, and negative energy is channelled into Marcato's home. Jamie Lee turns up dead, bursting through the wall as a rotten cadaver. George goes to see Marcato again, who tells him that he has substituted himself for Susie, and the curse is now upon him. That night Marcato is killed in a gory attack by the re-animated carcasses of his stuffed birds. George follows Marcato's advice and flings the amulet into the river.

About the production: Announced as forthcoming for the first time on 31 March 1982, in advance of the Cannes film market, *Manhattan Baby* began its promotional life as 'The Evil Eye' starring Christopher Connelly and Laura Lenzi (aka Martha Taylor). By this point the film had already started shooting, commencing in Rome on 15 March 1982. By May '82 its title had changed to *Manhattan Baby* for English-language territories, with 'L'occhio del male' as a short-lived Italian-language variant (eventually jettisoned in favour of *Manhattan Baby* worldwide). Yet something was amiss: picked up two years after completion by 21st Century Distribution in 1984, the film took another two years to emerge Stateside, finally crawling into theaters in 1986 when the horror boom was well and truly over. In the UK it skipped cinemas entirely, although it came out on video fairly quickly as *Possessed* in August 1983 (hot on the heels of the recent run of Fulci horrors in UK cinemas).

On 18 August 1982, under the headline *"No holiday for those who work on the sets of Rome – Cinecittà does not stop"*, *La Stampa* ran a story about the current workload at the city's major film studio, including *"Lucio Fulci, who is having to redo a pile of special effects, a particularly laborious job, for his new horror film* Manhattan Baby.*"* Fulci must have worked pretty fast, because the very next day the film received its first confirmed screening, in the Italian Alpine town of Aosta!

Review: Occupying the strangest position in the Fulci-Sacchetti period is this film, made at the tail-end of the team's enthusiasm. Forced into filming a desert-set prologue, presumably in order to trigger off memories of *The Exorcist* and *The Awakening*, Fulci here eschews the welter of gore for which his films of the period were renowned. However, all the other elements of the evolving style discussed in *The Beyond*, *City of the Living Dead* and *The House by the Cemetery* are here. Plot arrythmia, emphasis on emotionally unrevealing facial close-ups, even snatches of the same music, make *Manhattan Baby* feel like some sort of fractal digression from the previous movies, an abortive but fascinating curlicue, springing from the same terrain as the zombie films but straying dazedly past their promise to shock. Of course, this is only perceptible when the film is taken as part of a series; I imagine that *Manhattan Baby* could seem at best sullen and dysfunctional, or at worst unprepossessing and dull, to a viewer whose preferences haven't been stoked by *The Beyond* or *The House by the Cemetery*.

The Italian *'filone'* principle sometimes leads the industry to 'cash-in' on a movie that turns out not to be a hit; what one might call premature emulation. The speed with which these derivative productions could be mounted paid off in spades when the public's interest was in synch with the producers' ambitions. Fulci though fell foul of this risky practice a couple of times (with *Ænigma* for instance, which unwisely assumed there would be an audience for post-*Phenomena* imitation). *Manhattan Baby* makes sense now, when viewed as part of Fulci's own *oeuvre*, but it made scant impression on contemporary audiences, whose interest in Egyptology waned somewhere in the first half-hour of *The Awakening* (1980).

So if we turn away from *Manhattan Baby*'s mainstream model, where do we look to clarify the peculiarity of this film? It's as if Fulci and Sacchetti are dreaming about their recent work with each other, but the dream is permeated with an anxiety about where to go next. If anything, the film is reminiscent of controversial cult director Jess Franco in its vague, zoned-out assembly of loose themes and images.[24] *Manhattan Baby* is a lot more conventional – and expensive in appearance – than most Franco films, but despite the prosaic anchoring offered by its New York locations, and the efforts of a competent if hardly inspired cast, it still feels detached and unstable. We are faced with a film whose production reality – a quick follow-up to a series of commercial horror flicks – is at odds with the actual accomplishment served to the public.

Variety were probably doing their best when they reported that *"Fulci is hampered here with a rotten screenplay which cribs interesting elements from other films but fails to resolve them"*. Nonetheless *Manhattan Baby* may appeal to those for whom the denial of a resolution isn't necessarily a 'failing'. It is precisely the film's reluctance to 'wake up' that is most striking. Whether we consider this to be symptomatic of an inability to resolve its influences, or a denial of the process of dream analysis, where awakening precedes attempts to force sense from the free-floating dream state, is immaterial. The film just doesn't click into any kind of co-ordinating pattern. It's a Fulci film on quaaludes in fact, with many shots of people in bed supporting the sense of it being a soporific, semi-slumbering recollection of the earlier films. There's a character called Emily (as in *The Beyond*), Laurence Welles [Cosimo Cinieri] reappears after his stint as a decadent husband in *The New York Ripper* (discussed in the next chapter), and the

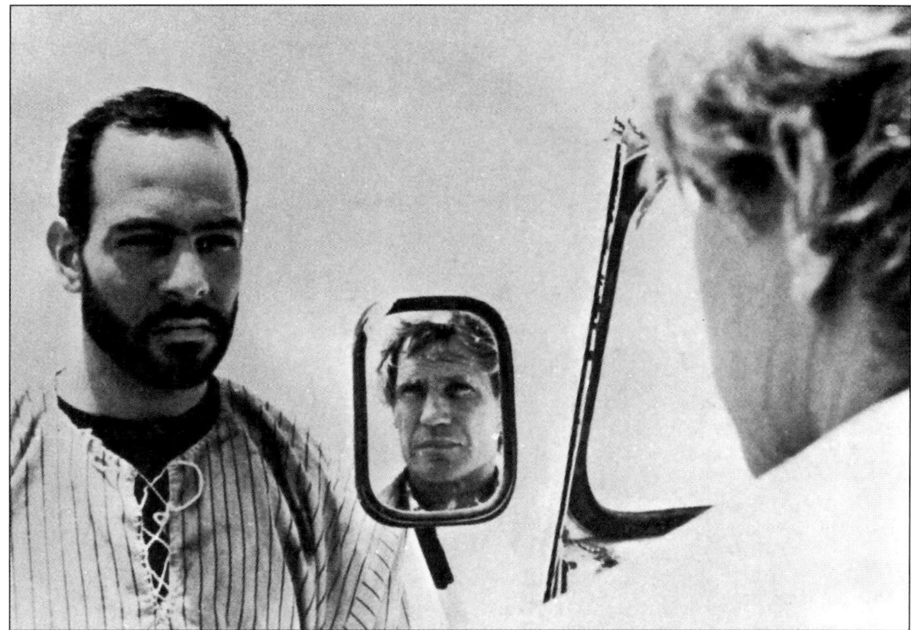

top:
George (Christopher Connelly) consults with an Egyptian colleague.

above:
George is comforted by his wife Emily (Laura Lenzi) after being blinded by a strange light whilst excavating a pyramid. (Note the credits which translate actress Cinzia De Ponti as Cinzia Bridge! Poor Giovanni Frezza suffers too; not only was he dubbed badly in *The House by the Cemetery* by a middle-aged woman trying to sound like a 12-year-old boy, but here he's feminized again as 'Faye Frezza'! Even Fulci's name is altered to 'Fulzy' although quite why is a mystery; surely the idea was to *Anglicize* the names?)

opposite main image:
Susie Hacker (Brigitta Boccoli) undergoes ineffectual medical testing in scenes reminiscent of *The Exorcist*.

opposite bottom left:
British video cover, as *Possessed*.

above:
Frezza and Connelly.

child actor playing Tommy (Giovanni Frezza) is familiar as 'Bob' from *The House by the Cemetery*. The enduring appeal of depicting the special, secret knowledge of children – a Sacchetti/Fulci favourite – is apparent again, whilst the scenes of a sick girl in hospital also recall *The New York Ripper*. As an extra nod and a wink, the script includes a scene where Frezza asks his sister Susie, who has been possessed by the Egyptian amulet, whether mummies are more scary than zombies!

Amongst all these self-referential details, elements from American horror films turn up too. *Poltergeist*, which featured trans-dimensional disappearances within the home of an American family, appears to have made an impact on the story development. Also, in parallel to the film's US title, an antique dealer called Adrian Marcato features in a *faux*-threatening role – the name is that of an acolyte of the Devil in *Rosemary's Baby*.

The only gruesome sequence bearing the Fulci trademark of excess occurs towards the end of the film, when the antique dealer meets his fate at the mercy of hordes of re-animated stuffed birds. These taxidermized terrors peck repeatedly at Marcato's

below:
Giovanni Frezza suffers an attack of Egyptian head-lice.

above:
Susie at the hospital.

right:
Susie starts to act strangely after her contact with an Egyptian mystic.

face, skewering his eyes. Even this is presented with somewhat less offal and orb mutilation than might be expected, although the sequence is very well edited and recalls a skilful bat attack sequence in the much earlier Fulci thriller *A Lizard in a Woman's Skin*. The scene embroiders the director's visceral preoccupations, so well expressed in the past four years of production. Earlier on, though, we see perhaps the first evidence of a change of mood, perhaps even a boredom (on the writing team's part), with the omnipresent violence of the recent films. A rather irritating character played by Carlo (*City of the Living Dead*) De Mejo turns up wearing a pair of 'comedy' glasses, with 'eyes' that pop out on springs and dangle ludicrously. *Molto buffo!* Taken on its own, this gag at the expense of previous gross-outs is merely dumb. As a hint of the ham-fisted levity to come though, in films like *Touch of Death* and *Nightmare Concert*, it is more depressing.

Still, there's something strange here. *Manhattan Baby* does achieve a weird air of its own, thanks to the supernatural conjuring of desert sands, and the denizens thereof, into the well-appointed New York apartment in which the protagonists live. (That's if they can truly be called protagonists – once again characters seem to be just reacting to events beyond their control, lending further oppressiveness to the film's drowsy ambience.) Black scorpions skitter across the rooms, the camera emulates a snake slithering across a light-slatted parquet floor, and sand piles up inexplicably in bedroom doorways. Although understated and almost thrown away, these images are genuinely surreal at times, carrying a whiff of Max Ernst and Dali, as well as echoing Clark Ashton Smith and H.P. Lovecraft, whose characters were often transported into the far-flung stygian realms of vast desert planets. A recurring image is that of sand falling away into itself, as if being sucked down from beneath by an unseen force. There's something disquieting about it, suggestive of both ebbing time and material collapse. The odd, undulating passivity of Fulci's modern Gothic horrors could be represented by the short-hand of these shots. We never see an end or a definite dramatic event aligned with them; instead they create the sensation of a slow, sinking collapse into the beyond. Nothing material or dramatically significant is revealed, but the film gains a lot from their eerie suggestion. Allied to the illogical way that events are shuttled between the banal and the fantastic, they offer the best-realised atmospherics of the film. *Manhattan Baby* perversely boils out the commercially essential violence and leaves us with just the distilled weirdness that its predecessors sneaked through, under the wing of horror's licence to shock.

Along with sterling work by Fabio Frizzi, whose new compositions here make one wish he'd been able to score the whole film with fresh material, there's further evidence of Fulci's sedate taste in jazz of the traditional variety. Acting performances verge upon the indifferent; if only the cast had included more accomplished Fulci veterans, such as Catriona MacColl or David Warbeck, instead of the less than memorable Christopher Connelly and Laura Lenzi. The lensing by Guglielmo Mancori fails to achieve quite the same poetic flair as Salvati's work on Fulci's true Gothic films, but despite all the reservations voiced so far, *Manhattan Baby* survives as a film that Fulci fans may find themselves revisiting long after their taste for hyperbolic gore has been sated. Best explored for a second or third time, after frequent viewings of the other titles in this chapter, and preferably very late at night, this is, to borrow a term from writer David Kerekes, a 'peaceful horror' film, perhaps even a 'transcendental nightmare'. Whatever you do, though, don't watch *Manhattan Baby* before seeing the others described here.

Footnotes

1 With an audience of 477,103.

2 Not, as Massaccesi stated (in an interview with Manlio Gomarasca for the magazine *aka: Joe D'Amato*), on 1973's *White Fang*. The full credits of these films indicate Massaccesi's presence on only the second of the two *White Fang* films.

3 Some of Massaccesi's films were edited by Fulci's long-time associate Ornella Micheli, who worked with Fulci as far back as 1962's *Le massaggiatrici*.

4 Umberto Lenzi is most notorious for a couple of extreme gore sagas which lift ideas from Ruggero Deodato's essential *Cannibal Holocaust*. He can, however, claim precedence, with his seminal if lacklustre 1972 film *Deep River Savages*. He would probably never have returned to his flesh-ripping inspiration if Deodato's far superior film hadn't been such an international succès-de-scandale. His subsequent panderings to the format he'd unwittingly instigated (*Eaten Alive* and *Cannibal Ferox*, both 1980) are amongst the eighties 'gore' genre's most visible, superficially celebrated titles. Yet ultimately they fail either to ignite the imagination or outrage the jaded sensibilities of hardened horror fans; Deodato's misanthropic *Cannibal Holocaust* completely stole Lenzi's thunder. (On a personal note, it's worth mentioning that Umberto Lenzi was one of Fulci's last remaining friends in the industry, one of the few industry figures to attend his funeral.)

5 De Paolis Studios sadly no longer exists.

6 *"UNRELENTING EXCITEMENT, a truly original haunted house thriller"* – Tobe Hooper, Director of POLTERGEIST. *"TERRIFYING...*

above:
Christopher Connelly (top) and Brigitta Boccoli (bottom) with the malefic amulet.

above:
Japanese video cover.

opposite:
City of the Living Dead was released Stateside as *The Gates of Hell*.

below:
George Hacker visits the shop run by Adrian Marcato.

UNIQUE... SURREAL, one of the most frightening films I have ever seen" – Kim Henkel, Author of THE TEXAS CHAIN SAW MASSACRE.

7 *Death Trap* aka *Eaten Alive* also revolves around a ramshackle hotel whose architecture is infected with the madness of its occupants and depicts action taking place on different layers of the building. Scenes set down in the crawl space beneath the hotel are amongst Hooper's strongest work.

8 It's of little discredit to Sacchetti, then, that the finished film was Argento's weakest of his early thrillers.

9 Although he did complete one more film for TV, the delicate supernatural tale *La Venere d'Ille* (1978).

10 The Sacchetti-Bava story has a tantalising but unhappy coda. In 1979, Sacchetti wrote a script called 'Anomalia' for Bava, which would have seen a production collaboration with that other great horror specialist, Roger Corman. Sadly this was not to be; Bava died in Rome on the 26th of April, 1980 while still preparing the project.

11 I refer here to the unfortunate experience of a British horror fanzine editor who agreed to attempt an on-camera defence of Lucio Fulci's *The New York Ripper* for a Channel 4 TV documentary, while the film played silently behind him. His stammering performance may well have been the result of selective editing on the part of the programme-makers, as the slant of the show was resolutely hostile to 'violence as entertainment'. Film journalist David Prothero (now sadly deceased), who was characteristically far more eloquent on the subject of censorship, had his offer of participation refused after a lengthy telephone conversation with the producers. Clearly their agenda was not best served by allowing more articulate fans to have their say.

12 *Film Art – An Introduction* by David Bordwell & Kristin Thompson.

13 *Variety*, 7 May 1980.

14 *Variety*, 4 June 1980.

15 "The tricks of the trade, according to Lucio Fulci", *l'Unità*, 1 May 1982. Note: Fulci is mixing his references here; 'Bombolo' was an Italian comedian who made numerous sexy comedies but *Le fichissime* – a sexy comedy directed in 1982 by Michele Tarantini starring Nadia Cassini and Carmen Russo – wasn't one of them.

16 The director who can best match Donaggio's overwrought style is the American Brian De Palma, for instance on *Carrie* (1976), *Dressed to Kill* (1980), *Blow Out* (1981), *Body Double* (1984) and *Raising Cain* (1992). De Palma's complex narratives synchronize closely with Donaggio's scores, whilst the more mercurial Italian directors, such as Fulci or Argento, seem to require greater elasticity between image and music.

17 Magee was Samuel Beckett's favourite actor, and interpreted many of his greatest works, including the one-character play *Krapp's Last Tape*, which Beckett wrote specially for Magee.

18 Post-Freudian linguistic psychoanalyst Jacques Lacan examined in detail Poe's short story "The Purloined Letter".

19 *Variety*, 9 May 1984.

20 *The Dark Side*, Lamberto Bava interview by Jay Slater.

21 "The tricks of the trade, according to Lucio Fulci", *l'Unità*, 1 May 1982.

22 Kubrick's extraordinary film paid far more attention to the hallucinations and/or spectral visitations of Jack Torrance, the writer/father.

23 However, the ultimate fates of the families in *Shock* and *The House by the Cemetery* are very different. For Bava, Sacchetti posited a supernatural link between a degenerate dead man and his living son. At the climax, both stepfather and mother are dead, and the boy bonds with his ghostly father. A weird sentimentality inflects this outcome, which turns away from the initial Oedipal drives of the tale towards a pact between murdered father and go-between son. In Fulci's film Bob's father, Norman, seems decent if work-obsessed; and at least he's alive. More than that, there is mutual respect between Bob's father and mother. They seem only peripherally antagonistic (a few details in the acting suggest that perhaps some of the magic has gone from their relationship).

24 Jess Franco, a Spanish director whose concerns sometimes overlap with Fulci but whose work-rate left Lucio looking like a prima donna, conducted his entire career in this sort of artfully somnabulent state.

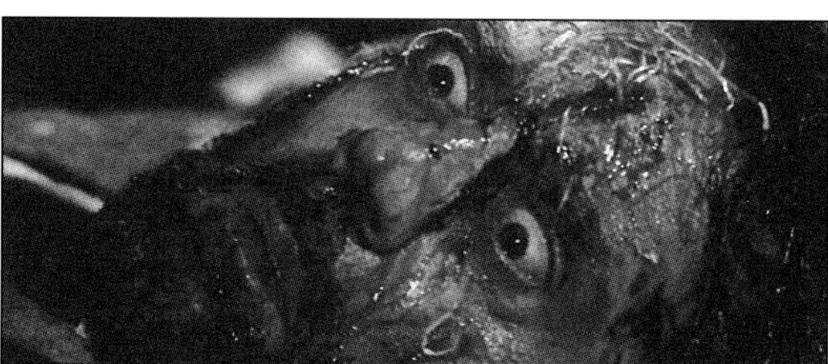

"THE DEAD SHALL RISE
AND WALK THE EARTH"

THE GATES OF HELL

JERRY ZIMMERMAN/MICHAEL FRANZESE PRESENT
"THE GATES OF HELL"
Starring CHRISTOPHER GEORGE • KATHERINE MAC COLL • ROBERT SAMPSON
Story and Screenplay by LUCIO FULCI & DANNY SACCHETTI
Directed by LUCIO FULCI • Color by MGM LABORATORIES
An MPM Release © 1983

THIS FILM CONTAINS SCENES WHICH MAY BE CONSIDERED SHOCKING. NO ONE UNDER 17 WILL BE ADMITTED.

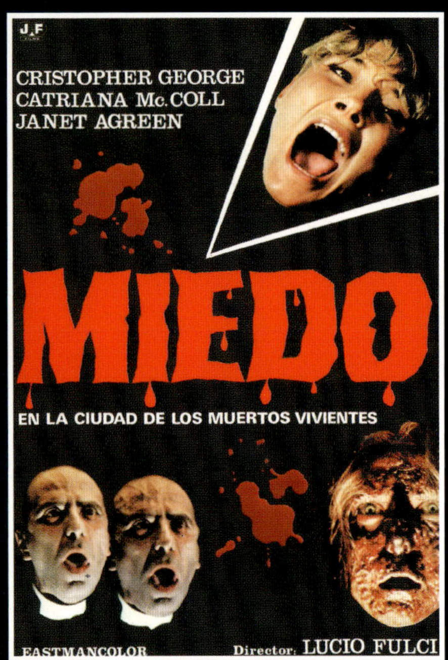

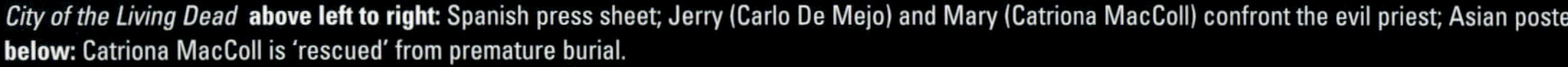

City of the Living Dead **above left to right:** Spanish press sheet; Jerry (Carlo De Mejo) and Mary (Catriona MacColl) confront the evil priest; Asian poster.
below: Catriona MacColl is 'rescued' from premature burial.

City of the Living Dead
facing page: Rose (Daniela Doria) suffers for Fulci's art

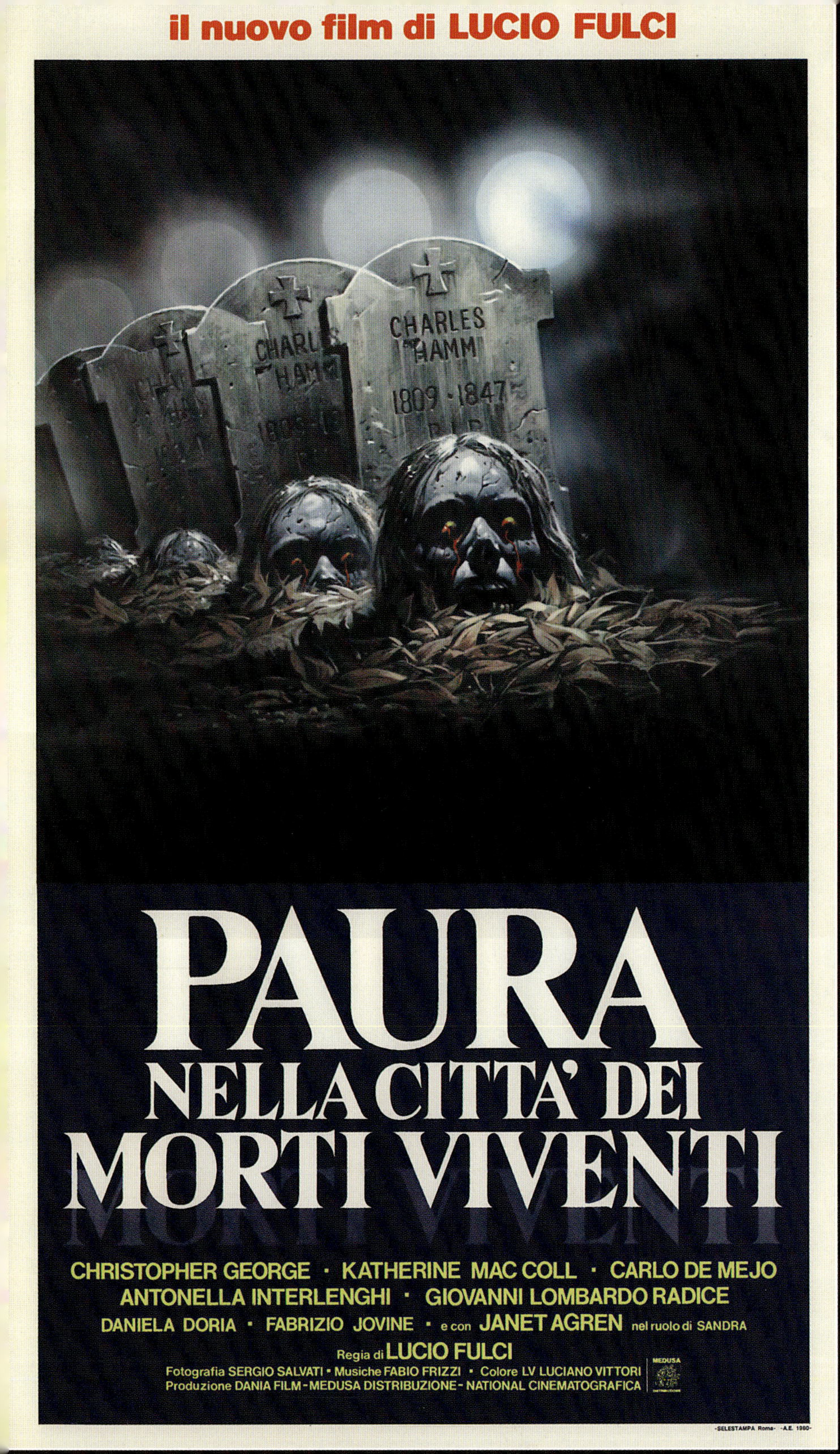

il nuovo film di LUCIO FULCI
CHARLES HAMM
1809 · 1847
PAURA
NELLA CITTA' DEI
MORTI VIVENTI
CHRISTOPHER GEORGE · KATHERINE MAC COLL · CARLO DE MEJO
ANTONELLA INTERLENGHI · GIOVANNI LOMBARDO RADICE
DANIELA DORIA · FABRIZIO JOVINE · e con JANET AGREN nel ruolo di SANDRA
Regia di LUCIO FULCI
Fotografia SERGIO SALVATI · Musiche FABIO FRIZZI · Colore LV LUCIANO VITTORI
Produzione DANIA FILM - MEDUSA DISTRIBUZIONE - NATIONAL CINEMATOGRAFICA
MEDUSA
-SELESTAMPA Roma- -A.E. 1980-

Regie: LUCIO FULCI
Hier wird der Kinosessel zum elektrischen Stuhl!
Ein ZOMBIE hing am Glockenseil
CHRISTOPHER GEORGE · CATRIONA McCALL · JANET AGREN · CARLO DE MEJO · ANTONELLA INTERLENGHI ·
GIOVANNI LOMBARDO RADICE · DANIELA DORIA Kamera: SERGIO SALVATI
Eine DANIA-Filmproduktion im / arabella - Filmverleih

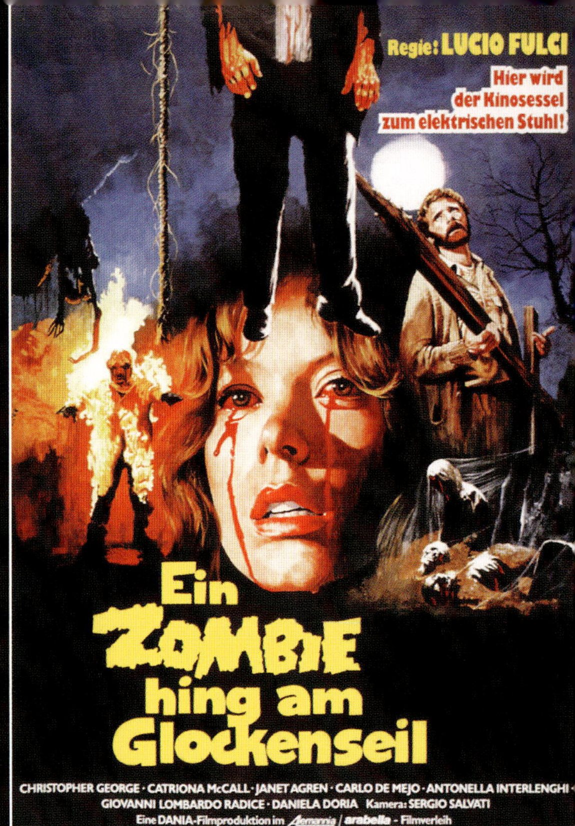

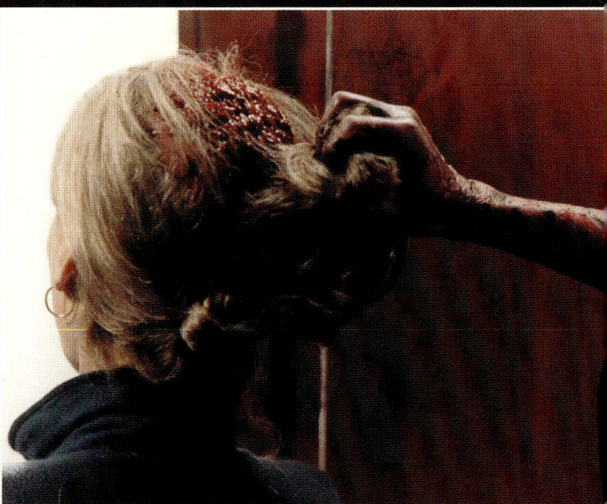

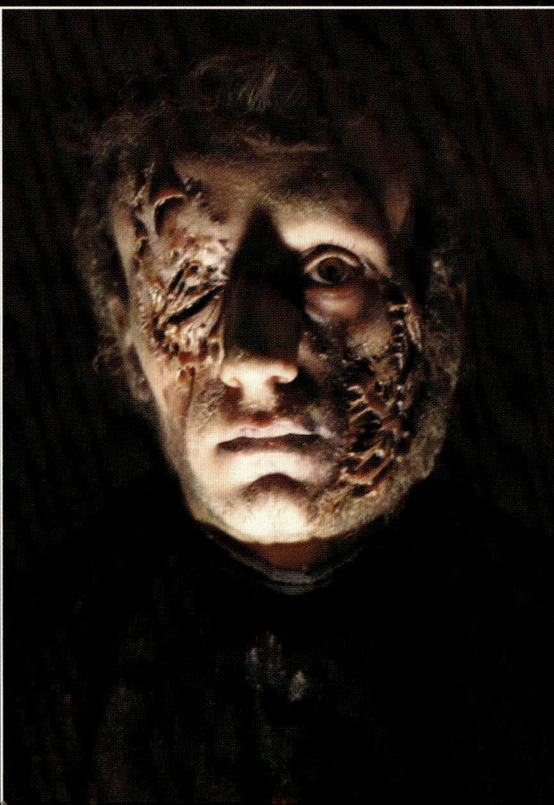

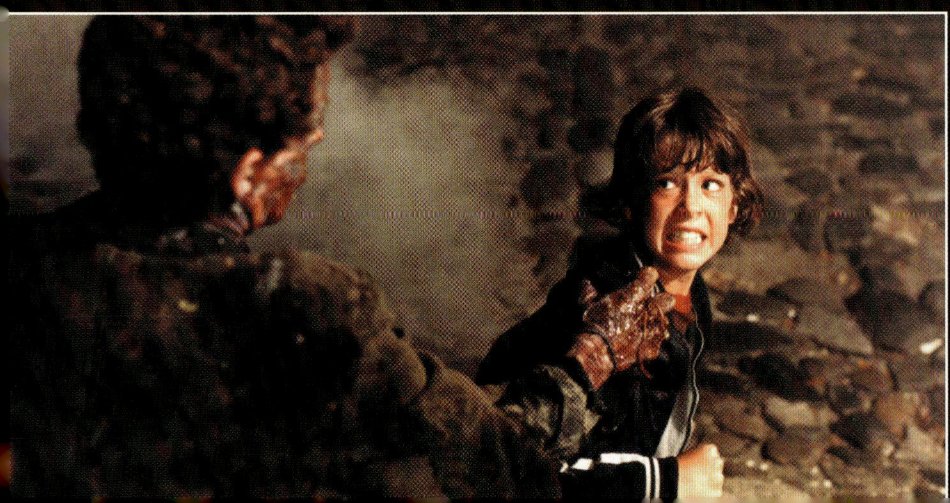

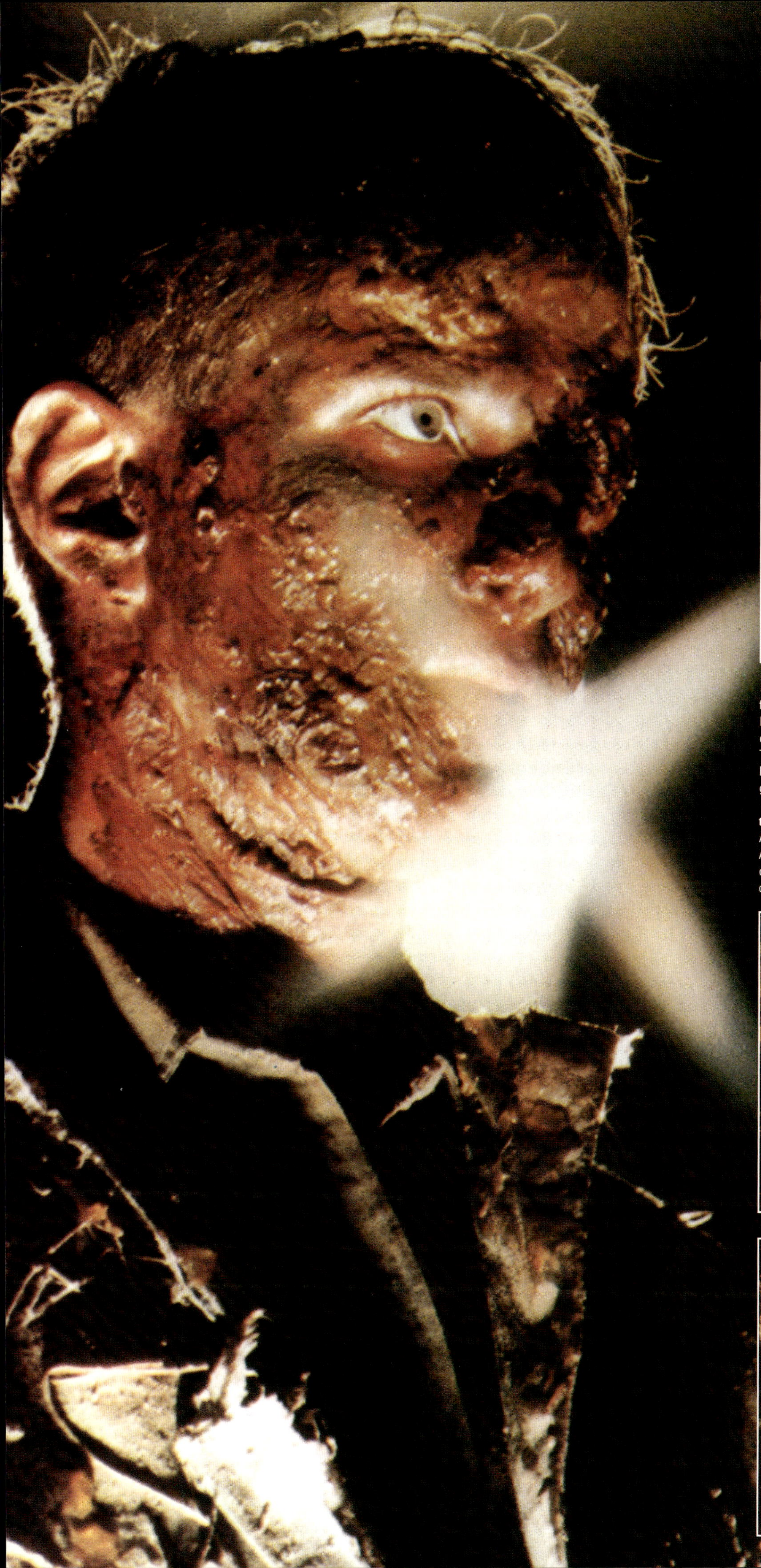

City of the Living Dead

facing page. clockwise from top left:

Italian locandina; German theatrical poster: "Here is the cinema seat to the electric chair!"; Sandra (Janet Agren) has a bad hair day, Dunwich-style; The zombie in this production still is not in the movie. The vestments suggest Father Thomas, but this isn't Fabrizio Jovine...; John-John (Luca Venantini) is grabbed by the zombiefied Tommy (Michele Soavi).

this page, clockwise from main picture:

A zombie (identity unknown) stops off at Junie's Lounge for a bite; Massimo Antonello Geleng's extraordinary art design for the caverns beneath the cemetery; Mary (Catriona MacColl) gets a little ratty, Jerry (Carlo De Mejo) looks on; Father Thomas goes up in flames; Cleansing fire defeats the living dead.

ประตูผีมันอยู่ดีๆมากว่า 5,000 ปี
วันนี้ตอนบ่ายๆคุณจะไปเปิดมันเล่นทำไม
คริสโตเฟอร์ ยอร์จ
จาเน็ต แอ็กเรน
แคธรีน แม็คโคลล์
ประตูผี
GATE OF HELL
ฉายที่
วันที่

City of the Living Dead

facing page, clockwise from top left: Catriona MacColl enjoys the glamour of the Italian film industry.
MacColl and an unidentified extra show off their dental work.
A gorgeous Thai poster for the film.
Mr. Ross (Venantino Venantini) prepares to radically ventilate Bob (Giovanni Lombardo Radice).

this page:
above: Denizens of the under-tomb.
below: The Robbins family mourn Emily (Antonella Interlenghi).
left: Mary and Peter (Christopher George) arrive at Dunwhich cemetery.

Ein ZOMBIE hing am Glockenseil
Alemannia | arabella -Filmverleih

Ein ZOMBIE hing am Glockenseil
Alemannia | arabella -Filmverleih

FRAYEURS
"LA PAURA"

above: Jerry and Mary open a tomb in search of the deceased Father Thomas.
below: I zombi del jukebox... the living dead invade the sanctity of Junie's lounge in *City of the Living Dead*.

LUCIO FULCI... le maître du macabre
L'
AU-DELA
FABRIZIO DE ANGELIS présente un film de LUCIO FULCI · avec KATHERINE MacCOLL
DAVID WARBECK · SARAH KELLER · ANTOINE SAINTJOHN
et VERONICA LAZAR produit par FABRIZIO DE ANGELIS • FULVIA FILM • TECHNICOLOR
INTERDIT AUX MOINS DE 18 ANS
L' AU DELA

The Beyond

above:
Liza (Catriona MacColl) is grabbed by a zombie (Roberto Dell'Acqua) in the climactic hospital battle.

right:
On a lonely causeway (across Lake Pontchartrain in Louisiana) Liza meets Emily (Cinzia Monreale) and her guide-dog Dickie.

facing page:
Emily's palms bleed after touching Schweik's painting. This alternative German title means 'Above the Beyond'.

ÜBER DEM JENSEITS
Alemannia | arabella -Filmverleih

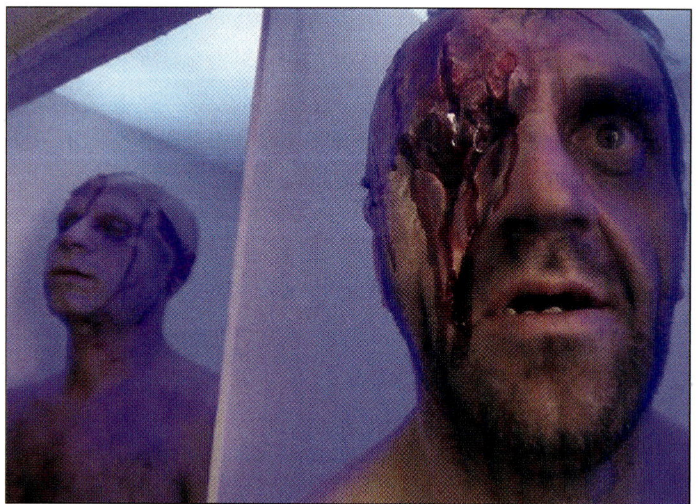

The Beyond

main picture:
Cinzia Monreale as Emily.

top left:
Jill's (Maria Pia Marsala) spectacular demise.

top right:
Zombies on the prowl at the hospital.

bottom left:
The refrigerated undead make their escape.

bottom right:
Liza finds herself in the morgue without a paddle.

DAIEI VIDEO
ルチオ・フルチ監督作品
ミステリアスな古書が闇の世界の死人を呼ぶ、地獄の門が今、開け放された。
ビヨンド

The Beyond

main picture: Locandina.

above from top:
Japanese video cover; German poster; American poster.

...E TU VIVRAI NEL TERRORE!

L'ALDILÀ

KATHERINE MacCOLL · DAVID WARBECK
SARAH KELLER · ANTOINE SAINT JOHN
e con VERONICA LAZAR
Prodotto da FABRIZIO DE ANGELIS per la FULVIA FILM srl
Regia di LUCIO FULCI

Technicolor

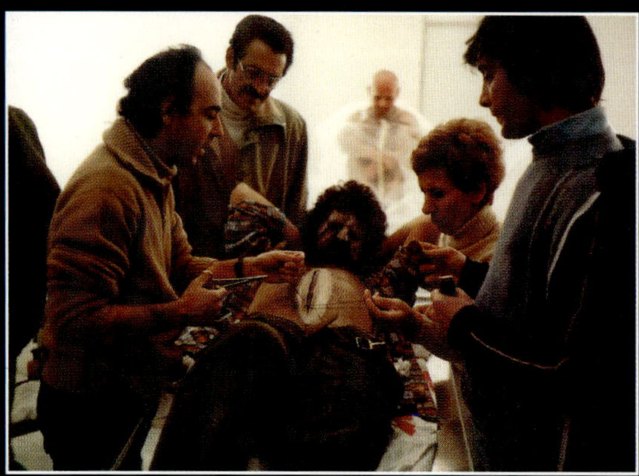

Views from the back of beyond, **from top:**
Lucio Fulci at work;
Extras relax on the morgue set;
Catriona MacColl (centre) and onlookers survey Massimo Lentini's beautiful set;
Tonino Pulci has his stitches applied by make-up artist Maurizio Trani, while stills photographer Alberto Cocchi observes;
The Beyond crew: (far left) Massimo Lentini; (to right of Fulci) cinematographer Sergio Salvati; (standing directly behind camera) Maurizio Trani; (far right) Alberto Cocchi.

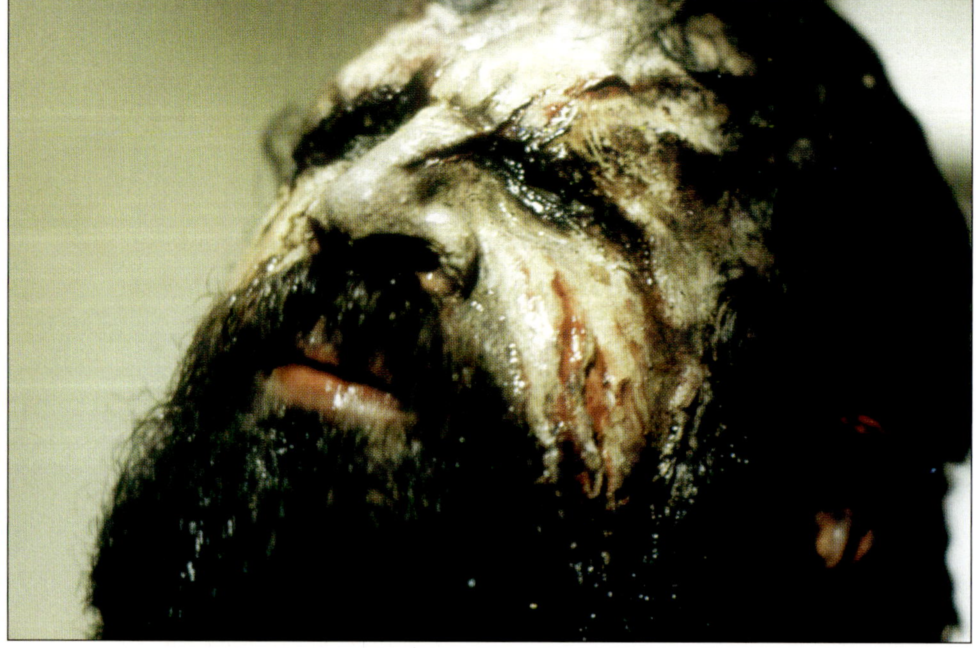

top: Martin (Michele Mirabella) enters an arachnophobe's nightmare.
middle: Emily (Cinzia Monreale, foreground) hints of mysteries at The Seven Doors Hotel to a bemused Liza (Catriona MacColl, reflected in mirror).
bottom: Joe the Plumber (Tonino Pulci) somewhat the worse for wear after his brush with the Beyond.

top: David Warbeck and Catriona MacColl find the hospital morgue a bad choice of hiding place.
middle: Warlock and painter Schweik (Antoine Saint-John) tortured in the cellar of The Seven Doors Hotel.
bottom: Catriona MacColl contemplates strange goings on at the hotel.

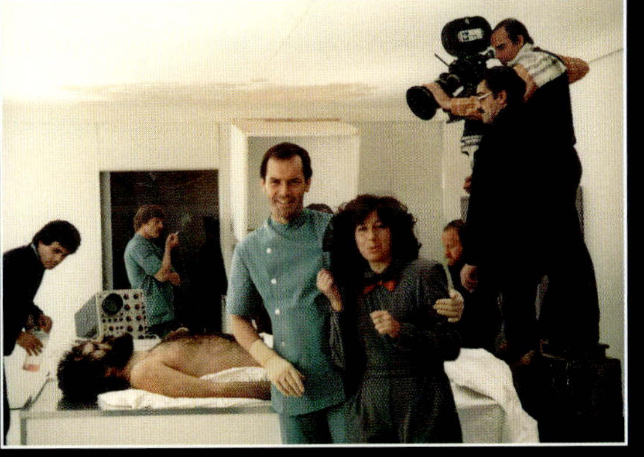

from top:
De Paolis studios at the time of shooting *The Beyond*;
Fulci and Salvati arrange a scene with Catriona MacColl;
Teabreak in Hell;
David Warbeck and Catriona MacColl in glamorous mood;
David and Al Cliver (background) wait for a shot in the morgue to be set up.

The Beyond
top: John (David Warbeck) defends Liza from a zombie in the hospital morgue.
below: "Attack, Dickie, attack!" Emily's guide-dog savages a zombie.

The Beyond
top: Jill (Maria Pia Marsala), an orphan with a secret.
bottom right: The corpse of Joe the Plumber (Tonino Pulci).
inset: Emily betrayed.
above: Mexican lobby card.

30ปี
ที่มันสะสมแรงอาฆาตไว้
เพื่อโผล่มาอาละวาดในปีนี้

สุดสยอง...เขย่าขวัญ
เหนือกว่า
มันมาจากหลุม
มันอยู่ในหุ่น
มันอยู่ในกระจก

มันอยู่ในโรงแรม
THE BEYOND

แคธรีน แม็คคอลล์
(ซอมบี้บุกนิวยอร์ค)

เดวิด วอร์แบ็ค
(ศึกนรกอำมหิต)

ลูซิโอ ฟุลซี่
กำกับ

ฉายที่

วันที่

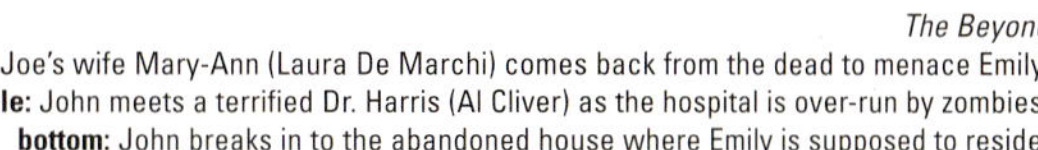

The Beyond
top: Joe's wife Mary-Ann (Laura De Marchi) comes back from the dead to menace Emily.
middle: John meets a terrified Dr. Harris (Al Cliver) as the hospital is over-run by zombies.
bottom: John breaks in to the abandoned house where Emily is supposed to reside.

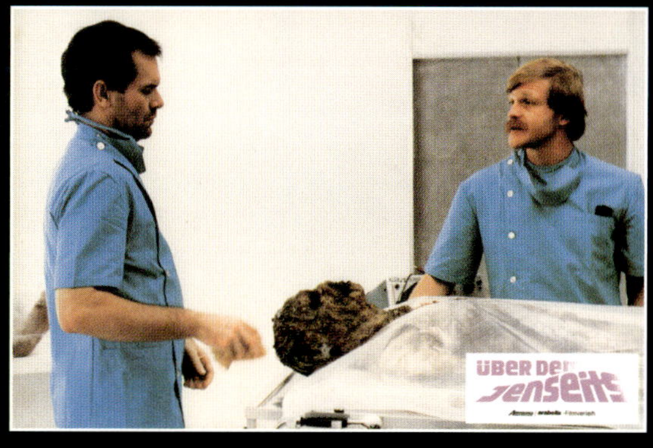

from top:
Catriona MacColl keeps a straight face while David Warbeck learns how to load a gun;
Liza and John confront "all therein that may be explored";
Hospital waiting times continued to worsen...;
Wacky Dr. Harris (Al Cliver, right) suggests wiring a decades-old corpse to an electro-encephalograph;
John and Liza find the climate a little stormy in the Seven Doors Hotel.

The House by the Cemetery
left: UK video company Vampix gave the film this memorable (and collectible) release.
above: Bob (Giovanni Frezza) and Mae (Silvia Collatina), seen here in a bizarre shot missing from the final edit of the film.
below: Fulci's favourite victim, Daniela Doria, is the first to die. **facing page:** Beautifully grisly French poster artwork.

...une expérience
DÉMONIAQUE...

LA MAISON PRES DU CIMETIERE

un film de LUCIO FULCI

avec

KATHERINE MACCOLL · PAOLO MALCO · ANIA PIERONI · GIOVANNI FREZZA · SILVIA COLLATINA
DAGMAR LASSANDER · PRODUIT PAR FABRIZIO DE ANGELIS · FULVIA FILM S.R.L. ROMA

INTERDIT AUX MOINS DE 18 ANS

S. E. LALANDE - COURBET 91 - WISSOUS
Visa de Contrôle n°9245

LA MAISON PRES DU CIMETIERE

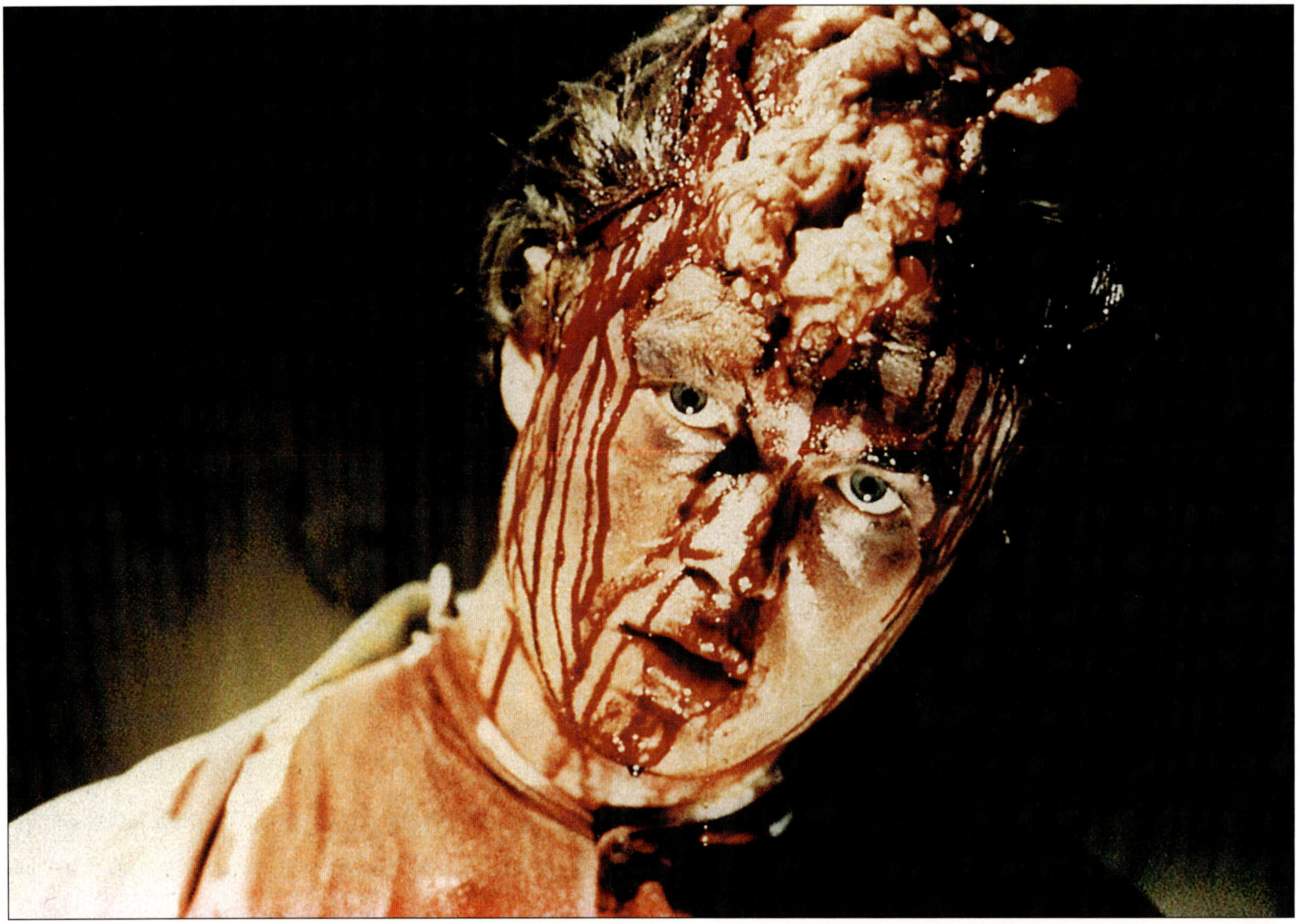

The House by the Cemetery

main picture:
Dr. Freudstein's first kill

above:
Italian fotobusta

right:
Lucy (Catriona MacColl) tries to protect her son in Dr. Freudstein's charnel-house lair.

far right:
Danish poster.

EAGLE FILMS present
KATHERINE MacCOLL in
THE HOUSE BY THE CEMETERY
X
directed by LUCIO FULCI

The House by the Cemetery

top:
British quad.

left:
Bob (Giovanni Frezza) caught between Dr. Freudstein and his father.

above:
Japanese video cover.

The House by the Cemetery

above, clockwise from top left: The Boyles find the bats in Boston a bit aggressive; Norman (Paolo Malco) and his wife Lucy (Catriona MacColl); Estate agent Mrs. Gittleson (Dagmar Lassander) pays dearly for her lies about 'Oak Mansion'; Norman investigates Dr. Freudstein's supposed grave.

facing page: German poster – 'The House at the Cemetery Wall'. Note the distributor, purveyor of erotica Erwin C. Dietrich, best known for his three-year spell as producer for Jess Franco.

below: Dr. Freudstein will see you now...

ERWIN C. DIETRICH
zeigt:
ASCOT
DAGMAR LASSANDER
KATHERINE MacCOLL
Regie: LUCIO FULCI
DIE NACHT
DES GRAUENS!
DAS HAUS AN
DER
FRIEDHOFMAUER
EINE FABRIZIO DE ANGELIS / FULVIA FILM-PRODUKTION IN EASTMANCOLOR IM VERLEIH DER ASCOT

DAL CAPOLAVORO DI

EDGAR ALLAN POE

"BLACK CAT" CON PATRICK MAGEE · MIMSY FARMER

DAVID WARBECK · AL CLIVER

DAL RACCONTO OMONIMO DI EDGAR ALLAN POE · DIRETTORE DELLA FOTOGRAFIA SERGIO SALVATI · MUSICHE DI PINO DONAGGIO

RIPRESE IN TECHNOVISION · COLORE DELLA TELECOLOR · UN FILM PRODOTTO DALLA SELENIA CINEMATOGRAFICA

DLE

REGIA DI LUCIO FULCI

IIF

PRIMA EDIZIONE ITALIANA 1981

GRAFOSERVICE – ROMA

IT'S LOOKING AT YOU...
...FROM HELL!
EYE OF THE
EVIL DEAD
Starring
CHRISTOPHER CONNELLY • MARTHA TAYLOR
Also Starring
BRIGITTA BOCCOLI • GEORGE FREZZA • CYNTHIA DE PONTI
Produced & Directed by LUCIO FULCI
21st CENTURY
21st CENTURY DISTRIBUTION CORP. ©1984
R
RESTRICTED
UNDER 17 REQUIRES ACCOMPANYING PARENT OR ADULT GUARDIAN

สร้อยคอผี
MANHATTAN BABY

un film de LUCIO FULCI
EXORCISMO
EN
MANHATTAN
BABY
CHRISTOPHER CONNELLY · MARTHA TAYLOR
BRIGITTA BOCCOLI · GIOVANNI FREZZA · CINZIA DE PONTI · DIRECCIÓN LUCIO FULCI

OČI ZLA
(Occhio del male)
Režija: Lucio Fulci
Distribucija: UNION
Uloge: Christopher Connelly, Martha Taylor

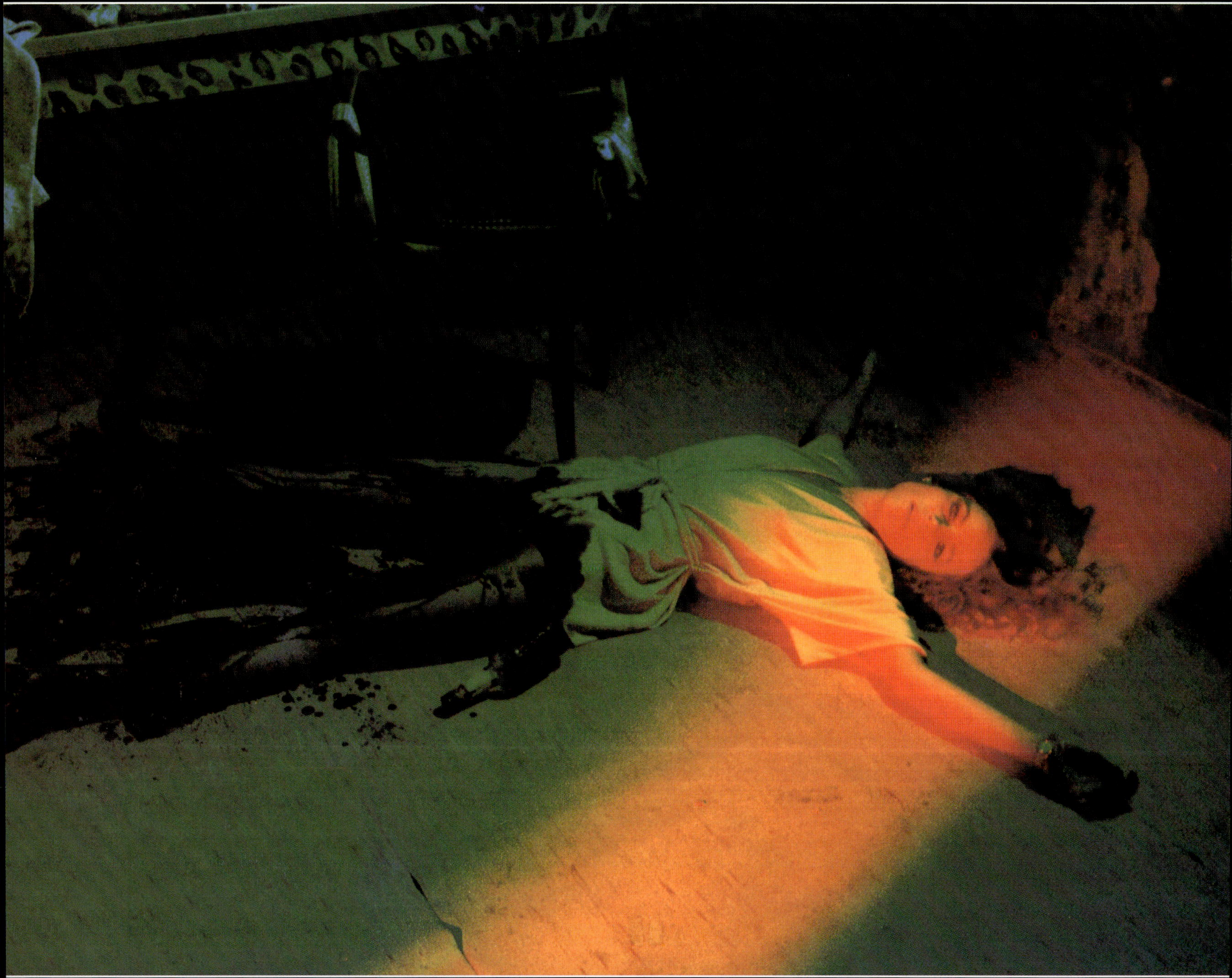

The New York Ripper

above: Jane (Alexandra Delli Colli), immersed in a sexual world. **below:** Argentinean, French and Yugoslavian theatrical posters.
facing page, top: Thai, Argentinean and Yugoslavian posters for *Manhattan Baby*. **facing page, bottom:** Eva (Zora Ulla Keslerová) dies horribly in *The New York Ripper*'s notorious 'bottle scene'.

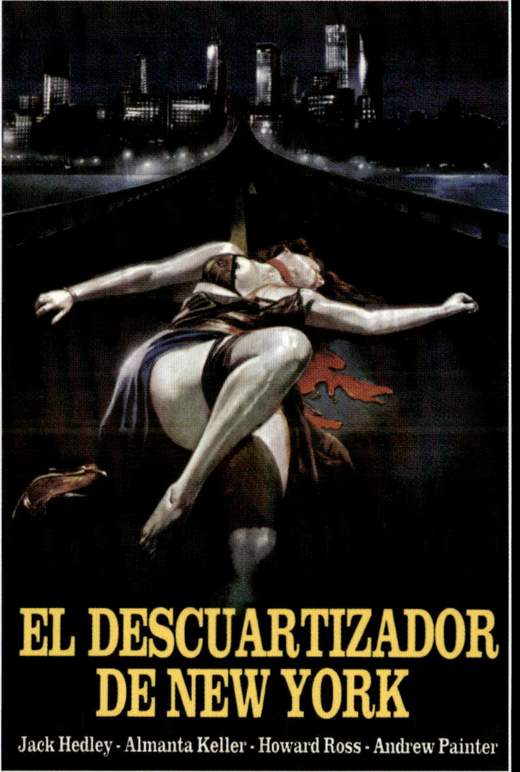

The New York Ripper

top left: Fay (Almanta Suska) man-handled by Mickey Scellenda (Howard Ross).

top right: Eva in danger, backstage at the strip-club.

middle row: French poster and Italian fotobusta.

bottom left: Lt. Williams (Jack Hedley) quizzes Scellenda's landlady (Rita Silva).

bottom right: Fay is attacked – but is it for real?

The New York Ripper

main picture: Jane (Alexandra Delli Colli) finds her latest S&M trip less fun than usual, thanks to Mickey Scellenda (Howard Ross).

above: Delli Colli relaxes in a Puerto Rican café.

ERWIN C. DIETRICH
zeigt:
DER
NEW YORK
RIPPER
mit:
JACK HEDLEY
ALMANTA KELLER
HOWARD ROSS · ANDREW PAINTER
ASCOT
REGIE: LUCIO FULCI
EINE FULVIA-FILMPRODUKTION IN EASTMANCOLOR IM VERLEIH DER ASCOT
ASCOT

chapter seven

Fulvia Film Proudly Goes Too Far...

featuring:

The New York Ripper aka *Lo squartatore di New York* (1982)

Murder-Rock Dancing Death aka *Murderock – Uccide a passo di danza* (1984)

The Devil's Honey aka *Il miele del diavolo* (1986)

Ænigma (1987)

Zombi 3 (1988)

Italy produced some shocking horror movies in the seventies and early eighties, but few appear to offer as many hostages to censorship fortune as Lucio Fulci's *The New York Ripper*. Filmed during April 1981 on location in New York, it was first screened in Italy in March 1982 after being touted to the international film markets with the outrageous banner, *'Fulvia Film Proudly Announces... Slashing Up Women Was His Pleasure!'* Even the timing of its attempted UK release was unfortunate. Public revulsion at the crimes of the recently incarcerated Peter Sutcliffe, the 'Yorkshire Ripper', was still fresh enough to be mobilized against any film touting the 'R' word in its title. Horror films in general were becoming the focus of mass-media scapegoating and the British censors were only too happy to extend their remit.

To viewers with a reasonable exposure to the genre, Fulci's early-eighties Gothics clearly resided within the *fantastique* wing of horror. Yet the British censors were unable or unwilling to distinguish their fantastical basis, with James Ferman, the BBFC's feudal baron, taking out his dislike of the form through the enforcement of drastic cuts. Then along came Fulci's first giallo for ten years, and his hardest, most bitter examination of sexual life in the big city. This was no Gothic spectacle, despite Fulci's tenuous remarks about the fantastical nature of the detection process required to root out the killer from a city of millions.[1] *The New York Ripper* is Fulci's bleakest and most cynical film, skilful and suspenseful in its construction, epic and alarming in its destruction. It is also one of his best, and I don't say this lightly – allied to its strengths and the ferocious nihilism of its approach is a queasy, savage attack on the female form, resulting in several murder scenes that present serious difficulties for impassioned defence.

left:
Attracting all the wrong kind of attention – Fabrizio De Angelis placed this trade show ad as part of the pre-release publicity for Fulci's *The New York Ripper...*

above:
Jane (Alexandra Delli Colli) is attacked by the Ripper, in a scene which shows the influence of Brian De Palma's *Dressed to Kill*.

The Ultimate Nasty?

In the spring of 1982, a media-co-ordinated campaign against the availability of so-called 'video nasties' in Britain was beginning to bite. The video revolution of 1980-82 had brought a huge wave of previously unseen, unreleased (or merely unreleasable) material into the public's living rooms. For a short, blissful period the industry was unregulated. Tiny fly-by-night companies could release a handful of obscure titles and make lots of money. The public were hungry for films to rent, and their choices veered wildly through areas that had never enjoyed such popular appeal in British cinemas. Strange things happened during this golden era. A micro-budgeted, ultra-violent, independently-produced horror film called *I Spit on Your Grave* hit the top of the video rental charts, ahead of the few major studio releases of the time. This raw, shocking presentation of multiple rape and bloody revenge is made all the more disturbing by its refusal of a whole cartload of structural norms.[2] The film has attracted appalled critics and vociferous admirers over the years, but its popularity as a video release and subsequent demonisation is interesting, as much for what it reveals about the film industry as for its relevance to debates around subject matter.

During the video nasty panic, the power to define what was 'obscene' and thus unacceptable resided not with the British censors (who were yet to gain the legal power to restrict video releases) but with the right-wing press and the police. Newspapers such as *The Daily Mail* peddled the notion that 'video nasties' were obscene, while the police capriciously seized horror films from the shelves. It's interesting to note, however, that as the definition of a video nasty was 'firmed up', movies released by 'respectable' film companies were dropped from the list of troublemakers. Thorn EMI's slasher movie *The Burning* was the only such title to make it to the ultimate banned list, the so-called 'DPP 39' (and they issued a statement claiming the uncut version had been released 'accidentally'). All other studio/ mainstream releases – 20th Century Fox's *Inferno*; CBS/Fox's *Visiting Hours*; Thorn EMI's *Dead and Buried*; Guild Home Video's *Terror Eyes*; CIC's *The Funhouse* – were dropped from the list during the period between the first list (July 1983) and the final list (December 1985).

Established film companies were happy to oblige the new moral guardians by sanctimoniously 'tidying up' the video market. How galling it must have been to see big studio flops like Barbra

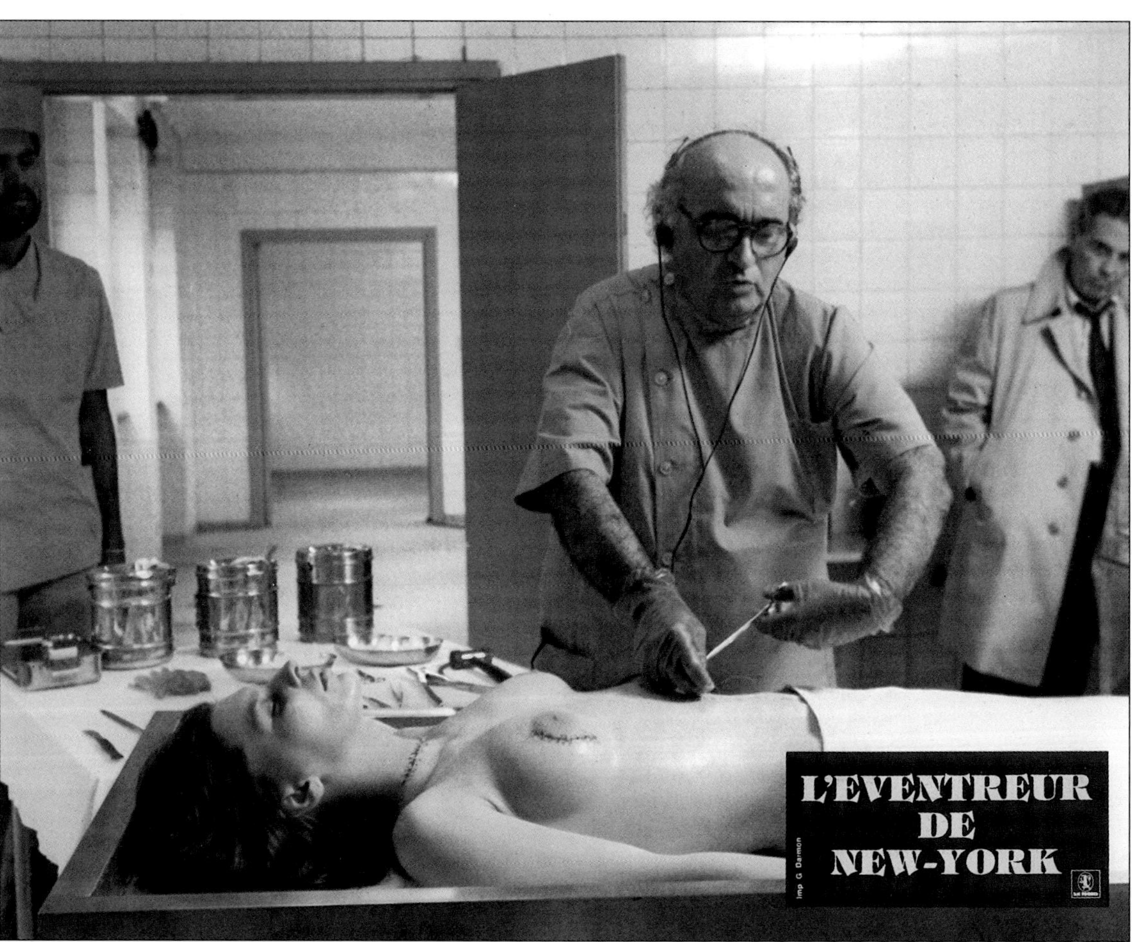

right:
"He used a blade. He stuck it up her joy trail and slit her wide open..." – professional banter from *The New York Ripper*.

Streisand's *Yentl* fail all over again in the video market, when no-budget backyard shockers like Wes Craven's *The Last House on the Left* made tiny video companies big profits for minimal outlay. To gain their accustomed market dominance on this new capitalist frontier, the major film companies knew they had to detach video from its proletarian, 'mom and pop' retail roots and move in the big guns to doctor the image of the industry – this unequal battle was the undertext of the video nasty saga.

Of the 39 titles on the final DPP banned list, thirteen were of Italian origin, and they were each successfully prosecuted under section 2 of the Obscene Publications Act. The films included Ruggero Deodato's *Cannibal Holocaust* (1980) and *House on the Edge of the Park* (1980), Luigi Batzella's *The Beast in Heat* (1977), Sergio Garrone's *SS Experiment Camp* (1976), Umberto Lenzi's *Cannibal Ferox* (1981), Antonio Margheriti's *Cannibal Apocalypse* (1980), Mario Bava's *Blood Bath* (1971), Dario Argento's *Tenebrae* (1982), Cesare Canevari's *The Gestapo's Last Orgy* (1977), and two films by Joe D'Amato, *Anthropophagous the Beast* (1980) and *Absurd* (1981). Fulci's *Zombie Flesh-Eaters* and *The House by the Cemetery* joined the list too, even though the latter was released only in its cinema-friendly 'X' certificate version.

That so many of the titles on the banned list were Italian is no accident (and there were a good many more from Spanish directors too). In the film industry's trade magazines and elsewhere, powerful multi-million dollar American interests milked the public's naive prejudices about the nature of 'quality' cinema (i.e. orthodox, expensive and made in Hollywood), joining forces with those in the media and in politics who already indulged in crass judgements of 'good' and 'bad' art. The Italian horror films, full of foreigners whose lips couldn't speak proper English even if their voices did, were easily defined as 'other'.

Arriving at the height of this frenzy of political expediency and moral humbug (and with a general election on its way), *The New York Ripper* earned itself a particular notoriety. Thanks to an increasing irritation at the BBFC with Fulci's violent Gothic films of the past three years, it was greeted with a veritable phalanx of repression, escorted from the BBFC's Soho offices and out of the country before a print could even be screened to the industry. The question of video release, in even the most truncated of forms, was never even near the agenda. However, the BBFC's director himself retained a copy of the film on video to show indecisive MPs and anti-censorship lobbyists exactly what he was protecting the nation against. (If only producer Fabrizio De Angelis could have brought a prosecution against Ferman for bootlegging and illegal display of an undistributed title!)

There is something about *The New York Ripper* that sends even those usually staunch in their regard for the genre into a panic. The violence in this film is strong meat; scenes such as the one where a prostitute has her nipples and eyeball bisected with a razor blade are enough to induce a tendency to denial among the most seasoned horror critics, fans and professionals. Dardano Sacchetti, Fulci's collaborator on *The Beyond*, *City of the Living Dead*, and numerous others, contributed to the screenplay when it was being developed under the working title 'The Beauty Killer'. In interviews Sacchetti has said that he feels Fulci tried to take too much credit for the writing of their films together; and yet ironically, when pressed on the origination of *The New York Ripper*'s alarming sequences of sadism, he unequivocally blames the perceived misogyny on Fulci alone.

Once again it was up to British critic Alan Jones to defend Fulci, and this time he really stuck his neck out, calling it *"The strongest and most powerful of all his films to date [...] a psychotic, erotic masterpiece [...] Art imitates life in all its many ugly forms. Fulci's approach to his source material has never been polite and* The New York Ripper *clinches his position as one of the most influential directors of the past decade."* Whilst it would be some time before fans were able to sneak a look at this soon-to-be-banned slasher, Jones fought the pariah-bashing mentality with a combative attitude of his own that few, even in the fan publications, have dared to voice since. Nowadays, with dubious sincerity, the common response is to suddenly come over all sensitive to 'feminist' rhetoric, condemning Fulci's shocker as a work of unrestrained misogyny. Meanwhile Joe D'Amato, H.G. Lewis and many more remain just a bit of fun – a hard line to draw, I'd say. Some reviewers have even reviled the film whilst at the same time claiming to find the actual gore scenes tacky and unbelievable.[3] This contrives to place them in a special position, combining moral superiority *and* technical disdain. It's now common for those who can't admit that an image troubles them to profess they are bored, unimpressed, unaffected by the violence, whilst maintaining enough dislike of it to harbour a moral revulsion. Is it possible to be bored and repulsed at the same time? I don't think so. This strategy of suspect jadedness deserves no further elaboration.

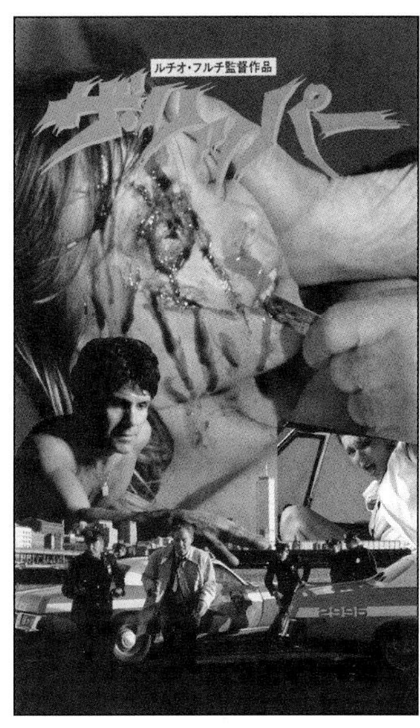

main picture:
The New York Ripper German DVD booklet artwork.

above:
Japanese video cover.

above:
Fay Majors (Almanta Suska) endures a nerve-wracking ride on the New York subway.

right:
Lobby card for *The New York Ripper*.

The New York Ripper is a film of relentless nihilism and cynical black humour which taunts and goads its viewers. The French writer Louis-Ferdinand Céline said of a character in his *Journey to the End of the Night*: *"The whole world for him was nothing but one mass of acid"*. Fulci's temperament is perilously close to this morbid loathing of life. (Interestingly, like Céline, Fulci also studied medicine in his early years). If his expression of misanthropy in *The New York Ripper* seems tilted excessively towards an attack on the feminine, that seems to be as much a part of the film's strategy to grate the viewer's nerves as an indulgence of misogyny. Every male character is tainted by hypocrisy of one sort or another; their actions treated with either casual mockery or outright contempt. And for the film to be truly misogynous, it would have to invest some sympathy in the killer himself; instead he is ridiculed, with his risible quacking duck's voice. His wholly self-serving, emotionally stunted rationale is condemned. Fulci's treatment of this supposed 'moral avenger' recaptures the blistering scorn of his earlier giallo *Don't Torture a Duckling*. His work shares Céline's paradoxical love of children and animals, yet rarely is this mere sentimentality. Certainly the end of *The New York Ripper* expresses horror at a child's dismal, lonely fate which is far too bleak to read as sentimental pity.

below:
Danish video release of *The New York Ripper* under the title *Bloody Rape*.

Note that the (highly effective) artwork for *The New York Ripper* stayed close to the original in releases all over the world (see several more examples on the following pages).

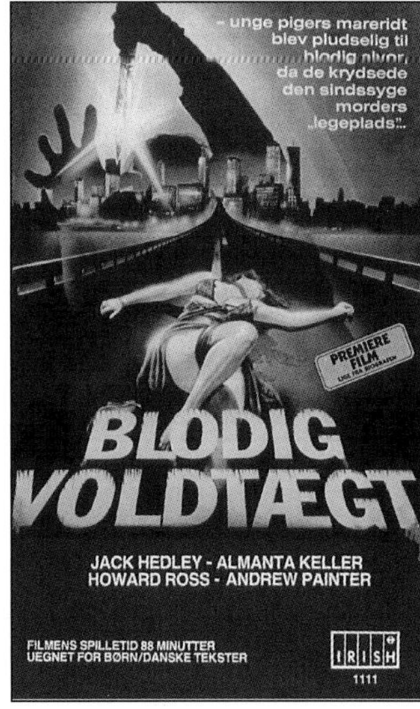

Sickness and devils

As the eighties progessed, the practice of featuring adults in horror films fell victim to the industry's relentless chasing of the dollar; to demographic consultancies, market research. If horror's prime audience is youthful, the reasoning went, teenagers should prefer watching characters their own age. Many successful horror films had enthralled audiences without having to be patronisingly tailored to their age-bracket, but the trend for teen-horror proliferated in the 1980s regardless. This kind of audience targeting was part of the strangulating influence of American studio interest in the modern horror genre.

Films like the independently produced *Halloween* (1978) and *Friday the 13th* (1980) may ironically have sounded the death-knell on audacious, unconventional horror film-making, merely by being so successful. Companies like Universal and 20th Century Fox probably felt distaste at the idea of embracing the modern breed of horror film, but they certainly weren't going to miss out on all the profits to be made. Early imitations of the independent slasher movies made by major studios looked embarrassed to be playing the game. Thereafter, the expensive look of big studio horror pictures insulated the squeamish money-men from the 'nastiness' they wanted to exploit.

At first, it was the low cost of producing an effective horror film that made them so worthy of investment. Unfortunately, it was also to prove the weak link as far as the possible manipulation of the genre was concerned. Audiences of all kinds were being coaxed into a new aesthetic of conspicuous expenditure as the eighties unfolded, and it was a style only the majors could maintain. Once the most dynamic (and success-hungry) film-makers were persuaded to smooth off their rough edges, with huge amounts of cash for their next projects, their brutal but lucrative films could be absorbed by the sponge of big-time Pop America.

Whatever their considerable individual merits, films like Tobe Hooper's *Poltergeist* (1982) and John Carpenter's *The Thing* (1982) helped to sell the inexpensive, grainy but gruelling style of horror down the river. Subsequent low-budget features had a new and incongruous requirement to meet if they were to succeed in a market redefined by the majors. They had to look expensive. Some independent producers found they could just afford the required gloss, but it left the atmosphere of the resulting mongrel decidedly limp. What's more, audiences were becoming skilled in judging the 'cash-status' of the films they were watching. The video market was making even the most casual viewer a film-buff. When the horror film got sucked into this highly polished straitjacket/chastity belt, wider audiences began to consider the rough-and-ready, guerilla-shot look of independently produced horrors cheap, unattractive and dated.

Grit was anathema to the new, style-obsessed directors. Rotor-fans, venetian blinds lit through with blue light, no-grain film-stock and persistent deep-focus – these were the filters that obsessed the eighties sensibility, to the detriment of raw energy. The emergence of the heavily over-determined plot, with characters pinned out like laboratory rats for the inspection of a generally more 'knowing' viewer, also nibbled away at the genre's penchant for illogic. Films like Tony Scott's *The Hunger* (1983) or Alan Parker's *Angel Heart* (1987) paid scant respect to the genre's dynamics, whilst having the unfortunate capacity to obsess other producers with the 'classy' sheen of their efforts. The majors had gambled well by getting involved with independent-style horror. Taking it out of the hands of the people who'd made it, or encouraging them into the commercial fold and then neutering their subsequent work, the studios brought the horror film into a new arena, the world of hip TV commercials and music video, and with a few exceptions that's where it languishes even today.

The first Lucio Fulci film to be affected by this malaise was *Murderock – Uccide a passo di danza/Murder-Rock Dancing Death* (1984), although it does at least fold the pre-occupation with advertising aesthetics into its plot and dialogue. The story has a woman's dreams over-run by Tony Scott slow-motion and gauzy filters, until she discovers that the killer she's dreaming of is currently occupying giant poster billboards all over New York, a mild parody of the Marlboro man. Signs of life above the leotard neck-line don't really save this disco-giallo though, because the film is over-run with other problems. One senses a director perhaps rather taken aback by the hostile reception for *The New York Ripper*, clutching at less threatening mainstream models for support and uncertain of where to go next. Fulci's inspiration for this film, believe it or not, was Adrian Lyne's damp-gussetted aerobathon *Flashdance* (1983), but the galumphing disco sequences and an unbelievably bad score from Keith Emerson (what was he thinking?) hamstring *Murder-Rock* almost as much as the indifferent acting and wimpish violence.

It's here, while attempting to land his next assignment in the summer of 1985, that Fulci suffered his first serious illness, a form of viral hepatitis which brought him very close to death. When he returned to directing with *Il miele del diavolo/The Devil's Honey* in February 1986 he was considerably frailer than before: in pictures taken during the shoot he looks alarmingly gaunt. Yet despite his health problems, Fulci made a decent go of the film, which featured beautiful Italian youngster Blanca Marsillach and, from the USA, grizzled character actor Brett Halsey. Adding more sex to an idea he'd already used in a script for Giuseppe Petroni Griffi (1985's *The Trap* starring Cristina Marsillach) Fulci turned in a trashy, often hilarious S&M fantasy with an undertow of melancholia for good measure. Part of the film's success is due to the attention it pays to adult intrigues and characters. It isn't a deep and meaningful character study, of course, but there's a refreshing vigor to its kinky lusts and pop-despair. You'd never guess it was made by a man who'd just recovered from a debilitating illness.

Lifting The Curse

Throughout 1986 Fulci struggled to find new directorial projects, probably because his recent health problems had compromised his bankability in the Darwinian world of film insurance. To make ends meet he took what was for him an unusual job: special effects supervisor. An American-Italian co-production was currently in Rome to shoot interiors and effects and Fulci landed a job helping out with the extensive horror fx scenes.

The film was *The Curse*, which had been part-shot in the USA by actor-turned-director David Keith, under the watchful eye of veteran producer/director Ovidio Assonitis. An adaptation of the classic H.P. Lovecraft short story 'The Colour Out of Space', it started out in July 1986 under the pre-production title 'The Well'. Lined up to star was Treat Williams, presumably in the role of family patriarch Nathan Crane. However, when Williams dropped out the film ended up headlining teenager Wil Wheaton as Nathan's son Zack (Wheaton was a hot property at the time thanks to a strong performance in the highly regarded Stephen King adaptation *Stand By Me*). Now labouring under the bland retitling *The Farm*, the film went into production during January and February 1987, shooting on location in Tellico Plains, Tennessee. It's interesting to note that cinematographer 'Robert D. Forges' (aka Roberto Forges Davanzati) had worked as camera operator on Fulci's *The Black Cat* and *City of the Living Dead* (as well as Pasolini's *Pigsty* and Ruggero Deodato's *Cannibal Holocaust*), while production designer 'Frank Danorio' (aka Franco Vanorio) worked on Fulci's *Rome 2033 – The Fighter Centurions* and would turn up again as art director on the upcoming *Touch of Death* and *The Ghosts of Sodom*.

Curious about Fulci's exact contribution to the film, I spoke to line producer Anselmo Parrinello, whose extensive film experience before *The Curse* included working as production supervisor on David Lynch's hugely complex *Dune*, and production manager on the hit comedy *Bill & Ted's Excellent Adventure*. He gave me this valuable information about the shoot: "*Lucio Fulci was a specialist in horror movies, he had a good reputation for that kind of film. He deserved a good credit. He basically directed a few difficult SFX sequences, such as the mother melting in the basement. I also remember Lucio working with the wrangler for the flies. Nothing more. The film was shot in Tellico Plains (one week more or less) and the rest in a studio in Rome. In Italy we only had David Keith and the cast from the USA. We had an American crew in the USA and an Italian crew in Italy. We built the interior of the farm in the studio, and the exterior of the farm in the backlot of the studio. We also shot the landing of the meteor in a valley near Rome. Ovidio was the leader of the project in many ways. He co-financed the film. He also helped with directing here and there. David Keith handled directing pretty well, sometimes here and there Assonitis was suggesting and helping. All the special effects were created and handled in Rome. Sometimes we had three units*

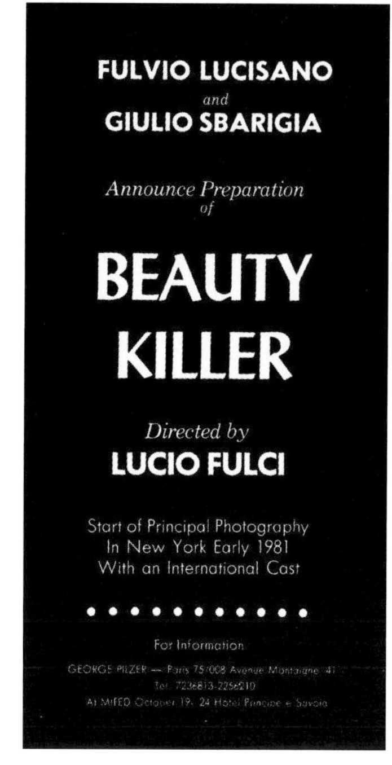

above:
The New York Ripper was announced in advance at the MIFED film market under this pre-production title.

below:
Lieutenant Borges (Cosimo Cinieri, middle) investigates the dance school killings in *Murder-Rock Dancing Death.*

above:
Kim (Sophie D'Aulan) and Tom (Dragan Bjelogrlic) pay for their mean practical jokes in *Ænigma*.

shooting simultaneously. Mario Ciccarella and myself were the SFX creators, we shot miniatures (the farm, the meteor etc.) and Assonitis was the master in charge of handling these effects. Most of the additional effects were shot by him with a mini unit after the wrap of the film. To me it was the most exciting part of the movie because we had a tiny budget for handling many effects, so we had to achieve a lot. Assonitis's experience was vital in this. David had left and Ovidio directed those miniature shots. For instance, the meteor was a 1k quartz lamp inside a wax globe tied to a swinging arm. The heat from the lamp melted the wax while the meteor passed over the farm miniature in the dark studio. Then we cut to the pre-filmed wide shot of the valley with the effect of the grass burning that is actually sawdust and gasoline. Assonitis was really 'the father' of the film. I remember he went from supervising the script to the final cut in Rome." I asked Parrinello if Fulci had displayed his infamous temper during his time on the picture; his response is emphatic: *"Totally wrong! Lucio Fulci was a gentleman. He did not like 'fake people', those who were trying to make things difficult just to show they could fix things. With his long experience it was difficult to cheat Lucio."*[4]

The finished film was shown at Cannes in May 1987, and received a glowing review in *Variety* (*"David Keith makes an auspicious film directing debut with 'The Farm', a well made and well-acted horror opus"*).[5] It opened Stateside in September 1987 as *The Curse* (another 'please forget about me' title that ought to have been nixed) and while it never received anything like the *Variety* thumbs-up again it's worth checking out for some genuine chills and some grisly moments courtesy of the maestro Lucio Fulci.

Snail's pace

Sadly, Fulci's next film as director, *Ænigma*, feels as tired as Fulci looks in his brief cameo role. It begs, borrows and steals from elsewhere in the horror genre (nothing new in that of course) but this time the sources are either beyond Fulci's reach as a director (*Carrie*, 1976), dubiously worth referring to anyway (*Patrick*, 1978), or poisoned at the well (*Phenomena*, 1985). Alongside these borrowings, in addition the film sees Fulci turning self-referential, a tendency he would indulge more and more in the years to come. *Ænigma* features a prolonged attack by garden snails on a 'helpless' victim that makes the the spider attack in *The Beyond* seem a paragon of plausibility. It's sad that even the self-quotations are fumbled, while the director's trademark violence – which made unlikely sequences electrifying in the best Fulci horrors – is conspicuous by its absence.

Ænigma was an Italian-Yugoslav co-production, made with a largely Yugoslav cast, although the exteriors were allegedly shot in Boston, Massachusetts. (I have my doubts...) It sat on the shelf for a year after completion before receiving limited exposure abroad, almost exclusively on video. According to Fulci it fell victim to a nervous producer who, doubting its chances of success in the home market, failed to distribute the film in Italy (although records show there were a couple of screenings in Rome and Milan). The only seasoned actor on hand was the American Jared Martin, who'd previously tried his best to breathe energy into Fulci's *Rome 2033 – The Fighter Centurions*. Born on 21 December 1943, Martin began in intriguing low-budget experimental features for the likes of Brian De Palma (*The Wedding Party*, 1963; *Murder à la Mod*, 1968) and Paul Morrissey (*Civilization and Its Discontents*, 1964), but then disappeared into a swamp of US TV pilots during the seventies, before finally netting sustained TV employment in *The Fantastic Journey* and *Dallas*. Apart from his Fulci assignments his only Euro-credits are Amando de Ossorio's monster movie *The Sea Serpent* (1984) and Fabrizio De Angelis's *Karate Warrior* (1987). *Ænigma* benefits from Martin's rugged appearance but fails to employ him with anything like vigour, making it two strikes and out for his collaboration with the director.

Zombie fails to revive...

This period of activity ended on the bitterest note of Fulci's career. After a gap of nine years, the trade papers announced a forthcoming Fulci *sequel* that, had it worked out, could have stimulated a fresh wave of enthusiasm for the Italian horror genre. In 1988 *Zombi 3*, first announced as *Zombi 3-D*, would go before the cameras. A follow-up to the wonderful *Zombie Flesh-Eaters* directed by the inimitable Fulci himself. It seemed perfect. The genre badly needed a grand showboat gore epic to counter the increasing trivialisation perpetrated by both American and Italian genre film-makers. MTV-horror (*Fright Night*, 1985; *The*

right:
Carol Simpson (Corinne Cléry) on the verge of divorcing her work and whore-obsessed husband (Brett Halsey); *The Devil's Honey*.

la DMV DISTRIBUZIONE presenta

a film directed by LUCIO FULCI

ZOMBI 3

with DERAN SERAFIAN • BEATRICE RING

Lost Boys, 1987), heavy-metal horror (*Trick or Treat*, 1986; *Prince of Darkness*, 1987) and cute-little-monster horror (*Ghoulies*, 1984; *Troll*, 1985) were bad enough: the emergence of Wes Craven's horror-franchise puppet Freddy Krueger as a figurehead for the genre was enough to make you burn your videotape of *The Last House on the Left* in disgust. Items like British writer Clive Barker's well-conceived but inconsistently directed *Hellraiser* (1987) offered a glimmer of hope that was swiftly snuffed out by American production aesthetics (*Hellbound: Hellraiser II* and so on). Perhaps most disappointingly of all, Italian horror also embraced a veritable horde of bad influences from the States. Dario Argento must take some of the blame: slapping puerile heavy metal onto his own soundtracks (*Phenomena* and *Opera*) and foisting it on his Lamberto Bava productions too. Bava's Argento-produced *Demons* was the start of a depressing rot in the quality of Italian horror. The pace and occasional weirdness did battle and lost against its idiotic elements. Breathtakingly stupid youth characters, macho posturing dragged in from US action blockbusters, make-up effects redolent of bad Heavy Metal album covers (Iron Maiden spring to mind), and a soundtrack mercilessly packed with pop-rock garbage all signalled the end for horror Italian style.

So the faithful were ready for a miracle. Unfortunately, Fulci's opportunity to act as saviour of the Italian horror film came to a sticky end; half-way through principal photography he was relieved of the director's post. Different accounts have been given as to why. Fulci once claimed to have directed just one scene in the existing film, leaving the production after three days of shooting. Subsequent testimony contradicted this, and he eventually confessed that he'd completed enough footage for a rough assembly of the film to be possible. Rumours that ill-health was to blame were also eventually scotched by Fulci himself, who admitted (some time afterwards) that his withdrawal was down to violent disagreements with the film's producer Franco Gaudenzi and scriptwriter Claudio Fragasso. Replacement director Bruno Mattei, who completed the picture, is often seen as the other villain of the piece, bringing his 'skills' to a movie as witless and excrutiating as his previous effort in the sub-genre, *Zombie Creeping Flesh* (1980).

It would be better if Fulci fans could believe the accounts that minimize his involvement, because *Zombi 3* as it eventually appeared, to a howling chorus of disappointment, is one of the worst films ever made in Italian horror cinema. But there's a problem; how can Mattei have transformed a film he wasn't involved in scripting into a carbon copy of his own pathetic zombie opus, when all he did was take over the reins on a project already in production? Script re-writes were no doubt part of the panicky handing-over process, but it's unlikely that a hack like Mattei would insist on complete redrafting. He probably just wanted to do the work, pick up the cheque and walk. Fulci himself blamed Franco Gaudenzi for the mangled, incoherently re-written script. Although there's really nothing to be gained by considering the film *truly* 'directed by Lucio Fulci' as the credits insist, one can't help but wonder quite what sort of miracle Fulci could have pulled off with such a stupid, feeble-minded storyline. That Fulci's big comeback went off the rails is regrettable, but perhaps the silver lining of the episode is that we never had to see what a dog's dinner Lucio Fulci's undisputed *Zombi 3* would have been.

above:
Fotobusta for *Zombi 3*.

below:
Bruno Mattei's *Zombie Creeping Flesh* was released to British cinemas the same year as Fulci's *City of the Living Dead*. Although it too featured zombies the resemblance ended there... Eight years later Fulci's sequel to *Zombie Flesh-Eaters* wound up being completed by Mattei and *Zombie Creeping Flesh* scriptwriter Claudio Fragasso in Fulci's absence.

Italian theatrical title
Lo squartatore di New York

Italy

Alternative titles
The Ripper (pre-shooting script title)
Manhattan Ripper (pre-shooting title)
Beauty Killer (pre-production title)
The Beauty Killers (pre-production title)

International theatrical titles
The New York Ripper (USA)
El destripador de Nueva York (SP)
L'eventreur de New York (FR)
El descuartizador de New York (ARG)
Njujorški Trbosek (YUG)
Blodig Voldtaegt (DEN) 'Bloody Rape'

Video/DVD titles
Der Schlitzer von New York (Austria)
Der New York Ripper (SWI video)

Production company
Fulvia Film S.r.l. (Rome)

Theatrical distributor
77 Cinematografica (Italy)

Theatrical running times
Italy 91m

Video/DVD/Blu-ray running times (adjusted)
Anchor Bay DVD (USA) 93m 01s
Shameless DVD (UK) 90m 45s

Shooting period
September-October 1981

Censorship
Italian censor certificate 77607 issued 18 February 1982

Release information
Bari/Brindisi 04 March 1982
Casale 24 March 1982
Rome 23 April 1982
Turin 06 May 1982
Rejected by the BBFC for UK release 15 February 1984 (submitted at 91m 06s)

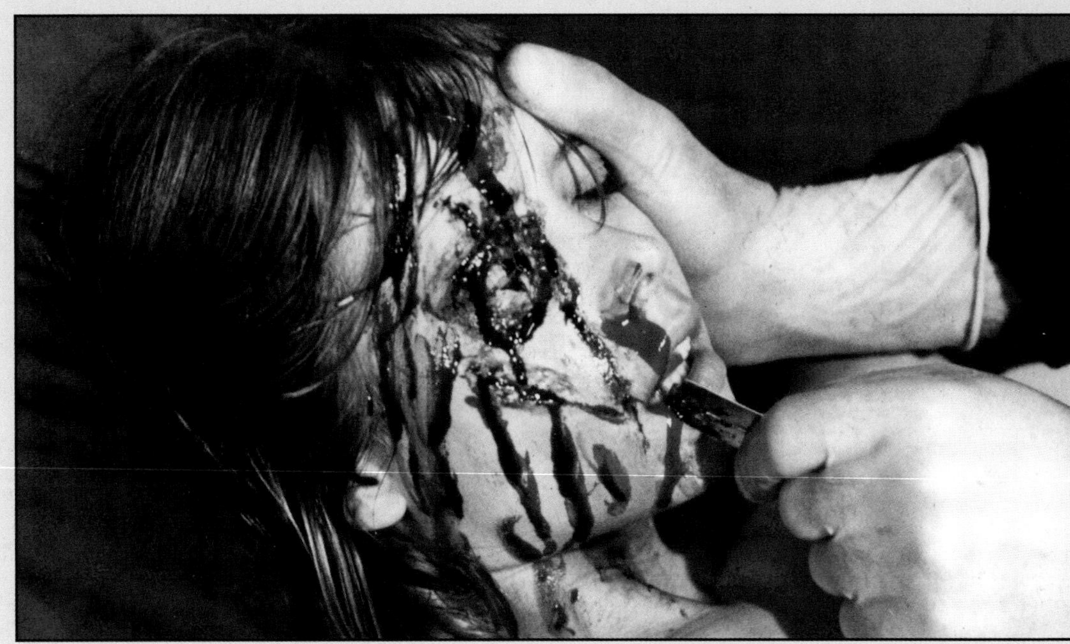

The New York Ripper

1982

Directed by Lucio Fulci. produced by Fabrizio De Angelis for Fulvia Film S.r.l. (Rome). story: Gianfranco Clerici, Vincenzo Mannino & Lucio Fulci. screenplay: Gianfranco Clerici, Vincenzo Mannino, Lucio Fulci & Dardano Sacchetti. director of photography: Luigi Kuveiller. music composed & conducted by Francesco De Masi, copyright: DEAF Edizioni Musicali S.r.l. editor: Vincenzo Tomassi. production design & costumes: Massimo Lentini. unit managers: Paolo Gargano & Fabrizio De Martino. assistant director: Roberto Giandalia. 2nd unit asst director: Marisa Agostini. continuity: Rita Agostini. stunt co-ordinator: Nazzareno Cardinali. 2nd unit dp: Guglielmo Mancori. cameraman: Ubaldo Terzano. asst cameramen: Antonio Annunziata & Renato Palmieri. 2nd unit asst cameramen: Aldo Marchiori & Marco Sperduti. key grip: Sergio Emidi. chief electrician: Sabatino Sperandeo. make-up: Manlio Rocchetti & Luigi Rocchetti. 2nd unit make-up: Franco Di Girolamo. hairstyles: Rosa Luciani. property master: Rodolio [Rodolfo] Ruzza. assistant designer: Mariangela Capuano. set construction: Fabio Traversari & Roberto Pace. 2nd unit make-up assistant: Rosario Prestopino. production assistants: Emilia Morale & Settimio Scacco. paymaster: Otello Tomassini. stills: Antonio Benetti. 2nd unit stills: Roberto Nicosia. assistant editors: Armando Pace & Massimo Cataldo. sound engineer: Eros Giustini. boom operator: Guglielmo Smeraldi. recording studios: N.C.. mixage: Bruno Moreal. camera equipment: Cinenoleggio. wigs: Rocchetti – Carboni. stills processing: Antonio Benetti. set dressing: Arredamenti Cineteatrali Grp., L'Immaginoteca, E. Rancati. set furnishing: D'Angelo. color by LV – Luciano Vittori. negatives: Eastmancolor. filmed in Gotham (New York City) interiors filmed at IN.CI.R. – De Paolis Studios (Rome).

Cast: Jack Hedley (Lt. Fred / Barnaby Williams). Almanta Suska [as 'Almanta Keller'] (Fay Majors). Renato Rossini [as 'Howard Ross'] (Mikos ['Mickey'] Scellenda). Andrea Occhipinti [as 'Andrew Painter'] (Peter Bunch). Alexandra Delli Colli (Jane Forrester Lodge). Paolo Malco (Dr. Paul Davis). Cinzia De Ponti (Rosie, ferry victim). Cosimo Cinieri [as 'Laurence Welles'] (Dr. Lodge). Daniela Doria (Kitty). Babette New (Mrs. Weissburger). Zora Ulla Keslerová [as 'Zora Kerowa'] (Eva, bottle victim). Paul E. Guskin [as 'Paul Guskin']. Antone Pagan [as 'Anthon Kagan'] (Chico). Josh Cruze [as 'Johs Cruze'] (Morales). Marsha MacBride. Rita Silva (Scellenda's Landlady). Giordano Falzoni (Dr. Barry Jones, Coroner). Lucio Fulci (Chief of Police). Barbara Cupisti (Heather, psychology trainee). Martin Sorrentino (black police detective at Scellenda's house). Violetta Jean. Cesare Di Vito (telephone technician). Elisa Cervi. Chiara Ferrari (Susy Bunch). *Uncredited:* Urs Althaus (male sex show performer). Sal Carollo (man walking dog).

below:
North European video re-release.

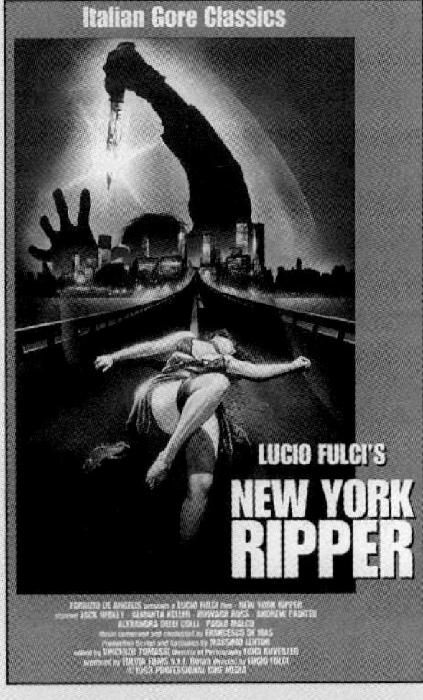

Synopsis: New York. A man out walking near Brooklyn Bridge discovers a decomposed human hand belonging to a missing prostitute. Lieutenant Williams interviews the victim's landlady, who says the girl had arranged to meet a man who spoke with a duck-like voice. A pretty young woman boards the Staten Island Ferry after an altercation with a boorish motorist. In the car-bay she's brutally murdered by a man with a 'Donald Duck' voice. Williams informs the press that a maniac is at large: soon after, a man sounding "just like a duck" tries to call him. Williams consults Doctor Davis, a psychotherapist, for help in tracing the murderer. On 42nd Street, Jane Lodge, an attractive wealthy woman, attends a live sex show. A dangerous looking man observes her. After the show, the female performer is attacked by a duck-voiced assailant who shoves a broken bottle into her vagina. Another young woman, Fay Majors, is menaced by the dangerous-looking man on a late night subway train. Fleeing, she is attacked in a dark alley by the quacking maniac. Recovering in hospital, Fay tells Williams that the man who followed her had two fingers missing on his right hand. Somewhere in New York, the owner of the mutilated hand binds Jane to a bed in readiness for S&M sex. By the end of the evening she will be dead. The police discover the man's identity – a Greek called Mikos Scellenda – and step up the search for him. Doctor Davis buys a gay magazine at a street-corner newstand, then visits Fay and Peter. Something about their story arouses his suspicions. Later, Fay is attacked again, when Scellenda breaks into her house. Peter arrives back and the man flees. Next, Kitty, William's lover, is horribly murdered. Davis discovers that Peter has a child from a previous marriage. She's in hospital, with a rare bone disorder which means she will never grow up to be a woman. Davis rushes to speak to Fay, but she has already deduced Peter's guilt after overhearing a phone-call to his daughter during which he quacked like a duck. Fay and Peter struggle on the stairs and Fay is stabbed, before a gunshot from the police blasts Peter's face off. In hospital, a lonely little girl calls for her father to telephone...

above:
Spanish pressbook cover.

left:
The only real affection anyone shows in the film; a man out walking his beloved dog gets a nasty surprise.

About the production: Lucio Fulci's infamous *The New York Ripper* was first announced in *Variety* on 8 October 1980 as 'The Beauty Killer', a project planned by Giulio Sbarigia of Selenia Cinematografica and Fulvio Lucisano of Italian International, to be directed by Fulci in New York. A week later, *Variety* announced: *"In May, Sbarigia and Lucisano will produce two products back to back in America – both action thrillers directed by Luigi [sic] Fulci. First to roll will be 'The Beauty Killers'; second is still untitled."*[6] Come May 1981, the film – now referred to as 'The Ripper' – was reportedly *"awaiting the green light"*. However, the same news item went on to say that the director would be 'Roger Deodato', *"whose own slate will keep him busy for almost a half dozen producers well into 1982."*[7] The name of course suggests *Ruggero* Deodato, director of *Cannibal Holocaust*, so was *he* penciled in to direct *The New York Ripper*? The notion is intriguing – after all, the *Ripper* script was written by Gianfranco Clerici and Vincenzo Mannino, who had recently penned *House on the Edge of the Park* for Deodato. Given the opprobrium heaped on Fulci when *The New York Ripper* came out, it's amusing to think that Deodato (already in the dog-house for *Cannibal Holocaust*) nearly added another of the most offensive horror films ever made to his resumé!

Whatever transpired in the parallel universe where Ruggero Deodato made *The New York Ripper*, here in our universe Fulci was back on board by September 1981, albeit with a different producer holding the reins.[8] *"Lucio Fulci jumps off next week on 'Manhattan Ripper' with a five-week location schedule in Gotham and wrap up sequences in Rome for producer Fabrizio DeAngelis of Fulvia Film,"* *Variety* reported.[9] In fact the film was delayed a couple of weeks longer, but it finally started a four week location shoot on 21 September, almost a year after it was first mooted in the trades.

There is one more date to note. 14 October 1981 saw the publication in *Variety* of a full-page ad for 'The Ripper', the crude and careless wording of which could only inflame the wrath of those in the industry already railing against depictions of violence against women. The film would be every bit as incendiary, but for sheer bad taste in marketing the advertisement was hard to beat. In rough-hewn type it read: *"Fulvia Film proudly announces – slashing up women was his pleasure."* Beneath these words, posing serenely in his director's chair and facing the camera, was Lucio Fulci himself...

Review: Some Big Apple this turns out to be. Fulci's New York is a town even Woody Allen would want to leave. A rancid, bitter, wormily corrupt place, teeming with the nasty germs of humanity; cold, barbarous and full of hate. *The New York Ripper* is Lucio Fulci's darkest work. No one emerges from its narrative as anything other than blighted. The standard of plotting is complex and unusual, marking a return to the tricky convolutions of the early seventies gialli. The film tempts us to make assumptions about the characters, assumptions which are then overturned by the unpleasant revelations that follow. It represents the vicious fusion of Fulci's horror films and his thrillers, being easily as over-the-top in its violence as the former, and as mind-bendingly plotted as the latter. Fulci's cynicism and bloody-minded tastelessness is astonishing, and the savagery of the razor-slashing, flesh-gouging special effects can offend even some hard-core fans of the horror genre.

It's a little like another New York scum-horror tale, William Lustig's *Maniac* (1980), in this respect. The early eighties saw a plethora of so-called 'slasher films' following in the wake of commercial successes like *Halloween* and *Friday the 13th*. Many were just mediocre, tarted-up thrillers interspersed with a fashionable quota of gory deaths. *Maniac* was an ugly

opposite page main image:
The Ripper does his worst to the luckless Kitty (Daniela Doria).

below:
Cinzia De Ponti, slashed to death on the Staten Island ferry.

above:
Alexandra Delli Colli as Jane, a woman whose S&M tastes lead her into deep trouble.

below:
Mickey Scellenda (Howard Ross) has a treat for a violent buddy that's "right up your perverted alley..."

cut above these tepid items, and it alienated substantial sections of the horror crowd by neglecting to make its horrors much fun to watch. Even Tom Savini, the special effects man on the film, known and adored by fans for his work on Romero's *Dawn of the Dead* and less prestigious films like *Friday the 13th*, was quoted as regretting his involvement in the Lustig project. *The New York Ripper* shares with the American film a gloomy, pessimistic atmosphere and a much queasier take on sexual violence. Both rub the audience's noses in scenes of vile butchery and nerve-squeaking grotesquerie.

At first glance, the film opens with a breathtakingly arbitrary murder scene. A girl on a bicycle – who initially embodies happy sexual freedom – becomes a victim of the Ripper. Dressed for the summer, she looks fresh and confident as she prepares to board the New York ferry. However, carelessly gliding along on her bicycle with hands off the handlebars, she scratches the paintwork of a misogynist's car. He justifiably reproaches her thoughtless driving, but in terms which reveal his own crass attitude to women. *"You women should stay at home where you belong. You've got the brains of a chicken"*, he gripes. Her response is understandably dominated not by contrition but defiance. *"And you're an asshole. Caio."* Fair enough; she even got the last word. Unfortunately she then compromises her defiant position by returning to the scene of the crime to underline her *ressentiment* with lipstick (entering the ferry's hold and daubing the word 'Shit' onto the chauvinist's windscreen). By 'winding back the sequence' of sex warfare she betrays an exaggerated desire to control and is then ensnared, not by the car's owner but by the killer whose lurking subjective-camera viewpoint we'd been sharing earlier.

Already the film is playing dangerously close to the bone by suggesting that she had some tiny part to play in her own grisly demise. It's a tricky approach to pull off. Stopping, I believe, just short of suggesting – as many critics have claimed – that she was 'asking for it', the film skates right up to the edge of such a grave offence and taunts the viewer with the question – a grim little game. This is followed through in the way that the violence is edited. For a few moments, Fulci pretends we're going to see nothing, then delivers in spades with a full-on depiction of a slashing razor attack. Cutaways to long shots of the ferry with distant screams on the soundtrack almost have us convinced that this first crime is not going to be explicitly shown.

The structure of *The New York Ripper* then begins to emerge. The sense of a plot with displaced or inadequate central characters is a key to the film's chilly effect, which makes the question of who is the leading character a vexed one. Because of this it may be appropriate to examine *The New York Ripper* in detail by separating out the individual characters and examining them one by one. It's fair to say that all the relationships between them are alienated, abusive or severely retarded. Despite the terrible isolation of their affairs with each other, they are all intertwined in a grippingly nasty downward spiral. These 'lost souls' make the sexually charged, psychotic mayhem of Fulci's urban hell truly memorable.

Jane, the decadent woman who turns up throughout the first part of the film, initially looks like a candidate for lead status. However, several factors interfere with this expectation. Although we see a lot of her – attending live sex shows, submitting to erotic humiliation in a downtown coffee-house, conducting veiled innuendos with her husband in their low-contact, high-sleaze relationship – she remains principally defined through her desires. She has no casual conversation, no commonplace, 'ordinary' activities. No context is established for her in conventional narrative terms. Interestingly enough, though, her *sexual* activities occupy a sort of relativistic normality; her husband is shown to be fully aware of her sleazy escapades and encourages them. His emotional remarks to the police after her murder bear this out. Their relationship, whilst cold and alienated in some respects, is organized and mutually agreed, tacitly at least. Their decadence is shown by the way they imply that each knows what the other's 'secret life' involves, whilst both choosing to go along with their cover-story tactics. Neither of them believes or expects to be believed – and they want the other to know they don't believe. Paradoxically, this is their bond of trust.

Jane enjoys making a spectacle of herself. She attends live sex shows alone, heavily made up and dressed in a chic raincoat. Immediately we are in a bind as we contemplate her character. Surely, we think, no woman would stray into such an environment without being aware of the kind of attention she could expect from the generally all-male clientele? The film presents her in this way as a knowing, sexually provocative character, and then voyeuristically focuses on her quivering lips as she becomes ardently aroused by the sex show. We, the film's viewers, are voyeurs by definition, and we are presented with the spectacle of another's voyeuristic arousal. Again the scene cuts close to the knuckle by playing with one of the standard chauvinistic attitudes to women; that they must want to be looked at lasciviously, otherwise they wouldn't do the things they do, dress the way they dress etc. But Jane is without doubt actively seeking sexual attention. Her preference for such thrills is part of a picture of modern sexual license which coldly admits to the fascination her behaviour causes.

Two things jostle in our minds as we contemplate the way she's being presented. We are aware of both the fact that domination by the sexual imperative is a fact of some people's lives (Jane might be ripe with actorly exaggerations but she's a recognisable type to anyone who's explored the sexual geography of cities like Amsterdam or Hamburg); and of the prevailing sexual fantasy entertained in pornography that the streets are awash with lubriciously over-stimulated rich-bitches desperate for a screw from all-comers. Are we watching a character whose sexual obsession can be accepted as fairly portrayed; or are we seeing a chauvinistic cliché plucked from the letters-page male fantasies of porn? Once again, I believe we are being taunted by the film, invited to snipe at it for being 'out-of-order'. And yet, by portraying Jane as a thrill-seeking voyeur, self-willed but reckless in the pursuit of excitement, Fulci forges a sneaky connection between her character and the audience. This wily invitation to hypocrisy is part of the film's nasty game. Any viewer who commits the double-standard of watching *The New York Ripper* for pleasure whilst reviling the

above: American VHS cover.

below: Jane meets the Ripper.

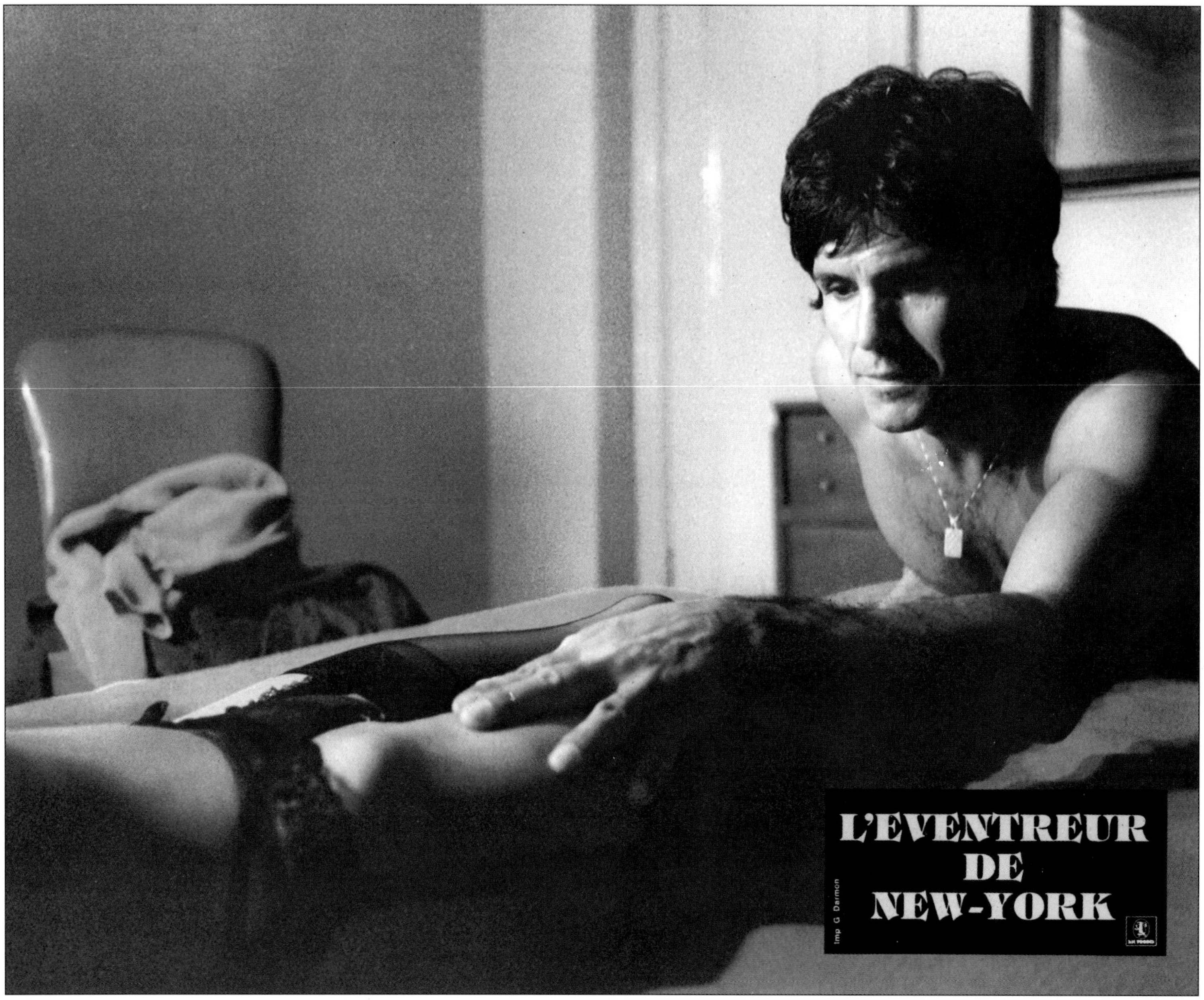

above:
Howard Ross (aka Renato Rossini) plays the villainous Mickey Scellenda, a sexual sadist and number one suspect in the Ripper case.

provocative hedonism of this woman is in for a bumpy ride. Her ultimate fate in the plot could twist even misogynist viewers into an uncomfortable identification with her plight. For those who have no reason or desire to condemn her sex-obsessed lifestyle, the end of the line for Jane is the film's most gut-wrenching sequence.

Fulci concocts a terrifying demise for her, as she encounters the Ripper's brutal procurer Mikos ('Mickey') Scellenda and submits to an S&M bondage session with him. He turns up the radio, signalling his intention to get very rough indeed, and we see in Jane's face a sinking sense of the terrible loneliness she's trying to fill, her suppressed dread of what she's letting herself in for, and a chilling resignation to extremes in her search for thrills. Jane is lost in a city about to swallow her into its darkness. When next we see her, still trussed up on the bed next to Scellenda in the aftermath of this brutal session, she hears a radio announcer describe the chief suspect in the Ripper case. The film attains a truly nightmarish intensity when Jane realizes that Scellenda, whose mutilated hand reaches sleepily out to grope her breasts, is the man being sought for the razor murders.

Her terror is now plainly intended to stimulate our concern for her safety, as we appreciate the terrible position she's in. Fulci handles the suspense here brilliantly, and no one could dispute the emphasis that he places on generating a sympathetic tension in the audience. Her predicament is simply too dire for the director to watch dispassionately, and her escape from her bonds is urged on by the film-technique and the viewer. When she escapes from Scellenda only to encounter the real Ripper in one of the corridors, the film has generated so much relief that her death is a shocking blow. We appreciate that her preferred sexual life-style is one fraught with dangers, and that she's been playing

right:
Lieutenant Williams (Jack Hedley), the moralistic cop investigating the Ripper case, in bed with the prostitute, Kitty.

with the risks involved quite consciously, but the film uses techniques worthy of Hitchcock himself to ensure that we are definitely rooting for Jane as she almost, but not quite, escapes the horror with her life. Although ringing in some considerable changes to *Psycho*, she is as much the 'heroine' of the film as Marion Crane was in Hitchcock's classic. By extinguishing this character after winning us over with her likeably decadent mannerisms, Fulci decentres the film just as Hitchcock did with the shower-room slaughter of Marion.

The other female candidate for lead status is Fay Majors, who doesn't come into the picture until half way. We are denied the comfort of an establishing context of normality with her too. We first see her as another potential victim being stalked on the New York subway – she narrowly escapes a vicious knife attack (in scenes which suggest the influence of Brian De Palma's highly controversial *Dressed to Kill* (1980) and the aforementioned *Maniac*). Later her conversation is dominated by the murder attempt. The way in which she perceives Peter, her boyfriend, as the killer – albeit dismissing the memory as a hallucination – even subverts narrative closure by occurring too early. (One is reminded of Carol Hammond in *A Lizard in a Woman's Skin*.)

After the initial horror of the attack, Fay's life seems as if it might be returning to normality. There's a brief gasp of apparently untainted air as we see her engaging in 'casual' conversation with her boyfriend. Fay seems to be emerging as a conventional female lead. But then Peter leaves on an 'errand' – and her face drops instantly into a depressed, unhappy scowl. The 'normality' was a brittle facade behind which Fay's suffering and alienation can clearly be seen. Her status as a potential female lead is complicated by this layered character construct. After being introduced as the next in a chain of female victims, followed by a spell of what looks like temporary madness, she is denied a comfortable place to go as a character. Like everyone else in the film, she cannot 'touch base' because her apparent domestic bliss is a sham. (Without wishing to be completely facetious, I'm reminded of the way that Robert Altman constructed narratives so that each person depicted would share an importance in the overall picture.)

Fay is an unhappy, emotionally repressed wretch, able to function only falsely in her failing relationship. We can surmise that she is already on the verge of a breakdown before the attack. The trauma of being attacked by her boyfriend results not in a blinding flash of revelation but in a very twisted form of denial. She constructs an elaborate dream of impossible physical attack in a darkened cinema; only then is she ready for a face-to-face confrontation with the man who wants to kill her. As cartoons play in a hallucinated movie-theatre, she 'sees' at last the image of her lover, attacking her with an open razor. Her subsequent revelation of this 'dream image' as she lies recovering from a minor knife-wound is made to the very person who stands to benefit most from her elaborately evasive confusion. She tells the killer she lives with. Fay is a fool to herself. Compared to Jane, she is slow on the uptake, and prone to self-deluding denial rather than (decadent) awareness. This is Fulci's toughest position in relation to character.

Conventional approaches to this film have tended to contrast her staid manner of dress and nice-girl surface with the sexually active/sexualized women who are murdered in the film. I think this would be a fair point if Fay was really given positive characteristics to go with her prosaic appearance. In fact she's a very uninvolving figure, whose blandness is a denial of her privileged perception of the killer's identity. He may be murdering sexually active women, but he's meant to be in a *relationship* with this one. Her blindness to what's going on, until it's almost too late, offers little in the way of empathy for audience appreciation. Fay is not the heroine of this film.

above:
Fay slips into a fugue state as she eludes Scellenda in the alleyways of New York.

In terms of distribution throughout the action of the film, there is only one figure – apart from the killer – who comes close to occupying centre-stage in *The New York Ripper*'s giddy narrative sickness...

The first thing you notice about Lieutenant Williams is an air of distaste. It's the same weariness, the same old 'seen it all before' that we're familiar with from countless American TV cop shows. We notice a similar attitude from a black female cop who points out the landlady of the first victim. She pronounces the eccentric old woman's name – *"Mrs. Weissburger"* – with dubious relish. Already we are assailed with the suggestion of contempt between one minority (a black woman) and another (a Jewish woman). When Fulci himself appears, in a characteristically terse and authoritarian cameo, even he appears to admit some distaste at the situation he's entered – letting go of a door handle as he enters, the director rubs his fingers together as if he's just encountered something sticky and abhorrent. Fulci – playing a top brass police exec – berates Williams for going to the press with the Ripper story, accusing him of starting a media scare. *"Is there anywhere private where we can talk?"*, he mutters. *"Sure, up at the church across the street"*, is Williams's bitter rejoinder. The exchange bodes badly for the development of this character, cynical, adversarial yet religious. It suggests that Williams feels the venal slaughter depicted in *The New York Ripper* has its roots in the collapse of the church's moral authority. We feel primed to pounce on the film for any displays of moral hypocrisy. Surely Fulci isn't going to lecture us about the absence of Christian values in a thriller with the ad-line *"Slashing up women was his pleasure!"*?

below and bottm:
The police make a futile attempt to catch the Ripper before he can slaughter Kitty.

above:
"Well, well, well... if it isn't the big chief person himself." Lt. Williams (Jack Hedley) greets his boss, played (here out of shot) by Lucio Fulci.

Williams, embittered and cynical in a way devoid of the leavening wit of say, Kojak, only takes the frontal narrative position because no one else has moral authority – his obnoxious character becomes the focus by default. In *The New York Ripper*, cops – like them or loathe them – are in the front-line of the fall-out of an amoral, grasping world. Fulci's gargantuan cynicism introduces, in a tellingly casual way, the fact that the Lieutenant regularly visits a prostitute, 'Kitty'. He is so dulled and corrupted that he barely recognises his own hypocrisy. One exchange with Kitty has him request a cup of coffee. *"Sweetheart! I'm a prostitute, not your wife. If you want coffee, make it yourself"*, she admonishes. In keeping with the sexual malaise and dearth of warm, loving relationships in the film, even the degraded 'comfort' of this mutually exploitative, respectless affair seems par for the course, rather than a heightened example of moral turpitude.

It isn't until fairly late in the film that we see the full extent of Williams's callousness and disregard for women. The killer has Kitty tied up at her flat. He announces by walkie-talkie to an impotent police unit that he is about to start butchering her on air. Williams (Jack Hedley), who knows where the call must be coming from, waits for an unconscionable length of time before announcing the location of the slaughter that they will hear taking place – thus trying to avoid admitting his own nefarious involvement. His hesitation to avoid exposing a corrupt relationship with a woman about to be razored to death is the grossest character trait we see in the film, the Ripper's vile activities excepted. It's a very nasty twist, and one which must stick in the craw of voyeuristic moralizers who may have identified with the cop's regular diatribes about the sleazy lives of others (and this razor-blade murder scene is surely the nastiest thing Fulci ever shot).

Searching for an angle on the Ripper's personality, Lt. Williams turns to psychoanalysis. Hence we meet the next character on our list.

Dr. Davis is well played by Paolo Malco as a quiet, slightly smug but highly intelligent young man. Emotionally reserved, he hides his particular brand of weariness behind a beaming smile. We first see him playing computer chess, 'taunting' the machine with the words *"Now don't tell me you're thinking of winning here"*. Lieutenant Williams fails to recognise Davis, allowing the young doctor to reproach him for expecting a bearded old man with a German accent. After checking that the Police Department can afford his consultation fees, Davis demonstrates his 'professional' dissociation from the horrible crimes. He readily admits that his initial prognosis of the killer's character is inadequate. Further insight will only come after more attacks; a fact Davis admits with a bland smile. His thumbnail profile of the killer

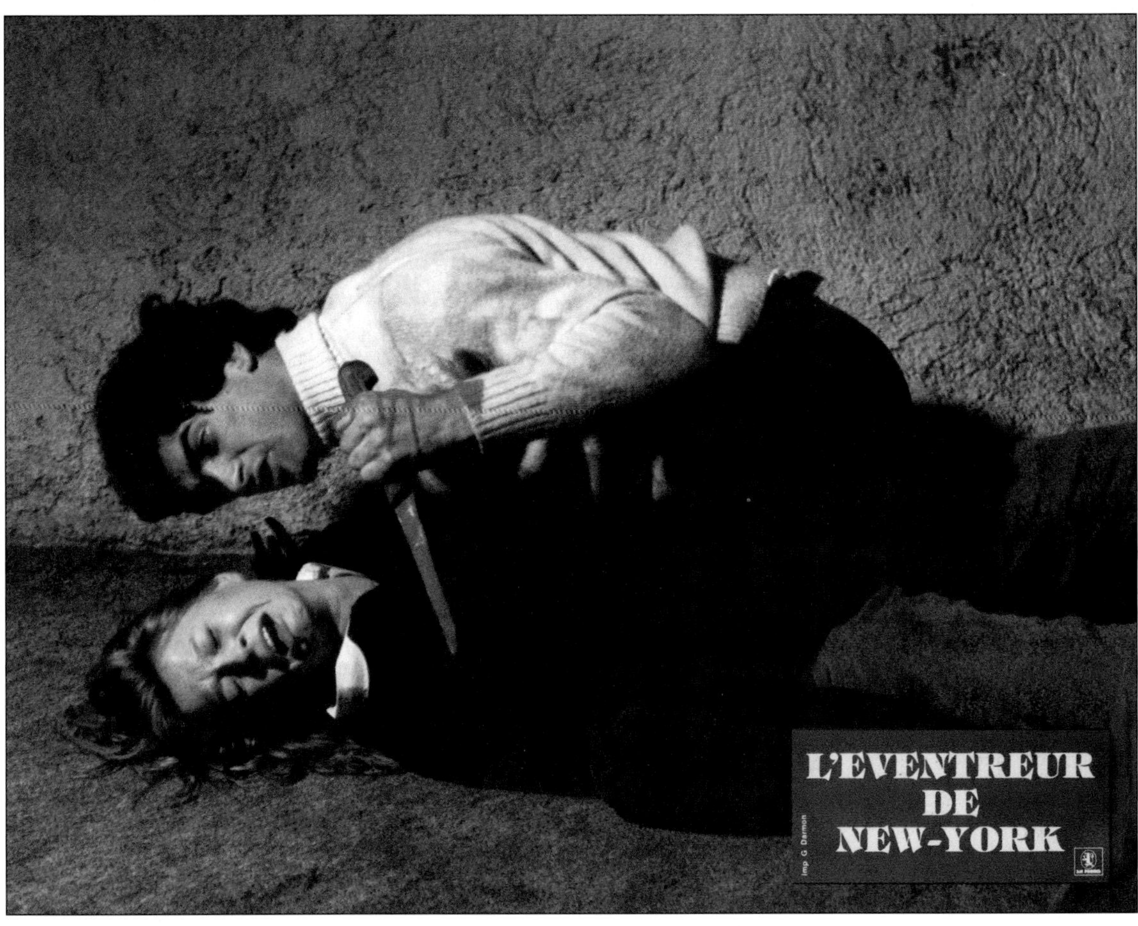

right:
Peter Bunch (Andrea Occhipinti) and his girlfriend Fay in a struggle to the death.

seems uncannily close to what we perceive Davis thinks of himself. Smart and keen to be noticed. *"You can be sure we're dealing with a very superior mind"*, he tells Williams. A later scene has him buying a gay porno magazine at a street news-stall. The vendor wraps the mag in a newspaper with a sly smile at Davis, who fails to object to the suggestion that he is ashamed to be seen buying it. These innuendos allow us to add the doctor to our list of possible suspects. Davis is eventually given credit for deducing the killer's identity, but his role remains a secondary one. His suspicions are aroused during a conversation with Fay Majors and her boyfriend Peter...

Peter Bunch (try, if you can, to forget that ridiculous surname) is one of the film's most important characters, although we see and hear him first through the typical obscurations of the giallo plot. He haunts the film with a psychopathic presence, but doesn't appear as a real 'character' until well into the story. When he turns up, at the bedside of his traumatized girlfriend, he seems a nice guy. Good-looking in a bland sort of way. Calm, concerned, almost an early version of the 'new man' as dreamt up by the media. He is also a liar. A cynic. A madman. The killer. Ever since *Psycho*, murder has been one of many innuendos made against the 'sensitive' man. At first glance this is recognisable as a function of male defensiveness. Hitchcock attempted to frighten women with the idea that the sensitivity they reputedly admire in a man is a lunatic's mask. Norman Bates carried off his deceit from behind the counter of his motel office. Here, the mask is persuasive enough to work inside a relationship.

Peter's work as a research physicist embodies the horror at the film's heart. *"Entropy at absolute zero"*, he replies when Dr. Davis inquires about his area of specialisation. Love and warmth are entirely absent in *The New York Ripper*. Jane and her husband have respect but show no affection. Fay and Peter have coasted blandly along whilst he commits the most vile and woman-hating crimes. And a little girl – Peter's daughter – deserted except for her father's psychotic role-playing phone-calls, lies in a hospital bed unwanted and alone.

The psychological 'reason' for his crimes is as nauseating as his actions. Not for Fulci the Thomas Harris-style sympathy for a maniac's tortured inner turmoils. This killer is presuming to act as a sick-hearted proxy for his physically deformed daughter, victim of a terrible bone disorder which is gradually robbing her of her limbs, and retarding her physical development. *"She'll never grow up to be a woman"*, muses Dr. Davis as he gazes into the children's ward at the tragic child. This is the killer's pathetic excuse for his actions. He's punishing women who 'abuse' their sexual maturity in one way or another, either through promiscuity, prostitution or merely by the exposure of their bodies to the casual attentions of passers-by. His daughter gets no hospital visits from this monster, just phone-calls where he adopts the voice of a duck (in imitation of her favourite toy). Even then he pours out his hatred and misogyny down the phone using the duck voice, into the uncomprehending ears of his lonely daughter.

Whilst there is generally no quarter in the depiction of the killer's ghastly male aggression, there are occasions when the violence challenges conventional codes of representation. One of Peter's victims, a stripper at a live sex show, dies when a broken bottle is plunged into her vagina. This twists the usual interpretation of such 'stabbings' in horror films as expressions of phallic aggression. The broken serrated edge of the wide part of the bottle is more vaginal than phallic, like the morbid phantasy of the *vagina dentata*. The bottleneck thus resembles the neck of the cervix. The hand holding the bottle belongs to Peter, the bitter father of a

'defective' little girl. He substitutes himself as attacker on his daughter's behalf, murdering women for their ability to conceive, have sex, to be women at all. Usually (if one can be so blasé about such things), a bottle is used in a rape by being thrust intact into the vagina, thus recreating a pathological version of phallic penetration by a probing shape. Peter's killing of the stripper is symbolically inter-vaginal, manipulated by a twisted male whose sense of potency has been problematized by the 'failure' of his genes to produce a daughter who can grow to womanhood. All the other killings are 'slashings'. This one gains if anything a greater degree of nauseating horror from its *conflating* of phallic and vaginal aggression. To further emphasize the divergence of this representation, during the attack we see one shot through the inside of the bottle, just as later we 'see' from inside the slashed throat of another female victim (ensconced within a hallucinogenic dream). The influence of Dario Argento can be discerned in these scenes, with their slightly absurd, blatantly anti-naturalistic technique.

It's typical of Fulci's approach to the psychology of murderous characters that there is not a shred of sympathy woven into the fabric of the film for the killer's self-justifications and 'traumas'. In *Don't Torture a Duckling* a rotten-hearted priest murdered young boys to prevent them growing into sinful puberty. Here a killer takes out a resentment against women because his daughter *can't* grow into womanhood. Both meet gory deaths with no hint of compassion. This is in marked contrast to the films of Dario Argento, who professes a sympathy so strong for his killers that he often stands in to perform off-camera stabbings and mutilations, with his own hand substituting for theirs.

Fulci has barely a speck of warmth for any of the characters (with the exception of Jane), and if after all the *killer* had been presented sympathetically then the film would be a deeply distasteful affair. But this is not the case, however difficult, bad-tempered and downright goading its attitude to the audience is at times. *The New York Ripper* is a nihilistic vision of Hell on Earth. No one matters. No one cares. A child dies a slow emotional death, alone in the septic aftermath of the killings, crying over shots of a callous New York. Fulci's film offers a powerful vision of a world where love has curdled away into poison and death. Life goes on alright, as the soundtrack suggests over the credits, with its 'just another day in the Big Bad Apple' inflections and junk-funk facelessness; but in a climate of absolute zero.

top:
Scellenda's body is found, leaving the identity of the real Ripper a mystery to the police.

above:
Dr. Davis (Paolo Malco) tries to comfort the devastated Fay.

below:
Fay and Peter.

Italian theatrical title
Murderock – Uccide a passo di danza

Translation
'Murderock – Killing Dance Steps'

Italy

Alternative title
Murder-Rock Dancing Death
(English language export title)

International theatrical titles
The Demon Is Loose (USA)
Murderock (FR)

Video/DVD titles
Murder Rock (ARG)
Rock de sangre (CHL)
'Blood Rock'
Nova York Cidade Violenta (BRZ)
'New York, City of Violence'
Moord op de academie (NL)
'Murder at the Academy'
Murder Rock (GER DVD)

Production company
Scena Films

Theatrical distributors
Compagnia Distribuzione Europa S.r.l.
(Italy)
BLC Services Inc. (USA)

Theatrical running time
Italy 88m

Video/DVD/Blu-ray running times (adjusted)
Media Blasters/Shriek Show DVD
(USA) 92m 40s

Shooting period
December to January 1983-84

Censorship
Italian censor certificate 79763
issued 05 April 1984

Release information
Rome 20 April 1984
Bari 01 May 1984
Turin 05 May 1984
USA (Saginaw, MI) 04 May 1990

Murder-Rock Dancing Death

1984

Directed by Lucio Fulci. executive producer: Gabriele Silvestri. producer: Augusto Caminito for Scena Film. story: Gianfranco Clerici, Vincenzo Mannino & Lucio Fulci. screenplay: Gianfranco Clerici, Vincenzo Mannino, Roberto Gianviti & Lucio Fulci. director of photography: Giuseppe Pinori. music composed & conducted by Keith Emerson; published by Bixio – C.E.M.S.A./ Another Music Co./ Artem Publishing. editor: Vincenzo Tomassi. art director: Paolo Biagetti. production supervisor: Sergio Iacobis. general organizer: Piero Lazzari. unit manager: Tullio Lullo. assistant director: Roberto Giandalia. continuity: Patrizia Zulini & Camilla Fulci. cameraman: Silvano Tessicini. assistant cameramen: Mariano Cafiero & Guido Tosi. costumes: Michela Gisotti. make-up: Franco Casagni. hair styles: Maura Turchi. set dressings: Mauro Passi. choreography: Nadia Chiatti. business administrators: Umberto Buffalo & Luigi Scardino. still photographer: Enrico Appetito. 1st assistant editor: Giancarlo Tiburzi. 2nd assistant editor: Massimo Cataldo. titles & opticals Penta Studio. sound: Eros Giustini. sound mixer: Fausto Ancillai & Cinecittà. sound effects: Cineaudio. dialogue director: Gene Luotto @ Filmatix Rome. voices: Associated Recording Artists (Rome). music recorded at Trafalgar Recording Studio. mixer: Eliano Negri. music soundtrack recorded on Bubble Records. laser lighting effects: "Rental Service" F. [Fratelli] Ciriciofolo. cinema equipment: Arco 2/Video Sincro TV/ Mabj Cinematografica. costume house: Russo. The production thanks Manlio Mallia, Fur Styles of Rome and Vito Bruno for dance sequences at the Roxy in New York. songs "You Are Not Alone Tonight" by Doreen Charter & Keith Emerson; "Tonight Is the Night" & "Are the Streets to Blame" by Doreen Charter & Keith Emerson, performed by Doreen Chanter; "Not So Innocent" by Doreen Charter & Keith Emerson, performed by Doreen Charter & Mike Sebbage. color by Telecolor S.p.A. filmed on location in New York (including the Roxy & the Arts for Living Center) with interiors at De Paolis Studios (Rome).

Cast: Olga Karlatos (Candice Norman). Ray Lovelock (George Webb). Claudio Cassinelli (Dick Gibson). Cosimo Cinieri (Lt. Borges). Giuseppe Mannajuolo (Prof. Davis). Berna Maria do Carmo (Joan). Belinda Busato (Gloria Weston, dancer with short blonde hair). Maria Vittoria Tolazzi (Jill, third victim). Geretta Geretta [sic] [as 'Geretta Marie Fields'] (Margie, dance instructor). Christian Borromeo [as 'Cristian Borromeo'] (Willy Stark). Robert Gligorov (Bert). Carlo Caldera (Bob, Jill's brother). Riccardo Parisio Perrotti (Steiner, co-administrator). Giovanni De Nava (Morris, co-administrator). *Uncredited:* Carla Buzzanca (Janice, 2nd victim). Pier Luigi Conti (voice analyst). Silvia Collatina (Molly, child in wheelchair). Lucio Fulci (Phil, theatrical agent). Angela Lemerman (Susan, 1st victim).

Synopsis: Candice Norman runs a dance class at the Arts for Living Center in New York. One evening after class a pupil called Susan is murdered in the changing rooms. The killer uses chloroform and a long needle pushed into the victim's heart. Lieutenant Borges heads the investigation: the suspects include Candice, Willy Stark (a young male student), Dick Gibson (the school governor), and several of Susan's bickering classmates. Word has leaked out about plans to select three students for a high-profile TV show. Could the murder have been committed by an ambitious dancer determined to narrow the odds? Another dancer, Janice, is killed. Meanwhile Candice is having nightmares in which she is terrorised by a handsome man wielding a long needle identical to the one used in the murders. After seeing her dream assailant on a real life advertising billboard she finds the man who modelled for the poster, George Webb, staying at a sleazy hotel. When she breaks in, Webb returns unexpectedly. He is drunk and dishevelled. Candice flees in terror, mixed with disappointment. Soon they meet again and begin a romantic liaison. More students are murdered, and an attempt is made on Candice's life by Margie, a dance tutor whose job Candice took. Margie tries to emulate the style of the other killings, but she cannot finish the job. Finally it's revealed that Candice is the killer – she was the victim of a hit and run accident which curtailed her dancing career and forced her into teaching. George was the driver who has haunted her dreams ever since. She persuades George to hold the pin against her breast, then impales herself on it, leaving him the apparent murderer. He acquiesces to the illusion out of a consuming guilt for having destroyed her ambitions.

About the production: *Murder-Rock Dancing Death* was mentioned in *Variety* for the first time on 25 October 1983, and a follow-up article in late November suggested that the film was due to enter production "imminently", so it's likely it was shot during December 1983 and into January 1984. It was declared "just completed" in *Variety* on 9 May '84, although the information seems to have been rather slow in coming, as by then the film was already in release across Italy!

Finance came from Scena Film, a production company set up by two screenwriters, Rodolfo Sonego and Augusto Caminito. The deal was also helped along by Scena Film's 'shadow-partner', the comic actor Alberto Sordi, whom Fulci knew from his days as a scriptwriter and assistant director in the 1950s on such films as *Un americano a Roma*. Interviewed after completion of *Murder-Rock*, Fulci told *l'Unità*'s Michele Anselme, *"[It] is a film improvised in a jiffy. The production company had earned too much money with Sordi's* Il tassinaro *and had an absolute need to unload the tax by November. So they called me, and they asked if I had some project in a drawer, and we decided to utilise an old subject that I had written a few years ago."*[10]

This was the first Lucio Fulci film since 1978's *Silver Saddle* to secure neither a theatrical nor video release in the UK, and in the USA it was ignored until 1989-90 (when it emerged, briefly, as *The Demon Is Loose*). The fact that *Murder-Rock* fared so badly in English-speaking markets was an indicator of tough times ahead. The American mainstream film companies were increasing their stranglehold on the industry, and in the meantime audience taste was being shaped and defined as much by the conspicuous expenditure of Hollywood blockbusters as by the stories themselves. Angela Pinton, head of Italian distribution giants Filman, defined Italy's problem succinctly when she told *Variety*, *"Quality at medium cost has always been a characteristic of Italian cinema, but the medium cost continues to rise from year to year."*[11] In May 1984 the same publication ran a feature examining the problems faced by Italian producers, concluding, *"Lucio Fulci, Antonio Margheriti and Enzo G. Castellari get a fairly wide US release these days on the action circuit, and by default are the only flag-bearers hereabouts for the once proud (and pervasive) Italian cinema."*[12] Sadly, even these old veterans were now finding the new environment inhospitable to their talents...

Interviewed in *l'Unità* just after the release of *Murder-Rock*, Fulci was pugnacious as ever but sounded tired of answering questions about violence in his movies, telling Michele Anselme, *"I like to shoot films that don't make people fall asleep. As far as brutality goes, I have had enough of hearing the same conversations, my horror films are not brutal, they are simply cruel. And even then not very much so. I've recently seen the Spielberg film,* Indiana Jones and the Temple of Doom*: that's really where there are horrific special effects and make-up, to the limits of disgust, but no one will say this. And you know why? Because Spielberg is mythical, so it's not discussed. Fulci though can easily be slapped in the face with fishes, be offended and ridiculed."*[13] The worsening state of the industry also seemed to vex him: *"I am the last zombie of Italian cinema, condemned to make three films in a year in order to survive and to shoot them in five weeks, including the American version, in order save costs. I earn the same as Celentano's butler, perhaps even less."*[14] Asked if he would shoot a love story he replied, *"Certainly, but do you have one ready? The truth is that Italian cinema is in crisis. They speak badly about my films, but it is with these products – often modest, I'll admit – that we manage to penetrate into international markets. Do you know that* The House by the Cemetery *has taken nearly 8 million dollars in the USA?"*[15]

top:
Fotobusta.

above:
Terror at the dance academy...

Review: Struggling beneath the multitude of faults that this film exhibits is a far more entertaining thriller, sadly ruined by Keith Emerson's appalling soundtrack and a host of awkward aerobic dancing scenes. The film follows on neatly from *The New York Ripper* in its determinedly Americanized aura, and as long as one approaches it without expecting any excessive violence, it can hold the attention as an amusingly tacky giallo. Despite the film's wish to be taken as American product, though, there are several bizarre giveaways that carry an unmistakeably Italian illogic. The ironically named Arts for Living Center is a good example, with its cool electronic voice announcements warning of the Center's imminent 'automatic closing'. The corridors are shown pulsating from light to darkness, whilst a synthesized tone completes the sci-fi ambience. It's a nice, typically nutty Italian touch, reminiscent of Bava's propensity for lighting scenes with flashing colour from defective neon signs – the sort of thing which was of course codified into horrendous cliché during the eighties designer-decade. Bava's use of such techniques was effective because of the way it threatened the story with its technical contrivance. Given such a flicker of Italianicity, it's a shame that the story is then allowed to drift haphazardly through so many nods to the American mainstream.

Compared to many of the American stalk-and-slash flicks around at the time, this is a fairly restrained little number, with the only really hideous violence perpetrated by Keith (ELP) Emerson's score. Fulci himself hated the music (although he dredged up some two-faced enthusiasm for it on the Japanese CD sleeve-notes!), and it's truly a sad and sorry wonder to hear the man who composed the marvellous, intertwining themes for Dario Argento's *Inferno* trotting out such lumpy, frumpy disco tracks for *Murder-Rock*. (How he came to be involved in the project is beyond me anyway – what on earth made a former progressive rocker with grandiose aspirations towards the classical music of the 18th and 19th centuries accept a commission to write tacky disco songs for a minor giallo film?) His songs are meant to give the film a fizz and sparkle of coke-driven disco nerviness; *"Paranoia's comin' your way!"* one track insists. Instead the music sounds like it was rejected for a satellite TV tampon commercial.

The world of advertising is represented in *Murder-Rock* as some sort of emerging subtext. One's suspicions are alerted fairly soon when Candice's first nightmare sequence unspools. It's like a parody of a shampoo commercial, all slow motion running

opposite top:
The cynical Inspector Borges (Cosimo Cinieri).

below:
After the razor-wielding excess of *The New York Ripper*, Fulci opted for a more discreet form of bodily violation in *Murder-Rock Dancing Death*.

above:
Margie (Geretta Geretta) is comforted by Bert (Robert Gligorov) while Gloria (Belinda Busato) looks on.

opposite:
Spanish theatrical poster for Fulci's 1986 movie, *The Devil's Honey.*

below:
After the grisly excesses of *The New York Ripper*, *Murder-Rock* sees Fulci reining in his taste for mutilation.

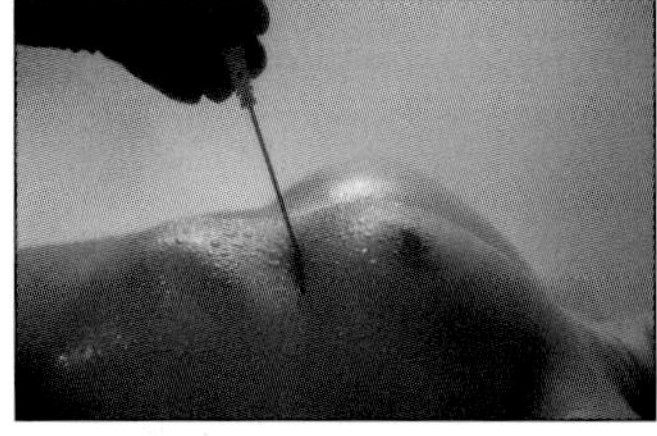

through hazy surroundings. A scene where ageing exploitation hunk Ray Lovelock chases Olga Karlatos with a giant ornamental pin looks like a dry run for a chic perfume ad – for a fragrance with a name like 'Nightshade' or 'Forbidden'. This intrusion of the commercial-shoot into the cinema dream-sequence was to become endemic throughout the eighties, with dreams the last unsold territory, a market-place of the unconscious. The disorientating technical effects (though never their emotional correlatives) created by directors like Nicolas Roeg, Dario Argento and even Ken Russell in the 1970s were relentlessly codified into the language of selling (and to compound the horror, all three have directed TV commercials). Films like Paul Verhoeven's *Basic Instinct* (1991) have taken this colonizing tendency, capitalism's remorseless expansion into the realm of psychology, and exposed the process by overdoing it. Over-determined plots and dialogue leave no room for suspicions that aren't immediately voiced and then thrown into the hyper-real mix.

This process occurs in a hesitant, blurry way in *Murder-Rock*. *"He's snuck into your subconscious"*, pronounces a friend as Candice obsesses over the man on the billboard who appears so like the man of her nightmare dreams. Later, George the model makes the surprising statement *"Maybe I should get into the dream market – nothing ever materializes in the movies."* The theme is scrappily explored but it turns up often enough to suggest that Fulci was aware of changing trends in the production of fiction in America, where *Murder-Rock* was almost entirely filmed. (Indeed Fulci seems to have been back and forth rather a lot between Rome and New York at this point in his career. *Manhattan Baby*, *The New York Ripper* and *Murder-Rock* were all heavily reliant on New York shooting.) Just to add a further glimmer of harsh irony, Fulci himself cameos as a friend of Candice's – an executive in the world of advertising.

Although working below-par, Fulci actually pre-empts here some of the characteristics of Michele Soavi's much-lauded debut, *Stagefright* (1987). The setting is the same, a dance/theatre troupe filled with the requisite bitchy queens and waspish girl 'friends', all angling for position in a plot which rewards the characters' talent for getting noticed with murder. Despite the superficial similarities of plot and *mise-en-scène* though, there is a definite difference between the two films – it's a matter of tone. Soavi's *Stagefright*, whilst tacky and occasionally toppling into silliness in its eagerness to create an effect, exudes the energy and panache of a lively young director out of the traps for the first time. There is a freshness to the way he marshals his hackneyed plot that gives the project wings. Fulci's film on the other hand is a further excursion into cynicism, following on from *The New York Ripper* and *Manhattan Baby*, both fraught with differing types of bleak nihilism (blatant and searing in the former case, casual and indolent in the latter).

Unfortunately, social authority makes an unwelcome return as the main focus of an eighties Fulci film. Once again we are in the hands of a bitter detective who is given the opportunity to pour scorn on the attitudes and lifestyles of other characters. At least in *The New York Ripper* Jack Hedley's cop was shown to be horribly corrupt. A good example of the tone of the investigation in *Murder-Rock* can be gleaned from the following dialogue: one of the dancers underlines for the police (and the audience) the significant fact that only three alumni of the dance classes will be chosen for stardom – *"Yeah, yeah, I get the gist"*, a dismissive Lieutenant Borges snaps. One can almost feel the underlying weariness, bordering on contempt, for the writers' own plotting techniques (perhaps even in the ironic choice of the name Borges). Furthermore, when someone speculates that the killer may have been a 'paranoid who hates dancers', Borges says *"He'd have my heartfelt approval"*. The result is a film that might casually appeal to the protagonist of Bret Easton Ellis's *American Psycho*.

La inconfesable pasión por la miel prohibida.

La Miel del Diablo

Con BRETT HALSEY - BLANCA MARSILLACH - STEFANO MADIA
CORINNE CLERY - PAULA MOLINA - BERNARD SERAY

Guión: JESUS BALCAZAR y VINCENZO SALVIANI Música: C. NATALI Director: LUCIO FULGI

Visión

Italian theatrical title
Il miele del diavolo

Italy & Spain

International theatrical titles
La miel del diablo (SP)
Plaisirs pervers (FR) 'Kinky Pleasures'
Le miel du diable (FR alt.)
Devil's Honey (Pakistan)

Video/DVD titles
The Devil's Honey (AUS)
Dangerous Obsession (USA)
Mrs Brown (GRE)
De lange negles nat (DEN)
'The Night of Long Nails'

Production companies
Selvaggia Film (Rome)
Producciones Balcazar s.a.s. (Barcelona)

Theatrical distributors
Selvaggia Film (Italy)
Bellparaiso, S.A. (Spain)

Theatrical running times
Italy 83m
Spain (SMC) 85m

Video/DVD/Blu-ray running time (adjusted)
Cecchi Gori DVD (Italy) 82m 38s

Shooting period
Shooting from 21 February 1986

Censorship
Italian censor certificate 81711 issued 01 August 1986

Release information
Rome 21 August 1986
Allesandria 21 August 1986
Bari 17 December 1986

The Devil's Honey

1986

Directed by Lucio Fulci. executive producers: Franco Casati & Sergio Martinelli. produced by Vincenzo Salviani for Selvaggia Film (Rome) / Producciones Balcazar S.a.s. (Barcelona). story & screenplay: Ludovica Marineo, Vincenzo Salviani, Jésus Balcazar [Granda] & Lucio Fulci. director of photography: Alessandra [Alejandro] Ulloa. music: Claudio Natili; published by Golden Grape S.a.s. editors: Vincenzo Tomassi & Emilio Ortiz. art director: Marta Cabeza [Villanueva]. production chief: Antonio Lisa. 1st assistant [director]: Juan Ramon Romani. continuity: Camilla Fulci. cameraman: Gaetano Valle. focus puller: Fulvio Martinelli. assistant cameraman: Gerardo Lopez. make-up: Jachin Navarro. hairdresser: Saturnino Merino. wardrobe: Elena Olgra. stills: Giuseppe Garibaldi Schwarze. press representative: Raffaele Striano. editor's assistants: Rita Antonelli & Massimo Cataldo. titles & visuals: Filmstudio 83. sound: Juan Quilis. recording studios: Santini (Rome). sound mixer: Claudio Pochini. with artists from ARA (Rome). Italian version mixer: Bruno Moreal. English version: John Gayford. dialogue [adaptation]: Sergio Patou. special effects: Alvaro Gremigna & Fernando Caso for Cine Audio Effects.

Cast: Brett Halsey (Dr. Wendell Simpson). Corinne Cléry (Carol Simpson). Blanca Marsillach (Jessica). Stefano Madia (Johnny). Paula Molina [as 'Paola Marina'] (Sandra). Bernard Seray (Nicky). *Uncredited:* Lucio Fulci (Bracelet Vendor). Eulàlia Ramon (Prostitute).

Synopsis: Johnny, a musician, and Jessica his lover are in the throes of a wild passion. Johnny is obsessed with sex, and carries the protesting but breathless Jessica along with his charm. Their torrid affair is brought to a premature end after Johnny hits his head falling from his motorbike. At first he appears fine, but later, in the recording studio, he collapses into a coma. Doctor Wendell Simpson, the surgeon who tries to save Johnny, has marital problems. He never makes love to his unhappy wife Carol, he regularly visits prostitutes, and is obsessed with his work. Carol demands a divorce just minutes before he's due to perform the operation. Simpson's mind wanders and Johnny dies under his hands. Jessica swears revenge on her lover's 'killer', sending threatening notes and making calls to his office. Simpson and his wife make one final attempt to patch things up. Entreating her husband to "treat me like a whore", Carol entices her husband to bed. But when the telephone rings he feels compelled to answer, despite the urgency of his wife's need. The phone rings off but the damage has been done. His wife walks out on him for good. Seconds later, the phone rings again. When Simpson answers, he hears Jessica's voice asking "Why did you let him die?" Jessica has become deranged by grief, spending hours watching home videos of Johnny. The next day she pulls a gun on Simpson and forces him to drive to her apartment. There she chloroforms him and ties him up in her cellar. Simpson regains consciousness to find an Alsation dog barking furiously at him, tied just inches away. Jessica informs her captive that she intends to kill him. In the meantime, she sets about humiliating the man, feeding him dog food and having him lick her abdomen, which is smeared with his own blood. Simpson finds himself perversely attracted to his tormentor. Jessica's sadistic games go further the following day, when she forces Simpson at gunpoint down to the sea. Whilst dragging him on a leash, she says she intends to drown him, and almost does, before changing her mind and reviving him. Her memories of her dead lover become gradually more ambivalent as she recalls some of the cruelties and excesses he was capable of. The baby she'd been carrying from her affair with Johnny miscarries at an early stage, and her periods resume. Her dog dies too, and she buries it on the beach. One final recollection changes her mind about Johnny. She'd gone to the cinema with him and his camp friend Nicky. During the film, the two lovers embraced but Jessica was horrified to see that Johnny was simultaneously letting Nicky go down on him. This memory is the last straw, and Jessica throws a bracelet symbolising their love, into the ocean. Going down to her prisoner's 'kennel', she unleashes him and lies down upstairs. Seconds later, the besotted victim walks willingly into her bedroom...

About the production: *The Devil's Honey*, Fulci's first film after recovering from viral hepatitis, was announced as 'in preparation' on 19 February 1986, with commencement of shooting scheduled for Rome just two days later. Production was handled by Selvaggia Film, run by veteran producer Franco Casati and his partners Sergio Martinelli and Massimo Pirri. Selvaggia had recently entered into co-production arrangements with Augusto Caminito's Scena Film, who had bankrolled Fulci's previous film *Murder-Rock* before he fell ill. Perhaps Caminito helped set up the deal with Selvaggia while Fulci was recovering?

Review: This erotic drama was allegedly conceived as 'Secrets of The Beyond', combining the story that became *The Devil's Honey* with a semi-sequel to Fulci's Gothic cornerstone. It's hard to credit this, although a trace of the notion of a 'living hell' is present in the soft-core S&M carry-on which Jessica's victim endures. The sexual kinks are perhaps rather tame, compared to earlier European sleaze like *Maîtresse* (1976) or *Salon Kitty* (1976), but the tale gets quite steamy for an aspiring commercial drama, and demonstrates Fulci's ability – not really seen since the 1970s – to engage with erotic material on a 'firmer' basis.

From the opening sequence we enter what must qualify as Fulci's campest territory. A machismo musician thrills his overheated girlfriend by playing a saxophone pressed tightly against her snatch. Like *9½ Weeks* (1986), or a cheesy spin on *Betty Blue* (1986), it depicts a delirious love affair that is quite clearly doomed to die in flames. The couple throw themselves into passion, roaring around on a motorbike and playing sex games of power and submission, all the while slinking through their emotions in a state of fatalistic celebration. The atmosphere is gloomy but lubricious, a Last Tango in Tatters. Political correctness is thrown gaily to the winds as Jessica embraces her lover's thrilling dominance, pushed deliriously over precipice after precipice of desire. The couple get into anal sex on the staircase, whilst their Alsation dog tries to batter down the door to join in. Animal heat and lovers' bliss combine in a plunging spiral of lust. Johnny flirts repeatedly with death, ordering Jessica to masturbate him to climax as he drives along on his motorbike at alarming speed. He closes his eyes as he climaxes, and the couple are nearly mashed by an oncoming truck. And yet, despite all this ecstatic morbidity, the temptation to end it all in a spasm of intertwining never quite finds the magic moment. Their relationship is doomed to decay into memories. Amidst extravagant life, tragedy strikes; Death claims Johnny after he hits his head falling from his motorbike. He expires under the surgeon's knife during a brain operation and Jessica is condemned to life without him.

Blanca Marsillach and Stefano Madia are compelling as the young couple consumed by obsessive lust, portraying passion and its overbearing shadow. Marsillach's ambivalence about her lover's appetite for sex is well captured. *"It's a mean thing you just did. You treat me like a piece of meat"*, she complains after Johnny has sodomized her on the stairs. Nevertheless, she continues to comply with his aggressive sexual demands. *The Devil's Honey* is by no means a howl of protest at the exploitation of women; the film shares its sympathies with both of these driven dionysiacs. Madia's energetic performance ensures that Johnny's sexual charisma is plausible to the viewer, and we feel a stab of horror at his sudden accident. First the crunching smack on the head and then the delayed reaction, as he attempts to play saxophone during a gruelling recording session; both scenes inject a painful note of loss into the tale. (It's a shame that Fulci has Marsillach press herself against the studio glass in anguish at the latter point, because it tips the sequence over into bathos.) Later, when we see flashback examples of Johnny's unpredictable kindness, his sexual bullying, and even his outright nastiness (he smashes a doll he'd given his lover as a present, sneering *"I love you, I love you; is that all you can say? It's a bore."*), we can believe that Jessica has been deranged by the loss of this powerful elemental force in her life.

The soon-to-be-enslaved Dr. Simpson, on the other hand, has a frigid relationship with his wife and joyless encounters with prostitutes. In a scene that's difficult not to laugh at, he compels one hooker to stimulate herself with a nail-varnish brush, before screwing her in a mess of red lacquer.

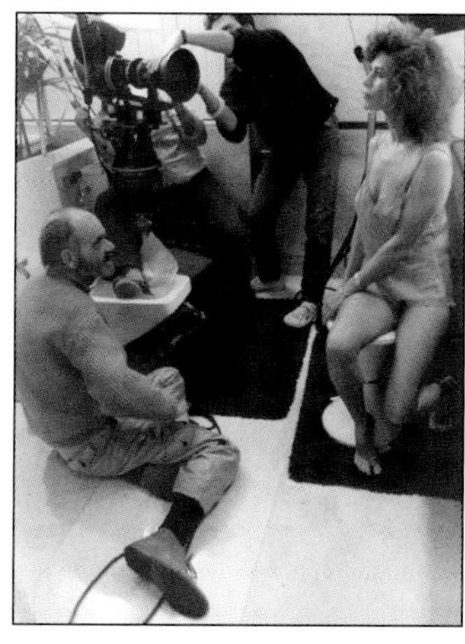

above:
"I'm sick of being respected! Treat me like a whore, that's what I am – your whore!" – Fulci directs the excellent Corinne Cléry.

opposite page main picture:
Jessica (Blanca Marsillach) taunts her prisoner Dr. Simpson (Brett Halsey) after nearly drowning him.

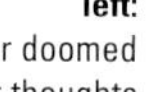

left:
As Jessica looks back at her doomed relationship with Johnny, her thoughts turn to suicide...

opposite bottom left and below:
The same key art was used across the globe. The Italian locandina poster is shown opposite bottom left, the rare Dutch VHS cover is below.

above:
Jessica and Johnny (Stefano Madia) enjoy a holiday in Venice.

below:
A distraught Jessica is comforted by Johnny's gay lover Nicky (Bernard Seray, right).

Our sympathy for his later predicament is tempered by recollections of the contemptuous way he spoke to the prostitute after ejaculating. *"Go away now"*, he snaps. The hooker calls him a freak, to which he responds *"What do you want, flowers? I should treat you like a lady or something?"* He returns home to his wife, well played by Corinne Cléry who gets some great lines: *"I thought tarts were your latest passion"*, she says, smearing on lipstick before a staid dinner engagement. Later, she explains her frustration to her husband in tones that sound fresh even though the lines are as old as the hills: *"I'm sick of being respected! Treat me like a whore, that's what I am – your whore!"* Despite the tackiness, Cléry still manages to bring a credible hurt and sorrow to the scene when her husband's insatiable desire to answer the phone over-rides his lust, trashing their attempt to start over.

The sequences between Marsillach and Halsey are charged as high as can be expected considering the 'vanilla' standard of degradation Fulci has Jessica exact on Simpson. An early humiliation – the bound captive pisses his pants in fear when Jessica seems about to set the vicious dog upon him – suggests a possible accumulation of sordid torments, but Fulci rushes through this stage and onto the more 'porno' aspects of the relationship, when Simpson begins to offer his obedience willingly to the vengeful beauty.

However, one sequence does depict a darker, more frightening aspect of dominance, when Jessica takes her prisoner down to the sea and holds the bound man's head under the waves with her foot. *"Death has given you to me"*, she pronounces, as he slumps unconscious beneath the water. He can't hear her, though, and there's the rub. The sadistic desire to kill is haunted by its own imminent success. She experiences a loathsome moment of emptiness in the wake of her action, and drags Dr. Simpson back to the shore to revive him. In a scene worthy of de Sade, she revives the drowned man with mouth-to-mouth resuscitation and, as he rises blearily into consciousness again, leans into his face and announces *"I hate you – I'm going to kill you"*.

The dark suggestions of malignant motherhood implicit here – supported by the detail of Jessica's failed pregnancy, her wish to have a baby as *"something of my own, that's all mine"*, and her fascination with a broken doll – are not followed up. Some of the other lines of dialogue also tend to dissipate the sadistic tension. After allowing her prisoner to lick his own blood from her lower belly, a submission the man makes assiduously, she pulls away saying *"That's enough! – I hate you – you murderer!"* Later, Marsillach tries to menace with lines like *"My name is Fear – but you can call me Jessica"*. And when the S&M 'highlight' of the film is Jessica dripping hot wax onto Simpson's back as he grovels at her feet, it's hard to be particularly shocked.

Nevertheless, a melancholia is successfully introduced to compensate, as Jessica recalls her love affair with Johnny through gradually less rose-tinted glasses. One particular flashback dabbles briefly – but highly imaginatively – with complex subjectivity on Jessica's part. Seeming to recall a day when Johnny insisted on filming her with a pistol stuck between her legs, she suddenly remarks, *"It's gross – even you weren't like that"*. *"What do you mean?"*, asks Johnny. Jessica's face expresses a confusion, but she replies, *"You know what I mean"*. This scene, impossible as a real exchange in the past, is more akin to Alain Resnais' or Nicolas Roeg's treatment of memory than anything we're accustomed to from Fulci. Is Jessica interrogating a false memory from within the frame of her mind's eye, or are we witnessing an attempt

to negate unpalatable facts about Johnny, re-writing selectively, as we are all wont to do, her memory of 'the truth'? Whatever, it's an unusual scene that makes one wish Fulci had dabbled with such labyrinths of representation more often.

So *The Devil's Honey* isn't hot as such, but it is 'hot'. It's good, sleazy fun, and perhaps Fulci's last truly enjoyable movie. A demented tackiness makes it a hard film to criticize. Few viewers are going to take seriously its catalogue of misfortune, and yet there is a dynamic quality to the tortured dramatics. Of course, Fulci studied for a while to become a doctor, so who knows – perhaps the role of Brett Halsey's distracted surgeon, thrown into erotic passivity by an avenging woman, was some sort of kinky wish-fulfillment. It's certainly a more upbeat romp than his early giallo, *One on Top of the Other*, which also examined the misfortunes of an inattentive husband-doctor. In place of that film's dominant melancholia, *The Devil's Honey* has a distinct air of lubricious celebration to it. Sadly, it would be one of the very last examples of Fulci's ebbing talent.

above:
High drama or high camp? Tears at the studio as Jessica sees Johnny collapse whilst recording a saxophone solo.

below:
Dr. Simpson and his wife try to mend their ways one last time...

Italian theatrical title
Ænigma

Italy & Yugoslavia

Alternative titles
Internado diabolico (ARG video)
'Evil Boarding School'
Dämonia (GER DVD)

Production companies
A.M. Trading International (Rome)
Sutjeska Film (Belgrade)

Theatrical distributors
By regional independents

Theatrical running time
Italy 90m

Video/DVD/Blu-ray running time (adjusted)
Image DVD (USA) 85m 27s

Shooting period
May-June 1987

Censorship
Italian censor certificate 83089
issued 19 November 1987

Release information
France 30 December 1987
Rome 1 September 1988
Milan 7 October 1988
Taranto & Savoia 25 January 1989

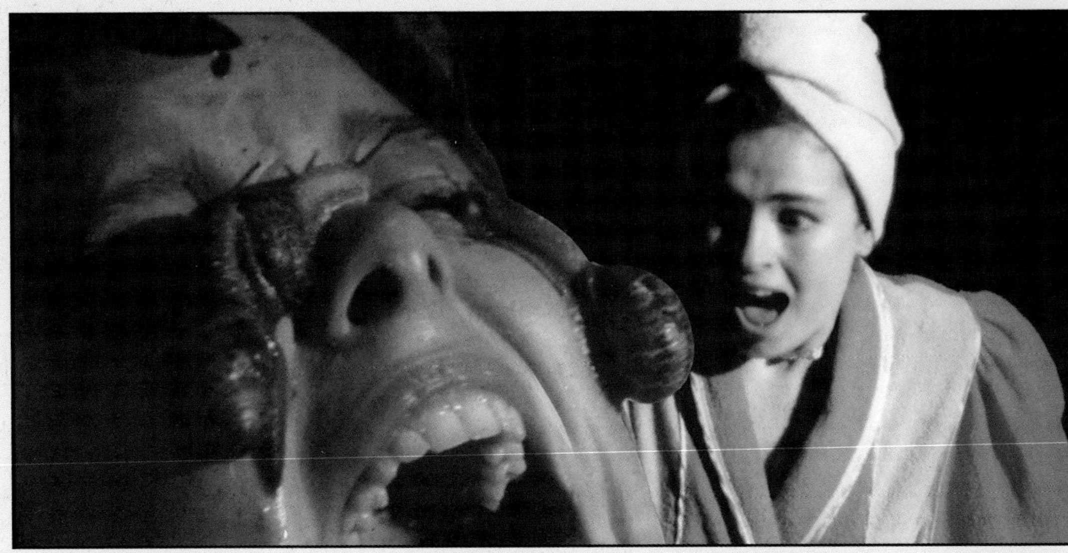

Ænigma

1987

Directed by Lucio Fulci. executive producer: Walter Bigari. a film produced by Ettore Spagnuolo for A.M. Trading International (Rome) in collaboration with Boro Banjack for Sutjeska Film (Sarajevo). story & screenplay: Giorgio Mariuzzo & Lucio Fulci. director of photography: Luigi Ciccarese. music composed & directed by Carlo Maria Cordio. film editor: Vanio Amici. production designer: Zijo Pasic'. set designer: Kemo Hrustanovic. set manager: Alessandra Spagnuolo. continuity: Camilla Fulci. cameraman: Daniel Sukalo. assistant cameraman: Fabio Lecni. gaffer: Marco Firmi. costume designer: Karlo Klemencic'. make-up artist: Giuseppe Ferranti. hair stylist: Maria Teresa Cerrera. special camera effects: Lucio Fulci. production secretary: Fulvio Onorati. assistant editor: Carlo Pulerà. sound recording: N.C. S.r.l. sound mixer: Bruno Monreal [Moreal]. sound effects: Walter Polini. special effects: production Film 82 S.N.C. technical equipment: Cineluce. furnishings: Cinears S.r.l. travel: Alien 1999. transport: Cinetrasport. insurance: Cinesicurtà. the song "Head Over Heels" by A.D. Meakin & Carlo Maria Cordio, performed by Douglas Meakin Giuliana & Schmidl S.r.l. color: Telecolor S.p.A. negative: Kodak. laboratory: Franco Appetito.

Cast: Jared Martin (Dr. Robert Anderson). Lara Lamberti [as 'Lara Naszinski'] (Eva Gordon). Ulli Reinthaler (Jennifer Clark). Sophie D'Aulan (Kim). Jennifer Naud (Grace O'Neal). Riccardo Acerbi (Fred Vernon). Kathi Wise (Virginia Williams). Milijana Zirojevic [as 'Mijlijana Zirojevic'] (Kathy). Dragan Bjelogrlic [as 'Dragan Ejelogrlic'] (Tom). Ljiljana Blagojevic [as 'Lijlijana Blagojevic'] (Ms. Jones). Franciska Spahic (Joanne). Dusica Zegarac (Mary). Zorica Lesic (Miss James). Zoran Lesic). Rade Colovic (Tom). *Uncredited:* Lucio Fulci (police inspector).

Synopsis: St. Mary's College Boston. A boarding school for girls. A lonely student, Kathy, is the butt of a cruel practical joke perpetrated by a gang of students and a sadistic gym teacher, Fred Vernon. Running away from her tormentors, she is hit by a car and admitted to hospital in a coma. Kathy's mother, Mary, continues working at the school as a cleaner. A new girl, Eva Gordon, arrives. She is given Kathy's old room and becomes acquainted with the perpetrators of the stunt. From the depths of her coma, Kathy's mind reaches out for revenge... First to die is the narcissistic Mr. Vernon, whose reflection steps through a mirror to crush him. Next is Virginia, who is suffocated by snails. Doctor Robert Anderson, the neurologist in charge of Kathy's case, notices that her vital signs increase in step with the mysterious deaths. When Eva has a violent fit, Anderson is called to the school to examine her: she seduces him. Another girl, Grace, is killed when a marble statue comes to life and crushes her. Anderson becomes apprehensive about Eva, and has a nightmare in which she eats his flesh during sex. He's relieved when Eva's mother comes to take her on vacation. She writes love letters to Anderson but he has already started a fling with another girl, Jennifer Clark, the only practical joker to show any remorse. Eva runs away from her parents and returns to the school. Tom and Kim, two of the cruellest of Kathy's tormentors, are the next victims: after suffering a vision of Tom stabbed through the neck, Kim plummets from a high window. Tom is decapitated by a falling blind. Jenny, who has gone to the hospital to be with Doctor Anderson, gets lost and encounters Eva, who is possessed by Kathy, in the morgue. Eva/Kathy threatens to kill Jenny, but Anderson intervenes and Eva slumps to the ground. In Kathy's hospital room, her mother has pulled out the intravenous drips, appalled at her daughter's malice. Kathy's soul rises into the night sky.

About the production: The death-knell for Italian horror was tolling loud and clear in 1987, but Lucio Fulci soldiered on. His next film, *Ænigma*, was an Italo-Yugoslav co-production, put together by Ettore Spagnuolo of A.M. Trading International. Spagnuolo had recently co-financed two Umberto Lenzi action pics, *War Time* and *Bridge to Hell*, with Sutjeska Film (the latter a longstanding cornerstone of Yugoslavian film production[16]) and had also recently worked as producer on *The Trap* (1985), directed by Giuseppe Patroni Griffi from a script by Fulci. However, *Ænigma* appears to have originated with Realta Cinematografica in October 1986, when it was mooted (with a November '86 commencement) as a directing project for one Peter Valenti, a mysterious individual who disappeared from the industry and never actually made a film. The intended producer at this stage was Pino Buricchi, an acquaintance of Spagnuolo's; they had worked together on a matching pair of 1982 muscleman pics, *The Invincible Barbarian* and *The Sword of the Barbarians* featuring erotic siren Sabrina Siani. Siani's name was also

below:
British video cover.

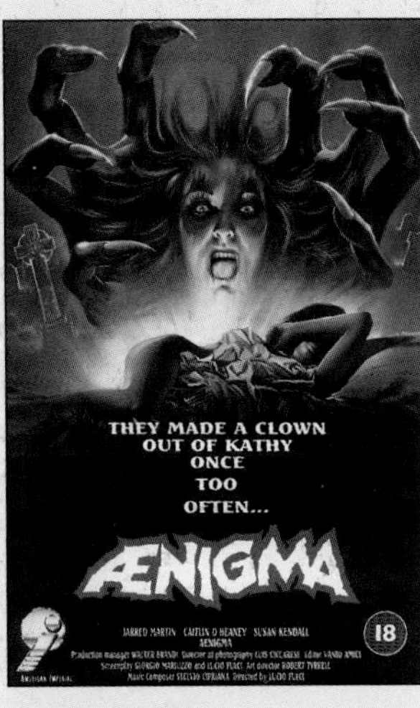

attached to the proposed Realta version of *Ænigma* alongside Andy J. Forest and Mimsy Farmer (although neither Siani nor the others ended up in the finished film). By 6 March 1987 Fulci was onboard, and shooting was expected to take place in England and the USA. At this stage the cast still included Farmer, Forest and Siani, along with *"Roberta Sarazzi aka Jane Keller, in the role of a reincarnated witch"*.[17] In May, however, with Spagnuolo instead of Buricchi steering the production, casting choices underwent a major overhaul. Yugoslavian finance meant a leading role went to Milijana Zirojevic, while location work switched to Belgrade. (Despite everyone running around wearing T-shirts emblazoned with 'St. Mary's College Boston' there's no way that any Stateside shooting took place; the exteriors are purposely evasive where one would expect them to capitalise on the available scenery, and the background in shots of Jared Martin driving looks Eastern-European.) *Ænigma*'s subsequent releases were sporadic. The film was selected for the Avoriaz Film Festival 1988, and scored a few play dates across Europe, doing as well as could be expected with the Italian horror genre in such steep decline...

opposite page main image: The scene *Ænigma* is most likely to be remembered for, as a character is besieged in her bedroom by hordes of ravening molluscs.

Review: When first announced, the supernaturally-themed *Ænigma* seemed to suggest a return to surrealistic horror after the minor giallo *Murder-Rock* and the failed genre digressions *Conquest* and *Rome 2033 – The Fighter Centurions*. Even the title was promising, its spelling defiantly out of the ordinary, perhaps to trigger associations with films like Argento's *Tenebrae* and *Suspiria*. It offered a tantalizing suggestion of the mysterious, so skilfully evoked in Fulci's early eighties work. The reality proved somewhat different; *Ænigma* borrowed heavily (no problem in itself) from American sources – the wrong American sources – but also tagged unwisely along with the girls' school setting and animal-horror daftness of Dario Argento's *Phenomena* (1985). As the eighties malaise sank deep into the texture of Italian horror, *Ænigma* came out like a dishevelled, if paradoxically smooth-looking amalgamation of tired American resources (*Carrie* – done to death – plus films like *Prom Night*, which surfaced in the wake of *Friday the 13th*) and grossly depleted Italian stock. Perhaps the most blatant steal comes from Richard Franklin's *Patrick* (1978), which had itself already been the subject of an amusingly sleazy Italian follow-up, Mario Landi's *Patrick vive ancora* (1980). *Ænigma* lifts from it the central notion of a telepathic, telekinetic accident-victim psychically manipulating events from a hospital bed.

Chiefly, *Ænigma* can be seen as Fulci's stab at an up-to-date eighties-style horror movie. The film-stock is bland, clean and micro-grained, while the lighting strives vainly for colour gel atmospherics. Caught between two stools, however, the film lacks the right sort of cast for the new aesthetic it's trying to match. The actresses simply aren't tacky enough. Instead of being a coiffured eighties sex kitten, the female lead looks rather plain. Not a problem if the film were playing its own game, but a cock-eyed miscast when judged by the standards of the airbrushed American product it wants to evoke.

The oddness that made Italian horror movies so compelling is here represented by steals from Argento's *Phenomena*. At least the female lead doesn't *talk* to the snails in the film's most bizarre death sequence (*Phenomena* depends upon psychic congress between insects and a blank, lousy actress for its plot development). In fact, the snail sequence almost breaks through the Americanised patina of *Ænigma* by dint of sheer ridiculousness. A girl is – well, *snailed* to death. No explanation is given as to what these slow-moving blobs are actually doing – no hissing to suggest caustic slime, no munching sounds to suggest toothy variants on the mollusc theme, and no gleeful inserts of unlikely but amusingly repulsive gore to match the spiders in *The Beyond*. (In case you think that harking back to *The Beyond* is just gratuitous nostalgia on my part, bear in mind that the hell-bound groans dubbed onto the end of the sequence explicitly recycle that film's sepulchral atmosphere.) It seems Fulci was struggling to find an alternative to the extreme violence he'd deployed so successfully before, but which was increasingly out of fashion in the film markets of the late 1980s. The snails are *almost* a triumph of the bizarre, but their silliness is inescapable. All they really do is crawl on the victim very slowly, and the effort required for the rampaging gastropods to invade the girl's mouth are entirely her own. Fulci's use of inexplicably pinnioned helpless victims has rarely seemed so nonsensical. Other death scenes suggest that Fulci was striving for a less-is-more approach to the horrors, but instead the cutting falls into ineptitude. One particular sequence, featuring a hapless teen being crushed by a supernaturally animated statue, initially looks as if the censor has been nibbling at it, but unfortunately the scene is merely a mess. Fulci might once have been able to lend the *Carrie*-derived story the emotional commitment it needed, but it's hard to sympathise with the put-upon drudge whose suffering sparks *Ænigma*'s story. Where Brian De Palma reinforced identification with the eponyous victim in *Carrie* by turning the heat of his contempt on the pranksters who bully her, Fulci seems unable to make even the childish cruelty of the girl's tormentors memorable. The result is a film as inexpressive and unendearing as its characters.

If the blasted emptiness of the land of death in *The Beyond* was an artistic triumph, both visually and conceptually, then what can we say about the 'vision' of a soul's point-of-view as it leaves the body, as shown in *Ænigma*? Knowing that Fulci had recently survived a life-threatening illness, one anticipates some kind of visual apotheosis here, and the eye strives to make something interesting of the uninspiring abstract surface that we see as the camera rises into the night. The nagging sense that it's probably just meant to be the nondescript roof of a hospital building, achieved as a model shot, ends the film on a note of anti-climax. Which might have been amusingly existential – 'Is that all there is?' – if it weren't a sign that Fulci was now unwilling or unable to conjure even the most basic of transmigratory fireworks.

above and below: Fotobuste produced for the film's limited January 1989 Italian theatrical release.

Italian theatrical title
Zombi 3

Italy

Alternative titles
Zombi 3 Revolta dos mortos vivos (POR video) 'Zombie 3 Revolt of the Living Dead'
El Zombi (MEX video)
Zombie III Atomverseucht und Untot Sie Kommen Wieder (WG video cover) 'Zombie 3 Radioactive and Undead, They Come Back'
Zombie Flesh-Eaters 2 (UK DVD)
Zombie Flesh Eaters II (UK TV transmission video-generated screen title)
Zombie: Hell on Earth (DEN DVD)

Production company
Flora Film

Theatrical distributors
DMV Distribuzione

Theatrical running time
Italy 88m

Video/DVD/Blu-ray running times (adjusted)
Media Blasters DVD (USA) 94m 49s
Nocturno/Cine-Kult DVD 94m 32s

Shooting period
Shooting November 1987

Censorship
Italian censor certificate 83666 issued 02 June 1988

Release information
Rome 'Rassegna internazionale del fantastico' 07 June 1988
Rome 29 July 1988
Turin 30 July 1988
Bari 18 August 1988

Zombi 3

1988

Directed by Lucio Fulci [completed by Bruno Mattei & Claudio Fragasso]. producer: Franco Gaudenzi for Flora Film. story & screenplay: Claudio Fragasso. script translation [uncredited]: John Dulaney. director of photography: Riccardo Grassetti. music composed & conducted by Stefano Mainetti. editor: Alberto Moriani. art director: Bart Scavia [Bartolomeo Scavia]. special effects make-up: Franco Di Girolamo. production supervisor: Rick Hasserot. production manager: Giovanni Paolucci. continuity: Mily Fulci & Liliane Hann [Liliana Ginanneschi]. stunt coordinator: Ottaviano Dell'Acqua. camera operator: John Richins. assistant cameramen: Ruben Hundit [Mauro Di Croce] & Raul Matthews [Raul Filippo Mattei]. key grips: Charles Kascioff & Alvit Hessar. gaffer: Bert Hessar [Umberto Chessari]. make-up: Franco Di Girolamo. special effects: Joseph Ross & Tony Cevi. make up assistant: Angelica Raf. Philippines crew Philippine coordinator: Benny Ternante. assistant production coordinator: Ernie Barredo. location manager: Roland Taino. assistant location manager: Edgard Taino. assistant stunt coordinator: Dante Abadessa. art director: Vic Dabao. camera assistant: Ed Sequerada. key grip: Fred Marquez. gaffer: Mario Ponce. set decorators: Leonardo Mediarito & Rene Mediarito. special effects: Rodolfo Torrente. wardrobe: Julie De Guzman. tailor: Eddy De Guzman. still photographer: Billy Carter. transportation manager: Francisco Taino. production secretary: Angel Valli. accountant: Mary Hope [Maria Spera]. 1st assistant editor: Lorenz Costanth. 2nd assistant editor: Cinthia Matthews. titles & opticals: Studio Mafera. sound: David Meel. boom operator: Clay Mc Paul. re-recording by N.C. (Rome). mixage: Bruno Moreal. dialogue editor: Jonh [John] Gayford. sound effects editors: Tullio Arcangeli, Roberto Sterbini & Gjika Sotir. music recorded at Rome Yeah Recording Studios. sound engineer: Davide Piccini. soundtrack released on Beat Records label – Variety Film. production equipment & facilities supplied by E.C.E. Technovision srl. Arriflex cameras supplied by E.C.E. Technovision srl. songs "Tumble Down", "The Sound of Fear", "Slow Think" & "Nature" by Zac & Stefano Mainetti, all recorded by Clue in the Crew. colour by Technicolor. filmed on location in the Philippines.

Cast: Deran Sarafian (Kenny). Beatrice Ring (Patricia). Ottaviano Dell'Acqua [as 'Richard Raymond'] (Roger). Massimo Vanni [as 'Alex McBride'] (Bo). Ulli Reinthaler (Nancy). Marina Loi (Carole). Deborah Bergamini (Lia). Luciano Pigozzi [as 'Alan Collins'] (Plant Director [scenes deleted]). *Uncredited:* Rene Abadeza (zombie). Mari Catotiengo (Suzanna). Roberto Dell'Acqua (zombie on footbridge). Claudio Fragasso (soldier at crematorium). Robert Marius (Doctor Holder). Bruno Mattei (soldier at crematorium). Mike Monty (General Morton).

Synopsis: Scientists at a top secret research centre are experimenting with a chemical compound called 'Death One' which can bring the dead back to life. The military are interested in its capabilities as a weapon; the substance causes tissue mutation and eventual death in living subjects. Doctor Holder requests permission to leave the project but before he can do so the centre is attacked by agents of another military power who make off with samples of 'Death One'. The box is damaged by gunfire and one of the thieves infects himself by touching it. Rotting away whilst still alive, he checks into a hotel and tries to stem the infection by cutting off his hand. Soldiers arrive and find him dead, but he has infected a bellhop and slaughtered a maid. Head of the military clean-up team General Morton orders everyone in the region killed to prevent the infection spreading. Bodies are burned, sending infected ash flying through the air. Three soldiers vacationing in an army jeep – Kenny, Roger and Bo – encounter a group of young people travelling by coach. Nancy, Carole and Lia flirt with the soldiers, but chaos strikes as the bus is attacked by birds. Nearby, a young couple, Patricia and Glenn, are out for a drive. They see dead birds strewn across the road and when Glenn investigates he's savagely pecked by one. He starts to feel ill and the couple stop at a disused garage for help. There, Patricia is attacked by zombies. The three soldiers and the coach party, meanwhile, seek help at the hotel where the infected agent died. Lia has fallen sick after being pecked by infected birds. Kenny and Roger explore the building and find a crate of firearms. Bo goes with Carole in the jeep to look for signs of life – the whole area seems deserted. The vehicle breaks down and Carole wanders off looking for water. As she explores an apartment block she is attacked by a zombie which pushes her into a swimming pool. Bo dives in after her but when he pulls her out she has no legs and tries to kill him. More zombies attack and Bo runs away. He flags down Patricia who is driving Glenn to hospital and persuades her to stop off at the hotel to check on his friends. Glenn suddenly attacks Patricia. Bo tries to defend her but a horde of zombies attack and kill him. Patricia escapes and heads for the hotel. There, two of the party are attacked by a flying severed head found lurking in a fridge. The sick girl, Lia, suddenly attacks Nancy. In the struggle Lia falls through a first floor window and drops dead at Kenny's feet. Patricia stumbles into the hotel and seeks refuge with the dwindling group but zombies attack and the group are forced to flee. After taking to canoes, the five survivors rest on a river bank. General Morton's clean-up squad arrive and open fire, killing the bus driver. Kenny, Roger, Nancy and Patricia hide in an abandoned hospital. The girls find a pregnant woman about to give birth. Nancy tries to deliver the child whilst Patricia wanders off and the two men get into a fight with Morton's soldiers. Nancy is attacked by a zombie as she tries to deliver the baby, which bursts from its mother's stomach and rips her face to pieces. Patricia encounters a zombiefied Glenn and has to behead him to save herself. Roger is attacked by zombies and shot dead by the clean-up squad. Kenny and Patricia manage to fly off in a helicopter and tune in to the radio. The DJ is a zombie who dedicates a record to "all the undead around the world". Patricia wonders if there's anything worth returning to.

About the production: In the mid-to-late 1980s, *Zombi 2* co-producer Gianfranco Couyoumdjian had taken to shooting numerous action movie projects on location in the Philippines. In 1987-88 his company Flora Film made four films there, all helmed by exploitation journeyman Bruno Mattei: *Double Target*, starring Miles O'Keefe and Bo Svenson, *Strike Commando 2* with Brent Huff and Richard Harris, *Cop Game* with Brent Huff and Werner Pochath, and *Robowar* with Reb Brown. Consequently, when the idea of a sequel to *Zombi 2* was suggested, the Philippines seemed to offer a viable location setting. Sadly, *Zombi 3* proved to be the biggest disaster of Fulci's career. Instead of a triumphant return to form, the film was a wreck of embarrassing proportions from which Fulci departed, in fury and despair, with shooting only two-thirds completed. Bruno Mattei, very much the man of the moment at Flora Film, stepped in to direct the rest.

The first mention of *Zombi 3* in *Variety* came on 21 October 1987: *"Variety Film, repped by Maria Rita Tuccio, has available Filmirage's "Killing Birds" and "Top Model" as well as Flora Film's "Zombie 3" and "Strike Commando 2."* This however was a pre-sales pitch by Flora, not an indication that the film was ready for release. A more reliable indication can be gleaned from an article dated 2 December 1987 announcing that Ulli Reinthaler was *"back from the Philippines where she played the leading role in Lucio Fulci's latest horror pic 'Zombies 3' [sic]"*. Given that the rainy season in the Philippines starts in June and lasts until October, with typhoons common in the latter month, shooting must have taken place during November 1987.

Afterwards, Fulci was frank in his dismissal of the film, telling Massimo F. Lavagnini: *"I don't repudiate any of my movies except* Zombi 3. *But that movie's not mine. It's the most foolish of my productions. It has been done by a group of idiots, who are Claudio Fragasso – natural born cretin; Bruno Mattei – who before becoming a 'director' was a house painter; and a guy named Mimmo* [aka Bartolomeo] *Scavia – the director of production, who arrived in the Philippines and his first thought was to just fuck some Oriental girls. I refused to finish* Zombi 3. *I took the plane and came back to Rome. On the screen you can only see fifty minutes directed by me, and that's because Fragasso continuously changed my screenplay. 'We can't do this, we can't do that...' I'm only proud of the scene of the biting skull."*[18]

Review: The film print and the posters for *Zombi 3* may bear the name of Lucio Fulci, but attribution of a director's credit to this troubled production has long been fraught with difficulty. As early as its inaugural screening at the Rome Fantafestival in 1988 rumours were afloat that Lucio Fulci had actually shot very little of the film. The first head to replace his on the chopping block was that of Bruno Mattei, director of 1980's *Zombie Creeping Flesh*. Mattei was said to have completed the film after Fulci was taken ill, with the latter having completed perhaps as little as five minutes of onscreen footage. Fulci, worried about his future and not wanting to seem an insurance risk, at first denied these stories about his illness. He eventually claimed to have shot virtually a feature's length of material before walking from the project, due to disagreements with producer Franco Gaudenzi and writer Claudio Fragasso.[19]

The most recent developments in the *Zombi 3* saga have seen Fragasso absolving Bruno Mattei from blame, by asserting it was he who made the film after illness forced Fulci to quit. It seems Fulci did actually shoot almost a complete feature, only to have it junked as unusable (save for a couple of short scenes) by the team of Gaudenzi, Fragasso and Mattei. Fragasso can hardly have expected any praise for the fiasco that was eventually released, so we must assume (for now at least) that his admission of culpability is the truth.[20]

For Lucio's fans there's always been overwhelming aesthetic evidence to consider too. Unlike even the least of Fulci's horror films before it, *Zombi 3* has no style, no atmosphere, no impact at all. It looks dreadful – everything is shot in labour-saving medium and long shots with barely a glimmer of ambition to the staging. And it sounds even worse – bombastic synthesizer music forms a poisonous collusion with Fragasso's totally asinine dialogue. The actors are either insipid or appalling and the gore effects, whilst bloody, are shot in disinterested, inept fashion. Everything that made Fulci's *Zombie Flesh-Eaters* so thrilling is absent in this supposed sequel, which fails even to work as a cash-in on the first film (surely the most basic requirement of such a project). It's astonishing the way this dull story completely betrays the first film's memory. Fulci was quite a celebrity in the horror field, but nothing could have been more calculated to sully his image. Instead of capitalizing on his notoriety and boldly playing to the gallery, the film cohabits with the lowly efforts of Bruno Mattei, whose absurd, disorganized *Zombie Creeping Flesh* it resembles far more than *Zombie Flesh-Eaters*.

As if already bored with its own reason for existing, *Zombi 3* ignores the precepts of its forebear and neglects even to revisit its influences. Instead of Romero's zombie trilogy the story uses themes from the same director's 1973 film *The Crazies*, 'borrowing' not only the idea of a bacteriological weapons spill in a populated area, and the depiction of excessive military action in response, but also the image of white suited, gas-masked soldiers sent to shoot down the infected citizenry. Here though, the General in charge takes such an idiotically brutal satisfaction in ordering soldiers to kill indiscriminately that we just shut down any credulity – the script can't be bothered to offer a believable villain, idly assuming we'll take this charade as a critique of military fascism.

Of course Fulci's horror films had certainly taken liberties with plausibility before, and to breathtaking effect. Here though, despite occasional gusts of dry ice wafted before the lens to obscure wretched special make-up fx, there's no sense of the supernatural to provide ingenious alibis for an abandonment of cause-and-effect. The relentlessly banal look of the film is completely at odds with the few moments of illogic – no excuses here for

above:
Locandina.

opposite main image:
Patricia (Beatrice Ring) is attacked by a fast-moving machete-wielding zombie when she stops for help at a roadside garage.

opposite bottom left:
Vipco, the company that made *Zombie Flesh-Eaters* a hit on the British video rental market in the early 1980s, could not resist cashing in on their earlier success by cheekily re-titling *Zombi 3* as *Zombie Flesh Eaters 2* in the UK.

below:
Kenny (Deran Sarafian) and Roger (Ottaviano Dell'Acqua) face an army of the undead.

this page:
Fire... zombies... guns... and the script is in the mail...

mistakes like the ones Catriona MacColl referred to in her comments about *The House by the Cemetery*. The scene Fulci always admitted to directing – in which a severed head flies through the air and savages a man's throat – is perhaps the closest to a pleasurably lunatic surprise in the film (it even has a reaction shot edited in, and a quick reverse zoom for impact). But as if to confirm Fulci's absence from the rest of the film it feels stranded, out of place, probably included as a sop to the Far Eastern market where *Zombi 3* was indeed able to secure a release. Indonesian films such as H. Tjut Jalil's *Mystics in Bali* and L. Sudjio's *Queen of Black Magic* (both 1981), and the self-explanatory 1977 Hong Kong weirdie *Witch with Flying Head*, let fly with similar scenes of supernatural madness. Fulci's success in the Far East – where many of his early eighties horror titles were enthusiastically received – can safely be assumed to have 'inspired' this bizarre but totally isolated sequence in *Zombi 3*.

Unfortunately, a much greater influence stems from Lamberto Bava's *Demons*, particularly on the soundtrack, with its cheap choral samples and crass

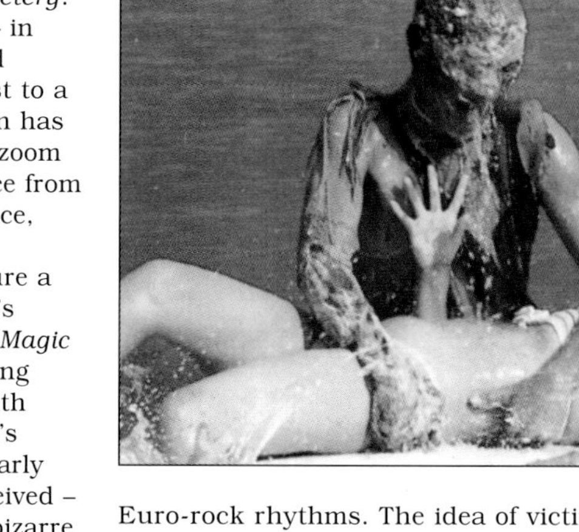

Euro-rock rhythms. The idea of victims' infected wounds pulsating visibly, rapidly transforming into suppurating boils, replaces the slower-acting infection transmitted by Romero-style zombies, but this is another idea – like the flying head – that requires a commitment to the fantastic. In *Demons*, the supernatural is smartly ensconced within a film inside the film, whilst the gruesome transformations erupt from the screen and into the cinema audience – playing with frames like this offers as much of an opportunity for illogic as the supernatural, and *Demons*, though full of irritations, has just such a clever double game at its core. In *Zombi 3* though, the mutations are 'explained' through pseudo-science, swerving the film relentlessly into the mundane. (Romero sensibly pushed the brief mention of 'radiation' out of the way in *Night of the Living Dead*'s script.)

In *Zombie Flesh-Eaters*, Richard Johnson's Doctor Menard is searching for a scientific explanation for the risen dead, whilst the locals are attributing their appearance to voodoo. There, Fulci's approach leant heavily on the latter implication (at least in the art design and photography), but here he unwisely signs up for a script which prefers the avenues taken by later zombie films, not least Dan O'Bannon's Romero spoof *Return of the Living Dead* (1985), based on a script by a co-writer of the original *Night of the Living Dead*, John Russo.

Amazingly, there's no understanding that for a straight-faced gore flick to borrow liberally from an avowed horror comedy is a mistake. *Return of the Living Dead* has its fun by suggesting Romero's first film was based on a real-life biological warfare situation, hushed up by the military. The next 'chemical spill' accident is then played out as comedy. (When a bullet to the brain fails to stop the marauding undead, a shocked character asks 'You mean the movie lied?') The process of becoming a zombie is a gradual (and painful) one caused by the chemical, which slowly extinguishes all vital signs until the still-conscious victim is locked in a 'dead' body. To allow the creation of a homicidal zombie horde, these unfortunates are then re-animated, driven by a desire to feed on 'fresh brains' (which means the potential horror of the process can be transmuted into ghoulish E.C. Comics fun). This accelerated slide into rigor-mortis and decay is swiped wholesale from the American film by Fragasso's script, but its clot-headed incorporation makes *Return of the Living Dead* look like a masterpiece in comparison. All *Zombi 3* can do with the idea is to confuse the viewer as to whether victims are really dead. The corpses are burnt and the contaminated ashes return their poison to the earth – another idea taken from O'Bannon and Russo – but without the American film's effective rainfall scenes, the supposed mass infection is rather less than cinematic.

Among the other similarities worth mentioning, shades of *The Evil Dead*'s snickering girl-ghouls may be detected in a scene where a female zombie calls to her friend to wake her before attacking. Closer to Rome, Gaudenzi's script unwisely ditches Fulci's effective slow, tottering ghouls and opts for the all-action brawling zombies of Umberto Lenzi's absurd *Nightmare City*; worse still, the film also shares *Nightmare City*'s blundering ecological platitudes. (It's a wry thought that Romero's fractionally over-earnest critique of materialism in *Dawn of the Dead* was probably the catalyst for these grotesquely tacked-on Italian displays of political/social/ecological conscience.)

However, most astonishing (and unwelcome) of all are the blatant similarities to Bruno Mattei's *Zombie Creeping Flesh*. Claudio Fragasso was the writer (and assistant director) of that dismal film too, and appears to have cynically recycled the previous storyline.[21] Considering that *Zombie Creeping Flesh* owed its paltry existence to the success of Romero's *Dawn of the Dead* and Fulci's *Zombie Flesh-Eaters*, his cuckoo-in-the-nest approach to the task shows that Fragasso took a contemptuous attitude to Fulci from the start. Given the job of scripting a sequel to Fulci's hit, he took advantage of the project to re-make his own dire zombie flick. At least Fulci smelled a rat somewhere down the line, but to add insult to injury it was Bruno Mattei that producer Franco Gaudenzi then drafted in to complete the film! No doubt this was undertaken at Fragasso's suggestion – the two had worked together several times as a writer-director team on films like *The Other Hell* and *The True Story of the Nun of Monza* (shot back-to-back in 1980) as well as *Zombie Creeping Flesh* (although Fragasso also now claims to have helmed several of Mattei's films too!) Why did Fulci ever get involved in such a mess? One can only assume that his prior ill-health, his gradual alienation from earlier, more reliable collaborators, and the rapidly evaporating pool of producer interest in the horror film all played their part. There is nothing else to mention in *Zombi 3*'s defence – certainly not its groan-inducing ecological 'subtext' – and little to be gained from dwelling further on this unfortunate film.

Footnotes

1 *"It's the story of a mad killer committing terrible murders in New York, but to some extent it's a fantastic film, if only because the police have to spot this madman among twenty million New Yorkers... I aim at making a new style of thriller, I want to pay a tribute to Hitchcock. The Ripper is in a way Hitchcock revisited, a fantastic film with a plot, violence and sexuality."* – Fulci to Robert Schlockoff, *Starburst* #48

2 Briefly: no music; no rapid editing, virtually no 'expressive' use of the camera; a concentration on 'real-time' sequences. The reader is referred to Carol J. Clover's book *Men, Women and Chainsaws* which contains a sterling examination.

3 *"A police lieutenant tracks this duck-voiced maniac across the Big Apple with disturbingly incompetent results. Any woman not dressed in a manner befitting a nun receives grotesque sexual mutilations. Even worse, the FX wouldn't scare your grandmother."* – 'Dr. Cyclops', *Fangoria* #69.

4 Interview with the author, 6 October 2015.

5 *Variety*, 20 May 1987.

6 *Variety*, 15 October 1980. It seems likely that the second title was the proposed Sbarigia/Fulci title 'Dirty Star' – see 'Unmade and Posthumous Projects'.

7 *Variety*, 13 May 1981. This reference to Deodato's busy schedule sounds strange: he shot *Cannibal Holocaust* and *House on the Edge of the Park* in 1979 and didn't make another film until *The Atlantis Interceptors* in May 1983; hardly a slate that would *"keep him busy for almost a half dozen producers well into 1982"*! One wonders if somebody was confusing Deodato with Fulci, whose own schedule was far more deserving of the description.

8 Selenia Cinematografica would go on to produce just one more film, Tinto Brass's *The Key*, before Giulio Sbarigia bowed to the inevitable and retired for the second and last time. He died on 25 May 2000 at the age of 86. For more about Sbarigia see review of *The Black Cat*.

9 *Variety*, 2 September 1981.

10 *l'Unità*, 29 June 1984.

11 *Variety*, 4 May 1983.

12 *Variety*, 9 May 1984.

13 *l'Unità*, 29 June 1984.

14 ibid.

15 ibid.

16 Sutjeska were veterans of over two hundred prior Yugoslav productions. They would make just three more films after *Ænigma* before the collapse of Yugoslavia and the civil war of the early 1990s ended their thirty-year run.

17 As reported in *La Gazzetta del Mezzogiorno*.

18 Lucio Fulci interviewed by Massimo Lavagnini for *Draculina* #24, 1995. Mimmo Scavia was credited as art director, not 'director of production' as Fulci says.

19 *"It's true that I didn't finish that movie, but that didn't have anything to do with my illness... During the making of* Zombi 3 *I had the usual arguments, but finished a cut of the film which was 75 minutes long. We had a problem with the script, which we couldn't change, because the useless writer was a good friend of the producer, Franco Gaudenzi, who's a nice guy but hasn't got a clue. While we were shooting the thing, in the Philippines, my daughter and I were surreptitiously changing the script, bit by bit, but eventually I had to ask the producer to let me drop the project..."* – Lucio Fulci to Luca Palmerini, printed in *Giallo Pages* #3, 1994.

20 *"Fulci finished directing... Unfortunately Fulci was ill and the end result wasn't as good as we had hoped for. In fact, we were 20 minutes-worth of footage short of completing a feature film. Gaudenzi was now very worried and asked me how we could save the film. After discussing the possibilities, Gaudenzi said that I could cut the existing scenes but was not allowed to make them longer. So, my wife and I wrote extra scenes, and Gaudenzi then said that I had to go to the Philippines to shoot the new footage. I filmed for 15 days with Mattei's help, although most of the directorial duties were mine. However, I really didn't want anyone to know what happened as I had the greatest respect towards Lucio Fulci. I knew that Fulci would have spoken badly about the film, and I preferred it if he thought Mattei was at fault, not me! (laughs). It wasn't a very lucky film, I think it was jinxed. I say this because of Fulci's illness and it was very difficult to reason with him at the time."* Claudio Fragrasso interviewed by Jason Slater in *The Dark Side* issue 73.

21 Mattei's *Zombie Creeping Flesh* also begins with a scientific experiment, called 'Operation Sweet Death' in this case; conducted in secret labs in Papua, New Guinea (rather than the Philippines), it too goes off the rails, causing an epidemic of the living dead. A small 'commando' team are sent in and manage to rescue a few people before being chased from one dreary location to another by the zombies. The film ends with the revelation that 'Operation Sweet Death' was secretly developed by industrialized nations to 'solve' Third World overcrowding, ending the film with a 'radical' political critique of the West.

below:
Japanese video cover.

Vittorio and Sara Corsini seem a harmless old couple. But they take any kind of disturbance bedly and quickly resort to murder if necessary. Vittorio's old clocks are his passion and something more. When three punks decide to make an easy robbery, they come up against Vittorio and the clocks that menacingly use time to alter "reality". Time transforms the victims into the hunters, and the hunters into victims...!

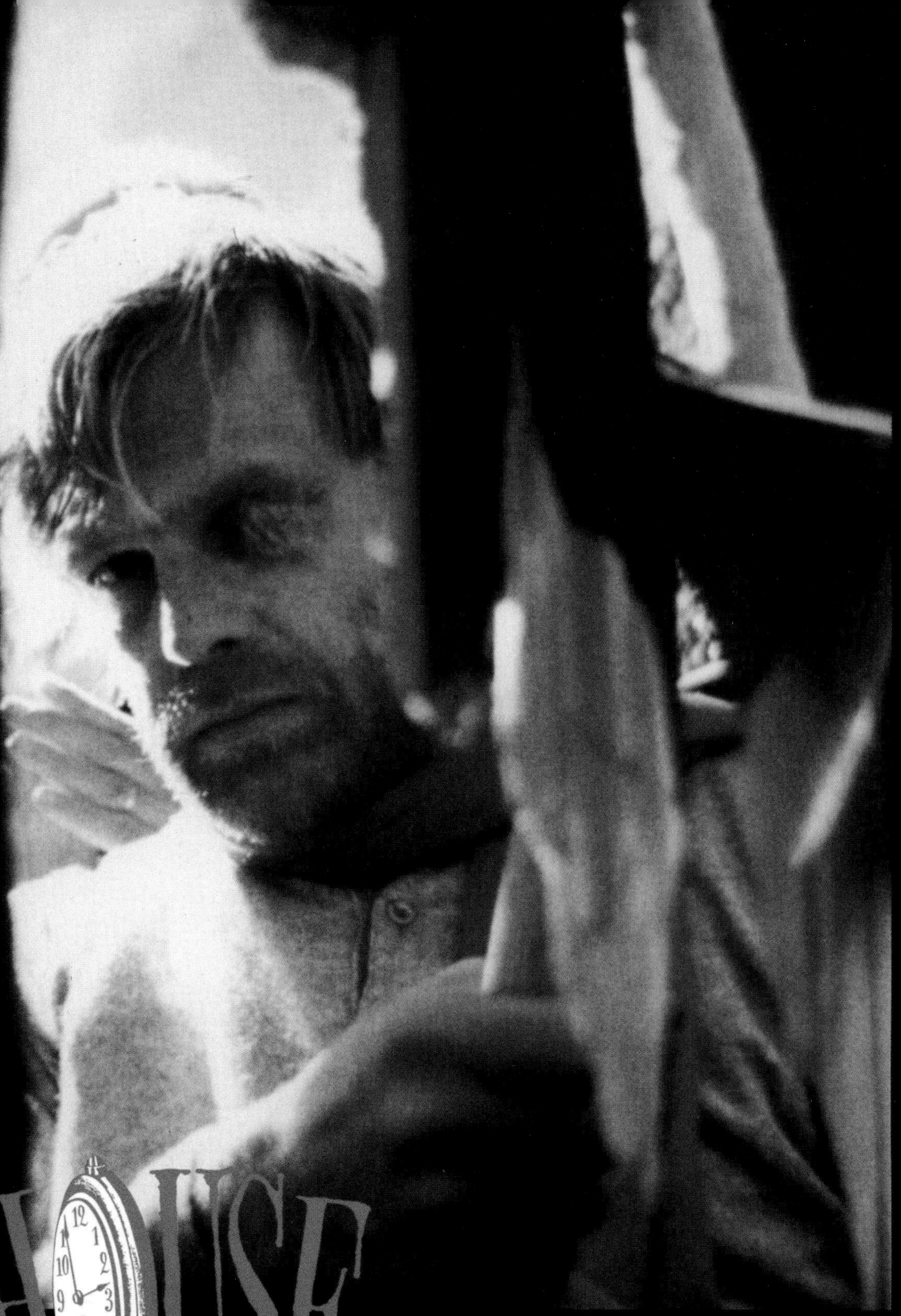

THE HOUSE OF CLOCKS

This film is part of the collection entitled:
HOUSES OF DOOM
The other titles are:
THE SWEET HOUSE OF HORROR
THE HOUSE OF WITCHCRAFT
THE HOUSE OF LOST SOULS

chapter eight

Adrift on Perversion...

Fulci's later horrors

Lucio Fulci moved swiftly on after the *Zombi 3* debacle, with two new horror films in production in 1988. But something had changed. The Italian film industry was scaling down, and Rome was home to fewer and fewer productions. Horror was in steep decline, and no other genre was rising to fill the studios of De Paolis and Cinecittà (a brief fling with post-apocalyptic adventure in the style of *Mad Max* made quick money but failed to last). The ground was shifting away from Italian production towards American studio output.

When exactly did Italian exploitation die? If you're looking for a precise date, try the 7th of March 1988. That was the day *Variety* published an article by Tom Bierbaum entitled "Age of Schlock Over". Although written from an American industry perspective, the points that are made apply equally to the Italian industry, and it's worth quoting at length for the sad picture it paints of the changing face of commercial genre cinema:

"The golden age of schlock is truly at an end, according to some of the video executives polled here at the American Film Market. They say the overseas vid business has begun to turn its back on the lowest-budget, extremely exploitive pix that have been delivering more buckets of blood and bared bodies than production values. That family of schlock product came to its own earlier this decade with the rise of programming-starved vid rental shops. But in recent years, the US vid business has given those films the boot, and now the overseas market – perhaps the last refuge for schlock – may be doing the same thing. That was one of a number of trends cited by vid execs here at the market. Others included: The emergence of censorship as a force that's hindering some US sales overseas and changing the nature of the product that can make big money internationally. While such terms as 'gore' and 'splatter' were the buzzwords in years past, this year many buyers wanted to hear none of it, and instead were talking almost exclusively about 'action' and 'action-adventure', according to some of the vid execs polled."

Fox/Lorber president Richard Lorber, speaking to Bierbaum, said, *"A lot of overseas companies are scrambling to bolster their credibility and leverage, and licensing excessively exploitive product is not the way to do it."*

Meanwhile RCA/Columbia International's senior vice president of marketing, Christopher Deering, suggested to Bierbaum that low-end product was confronting a natural stage in the evolution of the video market: *"There are millions of viewers now familiar with movies who'd never viewed them regularly before. And the more people experience films, the more they demand from them."* By June 1988, *Variety* were reporting: *"The domestic [Italian] market, once a supportive rockbed, is now only a pitiful shadow of its former strength and foreign markets have dried up."*[1]

Veteran Italian exploitation director Aristide Massaccesi (*aka* Joe D'Amato) survived during this period by concentrating on erotica and sex films. He had already dipped into hardcore porn in the early 1980s (*La voglia*, *Blue Erotic Climax*, *Le porno investigatrici*) and in the mid-eighties he added another string to his bow: softcore erotic thrillers in the American style. Modelled on Adrian Lyne's *9½ Weeks*, D'Amato's *Eleven Days, Eleven Nights* and its sequel (1987/88) were major money-spinners, doing great business on video around the world. Ever pragmatic, he churned out more in the same general style, with glossy artwork and titles like *Dirty Love* and *Blue Angel Cafe*, before eventually returning to hardcore (with a vengeance) in the mid-1990s.

Fulci had demonstrated some skill with erotic drama on *The Devil's Honey*, but unfortunately by now he was thoroughly typecast as a horror director. This meant he had little choice but to pack his production slate with contributions to what was then a declining genre. Despite *Zombi 3* there was still a reservoir of good-will towards Fulci among fans of the genre, and his greatest work was still pretty fresh in audiences' minds. The prospect of another run of violent horror pictures should therefore have been cause for fan celebration. But whilst they return to the extreme gore of his greatest triumphs, Lucio Fulci's later films lack credibility, feature few real thrills, and present too many occasions for disappointment and dismay.

The most immediate problem was money: all of Fulci's late-period films suffer from woefully meagre budgets. It's little wonder they cannot compete with *The House by the Cemetery* or *The New York Ripper*.

facing page:
Pressbook cover for Fulci's TV movie *The House of Clocks.*

below:
English-language video release for *The Ghosts of Sodom.*

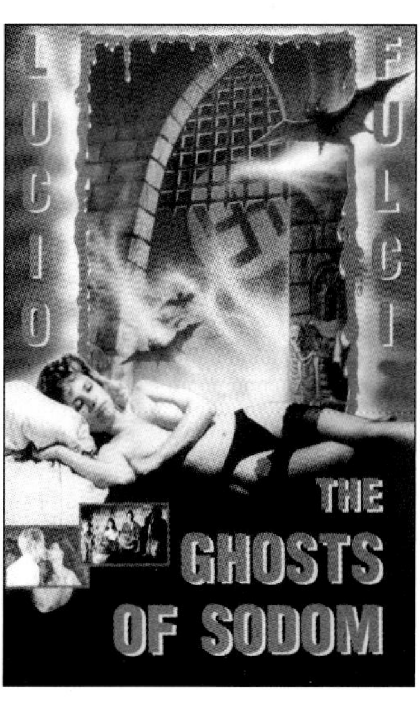

above:
The red monks pose monkishly, in red, in Gianni Martucci's The Red Monks.

They are films that Fulci made on budgets that would scarcely have bought the plane tickets for his previous productions. With money so hard to find, he was forced to hustle as never before, and the first indication of this came in 1988...

'Lucio Fulci presents...'

In late 1987 or early 1988, small-time film producer Pino Buricchi approached Lucio Fulci with a curious request: would he consider giving permission for the phrase 'Lucio Fulci presents' to be added to the credits of Buricchi's low-budget horror film production *I frati rossi* (*The Red Monks*), which had gone before the cameras in the Autumn of 1987 with Gianni ('Joe') Martucci in the director's chair? As Buricchi was a friend of a friend (namely *Ænigma* producer Ettore Spagnuolo), Fulci agreed to the request, in return for a small remunerative payment. Evidently intrigued by the idea of being, in effect, a brand name, Fulci came to a similar agreement with producers Luigi Nannerini and Antonino Lucidi (it's unclear who first suggested it) for a slate of ten low-budget horror films to be marketed under the banner "Lucio Fulci presents..." The plan was for Fulci to direct four of them, with the other six handled by different directors. Fulci would have no creative involvement in the other films but the use of his name across the whole slate would hopefully generate more sales and revenue. While Fulci set about writing the stories he would direct himself, the first film on the slate – *Bloody Psycho*, directed by Leandro Lucchetti – went into production. This was followed by *Massacre*, a gore-soaked serial-killer yarn by veteran horror-sleaze specialist Andrea Bianchi.

Production on the first three films went quickly and smoothly, but this was to change with the fourth film in the series, *Hansel and Gretel*, the sordid tale of a gang of child traffickers haunted by the vengeful ghosts of two children they murdered. What started out as another uncomplicated 'in name only' credit for Fulci turned into a co-directing gig, as the first director, Giovanni Simonelli, failed to finish the shoot. The producers begged Fulci to step in and complete the film, which he obligingly did, adding over half an hour of material to bring Simonelli's fifty minutes up to feature length. Production then rolled swiftly on, with two more films in the series – *Luna di sangue* (directed by Enzo Milioni) and *Non aver paura della zia Marta* (directed by Mario Bianchi) – shot in quick succession.

By now Fulci had decided upon the storylines for his four films as director. He kicked off with *Il fantasma di Sodoma*/*The Ghosts of Sodom*, about the spirits of sex-crazed Nazi soldiers haunting an isolated chateau in which a quartet of teenagers find themselves trapped. It was made in just a couple of weeks in May 1988, and shot back-to-back with the second of Fulci's directorial contributions, *Quando Alice ruppe lo specchio*/*Touch of Death*, which starred American actor Brett Halsey as a serial killer who brutally murders women with unusual physical or emotional defects. Neither film achieved anything

right:
A scene from Lamberto Bava's hit *Demons*.

below:
Japanese video cover for Lamberto Bava's *Graveyard Disturbance*, a made-for-TV film typical of the slipshod, undernourished horror productions made in Italy during the mid-to-late eighties.

memorable, with *The Ghosts of Sodom* based around a witless group of teenagers lacking the depth and plausible character shadings of the Scooby Doo kids, while *Touch of Death* found the director aiming for black humour but overstepping the line into bitterness and misogyny.

By now, having made two and a half films for Nannerini and Lucidi, Fulci was only too well aware of how little money there was in the pot. Irritated by the meagre funds and cynical about the entire arrangement, he pulled out of the remaining two projects. So what would these stories have been? Michele De Angelis, Fulci's assistant director at the time, sheds light on what we missed: *"I remember Lucio telling me an idea that later became* Voci dal profondo. *And I read the script for one of the films we didn't do that was called 'No Human Factor'. A sci-fi story with 'replicants', that was darn good. But, a sci-fi flick in two weeks? With no money? Seriously, I'm glad we didn't do it."*[2]

Gore TV

The next twist in Fulci's career was, on the face of it, the most unlikely so far: an invitation to direct two 'made-for-TV' horror films for Reteitalia ('Network Italy), a company owned by Italy's foremost television magnate...

In the 1980s the Italian film and TV industries were dominated by one man in particular, media mogul and future Italian prime minister Silvio Berlusconi. He first came to prominence in the Italian entertainment industry in 1978, when he established a financial holding company, Fininvest. In 1980 he moved into commercial TV, buying a disparate scattering of local TV stations and linking them into a chain showing the same programmes ('Canale-5'), in effect creating an independent rival to the official national network, RAI. Shortly afterwards, in 1982, Berlusconi bought another channel, Italia 1, from the Rusconi family, and in 1984 a third, Rete 4, from Mondadori, which further strengthened his media holdings.

Reteitalia, founded in 1979, was the acquisition and distribution wing of Berlusconi's empire, and its approach, to begin with, involved buying bulk programming from abroad, especially the USA (shows such as *Lou Grant*, *The Waltons*, *Diff'rent Strokes* and *The Dukes of Hazzard*). However, it wasn't long before the company began generating its own film and TV content. In May 1984, *Variety* reported, *"Berlusconi subsidiary Reteitalia, once fully engaged in foreign tv acquisitions and tv distribution programming in Italy, has now come to the forefront as the key media company for film feature coproductions."*[3] During this period, Reteitalia frequently struck co-production deals with existing Italian film companies. One such was Luciano Martino's Dania Film, which first entered co-production with Reteitalia in 1985 for a pair of 'telepics' directed by Luciano's brother Sergio Martino: *Doppio misto* ('Mixed Doubles') and *Ferragosto O.K.* ('August Hols O.K.').

Given that the Italian horror boom was on the wane in cinemas, it may seem surprising that horror was a serious contender for TV production money in the mid-to-late 1980s. The reason came down to one film: *Demons* (1985), directed by Lamberto Bava and produced by industry kingpin Dario Argento. The closest thing to an international smash the genre had produced in recent years, it galvanised interest and put producer and director on the radar for TV producers. In the spring of 1986 Reteitalia entered into discussions with Argento for a six-part TV horror series. This never came to pass, although a series of fifteen TV horror tales called 'Turno di notte' ('Night Shift') did emerge, in 1987, without Reteitalia's involvement. Produced by Argento for ADC Produzioni TV (probably a short-lived subsidiary of his own DAC Film company), these fifteen-minute 'mini-episodes' began with fleeting 'vignettes' directed by Argento, while the stories themselves were directed either by Luigi Cozzi (who made nine) or Lamberto Bava (who made six).

But if Reteitalia failed to net Argento, they did attract Lamberto Bava. He signed up with Reteitalia for a 1987-88 telefilm series called 'Brivido Giallo' ('Giallo Shivers') comprising four feature-length supernatural horror stories: *Una notte al cimitero* (aka *Graveyard Disturbance*), *Per sempre* (aka *Until Death*), *La casa dell'orco* (aka *The Ogre*), and *A cena*

top:
Karina Huff, star of Fulci's *Voices from Beyond*, seen here in the earlier *The House of Clocks*.

above and left:
Video covers for films 'presented by' Lucio Fulci.

Charles and Marcia come to take care of their cousins' children when the parents tragically die. The house is beautiful but strangely menacing and Marcia is worried about its effect on Mitch and Sarah when they return from boarding school Bloodstains suddenly appear in different rooms and there are unpleasant noises.
But after the children arrive home the house seems to quiet down. This lasts only until the couple decide to sell the house to take the kids to a "healthier" atmosphere. The house is reluctant to let the children go... is there some mystery behind their parents death?

the sweet house of horror

This film is part of the collection entitled:
HOUSES OF DOOM
The other titles are:
THE HOUSE OF WITCHCRAFT
THE HOUSE OF CLOCKS
THE HOUSE OF LOST SOULS

col vampiro (aka *Dinner with a Vampire*).[4] These aired successfully on Berlusconi's Canale 5, which led to further ideas being developed along similar lines. In June 1988 *Variety* announced that preparations were underway for a Reteitalia co-production deal with Hamster, a French television production company, to make ten telefilms under the umbrella title 'High Tension'. Lamberto Bava was pencilled in to direct two of the five Italian episodes, and to cooperate with Hamster on the production of five more in France. As things turned out, the co-production deal never came to fruition and the companies went their separate ways. Both, however, went on to produce their own versions of 'High Tension'. The Hamster side of the deal resulted in a 1988 Belgian-French-Swiss series, without Lamberto Bava, while Reteitalia's money went into an Italian TV series, 'Alta tensione', for which Bava directed four contributions: *Il maestro del terrore* (aka *The Prince of Terror*), *Il gioko* (aka *School of Fear*), *Testimone oculare* (aka *Eyewitness*) and *L'uomo che non voleva morire* (aka *The Man Who Didn't Want to Die*).

In March 1988 Reteitalia acquired complete control of the Cannon Management circuit, swallowing Cannon's 41-house cinema chain into an even bigger circuit, Cinema 5, and in October 1988 Berlusconi acquired 100% of Italy's leading indie distributor Medusa Distribuzione. Doing business in the Italian film industry without Berlusconi was now close to impossible. It was against this production backdrop that a four telefilm project called 'Le case maledette' ('Houses of Doom') was initiated, comprised of two films by Lucio Fulci (*La dolce casa degli orrori* and *La casa nel tempo*) and two by Umberto Lenzi (*La casa del sortilegio* and *La casa delle anime erranti*).

Ultimately, the 'Houses of Doom' films were deemed too violent for TV (which makes you wonder if anyone writing the cheques had ever actually seen a Lucio Fulci film) and although the films reportedly received cinema screenings in Japan they sank into obscurity for many years.

To the curtain call and beyond

Bloodied but unbowed, Fulci pressed on. The fact is, he had no chance to relax: he was being threatened with legal action by his producers on *The Ghosts of Sodom*, who were angry that he'd pulled out of directing the third and fourth films he'd promised them! The solution he devised was ingenious, and it generated what is certainly the most eccentric film of his latter years.

Un gatto nel cervello/Nightmare Concert (1990) is bizarrely entertaining but it's also a terrifically frustrating waste of a golden opportunity. Fulci took on the mantle of *auteur* with a vengeance for this would-be magnum opus, in which he stars as himself, a horror director plagued with terrifying visions. Reservations aside, he did at least manage to deliver the weirdest film of his later years. It offers fans a glimpse of the *maestro* at work, a trip through the highlights of his recent catalogue, and a peek, of sorts, into the brain of the tortured man himself. It is also notable as the last film by Fulci to receive a genuine theatrical release, however brief.

In the early 1990s things were looking bad for the one-time peer of Dario Argento and Mario Bava. 1990's *Demonia* seemed promising from the publicity materials, and the bare bones of the story could have provided Fulci with the right base from which to build another classic – but again something went wrong. Demoralised by the shaky nature of the production arrangements and the inevitable lack of money, Fulci let the project fall apart. He allowed actor Brett Halsey to re-write sections of the rough shooting script, and, thanks to his customary terseness in dealing with actors, the other performances have no spark that might have compensated for weak dialogue. At least the location is attractive: the ruined monastery at Monte Castello (near Sciacca on the south coast of Sicily) provides a pleasing respite from the blandness of recent films. But the outcome would be a waste of even this natural resource. *Demonia* feels hasty and disorganized, with scenes that could have worked, such as those in the crypt of a ruined monastery, rendered tiresome by too much wandering around, and the lack of anything dramatic for the actors to cut their teeth on. A climactic gore sequence involving a child and his father evokes the flagrant gruesomeness of the classic Fulci horrors; but even this is too late to rescue the film from joining *Touch of Death* and *The Ghosts of Sodom* in yet another minor production grave.

Fulci's most technically accomplished late film is *Voci dal profondo/Voices from Beyond* (1991). Based on his short story, originally published in the Italian newspaper *Gazzetta di Firenze*, it boasts a tightly controlled if soap-operatic plot by Daniele Stroppa (who would go on to script *The Wax Mask* after Fulci's death) and a modicum of invention in the development of atmosphere. Although it shares with the other efforts of this period a certain smallness, as if the intention was to stay within TV ratios despite working for the cinema, *Voices from Beyond* is distinguished from the surrounding films by the presence of a definite narrative 'motor'. It doesn't exactly roar along, but neither does it flounder like *The Ghosts of Sodom* or *Demonia*. There's conviction in the staging, the acting, and even the eccentric but effective score. It was also the only Fulci film after *Rome 2033 – The Fighter Centurions* to come out on video in the UK. It even got a thumbs-up from the trade mag *Variety* – *"a stylish Gothic thriller that features several novel scares... What sets "Voices" apart are Fulci's ingenious stagings, which make everyday objects threatening or downright scary"*.[5]

In 1992, director-producer Joe D'Amato expressed an interest in working with Fulci, and he suggested adapting a story from Fulci's recent short story collection, *Le lune nere*. Fulci was sceptical about the cinematic possibilities of the story, but agreed nevertheless. What transpired confirmed Fulci's scepticism...

After *Door to Silence*, Fulci's career entered a further period of decline and sadly, after three years trying to get a new project off the ground, he was to die without achieving his aim. Plans were afoot for him to direct a re-make of André De Toth's 1953 film *House of Wax*, itself a re-make of the earlier *Mystery of the Wax Museum* (Michael Curtiz, 1933). Fulci claimed to have re-thought the concept in a way that would transcend a mere re-make, perhaps akin to David Cronenberg's daring reformulation of venerable 1950s horror, *The Fly*. Dario Argento had been slated for over a year to act as producer. When I spoke to Fulci for this book in 1995, he was confident that the project, by then known as *The Wax Mask*, would soon be entering production. Unfortunately, because of Fulci's age and infirmity, not to mention his garrulous temperament, insurance could only be arranged for him on condition that Argento himself would 'supervise' the production and agree to be present on set. However, Argento's schedule on *The Stendhal Syndrome* made this a difficult requirement to meet. Fulci ended up hanging on the telephone for a call from the increasingly beleaguered Argento, whose priorities were inevitably first and foremost with his own work. After a long and active career packed with work on over 100 films, this drawn-out waiting game must have been torture. The events of Fulci's last few months were out of his hands.

above:
The Farm (aka *The Curse*) was an American film by actor turned director David Keith, based on H.P. Lovecraft's brilliant cosmic horror tale *The Colour Out of Space*. Fulci was credited as associate producer and special optical effects designer. The film is a mixture of the banal and the genuinely creepy, flawed but worth seeking out for anyone interested in Lovecraft.

facing page:
Pressbook cover for *The Sweet House of Horrors* (note that on the pressbook the title is given incorrectly).

below:
Italian video release of Leandro Lucchetti's *Nel nido del serpente* – one of the films billed as being 'presented by Lucio Fulci' – was plundered for extra gore to add to Fulci's cauldron of horrors in *Nightmare Concert*.

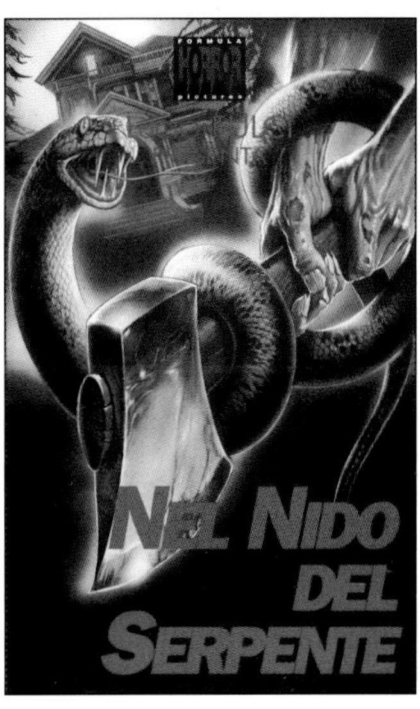

Original Italian title
Hansel e Gretel

Italy

Alternative titles
Non si seviziano i bambini (shooting title) 'Do Not Harm the Children'
Die Saat des Teufels (GER DVD) 'The Seed of the Devil'

Production company
Cine Duck

Theatrical distributor
None

Video/DVD/Blu-ray running times (adjusted)
AVO Film DVD (IT) 89m 56s

Shooting period
Early Spring 1988

No theatrical release

Hansel and Gretel

1988

Directed by Giovanni Simonelli [and Lucio Fulci (uncredited)]. story & screenplay: Giovanni Simonelli. producers: Antonio Lucidi [as 'Antonino Lucidi'] & Luigi Nannerini. music: Lanfranco Perini. cinematography: Silvano Tessicini. editor: Luigi Gorini. hairdresser: Maria Teresa Carrera. make-up artist: Giuseppe Ferranti [as 'Pino Ferrante']. production manager: Marco Alfieri. property master: Vincenzo Luzzi [as 'Vincenzo Lozzi']. boom operator: Aristide Bigliocchi [as 'Aristide Bagliocchi']. foley artist: Giulio De Angeli [as 'Giulio D'Angeli']. sound technician: Davide Magara [as 'Davide Macara']. mixage: Claudio Oliviero. camera operator: Luca Alfieri. grips: Gaetano Barbera, Nino Magostini. electrician: Massimo Rocchi. assistant camera: Rolando Stefanelli. generator operator: Roberto Stiffi. electrician: Marcello Tallone. seamstress: Mirella Pedetti. script supervisor: Camilla Fulci. supervisor: Lucio Fulci.

Cast: Elisabete Pimenta Boaretto (Silvia). Lucia Prato (Lina). Gaetano Russo [as 'Ronald Russo'] (Fred). Giorgio Cerioni (Mario). Mario Sandro De Luca. Renzo Robertazzi. Silvia Cipollone (Gretel). Massimiliano Cipollone (Hansel). Paul Muller (Inspector). Maurice Poli (Commissioner Roy). *Uncredited:* Brigitte Christensen (Solange). Zora Ulla Keslerová (woman in bath). Roberta Orlandi (Rosi).

Synopsis: Hansel and Gretel, aged around nine years old, are abducted after school by Jim and Dustin, two pig-farmers employed by a child-trafficking ring. The ring sells children as "thieves, beggars or prostitutes" but specialises in providing unwilling organ donors for the offspring of the unscrupulous rich. Inspector Roy suspects a woman called Solange of being the ringleader, but lacks conclusive evidence. Silvia Ruiz joins Roy's team and throws herself into the investigation. Meanwhile, Hansel and Gretel are murdered for their organs and their corpses buried on waste ground by Mario and Stanko, two of Solange's associates. The ghosts of the children rise up and begin a campaign of vengeance. Before each supernatural manifestation the victims hear a ghostly nursery rhythme. The first victim is Bruce, the stepfather who cared nothing for Hansel and Gretel. He is killed on his farm when a faulty rotavator springs to life and tears him to pieces. Second to die is the partly crippled Solange, who sees the children and topples into her swimming pool. Silvia confronts the rest of Solange's gang – Stanko, Mario and his wife Anna, Solange's husband Fred and her secretary Lina – who realise that someone is picking them off one by one. The children's next victim is Stanko, who falls into a slurry pit full of manure. Mario's mother backs away from the children and impales her head on a steel spike, which dislodges her eyeball. The arrival of Roy's superior resolves nothing, and Silvia calls in her old chaplain from the police academy. He too has little effect. Meanwhile, a woman planning to take over the running of Solange's business is terrorised by the children while taking a bath: she slips and bangs her head, dying from her injury. Two men sent to bury more child corpses are burned alive in a fire caused by the ghosts. Lina is killed when her shower turns boiling hot and scalds her to death. A heavy called Pat is induced to shoot himself in the face. Fred makes a run for it and heads for the local church but the children will not be denied: he falls to his death from the roof of a nearby buidling. With all the gang now dead, the children can rest in peace after waving goodbye to Silvia.

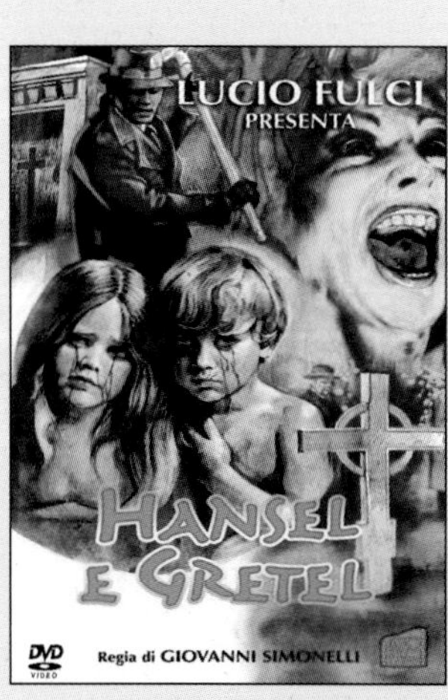

About the production: This 'Lucio Fulci presents' production was, according to assistant director Michele De Angelis, co-directed by Fulci himself. It turns out that the 'official' director, Giovanni Simonelli, was less than committed, as De Angelis explained to Adrien Clerc: *"Simonelli was an old man at the time, and he was not very interested in his own film. Actually, he didn't give a fuck! I remember one day we were on the set, ready to shoot, everything set up, and we were just waiting for the instructions of the director... who had disappeared. After some investigation, he was found in the basement of the villa where we shot, admiring old bottles of wine."*[6]

Although Simonelli had no prior directing credits, he was a long-standing screenwriter with over seventy films to his name. He'd also worked as assistant director on a handful of his own scripts, including *Il conquistatore di Maracaibo* (1961), *Samson* (1961) and *La furia di Ercole* (1962). Though never very fond of outright horror, he wrote a few giallo films in the 1970s: two for Antonio Margheriti (*Nude... si muore* and *La morte negli occhi del gatto*), one for Alfonso Balcázar (*La casa de las muertas vivientes*) and one for Sergio Pastore (*Crimes of the Black Cat*). Westerns, however, were more his style; he wrote eighteen between 1964 and 1972. His horror credits amount to three 'Lucio Fulci presents' projects – *Hansel e Gretel*, *Bloody Psycho* and *Luna di sangue* – plus Fulci's *Nightmare Concert* for which, according to De Angelis, he actually wrote very little.

Nowadays a director in his own right, De Angelis first met Fulci in 1988, when he gained work on the 'Lucio Fulci presents' project *Massacre*, directed by Andrea Bianchi. His sights, however, were set firmly on the film's charismatic 'supervisor': *"Well, I am fond of Andrea Bianchi because he gave my first shot at the movies. But you can't compare Lucio. He had the qualities of a master, he was a creative genius with great culture and taste. He knew how to trick an audience, how to seduce it. He also was a master technician in the use of long takes, dollies and tracks. I got along with almost everybody, when you are an assistant director you have to. But, Lucio was of another class."*[7] De Angelis found himself driving Fulci to the set every morning, and he got on very well with his new boss: *"We discussed many of his movies, I was always asking extensive questions about them. He told me the whole censorship problems with* The Eroticist *for instance, as I was interested in all of his films, not only horror, even if those were some I like the most. I realized also that Lucio, even if not credited in the scripts, was always reworking them, changing things, and sometimes even using just the original storyline. But we also discussed art that he was very fond of, and politics, as well as sports – tennis and football especially. He told me about his collaborators, of whom he was very fond, especially director of photography Sergio Salvati and his editor Vincenzo Tomassi, who was nicknamed 'il vermone' (the big worm) because of the 35mm film running into the editing machine that looked like a worm."*[8]

De Angelis was well placed to observe the production of *Hansel and Gretel*: *"Simonelli was an experienced screenwriter of mostly comedies. He probably accepted the job for the money; his son was also working in the production team, and disappearing every day. He didn't care at all, it was very easy to get along. He said always fine, it's okay, etc."* Fulci's involvement came after Simonelli's: *"Lucio did a week of extra shooting, because the film was too short. Once cut it was only fifty minutes long, and with a dramatic lack of punch in the gore zone. The week he took over we shot many scenes with special effects, including the death in the bathroom and the drowning and dismembering of two characters in the dam."* And how did Simonelli feel about the arrangement? *"He was fine with it, couldn't care less. The producers had the final decision about it."*[9]

Review: So, what to make of this late arrival in the Fulci canon? If you adjust your expectations to account for the terribly low budget, it's just about watchable and sometimes amusingly grisly, but it's very flimsy and certainly not a contender for reappraisal. A comparison between Fulci's scenes and Simonelli's reveals very little difference in style: it seems Lucio's priority was simply to match his footage with the rest, something he achieves with disappointing success.

Much of *Hansel and Gretel* is shot in labour-saving medium shots, without enough close-ups to enliven the dull expository scenes. Devoid of backstory, *Hansel and Gretel* lacks a sense of place. It's never clear where we are, given the anonymous countryside and bland interiors. We're in Anywherio, Italia, a place where police inspectors have Christian names but not surnames, where children go missing without parents reporting it, and where child traffickers can avail themselves of the facilities of a private clinic no questions asked.

A major hazard to enjoyment is Lanfranco Perini's score which, as in so many of the 'Lucio Fulci presents' titles, is cheap, tacky and poorly matched to the images. Built from generic synthesiser and bog-standard drum samples it's a constant thorn in the side of the film. More seriously, Simonelli's script misses several important narrative beats. For instance, the first victim of the ghostly children is their stepfather, and you would think that this would justify a little time setting the scene. Instead, all we get is a brief exchange between the children and their abductors in which the kids claim their stepfather won't be looking for them because "he doesn't like us". It's not much of a set-up for a gory revenge; we don't even meet the man before he's killed. The very least that we need is a scene in which the stepfather responds callously to news of the kids' abduction. Not only does the film lose clarity by omitting such contextualising details, it squanders genuine dramatic potential too.

More interesting is the depiction of some of the traffickers. Beset by misgivings, their squeamishness and cowardice adds colour to their villainy. *"It's not nice to look at them,"* says Mario, one of the 'disposal team', when Solange sneers at him for covering the face of a child corpse, *"I'll never get used to it."* Underlying the story is a hint of the way 'ordinary people' can become complicit in atrocity. Nazi Germany isn't referred to in the film but it seems as though it may have drifted through Simonelli's mind as he bashed out this script: for instance Silvia quizzes Lina about her role in Solange's sickening trade, and her explanations – I'm just a secretary, the boss's letters didn't go into detail, I needed a job – seem to echo the self-justifications of those who did the paperwork for the Final Solution.

Among the funnier failings of the film, we're treated to a surgical operation in which harvested human organs are kept in a cheap goldfish bowl, a cost-cutting device that wouldn't look amiss in the films of Ted V. Mikels. Clichés such as a surgeon having his profusely dripping brow repeatedly mopped by a nurse put one in mind of the *Airplane* films, and when Bill the cop finds a cassette recorder "still switched on" at the poolside, days after Solange died, it makes you marvel at the ineptitude of the police who first attended the scene. Meanwhile, as if to prevent anyone from wandering off and costing the production too much in location clearances, the cops keep the villains corralled at their 'base' while the spooky children pick them off one by one.

Pointlessly, the final scenes pull back from depicting children as vengeful spirits. Despite having seen the ghosts, Silvia speculates that the criminals were in fact killed by their own guilty consciences: an unsatisfying 'psychological' twist for a very unsatisfying film.

above:
Child-trafficker Stanko sinks into a pit of manure.

opposite:
Suffer the adults: Hansel (Massimiliano Cipollone) and Gretel (Silvia Cipollone), back from the grave with vengeance in mind.

below:
Zora Ulla Keslerová, best known to horror fans for her gruesome breast impalement scene in Umberto Lenzi's *Cannibal Ferox* and her death by broken bottle in *The New York Ripper*, steps in to assist Fulci during additional shooting on *Hansel e Gretel*, playing Solange's unnamed successor.

bottom:
Silvia (Elisabete Pimenta Boaretto) encounters the ghostly children.

Original Italian title
Il fantasma di Sodoma

Italy

Alternative titles
The Ghosts of Sodom (USA video)
Sodoma's Ghost (IT video/DVD)
Sodoma's tödliche Rache (GER DVD)
'Sodom's Deadly Revenge'

Production company
Distribuzione Alpha Cinematografica (Rome)
Sigma Eco [S.I.G.M.A. E.CO.] (Rome)

Video/DVD/Blu-ray running time (adjusted)
EC Entertainment DVD (Sweden)
87m 47s

Release information
No cinema release
TV screening on Italia 7 28 June 1991

The Ghosts of Sodom

1988

Directed by Lucio Fulci. producers: Luigi Nannerini & Antonino Lucidi for Distribuzione Alpha Cinematografica. story: Lucio Fulci. screenplay: Lucio Fulci & Carlo Alberto Alfieri. editor: Vincenzo Tomassi. original music: Carlo Maria Cordio © Artem Publishing. director of photography: Silvano Tessicini. camera operator: Luca Alfieri. production manager: Silvano Zignani. unit manager: Marco Alfieri. camera assistant: Rolando Stefanelli. set design: Franco Vanorio. seamstress: Mirella Pedetti. make-up: Giuseppe Ferranti. hairstylist: Maria Teresa Carrera. gaffer: Massimo Rocchi. key grip: Umberto Magostini. sound recordist: Roberto Barbieri. script supervisor: Camilla Fulci. special effects: Luca Vagni. generator operator: Roberto Stiffi. film stock: Fujicolor. prints, processing & technical equipment: Cinecittà S.p.A. electrical equipment: Stiffi srl. dubbing & post-synchronization: Technosound srl. foley: Giulio D'Angeli. insurance: "Il Sole Assicurazioni".

Cast: Claudio Aliotti [as 'Claus Aliot'] (Paul). Maria Concetta Salieri [as 'Mary Salier'] (Celine). Robert Egon [Spechtenhauser] (Willy, young SS officer). Luciana Ottaviani [as 'Jessica Moore'] (Marie). Teresa Razzaudi [aka 'Teresa Razzauti'] (Anne). *Uncredited:* Alan Johnson (Mark). Sebastian Harrison (John). Pier Luigi Conti (cocaine-snorting Nazi soldier). Domiziano Arcangeli (Klaus). Zora Ulla Keslerová (succubus).

Synopsis: In an isolated country house, as the Second World War ends, a group of Nazi soldiers indulge in orgiastic behaviour with whores – drinking, taking drugs, riding around on each other's backs, playing pool with a woman's vagina as the 'pocket'. As the party goes on the participants grow desperate to reach some nirvana that remains out of reach. The ringleader, a handsome androgynous young soldier called Willy, films the cavortings with a movie camera. The revels are brought to an end by Allied bombing...

The present. Six teenagers – Mark, Paul, John, Celine, Anne and Marie – are on their way back to Paris after a holiday in Italy. Mark, the driver, takes a short cut and gets lost. After a while they discover the house seen in the prologue. It's abandoned, so they break in and elect to stay for the night. The house is plush, fully furnished, and dotted with erotic paintings and photographs. It's also haunted by the ghosts of the sex-mad Nazis. That night, Willy, the young Nazi soldier seen earlier, emerges from a mirror and seduces one of the three girls, Maria, who aquiesces to his violent sexual overtures. When she wakes the next morning she discovers she's unmarked and assumes she was dreaming. The teens try to leave the next day, but their one attempt to drive away is thwarted when the route leads mysteriously back to the villa. Returning inside, they loiter around until dusk, finally deciding to try again. This time the vehicle won't start and they go back in to phone for help. They are met with sinister responses by the police station they call, and then discover that the phone line has actually been cut. What's more they are now locked in. The window shutters resist their minimal efforts to break through, and all the doors are shut tight. Claustrophobic attacks, bitter arguments, sexual tension and recriminations ensue. One youth, Mark, gets horribly drunk on the vintage wines found in the cellar. After obnoxiously taunting one of the girls, he wanders off to explore the house. Mark enters a room and sees a group of Nazi soldiers playing cards round a table. They invite the inebriated youth to join them. The others disappear and Mark plays Russian roulettte with Willy. He survives and wins his 'reward' – an assignation with a prostitute in a neighboring room. His desire turns to horror when his hands go right through the skin of her breasts and into a bloody pulp. Running out in horror, he meets Paul on the stairs, but hallucinates that his friend is a Nazi too. Mark lunges at Paul and in their struggle he is mortally injured. Paul calls the others and they drag Mark into the living room, but he dies there before their eyes. Further supernatural manifestations, including a lesbian ghost and a rotting version of Maria, harass the frightened teens. The two boys find a can of film in the cellar which holds the key to the ghosts' power. As Mark's corpse rots before their eyes, they hear soldier's footsteps approaching down the corridor. They barricade themselves into a drawing room and run the film of the orgy. It ends with the explosion that killed the Nazis, the marauding ghosts disappear and the youths black out. When they awake, they find themselves beside the ruined shell of the villa. The horror has melted away like a dream, and the teens are relieved to discover that Mark is alive after all.

About the production: *Il fantasma di Sodoma* was the first 'official' Fulci film in the production package that also included the 'Lucio Fulci presents' titles. Sadly, it holds the dubious distinction of being the first of his films never to have played in a cinema. It was shot (back-to-back with immediate successor *Quando Alice ruppe lo specchio*) for Distribuzione Alpha Cinematografica, a short-lived company who made just three other films: *Non aver paura della zia Marta* (Mario Bianchi, 1988), *The Hell's Gate* (Umberto Lenzi, 1989), and *Luna di sangue* (Enzo Milioni, 1989). Alpha Cinematografica belonged to Antonino Lucidi and Luigi Nannerini, who are credited as co-producers on all of the above except for the Lenzi film (*The Hell's Gate* has no production credit although Lucidi is credited as treasurer/cashier). Of the two men, Nannerini was the more experienced; he'd been production manager on some fairly sizeable productions in the 1960s (e.g. *Ulysses Against Hercules*, 1962) and served as production supervisor on Luigi Cozzi's *Starcrash* (1978). Lucidi's first credit was on *Teresa altri desideri*, a hardcore sex film by Bruno Vani, which he co-produced with Nannerini. Neither man appears to have worked on another film until 1988, when they pop up as the producers of *Il fantasma di Sodoma*.

Shooting of *Il fantasma di Sodoma* and *Quando Alice ruppe lo specchio* began in the early summer of 1988, recalls assistant director Michele De Angelis: *"It was probably late May, June and July. The shooting lasted two weeks each, maybe a few days more. They were made entirely on location, the budget didn't allow for any studio shooting. Many different villas were used; one near Via Trionfale, another one in Casal Palocco.* Sodoma *was shot mostly in Castel Di Decima, in an old kind of castle that had been transformed into a residence."*[10] Money was very limited, and Fulci was not in a strong position with regard to defining the boundaries of the production. De Angelis recalls, *"Unfortunately we were not more in charge. We had the bare minimum to shoot a movie. The producers wanted to keep costs down and didn't want to spend a single buck more."* What money there was came not from Alpha Cinematografica directly but from a third party financier, meaning that producers Luigi Nannerini and Antonino Lucidi were constantly referring Fulci's requests 'upwards': *"They were kind of executives, the money came from another company called Sigma Eco, owned by a producer named Alfieri."* De Angelis is referring to Carlo Alberto Alfieri, whose company Sigma started out as producers of the 1978 Luigi Batzella production *La bestia nello spazio*. Boasting few self-generated projects but with a sales library of 180 titles, Sigma's production hopes received a boost in 1985 when they scored a backing deal with RAI-TV. Their most significant production after this was the troubled *Nosferatu in Venice*, originally slated for Pasquale Squitieri to direct in 1986, which went into production a year later with Mario Caiano at the helm. Caiano was then fired and an astonishing four further individuals took his place at the wheel: Augusto Caminito, Luigi Cozzi, Maurizio Lucidi, and the star of the film, Klaus Kinski.[11] Carlo Alberto Alfieri was also the credited scriptwriter on *Il fantasma di Sodoma*, which must have made his tightness with the purse-strings even more frustrating for Fulci!

Review: Soft-core gropings and an attempt at that Italian exploitation standby, Nazi decadence[12], pad out this tedious teens-in-peril story. The title's reference to Sodom in the context of Nazism brings to mind Pasolini's *Salò, or The 120 Days of Sodom*, adapted from the Marquis de Sade's *The 120 Days of Sodom*, a film which explores the human capacity for destruction and cruelty through the example of the 3rd Reich. Pasolini had his four Sadean Nazis (corrupt representatives of State and Church authority dedicated to pleasure through torture) enact their atrocities in the village of Salò in Northern Italy, the scene of mass killings during the closing stages of the Second World War. For Fulci and script-writer Carlo Alberto Alfieri to connect their silly horror story to Pasolini and de Sade is bad enough – to make it a ghost story is the idiotic cherry on the cake, ignoring the principle of death in de Sade, death as inescapable, final, and irreversible.

The film introduces – or wheels on – three boys and three girls (a notion of symmetry drawn from Sade? – one shudders to think) holidaying in a remote country region. Their status as wild young tearaways is established as they leave a country trail and drive their Range Rover through a field 'as a joke'. Half-hearted cross-tensions between members of the group struggle limply to attain the status of 'characterisation'. Eventually the youths come across a large, apparently deserted chateau and, as horror film teens are wont to do, blunder in and make themselves at home for the night.

The supernatural manifestations that Fulci trots out during the following 'night of terror' are pathetic, and the level of decadent sexual kinkiness is likewise a joke. (For further elaboration see the review of *Nightmare Concert*). Suffice to say that this 'daring' dalliance with the sexual allure of fascism reaches its kinkiest extreme with the *implied* 'pocketing' of a ball in a girl's vagina as she lies drunkenly on a pool table. Fulci's half-hearted sauciness sends the exploitation fan's mind wandering wistfully back to the likes of *The Beast in Heat* (1977), and *SS Experiment Camp* (1976).

The Ghosts of Sodom would send even Fulci's sternest critics back to *The New York Ripper* with something like an appreciative eye. More than any of his other films, it commits the unpardonable crime of being dull. If the follow-up, *Touch of Death*, is the nadir of Fulci's morality, this one is the zero of his ambition.

If the film has a saving grace it's actor Robert Egon, who plays the lead Nazi, Willy. Born on 19 February 1966 in Sindelfingen, West Germany, he first popped up in Giuliana Gamba's *Bizarre* (1987) and Andrea Bianchi's 'Lucio Fulci Presents' film *Massacre*. In *The Ghosts of Sodom* he eclipses the main cast: his scenes with Claudio Aliotti, playing Russian Roulette, are the best in the film. He's a strikingly handsome youth whose eyes dance with energy and a plausible air of playful sadism. He deserved much better than this film, but success in the cinema eluded him. After small roles in *My Own Private Idaho* and the 1990 *Captain America* (playing 'Perfect Young Italian') he retired and turned to painting and photography. Sadly he died young, suffering a terrible accident in 2008, after which he moved to Torvaianica, Italy. He died on 30 January 2010.

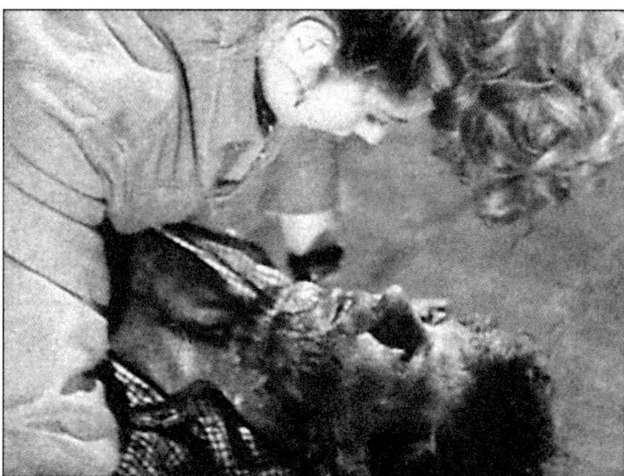

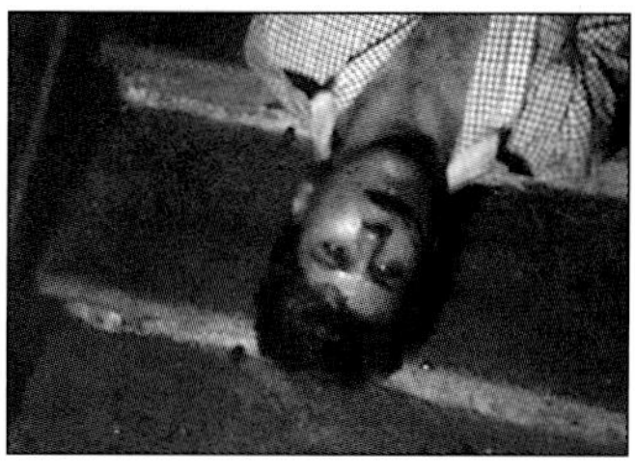

above, below and opposite: Scenes from *The Ghosts of Sodom*, with the Italian video cover at bottom right this page, and the Japanese video cover opposite bottom left.

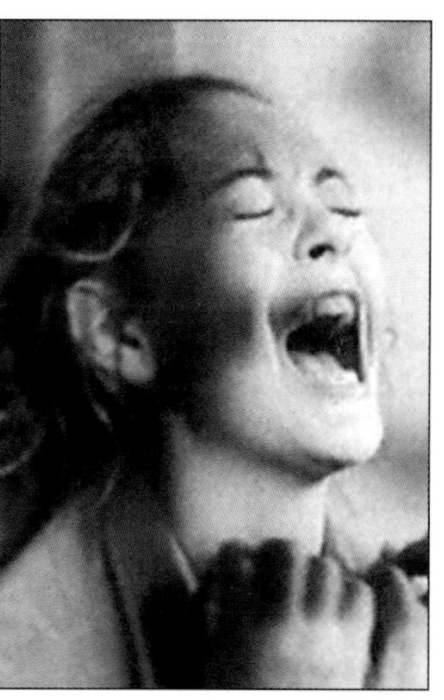

Original Italian title
Quando Alice ruppe lo specchio

Translation
'When Alice Broke the Mirror'

Italy

Alternative titles
Touch of Death
(English-language export title)
Soupçons de mort (FR video/DVD)
When Alice Broke the Mirror
(USA DVD)

Unconfirmed titles
El espejo roto (SP)
'The Broken Mirror'
O Espelho Partido (POR or BRZ)
'The Broken Mirror'
La sombra de Lester (SP)
'The Shadow of Lester'

Production company
Distribuzione Alpha Cinematografica

Video/DVD/Blu-ray running times (adjusted)
EC Entertainment DVD (Sweden)
84m 49s
Formula video (Italy) 84m 56s

Release information
No cinema release
TV screening on TCS 14 June 1991
TV screening on Teledue
06 August 1991

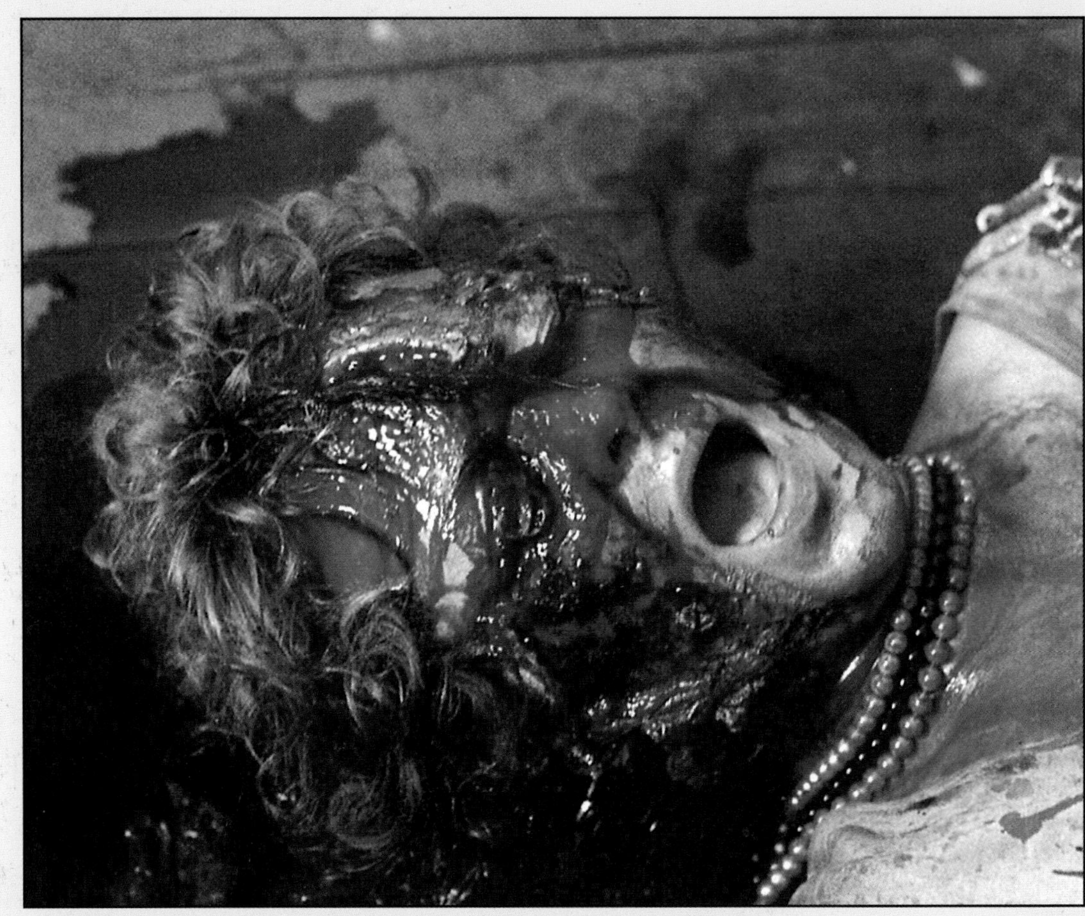

Touch of Death

1988

Directed by Lucio Fulci. produced by Luigi Nannerini & Antonino Lucidi for Distribuzione Alpha Cinematografica. story & screenplay by Lucio Fulci. director of photography: Silvano Tessicini. original music by Carlo Maria Cordio; published by Artem Publishing. editor: Vincenzo Tomassi. set designer: Franco Vanorio. production manager: Silvano Zignani. unit manager: Marco Alfieri. continuity: Camilla Fulci. cameraman: Luca Alfieri. assistant cameraman: Rolando Stefanelli. gaffer: Massimo Rocchi. key grip: Umberto Magostini. make-up: Pino Ferranti. hair stylist: Maria Teresa Carrera. wardrobe: Mirella Pedetti. special effects: Angelo Mattei. generator operator: Roberto Stiffi. sound recordist: Roberto Barbieri. re-recording & synchronization [Italian version]: Technosound S.r.l. sound studio [English language version]: Doppiaggio Internazionale (Rome). foley: Giulio D'Angeli. technical equipment: Cinecittà. generator: Stiffi S.r.l. insurance: "Il Sole Assicurazioni". colour processing by Cinecittà. raw stock: Fujicolor.

Cast: Brett Halsey (Lester Parson). Ria De Simone (Alice Shogun). Pier Luigi Conti (Randy). Sasha [Sacha Maria] Darwin (Maggie MacDonald). Zora Ulla Keslerová [as 'Zora Ulla Kesler'] (Virginia Field). Marco Di Stefano (the tramp). *Uncredited:* Maurice Poli (1st news reader).

Synopsis: Lester Parson is a cannibal psychopath who abducts and mutilates young women, eating parts of them and then disposing of the rest in his garden. Afterwards he talks to himself via tape recordings of his own voice. Living an apparently carefree life without a job, his crimes appear to be little more than the fulfillment of an idle hobby. Nevertheless he manages to make enemies and run down the inheritance left to him by his rich wife, now deceased. A careless and inept gambler, he is being hounded by Randy, a shady underworld acquaintance to whom he owes money due to bad debts. Parson kills his most recent pick-up, Maggie MacDonald, who is a hysterical, sexually frustrated alcoholic. He chooses her as a victim from a video she sent to a dating agency, selecting her to die because she has a moustache. When he gets her to his villa he tries to poison her but fails because she drunkenly spills the tainted glass and then mixes it up it with his. At last she swallows the poisoned drink, only to vomit before it can take effect. Parson tries to club her to death, but after feigning unconsciousness she makes a dash for the door. Furious and exhausted, Parson knocks her unconscious and then shoves her head into the oven. Her flesh slowly melts off the bone. Later he chops off the corpse's feet to get it in the boot of his car, and drives off to bury it in the woods.

A local tramp witnesses the burial and proceeds to attempt blackmail. Parson pursues him in the car and crushes him beneath the wheels ... Parson's next sexual encounter is with Alice Shogun, an annoying self-centred woman who sings opera during sex. He strangles her to death. One night a 'wrong number' caller invites him to 'come on over'. The caller is Virginia, a similarly bored and lonely younger woman. Though otherwise desirable, Virginia has a large, unattractive blemish on her lip. Parson is repulsed by her ugly scar. Eventually, this blighted angel (herself a Janus-faced nut) discovers the truth and shoots Parson in the chest. Crawling to his garage, Parson converses with his other self, a shadow on the wall, and dies as it converges with him...

About the production: In February 1988, stalwart American character actor Brett Halsey was in Rome touting for work. He was no stranger to the city, having lived and worked there in the 1960s, notching up numerous leading and supporting roles in westerns and spy stories. Among the projects he accepted in 1988 was a starring role as a psychopath in Lucio Fulci's *Quando Alice ruppe lo specchio* aka *Touch of Death*.

Assistant director Michele De Angelis has nothing but praise for the star: *"Brett Halsey is one the finest people I have worked with. He was a real gentleman and a professional. Never complained, never said a word. Always ready and on set in time. Always knew his lines. A real pleasure. We were at the end of the production and I thanked him and told him I was impressed by his behaviour. He answered 'It's normal, I'm a professional, I am here to do my job the best that I could'. He and Fulci loved each other. Lucio would keep repeating this me, he was just great and a true professional. I guess he liked Lucio as well."*[13]

Halsey's performance is highly exaggerated and comic, so I asked De Angelis if this approach was the actor's idea: *"No it was Lucio who wanted this over the top quality for the story, which was kind of bizarre. A man losing his shadow, there is nothing realistic about it. So he wanted to push the grotesque part of the story, with all the girls the guy was seducing having physical defects that made them unattractive. It was a very dark black comedy."*

The chief location, the killer's home, was a villa on the outskirts of Rome. As De Angelis recalls, *"We were also shooting in the Vides studios, which at the time were closed down. But we didn't built any sets, we just filmed a river there, and a construction pretending to be a stable."*

The production designer on the film, Franco Vanorio, was another person Fulci got along well with, says De Angelis: *"Vanorio was a very good set designer, he made things with nothing. Lucio liked him a lot for his ability. He was a very funny short guy, so Lucio called him 'Nanorio' (nano is dwarf in Italian) as a joke. But he didn't mean it in a bad way, it was a way to show his affection. Vanorio was a cool cat, he was fancy dressed and had an old sports car. But most of all, he knew how to do things with a nothing budget like we had."*

Indeed, the film's terribly low budget was a constant problem. De Angelis recalls that Luigi Nannerini and Antonino Lucidi struggled to keep up the cash-flow: *"Luigi Nannerini was kind of elegant and rounded, nicknamed 'the marquise'. He'd been in the movies for a long time. Lucidi was shorter than Nannerini, so they made a funny couple. He was kind of an accountant. One day, after a fight with Alfieri in the production offices because of the money (at this point* Alice *was stalling, we were supposed to start it two days after* Sodoma *wrapped, but there were money problems) Lucidi felt bad and had a light heart attack. I thought he was faking it or just pretending, but it was real. Thank God he recovered and production resumed for* Alice*."*

De Angelis found the experience of working for Nannerini and Lucidi challenging but rewarding: *"They were called 'the cat and the fox' since they were without scruples and very tricky. But I liked them, they gave me a shot with their movies. I had been attending a screenplay class and loved movies since I was seven, always dreamed of entering the film industry. Andrea Bianchi gave me the first opportunity, hiring me as his assistant on* Massacre*, which happened because he was amazed by the fact I'd seen most of his films. But when the movie was over, it was 'the cat and the fox' who wanted me to continue to work with them, since I had been good and tried to give my best, even contributing a few tricks that saved them money and face. So I cannot be anything other than fond of the couple. They even paid me – a little, but they paid me. One day on the set the chief electrician told us: 'The cat and the fox are coming, beware of your pockets!'"*

above and opposite:
As extreme as he wanted to be... Fulci certainly threw gore-hungry audiences a few armfuls of raw meat in *Touch of Death*. These scenes also made their way into *Nightmare Concert*, for obvious reasons.

In the end, just like *Il fantasma di Sodoma*, *Quando Alice ruppe lo specchio* failed to reach cinemas. Instead it received its Italian 'premiere' on late night television in 1991. Ultimately, however, although I would argue that both of these films are pretty terrible, it seems likely that the reason they failed to secure theatrical release was more to do with the financial problems of the production company than the intrinsic weakness of the material.

Review: *Touch of Death* opens with a prowling camera entering the house of Lester Parson (Brett Halsey) whom we first see sitting down in front of the TV to eat his lunch – a juicy piece of steak. He's middle-aged, relaxed and wealthy – the distinguished-looking type. Leaving him to his meal, the camera ventures down into the basement. There, laid out on a table, is a mutilated female cadaver, missing a large chunk of flesh from its thigh. All is not as it seems in this charming country retreat. We are in the lair of a cannibal psychopath whose urbanity masks a monstrous secret... Having completed his vile repast, Parson goes down to the cellar, picks up a chainsaw, and hacks the corpse into pieces, before grinding the remains into mincemeat and disposing of them in his garden.

Quite an opening sequence... And yet there's something wrong. As the events unfold, questions start to form in the mind. Why, despite all we're seeing, does the film feel so uninvolving? Could it be Brett Halsey's arch and prissy performance? The 'ironic' music? The fatuous, cynically disinterested direction? Or all three?

Although none of Fulci's films were over-stimulated with cash, this period marked a definite financial down-turn. *Touch of Death* looks dismayingly amateur – watched straight after a film like *A Lizard in a Woman's Skin* or even *The Black Cat* it looks like the work of a completely different director. According to the credits, *Touch of Death* was the only film Fulci ever wrote entirely by himself. What that says about the nature of his collaborations is unflattering to say the least. Fulci seems to have been aiming here for misanthropic comedy and damn-them-all bursts of misogyny aimed at the audience; an audience, one feels, that he really couldn't be bothered trying to engage any more. In terms of wit, the camp acting of Brett Halsey scarcely deserves to be considered 'ironical'. His movements, for instance when seasoning a chunk of human flesh for dinner, are like the pantomime gestures of an end-of-the-pier

below:
Lester (Brett Halsey) saws up a corpse.

bottom:
Virginia (Zora Ulla Keslerová, aka Zora Kerova) in seduction mode.

above:
Japanese VHS releases of Fulci's films are sought after on the collector's circuit; this is the cover for *Touch of Death*.

children's entertainer. An otherwise disgusting – and potentially impressive – sequence of corpse dismemberment is ruined by Halsey's continued arching of the brow, meant to indicate a casual workaday attitude to the grisly task he's performing, while his exaggerated precision is obviously meant to be hilarious. It's such a waste. Fans of Italian special effects may recall the shocking scenes of amputation in Mario Landi's *Giallo a Venezia* (1979) where a similarly realistic brand of mutilation make-up was achieved. There the tone was grimly serious; an attitude Fulci clearly felt disillusioned with at this point in his career. Just in case you were failing to pick up on the comedic intentions, the soundtrack provides cues to labour the point. The chainsawing scene, for instance, wilts under a handicap of synthesised Viennese waltzes from Carlo Maria Cordio, while the rest of the soundtrack consists of regulation droning synths and turgid pre-set 'atmospheres'.

As we learn more about Lester Parson, the film grudgingly picks up pace, although Fulci directs with all the enthusiasm of a man in need of an afternoon nap. The killer scans lonely hearts columns for loose females, who are encouraged to drink themselves silly and pose in the nude for his video camera. After the (invariably unsatisfying) sexual act has been performed, he poisons them, then disposes of the bodies in whatever way takes his fancy, occasionally eating parts of them or leaving severed heads lying around in public places. Later, he watches television, enjoying the spectacle of his murder-spree reported on the news. Just to get him out and about a bit, the script furnishes him with an addiction to illegal gambling. His debts have piled up, and the villains he plays with are on his case, but the story strand leads nowhere. Instead, a dearth of supporting characters and the paucity of *mise-en-scène* add to an increasing sense of creative impoverishment.

Fulci's appetite for violence inflicted upon female characters is well-documented, but in *Touch of Death* the frenzied special effects are insufficient: he has to ridicule his female characters too. Somehow this feels more hostile and unpleasant than the gore. The first victim, Maggie, is depicted as a ridiculous, simpering nympho. To begin with, she's given a fuzz of uneven hair on her cheeks and upper lip. This bizarre factor noted, she's then shown writhing around on the bed next to Parson, moaning hysterically (and for no reason) as if approaching a sexual climax. One gets the sense that the audience are being goaded into regarding the woman as stupid and disposable. Her cries are shrill and absurd, making her an object of derision. With her scruffy facial hair and annoying voice she's being sent up, without any redeeming flourish of performance to suggest that we view her as anything but a stupid, ridiculous waste of space. Parson's failed attempt at poisoning her could almost be amusing if it weren't for the fact that Maggie is still being relentlessly lampooned, by a film that can't achieve our identification, *à la* Hitchcock, with the murderer either. Oscar Wilde's line about fox-hunting – the unspeakable in pursuit of the uneatable – pretty much sums up the dynamic here.

The startling and accomplished special effects deluge the screen with gore during Maggie's protracted death throes, but once again a scene that could have been truly horrific is thrown away, as Parson mugs ludicrously to indicate camp relief at the success of his endeavours. He's at it again when he has to chop the corpse's feet off to get it in the boot of his car. Halsey's laboured face-pulling – 'hey-ho, the things a murderer has to do' – sinks the scene for good.

When Parson is threatened with blackmail by a local tramp, he runs him over in his car. Fulci shows with obvious satisfaction the wheels crushing the vagrant's mangled body. Here it's not that the sequence is so blatantly tagged-on that irritates. After all, episodic plot development never hurt the Gothic horrors of Fulci's classic period. What is annoying is the sheer stupidity of the chase, as the terrified vagrant insists on running away from an approaching vehicle down the middle of the road. He knows the driver intends to kill him, but elects to stay in the firing line when an avenue of trees lines the route on either side. This sort of nonsensical behaviour is all too common in exploitation cinema, and a director can only really get away with it by cranking up the pace and playing on the audience's taste for speed. If it feels too 'stick-in-the-mud' to object, we tend to ignore implausibilities, but this is hardly possible with the slug-like progress of *Touch of Death*!

Having dispensed with this digression, Fulci returns to the film's favoured theme, the contemptible absurdity of female desire. This time, Halsey mugs his way through a sexual encounter with a woman who sings opera during sex. She even continues in her sleep. Once again, the emphasis is on making the female victim look (and sound) ludicrous. An objectionable contrast is made in the film between irritating female characters and the wry weariness of the killer, whose responses are meant to match ours in the face of each victim's 'stupidity'. Instead it's the film that ends up looking foolish.

Fulci's half-assed return to comedy is nowhere more tiresome than in the sequence where Parson disposes of the opera singer's corpse. For reasons the script can't be bothered to elaborate as it clambers laboriously around in search of comedy business, the killer opts to fasten the body into the passenger seat of his car, passing her off as alive. Argento's *Two Evil Eyes* plays far more successfully with this idea, in black comic terms that are nonetheless bolstered by sound narrative requirements. Here, much hilarity is supposed to accompany the fact that the dead singer's mouth keeps dropping open, giving the corpse a slack-jawed, moronic expression. Fulci ladles more of Cordio's appalling music over these shots, smothering the life out of what could have been a moment of incidentally observed humour. As for the payoff, in which Halsey encounters a traffic cop who fails to notice the 'passenger' is a cadaver, suffice to say it makes the *Police Academy* films look like noble successors to the Marx Brothers.

The story is nudged on, here and there, by information ported in from technological devices. Radio bulletins, telephone calls and announcements on TV are all heavily leant upon by the writing, not to mention the tape-recorder conversations which expose Parson's schizophrenia. These devices do nothing but emphasise the 'armchair' laziness of plotting and conception. Narrative information has to be brought to our 'Couch-potato Killer' since he doesn't generate it himself. Even his demise occurs thanks to a girl who chats him up when he dials a wrong number. This middle-aged fantasy of seduction by accident is depressing enough: the film's inability to make the young woman compelling even more so.

Touch of Death is a dispiriting experience. Opting to play a serial killer narrative for laughs is an endeavour fraught with difficulties that Fulci in no way succeeds in addressing. For once, accusations of misogyny seem dismally appropriate when so many of the jokes backfire or depend on the mockery of the victims.

Surely there can have been no personal feeling invested by Fulci in this enervated buffoon of a killer? An early scene that leads nowhere depicts Parson gazing adoringly at a portrait of his dead wife, Eunice Parson, which conceals the door to his personal safe. Whether this is meant as a touching or cynical detail is unclear. Given the subsequent dislike incurred by the character, I can only hope it isn't meant to be the former. The idea that we may actually be meant to feel sorry for this dreary monster raises unfortunate collisions of fiction and biography that I am loathe to feel could be appropriate.

opposite:
Italian video cover.
Quando Alice ruppe lo specchio translates as 'When Alice Broke the Looking Glass', a poetic title somewhat at odds with the film itself.

FORMULA HORROR pictures

LUCIO FULCI PRESENTA

Original Italian title
La dolce casa degli orrori

Italy

Alternative titles
The Sweet House of Horrors
(English-language export title)
Das Haus des Bösen
(GER DVD) 'The House of Evil'

Production companies
Reteitalia s.p.a. (Rome)
Dania Film (Rome)

Video/DVD/Blu-ray running time (adjusted)
TCC DVD (Japan) 82m 39s

Shooting period
November-December 1988

Release information
TV screening on Quadrifoglio Odeon TV
13 January 2001

The Sweet House of Horrors

1989

Directed by Lucio Fulci. executive producers: Massimo Manasse & Marco Grillo Spina for Reteitalia S.p.A. / Dania Film S.r.l. / National Cinematografica S.r.l. story by Lucio Fulci. screenplay by Vincenzo Mannino & Gigliola Battaglini. director of photography: Nino [Sebastiano] Celeste. music by Vince Tempera; music copyright: Musica Italia Edizioni Musicali S.r.l. film editor: Albert Morris [Alberto Moriani]. set designer: Antonello Geleng. production manager: Renato Fiè. Reteitalia production representative: Renato Camarda. production supervisor: Alessandro Loy Donà. assistant director: Camilla Fulci. continuity: Egle Guarino. cameramen: Sandro Grossi & Sandro Tamborra. assistant cameramen: Camillo Sabatini & Luigi Conversi. gaffer: Armando Moreschini. key grip: Tarcisio Diamanti. costume designer: Valentina Di Palma. special make-up effects: Giuseppe Ferranti. hair stylist: Maria Teresa Carrera. wardrobe: Milena Pintus. assistant set designer: Paolo Faenzi. set decorator: Giacomo Calò Carducci. property master: Vincenzo Luzzi. set technician: Elio Terribili. accountant: Massimo Massimi. still photographer: Romolo Eucalitto. editor's assistant: Rosaria Bellu. titles & opticals: Videogamma. sound recordist: Giuliano Piermarioli. sound studio: Studio 16 (Rome). technical equipment: Ciak Italia. transportation: C.S. – Cinematografica Service. set effects: Ditta Ricci. wigs by Rocchetti – Carboni. set decor: G.R.P. Arredamenti Teatrali; Rancati; L'Immaginoteca. insurance consultant: Cinesicurtà. The production wishes to thank La Ditta Tabak S.r.l.; Il Gruppo Imec S.p.A.; L'Azienda Agrituristica; Il Covo di Ponte Pattoli; La Ditta Commoter di Ponte Pattoli; De Vecchis Fuoristrada (Rome). colour by Telecolor. raw stock: Agfacolor XT.

Cast: Jean Christophe Bretigniere (Uncle Carlo). Cinzia Monreale (Aunt Marcia). Lubka Cibulova (Mary Valdi, the children's mother). Lino Salemme (Guido the gardener). Franco Diogene (Mr. Colby, realtor). Alexander Vernon Dobtcheff ('Jack', the exorcist). Giuliano Gensini (Marco Valdi, the boy). Ilary Blasi (Sarah Valdi, the girl). Dante Fioretti (Father O'Toole). Pascal Persiano (Roberto Valdi, the children's father).

Synopsis: Mary and Roberto Valdi return home from a party to find an intruder ransacking their elegant country house. The masked man attacks and kills them, disguising their deaths as a motor accident. At their parents funeral, the Valdis' bereaved children Sarah and Marco exhibit a strange mixture of grief and hilarity, chewing gum whilst weeping and giggling at the elderly priest conducting the ceremony. Aunt Marcia and Uncle Carlo decide to stay with the children at the Valdi house whilst arrangements are made to sell it. Carlo is called away on business, and during the night Martha explores the attic and is frightened by a giant toy fly which seems to attack her. The children are adamant that they wish to continue living at the house and are openly hostile to Mr. Colby, the estate agent Uncle Carlo brings to visit. When Colby suffers an accident at the house, the children laugh. Meanwhile, a flashback alerts us to the fact that the masked assailant who murdered the Valdis was Guido, their gardener. Sarah and Marco are visited in their beds by floating flames which they suspect represent their dead parents. Guido is about to accept a generous cheque from Carlo for renovation of the house when a violent flashback shocks him into screaming his guilt for all to hear. He runs away and falls under an oncoming truck. The injured Mr. Colby returns, but is attacked by a violent wind and flames in the hallway. Terrified but defiant he leaves the house again. Sarah and Marco conduct a masked ritual to contact the spirit world. They ask their parents to manifest themselves. Their wish is granted and they are greeted by their parents' ghosts. Marsha and Carlo cannot see the ghosts and try to force the children to leave in the car. However, a ghostly fog makes it impossible to drive. The frightened couple bring in a medium, an arrogant, caped 'spirit challenger' who attempts to exorcise the house. After a brief skirmish, he returns with a giant bulldozer and commands the spirits of Mary and Roberto to leave as the building is smashed to rubble. For a while the children try to inhabit an old lean-to playhouse they'd constructed. The spirits of their parents enter two stones and the children pocket them. When the spiritualist tries to confiscate the stones, his hand melts. The family of living children and ghostly parents remain together.

About the production: The first 'House of Doom' to go before the cameras, in mid-November 1988, was Umberto Lenzi's *La casa del sortilegio* (aka *The House of Witchcraft*), and Fulci's two films began soon after. *La dolce casa degli orrori* went first, for which the production spent a month on location in the beautiful town of Perugia, north of Rome. Interviewed for the *Sweet House of Horrors* DVD, Gigliola Battaglini, co-writer of the screenplay with her partner Vincenzo Mannino, recalled that the story idea had been Fulci's and the screenplay was written very much on his instructions.[14] Once again, stories of Fulci's volatile temper emerged. Actor Lino Salemme, interviewed for the *Sweet House of Horrors* DVD, described his experience on the film with sadness: *"Lucio Fulci treated us awfully, both Pascal [Persiano] and me, and especially Pascal... We were young at the time, we had little experience, we'd made only a few films. It was the first time a director treated us like that and it made us nervous. We even found it difficult to concentrate on our scenes and our characters. We were just trying to understand the reasons for his behaviour. Fulci was always mad, he was always screaming, he treated everyone very poorly."*[15]

When I asked Fulci's assistant on these films, Michele De Angelis, for an insight into Fulci's temperament, he stressed the difficulties under which Fulci laboured, and advanced the following reasons for his short temper: *"I saw Lucio behave like that with actors. He was doing it with people he didn't like or he thought had no talent. Mostly he was doing it with people who were snobbish or not paying too much attention to what they were doing."* Could he perhaps have achieved better results if he'd treated the actors less harshly? De Angelis remains sceptical: *"I don't think that some of those so called 'actors' would have been better if treated in a nicer way. I don't believe in screaming, but a film set is a tricky place to be, especially when you are not in top form and you have a lot of pressure, and no time to do what you would like. I don't remember Lucio being particularly nasty. Indeed he would say something like 'You did a good job, you barked well', implying that they were dogs (in Italy we use to say 'dog' referring to a bad actor). Or 'Good, cut, a golden bone to everybody!' – again the dog metaphor. If they were offended, well they should have listened to what he was telling them! Lucio had this way to offend people or scream at them, trying to push them to give their best. But he was also very tender with actors he liked and respected. Nice moments like once when he said to some people involved in a scene, 'If you do it right, I will personally take you on a special tour to the city dog shelter!' I thought it was damn funny! Once he introduced me to a media professor who came on a set visit. This was Antonio Bruschini, the nicest man in film criticism in Italy – he's not with us anymore, unfortunately. Anyway, he came, and Lucio told him: 'This is my assistant, he does only one thing in life, watch horror movies and jerk off while doing it'. And that was the first time I met Antonio, as we were shaking hands! So I took it as a compliment."*[16]

Review: *The Sweet House of Horrors* combines a handful of strange ideas with a bunch of standard haunted house clichés and then sinks the result in a cloying sentimentality. Fulci, who wrote the story and guided the screenplay (by Vincenzo Mannino and Gigliola Battaglini), revives an old theme from previous films, that of the mysterious complicity of children with the supernatural, and for a while the tale is engaging. Bereaved kids Sarah and Marco are depicted in an unusually nuanced way, neither innocents nor monsters but somewhere in between. Insolently chewing gum at their parents' graveside, giggling at the solemnity of the proceedings yet shedding tears too, they are immediately interesting and compelling. Their disrespect for adults – a priest, a money-sniffing estate agent, a bullying medium – sets them apart, as does their easy acceptance of the spirit world. Their fervent wish to be reunited with their parents, and their parents' reappearance as ghosts, are certainly interesting ideas, but as things progress this 'house of horrors' turns just a little too sweet, a problem aggravated by pastel colour schemes and hazy soft-focus photography.

Sweet it may be, but Fulci didn't restrain himself when it came to his trademark gore scenes. Given that the film was subsequently deemed too violent for TV transmisison it's hard to figure out what Fulci thought he was doing. It's too sentimental for a teenage horror audience, yet even by Italian standards it's far too brutal for pre-teens. The murders of Mary and Roberto Valdi are particularly gruesome, with gross details such as Roberto's flesh sticking to the poker used to club him to death going way beyond the norm for TV horror. The special make-up, though, is often crude, at times resembling the amateur grue created by Herschell Gordon Lewis for his 1960s splatter films *Blood Feast* and *The Gruesome Twosome*.

In terms of construction, the story could have used more work. A good example is the treatment of Guido, the gardener who murders the Valdis. Although he commits the crime wearing a mask, his identity is revealed to us without fanfare at the thirty minute mark: evidently Fulci was not interested in making a thriller. It would have served the film better if Guido (decently played by Lino Salemme, who returned in Fulci's *Demonia*) had been visible from the start – it would have made his condolences to the children at the funeral more contemptible and created a stronger sense of tension in the otherwise leisurely scenes after the murders. Also lacking in guile is the crude manner in which Guido reveals his guilt, bellowing *"I have to murder the two of you!"* and staggering around in front of a startled Carlo looking at his outstretched hands.

While the benevolence of the spectres is certainly unusual for a film of this type, it also undercuts the drama during the second half of the film. With nasty Guido out of the way, what's left borders on the twee, a problem not helped by the typically poor dubbing performances allotted to child characters in Italian horror. The final confrontation between a pompous exorcist and a possessed earth-moving truck (no, I'm not making this up) lifts the proceedings with a dash of extreme weirdness, as does the random-as-you-like finale in which the parents are reincarnated as two large pebbles, but despite such oddities the film remains a minor excursion at best.

above:
Japanese video cover for *The Sweet House of Horrors*.

opposite top and this page bottom:
Sarah (Ilary Blasi) and Marco (Giuliano Gensini) are two children who make contact with the spirits of their dead parents (Lubka Cibulova and Pascal Persiano, pictured this page, bottom).

below:
A mystery intruder murders Roberto (Pascal Persiano).

Original Italian title
La casa nel tempo

Translation
'The House in Time'

Italy

Alternative titles
La casa del tempo (IT video cover)
'The House of Time'
The House of Clocks
(English-language export title/USA DVD)
Die Uhr des Grauens (GER DVD)
'The Clock of Evil'

Production companies
Reteitalia s.p.a. (Rome)
Dania Film (Rome)

Video/DVD/Blu-ray running time (adjusted)
Media Blasters DVD (USA) 83m 36s

Shooting period
November-December 1988

Release information
TV screening on Quadrifoglio Odeon TV
23 January 2001

The House of Clocks

1989

Directed by Lucio Fulci. executive producers: Massimo Manasse & Marco Grillo Spina for Reteitalia S.p.A. / Dania Film S.r.l. / National Cinematografica S.r.l. story by Lucio Fulci. screenplay by Gianfranco Clerici & Daniele Stroppa. director of photography: Nino [Sebastiano] Celeste. music by Vince Tempera; music copyright: Musica Italia Edizioni Musicali S.r.l. film editor: Albert Morris [Alberto Moriani]. set designer: Elio Micheli. production manager: Renato Fiè. Reteitalia production representative: Renato Camarda. production supervisor: Alessandro Loy Donà. assistant director: Camilla Fulci. continuity: Egle Guarino. cameraman: Sandro Grossi. assistant cameramen: Francesco Damiani & Camillo Sabatini. gaffer: Armando Moreschini. key grip: Tarcisio Diamanti. costume designer: Valentina Di Palma. special make-up effects: Giuseppe Ferranti. hair stylist: Maria Teresa Carrera. wardrobe: Milena Pintus. assistant set designer: Paolo Faenzi. property master: Vincenzo Luzzi. set technician: Elio Terribili. accountant: Massimo Massimi. still photographer: Romolo Eucalitto. editor's assistants: Rosaria Bellu & Nicoletta Leone. titles & opticals: Videogamma. sound recordist: Giuliano Piermarioli. sound studio: Studio 16 (Rome). transportation: C.S. – Cinematografica Service. wigs by Rocchetti – Carboni. set effects: Ditta Ricci. set decor: G.R.P. Arredamenti Teatrali; Rancati; L'Immaginoteca. insurance consultant: Cinesicurtà. the production wishes to thank La Ditta Tabak S.r.l.; Il Gruppo Imec S.p.A.; Il Park Hotel (Perugia); "Gruppo Conifili Lanciani". colour by Telecolor. raw stock: Agfacolor XT.

Cast: Keith Van Hoven (Tony). Karina Huff (Diana, Tony's girlfriend). Paolo Paoloni (Uncle Victor). Bettine Milne (Aunt Sarah). Peter Hintz (Paul, Tony's friend). Al Cliver [Pier Luigi Conti] (Peter, the handyman). Carla Cassòla (Maria, the housekeeper). Paolo Bernardi (Simon, the nephew). Francesca De Rose (the niece). Massimo Sarchielli (storekeeper). Vincenzo Luzzi (balding cop).

Synopsis: Victor and Sarah, a strange old couple with a murderous secret, live in a rambling country house filled with clocks. A groundsman, Peter, looks after the couple's vicious guard-dogs, which patrol the grounds after dark. Maria, the maid, discovers the bodies of the couple's money-grabbing nephew and niece lying in open coffins in the cellar. She announces she wishes to quit, so Sarah murders her ... Three hoodlums, Diana, Tony and Paul, are driving through the area and decide to rob the house after a tip-off about the wealth it contains and the decrepitude of the owners. Diana talks her way in by pretending her car has broken down and asking to use the phone. Tony and Paul cut the phone lines and climb in through a window. Their plan merely to rob the old couple goes awry when Peter intervenes with his shotgun. A bloodbath ensues and Peter, Victor and Sarah are killed. The hoodlums, horrified at this turn of events, hide the bodies in a cupboard. At first they fail to notice that each clock in the house has stopped at the exact time the couple were killed. When they do, they try to leave but are trapped by the dogs prowling the grounds. The clocks begin to move in reverse. The three decide to stay overnight. Diana and Tony head upstairs to make out and smoke joints while Paul wanders downstairs. He sees that the bloodstains have disappeared and the bodies are back where they'd fallen. Before he can alert the others he is shot by an unseen figure. Diana and Tony rush downstairs and see the old couple reanimating. In the kitchen Diana is trapped by Sarah and stabbed through the hand, pinning her to the kitchen table. A ring she'd stolen is retrieved from her finger. Diana and Tony find Paul hiding in the cellar severely wounded. Illogical time distortions continue as Diana's hand heals up whilst Paul's injuries remain. Diana and Tony escape through a window into the grounds. Paul is too injured to hoist himself up and is axed to death by the reanimated Peter. Tony is pulled into a shallow grave by the corpse of Maria. She sticks him through the stomach with a wooden spike. In the cellar, the niece and nephew revive and kill Victor and Sarah. Diana staggers away from the house... Diana, Tony and Paul awaken to find that everything that happened was just a dream brought on by the marijuana they've been smoking. Driving away, the three of them remark upon the astonishing similarity of their dreams, before their car crashes off the road and kills them (again?).

About the production: According to De Angelis, Fulci experienced no interference or guidance from Reteitalia during the shoots: *"I don't remember any Reteitalia people coming on the set. They just financed the project that was made at Dania film by Luciano Martino."*[17] With production running smoothly, shooting and post-production for the 'Houses of Doom' appears to have been completed within three months of the mid-November start date. The completed package was announced in a *Variety* advertisement for newly available product, dated 8 February 1989: *"Houses of Doom. There's no place like home, except when it holds lurking horrors. Directed by Lucio Fulci and Umberto Lenzi. A Reteitalia and Dania Film Production. Produced By Dania Film. 4 TV movies x 93'."* (In fact *La casa nel tempo* and *La dolce casa degli orrori* were both 83m long, while the Lenzi films were 84m and 86m.)

Looking back, it's sad to see that whereas Lamberto Bava's experience shooting for television kept him in regular work, at a time when the Italian film industry was being stripped to the bone, Fulci gained no such lifeline from 'Houses of Doom'. His brace of TV films went unseen, and his remaining film projects were financed for very little money without the support of Reteitalia. Fulci's brush with the Berlusconi empire failed to dislodge any low-hanging fruit and brought him nothing in the way of career advancement, at a time when alternative sources of funding were diminishing rapidly.

Review: Shot back-to-back with *The Sweet House of Horrors* is this little gem, which also concerns the relationship between generations of the same family. But whereas the niece and nephew in *Sweet House* were heroic little children, and their uncle and aunt kind-hearted nurturers, here the aunt and uncle are a malevolent old couple with arcane temporal powers, and the niece and nephew are money-grabbing ingrates seeking vengeance.

The House of Clocks is a much better film than *Sweet House of Horrors*, indeed it's the best thing Fulci had crafted since *The Devil's Honey*. Although padded outrageously, and lacking in internal logic, it is at least reasonably atmospheric and creepy, with the overall mood enhanced by Vince Tempera's dreamy, melancholic theme tune. As for the cast, admittedly the three 'hoodlums' leave a lot to be desired, with Karina Huff bland and uninteresting, Peter Hintz (the guru masseur from Leandro Lucchetti's *Bloody Psycho*) overacting atrociously, and hunky Keith Van Hoven looking like a confused ten-year-old when asked to do anything more complex than move his lips. Fortunately help is at hand from the older cast, who carry the film and give it lots of sinister charm. Dubbed, in the English-language version, by voices so plummy you'd think Christopher Lee and Princess Anne had stepped in to deliver the lines, Paolo Paoloni as 'Uncle Victor' and Bettine Milne as 'Aunt Sarah' are consistently intriguing and amusing, and get the film off to a great start. Where *Sweet House of Horrors* buckled with only two inexperienced child actors to support it, here the performers know precisely how to create menace whilst teasing out the hints of sly comedy.

Backstory, however, is *not* a strength of the film. We learn nothing about neither the source of the couple's skills nor their special relationship with time. (They seem unsurprised to be back from the dead, so perhaps they're adepts in some form of necromancy?) Much goes unsaid and we are simply left to wonder, given just a few tantalising hints of depravity like the scene in which Victor feeds toast-crumbs to a song-thrush on his windowsill then bashes it with his stick and tosses the crumpled bird to his cat. Likewise, the relationship between the couple and their staff is fraught with such unexplained intensity that one cannot help but chuckle at the deliberate absurdity. Full marks here to Carla Cassòla as Maria, who serves table with an air of looming portentousness, the latest in a distinguished line of sinister Fulci servants that includes Martha in *The Beyond* and Ann in *The House by the Cemetery*.

And yes, once again, as reliable as clockwork himself, Fulci provides his intended TV audience with some deliciously horrible gore. I particularly liked the scene in which Sarah 'dismisses' Maria by means of a sharpened stick in the crotch. *"I'm just going to have to do the housework myself,"* she sighs as the maid expires with a gaping hole in her nether regions.

The downside of the film is the way it squanders the rich potential of its central idea. Having established the notion of time reversing, Fulci neglects the fantasy logic that could have given shape to the drama. Indeed he violates it so often that it was hardly worth bothering with in the first place. The clocks run backwards at a ridiculously high speed and one would expect weeks to have whizzed by in the time it takes for the recently deceased to revive. Diana's hand heals up scant minutes after being speared by Sarah's knife, yet Paul's shotgun injuries stubbornly remain. A more precise sense of time would also have improved scenes like the one in which a visit from the police is replayed a second time. Essentially, the temporal aspect is picturesque but narratively redundant. (Character logic is similarly askew: quite why the revived Maria takes it upon herself to kill Paul, whose only crimes are against the people who murdered her, is anyone's guess. You'd think she'd be grateful!) To cap it all, the time reversal is eventually dropped in favour of a cop-out 'twist' ending that opts for one of the oldest clichés in the book. Still, it's worth taking time out to see this film, which proves that Fulci's decline in his later years was not immune to the occasional time-reversal itself.

above:
Cover of the American DVD release.

left:
Diana (Karine Huff) and her boyfriend Tony (Keith Van Hoven) find the past won't stay dead in *The House of Clocks*.

opposite page:
Victor (Paolo Paoloni) takes his revenge as time runs backwards in *The House of Clocks*.

below:
Peter (Pier Luigi Conti) defends his employers;
Sinister servant Maria (Carla Cassòla) suffers the last word in unfair dismissals;
Aunt Sarah (Bettine Milne) gets her guts blown out during the film's home invasion sequence. But she'll be back...

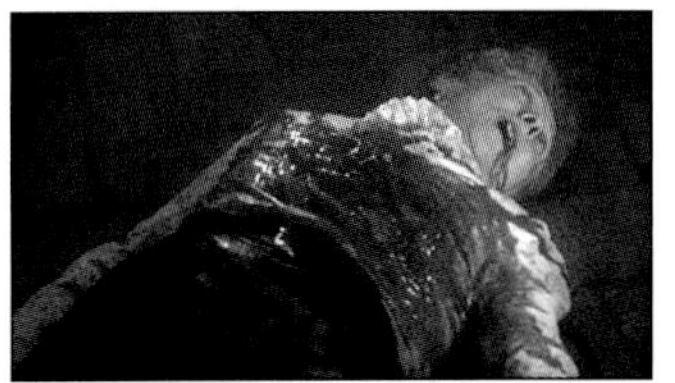

Original Italian title
Demonia

Italy

Alternative titles
Liza (mooted retitling, never used)
No Evil Deed Goes Undone (USA alt. DVD)

Production companies
Lanterna Editrice
A.M. Trading International (Rome)

Video/DVD/Blu-ray running time (adjusted)
Media Blasters DVD (USA) 84m 51s

Shooting period
Shooting from December 1989

Release information
No cinema or TV screenings

Demonia

1990

Directed by Lucio Fulci. produced by Ettore Spagnuolo for Lanterna Editrice & A.M. Trading International (Rome). original screenplay by Pietro [Piero] Regnoli & Lucio Fulci. director of photography: Luigi Ciccarese. music composed by Giovanni Cristiani; music © BEAT Records Company. film editor: Otello Colangeli. art director & costume designer: Massimo Bolongaro. special make up effects: Franco Giannini. production manager: Alessandra Spagnuolo. assistant production manager: Gianluca Bigari. director's assistant: Camilla Fulci. cameraman: Sandro Grossi. additional cameramen: Fabio Leoni & Gianluca Di Giacomo. gaffer: Ninuccio Tonnarini. generator operator: Francesco D'Agostino. key grip: Nazzareno Savini. grip: Fabrizio Pizzoferrato. make-up: Franco Giannini & Giuseppe Ferranti. hair dresser: Maria Teresa Carrera. special effects by Mario Ciccarella & Elio Terribili. set dresser: Cinzia Milani. property master: Vincenzo Luzzi. production secretary: Donatella De Guida. stills photographer: Carlotta Fenati. assistant editors: Giuliana Colangeli & Leonardo Kustermann. opticals & titles: Videogamma. sound director: Alberto Salvatori. mixage: Mario Lupi. sound recording: Cinemontaggio. sound effects: DA.MA. Sound. equipment: Cineluce. transport: Cinetrasport. wardrobe: Iacobelli. shoes: Arditi. decor: Rancati. wigs: Sexy Wig.

Cast: Brett Halsey (Professor Paul Evans). Meg Register (Liza). Lino Salemme (Turi DeSimone, the butcher). Christina Engelhardt (Susie). Pascal Druant (Kevin). Grady Thomas Clarkson (Sean). Ettore Comi (John). Carla Cassòla (woman with cats) also starring Michael J. Aronin (Lieutenant Andy, a cop). Al Clever [Pier Luigi Conti] (Porter). Isabella Corradini. Paola Cozzo. Bruna Rossi. Paola Calati. Antonio Melillo. Ruth Anderson. Gianfranco Bonavita. Francesco Biasini. Clorinda Pucci. Kerstin Soderberg. Francesco Cusimano. *Uncredited:* Lucio Fulci (Inspector Carter).

Synopsis: Sicily 1486. Villagers drag screaming nuns into a cavern beneath their convent, crucify them, and burn them. Toronto 1990. At a séance, Liza has a vision of the crucified nuns. Months later, she and Professor Paul Evans, a noted archaeologist, are with a team surveying Ancient Greek ruins on Sicily. Liza is fascinated by the ruined monastery which overlooks the dig. At the quayside, the professor talks to Porter, a colleague. Turi, the hot-headed local butcher, follows Liza into the crypt and warns her not to pry any further but she ignores him. Behind a wall she discovers a cavern containing charred human remains nailed to wooden crosses. The opening of the crypt sets in motion a series of supernatural events, beginning with the murder of Porter, who is shot with a harpoon gun by a ghostly nun. Liza pursues her investigations by checking the church records. There she meets a strange old woman who invites Liza to her house the following day to hear the story of what happened at the monastery. Two archaeologists, Sean and Kevin, get blind drunk and decide to wander the ruins at night. After hearing giggling female voices they fall to their deaths in a pit of metal spikes. Interpol's Inspector Carter arrives to investigate. Liza meets with the old woman, who tells her that the nuns practiced witchcraft and held orgies. Local youths would be invited for sex, then murdered as they reached orgasm; the nuns would drink their blood in a satanic frenzy. If they became pregnant the unwanted babies were burned. The old woman is the next victim, her eyes scratched out by her cats. Turi is found dead, locked in his cold-store with a meat-hook through his neck and his tongue nailed to the chopping board. Paul announces that the dig will be abandoned but Liza refuses to leave. As the townspeople mount an attack on the ruins, Paul tries to get his team clear but can't find Liza. John and Susie, a married couple in the team, realise their young son Robby is missing. His father sees the boy in the trees being abducted by a robed, faceless nun – Liza? The boy pulls free and discovers his father tied by the ankles between two bent saplings. Running to help, the boy trips a rope and the trees spring upright, ripping John's body in half. Paul finds Liza in the ruins; now possessed, she stabs him in the stomach, then disappears like a ghost. The townspeople converge on the hidden chamber, and Liza reappears, foaming at the mouth on one of the crosses. The mob set her alight. Liza materialises at the foot of the cross, no longer possessed but dead.

About the production: The opening production credits designate *Demonia* "An Ettore Spagnuolo film for Lanterna Editrice and A.M. Trading International, Rome". At the end of the film the copyright credit goes to "B.S.C." and Lanterna Editrice. Of these three companies, one is a total mystery; I've been unable to discover anything about 'B.S.C.', or 'B.S.C. International' as they were also named (just once) in *Variety*'s sparse *Demonia* coverage. Ettore Spagnuolo, producer of Fulci's *Ænigma*, was the head of A.M. Trading International but by the time *Demonia* was ready for sale at the Mifed film market in 1990, Giuseppe Massaro of Lanterna Editrice was hawking it. Unfortunately he was unable to secure a sale and the film went unreleased for many years. A video release from Japan (or a grey-market Italian tape ripped from the same source) was the only way to see *Demonia* until Shriek Show's 2001 DVD brought the film in from the cold.

Shot on location in Sciacca, Sicily, *Demonia* has some atmospheric charm, and some memorably nasty gore scenes, but unfortunately, behind it all, one can sense the truth in the words of supporting actor Grady T. Clarkson, who reminisced about his experience making the film to Alan Jones in *Eyeball* magazine: *"The whole film was a shambles. I'd heard all the stories about Fulci and now I know they're true. There was a vague semblance of a movie being made but the main problem was no producer support. On set he's disorganised and screams abusively a lot. Actually he screams at everyone all the time. It's not necessarily an angry scream, often it's tinged with humour, but it gets very tiring after a short while. The louder he gets the harder he is to understand, and none of the crew escapes the wrath of Fulci."*[18]

Review: If there's a morning after the night before in the Beyond, that's when and where *Demonia* was made. You'd swear there was a better film just over the horizon – the trouble is, we never reach it.

Although it's clearly a lot more inventive and atmospheric than *Touch of Death* or *The Ghosts of Sodom*, *Demonia* never really ignites. I certainly *wanted* to like it: the excellent poster artwork suggested that Fulci might have regained some concern for atmospheric design, a return to the successful stamping grounds of the early eighties; and the plot, when described briefly, seemed an ideal framework from which to hang a lurid Gothic fantasy, ripped open at the guts for the delectation of his most morbid of cameras. But it was not to be.

The chief drawback is the cast. They either sleepwalk through the proceedings or send up their meagre characterisations. If only Catriona MacColl, whose presence in Fulci's films lent a sympathetic quality often missing from his work, had not turned down his offer of the lead role in *Demonia*. Instead, in her place we have Meg Register. This Virginia-born actress strains to convey hauntedness but looks as though she's coping with indigestion. Brett Halsey is professional but forgettable as the male lead (to be fair the role is woefully underwritten), but the worst sinners are Grady Thomas Clarkson and Pascal Druant, playing drunken archaeologists who exchange improvised banter as they wander through their parts. When Clarkson's character hears a sound as the two of them explore a spookily-lit crypt, he berates his less attentive companion saying, *"If you'd take time to lay off your phony Irish accent maybe you'd hear it too."* True, they've both been indulging in absurd 'Oirish' brogues throughout the film, but the insincerity is disgraceful. Worse, it reveals the inattentiveness of the director; if Fulci had been more in control he would never have allowed it.

Demonia opens with shots of corpses stacked in layered tombs, before a sheet of flames engulfs the image. Two short sequences at the beginning sketch in the evil nuns' fate at the hands of the traditional mob of torch-waving villagers, and the 'contact' made by Liza during a séance in Toronto. The first of these scenes immediately invites comparison with the prologue of *The Beyond*, also set in an earlier time, and also depicting a crucifixion as punishment for black magic, performed by an angry posse in the bowels of a building. The second, with its recreation of the séance at the beginning of *City of the Living Dead*, is even more blatant a copy, down to the use of a revolving pan across the faces of the assembled occultists, and the use of an overhead shot to capture Liza's break from the circle. The recurrence of images from the prologue (in this case nuns being crucified) also recalls the same technique in *City* (the shots of Father Thomas's suicide). Sadly Luigi Ciccarese's camera fails to emulate the edginess of Sergio Salvati's technique in that film, and the acting performances are similarly lacking in eccentricity. Surely self-quotation is only a good idea if you can top or at least equal the source?

On the plus side, there are many grisly moments, even if the special effects recall Herschell Gordon Lewis more than Giannetto De Rossi. That really isn't the problem. What does matter is the level of energy and commitment; *Demonia* rarely feels *elated* with its gory apotheoses. Due to lack of money (and general tiredness), the death scenes feel rushed and scrappy instead of thrilling.

One sequence more than any other demonstrates what is wrong with *Demonia*. In it, a father is gruesomely split down the middle by the unwitting actions of his young son. It's a particularly nasty idea which, if handled well, could have had a powerful emotional impact as well as trading on the (here, very well designed) special effects. Instead it's merely inserted with no coherent set-up *at all*. It really isn't a case of provocative non-sequitur experimentation this time. Instead it appears that a handful of linking shots have been entirely omitted. Once again, lack of time and money have bitten into even the most basic of filmmaking considerations. We see the boy being abducted, led by the hand by a ghostly nun while his father gives chase through the woods. The boy pulls free – and in the next shot he sees his father tied by the ankles to two saplings! Presumably the father was overpowered by someone, but a few simple shots have gone missing. Was the negative spoiled? Did someone forget to include them in the shooting script as the film approached completion? The sad fact is that a scene which could have been really shocking has been bungled, failing even the most minimal requirements of editing. In terms of plot construction too the whole thing lacks elegance: it's bad storytelling to place so much weight upon the death of a peripheral character as the film is reaching a climax, especially when the whole thing would have worked so much better if we'd met the boy and his father earlier on: imagine how much more shocking it would have been if we'd got to know the characters, like Bob and his father in *The House by the Cemetery*! We could have been looking at one of Fulci's best set-pieces.

Demonia does have some amusement value for those willing to persist in the face of a general shoddiness. The restless nights of horror suffered by Liza have less to do with supernatural problems and more to do with her colleagues spending all night round a camp fire singing 'Molly Malone', and one has to admire the scene in which a ghostly nun manages the complicated business of nailing a strapping young butcher to a chopping block by his tongue. It's best, I suppose, to watch the film chiefly for laughs, and seen like this, it's a diverting enough way to spend ninety minutes. If you're in a more demanding mood, however, *Demonia* is a frustrating 'could've-been'. Lack of money, lack of time, and lack of effort all scuppered its chances of reaching its potential. Re-make, anyone?

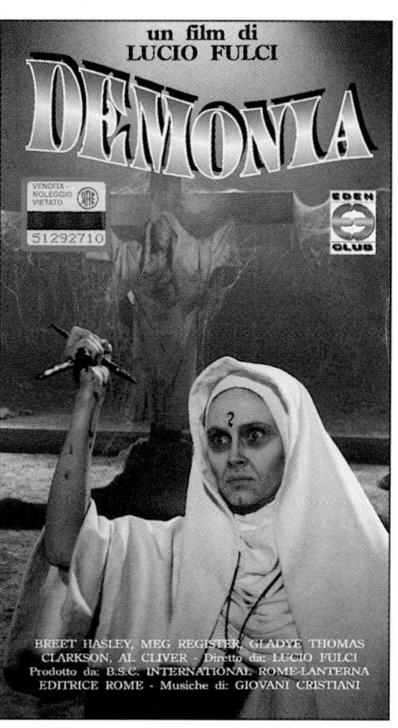

opposite top:
Pre-release artwork was circulated to promote *Demonia* on its completion, but it failed to secure a video release until 1998, early examples include the VHS tapes from Italy (above) and Japan (opposite bottom left).

below:
Nuns to the flame;
"Okay Inspector Carter, so you're from Interpol... but what are you doing around here?" Lucio Fulci (left), in a typical cameo role as a peripheral authority figure, offers guidance to Professor Evans (Brett Halsey);
The severed head of Porter (Pier Luigi Conti) is found at the quayside;
John (Ettore Comi) fails to pull himself together for the sake of his son.

Italian theatrical title
Un gatto nel cervello (I volti del terrore)

Translation
'A Cat in the Brain (The Faces of Terror)'

Italy

Alternative titles
Nightmare Concert (A Cat in the Brain)
Un gatto nel cervello (Nightmare Concert)
Cat in the Brain (onscreen alt. English-language DVD title)
Το κονσέρτο του τρόμου (GRE DVD)
'Concert of Terror'

Production companies
Executive Cine TV s.r.l. (Rome)

Theatrical distributors
Lucas Film (Italy)

Theatrical running time
Italy 89m

Video/DVD/Blu-ray running times (adjusted)
Grindhouse Releasing (USA) 92m 42s
Hardgore (UK) 92m 45s

Censorship
Italian censor certificate 85928
issued 08 August 1990

Release information
Rome 10 August 1990

Nightmare Concert

1990

Directed by Lucio Fulci. produced by Luigi Nannerini & Anthony Clear [Antonino Lucidi] for Executive Cine TV Srl. story & screenplay by Lucio Fulci & John Fitzsimmons with the collaboration of Antonio Tentori. director of photography: Alessandro Grossi. music by Fabio Frizzi © Ribot srl. film editor: Vincenzo Tomassi. production supervisor & script supervisor: Camilla Fulci. production manager: Silvano Zignani. assistant director: Roberto Lucidi. cameraman: Fabio Leoni. assistant cameraman: Alberto Cerchi. gaffers: Antonio La Barbera, Romano Martiri, Marcello Perricone & Giovanni Angeletti. grips: Vincenzo Luzzi, Marco Lucidi, Mario Occhioni & Massimo Galiano. make-up: Pino Ferranti. hair stylist: Maria Teresa Carrera. wardrobe: Milena Pintus. paymaster: Antonino Lucidi. production secretary: Maria Luisa Nannerini. generator operator: Roberto Stiffi. set photographer: Luca Spataro. assistant editors: Claudia Vivenzio & Paola Tomassi. sound technician: Roberto Barbieri. sound effects: G.J. ST. AR. Movie; Cine Sound. synchronization & mixage: Cooperativa di Lavoro Fono Roma srl. generators: C.S. Cinematografica srl. equipment furnished by Cinecittà. the production wishes to thank the following: interiors filmed at Cinecittà; restaurant: "Piazza vecchia"; restaurant "Tiro a volo"; the Petrini marina & the crew "Perversion". developing & printing: Cinecittà spa. film: Fuji Color. filmed on location at the Petrini Marina, at the 'Piazza Vecchia' restaurant & on board the yacht 'Perversion' with interiors at Cinecittà Studios (Rome).

Cast in the main story: Lucio Fulci (Dr. Lucio Fulci). David L. Thompson (Professor Egon Swharz, the psychiatrist). Jeoffrey Kennedy (Gabrielli, the policeman). Melissa Lang [Malisa Longo] (Katya Shwarz, Egon's wife). Shilett Angel (Filipo, the producer). Judy Morrow [Paola Cozzo] (Lilly, the nurse). Robert Egon [Spechtenhauser] (himself, actor playing young Nazi). *Uncredited:* Vincenzo Luzzi (man with chainsaw).

Cast from Lucio Fulci's Quando Alice ruppe lo specchio: Brett Halsey (Lester Parson, the cannibal killer). Zora Ulla Keslerová, Marco Di Stefano (the vagrant). Sacha Maria Darwin (the victim in the oven). Ria De Simone (the soprano).

Cast from Lucio Fulci's Il fantasma di Sodoma: Robert Egon [Spechtenhauser]. Klaus Aliot. Mary Salier. Luciana Ottaviani [as 'Georgia Moore'] (girl seduced by young Nazi). Pier Luigi Conti (Nazi pouring booze on woman).

Cast from Giorgio Simonelli and Lucio Fulci's Hansel e Gretel: Elisabete Pimenta Boaretto. Lucia Prato. Paul Muller. Maurice Poli.

from Andrea Bianchi's *Massacre*: Lubka Lenzi. Maurice Poli. Paul Muller.
from Leandro Lucchetti's *Bloody Psycho*: Peter Hintz. Marco Di Stefano. Paul Muller.
from Mario Bianchi's *Non aver paura della zia Marta*: Gabriele Tinti. Luciana Ottaviani. Maurice Poli. Sacha Maria Darwin.
from Enzo Millioni's *Luna di sangue*: Jacques Sernas. Pamela Prati. Zora Ulla Keslerová [as 'Zora Ulla Kesler']. Annie Belle.

Synopsis: Lucio Fulci wraps up shooting for the day on his latest film, *Touch of Death*, and goes to a restaurant. The friendly waiter recognises him and suggests a fillet of steak, or steak tartar, but Fulci can't look at meat without thinking back to the cannibalism scene he shot earlier, and leaves without ordering. The following day, checking an eye-popping effects shot from another movie (*Hansel and Gretel*), he irritably snaps at a technician to get the plate of animal eyeballs out of his sight. Returning home, he tries to sleep, but the noise of a handyman's chainsaw keeps him awake with recollections of his own recently shot chainsaw mayhem in *Touch of Death*. Fulci discovers that one of his neighbours is a psychiatrist, Professor Egon Swharz, and arranges to have a consultation with him. Swharz's nurse, Lilly, immediately phones a friend, saying *"Guess who just walked in as a patient!"* Swharz discusses Fulci's recent problems and suggests that he is *"breaking down the barrier, the boundary between what you film and what's real"*. The next day, at Cinecittà, Fulci's producer Filippo tells him that the pace has to be stepped up. Fulci is making two films at once (*Touch of Death* and *The Ghosts of Sodom*). Robert Egon, the young actor who plays a ghostly Nazi

seducer in *The Ghosts of Sodom*, approaches Fulci in a corridor to discuss his role. *"Your presence should make a deadly impression"*, Fulci tells him, *"You are after all a symbol of death. And you're also the whole horror of the Nazis. Get me?"* Fulci talks the actors through a seduction scene and then staggers ouside, muttering *"Sadism, Nazism; is there any point any more?"* His producer steers him into a studio suite for an interview with a Munich TV crew. The sight of the female interviewer's legs triggers a vision of sexual abandon in Nazi Germany from *The Ghosts of Sodom*. when Fulci recovers, Filippo informs him that he has just run amock, smashed the crew's camera and tried to rip off the interviewer's clothes. Swharz, having now watched all of Fulci's films, suggests hypnosis. Once Fulci is under, the psychiatrist inserts post-hypnotic commands to be triggered by the sound of a buzzer: *"You'll do everything I tell you when you hear this sound. Your mind will make you live scenes you think are real. You will slowly be possessed by madness. You'll think you've committed terrible crimes"*. Swharz then embarks on a chain of grisly murders, beginning with a gruesome attack on a prostitute. Fulci arrives at the scene and thinks he's done it. Rushing away, he heads off to a location film shoot but his car breaks down en route. When he arrives at the cemetery where the scene is to be filmed, he finds that the assistant director and producer have started without him. Back at home Fulci tries to relax, but is plagued by visions of violence. Fleeing the house, he goes for a drive, but Swharz follows and commits three more killings that Fulci believes himself to have committed. After hallucinating that he's run over the vagrant character from *Touch of Death*, the exhausted auteur returns home and phones his friend Inspector Gabrielli, intending to make a 'confession', but Gabrielli is out. Fulci drives to Gabrielli's home and Swharz follows with his buzzer device. Fulci lets himself into his friend's house, but suffers visions of Gabrielli's family being stabbed, chainsawed and decapitated. He staggers back outside to be greeted by the returning policeman, who reassures him that his family are safely on holiday in Sardinia. "If you're trying to create a sensation like you do in your films, this time you've goofed", the cheerful Inspector tells him. At home, Swharz strangles his contemptuous wife with piano wire: his plan to frame Fulci as a serial killer is just a cover to get away with killing her. Fulci suffers one more blast of violent imagery and faints in the middle of a field. He comes round to discover a cat digging up the loosely buried remains of another Swharz victim. As Fulci scrapes soil from the dead features, Inspector Gabrielli appears behind him. Before Fulci can protest his innocence, Gabrielli informs him that Swharz has been shot dead by police who were trailing Fulci and caught the mad psychiatrist in the act ... Fulci and the beautiful Nurse Lilly sail off in the yacht, 'Perversion'. He follows the girl into the cabin-quarters and we hear the sound of a chainsaw, followed by Lilly's terrified screams. Fulci emerges with a basket of body parts and attaches severed hands onto fishing hooks. Surely Lucio isn't really a mad killer after all? No of course not. It's the last shot of his new film, captured by a film crew sailing alongside. Bidding goodbye to his colleagues and the audience, Lucio happily sails off to sea with his leading lady.

About the production: Some time in 1989, Luigi Nannerini and Antonino Lucidi, producers of *Touch of Death* and *The Ghosts of Sodom*, decided to cease trading as Distribuzione Alpha Cinematografica. They re-emerged in 1990 with another short-lived company, Executive Cine TV s.r.l., and kicked off with the wildest and wooliest film of Lucio Fulci's later years, *Nightmare Concert*, a meta-horror tale about the trials and travails of an Italian goremonger. *"It's Eraserhead made by an old man,"* claimed Lucio Fulci to Howard Berger in 1996[19], offering what has to be the most damning indictment of old age ever defined by a major filmmaker. In truth, as noted by Fulci's then assistant Michele De Angelis[20], *Nightmare Concert*, far from being a vanity project or some kind of artistic statement, was created in a hurry in order to placate Nannerini and Lucidi, who were considering legal action after Fulci broke his contract by pulling out of 'No Human Factor'!

Nightmare Concert incorporates a bewildering amount of footage from other films, not all of it shot by Fulci. To begin with, we get copious clips from his recent films *Touch of Death* and *The Ghosts of Sodom*, but in addition the film culls the 'gory bits' from *Non aver paura della zia Marta* (Mario Bianchi, 1988), *Luna di sangue* (Enzo Milioni, 1989), *Hansel and Gretel* (Giovanni Simonelli and Lucio Fulci, 1988), *Bloody Psycho* (Leandro Lucchetti, 1989) and *Massacre* (Andrea Bianchi, 1989). All five of these were produced by Lucidi and Nannerini as part of the 'Lucio Fulci Presents' series, so there was no difficulty authorising use of the clips to spice up Fulci's new film. Fulci did not cannibalise his recently completed *Demonia* (presumably because Ettore Spagnuolo and Giuseppe Massaro hadn't yet given up hope of securing a proper release for it), nor was he granted permission to graverob the gory bits from his Dania-Reteitalia TV productions *The House of Clocks* and *The Sweet House of Horrors*, despite them having languished untransmitted for two years. Another of the 'Lucio Fulci presents' titles, Gianni Martucci's *Red Monks*, was passed over, as was a recent 'odd-one-out' for Distribuzione Alpha Cinematografica, Umberto Lenzi's *Le porte dell'inferno*, even though it plays very much like a tribute to Fulci, with its spider attacks, maggotty corpses and cobwebbed caverns leading to Hell. Perhaps Lenzi, a contemporary of Fulci's and a proud man with a long career behind him, looked askance at the idea of handing over his 'best bits' to another production, even one of Lucio Fulci's!

Review: *"A woman hacked to death with an axe, her face cleaved in half. Another strangled. Yet another hanged. Someone chopped to bits by a chainsaw. Or drowned in boiling water... throat torn out by a maddened cat... burned alive... buried alive... tortured... scalded... stabbed... sawn in two... crucified... decapitated..."* The humid imaginings of The Marquis de Sade? A National Viewers & Listeners Association report on a recent video release? No, we're hearing the troubled mind of Lucio Fulci as he sweats it out at the writing desk, letting his imagination run wild for the script of a new film. Simultaneously disappointing and hilarious, Fulci's grisliest film for eight years is packed with gratuitous carnage, but sadly it suffers from a near-complete absence of *cervello*. Anyone who found his earlier films beautiful and disturbing will probably consider this shambolic effort a severe let-down, bearing none of the haunting flourishes of his best work. On the other hand, only a fool would attempt to deny the appeal of the excessive scenes of violence in Lucio Fulci's films, and the audacity of *Nightmare Concert*'s relentless torrent of gore makes for often hysterical viewing. The lesson? Try not to take it too seriously.

above:
Promotional art for *Nightmare Concert* (as *Un gatto nel cervello* – literally translated as 'A Cat in the Brain').

top left:
Fulci aboard his yacht, 'Perversion'.

opposite page:
The Bracciano Chain Saw Massacre (these scenes were filmed just yards from Fulci's home at the time).

below:
Fulci's psychiatrist Professor Swharz (David L. Thompson) gives his wife (Melisa Longo) the benefit of his years of experience.

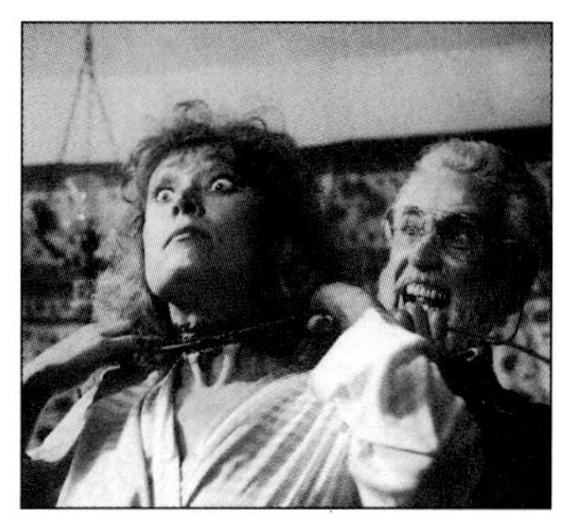

above:
Fulci fishes for ideas at the end of *Nightmare Concert*.

below:
After shooting scenes of extreme violence in a new movie, Fulci finds his usual plate of steak tartar impossible to face.

bottom:
A troubled Fulci sees a disabled neighbour whilst on his way to see a psychiatrist (an encounter which precipitates visions of yet more gruesome mutilation).

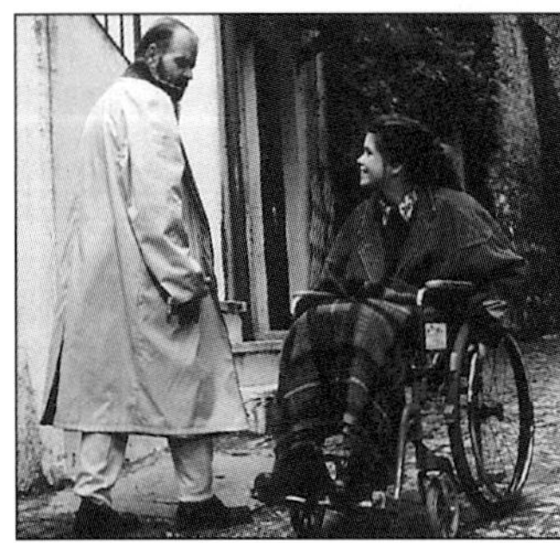

If violence isn't enough to maintain your interest, turning to the plot is unlikely to help. What we get is little more than a hasty sketch; Fulci consults a psychiatrist about the gory visions afflicting him away from the movie set but the psychiatrist is really a murderer, who uses his knowledge of Fulci's mental problems to frame him for the killings. Be prepared for disappointment, too, if the idea of Fulci waxing autobiographical piques your curiosity, because there's little in the way of personal analysis or revelation. Few directors, having chosen to play themselves in a movie, would leave their character so obstinately under-developed. Even a gratuitous display of narcissism would have been preferable to Fulci's disconsolate meandering. He seems satisfied just to mooch through his role with barely a desultory flicker of animation.

Although punctuated by grisly visions of death, putrefaction and dismemberment, the mood of the film is almost as facetious as *Touch of Death*. Insane psychiatrist Egon Swharz (David L. Thompson) is as much of a send-up and a caricature as Halsey's 'Lester Parson' in the earlier film. His 'crazy' grins and goggle-eyed mirth squander what could have been an interesting idea. Considering Fulci's defiantly downbeat approach throughout the preceding twenty years, such misplaced levity is extremely jarring. Frankly, there are Ray Dennis Steckler films with more gravitas than *Nightmare Concert*. Nevertheless, Fulci insists upon reminding us of his past glories, referencing earlier films which played the genre game straight: re-utilising music from *The Beyond*, for instance, and making a number of visual allusions to that film. Fun though the film may be when watched purely for its grisly scenes, it's hard not to feel quietly depressed by *Nightmare Concert*'s prosaic photography, graceless editing and complete lack of emotional impact.

The fact that Lucio Fulci saw fit to direct a self-portrait at this point, however rudimentary, suggests that he was aiming to capitalise on his increasing cult stature. After all, hadn't he recently been elevated to brand-name status by the 'Lucio Fulci presents' series? This seems to have been the seed from which *Nightmare Concert* grew. Sadly, though, I don't think this film will ever contribute towards the respect he so obviously craved.

In his last few years, Fulci would often assert that *Nightmare Concert* had been 'ripped off' by noted American horror specialist Wes Craven, as the uncredited inspiration for his reflexive horror film *Wes Craven's New Nightmare* (1994). Craven's film pulled a meta-move on the 'Freddy Krueger' franchise (which the director had set in motion with *A Nightmare on Elm Street* in 1984) by foregrounding the *Elm Street* film series itself within the fiction. What's more, it included Craven himself as 'Wes Craven', Freddy's writer-creator.

But of course Fulci didn't invent the idea of a film director appearing as himself in one of his fictions – Jean Cocteau played himself in *Le testament d'Orphée* (1960), Derek Jarman appeared as himself in his apocalyptic blast *The Last of England* (1987), and Alejandro Jodorowsky turns up in his mind-blowing film *The Holy Mountain* (1973) as a mystic guru leading the cast through his story-odyssey towards, if not enlightenment, then one hell of a wrap. And while Woody Allen's *Deconstructing Harry* (1998) doesn't literally star the director as himself, it does employ a highly reflexive onion-skin structure so that Allen may dissect his perceived role as a manipulator of personal relationships in both art and life. What these successful forays into reflexive cinema share is a commitment to lived experience, and a desire to invest modernist devices with passion and feeling. *Wes Craven's New Nightmare* peddles the idea that evil can escape from films into the real world... but only if they're cheap, badly made rip-offs of good work like his own. At least Fulci plays a director tormented by his *own* creations, instead of piously suggesting (as Craven does) that other people's 'lesser' work is to blame for the mayhem (Fulci certainly isn't including other directors' work as self-exculpation). *Nightmare Concert* is less self-serving than *Wes Craven's New Nightmare* but it's still a failure, because it has virtually nothing of personal importance invested in it. You have to wonder why Fulci bothered with a plot based around the psychiatrist's couch in the first place, because he's totally uninterested in revealing anything about himself. Here is a man who most certainly had demons, whose life was full of pain and trauma and difficulty, whose relations with the world seemed so often tense and fractious. Yet all we can glean is that he must have suffered depression relating to his work; a grudging revelation, fleetingly expressed, and laced (understandably, given recent efforts like *The Ghosts of Sodom*) with hints of a sense of futility. There is – quite amazingly, given the self-portrait format – no sense of personal reflection. Although the man in this film is a horror director responsible for extreme violent imagery, we never learn *why* he feels driven (or forced) to make this sort of film.

There is one scene that shows what *Nightmare Concert* could have been if Fulci had been more ambitious and more honest. Arriving late for a location shoot, he sees a sinister fog shrouding the road ahead, but in fact it's only the dry ice machine pumping out smoke: the producer and assistant director have started without him. There's something so melancholy about this, suggesting a deep insecurity on Fulci's part; as if he feared, at this stage in his career, despite playing the *auteur*, despite being a 'brand', that he might find himself dispensible, ready for the scrap-heap. The idea of the artist being shouldered out, made redundant, has the ring of truth to it as a genuine fear (it's a bad dream notion that drives key scenes in Peter Greenaway's *The Belly of an Architect* and Charlie Kaufman's *Synecdoche New York*). By revealing such a significant self-doubt in this context, Fulci comes closer to demonstrating artistic seriousness – and the irony otherwise so elusive to him – than anywhere else in his later work.

Federico Fellini had shown that to reveal personal angst and fantasy merely switches one game of appearances for another; his masterpiece *8½* (1963) demonstrated how to have your cake and eat it, creating entrancing (award-winning) drama out of the raw material of a director's self-consciousness and fear of failure. But Fellini was still a young man when he made *8½*; by the time the cameras rolled on *Nightmare Concert* Fulci was in his sixties. Perhaps he left it too late, but Fulci was never really an *auteur* in the accepted *Cahiers du Cinema* or Andrew Sarris fashion anyway. Arriving at the lowest ebb of his career, we should not, I suppose, subject the film to the sort of heightened expectation that would have made more sense in the early 1980s. Viewed in a lighter way, putting aside the desire for a more serious and revealing self-portrait, it's hard to watch *Nightmare Concert* without laughter, inspired not by ridicule of its flaws but enjoyment of its gory delights. Admittedly, when talking about a director fond of quoting Artaud or Balzac in interviews, settling for a barrel of gory laughs can seem to be setting your sights rather low: as though Luis Buñuel had played himself in a movie and then spent the whole film dropping his trousers in church. It would take a harder heart than mine, however, not to feel affection for Fulci as he sails off in his yacht, the good ship 'Perversion', at the end of the film, waving gaily to the camera with his arm around the buxom Paola Cozzo. Ciao Lucio! We didn't get to know you, but have a good trip...

Original Italian title
Voci dal profondo

Italy

Alternative titles
Voices from Beyond (UK video/DVD)
Voix profondes (FR DVD)
'Deep Voices'
Urla dal profondo (IT video)
'Screams from the Deep'
Voix d'outre tombe (FR video)
'Voices from Beyond the Grave'

Production companies
Executive Cine TV s.r.l.
Scena Group s.r.l.

Video/DVD/Blu-ray running times (adjusted)
ECV video (Italy) 91m 08s
Tr-State video (UK) 88m 47s

Censorship
Italian censor certificate 86776
issued 13 June 1991

Release information
Screened at the Cannes Film Festival Market 11 May 1991
No further cinema screenings

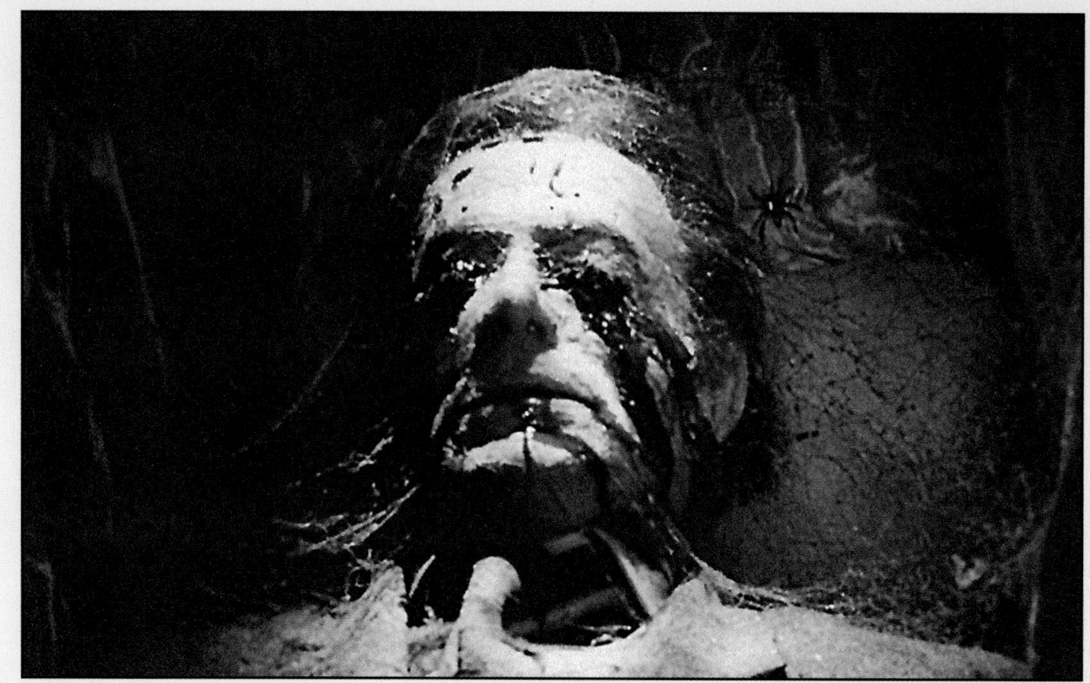

Voices from Beyond

1991

Directed by Lucio Fulci. executive producers: Luigi Nannerini & Antonino Lucidi for Executive Cine TV Srl. subject Lucio Fulci & Daniele Stroppa, from a story by Lucio Fulci, published in the Gazzetta di Firenze. screenplay: Lucio Fulci & Pietro [Piero] Regnoli. director of photography: Sandro Grossi. music by Stelvio Cipriani; published by B.M.G. Ariola. editor: Vincenzo Tomassi. production manager: Romualdo Buzzanca. unit manager: Stefano Bartolini. assistant director: Camilla Fulci. continuity: Anita Borgiotti. camera operator: Andrea Busiri Vici. assistant cameraman: Fabio Leoni. grips: Vincenzo Luzzi & Nello Putzu. electricians: Roberto Stiffi & Giovanni Biagiotti. costumes: Roberta Ciotti. make-up: Pino Ferranti. hairdressing: Maria Teresa Carrera. wardrobe: Lucia Viglino. props: Roberto Aneglucci & Paolo Sperati. paymaster: Antonino Lucidi. production secretaries: Roberto Lucidi & Marco Lucidi. stills: Luca Spataro. assistant editors: Pietro Tomassi & Paola Tomassi. boom: Roberto Barbieri. sound studios: Cooperativa di Lavoro; Fono Roma srl. mixage: Antonio Anastasi. sound effects: G.J.S.T.A.R. Movie. musical consultant: Gianluca Podio. equipment: Cine Luce. generators: C.S. Cinematografica srl. Scena Group srl and Executive Cine TV srl wish to thank Fiat spa; Brizimas Fashio (Rome); Ida Macallè (Rome); B.B. Mode (Florence); Boutique Matilde (Rome); Attica; Vittoria Colonna (Rome). processing laboratory: Telecolor spa. film stock: Fuji Color. 'this film is dedicated to my few real friends, in particular to Clive Barker and Claudio Carabba'.

Cast: Duilio Del Prete (Giorgio Mainardi). Karina Huff (Rosie Mainardi). Pascal Persiano (Mario Mainardi). Lorenzo Flaherty (Tommy, 'Gianni'). Bettina Giovannini (Lucy Mainardi). Frances Nacmen [Nacman] (Hilda Mainardi). Paolo Paoloni (Grandpa Mainardi). Sacha Maria Darwin (Dorie, the housekeeper). Antonella Tinazzo (Rita). Damiano Azzos (David). Rosamaria Grauso (young Rosie). *Uncredited:* Lucio Fulci (pathologist). Tomasso Felleghy (restaurant manager). Robert Daniels (doctor).

Synopsis: Giorgio Mainardi, a wealthy financier, collapses and dies of internal haemorrhage, possibly an ulcer. His daughter Rosie arrives for the reading of the will and finds the family squabbling over the estate. Giorgio's stepmother Hilda Mainardi refuses permission for an autopsy. Meanwhile, Hilda's son Mario is having an affair with Giorgio's wife Lucy. Giorgio's spirit remains conscious after death and from his coffin he tries to communicate with Rosie. He enters her dreams and begs her to discover who in the family was responsible for his death. She must hurry, for as his corpse rots away so too does his power to communicate. At the funeral, the mourners think back to their bitter relationships with the dead man. At the reading of the will, it's revealed that Giorgio has left his entire estate to Rosie. Lucy is to be allowed to remain at the house; she is furious that no provision has been made for their other child, David, a little boy Giorgio believed was not his. Despite Hilda's objections, an autopsy goes ahead. Rosie and her boyfriend Gianni (a medical student at the lab where Giorgio's autopsy was conducted) discover that bottles containing Giorgio's organs have been 'accidentally' smashed, but Gianni says he'd found minute splinters of glass in the intestines before the accident occurred. He suggests going to the police but Rosie insists they investigate themselves. Lucy tells Rosie that Giorgio had returned from a visit to his mistress the night of his collapse. Did Rita put broken glass in Giorgio's food? Rosie talks to the maitre d' at the restaurant but he tells her the couple ate and drank nothing, instead having a furious row. Rosie returns to the house and discovers her drink has been poisoned. She talks to Dorie, little David's nanny, who says only she, David and Rosie's mother were in the house the night of Giorgio's collapse. Rosie sees David playing with a mortar and pestle. She confronts her mother, who acts oddly. After a dream, Rose wakes with the answer. The glass shards had been concealed in the ice-cubes in Giorgio's late-night drink. Hilda admits plotting to kill Giorgio, adding that Rose's mother had also been involved. In case of discovery, David had been encouraged to play with the mortar and pestle, grinding a lightbulb into the water in the ice-tray as a 'game'. Thus Hilda hoped to explain away the murder as a tragic accident. Rosie tells Hilda she will leave the conspirators to fester in the Mainardi house instead of informing the police. As she leaves, she tells Hilda that Giorgio will haunt them to the grave.

About the production: At last persuading Fulci to deliver the fourth film he'd promised (after *Touch of Death*, *The Ghosts of Sodom* and *Nightmare Concert*), Luigi Nannerini and Antonino Lucidi (now trading as Executive Cine TV) joined forces with Augusto Caminito's Scena Group for *Voices from Beyond*, resulting in better production values and a slightly longer shooting period. However the game was nearly up for Nannerini and Lucidi, who made two more films before apparently quitting the industry – 1991's *Una donna da guardare*, a dire sex comedy directed by Michele Quaglieri about a pot-bellied middle-aged fashion designer and his steamy adventures with busty models, and *Le occasioni di una signora per bene* (dir: Pasquale Fanetti, 1993), a film that received a few Italian provincial playdates on the declining adult circuit. Fulci's daughter Camilla Fulci handled script supervision duties on *Una donna da guardare*, as she'd done on the 'Lucio Fulci presents' films and her father's own recent work, before settling in as assistant director on a slew of Joe D'Amato's hardcore films made between 1995 and 1997 (e.g. *Le bambole del führer*; *Irreparable Damage*; *Tarzan-X: Shame of Jane*; *120 Days of Anal*; *Provocation*).

Caminito was on firmer ground than Lucidi and Nannerini, having entered into an equity partnership with Silvio Berlusconi's Reteitalia in 1987. All was not plain sailing though – he had recently emerged from an acrimonious legal battle with Klaus Kinski over his film *Paganini* – but on a brighter note his flirtation with international co-production (via his company Scena International) had brought forth impressive results in the shape of Abel Ferrara's *King of New York*. (Caminito later worked with Ferrara again, producing his 2014 film *Pasolini*.)

Fulci was proud of *Voices from Beyond*, and he was not alone in seeing its qualities. *Variety* reviewed it positively, noting, *"Italian horror specialist Lucio Fulci takes a new tack with 'Voices from Beyond', a stylish Gothic thriller that features several novel scares."*[21] However, Fulci was reluctant to spread any of the love to his actors, telling interviewer Massimo Lavagnini: *"It's a wonderful movie with the wrong cast. Karina Huff is unpleasant, Del Prete is completely out of the role, the mother-in-law is too wicked and you understand immediately that she is the killer."*[22] Surely if we can guess that the mother-in-law is the villain, that's a flaw in the directing, not the acting? It's statements like this that make Fulci a difficult person to admire in his later years.

Review: After so many disappointments, *Voices from Beyond* is a marked improvement. A coherent plot and a skilful technical team combine to make this project Fulci's best since *The Devil's Honey*, and the last really watchable film he'd ever make. The tale is told without the intrusion of facile humour and elegant use is made of tracking shots, crane shots, focus-pulling and slow motion. This really is a return to a more stylish brand of filmmaking after the bare-bones mise-en-scène found in most of the late eighties films.

The story concerns businessman Giorgio Mainardi, whom we meet on his death bed, surrounded by his family and vomiting gouts of blood. As he dies, he gasps: *"Why?"* When he finally expires, the camera ascends above the body, gazing down at the bloodied sheets while nurses move in slow motion to uncouple the deceased from his drips (far more effective than the similar scenes in *Ænigma*). The film then charts the efforts of loving daughter Rosie to solve the mystery of her father's death, assisted by his spirit, which talks to her in her dreams...

The rest of the Mainardi family are a mixed bag of secretive, venal or downright hostile figures. We meet Lucy, Giorgio's frigid wife, Hilda, his wicked stepmother, and Mario, his sponging stepbrother. Then there's little David, Rosie's younger brother, who may not be Giorgio's real son. With three generations, a remarriage, and questionable paternity to deal with, not to mention two lots of infidelity (Lucy is having an illicit fling with Mario, Giorgio had been seeing a mistress, Rita) it takes some effort to gain a clear picture of the dysfunctional Mainardi clan. The confusion is not helped by the fact that Mainardi's stepmother looks barely older than he is; evidently his father remarried a much younger woman. This tangled melodrama, which unfolds like a macabre episode of the American TV soap *Dallas*, relies upon such ancient devices as the reading of the will and the murderous family plot. However, Fulci energises the standard motifs and stirs in a few new ideas, including an inventive murder technique worthy of Agatha Christie. An air of conviction redeems the clichés, and whilst the film isn't exactly jam-packed with outrageous violence, it feasts upon the grisly scenes with something like the relish we associate with vintage Fulci. He reserves a neat little gruesome cameo for himself as a pathologist lifting loops of intestine out of Mainardi's corpse, and best of all we see the progressive deterioration of Giorgio Mainardi's corpse in gratifyingly gross detail, with maggots and bubbling putrescence. (And it's here the film reveals its most imaginative twist. As the dead man decays, so too does his supernatural ability to communicate with his daughter. This limits the amount of time available and makes Rosie's investigation more compelling.) The decomposition of Giorgio's corpse, the shots of maggots and rotten eyeballs, and the spider hanging from a web between the dead man's face and the side of the coffin lend a 'Weird Tales' comic-strip vibe to the visuals, a welcome punctuation of the fantastique in what is essentially a soap-drama narrative. Fulci's zombies make a brief reappearance too, in a dream sequence experienced by the guilty Mario, whose grasping behaviour belies a tormented guilty conscience, and Fulci's trademark eye violence pops up again during a bizarre and well-designed nightmare in which Rita sees Giorgio cutting up eyeballs in a plate of scrambled eggs.

Voices from Beyond is a modest but mature work, and whereas *Nightmare Concert* gave nothing much away, it's tempting to speculate that Giorgio in *Voices from Beyond* is a closer glimpse of the director himself, in temperament if not in the precise detail of his personal relationships. Though not exactly a self-portrait, it's surely an example of certain facets. On the downside, it's a pity Fulci didn't see fit to show Giorgio's tender side. His daughter clearly loves him but frankly we're left wondering why: amid all the family flashbacks the only one from her point of view shows him berating her for entering a room without knocking! He's cruel, short-tempered, brusque and aggressive, and his callous treatment of his mistress, Rita, who really does love him, is frightful. Even his solicitous manner towards Rosie in her dreams could simply be a means to get her to investigate his death. One extra scene showing him capable of kindness and affection would have made a lot of difference.

There are other problems with the film, chiefly in the form of lead actress Karina Huff, a Linda McCartney lookalike with an awkward, low-energy acting style, and I have my reservations about the gauzy filters used for much of the film, something Fulci seems to have preferred in his later years. But it's good to see him firmly in control of a project, whatever the flaws. After the slump of his late 1980s output, this last peak on the oscilloscope of his career is perhaps the best way to remember Fulci's latter days.

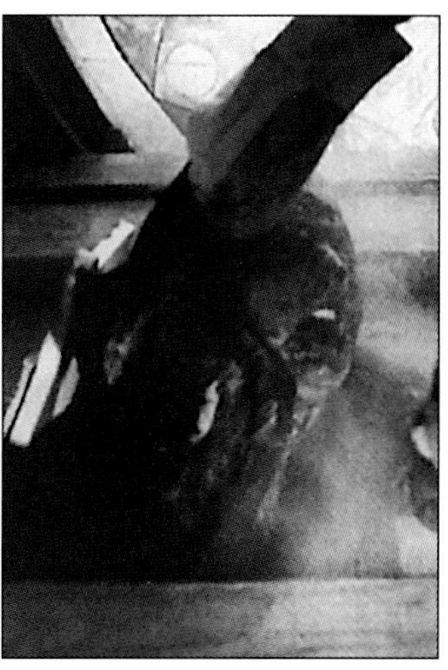

above:
Mario (Pascal Persiano) suffers from dreams in which the dead burst from their tombs to kill him.

below:
Giorgio's body undergoes an autopsy.

Giorgio Mainardi, a patriarch with many enemies... and a loyal daughter.

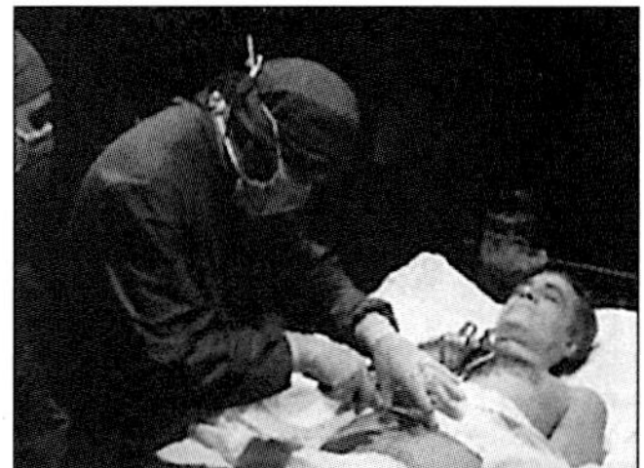

Original Italian title
Le porte del silenzio

Translation
'The Door to Silence'

Italy

Alternative titles
Door to Silence
(English-language export title)
Door to Silent (Eureka Film
International trade advert)
Door into Silence (USA alt. DVD)
El enigma de la muerte (ARG video)
'The Enigma of Death'

Production company
Filmirage (Rome)

Theatrical distributor
Eureka Film International
(no distribution deal struck)

Video/DVD/Blu-ray running times (adjusted)
Raging Thunder DVD (USA) 90m 39s
Severin DVD (USA) 87m 00s

Shooting period
Shooting April-May 1991

Release information
London Eurofest screening
11 December 1994
Rome Cine-club Detour screening
05 April 1998

Door to Silence

1991

Directed by Lucio Fulci [as H. Simon Kittay]. executive producer: John Gelardi [Aristide Massaccesi] for Filmirage S.r.l. story & screenplay: Jerry Madison [Lucio Fulci], from a short story published in Le lune nere. director of photography: John C. Fredericks [Giancarlo Ferrando]. music composed, arranged & conducted by Franco Piana. editor: Kathleen Stratton [Rosanna Landi]. production designer: Max Slowing [Massimo Lentini]. art director: William Jackson. casting: Diana Thomas. production supervisor: Dennis Curren. production manager [IT]: Vincenzo Gallo; [export]: Michelle Gelardi. production coordinator: Glenn Raynolds. 1st assistant director: Camille Folsom [Camilla Fulci]. 2nd assistant director: Marc White. script supervisor: Dawn Dreiling. stunt coordinator: Dave Golino. camera operator: Dan Slonisko [Daniele Massaccesi]. 1st assistant camera [IT]: Alessandro Capuccio, [export]: Peter Manno. 2nd assistant camera: Andrew W. Hoffman. key grip: Mat Giordano [Matteo Giordano]. best boy: Russ Zinneman. grips: Carlos Romero & John Rensen. gaffer [IT]: Armando Moreschini, [export]: Kurt Sterling. best boy generator operator: Jack Martin. electricians: Gene Baron & Ronald Martin. costume designer: Laurette M. Gemser [Laura Gemser]. make-up artist [IT]: Pietro Tenoglio, [export]: J.J. Kostic. hair dresser: Joan Ozment. special effects: Ross J. La Manta. property master: Rudy Roberts [Rodolfo Ruzza]. assistant art director: Diane O'Brian. wardrobe assistant: Julie Winn. production secretary: Paula Gonzales [Paola Bianchini]. production assistants: Jonathan Fuller & Connie Falco. transportation coordinator: Rose Scalisi. transportation captain: Roger Schmalberg. drivers: Kevin Grant & Julian Gardner. production accountant: Otello Thompson [Otello Tomassini]. still photographer: Martha Barbosa. catering by Benedict's Restaurant. assistant editors [IT]: Emanuela Fabrizi], [export]: Mary Abbene & [both] Chris Eber. titles & opticals by Studio Mafera. negative cutter: Tosca Spadaccioli. sound man: Peter Parish [Piero Parisi]. location sound: Richard Castleman. boom man: George Bertuccelli [Giorgio Bertuccelli]. re-recorded at Cinecittà. sound editor: Art Dooley. dialogue editor: Chris Taylor. supervising sound effects: Giulio De Angeli. sound effects by Bruno Verrazzo's Croma Film International Snc. original soundtrack music performed by Franco Piana Big Band and Piana – Valdambrini Sextet. music producer: Franco De Gemini. music recorded at Forum Studio (Rome). music released on Beat Records label. original publishers: Idra Music (S.I.A.E.); Beat Records (S.I.A.E.) – PA.GI. (S.I.A.E.). special thanks to Louisiana Film Commission; The Police of Madisonville.processing prints by Telecolor Spa. Kodacolor. filmed on location in Louisiana (U.S.A.).

Cast: John Savage (Melvin Devereux). Sandi Schultz (Death). Richard Castleman (hearse driver). Jennifer Loeb (Margie). Elizabeth Chugden (Sylvia Devereux, Melvin's wife). Joe 'Cool' Davis (minister). Bob Shreves (judge). Mary Coulson (Aunt Martha Devereux). Fred Lewis (bartender). Maureen Rocquin (juke box girl). Dunca Boyer (Cajun hunter).

Synopsis: New Orleans. Whilst attending the funeral of his father, Melvin Deveraux meets a beautiful young woman who addresses him by name, although he cannot remember having met her before. After an enigmatic exchange, Devereux drives away, motoring aimlessly before deciding to ignore warning barriers and head onto a closed freeway. Police follow and he is forced to turn aside. His car breaks down in a dilapidated area of town and the mysterious woman approaches again, suggesting that he try a mechanic located nearby. They then proceed to a motel, apparently for sex, but whilst Devereux is in the bathroom the woman disappears. A message written in lipstick on the bedroom mirror informs him that 'the time is not yet right'.

Having collected his repaired vehicle, Devereux encounters a hearse on the road ahead. When he attempts to overtake it, the driver (Richard Castleman) deliberately swerves to prevent him. Turning off onto progressively more treacherous country routes, he nearly gets stranded in muddy terrain and barely negotiates a rickety wooden bridge

At last finding his way back to the main road, he stops off at a pub where the hearse too is parked outside. In a drunken altercation Devereux challenges the driver to reveal whose body he is transporting. The folded ribbon adorning the casket seen inside the hearse bears a name tantalisingly similar to Devereux's own. The confused, now frightened man follows the hearse to a church where an all-black congregation is mourning at another funeral. Devereux drunkenly disrupts the proceedings attempting to look inside the casket. Eventually he ends up at a funeral home where all the corpses are labelled 'Melvin Devereux'. He finds his doppelgänger lying dead in one of the caskets and tries to touch it, but it disappears beneath his outstretched hand.

Back on the road, Devereux picks up a hitch-hiker and tries to respond to her seductive proposals, but he can't perform. He drives onto a river barge as it transports a handful of vehicles, including the omnipresent hearse, across to the other side. He rips open the hearse door and tries to open the casket which bears his name. The hearse driver intervenes and there is a struggle. Devereux is apprehended and arrested. Next we see him in court receiving a fine for defiling the casket. Driving away, he stops to visit a palmist who tells him he's been dead for several hours. She falls dead herself on receiving a telephone call from a Mr. Devereux.

Devereux is once more on the road, driving nowhere. He overtakes the hearse only to crash headlong into an oncoming lorry. His car clock stops at 7:29, the same time as in the film's prologue, where a briefly seen crash had appeared to be the cause of his father's death. The mysterious woman observes from a distance before driving off in her car; its numberplate is D.E.A.T.H.

About the production: The shooting of Fulci's last film *Door to Silence* began on 29 April 1991, and the film was ready for purchase at the Santa Monica film market in October that year. The production company Filmirage (run by director-producer Joe D'Amato) was still hawking it the following year but seems to have given up by the Spring of 1992. After another two years Filmirage itself would fold, but not before rattling off six more D'Amato productions. The first of these, *A Woman's Secret* (1992) was shot on location in Louisiana during the same production block as *Door to Silence* with many of the same crew. The remaining five films (*Una tenera storia*, *Sul filo del rasoio* aka *Instinct*, *Contamination .7*, *I racconti della camera rossa* and *China and Sex*) followed in the next two years, after which D'Amato shot exclusively on video, producing hardcore porn until his death in 1999.

As if Filmirage's failure to secure *Door to Silence* a theatrical release were not bad enough, Fulci suffered another insult: his directing credit was replaced on the English-language print by a ridiculous pseudonym, 'H. Simon Kittay'. Although Kittay is indeed a real name (there was a Seth Kittay working at the time for HBO and Disney), it's not one that should ever have been considered: it's a slap in the face for a director with so many successes behind him. Even the 'H', appended as if to avoid confusion with all the other Simon Kittays out there, feels like a sour joke at Fulci's expense. The director explained what happened, in colourful terms, to Massimo Lavagnini: *"It was the fault of a woman with shitty breath, a despicable being called Lucaroni. She told Aristide that 'Fulci isn't currently fashionable... let's call him Simon Kittay' [...] She isn't working for Massaccesi anymore, hah!"*[23] (The woman to whom Fulci is referring is Fiorella Lucaroni, sales manager for Eureka Film International who worked on *Door to Silence*'s marketing alongside assistant sales manager Francesca Massaccesi.)

Afterwards, Fulci's feelings about *Door to Silence* veered wildly across the highway, from pride to condemnation. To Lavagnini he was very positive: *"Recently I was invited to a festival in London where they screened the print with the original soundtrack. It has been an incredible success. It's an extraordinary movie."*[24] (I attended the screening Fulci describes, in London in 1994, and I can tell you that *Door to Silence* was not 'an incredible success'! At best, polite puzzlement greeted the film.) In America, to Howard Berger, Fulci struck a very different tone: "Door to Silence *was the last film I made before my accident. Never projected once. It was based on a short story I wrote [...] Aristide Massaccesi read it and said, 'Why don't we make this into a film?' I said, 'This film will be a flop! It's just the story of a man driving round in his car! The audience won't give a damn! He insists. We go into production [...] When we finish, Massaccesi says 'It's a good film'. I say, 'It's a flop! You'll still pay me, but it's a flop!'"*[25]

Review: Opening with aerial shots of a car driving across a long causeway, accompanied by Franco Piana's smooth but unadventurous jazz music, *Door to Silence* presents even the most avid fan of Lucio Fulci with a challenge to stay awake. Unlike *Zombi 3*, which we can afford to dismiss as a true Fulci film, this opus arrived on the fair winds of the director's self-endorsement. Sadly the admiration of its creator can't prevent it from landing with a dull thud on the screen as far as just about anyone else is concerned. *Door to Silence* wastes its wonderful title on a premise that would barely provide a mediocre half-hour's worth of television. At feature length it's impossible to avoid one's attention wandering, as the tale moves without grace to a predictable conclusion.

The unfortunate star, John Savage, once a striking actor who combined major league assignments for Michael Cimino (*The Deer Hunter*, 1978) with peculiar genre experiments for the likes of Curtis Harrington (*The Killing Kind*, 1973), here looks washed up and, in both senses of the word, wasted. Never mind his appearance though – actors on the skids can give strange, compelling performances – the problem lies in the astonishing idleness of the screenplay. His role requires him to drive, and drive, and drive... and drive. Down blandly photographed country roads, along partly overgrown dirt-tracks, over bridges. Sometimes he gets to go in reverse. *Duel* this ain't. A 'mysterious' woman is also on the road, sometimes ahead, sometimes behind. Who's following who? Who's looking for who? Why is it so hard to care? This movie makes going to the cinema feel like a bad joke, and one can't help resenting the experience. My response was partly to laugh – not at any wit in the film's doggedly dire construction, but at myself, poor sucker; sitting there trying to figure out if there was some reason for the persistent repetition, or if we were just (excuse me) being taken for a ride. It's as if Fulci had decided to mock the producer for offering him the money.

Door to Silence doesn't even look like it was shot on film, instead it resembles a high-band video project. The quality of the image is relentlessly flat and unimaginatively framed – like a low-grade car commercial, stripped of special effects and pretention. John Savage must have experienced a distinct unreality effect in this 'Tale of the Unexceptional' as he drove around with a camera-crew but no ideas. Fulci's input seems limited to the occasional 'Turn left at the traffic lights' or 'Check the rear-view and pull out'. Actress Sandi Schultz adds little but a whiff of the air-brush to her role as 'Death', like a minor fashion model filling in time before a perfume-ad. It's not her fault, she could have been the next Isabelle Adjani for all the viewer can tell...

It's sad to bring the reviews to a close on such a poor film – put this effort to the back of your minds and recall the many highlights of Lucio's career. This is not the real epitaph for a director whose legacy contains marvels and terrors utterly beyond this final mess.

above:
The cover of Severin's DVD release.

opposite:
A skirmish with the hearse driver (Richard Castleman).

below:
Death (Sandi Schultz) in the rear-view mirror;
Melvin (John Savage) finds himself at the funeral parlour;
Melvin stops off for a double scotch, adding drink-driving to his karmic burden.

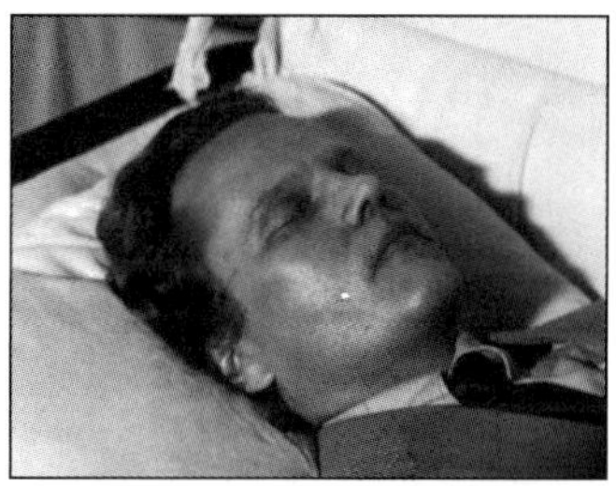

Posthumous Project

The Wax Mask

After ditching 'The Mummy', Fulci and Dario Argento decided upon a completely different source for a collaboration. Fulci suggested adapting a story by Gaston Leroux, Argento agreed, and so *The Wax Mask* was prepped as Fulci's next film. But which particular story by Leroux was Lucio Fulci thinking of? As the critic and film historian Tim Lucas explains at his Video Watchblog site, *"Articles sometimes link* [Wax Mask] *to a Gaston Leroux novel called* The Wax Museum *or* Mystery of the Wax Museum *depending on your reporter... but no such novel exists, and no screen credit was ultimately given. In the course of my collecting, I've now discovered that a short story exists, entitled* 'The Waxwork Museum', *which was collected in translation in a 1980 story compendium called* The Gaston Leroux Bedside Companion, *edited by Peter Haining. A foreword acknowledges that the translation by Alexander Peters first appeared in* Fantasy Book *in 1969, but no original French publication date is given. It very likely appeared in the 1910s-1920s, possibly prior to Paul Leni's classic silent picture* Waxworks *(1924)."*[26]

So, the source for *The Wax Mask* is Leroux's "The Waxwork Museum". Or is it? While puzzling over the question, I stumbled late at night upon "Wormwoodiana", a website for book collectors. There I found a fascinating discussion which sheds new light on the source of *The Wax Mask* while raising serious questions about the probity of anthologist Peter Haining. In a post dated 30 August 2012, Douglas A. Anderson (one of the creators of "Wormwoodiana") accuses Haining of fraudulently attributing rare tales by unknown or obscure writers to more established and collectable names, an allegation given further weight when another contributor to the site, Michel Parry, cites his own misgivings regarding Haining's Gaston Leroux anthology: *"When I read [Haining's] 1980 collection,* The Gaston Leroux Bedside Companion, *I had a nagging feeling that I had read one of the stories,* 'The Waxwork Museum', *somewhere else by another author. Eventually I realised I was thinking of a French play,* 'Figures de Cire', *by Andre de Lorde and Georges Montignac, the text of which I had read in the British Library. Intrigued, I did further research and found that Andre de Lorde had turned his play into a short story with the same title. Comparing the French text of that story with the 'Gaston Leroux translation' which appeared in Haining's book, I was able to establish that they were indeed the exact same story. The book's copyright page credits B.P. Singer Features Inc. (a syndication agency supplying 'fillers' to newspapers and magazines) for permission to reprint the translation by one Alexander Peters. It is entirely possible that Haining may have been convinced by the agency that he was buying bona-fide translations of Leroux stories. The president of B.P. Singer was, incidentally, Kurt Singer, himself the editor of many horror anthologies."*[27]

In a further posting, Douglas Anderson adds the coup de grâce: *"A little further digging shows that the 'Alexander Peters' translation is lifted word-for-word from the 1933 appearance under the title* 'Waxworks' *in the 1933* Creeps *volume,* 'Terrors', *where it is correctly attributed to Andre de Lorde."*[28]

To summarise, it's alleged that Peter Haining mis-attributed a story by a more obscure writer, Andre de Lorde, to the better-known author Gaston Leroux, as well as crediting another translator's work to one of his own pseudonyms. Leaving aside the allegations about Haining, this would seem to place the provenance of Fulci's *Wax Mask* project not with Gaston Leroux but instead with a far less celebrated playwright and author: Andre de Lorde, aka André de Latour, comte de Lorde (1869-1942).

However, it would be wrong to say that Andre de Lorde is a less significant figure than Leroux; indeed, when it comes to the films of Lucio Fulci he could hardly be more apropos. He worked by day as a librarian at the prestigious Bibliothèque de l'Arsenal in Paris, but in his free time he wrote tales of terror, murder, and madness that were then performed onstage by none other than the infamous Théâtre du Grand-Guignol in Paris, for whom he wrote at least a hundred plays between 1901 and 1926. Théâtre du Grand-Guignol performances were notorious for their extreme violence, presenting bloody eviscerations and dismemberments in so convincing a manner that audience members often fainted or vomited at the sight. It seems, therefore, quite delicious (especially for a film with the word 'mask' in the title) that beneath a veneer of literary respectability (Leroux) should lurk the spirit of a man whose work is synonymous with butcher-shop brutality of the most ghastly and revolting sort!

Of course the provenance of the 'Waxwork Museum' short story is just the tip of the iceberg when it comes to *The Wax Mask*'s inspiration. It's really André De Toth's film *House of Wax* (1953) which provides the strongest template for the project Fulci was planning. Nevertheless, it seems so very apt that the literary tale that first set Fulci's mind racing with the possibilities came from not from the pen of France's answer to Arthur Conan Doyle, but from the prince of Grand Guignol himself.

top right:
Fantastical set design in Paul Leni's *Waxworks* (1924), redolent of the bizarre catacombs in Fulci's *City of the Living Dead*.

below:
Vincent Price, diabolical inventor of a revolutionary new wax treatment, in André de Toth's *House of Wax* (1953). Note a young Charles Bronson in the background, as Igor.

Unmade Projects

1967
Sam Cooper's Gold

According to a news article in *Variety* dated 5 July 1967, this project was set to be directed by Fulci in Rome, August 1967, starring Gilbert Roland. However, within a week or two Fulci had departed the project and in August he began shooting *Operazione San Pietro*. 'Sam Cooper's Gold' was instead directed by Giorgio Capitani as *Ognuno per sé* ('Every Man for Himself') aka *The Ruthless Four*. Gilbert Roland did indeed play one of the major roles, alongside Van Heflin as the not-quite-eponymous Sam Cooper.

1972
Kamasutra at Fixed Prices

On 10 May 1972, a news article in *Variety* reported, *"Lucio Fulci is prepping 'Kamasutra at Fixed Prices' while filming 'Don't Torture a Duckling' for Medusa on exteriors down south."* The same project under a slightly different title ('Kamasutra at Fixed Rates') was mentioned again in *Variety* on 19 July 1972 and mooted for production in September. These are literally the only references to such a project I can find anywhere, and one can only speculate as to its subject. Perhaps, with one eye on Pasolini's *The Decameron* and *The Canterbury Tales*, or Bertolucci's *Last Tango in Paris* (which went before the cameras in February '72), Fulci was considering the Kama Sutra, the mother of all erotic source materials, for his own journey into sexual experimentation? On the other hand, the 'fixed prices' angle suggests a riff on the travails of the common man looking for exotic sex on a budget, in which case this would perhaps have been another Fulci comedy with Lando Buzzanca...

1972
Face of the Tiger

On 22 November 1972, *Variety* announced that Lucio Fulci *was "taking over from Carmello Bazzoni* [sic] *on the DC 7 project 'Face of the Tiger' probably paving the way for producer Giovanni Addessi to present Rod Steiger in the upcoming project."* However, it seems that Fulci did not in fact take control of the film...

'Face of the Tiger' was first announced in May 1971, when Italian producers DC 7 (a company run by Giovanni Addessi) told *Variety* that the film would start shooting in July. In August, Addessi announced that he was courting leading American character actor Rod Steiger for the project, with a *"tentative commitment"* from Steiger to begin shooting in September. However, by November production had still not started, although Addessi now claimed a February 1972 start date under Camillo Bazzoni's direction. At this point the project was put on ice for almost a year, until October 1972 when Bazzoni was once again announced as director. A few days later came the news that Fulci was taking over from Bazzoni, after which the story went cold for yet another year, until 3 October 1973, when commencement of production was announced in *Variety*: *"After a two-year wait, Giorgio Stegani finally started helming 'All the Faces of Violence' (originally called 'The Face of the Tiger') with Antonio Sabato topping the cast with Salvo Randone, Pier Paolo Capponi, Silvia Monti and 17-year-old beauty contest winner Monica Santorsola."* The film finally saw release in November 1974 under the Italian title *Milano: il clan dei Calabresi* (aka *The Last Desperate Hours*), with Camillo Bazzoni and Giovanni Addessi receiving co-scripting credit. Fulci's name does not appear and it would seem therefore that his involvement in this on-off production was abandoned when he found a more reliable project in 1973's *Zanna Bianca*.

1976
The Stepdaughter aka *La figliastra*

According to *Variety*, in June 1976 Lucio Fulci was due to begin directing a sex-comedy called *The Stepdaughter*, from a story and script by Luigi Angelo, Giuseppe Carbone and Piero Regnoli. Sonia Jeanine and Lucretia Love were lined up as the leads.**[29]** It wound up being directed by Edoardo Mulargia for the obscure and forebodingly named production company Austerity Film.

1980
The Mummy

A *Variety* article dated 23 January 1980 announced, *"When Lucio Fulci completes 'The Smugglers' in Naples for Primex Cinematografica, he helms 'The Mummy' for Pal Cinematografica."* Sadly this never happened, the only possible trace of it being the Egyptology theme of *Manhattan Baby* (a film regrettably short of marauding mummies) ... Maria Pia Gardini's short-lived company Pal Cinematografica (aka Pal International) made only two films, Umberto Lenzi's cross-dresser comedy *Scusi, lei è normale?* (1979) and an oddball Terry-Thomas/Gordon Mitchell comedy, *Febbre a 40* (1980). Something evidently went awry for Ms. Gardini after these two ... By September 1980 'The Mummy' had walked from Pal Cinematografica into the welcoming arms of Fulvio Lucisano's Italian International and Giulio Sbarigia's Selenia Cinematografica. Shooting was now apparently intended to start in May 1981 in the USA, back-to-back with another Fulci project, 'Bolero' (see below). However, much of Sbarigia's commitment was contingent on the success of another Fulci production waiting in the wings; *The Black Cat*. When *The Black Cat* did not perform as strongly as hoped, it seems 'The Mummy' was sent back to its sarcophagus...

I can find no connection between the aborted Fulci project and Frank Agrama's 1981 American-Egyptian-Italian co-production *Dawn of the Mummy*. Agrama, who moved from Italy to Hollywood in 1977, was back in Rome during April 1980 preparing his Mummy film, which ended up being shot on location in Cairo and New York.

1980
Bolero aka *They Call Him Bolero*

Announced on 3 September 1980 as a potential Selenia Cinematografica/Italian International co-production, 'Bolero', like 'The Mummy', was intended as a Fulci project to be shot in the USA in May 1981, but was contingent upon the commercial success of *The Black Cat*. Unlike 'The Mummy', it was still being mentioned as a possible production in May 1981, when it was referred to as 'They Call Him Bolero'. *Variety* explained, *"Both projects are mapped out but the final signal will come from box office at home and foreign sales on 'Black Cat.'"***[30]** Of course, as we know, that signal never came...

Quite what 'They Called Him Bolero' might have been about is anyone's guess, although it sounds reminiscent of spaghetti western titles like *They Call Me Trinity* (1972) and *They Call Him Veritas* (1972).

above:
The film that could have been Fulci's second western: *The Ruthless Four* (see *Sam Cooper's Gold*, opposite).

below:
Italian locandina for *Milano: il clan dei Calabresi* (see entry for *Face of the Tiger*).

Wednesday, May 12, 1982 VARIETY 225

THE SWORD OF SIEGFRIED

When the past meets the future

A FILM BY
LUCIO FULCI

Principal Photography starts October 1982

Produced by EMPIRE FILM s.r.l. · In association with ASTON FILMS Ltd.
4, Bream's Bldg.-Chancery Lane E.C.4 London · Telex 28778

At CANNES contact Hotel MARTINEZ · Rooms 257/258

However, it would have been eccentric, at best, to pitch a spaghetti western in 1980, as the genre had pretty much died out. Fulci's *Silver Saddle* (1978) was almost the last of its breed, and definitively the last to be directed by an Italian. Note: this unmade project was in no way associated with the 1981 Claude Lelouch film *Bolero*, nor did it presage the arrival in 1984 of the Bo Derek starring vehicle *Bolero* (although the latter did feature *New York Ripper* star Andrea Occhipinti in a steamy role as Bo's bullfighter lover).

1981
Dirty Star

With *The Black Cat* completed, producer Giulio Sbarigia announced plans for more Fulci films. *Variety* explained, *"If the Anglo-atmosphered thriller gets a good hand in the home market, Sbarigia will move ahead on [...] 'Dirty Star' – to roll in Georgia with a name actor from Hollywood."*[31] There's no indication of the type of film this might have been, although to me it suggests a western, with the 'star' being a sheriff's badge and the dirt being, possibly, a reference to 'dirty fighting'. Alternatively, perhaps 'Dirty Star' would have been an 'urban western' about a corrupt lawman? In any case, *The Black Cat* did not deliver the goods, and 'Dirty Star' bit the dust.

1982
Roman Black aka *Romano Nero*

In 1982, the French film magazine *L'Écran fantastique* published an illuminating interview with Fulci, conducted by Robert Schlockoff in January that year, just after Fulci had finished shooting *The New York Ripper* and a month or two before he started *Manhattan Baby*. In it he described a long cherished project: *"I have never been able to get it off the ground. I want to call it* Roman Black*; it's a study in power. Not a denunciation of power – this has been done so many times... but a thriller à la Chandler, Hammett or Irish, set in Ancient Rome at the end of the Empire. A new survey of the Fall of the Roman Empire in the form of a thriller."*[32]

1982
Siegried's Sword aka *The Sword of Siegfried*

'Siegfried's Sword' was first announced as a potential Lucio Fulci film in May 1982, and a mighty creation it promised to be. With heavyweight producer Edmondo Amati and his sons Sandro and Maurizio on board, and a budget set at a colossal ten to twelve million dollars, this sword-and-sorcery epic was clearly intended to make an impact. (Quite which of Amati's companies would have bankrolled the film is unclear: news reports in *Variety* named Regency Productions, whereas pre-release artwork listed two older Amati companies, Empire Films and Aston Films.) Location shooting was set for September or October 1982, and Amati let it be known that he was looking for an English or American leading man, preferably blond, to play the mythic hero. In early June he was "actively pre-selling" the film; and yet, by 23 June the project was dead.

So what would the story have been? Rather as *Zombie Flesh-Eaters* sought to sidestep criticism for ripping off George Romero by drawing upon earlier zombie imagery, perhaps Fulci and scriptwriter Gianfranco Clerici thought they could avoid flack for ripping off *Conan the Barbarian* by returning to the Norse Sigurd legends? Would Fulci have borrowed elements from Richard Wagner's epic opera *Der Ring des Nibelungen*? Would the art design have echoed Arthur Rackham's glorious illustrations? Or would Fulci have looked back to Fritz Lang's 1924 silent movie *Die Nibelungen: Siegfried*? It's possible. As for the project's sudden collapse, one wonders whether doubts crept in when *Conan the Barbarian* started attracting reviews sniffing racist and fascist subtexts. Perhaps this was what persuaded Edmondo Amati to invest his time and money elsewhere? America could get away with this sort of thing but Italy had skeletons in the closet; precisely the reason why Italian peplum producers of the 1960s featured Americans in the leading roles, being wary of home-grown brawn after the country's love affair with 'might makes right' during the days of Mussolini...

1982
Alibi

With Fulci on board for *Conquest*, producer Giovanni Di Clemente hurriedly pencilled in a second project, a chiller by the name of 'Alibi'. Needless to say, after the debacle of *Conquest* and the bad blood that followed, the project never happened. Fulci explained the situation to Luca Palmerini in a 1993 interview published in *Giallo Pages*: *"I had a contract to make two films with Giovanni Di Clemente, but he was such a terrible producer that, after Conquest, I refused to make the second one. Consequently, he tried to sue me, but I won the lawsuit because the Constitution says that if you don't wish to work you're not obliged to."*[33]

1982
Trance

In December 1982, a Turin-based businessman called Piermaria Romano who was seeking to expand into film production began prepping a project called 'Trance', intended to be the inaugural production of his new company Mara Cinematografica. Having made his wealth in auto manufacturing, and backed by private capital from three industrial investors, he asked Lucio Fulci to direct the film. Shooting was pencilled in for June 1983, with a cast to be headed by Franco Nero. Romano was expected to set up his production offices in Rome in the early weeks of 1983, but for reasons unknown nothing was heard from him again...

1983
Blastfighters

In May of 1983, Mino Loy, head of National Cinematografica, informed *Variety* of a forthcoming production called *Blastfighters*, with Lucio Fulci attached as director. It was to be a post-apocalyptic science fiction film and, as scriptwriter Dardano Sacchetti informed Fulci historian Lionel Grenier: *"The story took place in a future where all the energy left is in batteries. So, the one who owns a battery has a great treasure. It was a kind of western, with a ghost town full of end-of-life vehicles that drive in the snow."*[34] Fulci himself described the story to *L'Écran fantastique*'s Giuseppe Salza as *"a futuristic western in which I take all the traditional western themes and gather them together in a post-cataclysmic world."*[35] From this description it would seem that the story was heavily influenced by the *Mad Max* films, with a few careful tweaks to vary the scenery, and with the Macguffin changed from petrol to batteries. However, it was not to be. Complications in pre-production forced the scrapping of 'Blastfighters', and Fulci moved on to direct the futuristic gladiator movie *Rome 2033 – The Fighter Centurions*...

facing page:
Trade paper advert for an unmade Fulci film, *The Sword of Siegfried*. Obscure UK production company Aston Films Ltd. were previously co-producers on Alberto De Martino's *Holocaust 2000* (1977).

below:
The title that caused a permanent rift between Fulci and Dardano Sacchetti.

above:
Advertising artwork for *Blastfighter.*

National Cinematografica, however, had already sold the 'Blastfighters' project internationally, based on the title alone. This was not unusual at the time; such deals were known as pre-sales, in which films were sold to backers on the basis of a title or poster artwork before a single metre of film had been shot. With pre-sale agreements signed, but without a usable script, Sacchetti was asked to write a new story with the same name. 'Blastfighters' the post-apocalyptic sci-fi film became *Blastfighter*, a 'violent cop out for revenge' movie, and went into production in the Spring of 1984, as a co-production between National Cinematografica and Luciano Martino's Dania Film, with additional finance from Medusa Distribuzione. Lamberto Bava, fresh from another Dania/National co-production, *A Blade in the Dark*, was hired to direct. Editing took place in May 1984 and the film saw release in Rome in August that year. Unfortunately, when Fulci heard about this it seems he took the situation badly. According to Fulci's interpretation of events, he and Sacchetti worked together on the 'Blastfighters' script, and Sacchetti ripped off his ideas. He was furious, and it severely affected his relationship with Sacchetti. (See also *Per sempre*, below.)

Sadly it seems that Fulci, whose ego was sensitive and unstable at the best of times, took the matter to heart and never did change his attitude. To a dispassionate observer it appears absurd that an unmade film, based heavily on ideas 'borrowed' from the *Mad Max* movies, should inspire such rage, especially when even a cursory glance at the finished product shows how little similarity there really was to the original concept. One could even say that it demonstrates bad conscience on Fulci's part: Fulci was acting-out a role of decorum and moral rectitude regarding the sanctity of his original ideas, when in fact his entire career had been predicated on quite the opposite, namely the free mutation of ideas from source to variant. An unsympathetic observer might wonder, for instance, how Dario Argento was meant to have felt when Fulci's script 'The Cage' sprouted a distinctly Argento-esque new title, *A Lizard in a Woman's Skin*, in the wake of *The Bird with the Crystal Plumage* and *The Cat O'Nine Tails*; or how the directors of *Conan the Barbarian* (Con-) and *Quest for Fire* (-Quest) should have reacted if they watched (or tried to watch) Fulci's *Conquest*, which nicked ideas from both and then smirkingly referenced them in the title. Other examples, involving both content and presentation, are frankly legion in Fulci's career, making his outrage rather hypocritical.

As it transpired, the age of the pre-sale was drawing to an end. Adriana Chiesa, sales chief of Medusa Distribuzione, summed up the situation in late 1984, his terse summary capturing the chill wind then blowing through Italian production: *"Very careful buying, no more presales and few signed check deals"*.[36]

1983
Evil Comes Back aka *Per sempre*

Fulci's beef with Sacchetti over *Blastfighter* is so precisely reproduced in his remarks about *Per sempre* that one begins to wonder if he'd blurred the two stories together (see interview with Dardano Sacchetti). To summarise, Fulci claimed that he conceived this story (an admitted variation on *The Postman Always Rings Twice*) together with Sacchetti. He claimed that a treatment was co-written and he was set to direct, but the finance kept falling through. According to Fulci, Sacchetti later copyrighted the story himself, and in 1987 gave it to Lamberto Bava. Sacchetti however says that the story was always his, and his alone.

1983
Zombie 3D

In 1983, with horror at the vanguard of the eighties 3D boom (*Friday the 13th Part III*; *Amityville 3-D*; *Parasite*), it made perfect sense to suggest a 3D sequel to the literally eye-popping *Zombie Flesh-Eaters*. After all, the film was originally called *Zombi 2* in Italy, so after *Zombi 2* what could be more natural than 'Zombi 3D'? In August 1983, scriptwriters Gianfranco Clerici and Vincenzo Mannino, fresh from their work on *The New York Ripper* and *Conquest*, proposed just such a notion, under the auspices of their short-lived production venture Tandem Cinematografica, with production in Rome slated for September. If this fast turnaround was intended to whip-up pre-sales finance with a script to follow in short order it evidently failed, perhaps due to the inexperience of the two partners, whose writing credits were numerous but whose production skills were untested. In any case, the eighties 3D boom peaked in 1983 and had pretty much blown over by the end of 1984, and 'Zombie 3D' missed the boat. (Tandem Cinematografica's sole screen credit came five years later, on Ruggero Deodato's 1988 horror film *Phantom of Death*.)

1984
Killer-Samba

In 1984, while being interviewed by Corrado Mantoni on *Ciao Gente*, a popular TV show on Silvio Berlusconi's Canale 5, Fulci referred to *Murder-Rock* as the first film in a proposed 'trilogy of music', the second of which would have been called 'Killer-Samba'. Sounds improbable? See the next entry... (Note: the exact date of Fulci's appearance on *Ciao Gente* is unclear but it's likely to have been around April 1984; Fulci is promoting *Murder-Rock*, which opened that month.)

right:
German DVD cover for another disputed project that ended up being directed by Lamberto Bava; like *Blastfighter*, it was the subject of furious disagreement between Fulci and the writer Dardano Sacchetti.

1984

Thrilling-Blues

The third film in Fulci's proposed 'trilogy of music'was to have been called 'Thrilling-Blues'. Or was it? Watching the aforementioned *Ciao Gente* interview clip, it's clear that Fulci smiles when saying these titles, so it's possible they were just a joke. On the other hand, if 'Killer-Samba' were the real film in this 'trilogy' we'd just as likely think *Murder-Rock* was the joke... You can make up your own mind by searching YouTube for "Lucio Fulci e Maurizio Merli da Corrado"...

1984

Carnevale si legge M.O.R.T.E.

[translation: Carnival Spells D.E.A.T.H.]

Announced by producer/distributor Filman for shooting in Brazil, September 1984. No other information.

1984-1985

Towards the end of 1984 Lucio Fulci fell seriously ill with viral hepatitis and cirrhosis of the liver. For a while he was near death, and as a consequence he spent the next six to nine months recovering. This perhaps explains why he sold his script *La gabbia* ('The Trap') to Giuseppe Patroni Griffi instead of directing it himself. (It also explains why Fulci would direct *The Devil's Honey*, a strikingly similar story, just a few months later; it seems he regretted selling such a decent script to another director, and decided to make his own version once he was back on his feet.)

1985

La casa sull'Hudson aka *The House on the Hudson*

The House of Danwich

Two projects, announced within six weeks of each other, both with the word 'house' in the title, and both lined up for Lucio Fulci to direct... Could they in fact be the same project? 'The House on the Hudson' was announced in *Variety* on 20 March 1985, as a Fulci "thriller" being prepped by Ugo Tucci's Compagnia Generale (Tucci, of course, was co-producer of *Zombi 2*). Another news item dated 1 May 1985 had Fulci prepping "a horror pic" called 'The House of Danwich', a title which naturally brings to mind the H.P. Lovecraft story "The Dunwich Horror", already referenced in Fulci's *City of the Living Dead*. It's unclear which production company was to have made 'The House of Danwich', but one possible indication is a passing mention of Fulci in a list of directors signed up by Luciano Martino's Dania Film for their 1985-86 production roster.[37] Were Dania behind 'The House of Danwich'? They were after all co-producers of *City of the Living Dead*. *City* was written by Dardano Sacchetti, so was 'Danwich' also to have been a Sacchetti script? If so, it may have been scrapped when the dispute with Fulci exploded.

1985

Tashmad

Apparently slated for production by Film Export Group, a company run by Michel Freudenstein (see *The House by the Cemetery*), little is known about 'Tashmad', although it appears to have been a horror story with a 'hi-tech' element. The adline "It started as a game, but now evil was the opponent", in conjunction with an eighties computer font for the title, suggests inspiration may have been drawn from the satanic-computer horror of *Evilspeak*, with maybe a smattering of *Tron*! Interestingly, pre-sales artwork for 'Tashmad' features the menacing face used on the poster for *The House by the Cemetery*, so either Michel Freudenstein was in on the joke by now, or someone in the design department was thumbing his nose at the boss!

1987

Evil Messenger

Reputedly an unmade Fulci horror project. No other information.

1988

Adoration

Adoration was supposedly intended as a drama based on a novel by Juro Kara, although I've been unable to find such a book, nor verify that this project was ever mooted by Fulci. For the record, Juro Kara is an avant-garde Japanese playwright, theatre director, author, actor, and songwriter. His work formed the basis for *Violated Angels*, a film directed by controversial Japanese director Koji Wakamatsu in 1967.

1990

Nero per signora ('Black for the Lady')

If this was indeed planned as a feature, it was either drawn from, or ended up as, a short story written by Fulci and published posthumously by *Nocturno* in a 36-page volume called *I maestri del giallo: Racconti della paura di Fernando Di Leo, Lucio Fulci, Umberto Lenzi, Daniele Stroppa.*

1990

NHF – No Human Factor

This post-apocalyptic science fiction project was apparently intended to follow on from *Quando Alice ruppe lo specchio* and *The Ghosts of Sodom* as the third film in a four or five picture deal with Distribuzione Alpha Cinematografica. According to Michele De Angelis, Fulci's assistant at the time, *"NHF, No Human Factor should have been another film in the 'Lucio Fulci presents' series. Lucio would have directed the film [...] The story took place in the future, a kind of Blade Runner with characters that were not human but synthetic. [...] But with all the problems that we had with the production company, Alfa Cinematografica, it would have been impossible to make a good science-fiction movie without a significant budget."*[38]

1991

A Cat in the Brain Part 2

The mind boggles...

1991

Sembravano angeli ('They Looked Like Angels')

A proposed made-for-TV giallo, provenance uncertain.

1991

Diabolique Part 2

A proposed giallo, provenance uncertain.

above:
Lucio Fulci's *eXistenZ*? We can but dream...

1991

White Fang in New York

The success of the Walt Disney *White Fang* in 1991, directed by Randall Kleiser and starring Ethan Hawke, must have had Fulci sniffing the air for a possible third bite of the action. Sadly, nothing was to come of it.

1992 – DISPUTED PROJECT

Avanspettacolo

In July 1992 the Italian TV station Rai Tre launched a new TV series called *Avanspettacolo* featuring Lucio Fulci's old comrades Franco and Ciccio. Fulci however was far from pleased, believing that the show was plagiarised from a proposal he'd made to Rai Due two years earlier called "Luci del varietà" ('Variety Lights'). As he told the press, *"I deposited in 1990 a project for a TV variety programme and from 1991 I have been in discussion with Rai Due to bring it into realisation. Franco Franchi participated with me in the meetings with the department heads."*[39] Stefano Balassone, assistant to the director of Rai Tre, responded to the accusations, *"We are sorry for Fulci, but we do not know anything about his project.* Avanspettacolo *is an idea that Rai Tre presented to the general vice-director of Rai in 1989. There will be 10 episodes broadcast from 20:30 from the first week of July."*[40] Fulci was on the verge of involving lawyers when, on 9 December 1992, Franchi died.

'Avanspettacolo' (meaning 'before the show') is an Italian theatrical genre popular from the 1930s to the 1950s. A kind of variety revue, it incorporated songs, dancing, comedy and other forms of light entertainment, and was designed to entertain theatre audiences before the start of a movie programme. Avanspettacolo was a springboard for a great many famous Italian comics, including Totò and Franco and Ciccio.

1994

La Mummia (The Mummy)

The Mummy was mooted as a project to reunite Fulci and scriptwriter Dardano Sacchetti, under the wing of producer Dario Argento, but the bandages soon came undone after a bitter disagreement between Sacchetti and Argento. In Daniel Gouyette's video documentary *Ti ricordi di Lucio Fulci?* (2006), Sacchetti explained: *"The film was to be produced by Dario Argento. We sent the script to Argento who was in the USA. He didn't like it. I was insulted. That was our last disagreement. After that we stopped seeing each other."*

1990

The Beyond Part 2

A sequel to *The Beyond* was first suggested in 1996 when actor David Warbeck (in a commentary track for *The Beyond*) announced that he had begun working on a script – called 'Beyond the Beyond' – with original author Dardano Sacchetti. After Lucio Fulci died in 1996, there was talk of involving either Michele Soavi or Antonio Margheriti as director; however, when Warbeck himself died in 1997 his plans for a sequel died with him. Details of Warbeck's proposed storyline have never been revealed, although the idea appears to have been to establish 'Beyond the Beyond' as the third film in the 'Seven Gates Trilogy' (with *City of the Living Dead* the first and *The Beyond* the second). In 1998, Blackest Heart Media published a comic book adaptation of *The Beyond*, and in an essay contained within they announced plans to commission a comic-book adaptation of Warbeck's screenplay, renamed "Escape from The Beyond". Sadly this never materialised.

opposite:
John Savage as Melvin Devereux in *Door to Silence*: finding himself in all the wrong places...

Footnotes

1 *Variety*, 20 June 1988.
2 Michele De Angelis, interviewed by the author, October 2015.
3 *Variety*, 9 May 1984.
4 Note how the series title ignores the meaning of the word 'giallo' and instead refers to four supernatural stories!
5 *Variety* review of *Voices from Beyond*, 27 May 1991.
6 Michele De Angelis interviewed by Adrien Clerc for luciofulci.fr
7 Michele De Angelis, interviewed by the author, October 2015.
8 ibid.
9 ibid.
10 ibid.
11 Alfieri would go on to land himself in even deeper ordure in 1988 when he backed Kinski's vanity project *Paganini*.
12 The sleaziest extremes of Italian cinema were unleashed by the box-office success of Liliana Cavani's *The Night Porter*, although true exploitation encouragement was provided by the I-dare-you Canadian title *Ilsa, She Wolf of the SS* (Don Edmonds, 1974). Prior to this cheesy effort ("Even the SS feared her!", crowed the posters), there'd been just one sexploitational wet-dream spin on the Holocaust, Robert Frost's *Love Camp 7* (1968): but whereas the North American Nazi stories sanctimoniously emphasized the Allies' role in curtailing German evil, Italian variants indulged sex and sadism with varying degrees of nihilism. Even so, there is a shortfall in shock-value here. Despite the frequent depiction of torture and mutilation, one's most fearful expectations are often frustrated by these films, due to their clumsy, tasteless appropriation of the subject for mainly sexual purposes (the predominant topic is the 'love-camp' filled with unwilling 'prostitutes' for Nazi soldiers; not the death camps with their degraded human skeletons). Extreme though they are, they are as far removed from the realities of Buchenwald and Auschwitz as Spielberg's *Schindler's List*, albeit from the other side of the taste barrier. For the curious, the following top five is in order of grotesquerie: *The Beast in Heat* (Luigi Bazella), *Women's Camp 119* (Bruno Mattei), *SS Experiment Camp* (Sergio Garrone), *The Gestapo's Last Orgy* (Cesare Canevari), *SS Camp 5 – Women's Hell* (Sergio Garrone).
13 Michele De Angelis, interviewed by the author, October 2015.
14 Interviewed for the Shriek Show DVD release, released 2002.
15 ibid.
16 Michele De Angelis, interviewed by the author in October 2015.
17 Michele De Angelis, interviewed by the author in October 2015.
18 "On Set with Lucio Fulci: the filming of Demonia" by Alan Jones, in *The Eyeball Compendium*, 2003 (FAB Press).
19 Lucio Fulci interviewed by Howard Berger in *Fangoria* #154.
20 Michele De Angelis interviewed by Adrien Clerc for luciofulci.fr
21 *Variety*, 27 May 1991.
22 Lucio Fulci interviewed by Massimo Lavagnini for *Draculina* #24, 1995.
23 ibid.
24 ibid.
25 Lucio Fulci interviewed by Howard Berger for *Fangoria* #154.
26 "Unmasking the Wax Mask" by Tim Lucas, at Video Watchblog, 6 October 2011 (http://videowatchdog.blogspot.co.uk/2011/10/unmasking-wax-mask.html).
27 Michel Parry, 11 October 2012, responding to a post "Another Peter Haining Fraud" by Douglas A. Anderson at Wormwoodiana (http://wormwoodiana.blogspot.co.uk/2012/08/another-peter-haining-fraud.html).
28 Douglas A. Anderson, in an additional comment to his post "Another Peter Haining Fraud" at Wormwoodiana (http://wormwoodiana.blogspot.co.uk/2012/08/another-peter-haining-fraud.html).
29 *Variety*, 12 May 1976.
30 *Variety*, 13 May 1981.
31 *Variety*, 13 May 1981.
32 Interview with Lucio Fulci, by Robert Schlockoff, in *L'Écran Fantastique* #22.
33 Lucio Fulci interview, by Luca Palmerini, 1 June 1993, published in *Giallo Pages* #2
34 The interview appears on Grenier's marvellous website luciofulci.fr
35 Lucio Fulci interviewed by Giuseppe Salza for *L'Écran Fantastique* #44, April 1984.
36 *Variety*, 21 November 1984.
37 *Variety*, 22 May 1985.
38 Michele De Angelis, interviewed by Adrien Clerc for luciofulci.fr
39 "L'autore Fulci accusa Raitre di plagio" – *l'Unità*, 16 April 1992.
40 ibid.

Morto a Roma Lucio Fulci, artigiano dell'horror

E' morto ieri a Roma il regista Lucio Fulci. A dare la notizia, nel pomeriggio, è stato Dario Argento, con cui Fulci stava preparando da alcuni mesi il suo ritorno al cinema con un remake della «Maschera di cera». Nato a Roma il 17 giugno 1927, Fulci da tempo soffriva di diabete. Dalla sceneggiatura di «Un americano a Roma» di Steno con Sordi a «Paura nella città dei morti viventi», nella sua carriera durata più di 40 anni Fulci ha percorso tutti i generi del cinema italiano. Da buon artigiano vecchia maniera, ha iniziato facendo ridere con Totò, ha diretto molte parodie di Franchi e Ingrassia, ha provato il western e l'avventura, ma dal '75, aiutato anche dall'affermazione di Argento, si è dedicato alla sua vera passione, il film horror, con pellicole artigianalmente molto ben fatte come «Una lucertola con la pelle di donna» e «Non si sevizia un paperino».

Prima di dedicarsi al cinema, Fulci si era impegnato nelle milizie partigiane. Dopo la guerra, s'era iscritto al Centro sperimentale di cinematografia. Dopo aver diretto documentari per la Settimana Incom, Fulci cominciò con Steno come sceneggiatore e aiuto regista la carriera nel cinema.

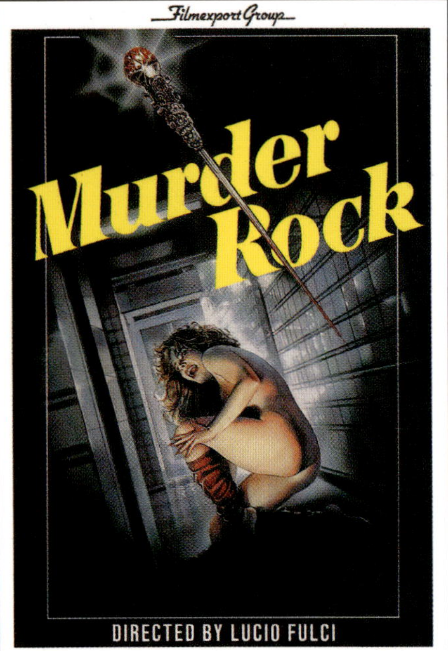

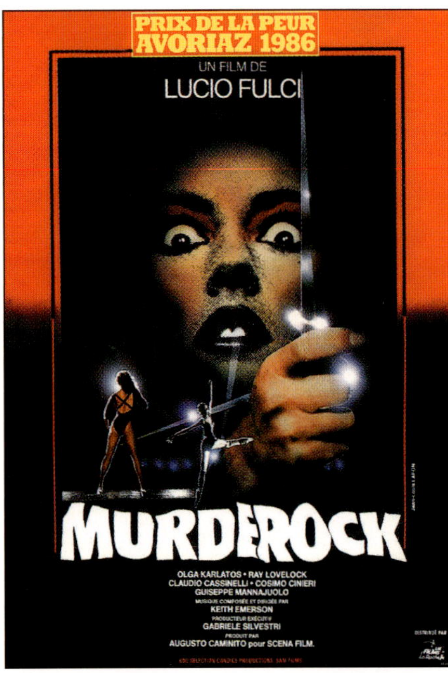

Murder-Rock Dancing Death
top: Sales brochure.
middle: French poster.
bottom: Italian promo sheet.

Ænigma
right: Locandina.

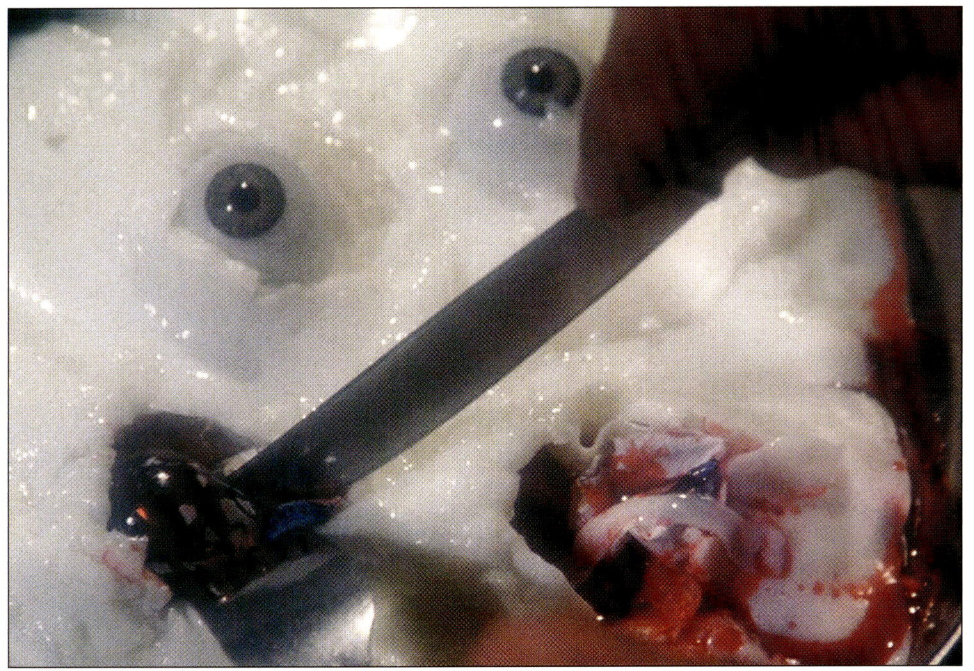

top: Eyeball violence makes a welcome return in Fulci's *Voices from Beyond*.

above: Very atmospheric artwork for *Voices from Beyond*; but why does it depict Klaus Kinski?

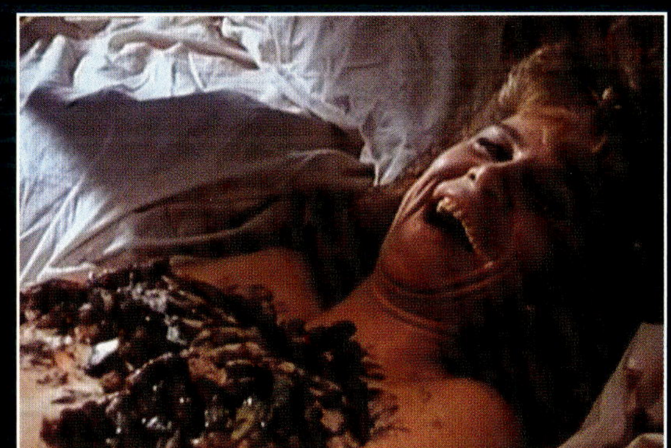

from top:
Duilio Del Prete as Giorgio Mainardi, a literally rotten patriarch in *Voices from Beyond*;
Uncle Carlo (Jean Christophe Bretigniere) and Aunt Marcia (Cinzia Monreale) try to rescue two children in *The Sweet House of Horrors*;
The ghosts fight back with fire, in *The Sweet House of Horrors*;
A supernatural seductress (Zora Ulla Keslerová) turns to unappetising gloop in *The Ghosts of Sodom*;
Jessica (Blanca Marsillach), the disturbed anti-heroine of *The Devil's Honey*.

CORINNE CLERY • BRETT HALSEY • BLANCA MARSILLACH

LE MIEL DU DIABLE

UN FILM DE
LUCIO FULCI

CORINNE CLERY • BRETT HALSEY • BLANCA MARSILLACH • STEFANO MADIA avec PAOLA MOLINA • BERNARD SERAY
scénario et dialogue LUDOVICA MARINEO - VINCENZO SALVIANI - JESUS BALKAZAR - musique de CLAUDIO NATALI • directeur de la photo ALESSANDRO ULLOA
une production SALVAGGIA FILMS • un film de LUCIO FULCI • distribué par EURODIS INTERNATIONAL

above: Jessica turns her dreams of vengeance into reality, in *The Devil's Honey.*

below: Locked in a prison of guilt and retribution: Olga Karlatos as Candice and Ray Lovelock as George in *Murder-Rock Dancing Death.*

top: Italian video cover artwork for *The Ghosts of Sodom.*
middle: Karina Huff as Diana, a criminal's moll, in *The House of Clocks.*
bottom: Mark (Alan Johnson) erupts with decay in *The Ghosts of Sodom.*

top: Lucio Fulci views *The Ghosts of Sodom* with dismay, in *Nightmare Concert.*
middle: Professor Swharz (David L. Thompson) about to cut up a whore in *Nightmare Concert.*
bottom: The discovery of one of Swharz's victims in *Nightmare Concert.*

NIGHTMARE CONCERT

starring: LUCIO FULCI
DAVID THOMPSON - JEOFFREY KENNEDY
and BRETT HALSEY as a Monster
directed by: LUCIO FULCI

chapter nine

Craft, Pain & Inspiration

Appreciating Lucio Fulci

In Italian exploitation cinema, as elsewhere in the arts, the question of authorship is fraught with ambiguity. It's little wonder that postmodernist filmmaker *in excelsis* Quentin Tarantino regards the Italian commercial cinema with such admiration. Cross-reference or rip-off? Italy's film industry made the distinction hard to call and probably irrelevant.

Italy's culture has always been alive to input from other countries. Early Roman art 'borrowed' liberally from Greek culture. But what is the value of the notion of an 'original'? Much has been written about this in the philosophical texts of the twentieth century. Today the artist has been 'de-centred', deposed from his/her privileged position as arbiter of their work. The most sophisticated critiques of single-source meaning – from Jacques Derrida, Michel Foucault, Jacques Lacan, Jean Baudrillard – ally significance to a shifting perspective, a restless becoming of symbolic relations that requires no authorial referent. Still, there is a fascination with the artist, and a wish to believe that we encounter his or her 'hand' in the work they've created. Hence the perennial popularity of the so-called auteur-theory, which seeks to discover the intentions of the film director in his/her work.

To search for a unique yet repeating personal 'stamp' throughout all the films of Lucio Fulci is to look in vain. Fulci does not fulfil the necessary criteria for inclusion in the category of 'auteur'. He is not possessed of a singular, metamorphosing yet consistent perspective; he does not return compulsively to the same themes explored in a variety of settings; he is hardly the sole creator of his films. Convenience, indifference and commercial necessity have all played significant parts in his career. When strings of his films do bear the stamp of a consistent world-view, that view is largely arrived at with his script-writer (e.g. Dardano Sacchetti, Roberto Gianviti) and significantly co-visualized by his cinematographers (e.g. Sergio Salvati, Luigi Kuveiller, Sergio D'Offizi). The subsequent absence of these collaborators brought about an immediate and lasting decrease in the quality of Fulci's work.

Nonetheless, Lucio Fulci has 'put his name' to a substantial number of striking, impressive and mesmerizing works over the years. If the efforts of collaborators are obscured by the priority given to his directorial credit, then maybe film writing is at fault. But must we ignore altogether Fulci's input, in furtherance of a de-centred perspective? For better or worse, our perception of the film-making process has incorporated an author-figure as part of the pleasurable experience of watching and thinking about a film. Auteurism cannot simply be dismissed; the pleasure of studying a man or woman's progress through a creative career is too strong to be dampened by academic disapproval.

Admiration of a fiction, the appreciation of its construction and emotional/visceral effect, is an experience we often seek in the cinema. But because we admire from *outside* the text, our involvement or immersion in the fiction isn't complete, so we insert the idea of a 'director/author' back in the space we left. We may then 'recognise' the author there and experience pleasure in his textual performance. This pleasure is, after all, partly why we seek out repeated exposure to someone's works, whether it be Alain Resnais and Jean-Luc Godard or Lucio Fulci and Jesús Franco. No one escapes this performative aspect of creativity, not even the deconstructionists. Roland Barthes, whose phrase 'the death of the author' became a semiotic clarion call in the seventies and eighties, is never more present on the stage of his work than when he silkily describes the decline of the authorial figure "diminishing like a figurine at the far end of the literary stage".

As a device for populating a pantheon of elite art, auteurism is highly suspect. It's been pointed out that the auteur theorist often ends up considering dreadful films by his favoured directors as more interesting than accomplished works by others. Is a bad film by Fellini more interesting *a priori* than a good film by Lucio Fulci? Fulci's wandering skills lead to failures as well as triumphs, and there can be no hiding the former behind an indulgent auteurism. Instead of demanding consistency, and then judging him lacking as an artist because of his occasional hack-work, we should appreciate the figure he cuts as an active contributor to various cinema genres. Perhaps by acknowledging Fulci as someone distorted into star status – subject of books – we may walk straight through the spectre of his 'signature', only to arrive gladly at a collection of individual films. Films that are fascinating without having to be read as the personal effluence of some mysterious, darkly inspired author.

below:
In 1953, Lucio Fulci was the assistant director and co-writer on *Un giorno in pretura* ('A Day in Court') directed by Steno [Stefano Vanzina]. Fulci contributed many ideas to his mentor's films, some of which were to reappear in his own work as director. *Gli imbroglioni*, Fulci's 1963 comedy starring Walter Chiari and Franco & Ciccio, took place, like *Un giorno in pretura*, during the course of a day in a Rome courtroom. (Fulci is standing behind the camera, Steno is in the foreground).

above:
Sarah Keller (aka Cinzia Monreale) as Emily – *The Beyond.*

below:
Lucio Fulci on the set of his 1975 black comedy *Young Dracula* aka *Dracula in the Provinces.*

Limits of auteur theory

In considering Lucio Fulci's position outside the 'auteur' category we should recall the way in which this dominant film-critical term became so important to debates about cinema. The romantic vision of the author as Magus of creative ceremonies, ring-master of rhetorics and spirit guide to the reading consciousness, was imported into cinema from literature. The first authors to add their names to their written texts did so at the insistence of the Catholic church – books were starting to disseminate the scourge of information and the Church was never happy to see texts interpreted by anyone but the ordained ministry. Just in case they were to transgress religious sacristy, writers, it was felt, had to be accountable. As literature developed, two versions of the artist's role were to emerge, characterized by literary critic M.H. Abrams as 'The Mirror' and 'The Lamp'. The word 'mirror' suggests an artist as an innocent conduit for the natural details of the world, whereas 'lamp' suggests an artist who illuminates the external world with his 'genius'. (The second category, often dismissed as hopelessly bourgeois, today ironically resides in the form of the critic-as-psychoanalyst, able to read the psyche of the artist through his work better than the artist himself).

In cinema, what became known as the 'auteur theory' began less categorically as 'le politique des auteurs', a term instigated by writers for the French film journal *Cahiers du Cinema* to oil the wheels of their polemic in favour of certain American directors conventionally dismissed as 'lowbrow'. The *Cahiers* writers lionized film-makers such as Alfred Hitchcock, John Ford and Howard Hawks: both in recognition of their ability to stamp personal authority on films, despite the constraints of the American studio system; and as a calculated attack on bourgeois criticism's snobbish esteem for 'serious' European films over 'frivolous' American ones. American critic Andrew Sarris then initiated a simplified form of reference when he reduced the phrase to 'the auteur theory'. The convention of 'the Director' as arbiter of a film's meaning took root, aided by Sarris's eulogies to personal favourites, and persists to this day. The auteur, then, was a 'lamp' artist, illuminating his chosen material with personal insight. (The change in terminology is significant; the word 'politique', dropped by Sarris, implies a polemical choice, facilitating a course of action. The '*Cahiers*' writers' strategy in coining the term was contingent rather than all-embracing; strategic, unfixed, and motivated by a drive towards change.)

Subsequently, attempts were made – by film theorists like Peter Wollen and others – to bring in structuralist methodology to prop up the auteur theory. (Structuralism, a mode of analysis inspired by Ferdinand de Saussure's theories on linguistics, attempted to reveal the underlying network of relationships governing textual artefacts and asserted that meaning was generated by the relations existing *between* elements in the network.) 'Auteur-structuralism' didn't really offer much of an advance: the structuralist system of decoding could not be grafted onto the contradictory auteurist position, and structuralism itself was flawed by its empirical strand and acceptance of an already constituted 'knowing subject'. (Michel Foucault in *The Order of Things*: *"Auteur structuralism allows the critic to offer an exegesis of the text, which allows the positing of a knowing subject (critic/reader) and textual object – implying that both are already constituted. This is empiricism."*)

Michel Foucault's hugely influential essay "What is an Author?" extends ideas from Roland Barthes' "The Death of the Author" and critiques the principle of unity in writing in a way which has been usefully applied to the idea of auteur works in the cinema. It is a commonplace to maintain that an auteur is one whose ideas and stylistic devices develop throughout their body of work; it's a view that can exclude from the auteurist pantheon those directors, like Fulci, whose careers vary wildly in subject matter, scope, temperament and artistic success. Considerations such as stylistic unity, coherence and consistency of quality, Foucault argues, are limits and constraints upon meaning in the works, a point which he shares with Barthes and Derrida. He also posits "a plurality of self" within such works allowing for multiple subject positions.

Jacques Derrida (a post-structuralist writer who has never actually written about cinema, but refers to literary and philosophical texts) amended structuralism by establishing text as process, not object. Process is determined by material conditions. One cannot analyze texts without looking at these material conditions, and they lie outside the text. Therefore the text can't be understood without reference to things outside of it. A text alone is unable to analyze itself as object. This reference outside serves to link up with surrounding discourses of meaning and interpretation. Any discourse that then studies the text changes the text as it does so; it is productive. In this relation the subject-object divide is crossed. A new text is produced, created by both text-process and discourse-modifier. This is intertextuality. The meaning of a piece of work, a film or a book, is not some glittering prize hidden at the work's core among the tendrils of technique, to be uncovered through interpretation of the author's brilliant displays of encoding. Meaning *occurs* through discursive enquiry. It can just as easily spring from consideration of a 'failed' moment of diegesis, a fragment of bizarrely disconnected dialogue, or an unexplained absence. The experience of looking at the films of Lucio Fulci offers many opportunities for such consideration, and the fruits of such are independent of his personal intentions.

There are those who protest about divergent readings of their work on principle; this is foolish. One mark of a mature artist is that he is alive and responsive to interpretations stimulated by his work. Film-makers can become convinced that they show, we watch; they talk, we pay attention. Fulci sometimes strayed into this attitude, dismissing attempts to discuss his work in terms which he had not set down. Of course, if a reading of someone's work becomes accusatory or dogmatic, hostility is a natural enough response. But to complain about a divergence of interpretation by reference to a privileged writerly position is naive.

The idea that consistency in a director's work is a sign of 'auteur' quality is further complicated by the artist's possible awareness of such expectations. This is a problem which, it could be argued, has been responsible for self-conscious but arid work by Fulci (*Nightmare Concert*) – and others, like Dario Argento (whose 1993 film *Trauma* seems to me an excess of textual self-consciousness in search of a theme). 'Authorial intertextuality' is a term devised in film semiotics to refer to a director's awareness of their own work, and their interpellation of this perception into a new film. We as viewers then recognise this and fold our awareness into the process of watching subsequent works by the director. Our position has been re-aligned by our perception, and by the authorial figure's anticipation of our spectatorship. All of which is potentially trapped in formalism (what some would call 'disappearing up your arse').

The most immediately useful aspect of an artist's name is the function of collection or categorisation. Thus do we assimilate diverse information into manageable groups. In fan terms, this is what we are doing when we identify a 'body of work' as the collected artistic output of one person. However, it must be remembered that information can be organized in any number of ways, and this is merely one of a range almost as bewildering as the raw data itself. (See the films of Peter Greenaway for example.) The director is believed to assume the mantle of responsibility when it comes to the 'vision thing', despite the presence of an army of collaborators. The splendors of cinema are therefore corralled under his or her name. For many fans of Italian exploitation cinema, the only way to make sense of the astonishing range of films made in the seventies and eighties was to allocate authorial credit willy-nilly to all directors. This enabled a sorting and streaming of material in the face of proliferating genres and sub-genres. It also lead to a naive optimism about the people thus accredited. As more information comes to light about the directors of Italian exploitation cinema, their roles often seem less and less like 'auteurs' – they are more like superintendents, journeymen, supervisors, sometimes of a lax and disorganized sort. The territory they are responsible for superintending isn't their own (or anyone else's). Films made by directors like Bruno Mattei or Umberto Lenzi are like lazily marshalled sporting events played out on a genre pitch. Whilst there is certainly fun to be had in spectating, there is – to extend the metaphor – no evidence of the formulation of new or improvised game structures in their work. This is partly the condition of genre; and yet some film-makers tease the parameters of their chosen genre and even escape from the ground altogether into a wider region of signification.

Genre is a complex of organized clichés, with artistic merit points for those who can cheat well, re-write the rules a bit without spoiling the game. But it isn't only genre film-making that can draw on cliché. For every Ingmar Bergman there are three or four tedious 'art-cinema' copyists, drawn to psychic collapse and existential angst more out of stolid adherence to a bourgeois notion of suffering as art than any genuine psychological or formal enquiry. Lucio Fulci's involvement with the cinema has been played almost entirely within genre boundaries. It's only after he scored a higher profile making a clutch of magnificent horror films between 1979-1983 that he started to choose a slightly different route – that of horror-auteur. It's unfortunate then that his work during the latter period dropped so drastically in quality.

A Face in the Sea of Darkness – Lucio Fulci

Having established that Fulci was not an auteur, and would not be best represented as such, it nonetheless matters to all who enjoyed his films to pay tribute to his intelligence and commitment to the cinema. Despite his notoriety as something of an awkward, bad-tempered man on the sets of his films, he commanded considerable loyalty from a number of regular collaborators over the years. He frequently stated that he'd given drastically of his self for the cinema (*"I ruined my life for it. I have no family, no wife, only daughters. All women left me because I never stop thinking of my job."* – to Robert Schlockoff, *Starburst* #48)

David Warbeck, the actor who worked with Fulci on *The Beyond* and *The Black Cat*, has frequently described Fulci as a rebel. This is perhaps the most appealing aspect of his persona and the one most suitable as an epitaph. The horror genre has always appealed to young audiences, something that the forbidding attitude of moralising elders does little to dispel. Quite the opposite. How many times have horror fans heard the exhortation to 'grow up'? What's really been demanded is that we abandon the genre's revelations of unconscious drives and fears, and instead join 'everyone else' in the 'adult' acceptance of repression. *Zombie Flesh-Eaters*, *The Beyond*, or *The New York Ripper* might be recognised as powerful, even magical experiences by some, but generally they are the sort of films detractors chide as 'immature'. They exist wilfully to show grotesque and extreme violence, whilst shunning characterization. Fulci's best work has a bloody-minded attitude that I believe will always ensure his work a reputation and audience, especially with young people. As I hope to have shown, there's a great deal more to Fulci's work, but what the hell... When all is said and done, Lucio will be remembered for his iconoclastic, outrageous scenes of violence. He dared to take horror to the limit – how many times in his films have we sat in a queasy state of awe, thinking "Is he really going to go through with this?"; only to realise that yes, the scene is going to pay off handsomely, *way* beyond the point where other directors would turn shy and cut away.

For a man who faced death scores of times through his films, and composed elaborate spectacles of painful demise, it is ironic that death should have arrived hidden within the cloak of a diabetic coma. Neither pain, terror, joy or resignation were enacted as Lucio Fulci expired, oblivious, unconscious, at his home 2pm, Wednesday the 13th of March 1996. Life had certainly gnawed enough chunks out of him, though – he always maintained that he was not afraid of Death, because Hell was already here on earth. Misfortune dogged him throughout his complicated life. Worst of all, Fulci suffered a terrible personal tragedy involving the suicide of his wife in 1969 followed not long after by the death of a daughter in a road accident.

After a suicide, a lover's tenderness survives beyond such loss only at a terrible price. Bruised, distorted, forced to continue, this love must constantly revisit its own trauma – and each return curdles the individual's spirit in the present. No wonder those who survive the suicide of a loved one feel so tormented and angry, so bitter. In the course of writing this book I've avoided making psychoanalytical speculation on Lucio Fulci's approach to his work. But I've also found that the knowledge of Fulci's private horror arrests the mind too much to pass without consideration.

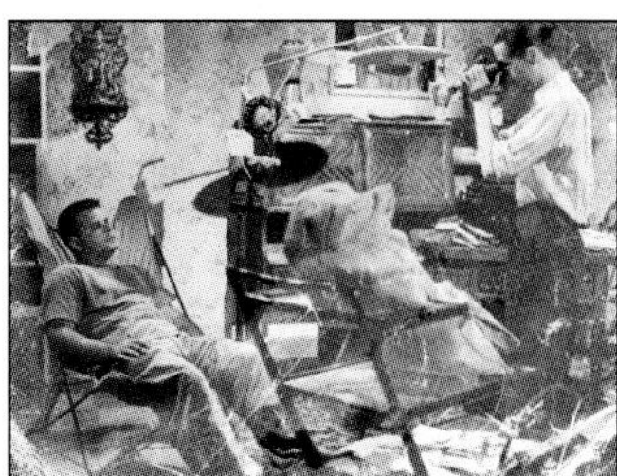

above:
This picture was taken on the set of *Un giorno in pretura* in 1953. Steno is filming Fulci, who probably sat in for one of the actors whilst the shot was being lined up.

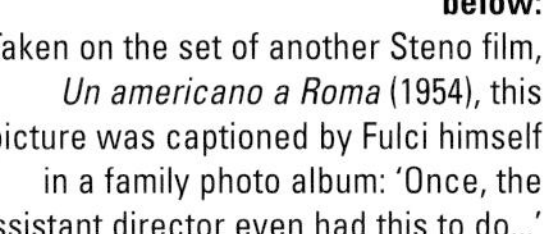

below:
Taken on the set of another Steno film, *Un americano a Roma* (1954), this picture was captioned by Fulci himself in a family photo album: 'Once, the assistant director even had this to do...'

above:
First day at high school, 1945...
"Dad had a huge passion for the sea, so he went to high school in Venezia, at the naval academy."
– Antonella Fulci

If Fulci's *One on Top of the Other* seems weirdly to anticipate the situation only to reshape it as a cruel plot against an inattentive lover, then it's not surprising that subsequent films should turn first fatalistic then uncanny in their world-view. One is reminded of the circumstances life has inflicted on Roman Polanski. Many went so far as to berate the director for somehow bringing evil down upon himself through his obsession with the macabre. In Fulci's case, his *fleur du mal* obsession with morbid themes only blossomed after the trauma of his wife's death.

Fulci suffered from a terrible neglect in his last few years – producers (and popular audiences) were no longer willing to venture through his domain. He became an embittered, isolated figure in Italian filmmaking. Dario Argento describes meeting the elderly director once pegged as his rival in Italian horror:

"I must be sincere. When I shot my first films, Lucio Fulci did some – I won't say exactly imitations – but something similar and I was a little unhappy with this. And we didn't see each other for many years. Then three years ago I was at a festival in Rome with Michele Soavi, and a man arrives, in a chair, an old man. Horrible. Christ, who is this? They say 'It's Lucio Fulci'. I say 'What has happened to him?' They say 'For a long time he was sick – for a year – and he disappeared. And nobody knew his address'. It was like... Edgar Allan Poe – when you go too much on the border, sometimes, a monster eats you. He was in bad condition – semi-paralyzed – poor, no house. Incredible. I don't like this and suddenly I become a big friend of his! Every day I went to see him."

Fulci lived for the excitement of filming, and trying to pull together a new version of the 1953 classic *House of Wax* was the passionate focus of his last months. Argento describes the effect that the planning of *The Wax Mask* had on Fulci:

"We started the preparation. The man was in the wheelchair – then he got up. There was an energy, he was becoming the old Fulci people knew. It was a great experience for us, for me especially. Sometimes the water is not sweet but bitter and he drank every last drop. We prepared this film, we do locations, we have lots of financing from the bank and we were happy. We were two months from starting and Lucio Fulci died. He was a good man, but when he died the newspapers didn't speak, no television... Mario Bava, for instance, was rich, a happy man, a big house, songs. For Lucio Fulci life was terrible: his wife committed suicide, his daughter was paralyzed because there was an accident. A different destiny".

Like Argento, Dardano Sacchetti – Fulci's closest ally on his best films – remains willing to praise him, stressing both the high quality of their collaborations and Fulci's consummate professionalism. Perhaps it is fitting that he should have the last word in appreciation of this troubled, difficult and driven man:

"Poor Lucio, he was right to be angry. He worked in the worst conditions. He had less and less money to do his movies and was forced to do anything in order to work. I think that Lucio was the greatest – his mastering of technique was almost unique. But he came to horror late in his career. Fulci had to start with a small producer, small distribution and small budgets. He used to claim he had two million dollars for a certain movie because he was ashamed of his microscopic budgets. Had he said the truth about the miracles he made with nothing, he would probably have been held in much greater esteem".

below:
Antoine Saint-John as the warlock artist Schweik, crucified in the basement of The Seven Doors Hotel in *The Beyond*.

chapter ten

Attack the Eye, Seduce the Ear

There are two schools of thought when it comes to film music. Some people say that you should scarcely notice it; others hang on every note. Personally I've always been staunchly in the latter camp. It's inconceivable to me that we should fail to notice something as profoundly affecting as a movie soundtrack, and that goes double for the horror genre. Insisting that film music should remain imperceptible to the conscious mind is a bit like criticising the stylistic flourishes of Brian De Palma or Dario Argento for 'snapping you out of the story' and reminding you that film is a construct. Such misgivings would seem to me to preclude enjoyment of Fulci's best work; the sensuous texture and extraordinary dissonance of Morricone's score for *A Lizard in a Woman's Skin*; the clangorous discords of Walter Rizzati's music for *The House by the Cemetery*, the grand melancholy of Frizzi's themes for *The Beyond*: these audio pleasures are deliberately seeking your attention.

Fulci was first and foremost a jazz fan, indeed in his younger days he'd played jazz trumpet himself. One of his earliest directorial jobs was to film the San Remo Jazz Festival in 1960 with Piero Vivarelli (*San Remo: la grande sfida*), and jazz would always remain his first and greatest musical love. And yet aside from the comedies of the 1960s he commissioned few outright jazz scores, the main exceptions being Riz Ortolani's music for *One on Top of the Other* (1969) and Franco Piana's work on *Door to Silence* (1991).

An increasing use of rock instrumentation during the 1970s and 80s was undoubtedly a response to the rising influence of Dario Argento, but by all accounts Fulci exerted a strong creative input on his scores whatever the idiom. Working with some of Italy's finest composers, he proved himself a canny listener with a nuanced musical sensibility and a definite ear for the unusual. Indeed it's the latter, more than his general 'good taste' in musical matters, which makes the films so aurally compelling. In his choice of collaborators he demonstrated an eclectic palate and a great deal of sensitivity, an aspect of his work which deserves greater recognition. What follows is a tour of the musical highlights of Fulci's filmography, with particular emphasis on his horror films and thrillers: two genres which tend to encourage a more daring and unusual approach to sound.

below:
Earworms? Putrefaction at the keyboard in *Zombie Flesh-Eaters*.

FABIO FRIZZI & BIXIO-FRIZZI-TEMPERA

The Four of the Apocalypse ~ Young Dracula ~ The Psychic ~ Silver Saddle ~ Zombie Flesh-Eaters ~ The Smuggler ~ City of the Living Dead ~ Manhattan Baby ~ A Cat in the Brain

Lucio Fulci's creative alliance with Fabio Frizzi outshines all of his other musical collaborations. Although Ennio Morricone and Riz Ortolani came up with marvellous work for the director, it's Frizzi who really *clicked* with him, just as Angelo Badalamenti did with David Lynch, or Daniel White with Jess Franco, or Goblin with Dario Argento. His ability to transcend the clichés of horror film scoring lends strange and elegant majesty to Fulci's most extravagantly gruesome creations. Films like *City of the Living Dead* and *The Beyond* are quite literally unthinkable without Frizzi's unique sense of melody, rhythm and texture.

Fabio Frizzi was born in Bologna in 1951 and joined his first band at the age of fourteen. After leaving school he became a jobbing musician, playing ultra-faithful covers of songs by popular acts like The Beatles, The Rolling Stones and Crosby Stills and Nash. Sidestepping his father Fulvio's intention to guide him towards a career in Law (Frizzi Sr. ran the Cineriz film company but was reluctant for his son to enter the business), Fabio managed to secure writing work with the prominent Italian publishing house Cinevox. It was run by Carlo Bixio, a man who would play a significant part in shaping the composer's early career.

Frizzi's first soundtrack credit was on *Amore libero – Free Love* (released in August 1974), a sun-soaked adventure shot in the Seychelles starring future 'black Emanuelle' Laura Gemser in her debut screen role.[1] Far more striking than the film itself, which is simply a milder-than-softcore travelogue romp, Frizzi's music is a mixture of exotica (stand-out track: "My Sweet Brown Sister") and sweet, sensuous pieces for strings, choir and a small electric band (notably "Ibo Lele" and "Janine"). Not just any band either: the musicians who played for Frizzi on *Amore libero* were Claudio Simonetti, Fabio Pignatelli, Massimo Morante and Walter Martino, four members of a young Italian rock group called Oliver, soon to change their name to Cherry Five, and then, famously, to Goblin.

Towards the end of 1974, Frizzi worked with Cherry Five (Claudio Simonetti, Fabio Pignatelli, Massimo Morante, Tony Tartarini and Walter Martino) on recordings that would find their way into a dire but very odd little sci-fi/sex-film called *Giro girotondo... con il sesso è bello il mondo* (1975), directed by Oscar Brazzi (younger brother of the actor Rossano Brazzi). Frizzi explains, *"This was born from an idea by Carlo Bixio, our publisher. Me, Claudio Simonetti, Fabio Pignatelli, Massimo Morante and others were all at*

below:
Fabio Frizzi performing in 2015.
photo copyright © Andrea Stevoli.

that time young composers of the Bixio 'team'. Carlo decided to entrust to me, Claudio and Fabio the creation of music for the movie. We wrote three themes, "Edda" (myself), "Ammoniaca" (Pignatelli) and "Epopea" (Simonetti). We produced them together, with great pleasure and fun, at Ortophonic Studios in Rome.[2] *A few weeks later, Fabio and Claudio's group was summoned by Dario Argento for his film* Profondo rosso. *We found ourselves again, in the same studio, for that historical recording – me, in this case, only as a friend and supporter."*

The onscreen credits of *Giro girotondo... con il sesso è bello il mondo* assert that the music was "performed by the group Goblin" (unsurprisingly, given the intervening success of *Profondo rosso*, which opened in March 1975 to rapturous acclaim). However, these compositions were not intended to be part of the official Goblin project. Consequently, when they later turned up as additional tracks on the 1976 Cinevox soundtrack LP for Mauro Macario's *Perché si uccidono*, the name of the project was changed to 'Il Reale Impero Britannico' (meaning 'The Royal British Empire', perhaps a tribute by the musicians to their predominantly British musical influences). The first side of this record features the *Giro girotondo* tracks by Frizzi, Pignatelli and Simonetti, plus "Kalu", a piece written solely by Frizzi from his soundtrack to *Amore libero – Free Love*. Side two features music written by composer Willy Brezza for *Perché si uccidono*, played by Simonetti, Pignatelli et al. Regardless of its patchwork history, fans of Goblin and Fabio Frizzi should try to obtain this rare disc as the music is quite extraordinary, ranging from the driving Minimoog melody of "Epopea" (which steals a lick from Van der Graaf Generator's "Theme One"), to the deliriously bizarre prog-pop of "R.I.B.", one of the equally excellent Willy Brezza numbers. Truly an obscurity worth investigating...

Whilst Cherry Five/Goblin were busy in the studio composing for Argento, Cinevox majordomo Carlo Bixio started planning another group, featuring his younger brother Franco Bixio. He suggested to Frizzi that he might like to team up with Franco, alongside Vincenzo Tempera, an older, more established composer already well known to him (he'd acted as musical director on the *Amore libero* sessions). Thus Bixio-Frizzi-Tempera was born. As Frizzi explains: *"Carlo Bixio had this idea to form another group. He had his brother Franco, who is a composer, and me, Fabio Frizzi, who's like a young horse, but I can write, and Vincenzo Tempera who was the oldest of us, a pop arranger from Milan. Vincenzo was a pianist, an arranger, a great musician, always conducting at the San Remo festival. He was there to make sure the work would go ahead. For me it was like a school. I could write, I could arrange, although I was very very young. I wanted to learn from Tempera, he was a man who knew everything about working in the studio. Franco Bixio and I were the artisans of the situation."*

One of the first film commissions involving all three – Frizzi, Bixio and Tempera – was *Fantozzi* (1975), a comedy based on a hugely popular series of short stories written by actor-comedian Paolo Villaggio for the magazines *L'Espresso* and *L'Europeo*. (A compendium of these tales, published by Rizzoli in 1971, sold over a million copies.) The film version starred Villaggio himself in the title role, and was a major hit, cementing the Fantozzi character in Italian culture and leading to several sequels. For a young composer like Frizzi it was a major catch, although he is quick to share the credit: *"The music for* Fantozzi *was born as my personal soundtrack (on the opening film titles and on the credits of the soundtrack 45 you will find only my name), but during that work my collaboration with Tempera was already ongoing. And Franco Bixio had long been my organizational support. Then, after the success of* Fantozzi*, Carlo asked me to join this working group/stable. Thus was born the trio Bixio-Frizzi-Tempera. Probably there was, in Carlo's head, the idea of us also becoming a kind of band, but it never happened that way."*

The first project for which Bixio-Frizzi-Tempera were fully credited saw the beginning of Frizzi's long and fruitful association with Lucio Fulci. Back in Rome after shooting in the foothills of Austria, Fulci was embroiled in post-production on a strange and violent spaghetti western: *The Four of the Apocalypse*. Frizzi recalls: *"We first met at the screening of a rough cut of* The Four of the Apocalypse. *Fulci had asked Carlo Bixio for musicians. This was at the very beginning of Bixio-Frizzi-Tempera, I think we had just done* Fantozzi. *Carlo knew we loved West Coast American music, like Crosby Stills and Nash, and Simon and Garfunkel. I loved the polyphony of the vocals in those groups. We were in a large screening room where we met everyone on the crew. We were seated in the middle rows, in the first rows were the bosses. Among them was Lucio, explaining and commenting. At the end of the screening we had our first 'face-to-face'. Fulci was a man with a strong personality, cultured and curious, with thousands of interests. Not an easy person at first sight, but if you could establish a confident connection then he was a positive and generous man. He used to study trumpet and he loved jazz. He'd been involved in the Italian music field, thanks to the "musicarelli", a kind of movie based on songs and singers in which Lucio worked as writer and director. He had a personal idea about music and was always my first reference point for the*

above: Italian poster for *Giro girotondo... con il sesso è bello il mondo* (Goblin members not pictured).

above left: Cinevox soundtrack LP for *Perché si uccidono*, featuring excellent music by Goblin members (aka Il Reale Impero Britannico) and Willy Brezza.

bottom left: Frizzi's first soundtrack, the onscreen title for which is *Amore libero – Free Love* (the same phrase repeated in Italian and English). The real title, irrespective of the odd decision to translate it onscreen, should probably be just *Amore libero* (certainly this is the title as shown in Italian cinema listings of the period).

below: Soundtrack LP for the hit comedy *Fantozzi* (in this case listing all three members of Bixio-Frizzi-Tempera).

above:
Greenfield & Cook, a Dutch vocal duo who sang and wrote the lyrics for "Movin' On", as featured in *The Four of the Apocalypse.*

themes and scores of his films. Now, at this stage, all the way through The Four of the Apocalypse, *they had put "Knockin' on Heaven's Door" by Bob Dylan! Oh! When we heard that this is what Lucio wants, we were horrified – this song is one of the greatest! We thought, well how? We thought we were lost! It fitted so well with the movie that it really influenced our writing. As I said, Franco, Vince and I loved that genre so we wrote many new songs, and in the end we did a pretty good job with it!"*

The music pleased Fulci immensely, and an LP of it was swiftly released by Cinevox. Oddly, however, it was credited on the cover as "Movin' On: original soundtrack to the film The Four of the Apocalypse" and credited to 'The Cook and Benjamin Franklin Group'. (Note: "Movin' On" was the name of a song which recurs throughout the film.) The back cover revealed that the music was composed by Franco Bixio, Fabio Frizzi and Vince Tempera whilst the lyrics and vocals were by Greenfield & Cook (real names Peter Kok and Rink Groeneveld), a Dutch singing duo on the Polydor label, with two albums and numerous singles under their belts. Evidently the disc was a temporary association between two distinct musical entities: Bixio-Frizzi-Tempera and Greenfield & Cook. The unwieldy 'Cook and Benjamin Franklin Group' monicker may have been decided upon as a compromise to avoid either group taking precedence (although Peter Kok/Cook seems to have won out overall!). Along with Frizzi, Bixio, Tempera, Cook and Greenfield, the line-up on the *Four of the Apocalypse* sessions also featured Massimo De Luca (guitar), occasional Morricone player Franco Di Lelio (harmonica), Michele 'Éra Di Acquario' Seffer (bass), and Toni Esposito (drums and percussion).

Bixio-Frizzi-Tempera's cues for Lucio Fulci's comedy *Young Dracula* (1976) are scarcely worth mentioning, as they're pushed down low in the mix and rarely attract attention, but their next Fulci assignment was another matter. Writing for *Sette note in nero* aka *The Psychic*, Fulci's return to the thriller after an absence of five years, the trio created some of their most indelible and exciting music. (See below.) When I discussed with Frizzi his musical influences, and the way they dovetail into his personal style, I said to him that I hear echoes of Morricone during parts of *Sette note in nero*. He laughed: *"Absolutely. Tempera was a master of pastiche. Not copying. He taught me that you have to inspire yourself, because music is there, already, and then you have to find your field. Tempera was a gifted pasticheur, and when you're a good musician you can play anything, you know? Before beginning to write music I was a friend of Morricone, in the beginning I loved him. My father was friends with Sergio Leone. I was just a boy then, but Sergio told my father, 'When your son wants to come to listen to our recording, he can.' So I went. On the day of recording "Shon"* [for Leone's *Giù la testa* aka *Duck You Sucker*] *I was there!"* So was it common for directors to ask him for music 'like Morricone' or 'like Nino Rota'? *"Oh! When I was young, always. Every time it happens. They ask me for Vangelis, they ask me for Morricone, and it was a weight on my shoulders. Then I grew, and I realised this can also be helpful. I began to prefer it when the director tells me where he wants to go like this. For instance, you meet a director, today, and you don't know him; you don't know how he thinks, what he eats, what he listens to. With music for movies, you have to find what is right for the project. It's not like it's just your own music, that you take to your mother and she says, 'Oh Fabio, bravo!' If you want to work with other people, you must meet them half way. Sometimes I was asked to play or to write like someone else. For instance, my music for* Blastfighter [dir: Lamberto Bava, 1984] *– now this is one that I love. I know where it comes from; I take the sound 'image' of Riz Ortolani, I change it, and it becomes the sound of Fabio Frizzi. The important thing is to use a style and to make it my style. Now I'm an older man, I know how to do it! And now that I'm older, I am asked to do it the Fabio Frizzi way!"*

After working on *The Psychic*, and then composing for Fulci's *Silver Saddle*, one of the last spaghetti westerns ever made (see below), Frizzi decided the time had come for him to work solo: *"I was growing. Franco was a publisher, still is, Vincenzo had a thousand and one other things to do. I thought to myself, my first daughter will soon be born, so I decided I had to try working on my own, although me and the guys remained absolutely friends. The cut-off point was when Maurizio Costanzo made a film called* Melodrammore [Maurizio Costanzo, 1977]. *It was signed by all three of us, but in fact I was the only one to do it. The same is true of* Manaos [dir: Alberto Vázquez Figueroa, 1979]; *this is also just Frizzi, although the credits say all three names."* Stylistically, Frizzi was beginning to hone a distinctive blend of styles and crossing the threshold between influence and personal expression, a process aided by the staggering breadth of his musical interests: *"I always had criss-cross passions in music, I mean that I cannot lock myself in a corral. I love baroque music, but rock as well. Strings, brass, Vienna waltzes, Scott Joplin, Debussy, Miles Davis, square dance, Philip Glass... And over all The Beatles, and the father of all musicians J.S. Bach. Every time I sit down and write music an enormous crowd is moving inside my head..."*

In 1979 Frizzi found himself working with Fulci again, and the special nature of the project, a horror film of unprecedented ferocity called *Zombi 2* aka *Zombie Flesh-Eaters*, would set the seal on their relationship for the next four years. *Zombie Flesh-Eaters* was such a huge success, both creatively and commercially, that the two men became artistically almost inseparable during a run of outstanding films: *The Smuggler*, *City of the Living Dead*, *The Beyond* and *Manhattan Baby* were all commissioned, written and released between 1979 and 1983. In each case, the working method was similar: *"Working with Lucio involved a certain routine: reading the script, a long talk with him on the specific movie's needs, writing down some thematic ideas. Then again we would sit down to listen and improve what I had done already, sometimes I would also go on set to get a real feel of the atmosphere surrounding the movie. Then at the end of shooting and editing images straight to moviola, noting duration and sense of each fragment of score."*

below:
Circa 1976, from left to right: Franco Bixio, Fabio Frizzi (partially obscured) and Vincenzo Tempera (plus unknown female friends) having dinner with actor-comedian Enrico Montesano, star of *Febbre da cavallo* (1976) for which Bixio-Frizzi-Tempera had recently composed the score.

above:
Fabio Frizzi recording at Cap Studios in Milan, circa 1975.

above left:
Fabio with Roberto Sbarigia (left) and Sergio Salvati (centre). Sbarigia (son of *The Black Cat* producer Giulio Sbarigia) was production manager on Fulci's *The Four of the Apocalypse*, executive producer of Fulci's *La pretora*, and producer of Enzo G. Castellari's *The Inglorious Bastards* (1978). Salvati of course was the director of photography on many of Fulci's most important films, including *The Beyond* and *City of the Living Dead*.

The sessions for *Zombie Flesh-Eaters* saw Frizzi joined, nominally at least, by a protegé of the film's producer Ugo Tucci, Giorgio Cascio (credited as Giorgio Tucci), who was given co-writing credit in return for acting as Frizzi's assistant on the project. The remaining instrumentation was handled by Goblin's Maurizio Guarini (keyboards and programming), session player Adriano Giordanella (percussion) and for one track with a Caribbean flavour, Tony Cicco on drums. Synthesised sounds and unusual textures were a distinctive aspect of the score: *"I tried some new effects during the recording of* Zombie Flesh-Eaters. *Connecting a Gibson 335 stereo guitar to a strange new box (can't remember the name) we had the opportunity of changing the guitar voice to a synthesised one. And overdriving one of the potentiometers we could get something like a high shriek. In the drill scene in* City of the Living Dead, *and some other scenes, we decided to use that same effect again."*

City of the Living Dead was the second Fulci horror film on which Frizzi worked, and this time he was joined by no less than three Goblin musicians – Maurizio Guarini (keyboards), Fabio Pignatelli (electric bass and guitar) and Agostino Marangolo (drums), plus session man Adriano Giordanella (percussion). Unsurprisingly, with this roster of talent Frizzi's passion for all things prog-rock found vivid expression in the score: *"Progressive rock was developing while I was growing up, as a boy and a musician. This musical virus was in my DNA and I was captivated by the many new kinds of sound: Pink Floyd, Genesis, Jethro Tull, Van der Graaf Generator, King Crimson. Especially Mike Oldfield's 'Tubular Bells' – this made a real impression on me. He used to play everything by himself, just like I was doing in my demos, and his talent bewitched me."*

One of the most important instruments in Frizzi's arsenal was the Mellotron, which can be heard on the themes for *Zombie Flesh-Eaters*, *City of the Living Dead*, *The Beyond* and *Manhattan Baby*. Frizzi fell in love with it: *"I had heard the sound of the Mellotron on The Beatles' "Sgt. Pepper" album and somewhere else, I think King Crimson or Genesis. Until that moment it was almost impossible to emulate real orchestra sounds, so I considered the birth of the Mellotron a real revolution. I knew a shop in Rome where you could hire one, and one day during* Zombie Flesh-Eaters, *when I understood that there was no other way to produce 'the voices of the dead', I rented one. It's not easy to use, always a bit out of tune, and so on... however the Mellotron is the one and only. A couple of years ago I actually bought one!"* Another influence on Frizzi's developing sound was the increasing sophistication of the recording studio, which became a creative tool in its own right: *"In those pre-computer days, the studio and the sound engineer certainly were tools in the production. Every sound, from Maurizio Guarini's keyboards, Fabio Pignatelli's basses, the guitars, percussion, effects, everything passed through the mixer in a creative way, giving a final and original shape to the score."*

The line-up remained fairly stable for the early-1980s Fulci scores, although the addition of a string section and choir demanded extra help. *"In* The Beyond *and* Manhattan Baby *there was an important orchestral contribution,"* says Frizzi. *"For the first of these I had the support of Giacomo Dell'Orso for arrangements and conducting. The orchestra was the Musicians Union of Rome, the chorus of four men and four women was by Nora Orlandi. Permanent staff, as always, Fabio Pignatelli and Maurizio Guarini. However, Maurizio was not available for* Manhattan Baby *and so the keyboards were played by a colleague, the composer and conductor Gianni Mazza, who is also a great friend of mine."*

Ultimately, what unites and defines Frizzi's music for Fulci is the emotional texture of the work. It's eerie and unsettling and mysterious but also somehow optimistic, uplifting even – a strange and unexpected response to Fulci's dark and nihilistic imagery. Was this something that emerged from Frizzi's preparatory conversations with the director? *"No I don't think so. It's my way of reading and translating, from images and stories to music. I think there is something nostalgic but positive in me, something that I can't stem, a point of view under which I metabolise reality. And maybe with Fulci's dramaturgy, this union-and-contrast is strong and decisive."* Several years ago I mentioned to Frizzi that I'm especially fond of a beautiful passage from the *City of the Living Dead* soundtrack that wasn't used in the film, a mid-section that occurs during the track "Paura e liberazioni". Clearly delighted, he laughed: *"Steve, you are the first person who noted it, congratulations! I prepared this theme expressly for the main title: a tracking shot in a cemetery. I felt something sweet in that scene, we aren't yet in the middle of fear. So I wrote the music you are talking about, a waiting and mesmerising music. I love it. However... When I'd finished recording the score, Lucio had heard a lot but not all of the final mixed music. Bruno Moreal, our mixing engineer, starts working. We are seated in the mixing room theatre, front row in front of the screen. The first images of the cemetery appear, with my first notes of music. Lucio gets up in a fury, shouting: 'What is this shit? What is this disgusting thing? This cannot be my main title music!! Back to the moviola!!!' I felt like dying! You can imagine – I was still a young guy. But even though I did not agree with his reaction and his artistic choice, from that moment on I realised that music written for images must tell the story that the director wants. And it's not always the beautiful piece of music that fits the scene."* Some years later, whilst talking to Frizzi after his sell-out concert in London, I pointed out that he'd had the last laugh by including "Paura e liberazioni" in his musical tribute to Lucio Fulci. He grinned: *"I still love that theme! And I'm sure he is smiling from beyond!"*

below:
CD soundtrack release: *The Four of the Apocalypse*.

above:
Fabio Frizzi (right) with his father Fulvio (standing) circa 1974. Fulvio was director-general of Rizzoli-Cineriz, one of Italy's largest and most successful film distribution companies, until May 1980 when he resigned following a clash over policy decisions. He died on 16 February 1983 at the age of just 59. Cineriz distributed the Italian releases of Fulci's *The Four of the Apocalypse, The Psychic* and *Silver Saddle*.

below: The original LP release of the score to *The Psychic* and the CD cover for the *Silver Saddle* soundtrack.

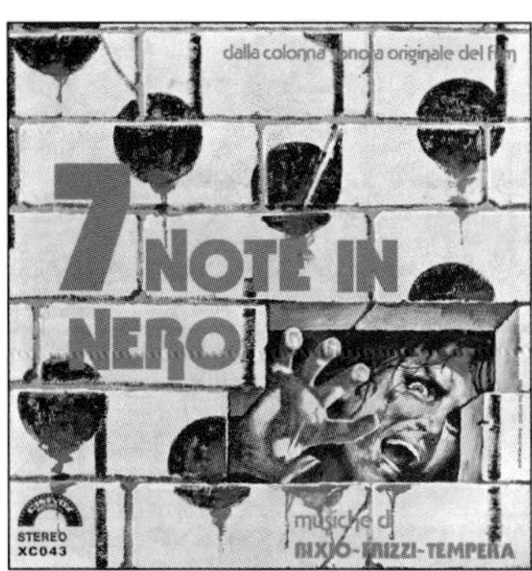

The Psychic

Sette note in nero aka *The Psychic* (1977) is one of Fulci's most accomplished films, and the Bixio-Frizzi-Tempera score boasts some outstanding compositions. Not that you would immediately agree if you dipped in to the opening credits and heard the theme song "With You", an MOR number that borrows liberally from the 1972 Johnny Pearson instrumental hit "Sleepy Shores" but adds a rather bland female vocal (the whole thing would be better served by the vocal talents of Demis Roussos, who would at least have sung it with gusto). Some of the other cues (for instance "Strane Visioni", "Allucinazioni" and "Abbatimento Del Muro") are effective in context of the film but sound rather wooden on disc; this is *not* the case, however, with the most famous pieces. The two leading musical themes in the film are "7 Note" and a piece called variously "Tracce Sul Muro" or "Ritrovamento Del Cadavere". "7 Note" is built around a simple yet implacable melody for piano and glockenspiel (which despite the film's title is *not* played entirely on the black notes!) over which a dreamily menacing string arrangement arcs into view like a creeping shadow of foreboding. Meanwhile "Tracce Sul Muro" is distinguished by an extraordinary bass line which remains a stubborn semitone flat in relation to the leading piano line. This weird tuning decision jars the nerves and perfectly represents the plot of the film, in which odd, disturbing details in a precognitive vision slowly come to bear on the protagonist's present day experience. Other standouts are "La Lettera", which bears the melodic hallmark of Frizzi's mature style in its eerie, insinuating flute motif, and "Aggressione", which could sit quite easily on the *City of the Living Dead* soundtrack. ("7 Note" and "Tracce Sul Muro" were issued as a 7" single by Cinevox in 1977. Although different to their movie versions, these recordings are easily superior. I'm usually disappointed when film soundtracks are re-recorded or messed around with for release on record, but the approach is more than vindicated here. Sadly, fans of the remaining cues had to wait until 1992 when they at last turned up on a compilation CD.)

Silver Saddle

Bixio-Frizzi-Tempera's second spaghetti western soundtrack for Fulci, *Silver Saddle*, continues in the West Coast American country-rock idiom established by *The Four of the Apocalypse*. The title theme (called, rather unadventurously, "Main Title Song" on the CD) is wistful, sweet and relaxed in a way that recalls Simon and Garfunkel (an admitted artistic touchstone for Frizzi in particular), although its hippie mellowness may challenge the palate of those brought up on grittier fare. The trio use the title theme melody in numerous variations in the film, for instance slowing it to a gentle ruminative pace and rescoring it for oboe, harmonica and strings on "Fear and Friendship" and "My Name Is Silver Saddle". Contrasting it is a piece first encountered on the CD as "Hot Lands". Beginning as a mock-menacing piece for harmonica and acoustic guitar, it shifts into another gear with a second melody for banjo and bass guitar. This has great charm, with a loping gait, a wry melody, and a pleasingly gritty production featuring dirty tremelo guitar that wouldn't sound out of place in a Link Wray rockabilly number. "Bandits", a pleasingly ominous piece for moody cor anglais, and doomy piano and strings, has hallmarks that would re-emerge in Frizzi's future horror soundtracks; glowering piano chords and a stately string ensemble, accompanied here by the inevitable wailing harmonica. "In the Desert" sends the string section galloping along to a cavalry snare drum, at a pace which, to be frank, the violins struggle to keep up with (the piece reappears several times, most notably in the extended "Silver Saddle Strikes Back"). Typically of course, for a soundtrack album, the basic themes are reshuffled and reprised, although the degree of repetition makes the CD hard to swallow as a sustained listening experience: a track like "A Cowboy and a Kid", for instance, merely shuffles "Silver Saddle", "Hot Lands" and "Bandits" into a medley without significant internal variations.

The CD concludes with two tracks from a 7" single released by Cinevox in 1978, featuring a radio friendly remix of "Silver Saddle" and the non-soundtrack B-side, "Two Hearts" (no relation to the earlier track "Two Friends" which was an MOR romantic variation on the title theme). Both of these cuts feature the vocal talents of Canadian singer-songwriter Ken Tobias (who receives a co-writing credit on the 7"). Tobias is best known for writing "Stay Awhile", a mellow smoocher by vocal group The Bells (aka The Five Bells) which hit the top spot in Canada in April 1971 and reached #7 in the American Billboard chart. The differences between the album version of "Silver Saddle" and the 7" version are slight, just a simple matter of editing the piece by fifty seconds and softening the clarity of the original with compression and some extra reverb. Interviewed in 2009 by Lionel Grenier (for his website luciofulci.fr), Tobias revealed, *"At the time, my record company, Attic Records, had published my music in Italy thanks to Cinevox Records [...] My manager and I were in Cannes for Midem, and we met Carlo and Franco Bixio ... We became friends and they asked me to participate in* Sella d'argento *... I had total freedom to write the lyrics because they respected my writing. It was difficult at first because I had this demo from Franco Bixio on which he played piano and hummed the melody on which I had to write. But when I finished the lyrics, I read and explained them to the trio and they were satisfied."*

Zombie Flesh-Eaters

Lucio Fulci brought to his groundbreaking *Zombie Flesh-Eaters* a sense of corporeal revulsion and malaise, feelings which seem to have sprung not only from Dardano Sacchetti's script but also from the pessimistic, haunted aspect of the director's psyche. Fabio Frizzi, a man with an altogether sunnier temperament, approached the music from an oblique angle, unleashing strange emotional undercurrents not immediately associated with gut-chomping gore.

His approach can be felt immediately in the justly celebrated title theme, which conveys first of all a sense of great age and solemnity. The sound is grandiose, corroded, antediluvian. But then, as if from behind a cloud of ancient dust, comes sunshine; a beautiful synthesiser melody with a bizarre sense of optimism and joy. What on earth is going on? For a film as relentlessly gruesome as *Zombie Flesh-Eaters*, this shift into ecstasy is one of the most off-the-wall twists ever to grace a movie soundtrack. And yet, what do we secretly feel as we watch a zombie apocalypse on the cinema screen? Could it be joy? Does a hidden pleasure in mankind's ruin lurk behind our gasps of horror? Apocalypse suggests a wiping of the slate, capitulation to the void, and there's something of joy in that, relief even, as the game is finally, irrevocably up. Frizzi's serene melodic counterpoint allows us to feel this strange existential pleasure.

Contemporary influences make their way into the mix too; echoes of disco can perhaps be discerned in the title theme's insistent pulse-beat (achieved, Frizzi told me, by simply tapping the palm of his hand on a directional microphone). However the dominant strand in the score's DNA is progressive rock, as represented by the Mellotron played by Frizzi himself, which provides the film's indelible 'voices of the dead'. (Much favoured by groups like King Crimson and The Moody Blues, the Mellotron was a keyboard containing a bank of tape loops, one for each key. The loops could carry any sound from strings to human voices, and since they were analogue rather than digital in origin they retained a murky, uniquely organic texture.) Among the other cues, "Eyeball" (which plays, of course, during the famous eye impalement) is built implacably on ascending chords, around which demented furies swirl. Agostino Marangolo's heavily phased drums are flung across the soundstage, a dissonant electric guitar wails, Maurizio Guarini's synthesiser hisses, and Fabio Pignatelli's propulsive bassline pushes us remorselessly towards the most staggering image in Lucio Fulci's career. (Note that this cue also appears, in a slightly remixed form, in the 1979 jungle adventure film *Manaos*.) "Escape from the Flesh Eaters" incorporates minimalist influences: Guarini's chugging Yamaha CS80 and Frizzi's insistent xylophone sound like Steve Reich jamming with Giorgio Moroder. "The Cab Ride" is pastiche Caribbean music, the backing track for a lost Boney M holiday hit, while "Menard's Duty" coaxes the film's tender emotions out of hiding.

Beneath the shock and awe of Fulci's incredible violence, *Zombie Flesh-Eaters* is at heart a melancholy tale, in which lovers rise from the grave to kill their partners, a daughter loses her father, marriages founder, friends die, and the decaying remnants of humanity perambulate joylessly. Frizzi's ability to capture all possible shades of feeling – horror, jollity, weird serenity, a tragic sense of loss – contributes immensely to the film's subliminal power.

In this music, eclecticism turns to ineffable magic, so personal to Frizzi that it may as well come with his signature attached. By choosing an oblique emotional approach to the horror, he gives the images a mythic dimension, a sense of awe and mystery, a delicious strangeness that lingers in the mind and stirs the heart.

above:
Fabio Frizzi (right) and Franco Bixio in Florence, 1975, teasing sounds from the inside of the piano for Pier Ludovico Pavoni's erotic drama *La peccatrice*. Unusual instrumental techniques would play a significant role in the soundtracks Frizzi recorded for Lucio Fulci's horror films.

The Smuggler

Jumping off at quite a different angle is this disco-funk soundtrack for Fulci's ultra-violent crime thriller, which sounds as though it would be right at home on a mid-seventies blaxploitation movie. Problems with the condition of the master tapes have restricted access to this score over the years, although a CD from Beat Records did eventually appear. The music's main achievement is to add some upbeat (and it must be said slightly cheesy) toe-tapping energy to what is frankly one of Fulci's nastiest films. The funky workout that plays during the Bunsen-burner sequence makes an already repellent scene even more stomach-churning by seeming almost to encourage the villlain, as he scorches a woman's face for selling him cut drugs. Perhaps the highlight is Frizzi's collaboration with Italo-disco act Cricket, for the song "You Are Not the Same". A sweet, gently melancholy tune under-pinned by bubbling bass and synthesiser, it has some of the feel of Roxy Music's "Same Old Scene" (if sung by Baccara rather than Bryan Ferry).

left:
CD soundtrack cover for *The Smuggler* under one of the film's alternative titles.

above:
Frizzi's soundtrack for *City of the Living Dead*, remastered and re-released in 2014 by Death Waltz, with stunning new artwork by Graham Humphreys.

City of the Living Dead

Although not directly a 'Lovecraft adaptation', *City of the Living Dead* owes much to the cosmic horror fiction of H.P. Lovecraft: the film's setting of Dunwich quotes "The Dunwich Horror", its 'book of Enoch' is obviously intended to sit beside the 'Necronomicon' in the bookcase of the damned, and the central image of a priest who hangs himself is drawn directly from Lovecraft's dream diaries, as conveyed in the short story 'The Evil Clergyman'. The New England scholar's taste for ancient gods, damned religions and transdimensional evil are ably echoed by Frizzi's scoring; choral Mellotron soaks the film in corroded liturgical menace, synthetic string glissandos promise impending dimensional catastrophe, while lunging rhythm motifs chase the listener along Escher staircases dogged by malevolent choristers and squealing apparitions. The incredible diversity of Frizzi's musical influences feeds the unpredictable emotions and oblique compositional strategies of his soundtracks for Fulci. When first you see *City of the Living Dead* the violence tends to stand out the most, but afterwards the film's haunting beauty lingers in the mind. It's a beauty one can also feel when listening to the score on its own.

We're given a tour through the scope of Frizzi's achievement on the opening track, "Introduzione". After a superlatively ominous arrangement for strings and flute we segue into a thrilling funeral march for piano and drums. Synthesiser and electric guitar radiate stealth and obscure menace, an implacable choir keeps faith with the beat, while the immaculate drumming and doom-laden piano say all there is to say about the straight-faced Gothic solemnity of Fulci's vision. "Irrealtà Di Suoni" introduces a gorgeous acoustic guitar figure, showing the influence of Mike Oldfield's "Tubular Bells" but made entirely Frizzi-esque by an exquisitely odd contrapuntal piano melody that adds a filament of lunacy. Meanwhile "Paura Vivente" pulses with danger and excitement, its simple ascending riff liberating all manner of eldritch disorder before slyly doubling back to the lower octaves. By combining the simplest of soundtrack structures (the ascending scale for tension is one of the oldest standbys in the book) with eruptions of the most extraordinary atonal squalling, Frizzi signals both his awareness of the established traditions of horror and a desire to push them forward.

"Apoteosi Del Mistero" is arguably Frizzi's crowning achievement for the film. Taking as his starting point the pulsing main theme for *Zombie Flesh-Eaters*, Frizzi delivers an even more potent variation. A serene Mellotron motif, a triumphant, optimistic synthesiser fanfare, and a uniquely stuttering drum pattern convey grandeur, excitement, and something more: this soaring, ecstatic music encourages us to feel somehow *affectionate* towards the risen dead. This is *their* music, and you can't help but adore them for it. It's this emotional dissonance, between the gruesome decay of Fulci's imagery and the exhilaration of Frizzi's music, that grants *City of the Living Dead* a life beyond its component parts; there's cinematic alchemy taking place here, as colliding emotions transcend the literal meaning of the images, leaving us with an ineffable compact of sadness, horror, warmth and adrenalin.

below:
The Beat Records soundtrack CD cover for *City of the Living Dead*.

The Beyond

It's almost impossible to think about *The Beyond* without the magic spell of the soundtrack in your mind as you do so. It's probably Frizzi's best work; one could argue that the ideas he poured into Fulci's earlier films reach their finest distillation and maturity in *The Beyond*. His music not only accompanies the dead, it rolls out the red carpet for them. Can you feel anything but thrilled for the zombies as they revive from their morgue slabs and stagnant cellar pools to the strains of Frizzi's glorious orchestration?

The Beyond confronts us with images of prolonged, extravagant violence. Vistas of rotten flesh, mouldering slime and suppurating wounds assault our senses and trouble our stomachs. And yet, with inspired perversity, Frizzi scores the film with a combination of melancholia and looming grandeur. "Liza, Sweet Liza" is as gentle and refined as Catriona MacColl herself, a lilting melody for strings, flute, and steel-string acoustic guitar. As the piece unfolds, Frizzi adds haunting cor anglais, and decorates the mix with harp, piano, fretless bass and recorder. The arrangement has a pastoral wistfulness that suggests the Englishness of Liza, before an ascending sequence sows the seed of disquiet. A second variant, "Liza, Damned Liza", adds an urgent drum pattern, a buzzing electric guitar, and a synthesiser which curls from the mix like whisps of smoke escaping from the cursed cellar of the Seven Doors Hotel. Meanwhile "Emily's Theme", for piano, flute and pizzicato strings, boasts a zig-zagging chromatic melody that steps back and forth across the black and white keys as easily as Emily steps across the divide between worlds (it's not too fanciful, either, to see its crazy-paved melody as representative of the fractured non-Euclidean geography in the film, with characters dying in one location only to pop up in another). This is one of Frizzi's most haunting and idiosyncratic tunes, as strange and evocative as anything in his canon. (Unusually, it was written after attending the shooting of the film, as Frizzi told me: *"Sometimes working from the moviola does not give you the emotion of the film. So I would try to go on the set. I was on set for* The Beyond, *during the scene where Emily is in the house alone. I must tell you, it was so cold! It was around Christmas time, and we were in De Paolis studios: they called 'Action!' and she entered the room and you could see her breath in the cold air! So they made her go and put ice in her mouth to bring down the temperature of her breath so you could not see the steam!"*)

If there's one track on this album which conveys the glorious lunacy of Fulci and Frizzi's work together it's "Acid Burn", an extraordinary combination of funkiness and morbidity. It proceeds paradoxically with a sort of straight-faced hysteria: shivering stabs of violin and slippery flourishes of bass guitar are joined by a decorous string ensemble, bringing a curious sense of propriety in the midst of madness. The effect is near-indescribable: bear in mind that these elements accompany a scene of the most surreal, preposterous carnage, as a woman's face is dissolved into bloody mulch by a supernatural acid deluge, and later a scene in which a man's eyes, nose and lips are chewed by marauding tarantulas!

"John and Liza's Blues" (for clarinet, trumpet and piano) accompanies a laid-back dialogue scene in a New Orleans jazz bar, in which David Warbeck and Catriona McColl's characters get to know each other; the piece has an old world charm that suits the New Orleans setting and complements the warmth of chivalrous Dr. McCabe and the gentility of our English rose heroine. By contrast there's the magnificent "Hotel Lament", a sound-portal hewn from the most portentous and granitic of choral Mellotrons, leading to the full-blown title theme in which female voices chant in Latin over a thrilling piece for the core ensemble of piano, flute, strings, bass and drums. The lyrics of the chorale – *"Cum resurget creatura"* ('All creation is awakening'), *"Quantus tremor est futurus"* ('Great trembling there will be') and *"Quando judex est venturus"* ('the judge will come') are taken from 13th century Gregorian chant "Dies Irae" ('The Day of Wrath') often, though not always, credited to Tommaso da Celano.[3]

"Schweik's Destiny" is another classic Frizzi cut: gloriously gloomy strings and an aching flute, with the metallic clank of a clavinet to add sinister weight to the payoff. Heavy with pain and the weight of sombre isolation, it reeks of the dirt, sweat and strain of Schweik's existence, but also rises in elegaic crescendos, representing perhaps the spirit of the artist whose vision unlocks the underworld. "Descent" begins with an exquisitely sad theme for piano, cor anglais and flute, backed with violins and a steel-stringed acoustic guitar. The return of the cor anglais from "Liza, Sweet Liza" adds a sorrowful note of regret to the depiction of Liza's fate. Some people claim to find Fulci's films simply nasty and crude, but if so they're emotionally colour-blind; his choice of this piece of music, as Liza and John enter the barren wasteland of death seen in Schweik's painting, emphasises tenderness, resignation and loss – not exactly the standard preoccupations of a gore-frazzled nihilist.

The latter stages of "Descent" and the whole of "Finale" lock into the same essential groove: thrilling, operatic, magisterial. Frizzi's spiralling violins, the soaring flute and vigorous choral singing, make it impossible to say what the dominant emotion should be at this point. The film climaxes with the saddest, most horrific scenario, a living death in a featureless dimension, surrounded by dust and smoke and crumbling cadavers... and yet the music pulls at the heartstrings, stirs the adrenalin, sends shivers of pleasure through the spirit, and pounds out a pulsebeat with a military snare drum for the chanting of the spirits of the dead. There's an air of triumph – but triumph for whom? For the demons of the beyond? Or death itself? One is pulled in opposing directions by this music: it aches with sadness for the fate of dear Liza and the good-hearted Dr. McCabe, yet it marches through one's mind like the soldiers of a new society; the society of the dead. Frizzi's genius is to leave us at a threshold between conflicting emotions. We cannot easily define the contradictory feelings he unleashes, and this dissonance between image and music creates a pervading sense of otherness. In a film concerned with Lovecraftian dimensions, with impossible gateways and dream logic, Frizzi gives *The Beyond* a non-Euclidean emotional life too.

Frizzi's great gift to Fulci was to emphasise not the cruelty of his vision but the grandeur. Where many composers would respond to a film as violent as this with shock effects and grating atonality, his master-stroke was to score to the elegance of Fulci's vision, to the decayed beauty of his film's rhapsodic violence. It's a poetic response, refusing to be coerced into simple repulsion. In tone and temperament, Frizzi's music speaks of the romance of death and the sadness of the flesh, the thrill of entering another reality and the mysterious joy of confronting the void. In *The Beyond*'s last image John and Liza's eyes are cataracted with the stigma of the undead, staring sightlessly into the camera; the music, however, rages with the fire of affirmation, sending the viewer out of the cinema not depressed, not desolate, but vibrating with excitement.

above:
Cover art for one of the many releases of Fabio Frizzi's masterful score to *The Beyond*.

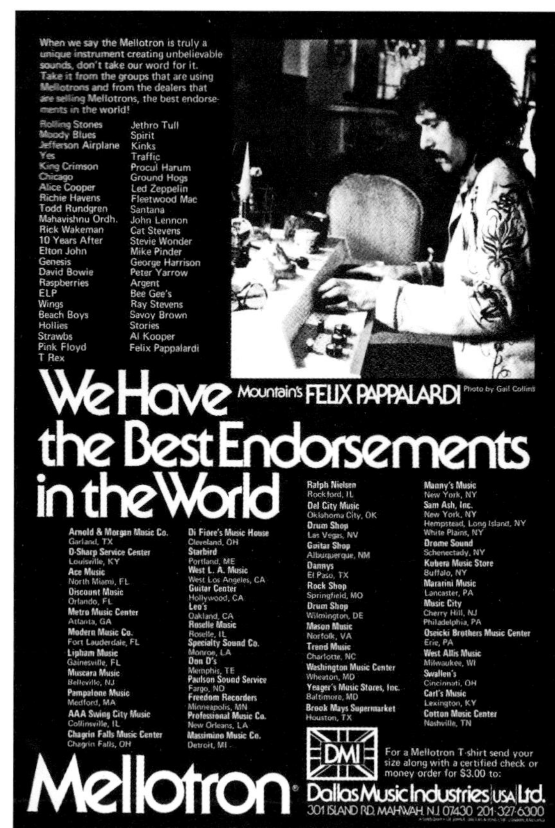

left:
A 1974 advertisement for the Mellotron, Fabio Frizzi's favourite keyboard.

below:
The Mellotron M400 (available in two finishes), a keyboard capable of playing specially recorded tape-loops, used extensively by Frizzi on the soundtracks for *Zombie Flesh-Eaters*, *City of the Living Dead*, *The Beyond* and *Manhattan Baby*.

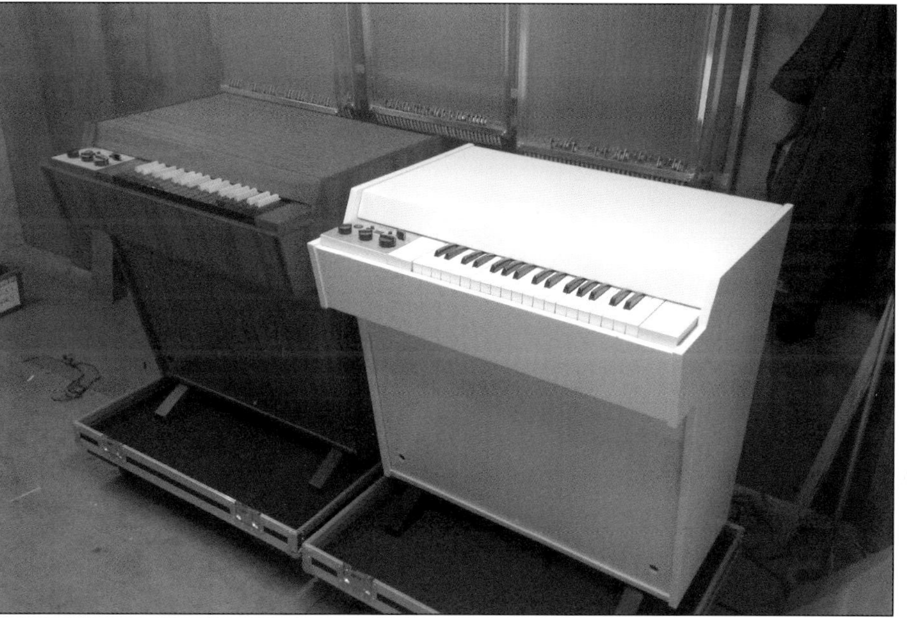

Manhattan Baby

Most fans would agree that *Manhattan Baby* is not one of Fulci's finest works. Made immediately after the scorching violence and thematic bleakness of *The New York Ripper*, it does not try to match such heights of horror, nor does it return to the mouldering Gothic splendor of *The Beyond* or *The House by the Cemetery*. It does, however, share a haunting atmosphere with those better films, credit for which must surely go to Fabio Frizzi, whose score is as good as anything he did on the earlier films. If Lucio Fulci had been as near to the top of his game as Frizzi clearly was at this point, *Manhattan Baby* would be another masterpiece.

The composer's unique approach is to use limpidly beautiful Mellotron themes to suggest unease, and gorgeous string glissandos both to suggest the middle-East and to evoke mortal dread at the dissolution of reality. The first piece, called, rather unappetisingly, "Baby Sequenzia One", is positively heroic in musical stature, with a sweeping sense of the geography of the dunes, a smoothness that speaks of centuries of erosion, and a tune that triggers mental images of ancient construction (filtered perhaps more through the romance of old silent movie epics than a sense of the real torment that went into building the pyramids). This is of course as it should be; *Manhattan Baby* is not a realist film by any stretch of the imagination, its Egypt is a place of dreams and fantasy, not political strife and hardship. Resisting the temptation to get carried away with cod-Arabic scales, Frizzi sidesteps ethno-kitsch and allows himself just a couple of string glissandos to hint at Eastern tunings (although "Sequenzia 5" does dabble with this approach, utilising a rather cheesy pan-pipe sample and some pitch-bend to suggest Arabic influences). "Sequenzia 2" features the kind of bubbling quasi-funk bass-playing that enlivens so much of his work for Fulci, and a melody that segues from delicate beauty to a soaring sense of exhilaration. "Sequenzia 3" is the music for a lysergically enhanced royal visit, marching through vast glittering pyramids like a sci-fi vision of 38th century Egypt. In other words, rather stranger and more magical than the film in which it resides. "Sequenzia 4" revisits the first 'sequenzia', in slower, more leisurely and melancholy mood, and the whole thing is over far too soon; what there is, though, is quality Frizzi through and through...

With the exception of "Sequenzia 11", a solo saxophone improvisation representing New York in the film, the remaining pieces on the Manhattan Baby soundtrack album either reshuffle already-heard musical elements into suites, or in one instance offer an earlier piece ("Sequenzia 1") in faster tempo. Finally, it's worth pointing out that many pieces heard in the film do not appear on the soundtrack album, because they were in fact lifted from Frizzi's previous work for *Zombie Flesh-Eaters*, *City of the Living Dead* and *The Beyond*, a strategy that would also make its mark on the next, and last, of Frizzi's alliances with Fulci, *Nightmare Concert* aka *A Cat in the Brain*.

Nightmare Concert
aka *A Cat in the Brain*

Made in 1990, this is a film that plays, deliberately and self-consciously, upon Fulci's role as purveyor of a certain kind of horror cinema, and therefore draws some of its music from *The Beyond* (namely "Hotel Lament" and "John and Liza's Blues"). The new material divides into three groupings: numerous variants of the main theme, a couple of romantic pieces, and a child's lullaby. The title theme is by far the strongest of these, built around a spiralling, chromatically unpredictable melody that gives off a decidedly oddball, absurdist sensation. Frizzi seems to have been picking up on the underlying attitude of sarcasm, perhaps the satire to which Fulci was groping on this project; the result is a sort of hectic comic menace that feels on the verge of laughing at itself. This madcap tune is then slowed down, rearranged and otherwise milked for variation through different samples and midi-setups. The romantic interludes are less successful, mainly because they lack the real instrumentation that would add emotional colour to the tunes. When played on samples, including some nasty pre-set brass sounds redolent of late 1980s *Doctor Who*, the tunes just sound trite and the potential in the arrangement is left untapped. The lullaby, on the other hand, is an effective take on the 'spooky child' motif that dominates so much of horror scoring. All in all, this is a score that cries out for reinvention by real instruments, which made it all the more welcome when Frizzi introduced the title theme into his live tribute to Fulci, a decision that proved that the tune was indeed of the same calibre as the pieces he wrote for the earlier films; it quite simply came to life on stage, suggesting that even the weakest tracks on the soundtrack album would benefit from real instrumentation.

top:
The Beat Records LP cover for Frizzi's *Manhattan Baby* soundtrack.

bottom right:
Fabio Frizzi.
photo copyright © Olivier Strecker.

below:
CD artwork for the soundtrack to *A Cat in the Brain* (released in 2014 by Mondo).

ENNIO MORRICONE

I maniaci ~ I due evasi di Sing Sing ~ A Lizard in a Woman's Skin

Ennio Morricone (1928–) is Italy's leading exponent of the art of film music, and one of the greatest soundtrack composers of all time. Innovative, prolific and hugely influential, he has helped to define entire movie genres, the spaghetti western and giallo film in particular. The world of cinema would be vastly poorer without him.

Morricone's first two brushes with Lucio Fulci are of minor interest. His music for *I maniaci* is limited to a chirpy title song and some functional comedy cues: with the exception of a strip-club number complete with exaggerated bordello trumpet, and an elegant faux-classical arrangement for a funeral cortège, Morricone's work is not so different here to that of any other jobbing composer of the day. For *I due evasi di Sing Sing*, in keeping with the pastiche aspect of the film, his title theme mimics the big band brass of American TV cop shows of the 1950s. There is very little music in the rest of the film; what music we do hear comes mainly from television shows watched by the characters, or else it plays unobtrusively in the background during nightclub scenes. None of this seems to me to bear the stamp of the maestro and may well have been piped in from elsewhere. (Note too that the credits mis-spell Morricone's name!)

In 1971, however, Fulci presented the composer with a stronger, more dynamic film: *A Lizard in a Woman's Skin*. The result was electrifying. Drawing on the innovative techniques he'd brought to Dario Argento's *The Bird with the Crystal Plumage* (1970), Morricone gave Fulci a score that was elegant, strident, melancholic, blaringly dissonant and calculatedly schizophrenic. *A Lizard in a Woman's Skin* features some of Fulci's most hallucinatory images, and Morricone responds with a score that seems to stretch space and time, with arcing trumpet wails, disorientating juxtapositions and acidic string clusters creating the aural equivalent of forced perspective.

In "Composing for the Cinema – The Theory and Praxis of Music in Film", Morricone had this to say about his more dissonant recordings: *"It is a type of writing that I inaugurated with the first film of Dario Argento, and then I used it in the second and third. I continued for a few other films, and then that was enough. Otherwise, I would have had to leave my profession, because the results were sufficiently difficult for spectators to listen to. I wrote the structure for various sections, and then, recording, I indicated the entrances, exactly as I said before. But all this would not have made any sense had I neglected the tone-color factor and the mixture of musical and other sounds."* Evidently, Morricone was receiving feedback from his peers suggesting that his more dissonant work was hard on the ears. But did anyone in the audience ever really complain that the sounds were too much to bear? I doubt it. It really is a pity that Morricone should have felt so discouraged. It's true that such is the popularity of the composer's jaunty, sardonic spaghetti western scores, and his Oscar-friendly work on films like *The Mission* and *The Untouchables*, that his skill with horror and thriller music often goes uncelebrated; but if his themes for Italian giallo films are not as whistleable as the westerns, they are easily as innovative.

From the first strains of track one ("La Lucertola"), we are in the hands of a master. Beginning with a delicate, echoing introduction for flute, piano, plucked strings and soft electronic whirring, we ascend through a series of ever more lovely extemporisations for bass, violins and steel-strung acoustic guitar, led by the exquisitely beckoning vocals of Edda Dell'Orso. Pieces such as "Magia Nera" resemble his pioneering work with

above:
Cover artwork of the original soundtrack LP for *A Lizard in a Woman's Skin.*

top right:
Ennio Morricone in 1976, recording with Gruppo di Improvvisazione di Nuova Consonanza, the improvisation group formed in 1964 with whom he pioneered many of the experimental techniques that would inform his scores for Lucio Fulci, Dario Argento and numerous giallo films of the 1970s.

below:
Morricone's soundtrack for *A Lizard in a Woman's Skin*: pictured is Jay Shaw's cover art for Death Waltz's essential double-album release.

Gruppo di Improvvisazione di Nuova Consonanza (1964–1980), such is the formidable avant-garde menace and challenging textural pallette on display. A composition like "Sfinge" is an exercise in atonality, with shimmering violin, rumbling piano and malignant yowling trumpet gnawing at the listener's nerves. Morricone lists Karlheinz Stockhausen and Luigi Nono as influences, and his flair for electronic sounds is very much in evidence, with screeches, whirrs, whistles and indescribable echo effects bounding and soaring across the soundstage like intimations of madness. He is fearless when it comes to dissonance; his dense tone clusters and strangulated trumpet can sound like the effusion of some deadly orchestral torture chamber (appropriately enough considering the 'split dogs' in Fulci's disturbing vivisection scene). Lurking in his sound paintings are elements of bold and startling 'ugliness'; fizzing and groaning fuzz guitar, branching harmonics from the wind instruments, eerily microtonal pitch bends from strings that drift woozily in and out of tune. On the other hand his melodic sense can be sardonic, sarcastic even, coming on so sweet it would make your teeth ache were it not for his immaculate sense of irony.

The qualities that make Morricone such a perfect match for the giallo film are his ultra-modernity and his cynical edge; his music revels in its effects, making him the ideal choice for a genre which gloatingly employs shock contrivances, outlandish set pieces and deliberately jarring twists and turns. What one remembers after a good giallo is not so much 'a satisfying story well told' as a kaleidoscope of lunatic detail; gruesome, sexy and shocking imagery, jaggedly assembled. The giallo film for Morricone is a playground for his maniacal wit, his taste for provocation, his predilection for the musical twist of the knife. Cool, confident, sly, deranged, playful, dangerous: his music defines all that is thrilling about the giallo experience. On a piece like "Anvora Ad Est" he layers wildly conflicting sound ideas as though shifting sonic

transparencies on top of one another in a psychedelic frenzy. And when you can take it no longer, along comes a cool, relaxing, elegant piece for flute, piano and organ ("Sole Sulla Pelle") which wafts through your mind like a mild breeze bearing a fragrance of vermouth and the tang of polished wood and leather furnishings, a world away from the frenzy of lust and madness elsewhere. Yet even this intensifies just a little more than it ought to, becoming almost orgasmically lush and luxurious before subsiding into peace and stillness.

"Giorno Di Notte" sounds like a groove ripped from a Can recording session, or *Live-Evil* period Miles Davis. Representing the wild abandon of next-door seductress Julia Durer's all-night sex and drug parties, it conveys reckless hedonism mixed with seething chaos as the boundaries of high-life and low-life blur and shift. It's a milieu for which Fulci's camera can barely contain its excitement, even plunging into split-screen at one point, a development that pre-empts Brian De Palma's experiments with the technique two years later in *Sisters* (1973). *Lizard* is indeed a 'schizoid' film (as the apt though rather boring American retitling insisted), inasmuch as it is both fascinated and repelled by the decadence it depicts. This push and pull between attraction and repulsion is embodied in the soundtrack's mixture of sweet alluring melodies and harsh atonalities. Parts of the score have a semi-improvised feel and flirt with a feeling of randomness, as the instruments are allowed to awaken alongside each other like drug-sozzled revellers after a wild party. Dyspeptic strings scrape at the nerves like the memory of last night's indulgence; fittingly enough for a film whose murderous protagonist has the mother of all "What did I *do* last night?" hangovers. "Mimetizzata" is a Penderecki nightmare wandering down avenues of chromatic oddity towards what could almost be a slurred rendition of the flute intro on "Strawberry Fields Forever", while internal conflict and clashing world-views are suggested by the mismatched elements of "Nenia Per Una Bambola" in which bass and drums fight for dominance against a snide flute motif which sidles along in a completely different tempo: meanwhile extraordinary sounds, as though a giant were brushing his teeth in an echo chamber, push the breakdown motif to the fore.

A Lizard in a Woman's Skin is a tour-de-force giallo bursting with searing images and curious emotional flavours, and Morricone's fantastical score matches it every step of the way. Beautiful and twisted, vivid and cruel, sad and strange and exciting, it's a no-holds-barred sonic adventure that belongs in the collection of anyone who treasures the work of this bone fide master composer.

RIZ ORTOLANI

One on Top of the Other ~ Don't Torture a Duckling ~ Rome 2033 – The Fighter Centurions

Riziero 'Riz' Ortolani (1926–2014) studied at the Conservatorio Statale di Musica in Pesaro and got his professional start as a musical arranger for the Italian TV network RAI. His first major success came with the international box-office smash *Mondo Cane* (1962) directed by Gualtiero Jacopetti, Franco Prosperi and Paolo Cavara. Ortolani's lush, melodious title theme lent a grandiose sweep to the titillatory travelogue, and such was its quality that in 1963 it was nominated for the Academy Award for Best Song (with the addition of words by British lyricist Norman Newell). The score was also nominated for a Grammy in 1964. Ortolani went on to score the same directorial team's *La donna nel mondo* (1963), *Africa addio* (1966), and their confrontational but massively misjudged slavery 'exposé' *Farewell Uncle Tom* (1971).

Elsewhere in Italian cinema Ortolani was in demand for his ability to combine brooding modernist string arrangements with jazz-inflected cues, talents especially suited to the giallo and horror films of the 1960s and '70s. He delivered classy material for Umberto Lenzi's *So Sweet... So Perverse* (1969) and *Seven Blood-Stained Orchids* (1972), and provided memorable soundtracks for Armando Crispino's *The Etruscan Kills Again* (1972), Maurizio Pradeaux's *Death Steps in the Dark* (1976) and Flavio Mogherini's *The Pyjama Girl Case* (1977). His chief collaborations, however, were with Antonio Margheriti, Damiano Damiani and Pupi Avati. For Margheriti he wrote an incongruous but deliciously cool jazz score for *The Virgin of Nuremberg* (1963) and intense, neurotic string arrangements for *Castle of Blood* (1964), *Web of the Spider* (1971) and *Seven Deaths in the Cat's Eye* (1973). For Damiani he scored eleven projects, including four of the director's signature dramas about corruption in the Italian establishment: *Confessions of a Police Captain* (1971), *How to Kill a Judge* (1975), *The Bodyguard* (1977) and *The Warning* (1980). From the 1980s onwards Ortolani became the composer of choice for Avati: horror fans are probably aware of his brilliantly alarming theme for the underappreciated *Zeder* (1983) but may be less familiar with the many other scores he wrote for the Emilia-Romagnian director, including their first collaboration, *Aiutami a sognare* (1981) and the TV mini-series *Un matrimonio* (2013 – Ortolani's last recorded work). As Italian commercial cinema all but died in the 1990s, he moved, like so many, into television, where his talents became perhaps less appreciable amid a slew of mundane asignments.

Ortolani's most notorious assignment came in 1979 when Ruggero Deodato signed him up for the brutal *Cannibal Holocaust* (released the following year). When a film is as cruel and upsetting as this one it can seem trite to discuss the beauty of the soundtrack, and yet, as anyone who's seen the film will attest, the score provides a vital emotional register for the film; one could go so far as to say that Ortolani's music is the conscience of *Cannibal Holocaust*. The same adeptness and spirit cannot be said to inform the two men's subsequent collaboration, *The House on the Edge of the Park* (1980); neither Deodato nor Ortolani are at the top of their game on this one, despite a few amusingly tacky Italo-disco moments.

below:
Two of Ortolani's most significant film scores, for two of Italy's most controversial films: the progenitor of the mondo film, *Mondo Cane* (1962); and the most troubling cannibal film of all, *Cannibal Holocaust* (1980).

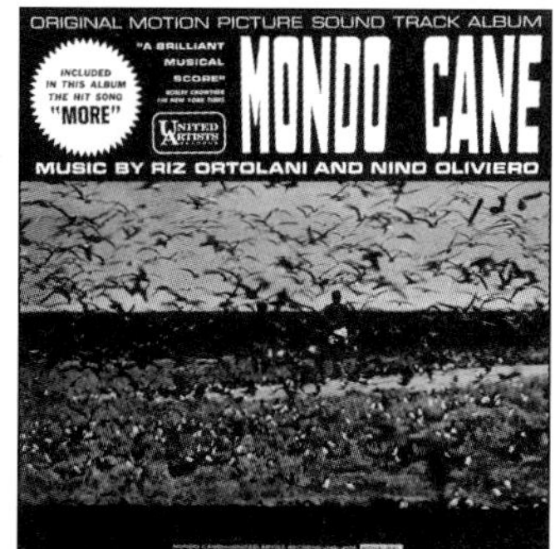

above:
The Dagored release of Ortolani's soundtrack to *One on Top of the Other*.

top right:
Jean Sorel and Marisa Mell as the alienated husband and wife in *One on Top of the Other*.

Ortolani wrote three scores for Lucio Fulci, beginning with *One on Top of the Other* (1969). For this elegant tale of deceit and betrayal he composed a modern (or as Ortolani preferred) "progressive" jazz score which drew on big band and be-bop styles, along with cool dinner-jazz cues and a few that one might almost tag 'easy listening'. However, 'easy listening' is certainly *not* the way to describe the title theme. It opens with a full-blooded jazz ensemble and some great tenor sax playing, bolstered by a fusion of gravelly baritone sax and squealing trumpets. The effect is a dense knot of controlled hysteria. It's fluent, confident, vivid and packs a hell of a punch. We then slide into a smooth finger-clicking passage for flute and upright bass, evoking the spirit of Henry Mancini, before the ensemble blasts again with the force of an aircraft engine. At the other end of the scale, "San Quentin" is perhaps the most sorrowful and beautiful piece ever used in a Fulci movie. Evoking a sense of intense longing and regret, it is quite simply breathtaking. Built around a hushed string section and a sensitive performance on muted trumpet, this is tender and mournful and so deeply evocative of loss that it could raise a lump in the throat of a clear blue sky. "San Francisco Railways" is built around the rarely used bass flute, a very haunting instrument which deserves mention for its husky tone and richness. The flautist was Ortolani's friend and frequent collaborator Gino Marinacci. As Ortolani explained, *"He played this bass flute and played it very well, although it is a very difficult instrument, it requires long, long breaths."* "Susan and Jane", a piece for sax and strings and more of Marinacci's bass flute, is lush and romantic, with an 'old-Hollywood' feel. The gently groovy "Lombard Street" and its uptempo sibling "The Roaring Twenties" are fun party froth with an easy-listening vibe, and "Sitar in Blues" delivers plentifully on its office-of-fair-trading approved title. Prowling upright bass and twanging sitar (the swinging sixties sound effect par excellence) occasionally give way to the blasting brass of the title track; the effect is cool and campy at the same time; Angelo Badalamenti meets Duke Ellington at an Andrew Loog Oldham soirée.

Ortolani's music for *Don't Torture a Duckling* takes a very different approach. The core is a string section, mainly violins, and the emphasis throughout is on modernist post-classical techniques. Herrmannesque chords shift subtly into microtonal variants glowering with nerviness and danger. This is not music to bop around your bachelor pad to; its closest precursors are Béla Bartók and György Ligeti. The main theme is built around stabbing violin chords, heavily echoed and filtered, creating a rhythmic sawing repetition of each phrase. For the sensuous moments in the film, as disturbing as they are, Ortolani opts for a slow-motion piece for alto sax, which sounds not unlike the work of Ornette Coleman in harmolodic mode; the instrument is sweet in tone but the melody is off-centre, with wide intervals pitched somewhere out of range of comfort and light. It underlines the amorality of the character played by Barbara Bouchet, who seduces young boys and exposes herself nude to them. Elsewhere, a cheerful melody is given a faintly Morricone-esque treatment, with harpsichord and organ, representing the carefree aspects of childhood. Ortolani revisits the tune with his string section later, only to segue into another disturbing 'detuned' arrangement which allows the melody to decay into malevolent microtonal clusters. There's also a sorrowful lament for recorder and strings which recalls the work of Gheorghe Zamfir (who made his soundtrack debut in 1972 and whose "Doina De Jale" became a UK hit in 1976 when it was used as the theme to a religious TV show, 'The Light of Experience').

The showstopper of course is "Quei giorni insieme a te" (translation: 'Those Days with You'), sung by Ornella Vanoni. Musically it's a rhapsodic evocation of sorrow, sweeping and full-blooded in delivery, with the emotional power of something like Ham and Evans's "Without You" (notably the Harry Nilsson version) or Neil Sedaka's "Solitaire" (with a few small similarities to the latter in the arrangement and melody). It's an example of a 'middle-of-the-road' ballad given such gusto that it transcends the triteness of the form. Lyrically, however, it's strangely oblique to the action in the film. The words (see below) speak of a love that died, from the perspective of a woman who looks back and sees how pointless it was but who mourns it all the same. The closest this comes to the feelings of anyone in *Don't Torture a Duckling* is the priest Don Alberto, whom one may suppose feels betrayed by the boys upon whom he lavishes affection, only to see them running off to have sex with a woman. It's a bit of a stretch though, so I find myself wondering instead if the lyric spoke to the recently bereaved Fulci on a level beyond the narrative requirements of the film...

"Quei giorni insieme a te"
(translation by Stephen Thrower)

Those days with you, I would not live again,
It was an odyssey, hard and useless.
We were a pair, and I adored you, I was one, the other was you
And you did not have the time to love me.

But I don't know why so little, in my eyes,
Seems more than I encountered then.
Those days with you I would erase: I repeat to myself,
'What a fool!' 'What a fool!'
And I'm a little ashamed I told you so.

Today I have more dignity, I would not accept the crumbs of love
you gave me then like charity.
But if it's so, I wonder why
I still think of those days with you?
But if it's so, I wonder why
I still think of those days with you?

Ortolani regarded Fulci highly and could see beyond the 'difficult' personal facade, telling *Nocturno*'s interviewer Davide Pulici, *"He was so... not surly, uncaring. If you were to say, 'Ah, but what a beautiful film you've done!', he would answer: 'What do I care ...' But it was all an attitude. A decent man, good, well-prepared."* [Interviewed by Davide Pulici, http://www.nocturno.it/intervista-riz-ortolani/] This ability to understand the deeper aspects of Fulci stood him in good stead on *Don't Torture a Duckling* and *One on Top of the Other*; sadly it seems to have done nothing for his creativity on the third and last of his Fulci collaboratrions, *Rome 2033 – The Fighter Centurions*. Characterised by dull rhythms and clichéd rock-disco arrangements, the score bathetically aims for grandeur while managing to sound as bargain-basement as the film's tinfoil chariots. Not a score for which a pro like Ortolani should be remembered, it was, one assumes, a reflection of the composer's disinterest in the material, and a mirror to Fulci's lack of suitability for the genre in which it resides.

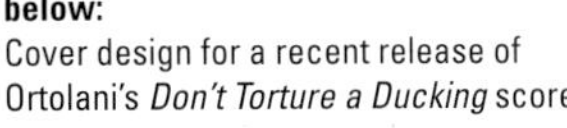

below:
Cover design for a recent release of Ortolani's *Don't Torture a Ducking* score.

WALTER RIZZATI & ALEXANDER BLONKSTEINER

The House by the Cemetery

Amid the non-linearity of Fulci's early-'80s work, *The House by the Cemetery* stands out for its fractionally more coherent plot, its emphasis on suspense, and also for its change of composer. Fabio Frizzi had scored eight out of Fulci's last ten films, but this time the job fell to a relatively new composer, Walter Rizzati.

Rizzati's previous credits gave no hint of his aptitude for horror: he'd scored two sex comedies for Giuliano Carnimeo (*L'insegnante balla... con tutta la classe* and *Mia moglie torna a scuola*), one for Marino Girolami (*Sesso profondo*, shot by Sergio Salvati), a Terence Hill/Bud Spencer flick (*Io sto con gli ippopotami*), and two projects written or directed by Joe D'Amato (*La voglia* and *Labbra vogliose*). Despite having made his home in sexploitation comedy, he revealed a definite talent for the dark side in *The House by the Cemetery*, composing a marvellously over-the-top soundtrack as lurid as the film it accompanies.

The score uses a basic ensemble of piano, drums, synthesiser, electric bass and guitar, a line-up similar to the one established by Fabio Frizzi in his scores for Fulci. The signature sound of *The House by the Cemetery* is a heavily flanged electric guitar, which seems to twist and curdle in the air like filaments of malevolent odour seeping from the cellar of "that Freudstein house... that *Freudstein* house". "Quella Villa", which underscores the film's opening scenes, is a Morricone-influenced piece for jagged rhythms, hammered into our nerves with syncopated drum and piano. It's not the most subtle approach but this *is* a Lucio Fulci film after all, and besides, Rizzati also delivers some breathtakingly beautiful passages, reflecting the sadness that permeates so much of Fulci's work, in particular the various incarnations of "Tema Bambino" which underscore the parallel universe of pretty little dead girl Mae (Silvia Collatina). A sorrowful elegy that tweaks at your heart-strings instead of pulling out the ventricles, this tune aches with the emotional weight of loss. "Chi Sta Arrivando" glooms across the soundstage like a spectre snooping around a favourite hunting ground, while "Incontro" melds curdling guitar with a piano motif that sounds like something played by ghosts in the back room of a dusty antique shop. Of course the title music "I Remember" is the centrepiece, resonating with all that is marvellous in Fulci's Gothic horror cinema. Like J.S. Bach scoring "The Hammer House of Horror", it's a gleefully macabre organ recital with phantasmal singers wordlessly flitting around the melody, the whole thing delivered with a slow pomp that suggests the funeral cortège of a deceased prog-rocker.

Also working on the soundtrack with Rizzati was the gloriously named Alexander Blonksteiner. He received no credit onscreen but he pops up, like a spirit that will not be denied, in the titles of three excellent tracks on the soundtrack album. "Blonk Suspense" hammers relentlessly at the most ominous two-note piano riff known to man, while heavily processed electric guitar and synthesiser stab and lunge at the listener. "Blonk Monster" unveils a killer guitar riff that early Pink Floyd and pre-showbiz Alice Cooper would have slit each other's throats for, before throwing us into a melée dominated by scourging synths and more of that deliciously menacing piano. "Blonk Fascia" is the most extreme track, and if like me you're a fan of the discordant music of the late 1970s 'No Wave' scene (Mars, DNA, Lydia Lunch) you might hear similarities. Sprawling over the soundstage like a rotten debauchee, it dispenses with regular tempo and throws us into a seething compost of sound. Designed to accompany the revolting excesses of Dr. Freudstein, it's an aural evocation of nausea; and yes, that *is* a recommendation.

Rizzati later scored Enzo Castellari's *1990: The Bronx Warriors* and two more films for Fulci's producer Fabrizio De Angelis; sadly *The House by the Cemetery* was Alexander Blonksteiner's last screen credit.

above:
The House by the Cemetery.
Evocative artwork by Graham Humphreys for the Death Waltz soundtrack LP.

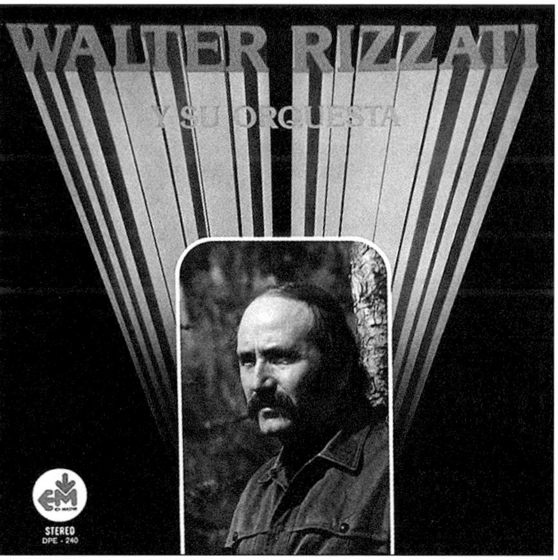

left:
This album of library music (called "Park Avenue") was written by Sergio Montori (who scored Walerian Borowczyk's 1978 film *Behind Convent Walls*), and performed by the Walter Rizzati Orchestra. Several tracks feature a distinctive flanged keyboard sound which Rizzati used extensively for *The House by the Cemetery.*

FRANCESCO DE MASI

The New York Ripper

Francesco De Masi (1930-2005) studied composition at the Neapolitan Conservatory San Pietro a Majella and orchestra direction at the Chigiana Academy in Siena. In 1968 he won an award for young conductors sponsored by the Italian TV company RAI, and in 1983 began teaching orchestra direction. He was the director of the Rome Symphonic Orchestra, and the composer of scores to more than 200 films. He was best known in the 1960s for his work on spaghetti westerns, but in the 1970s, among his many other commissions, he scored a giallo (*L'arma, l'ora, il movente* by Francesco Mazzei, 1972), a Spanish horror film (*La orgía de los muertos* by José Luis Merino, 1973), a cop thriller (*Napoli spara!* by Mario Caiano, 1977), a Nazisploitation fim (*Nazi Love Camp 27* by Mario Caiano, 1977), and a war film, *The Inglorious Bastards* (d: Enzo G. Castellari, 1978).

To prepare for *The New York Ripper* one suspects De Masi immersed himself in American TV cop shows: the music he created would work well in mainstream television hits like *Kojak* (1973-1978), *The Streets of San Francisco* (1972-1977), *Starsky and Hutch* (1975-1979) or *CHiPs* (1977-1983). These were turning up increasingly on Italian TV in the early 1980s, thanks to Silvio Berlusconi's Reteitalia TV company who imported numerous American shows for the first time. Such a drive towards American-style product was nothing new in Fulci's career: his horror films were all tailored to the USA, being nominally set there much of the time, but they retained a distinctive European identity. *The New York Ripper*, however, was far more 'Americanised', and De Masi's music was a vital component in that process.

As a listening experience divorced from the film, the score for *The New York Ripper* suffers from a tendency to repeat itself. By the end of an album's worth you will probably come to resent the ever-recycled title theme, even though it works well within a ninety minute film. So what can we observe about this theme, called "New York – One More Day" on the soundtrack LP? Scored for an electric rock ensemble plus horns and strings, with lead guitar carrying the melody, it incorporates jazz-funk shadings to indicate the racially mixed environment in which the film is set. Emotionally the piece is superficially cheerful, syncopated and purposeful yet tinged with fatalism: it's tailor-made to accompany shots of a cynical cop embarking on 'another day at the front-line'. The conventional design of this music, most definitely aiming within the bounds of 'mainstream entertainment', can be a touch off-putting after the majestic eccentricity of Fabio Frizzi's scores for Fulci, but the brief that De Masi has been given is quite clear: make the movie feel American!

"Phone Call" is gentle yet sinister, built on a two note ostinato and quivering flute (sounding not unlike the sort of music American director S.F. Brownrigg was enamored of in films like *Don't Look in the Basement* or *Keep My Grave Open*). It segues into a silky, mysterious passage for echoing, electronically filtered sax, slow and glutinous with a sensual druggy aura, before returning to the earlier ostinato. The main theme tune is then revisited in a more melancholic arrangement. "New York... One More Night" is brisk and effervescent, replaying the opening theme as a composition for trombone, sax, trumpet and strings. A curiously rattling electric guitar adds a sliver of menace before launching into an accomplished rock solo (it would be interesting to know who played this; perhaps Massimo Morante of Goblin? The technique is reminiscent of Pink Floyd's Dave Gilmour, one of Morante's chief influences). "Puertorico Club" is a rhythm workout with added sax

and casual scat vocal interjections, designed to give one of the film's most outrageous moments (the 'toe scene') a 'jungle fever' sexual frisson. In context of the film it's adequate, but on the soundtrack LP it outstays its welcome, and to make matters worse appears twice! "The Ripper" is more effective, slicing the key melody of the title theme into a series of fragments spread across a variety of instruments. This patchwork approach signifies both the maze of conflicting information about the killer's identity, the workings of the schizoid mind, and of course, the razor-slashing of victims' body parts! From a purely compositional point of view it's the strongest piece, with surprising variations and curious surreal passages redolent of Barry White's excellent score for the blaxploitation film *Together Brothers*.

By now, if you don't care for the lead melody, this soundtrack will be driving you crazy. Fortunately "Fay" brings a welcome expansion of melodic material, with a lovely new piece for trumpet and strings evoking the rich melancholy often found in the work of Ennio Morricone. "Where Is the Ripper?" opens with one of the best 'stings' in the film before coaxing shivers of unease from a string quartet and dissonant piano. The electric guitar motif returns, before passing the melody to the sax, thus blurring the line between the cop investigation and the sexual milieu (rather as Lieutenant Williams crosses the line from moralistic cop to whore's client). "Suspense and Murder" is yet another disassociation of the key melody, in the same vein as "The Ripper" but bringing nothing new to the table. "Waiting for the Killer' puts things back on the rails, revisiting the mid-section of "Phone Call" and pushing the velvet darkness further forward in the mix before dressing it with new melodic material. Slow, sensual, but woozily ominous, it suggests the flirtation with darkness implicit in the character Jane's sadomasochistic lifestyle.

De Masi's music for *The New York Ripper* is not as distinctive as the soundtracks for Fulci's other thriller and horror titles, but it's not without charm. In its slightly hokey attempt to evoke New York street life it manages, perhaps accidentally, to match the sleaziness of Fulci's scenario. And with all due respect to a long-standing professional of Italian film music, there's an almost kitsch aspect to this music which, in an odd kind of way, only serves to amplify the monumental tastelessness of Fulci's most shocking film.

top right:
This CD of Francesco De Masi's music for *The New York Ripper* also features tracks by Piero Piccioni from the Spanish/Italian giallo *La casa de las muertas vivientes* aka *Una tomba aperta... una bara vuota* (1972).

below:
Nick Percival's artwork for the Death Waltz soundtrack LP of *The New York Ripper*.

PINO DONAGGIO

The Black Cat

One of the finest film composers of the 1970s and 1980s, Pino Donaggio (1941–) is best known for his extraordinary work for Brian De Palma: *Carrie* (1976), *Home Movies* (1979), *Dressed to Kill* (1980), *Blow Out* (1981), *Body Double* (1984), *Raising Cain* (1992) and *Passion* (2012). He started out in 1973 with an exquisite score for Nicolas Roeg's *Don't Look Now*, which demonstrated all of his considerable strengths: a gift for sweet-and-sad melody, voluptuous-romantic string arrangements, and an ability, drawing on Bernard Herrmann's music for *Psycho*, to use the string section as a dangerous sonic weapon when required. (A native of Venice, he met Roeg by chance during the shooting of *Don't Look Now* and would go on to score another half-dozen or so films set in the 'city of bridges'.)

Always keen to work with new directors, Donaggio brought his gifts to bear on many smaller and less celebrated horror films in the next ten years: among the recipients of his talent were Herb Freed's moody little number *Haunts* (1977) and his not-so-special *Beyond Evil* (1980); Joe Dante's lively pulp horrors *Piranha* (1978) and *The Howling* (1981); Ugo Liberatore's *Nero veneziano* aka *Damned in Venice* (1978); and David Schmoeller's creepy and memorable *Tourist Trap* (1979) and *Crawlspace* (1986). Donaggio has worked three times with Dario Argento (*Two Evil Eyes* in 1990, *Trauma* in 1993 and *Do You Like Hitchcock?* in 2005) but his most sustained relationship with a filmmaker, other than De Palma, was with Marcello Aliprandi, for whom he scored five films until the director's death in 1997: the crime thriller *Corruzione al palazzo di giustizia* (1975), the subtle supernatural tale *Un sussurro nel buio* (1976), the erotic drama *Senza buccia* (1979), the ecclesiastical thriller *Morte in Vaticano* (1982) and the wartime ghost story *Soldato ignoto* (1995).

Donaggio worked with Lucio Fulci just once, but he gave him a magnificent score for *The Black Cat*. The title theme is a pure delight, as the composer responds creatively to the prowling black cat itself, and the pastoral country views over rolling fields and the village rooftops. The result is a piece of music that takes warmth and affection (I'm certain from this piece alone that Donaggio is a cat-lover) and marries it to a wistful celebration of rural beauty. The melody is carried by a cor anglais or 'English horn', a member of the oboe family, while the accompaniment is led by mandolin, harpsichord and acoustic guitar, instrumentation which establishes links to English medieval and folk music. Elsewhere, certain string passages feel as though they would just as easily grace De Palma's *Dressed to Kill*, such is their sumptuous elegance. (According to *Variety*, *Dressed to Kill* wrapped shooting some time in early April 1980 and came out in July that year, so Donaggio must have been tailoring the music to De Palma's film during April and May 1980: *The Black Cat* was shot just three months later, in August and September 1980, so it's little wonder that Donaggio still had *Dressed to Kill* in his system.) An occasional interjection from bass clarinet, and an indefinable imitation of a cat's querulous miaow (violin? singing saw?), introduces a quirky sense of menace just a whisker removed from the comedic, suggesting Donaggio's canny awareness that it doesn't do to be too straight-faced when scoring for a malevolent superfeline! Note also the recurrence of a 'sting' from *Don't Look Now*: a flute arabesque in *The Black Cat* which mimics a memorably uncanny synthesiser motif in the Roeg film.

Sadly this wonderful score remains criminally unavailable on CD or LP, except for a hard-to-find bootleg release. This is most puzzling, as in an interview conducted by Ottavia Da Re in August 2008, Donaggio commented favourably on his work with Fulci: *"Only one director has ever given me carte blanche... Lucio Fulci with whom I made 'The Black Cat'. I was also meant to make the music for his 'House of Wax' but then he passed away."*[4] Rumours abound that the original master tapes were lost or damaged: the bootleg version was evidently compiled by a person with access to all of the individual music cues (28 in total) but the sound quality is a little soft, as though lifted from a cassette tape. One hopes that someone else will manage to find the original recordings and give this soundtrack the prestige release it richly deserves.

Footnotes

1 Not, as the IMDb claims, the 1968 spaghetti western *And Now... Make Your Peace with God*: *"It's a false credit,"* he frowns. *"I was about sixteen! I think it was actually done by Franco Bixio."*

2 Rome's Ortophonic Studios (now the Forum Music Village), was founded in 1969 by Armando Trovajoli, Ennio Morricone, Luis Bacalov and Piero Piccioni, with studio manager and producer Enrico De Melis. It is built in the basement of a church, the Sacro Cuore di Maria, with special permits from the city and the Church of Rome. Consequently, an unusual feature of the studio, which would serve Goblin well during the *Profondo rosso* recording sessions, is the ability to record the church's on-site pipe organ directly to the studio.

3 Thanks to Mark Ashworth, who worked some of this out for me, and to Fabio Frizzi for confirming and providing the rest.

4 www.quellicheilcinema.com/interviste_detail.php?ptr=60

left:
Venetian resident Pino Donaggio at home in the City of Bridges.

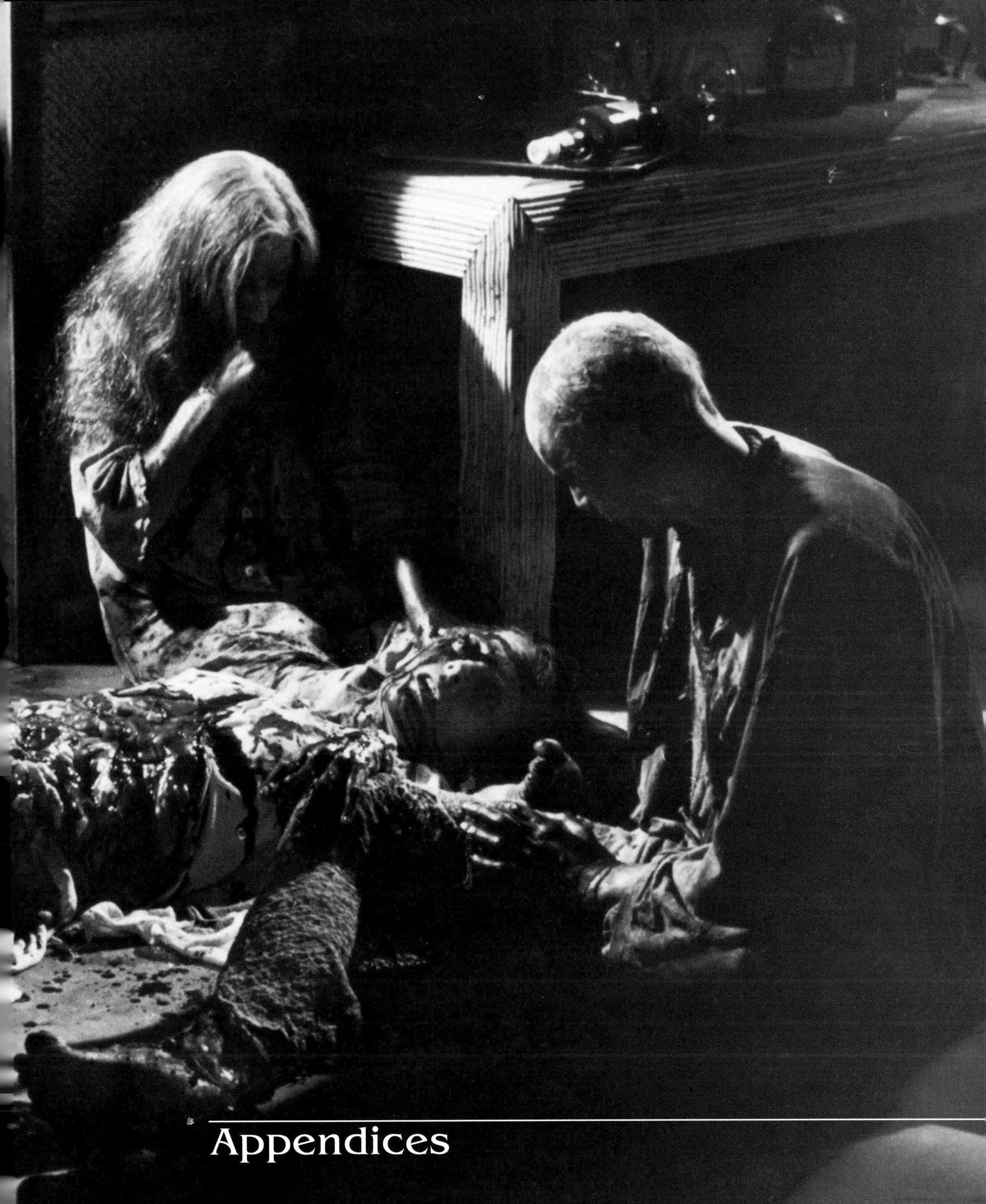

Appendices

Lucio Fulci at the BBFC

Lucio Fulci's relationship with the British Board of Film Censors was, to say the least, fraught. He resented them bitterly, and with good reason. Of the 54 movies he directed, ten were released theatrically in the UK, and at least nine were cut in some way. First to be tampered with was the religiously-themed comedy *Operation St. Peter's* (1968) – the censor's scissors claimed a chunk of comic imagery on the grounds of blasphemy. As Fulci's work grew more violent, the censors responded with their own methods of cutting and butchering, as if trying to outdo the director. This metaphorical arms race culminated in 1984 with a total ban on Fulci's most shocking and violent work, *The New York Ripper*. Meanwhile, two of his films – *Zombie Flesh-Eaters* and *The House by the Cemetery* – ended up on the so-called "video nasties list" of 39 banned titles, meaning that for many years one could be prosecuted for buying, selling, or even owning them.

The BBFC objected to the gory excesses of Fulci's zombie films, but as can be seen in the detailed notes that follow, the underlying attitude tended towards dry amusement. Despite demanding considerable cuts, the tone when addressing *Zombie Flesh-Eaters*, *City of the Living Dead* and *The House by the Cemetery* was something along the lines of a gentle rebuke. This was to change, however, when *The New York Ripper* arrived at the BBFC's offices in Soho House in December 1983. During the furore that followed, it's no exaggeration to say that Lucio Fulci became one of the most reviled film directors in British censorship history. Three years later his name was still sending shudders of disgust through the BBFC: in December 1986, when Elephant Video submitted Fulci's crime thriller *The Smuggler* for video release, one examiner remarked in his notes, *"For viewers of Fulci's loathsome* New York Ripper, *this boring and over-bloody gangster pic confirms our mistrust of his judgement. The now largely excised anal rape [...] itself establishes the case for some kind of censorship."* (*The Smuggler* was then ordered to be cut by 2m 52s.)

Fulci was no stranger to controversy. In Italy during the 1970s, he was in and out of court for a variety of reasons (see *The Eroticist*, *A Lizard in a Woman's Skin* and *Don't Torture a Duckling*) and as both an individual and a professional he contributed to various anti-authoritarian causes (adding his name to an official protest against the Vietnam War, for instance). He was against the imposition of state controls on creativity, and regarded all censorship as a form of political oppression. Many reviewers have laughed at his insistence that the killing by power drill of Bob in *City of the Living Dead* was intended as a statement "against a certain kind of fascism", but he was being sincere (if lacking a sense of humour about himself). After all, the scene involves a shy social misfit being blamed for a crime he didn't commit and then murdered by a brutally authoritarian patriarch, with the spectre of the Salem witch trials lurking in the story's undergrowth of allusions. That it was this scene which the BBFC cut from *City of the Living Dead* can only have added to Fulci's paranoid sense that all censorship is politically motivated.

However, the fury and vehemence of the response to *The New York Ripper* was certainly political; no paranoia required. The issues surrounding the film may have been thought of as moral ones by some at the Board, but the tenor of the debate was heavily informed by ideological viewpoints, namely those drawn from feminism. As can be seen from some of the comments reproduced here, the rise to prominence of feminist film theory (spurred by Laura Mulvey's influential essay "Visual Pleasure and Narrative Cinema" in 1975) was striking vivid echoes in the halls of the BBFC, and in the wider culture it was leading to an alliance between those who supported censorship on authoritarian grounds and those who took umbrage, ideologically, with certain kinds of images. Furthermore, the pot was being vigorously stirred by right-wing newspapers, who were drumming up hostility against the so-called video nasties. With 'moral campaigner' Mary Whitehouse always a force to be reckoned with in such matters, and right-wingers in the Church and Conservative Party joining the fray, 1983 was a pivotal year for the question of what was, and what was not, admissible as screen entertainment. *The New York Ripper* found itself at the centre of a perfect storm...

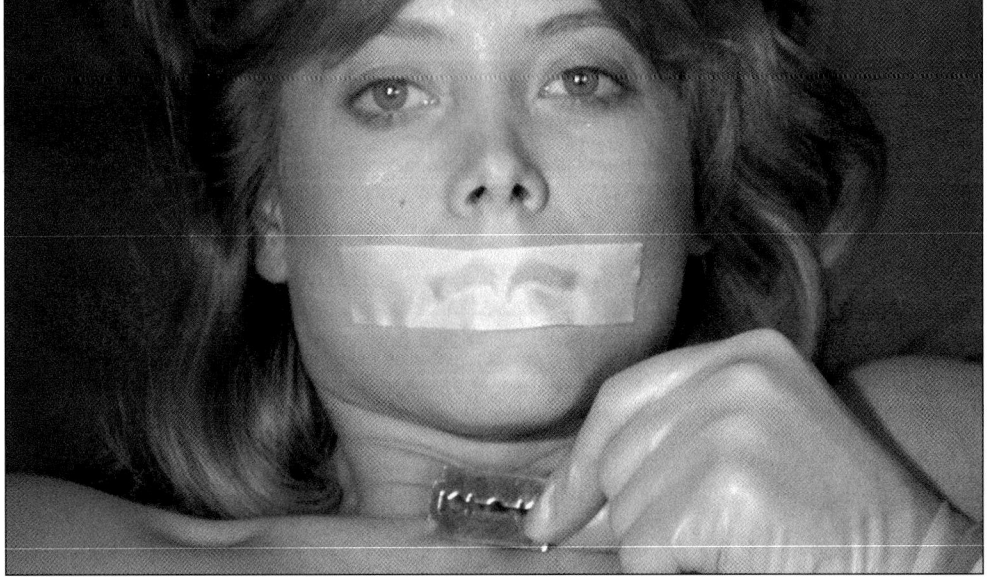

Theatrical releases

Operation St. Peter's

Date submitted: 25 November 1968
Company: Paramount Pictures
Running time on submission: 95m 53s (8630ft)
'A' certificate issued: 5 December 1968

Censorship requirements
"Reel 5 – Remove the whole incident in which a man poses as Christ, both when he is on the cross and when he descends from it."

Response
The scene in question was duly removed, as confirmed by a second screening at the BBFC on 5 December 1968. The film was then passed with an 'A' certificate.

One on Top of the Other

Date submitted: 23 November 1970
Company: Border Films
Running time on submission: 108m 06s (9729ft)
Re-submitted with cuts (length unknown): 7 January 1971
'X' certificate issued: 14 January 1971

Censorship requirements
Reel 1 – Shorten the lovemaking between Carol and George, in particular remove the shots that suggest cunnilingus and fellatio and the shots of him between her legs.
Reel 3 – Shorten the love scene between George and Monica, in particular remove the shots of her unzipping his fly-buttons and his hand between her legs.

Response
The film was resubmitted on 7 January 1971, and although the cuts to Reel 1 were deemed satisfactory, those in Reel 3 were not:

"We saw this reel. We doubt if any further cuts have been made, but if they have been the scene is still too long and strong. The first part of the scene must be drastically further reduced, particularly in view of the fact that the end part of the scene, which has not been mentioned, consists of the girl sitting astride the man."

Finally, after a complaint from Border Films that different changes were being asked for each time the film was submitted, the film was declared "not objectionable" and passed on 14 January 1971.

Additional notes
On 16 August 1989 the film was submitted for video release by Sheptonhurst Ltd., and offered a '15' certificate, uncut. However, on 9 January 1990, for undisclosed reasons, Sheptonhurst Ltd. withdrew the submission, along with three other titles – *Lovers Games*, *The Sex Bed* and *Sex Explosion*.

A Lizard in a Woman's Skin

Date submitted: 6 February 1973
Company: Gala Film Distributors
Running time on submission: 99m 16s (8934ft)
No cuts to the submitted version.
'X' certificate issued: 6 February 1973

Censorship requirements
There are no censor notes for this film in the BBFC archive.

White Fang

Date submitted: 13 November 1974
Company: Fox/Rank
Running time on submission: 103m 46s
Re-submitted 26 November 1974, with cuts of 2m 46s
'X' certificate issued: 9 December 1974

Censorship requirements
Reel 2: In fight where Kirk and Jason are against the townsfolk, reduce blows to neck and stomach.
Reel 3: Reduce fight between White Fang and black dog, removing bloodiest shots, in particular shot of black dog dead.
Reel 4: Reduce fight between dog and bear, again removing bloodiest shots. It is necessary, in plot terms, to have the shots of Jason picking up and carrying the apparently dead dog, but the bloodier shots should be removed.
Reel 5a: The savaging of the villain by White Fang as he is about to kill the sleeping Jason should be reduced, particularly removing bloody shots of neck.
Reel 5b: Blackbeard's savage hitting of Christa must be reduced.

Additional notes
The BBFC demanded *"some kind of account of how the animals were treated in the making of this film."* A letter from production company Oceania, dated 22 November 1974, confirmed that no animals were harmed or mistreated in the making of *White Fang*, as vouched for by the production's animal trainer the "well known zoologist" Luciano Spinelli (Spinelli, a Rome editor with a formidable private fortune, was indeed a minor celebrity in the field of zoology; in 1966 he had overseen the first two natural rearings of cheetahs in captivity, at his small private zoo in Cecchina, near Rome).

Zombie Flesh-Eaters

Alternative title on logging sheet:
Zombies 2
Date submitted: 29 November 1979
Company: Miracle Films
Running time on submission: 90m 42s
Re-submitted 6 December 1979 – further cuts required
Re-submitted 11 December 1979 with cuts totalling 1m 46s (new running time: 88m 56s)
'X' certificate issued: 2 January 1980

In terms of the examiner's own enjoyment, at least, *Zombie Flesh-Eaters* was warmly received. He declared himself impressed by *"the spectacularly gory special effects which outdo even Romero's zombies,"* adding that a fellow examiner *"yukked and squealed, and I squirmed and guffawed nervously."* He went on, *"We have made a number of cuts in the goriest sections although, as [my colleague] rightly said, it is the shock effects which are the raison d'être of this type of pic. We have left a considerable amount [...] No one in the least bit squeamish should cross the threshold of a cinema where this is showing, and if they do stray in they will probably have sacrificed willingly the price of admission by the time they get past Reel 1. Our cuts can do little to protect them, so who are we trying to protect? The horror buffs and ghoul-fanciers who will lap it up?"*

Reading this, one might suppose that the film was about to coast through the censorship process with ease. A browse through the list of required cuts however, tells a different story:

Censorship requirements

1. Remove aftermath of zombies bite to policeman's neck on boat – gaping wound and blood spurt.

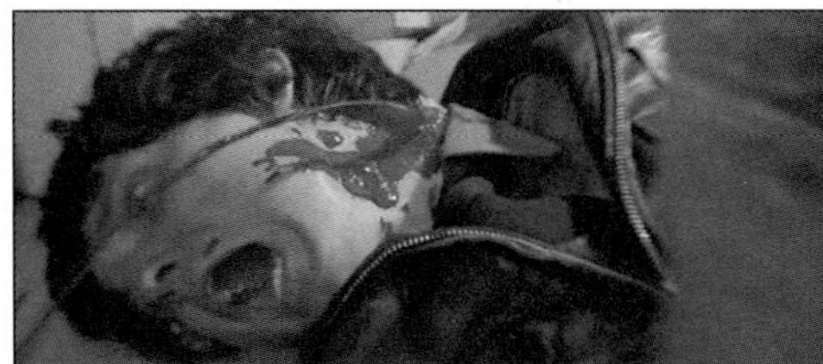

2. Remove sight of splinter of wood pushed into Mrs. Menard's eye.

3. Remove sight of zombie chewing Mrs. Menard's limbs and all sight of entrails please, when others arrive at the house.

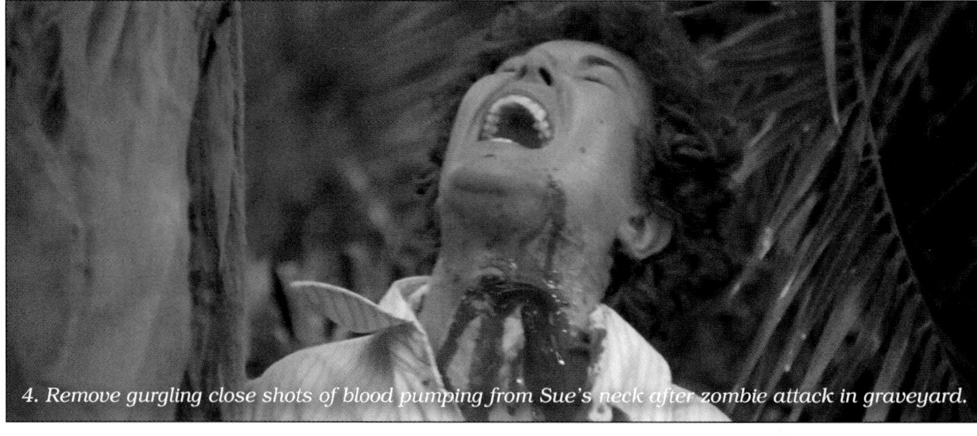

4. Remove gurgling close shots of blood pumping from Sue's neck after zombie attack in graveyard.

5. Remove bashing and decapitating of zombie with shovel.

6. Remove sight of zombie returning for a second chew at Menard's face.

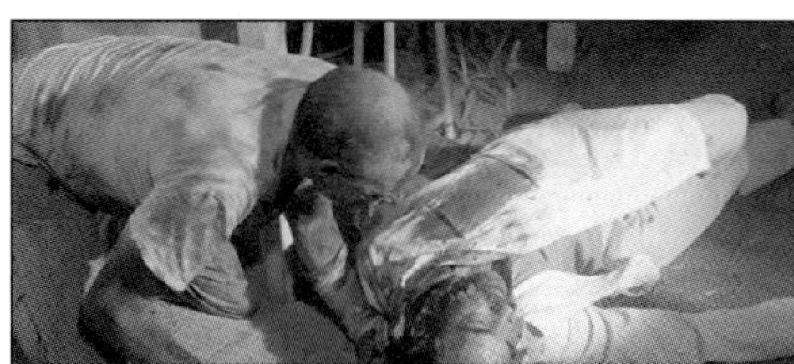

7. Remove sight of negress zombie biting an arm and resultant blood gout.

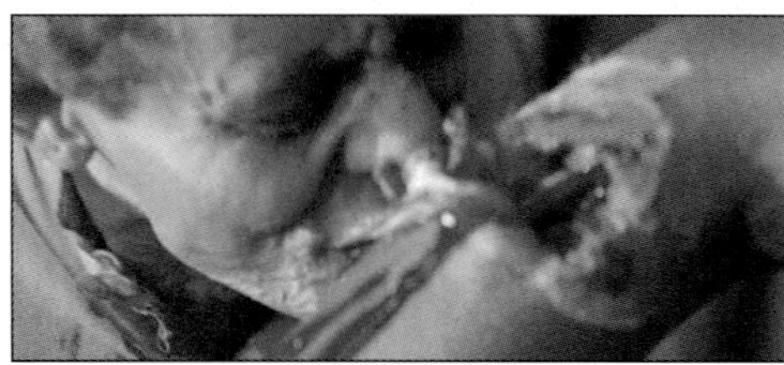

8. Remove close shot of zombie's head blown off through skylight.

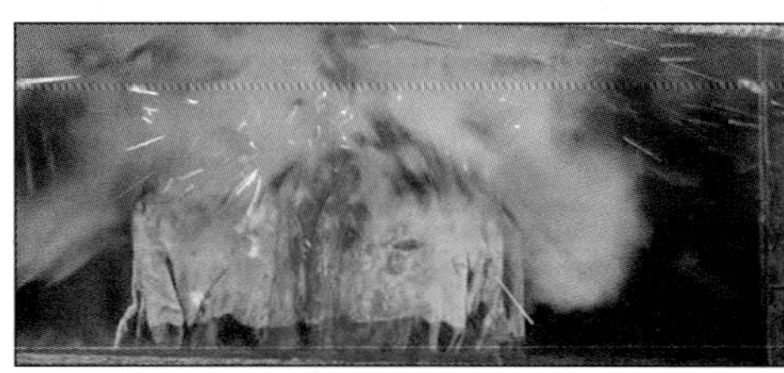

9. Remove close head shots of zombies battered by rifle butts.

10. Reduce to establish only zombie-Sue's cannibalistic attack on Brian.

By 6 December 1979 most of these cuts had been made, although a stray rifle-butt to a zombie face was extant, and the eye scene was still deemed too strong: *"Cuts made, but we consider that the last shot in sequence spoils it and should be removed."* It's unclear whether the examiner thought the last shot "spoiled it" because it was too gory, or because its presence created an editing glitch which betrayed the censor's scissors.

Additional notes

The UK video company VIPCO first released *Zombie Flesh-Eaters* in December 1980, and to begin with they put out the BBFC 'X' version. A year later, however, in November 1981, they released it again uncensored, with a sticker proclaiming the "Strong Uncut Version". It was a rental smash. Sadly, it was later ensnared in the media furore about violent horror films on video, becoming a prominent title in the so-called video nasties saga. Police seizures of the film were numerous, with individual store-owners and video collectors charged under the Obscene Publications Act. Successful convictions were obtained many times, although there were a significant number of acquittals where defendants registered a plea of not guilty. The last time anyone was prosecuted for owning or selling the film was on 30 July 1991, when a sentence of twelve weeks in prison suspended for two years, plus a fine of £20, was handed out by a court in Manchester.

The Beyond

Date submitted: 3 August 1981
Company: Eagle Lion Distribution Ltd.
Running time on submission: 87m 21s
Cut by 1m 49s
New running time: 85m 32s
'X' certificate issued: 27 August 1981

Censorship requirements

1. In sequence where warlock is dragged to cellar, reduce to establishing shots only his being beaten with chains.

2. Remove blood spurting from warlock's wrists as he is nailed to the wall.

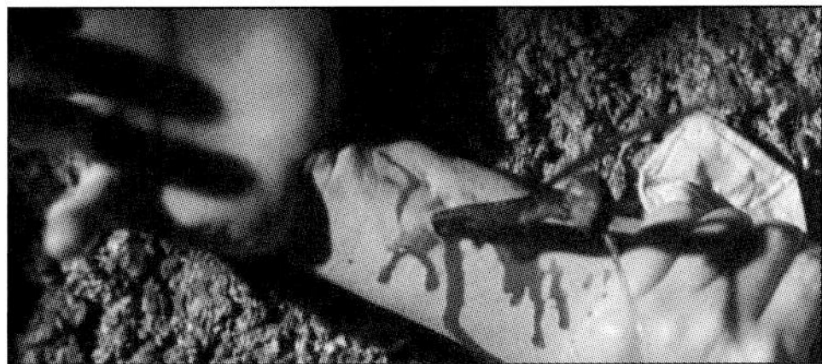

3. In scene where Joe's face is grabbed by zombie, remove sight of his eyeball hanging from its socket.

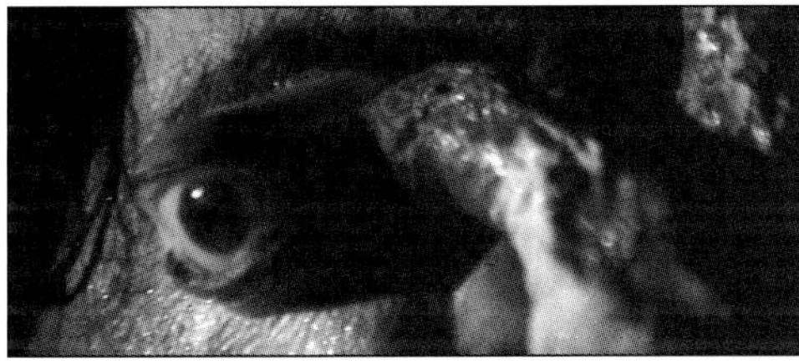

4. In sequence where tarantulas crawl on Martin, remove all shots of them tearing at facial flesh and pulling out his eye.

5. In scene where zombie Joe pushes Martha's head against nail, remove final shot where nail emerges through her eye and pushes eyeball out.

6. In scene where Emily is attacked by Alsation, remove all sight of flesh being torn and blood bubbling from big flesh wound.

7. In morgue, when John shoots zombies, remove shot of little Jill's exploding head as he shoots her.

City of the Living Dead

Date submitted: 13 November 1981
Company: Eagle Films
Running time on submission: unlisted
Cut by 45s (new running time: 91m 51s)
'X' certificate issued: 10 December 1981

Censorship requirements

The examiner remarked, *"Quite well made Italian schlock horror from director Fulci. The effects work is particularly nauseating and after showing the stronger sequences to the Secretary [James Ferman] it was agreed to considerably reduce the killing of Bob with the electric drill as, unlike the rest of the fantasy killings, this had a complete air of reality about it."*

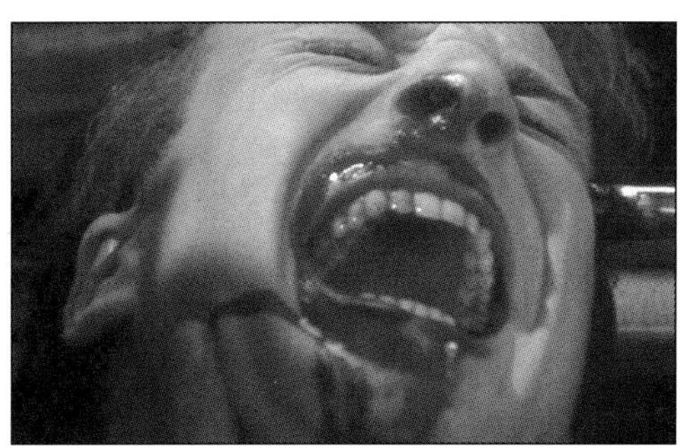

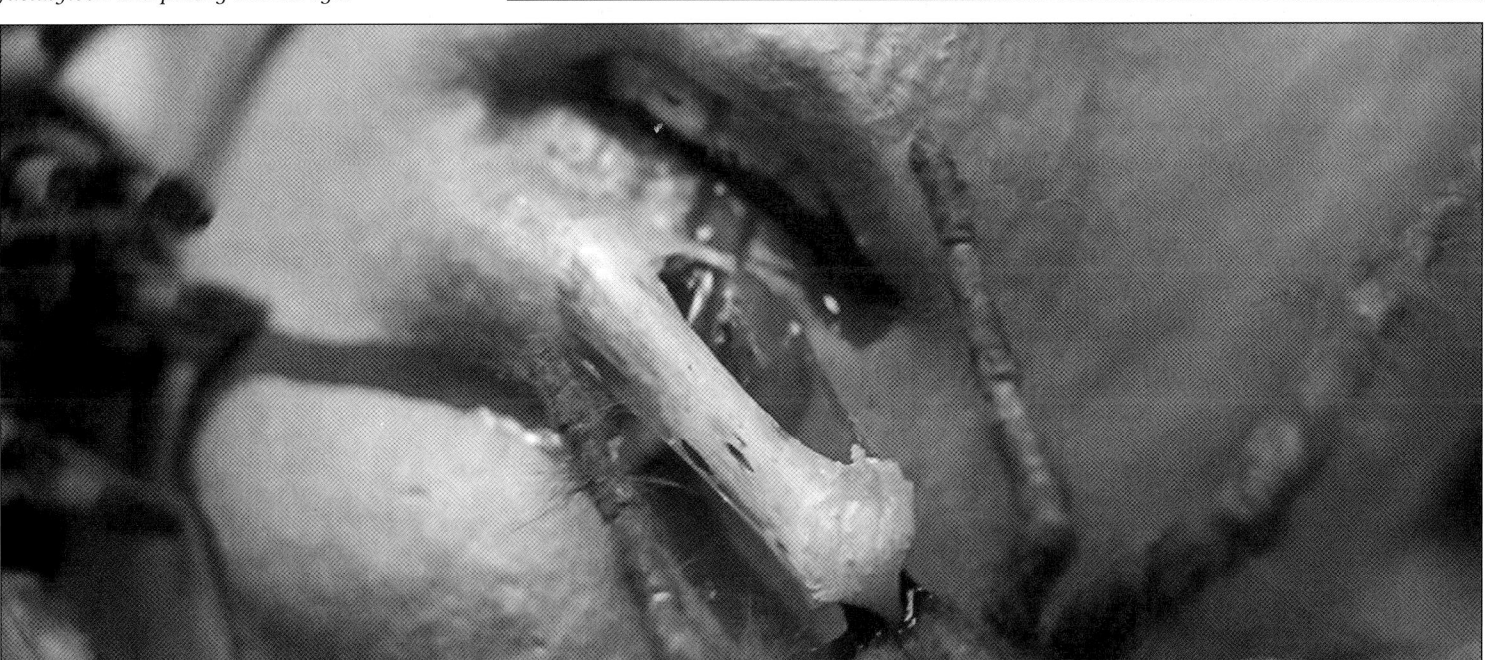

The House by the Cemetery

Date submitted: 17 November 1981
Company: Eagle Films, Ltd.
Running time on submission: 86m 15s
Re-submitted with cuts totalling 1m 25s (new running time: 84m 50s)
'X' certificate issued: 29 December 1981

Censorship requirements
The notes for this film are sketchy, but the following examiner's comment conveys the gist of the censor's requirements:

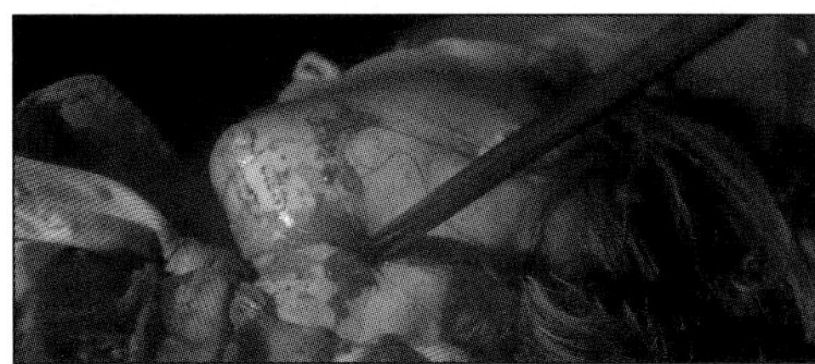

"Somewhat confused but nevertheless with very tense moments, this film again demonstrates director Fulci's ability in this field, particularly with gruesome special effects. In fact, these are so well done that it was necessary to reduce the killing of Laura in which she is stabbed twice in the body and then has her throat slashed, and in the throat slashing of Ann." (The throat-slashing of Laura to which the examiner refers is more accurately described as a throat stabbing, this being the third wound inflicted by a poker.)

Conquest

Date submitted: 1983
Company: Miracle Films
Running time on submission: 88m 15s
Re-submitted with cuts totalling 4m 08s (new running time: 84m 07s)
'X' certificate issued: 22 November 1983

Censorship requirements
Unavailable

The New York Ripper

Date submitted: 14 December 1983
Company: Eagle Films
Running time on submission: 91m 06s
Viewed at the BBFC seven times:
1. 14 December 1983
2. 16 December 1983
3. 6 January 1984
4. 10 January 1984
5. 11 January 1984
6. 12 January 1984
7. 14 February 1984

Rejection letter sent to Eagle Films:
15 February 1984

Of all of Lucio Fulci's films, *The New York Ripper* was by far the most contentious. The following material covers the film's torrid and turbulent encounter with the BBFC, which resulted in a total ban in 1984. To this day the film remains unavailable in its uncut form, despite cut-down versions being cleared for '18' certificate release in 2002 and 2011.

The New York Ripper was seen for the first time by four examiners. The record of their deliberations, conveyed here by a female examiner, is as follows:

"This is a nasty whodunit, the first time in a cinema that I've had to close my eyes. The murders are brutal, realistic, with the full impact of razors and knives going into flesh. It is relentless [...] There is a mixture of sex juxtaposed with the violence, and I feel that consequently there should be heavier cuts in, for instance, a masturbation scene than I would normally feel necessary at '18'. I would pass this film at '18' but with very heavy cuts; I would like to see what it looks like with only the suggestion of each murder. In some scenes such as the genital mutilation with the bottle, I would cut the attack completely. This makes it sound unredeemable, but there is sufficient in the plot, full of pop-psychology though it is, for me to feel that it is not a reject."

So far so typical; as with Fulci's previous horror films, it appeared that the censor would fillet out the nastier scenes before passing the film for release. The tenor of the response changed completely, however, when senior examiner Margaret Ford viewed the film. She was not only horrified by the film, but outraged on a moral level:

"I believe that this film displays a gross and distorted imagination and a hatred of women which I find hard to comprehend. The violence is gratuitous, excessive and sadistic. I have never been asked, in seven years at the board, to watch anything worse than the razoring of Kitty, the prostitute, and I believe that the sequence in the cafe bar when the rich woman is humiliated by the two young snooker players might have a depraving and corrupting effect on some of those likely to see it. Cuts would remove the excess, perhaps, but the sub-text to this so-called thriller is all about the punishment and humiliation of women for their sexuality and this would be hard to remove. Every one of the four victims is seen in a sexual context immediately prior to her killing: camera on crotch of girl in car, girl in live sex show, high class woman in porno show, in bar (described above), on a bed scared by supposed killer, and Kitty the prostitute. Even the blame for the killings rests ultimately with a female: the girl child mutilated by illness controls, through emotion, her killer father. I'm not trying to argue that male fear and hatred of women is necessarily illegitimate as a theme, only that in this film the fear and hatred is exposed in a way that unites sexual and violent excitement in a totally unacceptable way. N.B. I am also rather appalled at the title coming so soon after the Sutcliffe affair."

Another examiner, Guy Phelps, took a different view:

"What is basically a reasonably efficient and enjoyable thriller is interspersed with the most detailed and gratuitous killings imaginable. Knives or razor-blades cut through nipples and eyeballs in vivid close-up, and no knife plunges into throat, heart or crotch without repeating the movement three or four times. Yet outside the actual murders, there is not the unpleasant gloating atmosphere one notices in typical 'girls in peril' movies. The incursions of sexual violence are quite sudden and fit in not at all with the mood of the rest of the film, which is more or less TV-movie stuff. On this ground, I would suggest the film is cuttable: I think a version would remain that would not be at all morbid."

Geoffrey Wood, however, took against the film in a similar way to Margaret Ford (making the gender balance for and against the film equal at this juncture):

"I think this film must be rejected: it could indeed be cut but since the cuts would be severe they would leave little point in the film generally – which itself indicates how the film's rationale is in its sadism alone. It is a question not just of footage but of the premises of the film and this deserves some analysis [...] A further disturbing feature of the film is its association of sexuality with sadism and mutilation, directed against women [...] Jane the psychiatrist's wife, has a penchant for sexual humiliation but the long scene of her being aroused by the young man's foot under the table dwells on humiliation that goes beyond her desires ... Visually the context suggests links between female sexuality and mutilation, between red lips and red gashes. The final sequence of the child is one more recapitulation of this. The girl is mutilated (amputated arms) and bound (bandaged torso and hospital bed). The prior mutilation of the child is finally given narratively as the reason for all the murders, reinforcing the association of masochism and suggesting that the mutilations are ultimately the effects of the female. Aesthetically the film has little to offer as redeeming qualities. Such themes might be treated in meaningful ways (e.g. Peeping Tom*) but the focus of this film seems to be (1) Vicariously, to expect and enjoy sexual mutilation; (2) To identify this with female sexuality. This is therefore not a film to defend and not a film to cut."*

Examiner Sally Sampson then recorded her impressions:

"Stylishly made but excessively violent and bloodthirsty Italian whodunit. It's in the same genre (gloss and gore) as Tenebrae [a violent Italian murder mystery by Dario Argento]*, but Fulcio* [sic] *piles it on a lot more thickly than*

Argento. Some of the scenes are among the most objectionable I've seen during a year with the Board, and I would like to show them to people who oppose any censorship for adults. Strictly speaking though, the film isn't a nasty, and I think, with very heavy cutting, it could be transformed into a routine whodunit. But (given the present circumstances) it might be advisable to reject it [...] A ridiculous story – but it kept us guessing to the end. Like Pieces [a Spanish slasher horror film by Juan Piquer Simon], *its teeth could be drawn by heavy cutting, leaving a straightforward '18'. But, as I said above, I wouldn't protest very fiercely against a 'Reject'."*

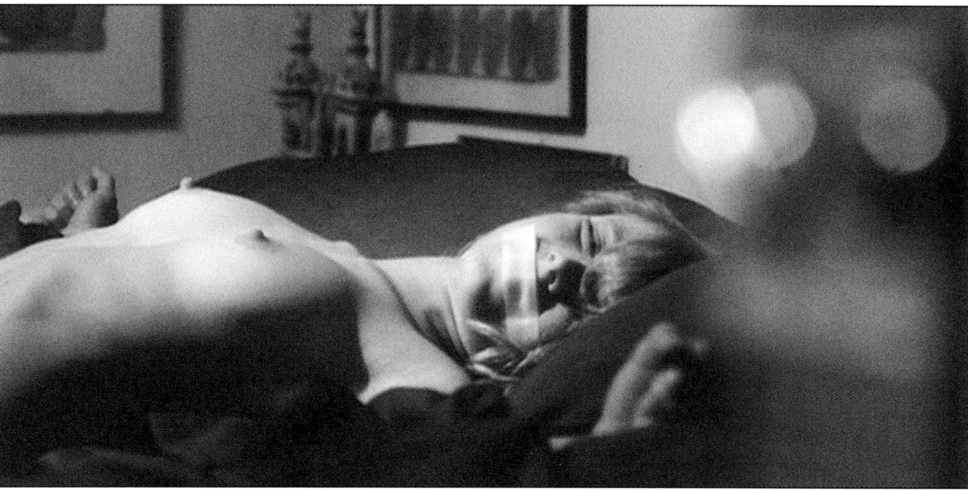

Examiner Tony Kerpel's report added some weight in favour of the film:

"Although I can understand the distressed attitude of some examiners towards this film, I approached it as both an examiner and an editor. In that frame of mind I felt that the intense violence which comes in blocks of shots could be entirely removed leaving us with an '18' murder mystery which was par for the course in violence terms [...] I don't think we should be vengeful about this film even though Fulci obviously revels in what he is making. We have professional judgements to make and editing skills which we can exercise – quite easily with the slow motion afforded by video – and I believe this film is salvageable for the '18'."

Examiner Maggie Mills reported her response as follows:

"This film is a reject on theme and treatment. It runs the risk of prosecution as it stands. I am pretty convinced that many juries would find the scene in the live sex joint where the girl is killed with a broken bottle up her, and the scene in the bar where the woman is masturbated by a man's foot to be depraving and corrupting. I certainly found them so ... The strident hatred and degradation of women in this film comes through loud and strong, which also we should not even consider as entertainment for adults. It is a cleverly constructed, tackily sensationalised and genuinely harmful piece of garbage which will find a ready-made consumer response in enough people who view it to make me genuinely afraid for its effects. This film, Salò [Pier Paolo Pasolini's 1975 adaptation of the Marquis de Sade's "The 120 Days of Sodom"] *and* Christiane F. [Uli Edel's 1981 film about the squalor and vice into which a young girl falls when addicted to heroin] *have given me the greatest emotional distress and revulsion in my seven years at the Board, but unlike the other two films, there is no moral, artistic or aesthetic merit in this film. We must reject it."*

Another female examiner, initials JF (not James Ferman), took perhaps the most extreme view of all:

"I don't think I've ever felt so viciously hated as I did throughout the viewing of this depraved film, and indeed for some time afterwards. It is painful even to contemplate the hostility present in a mind that can design the most effective way to film a woman's breast being sliced in half by a razor blade. I consider this film to be genuinely corrosive of anybody's consciousness in the way that it allows the audience to be enticed and allured by attractive female flesh and then invites the same, aroused audience to feast on the slashing, mauling and butchering of that flesh. It is not insignificant that the female flesh belongs to women who are worthy of punishment: that is, they are hookers, strippers, women of flexible morals – entirely deserving of their bloody fate. Their decadence is only emphasised by the regard in which the filmmaker holds them: they are dirty, depraved lumps of meat fit only for consumption. There is not a second of this film which I would preserve; in my short time on this Board I have seldom felt so sullied by a film – and so vindictive, finally, towards the filmmaker as I do now. The misogyny runs down the centre of the film, stick of rock fashion, and I have no doubts that the intermingling of sex with violence – how like a menstrual flow, the blood coursing down the inner thighs of the genitally bottled stripper – is truly depraving and corrupting."

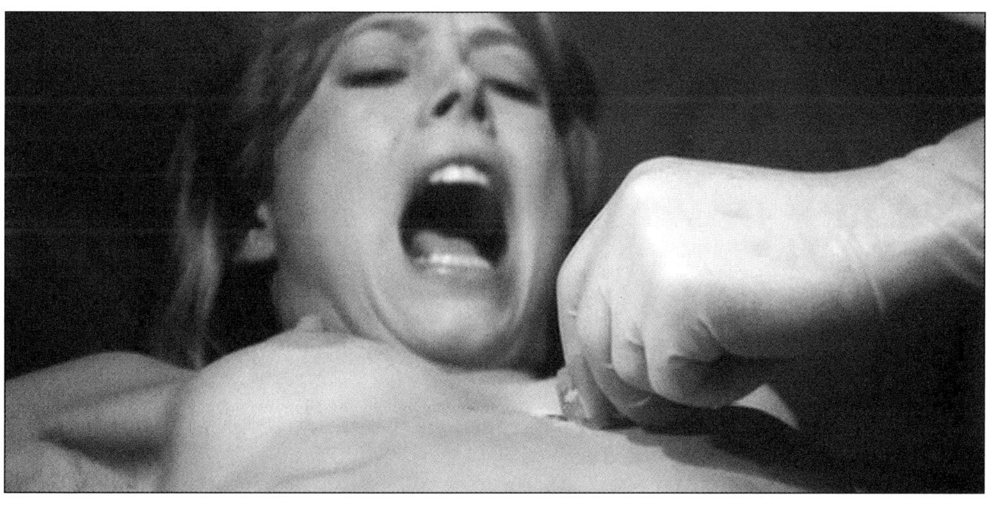

With so much conflicting feeling, and with such extreme responses from key examiners, there was a need for more consultation. On 11 January 1984 the matter was put before Lord Harlech, who saw *The New York Ripper* the next day and expressed strong doubts about the legality of releasing it. An unattributed note in the BBFC file (which may or may not convey Lord Harlech's own words but definitely carries the gist) states: *"Two years ago it might have been worth trying to cut this very heavily for 18. But now, the law of obscenity would seem to catch this material squarely. Monitor court cases and reply accordingly."*

After the film's seventh viewing, a note was appended to the film's file, stating: "Nightmares in a Damaged Brain [a similarly notorious slasher film directed by Romano Scavolini] *found obscene at Old Bailey. Lord Harlech advises absolute reject of* New York Ripper, *calling attention to legal vulnerability under 'Deprave and Corrupt' test."*

The fate of the film was now sealed. Secretary of the BBFC James Ferman wrote to Barry Jacobs of Eagle Films on 15 February 1984:

"The Board has now had an opportunity to consider the above film with great care, and to take legal advice on its liability under British obscenity law. I now have to tell you that we are unable to give a certificate to The New York Ripper *for cinema exhibition in the United Kingdom, and that it is our considered view that the film would be found obscene in British courts [...] In the light of the above, we must advise you that all copies of the film should be re-exported to Italy forthwith. Otherwise, your company would be liable to a charge of possessing an obscene article for publication for gain. I can only urge you in future not to seek to distribute in Britain films which link sex and violence in this unhealthy and sadistic manner. The fact that the film is technically well made makes it even more dangerous in that it seems to have little purpose other than to encourage audiences to expect and enjoy sexual mutilation of women. This is a theme which the board has always treated with the utmost caution, and we believe this film to be one of the most offensive exploitations of the subject the Board has ever seen."*

Lucio Fulci ~ other film credits

compiled by Julian Grainger & Stephen Thrower

1948

Una lezione di sistema – directed by Lucio Fulci (documentary)

Il sogno di Icaro – directed by Lucio Fulci (documentary)

Pittori italiana del dopoguerra – directed by Lucio Fulci (documentary)

1949

100.000 metri cubi – directed by Lucio Fulci (documentary – never completed)

Zona di porta fluviale – directed by Lucio Fulci (documentary – never completed)

Pittori in provincia – directed by Lucio Fulci (documentary)

1950

Gli ultimi giorni di Pompei – directed by Paolo Moffa, supervised by Marcel L'Herbier
French title: *Les derniers jours de Pompei*
2nd unit assistant director: Lucio Fulci. Production started 1948

1952

Totò a colori – directed by Steno [Stefano Vanzina]
Assistant director/co-screenplay [uncredited]: Lucio Fulci

Totò e i Re di Roma – directed by Mario Monicelli & Steno [Stefano Vanzina]
Assistant director: Lucio Fulci

Fratelli d'Italia – directed by Fausto Saraceni
Assistant director/[uncredited] co-screenplay: Lucio Fulci

Totò e le donne – directed by Mario Monicelli & Steno [Stefano Vanzina]
Assistant director: Lucio Fulci

1953

L'uomo, la bestia e la virtù – dir: Steno [Stefano Vanzina]
Assistant director: Lucio Fulci. starring Totò and Orson Welles
Ci troviamo in galleria – directed by Mauro Bolognini
Co-screenplay: Lucio Fulci

Cinema d'altri tempi – directed by Steno [Stefano Vanzina]
French title: *Drôle de bobines*
Spanish title: *Cine, amore y simpatia*
Assistant director/[uncredited] co-screenplay: Lucio Fulci

Madame de... – directed by Max Ophüls
Italian title: *I gioielli di Madame de...*
UK/US title: *The Earrings of Madame De...*
2nd assistant director [uncredited]: Lucio Fulci

1954

Un giorno in pretura – directed by Steno [Stefano Vanzina]
US title: *A Day in Court*
1st assistant director/co-screenplay: Lucio Fulci

Schiava del peccato – directed by Raffaello Matarazzo
Co-screenplay [uncredited]: Lucio Fulci

Un Americano a Roma – directed by Steno [Stefano Vanzina]
Spanish title: *Americano de Roma*
Assistant director/co-story/co-screenplay: Lucio Fulci

Io sono la Primula Rossa (Il sanculotto) – directed by Giorgio C. Simonelli
Co-screenplay: Lucio Fulci

1955

Totò all'Inferno – directed by Camillo Mastrocinque
Co-screenplay: Lucio Fulci

Buonanotte... avvocato! – directed by Giorgio Bianchi
Co-screenplay /2nd assistant director [both uncredited]: Lucio Fulci

Piccola posta – directed by Steno [Stefano Vanzina]
Assistant director/co-story/co-screenplay: Lucio Fulci

La ragazza di via Veneto – directed by Marino Girolami
Co-story/co-screenplay: Lucio Fulci

Le avventure di Giacomo Casanova – directed by Steno [Stefano Vanzina]
French title: *Casanova*
Assistant director/co-story/co-screenplay: Lucio Fulci

1956

Mio figlio Nerone – directed by Steno [Stefano Vanzina]
French title: *Les week-ends de Néron*
Asst. director/co-screenplay [uncredited]: Lucio Fulci

1957

Femmine tre volte – directed by Steno [Stefano Vanzina]
Spanish title: *Operacion Popoff*
Assistant director/[uncredited] co-screenplay: Lucio Fulci

Susanna tutta panna – directed by Steno [Stefano Vanzina]
Spanish title: *Susana, pura nata*
Assistant director/[uncredited] co-screenplay: Lucio Fulci

1958

Guardia, ladro e cameriera – directed by Steno [Stefano Vanzina]
Co-story/co-screenplay: Lucio Fulci

Totò nella luna – directed by Steno [Stefano Vanzina]
Co-story: Lucio Fulci

Pia de' Tolomei – directed by Sergio Grieco
French title: *La parole est à l'épée*
Co-screenplay [uncredited]: Lucio Fulci

1960

San Remo: la grande sfida – directed by Piero Vivarelli "The big challenge" – music by Piero Umiliani. Script clerk and continuity – Umberto Lenzi. Fulci is given the special credit of "collaborating director" and appears in a small part. He also wrote the song, "Blue Jeans Rock" with Piero Vivarelli and Leoni, sung by Adriano Celentano. (This song is performed by Celentano in Fulci's *Urlatori alla sbarra*, made the same year). The festival filmed was the Tenth Festival di San Remo.

Letto a tre piazze – directed by Steno [Stefano Vanzina]
Co-story/screenplay co-collaboration: Lucio Fulci. Winner of the Golden Olive Award, at the Festival del Film Comico e Umoristico at Bordighera

1961

Totò, Peppino e... la dolce vita – directed by Sergio Corbucci
German title: *Toto, Peppino und das süsse Leben*
Co-story: Lucio Fulci

1962

Nerone '71 – directed by Walter Filippi [Filippo Walter Ratti]
It has been suggested that Fulci directed this film, however, he receives no credit of any kind.

Il sangue e la sfida – directed by Nick [Nicola] Nostro.
It has been suggested that Fulci directed this film, however, he receives no credit of any kind.

1964

Il gaucho – directed by Dino Risi
Argentinean title: *Un Italiano en la Argentina*
It's been rumoured that this feature was begun by Lucio Fulci but completed by Risi. However, in an interview the author conducted with him in 1996 he claimed never to have failed to complete a film apart from *Zombi 3* in 1988. Fulci's daughter Antonella confirms that the rumour is false but suggests he may have been involved in the scripting.

1967

Due RRRingos nel Texas – directed by Marino Girolami
Actor [uncredited]: Lucio Fulci

1968

Il dolce corpo di Deborah – directed by Romolo Girolami
French title: *L'adorable corps de Deborah*
According to Italian scriptwriter Ernesto Gastaldi, Fulci may have written the original treatment (story outline) for this film but received no credit. However, Antonella Fulci says this is incorrect.

I due crociati – directed by Giuseppe Orlandini.
Story: Roberto Gianviti. Screenplay by Gianviti, Lucio Fulci and Dino Verde. With Franco & Ciccio. Also starring Janet Agren, Fabio Testi

1969

A doppia faccia – directed by Robert Hampton [Riccardo Freda]
German title: *Das Gesicht im Dunkeln*
French titles: *Liz et Hélèn / Chaleur et jouissance*
aka *Operazione allucianante*
aka *Double Face*
aka *Puzzle of Horrors*
Story: Romano Migliorini, Giovanbattista Musetto & Lucio Fulci, from the book "The Face in the Night" by Edgar Wallace. Screenplay: Freda and Paul Hengge

1971

Trois milliards sans ascenseur – director Roger Pigaut
Italian title: *Sette cervelli per un colpo perfetto*
German title: *Drei Milliarden ohne Lift*
Co-screenplay [apparently uncredited] by Lucio Fulci

1972

Ettore lo fusto – directed by Enzo G. Castellari [Enzo Girolami]
Spanish title: *El rapto de Elena, la decente italiana*
French titles: *Hector beau gosse / Les proxenetes*
UK title: *Hector the Mighty*
Screenplay: Alessandro Continenza, Lucio Fulci, Enzo G. Castellari & Leonardo Martin [Luciano Martino], based on the novel "Il re dei Mimiduti" [aka "King of the Troika"] by Viard & Zacharias

1978

Un uomo da ridere – directed by Lucio Fulci. TV documentary about Franco Franchi
translation: 'A Man To Laugh At'

Tecnica della regata – directed by Lucio Fulci. TV documentary on sailing races, with Franco Franchi

1985

La gabbia – directed by Giuseppe Petroni Griffi
Spanish title: *La jaula* / German title: *Der Käfig* / French title: *L'enchaîne* / UK video title: *The Trap*
US video title: *Collector's Item*
alternative title: *The Cage*
Story: Francesco Barili. Screenplay: Lucio Fulci, Alberto Silvestri & Concha Hombria. Starring Cristina Marsillach

1986

The Curse – directed by David Keith
aka *The Farm*
Associate producer/special optical effects designer: Lucio Fulci [credited as Louis Fulci]. Special make-up effects: Franco Ruffini, producer: Ovidio G. Assonitis. Filmed in the USA but post-produced in Rome.

1988

Non avere paura della zia Marta – directed by Robert Martin [Mario Bianchi]
export title: *The Murder Secret*
"A film supervised by Lucio Fulci"

1989

Night Club – directed by Sergio Corbucci
Story: Giovanni Fago (Fulci's asst. director on nine of his sixties comedies), Lucio Fulci & Luciano Martino.
Screenplay: Massimo Franciosa & Sergio Corbucci

I frati rossi – directed by Gianni Martucci
export title: *The Red Monks*
shooting title: *I monaci rossi*
The print and poster art proclaim "Lucio Fulci presents" however Fulci says "The producers begged me to help promote the film. I don't even know the director." (to Loris Curci & Antonio Tentori, *Splatting Image* 4 / *European Trash Cinema* vol2/no.4).

Massacre – directed by Andrea Bianchi
shooting title: *Remember Dottore Jekyll*
"Lucio Fulci presents..."

Nel nido del serpente – directed by Leandro Lucchetti
Italian video title: *The Snake House (Bloody Psycho)*
"Supervised by Lucio Fulci"

1997

M.D.C. Maschera di cera – directed by Sergio Stivaletti
export title: *The Wax Mask*
Based on "The Wax Museum" by Gaston Leroux.
Screenplay: Lucio Fulci & Daniele Stroppa

Lucio Fulci ~ actor filmographies

originally compiled by Julian Grainger, revised and updated by Francis Brewster

Janet Agren

born 6 April 1949 in Landskrona, Sweden

Sandra in ***City of the Living Dead***

1968 *Donne... botte e bersaglieri* (IT) aka *Un uomo piange solo per amore* – dir: Ruggero Deodato
1968 *I due crociati* (IT) – dir: Giuseppe Orlandini
1969 *Colpo di stato* (IT) aka *Coup d'état* – dir: Luciano Salce
1969 *Il giovane normale* (IT) – dir: Dino Risi
1969 *Du soleil plein les yeux* (FR) UK *I Want You Now* – dir: Michel Boisrond
1970 *Pussycat, Pussycat, I Love You* (US) [uncredited] – dir: Rod Amateau
1971 *Io non vedo, tu non parli, lui non sente* (IT) – dir: Mario Camerini
1971 *Io non spezzo... rompo* (IT/FR) FR *Deux trouillards pistonnés* – dir: Bruno Corbucci
1972 *La più bella serata della mia vita* (IT/FR) FR *La plus belle soirée de ma vie* – dir: Ettore Scola
1972 *Avanti!* (US/IT) IT *Che cosa e' successo tra mio padre e tua madre?* – dir: Billy Wilder
1972 *Pulp* (UK/IT) IT *Colpiscono senza pietà* – dir: Mike Hodges
1972 *La vita a volte è molto dura, vero Provvidenza?* (IT/FR/WG) FR *On m'appelle Providence* WG *Providenza! Mausefalle für zwei schräge Vögel* export title *Sometimes Life Is Hard-Right, Providence?* – dir: Giulio Petroni
1972 *Racconti proibiti... di niente vestiti* (IT) UK *Master of Love* – dir: Brunello Rondi
1972 *Fiorina la vacca* (IT) – dir: Vittorio De Sisti
1972 *Tecnica di un amore* (IT) – dir: Brunello Rondi
1973 *Ingrid sulla strada* (IT) – dir: Brunello Rondi
1974 *Il saprofita* (IT) – dir: Sergio Nasca
1974 *L'assassino ha riservato nove poltrone* (IT) export title *The Killer Reserved Nine Seats* – dir: Giuseppe Bennati
1974 *L'erotomane* (IT) – dir: Mario Vicario
1975 *Paolo Barca, maestro elementare, praticamente nudista* (IT) – dir: Flavio Mogherini
1975 *L'amaro caso della baronessa di Carini* (IT) (tv mini-series) – dir: Daniele D'Anza
1975 *La polizia interviene: ordine di uccidere!* (IT) US *The Left Hand of the Law* – dir: Giuseppe Rosati
1975 *Sensualidad* (SP) – dir: Germán Lorente

1976 *Vai col liscio* (IT) – dir: Giancarlo Nicotra
1976 *Chi dice donna, dice donna* (IT) – dir: Tonino Cervi
1976 *Stato interessante* (IT) – dir: Sergio Nasca
1976 *Per amore* (IT) – dir: Mino Giarda
1976 *Indagine su un delitto perfetto* (IT) UKvdt *Perfect Crime* – dir: Aaron Leviathan [Giuseppe Rosati] [released in 1978]
1978 *A chi tocca, tocca...!* (IT/WG/IS) WG *Agenten kennen keine Tränen* US *The Uranium Conspiracy* – dir: Frank G. Carroll [Gianfranco Baldanello] & Menahem Golan
1978 *Il commissario verrazzano* (IT) UKvdt *Deadly Chase* – dir: Franco Prosperi [Francesco Prosperi]
1978 *Il commissario di ferro* (IT) – dir: Stelvio Massi
1978 *Siete chicas peligrosas* (SP/IT) IT *Sette ragazze di classe* export title *Seven Dangerous Girls* – dir: Pedro Lazaga
1978 *Bermudas la cueva de los tiburones* (SP/IT) IT *Bermude la fossa maledetta* UKvdt *The Shark's Cave* – dir: Anthony Richmond [Tonino Ricci]
1979 *Aragosta a colazione* (IT/FR) FR *Une langouste au petit déjeuner* US *Lobster for Breakfast* – dir: Giorgio Capitani
1979 *Racconti fantastici* (IT) (tv mini-series) – dir: Daniele D'Anza
1980 *Vendetta napoletana (Maria)* (WG/IT) – dir: Herb Al Bauer [Ernst Hofbauer]
1980 *Paura nella città dei morti viventi* (IT) US *The Gates of Hell* UK ***City of the Living Dead*** – dir: Lucio Fulci
1980 *Prestami tua moglie* (IT) – dir: Giuliano Carnimeo
1980 *Mangiati vivi!* (IT) US *Doomed to Die* US *Emerald Jungle* UK *Eaten Alive!* – dir: Umberto Lenzi
1981 *L'onorevole con l'amante sotto il letto* (IT) – dir: Mariano Laurenti
1981 *La gatta da pelare* (IT) export title *A Hard Nut to Crack* – dir: Pippo Franco
1982 *Bakterion* (IT/SP) SP *Panico* UKvdt *Panic* – dir: Anthony Richmond [Tonino Ricci]
1982 *Ricchi, ricchissimi... praticamente in mutande* (IT) export title *Don't Play with Tigers* – dir: Sergio Martino
1982 *Sogni mostruosamente proibiti* (IT) – dir: Neri Parenti
1982 *L'inceneritore* (IT) – dir: Pier Francesco Boscaro dagli Ambrosi [unreleased, but screened at the Venice Film Festival in 1984]
1983 *Mystère* (IT) USvdt *Dagger Eyes / Murder Near Perfect* – dir: Carlo Vanzina
1983 *Questo e quello* (IT) aka *His and Her* segment *Questo... amore impossibile* – dir: Sergio Corbucci
1983 *Occhio malocchio prezzemolo e finocchio* (IT) segment *Il pelo della disgrazia* – dir: Sergio Martino
1984 *Vediamoci chiaro* (IT) aka *Let's See it Clear* – dir: Luciano Salce
1985 *Red Sonja* (US) – dir: Richard Fleischer
1985 *Vendetta dal futuro* (IT) US *Hands of Steel* UKvdt *Fists of Steel* FR *Atomic Cyborg* – dir: Martin Dolman [Sergio Martino]
1985 *Superfantagenio* (IT) UKvdt *Aladdin* – dir: Bruno Corbucci
1987 *Il ragazzo dal kimono d'oro* (IT) UKvdt *Karate Warrior* aka *Fist of Power* – dir: Larry Ludman [Fabrizio De Angelis]
1987 *La famiglia Brandacci* (IT) (tv movie) – dir: Sergio Martino
1988 *Quella villa in fondo al parco* (IT) export title *RatMan* – dir: Anthony Ascot [Giuliano Carnimeo]
1988 *La notte degli squali* (IT) UKvdt *Night of the Sharks* – dir: Anthony Richmond [Tonino Ricci]
1988 *Stille Nacht* (WG) US *Magdalene* export title *Silent Night* – dir: Monica Teuber
1990 *Forever (Per sempre)* (IT/BRA) – dir: Walter Hugo Khouri

Florinda Bolkan

born 15 February 1941 in Uruburetama, Brazil
real name **Florinda Soares Bulcão**

Carol Hammond in ***A Lizard in a Woman's Skin***
la maciara in ***Don't Torture a Duckling***

1968 *Candy* (FR/IT/US) IT *Candy e il suo pazzo mondo* – dir: Christian Marquand [collaborating director: Giancarlo Zagni]
1969 *Una ragazza piuttosto complicata* (IT) UK *Complicated Girl* – dir: Damiano Damiani
1969 *La caduta degli dei (Götterdämmerung)* (IT/WG) WG Die Verdammten UK *The Damned* – dir: Luchino Visconti
1969 *Un detective / Macchie di belletto* (IT) US *Detective Belli / A Detective* USvdt *Ring of Death* – dir: Romolo Guerrieri [Romolo Girolami]
1969 *Le voleur des crimes* (FR/IT) IT *Il ladro di crimini* – dir: Nadine Marquand Trintignant
1969 *Gli intoccabili* (IT) US/UK *Machine Gun McCain* – dir: Giuliano Montaldo
1969 *Metti, una sera a cena* (IT) UK/US *Love Circle* – dir: Giuseppe Patroni Griffi
1970 *Indagine su un cittadino al di sopra di ogni sospetto* (IT) UK/US *Investigation of a Citizen Above Suspicion* – dir: Elio Petri
1970 *...e venne il giorno dei limoni neri* (IT) UK *Those Who Kill* export title *Black Lemons* – dir: Camillo Bazzoni
1970 *Anonimo veneziano* (IT) US *The Anonymous Venetian* – dir: Enrico Maria Salerno
1970 *The Last Valley* (UK) – dir: James Clavell
1971 *Una lucertola con la pelle di donna* (IT/SP/FR) SP *Una lagartija con piel de mujer* FR Carole US/UK ***A Lizard in a Woman's Skin*** – dir: Lucio Fulci
1971 *Incontro* (IT) – dir: Piero Schivazappa
1971 *Una stagione all'inferno* (IT/FR) FR *Une saison en enfer* – dir: Nelo Risi
1972 *Le droit d'aimer* (FR/IT) IT *Diritto d'amare* US *The Right to Love* UKvdt *Brainwashed* – dir: Eric Le Hung
1972 *Non si sevizia un paperino* (IT) export title ***Don't Torture a Duckling*** – dir: Lucio Fulci
1972 *Un uomo da rispettare* (IT/WG) WG *Ein achtbarer Mann* US/USvdt *The Master Touch* UK *A Man to Respect* – dir: Michele Lupo
1973 *Cari genitori* (IT/FR) – dir: Enrico Maria Salerno
1973 *Una breve vacanza* (IT/SP) SP *Amargo despertar* UK *A Brief Vacation* – dir: Vittorio De Sica
1974 *Le mouton enragé* (FR/IT) IT *Il montone infuriato* – dir: Michel Deville
1974 *Flavia, la monaca musulmana* (IT/FR) FR *Flavia, la défroquée* UK *Rebel Nun* export title *Flavia, The Heretic* aka *Flavia, la nonne musulmane* – dir: Gianfranco Mingozzi
1974 *Le orme* (IT) export title *Footprints* aka *Footprints on the Moon* – dir: Luigi Bazzoni
1975 *Royal Flash* (UK) – dir: Richard Lester
1975 *Atentat u Sarajevo* (YUG) US/USvdt *The Day That Shook the World* UK *Assassination* – dir: Veljko Bulajic
1976 *Il comune senso del pudore* (IT) – dir: Alberto Sordi
1978 *Die Wölfin vom Teufelsmoor* (AT/WG) export title *The Devil's Bed* shooting titles *Tod im November / Death in November* – dir: Helmut Pfandler
1978 *La settima donna* (IT) UKvdt *Terror* export title *The Last House on the Beach* – dir: Franco Prosperi [Francesco Prosperi]
1978 *The Word* (US) (tv mini-series) – dir: Richard Lang
1980 *Manaos* (SP/IT/MEX) – dir: Alberto Vázquez-Figueroa
1981 *Habibi, amor mío* (SP/IT) – dir: Luis Gómez Valdivieso
1983 *Legati da tenera amicizia* (IT) (tv mini-series, shortened version shown theatrically) – dir: Alfredo Giannetti
1983 *Acqua e sapone* (IT) – dir: Carlo Verdone
1983 *La piovra* (IT) (tv mini-series) UK television title *The Octopus* – dir: Damiano Damiani
1985 *La gabbia* (IT/SP) SP *La jaula* US *The Trap* USvdt *Collector's Item* – dir: Giuseppe Patroni Griffi
1986 *La piovra 2* (IT) (tv mini-series) export title *The Octopus 2* – dir: Florestano Vancini
1987 *A rainha da vida* (BRA) (tv mini-series) – dir: Walter Campos
1987 *Prisoner of Rio* (BRA) – dir: Lech J. Majewski
1988 *Some Girls* (US) UKvdt *Sisters* – dir: Michael Hoffman
1989 *Affari di famiglia* (IT) (tv movie) – dir: Marcello Fondato
1989 *La trappola* (IT) (tv movie) – dir: Carlo Lizzani
1991 *Miliardi* (IT) UKvdt *Millions* – dir: Carlo Vanzina
1992 *Missione d'amore* (IT) – dir: Dino Risi
1992 *Gli uomini della sua vita* (IT/WG/FR) – dir: Michael Braun
1993 *La voyageuse du soir* (FR) – dir: Igaal Niddam
1993 *Tre passi nel delitto* (IT/WG) (3-part tv movie) WG television title *Die blondine in Schwarz* – dir: Fabrizio Laurenti
1994 *Delitto passionale* (IT) – dir: Flavio Mogherini
1994 *L'ombra abitata* (IT/FR) – dir: Mario Mazzucco
1995 *La strana storia di Olga "O"* (IT) export title *The Strange Story of Olga "O"* – dir: Antonio Bonifacio
1995 *Le Dernier des Pharoahs* (FR/IT/MOR) – dir: Souheil Ben Barka
1995 *La piovra 7* (IT) (tv mini-series) – dir: Luigi Perelli
1997 *Bela donna* (BRA) – dir: Fabio Barreto
1998 *Alice auf der Flucht* (GER) (tv mini-series) – dir: Axel de Roche
1999 *Ombre* (IT/GER) (tv movie) GER *Dem Mörder verfallen – Eine Frau in Gefahr* – dir: Cinzia Th. Torrini
2000 *Un bacio nel buio* (IT) (tv movie) – dir: Roberto Rocco
2000 *Eu não conhecia Tururu* (BRA) aka *I Didn't Know Tururu* (co-producer/director/screenplay/actor) – dir: Florinda Bolkan
2002 *Incantesimo 5* (IT) (tv series) – dir: Alessandro Cane & Leandro Castellani
2003 *Cattive inclinazioni* (IT) – dir: Pierfrancesco Campanella
2005 *La notte breve* (IT) (tv movie) – dir: Camilla Costanzo & Alessio Cremonini

Barbara Bouchet

born 15 August 1943 in Reichenburg (i.e. Liberec) in German occupied Czechoslovakia
birth name **Bärbel Goutscherola**
aka **Barbara Gutscher**

Patrizia in ***Don't Torture a Duckling***

1963 *Move Over, Darling* (US) [uncredited] – dir: Michael Gordon
1964 *Bedtime Story* (US) [uncredited] – dir: Ralph Levy
1964 *The Best Man* (US) – dir: Franklin J. Schaffner
1964 *Good Neighbor Sam* (US) [uncredited] – dir: David Swift
1964 *The Rogues* (US) (tv series) episode Plavonia, Hail and Farewell – dir: Robert Ellis Miller
1964 *What a Way to Go!* (US) – dir: J. Lee Thompson
1964 *Sex and the Single Girl* (US) [uncredited] – dir: Richard Quine
1964 *A Global Affair* (US) – dir: Jack Arnold
1965 *In Harm's Way* (US) – dir: Otto Preminger
1965 *Voyage to the Bottom of the Sea* (US) (tv series) episode *The Left-Handed Man* – dir: Jerry Hopper
1965 *John Goldfarb, Please Come Home* (US) [uncredited] – dir: J. Lee Thompson
1966 *Agent for H.A.R.M.* (US) – dir: Gerd Oswald
1966 *The Man from U.N.C.L.E.* (US) (tv series) episode *The Project Deephole Affair* – dir: Alex March
1967 *Casino Royale* (UK) – dir: John Huston, Ken Hughes, Val Guest, Robert Parrish & Joseph McGrath
1967 *The Virginian* (US) (tv series) episode *The Fortress* – dir: Abner Biberman
1968 *Danger Route* (UK) – dir: Seth Holt
1968 *Tarzan* (US) (tv series) episode *Jungle Ransom* – dir: Barry Shear
1968 *Star Trek* (US) (tv series) episode *By Any Other Name* – dir: Marc Daniels
1969 *Sweet Charity* (US) – dir: Bob Fosse
1969 *Gold Seekers / Deadly Game / Conspiracy* (US/PHI) US/UKvdt *The Surabaya Conspiracy* – dir: Wray Davis
1970 *Colpo rovente* (IT) US television title *The Syndicate: A Death in the Family* – dir: Piero Zuffi
1970 *L'asino d'oro: processo per fatti strani contro Lucius Apuleius cittadino romano* (IT) – dir: Sergio Spina
1970 *Il debito coniugale* (IT) – dir: Franco Prosperi [Francesco Prosperi]
1970 *Cerca di capirmi* (IT) – dir: Mariano Laurenti
1970 *Il prete sposato* (IT/FR) FR *Un prêtre à marier* US *The Married Priest / The Swinging Confessors* – dir: Marco Vicario
1971 *Le calde notti di Don Giovanni* (IT/SP) SP *Los amores de Don Juan* UKvdt *The Nights and Loves of Don Juan* – dir: Al Bradley [Alfonso Brescia]
1971 *La tarantola dal ventre nero* (IT/FR) FR *La tarentule au ventre noir* US *The Black Belly of the Tarantula* – dir: Paolo Cavara
1971 *Non commettere atti impuri* (IT) – dir: Giulio Petroni
1971 *Nokaut* (YUG/IT) IT *Donne sopra, femmine sotto* US *The Rogue* – dir: Barry Norton [Boro Draskovic]
1971 *Alla ricera del piacere* (IT) US *Amuck!* aka *Leather and Whips* shooting title *Replica di un delitto* – dir: Silvio Amadio
1971 *Forza "G"* (IT) US/UK *Winged Devils* – dir: Duccio Tessari
1972 *L'uomo dagli occhi di ghiaccio* (IT) aka *Man with Icy Eyes* shooting title *Black Day* – dir: Alberto De Martino

1972 *Milano calibro 9* (IT) UK/UKvdt *Contract* UKvdt *Calibre Nine* / *The Mikado Killers* – dir: Fernando Di Leo
1972 *Una cavalla tutta nuda* (IT) – dir: Franco Rossetti
1972 *Non si sevizia un paperino* (IT) export title ***Don't Torture a Duckling*** – dir: Lucio Fulci
1972 *Valeria dentro e fuori* (IT) – dir: Brunello Rondi
1972 *Finalmente le mille e una notte* (IT) UK *Bed of a Thousand Pleasures* US *House of 1,000 Pleasures* – dir: Anthony M. Dawson [Antonio Margheriti]
1972 *Casa d'appuntamento* (IT/WG) WG *Das Auge des Bösen* UKvdt *Murder in Paris* export title *The Bogey Man and the French Murders* – dir: F.L. Morris [Ferdinando Merighi]
1972 *Anche se volessi lavorare, che faccio?* (IT) – dir: Flavio Mogherini
1972 *Racconti proibiti... di niente vestiti* (IT) UK *Master of Love* – dir: Brunello Rondi
1972 *La calandria* (IT) – dir: Pasquale Festa Campanile
1972 *La dama rossa uccide sette volte* (IT/WG) WGvdt *Horror House* US *The Red Queen Kills Seven Times* / *Blood Feast* / *Feast of Flesh* – dir: Emilio P. Miraglia
1972 *Cool Million* (US) (tv movie) later shown as *The Mask of Marcella* – dir: Gene Levitt
1972 *Ancora una volta prima di lasciarci* (IT) aka *Conoscenza matrimoniale* – dir: Giuliano Biagetti
1973 *Il tuo piacere è il mio* (IT) – dir: Claudio Racca
1973 *Ricco (Ajuste de cuentas)* (SP/IT) IT *Un tipo con una faccia strana ti cerca per ucciderti* US *The Mean Machine* / *Cauldron of Death* / *Dirty Mob* UK *Ricco* – dir: Tulio Demicheli
1974 *Quelli che contano* (IT) US *Cry of a Prostitute – Love Kills* export title *Guns of the Bigshots* shooting title *The Bigshots* – dir: Andrea Bianchi
1974 *La badessa di Castro* (IT) – dir: Armando Crispino
1974 *La svergognata* (IT) – dir: Giulio Biagetti
1975 *Amore vuol dir gelosia* (IT/SP) SP *Yo no perdono un cuerno* – dir: Maurizio Severino
1975 *Per le antiche scale* (IT/FR) FR *Vertiges* US *Down the Ancient Staircase* – dir: Mauro Bolognini
1975 *To anghistri* (GRE/IT) IT *L'adultera* export title *The Hook* – dir: Eric Andrew [Erricos Andreou]
1975 *L'anatra all'arancia* (IT) US *Duck in Orange Sauce* – dir: Luciano Salce
1975 *L'amica di mia madre* (IT) – dir: Mario Ivaldi
1976 *40 gradi all'ombra del lenzuolo* (IT) UK *Sex with a Smile* segment *I soldi in banca* – dir: Sergio Martino
1976 *Con la rabbia agli occhi* (IT) UK *Death Rage* US *Anger in His Eyes* export title *Shadow of a Killer* – dir: Anthony M. Dawson [Antonio Margheriti]
1976 *Brogliaccio d'amore* (IT) – dir: Decio Silla
1976 *Tutti possono arricchire tranne i poveri* (IT) – dir: Maurizio Severino
1976 *Spogliamoci così senza pudor...* (IT) export title *Love in Four Easy Lessons* aka *Sex with a Smile 2* segment 3 – dir: Sergio Martino
1977 *L'appuntamento (Dove, come, quando?)* (IT) – dir: Giuliano Biagetti
1978 *Come perdere una moglie... e trovare un'amante* (IT) – dir: Pasquale Festa Campanile
1978 *Diamanti sporchi di sangue* (IT) export title *Blood and Diamonds* – dir: Fernando Di Leo
1978 *Travolto dagli affetti familiari* (IT) – dir: Mauro Severino
1979 *Sabato domenica e venerdì* (IT/SP) SP *Sábado, domingo y viérnes* segment *Domenica* – dir: Pasquale Festa Campanile [other dir's: [Franco] Castellano & Pipolo [Giuseppe Moccia] & Sergio Martino]
1979 *Liquirizia* (IT) – dir: Salvatore Samperi
1980 *Sono fotogenico* (IT/FR) FR *Je suis photogénique* [uncredited] – dir: Dino Risi
1980 *La moglie in vacanza... l'amante in città* (IT/FR) FR *Les zizis baladeurs* – dir: Sergio Martino
1981 *Per favore, occupati di Amelia* (IT/SP) SP *Por favor, ocúpate de Amelia* – dir: Flavio Mogherini
1981 *Perché non facciamo l'amore?* (IT/SP) SP *¿Por qué no hacemos el amor?* – dir: Maurizio Lucidi
1981 *Spaghetti a mezzanotte* (IT) – dir: Sergio Martino
1981 *Crema, cioccolato e pa...prika* (IT) – dir: Michele Massimo Tarantini
1983 *The Scarlet and the Black* (US/IT) (tv movie) – dir: Jerry London
1983 *The Beauty Center Show* (tv series) (IT) (hostess) – dir: Valerio Lazoron
1984 *Beklenmeyen randevu* / *Belali Elmaslar* (TUR/SWI/IT) IT *Diamond Connection (Diamanti che scottano)* – dir: Sergio Bergonzelli
1992 *L'ultimo dei buoni* (IT) aka *The Last of the Brave Men* – dir: Maurizio Gaudio
1992 *Quelli della speciale* (IT) (tv movie) – dir: Bruno Corbucci
2001 *Mari del sud* (IT/SP/UK) SP *Mi marido es una ruina* aka *Our Tropical Island* – dir: Marcello Cesena
2002 *Gangs of New York* (US/IT) – dir: Martin Scorsese
2003 *Incantesimo 6* (IT) (tv series)
2004 *Diritto di difesa* (IT) (tv series) – dir: Gianfrancesco Lazotti & Donatella Maiorca
2004 *Un posto al sole* (IT) (tv series)
2005 *Trailer for a Remake of Gore Vidal's Caligula* (IT/US) (short) – dir: Francesco Vezzoli
2006 *La provinciale* (IT) (tv movie) – dir: Pasquale Pozzessere
2008 *Bastardi* (IT) – dir: Federico Del Zoppo & Andres Alce Meldonado
2008 *Amiche mie* (IT) (tv series) episode *Giù la maschera* – dir: Paolo Genovese
2008 *Così vanno le cose* (IT) (tv movie) – dir: Francesco Bovino
2008 *Ho sposato uno sbirro* (IT) (tv series) aka *Married to a Cop*
2009 *La vita dispari* (IT) – dir: Luca Fantasia
2009 *Butterfly zone – Il senso della farfalla* (IT) – dir: Luciano Capponi
2009 *Giallo?* (IT) – dir: Antonio Capuano
2010 *Capri* (IT) (tv series) – dir: Dario Acocella
2010 *Crimini* (IT) (tv series) aka *Crimes episode Little Dream* – dir: Davide Marengo
2010 *Ho sposato uno sbirro 2* (IT) (tv series) aka *Married to a Cop* – dir: Andrea Barzini
2011 *Rewind* (IT) – dir: Massimo Spano
2012 *Double Swing* (IT) (tv series) episode *Io&Lui* – dir: Alessandro Tonda
2014 *Il tredicesimo apostolo – La rivelazione* (IT) (tv series) episode *Il pianto del demonio* – dir: Alexis Cahill
2014 *Come un morto ad Acapulco* (SWI) (short) – dir: Alessio Pizzicannella
2015 *Darkside Witches* (IT) – dir: Gerard Diefenthal
2015 *Madame & Monsieur* (IT) (short) – dir: Eleonora Albrecht
2015 *Das Wetter in geschlossenen Räumen* (GER) – dir: Isabelle Stever
2017 *Easy* (IT/UKR) – dir: Andrea Magnani
2017 *In Search of Fellini* (US/IT) – dir: Taron Lexton
2018 *Metti la nonna in freezer* (IT) aka *Put Grandma in the Freezer* – dir: Giancarlo Fontana & Giuseppe Stasi
2019 *Rome in Love* (US) – dir: Eric Bross
2020 *Tolo Tolo* (IT) – dir: Checco Zalone
2020 *Calibro 9* (IT/BEL) – dir: Toni D'Angelo
2021 *Una famiglia mostruosa* (IT) aka *Help! My In-Laws Are Vampires!* – dir: Volfango De Biasi
2023 *Diabolik chi sei?* (IT/FR) aka *Diabolik: Who Are You?* – dir: Antonio Manetti & Marco Manetti

Lando Buzzanca

born 24 August 1935 in Palermo, Italy
died 18 December 2022 in Rome, Italy
real name **Gerlando Buzzanca**

Napoleone in ***Operation St. Peter's***
Senator Gianni Puppis in ***The Eroticist***
Costante Nicosia in ***Young Dracula***

1959 *Ben-Hur* (US) [uncredited] – dir: William Wyler
1960 *Tutto da rifare pover'uomo* (IT) (tv series) – dir: Eros Macchi
1961 *La trincea* (IT) (tv movie) – dir: Vittorio Cottafavi
1961 *Divorzio all'italiana* (IT) UK/US *Divorce, Italian Style* – dir: Pietro Germi
1962 *Racconti dell'Italia di oggi – Una lapide in Via Mazzini* (IT) (tv movie) – dir: Mario Landi
1962 *I giorni contati* (IT) – dir: Elio Petri
1962 *Il mondo e una prigione* (IT) (tv movie) – dir: Vittorio Cottafava
1963 *La Parmigiana* (IT) – dir: Antonio Pietrangeli
1963 *La smania addosso* (IT/FR) FR *Viol à l'italienne* US *The Eye of the Needle* – dir: Marcello Andrei
1963 *Tutto il bello dell'uomo* (IT) – dir: Aldo Sinesio
1963 *Le monachine* (IT) US *The Little Nuns* – dir: Luciano Salce
1963 *I mostri* (IT/FR) FR *Les Monstres* US *Opiate 67* segment *Come un padre* – dir: Dino Risi
1964 *Sedotta e abbandonata* (IT/FR) FR *Séduite et abandonnée* US *Seduced and Abandoned* – dir: Pietro Germi
1964 *Amore in 4 dimensioni* (IT/FR) FR *L'amour en quatre dimensions* US *Love in 4 Dimensions* segment *Amore e alfabeto* – dir: Massimo Mida
1964 *I marziani hanno 12 mani* (IT/SP) SP *Llegaron los marcianos* – dir: [Franco] Castellano & Pipolo [Giuseppe Moccia]
1964 *Cadavere per signora* (IT) aka *Corpse for the Lady* – dir: Mario Mattoli
1964 *Senza sole né luna* (IT) – dir: Luciano Ricci
1964 *L'idea fissa* (IT) US *Love and Marriage* segment *La prima notte* – dir: Gianni Puccini [other dir: Mino Guerrini]
1964 *Il magnifico cornuto* (IT/FR) FR *Le cocu magnifique* US *The Magnificent Cuckold* [uncredited] – dir: Antonio Pietrangeli
1964 *Extraconiugale* (IT) segment *La doccia* – dir: Massimo Franciosa [other dir's: Mino Guerrini & Giuliano Montaldo]

1964 *Le lit à deux places* (FR/IT) IT *Racconti a due piazze* segment *Mourir pour vivre* – dir: Gianni Puccini [other dir's: François Dupont Midy, Jean Delannoy & Al World [Alvaro Mancori]]
1965 *Le corniaud* (FR/IT) IT *Colpo grosso, ma non troppo* UK *The Sucker* – dir: Gérard Oury
1965 *Su e giù* (IT) segment *Questione di principio* – dir: Mino Guerrini
1965 *Made in Italy* (IT/FR) FR *A l'italienne* – dir: Nanni Loy
1965 *Letti sbagliati* (IT) segment *Il complicato* – dir: Steno [Stefano Vanzina]
1965 *James Tont, operazione U.N.O.* (IT) – dir: Bruno Corbucci & Gianni [Giovanni] Grimaldi
1966 *James Tont, operazione D.U.E.* (IT/FR) – dir: Bruno Corbucci & Gianni [Giovanni] Grimaldi
1966 *I nostri mariti* (IT/FR) segment *Il marito di Olga* – dir: Luigi Zampa [other dir's: Luigi Filippo D'Amico & Dino Risi]
1966 *Per qualche dollaro in meno* (IT) – dir: Mario Mattòli
1966 *Ringo e Gringo contro tutti* (IT/SP) SP *Héroes a la fuerza* – dir: Bruno Corbucci
1966 *Caccia alla volpe* (IT/UK) UK/US *After the Fox* – dir: Vittorio De Sica
1966 *Spia spione* (IT/SP) SP *Una ladrona para un espía* – dir: Bruno Corbucci
1967 *Una rosa per tutti* (IT) export title *All on the Red* – dir: Franco Rossi
1967 *Don Giovanni in Sicilia* (IT) – dir: Alberto Lattuada
1967 *Le dolci signore* (IT) US *Anyone Can Play* – dir: Luigi Zampa
1968 ***Operazione San Pietro*** (IT/FR/WG) FR *Au diable les anges!* WG *Die Abenteuer des Kardinal Braun* export title *Operation St. Peter's* – dir: Lucio Fulci
1968 *Il cenerentolo* (IT) (tv movie) – dir: Flaminio Bollini
1968 *Meglio vedova* (IT/FR) US *Better a Widow* – dir: Duccio Tessari
1968 *7 uomini e un cervello (Criminal Symphony)* (IT/ARG) ARG *Il rubamento (El gran robo)* – dir: Edward Ross [Rossano Brazzi]
1968 *Colpo di sole* (IT) – dir: Mino Guerrini
1969 *Frau Wirtin hat auch eine Nichte* (AT/WG/IT/HUN) IT *Il trionfo della casta Susanna* UK *House of Pleasure* – dir: François Legrand [Franz Antel]
1969 *Warum hab ich bloß 2x ja gesagt?* (WG/IT) IT *Professione bigamo* UK *Confessions of a Bigamist* – dir: François Legrand [Franz Antel]
1969 *Puro siccome un angelo, papà mi fece... monaco di Monza* (IT) – dir: Gianni [Giovanni] Grimaldi
1969 *Quel negozio di Piazza Navona* (IT) (tv mini-series) – dir: Mino Guerrini
1969 *Gonflés a bloc* (FR/IT) IT *Quei temerari sulle loro pazze, scatenate, scalcinate carriole* UK *Monte Carlo or Bust!* US *Those Daring Young Men in Their Jaunty Jalopies* – dir: Ken Annakin
1969 *La donna ad una dimensione (La marcusiana)* (IT) [uncredited] – dir: Bruno Baratti
1970 *Signore e signora* (IT) (tv series) – dir: Carla Ragionieri
1970 *Un caso di coscienza* (IT) – dir: Gianni [Giovanni] Grimaldi
1970 *Fermate il mondo... voglio scendere* (IT) – dir: Giancarlo Cobelli
1970 *Il debito coniugale* (IT) – dir: Franco Prosperi [Francesco Prosperi]
1970 *Quando le donne avevano la coda* (IT) US *When Women Had Tails* – dir: Pasquale Festa Campanile
1970 *Il prete sposato* (IT/FR) FR *Un prêtre à marier* US *The Married Priest* / *The Swinging Confessors* – dir: Marco Vicario
1970 *La prima notte del Dottor Danieli industriale col complesso del giocattolo* (IT) export title *A Latin Lover on His Wedding Night* – dir: Gianni [Giovanni] Grimaldi
1970 *Nel giorno del Signore* (IT) – dir: Bruno Corbucci
1971 *Le belve* (IT) export title *The Beasts* segments *Il Salvatore* / *La voce del sangue* / *Il fachiro* / *Una bella famiglia* / *Il caso Apposito* / *Il cincillà* / *Il chirurgo* / *Processo a porte chiuse* – dir: Gianni [Giovanni] Grimaldi
1971 *Homo eroticus* (IT/FR) US *Man of the Year* – dir: Marco Vicario
1971 *Il merlo maschio* (IT) – dir: Pasquale Festa Campanile
1971 *Il vichingo venuto dal Sud* (IT) – dir: Steno [Stefano Vanzina]
1971 *Quando le donne persero la coda* (IT) US *When Women Lost Their Tales* – dir: Pasquale Festa Campanile
1972 *All'onorevole piacciono le donne* (IT/FR) FR *Obsédé malgré lui* US *The Senator Likes Women* UKvdt ***The Eroticist*** – dir: Lucio Fulci
1972 *La calandria* (IT) – dir: Pasquale Festa Campanile
1972 *Jus primae noctis* (IT) – dir: Pasquale Festa Campanile
1972 *Il sindacalista* (IT) – dir: Luciano Salce
1972 *L'uccello migratore* (IT) – dir: Steno [Stefano Vanzina]
1973 *Io e lui* (IT/FR) – dir: Luciano Salce
1973 *Il magnate* (IT) export title *Wife for Sale* – dir: Gianni [Giovanni] Grimaldi
1973 *La schiava io ce l'ho e tu no* (IT) UK *My Darling Slave* – dir: Giorgio Capitani
1974 *L'arbitro* (IT) US *The Referee* UK television title *Football Crazy* – dir: Luigi Filippo D'Amico
1974 *Bello come un arcangelo* (IT) – dir: Alfredo Giannetti
1974 *Il domestico* (IT) – dir: Luigi Filippo D'Amico
1975 *Il fidanzamento* (IT) export title *The Engagement* – dir: Gianni [Giovanni] Grimaldi
1975 *Il Cav. Costante Nicosia Demoniaco, ovvero: Dracula in Brianza* (IT) export title ***Young Dracula*** – dir: Lucio Fulci
1975 *Il gatto mammone* (IT) – dir: Nando [Fernando] Cicero
1976 *San Pasquale Baylonne protettore delle donne* (IT) – dir: Luigi Filippo D'Amico
1978 *Una noche enbarazosa* (SP/MEX) – dir: René Cardona Jr.
1978 *Travolto dagli affetti familiari* (IT) – dir: Mauro Severino
1980 *Prestami tua moglie* (IT) – dir: Giuliano Carnimeo
1981 *Los crápulas* (ARG/IT) – dir: Jorge Pantano
1982 *Vado a vivere da solo* (IT) – dir: Marco Risi
1983 *La pulce nell'orecchio* (IT) (tv movie) – dir: Vito Molinari
1987 *Secondo Ponzio Pilato* (IT) – dir: Luigi Magni
1988 *O diabo na cama* (BRA) – dir: Michele Massimo Tarantini
1989 *Cinema* (IT) (tv movie) – dir: Luigi Magni
1994 *Tutti gli anni, una volta l'anno* (IT/FR/BEL) FR *Même heure l'année prochaîne* – dir: Gianfrancesco Lazotti
1999 *Il popolo degli uccelli* (IT) – dir: Rocco Cesareo
1999 *Cornetti al miele* (IT) (tv movie) – dir: Sergio Martino
2000 *Il segreto del giaguaro* (IT) – dir: Antonello Fassari
2003 *Una famiglia per caso* (IT) (tv movie) – dir: Camilla Costanzo & Alessio Cremonini
2005 *Mio figlio* (IT) (tv movie) – dir: Luciano Odorisio
2005 *Incidenti* (IT) – dir: Ramón Alós Sanchez, Miloje Popovic & Toni Trupia
2005 *Il cielo può attendere* (IT) (tv movie) – dir: Bruno Gaburro
2007 *Chiara e Francesco* (IT) (tv movie) – dir: Fabrizio Costa
2007 *La baronessa di Carini* (IT) (tv movie) – dir: Umberto Marino
2007 *I vicerè* (IT/SP/GER/US) – dir: Roberto Faenza
2010 *Lo scandalo della Banca Romana* (IT) (tv movie) – dir: Stefano Reali
2010 *Achille* (IT) (short) – dir: Giorgia Farina
2010 *Capri* (IT) (tv series)
2010 *Io e mio figlio – Nuove storie per il commissario Vivaldi* (IT) (tv series) – dir: Luciano Odorisio
2012 *Terra ribelle – Il nuovo mondo* (IT) (tv series) – dir: Ambrogio Lo Giudice
2012-2014 *Il restauratore* (IT) (tv series)
2013 *Donne in gioco* (IT) (tv mini-series) – dir: Michelle Bonev
2017 *Chi salverà le rose?* (IT) – dir: Cesare Furesi
2019 *W gli sposi* (US/IT) – dir: Valerio Zanoli

Adriano Celentano

born 6 January 1938 in Milan, Italy

himself in ***I ragazzi del juke box***
Adriano in ***Urlatori alla sbarra***
Peppino / himself in ***Uno strano tipo***

1959 ***I ragazzi del juke box*** (IT) – dir: Lucio Fulci
1959 *Juke box urli d'amore* (IT) – dir: Mauro Morassi
1960 ***Urlatori alla sbarra*** (IT) export title *Howlers in the Dock* – dir: Lucio Fulci
1960 ***Sam Remo La grande sfida*** (IT) – dir: Piero Vivarelli [collaborating director: Lucio Fulci]
1960 *La dolce vita* (IT/FR) FR *La douceur de vivre* UK *The Sweet Life* [uncredited] – dir: Federico Fellini
1961 *Io bacio... tu baci* (IT) – dir: Piero Vivarelli
1961 *Hey, Let's Twist!* (US) [uncredited] – dir: Greg Garrison
1963 ***Uno strano tipo*** (IT) – dir: Lucio Fulci
1963 *Il monaco di Monza* (IT) – dir: Sergio Corbucci
1964 *I malamondo* (IT) – dir: Paolo Cavara
1964 *Super rapina a Milano* (IT) – (director/actor) [uncredited directorial supervision: Piero Vivarelli]
1966 *Por un puñado de canciones* (SP/IT) IT *Per un pugno di canzoni* aka *Europa canta* – dir: José Luis Merino
1968 *La più bella coppia del mondo* (IT) – dir: Camillo Mastrocinque
1968 *Serafino* (IT/FR) FR *Serafino, ou l'amour aux champs* – dir: Pietro Germi
1971 *Er più Storia d'amore e di coltello* (IT) (composer) – dir: Sergio Corbucci
1972 *Bianco, rosso e...* (IT/FR/SP) FR *Une bonne planque* SP *Blanco, rojo y...* US/UK *White Sister* – dir: Alberto Lattuada
1973 *L'emigrante* (IT/SP/WG) SP *Un trabajo tranquilo* WG *Der Kleine mit dem großen Tick* – dir: Pasquale Festa Campanile
1973 *Rugantino* (IT) – dir: Pasquale Festa Campanile
1973 *Le cinque giornate* (IT) – dir: Dario Argento
1975 *Di che segno sei?* (IT) segment *Aria* – dir: Sergio Corbucci
1975 *Yuppi du* (IT) (director/co-screenplay/actor)
1976 *Bluff storia di truffe e di imbroglioni* (IT) US/UK *Con Artists* UKvdt *The Con Men* USvdt *The Switch* – dir: Sergio Corbucci
1976 *Culastrisce nobile veneziano* (IT) US *Lunatics and Lovers* – dir: Flavio Mogherini
1977 *L'altra metà del cielo* (actor/composer) – dir: Franco Rossi
1977 *Ecco noi per esempio...* (IT) (composer/actor) – dir: Sergio Corbucci
1978 *Zio Adolfo in arte Führer* (IT) – dir: [Franco] Castellano & Pipolo [Giuseppe Moccia]
1978 *Geppo il folle* (IT) (director/story/screenplay/composer/actor)
1979 *Mani di velluto* (IT) – dir: [Franco] Castellano & Pipolo [Giuseppe Moccia]
1979 *Sabato domenica e venerdì* (IT/SP) SP *Sábado, domingo y viérnes* segment *Venerdì* – dir: [Franco] Castellano & Pipolo [Giuseppe Moccia] [other dir's: Sergio Martino & Pasquale Festa Campanile]
1980 *Qua la mano* (IT) segment *Il prete ballerino* – dir: Pasquale Festa Campanile
1980 *La locandiera* (IT) – dir: Paolo Cavara

1980 *Il bisbetico domato* (IT) (composer) – dir: [Franco] Castellano & Pipolo [Giuseppe Moccia]
1981 *Asso* (IT) – dir: [Franco] Castellano & Pipolo [Giuseppe Moccia]
1981 *Innamorato pazzo* (IT) (composer/actor) – dir: [Franco] Castellano & Pipolo [Giuseppe Moccia]
1982 *Bingo Bongo* (IT) – dir: Pasquale Festa Campanile
1982 *Grand Hotel Excelsior* (IT) – dir: [Franco] Castellano & Pipolo [Giuseppe Moccia]
1983 *Segni particolari: bellissimo* (IT) – dir: [Franco] Castellano & Pipolo [Giuseppe Moccia]
1983 *Sing Sing* (IT) – dir: Sergio Corbucci
1985 *Joan Lui – Ma un giorno nel paese arrivo io di lunedì* (IT/WG) WG *Joan Lui* (director/story/screenplay/composer/actor)
1985 *Lui è peggio di me* (IT) – dir: Enrico Oldoini
1986 *Il burbero* (IT) – dir: [Franco] Castellano & Pipolo [Giuseppe Moccia]
1992 *Jackpot (Classe speciale)* (IT) export title *Cybereden* shooting title *Tilt* (co-screenplay/actor) – dir: Mario Orfini
2016 *Mina Celentano: Se mi ami davvero* (IT) (short) (singer) – dir: Carlo Verdone
2019 *Adrian* (IT) (tv series) (director/writer/editor/voice)

Cosimo Cinieri

born 20 August 1938 in Taranto, Italy
died 19 August 2019 in Rome, Lazio, Italy
brother of director Francesco Cinieri
aka **Laurence Welles**

Doctor Lodge in ***The New York Ripper***
Adrian Marcato in ***Manhattan Baby***
Professor Towman in ***Rome 2033 – The Fighter Centurions***
Lieutenant Borges in ***Murder-Rock Dancing Death***

1961 *Cronache del '22* (IT) segment *La nuova legge* – dir: Francesco Cinieri [other dir's: Moraldo Rossi, Giuseppe Orlandini, Stefano Ubezio & Guidarino Guidi]
1966 *Atto senza parole 2* (IT) (short) – dir: Carlo Di Carlo
1969 *Tre nel mille* (IT) – dir: Franco Indovina [shown on Italian tv as *Storie dell'anno mille* in 4 parts in 1973]
1973 *La mano spietata della legge* (IT) US *The Bloody Hands of the Law* – dir: Mario Gariazzo
1974 *Il matrimonio di Rosa Palanca* (IT) – dir: Piero Panza
1975 *L'albero di Guernica* (IT/FR) FR *L'arbre de Guernica* – dir: Fernando Arrabal
1976 *Mosè* (IT/UK) (tv series, shortened version shown in cinemas) UK television title *Moses The Lawgiver* UK/US *Moses* – dir: Gianfranco De Bosio
1979 *Bloodline* (US/WG) – dir: Terence Young
1979 *Otello di Carmelo Bene* (IT) (tv movie) – dir: Carmelo Bene [shot in 1979, edited in 2001 and first shown in 2002]
1981 *La tragedia di un uomo ridicolo* (IT) UK *The Tragedy of a Ridiculous Man* [uncredited] – dir: Bernardo Bertolucci
1982 *Lo squartatore di New York* (IT) export title ***The New York Ripper*** – dir: Lucio Fulci
1982 ***Manhattan Baby*** (IT) USvdt *Eye of the Evil Dead* UKvdt *Possessed* – dir: Lucio Fulci
1984 *I guerrieri dell'anno 2072* (IT) USvdt *The New Gladiators* UKvdt ***Rome 2033 – The Fighter Centurions*** – dir: Lucio Fulci
1984 *Murderock uccide a passo di danza* (IT) US *The Demon Is Loose* export title ***Murder-Rock Dancing Death*** – dir: Lucio Fulci
1986 *I racconti del maresciallo* (IT) (tv movie) – dir: Giovanni Soldati
1986 *Il generale* (IT/FR/WG/YUG) (tv mini-series, shortened version shown theatrically) US television title *The General* UK television title *Garibaldi, the General* – dir: Luigi Magni
1987 *Secondo Ponzio Pilato* (IT) – dir: Luigi Magni
1989 *Rebus* (IT) – dir: Massimo Guglielmi
1990 *Eleonora Pimentel: The Jacobean Marquise* (IT) (tv movie) – dir: Ivana Massetti
1991 *Mia dolce Gertrude* (IT) – dir: Adriana Zanese
1991 *Antelope Cobbler* (IT) – dir: Antonio Falduto [released in 1993]
1992 *Felipe ha gli occhi azzurri 2* (IT) (tv movie) – dir: Felice Farina
1994 *Lucrezia Borgia* (IT) (tv movie) – dir: Tonino del Colle
1996 *Pizzicata* (IT/GER) – dir: Edoardo Winspeare
1996 *Intolerance* (IT) segment *Gruppo di famiglia in un esterno* – dir: Antonio Manzini
1997 *Consigli per gli acquisti* (IT) – dir: Sandro Baldoni
1997 *La tregua* (IT/GER/FR/SWI) FR *La trêve* aka *The Truce* – dir: Francesco Rosi
1997 *Ultimo bersaglio* (IT) aka *Last Target* – dir: Andrea Frezza
1999 *La vespa e la regina* (IT/SP) – dir: Antonello De Leo
1999 *Ombre* (IT/GER) (tv movie) – dir: Cinzia Th. Torrini
2002 *Vento di ponente* (IT) (tv series)
2002 *Fortezza Bastiani* (IT) – dir: Michele Mellara & Alessandro Rossi
2003 *La notte di Pasquino* (IT) (tv movie) – dir: Luigi Magni
2003 *Poco più di un anno fa* (IT) aka *Adored* [uncredited] – dir: Marco Filiberti
2003 *Il miracolo* (IT) aka *The Miracle* – dir: Edoardo Winspeare
2003 *Il ronzio delle mosche* (IT) – dir: Dario D'Ambrosi
2005 *Un anno a primavera* (IT) (tv movie) – dir: Angelo Longoni
2005 *San Pietro* (IT) (tv movie) aka *Imperium: Saint Peter* – dir: Giulio Base
2006 *Fratelli* (IT) (tv movie) – dir: Angelo Longoni
2006 *Don Matteo* (IT) (tv series) episode *Ultima preda* – dir: Giulio Base
2006 *Il padre delle spose* (IT) (tv movie) – dir: Lodovico Gasparini
2007 *Segretario particolare* (IT) – dir: Nicola Molino
2007 *Manuale d'amore 2 (Capitoli successivi)* (IT) – dir: Giovanni Veronesi
2007 *Tu chiamala musica* (IT) – dir: Michele Lastella
2007 *La terza verità* (IT) (tv movie) – dir: Stefano Reali
2008 *La formula* (IT) (short) – dir: Leonardo Cinieri Lombroso & Michele De Caro
2008 *I passi dell'anima* (IT) (short) aka *Soul Walking* – dir: Matteo Galante
2009 *L'altra metà* (IT) (short) – dir: Pippo Mezzapesa
2009 *Cavie* (IT) aka *Human Test* – dir: Antonio Manetti & Marco Manetti
2010 *Ho sposato uno sbirro* (IT) (tv series) aka *Married to a Cop* episode *Vigilia di Natale* – dir: Luca Miniero
2011 *Al di là del lago* (IT) (tv series)
2011 *Faccio un salto all'Avana* (IT) – dir: Dario Baldi
2011 *La penna di Hemingway* (IT) (short) – dir: Renzo Carbonera
2011 *Disinstallare un amore* (IT) (short) – dir: Alessia Scarso
2012 *Cesare Mori – Il prefetto di ferro* (IT) (tv movie) – dir: Gianni Lepre
2012 *Né con te né senza di te* (IT) (tv movie) – dir: Vincenzo Terracciano
2012 *La prima legge di Newton* (IT) (short) – dir: Piero Messina
2013 *Pasolini, la verità nascosta* (IT) – dir: Federico Bruno
2013 *Ritual – Una storia psicomagica* (IT) – dir: Giulia Brazzale & Luca Immesi
2013 *Alle corde* (IT) (short) – dir: Andrea Simonetti
2014 *Ameluk* (IT) – dir: Mimmo Mancini
2014 *Dura Pioggia Cadrà* (IT) (short) – dir: Giovanni Bufalini
2015 *I misteri di Laura* (tv series) episode *Il mistero della scena del crimine* – dir: Alberto Ferrari
2016 *Los Feliz* (AT) – dir: Edgar Honetschläger
2016 *Iaco* (IT) (short) – dir: Alessandro Zizzo
2017 *Le guerre horrende* (IT) – dir: Giulia Brazzale & Luca Immesi
2018 *Beyond the Mist* (IT/SWI) – dir: Giuseppe Varlotta

Corinne Cléry

born 23 March 1950 in Paris, France
real name **Corinne Piccoli**

Carol Simpson in ***The Devil's Honey***

1967 *Les poneyttes* (FR) [credited as Corinne Piccoli] – dir: Joël Le Moigné
1973 *Il sergente Rompiglioni* (IT) [credited as Corinne Piccolo] – dir: Pier Giorgio Ferretti
1975 *Histoire d'O* (FR/WG) WG *Geschichte der O* US/USvdt/UKvdt *Story of O* – dir: Just Jaeckin
1976 *Bluff storia di truffe e di imbroglioni* (IT) US/UK *Con Artists* UKvdt *The Con Men* USvdt *The Switch* – dir: Sergio Corbucci
1976 *Sturmtruppen* (IT/FR) FR *Le bataillon en folie* – dir: Salvatore Samperi
1976 *Strip-Tease* (SP) UK *Fade Out* UKvdt *Strip Tease* USvdt *Insanity* – dir: Germán Lorente
1976 *Natale in casa d'appuntamento* (IT) US *Love By Appointment / Holiday Hookers / Hollywood Hookers* USvdt *Christmas in a Whorehouse* – dir: Armando Nannuzzi
1976 *...E tanta paura* (IT) export title *Plot of Fear* aka *Bloody Peanuts* – dir: Paolo Cavara
1977 *Tre tigri contro tre tigri* (IT) aka *Three Tigers Against Three Tigers* – dir: Sergio Corbucci, Steno [Stefano Vanzina]
1977 *Autostop rosso sangue* (IT) US/UKvdt *Hitch-Hike* UKvdt *Death Drive* – dir: Pasquale Festa Campanile
1977 *Kleinhoff hotel* (WG/IT) USvdt/UKvdt *Kleinhoff Hotel* aka *The Passionate Strangers* – dir: Carlo Lizzani
1978 *Sono stato un agente* CIA (IT) UKvdt *Covert Action* – dir: Romolo Guerrieri
1978 *L'umanoide* (IT) UK/US/UKvdt *The Humanoid* – dir: George B. Lewis [Aldo Lado]
1979 *I viaggiatori della sera* (IT/SP) SP *Los viajeros del atardecer* aka *The Twilight Travellers* – dir: Ugo Tognazzi
1979 *Moonraker* (UK/FR) – dir: Lewis Gilbert
1980 *Odio le bionde* (IT/FR/WG) FR *Je hais les blondes* WG *Ich hasse Blondinen* USvdt *I Hate Blondes* – dir: Giorgio Capitani
1980 *Eroina* (IT) ITvdt *Tunnel* UKvdt *The Tunnel* USvdt *Fatal Fix* – dir: Massimo Pirri
1981 *L'ultimo harem* (IT/SP/WG) SP *El último harén* WG *Der letzte Harem* US/USvdt *The Last Harem* – dir: Willy S. Regan [Sergio Garrone]
1983 *Benedetta & Company* (IT) (tv movie) – dir: Alfredo Angeli
1983 *Il mondo di Yor* (IT/TUR) TUR *Yor* US/UKvdt *Yor: The Hunter from the Future* – dir: Anthony M. Dawson [Antonio Margheriti] [originally a four-part tv series]
1983 *Sotto le stelle '83* (IT) (tv series) (presenter)
1984 *Forte fortissimo tv top* (IT) (tv series) (presenter)
1984 *Giochi d'estate* (IT) – dir: Bruno Cortini
1985 *Yuppies I giovani di successo* (IT) – dir: Carlo Vanzina
1985 *Skipper* (IT) (tv movie) – dir: Roberto Malenotti
1986 *Affari di famiglia* (IT) (tv movie) – dir: Marcello Fondato
1986 *Il miele del diavolo* (IT/SP) SP *La miel del diablo* USvdt *Dangerous Obsession* export title ***The Devil's Honey*** – dir: Lucio Fulci
1987 *Via Montenapoleone* (IT) – dir: Carlo Vanzina
1988 *Rimini Rimini – Un anno dopo* (IT) – dir: Bruno Corbucci
1988 *Una vittoria* (IT) (tv movie) – dir: Luigi Perelli
1988 *La partita* (IT) export title *The Gamble* – dir: Carlo Vanzina
1988 *Ciak si muore* (IT) (tv movie) – dir: Luigi Cozzi [series *Giallo – Turno di notte*]
1989 *Disperatamente Giulia* (IT) (tv movie) – dir: Enrico Maria Salerno
1990 *Les mouettes* (FR) – dir: Jean Chapot
1990 *Forever (Per sempre)* (IT/BRA) – dir: Walter Hugo Khouri
1990 *Vita con i figli* (IT) (tv movie) aka *Vita coi figli* – dir: Dino Risi
1990 *Occhio alla perestrojka* (IT) – dir: [Franco] Castellano & Pipolo [Giuseppe Moccia]
1990 *Vacanze di natale '90* (IT) – dir: Enrico Oldoini
1991 *L'odissea* (IT) (tv movie) – dir: Giuseppe Recchia
1991 *L'avvoltoio può attendere* (IT) – dir: Gian Pietro Calasso
1991 *Errore fatale* (IT) (tv movie) export title *Condition Critical* shooting title *Non aver paura Giulia* – dir: Filippo De Luigi
1991 *28° minuto* (IT) shooting title *Quel violento desiderio* – dir: Paolo Frajoli
1992 *Non chiamarmi Omar* (IT) – dir: Sergio Staino
1992 *Donna di cuori* (IT) (tv movie) aka *Lady of Hearts* – dir: Dino Risi
1993 *L'ispettore anticrimine* (IT) (tv movie) – dir: Paolo Fondato
1993 *Moscacieca* (IT) (tv movie) – dir: Mario Caiano
1995 *Le roi de Paris* (FR) – dir: Dominique Maillet
1995 *A Dio piacendo* (IT) export title *God Willing* – dir: Filippo Altadonna
1996 *I ragazzi del muretto* (IT) (tv series) – dir: Gianfrancesco Lazotti & Gianluigi Calderone
1996 *La signora della città* (IT) (tv movie) aka *Witness Run* – dir: Beppe Cino
1997 *I misteri di Cascina Vianello* (IT) (tv series) episode *Un matrimonio e un funerale* – dir: Gianfrancesco Lazotti
1997 *Inquietudine* (IT) (tv movie) aka *Anxiety* – dir: Gianni Siragusa
1998 *La forza dell'amore* (IT) (tv mini-series) – dir: Vincenzo Verdecchi
1999 *Tre addii* (IT) (tv movie) – dir: Mario Caiano
1999 *L'ispettore Giusti* (IT) (tv series) episode *Per soldi o per amore* – dir: Sergio Martino
1999 *La vita in briciole* (IT) (tv movie) – dir: Mario Caiano
1999 *Stella di Mare – Hilfe, wir erben ein Schiff!* (GER/AT) (tv movie) – dir: Xaver Schwarzenberger
2000 *Alex l'ariete* (IT) – dir: Damiano Damiani
2001 *Prigionieri di un incubo* (IT) – dir: Franco Salvia
2002 *Non ho l'età 2* (IT) (tv movie) – dir: Giulio Base
2002 *Il diario di Matilde Manzoni* (IT) – dir: Lino Capolicchio
2002 *Don Matteo* (IT) (tv series) episode *Il passato ritorna* – dir: Enrico Oldoini
2007 *Incantesimo 9* (IT) (tv series)
2007 *Il peso dell'aria* (IT) – dir: Stefano Calvagna
2008 *Incantesimo 10* (IT) (tv series)
2008 *Ti stramo: Ho voglia di un'ultima notte da manuale prima di tre baci sopra il cielo* (IT) – dir: Pino Insegno & Gianluca Sodaro
2010 *Il ritmo della vita* (IT) (tv movie) – dir: Rossella Izzo
2012 *Pechino Express* (IT) (tv series)
2016 *Attesa e cambiamenti* (IT) – dir: Sergio Colabona
2018 *Beyond the Mist* (IT/SWI) – dir: Giuseppe Varlotta
2019 *W gli sposi* (US/IT) – dir: Valerio Zanoli
2019 *Preludio* (IT) (short) – dir: Stefania Rossella Grassi & Tommaso Scutari
2020 *Free – Liberi* (IT) – dir: Fabrizio Maria Cortese
2021 *Ritorno al crimine* (IT) – dir: Massimiliano Bruno
2021 *Io e Angela* (IT/ARG) – dir: Herbert Simone Paragnani

Christopher Connelly

born 8 September 1941 in Wichita, Kansas, USA
died 7 December 1988 in Burbank, California, USA
real name **Thomas Maume Connelly**

George Hacker in ***Manhattan Baby***

1963 *Move Over, Darling* (US) [uncredited] – dir: Michael Gordon
1963 *The Alfred Hitchcock Hour* (US) (tv series) episode *Starring the Defense* – dir: Joseph Pevney
1963-1964 *The Lieutenant* (US) (tv series) (4 episodes)
1963-1964 *My Three Sons* (US) (tv series) (2 episodes)
1964 *The Fugitive* (US) (tv series) episode *The End Game* – dir: Jerry Hopper
1964 *What a Way to Go!* (US) [uncredited] – dir: J. Lee Thompson
1964 *Voyage to the Bottom of the Sea* (US) (tv series) episode *Eleven Days to Zero* [uncredited] – dir: Irwin Allen
1964 *Gunsmoke* (US) (tv series) episode *The Warden* – dir: Andrew V. McLaglen
1964-69 *Peyton Place* (US) (tv series) (490 episodes)
1968 *Judd for the Defense* (US) (tv series) episode *The Grand Old Man* – dir: Boris Sagal
1969 *The Mod Squad* (US) (tv series) episode *Peace Now – Arly Blau* – dir: Gene Nelson
1969 *Love, American Style* (US) (tv series) season 1 episode 10 segment *Love and Mother* – dir: Bruce Bilson
1969 *In Name Only* (US) (tv movie) – dir: E.W. Swackhamer
1969 *Daniel Boone* (US) (tv series) episode *A Bearskin for Jamie Blue* – dir: William Wiard
1970 *Bonanza* (US) (tv series) episode *The Lady and the Mark* – dir: Leon Benson
1970 *The Interns* (US) (tv series) episode *Some Things Don't Change* – dir: William Hale
1970 *Mission: Impossible* (US) (tv series) episode *The Innocent* – dir: John Llewellyn Moxey
1971 *Dan August* (US) (tv series) episode *Circle of Lies* – dir: Richard Benedict
1971 *Incident in San Francisco* (US) (tv movie) – dir: Don Medford
1971 *Police Surgeon* (US) (tv series) episode *Death Holds an Auction...* – dir: John Meredyth Lucas, Brian Walker
1971 *The Man and the City* (US) (tv series) episode *I Should Have Let Him Die* – dir: Paul Henreid
1971 *Love, American Style* (US) (tv series) season 2 episode 20 segment *Love and the New Roommate* – dir: Allen Baron
1972 *They Only Kill Their Masters* (US) – dir: James Goldstone
1972 *Corky* (US) shooting title *Lookin' Good* – dir: Leonard Horn
1972 *Love, American Style* (US) (tv series) season 4 episode 1 segment *Love and the Triple Threat* – dir: Charles R. Rondeau
1972 *Night Gallery* (US) (tv series) episode *Spectre in Tap-Shoes* – dir: Jeannot Szwarc
1972 *Mannix* (US) (tv series) episode *One Step to Midnight* – dir: Don McDougall
1972 *Cannon* (US) (tv series) episode *Blood on the Vine* – dir: George McCowan
1973 *Owen Marshall, Counselor at Law* (US) (tv series) episode *Why Is a Crooked Letter*
1973 *Circle of Fear* (US) (tv series) episode *Spare Parts* – dir: Charles S. Dubin
1973 *A Touch of Grace* (US) (tv series) episode *The Lodge*
1973 *The ABC Afternoon Playbreak* (US) (tv series) episode *The Gift of Terror* – dir: Lela Swift
1973 *Gunsmoke* (US) (tv series) episode *Kitty's Love Affair* – dir: Vincent McEveety
1973 *Griff* (US) (tv series) episode *Her Name Was Nancy* – dir: Russ Mayberry
1973 *Ironside* (US) (tv series) episode *The Ghost of the Dancing Doll* – dir: Russ Mayberry
1973 *The Invasion of Carol Enders* (US) (tv movie) – dir: Burt Brinckerhoff & [uncredited] Dan Curtis
1973 *Benji* (US) – dir: Joe Camp
1974 *The Brian Keith Show* (US) (tv series) episode *Here Comes the What?*
1974 *Barnaby Jones* (US) (tv series) episode *The Deadly Jinx* – dir: Robert Douglas

1974 *Marcus Welby, M.D.* (US) (tv series) episode *The Fear of Silence* – dir: Randal Kleiser
1974 *Cannon* (US) (tv series) episode *The Hit Man* – dir: William Wiard
1974 *Ironside* (US) (tv series) episode *Speak No Evil* – dir: Don Weis
1974 *Police Story* (US) (tv series) episode *Wolf* – dir: Barry Shear
1974 *Paper Moon* (US) (tv series) (13 episodes)
1975 *The Last Day* (US) (tv movie) – dir: Vincent McEveety
1975 *Medical Story* (US) (tv series) episode *Wasteland*
1975 *Petrocelli* (US) (tv series) episode *The Sleep of Reason* – dir: Irving J. Moore
1975 *Police Story* (US) (tv series) episode *Company Man* – dir: Alexander Singer
1976 *Petrocelli* (US) (tv series) episode *Survival* – dir: Art Fisher
1976 *Hawmps!* (US) – dir: Joe Camp
1976 *Kit Carson and the Mountain Men* (US) (tv movie) – dir: Vincent McEveety [series *Walt Disney's Wonderful World of Color*]
1976 *The Quest* (US) (tv series) episode *The Captive* – dir: Barry Shear
1976 *Police Story* (US) (tv series) episode *The Jar: Part 1* – dir: Michael O'Herlihy
1976 *Police Story* (US) (tv series) episode *The Jar: Part 2* – dir: Michael O'Herlihy
1977 *Gibbsville* (US) (tv series) episode Manhood
1977 *Hawaii Five-O* (US) (tv series) episode *To Die in Paradise* – dir: Joseph Manduke
1977 *Quincy M.E.* (US) (tv series) episode *Valleyview* – dir: Ron Satlof
1977 *Charlie Cobb: Nice Night for a Hanging* (US) (tv pilot) – dir: Richard Michaels
1977 *The Hardy Boys/Nancy Drew Mysteries* (US) (tv series) episode *Nancy Drew's Love Match* – dir: Joseph Pevney
1977 *The Incredible Rocky Mountain Race* (US) (tv movie, also shown theatrically) – dir: James L. Conway
1977 *Murder in Peyton Place* (US) (tv movie) – dir: Bruce Kessler
1978 *Police Story* (US) (tv series) episode *No Margin for Error* – dir: Virgil W. Vogel
1978 *Fantasy Island* (US) (tv series) episode *The Funny Girl/Butch and Sundance* – dir: Cliff Bole
1978 *Crash* (US) (tv movie) aka *Crash of Flight 401* – dir: Barry Shear
1978 *The Norseman* (US) – dir: Charles B. Pierce
1978 *The Martian Chronicles* (US) (tv mini-series, shortened version shown theatrically) – dir: Michael Anderson
1978 *Martin Eden* (IT) (tv mini-series) – dir: Giacomo Battiato
1979 *Salvage 1* (US) (tv series) episode *Up, Up and Away* – dir: Les Green
1979 *Stunt Seven / Fantastic 7* (US) (tv pilot, also shown theatrically) – dir: John Peyser
1979 *The Love Boat* (US) (tv series) episode *The Brotherhood of the Sea / Letter to Babycakes / Daddy's Pride* – dir: George Tyne
1979 *Chief of Detectives* (US) (tv series) episode *The Dancer* – dir: Harvey S. Laidman
1979 *Trapper John, M.D.* (US) (tv series) episode *The Surrogate* – dir: Alex March
1979 *B.J. and the Bear* (US) (tv series) episode *Crackers* – dir: Michael Caffey
1979 *Fantasy Island* (US) (tv series) episode *Tattoo: the Love God / Magnolia Blossoms* – dir: Earl Bellamy
1980 *Eight Is Enough* (US) (tv series) episode *Memories* – dir: Vincent McEveety
1980 *Beyond Westworld* (US) (tv series) episode *My Brother's Keeper* – dir: Rod Holcomb
1981 *CHiPs* (US) (tv series) episode *New Guy in Town* – dir: Arnold Laven
1981 *B.J. and the Bear* (US) (tv series) episode *S.T.U.N.T.* – dir: Daniel Haller
1981 *Fantasy Island* (US) (tv series) episode *Basin Street / The Devil's Triangle* – dir: George W. Brooks
1981 *Return of the Rebels* (US) (tv movie) – dir: Noel Nosseck
1981 *Skyward Christmas* (US) (tv movie) – dir: Vincent McEveety
1981 *Liar's Moon* (US) – dir: David Fisher
1982 *Earthbound* (US) (tv special, also shown theatrically) – dir: James L. Conway
1982 *Simon & Simon* (US) (tv series) episode *Guessing Game* – dir: Vincent McEveety
1982 ***Manhattan Baby*** (IT) USvdt *Eye of the Evil Dead* UKvdt *Possessed* – dir: Lucio Fulci
1982 *1990 – I guerrieri del Bronx* (IT) UK/UKvdt *Bronx Warriors* US/USvdt *1990 The Bronx Warriors* – dir: Enzo G. Castellari [Enzo Girolami]
1983 *I predatori di Atlantide* (IT) UKvdt *The Atlantis Interceptors* USvdt *The Raiders of Atlantis* – dir: Roger Franklin [Ruggero Deodato]
1983 *Bring 'Em Back Alive* (US) (tv series) episode *The Shadow Women of Chung Tai* – dir: Peter H. Hunt
1983 *Fantasy Island* (US) (tv series) episode *What's the Matter with Kids? / Island of Horrors* – dir: Don Weis
1983 *Matt Houston* (US) (tv series) episode *China Doll* – dir: Charlie Picerni
1983 *The Fall Guy* (US) (tv series) episode *Inside, Outside* – dir: Don McDougall
1984 *Airwolf* (US) (tv series) (2 episodes)
1984 *La stagione delle piogge* (IT) (tv movie) – dir: Domenico Campana
1984 *Gli ultimi (SWI)* (tv movie) – dir: Matteo Bellinelli [series *Eva e dio*]
1985 *La leggenda del rubino malese* (IT) US *Jungle Raiders* UKvdt *Captain Yankee and the Jungle Raiders* – dir: Anthony M. Dawson [Antonio Margheriti]
1985 *Hollywood Beat* (US) (tv series) episode *Out in the Cold* – dir: Cliff Bole
1985 *Peyton Place – The Next Generation* (US) (tv movie) – dir: Larry Elikann
1986 *Foxtrap* (IT/US) – dir: Fred Williamson
1986 *Le miniere del Kilimangiaro (Afrikanter)* (IT) UKvdt/USvdt *The Mines of Kilimanjaro* – dir: Mino Guerrini
1986 *Cobra Mission (Cinque uomini contro tutti)* (IT/WG) WG *Die Rückkehr der Wildgänse* US/USvdt *Operation 'Nam* UKvdt *Cobra Mission* FR *Commando Cobra* – dir: Larry Ludman [Fabrizio De Angelis]
1986 *Strike Commando* (IT) – dir: Vincent Dawn [Bruno Mattei]
1986 *Il messaggero* (IT/US) US *The Messenger* UKvdt *Messenger of Death* – dir: Fred Williamson
1987 *Django 2 – Il grande ritorno* (IT) UKvdt *Django Strikes Again* – dir: Ted Archer [Nello Rossati]
1988 *La notte degli squali* (IT) UKvdt *Night of the Sharks* – dir: Anthony Richmond [Tonino Ricci]

Pier Luigi Conti

born 16 July 1951 in Alexandria, Egypt
aka **Al Cliver** / **Al Clever** / **Pierluigi Conti**

Brian Hull in ***Zombie Flesh-Eaters***
Sergeant Wilson in ***The Black Cat***
Doctor Harris in ***The Beyond***
Kirk in ***Rome 2033 – The Fighter Centurions***
voice analyst in ***Murder-Rock Dancing Death***
Randy in ***Touch of Death***
Peter in ***The House of Clocks***
a nazi soldier in ***The Ghosts of Sodom***
a nazi soldier in ***Nightmare Concert***
Porter in ***Demonia***

1969 *Le dieci meraviglie dell'amore* (IT/WG) WG *Libido – Das grosse Lexikon der Lust* – dir: Sergio Bergonzelli
1969 *La caduta degli dei (Götterdämmerung)* (IT/WG) WG *Die Verdammten* UK *The Damned* – dir: Luchino Visconti
1974 *Il saprofita* (IT) – dir: Sergio Nasca
1975 *Una ondata di piacere* (IT) export title *Waves of Lust* – dir: Ruggero Deodato
1975 *Blue Belle* (UK/IT) IT *La fine dell'innocenza* US *Annie* – dir: Massimo Dallamano
1976 *Laure* (IT/FR) – dir: uncredited [Emmanuelle Arsan]
1976 *Velluto nero* (IT) US *Black Velvet, White Silk* UK *Black Emanuelle, White Emanuelle* – dir: Brunello Rondi
1976 *Amore grande, amore libero* (IT) – dir: Luigi Perelli
1976 *Una donna chiamata Apache* (IT) UKvdt *Apache Woman* – dir: George McRoots [Giorgio Mariuzzo]
1976 *Big Pot* (AT/IT) IT *Il colpaccio Big Pot* – dir: John L. Huxley [Bruno Paolinelli]
1976 *I padroni della città* (IT/WG) WG *Zwei Supertypen räumen auf* US *Mister Scarface* UKvdt *Rulers of the City* USvdt *Scarface Killer* – dir: Fernando Di Leo
1977 *Un giorno alla fine di ottobre* (IT) – dir: Paolo Spinola
1977 *No alla violenza* (IT) export title *Death Hunt* – dir: Tano Cimarosa
1977 *Milano... difendersi o morire* (IT) export title *Blazing Bullets* UKvdt *Blazing Flowers* WG *Heroin* – dir: Gianni [Giovanni] Antonio Martucci
1978 *L'albero della maldicenza* (IT) – dir: Giacinto Bonacquisti
1978 *Provincia violenta* (IT) – dir: Robert Moore [Mario Bianchi]
1979 *Zombi 2* (IT) US *Zombie* UK ***Zombie Flesh-Eaters*** – dir: Lucio Fulci
1980 *Mondo cannibale* (FR/SP/IT/WG) WG *Mondo cannibale, 3.Teil Die blonde Göttin* FR *La déesse cannibale* FRvdt *Mangeurs d'hommes* ITvdt *La dea cannibale* USvdt *White Cannibal Queen* UKvdt *Cannibals* – dir: Jesús Franco Manera [Belgian version: *Une fille pour les cannibales* is credited to Franco Prosperi [Francesco Prosperi]]
1980 *Molto di più* (IT) – dir: Mario Lenzi
1980 *Sesso profondo* (IT) UKvdt *Flying Sex* – dir: Frank Martin [Marino Girolami]
1980 *Sexo caníbal* (SP/IT/WG) IT *Il cacciatore di uomini* WG *Jungfrau unter Kannibalen* US *The Man Hunter* USvdt *Mandingo Manhunter* UKvdt *The Devil Hunter* – dir: Clifford Brown [Jesùs Franco Manera]

1981 *Black cat* (IT) US/UKvdt ***The Black Cat*** – dir: Lucio Fulci
1981 *L'aldilà* (IT) US *Seven Doors of Death* UK ***The Beyond*** – dir: Lucio Fulci
1982 *Briganti* (IT) – dir: Giacinto Bonacquisti [released in 1983]
1983 *Notturno* (IT) aka *Spy Connection* [uncredited] – dir: Giorgio Bontempi
1983 *I paladini – Storia d'armi e d'amori* (IT) UKvdt *Hearts and Armour* – dir: Giacomo Battiato
1983 *Endgame – Bronx lotta finale* (IT) UKvdt *Endgame* – dir: Steve Benson [Aristide Massaccesi]
1984 *I guerrieri dell'anno 2072* (IT) USvdt *The New Gladiators* UKvdt ***Rome 2033 – The Fighter Centurions*** – dir: Lucio Fulci
1984 *Murderock uccide a passo di danza* (IT) US *The Demon Is Loose* export title ***Murder-Rock Dancing Death*** – dir: Lucio Fulci
1984 *Anno 2020 I gladiatori del futuro* (IT) UKvdt *2020 Texas Gladiators* aka *Texas 2000* – dir: Kevin Mancuso [Aristide Massaccesi & Luigi Montefiori]
1985 *L'alcova* (IT) UKvdt *The Alcove* – dir: Joe D'Amato [Aristide Massaccesi]
1986 *La piovra 2* (IT/FR/UK/WG) (tv mini-series) – dir: Florestano Vancini
1986 *Le miniere del Kilimangiaro (Afrikanter)* (IT) UKvdt/USvdt *The Mines of Kilimanjaro* – dir: Mino Guerrini
1986 *Lussuria* (IT) UKvdt *Lust* – dir: Joe D'Amato [Aristide Massaccesi]
1987 *Oggetto sessuale* (IT) aka *Laura* – dir: Bob Singer
1988 *Quando Alice ruppe lo specchio* (IT) export title ***Touch of Death*** – dir: Lucio Fulci
1988 *Sodoma's Ghost* (IT) export title ***The Ghosts of Sodom*** [uncredited] – dir: Lucio Fulci
1989 *La casa del tempo* (IT) export title The ***House of Clocks*** – dir: Lucio Fulci
1990 *Aquile* (IT) (tv movie) – dir: Antonio Bido & Nini Salerno
1990 Un gatto nel cervello (I volti del terrore) (IT) export title ***Nightmare Concert*** aka Nightmare Concert (A Cat in the Brain) [uncredited] – dir: Lucio Fulci
1990 ***Demonia*** (IT) – dir: Lucio Fulci

Carlo De Mejo

born 17 January 1945 in Rome, Italy
died 18 December 2015 in Rome, Italy
son of actress Alida Valli and painter/pianist/composer Oscar De Mejo
aka **Stewart May**

Dr. Jerry Hill in ***City of the Living Dead***
Mr. Wheatley in ***The House by the Cemetery***
Luke Anderson in ***Manhattan Baby***

1967 *L'oro di Londra* (IT) – dir: Bill Moore [Guglielmo Morandi]
1968 *Summit* (IT/FR) FR *Un corps, une nuit* – dir: Giorgio Bontempi
1968 *Teorema* (IT) – dir: Pier Paolo Pasolini
1969 *La battaglia del Sinai (5 giorni nel Sinai)* (IT/IS) IS *Hamisha Yamim B'Sinai* aka *The Battle of Sinai* – dir: Maurizio Lucidi
1970 *La colomba non deve volare* (IT/WG) export title *Skyriders Attack* – dir: Sergio Garrone
1970 *Microscopic Liquid Subway to Oblivion* (IT) – dir: John W. Shadow
1971 *Equinozio* (IT) aka *Equinox* – dir: Maurizio Ponzi
1972 *Ubica dolazi iz groba* (YUG/IT/WG) IT *L'etrusco uccide ancora* WG *Das Geheimnis des gelden Grabes* US *The Dead Are Alive* export title *The Etruscan Kills Again* – dir: Armando Crispino
1972 *I Nicotera* (IT) (tv mini-series) episode #1.4 – dir: Salvatore Nocita
1972 *Quando le donne si chiamavano 'Madonne'* (IT/WG) WG *Der Pfaffenspiegel* – dir: Aldo Grimaldi
1972 *Un homme est mort* (FR/IT) IT *Funerale a Los Angeles* UK/US *The Outside Man* – dir: Jacques Deray
1973 *L'ultima chance* (IT) UK *Last Chance* US *Stateline Motel* – dir: Maurizio Lucidi
1973 *Défense de savoir* (FR/IT) IT *L'uomo in basso a destra nella fotografia* – dir: Nadine Trintignant
1974 *Anna Karenina* (IT) (tv mini-series) episode #1.5 – dir: Sandro Bolchi

1974 *Orlando furioso* (IT) (tv mini-series) episode #1.3 – dir: Luca Ronconi
1975 *Das Netz* (WG) – dir: Manfred Purzer
1976 *Cassandra Crossing* (WG/IT) US/UK *The Cassandra Crossing* – dir: George Pan Cosmatos
1976 *La sposina* (IT) – dir: Sergio Bergonzelli
1977 *Un cuore semplice* (IT) – dir: Giorgio Ferrara
1978 *Porco mondo* (IT/SP) SP *Puerco mundo* Italian publicity title *Porco mondo (Porno)* UK – *Cindy's Love Games* UKvdt: *Tight Fit* – dir: Sergio Bergonzelli
1979 *Eros perversion* (IT) – dir: Ron Wertheim
1979 *Amanti miei* (IT) – dir: Aldo Grimaldi
1979 *La ragazza del vagone letto* (IT) UKvdt *Terror Express!* – dir: Ferdinando Baldi
1980 *Contamination – Alien arriva sulla terra* (IT/WG) WG *Astaron Brut des Schreckens* US *Alien Contamination* UKvdt *Contamination* USvdt *Toxic Spawn* – dir: Lewis Coates [Luigi Cozzi]
1980 *Paura nella città dei morti viventi* (IT) US *The Gates of Hell* UK ***City of the Living Dead*** – dir: Lucio Fulci
1980 *L'altro inferno* (IT) UKvdt *The Other Hell* export title *The Presence* aka *The Guardian of Hell* – dir: Stefan Oblowsky [Bruno Mattei]
1980 *La locanda della maladolescenza* (IT) – dir: Marco Sole
1981 *Quella villa accanto al cimitero* (IT) US/UK ***The House by the Cemetery*** – dir: Lucio Fulci
1982 ***Manhattan Baby*** (IT) USvdt *Eye of the Evil Dead* UKvdt *Possessed* – dir: Lucio Fulci
1982 *Violenza in un carcere femminile* (IT/FR) FR *Pénitencier de femmes* US/USvdt *Caged Women* USvdt *Women's Penitentiary* Italian shootitng title *Emanuelle reportage da un carcere femminile* – dir: Vincent Dawn [Bruno Mattei]

1983 *Blade Violent* (I violenti) (IT/FR) FR *Révolte au pénitencier des filles* export title *Blade Violent* US *Women's Prison Massacre* aka *Laura 2* – dir: Gilbert Roussel [Claudio Fragasso & Bruno Mattei]
1985 *Al limite, cioè, non glielo dico* (IT) – dir: Franco Rossetti
1985 *Quei trentasei gradini* (IT) (tv mini-series) – dir: Luigi Perelli
1988 *À notre regrettable époux* (FR) – dir: Serge Korber
1989 *Complotto internazionale* (IT) (tv movie) – dir: Florestano Vancini
1990 *Il giudice istruttore* (IT/FR) (tv series) episode *Complotto internazionale* – dir: Florestano Vancini
1999 *I fobici* (IT) segment *Frutto Proibito* – dir: Giancarlo Scarchilli
2013 *Two Left Arms* (IT) – dir: Domiziano Cristopharo [released in 2017]

Cinzia De Ponti

born 3 October 1960 in Pescara, Italy
former Miss Italy (1979)
real name **Cinzia Fiordeponti**

Rosie, ferry victim in ***The New York Ripper***
Jamie-Lee in ***Manhattan Baby***

1980 *La liceale al mare con l'amica di papà* (IT) – dir: Marino Girolami
1981 *Il marito in vacanza* (IT) – dir: Maurizio Lucidi
1981 *Perché non facciamo l'amore?* (IT/SP) SP *¿Por qué no hacemos el amor?* – dir: Maurizio Lucidi
1981 *Mia moglie torna a scuola* (IT) – dir: Giuliano Carnimeo
1981 *L'assassino ha le ore contate* (IT) (tv mini-series) – dir: Fernando Di Leo
1981 *La maestra... di sci* (IT) – dir: Sandro [Alessandro] Lucidi
1982 *Sballato, gasato, completamente fuso* (IT) aka *An Ideal Adventure* – dir: Steno [Stefano Vanzina]
1982 *Lo squartatore di New York* (IT) export title ***The New York Ripper*** – dir: Lucio Fulci
1982 *Sturmtruppen 2 (Tutti al fronte)* (IT) aka *Stormtroopers II* – dir: Salvatore Samperi
1982 *Notturno* (IT) export title *Spy Connection* – dir: Giorgio Bontempi
1982 *Vigili e vigilesse* (IT) – dir: Franco Prosperi [Francesco Prosperi]
1982 *1990 – I guerrieri del Bronx* (IT) UK/UKvdt *Bronx Warriors* US/USvdt *1990 The Bronx Warriors* – dir: Enzo G. Castellari [Enzo Girolami]
1982 ***Manhattan Baby*** (IT) USvdt *Eye of the Evil Dead* UKvdt *Possessed* – dir: Lucio Fulci
1983 *Il mondo di Yor* (IT/TUR) TUR *Yor* US/UKvdt *Yor: The Hunter from the Future* – dir: Anthony M. Dawson [Antonio Margheriti] [originally a four-part tv series]
1984 *Shark: Rosso nell'oceano* (IT/FR) FR *Apocalypse dans l'ocean rouge* UKvdt *Devouring Waves* WG *Monster Shark* aka *Devil Fish* – dir: John Old Jr. [Lamberto Bava]
1984 *Death Commando (Commando di morte)* (IT) shooting title *Killer contro Killer* – dir: Fernando Di Leo
1985 *Uccelli d'Italia* (IT) – dir: Ciro Ippolito

1985 *Carabinieri si nasce* (IT) – dir: Mariano Laurenti
1985 *Senza scrupoli* (IT) export title *Unscrupulous* aka *In Bed with a Killer* – dir: Tonino Valerii
1985 *I potere del male (Paradigma)* (IT) (tv movie) – dir: Kryzstof Zanussi
1986 *Yuppies I giovani di successo* (IT) – dir: Carlo Vanzina
1986 *Bianco Apache* (IT/SP) SP *Apache Kid* export title *White Apache* shooting title *L'apache bianco* – dir: Vincent Dawn [Bruno Mattei]
1986 *Fotoromanzo* (IT) – dir: Mariano Laurenti
1986 *Naso di cane (Dog Nose)* (IT/WG/FR) (tv mini-series) export title *Hit Man* shooting title *Camorra Killer* – dir: Pasquale Squitieri
1987 *L'estate sta finendo* (IT) – dir: Bruno Cortini
1987 *Ultimo minuto* (IT) – dir: Pupi Avati
1987 *Appuntamento a Trieste* (IT) (tv mini-series) – dir: Bruno Mattei
1988 *Diciottanni – Versilia 1966* (IT) (tv series) episode *Colpo di fulmine* – dir: Massimo Scaglione
1988 *Un amore di donna* (IT/WG) WG *Der Himmel ist fern* aka *Love of a Woman* – dir: Nelo Risi
1988 *Le due croci* (IT) – dir: Silvio Maestranzi
1989 *Sapore di Gloria* (tv series) – dir: Marcello Baldi
1991 *Processo di famiglia* (IT) (tv movie) – dir: Nanni Fabbri
1991 *Se non avessi l'amore* (IT) (tv movie) – dir: Leandro Castellani
1992 *La peur* (FR) – dir: Daniel Vigne
1992 *Prêcheur en eau trouble* (FR) (tv movie) – dir: Georges Lautner
1993 *Delitti privati* (IT) (4-part tv mini-series) UK television title *Private Crimes* – dir: Sergio Martino
1993 *Un commissario a Roma* (IT) (tv series) episode *Senza colpevole* – dir: Ignazio Agosta
1993 *L'amour assassin* (FR) – dir: Elisabeth Rappeneau
1993 *Gioco perverso* (IT) (tv movie) – dir: Italo Moscati

Daniela Doria

born 12 September 1956 in Rome, Italy

Rosie Kelvin in ***City of the Living Dead***
Maureen Grayson in ***The Black Cat***
First victim in ***The House by the Cemetery***
Jenny/Kitty in ***The New York Ripper***

1976 *Le seminariste* (IT) – dir: Guido Leoni
1976 *Classe mista* (IT) – dir: Mariano Laurenti
1976 *Il ginecologo della mutua* (IT) UKvdt *Ladies' Doctor* – dir: Joe D'Amato [Aristide Massaccesi]
1978 *Avere vent'anni* (IT) UKvdt *To Be Twenty* – dir: Fernando Di Leo
1980 *Paura nella città dei morti viventi* (IT) US *The Gates of Hell* UK ***City of the Living Dead*** – dir: Lucio Fulci
1981 *Black cat* (IT) US/UKvdt ***The Black Cat*** – dir: Lucio Fulci
1981 *Quella villa accanto al cimitero* (IT) US/UK ***The House by the Cemetery*** – dir: Lucio Fulci
1982 *Lo squartatore di New York* (IT) export title ***The New York Ripper*** – dir: Lucio Fulci
1982 *I camionisti* (IT/SP) SP *La camionera está como un tren* – dir: Flavio Mogherini

Mimsy Farmer

born 28 February 1945 in Chicago, Illinois, USA

Jill Travers in ***The Black Cat***

1961 *Gidget Goes Hawaiian* (US) [uncredited] – dir: Paul Wendkos
1962 *My Three Sons* (US) (tv series) episode *Steve Gets an A* – dir: Gene Reynolds
1962 *The Donna Reed Show* (US) (tv series) episode *The Swingin' Set* – dir: Gene Nelson
1962 *The Donna Reed Show* (US) (tv series) episode *The Father Image* – dir: Richard L. Bare
1963 *The Donna Reed Show* (US) (tv series) episode *Boys and Girls* – dir: Barry Shear
1963 *The Adventures of Ozzie & Harriet* (US) (tv series) episode *Rick's Wedding Ring* – dir: Ozzie Nelson
1963 *Spencer's Mountain* (US) – dir: Delmer Davies
1964 *The Outer Limits* (US) (tv series) episode *Second Chance* – dir: Paul Stanley
1964 *Kraft Suspense Theatre* (US) (tv series) episode *A Lion Amongst Men* – dir: Jack Smight
1964 *Perry Mason* (US) (tv series) episode *The Case of the Careless Kidnapper* – dir: Jesse Hibbs
1964 *Perry Mason* (US) (tv series) episode *The Case of the Tragic Trophy* – dir: Richard Donner
1964 *Lassie* (US) (tv series) episode *Lassie Works a Miracle* – dir: William Beaudine
1965 *Bus Riley's Back in Town* (US) – dir: Harvey Hart
1965 *Hank* (US) (tv series) episode *My Fair Co-Ed*
1966 *Honey West* (US) (tv series) episode *Like Visions and Omens... and All That Jazz* – dir: John Florea
1966 *Mister Roberts* (US) (tv series) episode *Damn the Torpedoes* – dir: Seymour Robbie
1966 *The F.B.I.* (US) (tv series) episode *The Animal* – dir: Christian Nyby
1966 *The F.B.I.* (US) (tv series) episode *The Price of Death* – dir: Paul Wendkos
1966 *Laredo* (US) (tv series) episode *The Calico Kid* – dir: Lawrence Dobkin
1966 *Laredo* (US) (tv series) episode *A Prince of a Ranger* – dir: Charles R. Rondeau
1966 *Devil's Angels* (US) – dir: Daniel Haller
1967 *Hot Rods to Hell* (US) – dir: John Brahm
1968 *The Wild Racers* (US) – dir: Daniel Haller
1968 *Riot on Sunset Strip* (US) – dir: Arthur Dreifuss
1968 *More* (US/LUX) – dir: Barbet Schroeder
1969 *Strogoff* (IT/FR/WG/Bulgaria) FR *Michel Strogoff* WG *Der Kurier des Zaren* – dir: Eriprando Visconti
1970 *La route de Salina* (FR/IT) IT *Quando il sole scotta* UK *Road to Salina* – dir: Georges Lautner
1971 *Quattro mosche di velluto grigio* (IT/FR) FR *Quatre mouches de velours gris* US/UK *Four Flies on Grey Velvet* – dir: Dario Argento
1972 *Les 1001 mains* (MOR/IT) – dir: Souheil Ben Barka
1972 *Corpo d'amore* (IT) – dir: Fabio Carpi
1972 *Majstor i Margarita* (YUG/IT) IT *Il maestro e Margherita* UK/US *The Master and Margarita* – dir: Aleksander Petrovic
1973 *La vita in gioco (Morire a Roma)* (IT) – dir: Gianfranco Mingozzi
1973 *Deux hommes dans la ville* (FR/IT) IT *Due contro la città* UK television title *Two Against the Law* – dir: José Giovanni
1973 *One Way / Un camino sin retorno* (MEX/IT) IT *La faccia violenta di New York* – dir: George Darnell [Jorge Eduardo Mauceri]
1974 *Allonsanfàn* (IT) – dir: Paolo & Vittorio Taviani
1974 *Il profumo della signora in nero* (IT) aka *The Perfume of the Lady in Black* – dir: Francesco Barilli
1974 *Les suspects* (FR/IT) IT *La polizia indaga: siamo tutto sospettati* US television title *The Suspects* working title *La pieuvre* – dir: Michel Wyn
1975 *Macchie solari* (IT) US *Autopsy* export title *The Victim* – dir: Armando Crispino
1975 *La traque* (FR/IT) IT *Il sapore della paura* export title *Gunman in the Streets* – dir: Serge R. Leroy
1977 *Antonio Gramsci – I giorni del carcere* (IT) – dir: Lino Del Fra
1977 *L'amant de poche* (FR) – dir: Bernard Queysanne
1978 *Ciao maschio* (IT/FR) FR *Rêve de singe* – dir: Marco Ferreri
1978 *Martin Eden* (IT) (tv mini-series) – dir: Giacomo Battiato
1978 *Les pieds poussent en novembre* (FR) (tv movie) – dir: Pierre Viallet
1979 *Concorde affaire '79* (IT) UKvdt *S.O.S. Concorde / Concorde Affair* – dir: Ruggero Deodato
1979 *La légion saute sur Kolwezi* (FR) – dir: Raoul Coutard
1980 *Il treno per Istambul* (IT) (tv movie) – dir: Gianfranco Mingozzi
1980 *Orient-Express* (SWI/SWE/IT/FR) (tv mini-series) episode *Maria* – dir: Daniele D'Anza
1980 *Même les mômes ont du vague à l'âme* (FR) – dir: Jean-Louis Daniel
1981 *Black cat* (IT) US/UKvdt ***The Black Cat*** – dir: Lucio Fulci
1981 *Quartetto Basileus* (IT/FR) – dir: Fabio Carpi
1982 *La déchirure* (FR) (tv movie) – dir: Franck Apprederis
1982 *La ragazza di Trieste* (IT) UKvdt *The Girl from Trieste* – dir: Pasquale Festa Campanile
1983 *Don Camillo* (IT/US) export title *The World of Don Camillo* – dir: Terence Hill [Mario Girotti]
1983 *La mort de Mario Ricci* (SWI/FR/WG) WG *Der Tod des Mario Ricci* UK/US *The Death of Mario Ricci* – dir: Claude Goretta
1983 *Arabesque* (IT) (tv mini-series) – dir: Roberto Guicciardini
1984 *Un foro nel parabrezza* (IT/YUG) (tv movie) – dir: Sauro Scavolini
1984 *Geheimcode Wildgänse* (WG/IT) IT *Arcobaleno selvaggio (Wild Rainbow)* US/UK *Codename Wildgeese* – dir: Anthony M. Dawson [Antonio Margheriti]
1984 *Mio figlio non sa leggere* (IT) (tv movie) – dir: Franco Giraldi
1984 *La bella Otero* (SP/IT/WG) (tv movie) – dir: José Maria Sanchez
1985 *Quando arriva il giudice* (IT) (tv movie) – dir: Giulio Questi
1985 *Fratelli* (IT) (tv movie) – dir: Loredana Dordi
1986 *Sensi* (IT) UKvdt *Evil Senses* – dir: Gabriele Lavia
1986 *Atelier* (IT) (tv movie) – dir: Vito Molinari
1986 *La ragazza dei lillà* (IT) shooting title *Thannia* – dir: Flavio Mogherini
1987 *Camping del terrore* (IT) US/UKvdt *BodyCount* shooting title *Camping della morte* – dir: Ruggero Deodato
1987 *Poisons* (SWI/FR) – dir: Pierre Maillard
1987 *La louve* (FR) (tv movie) – dir: José Giovanni

1987 *Her Fragrant Emulsion* (US) (short) – dir: Lewis Klahr [edited images from *Road to Salina* (1970)]
1988 *Sei delitti per padre Brown* (IT) (tv mini-series) episode *La sposa bugiarda* – dir: Vittorio De Sisti
1989 *Il segreto dell'uomo solitario* (IT) (tv movie) – dir: Ernesto Guida
1989 *Ceux de la soif* (FR) (tv movie) – dir: Laurent Heynemann
1990 *Safari* (FR/IT/GER) (tv movie) GER *Gefahr in der Savanne* – dir: Roger Vadim
2001 *Le pacte des loups* (FR) aka *Brotherhood of the Wolf* (sculptor) [uncredited] – dir: Christophe Gans
2004 *Five Children and It* (FR/UK/US) (sculptor) – dir: John Stephenson
2004 *Blueberry* (FR/MEX/UK) aka *Renegade* (sculptor) [uncredited] – dir: Jan Kounen
2004 *Troy* (US/MLT/UK) (sculptor) [uncredited] – dir: Wolfgang Petersen
2005 *Charlie and the Chocolate Factory* (US/UK/AUS) (sculptor) – dir: Tim Burton
2006 *Marie Antoinette* (US/FR/JAP) (sculptor) – dir: Sofia Coppola
2007 *The Golden Compass* (US/UK) (sculptor) – dir: Chris Weitz
2009 *Océans* (FR/SWI/SP/US/UAE) (documentary) (sculptor) – dir: Jacques Perrin & Jacques Cluzaud
2010 *Clash of the Titans* (US) (sculptor) [uncredited] – dir: Louis Leterrier
2011 *Pirates of the Caribbean: On Stranger Tides* (US/UK) (sculptor) – dir: Rob Marshall
2012 *Wrath of the Titans* (US/SP) (sculptor) – dir: Jonathan Liebesman
2014 *Guardians of the Galaxy* (US/UK) (sculptor) – dir: James Gunn
2017 *Beauty and the Beast* (US/UK) (sculptor) – dir: Bill Condon

Tisa Farrow

born 22 July 1951 in Los Angeles, California, USA
died 10 January 2024 in Rutland, Vermont, USA
daughter of Maureen O'Sullivan & John Farrow
real name **Theresa Magdalena Farrow**

Anne Bowles in ***Zombie Flesh-Eaters***

1970 *Homer* (CAN/US) – dir: John Trent
1972 *La course du lièvre à travers les champs* (FR/IT) IT *La corsa della lepre attraverso i campi* US/USvdt *...and Hope to Die* – dir: René Clément
1972 *Some Call It Loving* (US) – dir: James B. Harris
1974 *Only God Knows* (CAN) – dir: Peter Pearson
1976 *Una magnum special per Tony Saitta* (IT/CAN) CAN/US *Strange Shadows in an Empty Room* UK/UKvdt *Blazing Magnum* – dir: Martin Herbert [Alberto De Martino]
1977 *Fingers* (US) – dir: James Toback
1977 *The Initiation of Sarah* (US) (tv movie) – dir: Robert Day
1978 *Search and Destroy* (CAN) US *Striking Back* – dir: William Fruet
1979 *Winter Kills* (US) – dir: William Richert
1979 *The Ordeal of Patty Hearst* (US) (tv movie) – dir: Paul Wendkos
1979 *Manhattan* (US) – dir: Woody Allen
1979 *Zombi 2* (IT) US *Zombie* UK ***Zombie Flesh-Eaters*** – dir: Lucio Fulci
1980 *Antropophagus* (IT) US *The Grim Reaper* UKvdt *Anthropophagus the Beast* – dir: Joe D'Amato [Aristide Massaccesi]
1980 *L'ultimo cacciatore* (IT) US/UK *The Last Hunter* – dir: Anthony M. Dawson [Antonio Margheriti]

Edwige Fenech

born 24 December 1948 in Bône, French Algeria
real name **Edwige Sfenek**

Judge Viola Orlando/Rosa Orlando in ***La pretora***

1967 *Toutes folles de lui* (FR/IT) – dir: Norbert Carbonnaux
1967 *Die tolldreisten Geschichten – nach Honoré de Balzac* (WG) – dir: Joseph Zachar
1968 *Samoa Regina della giungla* (IT) – dir: James Reed [Guido Malatesta]
1968 *Frau Wirtin hat auch einen Grafen* (AT/WG/IT/HUN) IT *Susanna... ed i suoi dolci vizi alla corte del re* UK *Sexy Susan Sins Again* – dir: François Legrand [Franz Antel]
1968 *Il figlio di Aquila Nera* (IT) – dir: James Reed [Guido Malatesta]
1969 *Die nackte Bovary* (WG/IT) IT *I peccati di madame Bovary* UK *Play the Game or Leave the Bed* – dir: John Scott [Hans Schott-Schöbinger]
1969 *Top sensation* (IT) US *The Seducers* – dir: Ottavio Alessi
1969 *Testa o croce* (IT) aka *Heads or Tails* – dir: Peter E. Stanley [Piero Pierotti]
1969 *Frau Wirtin hat auch eine Nichte* (AT/WG/IT/HUN) IT *Il trionfo della casta Susanna* UK *House of Pleasure* – dir: François Legrand [Franz Antel]
1969 *Madame und ihre Nichte* (WG) – dir: Eberhard Schroeder
1969 *Alle Kätzchen naschen gern* (WG) – dir: Josef Zachar
1969 *Der Mann mit dem goldenen Pinsel* (WG/IT) IT *L'uomo dal pennello d'oro* export title *The Man with the Golden Brush* – dir: Franz Marischka
1969 *5 bambole per la luna d'agosto* (IT) export title *Five Dolls for an August Moon* – dir: Mario Bava
1970 *Le Mans – Scorciatoia per l'inferno* (IT) export title *Le Mans* – dir: Richard Kean [Osvaldo Civirani]
1970 *Don Franco e Don Ciccio nell'anno della contestazione* (IT) – dir: Marino Girolami
1970 *Satiricosissimo* (IT) – dir: Mariano Laurenti
1971 *Le calde notti di Don Giovanni* (IT/SP) SP *Los amores de Don Juan* UKvdt *The Nights and Loves of Don Juan* – dir: Al Bradley [Alfonso Brescia]
1971 *Lo strano vizio della signora Wardh* (IT/SP) SP *La perversa señora Ward* US *Next!* US/USvdt *The Next Victim* USvdt *Blade of the Ripper* aka *The Strange Vice of Mrs. Ward* – dir: Sergio Martino
1971 *Deserto di fuoco* (IT) aka *Desert of Fire* – dir: Renzo Merusi
1972 *Quel gran pezzo della Ubalda tutta nuda e tutta calda* (IT) – aka *Ubalda, All Naked and Warm* – dir: Mariano Laurenti
1972 *Quando le donne si chiamavano Madonne* (IT/WG) WG *Der Pfaffenspiegel* export title *When Women Were Called Madonna* – dir: Aldo Grimaldi
1972 *Il tuo vizio è una stanza chiusa e solo io ne ho la chiave* (IT) UK *Excite Me* aka *Gently Before She Dies* – dir: Sergio Martino
1972 *La bella Antonia, prima monica e poi dimonia* (IT) – dir: Mariano Laurenti
1972 *Perché quelle strane gocce di sangue sul corpo di Jennifer?* (IT) UK *Erotic Blue* – dir: Anthony Ascott [Giuliano Carnimeo]
1972 *Tutti i colori del buio* (IT/SP) SP *Todos los colores de la oscuridad* US *They're Coming to Get You / Demons of the Dead* USvdt *Day of the Maniac* – dir: Sergio Martino
1973 *Giovannona Coscialunga disonorata con onore* (IT) – dir: Sergio Martino
1973 *La vedova inconsolabile ringrazia quanti la consolarono* (IT) – dir: Mariano Laurenti
1973 *Anna, quel particolare piacere* (IT) UK *Secrets of a Call-Girl* – dir: Giuliano Carnimeo
1973 *Il suo nome faceva tremare... Interpol in allarme (Dio, sei proprio un padreterno!)* (IT/FR) FR *Johnny le fligeur* US *Power Kill / Mean Frank and Crazy Tony* – dir: Michele Lupo
1973 *Fuori uno sotto un altro, arriva il Passatore* (IT/SP) SP *Un casanova en apuros* – dir: Anthony Ascott [Giuliano Carnimeo]
1974 *La signora gioca bene a scopa?* (IT) UK *Poker in Bed* aka *The Good, the Bad and the Sexy* – dir: Giuliano Carnimeo
1974 *Innocenza e turbamento* (IT) – dir: Massimo Dallamano
1975 *Grazie nonna!* (IT) – dir: Franco Martinelli [Marino Girolami]
1975 *Il vizio di famiglia* (IT) UK *Vices in the Family* – dir: Mariano Laurenti
1975 *L'insegnante* (IT) – dir: Nando [Fernando] Cicero
1975 *La moglie vergine* (IT) UK *The Virgin Wife* US *Valentina... The Virgin Wife* aka *At Last, At Last* – dir: Franco Martinelli [Marino Girolami]
1975 *La poliziotta fa carriera* (IT) UK *Confessions of a Lady Cop* – dir: Michele Massimo Tarantini
1975 *Nude per l'assassino* (IT) export title *Strip Nude for Your Killer* – dir: Andrea Bianchi
1976 *40 gradi all'ombra del lenzuolo* (IT) UK *Sex with a Smile* segment *La cavallona* – dir: Sergio Martino
1976 *Cattivi pensieri* (IT) aka *Evil Thoughts* aka *Who Mislaid My Wife* – dir: Ugo Tognazzi
1976 ***La pretora*** (IT) export title *My Sister in Law* – dir: Lucio Fulci
1976 *La dottoressa del distretto militare* (IT) – dir: Nando [Fernando] Cicero
1977 *Taxi Girl* (IT) – dir: Michele Massimo Tarantini
1977 *Il grande attacco* (IT) USvdt *Battleforce* US tv title *The Great Battle* UKvdt *The Biggest Battle* – dir: Hank Milestone/Humphrey Logan [Umberto Lenzi]
1977 *La vergine, il toro e il capricorno* (IT) UK *The Erotic Exploits of a Sexy Seducer* UKvdt *Not Tonight Darling* – dir: Luciano Martino
1977 *La soldatessa alla visita militare* (IT/FR) FR *La toubib aux grandes manoeuvres* – dir: Nando [Fernando] Cicero
1978 *L'insegnante va in collegio* (IT/FR) FR *La prof et les cancres* – dir: Mariano Laurenti
1978 *La soldatessa alle grandi manovre* (IT/FR) FR *La toubib prend du galon* – dir: Nando [Fernando] Cicero
1978 *L'insegnante viene a casa* (IT/FR) FR *La prof connait la musique* – dir: Michele Massimo Tarantini
1978 *Amori miei* (IT) – dir: Steno [Stefano Vanzina]
1979 *La poliziotta della squadra del buoncostume* (IT) – dir: Michele Massimo Tarantini
1979 *Dottor Jekyll e gentile signora* (IT) export title *Dr. Jekyll Likes Them Hot* – dir: Steno [Stefano Vanzina]
1979 *La patata bollente* (IT) aka *It's Bad to Mix* – dir: Steno [Stefano Vanzina]

1979 *Sabato domenico e venerdi* (IT/SP) SP *Sábado, domingo y viérnes* segment *Sabato* – dir: Sergio Martino [other dir's: [Franco] Castellano & Pipolo [Giuseppe Moccia] & Pasquale Festa Campanile]
1980 *Sono fotogenico* (IT/FR) FR *Je suis photogénique* – dir: Dino Risi
1980 *Il ladrone* (IT/FR) FR *Le larron* export title *The Thief* – dir: Pasquale Festa Campanile
1980 *Il ficcanaso* (IT) – dir: Bruno Corbucci
1980 *Io e Caterina* (IT/FR) export title *Katherine and Me* – dir: Alberto Sordi
1980 *La moglie in vacanza... l'amante in città* (IT/FR) FR *Les zizis baladeurs* – dir: Sergio Martino
1980 *Zucchero, miele e peperoncino* (IT) – dir: Sergio Martino
1981 *Cornetti alla crema* (IT) – dir: Sergio Martino
1981 *Asso* (IT) – dir: [Franco] Castellano & Pipolo [Giuseppe Moccia]
1981 *La poliziotta a New York* (IT/FR) FR *Reste avec nous, on s'tire* – dir: Michele Massimo Tarantini
1981 *Tais-toi quand tu parles* (FR/TUN/IT) IT *Zitto quando parli* – dir: Philippe Clair
1982 *Ricchi, ricchissimi... praticamente in mutande* (IT) export title *Don't Play with Tigers* – dir: Sergio Martino
1982 *Sballato, gasato, completamente fuso* (IT) aka *An Ideal Adventure* – dir: Steno [Stefano Vanzina]
1982 *Il paramedico* (IT) export title *Luck... Bad Luck* – dir: Sergio Nasca
1984 *Vacanze in America* (IT) – dir: Carlo Vanzina
1984 *Bene, bravi, bis* (IT) (tv series) (hostess)
1987 *Rimini Rimini* (IT) – dir: Sergio Corbucci
1987 *Nel gorgo del peccato* (IT) (tv mini-series)
1987 *Immagina* (IT) (tv series)
1988 *Un delitto poco comune* (IT) UKvdt *Phantom of Death / Off Balance* – dir: Ruggero Deodato
1990 *Alta società* (IT) – dir: Giorgio Capitani
1992 *Il coraggio di Anna* (IT) (tv movie) aka *Surviving at the Top* – dir: Giorgio Capitani
1993 *Delitti privati* (IT) (4-part tv mini-series) UK television title *Private Crimes* – dir: Sergio Martino
1996 *Donna* (IT) (tv mini-series) – dir: Gianfranco Giagni
1997 *Sign of the Ape Adventure* (IT) (executive producer) aka *Sign of the Ape* – dir: Faliero Rosati
1998 *Commesse* (IT) (producer) – dir: Giorgio Capitani
1999 *Ferdinando e Carolina* (IT/FR) (co-producer) – dir: Lina Wertmüller
1999 *Le madri* (IT) (tv movie) (producer) – dir: Angelo Longoni
2000 *Il fratello minore* (IT) (co-producer/actor) – dir: Stefano Gigli
2000 *Aleph* (IT) (tv movie) (co-producer) – dir: Gianni Lepre
2001 *L'attentatuni* (IT) (tv movie) (producer) – dir: Claudio Bonivento
2002 *Le ragioni del cuore* (IT) (tv mini-series) (producer/actor) – dir: Luca Manfredi, Anna Di Francisca & Alberto Simone
2003 *La notte di Pasquino* (IT) (tv movie) (producer) – dir: Luigi Magni
2004 *Part Time* (IT) (tv movie) (producer) – dir: Angelo Longoni
2004 *Vite a perdere* (IT) (tv movie) (producer) – dir: Paolo Bianchini
2004 *The Merchant of Venice* (US/IT/LUX/UK) (co-producer) – dir: Michael Radford
2004 *La omicidi* (IT) (tv mini-series) (producer) – dir: Riccardo Milani
2005 *Angela* (IT) (tv movie) (co-producer) – dir: Andrea Frazzi & Antonio Frazzi
2005 *Matilde* (IT) (tv movie) (producer) – dir: Luca Manfredi
2005 *Lucia* (IT) (tv movie) (co-producer) – dir: Pasquale Pozzessere
2007 *Hostel: Part II* (US/CZE/IT/ICE/SVK) – dir: Eli Roth
2007 *La stella dei re* (IT) (tv movie) (producer) – dir: Fabio Jephcott
2008 *Per una notte d'amore* (IT) (tv movie) (co-producer) – dir: Vittorio Sindoni
2009 *Un amore di strega* (IT) (tv movie) (co-producer) – dir: Angelo Longoni
2009 *Le segretarie del sesto* (IT) (tv movie) (producer) aka *Top Secretaries* – dir: Angelo Longoni
2009 *Una sera d'ottobre* (IT) (tv movie) (co-producer) – dir: Vittorio Sindoni
2010 *Gorbaciof* (IT) (co-producer) – dir: Stefano Incerti
2011 *La ragazza americana* (IT) (tv movie) (co-producer) – dir: Vittorio Sindoni
2012 *La figlia del capitano* (IT) (tv movie) (co-producer/actor) – dir: Giacomo Campiotti
2015 *È arrivata la felicità* (IT) (tv mini-series) – dir: Riccardo Milani & Francesco Vicario

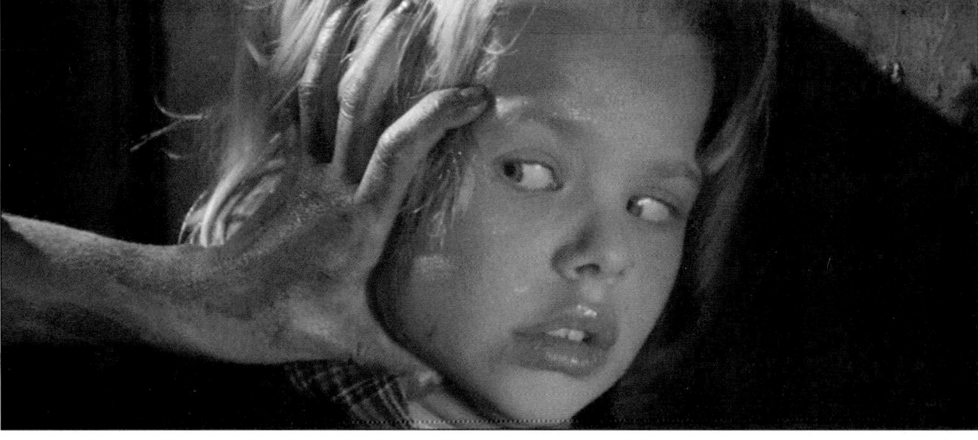

Giovanni Frezza

born 8 September 1972 in Potenza, Italy

Bob Boyle in ***The House by the Cemetery***
Tommy Hacker in ***Manhattan Baby***

1980 *Salto nel vuoto* (IT/FR) FR *Le saut dans le vide* US *Leap Into the Void / A Leap in the Dark* – dir: Marco Bellocchio
1981 *Quella villa accanto al cimitero* (IT) US/UK ***The House by the Cemetery*** – dir: Lucio Fulci
1982 *Testa o croce* (IT) – dir: Nanni Loy
1982 ***Manhattan Baby*** (IT) USvdt *Eye of the Evil Dead* UKvdt *Possessed* – dir: Lucio Fulci
1983 *I nuovi barbari* (IT) US *Warriors of the Wasteland* UK *The New Barbarians* – dir: Enzo G. Castellari [Enzo Girolami]
1983 *Cuando calienta el sol... vamos alla plaia* (IT) – dir: Mino Guerrini
1983 *Mani di fata* (IT) aka *The Magic Touch* – dir: Steno [Stefano Vanzina]
1983 *La casa con la scala nel buio* (IT) export title *A Blade in the Dark* [uncredited] – dir: Lamberto Bava
1985 *Dèmoni* (IT) export title *Demons* [uncredited] – dir: Lamberto Bava

Christopher George

born 25 February 1931 in Royal Oak, MI, USA
died 28 November 1983 in Los Angeles, CA, USA

Peter Bell in ***City of the Living Dead***

1965 *In Harm's Way* (US) [uncredited] – dir: Otto Preminger
1965 *Bewitched* (US) (tv series) episode *George the Warlock* – dir: William Asher
1965 *The Gentle Rain* (US/BRA) – dir: Burt Balaban
1966 *Thirteen Against Fate* (US) (tv series) episode *The Lodger* – dir: James Ferman
1966 *Ballad of Gavilan* (US) – dir: William J. Jugo [released in 1968]
1966 *El Dorado* (US) – dir: Howard Hawks
1966-68 *The Rat Patrol* (US) (tv series) (58 episodes)
1967 *Project X* (US) – dir: William Castle
1968 *Tiger By the Tail* (US) – dir: R.G. Springsteen
1968 *The 1,000 Plane Raid* (US) – dir: Boris Sagal
1968 *Massacre Harbour* (US) (tv movie, also shown theatrically) – dir: John Peyser [first shown as 3-part episode of *The Rat Patrol*]
1969 *Devil's 8* (US) – dir: Burt Topper
1969 *The Immortal* (US) (tv pilot) – dir: Joseph Sargent
1969 *The House on Greenapple Road* (US) (tv pilot) – dir: Robert Day
1970 *The F.B.I.* (US) (tv series) episode *Return to Power* – dir: Don Medford
1970 *The Delta Factor* (US) – dir: Tay Garnett
1970 *Chisum* (US) – dir: Andrew V. McLaglen
1970-71 *The Immortal* (US) (tv series) (15 episodes)
1971 *Escape* (US) (tv movie) – dir: John Llewellyn Moxey
1971 *Mission: Impossible* (US) (tv series) episode *Nerves* – dir: Barry Crane
1971 *Love, American Style* (US) (tv series) season 3 episode 1 segment *Love and Formula 26B* – dir: Charles R. Rondeau
1971 *Dead Men Tell No Tales* (US) (tv movie) – dir: Walter Grauman
1971 *Man on a String* (US) (tv pilot) – dir: Joseph Sargent
1972 *The Heist* (US) (tv movie) – dir: Don McDougall
1972 *Pushing Up Daisies* (US) UK *Their Breakfast Meant Lead* [uncredited] – dir: Ivan Nagy
1973 *The Train Robbers* (US) – dir: Burt Kennedy

1973 *Love, American Style* (US) (tv series) season 4 episode 20 segment *Love and the Burglar Joke* – dir: Charles R. Rondeau
1973 *Bad Charleston Charlie* (US) [uncredited] – dir: Ivan Nagy
1973 *I Escaped from Devil's Island* (US/MEX) – dir: William Witney
1974 *The Wide World of Mystery* (US) (tv series) episode *A Beautiful Killing*
1974 *Owen Marshall, Counselor at Law* (US) (tv series) episode *The Break In*
1974 *Police Story* (US) (tv series) episode *Cop in the Middle* – dir: Gary Nelson
1974 *The Innbreaker* (CAN) – dir: George McCowan
1974 *Thriller* (UK) (tv series) episode *The Next Scream You Hear* UStv *Not Guilty* – dir: Robert D. Cardona
1975 *Police Story* (US) (tv series) episode *The Execution* – dir: Alexander Singer
1975 *S.W.A.T.* (US) (tv series) episode *The Bravo Enigma* – dir: Phil Bondelli
1975 *S.W.A.T.* (US) (tv series) episode *Deadly Tide: Part 1* – dir: Gene Levitt
1975 *S.W.A.T.* (US) (tv series) episode *Deadly Tide: Part 2* – dir: Gene Levitt
1975 *The Last Survivors* (US) (tv movie) – dir: Lee H. Katzin
1975 *Sharks* (US) (tv movie) – dir: E.W. Swackhamer [series McCloud]
1976 *Grizzly / Killer Grizzly* (US) – dir: William Girdler
1976 *Dixie Dynamite* (US) – dir: Lee Frost
1976 *Day of the Animals / Something Is Out There* (US) – dir: William Girdler
1976 *The Shootist* (US) – dir: Don Siegel
1976 *Midway* (US) UK *The Battle of Midway* – dir: Jack Smight
1976 *Mayday at 40,000 Ft!* (US) (tv movie, also shown theatrically) – dir: Robert Butler
1976 *Wonder Woman* (US) (tv series) episode *Fausta, the Nazi Wonder Woman* – dir: Barry Crane
1977 *Questo sì che è amore* (IT) UKvdt *Last Touch of Love / Last Night of Christmas* – dir: Filippo Ottini
1977 *Whiskey Mountain* (US) – dir: William Grefe
1978 *Cruise Into Terror* (US) (tv movie) – dir: Bruce Kessler
1978 *VegaS* (US) (tv series) episode *Serve, Volley and Kill* – dir: Sutton Roley
1978 *The Love Boat* (US) (tv series) episode *The Business of Love / Crash Diet Crush / I'll Never Fall in Love Again* – dir: Roger Duchowny
1978 *Fantasy Island* (US) (tv series) episode *Lady of the Evening / The Racer* – dir: Don Weis
1978 *Fantasy Island* (US) (tv series) episode *The War Games / Queen of the Boston Bruisers* – dir: Earl Bellamy
1979 *Charlie's Angels* (US) (tv series) episode *Terror on Skis* – dir: Don Chaffey
1979 *The Misadventures of Sheriff Lobo* (US) (tv series) episode *The Day That Shark Ate Lobo* – dir: Dick Harwood
1979 *The Love Boat* (US) (tv series) episode *Alas, Poor Dwyer / After the War / Itsy Bitsy / Ticket to Ride / Disco Baby* – dir: Roger Duchowny
1979 *The Love Boat* (US) (tv series) episode *Cindy / Play By Play / What's a Brother For?* – dir: George Tyne
1980 *Fantasy Island* (US) (tv series) episode *The Love Doctor / Pleasure Palace / Possessed* – dir: Earl Bellamy & Cliff Bole
1980 *The Exterminator* (US) – dir: James Glickenhaus
1980 *Paura nella città dei morti viventi* (IT) US *The Gates of Hell* UK ***City of the Living Dead*** – dir: Lucio Fulci
1981 *Graduation Day* (US) – dir: Herb Freed
1981 *Enter the Ninja* (US) – dir: Menahem Golan
1981 *Mil gritos tiene la noche* (SP/PR) export title *Pieces* – dir: Juan Piquer Simón
1981 *Angkor* (TAI) UKvdt *Kampuchea Express / Brothers in Arms / Brothers in Arms – The Return* USvdt *Angkor: Cambodia Express* – dir: Lek Kitiparaporn
1982 *Fantasy Island* (US) (tv series) episode *The Magic Camera / Mata Hari / Valerie* – dir: Don Chaffey & Don Weis
1982 *Mortuary* (US) – dir: [Hikmet] Howard Avedis

Brett Halsey

born 20 June 1933 in Santa Ana, California, USA
real name **Charles Oliver Hand**
aka **Montgomery Ford**

Dr. Wendell Simpson in ***The Devil's Honey***
Lester Parson in ***Touch of Death***
'The Monster' in ***Nightmare Concert***
Professor Paul Evans in ***Demonia***

1953 *The Man from the Alamo* (US) [uncredited] – dir: Budd Boetticher
1953 *Walking My Baby Back Home* (US) [uncredited] – dir: Lloyd Bacon
1953 *The Glass Web* (US) – dir: Jack Arnold
1953 *All I Desire* (US) [uncredited] – dir: Douglas Sirk
1954 *Ma and Pa Kettle at Home* (US) – dir: Charles Lamont
1954 *Johnny Dark* (US) [uncredited] – dir: George Sherman
1954 *The Black Shield of Falworth* (US) [uncredited] – dir: Rudolph Maté
1954 *Waterfront* (US) (tv series) episode *Trestle Point* – dir: Frederick Stephani
1954 *Naked Alibi* (US) [uncredited] – dir: Jerry Hopper
1954 *Leave It to Harry* (US) (short) – dir: Will Cowan
1955 *To Hell and Back* (US) – dir: Jesse Hibbs
1955 *Revenge of the Creature* (US) [uncredited] – dir: Jack Arnold
1955 *Dr. Hudson's Secret Journal* (US) (tv series) episode *Hugh Adams Story* – dir: John Brahm
1955 *The Life of Riley* (US) (tv series) episode *Out to Pasture*
1956 *Three Bad Sisters* (US) [uncredited] – dir: Gilbert L. Kay
1956 *Brave Eagle* (US) (tv series) episode *The Spirit of Hidden Valley*
1956 *Brave Eagle* (US) (tv series) episode *The Gentle Warrior* – dir: Paul Landres
1956 *Brave Eagle* (US) (tv series) episode *Valley of Decision* – dir: George Blair
1956 *Gunsmoke* (US) (tv series) episode *Helping Hand* – dir: Charles Marquis Warren
1956 *The Girl He Left Behind* (US) [uncredited] – dir: David Butler
1956 *Tales of the 77th Bengal Lancers* (US) (tv series) episode *The Hostage*
1956 *The 20th Century-Fox Hour* (US) episode *Smoke Jumpers* – dir: Albert S. Rogell
1957 *Hot Rod Rumble* (US) – dir: Leslie H. Martinson
1957 *Lafayette Escadrille* (US) UK *Hell Bent for Glory* – dir: William A. Wellman
1957 *Matinee Theatre* (US) (tv series) episode *The Story of Joseph*
1957 *Schlitz Playhouse of Stars* (US) (tv series) episode *Sister Louise Goes to Town* – dir: John Brahm
1957 *West Point* (US) (tv series) episode *Start Running* – dir: James Sheldon
1957 *West Point* (US) (tv series) episode *Cold Peril* – dir: James Sheldon
1957 *West Point* (US) (tv series) episode *The Fight Back* – dir: Eddie Davis
1957 *The Silent Service* (US) (tv series) episode *The U.S.S. Tigrone Sets a Record* – dir: Jean Yarbrough
1957 *Highway Patrol* (US) (tv series) episode *Temptation* – dir: Henry S. Kesler
1958 *I Want to Live!* (US) [uncredited] – dir: Robert Wise
1958 *High School Hellcats* (US) – dir: Edward Bernds
1958 *Perry Mason* (US) (tv series) episode *The Case of the Cautious Coquette* – dir: Laslo Benedek
1958 *Studio 57* (US) (tv series) episode *The Terrible Discovery* – dir: Jus Addiss
1958 *Harbor Command* (US) (tv series) episode *Killer on My Doorstep* – dir: Derwin Abrahams
1958 *Target* (US) (tv series) episode *Police Doctor* – dir: Henry S. Kesler
1958 *The Millionaire* (US) (tv series) episode *The Susan Birchard Story* – dir: R.G. Springsteen
1958 *The Adventures of Jim Bowie* (US) (tv series) episode *Bad Medicine* – dir: Hollingsworth Morse
1958 *The Silent Service* (US) (tv series) episode *The U.S.S. Tinosa Story* – dir: Jean Yarbrough
1958 *The Silent Service* (US) (tv series) episode *The Bowfin Story* – dir: Jean Yarbrough
1958 *Flight* (US) (tv series) episode *Bombs in the Belfry* – dir: Jean Yarbrough
1958 *Highway Patrol* (US) (tv series) episode *Breath of a Child* – dir: Henry S. Kesler
1958 *Cry Baby Killer* (US) – dir: Jus Addiss
1958 *Gunman's Walk* (US) – dir: Phil Karlson
1958 *Submarine Seahawk* (US) – dir: Spencer Gordon Bennet
1958 *Speed Crazy* (US) – dir: William Hole Jr.
1959 *Mackenzie's Raiders* (US) (tv series) (3 episodes)
1959 *The Last Blitzkrieg* (US) [credited as Montgomery Ford] – dir: Arthur Dreifuss
1959 *Death Valley Days* (US) (tv series) episode *Eruption at Volcano* – dir: Paul Landres
1959 *Sea Hunt* (US) (tv series) episode *Diving for the Moon* – dir: Leon Benson
1959 *Bat Masterson* (US) (tv series) episode *River Boat* – dir: Walter Doniger
1959 *World of Giants* (US) (tv series) episode *Feathered Foe* – dir: Nathan Juran
1959 *Five Fingers* (US) (tv series) episode *Thin Ice* – dir: Lamont Johnson
1959 *Return of the Fly* (US) – dir: Edward Bernds
1959 *The Best of Everything* (US) – dir: Jean Negulesco
1959 *Blood and Steel* (US) – dir: Bernard L. Kowalski
1959 *Four Fast Guns* (US) – dir: William J. Hole Jr.
1959 *Jet Over the Atlantic* (US) – dir: Byron Haskin
1959 *Girl in Lover's Lane* (US) – dir: Charles R. Rondeau
1959 *The Silent Kill* (US) – dir: Don Siegel [unsold tv pilot entitled *Brock Callahan*, shown in cinemas]
1959 *The Atomic Submarine* (US) – dir: Spencer Gordon Bennet
1960 *Adventures in Paradise* (US) (tv series) episode *Passage to Tua* – dir: James Neilson
1960 *Desire in the Dust* (US) – dir: William F. Claxton
1961 *Return to Peyton Place* (US) – dir: José Ferrer
1961 *The Hunters* (US) (tv pilot) – dir: Robert Blees
1961-62 *Follow the Sun* (US) (tv series) (18 episodes)
1962 *Chalk One Up for Johnny* (US) (tv pilot) – dir: Leonard J. Horn
1962 *Le sette spade del vendicatore* (IT/FR) FR *Sept épées pour le Roi* US *The Seventh Sword* – dir: Riccardo Freda
1963 *Twice Told Tales* (US) – dir: Sydney Salkow
1963 *Jack und Jenny* (WG) – dir: Victor Vicas
1963 *Il magnifico avventuriero* (IT/SP/FR) SP *El magnifico aventurero* FR *L'aventurier magnifique* UK/US *The Magnificent Adventurer* – dir: Riccardo Freda
1964 *Il magnifico cornuto* (IT/FR) FR *Le cocu magnifique* US *The Magnificent Cuckold* [uncredited] – dir: Antonio Pietrangeli
1964 *L'heure de la vérité* (FR/IS) IS *Sha'at Emet* – dir: Henri Calef
1964 *Il ponte dei Sospiri* (IT/SP/FR) SP *El puente de los suspiros* FR *Le pont des Soupirs* aka *The Avenger of Venice* – dir: Piero Pierotti
1965 *Berlino, appuntamento per le spie (Operazione Polifemo)* (IT) US *Spy in Your Eye* – dir: Vittorio Sala
1965 *Misión Lisboa* (SP/FR/IT) IT *Da 077: intrigo a Lisbona* FR *077 intrigue à Lisbonne* – dir: Tulio Demicheli
1966 *Der Kongress Amusiert sich* (WG/AT) US *The Congress of Love* – dir: Geza von Radvanyl
1966 *Uccidete Johnny Ringo* (IT) UK *Kill Johnny Ringo* – dir: Frank G. Carroll [Gianfranco Baldanello]
1966 *Tre notti violente* (IT/SP) SP *Tres noches violentas* US *Web of Violence* – dir: Nick Nostro

1967 *Bang bang* (FR/IT) IT *O l'ammazzo o la sposo* – dir: Serge Piollet & Fernando Cerchio
1967 *Un día después de Agosto* (SP) aka *One Day After August* – dir: Germán Lorente
1967 *Le dolci signore* (IT) US *Anyone Can Play* – dir: Luigi Zampa
1967 *Oggi a me... domani a te* (IT) UK *Today It's Me... Tomorrow You!* USvdt *Today We Kill... Tomorrow We Die* [credited as Montgomery Ford] – dir: Tonino Cervi
1968 *Tutto sul rosso* (IT/WG) export title *All on the Red* – dir: Aldo Florio
1968 *L'ira di Dio* (IT/SP) SP *Hasta la última gota de sangre* UK *The Wrath of God* – dir: Albert Cardiff [Alberto Cardone]
1969 *20.000 dollari sporchi di sangue / Kidnapping: paga o uccidiamo tuo figlio* (IT/SP) SP *Forajidos implacables* UK *The Kidnapping* [credited as Montgomery Ford] – dir: Albert Cardiff [Alberto Cardone]
1969 *Las trompetas del apocalipsis* (SP/IT) IT *I caldi amori di una minorenne* UK *Again* aka *Perversion Story* US *Murder By Music* – dir: Julio Buchs
1969 *Roy Colt & Winchester Jack* (IT) – dir: Mario Bava
1971 *Quante volte... quella notte* (IT/WG) WG *Vier Mal heute Nacht* export title *Four Times That Night* – dir: Mario Bava
1971 *Where Does It Hurt?* (US) – dir: Rod Amateau
1971 *Alias Smith and Jones* (US) (tv series) episode *Return to Devil's Hole* – dir: Bruce Kessler
1971 *Death Lends a Hand* (US) (tv movie) – dir: Bernard L. Kowalski [feature-length episode of *Columbo*]
1972 *Alias Smith and Jones* (US) (tv series) episode *The Day the Amnesty Came Through* – dir: Jeff Corey
1973 *Love Is a Many Splendored Thing* (US) (tv series) episode #1.1430 – dir: Peter Levin & Portman Paget
1973 *Toma* (US) (tv series) episode *Crime Without Victim* – dir: Daniel Haller
1974 *CBS Daytime 90* (US) (tv series) episode *Once in Her Life* – dir: Robert J. Shaw
1975 *Search for Tomorrow* (US) (tv series)
1975 *Coonskin* (US) [uncredited] – dir: Ralph Bakshi
1976 *City of Angels* (US) (tv series) episode *The Losers* – dir: Barry Shear
1976-77 *General Hospital* (US) (tv series)
1978 *The Bionic Woman* (US) (tv series) episode *The Antidote* – dir: Don McDougall
1978 *The Love Boat* (US) (tv series) episode *Last of the Stubings / Million Dollar Man / The Sisters* – dir: Jack Arnold
1978 *Fantasy Island* (US) (tv series) episode *Let the Goodtimes Roll / Nightmare / The Tiger* – dir: George McCowan
1978 *Crash* (US) (tv movie) USvdt *The Crash of Flight 401* – dir: Barry Shear
1979 *Buck Rogers in the 25th Century* (US) (tv series) episode *Cruise Ship to the Stars* – dir: Sigmund Neufeld Jr.
1979 *Fantasy Island* (US) (tv series) episode *The Chain Gang / The Boss* – dir: Michael Vejar
1979 *The Dukes of Hazzard* (US) (tv series) episode *The Rustlers* – dir: Dick Moder
1980 *Power* (US) (tv movie) – dir: Barry Shear & Virgil W. Vogel
1980 *Hart to Hart* (US) (tv series) episode *Murder, Murder on the Wall* – dir: Tom Mankiewicz
1980-81 *The Young and the Restless* (US) (tv series)
1981 *Scruples* (US) (tv pilot) – dir: Robert Day
1981 *Charlie's Angels* (US) (tv series) episode *Attack Angels* – dir: Kim Manners
1981 *The Fall Guy* (US) (tv series) episode *The Meek Shall Inherit Rhonda* – dir: Sidney Hayers
1982 *Fantasy Island* (US) (tv series) episode *A Very Strange Affair / The Sailor* – dir: Cliff Bole
1982 *Fantasy Island* (US) (tv series) episode *Forget Me Not / The Quiz Masters* – dir: Cliff Bole
1982 *The Dukes of Hazzard* (US) (tv series) episode *Enos in Trouble* – dir: Paul Baxley
1983 *Knight Rider* (US) (tv series) episode *Give Me Liberty... or Give Me Death* – dir: Bernard L. Kowalski
1983 *Automan* (US) (tv series) episode *Club Ten* – dir: Kim Manners
1983 *Matt Houston* (US) (tv series) episode *Whose Party Is It Anyway?* – dir: Cliff Bole
1984 *Matt Houston* (US) (tv series) episode *Caged* – dir: Cliff Bole
1984 *Airwolf* (US) (tv series) episode *Sins of the Past* – dir: Donald A. Baer
1984 *Cagney & Lacey* (US) (tv series) episode *Insubordination* – dir: John Patterson
1984 *The Dukes of Hazzard* (US) (tv series) episode *The Dukes in Hollywood* – dir: George Bowers
1984 *The New Mike Hammer* (US) (tv series) episode *Sex Trap* – dir: James Frawley
1985 *Half Nelson* (US) (tv series) episode *Uppers and Downers*
1986 *The New Mike Hammer* (US) (tv series) episode *Murder in the Cards* – dir: Don Weis
1986 *Rose* (IT) (tv movie) – dir: Tomaso Sherman
1986 *Il miele del diavolo* (IT/SP) SP *La miel del diablo* USvdt *Dangerous Obsession* export title ***The Devil's Honey*** – dir: Lucio Fulci
1986 *Ratboy* (US) – dir: Sondra Locke
1988 *Sogno proibito* (IT/SP) SP *El vuelo de Venus* – dir: Vincenzo Salviani
1988 *La bahía Esmeralda* (SP/FR) FR *Esmeralda Bay* – dir: Jesús Franco
1988 *Der Commander* (WG/IT) IT *Il triangolo della paura* UKvdt *The Commander* – dir: Anthony M. Dawson [Antonio Margheriti]
1988 *Cop game (Giochi di poliotto)* (IT) export title *Cop Game* [uncredited] – dir: Bob Hunter [Bruno Mattei]
1988 *Quando Alice ruppe lo specchio* (IT) export title ***Touch of Death*** – dir: Lucio Fulci
1988 *L'impronta dell'assassino* (IT) (tv movie) – dir: Luigi Cozzi [series *Turno di notte*]
1989 *Black Cat* (US) aka *De Profundis / Out of the Depths* – dir: Lewis Coates [Luigi Cozzi]
1989 *Street Legal* (US) (tv series) episode *Blue Collar* – dir: Allan Harmon
1990 *Un gatto nel cervello (I volti del terrore)* (IT) export title ***Nightmare Concert*** aka *Nightmare Concert (A Cat in the Brain)* – dir: Lucio Fulci
1990 ***Demonia*** (IT) – dir: Lucio Fulci
1990 *The Godfather Part III* (US) – dir: Francis Ford Coppola
1990 *Back Stab* (US/CAN) – dir: Jim Kaufman
1990 *E.N.G.* (CAN) (tv series) (2 episodes)
1991 *Il principe del deserto* (IT) (tv movie, also shown theatrically) US *Beyond Justice* UKvdt *Desert Law* – dir: Duccio Tessari
1991 *Sweating Bullets* (CAN) (tv series) episode *Dead Men Tell* – dir: Timothy Bond
1991 *Counterstrike* (US/CAN/FR) (tv series) episode *Native Warriors* – dir: Alan Simmonds
1991 *Street Legal* (US) (tv series) episode *The Good Lawyer* – dir: Eleanor Lindo
1992 *Search for Diana* (CAN) – dir: Milad Bessada
1992 *To Catch a Killer* (CAN) (two-part tv movie) – dir: Eric Till
1992 *Forever Knight* (CAN/WG) (tv series) episode *Dying to Know You* – dir: Brad Turner
1992-93 *Top Cops* (US) (tv series) (3 episodes)
1992-93 *X-Men* (US/CAN) (tv series) (voice)
1993 *Almost Golden: The Jessica Savitch Story* (CAN/US) (tv movie) – dir: Peter Werner
1993 *Gregory K* (US) (tv movie) aka *Switching Parents* – dir: Linda Otto
1993 *Secret Service* (US) (tv series) episode *The Assassin*
1993 *Matrix* (CAN) (tv series) episode *Lapses in Memory* – dir: Jorge Montesi
1994 *First Degree* (CAN) – dir: Jeff Woolnough
1994 *TekWar* (CAN/US) (tv series) episode *Unknown Soldier* – dir: Allan Kroeker
1994 *Kung Fu: The Legend Continues* (US/CAN) (tv series) episode *The Possessed* – dir: Allan King
1995 *Kung Fu: The Legend Continues* (US/CAN) (tv series) episode *Plague* – dir: Mario Azzopardi
1995 *Kung Fu: The Legend Continues* (US/CAN) (tv series) episode *Target* – dir: Jon Cassar
1995 *Kung Fu: The Legend Continues* (US/CAN) (tv series) episode *Demons* – dir: Jon Cassar
1995 *Kissinger and Nixon* (US) (tv movie) – dir: Daniel Petrie
1995 *Expect No Mercy* (CAN) – dir: Zale R. Dalen
1996 *Terminal Rush* (CAN) – dir: Damian Lee
1998 *Mowgli: The New Adventures of the Jungle Book* (US) (tv series) episode *The Guardian* – dir: John Blizek
1999 *Free Fall* (US/CAN/GER) – dir: Mario Azzopardi
1999 *El barrio* (CRC) (tv series) (2 episodes) – dir: Óscar Castillo
1999 *La pensión* (CRC) (tv series) (3 episodes) – dir: Óscar Castillo
2001 *The Associates* (US) (tv series) episode *Disclosure* – dir: George Bloomfield
2001 *Asesinato en el Meneo* (CRC) aka *Murder at El Meneo* – dir: Óscar Castillo
2003 *Mujeres apasionadas* (CRC) – dir: Maureen Jiménez
2003 *Risk Factor* (CAN) shooting title *Into the Heat* – dir: Frank A. Caruso [released in 2015]
2008 *Cold Case* (US) (tv series) episode *Wings* – dir: David Von Ancken
2009 *Hierarchy* (US) [credited as Montgomery Ford] – dir: Michael Fredianelli
2011 *The Scarlet Worm* (US) [credited as Montgomery Ford] – dir: Michael Fredianelli
2013 *Club Utopia* (CAN) – dir: Frank A. Caruso

George Hilton

born 16 July 1934 in Montevideo, Uruguay
died 28 July 2019 in Rome, Lazio, Italy
real name **Jorge Hill Acosta y Lara**

Jeffrey Corbett in ***Massacre Time***

1956 *Los tallos amargos* (ARG) – dir: Fernando Ayala
1956 *Después del silencio* (ARG) – dir: Lucas Demare
1957 *Una viuda difícil* (ARG) – dir: Fernando Ayala
1958 *Alto Paraná* (ARG) – dir: Catrano Catrani
1960 *La procesión* (ARG) – dir: Francis Lauric
1960 *El bote, el río y la gente* (ARG) – dir: Enrique Cahen Salaberry

1963 *Los que verán a Dios* (ARG) – dir: Rodolfo Blasco
1963 *Las modelos* (ARG) – dir: Vlasta Lah
1964 *L'uomo mascherato contro i pirati* (IT) UKvdt *The Black Pirate* – dir: Vert Dean [Vetunnio De Angelis]
1965 *Dos caraduras en Texas* (SP/IT) IT *Per un pugno nell'occhio* – dir: Michele Lupo
1965 *Due mafiosi contro Goldginger* (IT/SP) SP *Operación relámpago* – dir: Giorgio C. Simonelli
1966 *Le colt cantarono la morte e fu... tempo di massacro* (IT) US *The Brute and the Beast* US/UKvdt ***Massacre Time*** – dir: Lucio Fulci
1966 *I due figli di Ringo* (IT) – dir: Giorgio Simonelli
1967 *Professionisti per un massacro* (IT/SP) SP *Los profesionales de la muerte* export title *Red Blood, Yellow Gold* – dir: Nando [Fernando] Cicero
1967 *Il tempo degli avvoltoi* (IT) UKvdt *Last of the Badmen* aka *Time of Vultures* – dir: Nando [Fernando] Cicero
1967 *Frontera al Sur* (SP/IT) IT *Kitosch, l'uomo che veniva dal Nord* export title *Kitosch, the Man Who Came from the North* – dir: Joseph Marvin [José Luis Merino]
1967 *La più grande rapina nel West* (IT) export titles *The Greatest Robbery in the West* / *Halleluja for Django* – dir: Maurizio Lucidi
1967 *Un poker di pistole* (IT) export title *Poker with Pistols* – dir: Joseph Warren [Giuseppe Vari]
1967 *Vado... l'ammazzo e torno* (IT) US/USvdt *Any Gun Can Play* USvdt *For a Few Bullets More* UKvdt *I Go... I'll Kill Him and I'll Be Back* – dir: Enzo G. Castellari [Enzo Girolami]
1967 *En Ghentar se muere con facil* (SP/IT) IT *A Ghentar si muore facile* – dir: Léon Klimovsky
1967 *L'harem* (IT/FR) FR *Le harem* aka *Her Harem* [uncredited] – dir: Marco Ferreri
1968 *Il momento di uccidere* (IT/WG) WG *Django Ein Sarg voll Blut* export title *The Moment to Kill* – dir: Anthony Ascott [Giuliano Carnimeo]
1968 *Ognuno per sé* (IT/WG) WG *Das Gold von Sam Cooper* US/UKvdt *The Ruthless Four* UK *Each Man for Himself* – dir: Giorgio Capitani
1968 *La battaglia di El Alamein* (IT/FR) FR *La bataille d'El Alamein* UK *Desert Tanks* US/UKvdt *Battle of El Alamein* – dir: Calvin Jackson Padget [Giorgio Ferroni]
1968 *Il dolce corpo di Deborah* (IT/FR) FR *L'adorable corps de Deborah* UK/US *The Sweet Body of Deborah* – dir: Romolo Guerrieri [Romolo Girolami]
1968 *T'ammazzo!... Raccomandati a Dio* (IT) aka *Fidarsi è bene, sparare è meglio* USvdt *Dead for a Dollar* aka *Trusting Is Good... Shooting Is Better* – dir: Osvaldo Civirani
1968 *Uno di più all'inferno* (IT/SP) SP *Los machos* export title *To Hell and Back* – dir: Giovanni Fago
1969 *Il dito nella piaga* (IT) US *Salt in the Wound* UKvdt *The Dirty Two* – dir: Tonino Ricci
1969 *La battaglia del deserto* (IT/FR) FR *Sette hommes pour Tobrouk* UK *The Desert Battle* UKvdt *Battle of the Desert* – dir: Mino Loy
1969 *Los desperados* (SP/IT) IT *Quei disperati che puzzano di sudore e di morte* UK *Vengeance Is Mine* US *A Bullet for Sandoval* – dir: Julio Buchs
1969 *Agente Howard: 7 minuti per morire* (IT/SP) SP *Siete minutos para morir* – dir: Ray Feder [Ramón Fernández]
1970 *C'è Sartana... vendi la pistola e comprati la bara!* (IT) export title *I am Sartana, Trade Your Guns for a Coffin* – dir: Anthony Ascott [Giuliano Carnimeo]
1971 *Lo strano vizio della Signora Wardh* (IT/SP) SP *La perversa señora Ward* US *Next!* US/USvdt *The Next Victim* USvdt *Blade of the Ripper* aka *The Strange Vice of Mrs. Ward* – dir: Sergio Martino
1971 *La coda dello scorpione* (IT/SP) SP *La cola del escorpión* export title *The Case of the Scorpion's Tail* – dir: John Hamilton [Sergio Martino]
1971 *Il diavolo a sette facce* (IT) US *The Devil Has Seven Faces* UKvdt *The Devil with Seven Faces* / *Nights of Terror* – dir: Osvaldo Civirani
1971 *Testa t'ammazzo, croce... sei morto! Mi chiamano Alleluja* (IT/FR/WG) FR *On m'appelle Allelulja* WG *...Man nennt mich Halleluja* export title *Heads You Die... Tails I Kill You* aka *Guns for Dollars* – dir: Anthony Ascott [Giuliano Carnimeo]
1972 *Mio caro assassino* (IT/SP) SP *Sumario sangriento de la pequeña Stefania* export title *My Dear Killer* Spanish shooting title *Mi querido asesino* – dir: Tonino Valerii
1972 *Coartada en disco rojo* (SP/IT) IT *I due volti della paura* UK *The Two Faces of Fear* – dir: Tulio Demicheli
1972 *Il West ti va stretto, amico... è arrivato Alleluja* (IT/FR/WG) FR *Alleluia défie l'Ouest* WG *Beichtet, Freunde, Halleluja kommt* – dir: Anthony Ascott [Giuliano Carnimeo]
1972 *Tutti i colori del buio* (IT/SP) SP *Todos los colores de la oscuridad* US *They're Coming to Get You* / *Demons of the Dead* USvdt *Day of the Maniac* – dir: Sergio Martino
1972 *Perché quelle strane gocce di sangue sul corpo di Jennifer?* (IT) UK *Erotic Blue* – dir: Anthony Ascott [Giuliano Carnimeo]
1973 *Fuori uno sotto un altro, arriva il Passatore* (IT/SP) SP *Un casanova en apuros* – dir: Anthony Ascott [Giuliano Carnimeo]
1973 *Contact – Contratto carnale* (IT/GHA) UKvdt *The African Deal – Contact* / *Only Love Defies* – dir: Giorgio Bontempi
1973 *Lo chiamavano Tresette... giocava sempre col morto* (IT) export title *Man Called Invincible* – dir: Anthony Ascott [Giuliano Carnimeo]
1973 *7 ore di violenza per una soluzione imprevista* (IT) export title *7 Hours of Violence* – dir: Michele Massimo Tarantini
1974 *Di Tresette ce n'è uno... tutti gli altri son nessuno* (IT) export title *Dick Luft in Sacramento* – dir: Anthony Ascott [Giuliano Carnimeo]
1974 *Il baco da seta* (IT) – dir: Mario Sequi
1975 *L'assassino è costretto a uccidere ancora* (IT/FR) export title *The Dark Is Death's Friend* Italian shooting title *Il ragno* – dir: Luigi Cozzi
1975 *Der kleine Schwarze mit dem roten Hut* (AT/IT/WG) IT *Prima ti suono e poi ti sparo* WG *Zwei tolle Hechte Wir sind die Grössten* export title *Trinity plus the Clown and a Guitar* – dir: François Legrand [Franz Antel]
1975 *Ah sí? E io lo dico a ZZZorro!* (IT/SP) SP *Nuevas aventuras del Zorro* export title *Who's Afraid of Zorro* – dir: Franco Lo Cascio
1976 *La llamada del sexo* (SP/COL) shooting title *Dulcemente moriras por amor* – dir: Tulio Demicheli
1977 *Taxi Girl* (IT) – dir: Michele Massimo Tarantini
1977 *El Macho* (IT) – dir: Mark Andrew [Marcello Andrei]
1977 *Torino violenta* (IT) export title *Double Game* – dir: Carlo Ausino
1977 *Milano... difendersi o morire* (IT) export title *Blazing Bullets* UKvdt *Blazing Flowers* WG *Heroin* – dir: Gianni [Giovanni] Antonio Martucci
1979 *El lugar del humo* (URU) – dir: Eva Landeck
1981 *Teste di quoio* (IT) – dir: Giorgio Capitani
1982 *Ricchi, ricchissimi... praticamente in mutande* (IT) export title *Don't Play with Tigers* – dir: Sergio Martino
1982 *Le notti segrete di Lucrezia Borgia* (IT/SP) SP *La noche segreta de Lucrecia Borgia* export title *The Secrets Nights of Lucrezia Borgia* – dir: Roberto Montero Bianchi
1983 *I predatori di Atlantide* (IT) UKvdt *The Atlantis Interceptors* USvdt *The Raiders of Atlantis* – dir: Roger Franklin [Ruggero Deodato]
1984 *College* (IT) – dir: [Franco] Castellano & Pipolo [Giuseppe Moccia]
1988 *Silvia è sola* (IT) (tv movie) – dir: Silvio Maestranzi
1988 *A cena col vampiro* (IT) export title *Dinner with the Vampire* aka *Una cena con il vampiro* – dir: Lamberto Bava [one of series *Brivido giallo*]
1989 *Il prato delle volpi* (IT) (tv movie) – dir: Piero Schivazappa
1989 *College* (IT) (tv mini-series) – dir: Lorenzo Castellano & Federico Moccia
1992 *Gli uomini della sua vita* (IT/GER/FR) (tv movie) – dir: Michael Braun
1993 *Abbronzatissimi 2 – Un anno dopo* (IT) – dir: Bruno Gaburro
1994 *Italian restaurant* (IT) (tv mini-series) – dir: Giorgio Capitani
1994 *Prestazione straordinaria* (IT) – dir: Sergio Rubini
1997 *Fuochi d'artificio* (IT) aka *Fireworks* – dir: Leonardo Pieraccioni
1999 *Cient' anne* (IT) – dir: Ninì Grassia
1999 *Tre addii* (IT) (tv movie) – dir: Mario Caiano
2007 *Natale in crociera* (IT) – dir: Neri Parenti
2009 *Un coccodrillo per amico* (IT) (tv movie) – dir: Francesca Marra
2015 *La promessa del sicario* (IT) – dir: Max Ferro

Olga Karlatos

born 20 April 1947 in Athens, Greece
real name **Olga Vlassopulos**

Paola Menard in ***Zombie Flesh-Eaters***
Candice Norman in ***Murder-Rock Dancing Death***

1966 *Per il gusto di uccidere* (IT/SP) SP *Cazador de recompensas* [uncredited] – dir: Tonino Valerii
1967 *Les pâtres du désordre* (FR/GRE) GRE *Oi voskoi* US *Thanos and Despina* aka *The Shepherds of Calamity* – dir: Nikos Papatakis
1971 *Eneide* (IT/FR/WG) (tv series) – dir: Franco Rossi
1972 *Paulina 1880* (FR) – dir: Jean-Louis Bertucelli
1974 *Le avventure di Enea* (IT/YUG) – dir: Franco Rossi [tv series, truncated version shown in cinemas]
1974 *Aufs Kreuz gelegt* (WG) (tv movie) – dir: Wolfgang Petersen
1975 *Amici miei* (IT) export title *All My Friends* – dir: Mario Monicelli
1976 *Gloria mundi* (FR) – dir: Nikos Papatakis
1976 *Keoma* (IT) UK *The Violent Breed* – dir: Enzo G. Castellari [Enzo Girolami]
1976 *Quelle strane occasioni* (IT) segment *Il cavalluccio svedese* – dir: Luigi Magni [other dir's: Nanny Loy & Luigi Comencini]
1976 *Ciclón* (MEX) IT/US/UKvdt *Cyclone* – dir: René Cardona Jr.
1977 *Per questa notte* (IT) – dir: Carlo Di Carlo
1977 *Mogliamante* (IT) – dir: Marco Vicario
1978 *Nero Veneziano* (IT) export title *Damned in Venice* – dir: Ugo Liberatore

1978 *Un poliziotto scomodo* (IT) UK *Convoy Busters* – dir: Stelvio Massi
1978 *Avere vent'anni* (IT) UKvdt *To Be Twenty* – dir: Fernando Di Leo
1978 *Diamanti sporchi di sangue* (IT) export title *Blood and Diamonds* – dir: Fernando Di Leo
1978 *Return of the Saint* (UK) (tv series) episode *The Judas Game* – dir: Jeremy Summers
1978 *I tembelides tis eforis kiladis* (GRE) aka *Idlers of the Fertile Valley* – dir: Nikos Panayotopoulos
1978 *Ridendo e scherzando* (IT) segment *Melodramma della gelosia* – dir: Marco Aleandri [Vittorio Sindoni]
1978 *Effetti speciali* (IT) (tv movie) – dir: Gianni Amelio
1979 *Senza buccia* (IT/SP) SP *Vacaciones al desnudo* export title *Skin Deep* – dir: Marcello Aliprandi
1979 *L'angelo dalle ali di cera* (IT) – dir: Gianni Siragusa [unreleased]
1979 *Agenzia Riccardo Finzi... praticamente detective* (IT) – dir: Bruno Corbucci
1979 *Belli e brutti ridono tutti* (IT) – dir: Domenico Paolella
1979 *Riavanti... marsch!* (IT) – dir: Luciano Salce
1979 *Il giocattolo* (IT) – dir: Giuliano Montaldo
1979 *Le rose di Danzica* (IT) US *The Roses of Danzig* – dir: Alberto Bevilacqua
1979 *Ege kai ni Sasagu* (JAP/IT) IT *Dedicato al mare egeo* – dir: Masuo Ikeda
1979 *Mani di velluto* (IT) – dir: [Franco] Castellano & Pipolo [Giuseppe Moccia]
1979 *Zombi 2* (IT) US *Zombie* UK ***Zombie Flesh-Eaters*** – dir: Lucio Fulci
1980 *Una moglie, due amici, quattro amanti* (IT/SP) SP *¿Doctor, estoy buena?* – dir: Michele Massimo Tarantini
1980 *Exodos kindynou* (GRE) – dir: Nikos Foskolos
1980 *Eleftherios venizelos* 1910-1927 (GRE) – dir: Pantelis Voulgaris
1980 *Scruples* (US) (tv movie) – dir: Robert Day
1981 *Peter and Paul* (US) (two-part tv movie) – dir: Robert Day
1981 *La storia vera della Signora dalle camelie* (IT/FR/WG) FR *La dame aux camélias* WG *Kameliendame* – dir: Mauro Bolognini
1981 *Der Schatz des Priamos* (WG) (two-part tv movie) – dir: Karl Fruchtmann
1981 *George Sand* (IT) (tv mini-series) – dir: Giorgio Albertazzi
1983 *Once Upon a Time in America* (US) – dir: Sergio Leone
1983 *The Scarlet and the Black* (US/IT) (tv movie) – dir: Jerry London
1983 *The Sins of Dorian Gray* (US) (tv movie) – dir: Tony Maylam
1984 *Murderock uccide a passo di danza* (IT) US *The Demon Is Loose* export title ***Murder-Rock Dancing Death*** – dir: Lucio Fulci
1984 *Purple Rain* (US) – dir: Albert Magnoli
1985 *Inganni* (IT) – dir: Luigi Faccini
1985 *Quo Vadis* (IT/FR/WG/SP/CAN) (tv mini-series) – dir: Franco Rossi
1986 *Miami Vice* (US) (tv series) episode *Forgive Us Our Debts* – dir: Jan Eliasberg
1987 *L'ingranaggio* (IT) – dir: Silverio Blasi

Zora Ulla Keslerová

born 11 August 1950 in Prague, Czechoslovakia
aka **Zora Kerova / Zora Keer / Zora Kerowa**

Eva, sex show performer in ***The New York Ripper***
Virginia Field in ***Touch of Death***
succubus in ***The Ghosts of Sodom***
woman in bath in ***Hansel and Gretel***
Virginia Field and Mary [two roles] in ***Nightmare Concert***

1976 *La casa dalle finestre che ridono* (IT) aka *The House with Laughing Windows* [uncredited] – dir: Pupi Avati
1978 *Fratello crudele* (IT) – dir: Mario De Rosa [unreleased]
1978 *American Fever* (IT) – dir: Claudio De Molinis
1978 *Le evase – Storie di sesso e di violenza* (IT) US *Escape from Women's Prison* UKvdt *Jail Birds / Sexual Freedom* – dir: Conrad Brueghel [Giovanni Brusadori]
1979 *Krehké vztahy* (CZ) – dir: Juraj Herz
1979 *La ragazza del vagone letto* (IT) UKvdt *Terror Express!* – dir: Ferdinando Baldi
1980 *Antropophagus* (IT) US *The Grim Reaper* UKvdt *Anthropophagus the Beast* – dir: Joe D'Amato [Aristide Massaccesi]
1980 *La vera storia della monaca di Monza* (IT) export title *The True Story of the Nun of Monza* – dir: Stefan Oblowsky [Bruno Mattei]
1980 *Contes pervers* (FR/IT) IT *Ragazze in affitto S.p.A.* UK *Erotic Tales / Tales of Erotic Fantasies* – dir: Régine Desforges [Michel Lemoine]
1981 *Krakonos a lyzníci* (CZ) – dir: Vera Plívová-Simková
1981 *Cannibal Ferox* (IT) US *Make Them Die Slowly* – dir: Umberto Lenzi
1981 *Retez* (CZ) – dir: Jiri Svoboda
1982 *Lo squartatore di New York* (IT) export title ***The New York Ripper*** – dir: Lucio Fulci
1982 *Sny o zambezi* (CZ) – dir: Stanlislav Strnad
1983 *I nuovi barbari* (IT) US *Warriors of the Wasteland* UK *The New Barbarians* – dir: Enzo G. Castellari [Enzo Girolami]
1983 *Vítr v kapse* (CZ) – dir: Jaroslav Soukup
1984 *Fesák Hubert* (CZ) – dir: Ivo Novák
1984 *Andel s dáblem v tele* (CZ) – dir: Václav Matejka
1985 *Skalpel, prosím* (CZ) – dir: Jirí Svoboda
1986 *Perinbaba* (CZ/WG/IT/AT) WG/ITvdt *Frau Hölle* – dir: Juraj Jakubisko
1986 *Operace me dcery* (CZ) – dir: Ivo Novák
1988 *Quando Alice ruppe lo specchio* (IT) export title ***Touch of Death*** – dir: Lucio Fulci
1988 *Andel svádí dábla* (CZ) – dir: Václav Matejka
1988 *Sodoma's Ghost* (IT) export title ***The Ghosts of Sodom*** [uncredited] – dir: Lucio Fulci
1988 *Hansel e Gretel* (IT) aka ***Hansel and Gretel*** [uncredited] – dir: Giovanni Simonelli & [uncredited] Lucio Fulci
1989 *Luna di sangue / Fuga dalla morte* (IT) – dir: Enzo Milioni
1990 *La luna nel pozzo* (IT) (tv movie) – dir: Enzo Balestrieri
1990 Un gatto nel cervello (I volti del terrore) (IT) export title ***Nightmare Concert*** aka Nightmare Concert (A Cat in the Brain) [uncredited] – dir: Lucio Fulci

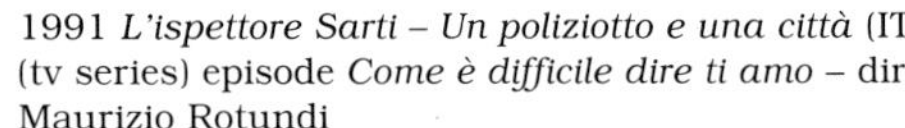

1991 *L'ispettore Sarti – Un poliziotto e una città* (IT) (tv series) episode *Come è difficile dire ti amo* – dir: Maurizio Rotundi
1995 *Mollo tutto* (IT) export title *I'll Leave It All Behind Me* – dir: José María Sánchez
1995 *Altrove* (IT) – dir: Enzo Balestrieri
1996 *Papà dice messa* (IT) – dir: Renato Pozzetto
2001 *Resurrezione* (IT/FR/GER) (tv movie) aka *Resurrection* – dir: Paolo Taviani & Vittorio Taviani
2006 *La radice del male* (IT) aka *The Root of Evil* – dir: Silvana Zancolo
2012 *Líbás jako dábel* (CZE) – dir: Marie Poledňáková

Sylva Koscina

born 22 August 1933 in Zagreb, Yugoslavia
died 26 December 1994 in Rome, Italy

Marisa in ***La massaggiatrici***
Mariù Nicosia in ***Young Dracula***

1955 *Siamo uomini o caporali* (IT) aka *Are We Men or Corporals?* – dir: Camillo Mastrocinque
1956 *Il ferroviere* (IT) UK *Man of Iron* US *The Railroad Man* – dir: Pietro Germi
1956 *Michel Strogoff* (FR/IT/YUG) IT *Michele Strogoff* US *Michael Strogoff* – dir: Carmine Gallone
1957 *Guendalina* (IT/FR) – dir: Alberto Lattuada
1957 *La nonna Sabella* (IT/FR) UK *Oh! Sabella* – dir: Dino Risi
1957 *La Gerusalemme liberata* (IT) US/UK *The Mighty Crusaders* – dir: Carlo Ludovico Bragaglia
1957 *I fidanzati della morte* (IT) – dir: Romolo Marcellini
1957 *Femmine tre volte* (IT/SP) SP *Operacíon Popoff* – dir: Steno [Stefano Vanzina]
1957 *Giovani mariti* (IT/FR) FR *Les jeunes maris* – dir: Mauro Bolognini
1957 *La naïf aux quarante enfants* (FR) – dir: Philippe Agostini
1957 *Non sono più guaglione (Oh, mia bella Carolina!)* (IT/FR) – dir: Domenico Paolella
1958 *Ladro lui, ladra lei* (IT) – dir: Luigi Zampa
1958 *Le fatiche di Ercole* (IT) US/UK *Hercules* – dir: Pietro Francisci
1958 *Racconti d'estate* (IT/FR) FR *Femmes d'un été* US *Love on the Riviera* UK *Girls for the Summer* – dir: Gianni Franciolini
1958 *Totò a Parigi* (IT/FR) FR *Parisien malgré lui* – dir: Camillo Mastrocinque
1958 *Quando gli angeli piangono* (IT) – dir: Marino Girolami
1958 *La nipote Sabella* (IT) – dir: Giorgio Bianchi
1958 *Mogli pericolose* (IT) – dir: Luigi Comencini
1958 *Totò nella luna* (IT) – dir: Steno [Stefano Vanzina]
1959 *Le confident de ces dames* (FR/IT) IT *Psicanalista per signora* – dir: Jean Boyer
1959 *Ercole e la regina di Lidia* (IT/FR) FR *Hercule et la reine de Lydie* US/UK *Hercules Unchained* – dir: Pietro Francisci
1959 *Poveri milionari* (IT) – dir: Dino Risi
1959 *La cambiale* (IT) – dir: Camillo Mastrocinque
1959 *Le sorprese dell'amore* (IT) – dir: Luigi Comencini
1959 *Tempi duri per i vampiri* (IT) US *Uncle Was a Vampire* – dir: Steno [Stefano Vanzina]
1960 *L'assedio di Siracusa (Archimede)* (IT/FR) FR *La charge de Syracuse* US/UK television title *The Siege of Syracuse* – dir: Pietro Francisci
1960 *Genitori in blue jeans* (IT) – dir: Camillo Mastrocinque
1960 *Les distractions* (FR/IT) IT *Le distrazioni* UK *Trapped By Fear* – dir: Jacques Dupont
1960 *Ravissante* (FR/IT) IT *Le mogli degli altri* – dir: Robert Lamoureux
1960 *Le pillole di Ercole* (IT) – dir: Luciano Salce
1960 *Il piacere dello scapolo* (IT) – dir: Giulio Petroni
1960 *Il vigile* (IT) – dir: Luigi Zampa
1960 *Crimen* (IT/FR) FR *Chacun son alibi* UK *Killing in Monte Carlo* US *...and Suddenly It's Murder!* – dir: Mario Camerini [cameo]
1960 *Femmine di lusso* (IT) US *Love, the Italian Way* – dir: George White [Giorgio Bianchi]
1960 *Mariti in pericolo* (IT) – dir: Mauro Morassi
1961 *Il sicario* (IT) – dir: Damiano Damiani

1961 *Mani in alto* (IT/FR) FR *En pleine bagarre* US *Destination Fury* – dir: Giorgio Bianchi
1962 *La congiura dei dieci (Lo spadaccino di Sienna)* (IT/FR) FR *Le Mercenaire* US/UK *Swordsman of Siena* – dir: Baccio Bandini
1962 *Jessica* (IT/FR) FR *La sage-femme... le curé et le bon Dieu* – dir: Oreste Palella (supervising dir: Jean Negulesco)
1962 *I giacobini* (IT) (tv mini-series) – dir: Giorgio Strehler
1962 *Copacabana Palace* (IT/FR) US *Girl Game* – dir: Steno [Stefano Vanzina]
1962 *Les quatre vérités* (FR/IT/SP) IT *Le quattro verità* SP *Las cuatro verdades* UK *The Three Fables of Love* segment *Le lièvre et la tortue* – dir: Alessandro Blasetti [other dir's: Hervé Bromberger, René Clair & Luis García Berlanga]
1962 *Le masque de fer* (FR/IT) IT *L'uomo dalla maschera di ferro* – dir: Henri Decoin
1962 *Le massaggiatrici* (IT/FR) FR *Les faux jetons* – dir: Lucio Fulci
1962 *La salamandre d'or* (FR/IT) IT *Il paladino della corte di Francia* [uncredited] – dir: Maurice Régamey
1963 *Il giorno più corto* (IT) US television title *The Shortest Day* – dir: Sergio Corbucci
1963 *Cyrano et d'Artagnan* (FR/IT/SP) IT *Cyrano e d'Artagnan* SP *Cyrano y D'Artagnan* – dir: Abel Gance
1963 *Hot Enough for June* (UK) US *Agent 8¾* aka *Agent Eight and Three Quarters* – dir: Ralph Thomas
1963 *Il fornaretto di Venezia* (IT/FR) FR *Le procès des Doges* – dir: Duccio Tessari
1963 *Judex* (FR/IT) IT *L'uomo in nero* – dir: Georges Franju
1963 *Le monachine* (IT) US *The Little Nuns* – dir: Luciano Salce
1963 *L'appartement des filles* (FR/IT/WG) IT *L'appartamento delle ragazze* WG *Gangster, Gold und flotte Mädchen* – dir: Michel Deville
1964 *Se permettete parliamo di donne* (IT/FR) FR *Parlons femmes* US *Let's Talk About Women* – dir: Ettore Scola
1964 *Amore in 4 dimensioni* (IT/FR) FR *L'amour en quatre dimensions* US *Love in 4 Dimensions* segment *Amore e vita* – dir: Jacques Romain [other dir's: Gianni Puccini, Massimo Mida & Mino Guerrini]
1964 *Cadavere per signora* (IT) – dir: Mario Mattòli
1964 *Le grain de sable* (FR/WG/IT/POR) IT *Il triangolo circolare* WG *Die Unmoralischen* – dir: Pierre Kast
1964 *L'idea fissa* (IT) US *Love and Marriage* segment *Sabato 18 luglio* – dir: Gianni Puccini [other dir: Mino Guerrini]
1964 *Una storia di notte* (IT) – dir: Luigi Petrini
1965 *L'arme à gauche* (FR/SP/IT) SP *Armas para el Caribe* IT *Corpo a corpo* UK *Guns for the Dictator* – dir: Claude Sautet
1965 *Le lit à deux places* (FR/IT) IT *Racconti a due piazze* segment *Un Monsieur de passage* – dir: François Dupont Midy [other dir's: Jean Delannoy, Alvaro Mancori & Gianni Puccini]
1965 *Giulietta degli spiriti* (IT/FR/WG) FR *Juliette des esprits* WG *Julia und die Geister* UK *Juliet of the Spirits* – dir: Federico Fellini
1965 *Estambul 65* (SP/IT/FR/WG) IT *Colpo grosso a Galata Bridge* FR *L'homme d'Istanbul* W. GER *Unser Mann aus Istanbul* US/UK *That Man in Istanbul* – dir: Anthony Isasi [Antonio Isasi-Isasmendi]
1965 *Thrilling* (IT) segment *Il vittimista* – dir: Carlo Lizzani [other dir's: Ettore Scola & Gian Luigi Polidoro]
1965 *Il morbidone* (IT/FR) – dir: Massimo Franciosa
1965 *Made in Italy* (IT/FR) FR *A l'italienne* – dir: Nanni Loy
1965 *I soldi* (IT) – dir: Gianni Puccini
1966 *Monnaie de singe* (FR/IT/SP) IT *I sette falsari* SP *La viuda soltera* UK *Monkey Money* – dir: Yves Robert
1966 *Baraka sur X 13* (FR/SP/IT) SP *Operación silencio* IT *Agente X 77 ordine di uccidere* – dir: [FR]: Maurice Cloche; dir [IT]: Edgar Lawson [Silvio Siano]
1966 *Io, io, io... e gli altri (Conferenza con proiezioni)* (IT/FR) – dir: Alessandro Blasetti
1966 *Three Bites of the Apple* (US) – dir: Alvin Ganzer
1966 *Deadlier Than the Male* (UK) – dir: Ralph Thomas

1966 *Carré de dames pour un as* (FR/SP/IT) SP *Demasiadas mujeres para Layton* IT *Layton... bambole e karaté* – dir: Jacques Poitrenaud
1966 *Les fables de La Fontaine* (FR) (tv series) episode *Le lièvre et la tortue* – dir: Alessandro Blasetti
1967 *Johnny Banco* (FR/IT/WG) WG *Jonny Banco – geliebter Taugenichts* – dir: Yves Allégret
1968 *I protagonisti* (IT) – dir: Marcello Fondato
1968 *The Secret War of Harry Frigg* (US) – dir: Jack Smight
1968 *A Lovely Way to Die* (US) – dir: David Lowell Rich
1968 *Kampf um Rom 1. Teil* (WG/IT/ROU) IT *La guerra per Roma Prima parte / La calata dei barbari* ROU *Lupta Pentru Roma* – dir: Robert Siodmak
1969 *Kampf um Rom 2. Teil Der Verrat* (WG/IT/ROU) IT *La guerra per Roma Seconda parte* ROU *Lupta Pentru Roma* – dir: Robert Siodmak
1969 *Marquis de Sade: Justine* (WG/IT/UK) IT *Justine ovvero le disavventure della virtù* UK *Justine and Juliet* US *Marquis de Sade: Justine / Justine* USvdt *Deadly Sanctuary* – dir: Jess Franco [Jesús Franco Manera]
1969 *Bitka na Neretvi* (YUG/US/IT/WG) US/UK *Battle of Neretva* IT *La battaglia della Neretva* WG *Die Schlacht an der Neretva* US *The Battle on the River Neretva* – dir: Veljko Bulajic
1969 *Fight for Rome / The Last Roman* [combined English language version of both *Kampf um Rom* films]
1969 *L'assoluto naturale* (IT) – dir: Mauro Bolognini
1969 *Vedo nudo* (IT) aka *I See It Naked* segment *La diva* – dir: Dino Risi
1970 *I lupi attaccano in branco* (IT/US) US *Hornet's Nest* – dir [IT]: Franco Cirino, [US]: Phil Karlson
1970 *Vertige pour un tueur* (FR/IT) IT *Vertigine per un assassino* export title *Nightmare for a Killer* – dir: Jean-Pierre Desagnat
1970 *Ninì Tirabusciò, la donna che inventò la mossa* (IT) – dir: Marcello Fondato
1970 *La colomba non deve volare* (IT/WG) export title *Skyriders Attack* – dir: Sergio Garrone
1970 *La modification* (FR/IT) IT *La moglie nuova* – dir: Michel Worms
1971 *Mazzabubù... Quante corna stanno quaggiù?* (IT) – dir: Mariano Laurenti
1971 *Sesso del diavolo (Trittico)* (IT) – dir: Oscar Brazzi
1971 *No desearás la mujer del vecino* (SP/IT) IT *La strana legge del dottor Menga* – dir: Fernando Merino
1971 *Homo eroticus* (IT/FR) US *Man of the Year* – dir: Marco Vicario
1971 *Les jambes en l'air* (FR/IT) IT *Week-end proibito di una famiglia quasi per bene* – dir: Jean Dewever
1971 *African story* (IT/ZA) ZA *The Manipulator* – dir: Fred Wilson [Marino Girolami]
1972 *Historia de una traición* (SP/IT) IT *Diabolicamente sole con il delitto / Nel buio del terrore* export title *A Treason Story: Carla and Nora* US *The Great Swindle* – dir: José Antonio Nieves Conde
1972 *Boccaccio* (IT/FR) – dir: Bruno Corbucci
1972 *Uccidere in silenzio* (IT) – dir: Giuseppe Rolando
1972 *Sette scialli di seta gialla* (IT) export title *The Crimes of The Black Cat* – dir: Sergio Pastore
1972 *Beati i ricchi* (IT) – dir: Salvatore Samperi
1972 *La mala ordina* (IT/WG) WG *Der Mafia-boß – Sie töten wie schakale* UK/US *Manhunt in Milan* US *Manhunt / The Italian Connection* UK *The Hit Men* USvdt *Hired to Kill* UKvdt *Man on the Run* – dir: Fernando Di Leo
1972 *Lisa e il diavolo* (IT/SP/WG) SP *El diablo se lleva a los muertos* UKvdt *Lisa and the Devil* – dir: Mario Bava [unreleased in Italy – re-edited, with added footage, and released circa 1975 as *La casa dell'escorcismo* UKvdt *The House of Exorcism* – credited to Mickey Lion [Bava & Alfredo Leone]]
1972 *Rivelazioni di un maniaco sessuale al capo della squadra mobile* (IT) US *The Slasher... Is the Sex Maniac* export title *So Sweet, So Dead* aka *Bad Girls* – dir: Roberto Montero [re-edited with additional hardcore material & released in the US as *Penetration* in 1976]
1973 *Il tuo piacere è il mio* (IT) – dir: Claudio Racca
1974 *Un par de zapatos del 32* (SP/IT) IT *Qualcuno ha visto uccidere... (Unica traccia un paio di scarpe n. 32)* US *The Student Connection* – dir: Rafael Romero Marchent
1974 *Delitto d'autore* (IT) – dir: Anthony Green [Mario Sabatini]
1974 *Las correrias del Vizconde Arnau* (SP) – dir: Joaquín Coll
1975 *Il Cav. Costante Nicosia Demoniaco, ovvero: Dracula in Brianza* (IT) export title ***Young Dracula*** – dir: Lucio Fulci
1977 *Casanova & Co.* (AT/IT/FR/WG) FR *Treize femmes pour Casanova* UK *The Rise and Rise of Casanova* US *Some Like It Cool* USvdt *Sex on the Run* – dir: François Legrand [Franz Antel]
1980 *Les séducteurs* (FR/IT) IT *I seduttori della domenica* US *Sunday Lovers* segment *Armando's Notebook* – dir: Dino Risi [other dir's: Bryan Forbes, Edouard Molinaro & Gene Wilder]
1981 *Asso* (IT) – dir: [Franco] Castellano & Pipolo [Giuseppe Moccia]
1982 *Cercasi Gesù* (IT/FR) FR *L'imposteur* – dir: Luigi Comencini
1982 *Stelle emigranti* (IT) (tv movie) – dir's: Francesco Bortolini & Claudio Masenza
1983 *Die Nacht der vier Monde* (WG/YUG) – dir: Jörg A. Eggers
1983 *E la vita continua* (IT) (tv movie) – dir: Dino Risi
1983 *Questo e quello* (IT) aka *His and Her* segment *Quello col basco rosso* – dir: Sergio Corbucci
1983 *Mani di fata* (IT) aka *The Magic Touch* – dir: Steno [Stefano Vanzina]
1983 *Cenerentola 80* (IT/FR) – dir: Roberto Malenotti
1987 *Rimini Rimini* (IT) – dir: Sergio Corbucci
1987 *Una grande storia d'amore* (IT) (tv mini-series) export title *A Great Love Story* – dir: DuccioTessari
1991 *L'odissea* (IT) (tv movie) – dir: Giuseppe Recchia
1992 *Ricky & Barabba* (IT) – dir: Christian De Sica
1994 *David e David* (IT) (tv movie) – dir: Giorgio Capitani
1994 *C'è Kim Novak al telefono* (IT) aka *Kim Novak Is on the Phone* – dir: Enrico Roseo

Dagmar Lassander

born 16 June 1943 in Prague, Czechoslovakia
real name **Dagmar Regine Hader**

Lillian Grayson in ***The Black Cat***
Laura Gittleson in ***The House by the Cemetery***

1966 *Sperrbezirk* (WG) – dir: Will Tremper
1967 *Der Mörderclub von Brooklyn* (WG) – dir: Werner Jacobs
1967 *Orgel und Rakete* (WG) (tv movie) – dir: Ferry Olsen
1967 *Strassenbekanntschaften auf St. Pauli* (WG) – dir: Werner Klingler
1968 *Quartett im Bett* (WG) – dir: Ulrich Schamoni
1968 *Andrea – Wie ein blatt auf nackter Haut* (WG) UK *Andrea / The Nympho* UKvdt *Andrea the Nympho* – dir: Hans Schott-Schöbinger
1969 *Femina ridens* (IT) US/UKvdt *The Frightened Woman* – dir: Piero Schivazappa
1969 *Von Haut zu Haut* (WG) re-release title *Nicki und Karin Von haut zu haut* UK *Skin to Skin* – dir: Hans Schott-Schöbinger
1969 *Il rosso segno della follia Un'accetta per la luna di miele* (IT/SP) SP *Un hacha para la luna de miel* UK *Blood Brides* US/USvdt *A Hatchet for the Honeymoon* – dir: Mario Bava
1969 *El gran crucero* (SP/ARG) – dir: José G. Maesso
1970 *Un caso di coscienza* (IT) – dir: Gianni [Giovanni] Grimaldi
1970 *Le foto proibite di una signora per bene* (IT/SP) SP *Días de angustia* export title *The Forbidden Photos of a Lady Above Suspicion* – dir: Luciano Ercoli
1971 *L'iguana dalla lingua di fuoco* (IT/FR/WG) export title *The Iguana with the Tongue of Fire* – dir: Willy Pareto [Riccardo Freda]
1972 *Guardami nuda* (IT) shooting title *Germoglio nera* – dir: Italo Alfaro
1973 *Il consigliori* (IT/SP) SP *El consejero* UK *The Counsellor* – dir: Alberto De Martino
1974 *Una donna per sette bastardi* (IT) export title *The Sewer Rats* – dir: Roberto Montero
1974 *Verginità* (IT) – dir: Marcello Andrei
1974 *Adolescence pervertie* (FR/IT) IT *Adolescenza perversa* [uncredited] – dir: José Benazeraf
1974 *Basta con la guerra... facciamo l'amore!* (IT) – dir: Andrea Bianchi
1974 *Pusteblume* (WG) UK *Hard to Remember / Dandelion* shooting title *Der wilde Blonde mit der heißen Maschine* – dir: Adrian Hoven
1975 *Lo stallone* (IT) aka *The Stallion* – dir: Tiziano Longo
1975 *Il vizio ha le calze nere* (IT) export title *Reflections in Black* – dir: Tano [Gaetano] Cimarosa
1975 *Frittata all'italiana* (IT) re-released as *La spacconata* – dir: Alfonso Brescia
1975 *Il torcinaso* (IT/FR) re-release title *Quando il sangue diventa bollente* shooting title *La venere del Piero* – dir: John Hencken [Giancarlo Romitelli]
1975 *Peccati di gioventù* (IT) UKvdt *So Young, Lovely and Vicious* – dir: Silvio Amadio
1976 *La lupa mannara* (IT) US/USvdt *Legend of the Wolf Woman* UK/UKvdt *Werewolf Woman* UKvdt *Naked Werewolf Woman* USvdt *Legend of the She-Wolf / She-Wolf* – dir: Rino Di Silvestro
1976 *L'adolescente* (IT) ITvdt *L'adolescente – La gioventù è bella* – dir: Alfonso Brescia
1976 *Il corsaro nero* (IT) US *The Black Pirate* – dir: Sergio Sollima
1976 *Gli amici di Nick Hezard* (IT) UK *Nick the Sting* – dir: Fernando Di Leo
1976 *Atti impuri all'italiana (Scherzando e ridendo... Che male to fo?)* (IT) – dir: Oscar Brazzi
1976 *Classe mista* (IT) – dir: Mariano Laurenti
1976 *La prima notte di nozze* (IT) – dir: Corrado Prisco
1976 *Il comune senso del pudore* (IT) – dir: Alberto Sordi
1976 *Puttana galera! / Colpo grosso al penitenziario* (IT) export title *The Hokey-Pokey Gang!* – dir: Gianfranco Piccioli
1976 *Sfida sul fondo* (IT) UKvdt *Sacha the Wonderdog / Duel of the Deep* – dir: Melchiade Coletti
1976 *Emanuelle nera n. 2* (IT) UK/UKvdt *The New Black Emmanuelle* export title *Black Emanuelle 2* – dir: Albert Thomas [Adalberto Albertini]
1977 *Zavrashtane ot Rim* (BUL) (tv series) – dir: Ilya Velchev
1977 *Ritornano quelli della calibro 38* (IT) USvdt *Gangsters* – dir: Joseph Warren [Giuseppe Vari]
1977 *Niñas... al salón* (SP) – dir: Vicente Escrivá
1977 *Piedone l'Africano* (IT/WG) WG *Platfuß in Afrika* export title *Knock-Out Cop* – dir: Steno [Stefano Vanzina]
1978 *I gabbiani volano basso* (IT) export title *Seagulls Fly Low* – dir: George Warner [Giorgio Cristallini]
1979 *Racconti fantastici* (IT) (tv mini-series) episode *Ligeia forever* – dir: Daniele D'Anza
1980 *Zucchero, miele e peperoncino* (IT) – dir: Sergio Martino
1981 *Black cat* (IT) US/UKvdt ***The Black Cat*** – dir: Lucio Fulci
1981 *Quella villa accanto al cimitero* (IT) US/UK ***The House by the Cemetery*** – dir: Lucio Fulci
1982 *S.A.S. Terreur a San Salvador* (FR/WG) WG *S.A.S. Malko Im Auftrag des Pentagon* UKvdt/US *S.A.S. Terminate with Extreme Prejudice* – dir: Raoul Coutard
1982 *W la foca* (IT) – dir: Nando [Fernando] Cicero
1983 *Occhio malocchio prezzemolo e finocchio* (IT) segment *Il pelo della disgrazia* – dir: Sergio Martino
1983 *E la vita continua* (IT) (tv movie) – dir: Dino Risi
1984 *Delitto in formula uno* (IT) – dir: Bruno Corbucci
1984 *Shark: Rosso nell'oceano* (IT/FR) FR *Apocalypse dans l'ocean rouge* UKvdt *Devouring Waves* WG *Monster Shark* aka *Devil Fish* – dir: John Old Jr. [Lamberto Bava]
1985 *Das Wunder* (WG) – dir: Eckhardt Schmidt
1985 *Il piacere* (IT) UK *The Pleasure* – dir: Joe D'Amato [Aristide Massaccesi]
1985 *Aeroporto internazionale* (IT) (tv series) – dir: Enzo Tarquini et al.
1986 *La piovra 2* (IT) (tv series) export title *The Octopus 2* – dir: Florestano Vancini
1987 *Cerco l'amore* (IT) (tv movie) – dir: Paolo Fondato
1987 *La famiglia* (IT/FR) FR *La famille* – dir: Ettore Scola
1987 *I ragazzi della 3aC* (IT) (tv series) – dir: Claudio Risi
1988 *Topo Galileo* (IT) – dir: Francesco Laudadio
1988 *L'igranaggio* (IT) (tv mini-series) – dir: Silvero Blasi
1989 *Affari di famiglia* (IT) (tv movie) – dir: Marcello Fondato
1991 *Passi d'amore* (IT) (tv mini-series) – dir: Sergio Sollima
1991 *I ragazzi del muretto* (IT) (tv series) – dir: Tomaso Sherman
1994 *Alles Glück dieser Erde* (GER) (tv series) – dir: Michael Werlin [Michael Meyer]
1994 *L'ispettore Sarti – Un poliziotto, una città* (IT) (tv series) episode *Il patto* – dir: Giulio Questi
2016 *Tommaso* (IT) – dir: Kim Rossi Stuart
2018 *Due piccoli italiani* (IT/ICE) aka *Two Little Italians* – dir: Paolo Sassanelli

Veronica Lazar

born 6 October 1938 in Bucharest, Romania
died 8 June 2014 in Rome, Italy

Martha in ***The Beyond***

1972 *Ultimo tango a Parigi* (IT/FR) FR *Dernier tango à Paris* UK/US *Last Tango in Paris* – dir: Bernardo Bertolucci
1978 *Le affinità elettive* (IT) (tv movie) – dir: Gianni Amico
1979 *La luna* (IT) – dir: Bernardo Bertolucci
1980 *Inferno* (IT) – dir: Dario Argento
1980 *Giacinta* (IT) (tv mini-series) – dir: Gianluigi Calderone
1981 *L'aldilà* (IT) US *Seven Doors of Death* UK ***The Beyond*** – dir: Lucio Fulci
1981 *Les ailes de la colombe* (FR/IT) IT *Storia di donne* aka *The Wings of the Dove* – dir: Benoît Jacquot
1982 *Identificazione di una donna* (IT/FR) FR *Identification d'une femme* US *Identification of a Woman* – dir: Michelangelo Antonioni
1984 *Un caso d'incoscienza* (IT) – dir: Emidio Greco [released in 1989]
1987 *Io e mia sorella* (IT) – dir: Carlo Verdone
1989 *Berlin-Jérusalem* (FR) – dir: Amos Gitai
1989 *Summer's Lease* (UK/US) (tv mini-series) – dir: Martyn Friend
1990 *Verso sera* (IT/FR) FR *Dans la soirée* – dir: Francesca Archibugi

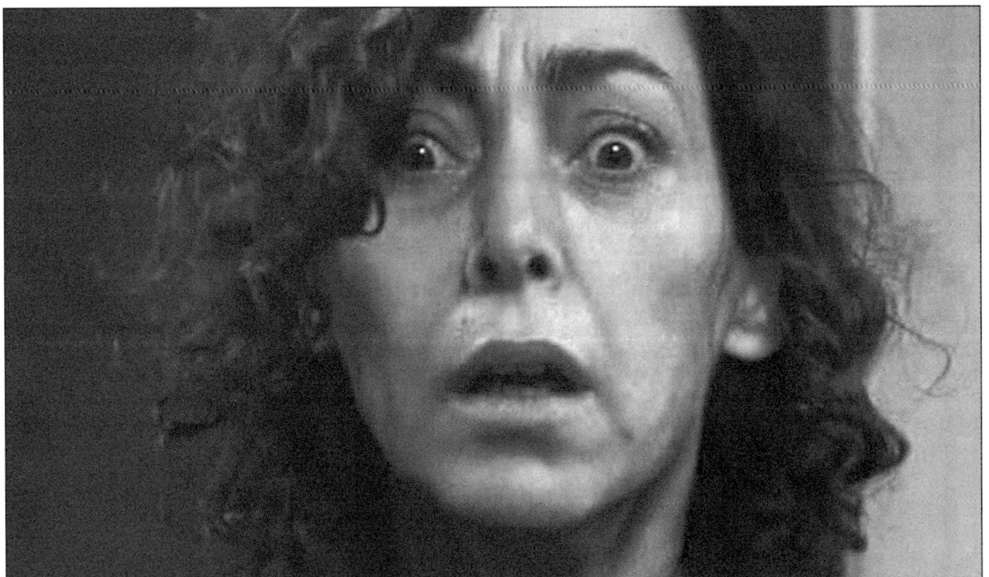

1990 *Il sole buio* (IT) – dir: Damiano Damiani
1990 *The Sheltering Sky* (UK/IT) IT *Tè nel deserto* – dir: Bernardo Bertolucci
1991 *La storia spezzata* (IT/GER) (tv movie) GER *Herzen im Sturm* aka *Sieg der Liebe* – dir: Andrea & Antonia Frazzi
1993 *La bionda* (IT) – dir: Sergio Rubini
1995 *Par-delà les nuages* (FR/IT/GER) IT *Al di là delle nuvole* GER *Jenseits der Wolken* UK *Beyond the Clouds* – dir: Michelangelo Antonioni & Wim Wenders
1995 *La storia di Chiara* (IT/GER) (tv movie) – dir: Andrea Frazzi & Antonio Frazzi
1996 *La sindrome di Stendhal* (IT) export title *The Stendhal Syndrome* – dir: Dario Argento
1998 *Besieged* (IT/UK) – dir: Bernardo Bertolucci
2000 *Il manoscritto del principe* (IT) aka *The Prince's Manuscript* – dir: Roberto Andò
2001 *L'impero* (IT) (tv mini-series) aka *Human Currency* – dir: Lamberto Bava
2002 *Ginostra* (FR/IT/US) – dir: Manuel Pradal
2002 *Lara* (BRA) – dir: Ana Maria Magalhães
2012 *6 passi nel giallo* (IT/MLT) (tv mini-series) episode *Gemelle* – dir: Fabrizio Bava
2012 *Io e te* (IT) aka *Me and You* – dir: Bernardo Bertolucci
2014 *Il giovane favoloso* (IT) aka *Leopardi* – dir: Mario Martone

Margaret Lee

born 4 August 1943 in Wolverhampton, England
died 24 April 2024 in Wolverhampton, England
real name **Margaret Gwendolyn Box**

Nurse Adelina in ***Gli imbroglioni***
Rosalynn in ***I maniaci***
Floriana in ***I due pericoli pubblici***

1962 *Maciste contro i mostri* (IT) UK *Colossus of the Stone Age* – dir: Guido Malatesta
1962 *I tre nemici* (IT) – dir: Giorgio C. Simonelli
1962 *Due samurai per cento geishe* (IT) – dir: Giorgio C. Simonelli
1962 *Totò di notte n. 1* (IT) – dir: Mario Amendola
1962 *Vino, whisky e acqua salata* (IT) – dir: Mario Amendola
1963 *Avventura al motel* (IT) – dir: Renato Polselli
1963 *Cleopatra* (UK/US/SWI) [uncredited] – dir: Joseph L. Mankiewicz, Rouben Mamoulian [uncredited] & Darryl F. Zanuck [uncredited]
1963 *Sansone contro i pirati* (IT) – dir: Amerigo Anton [Tanio Boccia]
1963 *La ballata dei mariti* (IT/SP) SP *La balada de los maridos* – dir: Fabrizio Taglioni
1963 ***Gli imbroglioni*** (IT/SP) SP *Los mangantes* – dir: Lucio Fulci
1963 *Siamo tutti pomicioni* (IT) – dir: Marino Girolami
1963 *I quattro tassisti* (IT) segment *Un'opera buona* – dir: Giorgio Bianchi
1964 *Due mattacchioni al Moulin Rouge* (IT) – dir: Carlo Infascelli
1964 ***I maniaci*** (IT) – dir: Lucio Fulci
1964 *La vedovella* (IT/FR) – dir: Silvio Siano
1964 *I marziani hanno 12 mani* (IT/SP) SP *Llegaron los marcianos* – dir: [Franco] Castellano & Pipolo [Giuseppe Moccia]
1964 *Questo pazzo, pazzo mondo della canzone* (IT) – dir: Bruno Corbucci & Gianni [Giovanni] Grimaldi
1964 *In ginocchio da te* (IT) – dir: Ettore Maria Fizzarotti
1964 *Un mostro e mezzo* (IT) – dir: Steno [Stefano Vanzina]
1964 *Adolescenti al sole* (IT) – dir: Rossaldo [Aldo Rossi]
1964 *Via Veneto* (IT) – dir: Giuseppe Lipartiti
1965 ***I due pericoli pubblici*** (IT) – dir: Lucio Fulci
1965 *Casanova '70* (IT/FR) FR Casanova – dir: Mario Monicelli
1965 *Questa volta parliamo di uomini* (IT) US *Let's Talk About Men* segment *Un uomo superiore* – dir: Lina Wertmüller
1965 *Io uccido, tu uccidi* (IT/FR) segment *La danza delle ore* – dir: Gianni Puccini
1965 *La ragazzola* (IT) – dir: Giuseppe Orlandini
1965 *Agente 077 Dall'Oriente con furore* (IT/FR/SP) FR *Fureur sur le Bosphore* SP *Paris-Estambul, sin regreso* UK *From the Orient with Fury* – dir: Terence Hathaway [Sergio Grieco]

1965 *Le tigre se parfume à la dynamite* (FR/IT/SP) IT *La tigre profumata alla dinamite* SP *El tigre se perfuma con dinamita* UK *An Orchid for the Tiger* – dir: Claude Chabrol
1965 *On a volé la Joconde* (FR/IT) IT *Il ladro della Gioconda* / *Le avventure di Golden Boy* – dir: Michel Deville
1965 *I due sergenti del generale Custer* (IT/SP) SP *Dos rivales en Fuerte Alamo (Dos evalidos de Fort Alamo)* – dir: Giorgio C. Simonelli
1965 *Letti sbagliati* (IT) segment *00-Sexy missione Bionda Platino* – dir: Steno [Stefano Vanzina]
1965 *Il morbidone* (IT/FR) – dir: Massimo Franciosa
1965 *Le lit à deux places* (FR/IT) IT *Racconti a due piazze* segment *Mourir pour vivre* – dir: Gianni Puccini [other dir's: Jean Delannoy, Alvaro Mancori & François Dupont Midy]
1966 *Lo scippo* (IT) – dir: Nando [Fernando] Cicero
1966 *New York chiama Superdrago* (IT/FR/WG) FR *New York appelle Super Dragon* WG *Höllenjagd auf heiße Ware* US television title *Secret Agent Super Dragon* – dir: Calvin Jackson Padget [Giorgio Ferroni]
1966 *Gern hab'ich die Frauen gekillt* (AT/IT/FR) IT *Spie contro il mondo* FR *Le Carnaval des barbouzes* US *Requiem for a Secret Agent* / *Killer's Carnival* UK *Carnival of Killers* – dir: Albert Cardiff [Alberto Cardone], Robert Lynn & Sheldon Reynolds
1966 *Circus of Fear* (UK) US *Psycho-Circus* / *Circus of Terror* – dir: John Moxey
1966 *Our Man in Marrakesh* (UK) US *Bang! Bang! You're Dead* – dir: Don Sharp
1966 *Se tutte le donne del mondo... Operazione Paradiso* (IT) US *Kiss the Girls and Make Them Die* – dir: Dino [Arduino] Maiuri
1966 *Tre notti violente* (IT/SP) SP *Tres noches violentas* US *Web of Violence* – dir: Nick Nostro
1966 *Djurado* (IT/SP) SP *Jim Golden Poker* – dir: John V. Narciss [Gianni Narzisi]
1967 *Da Berlino l'Apocalisse* (IT/FR/WG) FR *Le tigre sort sans sa mère* WG *Heisses Pflaster für Spione* UK *The Spy Pit* – dir: Mario Maffei
1967 *Dick Smart 2. 007* (IT) – dir: Frank Shannon [Francesco Prosperi]
1967 *Questi fantasmi* (IT/FR) FR *Fantômes à l'italienne* UK *Ghosts, Italian Style* – dir: Renato Castellani
1967 *Colpo maestro al servizio di sua Maestà Britannica* (IT/SP) SP *Gran golpe al servicio de su Majestad Británica* UK *The Great Diamond Robbery* US *Master Stroke* – dir: Michele Lupo
1967 *Arriva Dorellik* (IT) UKvdt *How to Kill 400 Dupont* – dir: Steno [Stefano Vanzina]
1967 *Five Golden Dragons* (UK/WG) WG *Die Pagode zum fünften Schrecken* – dir: Jeremy Summers
1967 *Le soleil des voyous* (FR/IT) IT *Il più grande colpo del secolo* WG *Action Man* US *Leather and Nylon* – dir: Jean Delannoy
1968 *Il cenerentolo* (IT) (tv movie) – dir: Flaminio Bollini
1968 *Coplan sauve sa peau* (FR/IT) IT *L'assassino ha le ore contate* US *Requiem for a Snake* UK *Devil's Garden* – dir: Yves Boisset
1968 *Banditi a Milano* (IT) US *The Violent Four* – dir: Carlo Lizzani
1968 *Franco, Ciccio e le vedove allegre* (IT/SP) segment *La vedova del nonno* – dir: Marino Girolami
1968 *Niente rose per OSS 117* (IT/FR) FR *Pas de roses pour OSS 117* UK *OSS 117 Murder for Sale* – dir: Renzo Cerrato & Jean-Pierre Desagnat
1968 *I bastardi* (IT/FR/WG) FR *Le bâtard* WG *Der Bastard* US *Sons of Satan* / *The Cats* – dir: Duccio Tessari
1969 *Paroxismus ...può una morta rivivere per amore?* (IT/WG) WG *Venus im Pelz* UK/US *Venus in Furs* – dir: Jess Franco [Jesús Franco Manera]; Italian prints credit 'Hans Billian'
1969 *Frau Wirtin hat auch eine Nichte* (AT/WG/IT/HUN) IT *Il trionfo della casta Susanna* UK *House of Pleasure* – dir: François Legrand [Franz Antel]
1969 *5 per l'Inferno* (IT) UK *Five for Hell* US *Five Into Hell* – dir: Frank Kramer [Gianfranco Parolini]
1969 *¡Viva America!* (SP/IT) IT *La vera storia di Frank Mannata* UK *Mafia Mob* – dir: Javier Setó
1969 *A doppia faccia* (IT/WG) WG *Das Gesicht im Dunkeln* US *Puzzle of Horrors* USvdt *Double Face* – dir: Robert Hampton [Riccardo Freda] (re-edited in 1976, with added hardcore footage and re-released as *Liz & Helen* / *Chaleur et jouissance* – dir: Claude Sendron)
1969 *Sai cosa faceva Stalin alle donne?* (IT) – dir: Maurizio Liverani
1969 *Un sudario a la medida* (SP/IT) IT *Candidato per un assassino* UK *Candidate for a Killing* – dir: José María Elorrieta
1969 *Appuntamento col disonore* (IT/YUG/WG) YUG *Sastanak sa necasnim* UKvdt *The Night of the Assassin* – dir: Robert McCahon [Adriano Bolzoni]
1970 *El proceso de las brujas (El juez sangriento)* (SP/IT/WG) IT *Il trono di fuoco* WG *Der Hexentöter von Blackmoor* US *Night of the Blood Monster* / *Throne of the Blood Monster* UK *The Bloody Judge* – dir: Jess Franco [Jesús Franco Manera]
1970 *Colpo rovente* (IT) aka *Red Hot Shot* – dir: Pietro Zuffi
1970 *Il dio chiamato Dorian* (IT/WG/LIE/UK) IT *Das Bildnis des Dorian Gray* UK/US *Dorian Gray* UKvdt *The Secret of Dorian Gray* aka *The Evils of Dorian Gray* – dir: Massimo Dallamano
1971 *Le belve* (IT) export title *The Beasts* segment *Il cincillà* – dir: Gianni [Giovanni] Grimaldi
1971 *La bestia uccide a sangue freddo* (IT) UK *The Cold-Blooded Beast* US *Slaughter Hotel* / *Asylum Erotica* – dir: Fernando Di Leo
1971 *Nokaut* (YUG/IT) IT *Donne sopra, femmine sotto* US *The Rogue* – dir: Barry Norton [Boro Draskovic]
1972 *The Protectors* (UK) (tv series) episode *The Numbers Game* – dir: Don Chaffey
1974 *Gli assassini sono nostri ospiti* (IT) export title *The Killers Are Our Guests* – dir: Vincenzo Rigo
1974 *La sensualità e... un attimo di vita* / *Un attimo di vita* (IT) – dir: Dante Marraccini
1975 *Scusi eminenza... posso sposarmi? (Papesatan)* (IT) aka *Excuse Me, Padre, Are You Horny?* – dir: Salvatore Bugnatelli
1982 *Sesso e volentieri* (IT) – dir: Dino Risi
1983 *Stangata napoletana (La trastola)* (IT) US *Neapolitan Sting* – dir: Vittorio Caprioli
1985 *Giorno dopo giorno* (IT) (tv series) – dir: Salvatore Nocita

Ray Lovelock

born 19 June 1950 in Rome, Italy
died 10 November 2017 in Trevi, Umbria, Italy
real name **Raymond Lovelock**

George Webb in ***Murder-Rock Dancing Death***

1965 *Darling* (UK) [uncredited] – dir: John Schlesinger
1967 *Se sei vivo spara* (IT/SP) SP *Oro maldito* US/UKvdt *Django Kill, If You Live Shoot* – dir: Giulio Questi
1968 *Banditi a Milano* (IT) US *The Violent Four* – dir: Carlo Lizzani
1968 *Häschen in der Grube* (WG) – dir: Roger Fritz
1968 *7 volte 7* (IT) US television title *Seven Times Seven* – dir: Michele Lupo [scenes deleted from English language version]
1968 *I giovani tigri* (IT) – dir: Antonio Leonviola
1969 *L'amica* (IT) – dir: Alberto Lattuada
1969 *Plagio* (IT/FR) FR *Un amour à trois* – dir: Sergio Capogna
1969 *Toh, è morta la nonna!* (IT) aka *Well, Grandma's Dead* – dir: Mario Monicelli
1971 *Il delitto del diavolo / Le regine* (IT/FR) FR *Les sorcières au bord du lac* UKvdt *Queens of Evil* – dir: Tonino Cervi
1971 *Fiddler on the Roof* (US) – dir: Norman Jewison
1971 *Un posto ideale per uccidere* (IT/FR) USvdt *Dirty Pictures* – dir: Umberto Lenzi
1973 *El mejor alcalde, el rey* (SP/IT) – dir: Rafael Gil
1973 *Il giorno del furore* (IT/UK) UK *Fury* aka *One Russian Summer* – dir: Antonio Calenda
1973 *Un modo di essere donna* (IT) – dir: Pier Ludovico Pavoni
1974 *No profanar el sueño de los muertos* (SP/IT) IT *Da dove vieni? / Non profanare i sogni dei morti / Zombi 3* UK *The Living Dead at Manchester Morgue* US *Don't Open the Window* – dir: Jorge Grau
1974 *Milano odia: la polizia non può sparare* (IT) US *The Kidnapping of Mary Lou* US/USvdt *Almost Human* export title *The Executioner* – dir: Umberto Lenzi
1974 *Squadra volante* (IT) export title *Emergency Squad* aka *Flying Squad* – dir: Stelvio Massi
1975 *Macchie solari* (IT) US *Autopsy* export title *The Victim* – dir: Armando Crispino
1975 *Roma violenta* (IT) export title *Violent Rome* UK *Street Killers* UKvdt *Forced Impact* – dir: Franco Martinelli [Marino Girolami]
1975 *La moglie vergine* (IT) UK *The Virgin Wife* US *Valentina... The Virgin Wife* aka *At Last, At Last* – dir: Franco Martinelli [Marino Girolami]
1976 *Cassandra Crossing* (WG/IT) UK/US *The Cassandra Crossing* – dir: George Pan Cosmatos
1976 *Pronto ad uccidere* (IT/WG) WG *Tote pflastern seinen Weg* UKvdt *Pronto / Risking...* – dir: Franco Prosperi [Francesco Prosperi]
1976 *Uomini si nasce poliziotti si muore* (IT) UK *Live Like a Cop, Die Like a Man* UKvdt *The Terminators* – dir: Ruggero Deodato
1977 *L'avvocato della mala* (IT) export title *Gangbuster* shooting titles *Vai e colpisci / Hit and Run* – dir: Alberto Marras
1977 *Il grande attacco* (IT) USvdt *Battleforce* US tv title *The Great Battle* UKvdt *The Biggest Battle* – dir: Hank Milestone/Humphrey Logan [Umberto Lenzi]
1977 *La vergine, il toro e il capricorno* (IT) UK *The Erotic Exploits of a Sexy Seducer* UKvdt *Not Tonight Darling* – dir: Luciano Martino
1978 *La settima donna* (IT) UKvdt *Terror* export title *The Last House on the Beach* – dir: Franco Prosperi [Francesco Prosperi]
1978 *Avere vent'anni* (IT) UKvdt *To Be Twenty* – dir: Fernando Di Leo
1979 *L'anello matrimoniale* (IT/SP) SP *Experiencia extramatrimonial de una esposa* – dir: Mauro Ivaldi
1979 *De Dunquerque à la victoire* (FR/IT/SP) IT *Contro 4 bandiere* SP *De Dunkerke a la victoria* US *From Hell to Victory* – dir: Hank Milestone [Umberto Lenzi]
1979 *Scusi, lei è normale?* (IT) – dir: Umberto Lenzi
1979 *Play Motel* (IT) – dir: Roy Garrett [Mario Gariazzo]
1980 *L'ebreo fascista* (IT) – dir: Franco Molè
1980 *La casa rossa* (IT) (tv mini-series) – dir: Luigi Perelli
1982 *Una tranquilla coppia di killer* (IT) (tv movie) – dir: Gianfranco Albano
1983 *L'amante dell'Orsa Maggiore* (IT) (tv mini-series) (7 episodes) – dir: Anton Giulio Majano
1984 *Murderock uccide a passo di danza* (IT) US *The Demon Is Loose* export title ***Murder-Rock Dancing Death*** – dir: Lucio Fulci
1984 *La ragazza dell'addio* (IT) (tv mini-series) (10 episodes) – dir: Daniele D'Anza
1985 *A viso coperto* (IT) (tv movie) – dir: Gianfranco Albano
1985 *Due prigionieri* (IT/YUG) (tv movie) – dir: Anton Giulio Majano
1986 *Mino* (SWI/WG/IT) (tv mini-series) (4 episodes) – dir: Gianfranco Albano
1987 *Manu* (FR) (tv movie) – dir: Alfredo Giannetti
1988 *Mak π 100* (IT) – dir: Antonio Bido
1988 *Uomo contro uomo* (IT) (tv movie) – dir: Sergio Sollima
1989 *Solo* (IT) (3-part tv mini-series) – dir: Sandro Bolchi
1990 *La piovra 5 – Il cuore del problema* (IT/WG/FR) (tv mini-series) – dir: Luigi Feltrinelli
1990 *Quattro piccole donna* (IT/GER) (tv movie) – dir: Gianfranco Albano
1991 *La stella del parco* (IT) (tv series) (20 episodes) – dir: Aldo Lado
1991 *Un bambino in fuga – tre anni dopo* (IT) (tv movie) – dir: Mario Caiano
1991 *La ragnatela* (IT) (tv mini-series) – dir: Alessandro Cane
1992 *Un posto freddo in fondo al cuore* (IT) (tv movie) – dir: Sauro Scavolini
1992 *Il coraggio di Anna* (IT) (tv movie) aka *Surviving at the Top* – dir: Giorgio Capitani
1992 *Softwar* (FR/GER) (tv movie) – dir: Michel Lang
1992 *Intrighi internazionali* (1992) (IT) (tv mini-series) aka *Europa Connection* – dir: Nando [Fernando] Cicero
1992 *Brigada central II: La guerra blanca* (SP/FR) (tv series) FR *La guerre blanche* – dir: Pedro Masó
1993 *Delitti privati* (IT) (4-part tv mini-series) UK television title *Private Crimes* – dir: Sergio Martino
1993 *La ragnatella 2* (IT) (tv movie) – dir: Alessandro Cane
1993 *Vite a termine* (IT) (tv movie) – dir: Giovanni Soldati
1993 *Moscacieca* (IT) (tv movie) – dir: Mario Caiano
1995 *Alta società* (IT) (tv mini-series) export title *Surviving at the Top* – dir: Giorgio Capitani
1995 *Addio e ritorno* (IT) (tv movie) – dir: Rodolfo Roberti
1996 *Voglio rivedere mio padre* (IT) – dir: Sergio Martino
1997 *Mamma per caso* (IT) (4-part tv mini-series) – dir: Sergio Martino
1997 *Dove comincia il sole* (IT/GER) (tv series) GER *Verwirrung des Herzens* – dir: Rodolfo Roberti
1998 *La vuelta de El Coyote* (SP) aka *The Return of El Coyote* – dir: Mario Camus
1998 *Primo cittadino* (IT) (tv series) – dir: Gianfranco Albano
1999 *Commesse* (IT) (tv series) (3 episodes)
1999 *A due passi dal cielo* (IT) (tv movie) – dir: Sergio Martino
1999 *Non lasciamoci più* (IT) (tv series) episode *Un caso di famiglia* – dir: Vittorio Sindoni
1999 *La vita in briciole* (IT) (tv movie) – dir: Mario Caiano
1999 *Una vita non violenta* (IT) [uncredited] – dir: David Emmer
1999 *Villa Ada* (IT) (tv movie) – dir: Pier Francesco Pingitore
1999-2000 *Turbo* (IT/GER) (tv series) GER *Mein Partner auf vier Pfoten* (4 episodes)
2000 *Ricominciare* (IT) (tv series)
2000 *Tequila & Bonetti* (IT) (tv series) episode *I coniugi Bonetti*
2000 *Il fratello minore* (IT) – dir: Stefano Gigli
2000 *Primetime Murder* (IT/CAN) – dir: Alessandro Capone
2001 *Incantesimo 4* (IT) (tv series)
2001 *Inviati speciali (Giulia e Marco)* (IT) (tv movie) – dir: Francesco Laudadio
2002 *Incantesimo 5* (IT) (tv series)
2002 *Lo zio d'America* (IT) (tv series)
2003 *Incantesimo 6* (IT) (tv series)
2004 *Don Matteo* (IT) (tv series) episode *L'amore rubato* – dir: Giulio Base
2005 *Caterina e le sue figlie* (IT) (tv series) aka *My Daughters*
2006 *L'ultimo rigore 2* (IT) (tv movie) – dir: Sergio Martino
2006 *L'onore e il rispetto* (IT) (tv mini-series)
2006-2007 *Raccontami* (IT) (tv series) (4 episodes)
2007 *Caterina e le sue figlie 2* (IT) (tv series) aka *My Daughters*
2008 *Capri* (IT) (tv series) (3 episodes) – dir: Andrea Barzini & Giorgio Molteni
2010 *Caterina e le sue figlie 3* (IT) (tv series) aka *My Daughters*
2011 *Il commissario Rex* (IT) (tv series) episode *I nomi delle stelle* – dir: Marco Serafini
2011 *Un amore e una vendetta* (IT) (tv mini-series) – dir: Raffaele Mertes
2012 *The World of Hemingway* (IT) – dir: Giuseppe Recchia
2014 *Controra* (IT/IRE) aka *House of Shadows* – dir: Rossella De Venuto
2015 *Mia and Me* (IT/NL/GER/CAN) (tv series) episode *Un Visitatore Misterioso* – dir: Marco Lonardo
2015 *Barbara ed io* (IT) – dir: Raffaele Esposito
2016 *My Father Jack* (IT) – dir: Tonino Zangardi
2016 *L'allieva* (IT) (tv series) – dir: Luca Ribuoli
2016 *My Father Jack* (IT) – dir: Tonino Zangardi
2016 *L'allieva* (IT) (tv series) (9 episodes) aka *The Good Apprentice* – dir: Luca Ribuoli

Catriona MacColl

born 3 October 1954 in London, England

Mary Woodhouse in ***City of the Living Dead***
Liza Merrill in ***The Beyond***
Lucy Boyle in ***The House by the Cemetery***

1977 *Brigade des mineurs* (FR) (tv series) episode *Incidents mineurs* – dir: Claude Loursais
1978 *Il était un musicien* (FR) (tv series) episode *Monsieur Berlioz* – dir: Roger Hanin
1978 *Lady Oscar* (FR/JAP) JAP *Berusaiyu no bara* – dir: Jacques Demy
1978 *Le dernier amant romantique* (FR) US *The Last Romantic Lover* – dir: Just Jaeckin
1979 *Le fils puni* (FR) – dir: Philippe Collin
1979 *Les moyens du bord* (FR) (tv movie) – dir: Bernard Toublanc-Michel
1980 *Sherlock Holmes and Doctor Watson* (POL/US) (tv series) episode *The Case of the Three Uncles* – dir: Val Guest
1980 *L'inspecteur mène l'enquête* (FR) (tv series) episode *Dossier à charge*
1980 *Hawk the Slayer* (UK) – dir: Terry Marcel
1980 *Paura nella città dei morti viventi* (IT) US *The Gates of Hell* UK ***City of the Living Dead*** – dir: Lucio Fulci
1981 *L'aldilà* (IT) US *Seven Doors of Death* UK ***The Beyond*** – dir: Lucio Fulci
1981 *Noires sont les galaxies* (FR) (tv movie) – dir: Daniel Moosmann
1981 *Quella villa accanto al cimitero* (IT) US/UK ***The House by the Cemetery*** – dir: Lucio Fulci
1982 *La amenaza* (SP) UKvdt *Power Game* aka *The Threat* – dir: Fausto Canel
1982 *Les amours des années grises* (FR) (tv series) episode *Histoire d'un bonheur* – dir: Marion Sarraut

1982 *Les diplômés du dernier rang* (FR) – dir: Christian Gion
1982 *Pleine lune* (FR) (tv movie) – dir: Jean-Pierre Richard
1982 *Squadron* (UK) (tv series)
1983 *The Spice of Wickedness* (UK) (short) – dir: Elka Tupiak
1983 *La peau de chagrin* (FR) (tv movie) – dir: Michel Favart
1984 *Sonntag* (WG) (tv movie) – dir: Stanislav Barabás
1984 *The Last Days of Pompeii* (UK/IT/WG) (tv mini-series) IT television title *Gli ultimi giorni di Pompei* WG television title *Die letzten Tage von Pompeji* – dir: Peter Hunt
1984 *The World Walk* (UK) (tv movie) – dir: Sarah Hellings
1984 *Mitch* (UK) (tv series) episode *Fit-Up* – dir: Terry Green
1985 *Dempsey and Makepeace* (UK) (tv series) episode *Hors de Combat* – dir: Christian Marnham
1986 *Lytton's Diary* (UK) (tv series) episode *The Ancien Regime* – dir: Derek Bennett
1988 *Trois places pour le 26* (FR) – dir: Jacques Demy
1988 *Man Eaters* (US) – dir: Daniel Colas
1989 *Jeniec Europy* (POL/FR) FR *L'otage de l'europe* – dir: Jerzy Kawalerowicz
1989 *Katts and Dog* (CAN) (tv series) FR *Rintintin Junior* US *Rin Tin Tin: K-9 Cop* episode *The Grand Hotel Caper*
1989 *Deadly Nightmares* (FR/CAN/US) (tv series) episode *Garter Belt* – dir: Roger Andrieux
1990 *Counterstrike* (US/CAN/FR) (tv series) episode *The Lady of the Rhine* – dir: Paolo Barzman
1990-1991 *Waterfront Beat* (UK) (tv series)
1991 *Afraid of the Dark* (UK/FR) FR *Double vue* – dir: Mark Peploe
1991 *Trainer* (UK) (tv series) episode *No Way to Treat a Lady* – dir: Tristan de Vere Cole
1992 *Le bal des casse-pieds* (FR) – dir: Yves Robert
1992 *Prova di memoria* (IT) export title *Crimson Dawn* – dir: Marcello Aliprandi
1992 *Cousin William* (FR) (tv series)
1994 *Poisoned Ink* (FR/US) (short) – dir: Jon Carnoy
1995 *The Hardy Boys* (CAN) (tv series) episode *The Last Laugh* – dir: Jon Cassar
1996 *Strangers* (FR/CAN) (tv series) episode *Touch*
1998 *A Soldier's Daughter Never Cries* (UK) – dir: James Ivory
2002 *Les filles du calendrier* (FR) (tv movie) – dir: Philippe Venault, Jean-Pierre Vergne
2004 *Les filles du calendrier sur scène* (FR) (tv movie) – dir: Jean-Pierre Vergne
2004 *Saint Ange* (FR) aka *House of Voices* – dir: Pascal Laugier
2006 *Sable noir* (BEL/FR) (tv series) episode *La villa du crépuscule* – dir: Doug Headline

2006 *Plus belle la vie* (FR) (tv series)
2006 *A Good Year* (US/UK) – dir: Ridley Scott
2006-2007 *Mafiosa* (FR) (tv series)
2011 *Employé du mois* (SWI) (short) – dir: Olivier Beguin
2011 *The Theatre Bizarre* (US/FR/CAN) segment *The Mother of Toads* – dir: Richard Stanley [other dir's: Douglas Buck, Buddy Giovinazzo, David Gregory, Karim Hussain, Tom Savini, Jeremy Kasten]
2012 *Caïn* (FR) (tv series) episode *Innocences* – dir: Bertrand Arthuys
2013 *Mourir d'aimer* (FR) (short) – dir: Alan Delabie
2013 *A Long Way from Home* (UK/FR) – dir: Virginia Gilbert
2013 *Chimères* (SWI) – dir: Olivier Beguin
2013 *The Love Punch* (FR/UK) – dir: Joel Hopkins
2014 *Horsehead* (FR) – dir: Romain Basset
2015 *Juliet* (FR) (short) – dir: Marc-Henri Boulier
2016 *Anatomy of an Antihero* (FR) (web series) episode *The Last Chance* – dir: Alan Delabie
2020 *Scarlett* (FR) (short) – dir: Sarah Tahraoui
2020 *Anatomy of an Antihero: Redemption* (US) – dir: Meosha Bean
2021 *Denard: Anatomy of an Antihero* (FR) aka *Borrowed Time 2* – dir: Alan Delabie & Louis-Henry Chambat
2022 *Borrowed Time III* (FR) – dir: Alan Delabie & David Worth
2023 *You and Eye* (US) (co-producer/actor) – dir: Przemyslaw Reut
2023 *Isaac* (UK) – dir: Tariq Sayed

Patrick Magee

born 31 March 1922 in Armagh, Northern Ireland
died 14 August 1982 in London, England

Professor Robert Miles in ***The Black Cat***

1955 *BBC Sunday-Night Theatre* (UK) (tv series) episode *The Adventurer*
1957 *BBC Sunday-Night Theatre* (UK) (tv series) episode *Juno and the Paycock*
1957 *BBC Sunday-Night Theatre* (UK) (tv series) episode *Teru*
1957 *ITV Television Playhouse* (UK) (tv series) episode *The Shadow of a Gun Man*
1958 *BBC Sunday-Night Theatre* (UK) (tv series) episode *Gracie*
1959 *BBC Sunday-Night Theatre* (UK) (tv series) episode *Mooney's Wreck*
1959 *Dial 999* (UK) (tv series) episode *The Great Gold Robbery* – dir: Terence Fisher
1959 *ITV Play of the Week* (UK) (tv series) episode *Parnell* – dir: David Boisseau
1959 *ITV Television Playhouse* (UK) (tv series) episode *Longitude 49* – dir: John Knight
1960 *Deadline Midnight* (UK) (tv series) episode #1.7
1960 *Here Lies Miss Sabry* (UK) (tv series) – dir: Ronald Mason
1960 *BBC Sunday-Night Play* (UK) (tv series) episode *The Ruffians*
1960 *ITV Television Playhouse* (UK) (tv series) episode *Who's Owen Stephens...?* – dir: David Boisseau
1960 *The Criminal* (UK) US *The Concrete Jungle* – dir: Joseph Losey
1960 *Rag Doll* (UK) US *Young, Willing and Eager* – dir: Lance Comfort
1961 *Never Back Losers* (UK) – dir: Robert Tronson
1961 *A Prize of Arms* (UK) – dir: Cliff Owen
1961 *No Hiding Place* (UK) (tv series) episode *Explosion Underground* – dir: James Ormerod & Richard Sidwell
1961 *About Religion* (UK) (tv series) episode *Inquest at Golgotha*
1961 *Armchair Theatre* (UK) (tv series) episode *Murder Club* – dir: Alan Cooke
1962 *The Boys* (UK) – dir: Sidney Furie
1962 *The Very Edge* (UK) – dir: Cyril Frankel
1962 *A Great Ship* (UK) (documentary short) (narrator) – dir: John Reeve
1962 *Operacija Ticijan* (YUG/US) US television title *Portrait in Terror* – dir: Rados Novakovic [some footage later used in *Blood Bath* / *Track of the Vampire* (US, 1966) – dir: Jack Hill & Stephanie Rothman]
1962 *Z Cars* (UK) (tv series) episode *Stab in the Dark* – dir: John McGrath
1962 *ITV Play of the Week* (UK) (tv series) episode *Miracle on Mano* – dir: John Hale
1962 *Antigone* (UK) (tv mini-series) episode #1.2
1963 *The Servant* (UK) – dir: Joseph Losey
1963 *Dementia 13* (US) UK *The Haunted and the Hunted* – dir: Francis Ford Coppola

1963 *The Young Racers* (US) – dir: Roger Corman
1963 *Ricochet* (UK) – dir: John L. Moxey
1963 *Too Old for Donkeys* (UK) (tv movie) – dir: Peter Potter [series *ITV Television Playhouse*]
1963 *Zulu* (UK) – dir: Cy Endfield
1963 *Moonstrike* (UK) (tv series) episode *The Escape* – dir: David Benedictus
1963 *Zero One* (UK) (tv series) episode *Stopover* – dir: Peter Graham Scott
1963 *The Sentimental Agent* (UK) (tv series) episode *Express Delivery* – dir: Charles Frend
1963 *The Avengers* (UK) (tv series) episode *Killer Whale* – dir: Kim Mills
1963 *The Avengers* (UK) (tv series) episode *The Gilded Cage* – dir: Bill Bain
1963 *The Plane Makers* (UK) (tv series) episode *The Old Boy Network* – dir: John Cooper
1964 *The Masque of the Red Death* (UK/US) – dir: Roger Corman
1964 *Seance on a Wet Afternoon* (UK) – dir: Bryan Forbes
1964 *Dixon of Dock Green* (UK) (tv series) episode *The Fire Raiser* – dir: Robin Nash
1964 *Dixon of Dock Green* (UK) (tv series) episode *The Witness* – dir: Ronald Marsh
1964 *Theatre 625* (UK) (tv series) episode *Carried By Storm* – dir: Donald McWhinnie
1964 *The Plane Makers* (UK) (tv series) episode *The Smiler* – dir: Bill Stewart
1965 *The Skull* (UK) – dir: Freddie Francis
1965 *Monster of Terror* (UK) US *Die, Monster, Die* – dir: Daniel Haller
1965 *Dr. Finlay's Casebook* (UK) (tv series) episode *Beware of the Dog* – dir: Prudence Fitzgerald
1965 *BBC Play of the Month* (UK) (tv series) episode *Luther* – dir: Alan Cooke
1966 *The Persecution and Assassination of Jean-Paul Marat as Performed By the Inmates of the Asylum of Charenton Under the Direction of the Marquis de Sade* (UK) – dir: Peter Brook
1967 *Jonathan Swift* (IRE) (documentary short) – dir: Kieran Hickey
1967 *The Wednesday Play* (UK) (tv series) episode *Message for Posterity* – dir: Gareth Davies
1968 *Decline and Fall... of a Birdwatcher!* (UK) – dir: John Krish
1968 *The Birthday Party* (UK) – dir: William Friedkin
1968 *Lo sbarco di Anzio* (IT) UK *The Battle for Anzio* US *Anzio* – dir: Edward Dmytryk & Duilio Coletti
1968 *The Wednesday Play* (UK) (tv series) episode *Nothing Will Be the Same* – dir: Peter Hammond
1968 *The Champions* (UK) (tv series) episode *The Iron Man* – dir: John Llewellyn Moxey
1968 *ITV Playhouse* (UK) (tv series) episode *Neutral Ground* – dir: Piers Haggard
1968 *Thirty-Minute Theatre* (UK) (tv series) episode *A Private Place* – dir: Gerald Blake
1969 *Hard Contract* (UK) UKvdt *The Manipulator* – dir: S. Lee Pogostin
1969 *Destiny of a Spy* (US) (tv movie) – dir: Boris Sagal
1969 *King Lear* (UK) – dir: Peter Brook
1969 *Canterbury Tales* (UK) (tv series) episode #1.4 – dir: Michael Bakewell & Roderick Graham
1970 *You Can't Win 'Em All* (UK) – dir: Peter Collinson
1970 *The Fiend* (UK) US *Beware My Brethren* aka *Beware of the Brethren* – dir: Robert Hartford-Davis
1970 *Cromwell* (UK) – dir: Ken Hughes
1971 *A Clockwork Orange* (UK) – dir: Stanley Kubrick
1971 *The Trojan Women* (US) – dir: Michael Cacoyannis
1971 *Young Winston* (UK) – dir: Richard Attenborough
1971 *Demons of the Mind* (UK) – dir: Peter Sykes
1972 *Asylum* (UK) US *House of Crazies* – dir: Roy Ward Baker
1972 *Tales from the Crypt* (UK) segment *Blind Alleys* – dir: Freddie Francis
1972 *Pope Joan* (UK) – dir: Michael Anderson
1972 *Thirty-Minute Theatre* (UK) (tv series) episode *Thrills Galore* – dir: Donald McWhinnie
1972 *Thirty-Minute Theatre* (UK) (tv series) episode *Krapp's Last Tape* – dir: Donald McWhinnie
1973 *Lady Ice* (US) – dir: Tom Gries
1973 *Simona* (IT/BEL) – dir: Patrick Longchamps
1973 *...and Now the Screaming Starts!* (UK) – dir: Roy Ward Baker

1973 *The Caucasian Chalk Circle* (UK) (tv movie) – dir: Bill Hays [series *BBC Play of the Month*]
1973 *Eh Joe!* (UK) [short] – dir: D.R. Clark
1973 *The Final Programme* (UK) US *The Last Days of Man on Earth* – dir: Robert Fuest
1973 *Luther* (US/UK/CAN) – dir: Guy Green
1973 *The Protectors* (UK) (tv series) episode *Chase* – dir: Harry Booth
1973 *Great Mysteries* (UK) (tv series) episode *The Monkey's Paw* – dir: Alan Gibson
1973 *BBC Play of the Month* (UK) (tv series) episode *Caucasian Chalk Circle* – dir: Bill Hays
1974 *Thriller* (UK) (tv series) episode *A Killer in Every Corner* – dir: Malcolm Taylor
1974 *Galileo* (UK/CAN) – dir: Joseph Losey
1974 *The Adventures of Black Beauty* (UK) (tv series) episode *The Last Charge* – dir: Freddie Francis
1974 *King Lear* (UK) (tv series) – dir: Tony Davenall
1975 *Barry Lyndon* (UK) – dir: Stanley Kubrick
1975 *Thriller* (UK) (tv series) episode *Where the Action Is* UStv *The Killing Game* [uncredited] – dir: Don Leaver
1975 *Quiller* (UK) (tv series) episode *Mark the File Expendable* – dir: Alan Gibson
1976 *What Big Eyes* (UK) (tv pilot of series *Beasts*) – dir: Donald McWhinnie
1977 *BBC Play of the Month* (UK) (tv series) episode *You Never Can Tell* – dir: James Cellan Jones
1977 *Telefon* (US) – dir: Don Siegel
1977 *Who Pays the Ferryman?* (UK) (tv mini-series) episode *The Well*
1978 *Die Abenteuer des David Balfour* (WG/FR/UK) (tv mini-series) UK *Kidnapped* – dir: Jean-Pierre Decourt
1978 *Ondskans vårdshus* (SWE/IRE) UKvdt *The Sleep of Death* / *Devil Sleep* aka *Flygande draken* – dir: Calvin Floyd
1979 *Les soeurs Brontë* (FR) US *The Bronte Sisters* – dir: André Téchiné
1979 *Churchill and the Generals* (UK/AT) (tv movie) – dir: Alan Gibson
1979 *The Last Window Cleaner* (UK) (tv movie) – dir: Bill Craske [series *Play for Today*]
1979 *Oresteia* (UK) (tv mini-series) episode *Agamemnon* – dir: Bill Hays
1980 *The Flipside of Dominick Hide* (UK) (tv movie) – dir: Alan Gibson [series *Play for Today*]
1980 *Rough Cut* (US) – dir: Don Siegel
1980 *The Monster Club* (UK) – dir: Roy Ward Baker
1980 *Hawk the Slayer* (UK) – dir: Terry Marcel
1980 *Sir Henry at Rawlinson End* (UK) – dir: Steve Roberts
1980 *The Greeks: A Journey in Space and Time* (UK) (tv series) episode *The Greek Beginning* – dir: Christopher Burstall
1981 *Dr. Jekyll et les femmes* (FR) UK *The Blood of Dr. Jekyll* / *The Strange Case of Dr. Jekyll and Miss Osborne* UKvdt *Bloodbath of Dr. Jekyll* – dir: Walerian Borowczk
1981 *Black cat* (IT) US/UKvdt ***The Black Cat*** – dir: Lucio Fulci
1981 *Chariots of Fire* (UK) – dir: Hugh Hudson
1982 *Another Flip for Dominick* (UK) (tv movie) – dir: Alan Gibson [series *Play for Today*]
1982 *Horace* (UK) (tv series) episode *Horace Finds a Friend* – dir: James Cellan Jones

Paolo Malco

born 10 April 1947 in La Spezia, Italy

Dr. Norman Boyle in ***The House by the Cemetery***
Dr. Paul Davis in ***The New York Ripper***

1973 *Number One* (IT) – dir: Gianni Buffardi
1973 *Noa noa* (IT) – dir: Ugo Liberatore
1973 *Le scomunicate di San Valentino* (IT) export title *The Sinful Nuns of St. Valentine* – dir: Sergio Grieco
1974 *Lucrezia giovane* (IT) – dir: André Colbert [Luciano Ercoli]
1974 *Orlando furioso* (IT) (tv mini-series) episode #1.3 – dir: Luca Ronconi
1975 *La traccia verde* (IT) (tv mini-series) – dir: Silvio Maestranzi
1977 *La gabbia* (IT) (tv movie) – dir: Carlo Tuzii
1977 *Il gatto dagli occhi di giada* (IT) UKvdt *The Cat's Victims* aka *Watch Me When I Kill* – dir: Antonio Bido
1977 *Io ho paura* (IT) export title *I'm Afraid* – dir: Damiano Damiani
1977 *Dove volano i corvi d'argento* (IT) – dir: Piero Livi
1979 *Return of the Saint* (UK) (tv series) episode *Dragonseed* – dir: Leslie Norman
1980 *Dolly – Il sesso biondo* (IT) – dir: Luigi Russo
1980 *Masoch* (IT) – dir: Franco Brogi Taviani
1981 *Le ali della colomba* (IT) (tv mini-series) – dir: Gianluigi Calderone
1981 *Quella villa accanto al cimitero* (IT) US/UK ***The House by the Cemetery*** – dir: Lucio Fulci
1982 *Lo squartatore di New York* (IT) export title ***The New York Ripper*** – dir: Lucio Fulci
1982 *Il mistero degli Etruschi* (IT/FR) (tv mini-series, shortened version shown theatrically) IT *Assassinio al cimitero etrusco* FR *Crime aux cimetière éstrusque* USvdt *Scorpion with Two Tails* – dir: Christian Plummer [Sergio Martino]
1983 *Fuga dal Bronx* (IT) US *Escape from the Bronx* UKvdt *Bronx Warriors 2* – dir: Enzo G. Castellari [Enzo Girolami]
1983 *Thunder* (IT) USvdt *Thunder Warrior* – dir: Larry Ludman [Fabrizio De Angelis]
1984 *Tuareg – Il guerriero del deserto* (IT/SP) SP *Tuareg* UKvdt *Tuareg: Desert Warrior* – dir: Enzo G. Castellari [Enzo Girolami]
1984 *I racconti del maresciallo* (IT) (tv series) episode *La fine di Flok* – dir: Giovanni Soldati
1985 *The Assisi Underground* (US) – dir: Alexander Ramati
1986 *Morirai a mezzanotte* (IT) export title *You'll Die At Midnight* – dir: John Old Jr. [Lamberto Bava]
1987 *C'era una volta l'orco* / *La casa dell'orco* (IT) (tv movie) UKvdt *Demons 3: The Ogre* aka *The Ogre* – dir: Lamberto Bava [series *Brivido giallo*]
1987 *Portami la luna* (IT) (tv movie) – dir: Carlo Cotti
1988 *Giallo alla regola* (IT) – dir: Stefano Roncoroni
1990 *Tre colonne in cronaca* (IT) – dir: Carlo Vanzina
1993 *Delitti privati* (IT) (4-part tv mini-series) UK television title *Private Crimes* – dir: Sergio Martino
1997 *L'avvocato delle donne* (IT/GER) (tv mini-series) GER *Für Liebe und Gerechtigkeit* episode *Adriana* – dir: Andrea Frazzi & Antonio Frazzi

1998 *Il mastino* (IT) (tv series) episode *Tradimenti* – dir: Francesco Laudadio & Ugo Fabrizio Giordani
1998 *Incantesimo* (IT) (tv series) – dir: Alessandro Cane & Gianni Lepre
1998 *Incantesimo 2* (IT) (tv series) – dir: Alessandro Cane & Tomaso Sherman
2000 *Don Matteo* (IT) (tv series) episode *Il ricatto* – dir: Enrico Oldoini
2000 *Turbo* (IT/GER) (tv series) GER *Mein Partner auf vier Pfoten* – dir: Antonio Bonifacio
2002 *Incantesimo 5* (IT) (tv series) – dir: Alessandro Cane & Leandro Castellani
2002 *La casa dell'angelo* (IT) (tv movie) aka *The Angel's House* – dir: Giuliano Gamba
2003 *Chiaroscuro* (IT) (tv movie) – dir: Tomaso Sherman
2003 *Incantesimo 6* (IT) (tv series) – dir: Alessandro Cane & Tomaso Sherman
2003 *Claras Schatz* (GER) (tv movie) – dir: Hans-Erich Viet
2004 *Incantesimo 7* (IT) (tv series) – dir: Alessandro Cane
2005 *Incantesimo 8* (IT) (tv series) – dir: Ruggero Deodato & Tomaso Sherman
2006 *Giorni da Leone 2* (IT) (tv mini-series) – dir: Francesco Barilli
2007 *Barbara Wood: Sturmjahre* (GER) (tv movie) – dir: Marco Serafini
2007 *Ma chi l'avrebbe mai detto...* (IT) (tv movie) – dir: Giuliana Gamba & Alessio Inturri
2007 *A Room with a View* (UK) (tv movie) – dir: Nicholas Renton
2008-2010 *Cento vetrine* (IT) (tv series)
2015 *Solo per amore* (IT) (tv series) – dir: Raffaele Mertes

Jared Martin

born 21 December 1941 in Manhattan, NY, USA
died 24 May 2017 in Philadelphia, Pennsylvania, USA

Drake in ***Rome 2033 – The Fighter Centurions***
Dr. Robert Anderson in **Ænigma**

1963 *The Wedding Party* (US) – dir: Brian De Palma, Wilford Leach & Cynthia Munroe [released in 1969]
1964 *Civilization and Its Discontents* (US) – dir: Paul Morrissey
1968 *Murder à la Mod* (US) – dir: Brian De Palma
1970 *The Young Lawyers* (US) (tv series) episode *Is There a Good Samaritan in the House?* – dir: John Newland
1970 *The Partridge Family* (US) (tv series) episode *See Here, Private Partridge* – dir: Claudio Guzmán
1970 *The Silent Force* (US) (tv series) episode *The Wax Jungle*
1970 *The Bold Ones: The Lawyers* (US) (tv series) episode *Trial of a PFC* – dir: Alexander Singer
1970 *Mississippi Summer* (US) – dir: William Bayer
1971 *Dan August* (US) (tv series) episode *The Law* – dir: Ralph Senensky
1971 *The Bold Ones: The Lawyers* (US) (tv series) episode *Justice Is a Sometime Thing* – dir: Jeffrey Hayden
1971 *Night Gallery* (US) (tv series) season 2 episode 14 segment *Tell David...* – dir: Jeff Corey
1972 *Lapin 360* (US) – dir: Robert Michael Lewis [unreleased]

1972 *Medical Center* (US) (tv series) episode *Deadlock* – dir: Michael Caffey
1972 *Cannon* (US) (tv series) episode *The Shadow Man* – dir: Robert Douglas
1972 *The Rookies* (US) (tv series) episode *A Bloody Shade of Blue* – dir: E.W. Swackhamer
1973 *A Stitch in Time* (US) – dir: Hy Averback [feature-length episode of *Columbo*]
1973 *Westworld* (US) – dir: Michael Crichton
1973 *Griff* (US) (tv series) episode *Death By Prescription* – dir: Robert Michael Lewis
1973 *Toma* (US) (tv series) episode *Stakeout* – dir: Nicholas Colasanto
1973 *Shaft* (US) (tv series) episode *The Killing* – dir: Nicholas Colasanto
1973 *The Rookies* (US) (tv series) episode *Sound of Silence* – dir: Richard Newton
1974 *Men of the Dragon* (US) (tv pilot) – dir: Harry Falk
1974 *The Second Coming of Suzanne* (CAN) – dir: Michael Barry
1974 *Get Christie Love!* (US) (tv series) episode *Fatal Damage* – dir: Richard Compton
1974 *Nakia* (US) (tv series) episode *A Matter of Choice*
1974 *The Rookies* (US) (tv series) episode *Key Witness* – dir: Phil Bondelli
1975 *The Rookies* (US) (tv series) episode *Reign of Terror* – dir: Fernando Lamas
1975 *Switch* (US) (tv series) episode *The Cruise Ship Murders* – dir: Bruce Kessler
1977 *The Fantastic Journey* (US) (tv series) (10 episodes)
1977 *Logan's Run* (US) (tv series) episode *Fear Factor* – dir: Gerald Mayer
1978 *The Six Million Dollar Man* (US) (tv series) episode *The Lost Island* – dir: Cliff Bole
1978 *How the West Was Won* (US) (tv mini-series)
1978 *The American Girls* (US) (tv series) UK *Have Girls Will Travel* episode *A Crash Course in Survival* – dir: John Peyser
1978 *Project U.F.O.* (US) (tv series) episode *Sighting 4017: The Devilish Davidson Lights Incident* – dir: John Patterson
1978 *The Waltons* (US) (tv series) episode *The Portrait* – dir: Ralph Senensky
1979 *Wonder Woman* (US) (tv series) episode *Phantom of the Roller Coaster, Part 1* – dir: John Newland
1979 *Wonder Woman* (US) (tv series) episode *Phantom of the Roller Coaster, Part 2* – dir: John Newland
1979 *Big Shamus, Little Shamus* (US) (tv series) episode *The Canary*
1979 *CHiPs* (US) (tv series) episode *Hot Wheels* – dir: John Florea
1979-91 *Dallas* (US) (tv series) (34 episodes)
1980 *Willow B: Women in Prison* (US) (tv pilot) – dir: Jeff Bleckner
1980 *M Station: Hawaii* (US) (tv pilot) – dir: Jack Lord
1980 *Disney's Wonderful World* (US) (tv series) episode *The Kids Who Knew Too Much* – dir: Robert Clouse
1980 *The Incredible Hulk* (US) (tv series) episode *Free Fall* – dir: Reza Badiyi
1981 *Aloha Paradise* (US) (tv series) episode *Letter from Broadway / Letter from Cyrano / Letter from a Secret Admirer* – dir: Bruce Bilson
1981 *Hart to Hart* (US) (tv series) episode *Operation Murder* – dir: John Patterson
1982 *The Big Easy* (US) (tv pilot) – dir: Jud Taylor
1982 *The Lonely Lady* (US) – dir: Peter Sasdy
1982 *Tales of the Gold Monkey* (US) (tv series) episode *Trunk from the Past* – dir: Christian I. Nyby II
1982 *The Love Boat* (US) (tv series) episode *Burl of My Dreams / Meet the Author / Rhymes, Riddles, and Romance* – dir: Richard Kinon
1983 *Fantasy Island* (US) (tv series) episode *What's the Matter with Kids? / Island of Horrors* – dir: Don Weis
1983 *A Rose for Emily* (US) (short) – dir: Lyndon Chubbuck
1983 *The Love Boat* (US) (tv series) episode *Call Me Grandma / A Gentleman of Discretion / The Perfect Divorce / Letting Go* – dir: Robert Scheerer
1984 *I guerrieri dell'anno 2072* (IT) USvdt *The New Gladiators* UKvdt ***Rome 2033 – The Fighter Centurions*** – dir: Lucio Fulci
1984 *Serpiente de mar* (SP/US) USvdt *The Sea Serpent* – dir: Gregory Greens [Amando de Ossorio]
1984 *Scarecrow and Mrs. King* (US) (tv series) episode *The Artful Dodger* – dir: Christian I. Nyby II
1984 *Knight Rider* (US) (tv series) episode *Knight of the Drones* – dir: Sidney Hayers
1984 *Murder, She Wrote* (US) (tv series) episode *It's a Dog's Life* – dir: Seymour Robbie
1985 *Airwolf* (US) (tv series) episode *Santini's Millions* – dir: Sutton Roley
1985 *Finder of Lost Loves* (US) (tv series) episode *Tricks* – dir: Allen Reisner
1985 *Hotel* (US) (tv series) episode *Fallen Idols* – dir: Bruce Bilson
1986 *Quiet Cool* (US) – dir: Clay Borris
1986 *Magnum, P.I.* (US) (tv series) episode *Novel Connection* – dir: Harry Harris
1986 *Murder, She Wrote* (US) (tv series) episode *Magnum on Ice* – dir: Peter Crane
1986 *Hotel* (US) (tv series) episode *Forsaking All Others* – dir: Alan Cooke
1987 *Il ragazzo dal kimono d'oro* (IT) UKvdt *Karate Warrior* aka *Fist of Power* – dir: Larry Ludman [Fabrizio De Angelis]
1987 *The New Mike Hammer* (US) (tv series) episode *Who Killed Sister Lorna?* – dir: Frank Beascoechea
1987 *Hunter* (US) (tv series) episode *Hunter* – dir: Michael Preece
1987 *Ænigma* (IT/YUG) – dir: Lucio Fulci
1987-88 *One Life to Live* (US) (tv series)
1988 *War of the Worlds* (CAN/US) (tv series) (43 eps.)
1993 *Silk Stalkings* (US) (tv series) episode *Crush* – dir: Linda Hassani
1993 *L.A. Law* (US) (tv series) episode *How Much Is That Bentley in the Window* – dir: Elodie Keene
1994 *Twinsitters* (US) aka *The Babysitters* – dir: John Paragon
2003 *The Sun Is One Foot Wide* (US) (short) (narrator) – dir: Joey Grossfield
2016 The Congressman (US) (co-producer/co-director) – dir: Jared Martin, Robert Mrazek

Marisa Mell

born 24 February 1939 in Graz, Austria
died 16 May 1992 in Vienna, Austria
born **Marlies Theres Moitzi**

Susan Dumurrier/Monica Weston in
One on Top of the Other

1954 *Das Licht der Liebe* (AT) [uncredited] – dir: Robert A. Stemmle
1959 *Das Nachtlokal zum Silbermond* (WG) – dir: Wolfgang Glück
1960 *The Good Soldier Schweik* (WG) [uncredited] – dir: Axel von Ambesser
1960 *Am Galgen hängt die Liebe* (WG) – dir: Edwin Zbonek
1960 *Wegen verführung Minderjähriger...* (AT) – dir: Hermann Leitner
1960 *Lebensborn* (WG) – dir: Werner Klingler
1961 *Das Rätsel der roten Orchidee* (WG) UStv *The Secret of the Red Orchid* – dir: Helmut Ashley
1961 *Der Ruf der Wildgänse* (AT) – dir: Hans Heinrich
1962 *Dr* (YUG) – dir: Soja Jovanovic
1963 *Der grüne Kakadu* (WG) – dir: Michael Kehlmann
1963 *Ein Mann im schönsten Alter* (WG) – dir: Franz Peter Wirth
1963 *Venusberg* (WG) – dir: Rolf Thiele

1963 *French Dressing* (UK) – dir: Ken Russell
1964 *Diamond Walkers* (ZA) – dir: Paul Martin
1964 *Der Letzte Ritt nach Santa Cruz* (AT/WG/FR) FR *La chevauchée vers Santa Cruz* US *Last Stage to Santa Cruz* – dir: Rolf Olsen
1965 *Casanova '70* (IT/FR) FR *Casanova* – dir: Mario Monicelli
1965 *Train d'enfer* (FR/SP) SP *Trampa bajo el sol* – dir: Gilles Grangier
1965 *Masquerade* (UK) – dir: Basil Dearden
1966 *New York chiama Superdrago* (IT/FR/WG) FR *New York appelle Super Dragon* WG *Höllenjagd auf heiße Ware* US television title *Secret Agent Super Dragon* – dir: Calvin Jackson Padget [Giorgio Ferroni]
1966 *City of Fear* (UK) – dir: Peter Bezencenet
1966 *Objectif cinq cents millions* (FR) – dir: Pierre Schoendoerffer
1966 *Che notte, ragazzi!* (IT/SP) SP *¡Que noche, muchachos!* export title *What a Night!* – dir: Giorgio Capitani
1967 *Le dolci signore* (IT) US *Anyone Can Play* – dir: Luigi Zampa
1968 *Diabolik* (IT/FR) FR/UK/US *Danger: Diabolik* – dir: Mario Bava
1968 *Stuntman* (IT/FR) FR *Le cascadeur* – dir: Marcello Baldi
1969 *Una sull'altra* (IT/FR/SP) FR *Perversion Story* SP *Una historia perversa* US/UK ***One on Top of the Other*** – dir: Lucio Fulci
1969 *Les libertines* (FR/IT/SP) IT *L'intreccio* SP *Las bellas del bosque* UK *Versatile Lovers* aka *Les belles au bois dormantes* – dir: Dave Young [Pierre Chenal]
1971 *Marta* (SP/IT) IT *...Dopo di che, uccide il maschio e lo divora* export title *Marta* – dir: José Antonio Nieves Conde
1971 *Senza via d'uscita* (IT/FR/SP) FR *Les victimes* SP *Las victimas* – dir: Piero Sciumé
1972 *Historia de una traición* (SP/IT) IT *Diabolicamente sole con il delitto / Nel buio del terrore* export title *A Treason Story: Carla and Nora* US *The Great Swindle* – dir: José Antonio Nieves Conde
1972 *Amico, stammi lontano almeno un palmo* (IT) US *The Ballad of Ben and Charlie* – dir: Michele Lupo
1972 *Alta tension* (SP/IT) IT *Doppia coppia con regina* – dir: Julio Buchs
1972 *Sette orchidee macchiate di rosso* (IT/WG) WG *Das Rätsel des silbernen Halbmonds* export title *Seven Blood-Stained Orchids* – dir: Umberto Lenzi
1972 *Tutti fratelli nel West... per parte di padre* (IT/SP) SP *Todos hermanos... en el Oeste* FR *Miss Dynamite* UKvdt *Where the Bullets Fly* – dir: Sergio Grieco
1972 *Elisabeth Kaiserin von Österreich* (AT) (tv movie) – dir: Jörg A. Eggers, Theodor Grädler
1973 *Bella, ricca, lieve difetto fisico, cerca anima gemella* (IT) – dir: Nando [Fernando] Cicero
1973 *Milano rovente* (IT) export title *Burning City* aka *Gang War in Milan* – dir: Umberto Lenzi
1973 *Pena de muerte* (SP) USvdt *Violent Bloodbath* UScbt *Night Fiend* – dir: Jorge Grau
1973 *La encadenada* (SP/IT) IT *Perversione* export title *The Diary of a Murderess* shooting title *Diario de una asesina* – dir: Manuel Mur Oti
1974 *Parapsycho – Spektrum der Angst* (AT/WG) segment 1 – dir: Peter Patzak
1975 *La moglie giovane* (IT/SP) SP *Infamia* – dir: Giovanni D'Eramo
1975 *Mahogany* (US) – dir: Berry Gordy
1976 *L'ultima volta / Gli scippatori* (IT) UKvdt *Born Winner* – dir: Aldo Lado
1976 *Amori, letti e tradimenti* (IT) – dir: Alfonso Brescia
1977 *Un ombra nell'ombra* (IT) UKvdt *Ring of Darkness* – dir: Pier Carpi [released in 1979]
1977 *Taxi-Love, servizio per signora* (IT/SP) SP *Taxista para señoras* – dir: Sergio Bergonzelli
1977 *Casanova & Co.* (AT/IT/FR/WG) FR *Treize femmes pour Casanova* UK *The Rise and Rise of Casanova* US *Some Like It Cool* USvdt *Sex on the Run* – dir: François Legrand [Franz Antel]
1977 *La belva col mitra* (IT) UKvdt *Street Killers* aka *Mad Dog Murderer* shooting title *Feroce* – dir: Sergio Grieco
1977 *Es muß nicht immer Kaviar sein* (WG) (tv series) – dir: Thomas Engel
1978 *L'osceno desiderio* (IT/SP) SP *Poseída* – dir: Jeremy Scott [Giulio Petroni]
1978 *Fratello crudele* (IT) – dir: Mario De Rosa [unreleased]
1979 *Sam et Sally* (FR) (tv series) episode *Bedelia* – dir: Robert Pouret
1980 *Peccati a Venezia* (IT) – dir: Amasi Damiani
1980 *La compagna di viaggio* (IT) – dir: Ferdinando Baldi
1980 *Fabricantes de pánico* (MEX/SP/IT/VEN/PAN) IT *I guerrieri del terrore* US *Hostages!* UKvdt *Under Siege* aka *Panic Makers* – dir: René Cardona Jr.
1980 *La liceale al mare con l'amica di papà* (IT) – dir: Marino Girolami
1980 *Buon compleanno, Harry* (IT/WG) aka *Happy Birthday, Harry* – dir: Marius Mattei
1981 *La dottoressa preferisce i marinai* (IT) – dir: Michele Massimo Tarantini
1981 *Peccati di giovani mogli* (IT/FR) aka *Petite culotte mouillée* – dir: Angel Valery [Angelo Pannacciò]
1983 *In Zeiten wie diesen* (AT) (tv movie) – dir: Wolfgang Bauer
1983 *Corpi nudi (Nude Strike)* (IT) – dir: Joseph Mallory [Amasi Damiani] [released in 1986]
1983 *Il commissionario* (IT/SWI/FR/AT) (tv movie) aka *Der Kommissionär* – dir: Florestano Vancini
1983 *Kottan ermittelt* (AT) (tv series) episode *Smokey und Baby und Bär* – dir: Peter Patzak
1984 *Heiße Wickel kalte Güsse* (WG) (tv series) – dir: Franz Josef Gottlieb
1985 *Simsalabim – Bam – Bum* (AT/WG) (tv series) – dir: Ernst Wolfram Marboe
1985 *Seifenblasen* (AT) – dir: Alfred Ninaus
1985 *Passaporto segnalato* (IT) – dir: Sergio Martino
1988 *La tempesta* (IT) – dir: Giovanna Lenzi
1990 *Il signore di Akili* (IT) UKvdt *Quest for the Mighty Sword* aka *Ator III: The Hobgoblin* – dir: David Hills [Aristide Massaccesi]
1990 *Sensazioni d'amore* (IT) – dir: Ninì Grassia
1992 *I Love Vienna* (AT) – dir: Houchang Allahyari

Tomas Milian

born 3 March 1933 in Havana, Cuba
died 22 March 2017 in Miami, Florida, USA
full name **Tomás Quintín Rodríguez Varona y Milián**

Olimpio Calvetti in ***Beatrice Cenci***
Andrea Martelli in ***Don't Torture a Duckling***
Chaco in ***The Four of the Apocalypse***

1958 *Decoy* (US) (tv series) episode *Fiesta at Midnight* – dir: Michael Gordon
1959 *The Millionaire* (US) (tv series) episode *The Louise Benson Story* – dir: James Sheldon
1959 *La notte brava* (IT/FR) FR *Les garçons* US *Night Heat* aka *On Any Street / Bad Girls Don't Cry* – dir: Mauro Bolognini
1960 *I delfini* (IT) – dir: Francesco Maselli
1960 *Il bell'Antonio* (IT/FR) FR *Le bel Antonio* – dir: Mauro Bolognini
1961 *L'imprevisto* (IT/FR) FR *L'imprevu* UK *Unexpected* – dir: Alberto Lattuada
1961 *Un giorno da leoni* (IT) aka *Bridge to Glory* – dir: Nanni Loy
1961 *Laura nuda* (IT/FR) FR *Laura nue* – dir: Nicolò Ferrari
1961 *Giorno per giorno, disperatamente* (IT) – dir: Alfredo Giannetti
1961 *Boccaccio '70* (IT/FR) FR *Boccace 70* segment *Il lavoro / Le travail / The Job* – dir: Luchino Visconti
1962 *La banda Casaroli* (IT/FR) – dir: Florestano Vancini
1962 *L'attico* (IT) – dir: Gianni Puccini
1962 *Il disordine* (IT/FR) FR *Le désordre* – dir: Franco Brusati
1962 *Mare matto* (IT/FR) FR *La mer à boire* – dir: Renato Castellani
1963 *Il giorno più corto* (IT) US television title *The Shortest Day* – dir: Sergio Corbucci
1963 *Gli indifferenti* (IT/FR) FR *Désirs pervers* US *Time of Indifference* – dir: Francesco Maselli
1963 *Il gattopardo* (IT/FR) FR *Le guépard* UK/US *The Leopard* – dir: Luchino Visconti
1963 *RO.GO.PA.G / Laviamoci il cervello* (IT/FR) segment *La ricotta / Le fromage blanc* [uncredited] – dir: Pier Paolo Pasolini [other dir's: Jean-Luc Godard, Ugo Gregoretti, Roberto Rossellini]
1964 *L'uomo* (IT) (tv movie) – dir: Vittorio Cottafavi
1965 *Le soldatesse* (IT/FR/WG/YUG) FR *Des filles pour l'armee* – dir: Valerio Zurlini
1965 *Io uccido, tu uccidi* (IT/FR) segment *Il plenilunio* – dir: Gianni Puccini
1965 *The Agony and the Ecstasy* (US/IT) IT *Il tormento e l'estasi* – dir: Carol Reed
1965 *Madamigella di Maupin* (IT/FR/SP/YUG) FR *Le chevalier de Maupin* SP *Mademoiselle de Maupin* – dir: Mauro Bolognini
1965 *I soldi* (IT) segments *La belva / Lui* – dir: Gianni Puccini
1966 *The Bounty Killer* (IT/SP) SP *El precio de un hombre* US/UK *The Ugly Ones* – dir: Eugenio Martín
1966 *La resa dei conti* (IT/SP) SP *El halcón y la presa* US *The Big Gundown* – dir: Sergio Sollima
1967 *Faccia a faccia* (IT/SP) SP *Cara a cara* UK *Face to face* – dir: Sergio Sollima
1967 *Se sei vivo spara* (IT/SP) SP *Oro maldito* US/UKvdt *Django Kill, If You Live Shoot* – dir: Giulio Questi
1967 *Sentenza di morte* (IT) UK *Death Sentence* – dir: Mario Lanfranchi
1967 *Corri uomo corri* (IT) export title *Run, Man, Run* – dir: Sergio Sollima
1967 *Crónica de un atraco* (SP/IT) IT *La lunga notte di Tombstone* UK/US *Night of Hate* – dir: Jaime Jesús Balcázar
1968 *Banditi a Milano* (IT) US *The Violent Four* – dir: Carlo Lizzani
1968 *Ruba al prossimo tuo* (IT/US) US *A Fine Pair* – dir: Francesco Maselli
1969 *Tepepa* (IT/SP) US/UKvdt *Blood and Guns* – dir: Giulio Petroni
1969 *Dove vai tutta nuda?* (IT) – dir: Pasquale Festa Campanile
1969 *I cannibali* (IT) UK *The Cannibals* – dir: Liliana Cavani
1969 ***Beatrice Cenci*** (IT) US/USvdt *The Conspiracy of Torture* export title *Conspiracy* – dir: Lucio Fulci
1969 *O' cangaçeiro* (IT/SP) UK *The Magnificent Bandits* – dir: Giovanni Fago
1970 *L'amore coniugale* (IT) – dir: Dacia Maraini
1970 *Vamos a matar, compañeros* (IT/SP/WG) SP *Los campañeros* WG *Laßt uns töten, Companeros* UK/US *Companeros* – dir: Sergio Corbucci
1971 *La vittima designata* (IT) export titles *Slam Out / Murder By Design* – dir: Maurizio Lucidi
1971 *The Last Movie* (US) – dir: Dennis Hopper
1972 *Un uomo dalla pelle dura* (IT) US *Ripped Off* USvdt *The Boxer* export title *Tough Guy* – dir: Franco Prosperi [Francesco Prosperi]
1972 *Non si sevizia un paperino* (IT) export title ***Don't Torture a Duckling*** – dir: Lucio Fulci
1972 *La vita a volte è molto dura, vero Provvidenza?* (IT/FR/WG) FR *On m'appelle Providence* WG *Providenza! Mausefalle für zwei schräge Vögel* export title *Sometimes Life Is Hard-Right, Providence?* – dir: Giulio Petroni
1972 *La banda J. & S. cronaca criminale del Far West* (IT/SP/WG) SP *Los hijos del día y de la noche* WG *Die rote Sonne der Rache* US *Sonny & Jed* UKvdt *Bandits!* FR *Far West Story* – dir: Sergio Corbucci
1973 *Il consigliori* (IT/SP) SP *El consejero* UK *The Counsellor* – dir: Alberto De Martino
1973 *Ci risiamo, vero Provvidenza?* (IT/SP/FR) SP *El bruto, el listo y el capitán* export title *Here We Go Again, Eh Providence?* – dir: Alberto De Martino
1974 *Il bianco, il giallo, il nero* (IT/FR/SP) FR *Le blanc, le jaune et le noir* – dir: Sergio Corbucci
1974 *Squadra volante* (IT) export title *Emergency Squad* aka *Flying Squad* – dir: Stelvio Massi
1974 *Milano odia: la polizia non può sparare* (IT) US *The Kidnapping of Mary Lou* US/USvdt *Almost Human* export title *The Executioner* – dir: Umberto Lenzi
1974 *La polizia accusa: il servizio segreto uccide* (IT/FR) FR *La ville accuse* UKvdt *Silent Action* – dir: Sergio Martino
1975 *Il giustiziere sfida la città* (IT) US *Syndicate Sadists* UKvdt *One Just Man* export title *Rambo's Revenge* – dir: Umberto Lenzi
1975 *I quattro dell'apocalisse* (IT) export title ***The Four of the Apocalypse*** – dir: Lucio Fulci
1975 *Folle à tuer* (FR/IT) IT *Una donna da uccidere* export title *Evil Trap* aka *Mad Enough to Kill* – dir: Yves Boisset
1976 *40 gradi all'ombra del lenzuolo* (IT) UK *Sex with a Smile* segment *La cavallona* – dir: Sergio Martino

1976 *Liberi, armati e pericolosi* (IT) export title *Young, Desperate, Violent* – dir: Romolo Guerrieri [Romolo Girolami]
1976 *Folies bourgeoises* (FR/WG/IT) WG *Die Verrückten Reichen* IT *Pazzi Borghesi* – dir: Claude Chabrol
1976 *Il trucido e lo sbirro* (IT) export title *Free Hand for a Tough Cop* aka *Tough Cop* – dir: Umberto Lenzi
1976 *Roma a mano armata* (IT) US *Brutal Justice / Assault with a Deadly Weapon* export title *The Tough Ones* – dir: Umberto Lenzi
1976 *Squadra antiscippo* (IT) UK *The Cop in Blue Jeans* – dir: Bruno Corbucci
1976 *Squadra antifurto* (IT) export title *Hit Squad* – dir: Bruno Corbucci
1977 *Messalina, Messalina!* (IT) – dir: Bruno Corbucci
1977 *Squadra antitruffa* (IT) US *Swindle* – dir: Bruno Corbucci
1977 *Il cinico, l'infame, il violento* (IT) UKvdt *The Cynic, the Rat and the Fist* – dir: Umberto Lenzi
1977 *La banda del Gobbo* (IT) export title *Brothers Till We Die* aka *Angry Vengeance / The Unforgettable Gang* – dir: Umberto Lenzi
1977 *La banda del trucido* (IT) UKvdt *Dirty Gang / Destruction Force* – dir: Stelvio Massi
1978 *Il figlio dello sceicco* (IT) – dir: Bruno Corbucci
1978 *Squadra antimafia* (IT) – dir: Bruno Corbucci
1979 *Squadra antigangsters* (IT) export title *The Gang That Sold America* – dir: Bruno Corbucci
1979 *Assassinio sul Tevere* (IT) – dir: Bruno Corbucci
1979 *La luna* (IT) – dir: Bernardo Bertolucci
1979 *The Day Christ Died* (US) – dir: James Cellan Jones
1979 *Winter Kills* (US) – dir: William Richert
1980 *Delitto a Porta Romana* (IT) – dir: Bruno Corbucci
1980 *Il lupo & l'agnello* (IT/FR) FR *Le coucou* US *The Wolf and the Lamb* – dir: Francesco Massaro
1980 *Uno contro l'altro, praticamente amici* (IT) – dir: Bruno Corbucci
1980 *Manolesta* (IT) aka *The Pick-Pocket* – dir: Pasquale Festa Campanile
1981 *Delitto al ristorante cinese* (IT) – dir: Bruno Corbucci
1981 *Delitto sull'autostrada* (IT) – dir: Bruno Corbucci
1982 *Cano e gatto* (IT) UKvdt *Thieves and Robbers* – dir: Bruno Corbucci
1982 *Monsignor* (US) – dir: Frank Perry
1982 *Identificazione di una donna* (IT/FR) FR *Identification d'une femme* US *Identification of a Woman* – dir: Michelangelo Antonioni
1983 *Il diavolo e l'acquasanta* (IT) – dir: Bruno Corbucci
1984 *Delitto in formula uno* (IT) – dir: Bruno Corbucci
1984 *Delitto al Blue Gay* (IT/WG) WG *Ein Superesel auf dem Ku'Damm* export title *Cop in Drag* – dir: Bruno Corbucci
1985 *Salomé* (IT/FR) – dir: Claude D'Anna
1985 *King David* (US) [uncredited] – dir: Bruce Beresford
1985 *Miami Vice* (US) (tv series) episode *Bought and Paid For* – dir: John Nicolella
1985 *The Equalizer* (US) (tv series) episode *Reign of Terror* – dir: Richard Compton
1987 *Una casa a Roma* (IT) – dir: Bruno Cortini
1987 *Luci lontane* (IT) export title *Distant Lights* – dir: Aurelio Chiesa
1987 *The Equalizer* (US) (tv series) episode *Shadow Play* – dir: Russ Mayberry
1988 *Cat Chaser* (US) – dir: Abel Ferrara
1989 *Gioco al massacro* (IT) aka *The Killing Game* – dir: Damiano Damiani
1989 *Drug Wars: The Kiki Camarena Story* (US) (tv mini-series) UK television title *The Drug Wars – Camarena* – dir: Brian Gibson
1989 *Revenge* (US/MEX) – dir: Tony Scott
1990 *Havana* (US) – dir: Sydney Pollack
1990 *Voglia da vivere* (IT) (tv movie) aka *The Will to Live / To Touch a Star* – dir: Lodovico Gasparini
1991 *Money* (FR/IT/CAN) IT *Money (intrigo in nove mosse)* – dir: Steven H. Stern
1991 *JFK* (US) – dir: Oliver Stone
1991 *L.A. Law* (US) (tv series) episode *The Gods Must Be Lawyers* – dir: Tom Moore
1992 *Nails* (US) (cbm) – dir: John Flynn
1992 *Bitter Harvest* (UK) (tv movie) – dir: Simon Cellan Jones [season 7 episode 4 of *ScreenPlay*]
1992 *Frannie's Turn* (US) (tv series) – dir: Sam Weisman
1992 *Murder, She Wrote* (US) (tv series) episode *Day of the Dead* – dir: Anthony Pullen Shaw
1993 *Marilyn and Bobby Her: Final Affair* (US) (tv movie) – dir: Bradford May
1993 *Love, Honour and Obey: The Last Mafia Marriage* (US) (tv movie) – dir: John Patterson
1994 *The Burning Season* (US) (cbm) – dir: John Frankenheimer
1994 *The Cowboy Way* (US) – dir: Gregg Champion
1997 *Dear Antonioni* (UK/IT) (tv documentary) – dir: Gianni Massironi
1997 *Fools Rush In* (US) – dir: Andy Tennant
1997 *Amistad* (US) – dir: Steven Spielberg
1997 *Oz* (US) (tv series) episode *Visits, Conjugal and Otherwise* – dir: Nick Gomez
1997 *Oz* (US) (tv series) episode *To Your Health* – dir: Alan Taylor
2000 *The Yards* (US) – dir: James Gray
2000 *Law & Order* (US) (tv series) episode *Vaya Con Dios* – dir: Christopher Misiano
2000 *For Love or Country: The Arturo Sandoval Story* (US) (tv movie) – dir: Joseph Sargent
2000 *Traffic* (US/GER) – dir: Steven Soderbergh
2001 *Ambush* (US) (short) – dir: John Frankenheimer
2001 *UC: Undercover* (US) (tv series) episode *Of Fathers and Sons* – dir: Lou Antonio
2002 *Washington Heights* (US) – dir: Alfredo Rodriguez de Villa
2005 *The Lost City* (US) – dir: Andy Garcia
2005 *La fiesta del Chivo* (DOM/SP/UK) aka *The Feast of the Goat* – dir: Luis Llosa
2013 *Roma nuda* (IT) – dir: Giuseppe Ferrara
2014 *Fugly!* (US) – dir: Alfredo Rodriguez de Villa

Cinzia Monreale

born 22 June 1957 in Genoa, Italy
real name **Cinzia Moscone**
aka **Sarah Keller**

Miss Margaret Barrett in ***Silver Saddle***
Emily in ***The Beyond***
Linda Summers in ***Rome 2033 – The Fighter Centurions***
Marcia in ***The Sweet House of Horrors***

1975 *Son tornate a fiorire le rose* (IT) [uncredited] – dir: Vittorio Sindoni
1976 *Perdutamente tuo... mi firmo Macaluso Carmelo fu Giuseppe* (IT) – dir: Vittorio Sindoni
1976 *Quel movimento che mi piace tanto (Dimmi che illusione non è...)* (IT) – dir: Franco Rossetti
1976 *Per amore di Cesarina* (IT) – dir: Vittorio Sindoni
1978 *Bermudas la cueva de los tiburones* (SP/IT) IT *Bermude la fossa maledetta* UKvdt *The Shark's Cave* – dir: Anthony Richmond [Tonino Ricci]
1978 *Sella d'argento* (IT) export title ***Silver Saddle*** – dir: Lucio Fulci
1979 *Buio omega / In quella casa buio omega* (IT) US *Buried Alive* FR *Blue Holocaust* UKvdt *Beyond the Darkness* – dir: Joe D'Amato [Aristide Massaccesi]
1980 *Piedone d'Egitto* (IT) – dir: Steno [Stefano Vanzina]
1981 *L'aldilà* (IT) US *Seven Doors of Death* UK ***The Beyond*** – dir: Lucio Fulci
1984 *I guerrieri dell'anno 2072* (IT) USvdt *The New Gladiators* UKvdt ***Rome 2033 – The Fighter Centurions*** – dir: Lucio Fulci
1984 *Illusione* (IT) – dir: Alex Carmeno
1984 *Passione coniugale* (IT) – dir: Mario Forges Davanzati [unreleased]
1986 *Cat's* (IT) – dir: Alex Carmeno
1986 *La vallée des peupliers* (tv series) (FR/IT/SWI)
1987 *Sotto il ristorante cinese* (IT) – dir: Bruno Bozzetto
1987 *Aeroporto internazionale* (IT) (tv series) episode *Una in meno* – dir: Enzo Tarquini
1988 *Il ferro contro il viso* (IT) (short) – dir: Gianluca Maria Tavarelli
1988 *Zanzibar* (IT) (tv series) – dir: Marco Mattolini
1989 *I-taliani* (IT) (tv series) – dir: Roberto Valentini
1989 *La dolce casa degli orrori* (IT) export title ***The Sweet House of Horrors*** – dir: Lucio Fulci
1990 *Return from Death (Frankenstein 2000)* (IT) shooting title *Ritorno dalla morte* – dir: David Hills [Aristide Massaccesi]
1991 *Chiara e gli altri* (IT) (tv series) – dir: Gianfrancesco Lazotti
1991 *I vicini di casa* (IT) (tv series) – dir: Silvia Arzuffi
1992 *Nel continente nero* (IT) – dir: Marco Risi
1993 *Kreola* (IT) – dir: Antonio Bonifacio
1993 *Diario di un vizio* (IT) aka *Diary of a Maniac* – dir: Marco Ferreri
1996 *La sindrome di Stendhal* (IT) export title *The Stendhal Syndrome* – dir: Dario Argento
1996 *Festival* (IT) – dir: Pupi Avati
1997 *Mamma per caso* (IT) (4-part tv mini-series) – dir: Sergio Martino
1999 *Commesse* (IT) (tv series) episode *Paola* – dir: Giorgio Capitani
1999 *Il popolo degli uccelli* (IT) – dir: Rocco Cesareo
2000 *Quando una donna non dorme* (IT) aka *When a Man Loves a Woman* – dir: Nino Bizzarri
2000 *La donna del delitto* (IT) aka *Under the Skin* – dir: Corrado Colombo
2000 *Turbo* (IT/GER) (tv series) GER *Mein Partner auf vier Pfoten* – dir: Antonio Bonifacio
2001 *L'accertamento* (IT) – dir: Lucio Lunerti
2002 *La casa dell'angelo* (IT) (tv movie) aka *The Angel's House* – dir: Giuliana Gamba
2003 *Ilaria Alpi – Il più crudele dei giorni* (IT) – dir: Ferdinando Vicentini Orgnani
2004 *Madre come te* (IT) (tv movie) – dir: Vittorio Sindoni
2009 *Il commissario Rex 2* (IT) (tv series) episode *La mamma è sempre la mamma* – dir: Marco Serafini
2010 *La mia casa è piena di specchi* (IT) (tv movie) aka *My House Is Full of Mirrors* – dir: Vittorio Sindoni
2011 *Il giorno del mio compleanno* (IT) (short) – dir: Roberto Capucci
2012 *Il commissario Rex 5* (IT) (tv series) – dir: Fernando Muraca
2013 *La festa* (IT) – dir: Simone Scafidi
2016 *Dark Signal* (UK) – dir: Edward Evers-Swindell
2019 *Everybloody's End* (IT) – dir: Claudio Lattanzi

Franco Nero

born 23 November 1941
in San Prospero Parmense, Parma, Italy
real name **Francesco Clemente Guiseppe Sparanero**

Tom Corbett in ***Massacre Time***
Jason Scott in ***White Fang***
Jason Scott in ***Challenge to White Fang***

1962 *Pelle viva* (IT) aka *Scorched Skin* – dir: Giuseppe Fina
1963 *Un delitto* (IT) (short) – dir: Luigi Bazzoni
1963 *La noia* (IT/FR) FR *L'ennui* US *The Empty Canvas* – dir: Damiano Damiani
1964 *La ragazza in prestito* (IT/FR) FR *Une femme disponible* US *Engagement Italiano* – dir: Alfredo Giannetti
1964 *Io la conoscevo bene* (IT/FR/WG) FR *Je la connaissais bien* WG *Ich hab sie gut gekannt* – dir: Antonio Pietrangeli
1965 *La celestina P... R...* (IT/FR) aka *Celestial Maid at Your Service* – dir: Carlo Lizzani
1965 *I criminali della galassia* (IT) US *Wild, Wild Planet* – dir: Anthony M. Dawson [Antonio Margheriti]
1965 *I diafanoidi vengono da Marte* (IT) UK television title *War of the Planets* – dir: Anthony M. Dawson [Antonio Margheriti]
1965 *Gli uomini dal passo pesante* (IT/FR) FR *Les forcenés* US *The Tramplers* – dir: Albert Band & Anthony Wileys [Mario Sequi]
1966 *Il terzo occhio* (IT) – dir: James Warren [Mino Guerrini]
1966 *La Bibbia* (IT) US/UK *The Bible... in the Beginning* – dir: John Huston
1966 *Le colt cantarono la morte e fu... tempo di massacro* (IT) US *The Brute and the Beast* US/UKvdt ***Massacre Time*** – dir: Lucio Fulci
1966 *Django* (IT/SP) – dir: Sergio Corbucci
1966 *Tecnica di un omicidio* (IT/FR) FR *Technique d'un muertre* US *The Hired Killer* UK *No Tears for a Killer* export title *Professional Killer* – dir: Franco Prosperi [Francesco Prosperi]
1966 *Texas, addio* (IT/SP) SP *Adiós, Texas* UK *The Avenger* – dir: Ferdinando Baldi
1967 *Camelot* (US) – dir: Joshua Logan
1967 *L'uomo, l'orgoglio, la vendetta* (IT/WG) WG *Mit Django kam der Tod* US *Man, Pride and Vengeance* – dir: Luigi Bazzoni
1968 *Il giorno della civetta* (IT/FR) UK/US *The Day of the Owl* USvdt *Mafia* – dir: Damiano Damiani
1968 *Un tranquillo posto di campagna* (IT/FR) FR *Un coin tranquille à la campagne* US/UK *A Quiet Place in the Country* – dir: Elio Petri
1968 *Il mercenario* (IT/SP) SP *Salario para matar* US *The Mercenary* UK *A Professional Gun* – dir: Sergio Corbucci
1968 *Sequestro di persona* (IT) US/UK *Island of Crime* USvdt *Sardinia Kidnapped* – dir: Gianfranco Mingozzi
1969 *Bitka na Neretvi* (YUG/US/IT/WG) US/UK *Battle of Neretva* IT *La battaglia della Neretva* WG *Die Schlacht an der Neretva* US *The Battle on the River Neretva* – dir: Veljko Bulajic
1969 *The Virgin and the Gypsy* (UK) – dir: Christopher Miles
1969 *Un detective* (IT) US *Detective Belli / A Detective* USvdt *Ring of Death* – dir: Romolo Guerrieri [Romolo Girolami]
1970 *Gott mit uns (Dio è con noi)* (IT/YUG) USvdt/UKvdt *The Fifth Day of Peace* UKvdt *Crime of Defeat* – dir: Giuliano Montaldo
1970 *Tristana* (SP/IT/FR) – dir: Luis Buñuel
1970 *Drop-out* (IT) (co-producer/actor) – dir: Tinto Brass
1970 *Vamos a matar, compañeros* (IT/SP/WG) SP *Los compañeros* WG *Laßt uns töten, Companeros* UK/US *Companeros* – dir: Sergio Corbucci
1971 *La vacanza* (IT) (co-producer/actor) – dir: Tinto Brass
1971 *Giornata nera per l'ariete* (IT) UK *Evil Fingers* UKvdt *The Fifth Cord* – dir: Luigi Bazzoni
1971 *Confessione di un commissario di polizia al Procuratore della Repubblica* (IT) UK/US *Confessions of a Police Captain* – dir: Damiano Damiani
1971 *L'istruttoria è chiusa: dimentichi (Tante sbarre)* (IT) – dir: Damiano Damiani
1971 *Viva la muerte... Tua!* (IT/SP/WG) SP *Viva la muerte... tuya* WG *Zwei wilde Companeros* US *Don't Turn the Other Cheek* UK *Long Live Your Death* – dir: Duccio Tessari
1972 *Le moine* (FR/IT/WG) IT *Il monaco* WG *Der Mönch und die Frauen* US/UK *The Monk* – dir: Ado Kyrou
1972 *Pope Joan* (UK) – dir: Michael Anderson
1972 *Squadra volante uccideteli... senza ragione* (IT/UK) UK/US *Redneck* – dir: Silvio Narizzano
1973 *Il delitto Matteotti* (IT) US *The Assassination of Matteotti* – dir: Florestano Vancini
1973 *Los amigos* (IT) US/UK *Deaf Smith & Johnny Ears* – dir: Paolo Cavara
1973 *La polizia incrimina, la legge assolve* (IT/SP) SP *La policía detiene, la ley juzga* US/UK *High Crime* UKvdt *The Marseilles Connection* – dir: Enzo G. Castellari [Enzo Girolami]
1973 *Zanna Bianca* (IT/SP/FR) SP *Colmillo Blanco* FR *Croc-blanc* UK/USvdt ***White Fang*** – dir: Lucio Fulci
1974 *I guappi* (IT) UKvdt *Blood Brothers* – dir: Pasquale Squitieri
1974 *Il ritorno di Zanna Bianca* (IT/WG/FR) WG *Die Teufelsschlucht der wilden Wölfe* FR *Le retour de Buck le loup* US/UK ***Challenge to White Fang*** – dir: Lucio Fulci
1974 *Il cittadino si rebella* (IT) US *Street Law / The Anonymous Avenger* UKvdt *Revenge / Vigilante 2* – dir: Enzo G. Castellari [Enzo Girolami]
1974 *Mussolini ultimo atto* (IT/US) UK/US *Last Days of Mussolini* – dir: Carlo Lizzani
1974 *Corruzione al palazzo di giustizia* (IT) US *The Smiling Maniacs* – dir: Marcello Aliprandi
1974 *Perché si uccide un magistrato* (IT) export title *How to Kill a Judge* – dir: Damiano Damiani
1975 *Cipolla colt* (IT/SP/WG) SP *Los ocos del oro negro* WG *Zwiebel-Jack räumt auf* US/UK *Cry Onion* US *Spaghetti Western* – dir: Enzo G. Castellari [Enzo Girolami]
1975 *Gente di rispetto* (IT) US *The Flower in His Mouth* UKvdt *A Man to Respect / The Masters* – dir: Luigi Zampa
1975 *The Legend of Valentino* (US) (tv movie) – dir: Melville Shavelson
1975 *Les magiciens* (FR/IT/WG) IT *Profezia di un delitto* – dir: Claude Chabrol
1976 *Scandalo* (IT) USvdt *Submission* – dir: Salvatore Samperi
1976 *Marcia trionfale* (IT/FR/WG) WG *Triumph-marsch* US *Victory March* – dir: Marco Bellocchio
1976 *Keoma* (IT) UK *The Violent Breed* – dir: Enzo G. Castellari [Enzo Girolami]
1976 *21 Hours at Munich* (US) (tv movie, also shown theatrically) IT *21 Ore a Monaco* – dir: William A. Graham
1977 *Autostop rosso sangue* (IT) US/UKvdt *Hitch-Hike* UKvdt *Death Drive* – dir: Pasquale Festa Campanile
1977 *Sahara Cross* (IT/TUN) UKvdt *Desert Chase* – dir: Tonino Valerii
1978 *Force Ten from Navarone* (UK) – dir: Guy Hamilton
1978 *The Pirate* (US) (tv movie) – dir: Ken Annakin
1979 *Stridulum* (IT/US) aka *The Visitor* [uncredited] – dir: Michael J. Paradise [Giulio Paradisi]
1979 *Le rose di Danzica* (IT) US *The Roses of Danzig* – dir: Alberto Bevilacqua
1979 *The Man with Bogart's Face* (US) – dir: Robert Day
1979 *Il cacciatore di squali* (IT/SP) SP *El cazador de tiburones* US *The Shark Hunter / The Jaws Hunter* UKvdt *Guardians of the Deep / Tearing Jaws* (co-producer/actor) – dir: Enzo G. Castellari [Enzo Girolami]
1979 *Un dramma borghese* (IT) US *Mimi* (co-producer/actor) – dir: Florestano Vancini
1980 *Il giorno del Cobra* (IT) US *The Day of the Cobra* – dir: Enzo G. Castellari [Enzo Girolami]
1980 *Il bandito dagli occhi azzurri* (IT) export title *The Blue-Eyed Bandit* (co-producer/actor) – dir: Alfredo Giannetti
1980 *Kamikaze 1989* (WG) US *Kamikaze '89* – dir: Wolf Greem
1981 *The Salamander* (UK/IT/US) IT shooting title *La salamandre* – dir: Peter Zinner
1981 *Banovic strahinja* (YUG/WG) WG *Der Falke* US *The Falcon* – dir: Vatroslav Mimica
1981 *Enter the Ninja* (US) – dir: Menahem Golan
1982 *Grog* (IT) – dir: Francesco Laudadio
1982 *Wagner* (UK/HUN/AT) – dir: Tony Palmer
1982 *Querelle ein Pakt mit dem Teufel* (WG/FR) US/UK *Querelle* – dir: Rainer Werner Fassbinder
1982 *Krasnie Kolokola Meksika v ogne* (USSR/MEX/IT) IT *Messico in fiamme* MEX *Campañas rojas* US *Mexico in Flames* – dir: Sergei Bondarchuk
1982 *Der Bauer von Babylon* (WG) US *The Wizard of Babylon* – dir: Dieter Schidor
1983 *Krasnie Kolokola Ja videl rozdenie novogo mira* (USSR/MEX/IT) IT *I dieci giorno che sconvolsero il mondo* MEX *Campañas rojas* US *I Saw the New World Born* – dir: Sergei Bondarchuk
1983 *Die Försterbuben* (AT/WG) US *The Forester's Son* – dir: Peter Patzak
1984 *The Last Days of Pompeii* (UK/IT/WG) (tv mini-series) IT television title *Gli ultimi giorni di Pompei* WG television title *Die letzten Tage von Pompeji* – dir: Peter Hunt
1984 *André schafft sie alle* (WG/AT) aka *Girl's Favorite Sport* – dir: Peter Fratzscher
1985 *Il pentito* (IT) US *The Repenter* – dir: Pasquale Squitieri
1985 *The Hitchhiker* (FR/CAN/US) (tv series) UK *Deadly Nightmares* episode *Murderous Feelings* – dir: Mai Zetterling
1985 *Glykeia patrida* (GRE) US/UKvdt *Sweet Country* – dir: Michael Cacoyannis
1985 *Un marinaio e mezzo* (IT) export title *Fight for Your Life* shooting title *Un solitario e mezzo* – dir: Tommaso Dazzi

1986 *Il generale* (IT/FR/WG/YUG) (tv mini-series, shortened version shown theatrically) US television title *The General* UK television title *Garibaldi, the General* – dir: Luigi Magni
1986 *The Girl* (UK) – dir: Arne Mattson
1986 *Un altare per la patria* (IT) (tv movie) aka *Un altare per la madre* – dir: Edith Bruck
1987 *Tre giorni a Tropici* / *Grosso guaio a Cartagena* (IT/WG) WG *Grüne Hölle von Cartagena* export title *Race to Danger* shooting title *Sbarco a Cartagena* – dir: Tommaso Dazzi
1987 *Django 2 – Il grande ritorno* (IT) UKvdt *Django Strikes Again* – dir: Ted Archer [Nello Rossati]
1987 *Run for Your Life* (US/IT) FRvdt *Marathon* export title *Sweet Revenge* – dir: Terence Young
1988 *Top Line* (IT) UKvdt *Alien Terminator* / *Top Line* – dir: Nello Rossati
1988 *Windmills of the Gods* (US) (tv mini-series) – dir: Lee Philips
1988 *Stille Nacht* (WG) US *Magdalene* export title *Silent Night* – dir: Monica Teuber
1988 *Il giovane Toscanini* (IT/FR) FR *Le jeune Toscanini* US *Toscanini, the Young Maestro* – dir: Franco Zeffirelli
1988 *I promessi sposi* (IT/WG) (tv mini-series) US television title *The Betrothed* – dir: Salvatore Nocita
1988 *Blaues blut* (WG) (tv mini-series) aka *Scandalous* / *Blue Blood* episode *Gegen die Uhr* – dir: Sidney Hayers
1988 *Patrizia* (IT) (tv movie) aka *Pygmalion 88* – dir: Flavio Mogherini
1989 *Oggi ho vinto anch'io* (IT) (tv movie) aka *Stasera ho vinto anch'io* / *A Double Victory* – dir: Ludovico Gasparini
1989 *The Magistrate* (UK/AUS/IT) (tv mini-series) IT *Il magistrato* – dir: Kathy Mueller
1990 *Diceria dell'untore* (IT) export title *The Plague Sower* (co-producer/actor) – dir: Beppe Cino
1990 *Die Hard 2* (US) – dir: Renny Harlin
1990 *Amélia Lópes O'Neill* (CHI/FR/SP/SWI) – dir: Valeria Sarmiento
1990 *Young Catherine* (US/USSR) – dir: Michael Anderson
1991 *Chi tocca muore* (UK/IT/GER) (tv movie) export title *Touch and Die* – dir: Piernico Solinas
1991 *I Julianus barát* (IT/HUN) IT *Frate Julianus* – dir: Gábor Koltay [released in three parts]
1992 *Fratelli e sorelle* (IT) export title *Brothers and Sisters* – dir: Pupi Avati
1992 *Le Visionarium* (FR/US) US *From Time to Time* aka *Timekeeper* – dir: Jeff Blyth
1992 *Azzurro profondo* (IT) (tv movie) aka *The Dolphin Girl* – dir: Filippo De Luigi
1992 *Prova di memoria* (IT) export title *Crimson Dawn* (uncredited co-producer) – dir: Marcello Aliprandi
1993 *Das Babylon Komplott* (AT) – dir: Peter Patzak
1993 *Oro* (IT) – dir: Fabio Bonzi
1993 *Jonathan degli orsi* (IT/USSR/US) USvdt *Jonathan of the Bears* (co-producer/co-screenplay/actor) – dir: Enzo G. Castellari [Enzo Girolami]
1993 *Der Fall Lucona* (GER/IT/AT) (tv movie) export title *The Lucona Affair* – dir: Jack Gold
1994 *Nemici intimi* (IT) (tv movie) – dir: Piernico Solinas
1994 *Desideria e l'anelio del drago* (IT) (tv movie) export title *The Dragon Ring* – dir: Lamberto Bava
1995 *The Innocent Sleep* (UK) – dir: Scott Michell
1995 Talk of Angels (US) – dir: Nick Hamm
1995 *Io e il re* (IT) – dir: Lucio Gaudino
1995 *Ha-Italkim Ba'im* (IT) shooting title *Arrivano gli italiani* – dir: Eyal Halfon
1996 *Il ritorno di Sandokan* (IT/GER) (tv mini-series) aka *The Return of Sandokan* – dir: Enzo G. Castellari
1996 *Il tocco* (IT/SP) SP *A tres bandas* export title *Rack-Up* aka *The Touch* / *The Cuemaster* – dir: Enrico Coletti
1996 *Action* (CIS) – dir: Vsevolod Plotkin
1996 *La medaglia* (IT) – dir: Sergio Rossi
1997 *Honfoglalás* (HUN) aka *The Conquest* – dir: Gabor Koltay
1997 *David* (US/IT/GER) (tv movie) – dir: Robert Markowitz [feature-length episode of *The Bible*]
1997 *Il deserto di fuoco* (IT) (tv movie) – dir: Enzo G. Castellari [Enzo Girolami]
1997 *Painted Lady* (UK/US) (tv mini-series) – dir: Julian Jarrold
1997 *Nessuno escluso* (IT) (tv movie) – dir: Massimo Spano
1997 *Bella Mafia* (US/UK) (tv mini-series) – dir: David Greene
1998 *The Versace Murder* (US) – dir: Menahem Golan
1998 *Il tesoro di Damasco* (IT) (tv movie) – dir: José María Sánchez
1999 *Uninvited* (US/IT) IT *L'escluso* (co-producer/actor) – dir: Carlo Gabriel Nero [Sparanero]
1999 *La voce del sangue* (IT) (tv movie) – dir: Alessandro Di Robilant
1999 *Li chiamarono... briganti!* (IT) aka *Brigands* – dir: Pasquale Squitieri
2000 *Mirka* (IT/FR/SP/UK) – dir: Rachid Benhadj
2000 *Maestrale* (IT) aka *Winds of Passion* – dir: Sandro Cecca
2000 *San Paolo* (IT/CZE/GER) (tv movie) aka *St. Paul* – dir: Roger Young
2001 *Chimera* (IT) – dir: Pappi Corsicato
2001 *Sacra Corona* (HUN) aka *The Legend of the Holy Crown* – dir: Gábor Koltay
2001 *La ragion pura* (IT) aka *The Sleeping Wife* – dir: Silvano Agosti
2001 *Megiddo: The Omega Code 2* (US) – dir: Brian Trenchard-Smith & [uncredited] Paul J. Lombardi
2001 *Gli angeli dell'isola verde* (IT) (tv series) – dir: Enzo G. Castellari
2001 *Crociati* (IT/GER) (tv movie) – dir: Dominique Othenin-Girard
2002 *Fumata blanca* (SP) aka *White Smoke* – dir: Miquel García Borda
2002 *Ultimo stadio* (IT) – dir: Ivano De Matteo
2002 *Die 8. Todsünde: Das Toskana-Karussell* (GER) – dir: Peter Patzak
2002 *L'ultimo pistolero* (IT) (short) – dir: Alessandro Dominici
2003 *Liebe, Lügen, Leidenschaften* (GER/AT) (tv mini-series) aka *Love, Lies, Passions* – dir: Marco Serafini
2003 *Herz ohne Krone* (GER) (tv movie) aka *The Uncrowned Heart* – dir: Peter Patzak
2003 *Cattive inclinazioni* (IT) – dir: Pierfrancesco Campanella
2004 *Post coitum* (CZE) – dir: Juraj Jakubisko
2004 *Guardiani delle nuvole* (IT) – dir: Luciano Odorisio
2005 *Forever Blues* (IT) (producer/director/co-screenplay/actor) – dir: Franco Nero
2005 *Summer Solstice* (GER/UK) (tv movie) – dir: Giles Foster
2006 *Hans* (IT) – dir: Louis Nero
2006 *Amore e libertà – Masaniello* (IT) – dir: Angelo Antonucci
2006 *La sacra famiglia* (IT) (tv movie) aka *The Holy Family* – dir: Raffaele Mertes
2007 *Mineurs* (IT/BEL) – dir: Fulvio Wetzl
2007 *Der Fürst und das Mädchen* (GER) (tv series)
2007 *Two Families* (UK/IT) – dir: Romano Scavolini
2007 *Una roccia spezzata* (IT) – dir: Carlo Fusco
2008 *Márió, a varázsló* (HUN/IT) IT *Mario il Mago* (co-producer/actor) – dir: Tamás Almási
2008 *Bastardi* (IT) – dir: Federico Del Zoppo & Andres Alce Meldonado
2008 *La rabbia* (IT) (co-producer/actor) – dir: Louis Nero
2008 *Bathory* (SVK/HUN/CZE/UK/FR) aka *Bathory: Countess of Blood* – dir: Juraj Jakubisko
2008 *Una storia di lupi* (IT) (short) – dir: Cristiano Donzelli
2008 *Il sangue e la rosa* (IT) (tv series) episode *Prima puntata*
2008 *Mein Herz in Chile* (GER) (tv movie) – dir: Jörg Grünler
2008 *Eine Nacht im Grandhotel* (GER) (tv movie) aka *A Night at the Grand Hotel* – dir: Thorsten Näter
2008 *Ti stramo: Ho voglia di un'ultima notte da manuale prima di tre baci sopra il cielo* (IT) – dir: Pino Insegno, Gianluca Sodaro
2008 *Four Seasons* (UK/GER) (tv mini-series) GER *Rosamunde Pilcher – Vier Jahreszeiten* – dir: Giles Foster
2008 *Elena* (IT) (short) – dir: Salvo Bitonti
2009 *Mord ist mein Geschäft, Liebling* (GER) aka *Killing Is My Business, Honey* – dir: Sebastian Niemann
2009 *Lullaby* (IT) (short) – dir: Louis Nero
2009 *Palestrina – princeps musicae* (GER/IT) – dir: Georg Brintrup
2010 *Sant'Agostino* (IT/GER) (tv movie) aka *Augustine: The Decline of the Roman Empire* – dir: Christian Duguay
2010 *Angelus Hiroshimae* (IT) – dir: Giancarlo Planta
2010 *Letters to Juliet* (US) – dir: Gary Winick
2010 *Prigioniero di un segreto* (IT) – dir: Carlo Fusco
2010 *Rasputin* (IT) – dir: Louis Nero
2010 *Calibro 10 – Il decalogo del crimine* (IT) – dir: Massimo Ivan Falsetta [released in 2015]
2011 *Father* (IT) – dir: Pasquale Squitieri
2011 *Cars 2* (US) (voice) – dir: John Lassete & Brad Lewis
2011 *Law & Order: Special Victims Unit* (US) (tv series) episode *Scorched Earth* – dir: Michael Slovis
2012 *New Order* (US) (producer/actor) – dir: Marco Rosson
2012 *Canepazzo* (IT) – dir: David Petrucci
2012 *A Memória que me Contam* (BRA/ARG) – dir: Lúcia Murat
2012 *The Woods* (US) – dir: Michael Mandell
2012 *Django Unchained* (US) – dir: Quentin Tarantino
2012 *The Last Alchemist* (IT) (short) – dir: Michele Massari
2013 *Handy* (IT) – dir: Vincenzo Cosentino
2013 *Cadences obstinées* (FR/POR) aka *Obsessive Rhythms* – dir: Fanny Ardant
2014 *Mamula* (SRB/MNE) aka *Nymph* – dir: Milan Todorovic
2014 *Love Island* (CRO/GER/BIH/SWI) (co-producer/actor)– dir: Jasmila Zbanic
2014 *Dante's Hell Animated* (US) (short) (voice, Italian version) – dir: Boris Acosta
2014 *Figli di MAAM* (IT) – dir: Paolo Consorti
2015 *Il Buio* (IT) (short) – dir: Giuliano Oppes
2015 *Gemma di Maggio* (IT) (short) – dir: Giuliano Giacomelli & Lorenzo Giovenga
2015 *The Kid* (US) (short) – dir: Vladislav Kozlov
2016 *Along the River* (IT) (short) – dir: Daniele Nicolosi
2016 *Il ragazzo della Giudecca* (IT) – dir: Alfonso Bergamo
2016 *The Lost City of Z* (US) – dir: James Gray
2017 *John Wick: Chapter 2* (US/HK/IT/CAN) – dir: Chad Stahelski
2017 *The Time of Their Lives* (UK) – dir: Roger Goldby
2017 *Death of the Sheik* (US) aka *Silent Life* – dir: Vladislav Kozlov
2017 *Iceman* (GER/IT/AT) – dir: Felix Randau
2017 *The Executrix* (US) – dir: Michele Civetta & Joseph Schuman
2017 *The Neighborhood* (CAN) – dir: Frank D'Angelo
2017 *The Broken Key* (IT) – dir: Louis Nero
2019 *Inferno Dantesco Animato* (US) (voice, Italian version) – dir: Boris Acosta
2018 *Delicious* (UK) (tv series) – dir: Clare Kilner & John Hardwick
2018 *Buon lavoro* (IT) – dir: Marco Demurtas
2018 *Red Land* (*Rosso Istria*) (IT) – dir: Maximiliano Hernando Bruno
2018 *A Rose in Winter* (UK) – dir: Joshua Sinclair
2019 *Ed è subito sera* (IT) – dir: Claudio Insegno
2019 *Der Fall Collini* (GER) aka *The Collini Case* – dir: Marco Kreuzpaintner
2019 *The Killers* (US) (co-producer/actor) – dir: Vladislav Kozlov
2019 *Peace* (US) – dir: Robert David Port
2019 *Christmas in Rome* (US) (tv movie) – dir: Ernie Barbarash
2019 *The Duel* (US) (short) – dir: Vladislav Kozlov
2020 *Havana Kyrie* (IT/CUB/US) – dir: Paolo Consorti
2020 *Harmonie* (AT) – dir: Juana Jimenez, Jaime Gómez & Juan Diego Puerta Lopez
2020 *The Divine Comedy: Inferno, Purgatory and Paradise* (US) (tv series) (voice) – dir: Boris Acosta
2020 *The Match* (CRO) – dir: Dominik Sedlar & Jakov Sedlar
2020 *On Our Way* (US) (short) – dir: Livia Coullias Blanc & Sophie Lane Curtis
2020 *Off the Rails* (UK) – dir: Jules Williamson
2020 *La danza nera* (IT) – dir: Mauro John Capece
2020 *Immortalist* (US) – dir: Vladislav Kozlov
2020 *The Executrix* (US) aka *Agony* – dir: Michele Civetta
2020 *Il suggeritore – Nil difficile volenti* (IT) – dir: Fabio D'Avino
2022 *The Man from Rome* (SP/IT/COL) aka *La piel del tambor* – dir: Sergio Dow
2022 *L'uomo che disegnò Dio* (IT) aka *The Man Who Drew God* – dir: Franco Nero
2023 *Silent Life: The Story of the Lady in Black* (US) – dir: Vladislav Alex Kozlov
2023 *Django* (IT/FR) (tv series) (2 episodes) – dir: Francesca Comencini, David Evans
2023 *The Pope's Exorcist* (US/SP/UK) – dir: Julius Avery
2023 *Giorni felici* (IT) – dir: Simone Petralia
2024 *The Jester from Transylvania* (ROU) – dir: Adrian Popovici

Andrea Occhipinti

born 12 September 1957 in Milan, Italy
aka **Andrew Painter**

Peter Bunch in ***The New York Ripper***
Ilias in ***Conquest***

1979 *Return of the Saint* (UK) (tv series) episode *Dragonseed* – dir: Leslie Norman
1980 *Quaderno proibito* (IT) (tv mini-series) – dir: Marco Leto
1980 *Augh! Augh!* (IT) – dir: Marco Toniato
1980 *Priest of Love* (UK) – dir: Christopher Miles
1981 *Vita di Antonio Gramsci* (IT) (tv mini-series) episode *Prima parte: L'educazione politica* – dir: Raffaele Maiello
1981 *La settimana al mare* (IT) – dir: Mariano Laurenti
1982 *La certosa di Parma* (IT/WG/FR) (tv movie) FR television title *La chartreuse de Parme* UK television title *The Charterhouse of Parma* – dir: Mauro Bolognini
1982 *Lo squartatore di New York* (IT) export title ***The New York Ripper*** – dir: Lucio Fulci
1983 ***Conquest*** (IT/SP/MEX) SP *La conquista de la tierra perdida* MEX *El Bárbaro – La conquista de la tierra perdida* – dir: Lucio Fulci
1983 *The Innocents Abroad* (US/AT/IT/WG/FR) (tv movie) WG *Arglosen im Ausland* IT *Gli innocenti vanno all'estero* – dir: Luciano Salce
1983 *La casa con la scala nel buio* (IT) export title *A Blade in the Dark* – dir: Lamberto Bava
1983 *Occhéi, occhéi* (IT) – dir: Claudia Florio
1984 *Bolero* (US) – dir: John Derek
1984 *The Sun Also Rises* (US) (tv movie) – dir: James Goldstone
1985 *Miranda* (IT) – dir: Tinto Brass
1985 *Finalmente morta* (IT) – dir: Elisabetta Valgiusti [unreleased]
1986 *Lulù* (IT/FR) – dir: Sandro Bolchi
1986 *Un metier de seigneur* (FR) (tv movie) – dir: Edouard Molinaro
1986 *Il giorno prima* (IT/FR/CAN/US) (tv movie) US television title/UKvdt *Control* shooting title *The Day Before* – dir: Giuliano Montaldo
1987 *La famiglia* (IT/FR) FR *La famille* – dir: Ettore Scola
1988 *Carla* (IT) (tv movie) – dir: Dino Risi [series *Quattro storie di donne*]
1988 *La ciociara* (IT) (two-part tv movie) aka *Two Women* – dir: Dino Risi
1989 *Il vizio di vivere* (IT) (tv movie) – dir: Dino Risi [series Amori]
1989 *The Jeweller's Shop* (CAN/IT/FR/AT/WG) (tv movie, shortened version shown theatrically) IT *La bottega dell'orefice* FR *La boutique de l'orfèvre* WG *Der Laden des Goldschmieds* – dir: Michael Anderson
1990 *Tracce di vita amorosa* (IT) – dir: Peter Del Monte
1990 *Night of the Fox* (US/UK/FR/GER) (tv movie) – dir: Charles Jarrott
1991 *Ti ho adottato per simpatia* (IT) (tv movie) – dir: Paolo Fondato
1991 *Appartamento all'ultimo piano* (IT) – dir: Liliana Ginanneschi
1991 *La ragnatella* (IT) (tv movie) – dir: Alessandro Cane
1993 *La ragnatella 2* (IT) (tv movie) – dir: Alessandro Cane
1993 *Alexandra* (IT/FR/GER) (tv movie) – dir: Denis Amar
1993 *La voyageuse du soir* (FR) – dir: Igaal Niddam
1993 *Caccia alle mosche* (IT) – dir: Angelo Longoni
1993 *Amour fou* (FR) (tv movie) – dir: Roger Vadim
1995 *Pasolini un delitto italiano* (IT/FR) FR *Pasolini, mort d'un poète* – dir: Marco Tullio Giordana
1995 *L'amore molesto* (IT) (co-producer) – dir: Mario Martone
1996 *RDF Rumori Di Fondo* (IT) (co-producer/actor) – dir: Claudio Camarca
1997 *Mas alla del jardin* (SP) – dir: Pedro Olea
1997 *L'amico di Wang* (IT) (co-producer) – dir: Carl Haber
1997 *Amor de hombre* (SP) – dir's: Yolanda G. Serrano & Juan Luis Iborra
1997 *Don Juan* (SP/FR/GER) (tv movie) – dir: Jacques Weber
1997 *Abre los ojos* (SP/FR/IT) aka *Open Your Eyes* (associate producer) – dir: Alejandro Amenábar
1998 *Teatro di guerra* (IT) (co-producer) – dir: Mario Martone
1998 *Indiscretion of an American Wife* (US) (tv movie) – dir: George Kaczender
1998 *Jeremiah* (IT/GER/US) (tv movie) – dir: Harry Winer
1999 *La vita che verrà* (IT) (tv mini-series) – dir: Pasquale Pozzessere
1999 *A las once en casa* (SP) (tv series)
1999 *Il guerriero Camillo* (IT) (producer) – dir: Claudio Bigagli
1999 *Questo è il giardino* (IT) (producer) – dir: Giovanni Davide Maderna
2000 *Preferisco il rumore del mare* (IT/FR) – dir: Mimmo Calopresti
2001 *Sin noticias de Dios* (SP/FR IT/MEX) aka *Don't Tempt Me* (co-producer) – dir: Agustín Díaz Yanes
2001 *Le peuple migrateur* (FR/IT/GER/SP/SWI) (documentary) aka *Winged Migration* (associate producer) – dir: Jacques Perrin, Jacques Cluzaud & Michel Debats
2002 *Incantesimo napoletano* (IT) (producer) – dir: Paolo Genovese & Luca Miniero
2002 *L'amore imperfetto* (IT/SP) (producer) – dir: Giovanni Davide Maderna
2002 *The Magdalene Sisters* (IRE/UK) (executive producer) – dir: Peter Mullan
2002 *Los lunes al sol* (SP/FR/IT) aka *Mondays in the Sun* (co-producer) – dir: Fernando León de Aranoa
2003 *Ballo a tre passi* (IT) aka *Three-Step Dance* (producer) – dir: Salvatore Mereu
2004 *Mar adentro* (SP/FR/IT) aka *The Sea Inside* – dir: Alejandro Amenábar
2004 *Sogni di cuoio* (IT) (documentary) (producer) – dir: César Meneghetti & Elisabetta Pandimiglio
2004 *La femme de Gilles* (BEL/FR/LUX/IT/SWI) aka *Gilles' Wife* (co-producer) – dir: Frédéric Fonteyne
2004 *Come inguaiammo il cinema italiano – La vera storia di Franco e Ciccio* (IT) (documentary) aka *How We Got the Italian Movie Business Into Trouble: The True Story of Franco and Ciccio* (producer) – dir: Daniele Ciprì & Franco Maresco
2005 *Reinas* (SP/NL/IT) aka *Queens* – dir: Manuel Gómez Pereira
2005 *Viva Zapatero!* (IT) (documentary) (producer) – dir: Sabina Guzzanti
2006 *Azur et Asmar* (FR/BEL/SP/IT) aka *Azur & Asmar: The Princes' Quest* (co-producer) – dir: Michel Ocelot
2006 *L'orchestra di Piazza Vittorio* (IT) (documentary) aka *The Orchestra of Piazza Vittorio* (producer) – dir: Agostino Ferrente
2007 *Funny Games* (US/FR/UK/AT/GER/IT) (co-producer) – dir: Michael Haneke
2007 *Angeli distratti* (IT) (producer) – dir: Gianluca Arcopinto
2008 *Sonetàula* (IT/FR/BEL) (producer) – dir: Salvatore Mereu
2008 *Il divo: La spettacolare vita di Giulio Andreotti* (IT/FR) aka *Il Divo* (producer) – dir: Paolo Sorrentino
2009 *Antichrist* (DEN/GER/FR/SWE/IT/POL) (co-producer) – dir: Lars von Trier
2009 *Das weiße Band – Eine deutsche Kindergeschichte* (GER/AT/FR/IT) aka *The White Ribbon* (producer) – dir: Michael Haneke [producer]
2009 *L'amore e basta* (IT) aka *Hymn to Love* (producer) – dir: Stefano Consiglio
2009 *Io, Don Giovanni* (IT/SP/FR) aka *I, Don Giovanni* (producer) – dir: Carlos Saura
2009 *La prima linea* (IT/BEL/UK/FR) aka *The Front Line* (producer) – dir: Renato De Maria
2011 *Cavalli* (IT) aka *Horses* – dir: Michele Rho
2011 *Le gamin au vélo* (BEL/FR/IT) aka *The Kid with a Bike* (co-producer) – dir: Jean-Pierre Dardenne & Luc Dardenne
2011 *This Must Be the Place* (IT/FR/IRE) (producer) – dir: Paolo Sorrentino
2012 *Astérix & Obélix: Au service de sa Majesté* (FR/SP/IT/HUN) aka *Astérix and Obélix: God Save Britannia* (co-producer) – dir: Laurent Tirard
2014 *Grace of Monaco* (FR/US/BEL/IT/SWI) (co-producer) – dir: Olivier Dahan
2015 *Il nome del figlio* (IT) aka *An Italian Name* (producer) – dir: Francesca Archibugi
2015 *Io e lei* (IT) (producer) – dir: Maria Sole Tognazzi
2017 *Gli sdraiati* (IT) aka *Couch Potatoes* (producer) – dir: Francesca Archibugi
2017 *Todos lo saben* (SP/FR/IT/ARG/GER) aka *Everybody Knows* (co-producer) – dir: Asghar Farhadi
2018 *Sulla mia pelle* (IT) aka *On My Skin: The Last Seven Days of Stefano Cucchi* (producer) – dir: Alessio Cremonini
2018 *Ride* (IT) (producer) – dir: Jacopo Rondinelli
2018 *Natale a 5 stelle* (IT) (producer) – dir: Marco Risi
2018 *La befana vien di notte* (IT/SP) aka *The Legend of the Christmas Witch* (producer) – dir: Michele Soavi
2019 *Un'avventura* (IT) (producer) – dir: Marco Danieli
2019 *Il processo* (IT) (tv series) aka *The Trial* (producer) – dir: Stefano Lodovichi
2020 *18 regali* (IT) aka *18 Presents* (producer) – dir: Francesco Amato
2020 *D.N.A.: Decisamente non adatti* (IT) (producer) – dir: Claudio Gregori & Pasquale Petrolo
2020 *Sotto il sole di Riccione* (IT) (producer) – dir: Younuts
2021 *Freaks Out* (IT/BEL) (producer) – dir: Gabriele Mainetti
2021 *La stanza* (IT) aka *The Room* (producer) – dir: Stefano Lodovichi
2021 *La donna per me* (IT) (producer) – dir: Marco Martani
2021 *Io sono Babbo Natale* (IT) (producer) – dir: Edoardo Maria Falcone
2021 *La Befana vien di notte: Le origini* (IT) aka *The Legend of the Christmas Witch 2: The Origins* (producer) – dir: Paola Randi
2022 *...Altrimenti ci arrabbiamo!* (IT) (producer) – dir: YouNuts! (Niccolò Celaia & Antonio Usbergo)
2022 *Gli idoli delle donne* (IT) (producer) – dir: Claudio Gregori, Pasquale Petrolo, Eros Puglielli
2022 *Con chi viaggi* (IT) (producer) aka *Drive Me Crazy* – dir: YouNuts! (Niccolò Celaia & Antonio Usbergo)
2022 *Sotto il sole di Amalfi* (IT) aka *Under the Amalfi Sun* (producer/actor) – dir: Martina Pastori & Valeria Zunzun
2022 *Il principe di Roma* (IT) (producer) – dir: Edoardo Maria Falcone
2022 *Lillo e Greg Comedy Show* (IT) (producer) – dir: Cristiano D'Alisera
2022 *Christian* (IT) (tv series) (producer) – dir: Roberto Cinardi & Stefano Lodovichi
2023 *Sono Lillo* (IT) (tv series) (producer) – dir: Eros Puglielli
2023 *Profeti* (IT) (producer) – dir: Alessio Cremonini
2023 *Grosso guaio all'Esquilino – La leggenda del kung fu* (IT) (producer) – dir: YouNuts! (Niccolò Celaia & Antonio Usbergo)
2023 *Shake* (IT) (tv series) (producer) – dir: Giulia Gandini
2023 *Denti da squalo* (IT) (producer) – dir: Davide Gentile
2023 *La voce che hai dentro* (IT) (tv series) (producer) – dir: Eros Puglielli
2023 *Dall'alto di una fredda torre* (IT) (producer) – dir: Francesco Frangipane
2023 *Elf Me* (IT) (producer) – dir: YouNuts! (Niccolò Celaia & Antonio Usbergo)
2023 *Gigolò per caso* (IT) (tv series) (producer) – dir: Eros Puglielli
2024 *Gli addestratori* (IT) aka *The Trainers* (producer) – dir: Andrea Jublin
2024 *Marcello mio* (FR/IT) (co-producer) – dir: Christophe Honoré

Jennifer O'Neill

born 20 February 1948 in Rio de Janeiro, Brazil

Virginia Ducci in ***The Psychic***

1968 *For Love of Ivy* (US) – dir: Daniel Mann
1969 *Some Kind of a Nut* (US) [uncredited] – dir: Garson Kanin
1969 *Futz* (US) [uncredited] – dir: Tom O'Horgan
1970 *Glass Houses* (US) – dir: Alexander Singer [released in 1972]
1970 *Rio Lobo* (US) – dir: Howard Hawks
1971 *Summer of '42* (US) – dir: Richard Mulligan
1971 *Such Good Friends* (US) – dir: Otto Preminger
1972 *The Carey Treatment* (US) – dir: Blake Edwards
1973 *Lady Ice* (US) – dir: Tom Gries
1975 *The Reincarnation of Peter Proud* (US) – dir: J. Lee Thompson
1975 *Gente di rispetto* (IT) US *The Flower in His Mouth* UKvdt *A Man to Respect / The Masters* – dir: Luigi Zampa
1975 *Whiffs* (US) – dir: Ted Post
1976 *L'innocente* (IT/FR) FR *L'innocent* UK/US *The Innocent* – dir: Luchino Visconti
1977 *Sette note in nero* (IT) US ***The Psychic*** export title *Murder to the Tune of the Seven Black Notes* – dir: Lucio Fulci
1978 *A Force of One* (US) – dir: Paul Aaron
1978 *Caravans* (US/IRN) – dir: James Fargo
1979 *Love's Savage Fury* (US) (tv movie) – dir: Joseph Hardy
1979 *Cloud Dancer* (US) – dir: Barry Brown
1980 *Steel* (US) – dir: Steve Carver
1981 *Scanners* (CAN) – dir: David Cronenberg
1981 *The Other Victim* (US) (tv movie) – dir: Noel Black
1983 *Bare Essence* (US) (tv series) (11 episodes) – dir: Walter Grauman
1984 *A.D. – Anno Domini* (US/IT) (tv mini-series) – dir: Stuart Cooper
1984-85 *Cover Up* (US) (tv series) (14 episodes)
1985 *Chase* (US) (tv movie) – dir: Rod Holcomb
1986 *I Love N.Y.* (US/IT) – dir: Gianni Bozzacchi
1986 *Perry Mason: The Case of the Shooting Star* (US) (tv movie) – dir: Ron Satlof
1988 *The Red Spider* (US) (tv movie) – dir: Jerry Jameson
1988 *Glory Days* (US) (tv movie) – dir: Robert Conrad
1988 *Committed* (US) – dir: William Levey
1989 *Full Exposure: The Sex Tapes Scandal* (US) (tv movie) – dir: Noel Nosseck
1990 *Personals* (US) – dir: Steven Hilliard Stern
1992 *Love Is Like That* (US) – dir: Jill Goldman
1992 *Invasion of Privacy* (US) (tv movie) – dir: Kevin Meyer
1992 *Perfect Family* (US) (tv movie) – dir: E.W. Swackhamer
1993 *Discretion Assured* (US) – dir: Odorico Mendes
1993 *The Cover Girl Murders* (US) (tv movie) – dir: James A. Contner
1994 *Jonathan Stone: Threat of Innocence* (US) (tv movie) aka *Frame-up* – dir: Michael Switzer
1994 *The Visual Bible: Acts* (US) – dir: Regardt van den Bergh
1995 *The Silver Strand* (US) (tv movie) – dir: George Miller
1996 *The Corporate Ladder* (US) – dir: Nick Vallelonga
1996 *Voyeur II* (US) (full motion video game) (voice) – dir: Robert Weaver
1996 *Poltergeist: The Legacy* (CAN/US) (tv series) episode *Revelations* – dir: Allan Eastman
1997 *Raney* (US) – dir: Alan Gay
1997 *The Ride* (US) – dir: Michael O. Sajbel
1997 *Nash Bridges* (US) (tv series) episode *Shake, Rattle & Roll* – dir: John McPherson
1999 *The Prince and the Surfer* (US) – dir: Arye Gross & Gregory Gieras
2000 *On Music Row* (US) (tv movie) – dir: Armanda Costanza
2002 *Time Changer* (US) – dir: Rich Christiano
2008 *Billy: The Early Years* (US) – dir: Robby Benson
2009 *Set Apart* (US) – dir: Ralph E. Portillo
2012 *Last Ounce of Courage* (US) – dir: Darrel Campbell & Kevin McAfee
2013 *Doonby* (US/IRE) – dir: Peter Mackenzie
2016 *I'm Not Ashamed* (US) – dir: Brian Baugh

Marc Porel

born 3 January 1949 in Lausanne, Switzerland
died 15 August 1983 in Casablanca, Morocco
real name **Marc Landry**

Don Alberto Avallone in ***Don't Torture a Duckling***
Luca Fattori in ***The Psychic***

1967 *Un homme de trop* (FR/IT) IT *Il 13° uomo* aka *Shock Troops* – dir: Costa-Gavras
1967 *Des garçons et des filles* (FR/BEL) aka *Boys and Girls* – dir: Etienne Périer
1968 *La promesse* (FR) export title *Secret World* – dir: Paul Feyder
1968 *Le clan des Siciliens* (FR) UK *The Sicilian Clan* – dir: Henri Verneuil
1969 *Une fille nommée Amour* (FR/IT) IT *Una ragazza chiamata Amore* [uncredited] – dir: Sergio Gobbi
1970 *La horse* (FR/IT/WG) IT *Il clan degli uomini violenti* WG *Der Erbarmungslose* – dir: Pierre Granier-Deferre
1970 *Le dernier saut* (FR/IT) FR *Indagine su un "parà" accusato d'omicidio* aka *Last Leap* – dir: Édouard Luntz
1970 *La route de Salina* (FR/IT) IT *Quando il sole scotta* UK *Road to Salina* – dir: Georges Lautner
1970 *Tumuc-Humac* (FR) – dir: Jean-Marie Périer
1971 *Les aveux les plus doux* (FR/ALG/IT) IT *Ricatto di un commissario di polizia a un giovane indiziato di reato* – dir: Edouard Molinaro
1971 *Un peau de soleil dans l'eau froide* (FR/IT) IT *Un pò di sole nell'acqua gelida* – dir: Jacques Deray
1972 *Non si sevizia un paperino* (IT) export title ***Don't Torture a Duckling*** – dir: Lucio Fulci
1972 *Un officier de police sans importance* (FR) – dir: Jean Larriaga

1973 *Ludwig* (IT/FR/WG) FR *Ludwig... ou le crépuscule des dieux* WG *Ludwig II* – dir: Luchino Visconti
1973 *Tony Arzenta* (IT/FR) FR *Big Guns – Les grands fusils* export title *Big Guns* aka *No Way Out* – dir: Duccio Tessari
1974 *Colpo in canna* (IT) UK *Stick 'Em Up, Darlings!* US *Loaded Guns / Stick Them Up, Darlings!* – dir: Fernando Di Leo
1974 *Die Ameisen kommen* (WG) – dir: Jochen Richter
1974 *Nipoti miei diletti* (IT) – dir: Franco Rossetti
1974 *Virilità* (IT) US *Virility* – dir: Paolo Cavara
1975 *Quand la ville s'eveille* (FR) – dir: Pierre Grasset
1975 *Il marsigliese* (IT) (tv mini-series) – dir: Giacomo Battiato
1976 *Il soldato di ventura* (IT/FR) FR *La grande bagarre* UKvdt *Soldier of Fortune* – dir: Pasquale Festa Campanile
1976 *Uomini si nasce poliziotti si muore* (IT) UK *Live Like a Cop, Die Like a Man* UKvdt *The Terminators* – dir: Ruggero Deodato
1976 *L'innocente* (IT/FR) FR *L'innocent* UK/US *The Innocent* – dir: Luchino Visconti
1977 *Una spirale di nebbia* (IT/FR) FR *Caresses bourgeoises* – dir: Eriprando Visconti
1977 *Difficile morire* (IT) – dir: Umberto Silva
1977 *Sette note in nero* (IT) US ***The Psychic*** export title *Murder to the Tune of the Seven Black Notes* – dir: Lucio Fulci
1977 *Milano... difendersi o morire* (IT) export title *Blazing Bullets* UKvdt *Blazing Flowers* WG *Heroin* – dir: Gianni [Giovanni] Antonio Martucci
1978 *La sorella di Ursula* (IT) – dir: Enzo Milioni
1978 *Porci con la P 38* (IT) – dir: Gianfranco Pagani
1978 *L'albero della maldicenza* (IT) – dir: Giacinto Bonacquisti
1978 *Le Venere d'Ille* (IT) (tv movie) – dir: Mario Bava & Lamberto Bava [series *I giochi del diavolo Storie fantastiche dell'ottocento*]
1979 *Histoires insolites* (FR) (tv series) episode *Une dernière fois Catherine* – dir: Pierre Grimblat
1980 *La via del silenzio* (IT) – dir: Franco Brocani
1980 *La pagella* (IT) – dir: Ninì Grassia
1980 *Je vais craquer* (FR) – dir: François Leterrier
1981 *Habibi, amor mío* (SP/IT) – dir: Luis Gómez Valdivieso
1981 *La disubbidienza* (IT/FR) FR *La désobéissance* – dir: Aldo Lado
1981 *Il marchese del Grillo* (IT/FR) FR *Le marquis s'amuse* – dir: Mario Monicelli
1982 *Progetti di allegria* (IT) (tv mini-series) – dir: Vittorio De Sisti
1982 *Perdóname, amor* (SP) – dir: Luis Gómez Valdivieso
1982 *La certosa di Parma* (IT/WG/FR) (tv movie) FR television title *La chartreuse de Parme* UK television title *The Charterhouse of Parma* – dir: Mauro Bolognini
1982 *Delitto carnale* (IT) – dir: Cesare Canevari

Giovanni Lombardo Radice

born 23 September 1954 in Rome, Italy
died 27 April 2023 in Rome, Italy
aka **John Morghen**

Bob in ***City of the Living Dead***

1973 *Non ho tempo* (IT) aka *No More Time* [uncredited extra] – dir: Ansano Giannarelli
1980 *La casa sperduta nel parco* (IT) export title *House on the Edge of the Park* – dir: Ruggero Deodato
1980 *Apocalypse domani* (IT/SP) SP *Virus* US *Cannibals in the Streets / Invasion of the Flesh Hunters* UKvdt *Cannibal Apocalypse* – dir: Anthony M. Dawson [Antonio Margheriti]
1980 *Paura nella città dei morti viventi* (IT) US *The Gates of Hell* UK ***City of the Living Dead*** – dir: Lucio Fulci
1981 *Cannibal Ferox* (IT) US *Make Them Die Slowly* – dir: Umberto Lenzi
1981 *Greggio e pericoloso* (IT) (tv mini-series) – dir: Enzo Tarquini
1982 *Incontro nell'ultimo paradiso* (IT) GREvdt *Daughter of the Jungle* (co-story/co-screenplay) – dir: Umberto Lenzi
1982 *Il mistero degli Etruschi* (IT/FR) (tv mini-series, shortened version shown theatrically) IT *Assassinio al cimitero etrusco* FR *Crime aux cimetière éstrusque* USvdt *Scorpion with Two Tails* – dir: Christian Plummer [Sergio Martino]
1983 *Flipper* (IT) – dir: Andrea Barzini
1983 *Il momento dell'avventura* (IT) (tv movie) (co-writer) – dir: Falerio Rosati
1983 *The Scarlet and the Black* (US/IT) (tv movie) – dir: Jerry London
1983 *Progetto Atlantide* (IT) (tv movie) – dir: Gianni Serra
1983 *Nata d'amore* (IT) (tv movie) – dir: Duccio Tessari
1984 *Impatto mortale* (IT) UKvdt *Deadly Impact* WG *Giant Killer* shooting title *The Believer* – dir: Larry Ludman [Fabrizio De Angelis]
1984 *Majakowski* (IT) (tv movie) – dir: Gianni Toti
1985 *Aeroporto internazionale* (IT) (tv series) (screenplay – various episodes) – dir: Enzo Tarquini
1985 *I soliti ignoti vent'anni dopo* (IT) – dir: Amanzio Todini
1985 *Il calice di murano* (IT) (tv movie) – dir: Sergio Martino [series *Caccia al ladro d'autore*]
1985 *Quando arriva il giudice* (IT) (tv movie) – dir: Giulio Questi
1986 *Ciao ma'...* (IT) – aka *Baci da Roma* – dir: Giandomenico Curi
1987 *Deliria* (IT) UKvdt *Stagefright – Aquarius* FR *Bloody Bird* – dir: Michele Soavi
1987 *L'isola del tesoro* (IT/FR/WG) (tv mini-series) UKvdt *Space Island* UK television title *Treasure Island in Space* – dir: Antonio Margheriti
1987 *Che gioia vivere* (IT) (tv movie) – dir: Stelio Bergamo
1988 *Un delitto poco comune* (IT) UKvdt *Phantom of Death / Off Balance* – dir: Ruggero Deodato
1988 *Sei delitti per padre Brown* (IT) (tv mini-series) – dir: Vittorio De Sisti
1988 *La parola segreta* (IT) – dir: Stelio Fiorenza
1989 *La chiesa* (IT) UKvdt *The Church* – dir: Michele Soavi
1990 *I ragazzi del muretto* (IT) (tv series) (co-screenplay – 26 episodes) – dir's: Paolo Poeti & Tomaso Sherman
1990 *La setta* (IT) US *The Devil's Daughter* UKvdt *The Sect* – dir: Michele Soavi
1992 *Body Puzzle / Misteria* (IT) – dir: Lamberto Bava
1992 *Un posto freddo in fondo al cuore* (IT) (tv movie) – dir: Sauro Scavolini

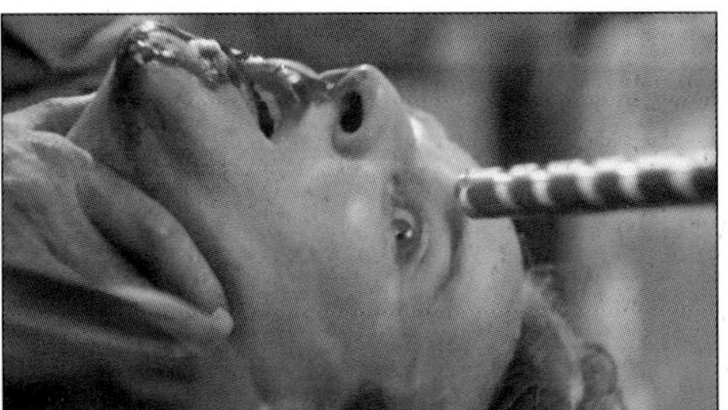

1992 *Ricky & Barabba* (IT) – dir: Christian De Sica
1993 *Amico mio* (IT) (tv series) (story/screenplay – 2 episodes) – dir: Paolo Poeti
1997 *L'avvocato delle donne* (IT/GER) (tv mini-series) GER *Für Liebe und Gerechtigkeit* (story/screenplay – 2 episodes) – dir: Andrea Frazzi & Antonio Frazzi
1997 *Mamma per caso* (IT) (4-part tv mini-series) (co-writer) – dir: Sergio Martino
1998 *Il cuore e la spada* (IT/FR/GER) (tv movie) GER *Tristan und Isolde – Eine Liebe für die Ewigkeit* – dir: Fabrizio Costa
1999 *Michele Strogoff – il corriere dello zar* (IT/GER) (tv movie) – dir: Fabrizio Costa
2000 *San Paolo* (IT/CZE/GER) (tv movie) aka *St. Paul* – dir: Roger Young
2000 *Padre Pio: Tra cielo e terra* (IT) (tv movie) – dir: Giulio Base
2000 *Sei forte, maestro* (IT) (tv series) (co-screenplay – 13 episodes)
2001 *Honolulu Baby* (IT) – dir: Maurizio Nichetti
2001 *Inviati speciali (Giulia e Marco)* (IT) (tv movie) (co-screenplay) – dir: Francesco Laudadio
2002 *Prendimi l'anima* (IT/FR/UK) aka The Soul Keeper – dir: Roberto Faenza
2002 *Don Matteo* (IT) (tv series) episode *Paura in palcoscenico* – dir: Andrea Barzini
2002 *Gangs of New York* (US/IT) – dir: Martin Scorsese
2003 *La notte di Pasquino* (IT) (tv movie) – dir: Luigi Magni
2003 *La squadra* (IT) (tv series) episode #3.31 (co-story) – dir: Marcantonio Graffeo
2006 *The Omen* (US) – dir: John Moore
2007 *Il nascondiglio* (IT/US) aka *The Hideout* – dir: Pupi Avati
2008 *Schifanosaurus rex* (IT) (documentary) – dir: Franco Brocani
2009 *Cemento* (IT) (short) – dir: Sebastiano Melloni
2009 *House of Flesh Mannequins* (US) – dir: Domiziano Cristopharo
2010 *A Day of Violence* (UK) – dir: Darren Ward
2011 *The Reverend* (UK) – dir: Neil Jones
2012 *The Infliction* (US) aka *The Inflicted* – dir: Matthan Harris
2012 *Dolor, Doloris, Dolore* (IT) (short) – dir: Simone Valentini
2013 *Viva la libertà* (IT) aka *Long Live Freedom* – dir: Roberto Andò
2013 *L'invito* (IT) (short) – dir: Sergio Stivaletti
2015 *Sfida al cielo – La narcotici 2* (IT) (tv series) – dir: Michele Soavi
2015 *Violent Shit: The Movie* (IT/GER) – dir: Luigi Pastore
2015 *The Three Sisters* (IRE) – dir: Dáire McNab
2015 *Flesh Mannequins: Totally Uncut* (US) – dir: Domiziano Cristopharo
2016 *Moderation* (UK/GRE) – dir: Anja Kirschner
2017 *Una gita a Roma* (IT) – dir: Karin Proia
2017 *Carly & Paolo* (UK) – dir: Spencer Hawken
2018 *Lycanimator* (US) (voice) – dir: Sébastien Godin
2018 *Rabbia furiosa* (IT) aka *Dogman's Rabies* – dir: Sergio Stivaletti
2019 *Beyond Fury* (UK) – dir: Darren Ward
2019 *Everybloody's End* (IT) – dir: Claudio Lattanzi
2021 *Baphomet* (US) – dir: Matthan Harris
2023 *The Well* (IT) – dir: Federico Zampaglione
2024 *Delirio Cremisi* (IT) (short) – dir: Leopoldo Medugno

Renato Rossini

born 10 January 1941 in Rome, Italy
aka **Howard Ross / Red Ross**

Mikos ('Mickey') Scellenda in ***The New York Ripper***
Raven in ***Rome 2033 – The Fighter Centurions***

1961 *Esther and the King* (US/IT) IT *Ester ed il re* [uncredited] – dir: Raoul Walsh & Mario Bava
1962 *La notte dell'innominato* (IT) – dir: Luigi Demar [Luigi Latini de Marchi]
1963 *Maciste contro i Mongoli* (IT) – dir: Domenico Paolella
1964 *Ercole l'invincibile* (IT) UK *Hercules the Invincible* – dir: Al World [Alvaro Mancori]
1964 *Maciste alla corte dello Zar* (IT) – dir: Amerigo Anton [Tanio Boccia]
1964 *Il trionfo di Ercole* (IT/FR) FR *Le triomphe d'Hercule* UK *The Triumph of Hercules* – dir: Alberto De Martino
1964 *Anthar l'invincibile* (IT/FR/SP) FR *Marchands d'esclaves* SP *Soraya, reina del desierto* – dir: Anthony Dawson [Antonio Margheriti]
1964 *Ercole, Sansone, Maciste e Ursus gli invincibili* (IT/FR/SP) FR *Le grand défi* SP *Combate de gigantes* – dir: Giorgio Capitani
1964 *Maciste nell'inferno di Gengis Khan* (IT) – dir: Domenico Paolella
1964 *Una spada per l'Impero* (IT) – dir: Sergio Grieco
1964 *La rivolta dei sette* (IT) UK *The Spartan Gladiators* – dir: Alberto De Martino
1965 *Kindar, l'invulnerabile* (IT/EGY) aka *Kindar the Invulnerable* – dir: Anthony Dawson [Antonio Margheriti]
1965 *El halcón del desierto* (SP/IT) IT *La magnifica sfida* US *Magnificent Challenge* – dir: Miguel Lluch [actually Osvaldo Civirani]
1965 *I quattro inesorabili* (IT/SP) SP *Los cuatro implacables* – dir: Primo Zeglio
1966 *Ringo del Nebraska* (IT/SP) SP *Ringo de Nebraska (El rancho maldido)* export title *Savage Gringo* – dir: Anthony Roman [Antonio Roman] & [uncredited] Mario Bava
1966 *Starblack* (IT/WG) WG *Django schwarzer Gott des Todes* export title *Johnny Colt* – dir: Gianni [Giovanni] Grimaldi
1966 *Zorro il ribelle* (IT) – dir: Piero Pierotti
1966 *Missione sabbie roventi* (IT/SP) SP *Misión arenas ardientes* – dir: Alfonso Brescia
1967 *Dalle Ardenne all'inferno* (IT/WG/FR) WG *...Und morgan fahrt ihr zur Hölle* FR *La gloire des canailles* US/UK *The Dirty Heroes* – dir: Alberto De Martino
1967 *El 'Che' Guevara* (IT) US/UK *Rebel with a Cause* – dir: Paolo Heusch
1967 *Attentato ai tre Grandi* (IT/WG/FR) WG *Fünf gegen Casablanca* FR *Les chiens verts du désert* USvdt *Desert Commandos* – dir: Umberto Lenzi
1967 *Wanted Johnny Texas* (IT) – dir: Emimmo Salvi
1967 *15 forche per un assassino* (IT/SP) SP *Quince horcas para un asesino* – dir: Nunzio Malasomma
1968 *L'ira di Dio* (IT/SP) SP *Hasta la última gota de sangre* UK *The Wrath of God* – dir: Albert Cardiff [Alberto Cardone]
1968 *Lady Hamilton – Zwischen Schmach und Liebe* (WG/IT/FR) IT *Le calde notti di Lady Hamilton* FR *Les amours de Lady Hamilton* US *Lady Hamilton* – dir: Christian-Jaque
1969 *Kidnapping! Paga o uccidiamo tuo figlio* (IT/SP) aka *Twenty Thousand Dollars for Seven* – dir: Alberto Cardone
1969 *Bitka na Neretvi* (YUG/US/IT/WG) US/UK *Battle of Neretva* IT *La battaglia della Neretva* WG *Die Schlacht an der Neretva* US *The Battle on the River Neretva* – dir: Veljko Bulajic
1969 *No importa morir* (SP/IT) IT *Quel maledetto ponte sull'Elba* UK *The Legion of No Return* – dir: Leon Klimowsky
1969 *Le calde notti di Poppea* (IT) – dir: James Reed [Guido Malatesta]
1969 *O' cangaçeiro* (IT/SP) UK *The Magnificent Bandits* – dir: Giovanni Fago
1969 *5 bambole per la luna d'agosto* (IT) export title *Five Dolls for an August Moon* – dir: Mario Bava
1970 *La colomba non deve volare* (IT/WG) export title *Skyriders Attack* – dir: Sergio Garrone
1971 *Il sergente Klems* (IT) – dir: Sergio Grieco
1971 *Quando gli uomini armarono la clava e... con le donne fecero din don* (IT) export title *When Men Carried Clubs... Women Played Ding Dong!* – dir: Bruno Corbucci
1971 *Marta* (SP/IT) IT *...Dopo di che, uccide il maschio e lo divora* export title *Marta* – dir: José Antonio Nieves Conde
1972 *Ragazza tutta nuda assassinata nel parco* (IT/SP) SP *Joven de buena familia, sospechosa de asesinato* export title *Naked Girl Killed in Park* – dir: Alfonso Brescia
1972 *Historia de una traición* (SP/IT) IT *Diabolicamente sole con il delitto / Nel buio del terrore* export title *A Treason Story: Carla and Nora* US *The Great Swindle* – dir: José Antonio Nieves Conde
1972 *A.A.A. Massaggiatrice bella presenza offresi...* (IT) – dir: Demofilo Fidani
1972 *Poppea... una prostituta al servizio dell'Impero* (IT) – dir: Alfonso Brescia
1972 *Il Boss* (IT) UK/US *Murder Inferno* UKvdt *The Boss* US television title *Wipe Out* – dir: Fernando Di Leo

1973 *The Man Called Noon* (UK/SP/IT) SP *Un hombre llamado Noon* IT *Lo chiamavano mezzogiorno* – dir: Peter Collinson
1973 *Campa carogna... la taglia cresce* (IT/SP) SP *Los cuatro de Fort Apache* US *Those Dirty Dogs* export title *Charge* – dir: Giuseppe Rosati
1973 *Number One* (IT) – dir: Gianni Buffardi
1973 *L'ultima chance* (IT) UK *Last Chance* US *Stateline Motel* – dir: Maurizio Lucidi
1973 *Elena sì, ma... di Troia* (IT) – dir: Alfonso Brescia
1973 *El clan de los inmorales* (SP/IT/DOM) IT *La testa del serpente* UK *Order to Kill* – dir: José G. Maesso
1974 *5 donne per l'assassino* (IT/FR) – dir: Stelvio Massi
1974 *L'assassino ha riservato nove poltrone* (IT) export title *The Killer Reserved Nine Seats* – dir: Giuseppe Bennati
1975 *L'uomo che sfidò l'organizzazione* (IT/FR/SP) SP *El hombre que desafío a la organización* US *One Man Against the Organization* export title *Counteragent Against the Organization* aka *Challenge to the Mafia* – dir: Sergio Grieco
1976 *La lupa mannara* (IT) US/USvdt *Legend of the Wolf Woman* UK/UKvdt *Werewolf Woman* UKvdt *Naked Werewolf Woman* USvdt *Legend of the She-Wolf / She-Wolf* – dir: Rino Di Silvestro
1976 *Philemon* (US) (tv movie) – dir: Norman Lloyd
1976 *Genova a mano armata* (IT) export title *The Merciless Man* – dir: Mario Lanfranchi
1976 *Oh, Serafina!* (IT) – dir: Alberto Lattuada
1976 *Sfida sul fondo* (IT) UKvdt *Sacha the Wonderdog / Duel of the Deep* – dir: Melchiade Coletti
1977 *La ragazza dal pigiama giallo* (IT/SP) SP *La chica del pijama amarillo* US *The Girl in the Yellow Pyjamas* – dir: Flavio Mogherini
1977 *L'immoralità* (IT) – dir: Massimo Pirri
1978 *I problemi di Don Isidro Parodi* (IT/FR) (tv series) – dir: Andrea Frezza
1979 *Interno di un convento* (IT/WG) WG *Unmoralische Novizzinnen* UK *Behind Convent Walls* – dir: Walerian Borowczyk
1980 *Vendetta napoletana (Maria)* (WG/IT) – dir: Herb Al Bauer [Ernst Hofbauer]
1980 *Champagne e fagioli* (IT) – dir: Oscar Brazzi
1981 *Napoli Palermo New York: il triangolo della camorra* (IT) export title *The Mafia Triangle* – dir: Alfonso Brescia
1981 *Teste di quoio* (IT) – dir: Giorgio Capitani
1982 *Lo squartatore di New York* (IT) export title ***The New York Ripper*** – dir: Lucio Fulci
1982 *Briganti* (IT) – dir: Giacinto Bonacquisti [released in 1983]
1984 *I guerrieri dell'anno 2072* (IT) USvdt *The New Gladiators* UKvdt ***Rome 2033 – The Fighter Centurions*** – dir: Lucio Fulci
1985 *I giorni dell'inferno* (IT) UKvdt *Days of Hell* – dir: Anthony Richmond [Tonino Ricci]
1987 *Appuntamento a Trieste* (IT) (tv mini-series) – dir: Bruno Mattei
1987 *Giallo* (IT) (tv series) – dir: Enzo Gatta
1987 *Turno di notte* (IT) (tv series) episode *Giallo Natale* – dir: Luigi Cozzi
1987 *Tutti in palestra* (IT) (tv mini-series) – dir: Vittorio De Sisti
1989 *Affari di famiglia* (IT) (tv movie) – dir: Marcello Fondato
1989 *Quelli del college* (IT) (tv movie) – dir: Lorenzo Castellano
1990 *Safari* (FR/IT/GER) (tv movie) GER *Gefahr in der Savanne* – dir: Roger Vadim
1991 *Liberate mio figlio* (IT) (tv movie) – dir: Roberto Malenotti
1993 *Il mago* (IT) (tv movie) – dir: Ezio Pascucci
1993 *Passioni* (IT) (tv series) – dir: Fabrizio Costa
1995 *Vacanze di natale '95* (IT) – dir: Neri Parenti
1996 *Il maresciallo Rocca* (IT) (tv series) episode *Senso di colpa* – dir: Giorgio Capitani

John Savage

born 25 August 1949 in Old Bethpage, NY, USA
real name **John Smeallie Youngs**

Melvin Devereux in ***Door to Silence***

1969 *The Master Beater* (US) aka *The Dirty Hawk / Hot Sex Tramp* – dir: Charles Carmello
1970 *Love Is a Carousel* (US) UKvdt *Love Games* – dir: Roy P. Cheverton
1971 *Cade's County* (US) (tv series) episode *Gray Wolf* – dir: Alf Kjellin
1972 *Steelyard Blues / Final Crash* (US) – dir: Alan Myerson
1972 *Bad Company* (US) – dir: Robert Benton
1973 *The Killing Kind* (US) UKvdt *The Psychopath* – dir: Curtis Harrington
1973 *There Was a Little Girl* (US) USvdt *Midnight Intruder* – dir: Gary Graver
1974 *The Sister-in-Law* (US) – dir: Joseph Ruben
1974 *All the Kind Strangers* (US) (tv movie) – dir: Burt Kennedy
1975 *The Turning Point of Jim Malloy* (US) (tv pilot) – dir: Frank D. Gilroy
1975 *Eric* (US) (tv movie) – dir: James Goldstone
1976 *John O'Hara's Gibbsville* (tv series) (13 episodes)
1978 *The Deer Hunter* (US) – dir: Michael Cimino
1978 *Hair* (US) – dir: Milos Forman
1979 *The Onion Field* (US) – dir: Harold Becker
1980 *Cattle Annie and Little Britches* (US) – dir: Lamont Johnson
1980 *Inside Moves* (US) – dir: Richard Donner
1981 *The Amateur* (US) – dir: Charles Jarrott
1982 *Coming Out of the Ice* (US) (tv movie) – dir: Waris Hussein
1983 *Hosszú vágta* (HUN) export title *The Long Ride* aka *Brady's Escape* – dir: Pál Gábor
1984 *The Little Sister* (US) USvdt *Forbidden* UKvdt *The Tender Age* – dir: Jan Egleson [series *American Playhouse*]
1984 *The Nairobi Affair* (US) (cable tv movie) UKvdt *Nairobi* – dir: Marvin J. Chomsky
1984 *Maria's Lovers* (US) – dir: Andrei Konchalovsky
1984 *La venganza de un soldado* (ARG/US) US *Soldier's Revenge* – dir: David Worth
1985 *Silent Witness* (US) (tv movie) – dir: Michael Miller
1985 *Salvador* (US) – dir: Oliver Stone
1986 *Beauty and the Beast* (US) – dir: Eugene Marner [series *Fairy Tales*]
1987 *Dear America, Letters Home from Vietnam* (US) – dir: Bill Couturie
1987 *Hotel Colonial* (IT/US) – dir: Cinzia TH Torrini
1987 *Nekudat Re'Ut* (IS) US *Point of View* UKvdt *War Shepherds* – dir: Noam Yavor
1987 *Caribe* (CAN) – dir: Paul Donovan
1987 *Desperate* (US) (tv movie) – dir: Peter Markle
1988 *The Beat* (US) aka *The Conjuror* – dir: Paul S. Mones
1988 *Any Man's Death* (US/ZA) – dir: Tom Clegg
1988 *Date Rape* (US) (tv special) – dir: Jesus Trevino
1989 *Do the Right Thing* (US) – dir: Spike Lee
1989 *Hunting* (AUS) US *My Forgotten Man* – dir: Frank Howson
1989 *Voice in the Dark* (ZA) – dir: Vincent G. Cox
1990 *The Godfather Part III* (US) – dir: Francis Ford Coppola
1990 *Primary Motive* (US) – dir: Daniel Adams [released in 1992]
1990 *Ottobre rosa all'Arbat* (IT) – dir: Adolfo Lippi
1991 *My Forgotten Man / Flynn* (AUS) – dir: Frank Howson

1991 *Favola crudele* (IT) aka *Dark Tale* – dir: Roberto Leoni
1991 *Great Expectations* (US/UK) (tv mini-series) episode *Chapter One* – dir: Kevin Connor
1991 *Scoop* (SP/IT) – dir: José Maria Sanchez
1991 *Notti di paura* (IT) export title *Across the Red Night* – dir: Francesca Archibugi & Maurizio Bonuglia
1991 *La montagna di diamanti* (IT/FR/WG) (tv mini-series) export title *The Burning Shore* aka *La signora dei diamanti / Mountain of Diamonds* – dir: Jeannot Szwarc
1991 *Buck ai confini del cielo* (IT/SWI) export title *Buck at the Edge of Heaven* aka *The Invincible Buck* – dir: Anthony Richmond [Tonino Ricci]
1991 *Le porte del silenzio* (IT) export title ***Door to Silence*** – dir: Humphrey S. Kittay [Lucio Fulci]
1992 *Berlino '39* (IT) – dir: Sergio Sollima
1993 *CBS Schoolbreak Special* (US) (tv series) episode *Love Off Limits* – dir: Steve Guttenberg
1993 *The Accident* (US) (tv movie) – dir: Kostas Iannios
1993 *C.I.A. II: Target Alexa* (US) – dir: Lorenzo Lamas
1993 *Hellmaster* (US) – dir: Douglas Schulze
1993 *The Dangerous* (US) – dir: Rod Hewitt
1993 *Centurion Force* (US)
1993 *A Killing Obsession* (US) – dir: Paul Leder
1993 *Daybreak* (US) (cable tv movie) – dir: Stephen Tolkin
1994 *Birdland* (US) (tv series) episode #1.1 – dir: Peter Horton
1994 *Tales from the Crypt* (US) (tv series) episode *Revenge Is the Nuts* – dir: Jonas McCord
1994 *Red Scorpion 2* (US) – dir: Michael Kennedy
1994 *Carnosaur 2* (US) – dir: Louis Morneau
1994 *Shattered Image* (US) (tv movie) – dir: Fritz Kiersch
1994 *The Takeover* (US) – dir: Troy Cook
1995 *Markus 4* (US) UKvdt *Firestorm* – dir: John Shepphird
1995 *American Strays* (US) aka *From the Edge* – dir: Michael Covert
1995 *Tuono di proiettile* (IT) export title *Deadly Weapon* – dir: James Lloyd
1995 *Tom Clancy's Op Center* (US) (tv movie) – dir: Lewis Teague
1995 *The Crossing Guard* (US) – dir: Sean Penn
1995 *One Good Turn* (US) – dir: Tony Randel
1995 *The X-Files* (US/CAN) (tv series) episode *Død Kalm* – dir: Rob Bowman
1995 *The Outer Limits* (CAN/US) (tv series) episode *The Conversion* – dir: Rebecca De Mornay
1995 *Fatal Choice* (US) – dir: Jenö Hodi
1996 *Where Truth Lies* (US) – dir: William H. Molina
1996 *White Squall* (US) – dir: Ridley Scott
1996 *Walker, Texas Ranger* (US) (tv series) episode *Patriot* – dir: Tony Mordente
1996 *The Mouse* (US) shooting title *Upper Cut* (producer/actor) – dir: Daniel Adams
1996 *Amnesia* (US) – dir: Kurt Voss
1996 *Managua* (US/CAN/UK) – dir: Michele Taverna
1997 *Hjørne af paradis* (DEN) US *A Corner of Paradise* – dir: Peter Ringgard
1997 *Little Boy Blue* (US) – dir: Antonio Tibaldi
1997 *Burning Down the House* (US) – dir: Philippe Mora
1997 *Immagini* (IT) – dir: Danilo També
1997 *Before Women Had Wings* (US) (tv movie) – dir: Lloyd Kramer [series *Oprah Winfrey presents*]
1997 *Club Vampire* (US) – dir: Andy Ruben
1997 *Hollywood Safari* (US) – dir: Henri Charr
1997 *Ultimo taglio* (IT/VEN) aka *Last Cut* – dir: Marcello Avallone
1997 *Hostile Intent* (US) – dir: Jonathan Heap
1998 *The Thin Red Line* (US) – dir: Terrence Malick
1998 *Message in a Bottle* (US) – dir: Luis Mandoki
1998 *Mia per sempre* (IT/GER) (tv mini-series) GER *Mia, Liebe meines Lebens* – dir: Giovanni Soldati
1998 *Nightworld: Lost Souls* (CAN/LUX) (tv movie) aka *Lost Souls* – dir: Jeff Woolnough
1999 *Frontline* (US) – dir: Quinton Peeples
1999 *Message in a Bottle* (US) – dir: Luis Mandoki
1999 *The Jack Bull* (US) (tv movie) – dir: John Badham
1999 *Summer of Sam* (US) – dir: Spike Lee
1999 *Star Trek: Voyager* (US) (tv series) episode *Equinox: Part 1* – dir: David Livingston
1999 *Star Trek: Voyager* (US) (tv series) episode *Equinox: Part 2* – dir: David Livingston
1999 *Ghost Soldier* (US) – dir: Ken Hanada

1999 *Something Between Us* (US) (short) – dir: Nayef Yassine
2000-2001 *Dark Angel* (US) (tv series) (24 episodes)
2000 *The Virginian* (US) (tv movie) – dir: Bill Pullman
2000 *Christina's House* (CAN) – dir: Gavin Wilding
2000 *They Nest* (US/CAN) (tv movie) – dir: Ellory Elkayem
2001 *Dead Man's Run* (US) – dir: Robert Hyatt
2001 *Burning Down the House* (US) – dir: Philippe Mora
2001 *Touched By an Angel* (US) (tv series) episode *When Sunny Gets Blue* – dir: Frank E. Johnson
2002 *Redemption of the Ghost* (US) – dir: Richard Friedman
2002 *The Anarchist Cookbook* (US) – dir: Jordan Susman
2002 *Ground Bloom Flower* (US) (short) – dir: Hso Hkam & James Binaski
2002 *Everwood* (US) (tv series) episode *A Thanksgiving Tale* – dir: David Petrarca
2003 *Intoxicating* (US) – dir: Mark David
2003 *Easy Six* (US) – dir: Chris Iovenko
2003 *The District* (US) (tv series) episode *Jupiter for Sale* – dir: Oz Scott
2003 *The Devil and Daniel Webster* (US) aka *Shortcut to Happiness* – dir: Harry Kirkpatrick [Alec Baldwin]
2003-2005 *Carnivàle* (US) (tv series) (15 episodes)
2004 *Alien Lockdown* (US) (tv movie) – dir: Tim Cox [Abram Cox]
2004 *Fallacy* (US) – dir: Jeff Jensen
2004 *Law & Order: Criminal Intent* (US) (tv series) episode *Conscience* – dir: Alex Chapple
2004 *Sucker Free City* (US) (tv movie) – dir: Spike Lee
2004 *Admissions* (US) – dir: Melissa Painter
2004 *Downtown: A Street Tale* (US) – dir: Rafal Zielinski
2005 *Law & Order: Special Victims Unit* (US) (tv series) episode *Quarry* – dir: Constantine Makris
2005 *Aimée Price* (US) (short) – dir: Julien Roussel
2005 *Iowa* (US) – dir: Matt Farnsworth
2005 *Everwood* (US) (tv series) episode *Where the Heart Is* – dir: David Petrarca
2005 *Confessions of a Pit Fighter* (US) – dir: Art Camacho
2005 *Love's Long Journey* (US) (tv movie) – dir: Michael Landon Jr.
2005 *The New World* (US/UK) – dir: Terrence Malick
2005 *King's Echo* (US) (short) – dir: Haim Silberstein
2006 *Kill Your Darlings* (SWE/US) – dir: Björne Larson
2006 *The Drop* (US) – dir: Kevin Lewis
2006 *Shut Up and Shoot!* (US) – dir: Silvio Pollio
2006 *Falling from Grace* (US) (short) – dir: Claudia Strepp
2006 *Father and Son* (US) (short) – dir: Michael C. Edwards
2007 *The Golden Age* (US) (short) – dir: Travis Huff
2007 *No Destination* (US) (short) – dir: Shannah Laumeister
2007 *The Attic* (US) – dir: Mary Lambert
2008 *The Grift* (US) – dir: Ralph E. Portillo
2008 *From a Place of Darkness* (US) – dir: Douglas A. Raine
2008 *Boiler Maker* (US) – dir: Paul T. Murray
2008 *The Coverup* (US) – dir: Brian Jun
2008 *The Golden Boys* (US) – dir: Daniel Adams
2008 *The Violent Kind* (US) – dir: Geoffrey Pepos
2009 *Anytown* (US) – dir: Dave Rodriguez
2009 *Redemption* (US) (short) – dir: Bruce Caulk
2009 *Handsome Harry* (US) – dir: Bette Gordon
2009 *Qi chuan xu xu* (CHN) – dir: Zhong Zheng
2009 *Fringe* (US/CAN) (tv series) episode *Night of Desirable Objects* – dir: Brad Anderson
2009 *Buffalo Bushido* (US) – dir: Peter McGennis
2009 *First Time Long Time* (US) (short) – dir: James Demo
2010 *Dreamkiller* (US) – dir: Catherine C. Pirotta
2010 *Bereavement* (US) – dir: Stevan Mena
2010 *A Small Town Called Descent* (ZA) – dir: Jahmil X.T. Qubeka
2010 *Bed & Breakfast: Love Is a Happy Accident* (US) – dir: Marcio Garcia
2010 *The Right to Bear Arms* (US) – dir: O.W. Tuthill
2011 *Colombian Interviews* (US) – dir: Haim Silberstein
2011 *The Last Gamble* (US) – dir: Joe E. Goodavage
2011 *Nichirin no isan* (JAP) aka *The Legacy of the Sun* – dir: Kiyoshi Sasabe
2011 *The Orphan Killer* (US) – dir: Matt Farnsworth
2011 *Hit List* (US) – dir: Minh Collins
2011 *Assassins' Code* (US) – dir: Lawrence Riggins
2011 *Summer Song* (US) – dir: A. Rappaport
2011 *Checking Under the Hood* (US) (short) – dir: Michael G. Kehoe
2012 *Sweetwater* (US) aka *The Jonas Project* – dir: Brian Skiba
2012 *Sins Expiation* (IT/ROU/US) – dir: Carlo Fusco
2012 *Art of Submission* (US) aka *Money Fight* – dir: Adam Boster & Kenneth Chamitoff
2012 *The Black Dove* (US) – dir: Michael Caporale
2012 *Spinning Dry* (US) – dir: James Avallone
2013 *Open Road* (BRA/US) – dir: Marcio Garcia
2013 *The Sorrow* (US) aka *A Sierra Nevada Gunfight* – dir: Vernon E. Mortensen
2013 *Real Gangsters* (CAN) – dir: Frank D'Angelo
2013 *Gemini Rising* (US/GER) aka *Alien Rising* – dir: Dana Schroeder
2013 *Awakened* (US) – dir: Joycelyn Engle & Arno Malarone
2013 *A Star for Rose* (US) – dir: Daniel Yost
2013 *Defending Santa* (CAN/US) – dir: Brian Skiba
2013 *7E* (US) – dir: Teddy Schenck
2013 *Discarded* (US) – dir: Jeffrey Elmont
2014 *Spreading Darkness* (US) – dir: Josh Eisenstadt [released in 2017]
2014 *Bullet* (US) – dir: Nick Lyon
2014 *Bermuda Tentacles* (US) (tv movie) – dir: Nick Lyon
2014 *Fort Bliss* (TUR/US) – dir: Claudia Myers
2014 *See How They Run* (US) aka *Demon Legacy* – dir: Rand Vossler
2014 *The Lookalike* (US) – dir: Richard Gray
2014 *Cry of the Butterfly* (US) – dir: Mihailo Stanich
2014 *Cleaners* (US) (tv series) – dir: Paul Leyden
2014 *Whitey* (US) (tv series) episode *Girlfriend* – dir: Jeff Hennessy & Donald Watson
2014 *The Big Fat Stone* (CAN) – dir: Frank D'Angelo
2014 *On Air* (US) (tv series) – dir: Ivan Lowenberg
2015 *The Sparrows: Nesting* (US) – dir: Nancy Criss, Josh Hodgins
2015 *Bicemo prvaci sveta* (SRB/CRO/SLO/BIH/MKD) aka *We Will Be the World Champions* – dir: Darko Bajic
2015 *Rise Again* (US) – dir: Craig Ross Jr.
2015 *Tales of Halloween* (US) segment *Bad Seed* – dir: Neil Marshall [other dir's: Darren Lynn Bousman, Axelle Carolyn, Adam Gierasch, Andrew Kasch, Lucky McKee, Mike Mendez, Dave Parker, Ryan Schifrin, John Skipp, Paul Solet]
2015 *Beverly Hills Christmas* (US) – dir: Brian Skiba
2015 *Last Call at Murray's* (US) – dir: Linda Palmer
2016 *American Romance* (US) – dir: Zackary Adler
2016 *In Dubious Battle* (US) – dir: James Franco
2016 *Texas Heart* (US) – dir: Mark David
2016 *Teen Star Academy* (UK) – dir: Cristian Scardigno
2017 *Nephilim* (US) (voice) – dir: Danny Wilson
2017 *Povratak* (SRB) export title *The Return* – dir: Predrag Jaksic
2017 *Hold On* (US) – dir: Tarek Tohme
2017 *Heavenly Deposit* (US) – dir: Rick Irvin & George Vincent
2017 *Fake News* (US) – dir: Craig Edwards & Samuel Morris
2017 *Three Seconds* (RUS) – dir: Anton Megerdichev
2017 *Insight* (US) – dir: Livi Zheng
2017 *Impuratus* (US) – dir: Mike Yurinko
2017 *Empire of the Sharks* (US) (tv movie) – dir: Mark Atkins
2017 *Twin Peaks* (US) (tv series) – dir: David Lynch
2017 *The Neighborhood* (CAN) – dir: Frank D'Angelo
2017 *Spreading Darkness* (US) – dir: Josh Eisenstadt
2018 *Easy Way Out* (US) (short) – dir: Jeffery T. Schultz
2018 *Goliath* (US) (tv series) episode *Diablo Verde* – dir: Lawrence Trilling
2018 *Mission Possible* (UK) – dir: Onysha D. Collins & Bret Roberts
2018 *Betrayed* (US) – dir: Harley Wallen
2018 *Torque* (BUL/IT/FR) (tv series) – dir: Martin Makariev, Dimitar Mitovski & Zoran Petrovski
2018 *Six Children and One Grandfather* (UK) – dir: Yann Thomas
2018 *Torch* (US) – dir: Christopher Coppola
2019 *Sensory Perception* (US) – dir: Alessandro Signore
2019 *40 and Single* (US) (tv series) – dir: Leila Djansi
2019 *American Exit* (US) – dir: Tim McCann & Ingo Vollkammer
2019 *Heavenly Deposit* (US) – dir: Rick Irvin & George Vincent
2019 *A Medicine for the Mind* (US) (short) – dir: David Xarach
2019 *Down's Revenge* (US) – dir: Lekhraj Patel
2019 *Ovid and the Art of Love* (US) – dir: Esmé von Hoffman
2019 *The Last Full Measure* (US) – dir: Todd Robinson
2019 *Spinning Dry* (US) – dir: James Avallone & Elana Krausz
2019 *Gates of Darkness* (US/FR/NEP) – dir: Don E. FauntLeRoy
2019 *The Islands* (US) – dir: Timothy A. Chey
2019 *Hold On* (US) – dir: Tarek Tohme
2020 *SEAL Team* (US) (tv series) episodes *Last Known Location, Drawdown, Edge of Nowhere, In the Blind* – dir: Larry Teng, Max Thieriot, Christine Moore & Allison Liddi-Brown
2020 *Followed* (US) – dir: Antoine Le
2020 *A Medicine for the Mind* (US) (short) – dir: David Xarach
2020 *Ain't That a Kick in the Head* (US) (short) – dir: K.C. Osterberg
2021 *The Dog of Christmas* (UK) – dir: Bret Roberts
2021 *Insight* (US) – dir: Ken Zheng & Livi Zheng
2021 *Torch* (US) – dir: Christopher Coppola
2022 *A Cloud So High* (US) – dir: Christopher L. Parson
2022 *Eye for Eye* (US) – dir: L.J. Martin
2022 *Bosch: Legacy* (US) (tv series) episode *Plan B* – dir: Alex Zakrzewski
2022 *The Right to Bear Arms* (US) – dir: O.W. Tuthill
2022 *The Audition* (UK) (narrator) – dir: Bizhan M. Tong
2023 *Showdown at the Grand* (US) – dir: Orson Oblowitz
2024 *The Man with the Camera* (IT/GER) – dir: B.K. Wunder
2024 *Beyond the Rush* (US) – dir: Robert Sayegh

Elke Sommer

born 5 November 1940 in Berlin-Spandau, West Germany
real name **Elke Schletz**

Giulia Cesari in ***I ragazzi del juke box***
Giulia Giommarelli in ***Urlatori alla sbarra***

1958 *Das Totenschiff* (WG/MEX) – dir: Georg Tressler
1959 *L'amico del giaguaro* (IT) – dir: Giuseppe Bennati
1959 *Uomini e nobiluomini* (IT) – dir: Giorgio Bianchi
1959 *Am Tag, als der Regen kam* (WG) US *The Day It Rained* – dir: Gerd Oswald
1959 ***I ragazzi del juke box*** (IT) – dir: Lucio Fulci
1959 *La Pica sul Pacifico* (IT) – dir: Roberto Montero [Bianchi]
1960 ***Urlatori alla sbarra*** (IT) export title *Howlers in the Dock* – dir: Lucio Fulci
1960 *Lampenfieber* (WG) – dir: Kurt Hoffmann
1960 *Femmine di lusso* (IT) US *Love, the Italian Way* – dir: George White [Giorgio Bianchi]
1960 *Himmel, Amor und Zwirn* (WG) US *Heaven and Cupid* – dir: Ulrich Erfurth
1960 *Saffo, Venere di Lesbo* (IT/FR) FR *Sapho* US/UK *The Warrior Empress* – dir: Pietro Francisci
1960 *Und so was nennt sich Leben* (WG) – dir: Geza von Radvanyi
1961 *Don't Bother to Knock* (UK) US *Why Bother to Knock?* – dir: Cyril Frankel
1961 *De quoi tu te mêles, Daniela!* (FR/WG) WG *Zarte Haut in schwarzer Seide* UK/US *Daniella By Night* – dir: Max Pecas
1961 *Douce violence* (FR) US *Sweet Ecstasy / Sweet Violence* – dir: Max Pecas
1961 *Geliebte Hochstaplerin* (WG) – dir: Akos von Ratony
1961 *Auf Wiedersehen* (WG) – dir: Harald Philipp
1961 *Café Oriental* (WG) – dir: Rudolf Schündler
1961 *Das Mädchen und der Staatsanwalt* (WG) – dir: Gustav Ucicky
1962 *Le chien* (FR) (tv movie) – dir: François Chalais
1962 *Les bricoleurs* (FR) UK *Who Stole the Body?* – dir: Jean Girault
1962 *Un chien dans un jeu de quilles* (FR/IT) IT *Uno sconosciuto nel mio letto* – dir: Fabien Collin
1962 *Nachts ging des Telefon* (WG) US *The Phone Rings Every Night* – dir: Geza von Cziffra
1962 *Bahía de Palma* (SP) – dir: Juan Bosch
1963 *The Victors* (UK) – dir: Carl Foreman

1963 *The Inheritance* (UK) – dir: Euan Lloyd [short on the making of *The Victors*]
1963 *...denn die Musik und die Liebe in Tirol* (WG) – dir: Werner Jacobs
1963 *Ostrva* (YUG/WG) WG *Verführung am Meer* US *Island of Desire* – dir: Jovan Zivanovic
1963 *The Prize* (US) – dir: Mark Robson
1964 *Parmi les vautours* (FR/IT/WG/YUG) IT *Là dove scende il sole* WG *Unter Geiern* UK *Among Vultures* US *Frontier Hellcat* – dir: Alfred Vohrer
1964 *Le bambole* (IT/FR) FR *Les poupées* US *Bambole / The Dolls* UK *Four Kinds of Love* segment *Il trattato di eugenetica* – dir: Luigi Comencini [other dir's: Dino Risi, Franco Rossi & Mauro Bolognini]
1964 *A Shot in the Dark* (UK/US) – dir: Blake Edwards
1964 *Wenn man baden geht auf Teneriffa* (WG) – dir: Helmuth M. Backhaus
1965 *The Art of Love* (US) – dir: Norman Jewison
1965 *Hotel der toten Gäste* (WG/SP) SP *El enigma de los Cornell* – dir: Eberhard Itzenplitz
1965 *The Money Trap* (US) – dir: Burt Kennedy
1965 *The Oscar* (US) – dir: Russell Rouse
1966 *Die Hölle von Macao* (WG/FR/IT) FR *Les corrompus* IT *Il sigillo de Pechino* US *The Corrupt Ones* UK *The Peking Medallion* – dir: Frank Winterstein & James Hill
1966 *Boy, Did I Get a Wrong Number!* (US) – dir: George Marshall
1966 *Deadlier Than the Male* (UK) – dir: Ralph Thomas
1966 *The Venetian Affair* (US) – dir: Jerry Thorpe
1967 *Las Vegas 500 milliones* (SP/IT/WG/FR) IT *Radiografia di un colpo d'oro* FR *Les hommes de Las Vegas* WG *An einem Freitag in Las Vegas* US/UK *They Came to Rob Las Vegas* – dir: Antonio Isasi Isasmendi
1967 *The Wicked Dreams of Paula Schultz* (US) – dir: George Marshall
1968 *The Wrecking Crew* (US) – dir: Phil Karlson
1968 *The Invincible Six* (US/IRN) – dir: Jean Negulesco
1970 *Percy* (UK) – dir: Ralph Thomas
1971 *Zeppelin* (UK) – dir: Etienne Perier
1971 *Perlico – Perlaco* (WG) (tv movie) – dir: Michael Pfleghar
1971 *Elke* (US) (tv pilot) – dir: Melville Shavelson
1972 *Probe / Search* (US) (tv pilot) – dir: Russ Mayberry
1972 *Gli orrori del castello di Norimberga* (IT/WG/US) UK/US *Baron Blood* USvdt *The Torture Chamber of Baron Blood* – dir: Mario Bava
1972 *Lodynskis Flohmarkt Company* (AT) (tv series) episode #1.7 – dir: Peter Lodynski
1972 *Lisa e il diavolo* (IT/SP/WG) SP *El diablo se lleva a los muertos* UKvdt *Lisa and the Devil* – dir: Mario Bava [unreleased in Italy]
1973 *Die Reise nach Wien* (WG) – dir: Edgar Reitz
1973 *Einer von uns Beiden* (WG) – dir: Wolfgang Petersen
1973 *The Most Dangerous Match* (US) (tv movie) – dir: Edward Abroms [series *Colombo*]
1974 *Percy's Progress* (UK) US *It's Not the Size That Counts* – dir: Ralph Thomas
1974 *Ein unbekannter rechnet ab* (WG/IT/SP/FR/UK) IT *...E poi, non ne rimase nessuno* SP *Diez negritos* FR *Dix petits nègres* UK *And Then There Were None* US *Ten Little Indians* shooting title *Death in Persepolis* – dir: Peter Collinson
1975 *La casa dell'esorcismo* (IT/SP/WG) WG *Der Teuflische* UK/US *House of Excorism* – dir: Mickey Lion [Mario Bava & Alfredo Leone] [re-edited version of *Lisa e il diavolo*, 1972, with new footage of Sommer]
1975 *Carry On Behind* (UK) – dir: Gerald Thomas
1975 *The Swiss Conspiracy* (FR/WG) WG *Per Saldo Mord* – dir: Jack Arnold
1975 *Das Netz* (WG) – dir: Manfred Purzer
1976 *The Six Million Dollar Man* (US) (tv series) episode *H+2+O = Death* – dir: John Meredyth Lucas
1976 *One Away* (UK) UKvdt *Gitano's Escape from Apartheid* – dir: Sidney Hayers
1976 *Pronto ad uccidere* (IT/WG) WG *Tote pflastern seinen Weg* UKvdt *Pronto / Risking...* – dir: Franco Prosperi [Francesco Prosperi]
1976 *The Astral Factor* (US) UKvdt *Silent Kill* – dir: John Florea [re-edited, with added footage, and re-released as *The Invisible Strangler* (US 1981)]
1976 *Forty Million Bucks on a Dead Man's Chest* (US) UKvdt *The Treasure Seekers / Contraband / Treasure of Death* – dir: Henry Levin
1977 *Nicht von gestern* (WG) (tv movie) – dir: Ludwig Cremer
1978 *I Miss You, Hugs and Kisses* (CAN) USvdt *Left for Dead* UKvdt *Drop Dead Dearest* – dir: Murray Markowitz
1978 *The Prisoner of Zenda* (UK) – dir: Richard Quine
1978 *The Double McGuffin* (US) – dir: Joe Camp
1979 *Stunt Seven / Fantastic 7* (US) (tv pilot, also shown theatrically) – dir: John Peyser
1979 *The Top of the Hill* (US) (tv movie) – dir: Walter Grauman
1980 *The Bank Robbery / A Nightingale Sang in Berkeley Square* (US) (tv movie, also shown theatrically) USvdt *The Big Scam / The Mayfair Bank Caper* – dir: Ralph Thomas
1980 *Exit Sunset Boulevard* (WG) – dir: Bastian Clevé
1981 *Der Mann in Pyjama* (WG) – dir's: Christian Rateuke & Hartmann Schmige
1981 *Fantasy Island* (US) (tv series) episode *Night in the Harem / Druids* – dir: Don Weis
1981 *The Love Boat* (US) (tv series) episode *A Model Marriage / This Year's Model / Original Sin / Vogue Rogue / Too Clothes for Comfort: Part 1 / Too Clothes for Comfort* – dir: Roger Duchowny
1982 *Inside the Third Reich* (US) (tv mini-series) – dir: Marvin J. Chomsky
1984 *Játszani Kell* (HUN/US) US *The Loves of Lily* UKvdt *Double Play* UK television title *Lily in Love* – dir: Karoly Makk
1984 *Niemand weint für immer* (WG/ZA) USvdt *No One Cries Forever* UKvdt *Death Threat* – dir: Jans Rautenback
1984 *The Love Boat* (US) (tv series) episode *Vicki and the Fugitive / Lady in the Window / Stolen Years / Dutch Treat: Part 1 / Dutch Treat* – dir: Robert Scheerer
1985 *Peter the Great* (US/USSR) (tv mini-series) – dir: Marvin J. Chomsky & Lawrence Schiller
1985 *Jenny's War* (UK/US) (tv movie) – dir: Steven Gethers
1986 *St. Elsewhere* (US) (tv series) episode *Brand New Bag* – dir: Beth Hillshafer [Bethany Rooney]
1986 *Anastasia: The Mystery of Anna* (US/IT/WG) (tv mini-series) UKvdt *Anastasia* – dir: Marvin J. Chomsky
1986 *Der Stein der Todes* (WG/COL) USvdt *Death Stone* (WG) aka *In der Hitze des Dschungels* – dir: Franz Josef Gottlieb
1986 *Neat and Tidy* (UK) [pilot *Adventures Beyond Belief*] – dir: Marcus Thompson
1989 *Himmelsheim* (WG) – dir: Manfred Stelzer
1991 *Severed Ties* (US) shooting title *Army* – dir: Damon Santostefano
1992 *Counterstrike* (US/CAN/FR) (tv series) episode *No Honour Among Thieves* – dir: Jean-Pierre Prévost
1993 *Happy Holiday* (GER) (tv series) episode *Der Star*
1993 *Destiny Ridge* (CAN) (tv series)
1994 *Florian III* (GER) (tv series)
1996 *Alles nur tarnung* (GER) aka *Life Is a Bluff* – dir: Peter Zingler
1996 *Dangerous Cargo* (US) – dir: Eric Louzil
1998 *Gotta Have It* (GER) (tv movie) – dir: Donald Kraemer
1999 *Unser Herr Gisbert* (GER) (tv series) aka *Gisbert* episode *Gute Reise*
1999 *Doppeltes Spiel mit Anne* (GER) – dir: Donald Kraemer
2000 *Flashback – Mörderische Ferien* (GER) – dir: Michael Karen
2000 *Nicht mit uns* (GER) (tv movie) – dir: Bernd Fischerauer
2005 *Reblaus* (GER) (tv movie) – dir: Klaus Gietinger
2005 *Ewig rauschen die Gelder* (GER) (tv movie) – dir: René Heinersdorff
2010 *Das Leben ist zu lang* (GER) – dir: Dani Levy
2017 *A Thousand Kisses* (US) (short) (voice) – dir: Richard Goldgewicht

Jean Sorel

born 25 September 1934 in Marseille, France
real name **Jean Bernard Antoine de Chieusses de Combaud Roquebrune**

George Dumurrier in ***One on Top of the Other***
Frank Hammond in ***A Lizard in a Woman's Skin***

1959 *J'irai cracher sur vos tombes* (FR) – dir: Michel Gast
1959 *Les lionceaux* (FR) – dir: Jacques Bourdon
1960 *La giornata balorda* (IT/FR) FR *Ça s'est passé à Rome* – dir: Mauro Bolognini
1960 *I dolci inganni* (IT/FR) FR *Les adolescentes* – dir: Alberto Lattuada
1961 *Amélie ou le temps d'aimer* (FR) – dir: Michel Drach
1961 *L'oro di Roma* (IT/FR) FR *Traqués par la Gestapo* – dir: Carlo Lizzani
1961 *Vu du pont* (FR/IT) IT *Uno sguardo dal ponte* US/UK *A View from the Bridge* – dir: Sidney Lumet [Italian prints also credit Roberto Savarese]
1961 *Vive Henri IV, vive l'amour!* (FR/IT) IT *I celebri amori di Enrico IV* – dir: Claude Autant-Lara
1962 *Il disordine* (IT/FR) FR *Le désordre* – dir: Franco Brusati
1962 *Le quattro giornate di Napoli* (IT) US *The Four Days of Naples* – dir: Nanni Loy
1962 *Hipnosis* (SP/IT/WG) IT *Ipnosi* WG *Nur tote Zeugen schweigen* aka *Dummy of Death* – dir: Eugenio Martín
1962 *Julia, du bist Zauberhaft* (AT/FR) FR *Adorable Julia* export title *The Seduction of Julia* – dir: Alfred Weidenmann
1963 *Chair de poule* (FR/IT) IT *Pelle d'oca* – dir: Julien Duvivier
1963 *Germinal* (FR/IT/HUN) IT *La furia degli uomini* – dir: Yves Allégret
1963 *Un marito in condominio* (IT) – dir: Angelo Dorigo
1964 *Amori pericolosi* (IT/FR) segment *La ronda* – dir: Carlo Lizzani [other dir's: Alfredo Giannetti & Giulio Questi]
1964 *La Ronde* (FR/IT) IT *Il piacere e l'amore* – dir: Roger Vadim
1964 *Vaghe stelle dell'Orsa* (IT) – dir: Luchino Visconti
1964 *Le bambole* (IT/FR) FR *Les poupées* US *Bambole / The Dolls* UK *Four Kinds of Love* segment *Monsignor Cupido* – dir: Mauro Bolognini [other dir's: Dino Risi, Luigi Comencini & Franco Rossi]
1964 *De l'amour* (FR/IT) IT *La calda pelle* UK *All About Loving* – dir: Jean Aurel

1965 *Made in Italy* (IT/FR) FR *A l'italienne* – dir: Nanni Loy
1965 *L'uomo che ride* (IT/FR) FR *L'homme qui rit* UK *The Man with the Golden Mask* – dir: Sergio Corbucci
1966 *L'ombrellone* (IT/FR/SP) FR *Play Boy Party* SP *El parasol* – dir: Dino Risi
1966 *Belle de jour* (FR/IT) IT *Bella di giorno* – dir: Luis Buñuel
1966 *Le fate* (IT/FR) – dir: Mauro Bolognini [other dir's: Mario Monicelli, Luciano Salce & Antonio Pietrangeli]
1966 *Fai in fretta ad uccidermi... ho freddo!* (IT/FR) FR *Tue-moi vite, j'ai froid* – dir: Francesco Maselli
1968 *I protagonisti* (IT) – dir: Marcello Fondato
1968 *Il dolce corpo di Deborah* (IT/FR) FR *L'adorable corps de Deborah* UK *The Sweet Body of Deborah* – dir: Romolo Guerrieri [Romolo Girolami]
1968 *L'età del malessere* (IT) – dir: Giuliano Biagetti
1968 *Adélaïde* (FR/IT) IT *Fino a farti male* UK *The Depraved* – dir: Jean-Daniel Simon
1969 *Una ragazza piuttosto complicata* (IT) UK *Complicated Girl* – dir: Damiano Damiani
1969 *L'amica* (IT) – dir: Alberto Lattuada
1969 *Uccidete il vitello grasso e arrostitelo* (IT) – dir: Salvatore Samperi
1969 *Una sull'altra* (IT/FR/SP) FR *Perversion Story* SP *Una historia perversa* US/UK ***One on Top of the Other*** – dir: Lucio Fulci
1970 *Paranoia* (IT/SP) SP *Una droga llamada Helen* export title *A Quiet Place to Kill* – dir: Umberto Lenzi
1970 *No desearás al vecino del quinto* (SP/IT) IT *Due ragazzi da marciapiede* – dir: Ramón Fernández
1971 *Una lucertola con la pelle di donna* (IT/SP/FR) SP *Una lagartija con piel de mujer* FR Carole US/UK ***A Lizard in a Woman's Skin*** – dir: Lucio Fulci
1971 *La controfigura* (IT) – dir: Romolo Guerrieri [Romolo Girolami]
1971 *La corte notte delle bambole di vetro* (IT/WG/YUG) WG *Malastrana* YUG *Kratka noc leptira* export title *Short Night of Glass Dolls* – dir: Aldo Lado
1971 *El ojo del huracán* (SP/IT) IT *La volpe dalle coda di velluto* UK *Lusty Lovers* aka *In the Eye of the Hurricane* – dir: José María Forqué
1972 *Mil millones para una rubia* (SP) – dir: Pedro Lazaga
1973 *Una gota de sangre para morir amando* (SP/FR) FR *Un ba du vaudou* UKvdt *Clockwork Terror* – dir: Eloy de la Iglesia
1973 *La polizia sta a guardare* (IT) UKvdt *The Great Kidnapping* – dir: Roberto Infascelli
1973 *Trader Horn* (US) – dir: Reza S. Badiyi
1973 *The Day of the Jackal* (UK/FR) – dir: Fred Zinnemann
1974 *La profanazione* (IT) – dir: Tiziano Longo
1975 *Une vieille maîtresse* (FR) (tv movie) – dir: Jacques Trébouta
1976 *La muerte ronda a Monica* (SP) – dir: Ramón Fernández
1977 *Les enfants du placard* (FR) UK *Closet Children* – dir: Benoît Jacquot
1978 *Der Mann im Schilf* (WG) – dir: Manfred Purzer
1978 *L'affaire Suisse* (SWI/IT/FR) – dir: Max Peter Ammann
1979 *Les soeurs Brontë* (FR) US *The Bronte Sisters* – dir: André Techiné
1980 *Aimée* (FR) – dir: Joël Farges
1981 *La naissance du jour* (FR) – dir: Jacques Demy
1981 *Un mère russe* (FR) – dir: Michel Mitrani
1981 *Quatre femmes, quatre vies: La belle alliance* (FR) (tv movie) – dir: Renaud de Dancourt
1981 *Les ailes de la colombe* (FR/IT) IT *Storia di donne* aka *The Wings of the Dove* – dir: Benoît Jacquot
1981 *Aspern* (POR) – dir: Eduardo de Gregorio
1982 *Le cercle fermé* (FR) (tv movie) – dir: Philippe Ducrest
1982 *La démobilisation générale* (FR) (tv movie) – dir: Hervé Bromberger
1983 *Bonnie e Clyde all'italiana* (IT) – dir: Steno [Stefano Vanzina]
1983 *Par ordre du Roy* (FR) (tv movie) – dir: Michel Mitrani
1985 *Elisabeth* (FR) (short) – dir: Pierre-Jean de San Bartolomé
1985 *L'herbe rouge* (FR) – dir: Pierre Kast
1985 *Rosa la rose fille publique* (FR) – dir: Paul Vecchiali
1986 *Il burbero* (IT) – dir: [Franco] Castellano & Pipolo [Giuseppe Moccia]
1988 *Le crépuscule des loups* (FR) (tv movie) – dir: Jean Chapot
1988 *Le clan* (FR) (tv mini-series) – dir: Claude Barma
1989 *Affari di famiglia* (IT) (tv movie) – dir: Marcello Fondato
1989 *Casablanca Express* (IT/MOR) – dir: Sergio Martino
1990 *Un piede in paradiso* (IT) export title *Speaking of the Devil* – dir: E.B. Clucher [Enzo Barboni]
1990 *Come una mamma* (IT) (tv movie) aka *Vostra per sempre, Elvira* – dir: Vittorio Sindoni
1990 *Prigioniera di una vendetta* (FR/IT) (tv mini-series) aka *Maximum Exposure* – dir: Vittorio Sindoni & Jeannot Szwarc
1991 *Miliardi* (IT) UKvdt *Millions* – dir: Carlo Vanzina
1993 *La scalata* (IT/GER/FR) (tv mini-series) – dir: Vittorio Sindoni
1994 *Les yeux d'Hélène* (FR) (tv series) – dir: Jean Sagols
1995 *Il prezzo della vita* (IT) (tv movie) – dir: Stefano Reali
1995 *Butterfly* (IT) (tv mini-series) – dir: Tonino Cervi
1995 *Fils unique* (FR) (short) – dir: Philippe Landoulsi
1997 *Dove comincia il sole* (IT/GER) (tv mini-series) GER *Verwirrung des Herzens* – dir: Rodolfo Roberti
1997 *Mamma per caso* (IT) (4-part tv mini-series) – dir: Sergio Martino
1997 *Il deserto di fuoco* (IT) (tv movie) – dir: Enzo G. Castellari [Enzo Girolami]
1997 *À nous deux la vie* (BEL/FR) – dir: Alain Nahum
2001 *Tout va bien c'est Noël!* (FR) (tv movie) – dir: Laurent Dussaux
2005 *I colori della vita* (IT) (tv movie) – dir: Stefano Reali
2008 *L'ultimo Pulcinella* (IT) – dir: Maurizio Scaparro
2014 *Una buona stagione* (IT) (tv mini-series)
2014 *Il teatro dei ricordi* (IT) (short) aka *The Theatre of Memories* – dir: Angela Bevilacqua, Giorgia Randolfi, Francesca Saracino
2016 *L'origine de la violence* (GER/FR) – dir: Élie Chouraqui
2017 *Drôles d'oiseaux* (FR) export title *Strange Birds* – dir: Élise Girard

John Steiner

born 7 January 1941 in Chester, England
died 31 July 2022 in La Quinta, California, USA

Charles 'Beauty' Smith in ***White Fang*** and ***Challenge to White Fang***
Count Dragulescu in ***Young Dracula***

1965 *Front Page Story* (UK) (tv series) episode *The £150,000 Win* – dir: Ian Curteis
1965 *Alice* (UK) (tv movie) – dir: Gareth Davies [series *The Wednesday Play*]
1966 *Public Eye* (UK) (tv series) episode *You're Not Cinderella, Are You?* – dir: Quentin Lawrence
1966 *Orlando* (UK) (tv series) (6 episodes) – dir: Bryan Shiner
1967 *The Saint* (UK) (tv series) episode *The Death Game* – dir: Leslie Norman
1966 *The Persecution and Assassination of Jean-Paul Marat as Performed By the Inmates of the Asylum of Charenton Under the Direction of the Marquis de Sade* (UK) – dir: Peter Brook
1967 *Sanctuary* (UK) (tv series) episode *A Cup of Tea with the Fullers* – dir: Tania Lieven
1967 *The Troubleshooters* (UK) (tv series) episode *Mr. Know-How* – dir: Ian MacNaughton
1967 *ITV Playhouse* (UK) (tv series) episode *Lady Windermere's Fan* – dir: Joan Kemp-Welch
1967 *Bedazzled* (UK) [uncredited] – dir: Stanley Donen
1968 *The Franchise Trail* (UK) (tv movie) – dir: James MacTaggart
1968 *Armchair Theatre* (UK) (tv series) episode *The Wind in a Tall Paper Chimney* – dir: Peter Sasdy
1968 *Work Is a Four Letter Word* (UK) – dir: Peter Hall
1969 *Tepepa* (IT/SP) US/UKvdt *Blood and Guns* – dir: Giulio Petroni
1969 *Alba pagana / Delitto a Oxford* (IT) export title *May Morning* – dir: Ugo Liberatore
1969 *Armchair Theatre* (UK) (tv series) episode *What's a Mother For?* – dir: Charles Jarrott
1969 *ITV Sunday Night Theatre* (UK) (tv series) episode *Pig in a Poke* – dir: James MacTaggart
1969 *ITV Playhouse* (UK) (tv series) episode *The Marrying Kind*
1969 *Una su tredici* (IT/FR) FR *12 + 1* US *12 Plus One* USvdt *13 Chairs* – dir: Nicolas Gessner
1970 *L'asino d'oro: processo per fatti strani contro Lucius Apuleius cittadino romano* (IT) – dir: Sergio Spina
1970 *El bosque del lobo* (SP) aka *El bosque de ancines / The Wolfman of Galicia* – dir: Pedro Olea
1970 *Department S* (UK) (tv series) episode *A Ticket to Nowhere* – dir: Cyril Frankel
1970 *La ragazza di nome Giulio* (IT) UKvdt *A Girl Called Jules / Model Love* – dir: Tonino Valerii
1971 *Hine* (UK) (tv series) (10 episodes)
1970 *Bali* (IT/WG) aka *Avventura a Bali* – dir: Ugo Liberatore [re-edited & re-released in 1975 as *Incontro d'amore a Bali* with Paolo Heusch credited as co-director]
1971 *L'istruttoria è chiusa: dimentichi (Tante sbarre)* (IT) FR *Nous sommes tous en liberté provisoire* – dir: Damiano Damiani
1972 *The Sextet* (UK) (tv series) episode *A Question of Degree* – dir: James Ferman
1972 *Sbatti il mostro in prima pagina* (IT/FR) aka *Slap the Monster on First Page* – dir: Marco Bellocchio
1972 *Rads 1000* (IT) (short) – dir: Giorgio Treves
1972 *La polizia é al servizio del cittadino?* (IT/FR) FR *La police au service du citoyen* US/UK *The Police at the Service of the Citizen* – dir: Romolo Guerrieri [Girolami]
1973 *L'invenzione di Morel* (IT) – dir: Emidio Greco
1973 *Zanna Bianca* (IT/SP/FR) SP *Colmillo Blanco* FR *Croc-blanc* UK/USvdt ***White Fang*** – dir: Lucio Fulci
1973 *ITV Playhouse* (UK) (tv series) episode *Professional* – dir: David Cunliffe
1973 *Rappresaglia* (IT/FR) FR *S.S. Représailles* US/UK *Massacre in Rome* – dir: George Pan Cosmatos
1973 *La villeggiatura* (IT) UK *Black Holiday* – dir: Marco Leto
1973 *Professional* (UK) (tv movie) – dir: David Cunliffe
1974 *Occupations* (UK) (tv movie) – dir: Michael Lindsay-Hogg

1974 *L'ultimo giorno di scuola prima delle vacanze di Natale* (IT) – dir: Gian Vittorio Baldi
1974 *Il ritorno di Zanna Bianca* (IT/WG/FR) WG *Die Teufelsschlucht der wilden Wölfe* FR *Le retour de Buck le loup* US/UK ***Challenge to White Fang*** – dir: Lucio Fulci
1975 *Una ondata di piacere* (IT) export title *Waves of Lust* – dir: Ruggero Deodato
1975 *Le guêpier* (FR/IT) IT *Sleeping Car – supplemento rapido con cadavere* – dir: Roger Pigaut
1975 *Roma violenta* (IT) export title *Violent Rome* UK *Street Killers* UKvdt *Forced Impact* – dir: Franco Martinelli [Marino Girolami]
1975 *Il Cav. Costante Nicosia Demoniaco, ovvero: Dracula in Brianza* (IT) export title ***Young Dracula*** – dir: Lucio Fulci
1975 *The Monster* (UK) US *The Devil Within Her* UKvdt *I Don't Want to Be Born* – dir: Peter Sasdy
1976 *Salon Kitty* (IT/WG/FR) aka *Madame Kitty* – dir: Tinto Brass
1976 *Mark colpisce ancora* (IT) UKvdt *The Specialist* US *The 44 Specialist* – dir: Stelvio Massi
1976 *Le deportate della sezione speciale SS* (IT) US *Deported Women of the SS Special Section* aka *Special SS Women* / *Deported Women* – dir: Rino Di Silvestro
1976 *...E tanta paura* (IT) export title *Plot of Fear* – dir: Paolo Cavara
1976 *Milano violenta* (IT) UKvdt *Bloody Payroll* – dir: Mario Caiano
1977 *La gabbia* (IT) (tv movie) – dir: Carlo Tuzii
1977 *L'avvocato della mala* (IT) export title *Gangbuster* shooting titles *Vai e colpisci* / *Hit and Run* – dir: Alberto Marras
1977 *Mannaja* (IT/SP) SP *Un hombre llamada hacha* UKvdt *A Man Called Blade* – dir: Sergio Martino
1977 *La malavita attacca... la polizia risponde* (IT) UKvdt *Bloody Payroll* – dir: Mario Caiano
1977 *Antonio Gramsci – I giorni del carcere* (IT) – dir: Lino Del Fra
1977 *Goodbye & Amen* (IT) – dir: Damiano Damiani
1977 *Von Buttiglione Sturmtrüppenführer* (IT) – dir: Mino Guerrini
1977 *Shock* (IT) US/USvdt *Beyond the Door II* Italian publicity title *Shock Transfert Suspense Hypnosis* shooting title *Al 33 via dell'orologia fa sempre freddo* – dir: Mario Bava
1978 *Il prigioniero* (IT) (tv movie) – dir: Aldo Lado
1978 *Effetti speciali* (IT) (tv movie) – dir: Gianni Amelio
1979 *Caligola* (IT) ITvdt *Io, Caligola* US/UK *Caligula* – dir: Tinto Brass & Bob Guccione
1979 *Design for Living* (UK) (tv movie) – dir: Philip Saville [series *Play of the Month*]
1979 *Action* (IT) – dir: Tinto Brass
1979 *Il piccolo Archimede* (IT) (tv movie, also shown theatrically) – dir: Gianni Amelio
1979 *L'amour en question* (FR) – dir: Andre Cayatte
1979 *BBC Play of the Month* (UK) (tv series) episode *The Voysey Inheritance* – dir: Robert Knights
1979 *BBC Play of the Month* (UK) (tv series) episode *Design for Living* – dir: Philip Saville
1980 *El gran choque* (IT/SP/MEX) SP *Carrera salvaje* MEX *Bólidas salvajes* UKvdt *Car Crash* – dir: Antonio Margheriti
1980 *The Sandbaggers* (UK) (tv series) episode *All in a Good Cause* – dir: Peter Cregeen
1980 *L'ultimo cacciatore* (IT) US/UK *The Last Hunter* – dir: Anthony M. Dawson [Antonio Margheriti]
1981 *The Salamander* (UK/IT/US) IT shooting title *La salamandre* – dir: Peter Zinner
1982 *I cacciatori del cobra d'oro* (IT) US *The Hunters of the Golden Cobra* – dir: Anthony M. Dawson [Antonio Margheriti]
1982 *Tenebre* (IT) US *Unsane* export title *Tenebrae* – dir: Dario Argento
1983 *Mystère* (IT) USvdt *Dagger Eyes* / *Murder Near Perfect* – dir: Carlo Vanzina
1983 *Il mondo di Yor* (IT/TUR) TUR *Yor* US/UKvdt *Yor: The Hunter from the Future* – dir: Anthony M. Dawson [Antonio Margheriti] [originally a four-part tv series]
1983 *I sopravvisati della città morta* (IT/TUR) TUR *Gunes imparatorunun hazinesi* US *The Ark of the Sun God* USvdt *Ark of the Sun God... the Temple of Hell* – dir: Anthony M. Dawson [Antonio Margheriti]
1984 *I racconti del maresciallo* (IT) (tv series) episode *In Loving Memory* – dir: Giovanni Soldati
1984 *I due carabinieri* (IT) – dir: Carlo Verdone
1984 *A.D. – Anno Domini* (US/IT) (tv mini-series) – dir: Stuart Cooper
1984 *Un caso d'incoscienza* (IT) – dir: Emidio Greco [released in 1989]
1985 *Inferno in diretta* (IT) FR *Amazonia* US/UK *Cut and Run* USvdt *Savage Amazon Adventure* – dir: Ruggero Deodato
1985 *Kommando Leopard* (IT/WG) IT/UK *Commando Leopard* – dir: Anthony M. Dawson [Antonio Margheriti]
1985 *Interno Berlinese* (IT/WG) WG *Leidenschaften* UK *The Berlin Affair* – dir: Liliana Cavani
1985 *Troppo forte* (IT) – dir: Carlo Verdone & [uncredited] Sergio Leone
1986 *Cobra Mission (Cinque uomini contro tutti)* (IT/WG) WG *Die Rückkehr der Wildgänse* US/USvdt *Operation 'Nam* UKvdt *Cobra Mission* FR *Commando Cobra* – dir: Larry Ludman [Fabrizio De Angelis]
1986 *Notte d'estate con profilo greco, occhi a mandorla e odore di basilico* (IT) – dir: Lina Wertmüller
1986 *The Lone Runner* (IT) (tv movie) aka *Flashfighter* shooting title *Un pugno di diamanti* – dir: Ruggero Deodato
1987 *Camping del terrore* (IT) US/UKvdt *BodyCount* shooting title *Camping della morte* – dir: Ruggero Deodato
1987 *Giulia e Giulia* (IT) UKvdt *Julia & Julia* – dir: Peter Del Monte
1987 *Striker* (IT) shooting title *Combat Force* – dir: Enzo G. Castellari [Enzo Girolami]
1987 *Appuntamento a Liverpool* (IT) aka *Appointment in Liverpool* – dir: Marco Tullio Giordana
1988 *La notte degli squali* (IT) UKvdt *Night of the Sharks* – dir: Anthony Richmond [Tonino Ricci]
1988 *Portami la luna* (IT) (tv movie) – dir: Carlo Cotti
1988 *Der Commander* (WG/IT) IT *Il triangolo della paura* UKvdt *The Commander* – dir: Anthony M. Dawson [Antonio Margheriti]
1988 *Big Man – Boomerang* (IT/WG/FR/AT/NOR) (tv movie) WG *Big Man – Strahlen des Todes* – dir: Steno [Stefano Vanzina]
1989 *Sinbad of the Seven Seas* (US) IT *Sinbad dei sette mari* shooting title *Sinbad il marinario* – dir: Enzo G. Castellari [Enzo Girolami & [uncredited] Luigi Cozzi] (production commenced in 1986)
1989 *Gioco al massacro* (IT) aka *The Killing Game* – dir: Damiano Damiani
1989 *The Nightmare Years* (UK/FR/IT/AUS/HUN) (tv mini-series) – dir: Anthony Page
1990 *Paprika* (IT) – dir: Tinto Brass
1991 *A Season of Giants* (US) (tv movie) aka *Michelangelo – The Last Giant* – dir: Jerry London

Anita Strindberg

born 19 June 1937 in Sweden
real name **Anita Edberg**

Julia Durer in ***A Lizard in a Woman's Skin***
French Ambassador's wife in ***The Eroticist***

1957 *Blondin i fara* (SWE) US *Blonde in Bondage* UK *Nothing But Blondes* [credited as Anita Edberg] – dir: Robert Brandt
1959 *Sköna Susanna och gubbarna* (SWE) [credited as Anita Edberg] – dir: Erik Strandmark
1970 *Quella chiara notte d'ottobre* (IT) [credited as Anita Edberg] – dir: Massimo Franciosa
1971 *Una lucertola con la pelle di donna* (IT/SP/FR) SP *Una lagartija con piel de mujer* FR *Carole* US/UK ***A Lizard in a Woman's Skin*** – dir: Lucio Fulci
1971 *La coda dello scorpione* (IT/SP) SP *La cola del escorpión* export title *The Case of the Scorpion's Tail* – dir: John Hamilton [Sergio Martino]
1971 *Forza "G"* (IT) US/UK *Winged Devils* – dir: Duccio Tessari

1972 *Coartada en disco rojo* (SP/IT) IT *I due volti della paura* UK *The Two Faces of Fear* – dir: Tulio Demicheli
1972 *Al tropico del Cancro – Peacock's Place* (IT) export title *Tropic of Cancer* Irish vdt *Death in Haity* [sic] – dir: Giampoalo Lomi & Edward G. Muller [Edoardo Mulargia]
1972 *All'onorevole piacciono le donne* (IT/FR) FR *Obsédé malgré lui* US *The Senator Likes Women* UKvdt ***The Eroticist*** – dir: Lucio Fulci
1972 *Malastrana* (WG/IT) IT *Chi l'ha vista morire* export title *Who Saw Her Die?* – dir: Aldo Lado
1972 *Il tuo vizio è una stanza chiusa e solo io ne ho la chiave* (IT) UK *Excite Me* aka *Gently Before She Dies* – dir: Sergio Martino
1973 *Partirono preti, tornarono... curati* (IT) aka *Halleluja to Vera Cruz* – dir: Newman Rostel [Stelvio Massi]
1973 *Diario segreto da un carcere femminile* (IT) re-released as *Diario erotico da un carcere femminile* US *Women in Cell Block 7* aka *Love in a Women's Prison / Behind Bars* – dir: Rino Di Silvestro
1973 *Contact – Contratto carnale* (IT/GHA) UKvdt *The African Deal – Contact / Only Love Defies* – dir: Giorgio Bontempi
1973 *L'anticristo* (IT) US/UK/USvdt/UKvdt *The Tempter* export title *The Antichrist* – dir: Alberto De Martino
1974 *L'uomo senza memoria* (IT) export title *Puzzle* – dir: Duccio Tessari
1974 *Milano odia: la polizia non può sparare* (IT) US *The Kidnapping of Mary Lou* US/USvdt *Almost Human* export title *The Executioner* – dir: Umberto Lenzi
1974 *La profanazione* (IT) – dir: Tiziano Longo
1975 *La verginella* (IT) – dir: Anthony Whiles [Mario Sequi]
1976 *La segretaria privata di mio padre* (IT) – dir: Mariano Laurenti
1976 *L'inconveniente* (IT) – dir: Pupo De Luca
1980 *Murder obsession (Follia omicidia)* (IT) US Fear UKvdt *The Wailing / Satan's Altar* export title *Murder Obsession* aka *L'ossessione che uccide / Deliria / Unconscious* – dir: Robert Hampton [Riccardo Freda]
1980 *L'eredita' della priora* (IT) (tv mini-series) – dir: Anton Giulio Majano
1981 *The Salamander* (UK/IT/US) IT shooting title *La salamandre* – dir: Peter Zinner

Fabio Testi

born 2 August 1941 in Peschiera del Garda, Italy

Stubby Preston in ***The Four of the Apocalypse***
Luca Di Angelo in ***The Smuggler***

1967 *Giurò e li uccise ad uno ad una (Piluk il timido)* (IT) [uncredited] – dir: William First [Guido Celano]
1968 *Straniero... fatti il segno della croce!* (IT) – dir: Miles Deem [Demofilo Fidani]
1968 *Due occhi per uccidere* (IT) [uncredited] – dir: Renato Borraccetti
1968 *I due crociati* (IT) – dir: Giuseppe Orlandini
1968 *C'era una volta il west* (IT) US/UK *Once Upon a Time in the West* [uncredited] – dir: Sergio Leone
1968 *Ed ora... raccomanda l'anima a dio!* (IT) export title *And Now Make Peace with God* – dir: Miles Deem [Demofilo Fidani]
1968 *Barbarella* (IT/FR) [uncredited] – dir: Roger Vadim
1968 *Un posto all'inferno* (IT) UKvdt *A Place in Hell* – dir: Joseph Warren [Giuseppe Vari]
1969 *Zingara* (IT) – dir: Mariano Laurenti
1969 *Blonde Köder für den Morder* (WG/IT) IT *La morte bussa due volte* US *Death Knocks Twice* – dir: Harald Philipp
1969 *Quella dannata pattuglia* (IT) UKvdt *The Battle of the Damned* – dir: Roberto B. Montero
1970 *Il giardino dei Finzi Contini* (IT/WG) WG *Der Garten der Finzi Contini* UK *The Garden of the Finzi Continis* – dir: Vittorio De Sica
1971 *Addio, fratello crudele* (IT) UKvdt/USvdt *Tis Pity She's a Whore* – dir: Giuseppe Patroni Griffi
1971 *Quel maledetto giorno d'inverno* (IT) re-release title *Quel maledetto giorno d'inverno Django e Sartana... all' ultimo sangue* export title *One Damned Day at Dawn... Django Meets Sartana* [credited as Stet Carson on some prints] – dir: Miles Deem [Demofilo Fidani]
1971 *Cosa avete fatto a Solange?* (IT/WG) WG *Das Geheimnis der grünen Stecknadel* US *Terror in the Woods / The School That Couldn't Scream* UKvdt *What Have You Done to Solange?* aka *Solange* – dir: Massimo Dallamano
1971 *Anda muchacho, spara!* (IT/SP) SP *El sol bajo la tierra* export title *At the End of the Rainbow* – dir: Aldo Florio
1972 *Le tueur* (FR/IT/WG) IT *Il commissario Le Guen e il caso Gassot* WG *Der Killer und der Kommissar* – dir: Denys de la Patellière
1972 *Camorra* (IT/FR) FR *Les tueurs à gages* export title *Gang War in Naples* – dir: Pasquale Squitieri
1972 *El Zorro justiciero* (SP/IT) IT *E continuavano a chiamarlo figlio di...* export title *And They Continued to Call Him a Son of a...* – dir: Rafael Romero Marchent
1973 *Un amore così fragile, così violento* (IT) – dir: Leros Pittoni
1973 *L'ultima chance* (IT) UK *Last Chance* US *Stateline Motel* – dir: Maurizio Lucidi
1973 *Revolver* (IT/FR/WG) FR *La poursuite implacable* US *Blood in the Streets* – dir: Sergio Sollima
1973 *La musica nelle vene / Viaggia ragazza, viaggia, hai la musica nelle vene* (IT) – dir: Pasquale Squitieri
1974 *I guappi* (IT) UKvdt *Blood Brothers* – dir: Pasquale Squitieri
1974 *Nada* (FR/IT) IT *Sterminate "Gruppo zero"* – dir: Claude Chabrol
1974 *L'important c'est d'aimer* (FR/IT/WG) IT *L'importante è amare* WG *Nachtblende* US *The Main Thing Is to Love* – dir: Andrzej Zulawski
1974 *Dieci bianchi uccisi da un piccolo indiano* (IT/SP) SP *Pasión salvaje* US *Ten Whites Killed By One Little Indian* – dir: Gianfranco Baldanello
1975 *Giubbe rosse* (IT) UKvdt *Cormack of the Mounties* – dir: Joe D'Amato [Aristide Massaccesi]
1975 *I quattro dell'apocalisse* (IT) export title The ***The Four of the Apocalypse*** – dir: Lucio Fulci
1975 *Vai gorilla* (IT) UKvdt *Go, Gorilla Go! / G Man Go / Streets of Blood* – dir: Tonino Valerii
1976 *L'eredità Ferramonti* (IT) UK *The Inheritance* US *The Inheritors* – dir: Mauro Bolognini
1976 *Il grande racket* (IT) – dir: Enzo G. Castellari [Enzo Girolami]
1977 *Clayton Drumm* (SP/IT) IT *Amore, piombo e furore* UK *China 9, Liberty 37* – dir: Monte Hellman (Spanish prints credit Tony Brandt [Antonio Brandt])
1977 *La via della droga* (IT) export title *The Heroin Busters* – dir: Enzo G. Castellari [Enzo Girolami]
1978 *A chi tocca, tocca...!* (IT/WG/IS) WG *Agenten kennen keine Tränen* US *The Uranium Conspiracy* – dir: Frank G. Carroll [Gianfranco Baldanello] & Menahem Golan
1978 *Enigma rosso* (IT/WG/SP) export title *Rings of Fear* WG *Orgie des Todes* SP *Tráfico de Menores* US *Trauma* UKvdt *Red Rings of Fear / Virgin Terror* – dir: Alberto Negrin
1980 *Luca il contrabbandiere* (IT) USvdt *Contraband* UKvdt *The Naples Connection / **The Smuggler*** – dir: Lucio Fulci
1980 *Manaos* (SP/IT/MEX) – dir: Alberto Vázquez-Figueroa
1980 *S*H*E* (US/IT) IT *S*H*E La volpe, il lupo e l'oca selvaggia* – dir: Robert Lewis
1980 *Speed Driver* (IT/WG/SP) SP *Vértigo en la pista* – dir: Stelvio Massi
1980 *Speed Cross* (IT) – dir: Stelvio Massi
1980 *La mano negra* (SP) aka *The Black Hand* – dir: Fernando Colomo
1981 *Il falco e la colomba* (IT) export title *The Hawk and the Dove* – dir: Fabrizio Lori
1981 *L'ultima volta insieme* (IT) – dir: Ninì Grassia
1981 *Il carabiniere* (IT) export title *A Gun for a Cop* – dir: Silvio Amadio
1983 *Ophiria* (IT) (tv mini-series) – dir: Tommaso Dazzi
1984 *Giochi d'estate* (IT) – dir: Bruno Cortini
1984 *The Ambassador* (US) aka *Peacemaker* – dir: J. Lee Thompson
1985 *Skipper* (IT) (tv movie) – dir: Roberto Malenotti
1985 *Giorno dopo giorno* (IT) (tv series) – dir: Salvatore Nocita
1985 *Scemo di guerra* (IT/FR) FR *La fou de guerre* – dir: Dino Risi
1985 *Io e il Duce* (IT/US/FR/WG) (tv movie, also shown in cinemas) US cable tv title *Mussolini and I* – dir: Alberto Negrin
1985 *Deceptions* (US) (tv mini-series) – dir: Robert Chenault
1985 *Se un giorno busserai alla mia porta* (IT) (tv movie) – dir: Luigi Perelli
1985 *I figli dell'ispettore* (IT) (tv series) – dir: Aldo Lado and others
1987 *Adios, pequeña* (SP) US *Goodbye Little Girl* – dir: Imanol Uribe
1987 *Iguana* (SWI/IT) – dir: Monte Hellman
1987 *Top Kids* (US/NOR) (tv movie) – dir: Michael Pfleghar

1988 *Sei delitti per padre Brown* (IT) (tv mini-series) episode *Il delitto del signore di Marne* – dir: Vittorio De Sisti
1988 *Il colpo* (IT) (tv movie) – dir: Sauro Scavolini
1989 *Domino* (IT) – dir: Ivana Massetti
1989 *Disperatamente Giulia* (IT) (tv movie) – dir: Enrico Maria Salerno
1990 *Le gorille* (FR/GER/IT) episode *Le Gorille chez les Mandinguez* – dir: Denys Granier-Deferre
1991 *Manuela* (ARG/IT) (tv series) – dir: Carlos Escalada & Rodolfo Hoppe
1991 *El sueño de Tánger* (SP) – dir: Ricardo Franco
1991 *Cacciatori di navi* (IT/US) (tv movie, also shown in cinemas) US tv title *Only One Survived* – dir: Folco Quilici
1991 *Gioco perverso* (IT) (tv movie) – dir: Italo Moscati
1991 *Money* (FR/IT/CAN) IT *Money (intrigo in nove mosse)* – dir: Steven H. Stern
1992 *Solo per dirti addio* (IT) (tv movie) – dir: Sergio Sollima
1992 *Un posto freddo in fondo al cuore* (IT) (tv movie) – dir: Sauro Scavolini
1992 *Micaela* (IT/ARG) (tv series) – dir: Rodolfo Hoppe
1992 *Due vite un destino* (IT) (tv movie) export title *The Final Contract* – dir: Romolo Guerrieri
1993 *Piazza di Spagna* (IT) (five-part mini-series) export title *The Spanish Steps* – dir: Florestano Vancini
1993 *Flash – Der Fotoreporter* (GER) (tv series) episode *Gift für die Welt*
1994 *Il burattinaio* (IT) UK cable tv title *First Action Hero* – dir: Ninì Grassia
1994 *Delitto passionale* (IT) – dir: Flavio Mogherini
1995 *Dottoressa Giò* (IT) (tv movie) – dir: Marcello Cesena
1995 *I ragazzi della notte* (IT) – dir: Jerry Calà
1995 *La storia di Frank* (IT) – dir: Leandro Lucchetti
1997 *Il ritorno di Sandokan* (IT) (tv movie) – dir: Enzo G. Castellari [Enzo Girolami]
1997 *Il deserto di fuoco* (IT) (tv movie) export title *Desert of Fire* – dir: Enzo G. Castellari [Enzo Girolami]
1997 *La dottoressa Giò* (IT) (tv mini-series) – dir: Filippo De Luigi
1998 *La dottoressa Giò 2* (IT) (tv mini-series) – dir: Filippo De Luigi
1998 *Annaré* (IT) – dir: Ninì Grassia
1999 *Tre stelle* (IT) (tv movie) – dir: Pier Francesco Pingitore
2001 *Sotto il cielo* (IT) – dir: Angelo Antonucci
2002 *Don Matteo* (IT) (tv series) episode *Beauty Farm* – dir: Andrea Barzini
2002 *Inseguito* (IT) – dir: Luca Guardabascio
2004 *Suherio* (IT) (tv movie) – dir: Giuseppe La Rosa
2005 *Torrente 3: El protector* (SP) – dir: Santiago Segura
2006 *Sottocasa* (IT) (tv series)
2007 *Mi último verano con Marián* (SP) (tv movie) – dir: Vicent Monsonís
2007-2008 *Herederos* (SP) (tv series)
2008 *La conjura de El Escorial* (SP) aka *The Conspiracy* – dir: Antonio del Real
2009 *Il falco e la colomba* (IT) (tv series) aka *The Falcon and the Dove* (6 episodes) – dir: Giorgio Serafini
2010 *Colpo di fulmine* (IT) (tv movie) – dir: Roberto Malenotti
2010 *Letters to Juliet* (US) – dir: Gary Winick
2010 *Road to Nowhere* (US) – dir: Monte Hellman
2010-2011 *Al di là del lago* (IT) (tv series) – dir: Raffaele Mertes
2011 *La donna che ritorna* (IT) (tv mini-series) aka *The Lady Who Returns* – dir: Gianni Lepre
2012 *Il commissario Rex* (IT) (tv series) episode *Superstar* – dir: Marco Serafini
2013 *King of the Sands* (SYR) – dir: Najdat Anzour
2015 *I Paranoidi* (IT) (short) – dir: Camillo Brena & Matteo Mercanti
2019 *Very Valentine* (US) (tv movie) – dir: Menhaj Huda
2020 *Curse of the Blind Dead* (IT) – dir: Raffaele Picchio
2023 *800 giorni* (IT) – dir: Dennis Dellai

David Warbeck

born 17 November 1941 in Christchurch, New Zealand
died 23 July 1997 in London, England
real name David Mitchell

Inspector Gorley in ***The Black Cat***
Dr. John McCabe in ***The Beyond***

1961 *Call Me a Liar* (AUS) (tv movie) – dir: William Sterling
1964 *Runaway* (NZ) UK *Runaway Killer* – dir: John O'Shea
1967 *30 Is a Dangerous Age, Cynthia* (UK) [uncredited] – dir: Joseph McGrath
1968 *Passport* (UK) – dir: Mira Coopman
1968 *Journey to the Unknown* (UK) (tv series) episode *Do Me a Favor and Kill Me* – dir: Gerry O'Hara
1968 *Treasure Island* (UK) (tv series) (9 episodes) – dir: Peter Hammond
1968 *BBC Play of the Month* (UK) (tv series) episode *Cyrano de Bergerac* – dir: James MacTaggart
1969 *The Elusive Pimpernel* (UK) (tv series) episode *The Challenge* – dir: Gerald Blake
1969 *The Borderers* (UK) (tv series) episode *Giant* – dir: James Gatward
1969 *ITV Saturday Night Theatre* (UK) (tv series) episode *Aren't We All* – dir: Michael Currer-Briggs
1969 *Wolfshead – The Legend of Robin Hood* (UK) (tv movie, also shown theatrically) – dir: John Hough
1969 *Tam Lin* (UK) US *The Devil's Widow* (voice) [uncredited] – dir: Roddy McDowell
1970 *My Lover My Son* (UK) – dir: John Newland
1970 *Trog* (UK) – dir: Freddie Francis
1970 *The Mating Machine* (UK) (tv series) episode *All About Little Eve* – dir: Howard Ross
1970 *UFO* (UK) (tv series) episode *Destruction* – dir: Ken Turner
1971 *UFO* (UK) (tv series) episode *Reflections in the Water* – dir: David Tomblin
1971 *Armchair Theatre* (UK) (tv series) episode *Will Amelia Quint Continue Writing 'A Gnome Called Shorthouse'?* – dir: James Gatward
1971 *Twins of Evil* (UK) – dir: John Hough
1971 *Giu la testa* (IT) UK *A Fistful of Dynamite* US *Duck! You Sucker* – dir: Sergio Leone
1972 *Give Me a Ring Sometime* (UK) (tv pilot for series *Go Girl*) aka *Passport to Murder* – dir: Steve Collins
1973 *Craze* (UK) aka *The Infernal Idol* – dir: Freddie Francis
1973 *The Sex Thief* (UK) – dir: Martin Campbell
1973 *Blacksnake / Sweet Suzy* (US) UK *Slaves* – dir: Russ Meyer
1973 *Spy Trap* (UK) (tv series) episode *The National Interest* – dir: Julia Smith
1973 *Spy Trap* (UK) (tv series) episode *Areas of Guilt* – dir: Viktors Ritelis
1973 *Spy Trap* (UK) (tv series) episode *Desperate Men* – dir: Viktors Ritelis
1973 *Voices* (UK) [uncredited] – dir: Kevin Billington
1974 *Thriller* (UK) (tv series) episode *Only a Scream Away* – dir: Peter Jefferies
1974 *Marked Personal* (UK) (tv series) episode #1.23 – dir: Joe Boyer
1974 *Marked Personal* (UK) (tv series) episode #1.24 – dir: Joe Boyer
1974 *Not on Your Nellie* (UK) (tv series) episode *The Apartment* – dir: Bryan Izzard
1974 *Notorious Woman* (UK) (tv mini-series) episode *Misalliance* – dir: Waris Hussein
1975 *Cipolla Colt* (IT/SP/WG) SP *El cibollero* WG *Zwiebel-Jack räumt auf* [uncredited] – dir: Enzo G. Castellari [Enzo Girolami]
1976 *Il comune senso del pudore* (IT) – dir: Alberto Sordi
1979 *L'argent du ministre* (FR) – dir: Michel Garnier
1980 *L'ultimo cacciatore* (IT) US/UK *The Last Hunter* – dir: Anthony M. Dawson [Antonio Margheriti]
1981 *Black cat* (IT) US/UKvdt ***The Black Cat*** – dir: Lucio Fulci
1981 *L'aldilà* (IT) US *Seven Doors of Death* UK ***The Beyond*** – dir: Lucio Fulci
1982 *Bakterion* (IT/SP) SP *Panico* UKvdt *Panic* – dir: Anthony Richmond [Tonino Ricci]
1982 *Fuga dall'arcipelago maledetto* (IT) US *Tiger Joe* – dir: Anthony M. Dawson [Antonio Margheriti]
1982 *I cacciatori del cobra d'oro* (IT) US *The Hunters of the Golden Cobra* – dir: Anthony M. Dawson [Antonio Margheriti]
1983 *I sopravvisati della città morta* (IT/TUR) TUR *Gunes imparatorunun hazinesi* US *The Ark of the Sun God* USvdt *Ark of the Sun God...the Temple of Hell* – dir: Anthony M. Dawson [Antonio Margheriti]
1983 *Lassiter* (UK) – dir: Roger Young
1984 *Minder* (UK) (tv series) episode *Second Hand Pose* – dir: Roy Ward Baker
1985 *7, Hyden Park: La casa maledetta* (IT) USvdt *Formula for a Murder* – dir: Martin Herbert [Alberto De Martino]
1985 *Miami Golem* (IT) USvdt *Miami Horror* aka *Alien Killer* – dir: Martin Herbert [Alberto De Martino]
1987 *L'isola del tesoro* (IT/FR/WG) (tv mini-series) UKvdt *Space Island* UK television title *Treasure Island in Space* – dir: Antonio Margheriti
1988 *Quella villa in fondo al parco* (IT) export title *RatMan* – dir: Anthony Ascot [Giuliano Carnimeo]
1988 *Domino* (IT) – dir: Ivana Massetti
1990 *Karate Rock (Il ragazzo dalle mani d'acciaio)* (IT) – dir: Larry Ludman [Fabrizio De Angelis]
1991 *Fuga da Kayenta (Tortilla Road)* (IT) – dir: Larry Ludman [Fabrizio De Angelis]
1991 *Tobacco Road* (IT) export title *Arizona Road* – dir: Fabrizio De Angelis
1991 *Il ragazzo dal kimono d'oro 3* (IT) export title *Karate Warrior 3* – dir: Larry Ludman [Fabrizio De Angelis]
1991 *Il ragazzo dal kimono d'oro 4* (IT) export title *Karate Warrior 4* – dir: Larry Ludman [Fabrizio De Angelis]
1991 *Il ragazzo dal kimono d'oro 5* (IT) export title *Karate Warrior 5* – dir: Larry Ludman [Fabrizio De Angelis]
1992 *Hornsby e Rodriguez sfida criminale* (IT) export title *Mean Tricks* – dir: Umberto Lenzi
1993 *Breakfast with Dracula: A Vampire in Miami* (IT) – dir: Fabrizio De Angelis
1993 *Il ragazzo dal kimono d'oro 6* (IT) (tv movie) aka *Karate Warrior 6* – dir: Larry Ludman [Fabrizio De Angelis]
1994 *Attrazione pericolosa* (IT) export title *Dangerous Attraction* – dir: Pierre Le Blanc [Bruno Mattei]
1995 *Fotogrammi mortali* (IT) export title *Fatal Frames* – dir: Al Festa [Alberto Festa]
1995 *Sick-O-Pathics* (IT) – dir: Massimo Lavagnini
1995 *Favola* (IT) – dir: Fabrizio De Angelis
1996 *Pervirella* (UK) – dir: Alex Chandon
1997 *Sudden Fury* (UK) – dir: Darren Ward
1998 *Razor Blade Smile* (UK) – dir: Jake West

index

Compiled by Francis Brewster.

Page references in **bold** refer exclusively to illustrations, though pages referenced as text entries may also feature relevant illustrations.

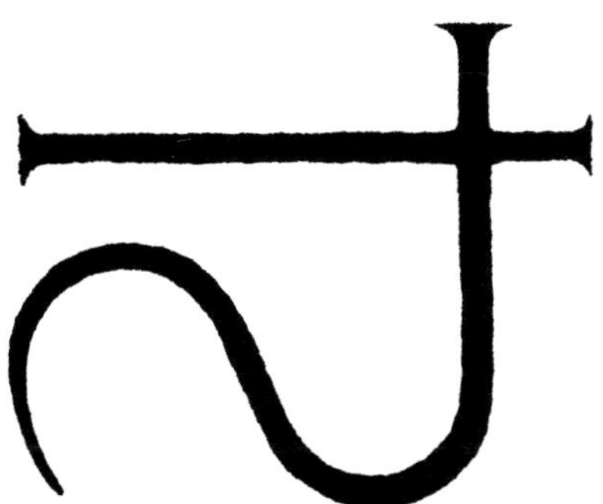

I LADRI
I RAGAZZI DEL JUKE BOX
URLATORI ALLA SBARRA
COLPO GOBBO ALL'ITALIANA
I DUE DELLA LEGIONE
LE MASSAGGIATRICI
UNO STRANO TIPO
GLI IMBROGLIONI
I MANIACI
I DUE EVASI DI SING SING
00-2 AGENTI SEGRETISSIMI
I DUE PERICOLI PUBBLICI
COME INGUAIAMMO L'ESERCITO
002 OPERAZIONE LUNA
I DUE PARÀ
COME SVALIGIAMMO LA BANCA D'ITALIA
MASSACRE TIME
COME RUBAMMO LA BOMBA ATOMICA
IL LUNGO IL CORTO IL GATTO
OPERATION ST. PETER'S
ONE ON TOP OF THE OTHER
BEATRICE CENCI
A LIZARD IN A WOMAN'S SKIN
THE EROTICIST
DON'T TORTURE A DUCKLING
WHITE FANG
CHALLENGE TO WHITE FANG
YOUNG DRACULA
THE FOUR OF THE APOCALYPSE
LA PRETORA
THE PSYCHIC
SILVER SADDLE
ZOMBIE FLESH-EATERS
THE SMUGGLER
CITY OF THE LIVING DEAD
THE BLACK CAT
THE BEYOND
THE HOUSE BY THE CEMETERY
THE NEW YORK RIPPER
MANHATTAN BABY
CONQUEST
ROME 2033 – THE FIGHTER CENTURIONS
MURDER-ROCK DANCING DEATH
THE DEVIL'S HONEY
ÆNIGMA
TOUCH OF DEATH
HANSEL AND GRETEL
ZOMBI 3
THE SWEET HOUSE OF HORRORS
THE HOUSE OF CLOCKS
DEMONIA
NIGHTMARE CONCERT
VOICES FROM BEYOND
DOOR TO SILENCE

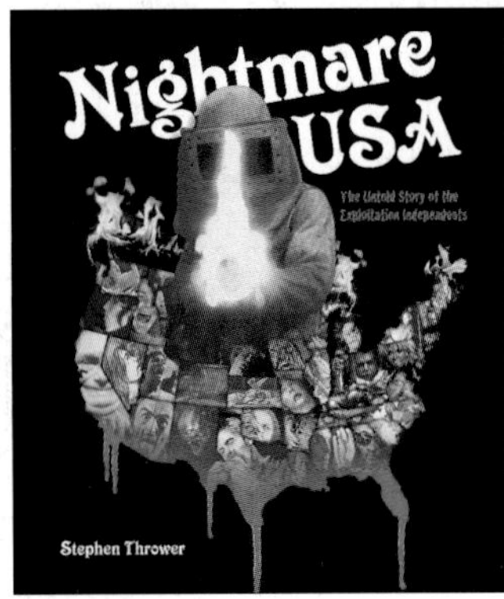

Nightmare USA: Exploitation Independents
Stephen Thrower

The Ghastly One: Andy Milligan
Jimmy McDonough

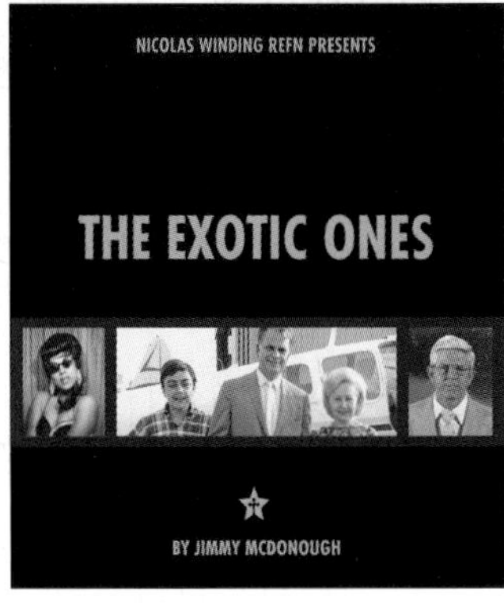

The Exotic Ones
Jimmy McDonough

Scala Cinema 1978-1993
Jane Giles

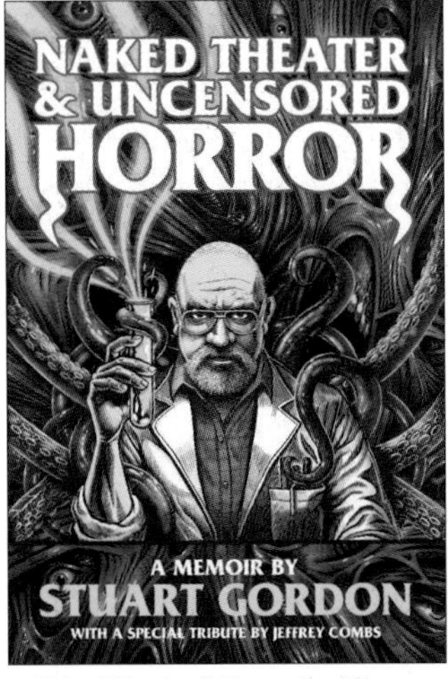

Naked Theater & Uncensored Horror
A Memoir by Stuart Gordon
With a Special Tribute by Jeffrey Combs

American Exxxtasy
My 30-Year Search for a Happy Ending
John Amero

Cinema Sewer
Volume Eight
Edited by Robin Bougie

Sonic Sewer
Volume One
Edited by Robin Bougie

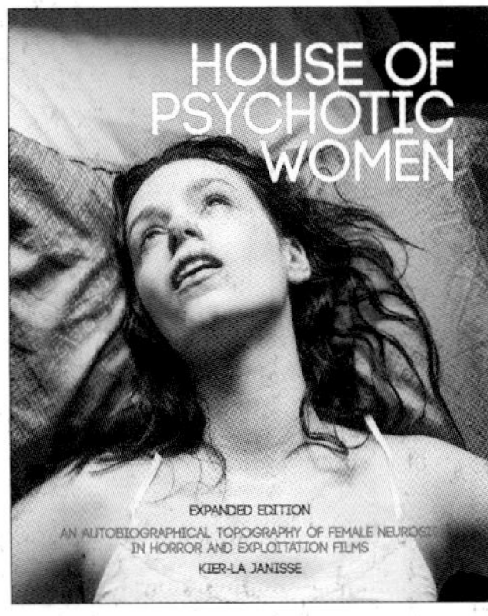

House of Psychotic Women
Kier-La Janisse

Cockfight: A Fable of Failure
Kier-La Janisse

Starburst: The Complete Alan Jones Film Reviews 1977-2008

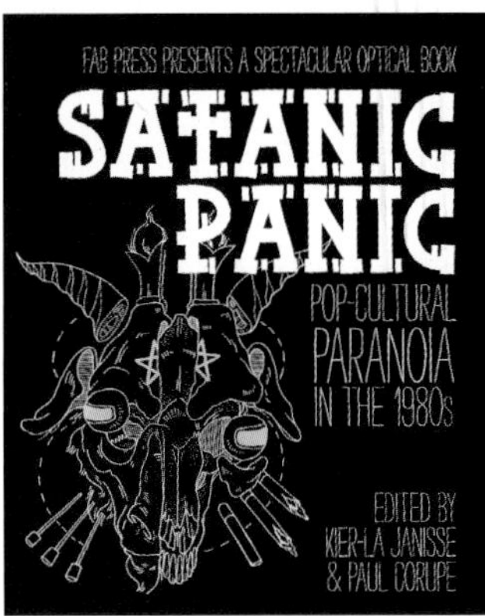

Satanic Panic
Edited by Kier-La Janisse & Paul Corupe

FrightFest Guide to Exploitation Movies
Alan Jones

FrightFest Guide to Grindhouse Movies
Alan Jones

FrightFest Guide to Vampire Movies
Nathaniel Thompson

FrightFest Guide to Mad Doctor Movies
Dr. John Llewellyn Probert